HEALTH PSYCHOLOGY

Biopsychosocial Interactions

Seventh Edition

HEALTH PSYCHOLOGY

Biopsychosocial Interactions   Seventh Edition

International Student Version

Edward P. Sarafino
The College of New Jersey

Timothy W. Smith
University of Utah

WILEY

JOHN WILEY & SONS, INC.

In memory of my mother and father. They gave me life, loved and nurtured me, and helped me be healthy. (Edward P. Sarafino)

For Paula, Wyatt, and Elliott. (Timothy W. Smith)

ABOUT THE AUTHORS

Edward P. Sarafino received his Ph.D. from the University of Colorado, and he began his affiliation with the Department of Psychology at The College of New Jersey more than three decades ago. He is now Professor Emeritus there. His scholarship has combined areas of health, developmental, and behavioral psychology, particularly with regard to the study of asthma. In addition to having published dozens of research articles and chapters, he is the author of six books. He is a fellow of Division 38 (Health Psychology) of the American Psychological Association, served as an officer (Secretary) of that division, and has been a member of several committees of Division 38 and of the Society of Behavioral Medicine. When he is not working, he enjoys being with friends, traveling, hiking and other outdoor activities, and going to cultural events, especially music and visual arts.

Timothy W. Smith received his PhD from the University of Kansas. After both a pre-doctoral internship in clinical psychology and a post-doctoral fellowship in behavioral medicine at the Brown University Medical School, he joined the faculty of the Department of Psychology at the University of Utah, where he has remained for nearly thirty years. He has published over two hundred articles and chapters, and three books, most in personality and social psychology, clinical psychology, and health psychology and behavioral medicine, particularly in the area of psychosocial issues

in cardiovascular disease. He is a Fellow in Division 38 (Health Psychology) of the American Psychological Association and in the Society of Behavioral Medicine. He has served as President of Division 38, and the Academy of Behavioral Medicine Research. He has also served as a member of the Behavioral Medicine Study Section of the National Institutes of Health, and as an Associate Editor or on the editorial boards of a variety of journals, including the *Journal of Consulting and Clinical Psychology*, *Health Psychology*, *Annals of Behavioral Medicine*, and the *American Psychologist*. His research has been supported by the National Institute on Aging and the National Heart, Lung, and Blood Institute of NIH, and has been recognized in awards from the Division 38, the American Psychosomatic Society, and the Society of Behavioral Medicine. He has supervised the graduate studies of over twenty-five PhD students in clinical and health psychology, including two past recipients of the American Psychological Association's award for early career contributions to health psychology. He enjoys skiing, backpacking, mountain biking, exercise, and spending time with family and friends.

TO CONTACT THE AUTHORS

We would be pleased to receive comments and suggestions about this book from students and instructors so that we may consider those ideas for future editions. You may contact us at sarafino@tcnj.edu.

PREFACE

"The first wealth is health," wrote the poet/philosopher Ralph Waldo Emerson in the 19th century. Although people have probably always valued good health, they are becoming increasingly health conscious. This heightened consciousness generally reflects two beliefs: that we can do things to protect our health and that being sick is unpleasant. As Emerson put it, "Sickness is poor-spirited, and cannot serve anyone." Serious health problems can be quite distressing to a patient and his or her family and friends. These beliefs underlie psychologists' interests in helping people behave in ways that promote wellness, adjust to health problems that develop, and participate effectively in treatment and rehabilitation programs.

The goal for each edition of this text has been to create a teaching instrument that draws from the research and theory of many disciplines to describe how psychology and health are interconnected. The resulting book is a comprehensive text that is appropriate for several courses, especially those entitled either Health Psychology or Behavioral Medicine. Two objectives were central regarding the likely audience in these courses. First, although we aimed to make the content appropriate for upper-division students, we wrote in a straightforward style to make the material accessible to most sophomores. The content assumes that the student has already completed an introductory psychology course. Second, we tried to make the material relevant and interesting to students from diverse disciplines—particularly psychology, of course, but also fields such as sociology, medicine, allied health, and health and physical education. Training in health psychology has developed rapidly and can play an important role in helping students from many disciplines understand the interplay of biological, psychological, and social factors in people's health.

The field of health psychology is enormously exciting, partly because of its relevance to the lives of those who study it and individuals the students know or will work with in the future. The field is also exciting because it is so new, and researchers from many different disciplines are finding fascinating and important relationships between psychology and health every day. Keeping up to date in each area of such a complex field presents quite a challenge, which begins with culling from thousands of new abstracts, articles, and books to prepare for the current revision. Most of the more than 2,700 references this edition cites were published within the last 10 years, and hundreds are new, published since the last edition of this book went to press.

NEW TO THIS EDITION

The most important new feature for this edition is the addition of a coauthor, Timothy W. Smith, a noted researcher and leader in the field of clinical health psychology. He brings a wealth of knowledge and a new perspective to the book.

The new edition retains the overall organization and the pedagogy that students and instructors have praised in the last edition. It also retains the *modular* structure of the chapter. The Body's Physical Systems, which has now been moved to the end of the book as an appendix. This appendix allows instructors to *choose* to cover *all of the systems at once* (assign the whole appendix) or *distribute* them to other chapters. For students using the distributed approach, appropriate chapters have salient notices that tell students when to read a specific module that is relevant to the current material. For example, a notice to read Module 4 (The Respiratory System) appears early in Chapter 6 at the start of the discussion of smoking tobacco, and a notice with the Key Terms list for that chapter reminds the students to study Module 4. In addition, we have retained the *interactive animations* of physiological systems in the Student Companion Website and notices in the book that prompt students to use them. Each animation takes 5 to 10 minutes to do and is accessed at http://www.wiley.com/go/global/sarafino.

Two features of the book were enhanced across chapters in the new edition. The most obvious enhancements are to:

- *Cross-cultural data*. To give students a broader picture of health psychology, we have found the latest available data on health and lifestyles and presented them concisely, typically in tables, for 14 countries: Australia, Brazil, Canada, China, Germany, India, Italy, the Netherlands, Singapore, South Africa, Sweden, Turkey, the United Kingdom, and the United States. For example, *Table* 5.7 gives data on infant mortality and low birth weight in these countries.

- *Illustrations*. We updated data in many figures and developed new ones to clarify physiological processes and to present interesting and important data. Figures 1-2, 5-4, 6-1, 7-1, 8-2, 13-2, and 14-1 are examples.

Every chapter has been updated, and we substantially revised or expanded the coverage of the following topics:

- How stress affects health
- Religiosity, positive emotions, and health
- Stages of change and motivational interviewing in health promotion
- Processes in and prevention and treatment of tobacco and alcohol use
- Weight control and exercise
- Health care systems around the world
- Pain conditions and treatment
- Diabetes and arthritis conditions and psychosocial interventions
- Cardiovascular, cancer, and AIDS conditions and treatments
- Technological approaches for health promotion

THEMES

A commonly stated goal in psychology is to understand the "whole person." To approach this goal, this book adopts the *biopsychosocial model* as the basic explanatory theme. We have tried to convey a sense that the components of this model interrelate in a dynamic and continuous fashion, consistent with the concept of *systems*. The psychological research cited reflects an eclectic orientation and supports a variety of behavioral, physiological, cognitive, and social–personality viewpoints. In addition, *gender and sociocultural differences* in health and related behaviors are addressed at many points in the book. In these ways, this book presents a balanced view of health psychology that is squarely in the mainstream of current thinking in the field.

One additional theme makes this book unique. We have integrated a focus on *life-span development* in health and illness throughout the book, and each chapter contains information dealing with development. For example, the book discusses how health and health-related behavior change with age and describes health care issues and examples that pertain to pediatric and elderly patients. Sometimes this information is organized as a separate unit, as with the sections "Development and Health-Related Behavior," "When the Hospitalized Patient Is a Child," "Assessing Pain in Children," and "Alzheimer's Disease."

ORGANIZATION

This text examines the major topics and problem areas in health psychology by using an overall organization that progresses in main focus across chapters from *primary*, to *secondary*, to *tertiary* prevention and care. As the table of contents shows, the book is divided into 14 chapters in the following seven parts, with an additional appendix

- **Part I.** Chapter 1 presents the history and focus of health psychology and introduces the major concepts and research methods used in the field.
- **Part II.** Chapters 2, 3, and 4 discuss stress, its relation to illness, and methods for coping with and reducing it. Some modules on body systems in the Appendix connect directly to discussions in Chapters 2 and 3, such as the sections entitled "Biological Aspects of Stress," "Physiological Arousal," "Stress, Physiology, and Illness," and "Psychoneuroimmunology." This connection is one reason why stress is covered early in the book. A reviewer recognized a second reason and wrote: "The issue of stress permeates all of the other topics, and it would be useful to have the students read about this first." Chapter 4 includes information on psychosocial methods in helping people cope better.
- **Part III.** The third part of the book examines issues involved in enhancing health and preventing illness. Chapters 5, 6, and 7 discuss how health-related behaviors develop and are maintained, can affect health, and can be changed via psychosocial and public health efforts. Chapter 6 gives special attention to the topics of tobacco, alcohol, and drug use, and Chapter 7 discusses nutrition, weight control, exercise, and safety. The role of stress in health behaviors and decision making is considered in these chapters. The book up to this point focuses mainly on primary prevention.
- **Part IV.** In Chapter 8, the main focus shifts to secondary prevention by describing the kinds of health services that are available and considering why people use, do not use, and delay using these services. This chapter also examines patients' relationships to practitioners and problems in adhering to medical regimens. Chapter 9 discusses the hospital setting and personnel, how people react to being hospitalized and cope with stressful medical procedures, and the role psychologists play in helping patients cope with their illnesses and medical treatments.
- **Part V.** Chapters 10 and 11 explore the physical and psychological nature of pain, ways to assess

patients' discomfort, the psychosocial impact pain, and methods for managing and controlling pain.

- **Part VI.** The two chapters in this part of the book emphasize tertiary prevention. They examine different chronic health problems, their impact on patients and their families, and medical and psychosocial treatment approaches. The chapters separate illnesses on the basis of mortality rates. Chapter 12 focuses on health conditions, such as diabetes and arthritis, that have either very low or moderate rates of mortality and may lead to other health problems or disability. In contrast, Chapter 13 examines four high-mortality illnesses—heart disease, stroke, cancer, and AIDS—and people's reactions to losing a loved one.

- **Part VII.** Chapter 14 discusses goals and issues for the future of health psychology.

- **Appendix.** Chapter 2 describes the physical systems of the body in an engaging manner a reviewer called "a pleasant surprise." This chapter is now divided into six modules that instructors can assign in two ways—all together or distributed to later chapters—depending on how they like to organize the course. Instructors who cover the modules all together want to present the body systems as an integrated and basic topic that underlies all later topics. They also want students to have a single place to refer to if needed, such as when reading about the neural transmission of pain signals in Chapter 10. Instructors who distribute the modules want to introduce important physiological principles as they become relevant. Either approach works easily now.

OPTIONAL ORGANIZATION

Because some instructors might like some *flexibility in the organization of chapters*, Chapters 9 through 13 were written with this possibility in mind. Chapter 9, Part V, and Part VI are written as three independent units that may be covered in any order. Two examples of alternate sequences that would work nicely after Chapter 8 are: (1) Part V, Part VI, and then Chapter 9; and (2) Part VI, Chapter 9, and then Part V.

LANGUAGE AND STYLE

The field of health psychology involves complex issues and technical information that require extra efforts to make the material readable and clear without sacrificing content. To accomplish this, we have limited the use of jargon in this book and have sought to write in a concrete and engaging fashion. The gradual progression of concepts, choice of words, and structure of each sentence were all designed to help students master and retain the material. When introducing new terms, we define them immediately. Many examples and case studies are included to clarify concepts and to bring them to life.

LEARNING AIDS

This book contains many pedagogical features. Each chapter begins with a *contents* list, giving students an overview of the progression of major topics and concepts. Then a *prologue* introduces the chapter with (1) a lively and engaging vignette that is relevant to the chapter material and (2) an overview of the basic ideas to be covered. The body of each chapter includes many *figures*, *tables*, and *photographs* to clarify concepts or research findings. For example, special figures were created to show how the immune system functions and how gate-control theory explains pain perception. Important terms are **boldfaced**, and *italics* are used liberally for other terms and for emphasis.

Throughout the book, three types of boxed material are presented to fit with the surrounding content. They are identified in the text with the corresponding icons:

- **Highlight.** This type of box focuses on high-interest and in-depth topics. Some of these topics are careers relating to health and psychology, breast and testicular self-examination, the effects of second-hand smoke, acute pain in burn patients, and the complex medical regimens for diabetes.

- **Assess Yourself.** This boxed feature has students actively examine their own health-related characteristics, such as their lifestyles, typical daily hassles, ways of coping with stress, knowledge about the transmission of HIV, beliefs about alcohol use, and symptoms of health problems.

- **Clinical Methods and Issues.** The third type of boxed material focuses on methods and issues in application efforts in clinical health psychology, medicine, public health, and rehabilitation. We examine, for instance, cognitive and behavioral methods that can help people reduce stress, stop smoking, and eat healthfully; biofeedback and relaxation techniques for treating asthma and some forms of paralysis; and procedures to prepare children for being hospitalized.

Each chapter ends with a substantial *summary* and a list of *key terms*. All these terms are redefined in the *glossary* at the back of the book.

ONLINE SUPPLEMENTS

Instructors who are using this text can access a companion website at www.wiley.com/go/global/sarafino after registering and obtaining a password. It contains:

- An *instructor's manual* with information to help instructors organize and present the subject matter effectively and enrich the classroom experience through activities and discussion.
- A *test bank*.
- *Powerpoint slides* with figures and tables from the text are available for download.
- Access to *Psychology Select*, a custom-publishing program that provides a database of materials from which you can create your own custom course-pack of readings, journal articles, and research articles.

The book's companion website also includes features specifically for students, such as a substantial *study guide* and more than a dozen *interactive animations* that show how physiological systems work, describe the effects of homeostatic imbalances on them, and present case studies of people with health problems and their diagnostic signs and symptoms.

ACKNOWLEDGMENTS

Writing this book and revising it have been enormous tasks. We are indebted first of all to the thousands of researchers whose important and creative work we have cited. There would be no health psychology without their work. We also received a great deal of direct help and encouragement from a number of people whose contributions we gratefully acknowledge.

Our thanks go to our editors at John Wiley & Sons, Christopher Johnson, Robert Johnston, and Eileen McKeever, who made valuable suggestions and oversaw and guided the revision process for this edition. We also appreciate the fine work of Wiley production editor Yee Lyn Song; designer, Seng Peng Ngieng; and photo editors, Hilary Newman and Kathleen Pepper.

The textbook review process generated many helpful suggestions that have made this a better book. Reviewers of the present and past editions of the book deserve our heartfelt thanks for their ideas and favorable comments regarding plans for the book and the major parts of the manuscript they read. The new edition has benefited greatly from the cover-to-cover review process and the excellent perspectives of the following colleagues:

Brian P. Daly, Temple University
Carla Messenger, George Washington University
Michael Kirkpatrick, Wheeling Jesuit University
Josephine Wilson, Wittenberg University
Paige Muellerleile, Marshall University
Marguerite Kermis, Canisius College

Because the new edition retains many of the features of earlier editions of the book, we continue to be indebted to the reviewers for those editions. Their names and affiliations (at the time the reviews were completed) are given on the book's companion website.

Very personal thanks go to the closest people in our lives—family, friends, and colleagues—for encouraging and supporting our efforts to complete this book and for tolerating our preoccupation.

Edward P. Sarafino and Timothy W. Smith

Wiley also acknowledges the assistance of Tara Foss in the preparation of this International Student Version.

TO THE STUDENT

"I wish I could help my father stop smoking," a health psychology student said at the start of the semester. Maybe she did help—he quit by the end of the course. This example points out two things that will probably make health psychology interesting to you: (1) the material is *personally relevant* and (2) many of the things you learn can actually be *applied* in your everyday life. Studying health psychology will also help you answer important questions you may have considered about health and psychology in the past. Does the mind affect our health—and if so, how? What effect does stress have on health and recovery from illness? What can be done to help people lead more healthful lives than they do? Why don't patients follow their doctors' advice, and what can health care workers do to help? What special needs do children have as patients, and how can parents and health care workers address these needs? How can families, friends, and health care workers help patients adjust to disabling or life-threatening health problems?

As these questions indicate, knowledge of health psychology can be relevant both now and later when you enter *your future career*. This is so whether you are studying to be a psychologist, medical social worker, nurse or physician, physical or occupational therapist, public health worker, or health educator. You will learn in this course that the relationship between the person's health and psychology involves a "two-way street"—each affects the other. Psychological factors go hand in hand with medical approaches in preventing and treating illness and in helping patients adjust to the health problems they develop.

THE BOOK AND WEBSITE

This book was designed for you, the reader. First and foremost, it provides a thorough and up-to-date presentation of the major issues, theories, concepts, and research in health psychology. Throughout the book, the major point of view is "biopsychosocial"—that is, that health and illness influence and result from the interplay of biological, psychological, and social aspects of people's lives. Because integrating these aspects involves complex concepts and technical material, we have made special efforts to write in a straightforward, clear, and engaging fashion.

FEATURES OF THE BOOK

To help you master the material and remember it longer, the book includes the following learning aids:

- **Chapter Contents and Prologue.** Each chapter begins with a contents list that outlines the major topics in the order in which they are covered. The prologue then introduces the chapter with a vignette that is relevant to the material ahead and gives an overview of the basic ideas you will read about.

- **Illustrations.** The many figures, tables, and photographs in each chapter are designed to clarify concepts and research findings and help them stick in your mind.

- **Boxed Material.** Three types of boxed material are included in the chapters. Each type of box has a special icon that is used in "Go to … " instructions, prompting you to read the appropriate box at the right point in the text.

- **Summary and Key Terms.** Each chapter closes with two features: (1) the summary, which presents the most important ideas covered, and (2) the key terms—a list of the most important terms in the chapter, arranged in order of their appearance.

- **Glossary.** The glossary at the back of the book gives definitions of important terms and concepts, along with pronunciation keys for the most difficult words. It will be useful when you are studying or reading and are not sure of the exact meaning or pronunciation of a term.

THE WEBSITE

To enhance your learning experience, you can access this book's *companion website* at www.wiley.com/go/global/sarafino. This website contains *links to websites* of illness-related organizations and:

- A *study guide*, which contains multiple-choice items, separated by chapter. For each item, the approximate page number of the textbook where the topic was discussed is given. For the Appendix, the items are separated also by modules, enabling easy use for students who are covering the entire chapter at once or are distributing the modules to other chapters. The software provides feedback, telling you how well you performed for each chapter and module and which items you missed.

- *Interactive animations* that will (1) help you learn how each physiological system of the body operates and (2) describe case studies of people with serious health problems. Announcements of the animations are given in the text with the relevant material, telling you that they are available and how to access them. When you use the website, click on Health Psychology Animations and Interactions and then on the title of the animation you want to do. The animations provide instructions—voice and written (which has the icon □)—and a bar at the bottom of the screen to control the progress and sound. Each animation takes 5 to 10 minutes to do.

STUDY HINTS

There are many ways you can use the features of this book to learn and study well, and you may want to experiment to find the best way for you. We will describe one method that works well for many students.

Survey the chapter first. Read the contents list and browse through the chapter, examining the figures, tables, and photographs. Some students also find it useful to read the summary first, even though it contains terms they may not yet understand. Then read the prologue. As you begin each new section of the chapter, look at its title and turn it into a *question*. Thus, the heading early in Chapter 1, "An Illness/Wellness Continuum," might become "What is an illness/wellness continuum?" Doing this helps you focus on your reading. After reading the section, *reflect* on what you have just read. Can you answer the question you asked when you reworded the title?

When you have finished the body of the chapter, *review* what you have read by reading the summary and trying to define the items in the list of key terms. If there is something you do not understand, look it up in the chapter or glossary. Last, *reread* the chapter at least once, concentrating on the important concepts or ideas. You may find it helpful to underline or highlight selected material now that you have a good idea of what is important. If your exam will consist of "objective" questions, such as multiple choice, using this approach intensively should be effective. If your exam will have essay items, you will probably find it helpful to develop a list of likely questions and write an outline or a complete answer for each one.

We hope that you enjoy this book, that you learn a great deal from it, and that you will share our enthusiasm and fascination for health psychology by the time you finish the course.

Edward P. Sarafino and Timothy W. Smith

BRIEF CONTENTS

CONTENTS

1

AN OVERVIEW OF PSYCHOLOGY AND HEALTH

PROLOGUE

Lisa has always been an attractive girl. She was long-legged and slender, blonde and blue-eyed. Like other girls of her age, looking like the supermodels in magazines or the young actresses on television was important to Lisa. So was wearing designer-label clothing for which she had the ideal body shape.

Other girls envied Lisa's great looks. For them it was hard work to keep the kilograms off. What did she eat, they wondered, not to have an ounce of flab? They knew that she was not athletic. Lisa did not play sports or go to the gym, thinking that if she did so, she would develop muscles, which she considered unfeminine.

Although her parents were not overweight, Lisa's body shape, it seems, was due to the very restricted range of foods she ate. When she was younger, she would eat cereals for breakfast, but after she started going to university, she skipped breakfast most mornings. Around 11.00 a.m. she would feel hungry and would have an apple or a tub of yoghurt. She did not eat lunch most days, preferring to have a chocolate or energy bar in the mid-afternoons. Sometimes she would go for coffee—a skinny latte—with her friends at the university cafe. She did not consider herself to be a smoker, but would often share her boyfriend's cigarettes, after which she would not feel like eating. At dinner, Lisa often picked at her food. She liked to eat salads, preferring raw vegetables to cooked ones. Some vegetables she did not eat, for instance, broccoli, cabbage, cauliflower, turnips, and radishes. Lisa also did not eat dessert or cake, although she would sometimes indulge in an ice-cream while out shopping. Lisa's mother rarely served dessert with dinner.

Though Lisa still lived with her parents, she was saving her income from a part-time job so that she could share rental accommodation. During the weeknights Lisa did not drink alcohol, but on weekends she would go out nightclubbing with friends, trying out the different cocktails during happy hour and drinking throughout the night. Lisa, like most people, has both good and bad health habits.

This story illustrates important issues related to health. For instance, the things a person does, such as skipping a meal, not having a balanced diet, or not engaging in physical activity, can affect their health. Also, an individual's social relations may encourage unhealthy behaviour, as we see in Lisa's drinking on weekends and sharing a smoke with her boyfriend. In this book, we will examine the relationships between health and a wide variety of psychological, biological, and social factors in people's lives.

This chapter introduces a relatively new and very exciting field of study called *health psychology*. We will look at its scope, history, and research methods, and discuss how it draws on and supports other sciences. As we study these topics, you will begin to see how a health psychologist would answer such questions as: Does the mind affect our health? What role does the cultural background of individuals play in their health? Does the age of a person affect how he or she deals with issues of health and illness?

But first let's begin with a definition of health.

WHAT IS HEALTH?

You know what health is, don't you? How would you define it? You would probably mention something about health being a state of feeling well and not being sick. We commonly think about health in terms of an absence of (1) objective *signs* that the body is not functioning properly, such as measured high blood pressure, or (2) subjective *symptoms* of disease or injury, such as pain or nausea (Kazarian & Evans, 2001; Thoresen, 1984). Dictionaries define health in this way, too. But there is a problem with this definition of health. Let's see why.

AN ILLNESS/WELLNESS CONTINUUM

Consider Lisa, the girl in the opening story. You've surely heard people say, "It's not healthy to be underweight." Is Lisa healthy? What about someone who feels fine but whose lungs are being damaged from smoking cigarettes or whose arteries are becoming clogged from eating foods that are high in saturated fats? These are all signs of improper body functioning. Are people with these signs healthy? We probably would say they are not "sick"—they are just *less* healthy than they would be without the unhealthful conditions.

This means health and sickness are not entirely separate concepts—they overlap. There are degrees of wellness and of illness. Medical sociologist Aaron Antonovsky (1979, 1987) has suggested that we consider these concepts as ends of a continuum, noting that "We are all terminal cases. And we all are, so long as there is a breath of life in us, in some measure healthy" (1987, p. 3). He also proposed that we revise our focus, giving more attention to what enables people to stay well than to what causes people to become ill. Figure 1-1 presents a diagram of an **illness/wellness continuum**, with *death* at one end and *optimal wellness* at the other.

We will use the term **health** to mean a positive state of physical, mental, and social well-being—not simply the absence of injury or disease—that varies over time along a continuum. At the wellness end of the continuum, health is the dominant state. At the other end of the continuum, the dominant state is illness or injury, in which destructive processes produce characteristic signs, symptoms, or disabilities.

ILLNESS TODAY AND IN THE PAST

People in developed, industrialized nations live longer, on the average, than they did in the past, and they suffer from a different pattern of illnesses. During the 17th, 18th, and 19th centuries, people in North America suffered and died chiefly from two types of illness: dietary and infectious (Grob, 1983). *Dietary diseases* result from malnutrition—for example, beriberi is caused by a lack of vitamin B_1 and is characterized by anemia, paralysis, and wasting away. **Infectious diseases** are acute illnesses caused by harmful matter or microorganisms, such as bacteria or viruses, in the body. In most of the world today, infectious diseases continue to be a main cause of death (WHO, 2009).

A good example of the way illness patterns have changed in developed nations comes from the history of diseases in the United States. From the early colonial days in America through the 18th century, colonists experienced periodic epidemics of many infectious

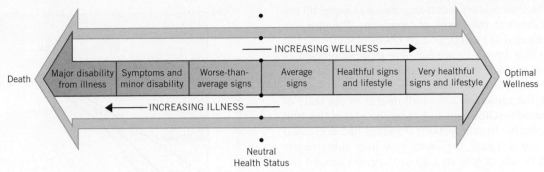

Death ← | Major disability from illness | Symptoms and minor disability | Worse-than-average signs | Average signs | Healthful signs and lifestyle | Very healthful signs and lifestyle | → Optimal Wellness

—— INCREASING WELLNESS ——→

←—— INCREASING ILLNESS ——

Neutral
Health Status

Figure 1-1 An illness/wellness continuum to represent people's differing health statuses. Starting at the center (neutral level) of the diagram, a person's health status is shown as progressively worse to the left and progressively healthful as it moves to the right. The segments in the central band describe dominant features that usually characterize different health statuses, based on the person's *physical condition*—that is, his or her signs (such as blood pressure), symptoms, and disability—and *lifestyle*, such as his or her amount of regular exercise, cholesterol consumption, and cigarette smoking. Medical treatment typically begins at a health status to the left of the neutral level and intensifies as the physical condition worsens. Medical treatment can bring the person's health status back to the mid-range of the continuum, but healthful lifestyles can help, too. Increasing wellness beyond the mid-range can be achieved through lifestyle improvements. (Based on information in Antonovsky, 1987; Bradley, 1993; Ryan & Travis, 1981.)

diseases, especially smallpox, diphtheria, yellow fever, measles, and influenza. It was not unusual for hundreds, and sometimes thousands, of people to die in a single epidemic. Children were particularly hard hit. Two other infectious diseases, malaria and dysentery, were widespread and presented an even greater threat. Although these two diseases generally did not kill people directly, they weakened their victims and reduced the ability to resist other fatal diseases. Most, if not all, of these diseases did not exist in North America before

the European settlers arrived—the settlers brought the infections with them—and the death toll among Native Americans skyrocketed. This high death rate occurred for two reasons. First, the native population had never been exposed to these new microorganisms, and thus lacked the natural immunity that our bodies develop after lengthy exposure to most diseases (Grob, 1983). Second, Native Americans' immune functions were probably limited by a low degree of genetic variation among these people (Black, 1992).

Epidemics of deadly infectious diseases have occurred throughout the world. Before the 20th century, there were no effective methods for prevention or treatment of the plague, for instance, which is the disease illustrated in this engraving.

In the 19th century, infectious diseases were still the greatest threat to the health of Americans. The illnesses of the colonial era continued to claim many lives, but new diseases began to appear. The most significant of these diseases was tuberculosis, or "consumption," as it was often called. In 1842, for example, consumption was listed as the cause for 22% of all deaths in the state of Massachusetts (Grob, 1983). But by the end of the 19th century, deaths from infectious diseases had decreased sharply. For instance, the death rate from tuberculosis declined by about 60% in a 25-year period around the turn of the century.

Did this decrease result mostly from advances in medical treatment? Although medical advances helped to some degree, the decrease occurred long before effective vaccines and medications were introduced. This was the case for most of the major diseases we've discussed, including tuberculosis, diphtheria, measles, and influenza (Grob, 1983; Leventhal, Prohaska, & Hirschman, 1985). It appears that the decline resulted chiefly from *preventive* measures such as improved personal hygiene, greater resistance to diseases (owing to better nutrition), and public health innovations, such as building water purification and sewage treatment facilities. Many people had become concerned about their health and began to heed the advice of health reformers like William Alcott, an advocate of moderation in diet and sexual behavior (Leventhal, Prohaska, & Hirschman, 1985). Fewer deaths occurred from diseases because fewer people contracted them.

The 20th century witnessed great changes in the patterns of illness afflicting people. The death rate from life-threatening infectious diseases declined, and people's average life expectancy increased dramatically. For example, in 1900 in the United States, the life expectancy of babies at birth was about 48 years (USDHHS, 1987); today it is nearly 78 years (USBC, 2010). Figure 1-2 shows this change and an important reason for it: the death rate among children was very high many years ago. Babies who survived their first year in 1900 could be expected to live to about 56 years of age, adding 7 years to their expected total life span. Moreover, people in 1900 who had reached the age of 20 years could expect to live to almost 63 years of age. Today the death rate for American children is much lower, and only a small difference exists in the expected total life span for newborns and 20-year-olds. Developed countries around the world experienced similar histories.

Death is still inevitable, of course, but people die at later ages now and from different causes. The main health problems and causes of death in developed countries today are **chronic diseases**—that is, degenerative illnesses, such as heart disease, cancer, and

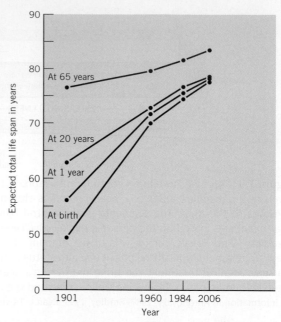

Figure 1-2 Expected total life span for people in the United States at various years since 1900 who were born in the specified year or had reached 1 year, 20 years, or 65 years of age. (Data from USDHHS, 1987, p. 2, for years 1900–1902, 1959–1961, and 1984; USBC, 2010, Table 105, for 2006.)

stroke—that develop or persist over a long period of time. And worldwide, chronic illnesses account for more than half of all deaths (WHO, 2009). These diseases are not new, but they were responsible for a much smaller proportion of deaths before the 20th century. Why? One reason is that people's lives are different today. For example, the growth of industrialization increased people's stress and exposure to harmful chemicals. In addition, more people today survive to old age, and chronic diseases are more likely to afflict older than younger individuals. Thus, another reason for the current prominence of chronic diseases is that more people are living to the age when they are at high risk for contracting them.

Are the main causes of death in childhood and adolescence different from those in adulthood? Yes. In the United States, for example, the leading cause of death in children and adolescents, by far, is not an illness, but accidental injury (USBC, 2010). In the age range from 1 to 24 years, over 42% of deaths result from accidents, frequently involving automobiles. In this age group, the next four most frequent causes of death are homicide, suicide, cancer, and cardiovascular diseases. All five of these causes of death are far more common among 15- to 24-year-olds than for younger ages. Clearly, the role of disease in death differs greatly at different points in the life span.

VIEWPOINTS FROM HISTORY: PHYSIOLOGY, DISEASE PROCESSES, AND THE MIND

Is illness a purely physical condition? Does a person's mind play a role in becoming ill and getting well? People have wondered about these questions for thousands of years, and the answers they have arrived at have changed over time.

EARLY CULTURES

Although we do not know for certain, it appears that the best educated people thousands of years ago believed physical and mental illness were caused by mystical forces, such as evil spirits (Stone, 1979). Why do we think this? Researchers found ancient skulls in several areas of the world with coin-size circular holes in them that could not have been battle wounds. These holes were probably made with sharp stone tools in a procedure called *trephination*. This procedure was done presumably for superstitious reasons—for instance, to allow illness-causing demons to leave the head. Because there are no written records from those times, we can only speculate about the reasons for the holes.

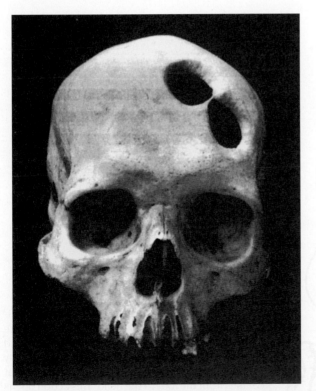

A skull with holes probably produced by trephination. This person probably survived several of these procedures.

ANCIENT GREECE AND ROME

The philosophers of ancient Greece produced the earliest written ideas about physiology, disease processes, and the mind between 500 and 300 B.C. Hippocrates, often called "the Father of Medicine," proposed a *humoral theory* of illness. According to this theory, the body contains four fluids called *humors* (in biology, the term *humor* refers to any plant or animal fluid). When the mixture of these humors is harmonious or balanced, we are in a state of health. Disease occurs when the mixture is faulty (Stone, 1979). Hippocrates recommended eating a good diet and avoiding excesses to help achieve humoral balance.

Greek philosophers, especially Plato, were among the first to propose that the mind and the body are separate entities (Marx & Hillix, 1963; Schneider & Tarshis, 1975). The mind was considered to have little or no relationship to the body and its state of health. This remained the dominant view of writers and philosophers for more than a thousand years, and the body and the mind are conceptually separate today. The *body* refers to our physical being, including our skin, muscles, bones, heart, and brain. The *mind* refers to an abstract process that includes our thoughts, perceptions, and feelings. Although we can separate the mind and body conceptually, an important issue is whether they function independently. The question of their relationship is called the **mind/body problem**.

Galen was a famous and highly respected doctor and writer of the 2nd century A.D. who was born in Greece and practiced in Rome. Although he believed generally in the humoral theory and the mind/body split, he made many innovations. For example, he "dissected animals of many species (but probably never a human), and made important discoveries about the brain, circulatory system, and kidneys" (Stone, 1979, p. 4). From this work, he became aware that illnesses can be localized, with pathology in specific parts of the body, and that different diseases have different effects. Galen's ideas became widely accepted.

THE MIDDLE AGES

After the collapse of the Roman Empire in the 5th century A.D., much of the Western world was in disarray. The advancement of knowledge and culture slowed sharply in Europe and remained stunted during the Middle Ages, which lasted almost a thousand years. The influence of the Church in slowing the development of medical knowledge during the Middle Ages was enormous. According to historians, the Church regarded the human being

as a creature with a soul, possessed of a free will which set him apart from ordinary natural laws, subject only to his own willfulness and perhaps the will of God. Such a creature, being free-willed, could not be an object of scientific investigation. Even the body of man was regarded as sacrosanct, and dissection was dangerous for the dissector. These strictures against observation hindered the development of anatomy and medicine for centuries. (Marx & Hillix, 1963, p. 24)

The prohibition against dissection extended to animals as well, since they were thought to have souls, too.

People's ideas about the cause of illness took on pronounced religious overtones, and the belief in demons became strong again (Sarason & Sarason, 1984). Sickness was seen as God's punishment for doing evil things. As a result, the Church came to control the practice of medicine, and priests became increasingly involved in treating the ill, often by torturing the body to drive out evil spirits.

It was not until the 13th century that new ideas about the mind/body problem began to emerge. The Italian philosopher St. Thomas Aquinas rejected the view that the mind and body are separate and saw them as interrelated (Leahey, 1987). Although his position did

not have as great an impact as others had had, it renewed interest in the issue and influenced later philosophers.

THE RENAISSANCE AND AFTER

The word *renaissance* means rebirth—a fitting name for the 14th and 15th centuries. During this period in history, Europe saw a rebirth of inquiry, culture, and politics. Scholars became more "human-centered" than "God-centered" in their search for truth and "believed that truth can be seen in many ways, from many individual perspectives" (Leahey, 1987, p. 80). These ideas set the stage for important changes in philosophy once the scientific revolution began after 1600.

The 17th-century French philosopher and mathematician René Descartes probably had the greatest influence on scientific thought of any philosopher in history (Schneider & Tarshis, 1975). Like the Greeks, he regarded the mind and body as separate entities, but he introduced three important innovations. First, he conceived of the body as a machine and described the mechanics of how action and sensation occurred. For example, Figure 1-3 shows his concept of how we experience pain. Second,

Figure 1-3 Descartes' concept of the pain pathway. Descartes used this drawing to illustrate the mechanisms by which people experience and respond to pain: The heat of the fire (at A) sends tiny particles to the foot (B) that pull on a thread that courses from the foot to the head. This action opens a pore (de), releasing spirits from a cavity (F) that travel to the parts of the body that respond (e.g., the leg moves away). (From Descartes, 1664, Figure 7.)

he proposed that the mind and body, although separate, could *communicate* through the pineal gland, an organ in the brain (Leahey, 1987). Third, he believed that animals have no soul and that the soul in humans leaves the body at death (Marx & Hillix, 1963). This belief meant that dissection could be an acceptable method of study—a point the Church was now ready to concede (Engel, 1977).

In the 18th and 19th centuries, knowledge in science and medicine grew quickly, helped greatly by improvements in the microscope and the use of dissection in autopsies. Once scientists learned the basics of how the body functioned and discovered that microorganisms cause certain diseases, they rejected the humoral theory of illness and proposed new theories. The field of surgery flourished after antiseptic techniques and anesthesia were introduced in the mid-19th century (Stone, 1979). Before then, hospitals were "notorious places, more likely to spread diseases than cure them" (Easterbrook, 1987, p. 42). Over time, the reputation of doctors and hospitals began to improve, and people's trust in the ability of doctors to heal increased.

These advances, coupled with the continuing belief that the mind and body are separate, laid the foundation for a new approach, or "model," for conceptualizing health and illness. This approach—called the **biomedical model**—proposes that all diseases or physical disorders can be explained by disturbances in physiological processes, which result from injury, biochemical imbalances, bacterial or viral infection, and the like (Engel, 1977; Leventhal, Prohaska, & Hirschman, 1985). The biomedical model assumes that disease is an affliction of the body and is separate from the psychological and social processes of the mind. This viewpoint became widely accepted during the 19th and 20th centuries and still represents the dominant view in medicine today.

SEEING A NEED: PSYCHOLOGY'S ROLE IN HEALTH

The biomedical model has been very useful. Using it as a guide, researchers have made enormous achievements. They conquered many infectious diseases, such as polio and measles, through the development of vaccines. They also developed antibiotics, which made it possible to cure illnesses caused by bacterial infection. Despite these great advances, the biomedical model needs improvement. Let's see why.

PROBLEMS IN THE HEALTH CARE SYSTEM

Scarcely a week goes by when we don't hear through the mass media that health care costs are rising rapidly,

particularly for prescription drugs and for hospital and nursing home care. Countries worldwide have been facing escalating costs in health care. For example, between 1960 and today the United States saw a 49-fold increase to over $7,200 in the amount of money spent per capita on health care, and the economic burden of health costs increased from about 5% to 16% of the gross domestic product (NCHS, 2009). In Canada and most European countries, per capita health costs are now at about 8% to 10% of their gross domestic products (WHO, 2009). Because medical costs continue to rise rapidly, we need to consider new approaches for improving people's health.

We've seen that the patterns of illness affecting people have changed, particularly in developed nations where the main health problems now are chronic diseases. Consider cancer, for example. Although a great deal of progress is being made in understanding the causes of cancers, improvements in techniques for treating them have been modest: gains in cancer survival rates from the 1950s to the 1980s, for instance, resulted more from earlier detection of the disease than from improved treatments (Boffey, 1987). Although detection occurs earlier today partly because diagnostic methods have improved, another part of the reason is that *people* have changed. Many individuals are more aware of signs and symptoms of illness, more motivated to take care of their health, and better able to afford visits to doctors than they were in the past. These factors are clearly important and relate to psychological and social aspects of the person. But *the person* as a unique individual is not included in the biomedical model (Engel, 1977, 1980).

"THE PERSON" IN HEALTH AND ILLNESS

Have you ever noticed how some people are "always sick"—they get illnesses more frequently than most people do and get well more slowly? These differences between people can result from biomedical sources, such as variations in physiological processes and exposure to harmful microorganisms. But psychological and social factors also play a role. Let's look briefly at two of these factors: the lifestyle and personality of the person. (Go to ●—as described in the Preface, this instruction prompts you to read the nearby boxed material that has the same icon.)

Lifestyle and Illness

Earlier we saw that the occurrence of infectious diseases declined in some nations in the late 19th century chiefly because of preventive measures, such as improved nutrition and personal hygiene. These measures involved changing people's *lifestyles*—their everyday patterns of

ASSESS YOURSELF

What's Your Lifestyle Like?

At various points in this book, you'll find brief self-assessment surveys like this one that you should try to fill out as accurately as you can. These surveys relate to the nearby content of the chapter, and most of them can be completed in less than a minute or two.

This survey assesses seven aspects of your *usual* lifestyle. For each of the listed practices, put a check mark in the preceding space if it describes your usual situation.

_____ I sleep 7 or 8 hours a day.

_____ I eat breakfast almost every day.
_____ I rarely eat between meals.
_____ I am at or near the appropriate weight for my height (see Table 8.3 on page 202)
_____ I never smoke cigarettes.
_____ I drink alcohol rarely or moderately.
_____ I regularly get vigorous physical activity.

Count the check marks—six or seven is quite good. The more of these situations that describe your lifestyle now and in the future, the better your health is likely to be, particularly after the age of 50.

---

behavior, such as in washing, preparing, and eating healthful foods. Changes in people's lifestyles can also reduce chronic illnesses. Let's see how.

Characteristics or conditions that are associated with the development of a disease or injury are called **risk factors** for that health problem. Although some risk factors are *biological*, such as having inherited certain genes, others are *behavioral*. For example, it is well known that people who smoke cigarettes face a much higher risk of developing cancer and other illnesses than nonsmokers do. Other risk factors for cancer include eating diets high in saturated fat and having a family history of the disease. People who "do more" or "have more" of these characteristics or conditions are more likely to contract cancer than people who "do less" or "have less" of these factors. Keep in mind that a risk factor is *associated* with a health problem—it does not necessarily *cause* the problem. For example, being an African American man is a risk factor for prostate cancer (ACS, 2009), but that status does not cause the disease—at least, not directly.

Many risk factors result from the way people live or behave, such as smoking cigarettes and eating unhealthful diets. Some behavioral risk factors associated with the five leading causes of death in the United States are:

1. *Heart disease*—smoking, high dietary cholesterol, obesity, and lack of exercise.
2. *Cancer*—smoking, high alcohol use, and diet.
3. *Stroke*—smoking, high dietary cholesterol, and lack of exercise.
4. COPD (chronic lung diseases, e.g., emphysema)—smoking.

5. *Accidents* (including motor vehicle)—alcohol/drug use and not using seat belts. (ACS, 2009; AHA, 2010; NCHS, 2009a; USBC, 2010)

Many of the people who are the victims of these illnesses and accidents live for at least a short while and either recover or eventually succumb. Part of today's high medical costs result from people's lifestyles that contribute to their health problems, and society, not the individual, often bears the burden of medical costs through public and private health insurance programs.

How influential are lifestyle factors on health? Researchers studied this question by surveying nearly 7,000 adults who ranged in age from about 20 to over 75, asking them two sets of questions. One set asked about the health of these people over the previous 12 months—for instance, whether illness had prevented them from working for a long time, forced them to cut down on other activities, or reduced their energy level. The second set of questions asked about seven aspects of their lifestyles: sleeping, eating breakfast, eating between meals, maintaining an appropriate weight, smoking cigarettes, drinking alcohol, and getting physical activity. The questions you answered above are similar to those in this research. When the researchers compared the data for people in different age groups, they found that at each age health was typically better as the number of healthful practices increased. In fact, the health of those who "reported following all seven good health practices was consistently about the same as those 30 years younger who followed few or none of these practices" (Belloc & Breslow, 1972, p. 419). And these health practices were also important in the future health of these people. Breslow (1983) has described later studies of the same people, such as to find out which of them had died in the 9 1/2 years after the original survey. The data revealed that the percentage dying generally decreased with increases in the number of healthful behaviors practiced, and this impact was greater for older than younger people, especially among males. These findings suggest that people's practicing healthful behaviors can reduce their risk of illness and early death substantially.

You've surely heard someone ask, "Why don't people do what's good for them?" There's no simple answer to that question—there are many reasons. One reason is that less healthful behaviors often bring immediate pleasure, as when the person has a "good-tasting" cigarette or ice cream. Long-range negative consequences seem remote, both in time and in likelihood. Keep in mind that pleasurable lifestyles can benefit health: some evidence suggests that engaging in enjoyable activities, such as vacationing or attending concerts, may lead to better health (Bygren et al., 2009; Pressman et al., 2009). Another reason why people don't do what's good for them is that they may feel social pressures to engage in unhealthful behavior, as when an adolescent begins to use cigarettes, alcohol, or drugs. Also, some behaviors can become very strong habits,

perhaps involving a physical addiction or psychological dependency, as happens with drugs and cigarettes. Quitting them becomes very difficult. Lastly, sometimes people are simply not aware of the dangers involved or how to change their behavior. These people need information about ways to protect their health.

Personality and Illness

Do you believe, as many do, that people who suffer from ulcers tend to be worriers or "workaholics"? Or that people who have migraine headaches are highly anxious? If you do, then you believe there is a link between personality and illness. The term **personality** refers to a person's cognitive, affective, or behavioral tendencies that are fairly stable across time and situations.

Researchers have found evidence linking personality traits and health. For example, people whose personalities include:

- Low levels of *conscientiousness* measured in childhood or adulthood are more likely to die at earlier ages, such as from cardiovascular diseases, than individuals high in conscientiousness (Kern & Friedman, 2008; Terracciano et al., 2008).

What risk factors for disease does this photo suggest this boy has developed?

- High levels of *positive emotions*, such as happiness or enthusiasm, tend to live longer than individuals with low levels of these emotions (Chida & Steptoe, 2008; Xu & Roberts, 2010).

- High levels of *anxiety*, *depression*, *hostility*, or *pessimism* are at risk for dying early and developing a variety of illnesses, particularly heart disease (Grossardt et al., 2009; Smith & Gallo, 2001).

Anxiety, depression, hostility, and pessimism are reactions that often occur when people experience stress, such as when they have more work to do than they think they can finish or when a tragedy happens. Many people approach these situations with relatively positive emotions. Their outlook is more optimistic than pessimistic, more hopeful than desperate. These people are not only less likely to become ill than are people with less positive personalities, but when they do, they tend to recover more quickly (Scheier & Carver, 2001; Smith & Gallo, 2001).

The link between personality and illness is not a one-way street: illness can affect one's personality, too (Cohen & Rodriguez, 1995). People who suffer from serious illness and disability often experience feelings of anxiety, depression, anger, and hopelessness. But even minor health problems, such as the flu or a toothache, produce temporary negative thoughts and feelings (Sarason & Sarason, 1984). People who are ill and overcome their negative thoughts and feelings can speed their recovery. We will examine this relationship in more detail later in this book.

Our glimpse at the relationships of the person's lifestyle and personality in illness demonstrates why it is important to consider psychological and social factors in health and illness. Next we will see how this recognition came about.

HOW THE ROLE OF PSYCHOLOGY EMERGED

The idea that medicine and psychology are somehow connected has a long history, dating back at least to ancient Greece. It became somewhat more formalized early in the 20th century in the work of Sigmund Freud, who was trained as a doctor. He noticed that some patients showed physical symptoms with no detectable organic disorder. Using his *psychoanalytic theory*, Freud proposed that these symptoms were "converted" from unconscious emotional conflicts (Alexander, 1950). He called this condition *conversion hysteria*; one form it can take is called *glove anesthesia* because only the hand has no feeling. Symptoms like these occur less often in urban than in backwoods areas, perhaps because urbanites realize that medical tests can generally determine if an

organic disorder exists (Kring et al., 2010). The need to understand conditions such as conversion hysteria led to the development of psychosomatic medicine, the first field dedicated to studying the interplay between emotional life and bodily processes.

Psychosomatic Medicine

The field called **psychosomatic medicine** was formed in the 1930s and began publishing the journal *Psychosomatic Medicine* (Alexander, 1950). Its founders were mainly trained in medicine, and their leaders included psychoanalysts and psychiatrists. The field was soon organized as a society now called the American Psychosomatic Society.

The term *psychosomatic* does not mean a person's symptoms are "imaginary"; it means that the mind and body are both involved. Early research in psychosomatic medicine focused on psychoanalytic interpretations for specific, real health problems, including ulcers, high blood pressure, asthma, migraine headaches, and rheumatoid arthritis. For example, Alexander (1950) described the case of a 23-year-old man with a bleeding ulcer and proposed that the man's relationship with his mother created feelings of insecurity and dependence that caused the ulcer. The man's stomach problems later decreased, presumably because he overcame these feelings through therapy. Over the years, the field's approaches and theories evolved (Duberstein, 2004). It is currently a broader field concerned with interrelationships among psychological and social factors, biological and physiological functions, and the development and course of illness.

Behavioral Medicine and Health Psychology

Two new fields emerged in the 1970s to study the role of psychology in illness: one is called behavioral medicine, and the other is called health psychology.

The field of **behavioral medicine** formed an organization called the Society of Behavioral Medicine, which publishes the *Annals of Behavioral Medicine*. This field has two defining characteristics (Gentry, 1984): First, its membership is *interdisciplinary*, coming from a wide variety of fields, including psychology, sociology, and various areas of medicine. Second, it grew out of the perspective in psychology called *behaviorism*, which proposed that people's behavior results from two types of learning:

- *Classical (or respondent) conditioning*, in which a stimulus (the conditioned stimulus) gains the ability to elicit a response through association with a stimulus (the unconditioned stimulus) that already elicits that response.

- *Operant conditioning*, in which behavior is changed because of its consequences: *reinforcement* (reward) strengthens the behavior; *punishment* suppresses it.

Conditioning methods had shown a good deal of success as therapeutic approaches in helping people modify problem *behaviors*, such as overeating, and *emotions*, such as anxiety and fear (Sarafino, 2001). By the 1970s, physiological psychologists had clearly shown that psychological events—particularly emotions—influence bodily functions, such as blood pressure. And researchers had demonstrated that people can learn to control various physiological systems if they are given *feedback* as to what the systems are doing (Miller, 1978).

Why were these findings important? They revealed that the link between the mind and the body is more direct and pervasive than was previously thought. Soon they led to an important therapeutic technique called *biofeedback*, whereby a person's physiological processes, such as blood pressure, are monitored by the person so that he or she can gain voluntary control over them. This process involves operant conditioning: the feedback serves as reinforcement. As we shall see in later chapters, biofeedback has proven to be useful in treating a variety of health problems, such as headaches.

Behaviorism also served as an important foundation for **health psychology**, a field that is principally within the discipline of psychology. The American Psychological Association has many divisions, or subfields; the Division of Health Psychology was introduced in 1978 (Sarafino, 2004b) and soon began publishing the journal *Health Psychology*. Joseph Matarazzo (1982), the first president of the Division, outlined four goals of health psychology.

Let's look at these goals and some ways psychologists can contribute to them.

- To *promote and maintain health.* Health psychologists study such topics as why people do and do not smoke cigarettes, exercise, drink alcohol, and eat particular diets. As a result, these professionals can help in the design of school health education programs and media campaigns to encourage healthful lifestyles and behaviors.

- To *prevent and treat illness.* Psychological principles have been applied effectively in preventing illness, such as in reducing high blood pressure. For people who become seriously ill, psychologists with clinical training can help them adjust to their current condition, rehabilitation program, and future prospects, such as reduced work or sexual activity.

- To *identify the causes and diagnostic correlates of health, illness, and related dysfunction.* Health psychologists study the causes of disease; the research we saw earlier showing the importance of personality factors in the development of illness is an example of the work toward this goal. Psychologists also study physiological and perceptual processes, which affect people's experience of physical symptoms.

- To *analyze and improve health care systems and health policy.* Health psychologists contribute toward this goal by studying and advising medical professionals on ways by which characteristics or functions of hospitals, nursing homes, medical personnel, and medical costs affect patients and their likelihood of following medical advice.

Psychologists work to achieve these goals in a variety of ways, some of which involve applying techniques that were derived from behaviorism. (Go to ♠.)

CLINICAL METHODS AND ISSUES

Behaviorism's Legacy: Progress in Health Psychology's Goals

The perspective of behaviorism led to the development of *behavior modification* techniques, which use principles of learning and cognition to understand and change people's behavior (Sarafino, 2001). These techniques can be grouped into two categories: **Behavioral methods** apply mainly principles of operant and classical conditioning to change behavior. **Cognitive methods** are geared toward changing people's feelings and thought processes, such as by helping individuals identify and alter problematic beliefs; most cognitive methods were developed after the mid-1960s.

How can professionals use behavioral and cognitive methods to promote and maintain people's health and to prevent and treat illness? Let's consider two examples. Using behavioral methods, psychologists reduced work-related injuries at worksites with high accident rates by applying a program of reinforcement for safety behaviors (Fox, Hopkins, & Anger, 1987). In an example that used cognitive methods with patients suffering from chronic back pain, a psychologist reduced their degree of pain, depression, and disability by providing training in ways to relax and think differently about the pain (Turner, 1982).

An Integration

By now you may be wondering, "Aren't psychosomatic medicine, behavioral medicine, and health psychology basically the same?" In a sense they are—they have very similar goals, study similar topics, and share the same knowledge. The three fields are separate mainly in an organizational sense, and many professionals are members of all three organizations. The main distinctions among the fields are the degree of focus they give to specific topics and viewpoints, and the particular disciplines and professions involved. Psychosomatic medicine is closely tied to medical disciplines, including psychiatry, but works with behavioral scientists to understand and treat physical illness. Behavioral medicine involves professionals in several disciplines and tends to focus on studying and applying methods to promote healthy lifestyles without the use of drugs or surgery. Health psychology is based in psychology and draws heavily on other subfields—clinical, social, developmental, and physiological—to identify and alter lifestyle and emotional processes that lead to illness and to improve recovery for people who are sick. Although this book focuses mainly on health psychology, all three fields share the view that health and illness result from the interplay of biological, psychological, and social forces.

HEALTH PSYCHOLOGY: THE PROFESSION

Because the field of health psychology is so new, the profession is expanding quickly. Most health psychologists work in hospitals, clinics, and academic departments of colleges and universities. In these positions, they either provide direct help to patients or give indirect help through research, teaching, and consulting activities.

The direct help health psychologists provide generally relates to the patient's psychological adjustment to and management of health problems. Health psychologists with clinical training can provide therapy for emotional and social adjustment problems that being ill or disabled can produce—for example, in reducing the patient's feelings of depression. They can also help patients manage the health problem by, for instance, teaching them psychological methods, such as biofeedback, to control pain.

Health psychologists provide indirect help, too. Their research provides information about lifestyle and personality factors in illness and injury. They can apply this and other knowledge to design programs that help people practice more healthful lifestyles, such as by preventing or quitting cigarette smoking.

They can also educate health professionals toward a fuller understanding of the psychosocial needs of patients.

The qualifications for becoming a health psychologist vary across countries, but they usually include completion of the doctoral degree in psychology (Belar & McIntyre, 2004). Additional study may be needed if the doctoral program contained little training in health psychology. *Clinical health psychology* is a recognized specialty of the American Psychological Association. State licensing is required to practice clinical techniques in the United States, and board certification is available (Belar & McIntyre, 2004).

CURRENT PERSPECTIVES ON HEALTH AND ILLNESS

Once we add the person to the biomedical model, we have a different and broader picture of how health and illness come about. This new perspective, called the **biopsychosocial model**, expands the biomedical view by adding to *biological* factors connections to *psychological* and *social* factors (Engel, 1977, 1980; Kazarian & Evans, 2001). This new model proposes that all three factors *affect* and *are affected by* the person's health.

THE BIOPSYCHOSOCIAL PERSPECTIVE

Let's look at the elements of the biopsychosocial model in more detail.

The Role of Biological Factors

What is included in the term *biological factors*? This term includes the genetic materials and processes by which we inherit characteristics from our parents. It also includes the function and structure of the person's physiology. For example, does the body contain structural defects, such as a malformed heart valve or damage in the brain, that impair the operation of these organs? Does the body respond effectively in protecting itself, such as by fighting infection? Does the body overreact sometimes in the protective function, as happens in many allergic reactions to harmless substances, such as pollen or dust?

The body is made up of enormously complex physical systems. For instance, it has organs, bones, and nerves, and these are composed of tissues, which in turn consist of cells, molecules, and atoms. The efficient, effective, and healthful functioning of these systems depends on the way these components operate and interact with each other.

The Role of Psychological Factors

When we discussed the role of lifestyle and personality in health and illness earlier, we were describing behavior and mental processes. Behavior and mental processes are the focus of psychology, and they involve cognition, emotion, and motivation.

Cognition is a mental activity that encompasses perceiving, learning, remembering, thinking, interpreting, believing, and problem solving. How do these cognitive factors affect health and illness? Suppose, for instance, you strongly believe, "Life is not worth living without the things I enjoy." If you enjoy smoking cigarettes, would you quit to reduce your risk of getting cancer or heart disease? Probably not. Or suppose you develop a pain in your abdomen and you remember having had a similar symptom in the past that disappeared in a couple of days. Would you seek treatment? Again, probably not. These examples are just two of the countless ways cognition plays a role in health and illness.

Emotion is a subjective feeling that affects and is affected by our thoughts, behavior, and physiology. Some emotions are positive or pleasant, such as joy and affection, and others are negative, such as anger, fear, and sadness. Emotions relate to health and illness in many ways. For instance, people whose emotions are relatively positive are less disease-prone and more likely to take good care of their health and to recover quickly from an illness than are people whose emotions are relatively negative. We considered these relationships when we discussed the role of personality in illness. Emotions can also be important in people's decisions about seeking treatment. People who are frightened of doctors and dentists may avoid getting the health care they need.

Motivation is the process within individuals that gets them to start some activity, choose its direction, and persist in it. A person who is motivated to feel and look better might begin an exercise program, choose the goals to be reached, and stick with it. Many people are motivated to do what important people in their lives want them to do. Parents who quit smoking because their child pleads with them to protect their health are an example.

The Role of Social Factors

People live in a social world. We have relationships with individual people—a family member, a friend, or an acquaintance—and with groups. As we interact with people, we affect them, and they affect us. For example, adolescents often start smoking cigarettes and drinking alcohol as a result of peer pressure (Murphy & Bennett, 2004). They want very much to be popular and to look "cool" or "tough" to schoolmates and others. These social processes provide clear and powerful motivational forces. But our social world is larger than just the people we know or meet.

On a fairly broad level, our *society* affects the health of individuals by promoting certain values of our culture, such as that being fit and healthy is good. The mass media—television, newspapers, and so on—often reflect these values by setting good examples and urging us to eat well, not to use drugs, and not to drink

Society can help prevent disease or injury in many ways, such as through advertisements against smoking.

and drive. The media can do much to promote health, but sometimes they encourage unhealthful behavior, such as when children see jazzy TV commercials for sweet, nutrient-poor foods (Harris et al., 2009). Can individuals affect society's values? Yes, by writing our opinions to the mass media and lawmakers, selecting which television shows and movies to watch, and buying healthful products, for example.

Our *community* consists of individuals who live fairly near one another, such as in the same town or county, and organizations, such as government. The influence of communities is suggested in the research finding that they differ in the extent to which their members practice certain health-related behaviors, such as smoking cigarettes or consuming fatty foods (Diehr et al., 1993). There are many reasons for these differences. For instance, a community's environmental characteristics seem to influence residents' physical activity and diets (Sallis et al., 2006; Story et al., 2008). Residents tend to be more physically active and have healthier diets in communities that have parks, are safe, and have stores and restaurants with large selections of high-quality fruits, vegetables, and low-fat products.

The closest and most continuous social relationships for most people occur within the *family*, which can include nonrelatives who live together and share a strong emotional bond. As individuals grow and develop in childhood, the family has an especially strong influence (Murphy & Bennett, 2004). Children learn many health-related behaviors and ideas from their parents, brothers, and sisters. Parents can set good examples for healthful behavior by using seat belts, serving and eating nutritious meals, exercising, not smoking, and so on. Families can also encourage children to perform healthful behaviors and praise them when they do. And as we have said, an individual can influence the larger social unit. A family may stop eating certain nutritious foods, such as broccoli or fish, because one member has a tantrum when these foods are served.

The role of biological, psychological, and social factors in health and illness is not hard to see. What is more difficult to understand is how health is affected by the *interplay* of these components, as the biopsychosocial model proposes. The next section deals with this interplay.

The Concept of "Systems"

"We need to understand the whole person," you've probably heard a professional say. This statement reflects the recognition that people and the reasons for their behavior are very complex. Many health professionals strive to consider all aspects of people's lives in understanding health and illness. This approach uses the biopsychosocial model and is sometimes called *holistic*, a term many people use and define to include a wide range of "alternative" approaches to promote health, such as treatments that use aromas and herbs to heal.

We can conceptualize the whole person by applying the biological concept of "systems" (Engel, 1980). A **system** is a dynamic entity with components that are continuously interrelated. By this definition, your body qualifies as a system, and it includes the immune and nervous systems, which consist of tissues and cells. Your family is a system, too, and so are your community and society. There are levels of systems, as Figure 1-4 depicts. If we look at levels within the person, illness in one part of the body can have far-reaching effects: if you fell and

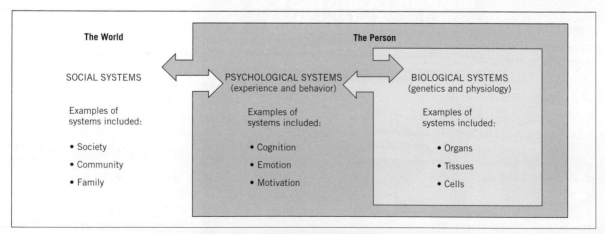

Figure 1–4   A diagram of the interplay of systems in the biopsychosocial model. The person consists of biological and psychological systems, which interrelate; and each of the systems includes component systems. The person interrelates with the social systems of his or her world. Each system can affect and be affected by any of the other systems.

seriously injured your leg, your internal systems would be automatically mobilized to help protect the body from further damage. In addition, the discomfort and disability you might experience for days or weeks might affect your social relations with your family and community. As systems, they are entities that are constantly changing, and they have components that interrelate, such as by exchanging energy, substances, and information.

To illustrate how the systems concept can be useful, let's use it to speculate how a teenage girl's weight problem might have come about. Let's assume that she inherited some factor that affects her weight, such as a liking for sweet foods. When she was a toddler, her parents were not concerned that she was getting heavy because they believed a popular misconception: "A chubby baby is a healthy baby." The meals the family ate usually contained lots of high-fat, high-calorie foods and a sweet dessert. Because this girl was heavy, she was less agile, tired more easily than children who were not overweight, and preferred to engage in sedentary activities, such as playing with dolls or watching television, rather than sports. She and her friends snacked on cookies while watching television commercials that promoted high-fat, sweet breakfast and snack foods, which she got her parents to buy. Thus, interacting biopsychosocial systems can contribute to a person's weight problem.

Using the biopsychosocial model as a guide, researchers have discovered new and important findings and ways to promote people's health and recovery from illness. Here is a sample of discoveries that we will discuss in later chapters:

- Using psychological methods to reduce anxiety of patients who are awaiting surgery enables them to recover more quickly and leave the hospital sooner.
- Programs that teach safer sex practices have dramatically reduced risky sexual behavior and the spread of HIV infection.
- People who have a high degree of social support from family and friends are healthier and live longer than people who do not.
- Stress impairs the functioning of the immune system.
- Applying psychological and educational programs for heart disease patients reduces their feelings of depression and enables them to live longer.
- Biofeedback and other psychological techniques can reduce the pain of people who suffer from chronic, severe headaches.

LIFE-SPAN AND GENDER PERSPECTIVES

People change over time through the process called "development," and each portion of the life span is affected by happenings in earlier years and affects the happenings in years that will come. Throughout people's lives, health, illness, and the role of different biopsychosocial systems change. Gender also plays a role, such as in the health-related behaviors people perform and the illnesses they develop. This is why it's important to keep the life span and gender perspectives in mind when we examine health psychology.

In the *life-span perspective*, characteristics of a person are considered with respect to their prior development, current level, and likely development in the future (Hayman, 2007). Health and illness characteristics vary with development. For instance, the kinds of illnesses people have tend to change with age. Compared with older people, children are less likely to experience activity limitations from chronic diseases (USBC, 2010). Illnesses that keep children out of school tend to be short-term infectious diseases, such as colds or the flu. In contrast, many people in late adulthood and old age suffer from heart disease, cancer, and stroke, which often result in disability and death. *Pediatrics* and *geriatrics* are branches of medicine that deal with the health and illness of children and the elderly, respectively.

How do the roles of different biopsychosocial systems change as we develop? Biological systems change in many ways. Virtually all systems of the body grow in size, strength, and efficiency during childhood and decline in old age. The decline can be seen in the slowing down that older people notice in their physical abilities. They have less stamina because the heart and lungs function less efficiently and the muscles are weaker (Tortora & Derrickson, 2009). They also recover from illness and injury more slowly.

Changes occur in psychological systems, too—for example, in cognitive processes. Children's knowledge and ability to think are limited during the preschool years but grow rapidly during later childhood. Before children can assume responsibility for their health, they need to understand how their behavior can affect it. As children get older and their cognitive skills improve, they are better able to understand the implications of their own illness when they are sick and the rationales for behaviors that promote their health and safety (Murphy & Bennett, 2004).

How do people's social relationships and systems change with development? For one thing, there are some usual progressions: children usually progress through levels of education, enter a career in adulthood, become parents and grandparents, and retire in old age. Changes in social relationships also relate to health and illness. Children's health is largely the responsibility of adult caregivers—parents and teachers. During the teenage years, adolescents take on more and more of these responsibilities. But age-mates in the community have a powerful influence, and the need to be accepted by peers sometimes leads teens toward unhealthful or unsafe behavior. For example, an adolescent who has a chronic illness that can be controlled—as diabetes can—may neglect his or her medical care to avoid looking and feeling different from other teens (La Greca & Stone, 1985).

The *gender perspective* also adds an important dimension to the biopsychosocial perspective in our effort to understand how people deal with issues of health and illness. Males and females differ in their biological functioning; their health-related behaviors and social relationships, such as drinking, dieting, and using safer-sex practices; and the risk of specific illnesses, such as breast cancer.

RELATING HEALTH PSYCHOLOGY TO OTHER SCIENCE FIELDS

Knowledge in health psychology is greatly enriched by information from many other disciplines, including some disciplines within *psychology*, such as the clinical and social areas; *medicine*, including psychiatry and pediatrics; and *allied fields*, such as nursing, nutrition, pharmacology, biology, and social work. We will look at four fields that are very important because they provide information and a context for health psychology.

RELATED FIELDS

To understand health psychology fully, we need to know the context in which health and illness exist. The field of *epidemiology*—the scientific study of the distribution and frequency of disease and injury—provides part of this context. Researchers in this field determine the occurrence of illness in a given population and organize these data in terms of when the disease or injury occurred, where, and to which age, gender, and racial or cultural groups. Then they attempt to discover why specific illnesses are distributed as they are. You have probably seen the results of epidemiologists' work in the mass media. For example, news reports have described areas of the United States where Lyme disease, a tick-borne illness, occurs at high levels and where certain forms of cancer are linked to high levels of toxic substances in the environment.

Epidemiologists use several terms in describing aspects of their findings (Gerace & Vorp, 1985; Runyan, 1985). We will define five of these terms:

- **Mortality** means death, generally on a large scale. An epidemiologist might report a decrease in mortality from heart disease among women, for instance.
- **Morbidity** means illness, injury, or disability—basically any detectable departure from wellness.
- **Prevalence** refers to the number of cases, such as of a disease or of persons infected or at risk. It includes both continuing (previously reported) and new cases at a given moment in time—for example, the number of cases of asthma as of the first day of the current year.
- **Incidence** refers to the number of *new* cases, such as of illness, infection, or disability, reported during a period of time. An example is the number of new tuberculosis cases in the previous year.
- **Epidemic** usually refers to the situation in which the incidence, generally of an infectious disease, has increased rapidly.

Some of these terms are used with the word *rate*, which adds relativity to the meaning. For instance, the mortality rate gives the number of deaths per number of people in a given population during a specified period of time. An example might be a mortality rate of 5 babies per 1,000 births dying in their first year of life in the current year in Canada.

Another discipline of importance to health psychology is *public health*, the field concerned with protecting, maintaining, and improving health through organized effort in the community. People who work in public health do research and set up programs to promote or provide inoculations, sanitation, health education and awareness, and community health services (Runyan, 1985). This field studies health and illness in the context of the community as a social system. The success of public health programs and the way individual people react to them are of interest to health psychologists.

Two other related fields are sociology and anthropology (Adler & Stone, 1979). *Sociology* focuses on human social life; it examines groups or communities of people and evaluates the impact of various social factors, such as the mass media, population growth, epidemics, and institutions. *Medical sociology* is a subfield that studies a wide range of issues related to health, including the impact of social relationships on the distribution of illness, social reactions to illness, socioeconomic factors of health care use, and the way hospital services and medical practices are organized. *Anthropology* includes the study of human cultures. Its subfield, *medical anthropology*, examines differences in health and health care across cultures: How do the nature and definition of illness vary across different cultures? How do people in these cultures react to illness, and what methods do they use to treat disease or injury? How do they structure health care systems? Without the knowledge from sociology and anthropology, health psychologists would have a very narrow view. Knowledge from sociology and anthropology gives us a broad social and cultural view of medical issues and allows us to consider different ways to interpret and treat illness.

The combined information health psychologists obtain from epidemiology, public health, sociology, and anthropology paints a broad picture for us. It describes the social systems in which health, illness, and the person exist and develop. (Go to 💡.)

HIGHLIGHT

Related Nonpsychology Careers

The process of providing care for a patient who is suffering from a chronic illness, serious injury, or disability involves a variety of professionals working together with doctors as a team. Each professional has specific training for a special role in the treatment or rehabilitation process. Most of them have some education in psychology. We've already seen how health psychologists can play a role. Let's look at some careers outside of psychology.

Nurses and Medical Care Practitioners

There are two overall categories of nurses: *registered nurses* (RNs) and *state enrolled nurses* (SENs). RNs work in hospitals, community health clinics, doctors offices, and industrial settings. They assess and record patients' symptoms and progress, conduct tests, administer medications, assist in rehabilitation, provide instructions for self-treatment, and instruct patients and their families in ways to improve or maintain their health. RNs often deal with mental and emotional aspects of the patient as well. RNs must be licensed to practice, have graduated from an approved training program in nursing, and have passed a national examination. RN training programs vary in structure and length; college and university programs take about 4 years and lead to a baccalaureate degree.

SENs work in hospitals, clinics, doctors' offices, and patients' homes. They perform nursing activities that require less training than those performed by RNs. For example, they take and record temperatures and blood pressures, administer certain medications, change dressings, assist doctors or RNs, and help patients with personal hygiene. Like RNs, SENs must be licensed to practice and have graduated from an approved practical nursing program. Training programs for SENs take about a year to complete and are offered through various types of institutions, such as trade and vocational schools, community and junior colleges, and hospitals.

Medical care practitioners and *nurse practitioners* usually work closely with medical doctors, performing routine tasks that doctors ordinarily did in the past, such as examining patients with symptoms that do not appear serious and explaining treatment details. Training involves a program of about 2 years of study; admission often requires that applicants have had at least 2 years of college and health care experience.

Dietitians

Dietitians study and apply knowledge about food and its effect on the body. They do this in a variety of settings, such as hospitals, clinics, nursing homes, colleges, and schools. Some dietitians are administrators; others work directly with patients in assessing nutritional needs, implementing and evaluating dietary plans, and instructing patients and their families on ways to adhere to needed diets after discharge from the hospital. Some dietitians work for social service agencies in the community, where they counsel people on nutritional practices to help maintain health and speed recovery when they are ill.

Becoming a dietitian requires a bachelor's or master's degree specializing in nutrition sciences or institutional management. To become a Registered Dietitian, the individual must complete a supervised internship and pass an exam.

Physical Therapists

Many patients need help in restoring functional movement to parts of their body and relieving pain. If they have suffered a disabling injury or disease, treatment may be needed to prevent or limit permanent disability. *Physical therapists* plan and apply treatment for these goals in rehabilitation.

To plan the treatment, physical therapists review the patient's records and perform tests or measurements of muscle strength, motor coordination, endurance, and range of motion of the injured body part. Treatment is designed to increase the strength and function of the injured part and aid in the patient's adaptation to having reduced physical abilities, which may be quite drastic. People who have suffered severe strokes are sometimes

(continued)

left partially paralyzed, for instance. The most universal technique used in physical therapy involves exercise, generally requiring little effort initially and becoming more and more challenging. Another technique involves electrical stimulation to move paralyzed muscles or reduce pain. Physical therapists also give instructions for carrying out everyday tasks, such as tying shoelaces or cooking meals. If the patient needs to use adaptive devices, such as crutches or a prosthesis (replacement limb), the therapist provides training.

Physical therapists must have completed an approved training program and be licensed by passing an exam.

Occupational Therapists

Occupational therapists help physically, mentally, and emotionally disabled individuals gain skills needed for daily activities in a work setting, at school, in the community, and at home. Their patients are often people who had these skills at one time, but lost them because of an injury or disease, such as muscular dystrophy. These professionals usually specialize in working with a particular age group, such as the elderly, and a type of disability—physical, for example. They design and implement educational, vocational, and recreational activities based on the patient's age and the type and

degree of disability. The program for a child, for instance, might involve academic tasks and crafts; for an adult, it might involve typing, driving a vehicle, and using hand and power tools.

Occupational therapists must be licensed by passing an exam.

Social Workers

The field of *social work* is quite broad. Probably most social workers are employed in mental health programs, but many others work in hospitals, nursing homes, rehabilitation centers, and public health programs. When working with people who are physically ill or disabled, social workers help patients and their families make psychological and social adjustments to the illness and obtain needed community services, including income maintenance. Thus, social workers may arrange for needed nursing care at home after a patient leaves the hospital or refer a patient for vocational counseling and occupational therapy if the illness or disability requires a career change.

Social workers must be licensed or certified to practice. Training requires a bachelor's degree in a social science field, usually social work, but often a degree in psychology or sociology is sufficient. Many positions require a master's degree in social work, the MSW degree.

HEALTH AND PSYCHOLOGY ACROSS CULTURES

Health and illness have changed across the history and cultures of the world, as the following excerpt shows:

> Less than a hundred years ago the infant mortality rate in Europe and North America was as high as it is in the developing world now. In New York City in the year 1900, for example, the IMR [infant mortality rate] was approximately 140 per 1,000—about the same as in Bangladesh today. In the city of Birmingham, England a survey taken in 1906 revealed an IMR of almost 200 per 1,000—higher than almost any country in the world in the 1980s. A look behind these statistics also shows that the main causes of infant death in New York and Birmingham *then* were much the same as in the developing world *now*—diarrheal disease and malnutrition, respiratory infections, and whooping cough. (UNICEF, cited in Skolnick, 1986, p. 20)

The world view we get from historical–cultural comparisons can be quite dramatic. Each country's

present culture is different from every other's and from the culture it had 200 years ago. Lifestyles have changed in each culture, and so has the pattern of illnesses that afflict its citizens.

Sociocultural Differences in Health

The term **sociocultural** means involving or relating to social and cultural factors, such as ethnic and income variations within and across nations. The World Health Organization collects epidemiological data on sociocultural differences in health by regions of the world (WHO, 2008). They reported, for instance, that the incidence rates (per 100,000 population) for certain forms of cancer are much higher for some regions than others. The incidence rates for lung and colon cancers are low for Eastern Mediterranean nations (21 countries, including Morocco, Pakistan, and Saudi Arabia) and high for Western Pacific nations (27, including China, Japan, New Zealand, and Singapore). Sociocultural health differences also occur within specific countries. In the

United States, for example, Whites and American Indians have about 2 1/2 times the incidence rate for kidney cancer as Asian Americans (ACS, 2009). And among males, African Americans have far higher rates of lung and prostate cancer than any other ethnic group. The differences we see in illness patterns between countries, regions, or ethnic groups result from many factors, including heredity, environmental pollution, economic barriers to health care, discrimination-based negative emotions, and cultural differences in people's diets, health-related beliefs, and values (Mays, Cochran, & Barnes, 2007; Whitfield et al., 2002). Although people around the world value good health, not all people have the attitudes, environments, and access to health care that promote good health.

Sociocultural Differences in Health Beliefs and Behavior

Differences across history and culture can also be seen in the ideas people have about the *causes* of illness. Recall our discussion of the widespread beliefs in the Middle Ages that evil spirits caused illness. Today, educated people in technological societies generally reject such ideas. But less sophisticated people often do not, as the following excerpt shows:

> I've heard of people with snakes in their body, how they got in there I don't know. And they take 'em someplace to a witch doctor and snakes come out. My sister, she had somethin', a snake that was in her arm. She was a young woman. I can remember her bein' sick, very sick … This thing was just runnin' up her arm, whatever it was, just runnin' up her arm. You could actually *see* it. (Snow, 1981, p. 86)

A disadvantaged person in the United States gave this account, which is typical of the level of knowledge generally found in people in underdeveloped regions or countries. This is important to recognize because the large majority of people in the world live in underdeveloped societies.

The United States has been described as a melting pot for immigrants from every corner of the world. Immigrants carry with them health ideas and customs from their former countries. For example, many Chinese immigrants have entered their new country with the belief that illness results from an imbalance of two opposing forces, *yin* and *yang*, within the body (Campbell & Chang, 1981). According to this view, too much *yin* causes colds and gastric disorders, for instance, and too much *yang* causes fever and dehydration. Practitioners of traditional Chinese medicine try to correct an imbalance by prescribing special herbs and foods or by using *acupuncture*, in which fine needles are inserted under the skin at special locations of the body. Immigrants and others with these beliefs often use these methods when sick instead of, or as a supplement to, treatment by an American doctor. They may also pressure their family members to do this, too: a pregnant Chinese woman who was a registered nurse "followed her obstetrician's orders, but at the same time, under pressure from her mother and mother-in-law, ate special herbs and foods to insure birth of a healthy baby" (Campbell & Chang, 1981, p. 164).

Religion is an aspect of culture. Many religions include beliefs that relate to health and illness. For instance, Jehovah's Witnesses reject the use of blood and blood products in medical treatment (Sacks & Koppes, 1986). Christian Scientists reject the use of medicine, believing that only mental processes in the sick person can cure the illness. As a result, sick persons need prayer and counsel as treatment to help these processes along (Henderson & Primeaux, 1981). These beliefs are controversial and have led to legal conflicts between members of these religions and health authorities in the United States, particularly when parents reject medical treatments for life-threatening illnesses for their children. In such cases, the doctor and hospital can move quickly to seek an immediate judicial decision (Sacks & Koppes, 1986).

Some religions include specific beliefs that promote healthful lifestyles. Seventh-day Adventists, for example, believe that the body is the "temple of the Holy Spirit" and cite this belief as the reason people should take care of their bodies. Adventists abstain from using tobacco, alcohol, and nonmedically prescribed drugs. In addition, they promote in fellow members a concern for exercise and eating a healthful diet (Henderson & Primeaux, 1981). Although it is clear that cultural factors play a role in health, our knowledge about this role is meager and needs to be expanded through more research.

RESEARCH METHODS

Contemporary mass media present lots of scientific findings. Diets high in fiber and low in saturated fats are good for your health. Smoking is not. Dozens of toxic, or poisonous, chemicals can cause cancer. How do scientists discover these relationships? What methods do they use?

Scientists do research. Often their research is planned and conducted to test a **theory**—a *tentative explanation* of why and under what circumstances certain events occur (Michie & Prestwich, 2010). For example, a leading theory of the cause of heart disease is that excess *cholesterol*, a fatty substance in the blood, is deposited in artery walls. This buildup hardens and narrows the diameter of the artery, thereby causing tissue damage to the heart if the flow of blood in an artery becomes blocked. Cholesterol comes from two sources. Most cholesterol in the blood is manufactured by the body; the rest of it comes from the foods we eat—especially red meats, egg yolks, butter and some oils, and most cheeses.

The cholesterol theory is one of several useful theories of heart disease. By useful we don't necessarily mean that it is correct. We mean that it:

- Is clearly stated.
- Brings together or organizes known facts.
- Relates information that previously seemed unrelated.
- Enables us to make predictions, such as what would happen if cholesterol levels were reduced.

Useful theories play an important role in all sciences. Because theories offer predictions, they guide research programs by suggesting a "road map" of relationships to study.

As you think about the causes of heart disease, you'll realize that both the illness and the theoretical cause—in this case, high levels of cholesterol—can change or vary from one time to another and from one individual to another. That is, the condition of the heart and arteries and the amount of cholesterol in the blood are not constant. Because these things *vary*, they are called *variables*. A **variable** is any measurable characteristic of people, objects, or events that may change. The variables studied in research are of two types: an *independent variable* is studied for its potential or expected influence, as in the case of cholesterol levels; a *dependent variable* is assessed because its value, such as the condition of the heart, is expected to "depend" on the independent variable.

Researchers use a variety of *experimental* and *nonexperimental* methods to study health-related variables like the ones we've discussed (Sarafino, 2005).

EXPERIMENTS

An **experiment** is a controlled study in which researchers manipulate an independent variable to study its effect on a dependent variable. In a well-designed experiment—which is often called a *trial* in health research—all other variables are controlled or held constant. The term *manipulate* means that the researchers produce or introduce the levels of the independent variable they are studying.

The Experimental Method: A Hypothetical Example

To illustrate the experimental method, let's see how researchers might test the cholesterol theory of heart

disease. One prediction, or *hypothesis*, from the theory is that people's incidence of heart disease should decrease if they reduce their cholesterol levels. We could test this hypothesis by lowering some people's cholesterol levels and seeing if these people develop fewer heart attacks over a suitable period of time than they otherwise would. How can we lower their cholesterol levels? There are two ways to manipulate this independent variable, both of which would require including medical professionals in the research team. One way is to alter the people's diets, and the other is to have them take a cholesterol-lowering drug regularly. We will use the latter approach and assume, for our example, that the drug is new and the only one available.

We'd start the research by selecting a fairly large sample of people—preferably at least middle-aged, because they have a relatively high risk of having a heart attack in the near future. Then we assign them *randomly* to the conditions or groups in the experiment. One way to assign them randomly is to put their names on cards in a bowl, mix up the cards, and draw the cards out one at a time. The first name drawn would be assigned to one group, the second name to another group, and so on. By doing this, we can *equate the groups*, distributing the people's existing characteristics, such as personality and genetic factors, fairly equally across groups. As a result, the characteristics will have about the same impact on the dependent variable (heart attacks) for each of the groups.

To test the hypothesis, we will need two groups of people. One group receives the experimental treatment, the cholesterol-lowering pills, and is called the *experimental group*. The other group receives their usual care without the drug, and is called the *control group* (or *comparison* group). By administering the drug to and lowering the cholesterol level of one group, but not the other, we are manipulating the independent variable. We then observe over several years the incidence of heart attacks. If the experimental group has fewer heart attacks than the control group, the hypothesis is supported.

You may be wondering, "Isn't it possible that a decrease in heart attacks for the experimental group could result *not* from the drug per se, but simply from taking *any* substance a medical person prescribes?" Sometimes people's beliefs or expectations can affect their health (Ader, 1997; Rehm & Nayak, 2004). To control for this possibility, we would have a third group: they'd receive an inert, or inactive, substance or procedure—called a **placebo**—in the form of pills that look like medicine. The placebo group would be given the same instructions as the experimental group, and both would have equal expectations about the effectiveness of the pills. Any influence the placebo has on the dependent variable is called a *placebo effect*.

One other control procedure is needed: the person who distributes the pills should not know which pills contain the active drug. Why? This person could inadvertently bias the outcome of the experiment, such as by giving instructions offhandedly to the placebo group but emphatically and precisely to the experimental group. Being unaware of which individuals are getting which treatment is called being *blind* as to the treatment. Since both the individuals receiving and distributing the pills are unaware, the method we are using is called the **double-blind** procedure.

Now that we have included these control procedures, let's look at the outcome of our hypothetical experiment. As Figure 1-5 shows, the people in the experimental group had far fewer heart attacks than those in the other groups. Thus we can conclude that lowering cholesterol levels in the blood causes a decrease in heart disease, as the theory predicts. Notice also in the graph that the people in the placebo group had somewhat fewer heart attacks than the controls. This suggests a placebo effect, with expectancy having some effect on heart disease, but not nearly as much as the active ingredient in the cholesterol-lowering drug.

You may have noticed that our conclusion used the word *causes*: lowering cholesterol "causes" a decrease in heart disease. To make a *cause-effect* conclusion, it must be clear that three criteria have been met:

- The levels of the independent and dependent variables corresponded or varied together.
- The cause preceded the effect.
- All other plausible causes have been ruled out.

Well-designed experiments, usually called *randomized controlled trials*, meet these requirements because the researchers use random assignment to equate the groups, manipulate the independent variable, and control variables that are not being studied. Other research approaches do not use experimental methods and do not provide the ability to determine what causes what.

Comparing Experimental and Nonexperimental Methods

Research always involves the study of variables, but in *nonexperimental methods*, the researchers either *do not manipulate an independent variable* and/or *do not equate the groups*. In addition, there is frequently less opportunity for precise measurement and for control of variables not being studied. As a result, although nonexperimental methods may be used to point out relationships between variables, they do *not* provide direct and unambiguous tests of cause-effect relationships.

Nonexperimental methods are nevertheless very valuable and have some important advantages. Sometimes it is simply not possible or feasible to assign subjects randomly and manipulate the variable of interest. We cannot manipulate the past lifestyles of people, for instance; the past has already happened. Nor can we have individuals in one group of a study do harmful things they would ordinarily not do simply to test an important theory. For instance, it would be unethical to assign people of a sample to a group in which they must smoke cigarettes for the next 5 years if some of these people do not smoke or want to quit. Even if it were ethical, nonsmokers might refuse to do it. What if we didn't

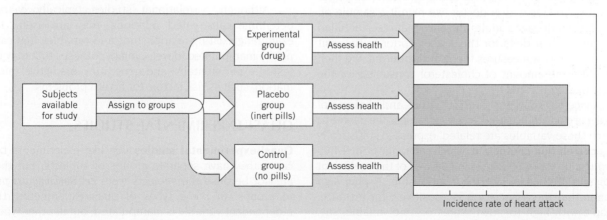

Figure 1-5   The left-hand portion of this diagram shows how the study would be carried out. Subjects (also called participants) are assigned to groups and, after a suitable period of time, the researcher checks whether they have had heart attacks. The right-hand portion illustrates how the results might appear on a graph: participants who received the anticholesterol drug had far fewer heart attacks than subjects in the placebo group, who had somewhat fewer attacks than those in the control group.

randomly assign individuals to groups? If we do not randomly assign them, the groups are not likely to be equal at the start of the study with respect to characteristics, such as genetics or past lifestyle, that could affect the outcome of the research. In situations like this in which ethical considerations prevent the study of humans in research, animals are sometimes used.

In many cases, the aim of a research project requires only that an association between variables be demonstrated. We may want to know, for instance, which people are at greatest risk for a disease so that we may help them avert it. Studies to determine risk factors are examples, which have revealed that people who are among the most likely to develop heart disease are male and/or over 50 years old (AHA, 2010). Researchers can determine this relationship without manipulating gender or age, and a nonexperimental method is, in fact, the most appropriate technique.

The rest of our examination of research methods will focus on nonexperimental approaches in research relating to health psychology and continue to use the cholesterol theory of heart disease as the basis for research examples. Let's turn to correlational studies as the first of these methods.

CORRELATIONAL STUDIES

The term *correlation* refers to the *co* or joint relation that exists between variables—changes in one variable correspond with changes in another variable. Suppose, for example, we did a study of two variables: heart function and people's diets, particularly the amount of cholesterol they consume. A measure of heart function is *cardiac output*, the amount of blood the heart pumps per minute. Working with a doctor, we recruit a sample of, say, 200 middle-aged adults and have them keep detailed records of their diets for the 2 weeks prior to the visit when the doctor measures their cardiac output. We then calculate the amount of cholesterol consumed on the basis of their records.

Once we know the cardiac output and cholesterol intake of each of the subjects, we can assess the degree to which these variables are related, expressed statistically as a **correlation coefficient**, which can range from $+1.00$ through .00 to -1.00. The sign ($+$ or $-$) of the coefficient indicates the *direction* of the relationship. A plus sign means that the association is "positive": for instance, people with high (or low) scores on one variable, say, cardiac output, tend to have high (low) scores on the other variable, such as blood pressure. Conversely, a minus sign means that the association is "negative": *high* scores on one variable tend to be associated with *low* scores on the other variable. For example, high cardiac

output is correlated with low concentrations of cells in the blood, because cells thicken the blood (Rhoades & Pflanzer, 1996). Thus, there is a negative correlation between cardiac output and concentration of blood cells.

Disregarding the sign of the correlation coefficient, the absolute value of the coefficient indicates the *strength* of association between variables. The higher the absolute value (that is, the closer to either $+1.0$ or -1.0), the stronger the correlation. As the absolute value decreases, the strength of the relationship declines. A coefficient approximating .00 means that the variables are not related. From the information we have just covered, we can now state a definition: **correlational studies** are nonexperimental investigations of the degree and direction of statistical association between two variables.

Let's suppose that our study revealed a strong negative correlation—a coefficient of $-.72$—between cardiac output and cholesterol intake. This would support the cholesterol theory, because low cholesterol intake should produce less fatty buildup to clog the arteries, thereby allowing the heart to pump more blood per minute. But we cannot say on the basis of our study that these events occurred, and we cannot conclude that low cholesterol intake *causes* high cardiac output. Why? Because we did not manipulate any variable—we simply measured what was there. It may be that some variable we did not measure was responsible for the correlation. For example, the people with low cholesterol intake may also have had low concentrations of blood cells, and it may have been this latter factor that was responsible for their high cardiac output. We don't know. We would only know for sure that the two variables have a strong negative relationship.

Although correlational studies typically cannot determine cause-effect relations, they are useful for examining existing relationships and variables that cannot be manipulated, developing hypotheses that may be tested experimentally, and generating predictive information, such as risk factors for health problems.

QUASI-EXPERIMENTAL STUDIES

Quasi-experimental studies *look* like experiments because they have separate groups of subjects, but they are not because the subjects were *not randomly assigned* to groups. In some types of quasi-experiments, the independent variable is manipulated, but in other types, it is not. A commonly used quasi-experimental approach is called an *ex post facto study*, in which subjects are categorized and placed in groups on the basis of an existing variable or circumstance. Groups based on gender (males and females), cholesterol level (high, moderate, and low), or diet (high-fat and low-fat) in the past year are examples.

We could do a quasi-experimental study relating to the cholesterol theory of heart disease in the following way. Suppose we wanted to see if people's cholesterol level at the time of a heart attack is associated with the severity of the attack. For this study, we could just consult the medical records of heart disease patients, since it is standard practice to assess both variables. We could categorize the patients as having a high or low cholesterol level at the time they were admitted to the hospital. Then we would determine whether the attacks were more severe for one group than for the other.

If we found that the high-cholesterol patients had the more severe heart attacks, could we conclude that higher levels of cholesterol in the blood cause more severe attacks? No—for the same reasons we've discussed before. We cannot tell what caused what. In fact, this particular study could have been turned around. We could have categorized the patients on the basis of the severity of their attacks and then compared these groups for cholesterol levels. We would have found the same relationship: severe heart attacks are associated with a high level of cholesterol in the blood.

In general, the conclusions from quasi-experimental studies are basically correlational. The relationships they reveal do not become causal simply because we categorize subjects. There are many variations to the quasi-experimental method. We will look at a few of the more important ones, beginning with retrospective and prospective approaches.

Retrospective and Prospective Approaches

The prefix *retro* means "back" or "backward," and *spective* comes from the Latin word meaning "to look." Thus, the **retrospective approach** uses procedures that look back at the histories of subjects, such as individuals who do or do not have a particular disease. The purpose of this approach is to find commonalities in the people's histories that may suggest why they developed the disease.

How is the retrospective approach used in a quasi-experimental study? We might identify two groups of individuals. One group would consist of people who have already developed a particular illness, such as heart disease. They would be compared against a control group, consisting of similar people without the disease. We would then examine the two groups for characteristics of their histories that are common to one group, but not the other. We might find, for example, that the heart disease victims reported having eaten higher-cholesterol diets during the preceding 10 years than the controls

did. Although the retrospective approach is relatively easy to implement, it has a potential shortcoming: when the procedures rely on people's memories, especially of long-past happenings, the likelihood of inaccurate reports increases.

The **prospective approach** uses procedures that look *forward* in the lives of individuals, by studying whether differences in a variable at one point in time are related to differences in another variable at a later time. We could do this to see whether certain characteristics or events in people's lives are associated with their eventual development of one or more diseases. In using the prospective approach, we would start by recruiting a large group of people—say, 2,000—who did not yet have the illness in question, heart disease. Periodically over several years we would interview them, have a doctor examine them, and check their medical records. The interviews would inquire about various events and characteristics, such as cholesterol intake. Then we would categorize the people—for instance, as having or not having had a heart attack—and determine whether these groups differed in some earlier aspects of their lives.

What might our study show? We might find that, compared with people who did not have heart attacks, those who did had eaten diets that were much higher in cholesterol. We might also find that changes in people's diets, becoming higher or lower in cholesterol content over the years, corresponded with their suffering an attack. That is, those who consumed increasing amounts of cholesterol had more heart attacks than those whose cholesterol intake decreased. Because this is a quasi-experimental study, we cannot be certain that high-cholesterol diets caused the heart disease. But the prospective approach gives greater plausibility to a causal link than the retrospective approach would. This is because the diets, and changes in them, clearly preceded the heart attacks.

Retrospective and prospective approaches to study health were developed by epidemiologists. These approaches have been useful in identifying risk factors for specific illnesses.

Developmental Approaches

We saw earlier that the life-span perspective adds an important dimension to the study of health and illness. An essential research approach in studying life-span development is to examine and compare subjects at different ages. Of course, the age of the subjects cannot be manipulated; we can assign individuals to groups based on their age, but this assignment is not random. This approach is quasi-experimental, and, therefore, *age* itself cannot be viewed as a cause of health or behavior.

Two basic approaches are used for studying the age variable. In the **cross-sectional approach**, different individuals of different ages are observed at about the same time. The **longitudinal approach** involves the repeated observation of the *same* individuals over a long period of time. The longitudinal approach is like the prospective method, but it focuses specifically on age as a variable. Let's see how the cross-sectional and longitudinal approaches are used.

Suppose we were interested in examining age-related changes in dietary intake of cholesterol among middle-aged adults. If we use a *cross-sectional* approach, we might evaluate the diets of, say, 50 adults at each of three approximate ages—for example, 35, 45, and 55 years—during the current month. On the other hand, if we use a *longitudinal* approach to examine the same age range, we would evaluate the diets of 50 35-year-olds during the current month, and again when they are 45 and 55 years of age. This longitudinal study would take 20 years to complete.

Not all longitudinal studies take so long to do. Often a shorter span of ages—sometimes only a few months—is appropriate, depending on the question or issue the researcher wants to resolve. But the longitudinal approach, and the prospective approach in general, is typically more costly in time and money than the cross-sectional approach. Also the longer a study lasts, the greater the likelihood that subjects in the sample will be lost. Some will move away, others will lose interest in participating, and still others may die. Despite these difficulties, it is a valuable research approach that is unique in its ability to examine *change and stability in the lives of individuals* across time. For example, our longitudinal study could tell us whether individuals who eat a high-cholesterol diet at age 35 will generally continue to do so many years later. In contrast, a cross-sectional approach loses sight of stability and individual changes.

Now, let's suppose we did our cross-sectional study and found that the cholesterol content of adults' diets decreased with age. We would then like to know why this is so. One possible answer is that people change their diets as they get older because they feel more vulnerable to heart disease. So we asked the oldest group, using the retrospective approach, if they feel more vulnerable and eat less high-cholesterol food today than they used to. Sure enough, they said yes. But another reason for the current age differences in diet could be that the older adults never ate diets as high in cholesterol as those of the younger adults. So we asked the oldest group to describe the diets they ate 10 or 20 years ago. The diets they described contained less cholesterol than their current diets (which we already knew) *and* the current diets of the 35- and 45-year-olds in our study! This

finding reflects the fact that the older subjects grew up at a different time, when food preferences or availability may have been different.

The influence of having been born and raised at a different time is called a *cohort effect*. The term *cohort* refers to a group of people who have a demographic factor in common, such as age, generation, or social class. As a result, they share a set of experiences that are distinct from those of other cohorts. Researchers can examine cohort effects by combining the two developmental approaches. Looking back at our study with middle-aged adults, the combined approach could be carried out by selecting and testing 35-, 45-, and 55-year-olds initially. So far the study is cross-sectional, but we would follow most of these same adults longitudinally and add younger subjects along the way. By doing this in a planned and systematic way, we'll have data on cross-sectional differences, changes within each cohort, and differences between cohorts.

Single-Subject Approaches

Sometimes studies are done with just one subject. One type of research that uses this approach is the *case study*, in which a trained researcher constructs a systematic biography from records of the person's history, interviews, and current observation. This kind of research is useful in describing, in depth, the development and treatment of an unusual medical or psychological problem. Other types of research that use one subject are called *single-subject designs*. This approach is often used for demonstrating the usefulness of a new treatment method for a specific medical or behavioral problem. In the simplest of these designs, data on the subject's problem at the beginning and end of treatment are compared. Often, follow-up assessments are made weeks or months later to see if the person's condition has regressed. Some single-subject designs have additional phases or features that enable them to provide evidence for cause-effect relationships.

The principal disadvantage of single-subject approaches is that information on only one subject, no matter how detailed it is, may not describe what would be found with other individuals. A major purpose of psychological research is to collect information that can be applied or generalized to other people. Nevertheless, studies using one subject stimulate the development of new treatment procedures and suggest topics for further research.

GENETICS RESEARCH

In the 19th century, Charles Darwin speculated that unseen particles called "gemmules" were present in the sperm and ovum. Darwin's concept of gemmules formed the basis for the search for genetic materials. What did this search yield?

Genetic Materials and Transmission

Researchers discovered threadlike structures called *chromosomes* and proposed that these structures contained units called *genes*. Soon they determined the basic substance in all genetic material—*deoxyribonucleic acid*, or DNA for short—and described its structure. Today we know that DNA determines our growth patterns and physical structures (Tortora & Derrickson, 2009). We also know that genes are discrete particles of DNA that are strung together in chromosomes and transmitted from parent to child. Each parent contributes half of the genetic information we inherit.

Chromosomes have identifying features. Photographs taken through a microscope can be arranged according to the size and shape of chromosome pairs. One pair is called the *sex chromosomes* because they carry the genes that will determine whether an individual will be female or male. The normal sex chromosomes for males consist of one large chromosome (called an X chromosome) and one small chromosome (called a Y chromosome); females have two X chromosomes. As with chromosomes, genes come in pairs. Although a single pair of genes may determine some traits a person inherits, others require many genes. Some traits occur in the presence of a single *dominant* gene, with the paired gene making little or no contribution. But when a trait occurs only if two identical genes make up the pair, these genes are called *recessive*.

Twin and Adoption Studies

How do psychologists and other scientists determine whether hereditary factors influence people's health and illness? The methods are based on a distinction between two types of twins. *Monozygotic* (MZ), or identical, twins are conceived together and have the same genetic inheritance; *dizygotic* (DZ), or fraternal, twins are conceived separately and are no more genetically similar than singly born siblings and may, of course, be of different sex.

Much of the research on hereditary factors has focused on the differences in characteristics shown in MZ twins as compared with DZ twins. Investigations using this approach are called **twin studies**. The rationale for making these comparisons, although statistically complex, is logically simple. Because the two individuals in an MZ pair are genetically identical, we can assume that differences between them are environmentally determined. Conversely, the greater the similarity between MZ

twins, the more likely it is that the characteristic is genetically influenced. Differences between DZ twins, on the other hand, are due to both genetic and environmental factors, even when they are the same sex. If we could assume that both members of each MZ and same-sex DZ pair that we study have had equal environmental experiences, we could measure genetic influence simply by subtracting the differences for MZ from the differences for DZ twins. Even though both members of each MZ and DZ pair may not have had equal environmental experiences, researchers can take the differences into account—and when they do, important genetic forces are still found (Scarr & Kidd, 1983).

Another way to examine hereditary influences is to study children adopted at very early ages. **Adoption studies** compare traits of adopted children with those of their natural parents and their adoptive parents. Why? Adoptive parents contribute greatly to the rearing environment, but are genetically unrelated to the children; the natural parents are genetically related to the children, but play little or no role in rearing them. So, if adopted children are more similar to their natural parents than to their adoptive parents, we then have evidence for heredity's influence.

Let's look at a few conclusions relevant to health psychology that have come from twin and adoption studies. First, heredity affects not only physical characteristics, such as height and weight, but also physiological functions, including heart rate and blood pressure (Ditto, 1993). Second, genetic disorders can produce very high levels of cholesterol in the blood, making their victims susceptible to heart disease at very early ages (AMA, 2003). Third, some evidence indicates that heredity has its greatest impact on people's health early in life, and by old age the role of habits and lifestyle become increasingly important (Harris et al., 1992). Fourth, although genetic factors affect people's risk of developing cancer, environmental factors appear to play a stronger role for most people (Lichtenstein et al., 2000).

Linking Specific Genes with Diseases

After having identified which disorders have a genetic basis, researchers began looking for links to specific genes. We now know that every human cell contains 30,000–40,000 genes, and almost all of the human system of genes have been identified and mapped (IHGSC, 2001). Genes influence a vast number of traits, including more than 3,000 diseases. For some diseases, researchers have even pinpointed the exact gene locations. We will look at a few of these traits and diseases.

Sickle-cell anemia is a hereditary disease whose victims are usually Black people. The body of a person who has two of these genes manufactures large quantities of sickle-shaped red blood cells that carry little oxygen and tend to clump together in the bloodstream—often they cannot pass through capillaries. As a result, the vital organs of people with sickle-cell anemia receive inadequate amounts of oxygen and incur tissue damage. The condition, which usually develops in childhood, produces painful episodes, progressive organ failure, and brain damage.

Another recessive disease is *phenylketonuria* (PKU). In this disease, which occurs more frequently among Whites than other racial groups, the baby's body fails to produce a necessary enzyme for metabolizing phenylalanine, a toxic amino acid present in many common foods (AMA, 2003). If the disease is not treated, the amino acid builds up and causes brain damage. Placing PKU babies on special diets as soon as possible after birth can prevent this. When the brain is more fully developed after about 5 years of age, many PKU children can switch to normal diets. PKU provides a good example of an inherited disease that can be controlled by modifying the victim's behavior.

Researchers are also closing in on certain *oncogenes*, which are genes that can cause cancer. Researchers have, for example, found oncogenes for certain types of cancers of the colon (Bodmer et al., 1987), breast (Chen et al., 1995; Wooster et al., 1995), skin (Hussussian et al., 1994), lung (Rodenhuis et al., 1987), and prostate (Lee et al., 1994). Oncogenes can be normal genes or mutations that may result from exposure to harmful environmental agents, such as tobacco smoke.

Epigenetic Effects

Epigenetics is a process in which chemical structures within or around the DNA govern how, when, and how much a gene acts. These structures typically suppress the gene's usual activity, can change, and can be passed on to one's offspring (Foley et al., 2009; Zhang & Meaney, 2010). Epigenetics operates in normal development, such as when cells specialize to become heart or brain cells. But environmental events can change epigenetic processes, especially during prenatal, early childhood, and puberty periods. Environmental factors that can lead to epigenetic changes include exposure to toxic chemicals, bacterial and viral infection, dietary elements, tobacco, alcohol, and drugs.

For both members of an MZ twin pair, gene activity is highly similar in childhood and becomes less and less similar as they get older, especially when their lifestyles differ and the resulting epigenetic changes accumulate. Evidence today suggests that epigenetic changes can influence an individual's response to stress, ability to learn and remember, and development of health problems, such as cancer, heart disease, obesity, asthma, and diabetes. The study of epigenetics is fairly new, and there's a lot we don't yet know about it. Given that most of the research on epigenetics has been conducted with animals, to what extent do the same specific effects occur in humans? What determines the likelihood that an epigenetic change will be inherited? Can epigenetic processes that lead to health problems be reversed, such as by taking medication?

Which Research Method Is Best?

In this chapter, we have discussed a variety of research methods that are useful in health psychology. Which one is best? Some scientists might say that randomized controlled trials are best because they can uncover cause-effect relationships. But precise control and manipulation do not always yield results that help us understand real-life behavior. For example, studying behavior in experimental settings sometimes involves artificial conditions, such as precisely occurring events and special equipment. To the extent that these conditions are unlike the subjects' real world, their behavior may be influenced. As a result, when reading about an experiment, it is useful to keep two questions in mind: Does the experimental situation approximate anything the subjects might experience in real life? If the experimental situation is highly artificial, what specific effect might this have on the outcome of the experiment? New techniques may help avoid these and other problems. For example, a method called *ecological momentary assessment* uses devices, such as pagers, to cue and collect data on individuals periodically in their regular day-to-day living (Shiffman & Stone, 1998).

In a sense, all the research methods we discussed are "best," since the investigator must select the most suitable method(s) to answer the specific question(s) under study. This leads us to a final point: it is possible and desirable to use experimental and nonexperimental methods *simultaneously* in one study. For instance, if we wanted to find out whether people's reading information about the health effects of excessive cholesterol would induce them to modify their diets we could manipulate the independent variable by having the experimental group, but not the control group, read the health information. We might also want to test people of different ages: people who are 50 years of age might be more easily persuaded to lower their cholesterol levels than people who are 20. We could examine both variables by randomly assigning people of each of the two age groups to experimental and control groups and later examining their diets and blood cholesterol levels.

Note, however, that the kinds of conclusions yielded by each variable (information and age) will differ; only the manipulated variable can yield unambiguous causal statements.

SUMMARY

Health and illness are overlapping concepts that exist along a continuum. One end of the illness/wellness continuum is dominated by health—a positive state of physical, mental, and social well-being that varies over time; the other end is dominated by illness, which produces signs, symptoms, and disabilities. The patterns of illness affecting people have changed across history, especially in the 20th century. Compared with earlier times, today people die at later ages and from different causes. Infectious diseases are no longer the principal cause of death in technological societies around the world. Chronic illnesses now constitute the main health problem in developed nations.

Ideas about physiology, disease processes, and the mind have changed since the early cultures thousands of years ago, when people apparently believed that illness was caused by evil spirits and the like. Greek philosophers produced early written ideas about health and illness, considering how sickness happens and the mind/body problem. During the Middle Ages, the Church had an enormous influence on ideas about illness, and the belief in mystical causes of disease became strong again. Philosophers and scientists from the 17th to the 20th centuries provided the foundation for the biomedical model as a way to conceptualize health and illness.

The biomedical model has been extremely useful, enabling researchers to make great advances in conquering many infectious diseases through the development of vaccines and treatments. But many researchers today have come to recognize that aspects of individual patients—their histories, social relationships, lifestyles, personalities, mental processes, and biological processes—must be included in a full conceptualization of risk factors for illness. As a result, the biopsychosocial model has emerged as an alternative to the biomedical approach and proposed a constant interplay of biological, psychological, and social systems—each interrelated with and producing changes in the others. Psychosomatic medicine, behavioral medicine, and health psychology have introduced new techniques, such as behavioral and cognitive methods, to promote health. Life-span, gender, and sociocultural perspectives add important dimensions to this model by considering the role of people's development, sex, and culture in health and illness. Health psychology draws on knowledge from a variety of other psychology fields and nonpsychology fields, such as medicine, biology, social work, epidemiology, public health, sociology, and anthropology. Epidemiology examines the mortality, morbidity, prevalence, incidence, and epidemic status of illnesses.

The study of important variables in health psychology involves the use of experimental and nonexperimental research methods, often testing a theory. A well-designed experiment can lead to cause-effect conclusions because it involves rigorous control, such as with placebo and double-blind methods, and manipulation of variables. Correlational studies test relationships between variables; a correlation coefficient describes an association between variables but does not indicate whether it is a causal relation. Quasi-experimental studies are useful when subjects cannot be randomly assigned to groups or independent variables cannot be manipulated, such as the subjects' history, age, and gender; quasi-experiments often use retrospective and prospective approaches. To study people at different ages, researchers use cross-sectional and longitudinal approaches. The role of heredity in health and illness can be examined through twin and adoption studies and by examining epigenetics.

KEY TERMS

illness/wellness
   continuum
health
infectious diseases
chronic diseases
mind/body problem
biomedical model
risk factors
personality
psychosomatic medicine

behavioral medicine
health psychology
behavioral methods
cognitive methods
biopsychosocial model
system
mortality
morbidity
prevalence
incidence

epidemic
sociocultural
theory
variable
experiment
placebo
double blind
correlation coefficient
correlational studies

quasi-experimental
   studies
retrospective approach
prospective approach
cross-sectional approach
longitudinal approach
twin studies
adoption studies
epigenetics

2

STRESS—ITS MEANING, IMPACT, AND SOURCES

PROLOGUE

"Mum! Dad! I got in. I'm going to university! And my first choice!" exclaimed Claire when the letter arrived in the post. Claire had been agonising over her decision to apply to a course so far away from home, but her initial reaction to the letter shows she made the right choice for herself.

The happiness and excitement of going to university is book-ended by many different fears, stresses, and concerns. For example, students wanting to go to university have to make certain marks in their exams, which means long hours of study, too little sleep, low amounts of socialising, and sometimes poor diets if you eat on the run. And after the acceptance comes the stress of leaving your school friends and your parents, the packing, and wondering if you'll fit in and meet new friends. All of these issues can cause stress and tension. Some people react in productive ways, for example, by making lists to ensure they don't forget anything when packing; others react negatively by allowing themselves to become run-down and ill. Stress can affect your immune system and make you more vulnerable to infections, or it can cause muscle aches and headaches. While some people react to stress this way, others thrive on stress and stressful situations.

In our story, Claire is not only leaving her parents, but is also leaving behind her boyfriend, Max. She worries that she won't see Max enough because he's going to a university closer to home.

"He'll probably find someone else in the first week and forget all about me," she told a friend, who suggested that Claire to speak to Max about her concerns. However, Claire's parents are hoping that Claire will meet more boys at university rather than remain in a serious long-distance relationship, which they think is unhealthy and can be socially isolating. They are pressuring her to break it off with Max, but Max keeps saying that he'll visit "every weekend". How will this promise affect Claire? If Max does visit every weekend, will she feel pressured to not study because he had come such a long distance? How will the visits affect Claire's social life? What kind of stress will Claire be under if Max *doesn't* visit all the time?

Claire's situation is not uncommon. We all experience stress in our everyday lives, probably more than we would like. It occurs in a wide variety of situations and settings—in the family, in school, and on the job, for example. Sometimes the stress experienced is brief, and sometimes it continues for a long time and becomes chronic. Sometimes it is intense, and sometimes it is mild. It varies between individuals, and even across a particular person's life. An experience that is stressful for one person—such as taking a difficult examination—may not be stressful for another, and may even be exciting or challenging for someone else.

In this chapter we discuss what stress is, where it comes from, and what impact it has. In the course of the discussion, you will find answers to questions you may have about stress. What makes an event stressful? Why does a particular event produce more stress in one person than in another? How does stress affect our bodies and our behaviour? Does the experience of stress change across the lifespan?

This man's face reveals that he appraises the pain in his chest as stressful.

EXPERIENCING STRESS IN OUR LIVES

When you hear people say they are "under a lot of stress," you have some idea of what they mean. Usually the statement means they feel unable to deal with the demands of their environment, and they feel tense and uncomfortable. Because of the pervasiveness and commonality of these experiences in our lives, you might expect that defining the concept of stress would be simple. But it isn't. Let's see how psychologists have conceptualized stress and what the prevailing definition is today.

WHAT IS STRESS?

The condition of stress has two components: *physical*, involving direct material or bodily challenge, and *psychological*, involving how individuals perceive circumstances in their lives (Lovallo, 2005). These components can be examined in three ways (Dougall & Baum, 2001). One approach focuses on the environment: stress is seen as

a *stimulus*, as when we have a demanding job or experience severe pain from arthritis or a death in the family. Physically or psychologically challenging events or circumstances are called **stressors**. The second approach treats stress as a *response*, focusing on people's reactions to stressors. We see an example of this approach when people use the word *stress* to refer to their state of tension. Our responses can be psychological, such as your thought patterns and emotions when you "feel nervous," and physiological, as when your heart pounds, your mouth goes dry, and you perspire. The psychological and physiological response to a stressor is called **strain**.

The third approach describes stress as a *process* that includes stressors and strains, but adds an important dimension: the relationship between the person and environment (Lazarus, 1999; Lazarus & Folkman, 1984). This process involves continuous interactions and adjustments—called **transactions**—with the person and environment each affecting and being affected by the other. According to this view, stress is not just a stimulus or a response, but rather a process in which the person is

Table 2.1 *Components of the Definition of Stress*

Component	Description/Example
Resources	Stress taxes the person's biopsychosocial *resources* for coping with difficult events or circumstances. These resources are limited. Sometimes the impact is focused mainly on our biological system—for instance, when we tax our physical strength to lift something heavy. More typically, however, the strain has an impact on all three systems.
Demands	The phrase *"demands of a situation"* refers to the amount of our resources the stressor appears to require.
Discrepancy	When there is a poor fit, or a mismatch, between the demands of the situation and the resources of the person, a *discrepancy* exists. This generally takes the form of the demands taxing or exceeding the resources. But the opposite discrepancy also occurs—that is, our resources may be underutilized—and this can be stressful, too. A worker who is bored by a lack of challenge in a job may find this situation stressful.
Transactions	In our *transactions* with the environment, we assess demands, resources, and discrepancies between them. These transactions are affected by many factors, including our prior experiences and aspects of the current situation.

an active agent who can influence the impact of a stressor through behavioral, cognitive, and emotional strategies. People differ in the amount of strain they experience from the same stressor. One person who is stuck in traffic and late for an important appointment keeps looking at his watch, honking his horn, and getting angrier by the minute; another person in the same circumstances stays calm, turns on the radio, and listens to music.

We will define **stress** as the circumstance in which *transactions* lead a person to *perceive a discrepancy* between the physical or psychological *demands* of a situation and the *resources* of his or her biological, psychological, or social systems (Lazarus & Folkman, 1984; Lovallo, 2005). Table 2.1 gives descriptions and examples of the four components of this definition, starting at the end. An important point to keep in mind is that a demand, resource, or discrepancy may be either *real* or just *believed* to exist. As an example, suppose you had to take an exam and wanted to do well, but worried greatly that you would not. If you had procrastinated and did not prepare for the test, the discrepancy you see between the demands and your resources might be real. But if you had previously done well on similar exams, prepared thoroughly for this one, and scored well on a pretest in a study guide yet still thought you would not do well, the discrepancy you see would not reflect the true state of affairs. Stress often results from inaccurate perceptions of discrepancies between environmental demands and the actual resources. Stress is in the eye of the beholder.

APPRAISING EVENTS AS STRESSFUL

Transactions in stress generally involve an assessment process that Richard Lazarus and his coworkers call **cognitive appraisal** (Lazarus, 1999; Lazarus & Folkman, 1984). Cognitive appraisal is a mental process by which people assess two factors: (1) whether a demand threatens their physical or psychological well-being and (2) the resources available for meeting the demand. These are called primary and secondary appraisal.

Primary and Secondary Appraisal

When we encounter a potentially stressful circumstance—for example, feeling symptoms of pain or nausea—we first try to assess the meaning of the situation for our well-being. This assessment process is called **primary appraisal**. This appraisal seeks answers to such questions as, "What does this mean to me?" and "Will I be okay or in trouble?" Your primary appraisal regarding the pain or nausea could yield one of three judgments:

- It *is irrelevant*—as you might decide if you had had similar symptoms of pain and nausea before that lasted only a short while and were not followed by illness.

- It *is good* (called "benign-positive")—which might be your appraisal if you wanted very much to skip work or have a college exam postponed.

- It *is stressful*—as you might judge if you feared the symptoms were of a serious illness, such as botulism (a life-threatening type of food poisoning).

Circumstances we appraise as stressful receive further appraisal for three implications: harm-loss, threat, and challenge.

Harm-loss refers to the amount of damage that has already occurred, as when someone is incapacitated and in pain following a serious injury. Sometimes people who experience a relatively minor stressor think of it as a "disaster," thereby exaggerating its personal impact and increasing their feelings of stress (Ellis, 1987). *Threat* involves the expectation of future harm—for example, when hospitalized patients contemplate their medical bills, difficult rehabilitation, and loss of income. Stress appraisals seem to depend heavily on harm-loss and threat (Hobfoll, 1989). *Challenge* is the opportunity to achieve growth, mastery, or profit by using more than routine resources to meet a demand. For instance, a worker might view an offer of a higher-level job as demanding, but see it as an opportunity to expand her skills, demonstrate her ability, and make more money. Many people are happiest when they face challenging but satisfying activities.

Appraisals can influence stress even when the stressor does not relate to us directly—even that is, when the transaction is *vicarious*. If we see other people in stressful circumstances, such as suffering from pain, we may empathize with their feelings and feel vulnerable ourselves, but our responses are still influenced by appraisals. A classic experiment demonstrated empathic appraisal by showing college students a film called *Subincision* (Speisman et al., 1964). The film showed a rite of passage for young adolescent boys in a primitive society in which the underside of the penis is cut deeply from the tip to the scrotum, using a sharp stone. Before seeing the film, the students were divided into four groups, so that each group would see the film a different way. Each group saw the film with either:

1. No sound track.
2. A sound track with a "trauma" narrative that emphasized the pain, danger, and primitiveness of the operation.
3. A narration that denied any pain and potential harm to the boys, describing them as willing participants in a joyful occasion who "look forward to the happy conclusion of the ceremony."
4. A "scientific" narration that encouraged the viewers to watch in a detached manner—for example, the narrator commented, "As you can see, the operation is formal and the surgical technique, while crude, is very carefully followed."

Did the different sound tracks affect the subjects' stress appraisals? Physiological (such as heart rate) and self-report measures of stress showed that, compared with the subjects who saw the film with no sound track, those who heard the trauma narration reacted with more stress during the film; those who heard the denial and scientific tracks displayed less stress. Thus, people can experience stress vicariously, and their reactions depend on the process of primary appraisal. As a dramatic real-life confirmation of this process, researchers found heightened stress reactions among people across the United States a few days after the September 11 terrorist attacks (Schuster et al., 2001).

Secondary appraisal refers to our assessment of the resources we have available for coping. Although these assessments occur continuously in our transactions, we are especially aware of our secondary appraisals when we judge a situation as potentially stressful and try to determine whether our resources are sufficient to meet the harm, threat, or challenge we face. Examples of secondary appraisal judgments include:

• I can't do it—I know I'll fail.
• I'll try, but my chances are slim.
• I can do it if Ginny will help.
• If this method fails, I can try a few others.
• I can do it if I work hard.
• No problem—I can do it.

The condition of stress that we experience often depends on the outcome of the appraisals we make. When we judge our resources as sufficient to meet the demands, we may experience little or no stress; but when we appraise demands as greater than our resources, we may feel a great deal of stress. These processes determine everyday stress responses, but also influence much more severe reactions, such as the development of post-traumatic stress disorder (Carek et al., 2010; Meiser-Stedman et al., 2009). (Go to 👤.)

What Factors Lead to Stressful Appraisals?

Appraising events as stressful depends on two types of factors—those that relate to the person and those that relate to the situation (Lazarus & Folkman, 1984). Let's begin by looking at how personal factors can affect appraisals of stress.

Personal factors include intellectual, motivational, and personality characteristics. One example is self-esteem: people who have high self-esteem are likely to believe they have the resources to meet demands that require the strengths they possess. If they perceive an event as stressful, they may interpret it as a challenge rather than a threat. Another example relates to motivation: the more important a threatened goal, the more stress the person is likely to perceive (Paterson & Neufeld, 1987). One other example involves the person's belief system: as psychologist Albert Ellis has noted, many people have irrational beliefs that increase their stress, for instance:

> Because I strongly desire to have a safe, comfortable, and satisfying life, the conditions under which I live *absolutely must* be easy, convenient and gratifying (and it is *awful* and I *can't bear it* and *can't be happy at all* when they are unsafe and frustrating)! (1987, p. 373)

A person who holds such beliefs is likely to appraise almost any sort of inconvenience as harmful or

CLINICAL METHODS AND ISSUES

Posttraumatic Stress Disorder (PTSD)

Experiencing an extremely severe stressor that creates intense fear and horror can lead to a psychiatric condition called *post-traumatic stress disorder*. PTSD is marked by being highly aroused (with difficulty sleeping or concentrating), reliving the event often, and being unresponsive to other people (Kring et al., 2010). Many individuals develop this disorder after being injured in a car accident, exposed to war or terrorism, sexually assaulted, or suffering serious medical illnesses (Cordova & Ruzek, 2004; Jacobsen et al., 1998). Being a victim of PTSD may affect people's health: for instance, veterans and others with PTSD are more likely than those without the disorder to develop various serious illnesses (Dedert et al., 2010), such as heart disease, in the years after such trauma (Kubzansky et al., 2007; 2009). Studies have shown that behavior modification therapy with behavioral and cognitive methods can prevent this disorder after a trauma and help people overcome it if it develops (Cordova & Ruzek, 2004; Kring et al., 2010).

threatening. The tendency to appraise even minor issues as major problems is often called *perfectionism*, and this thinking style not only often causes emotional distress but also can pose a serious threat to long-term health (Fry & Debats, 2009).

What is it about situations that make them stressful? One answer is that events that involve very *strong demands* and are *imminent* tend to be seen as stressful (Paterson & Neufeld, 1987). Thus, patients who expect to undergo a physically uncomfortable or painful medical procedure, such as surgery, tomorrow are likely to view their situation as being more stressful than, say, expecting to have a blood pressure test next week. Table 2.2 presents several other characteristics of events that make them stressful.

DIMENSIONS OF STRESS

Psychologists who study stress or perform therapy to help people manage it assume that the amount of stress a person experiences increases with stressor frequency, intensity, and duration (Sarafino & Ewing, 1999). Evidence supports this assumption. Research has shown that stronger stressors produce greater physiological strain (Steptoe, Cropley, & Joekes, 2000). Many people experience *chronic stress*—that is, it occurs often or lasts a long time, such as when many stressors happen or thoughts about a trauma recur often over time (Dougall & Baum, 2001). Chronic stress makes people more susceptible to catching cold when exposed to infection than occasional stress (Cohen et al., 1998).

Table 2.2 *Characteristics of Stressful Situations*

Characteristic	Description/Example
Life transitions	Passing from one life condition or phase to another. Examples: starting day care or school, moving to a new community, becoming a parent, and retiring from a career.
Difficult timing	Events that happen earlier or later in life than usual or expected. Examples: having a child at 15 years of age and entering college at 40.
Ambiguity	A lack of clarity in a situation. Examples: unclear information for a worker about a function or task and for a patient about his or her health status, treatment options, or prognosis.
Low desirability	Some circumstances are undesirable to most people in virtually all respects. Examples: losing one's house in a fire and getting a traffic ticket.
Low controllability	Circumstances that seem to be outside the person's behavioral or cognitive influence. Examples: low *behavioral control*, such as not being able to do anything to prevent instances of back pain; low *cognitive control*, such as not being able to stop thinking about a traumatic experience.

Sources: Lazarus & Folkman, 1984; Moos & Schaefer, 1986; Paterson & Neufeld, 1987; Quick et al., 1997; Suls & Mullen, 1981; Thompson, 1981.

If your course has you read the modules from the Appendix, The Body's Physical Systems, distributed to the chapters, read now **Module 1** (The Nervous System) and **Module 2** (The Endocrine System).

BIOPSYCHOSOCIAL ASPECTS OF STRESS

We've seen that stressors can produce strain in the person's biological, psychological, and social systems. Let's examine biopsychosocial reactions to stress more closely.

BIOLOGICAL ASPECTS OF STRESS

Anyone who has experienced a very frightening event, such as a near accident or other emergency, knows that there are physiological reactions to stress—for instance, almost immediately our heart begins to beat more rapidly and more forcefully, and the skeletal muscles of our arms and legs may tremble. The body is aroused and motivated to defend itself, and the sympathetic nervous system and the endocrine system cause this arousal to happen. After the emergency passes, the arousal subsides. The physiological portion of the response to a stressor—or strain—is called **reactivity**, which researchers measure by comparison against a baseline, or "resting," level of arousal (Lovallo, 2005). Genetic factors influence people's degree of reactivity to stressors (Williams, Marchuk et al., 2001). People who are under chronic stress often show heightened reactivity when a stressor occurs, and their arousal may take more time to return to baseline levels (Gump & Matthews, 1999).

Many years ago the distinguished physiologist Walter Cannon (1929) provided a basic description of how the body reacts to emergencies. He was interested in the physiological reaction of people and animals to perceived danger. This reaction has been called the *fight-or-flight* response because it prepares the organism to attack the threat or to flee. In the fight-or-flight response,

Physical exertion, such as in athletic competition, is a stressor that produces strain in the body.

the perception of danger causes the sympathetic nervous system to stimulate many organs, such as the heart, directly, and stimulates the adrenal glands of the endocrine system, which secrete adrenaline, arousing the body still further. Cannon proposed that this arousal could have positive or negative effects: the fight-or-flight response is adaptive because it mobilizes the organism to respond quickly to danger, but this high arousal can be harmful to health if it is prolonged.

General Adaptation Syndrome

What happens to the body when high stress levels are prolonged? Hans Selye studied this issue by subjecting laboratory animals to a variety of stressors—such as very high or low environmental temperatures, X-rays, insulin injections, and exercise—over a long period of time. He also observed people who experienced stress from being ill. Through this research, he discovered that the fight-or-flight response is only the first in a series of reactions the body makes when stress is long-lasting (Selye, 1956, 1976, 1985; Weinrib, 2004). Selye called this series of physiological reactions the **general adaptation syndrome** (GAS). As Figure 2-1 shows, the GAS consists of three stages:

1. **Alarm reaction.** The first stage of the GAS is like the fight-or-flight response to an emergency—its function is to mobilize the body's resources. This fast-acting arousal results from the sympathetic nervous system, which activates many organs through direct nerve connections, including the adrenal glands, which when stimulated release adrenaline and noradrenaline into the bloodstream, producing further activation. Somewhat less quickly, the *hypothalamus–pituitary–adrenal axis* (HPA) of the stress response is activated, and this component of the stress response was Selye's novel and main emphasis. Briefly, the hypothalamus triggers the pituitary gland to secrete ACTH, which causes the adrenal gland to release cortisol into the bloodstream, further enhancing the body's mobilization.

2. **Stage of resistance.** If a strong stressor continues, the physiological reaction enters the stage of resistance. Here, the initial reactions of the sympathetic nervous system become less pronounced and important, and HPA activation predominates. In this stage, the body tries to adapt to the stressor. Physiological arousal remains higher than normal, and the body replenishes the hormones the adrenal glands released. Despite this continuous physiological arousal, the organism may show few outward signs of stress. But the ability to resist new stressors may become impaired. According to Selye, this impairment may eventually make the individual vulnerable to the health problems he called *diseases of adaptation*. These health problems include

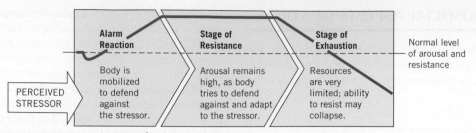

Figure 2-1   General adaptation syndrome with three stages. The superimposed graph (dark color) illustrates changes in the body's degree of resistance against disease.

ulcers, high blood pressure, asthma, and illnesses that result from impaired immune function.

3. **Stage of exhaustion.** Prolonged physiological arousal produced by severe long-term or repeated stress is costly. It can weaken the immune system and deplete the body's energy reserves until resistance is very limited. At this point, the stage of exhaustion begins. If the stress continues, disease and damage to internal organs are likely, and death may occur.

The effects of the body's having to adapt repeatedly to stressors—such as with fluctuations in levels of hormones like cortisol and adrenaline, blood pressure, and immune function—that accumulate over time are called **allostatic load**, which creates wear and tear on the body and impairs its ability to adapt to future stressors (McEwen & Stellar, 1993). Studies of chronic stress have confirmed that high levels of allostatic load are related to poor health in children and the elderly (Johnston-Brooks et al., 1998; Seeman et al., 1997). The concept of allostatic load highlights the importance of considering the overall accumulation of physiological strain over time. In this view, the cumulative amount of strain typically has a greater influence on health than the degree of activation in response to any one stressor. Four factors are important in the overall amount of bodily activation or physiological stress (Uchino et al., 2007; Williams et al., 2009):

1. *Amount of exposure.* This is obviously key: when we encounter more frequent, intense, or prolonged stressors, we are likely to respond with a greater total amount of physiological activation.

2. *Magnitude of reactivity.* In response to any particular stressor, such as taking a major academic exam, some individuals will show large increases in blood pressure or stress hormones while others show much smaller changes.

3. *Rate of recovery.* Once the encounter with a stressor is over, physiological responses return to normal quickly for some people, but stay elevated for a longer time for others. Continuing to think about a stressor after

it is over, revisiting it mentally, or worrying about it recurring in the future can delay physiological recovery and add to the accumulated toll through prolonged physiological activation (Brosschot, 2010).

4. *Resource restoration.* The resources used in physiological strain are replenished by various activities (Smith & Baum, 2003), and sleep may be the most important of them. Sleep deprivation can be a source of stress, and contributes to allostatic load directly (McEwen, 2006). What's more, poor sleep quality or reduced amounts of sleep predict the development of serious health problems, such as heart disease (Shankar et al., 2008).

During sleep, some aspects of physiological activity typically drop below daytime levels, as happens with blood pressure; the larger the drop, the more beneficial it is for health, but this can be disrupted by daily stressors (Tomfohr et al., 2010). The restoration of stress resources has a major impact on allostatic load and related health consequences. When combined, the above four factors determine our overall physiological stress burden. Any conditions that contribute to increased exposure to stressors, greater reactivity, delayed recovery, or reduced restoration can have important influences on health.

WEB ANIMATION: General Adaptation Syndrome

Access: www.wiley.com/go/global/sarafino. This interactive animation describes the phases and physiological effects of prolonged high stress.

Do All Stressors Produce the Same Physical Reactions?

Many studies have demonstrated that stressors of various types increase the secretion of hormones by the adrenal glands (Lovallo, 2005), including cold temperatures, noise, pain, athletic competition, taking examinations, flying in an airplane, and being in crowded situations. Selye (1956) believed that the GAS is *nonspecific* with regard to the type of stressor. That is, the physiological reactions the GAS describes will occur regardless of whether the stress results from very cold temperature, physical exercise, illness, conflicts with other people, or the death of a loved one. However, the notion of nonspecificity does not take important psychosocial processes into account. Three lines of evidence suggest this is a problem.

First, some stressors appear to elicit a stronger *emotional* response than others do. This is important because the amount of hormone released in reaction to a stressor that involves a strong emotional response, as a *sudden* increase in environmental temperature might produce, appears to be different from the amount released with a less emotional stressor, such as a *gradual* increase in temperature. After conducting extensive studies of various stressors and hormones, John Mason concluded that he and his colleagues "have not found evidence that any single hormone responds to *all* stimuli in *absolutely* nonspecific fashion" (1975, p. 27). For instance, some stressors led to increases in adrenaline, noradrenaline, and cortisol, but other stressors increased only two of these hormones. He also pointed out that research conducted since Selye first described the GAS has shown that stressors are most likely to trigger the release of large amounts of all three of these hormones if the individual's response includes a strong element of emotion.

Second, findings of many studies Marianne Frankenhaeuser and other researchers have conducted on stress led her to propose that the pattern of physiological arousal under stress depends on two factors: effort and distress. E*ffort* involves the person's interest, striving, and determination, and *distress* involves anxiety, uncertainty, boredom, and dissatisfaction. She has described that:

> E*ffort with distress* tends to be accompanied by an increase of both catecholamine *and* cortisol excretion. This is the state typical of daily hassles. In working life, it commonly occurs among people engaged in repetitious, machine-paced jobs on the assembly line or … at a computer terminal.
>
> E*ffort without distress* is a joyous state, characterized by active and successful coping, high job involvement, and a high degree of personal control. It is accompanied by increased catecholamine secretion, whereas cortisol secretion may be suppressed.
>
> D*istress without effort* implies feeling helpless, losing control, giving up. It is generally accompanied primarily by increased cortisol secretion, but catecholamines may be elevated, too. (1986, p. 107)

Because distress is an emotion, her view ties in with and extends that of Mason.

Third, evidence suggests that cognitive appraisal processes play a role in people's physiological reaction to stressors. For example, researchers assessed elementary school children's cortisol levels in urine samples taken on regular school days and on days when achievement tests were given (Tennes & Kreye, 1985). The expected increase in cortisol on test days was found, but not for all children—their intellectual ability was an important factor. Intelligence test scores were obtained from school records. Cortisol levels increased on test days for children with above-average intelligence, but not for children with low to average intelligence. The influence of intelligence suggests that the brighter children were more concerned about academic achievement and, as a result, appraised the tests as more important and threatening than did the other children.

So, the basic structure of the GAS appears to be valid, but it assumes that all stressors produce the same physiological reactions and fails to include the role of psychosocial factors in stress. Whether physiological stress responses are general, as Selye suggested, or show more specific patterns influenced by psychological processes remains a current debate and focus of stress research (Denson et al., 2009; Miller, 2009). Also, as we will see later in this chapter and in others, the range of physiological responses involved in stress has expanded well beyond those described by Cannon and Selye, and this "cutting edge" of stress research helps us understand its effects on health.

PSYCHOSOCIAL ASPECTS OF STRESS

At this juncture, we can begin to see how interwoven our biological, psychological, and social systems are in the experience of stress. To give a more complete picture of the interplay among these systems, we will now examine the impact of stress on people's cognitive, emotional, and social systems.

Cognition and Stress

Many students have had this experience: While taking a particularly stressful exam in school, they may neglect or misinterpret important information in a question or have difficulty remembering an answer they had studied well. It is frustrating when an answer is "on the tip of your tongue," especially since you will probably remember it after the test is over. High levels of stress affect people's memory and attention. Let's see how.

In the example of stress during exams, preoccupation with worries about failure can interfere with memory and attention that are required for good performance on the exam (Putwain et al., 2010). Stress can also impair cognitive functioning by distracting our attention. Noise can be a stressor, which can be chronic for people who live in noisy environments, such as next to train tracks or highways (Lepore, 1997). How does chronic noise affect cognitive performance? Many people try to deal with this kind of stress by changing the focus of their attention from the noise to relevant aspects of a cognitive task—they "tune out" the noise. Evidence suggests that children who try to tune out chronic noise may develop generalized cognitive deficits because they have difficulty knowing which sounds to attend to and which to tune out (Cohen et al., 1986).

Not only can stress affect cognition, but the reverse is true, too. In the opening story about Claire, she was worrying about how going to university would affect her relationship with Max which was very distressing for her. Worry about future threats and ruminating about past difficulties can maintain elevated physiological stress responses, even in the absence of actual stressful situations (Brosschot, 2010). Andrew Baum (1990) has studied this kind of thinking in individuals who were living near the Three Mile Island nuclear power plant in Pennsylvania when a major nuclear accident occurred. He found that years later some of these people still experienced stress from the incident, but others did not. One of the main factors differentiating these people was that those who continued to feel this stress had trouble keeping thoughts about the accident and their fears out of their minds. It seems likely that these thoughts perpetuated their stress and made it chronic.

The two-way connection between cognition and stress is particularly important in the group of cognitive processes called *executive functioning*. Executive functions refer to a set of cognitive abilities involved in the regulation and direction of our ongoing behavior (Suchy, 2009), such as maintaining and shifting attention as needed; inhibiting unhelpful or inappropriate responses or impulses; current or working memory capacity; and selecting among alternative responses under consideration. These are the cognitive processes that enable us to direct or guide our behavior intentionally. Better executive cognitive functioning obviously can help one manage the demands of stressful situations, but stressful experiences can also temporarily disrupt these same cognitive processes (Williams et al., 2009). That is, difficulties with concentration, memory, problem-solving, and impulse control during stressful experiences may reflect the fact that stress has temporarily depleted or fatigued these cognitive resources. Depleted executive cognitive resources can then lead to more difficulty dealing with stressful situations, creating a possible "vicious cycle" of stress and impaired cognition. These same aspects of cognitive functioning are supported by

structures and circuits in the pre-frontal cortex of the brain that also support the parasympathetic "brake" on physiological stress responses (Thayer et al., 2009). So, difficulties thinking clearly during stress might be accompanied by poor physiological control or regulation of the stress response.

Emotions and Stress

Long before infants can talk, they display what they feel by their motor, vocal, and facial expressions. You can test this with a little experiment: place a bit of a bitter food, such as unsweetened chocolate, in a newborn's mouth and watch the baby's face—the eyes squint, brows drop and draw together, the mouth opens, and tongue juts out. This is the facial expression for the emotion of disgust. Each emotion has a specific facial pattern. Using procedures like this one, researchers have shown that newborn babies express several specific emotions, such as disgust, distress, and interest (Izard, 1979).

Emotions tend to accompany stress, and people often use their emotional states to evaluate their stress. Cognitive appraisal processes can influence both the stress and the emotional experience (Lazarus, 1999; Scherer, 1986). For example, you might experience stress and fear if you came across a snake while walking in the woods, particularly if you recognized it as poisonous. Your emotion would not be joy or excitement, unless you were studying snakes and were looking for this particular type. Both situations would involve stress, but you might experience fear if your appraisal was one of threat, and excitement if your appraisal was one of challenge.

Fear is a common emotional reaction that includes psychological discomfort and physical arousal when we feel threatened. Of the various types and intensities of fears people experience in everyday life, psychologists classify many into two categories: phobias and anxiety. *Phobias* are intense and irrational fears that are directly associated with specific events and situations. Some people are afraid of being enclosed in small rooms, for instance, and are described as claustrophobic. *Anxiety* is a vague feeling of uneasiness or apprehension—a gloomy anticipation of impending doom—that often involves a relatively uncertain or unspecific threat. That is, the person may not be aware either of the situations that seem to arouse anxiety or of exactly what the "doom" entails. Patients awaiting surgery or the outcome of diagnostic tests generally experience high levels of anxiety. In other situations, anxiety may result from appraisals of low self-worth and the anticipation of a loss of either self-esteem or the esteem and respect of others.

Stress can also lead to feelings of sadness or *depression*. We all feel sad at times, and when we do, we often say we're "depressed." These feelings are a normal part of life for children and adults. The difference between these feelings and depression as a serious *disorder* is a matter of degree. Depression meets the criteria for a psychological disorder when it is severe and prolonged, lasting at least two weeks (Kring et al., 2010). People with this disorder tend to:

- Have a mostly sad mood nearly every day
- Appear listless, with loss of energy, pleasure, concentration, and interest
- Show poor sleeping habits and either poor appetite or markedly increased appetite.
- Have thoughts of suicide, feeling hopeless about the future
- Have low self-esteem, often blaming themselves for their troubles

Having long-term disabling health problems, such as being paralyzed by a stroke, often leads to depressive disorders.

Another common emotional reaction to stress is *anger*, particularly when the person perceives the situation as harmful or frustrating. You can see this in the angry responses of a child whose favorite toy is taken away or an adult who is stuck in a traffic jam. Anger has important social ramifications, including aggressive behavior.

Social Behavior and Stress

Stress changes people's behavior toward one another. In some stressful situations, such as train crashes, earthquakes, and other disasters, people may work together to help each other survive. Some stressful circumstances lead people to seek the comfort of others for support or companionship. In other stressful situations, people may become less sociable and more hostile and insensitive toward the needs of others (Cohen & Spacapan, 1978).

When stress and anger join, negative social behaviors often increase. Research has shown that anger in response to stress often leads to aggressive behavior, and these negative effects continue after the stressful event is over (Wilkowski & Robinson, 2008). The stress of social rejection, for example, can lead to increased aggressive behavior, even toward the source of that rejection (Leary et al., 2006). Stress-related aggressive behavior has important implications in real life. For example, stress can undermine the quality of marriage and other close relationships, and in some cases can increase levels of conflict and the potential for spouse abuse (Randall & Bodenmann, 2009). Child abuse is a

major social problem that poses a serious threat to children's physical and emotional health, and parental stress is often a contributing factor (Rodriguez & Richardson, 2007). Prior to an act of battering, frequently the parent has experienced a stressful crisis, such as the loss of a job or other difficulties. A parent under high stress is at risk of losing control. If, for example, a child runs around the house making a racket, a stressed parent may become angry, lose control, and strike the child, perhaps reflecting the temporary depletion of psychological resources required for self-restraint (DeWall et al., 2007).

Gender and Sociocultural Differences in Stress

Does the experience of stress depend on a person's gender and sociocultural group membership? Apparently so. Women generally report experiencing more major and minor stressors than men do (Davis, Matthews, & Twamley, 1999). This difference could result partly from women's greater willingness to say they experienced stress; it probably also reflects real variations in experiences. Because in today's two-income households mothers still do most of the chores, they often have heavier daily workloads than men and greater physiological strain than women without children (Luecken et al., 1997; Lundberg & Frankenhaeuser, 1999). Women's greater domestic burden also includes greater effort attending to the emotional needs of family members (Erickson, 2005).

Being a member of a minority group or being poor appears to increase the stressors people experience. Research in the United States has shown that individuals with these sociocultural statuses report experiencing a disproportionately large number of major stressors, and not surprisingly they experience far greater health difficulties (Adler & Rehkopf, 2008; Gallo & Matthews, 2003). For example, Black Americans report far more stressors than Hispanics, who report more stress as than do nonminority people. A prospective study spanning 7 1/2 years found that income and educational attainment are also important factors (Lantz et al., 2005). Adults with low income and education reported more chronic stress and major stressors, such as divorce or the death of a child, than adults with higher income and education. And the greater the stress they had experienced earlier, the more likely they were to have died or to have poor health in the next several years. Other research found that the lower people's income and education, the greater their daily levels of stress hormones, such as adrenaline and cortisol (Cohen, Doyle, & Baum, 2006). Later in this chapter, we will discuss how discrimination is a major source of stress for ethnic minorities, with negative effects on health.

There appear to be gender and sociocultural differences in physiological strain from stressors, too. Many studies have found that men show more reactivity than females when psychologically stressed (Collins & Frankenhaeuser, 1978; Kudielka et al., 1998; Ratliff-Crain & Baum, 1990). Men also seem to take longer for their physiological arousal to return to baseline levels after the stressor has ended (Earle, Linden, & Weinberg, 1999). But some evidence suggests that men and women differ in the events they find stressful, and the strength of reactivity compared with that of the opposite sex may be greater when the stressor is relevant to the person's gender (Weidner & Messina, 1998). For instance, men show greater reactivity than women do when their competence is challenged, and women show greater reactivity than men when their friendship or love is challenged (Smith et al., 1998). Taylor and her colleagues (2000) have suggested that the "fight or flight" response is an accurate description of men's stress reactions, whereas women's responses might be better characterized as a "tend and befriend" reaction in which they increase their efforts to maintain their close social connections and ties.

Regarding sociocultural differences, some studies in the United States have found that Blacks show greater reactivity than Whites when under stress (McAdoo et al, 1990; Miller et al., 1995). But other findings suggest that differences between Blacks and Whites vary depending on the stressor and the subjects' gender (Saab et al., 1997; Sherwood et al., 1995). For instance, Black women show greater reactivity than White women when a stressor is perceived as racist (Lepore et al., 2006).

We've seen that the effects of stress are wide ranging and involve an interplay among our biological, psychological, and social systems. Even when the stressor is no longer present, the impact of the stress experience can continue. Some people experience more stress than others do, but we all find sources of stress somewhere in our lives.

SOURCES OF STRESS THROUGHOUT LIFE

Babies, children, and adults all experience stress. The sources of stress may change as people develop, but stress can occur at any time throughout life. Where does stress come from, and what are its sources? To answer this question, we will examine sources that arise within the *person*, in the *family*, and in the *community* and *society*.

SOURCES WITHIN THE PERSON

Sometimes the source of stress is within the person. *Illness* is one way stress arises from within the individual.

Being ill creates physical and psychological demands on the person, and the degree of stress these demands produce depends on the seriousness of the illness and the age of the individual, among other things. Why is the person's age important? For one thing, the ability of the body to fight disease normally improves in childhood and declines in old age (Coico & Sunshine, 2009; Gouin et al., 2008). Another reason is that the meaning of a serious illness for the individual changes with age. For adults, stress appraisals of an illness typically include both current difficulties and concerns for the future, such as whether they may be disabled or may die. But because young children have a limited understanding of disease and death, their appraisal of stress that arises from their illness is likely to focus on current, rather than future, concerns—such as how well they feel at the moment and whether their activities are impaired (La Greca & Stone, 1985).

Another way stress arises within the person is through the appraisal of opposing motivational forces, when a state of *conflict* exists. Suppose you are registering for next semester and find that two courses you need meet at the same time. You can take only one. Which will you choose? You have a conflict—you are being pushed and pulled in two directions. Many conflicts are more momentous than this one. We may need to choose between two or more job offers, or different medical treatments, or expensive purchases. The pushes and pulls of conflict produce opposing tendencies: *approach* and *avoidance* (Miller, 1959). Table 2.3 describes the three types of conflict these tendencies produce. But conflicts can be more complicated, having several alternatives, with many attractive and unattractive features. In general, people find conflict stressful when choices involve many features, when opposing motivational forces have fairly equal strength, and when the "wrong" choice can lead to very negative and permanent consequences. These conditions often apply when people face major decisions about their health.

Some of our most common and significant stressors arise from motives or goals, especially motives about social interactions and relationships with other people. Social motives include the need to be connected to and valued by others, and concerns about achievement and status (Baumeister & Leary, 1995; Leary et al., 2001, Newton, 2009). As a result, experiences of rejection, isolation, conflict with others, competition, failure, and disrespect are central sources of stress (Miller et al., 2009; Newsom et al., 2008; Richman & Leary, 2009; Smith et al., 2003). For example, the threat of being rejected or evaluated negatively by others can evoke large stress responses, including increase in blood pressure, cortisol, and other stress hormones (Bosch

Table 2.3 *Three Main Types of Conflict*

Type	Definition/Example/Effect
Approach/approach	Choice involves two appealing goals that are incompatible. For example, individuals trying to lose weight to improve their health or appearance experience frequent conflicts when delicious, fattening foods are available. Although people generally resolve an approach/approach conflict fairly easily, the more important the decision is to them, the greater the stress it is likely to produce.
Avoidance/avoidance	Choice between two undesirable situations. For example, patients with serious illnesses may be faced with a choice between two treatments that will control or cure the disease, but have very undesirable side effects. People in avoidance/avoidance conflicts usually try to postpone or escape from the decision; when this is not possible, people often vacillate between the two alternatives, changing their minds repeatedly, or get someone else to make the decision for them. People generally find avoidance/avoidance conflicts difficult to resolve and very stressful.
Approach/avoidance	A single goal or situation has attractive and unattractive features. This type of conflict can be stressful and difficult to resolve. Consider, for instance, individuals who smoke cigarettes and want to quit. They may be torn between wanting to improve their health and wanting to avoid the weight gain and cravings they believe will occur.

et al., 2009; Dickerson et al., 2008; Rohleder et al., 2008). Also, interacting with other people who are perceived as higher in status, competing with others, and making an active effort to influence or control other people also evoke physiological stress responses (Mendelson et al., 2008; Newton, 2009; Smith et al., 2003).

SOURCES IN THE FAMILY

Given the important role of social motives in stress, it is not surprising that our closest relationships can be major sources of stress. Families provide great comfort, but can be sources of tension and conflict, as well. Interpersonal discord can arise from financial problems; inconsiderate behavior; use of household resources; opposing goals, such as which television program to watch. Of the many sources of stress in the family, we will focus on three: adding a new family member, marital conflict and divorce, and illness and death in the family.

An Addition to the Family

A new child in the family is typically a joyful event, but it also brings stress—particularly to the mother, of course, during pregnancy and after the birth. But an addition to the family is stressful to other family members, too. For instance, the father may worry about the health of his wife and baby or fear that his relationship with his wife may deteriorate, and both parents may feel the need to earn more money. The arrival of a new baby can also be stressful to other children in the family.

An important factor in parental stress relates to the child's emerging personality. Each baby has personality dispositions, which are called **temperaments** (Buss & Plomin, 1975). Pediatric nurses and doctors, well aware of the unique combinations of temperaments that babies show right from birth, describe infants broadly as "easy"

babies and "difficult" ones. Temperamentally difficult babies tend to cry a great deal, and efforts to soothe them do not work very well. They resist being introduced to new foods, routines, and people, and their patterns of sleeping and eating are hard to predict from day to day. These behaviors are stressful for parents. Although only about 10% of babies are classified as "difficult," displaying most or all of these traits fairly consistently, many others show some of these traits at least occasionally. Although temperaments are fairly stable across time, with aspects of these traits continuing for many years, many difficult children show changes toward the development of easy traits (Carey & McDevitt, 1978).

When women experience high levels of stress during pregnancy, the baby can be adversely affected. Pregnant women who experience higher levels of stress and negative emotion during pregnancy are more likely to give birth prematurely, and their babies are more likely to be below normal weight (Kramer et al., 2009; Lobel et al., 2008). These pre-term births increase the risk of future health problems and other difficulties for the child, which can cause further stress for the family.

Marital Strain and Divorce

Conflict in marriage is nearly universal, but when it becomes frequent and severe, it is a major source of stress with important consequences for health. When couples discuss issues that are sources of disagreement or conflict, such as household finances or chores, they show increases in blood pressure, cortisol and other stress hormones, and other physiological stress responses (Kiecolt-Glaser et al., 2005; Nealey-Moore et al., 2007; Smith et al., 2009). These stress responses are especially evident in couples who are experiencing chronic marital strain and in those whose disagreements include more hostile comments toward each other

(Kiecolt-Glaser et al., 2005; Robles & Kiecolt-Glaser, 2003). Marital unhappiness is also associated with sleep difficulties (Troxel et al., 2009), perhaps interfering with restorative processes.

These physiological effects of conflict in marriage and other close relationships are likely to contribute to the long-term negative effects of family problems on physical health (De Vogli et al., 2007). Couples who have frequent disagreements and greater negative behavior during those conflicts are more likely to separate or divorce eventually (Snyder et al., 2005), and marital disruptions also increase one's risk of serious health problems (Matthews & Gump, 2002).

A divorce produces many stressful transitions for all members of the family as they deal with changes in their social, residential, and financial circumstances (Cooper et al., 2009). In the case of the children, they may move to a new neighborhood, be left with new sitters, or have to take on new chores at home. The custodial parent may not be very available to the children because of work or other preoccupations. Adapting to divorce usually takes several years, and some children show long-term effects, although it is often difficult to distinguish negative effects of a divorce from the continuing effects of family conflict that preceded it (Kushner, 2009). Some evidence suggests that the stress of divorce and the family changes that result can contribute to health problems in children (Troxel & Matthews, 2004). Psychological interventions for children in divorcing families and their parents can reduce and even prevent these difficulties (Wolchik, Schenck, & Sandler, 2009). Parents can help their children adjust to a divorce by maintaining a loving, secure home life and (Sarafino & Armstrong, 1986):

- Telling the children in advance of the impending separation.
- Encouraging open communication and answering the children's questions truthfully, but sensitively.
- Giving information, such as what changes will happen, at the children's levels of understanding.
- Recruiting help and advice from others, such as relatives, parent organizations, counselors, and the children's school personnel.
- Encouraging the children to have contact with both parents.

Family Illness, Disability, and Death

The following is a familiar story to many parents: In the middle of a frantic day at work, the parent receives a call from the school nurse, who says, "Your child is sick. You'll have to come and pick him up." Having a sick child adds to the stress in an already stressful day.

When children have a serious chronic illness, their families must adapt to unique and long-term stress (Quittner et al., 1998). Sometimes this stress is enough to cause symptoms of post-traumatic stress disorder in these parents (Cabizuca et al., 2009). Part of the stress stems from the amount of time needed to care for the child and from the reduced freedom family members have in their schedules. For example, a child with the respiratory disease called cystic fibrosis may need to have an adult thump his or her back two or three times a day to reduce the mucus that collects in the lungs (AMA, 2003). The family also faces many difficult decisions and must learn about the illness and how to care for the child. The medical needs of chronically ill children are expensive, and this burden adds to the family's stress. Relationships between family members may also suffer. The parents are likely to feel that having a chronically ill child reduces the time they have to devote to each other. In addition, other children in the family may feel isolated and deprived of parental attention.

Adult illness or disability is another source of family stress. The strain on their financial resources can be severe if the sick adult is a principal breadwinner. Having a physically ill or disabled adult in the family restricts the family's time and freedom, and produces very important changes in interpersonal relationships. The demands of related medical care can place burdens on both patients and their spouses (Berg & Upchurch, 2007). For example, suppose a man has a heart attack. His spouse may experience stress from fears that he may have another attack and from changes in his behavior, such as being more irritable and dependent. The spouse might also worry about whether her husband is making all of the behavioral changes suggested by his doctor. Although the couple may show increased affection for one another during convalescence, their sexual relations are often curtailed—sometimes because of fears that sex could induce another attack. And the roles of family members change: the healthy spouse and the children who are old enough take on many of the responsibilities and tasks of the recovering spouse.

Often the stress a family experiences when an adult is seriously ill depends on the sick person's age (Berg & Upchurch, 2007). For instance, advanced cancer in an elderly person has a very different meaning from the same illness in someone at 30 years of age, especially if the young adult has one or more children. In the latter case, the disease is inconsistent with the person's roles and threatens the family unit. But if an elderly person who is ill or disabled must live with and be cared for by relatives, the stress for all those in the household can be severe, especially if the person requires constant care and shows mental deterioration (Martire & Schulz, 2001). Elderly

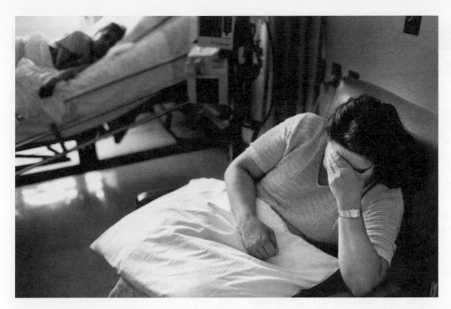

A mother overcome by the stress of dealing with her daughter's recurrent leukemia episodes and hospital treatments. Family stressors increase when children require special attention.

spouses who provide such care are often emotionally distressed and show heightened physiological strain, making them more susceptible to infectious disease (Gouin et al., 2008; Vedhara et al., 1999).

Age is also an important factor in the experience of stress when a family member dies. Some children suffer the loss of a parent during the childhood years—one of the most traumatic events a child can face. Young children may not grieve strongly for a lost parent because their understanding of death is incomplete: they often think death is reversible—the person is simply living somewhere else and can come back (Lonetto, 1980; Speece & Brent, 1984). By about 8 years of age, most children understand that death is final. An adult whose child or spouse dies suffers a tremendous loss (Kosten, Jacobs, & Kasl, 1985), and losing a child creates other losses—for example, bereaved mothers reported that they had lost important hopes and expectations for the future (Edelstein, 1984). These parents lose their identity and role as mothers and fathers, too. When a spouse dies, the surviving spouse also loses important hopes, expectations, and roles—as well as the one companion who made him or her feel loved, wanted, special, and safe. The experience of such losses can alter stress physiology and pose a clear threat to long-term health (Cankaya et al., 2009; Elwert & Christakis, 2008). (Go to 💡.)

SOURCES IN THE COMMUNITY AND SOCIETY

Contacts with people outside the family provide many sources of stress. For instance, children experience stress at school and in competitive events, such as in sports and talent performances. Much of the stress adults experience is associated with their jobs and the environmental conditions where they live; we'll focus on these sources of stress.

Jobs and Stress

Almost all people at some time in their lives experience stress that relates to their occupations. Often these stressful situations are minor and brief and have little impact on the person. But for many people, the stress is intense and continues for long periods of time. What factors make jobs stressful?

The *demands of the task* can produce stress in two ways. First, the workload may be too high. Some people work very hard for long hours over long periods of time because they feel required to do so—for example, if they need the money or think their bosses would be unhappy if they did not. Studies have found that excessive workloads are associated with increased rates of accidents and health problems (Mackay & Cox, 1978; Quick et al., 1997). Second, some kinds of job activities are more stressful than others. For example, repetitive manual action, as in cashier work, can be stressful and is linked to physical symptoms, such as neck and shoulder pain (Lundberg et al., 1999). Also, jobs that underutilize workers' abilities can produce stress. As one worker put it:

> I sit by these machines and wait for one to go wrong, then I turn it off, and go and get the supervisor. They don't go wrong very much. Sometimes I think I'd like them to keep going wrong, just to have something to do…. It's bloody monotonous. (Mackay & Cox, 1978, p. 159)

HIGHLIGHT

Gender Differences in Caregiving?

If I mentioned to you that an elderly friend was receiving care at home from family members, would you picture most of those caregivers as women? Probably most people would, and studies have typically found more women than men are caregivers (Vitaliano, Zhang, & Scanlan, 2003). But some researchers have questioned the societal image of women being the main caregivers among family members.

To examine this issue, Baila Miller and Lynda Cafasso (1992) did a **meta-analysis**, a statistical research method that pools the results of prior studies to create an integrated overview of their findings. No new data are collected. The prefix *meta* means "after" or "among"—thus, researchers apply this method *after* a series of studies has been done and assess the overall relationships these studies found *among* relevant variables. Meta-analysis is a useful technique for revealing patterns in relationships and clarifying what has been found, *especially* when some studies found different results from others. This meta-analysis was based on 14 published studies that had investigated gender differences in caregiving for elderly individuals.

Miller and Cafasso decided to examine the data from these studies for gender differences in several aspects of the caregiving experience. These analyses revealed that female caregivers were somewhat more likely than males to:

- Carry out personal care activities, such as dressing, bathing, and grooming the elderly person.
- Do the household chores in the elderly person's dwelling.
- Report experiencing greater degrees of stress from the caregiving.

But these differences were not very great, and no gender differences were found for any of the other aspects of caregiving, including:

- The degree of caregiving involvement, which was based on the number of tasks the caregiver had to do, the extent of assistance the elderly person needed to perform tasks, and the number of hours spent in caregiving.
- The extent to which the elderly person was functionally impaired, or unable to carry out activities of daily living.
- The caregiver's involvement in managing the elderly person's finances.

The researchers concluded that their results contradict gender-role stereotypes of Western societies and indicate that females and males are fairly similar in the degree to which they provide care for elderly relatives, the types of caregiving tasks they do, and the stress they experience from caregiving.

Another kind of activity that can produce stress is the evaluation of an employee's job performance—a process that can be difficult for both the supervisor and the employee.

Jobs that involve a *responsibility for people's lives* can be very stressful. Medical personnel have heavy workloads and must deal with life-or-death situations frequently. Making a mistake can have dire consequences. In an intensive care unit of a hospital, emergency situations are common; decisions must be made instantly and carried out immediately and accurately. As part of the job, nurses must comfort and deal with the wounds of a seriously injured person, try desperately to keep alive someone who is dying, and cope with more patients than the hospital can accommodate effectively. These and other conditions health professionals experience take their toll, often leading to emotional exhaustion (Maslach, Schaufeli, & Leiter, 2001). Similar stressors exist in the jobs of police and fire personnel.

Several other aspects of jobs can increase workers' stress (Cottington & House, 1987; Mackay & Cox, 1978; Quick et al., 1997). For example, stress can result from:

- *The physical environment* of the job. Stress increases when the job involves extreme levels of noise, temperature, humidity, or illumination (McCoy & Evans, 2005).

- *Perceived insufficient control* over aspects of the job. People experience stress when they have little opportunity to learn new skills and to make decisions on their own (Fitzgerald et al., 2003).

- *Poor interpersonal relationships*. People's job stress increases when a co-worker or customer is socially abrasive or treats them unfairly (Fitzgerald et al., 2003).

- *Perceived inadequate recognition or advancement*. Workers feel stress when they feel they are treated unfairly, as when they do not get the recognition or promotions they believe they deserve (Steptoe & Ayers, 2004).

Firefighters have stressful jobs, partly because of their responsibility for people's lives.

- *Job loss and insecurity.* People experience stress when they lose their jobs or think they are likely to be fired or laid off.

Research has linked these aspects of jobs to emotional distress, physiological strain, and sleep loss (Burgard & Ailshire, 2009; Kalil et al., 2010; Melin et al., 1999; Schnall et al., 1998; Steptoe, Cropley, & Joekes, 2000)—and the eventual development of cardiovascular disease (Burgard et al., 2007; Eller et al., 2009; Gallo et al., 2006; Tsutsumi et al., 2009). Also, job stress can "spill over" to family life, creating stress at home (Bakker et al., 2009; Eby et al., 2010).

Many elderly people approach *retirement* with expectations of blissful freedom and leisure. But retirees often find that they have lost opportunities for social interaction and an important part of their identity. They may miss the status and influence they once had, the structure and routines of a job, and the feeling of being useful and competent (Bohm & Rodin, 1985; Bradford, 1986). The stress from these circumstances and from reduced income can affect not only the retirees, but their spouses, too.

Environmental Stress

People's environments can be a source of stress. Some of these stressors are of only moderate levels, such as when we are at an event in a noisy, crowded arena (Evans, 2001). Crowding reduces our control over social interaction and restricts our ability to move about freely. Other environmental conditions create much more intense and chronic stressors, such as when a constant threat of violence or serious harm exists—as occurs in many areas of the world today. Even in areas as yet spared from war or terrorism in nearby communities, people feel threatened, and the resulting stress can influence their physical health (Levy & Sidel, 2009; Llabre & Hadi, 2009; Shalev et al., 2006).

Imagine how you would react to learning that a hazardous substance has seeped into the water supply where you live. How much of it have you and your family already drunk? Will you develop serious illnesses because of it in the future? Can the substance be removed? And after it is, will you believe there is no more danger? Can you sell your house now without suffering a great financial loss? Many people who are exposed to hazardous substances or other continuous threats in their environment worry for years about what will happen to them (Baum, 1988; Bland et al., 1996; Specter, 1996). Natural disasters, such as earthquakes, also create long-term disruptions in social relationships, which worsen the stress (Bland et al., 1997).

In the late 1970s, attention was focused on this type of situation at Love Canal in New York State, where a chemical dump site had contaminated a residential community. By comparison, natural disasters—such as a tornado or hurricane—end quickly, and much of the damage can be repaired in time. At Love Canal, however, "the nightmare goes on and on" (Holden, 1980). Another example of the psychological effects of living in a hazardous environment comes from the nuclear accident at the Three Mile Island power plant in Pennsylvania. More than a year after the accident, researchers compared the stress of nearby residents to that of people who lived near a different nuclear facility that had not had an accident. This comparison revealed greater psychological and physiological evidence of stress among the residents around Three Mile Island than among those near the other facility (Fleming et al., 1982).

The relative wealth versus poverty of a neighborhood is another important source of stress. It is very well established that low socio-economic status (SES)—reflected in lower household income and lower levels of education—is associated with reduced life expectancy and an increased risk of many life-threatening diseases (Adler & Rehkopf, 2008). Lack of health insurance or limited access to adequate health care contributes to some of this effect of low SES on health (Wilper et al., 2009), but much of it seems to involve the many sources of stress associated with low SES (Gallo & Matthews, 2003). But aside from an *individual's* income or level of education, the average SES of the *neighborhood* is a separate influence on important health outcomes, including cardiovascular disease, diabetes, and pre-term births (Chaix, 2009; O'Campo et al., 2008; Schootman et al., 2007). In many low SES neighborhoods, social relationships among people living there may be more stressful or less supportive, and residents may feel less safe and less able to influence or control their everyday experiences (Chaix, 2009).

Apart from objective indications of SES, such as income and education, an individual's subjective or perceived social status or rank in a community is a separate influence on stress and physical health (Cohen et al., 2008; Ghaed & Gallo, 2007). Beyond actually being relatively poor or uneducated and living in neighborhoods where that is generally true of the residents, simply feeling like a lower-status person apparently can be stressful and unhealthy. Also, living in low SES environments during childhood can have negative effect on stress responses and physical health that persist well into adulthood (Loucks et al., 2009; Miller et al., 2009).

Because of their income or occupation, the neighborhood where they reside, race or ethnicity, or their sexual orientation, many people experience discrimination and other forms of mistreatment—often on a daily basis (Pascoe & Richman, 2009; Richman & Leary, 2009). These recurring experiences can increase stress responses and the risk of health problems, including earlier death, cancer, cardiovascular disease (Barnes et al., 2008; Huebner & Davis, 2007; Taylor et al., 2000). Pregnant women exposed to discrimination are more likely to give birth to babies with low birth weight (Dominguez et al., 2008), and racial discrimination can interfere with otherwise beneficial nighttime decreases in blood pressure (Brondolo et al., 2008; Beatty & Matthews, 2009).

So far in this chapter we have seen that stress involves biopsychosocial reactions, and that all sorts of circumstances can be stressors, including noise, taking an exam, mistreatment, traffic jams, having a painful medical test, getting divorced, and losing a job. The possible stimuli and reactions, and the appraisal processes that link them, make for an interesting question: If you were doing research and needed to know the amount of stress different people had experienced, how could you assess this variable? (Go to 💡.)

MEASURING STRESS

Researchers have used several different approaches for measuring stress. Commonly used approaches involve assessing people's physiological arousal, life events, daily hassles, and exposure to many of the sources of stress reviewed previously.

HIGHLIGHT

Does Environmental Stress Affect Reactivity to New Stressors?

Psychologist Brooks Gump and his colleagues (2005) had already begun collecting data on cardiovascular functioning in 9½-year-old boys and girls in upstate New York when the 9/11/2001 terrorist attacks occurred. Although the original study design had another purpose, the researchers quickly changed their plans to examine the impact of the attacks on the children's cardiovascular reactivity to new stressors, such as a task in which they had to respond as fast as possible to one of two tones that were repeatedly presented in random order. Some of the children in 2001 were tested for reactivity before the attacks, and some were tested after; all of them were retested a year later.

What did this study find? The children tested prior to 9/11 showed relatively low reactivity in 2001, but moderately high reactivity a year later. For the children tested soon after 9/11, their reactivity was very high at that time, but it decreased to a moderately high level a year later. It seems that the terrorist attacks increased the children's reactivity to new stressors, but over the next year their reactivity decreased. The researchers noted that the impact of 9/11 was "relatively short-lived" for these children, and speculated that chronic threats of terrorism might lead to a stable heightened reactivity or to fatigue and a reduced ability of the body to react to new stressors.

PHYSIOLOGICAL AROUSAL

Stress produces physiological arousal, reflected in the functioning of many of our body systems. One way to assess arousal is to use electrical/mechanical equipment to take measurements of blood pressure, heart rate, respiration rate, or galvanic skin response (GSR). Each of these indexes of arousal can be measured separately, or they can all be measured and recorded simultaneously by one apparatus called the **polygraph** (Figure 2-2). Miniaturized versions of these devices are available with recording units that can fit in a pocket, thereby allowing assessments during the person's daily life at home, at work, or in a stressful situation. For example, using one of these devices, researchers have shown that paramedics' blood pressure is higher during ambulance runs and at the hospital than during other work situations or at home (Goldstein, Jamner, & Shapiro, 1992).

Another way to measure arousal is to do biochemical analyses of blood, urine, or saliva samples to assess the level of hormones that the adrenal glands secrete during stress (Mills & Ziegler, 2008; Nicolson, 2008). Using this approach, researchers can test for two classes of hormones: **corticosteroids**, the most important of which is cortisol, and **catecholamines**, which include adrenaline and noradrenaline.

There are several advantages to using measures of physiological arousal to assess stress (Luecken & Gallo, 2008). Physiological measures are reasonably direct and objective, quite reliable, and easily quantified. But there are disadvantages as well. Assessing physiological arousal can be expensive, and the measurement technique may itself be stressful for some people, as may occur when blood is drawn or when electrical sensors and other recording devices are attached to the body.

(a)

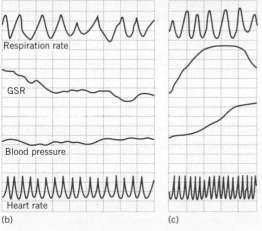

(b)   (c)

Figure 2-2 A typical polygraph (a) makes a graphical record of several indexes of arousal, including blood pressure, heart rate, respiration rate, and the galvanic skin response (the GSR measures skin conductance, which is affected by sweating). A comparison of the two graphs depicts the difference in arousal between someone who is calm (b) and someone who is under stress (c).

Lastly, measures of physiological arousal are affected by the person's gender, body weight, activity prior to or during measurement, and consumption of various substances, such as caffeine. Nonetheless, physiological assessments are used widely in research.

LIFE EVENTS

If you wanted to know whether people were feeling stress, you might simply ask them. Using a self-report method is easy to do. But in doing research, you would probably want to get a more precise answer than, "Yes, I am," or even, "Yes, I'm under a lot of stress." For this reason, a number of different scales have been developed to measure people's stress and assign it a numerical value. One approach many scales have used is to develop a list of **life events**—major happenings that can occur in a person's life that require some degree of psychological adjustment. The scale assigns each event a value that reflects its stressfulness.

The Social Readjustment Rating Scale

A widely used scale of life events is the *Social Readjustment Rating Scale* (SRRS) developed by Thomas Holmes and Richard Rahe (1967). To develop this scale, these researchers constructed a list of events they derived from clinical experience. Then they had hundreds of men and women of various ages and backgrounds rate the amount of adjustment each event would require, using the following instructions:

> *Use all of your experience* in arriving at your answer. This means personal experience where it applies as well as what you have learned to be the case for others. Some persons accommodate to change more readily than others; some persons adjust with particular ease or difficulty to only certain events. Therefore, strive to give your opinion of the average degree of readjustment necessary for each event rather than the extreme. (p. 213)

The researchers used these ratings to assign values to each event and construct the scale shown in Table 2.4.

As you can see, the values for the life events in the SRRS range from 100 points for death of a spouse to 11 points for minor violations of the law. To measure the amount of stress people have experienced, respondents are given a survey form listing these life events and asked to check off the ones that happened to them during a given period of time, usually not more than the past 24 months. The researcher sums the values of the checked items to get a total stress score. How commonly do life events like those in the SRRS occur? A study of nearly

Table 2.4 *Social Readjustment Rating Scale*

Rank	Life Event	Mean Value
1	Death of spouse	100
2	Divorce	73
3	Marital separation	65
4	Jail term	63
5	Death of close family member	63
6	Personal injury or illness	53
7	Marriage	50
8	Fired at work	47
9	Marital reconciliation	45
10	Retirement	45
11	Change in health of family member	44
12	Pregnancy	40
13	Sex difficulties	39
14	Gain of new family member	39
15	Business readjustment	39
16	Change in financial state	38
17	Death of close friend	37
18	Change to different line of work	36
19	Change in number of arguments with spouse	35
20	Mortgage over $10,000	31
21	Foreclosure of mortgage or loan	30
22	Change in responsibilities at work	29
23	Son or daughter leaving home	29
24	Trouble with in-laws	29
25	Outstanding personal achievement	28
26	Wife begin or stop work	26
27	Begin or end school	26
28	Change in living conditions	25
29	Revision of personal habits	24
30	Trouble with boss	23
31	Change in work hours or conditions	20
32	Change in residence	20
33	Change in schools	20
34	Change in recreation	19
35	Change in church activities	19
36	Change in social activities	18
37	Mortgage or loan less than $10,000	17
38	Change in sleeping habits	16
39	Change in number of family get-togethers	15
40	Change in eating habits	15
41	Vacation	13
42	Christmas	12
43	Minor violations of the law	11

Source: From Holmes & Rahe, 1967, Table 3.

2,800 American adults used a modified version of the SRRS and found that 15% of the subjects reported having experienced none of the events during the prior year, and 18% reported five or more (Goldberg & Comstock, 1980). The three most frequent events reported were "took a vacation" (43%), "death of a loved one or other important person" (22%), and "illness or injury" (21%).

Table 2.5 *Other Life Events Scales*

Scale Name	Description (reference)
Life Experiences Survey (LES)	Contains 57 items that are stated relatively precisely—for example, "major change in financial status (a lot better off or a lot worse off)." Respondents rate each event on a 7-point scale, ranging from extremely negative (−3) to extremely positive (+3). The items perceived as positive or as negative can be examined separately or combined for a total score (Sarason, Johnson, & Siegel, 1978).
PERI Life-Events Scale	Contains 102 items that describe events involving either a gain, a loss, or an ambiguous outcome (Dohrenwend et al., 1978).
Unpleasant Events Schedule (UES)	Contains 320 items; takes an hour to complete, although a shorter, 53-item form is also available (Lewinsohn et al., 1985).

Strengths and Weaknesses of the SRRS

When you examined the list of life events included in the SRRS, you probably noticed that many of the events were ones we have already discussed as stressors, such as the death of a spouse, divorce, pregnancy, and occupational problems. One of the strengths of the SRRS is that the items it includes represent a fairly wide range of events that most people do, in fact, find stressful. Also, the values assigned to the events were carefully determined from the ratings of a broad sample of adults. These values provide an estimate of the relative impact of the events, distinguishing fairly well between such stressors as "death of a close family member" and "death of a close friend." Another strength of the SRRS is that the survey form can be filled out easily and quickly.

One of the main uses of the SRRS has been to relate stress and illness. These studies have generally found that people's illness rates tend to increase following increases in stress (Holmes & Masuda, 1974; Johnson, 1986). But the correlation between subjects' scores on the SRRS and illness is only about .30—which means that the relationship is not very strong (Dohrenwend & Dohrenwend, 1984). One reason that the relationship is not stronger is that people get sick and have accidents for many reasons other than stress. But another factor is that the SRRS and similar approaches have several weaknesses (Monroe, 2008).

For example, the items in the SRRS can seem vague or ambiguous. The item, "change in responsibilities at work" fails to indicate how much change and whether it involves more or less responsibility. As a result, someone whose responsibility has decreased a little gets the same score as someone whose responsibility has increased sharply. Similarly, "personal injury or illness" does not indicate the seriousness of the illness—someone who had the flu gets the same score as someone who became paralyzed. Vague or ambiguous items reduce the precision of an instrument, and the correlation it is likely to have with other variables.

Another criticism is that the scale does not consider the meaning or impact of an event for the individual. For example, the score people get for "death of spouse" is the same regardless of their age, dependence on the spouse, and the length and happiness of the marriage. These items do not take the person's subjective appraisal into account, reducing the precision of the scale. The SRRS also does not distinguish between desirable and undesirable events. Some events, such as "marriage" or "outstanding personal achievement," as usually desirable; but "sex difficulties" and "jail term" are undesirable. Other items could be either desirable or undesirable, for example, "change in financial state"; the score people get is the same regardless of whether their finances improved or worsened. This is important because studies have found that undesirable life events are correlated with illness, but desirable events are not (Sarason et al., 1985).

The SRRS and similar life event checklists also emphasize acute stressors involving single events rather than chronic stress, and the latter may be the more important influence on some health problems (Monroe, 2008). Further, the self-report checklist format is susceptible to difficulties surrounding the respondent's ability to recall events accurately and their willingness to report them honestly. Newer, interview-based measures have been developed that derive from the ground-breaking, basic work of Holmes and Rahe (1967) but are intended to address these weaknesses (Monroe, 2008). Table 2.5 describes three other life event scales for adults intended to address weaknesses with the SRRS; other instruments have been developed to measure life events in children and adolescents (Coddington, 1972; Johnson, 1986).

DAILY HASSLES

If we consider the sources of stress we experience in a typical week or month, lesser events will quite likely come to mind, as when we give a speech, misplace our keys during a busy day, or have our quiet disrupted by a loud party next door. These are called **daily hassles**. Some people experience more daily hassles than others do.

Richard Lazarus and his associates developed a scale to measure people's experiences with day-to-day unpleasant or potentially harmful events (Kanner et al., 1981). This instrument—called the *Hassles Scale*—lists 117 of these events that range from minor annoyances, such as "silly practical mistakes," to major problems or difficulties, such as "not enough money for food." Respondents indicate which hassles occurred in the past month and rate each event as "somewhat," "moderately," or "extremely" severe. Because the researchers felt that having *desirable* experiences may make hassles more bearable and reduce their impact on health, they also developed the *Uplifts Scale*, which lists 135 events that bring peace, satisfaction, or joy. The researchers tested 100 middle-aged adults monthly over a 9-month period and identified the most frequently occurring items. For hassles, they included "concerns about weight," "health of a family member," "too many things to do," and "misplacing or losing things"; for uplifts, they included "relating well to your spouse or lover" and "completing a task."

Are hassles and uplifts related to health? Studies have examined this issue. One study tested middle-aged adults, using four instruments: (1) the Hassles Scale; (2) the Uplifts Scale; (3) a life events scale that includes no desirable items; and (4) the Health Status Questionnaire, which contains questions regarding a wide variety of bodily symptoms and overall health (DeLongis et al., 1982). Hassles scores and life events scores were associated with health status—both correlations were weak, but hassles were more strongly associated with health than life events were. Uplifts scores had virtually no association with health status. Other studies generally support these findings regarding the relationship of hassles and uplifts to health (Gortmaker, Eckenrode, & Gore, 1982; Holahan, Holahan, & Belk, 1984; Zarski, 1984). (Go to 🍎.)

CHRONIC STRESSORS IN SPECIFIC DOMAINS

As we saw earlier, potential sources of chronic or recurring stress exist in many specific domains of life experience, such as in our jobs, family conflicts, and neighborhoods. Life events and hassles scales have items that tap these sources of stress, but not extensively or specifically. Current research on stress and health often measures stressors in specific domains. In such cases, researchers are typically pursuing a more focused question about the role of a particular source of stress in health. All measures of stress have strengths and shortcomings, but they have generally been effective in demonstrating that stress is linked to an increased risk of future health problems, some of them major.

CAN STRESS BE GOOD FOR YOU?

Another reason why measures of stress do not correlate very highly with illness may be that not all stress is unhealthy. Is it possible that some types or amounts of stress are neutral or, perhaps, *good* for you? There is reason to believe this is the case (McGuigan, 1999).

How much stress may be good for people? Some theories of motivation and arousal propose that people function best, and feel best, at what is, *for them*, an optimal level of arousal (Fiske & Maddi, 1961; Hebb, 1955). People differ in the amount of arousal that is optimal, but too much or too little arousal impairs their

---

ASSESS YOURSELF

Hassles in Your Life

Table 2.6 gives a list of common events you may sometimes find unpleasant because they make you irritated, frustrated, or anxious. The list was taken from the Hassles Assessment Scale for Students in College, which has respondents rate the *frequency* and *unpleasantness* of and *dwelling* on each event.

For this exercise, rate only the *frequency* of each event. Beside each item estimate how often it occurred during the past month, using the scale:

0 = never, **1** = rarely, **2** = occasionally, **3** = often, **4** = very often, **5** = extremely often

Then add all of the ratings for a total score. You can evaluate your relative hassles with the following schedule: compared to the stress other college students have from hassles, a total score of 105 is about average, above 135 indicates much more stress, and below 75 indicates much less stress.

(continued)

ASSESS YOURSELF *(Continued)*

Table 2.6   *Hassles Assessment Scale for Students in College (HASS/Col)*

———— Annoying social behavior of others (e.g., rude, inconsiderate, sexist/racist)
———— Annoying behavior of self (e.g., habits, temper)
———— Appearance of self (e.g., noticing unattractive features, grooming)
———— Accidents/clumsiness/mistakes of self (e.g., spilling beverage, tripping)
———— Athletic activities of self (e.g., aspects of own performance, time demands)
———— Bills/overspending: seeing evidence of
———— Boredom (e.g., nothing to do, current activity uninteresting)
———— Car problems (e.g., breaking down, repairs)
———— Crowds/large social groups (e.g., at parties, while shopping)
———— Dating (e.g., noticing lack of, uninteresting partner)
———— Environment (e.g., noticing physical living or working conditions)
———— Extracurricular groups (e.g., activities, responsibilities)
———— Exams (e.g., preparing for, taking)
———— Exercising (e.g., unpleasant routines, time to do)
———— Facilities/resources unavailable (e.g., library materials, computers)
———— Family: obligations or activities
———— Family: relationship issues, annoyances
———— Fears of physical safety (e.g., while walking alone, being on a plane or in a car)
———— Fitness: noticing inadequate physical condition
———— Food (e.g., unappealing or unhealthful meals)
———— Forgetting to do things (e.g., to tape TV show, send cards, do homework)
———— Friends/peers: relationship issues, annoyances
———— Future plans (e.g., career or marital decisions)
———— Getting up early (e.g., for class or work)
———— Girlfriend/boyfriend: relationship issues, annoyances
———— Goals/tasks: not completing enough
———— Grades (e.g., getting a low grade)
———— Health/physical symptoms of self (e.g., flu, PMS, allergies, headaches)
———— Schoolwork (e.g., working on term papers, reading tedious/hard material, low motivation)
———— Housing: finding/getting or moving
———— Injustice: seeing examples or being a victim of
———— Job: searching for or interviews
———— Job/work issues (e.g., demands or annoying aspects of)
———— Lateness of self (e.g., for appointment or class)
———— Losing or misplacing things (e.g., keys, books)
———— Medical/dental treatment (e.g., unpleasant, time demands)
———— Money: noticing lack of
———— New experiences or challenges: engaging in
———— Noise of other people or animals
———— Oral presentations/public speaking
———— Parking problems (e.g., on campus, at work, at home)
———— Privacy: noticing lack of
———— Professors/coaches (e.g., unfairness, demands of, unavailability)
———— Registering for or selecting classes to take
———— Roommate(s)/housemate(s): relationship issues, annoyances
———— Sexually transmitted diseases (e.g., concerns about, efforts to reduce risk of STDs/HIV)
———— Sports team/celebrity performance (e.g., favorite athlete or team losing)
———— Tedious everyday chores (e.g., shopping, cleaning apartment)
———— Time demands/deadlines
———— Traffic problems (e.g., inconsiderate or careless drivers, traffic jams)
———— Traffic tickets: getting (e.g., for moving or parking violations)
———— Waiting (e.g., for appointments, in lines)
———— Weather problems (e.g., snow, heat/humidity, storms)
———— Weight/dietary management (e.g., not sticking to plans)

Source: Sarafino & Ewing, 1999.

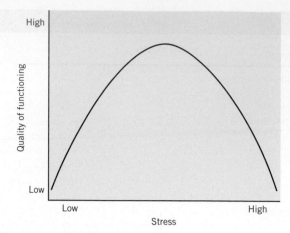

Figure 2-3 Quality of functioning at varying levels of stress. Functioning is poor at very low and very high levels of stress, but is best at some moderate, "optimal" level. (Based on material in Hebb, 1955.)

functioning. Figure 2-3 gives an illustration of how stress, as a form of arousal, relates to the quality of functioning. How might different levels of stress affect functioning? Imagine that you are in class one day and your instructor passes around a surprise test. If the test would not be collected or count toward your final grade, you might be underaroused and answer the questions carelessly or not at all. But if it were to count as 10% of your grade, you might be under enough stress to perform well. And if it counted a lot, you might be overwhelmed by the stress and do poorly.

Are some types of stress better than others for people? Three prominent researchers on stress have taken very similar positions on this question, claiming that there are at least two kinds of stress that differ in their impact. Selye (1974, 1985), for instance, claimed one kind of stress is harmful and damaging, and is called *distress*; another kind is beneficial or constructive, and is called *eustress* (from the Greek *eu*, which means

"good"). Similarly, as we saw earlier, Frankenhaeuser (1986) has described two components of stress: *distress* and *effort*. Distress with or without effort is probably more damaging than effort without distress. And Lazarus has described three types of stress appraisals—*harm-loss*, *threat*, and *challenge*—and noted:

> Challenged persons are more likely to have better morale, because to be challenged means feeling positive about demanding encounters, as reflected in the pleasurable emotions accompanying challenge. The quality of functioning is apt to be better in challenge because the person feels more confident, less emotionally overwhelmed, and more capable of drawing on available resources than the person who is inhibited or blocked. Finally, it is possible that the physiological stress response to challenge is different from that of threat, so that diseases of adaptation are less likely to occur. (Lazarus & Folkman, 1984, p. 34.)

There is a commonality to these three positions: to state it in its simplest form, there is good stress and bad stress—bad stress generally involves a strong negative emotional component. Cognitive appraisal processes play an important role in determining which kind of stress we experience.

Finally, in discussing whether stress is harmful, one other point should be made: individuals seem to differ in their susceptibility to the effects of stress. John Mason (1975) has proposed that these differences are like those that people show to the effects of viruses and bacteria. That is, not all people who are exposed to a disease-causing antigen, such as a flu virus, develop the illness—some individuals are more susceptible than others. Susceptibility to the effects of antigens and to stress varies from one person to the next and within the same individual across time. These differences result from biological variations within and between individuals, and from psychosocial variations, as we will see in the next chapter.

SUMMARY

Researchers have conceptualized stress in three ways. In one approach, stress is seen as a stimulus, and studies focus on the impact of stressors. Another approach treats stress as a response and examines the physical and psychological strains that stressors produce. The third approach proposes that stress is a process that involves continuous interactions and adjustments—or transactions—between the person and the environment. These three views lead to a

definition of stress: the condition that results when person-environment transactions lead to a perceived discrepancy between the demands of a situation and the resources of the person's biological, psychological, and social systems.

Transactions that lead to the condition of stress generally involve a process of cognitive appraisal, which takes two forms: *primary appraisal* focuses on whether a demand threatens the person's well-being, and *secondary appraisal* assesses the resources available for meeting the demand. Primary appraisal produces one of three judgments: the demand is irrelevant, it is good, or it is stressful. A stressful appraisal receives further assessment for the amount of harm or loss, the threat of future harm, and the degree of challenge the demand presents. When primary and secondary appraisals indicate that our resources are sufficient to meet the demands, we may experience little stress. But when we appraise a discrepancy where the demands seem greater than our resources, we may feel a substantial amount of stress.

Whether people appraise events as stressful depends on factors that relate to the person and to the situation. Factors of the person include intellectual, motivational, and personality characteristics, such as the person's self-esteem and belief system. With regard to situational factors, events tend to be appraised as stressful if they involve strong demands, are imminent, are undesirable and uncontrollable, involve major life transitions, or occur at an unexpected time in the life span.

Stressors produce strain in the person's biological, psychological, and social systems. Emergency situations evoke a physiological fight-or-flight reaction, by which the organism prepares to attack the threat or flee. When stress is strong and prolonged, the physiological reaction goes through three stages: the alarm reaction, the stage of resistance, and the stage of exhaustion. This series of reactions is called the general adaptation syndrome. According to Selye, continuous high levels of stress can make the person vulnerable to diseases of adaptation, including ulcers and high blood pressure. The overall total of physiological reaction to stressors, sometimes called allostatic load, may be a more important influence on health than the magnitude of the response to any single stressor. Factors that affect allostatic load include exposure to stressors, reactivity, recovery, and restoration.

Stress is linked to psychosocial processes. It can impair cognitive functioning, reduce people's helping behavior, and increase their aggressiveness. Various emotions can accompany stress—these emotions include fear, anxiety, depression, and anger. Although the sources of stress may change as people develop, the condition of stress can occur at any time in the life span. Sometimes stress arises from within the person, such as when the person is ill or experiences conflict. Another source of stress is the family, such as in marital conflicts and serious illnesses or death in the family. Although women are more likely than men to be caretakers of elderly relatives, a meta-analysis found that the amount of care men and women give is similar. A new baby with a difficult temperament can be stressful for parents, and stress during pregnancy can lead to premature births. Other sources of stress include the community and society—for example, from problems related to people's jobs, environmental conditions, the qualities of their neighborhoods, and the experience of discrimination.

Researchers measure stress in several ways. One way assesses physiological arousal, such as changes in blood pressure and heart rate, with various sensors attached to the body. Biochemical analyses of blood or urine samples can test for corticosteroids (for example, cortisol) and catecholamines (for example, adrenaline and noradrenaline). Other methods to measure stress use surveys of people's experience of life events, daily hassles, and experience of different chronic stressors. Although stress can contribute to the development of illness, many psychologists believe that not all stress is harmful.

KEY TERMS

stressors	secondary appraisal	stage of resistance	polygraph
strain	reactivity	stage of exhaustion	corticosteroids
transactions	general adaptation	temperaments	catecholamines
stress	syndrome	allostatic load	life events
cognitive appraisal	alarm reaction	meta-analysis	daily hassles
primary appraisal			

Note: If you read **Modules 1** and **2** (from the Appendix) with the current chapter, you should include the key   terms for those modules.

3

STRESS, BIOPSYCHOSOCIAL FACTORS, AND ILLNESS

Psychosocial Modifiers of Stress
Social Support
A Sense of Personal Control
Personality as Resilience and Vulnerability
Type A Behavior and Beyond

How Stress Affects Health
Stress, Behavior, and Illness
Stress, Physiology, and Illness
Psychoneuroimmunology

Psychophysiological Disorders
Digestive System Diseases
Asthma
Recurrent Headache
Other Disorders

Stress and Cardiovascular Disorders
Hypertension
Coronary Heart Disease

Stress and Cancer

PROLOGUE

Two cataclysmic events riveted the world's attention within a year of each other—the enormous tsunami that affected Indonesia in the Indian Ocean in December 2004, and Hurricane Katrina, which nearly destroyed New Orleans, Louisiana and surrounding areas in August 2005. Together, these events killed over 200,000 people and left even more injured and homeless. Hundreds of thousands of people were relocated, and very often family members were separated, at least temporarily.

Let us contrast the aftermath of the tsunami on Budi and Atin, two friends from a village whose families were relocated far apart. The initial impact of the tsunami on them was similar, but the amount of stress that followed was different. Budi's stress levels were not as severe as Atin's—one thing that helped Budi cope was that his whole family remained together when they were relocated to a nearby village where they had relatives. Being with relatives provided consolation for Budi's loss, an environment for him to socialise in, help in getting jobs for his parents, and assistance in getting a new home built. How was he coping two years later? He missed Atin, whom he hadn't seen in over a year, but Budi was making a good adjustment in his new community; he was in good health; he had a good relationship with his family; and he was working to help build more homes for other families in his situation.

Atin was not so fortunate, and her situation differed from Budi's in several major ways. Her immediate family had been split up for several months until they were relocated to a distant province where one of her parents managed to get a job. Atin had no extended family to help her and her parents, or to provide them with emotional support in their grief. Her family lived in a cramped, city-centre flat at their new location, and their financial situation was very difficult. Atin had never been as outgoing as Budi—she felt awkward and insecure in making friends of either sex. Two years after the tsunami, she felt isolated and lonely. Although she graduated from school, Atin only managed to get a low-paying, mundane job that required a lot of overtime and left her with little time or money to socialise. The stress was taking its toll on Atin; she and her parents argued often, and her health was deteriorating. She developed two illnesses—migraine headaches, and a digestive system condition that caused abdominal pain—that worsened when she felt stressed.

Continuing with issues introduced in Chapter 2, this chapter examines in more detail the effects of stress on health. We begin by looking at the psychosocial factors that can modify the stress people experience. Then we consider how stress affects one's health and the development of specific illnesses. In this chapter, we address many questions about stress and illness that are of great concern today. Why is it that some people can experience one traumatic event after another without suffering any ill effects, while others cannot? Are angry and hardworking people more likely to have a heart attack than people who are easy-going? Can stress delay a person's recovery from illness?

PSYCHOSOCIAL MODIFIERS OF STRESS

People's reactions to stress vary from one person to the next and from time to time for the same person. These variations often result from psychological and social factors that seem to *modify* the impact of stressors on the individual. Let's look at some of these modifiers, beginning with the role of social support.

SOCIAL SUPPORT

We saw in the experiences of Budi and Atin how important social ties and relationships can be during troubled times. The social support Budi got from his family tempered the impact of his stressful loss and probably helped him adjust. **Social support** refers to comfort, caring, esteem, or help available to a person from other people or groups (Uchino, 2004). Support can come from many sources—the person's spouse or lover, family, friends, doctor, or community organizations. People with social support believe they are loved, valued, and part of a *social network*, such as a family or community organization, that can help in times of need. So, social support refers to actions actually performed by others,

or *received support*. But it also refers to one's sense or perception that comfort, caring, and help are available if needed—that is, *perceived support*. As will we see later, received and perceived support can have different effects on health.

Types of Social Support

What specifically does social support provide to the person? It appears to provide four basic functions (Cutrona & Gardner, 2004; Uchino, 2004). *Emotional or esteem support* conveys empathy, caring, concern, positive regard, and encouragement toward the person. It provides comfort and reassurance with a sense of belongingness and of being loved in times of stress, as Budi received from his immediate and extended family after the Indian Ocean tsunami. *Tangible or instrumental support* involves direct assistance, as when people give or lend the person money or help out with chores in times of stress. Budi's relatives helped his parents get jobs and set up the new house. *Informational support* includes giving advice, directions, suggestions, or feedback about how the person is doing. For example, a person who is ill might get information from family or a doctor on how to treat the illness. *Companionship support* refers to the availability of others to spend time with the person, thereby giving a feeling of membership in a group of people who share interests and social activities.

What type of support do people generally need and get? The answer depends on the stressful circumstances. For instance, Figure 3-1 shows that cancer patients find emotional and esteem support to be especially helpful, but patients with less serious chronic illnesses find the different types of support equally helpful (Martin et al., 1994). Another study had college students fill out a questionnaire, rating the degree to which their

A patient receiving informational support from her doctor.

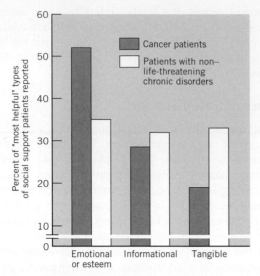

Figure 3-1   Percentage of patients with cancer and with non-life-threatening disorders (chronic headache or irritable bowel syndrome) whose reports of the "most helpful" social support they received described the emotional/esteem, instrumental, or tangible types of support. Notice that the cancer patients found emotional or esteem support especially helpful. (Data from Martin et al., 1994, Figure 1.)

current relationships provided them with different types of support, and then keep a daily record of their stress and social experiences for 2 weeks (Cutrona, 1986). The daily records revealed that most of the stressors were relatively minor, such as having car trouble or an argument with a roommate, but one-fifth of the students reported a severe event, such as a parent's diagnosis of cancer or the ending of a long-term romantic relationship. As you might expect, individuals received more social support following stressful events than at less stressful times. Tangible support occurred very infrequently, but informational and emotional/esteem support occurred often. Emotional/esteem support appeared to protect individuals from negative emotional consequences of stress.

Who Gets Social Support?

Not everyone gets the social support they need. Many factors determine whether people receive support (Antonucci, 1985; Broadhead et al., 1983; Wortman & Dunkel-Schetter, 1987). Some factors relate to the potential *recipients* of support. People are unlikely to receive support if they are unsociable, don't help others, and don't let others know that they need help. Some people are not assertive enough to ask for help, or feel that they should be independent or not burden others,

or feel uncomfortable confiding in others, or don't know whom to ask. Other factors relate to the potential *providers* of support. For instance, they may not have the resources needed, or may be under stress and in need of help themselves, or may be insensitive to the needs of others. Old age is a time when social support sometimes declines: the elderly may exchange less support because of the loss of a spouse or because they may feel reluctant to ask for help if they become unable to reciprocate. Whether people receive social support also depends on the size, intimacy, and frequency of contact of individuals in their *social network*—the people a person knows and contacts (Cutrona & Gardner, 2004; Wills & Fegan, 2001).

How can we assess people's social support, given the different types of support and the complex relationships that are involved? One highly regarded instrument is the *Social Support Questionnaire*, which consists of items, such as, "Who helps you feel that you truly have something positive to contribute to others?" (Sarason et al., 1983). For each item, the respondents list the people they can rely on and then indicate their overall degree of satisfaction with the support available. Using this instrument, these researchers have found that some people report high levels of satisfaction with support from a small number of close friends and relatives, but others need a large social network. (Go to 🍎 .)

Gender and Sociocultural Differences in Receiving Support

The amount of social support individuals receive appears to depend on their gender and sociocultural group membership. Some evidence suggests that women receive less support from their spouses than men do and seem to rely heavily on women friends for social support (Greenglass & Noguchi, 1996). These gender differences may result from the greater intimacy that seems to exist in the friendships of females than males and may reflect mainly differences in the emotional and esteem support males and females seek out and give (Heller, Price, & Hogg, 1990). Such gender differences could also reflect the fact that women generally respond to their own and others' stress with greater attention to personal relationships (Taylor et al., 2000). Research on social networks in the United States has revealed interesting gender and sociocultural relationships (Gottlieb & Green, 1987): Black Americans have smaller social networks than Whites and Hispanics, and men's networks are larger than women's among Black and Hispanic groups but not among nonminority people. Hispanics tend to focus mainly on extended families as their networks, Whites have broader networks of friends and coworkers, and Blacks focus on family and church groups.

ASSESS YOURSELF

How Much Emotional Support Do You Get?

Think of the 10 people to whom you feel closest. For some of them, you may not feel a strong bond—but they are still among the closest 10 people in your life. Write their initials in the following spaces:

—— —— —— —— —— —— —— —— —— ——

In the *corresponding* spaces below each of the following four questions, rate each person on a 5-point scale, where **1** = "not at all" and **5** = "extremely."

- How reliable is this person; is this person there when you need him or her?

—— —— —— —— —— —— —— —— —— ——

- How much does this person boost your spirits when you feel low?

—— —— —— —— —— —— —— —— —— ——

- How much does this person make you feel he or she cares about you?

—— —— —— —— —— —— —— —— —— ——

- How much do you feel you can confide in this person?

—— —— —— —— —— —— —— —— —— ——

Add together all of the ratings you gave across all of the people and questions. A total score between 120 and 150 is fairly typical and suggests that you can get a reasonably good level of emotional support when you need it. (Based on material in Schaefer, Coyne, & Lazarus 1981.)

Social Support, Stress, and Health

A favorite fortune cookie read, "Friendship is to people what sunshine is to flowers." Does the social support of friends, relatives, and other people affect our stress and health? Social support may reduce the stress people experience. For example, studies of job stress have shown that the greater the social support available to employees, the lower the psychological strain they report (Cottington & House, 1987; LaRocco, House, & French, 1980). Other research has found that blood pressure during work is lower for workers who have high social support than for those with less support (Karlin, Brondolo, & Schwartz, 2003), and positive interactions with spouses can reduce the effects of job stress on cortisol levels (Ditzen et al., 2008). People with better social support also have larger nighttime decreases in blood pressure, suggesting better restorative processes (Troxel et al., 2010). And social support has been associated with reduced stress from a variety of other sources, such as living near the damaged nuclear power plant at Three Mile Island (Fleming et al., 1982).

Experiments have assessed people's physiological strain while they were engaged in a stressful activity (such as giving a speech or performing mental arithmetic) either alone or in the presence of one or more individuals. Strain in these experiments is often assessed as *cardiovascular reactivity*—that is, an increase in blood pressure and/or heart rate from a baseline level. However, other aspects of the physiological stress response, including stress hormones such as cortisol, have been

examined as well (Uchino, 2006). We'll consider a few findings. First, while giving a speech, people often show less reactivity if a supportive person is present than if speaking alone (Lepore, Allen, & Evans, 1993; Uchino & Garvey, 1997). Second, reactivity is lower with a friend present than with a supportive stranger (Christenfeld et al., 1997). Third, sometimes the presence of supportive people can *increase* reactivity, especially if their presence functions as an audience that increases the support recipient's worries about being evaluated negatively (Taylor et al., 2010). Fourth, reactivity is also lower in the presence of the person's pet than alone (Allen, Blascovich, & Mendes, 2002). Fifth, other findings suggest that the benefits of social support on reactivity may depend on the person's personality: people who are defensive—they avoid information or feelings that threaten their self-concept—show *higher* reactivity under stress when social support is given (Westmaas & Jamner, 2006). Similarly, hostile individuals can also show increased reactivity during stressful activities when accompanied by friends, perhaps because they mistrust their friends or are concerned about being evaluated (Holt-Lunstad et al., 2008). Finally, simply thinking about supportive relationships before encountering a stressor can reduce cardiovascular stress responses (Smith et al., 2004). So, looking at the pictures of loved ones on your desk during a stressful day at work might be more than just a pleasant distraction.

Having social support also seems to benefit people's health (Cutrona & Gardner, 2004; Uchino, 2004). For instance, a prospective study had more than 4,700 men and women between 30 and 69 years of age report on four aspects of social support: marital status, contacts with family and friends, church membership, and formal and informal group associations (Berkman & Syme, 1979). Mortality data collected over the next 9 years revealed that the greater the degree of social support the subjects had, the lower the likelihood of their dying during the period of the study. Figure 3-2 shows an example of these findings. In each age category, individuals who had few contacts with friends and relatives had higher mortality rates than those with many contacts. This relationship applied to deaths from all causes and deaths from several specific diseases, including cancer and heart disease. This association is also quite strong in the case of coronary heart disease, a leading cause of mortality in industrialized nations. Specifically, social support is associated with a lower risk of developing heart disease, and among people who have already developed heart disease social support is associated with lower risk of additional heart attacks and death from heart disease (Lett et al., 2005).

Because this research is quasi-experimental, the relationship found between social support and mortality is correlational. How do we know whether social support leads to better health or whether the influence is the other way around? That is, could the people who had less social support be less active socially because they were already sick at the start of the study? Berkman and Syme provided some evidence that this was not the case. For instance, the subjects had been asked about past illnesses at the initial interview, and those with high levels of social support did not differ from those with low levels of support. But better evidence comes from a similar study of more than 2,700 adults who were medically examined at the start of the research (House, Robbins, & Metzner, 1982). This research found that people with less social support had higher mortality rates and that the initial health of those with low social support was the same as that of those with high support. Many studies of social support and future health have made sure that initial differences in health do not explain the prospective association between support and health. However, the correlational design still means that we cannot be certain that good support *causes* good health. Unexamined third variables could still play a role. For example, twin studies demonstrate that social support and the quality of our personal relationships are at least partially influenced by genetic factors (Spotts, Prescott, & Kendler, 2006). So, it is possible that genetic factors influence both the development of social support and future health, without support playing a direct causal role in health.

Researchers have also studied the association between social support and the likelihood that people will recover quickly from serious illness. Early findings were inconsistent—probably because of variations in research methods, such as in the way support was defined and measured (Wallston et al., 1983; Wortman & Dunkel-Schetter, 1987). Newer research has found more consistently positive results, showing, for example, that heart disease and surgery patients with high levels of social support recover more quickly than comparable patients with less support (Cutrona & Gardner, 2004; Kulik & Mahler, 1989; Wills & Fegan, 2001). Although these findings suggest that social support reduces the likelihood of illness and speeds recovery, the connection between social support and health is not always very strong, probably because support is only one of many factors involved (Kobasa et al., 1985; Smith et al., 1994). Social support appears to have a strong impact on the health of some individuals, and a weak influence on the health of others. For instance, some evidence indicates that the recovery of many patients who believe they can cope with the emotional demands of their illness does not benefit from social support (Wilcox, Kasl, & Berkman, 1994).

How May Social Support Affect Health?

We have seen that prolonged exposure to high levels of stress can lead to illness. To explain how social support may influence health, researchers have proposed two

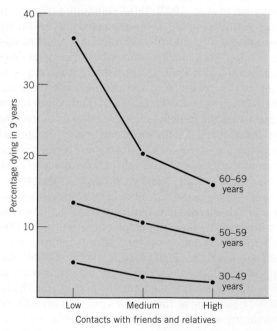

Figure 3-2 Percentage of adults who died within 9 years as a function of the number of contacts with friends and relatives and the subjects' ages at the start of the study, in 1965. (Data from Berkman & Syme, 1979, Table 2.)

theories: the "buffering" and the "direct effects" (or "main effects") hypotheses (Cutrona & Gardner, 2004; Wills & Fegan, 2001). According to the **buffering hypothesis**, social support affects health by *protecting* the person against the negative effects of high stress. A graphical illustration of the buffering hypothesis appears in Figure 3-3a. As the graph shows, this protective function is effective only or mainly when the person encounters a strong stressor. Under low-stress conditions, little or no buffering occurs. Research has shown that the buffering process does occur (Wills & Fegan, 2001). For example, a study of job stress found that social support had a much stronger association with lower blood pressure during stressful than nonstressful work times (Karlin, Brondolo, & Schwartz, 2003).

How may buffering work? Here are two ways. First, when people encounter a strong stressor, such as a major financial crisis, those who have high levels of social support may be less likely to appraise the situation as stressful than those with low levels of support. Individuals with high social support may expect that someone they know will help them, such as by lending money or giving advice on how to get it. Second, social support may modify people's response to a stressor after the initial appraisal. For instance, people with high social support might have someone provide a solution to the problem, convince them that the problem is not very important, or cheer them on to "look on the bright side." People with little social support are much less likely to have any of these advantages—so the negative impact of the stress is greater for them.

The **direct effects hypothesis** maintains that social support benefits health and well-being regardless of the amount of stress people experience—the beneficial effects are similar under high and low stressor intensities, as depicted in Figure 3-3b. How do direct effects work? One way is that people with high levels of social support may have strong feelings of belongingness and self-esteem. The positive outlook this produces may be beneficial to health independently of stress: studies have found lower blood pressures in daily life and in laboratory tests among middle-aged and younger adults with higher levels of social support regardless of stress levels (Carels, Blumenthal, & Sherwood, 1998; Uchino et al., 1999). Other evidence suggests that high levels of support may encourage people to lead healthful lifestyles (Broman, 1993; Peirce et al., 2000). People with social support may feel, for example, that because others care about them and need them, they should exercise, eat well, and not smoke or drink heavily.

Does Social Support Always Help?

Social support does not always reduce stress and benefit health. Why not? For one thing, although support may be offered or available to us, we may not *perceive* it as supportive (Dunkel-Schetter & Bennett, 1990; Wilcox, Kasl, & Berkman, 1994). This may happen because the help is insufficient or the wrong kind, or we may not want help. When we do not perceive help as supportive, it is less likely to reduce our stress. For example, when people feel the need for tangible help or instrumental support but receive emotional support, they find that support unhelpful and ineffective. Similarly, when people feel the need for emotional support but

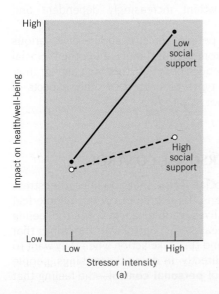

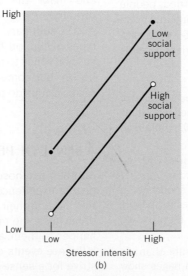

Figure 3–3 Illustration of two ways social support may benefit health and well-being. Graph (a) illustrates the buffering hypothesis, which proposes that social support modifies the negative health effects of high levels of stress. Graph (b) depicts the direct effects hypothesis, which proposes that the health benefits of social support occur regardless of stress.

receive offers of instrumental support, they also find that support unhelpful (Horowitz et al., 2001). Support that is responsive to the recipient's needs is the most beneficial (Maisel & Gable, 2009). Further, receiving support can sometimes convey the message to the recipient that they are inadequate to handle their problems on their own, resulting in lower self-esteem (Lepore et al., 2008). These possible negative consequences of received support may be the reason that overall the health benefits of the general sense or perceptions that one has support is a better predictor of future good health than is actual received support (Uchino, 2009).

Despite the advantages of perceived support, some intriguing research suggests that "invisible support" is best. By studying couples and asking each partner separately whether they gave or received support on a given day, Niall Bolger and his colleagues (2000) found the most beneficial effects of support on reducing negative mood during high stress days when the partner reported giving support but the recipient was unaware of it. Experimental studies have shown similar advantages of receiving support without being aware of it (Bolger & Amarel, 2007). Perhaps a "light touch" that is responsive to the recipients' needs without making them feel less competent or as though they are a burden on the support providers can maximize the benefits of support in some instances.

Marriage is often thought to convey protective health benefits by providing social support. Consistent with this idea, studies have found that married people live longer than divorced and never-married individuals (Kaplan & Kronick, 2006; Murphy & Bennett, 2004). James Lynch (1990) has argued that being lonely or having a "broken heart" is a risk factor for heart disease because widowed, divorced, and never-married individuals have higher death rates from heart disease than married people do. Some evidence indeed suggests that loneliness can increase the risk of heart disease (Thurston & Kubzansky, 2009). But other findings suggest that marriage itself is not the crucial factor:

- Studies have found that a health protective role of marriage occurs mainly for men and women who think their marital quality is high (Gallo et al., 2003; Umberson et al., 2006).
- Research on middle-aged men and women with no symptoms of heart disease found similar low rates of atherosclerosis in people living with a spouse or a partner (unmarried), but much higher rates for people living alone, either single or widowed (Kop et al., 2005).
- Married people show lower blood pressure than do single people, but people in unhappy marriages show

higher blood pressure than single individuals (Holt-Lunstad et al., 2009).

- Frequent contact with a spouse, presumably a source of social support, can protect against worsening atherosclerosis over time, unless the marriage is perceived as low in quality (Janicki et al., 2005).

These findings suggest that social support, and not specifically marriage, is the crucial factor. When it comes to marriage and health, simply being married is not everything; quality matters.

Last, sometimes social ties can harm a person's health. For one thing, strain or conflict in relationships can increase chances of developing serious illness (De Vogli et al., 2007), probably because, as discussed in Chapter 2, conflict in relationships evokes a strong physiological stress response. Further, people with high levels of stress and frequent social contacts are more likely than others to develop infectious illnesses, such as colds (Hamrick, Cohen, & Rodriguez, 2002). Also, social ties harm health when people encourage unhealthful behavior (Burg & Seeman, 1994; Kaplan & Toshima, 1990; Suls, 1982). We'll look at three examples. First, people may set a bad example—for instance, children are more likely to start smoking and drinking if their friends and family engage in these behaviors and less likely to use seat belts and eat a balanced diet if friends and family don't. Second, people may encourage individuals who are overweight or have high blood pressure to eat prohibited foods, saying, "A little more cheesecake can't hurt" or "You can make up for it by dieting next week." Third, families may be overprotective toward a person with a serious illness, such as heart disease, and discourage the patient's need to become more active or to go back to work. This can interfere with rehabilitation and make the patient increasingly dependent and disabled.

In summary, people perceive and receive various types of support from friends, family, and others. Social support tends to reduce people's stress and benefit their health, but some types of support or other aspects of relationships do not. (Go to 🧑.)

A SENSE OF PERSONAL CONTROL

Another psychosocial factor that modifies the stress people experience is the degree of control people feel they have in their lives. People generally like the feeling of having some measure of control over the things that happen to them, and they take action when they want to influence events directly. In doing these things, people strive for a sense of **personal control**—the feeling that

CLINICAL METHODS AND ISSUES
Social Support, Therapy, and Cognitive Processes

Years ago, a reporter asked actress Melina Mercouri about psychotherapy in her native country; she replied that in Greece people don't need therapists, they have friends. Although her view oversimplifies the therapy process, therapy does include two features friends can provide: social support and the opportunity for *disclosure* of negative experiences and feelings. James Pennebaker and other researchers have found that people's talking or writing about traumatic or very emotional experiences for a few sessions of 15- to 30-minutes has beneficial effects that last for months. This reduces their stress and negative feelings and seems to improve their health, as reflected in the number of doctor visits and episodes of chronic illness symptoms (Pennebaker, 1990; Smyth & Pennebaker, 2001). Although the effects of disclosure on psychological and physical health are not very large, they have been confirmed in a meta-analysis of over 140 studies (Frattaroli, 2006). Other research has shown that simply describing the benefits gained from traumatic events or the success in managing one's stress, can have similar effects (King & Miner, 2000; Leake, Friend, & Wadhwa, 1999). Why does disclosure help? An experiment tested this issue with breast cancer patients and found that the benefits of disclosure are linked to the reduced autonomic arousal, such as heart rate, that occurs when people express negative memories (Low, Stanton, & Danoff-Burg, 2006).

they can make decisions and take effective action to produce desirable outcomes and avoid undesirable ones (Contrada & Goyal, 2004). Studies have found that people who have a strong sense of personal control report experiencing less strain from stressors (McFarlane et al., 1983; Suls & Mullen, 1981).

Types of Control

How can feelings of personal control reduce the stress people experience? People can use several types of control to influence events in their lives and reduce their stress (Cohen et al., 1986; Thompson, 1981). We'll focus on two. **Behavioral control** involves the ability to take concrete action to reduce the impact of a stressor. This action might reduce the intensity of the event or shorten its duration. For example, a pregnant woman who has taken natural childbirth classes can use special breathing techniques during delivery that reduce the pain of labor. **Cognitive control** is the ability to use thought processes or strategies to modify the impact of a stressor, such as by thinking about the event differently or focusing on a pleasant or neutral thought. While giving birth, for instance, the mother might think about the positive meanings the baby will give to her life, or she could focus her mind on an image, such as a pleasant day she had at the beach. Cognitive control appears to be especially effective in reducing stress (Cohen et al., 1986). For example, cognitive reappraisal of stressful stimuli or events as less threatening can reduce negative emotions and physiological stress responses (John & Gross, 2004).

Beliefs About Oneself and Control

People differ in the degree to which they believe they have control over their lives. Most people believe they have at least some control, but others think they have almost none. The latter is shown in the case study of a chronically unemployed man named Karl, who was referred to therapy by the Veterans Administration and with some help

> applied for a job and got it. But this did not raise his expectancies of being able to get another job should he have to do so. Indeed, he attributed his success entirely to good fortune. He believed that the employer probably was partial to veterans or just happened to be in a good mood that day ... [and] that the occurrence of reinforcement was outside his own personal control. (Phares, 1984, pp. 505–506)

People who believe they have control over their successes and failures are described as possessing an *internal* **locus of control**. That is, the control for these events lies within themselves—they are responsible. Other people, like Karl, who believe that their lives are controlled by forces outside themselves, for example, by luck, have an *external* locus of control (Rotter, 1966). A questionnaire called the I-E *Scale* is used for measuring the degree of internality or externality of a person's beliefs about personal control

Another important aspect of personal control is our sense of **self-efficacy**—the belief that we can succeed at a specific activity we want to do (Bandura, 1986, 2004). People estimate their chances of success in an activity, such as quitting smoking or running a mile, on the basis of their prior observations of themselves and others. They decide whether to attempt the activity according to two expectations:

1. *Outcome expectancy*—that the behavior, if properly carried out, would lead to a favorable outcome.

2. *Self-efficacy expectancy*—that they can perform the behavior properly.

For example, you may know that by taking and doing well in a set of college honors courses you can graduate with a special diploma or certificate. But if you think the likelihood of achieving that feat as "zilch," you're not likely to try. For people engaged in a stressful activity, increases in heart rate and blood pressure generally correspond to their level of mental effort in dealing with the demands of the situation—the greater their effort, the greater the cardiovascular reactivity (Gendolla & Wright, 2005). People with strong self-efficacy for the activity may be less threatened and exert less mental effort because they know they can manage the demands of the situation more easily. Hence, they generally show less psychological and physiological strain than do those with a weaker self-efficacy (Bandura, Reese, & Adams, 1982; Bandura et al., 1985; Holahan, Holahan, & Belk, 1984).

Determinants and Development of Personal Control

On what basis do people judge that they have control over things that happen in their lives? We make these assessments by using information we gain from our successes and failures throughout life (Bandura, 1986, 2004; DeVellis & DeVellis, 2001). Our sense of control also develops through *social learning*, in which we learn by observing the behavior of others (Bandura, 1969, 1986). During childhood, people in the family and at school are important others, serving as models of behavior, agents of reinforcement, and standards for comparison. At the other end of the life span, people tend to be relatively external in locus of control—that is, beliefs that chance and powerful others affect their lives are greater in the elderly than in younger adults (Lachman, 1986). So, among adults who develop serious illnesses, those who are elderly are more inclined to prefer having professionals make health-related decisions for them (Woodward & Wallston, 1987).

Gender and Sociocultural Differences in Personal Control

Gender and sociocultural differences in personal control often develop, depending on the social experiences individuals have. Sometimes parents and teachers inadvertently lead girls more than boys toward beliefs in external control and in low self-efficacy for certain activities (Dweck & Elliott, 1983). This socialization may carry over to old age: among elderly cardiac patients, men report greater self-efficacy than women for being able to walk various distances, a common rehabilitation behavior (Jenkins & Gortner, 1998). Self-efficacy beliefs generally can play an important role in the process of rehabilitation for heart patients (Woodgate & Brawley, 2008). Because minority groups and poor people generally have limited access to power and economic advancement, they tend to have external locus of control beliefs (Lundin, 1987).

When People Lack Personal Control

What happens to people who experience high levels of stress over a long period of time and feel that nothing they do matters? They feel helpless—trapped and unable to avoid negative outcomes. A worker who cannot seem to please her boss no matter what she does, a student who cannot perform well on exams, or a patient who is unable to relieve his severe low back pain—each of these situations can produce apathy. As a result, these people may stop striving for these goals, come to believe they have no control over these and other events in their lives, and fail to exert control even when they could succeed. This is the condition Martin Seligman (1975) has called **learned helplessness**—which he describes as a principal characteristic of depression. Research has shown that people can learn to be helpless by being in uncontrollable situations that lead to repeated failure, such as in trying to stop an unpleasant noise (Hiroto & Seligman, 1975).

Seligman and his colleagues have extended the theory of learned helplessness to explain two important observations (Abramson, Seligman,& Teasdale, 1978). First, being exposed to uncontrollable negative events does not always lead to learned helplessness. Second, depressed people often report feeling a loss in self-esteem. The revised theory proposes that people who experience uncontrollable negative events apply a cognitive process called *attribution*, in which they make judgments about three dimensions of the situation:

1. *Internal-external*. People consider whether the situation results from their own personal inability to control outcomes or from external causes that are beyond anyone's control. For example, suppose a boy receives physical therapy for a serious injury but cannot seem to meet the goals each week, which he might attribute either to his own lack of fortitude or to the rehabilitation program design. Either judgment may make him stop trying. He is likely to suffer a loss of self-esteem if he

This homeless woman probably sees little personal control in her life and feels very helpless.

attributes the difficulty to a lack of personal strength, but not if he attributes the difficulty to external causes.

2. *Stable-unstable.* People assess whether the situation results from a cause that is long-lasting (stable) or temporary (unstable). If they judge that it is long-lasting, as when people develop a chronic and disabling disease, they are more likely to feel helpless and depressed than if they think their condition is temporary.

3. *Global-specific.* People consider whether the situation results from factors that have global and wide-ranging effects or specific and narrow effects. Individuals who fail at stopping smoking cigarettes and make a *global* judgment—for example, "I'm totally no good and weak-willed"—may feel helpless and depressed. But others who fail and make a *specific* judgment, such as "I'm not good at controlling this part of my life," are less likely to feel helpless.

Thus, people who tend to attribute negative events in their lives to *stable* and *global* causes are at high risk for feeling helpless and depressed. If their judgments are also *internal*, their depressive thinking is likely to include a loss of self-esteem as well. People who believe bad events result from internal, stable, and global factors while good events result from external, unstable, and specific factors have a *pessimistic explanatory style* (Kamen & Seligman, 1989). Attributing negative events to external, unstable, and specific causes, in contrast, reflects an optimistic explanatory or attributional style.

How does lacking personal control affect people in real-life stressful conditions? Studies have examined this question with college students and children. For instance, of college students in dormitories, those who lived on crowded floors reported more stress and less ability to control unwanted social interaction and showed more evidence of helplessness, such as giving up in competitive games, than those on uncrowded floors (Baum, Aiello, & Calesnick, 1978; Rodin & Baum, 1978). In a study of fifth-graders, students were given an impossible task to arrange blocks to match a pictured design (Dweck & Repucci, 1973). Children who attributed their failure to stable, uncontrollable factors, such as their own lack of ability, showed poorer performance on subsequent problems than those who attributed failure to unstable, modifiable factors, such as a lack of effort. Thus, the children's attributions were linked to their feelings of helplessness.

Personal Control and Health

There are two ways in which personal control and health may be related. First, people who have a strong sense of personal control may be more likely or able to maintain their health and prevent illness than those who have a weak sense of control. Second, once people become seriously ill, those who have a strong sense of control may adjust to the illness and promote their own rehabilitation better than those who have a weak sense of control. Both types of relationships have been examined.

To study these relationships, researchers have used several approaches to measure people's personal control. One of the best-developed health-related measures of personal control is the *Multidimensional Health Locus of Control Scales* (Wallston, Wallston, & DeVellis, 1978). This instrument contains 18 items divided into three scales that assess:

1. *Internal health locus of control,* the belief that control for one's health lies within the person.

2. *Powerful-others' health locus of control,* the belief that one's health is controlled by other people, such as doctors.

3. *Chance locus of control,* the belief that luck or fate controls health.

As you can see, the powerful-others and chance scales are directed toward assessing the degree to which people believe important external sources have control over their health.

Does a sense of personal control influence people's health? Studies have shown that pessimistic and hopeless people—those who believe they have little control—have poorer health habits, have more illnesses, and are less likely to take active steps to treat their illness than are people with a greater sense of control (Kamen & Seligman, 1989; Lin & Peterson, 1990; Rasmussen, Scheier, & Greenhouse, 2009; Whipple et al., 2009). Personal control can also help people adjust to becoming seriously ill (Thompson & Kyle, 2000). Patients with illnesses such as kidney failure or cancer who score high on internal or powerful-others' health locus of control suffer less depression than those with strong beliefs in the role of chance (Devins et al., 1981; Marks et al., 1986). The belief that either they or someone else can influence the course of their illness allows patients to be hopeful about their future. Moreover, patients with strong internal locus of control beliefs probably realize they have effective ways for controlling their stress.

Personal control also affects the efforts patients make toward rehabilitation—in particular, feelings of self-efficacy enhance their efforts. A study demonstrated this with older adult patients who had serious respiratory diseases, such as chronic bronchitis and emphysema (Kaplan, Atkins, & Reinsch, 1984). The patients were examined at a clinic and given individualized prescriptions for exercise. And they rated on a survey their self-efficacy—that is, their belief in their ability to perform specific physical activities, such as walking different distances, lifting objects of various weights, and climbing stairs. Correlational analyses revealed that the greater the patients' self-efficacy for doing physical activity, the more they adhered to the exercise prescription.

Health and Personal Control in Old Age

Here are two things we know about elderly people who live in nursing homes: First, they often show declines in their activity and health after they begin living in nursing homes. Second, residents of nursing homes frequently have few responsibilities or opportunities to influence their everyday lives. Could it be that the declines in activity and health among nursing-home residents result in part from their dependency and loss of personal control that the nursing home procedures seem to encourage?

Ellen Langer and Judith Rodin (1976) studied this issue by manipulating the amount of responsibility allowed residents of two floors of a modern, high-quality nursing home. The residents on the two floors were similar in physical and psychological health and prior socioeconomic status. On one floor, residents were given opportunities to have responsibilities—for example, they could select small plants to care for and were encouraged to make decisions about participating in activities and rearranging furniture. In comparison, residents of the other floor continued to have little personal control. For example, they were assigned to various activities without choice, and when they were given plants, they were told that the staff would take care of them. Assessments revealed that the residents who were given more responsibility became happier and more active and alert than the residents who had little control. A year and a half later the residents who were given responsibility were still happier and more active than those who had little control (Rodin & Langer, 1977). Moreover, comparisons of health data during these 18 months showed that the residents with responsibility were healthier and had half the rate of mortality than the residents with little control.

Other research with residents of a retirement home also demonstrated the importance of personal control for physical and psychological well-being and showed that withdrawing opportunities for personal control may impair people's health (Schulz, 1976; Schulz & Hanusa, 1978). The results of these studies suggest two important conclusions. First, personal control—even over relatively simple or minor events—can have a powerful effect on people's health and psychological condition. Second, health care workers and researchers need to consider the nature of the personal control they introduce and what the impact will be if it is removed.

To summarize the material on personal control, people differ in the degree to which they believe they have control over the things that happen in their lives. People who experience prolonged, high levels of stress and lack a sense of personal control tend to feel helpless. Having a strong sense of control seems to benefit people's health and help them adjust to becoming seriously ill. A sense of personal control contributes to people's hardiness, which is the next psychosocial modifier of stress we will examine.

PERSONALITY AS RESILIENCE AND VULNERABILITY

Researchers have long been interested in the ways in which some personality traits can make individuals more resilient in the face of stressful life circumstances, whereas other personality characteristics are sources of vulnerability. That is, some personality factors make the individual more able to withstand high levels of stressful experience without becoming emotionally distressed or physically ill, and other aspects of personality make them *more* susceptible to those problems.

Early in the development of the field of health psychology, researchers Suzanne Kobasa and Salvatore Maddi suggested that individual differences in personal control provide only part of the reason why some people who are under stress get sick whereas others do not. They proposed that a broader array of personality traits—called **hardiness**—differentiates people who do and do not get sick under stress (Kobasa & Maddi, 1977). Hardiness includes three characteristics: (1) *Control* refers to people's belief that they can influence events in their lives—that is, a sense of personal control. (2) *Commitment* is people's sense of purpose or involvement in the events, activities, and people in their lives. For instance, people with a strong sense of commitment tend to look forward to starting each day's projects and enjoy getting close to people. (3) *Challenge* refers to the tendency to view changes as incentives or opportunities for growth rather than threats to security. The concept of hardiness has been highly influential, although more recent studies have found conflicting results, and some evidence indicates that tests used to measure hardiness may simply be measuring the tendency to experience negative affect, such as the tendency to be anxious, depressed, or hostile (Funk, 1992). Nonetheless, the basic idea that some personality traits make the individual resilient has continued to be a major focus in the field, and research supports this general hypothesis.

Sense of Coherence, Mastery, Optimism, and Resilience

One example of a personality concept similar to hardiness is *sense of coherence*, developed by Aaron Antonovsky (1979, 1987). This trait involves the tendency of people to see their worlds as comprehensible, manageable, and meaningful. People's sense of coherence has been linked to reduced levels of stress and illness symptoms (Jorgensen, Frankowski, & Carey, 1999). A related personality characteristic is *sense of mastery* (Pearlin & Schooler, 1978), which refers to people's general belief that they are able to deal effectively with the events of life, rather than being subjected to forces beyond their control. This trait is obviously quite similar to the belief in personal control or a general sense of self-efficacy as described previously. *Optimism* is the point of view that good things are likely to happen, and has similarities to the optimistic versus pessimistic explanatory style described previously. Optimists tend to experience life's difficulties with less distress than do pessimists (Scheier, Carver, & Bridges,

2001). They also tend to have better health habits, better mental and physical health, and faster recovery when they become ill than pessimists (Ouellette & DiPlacido, 2001).

Finally, *resilience refers to* high levels of three inter-related positive components of personality: self-esteem, personal control, and optimism (Major et al., 1998). Resilient people appraise negative events as less stressful; they bounce back from adversities and recover their strength and spirit. For example, resilient children develop into competent, well-adjusted individuals even when growing up under extremely difficult conditions (Garmezy, 1983; Werner & Smith, 1982). The following case shows what this means:

> In the slums of Minneapolis … is a 10-year-old boy who lives in a dilapidated apartment with his father, an ex-convict now dying of cancer, his illiterate mother, and seven brothers and sisters, two of whom are mentally retarded. Yet his teachers describe him as an unusually competent child who does well in his studies and is loved by almost everyone in the school. (Pines, 1979, p. 53)

Even when facing adversity, resilient people seem to make use of positive emotions and find meaning in the experience (Ong et al., 2006; Tugade & Fredrickson, 2004). Although such resilience was once considered rare, it now appears that probably most adults move on with their lives and do not suffer serious depression after a trauma, such as the loss of a close relative or friend (Bonanno, 2004).

Why are some individuals resilient and others not? Part of the answer may lie in their genetic endowments. Resilient people may have inherited traits, such as relatively easy temperaments, that enable them to cope better with stress and turmoil. Another part lies in their experiences. Resilient people who overcome a history of stressful events often have compensating experiences and circumstances in their lives, such as special talents or interests that absorb them and give them confidence, and close relationships with friends or relatives. The concepts of hardiness, resilience, optimism, mastery, and coherence have a great deal in common, and research scales used to measure these traits may be tapping overlapping personality strengths.

Personality Strengths and Health

In theory, the personality strengths we've discussed make people better able to deal with stressors and less likely to become emotionally distressed and physiologically aroused by stressful events, leading them to remain healthier. Given the personality assets or strengths reflected in a sense of coherence, mastery, and optimism, the spiraling process that can lead from stress to illness should not take hold. Studies have generally supported the prediction that these traits should be associated with lower risks of physical illness. For example, a meta-analysis of several studies of a variety of health conditions found that, as expected, optimism is associated with a reduced risk of developing physical illnesses and with a more positive outcome of illness among individuals who are already suffering from disease (Rasmussen, Scheier, & Greenhouse, 2009). Prospective studies have shown that optimistic people are at lower risk of life-threatening medical conditions, such as heart disease (Tindle et al., 2009). And a prospective study found that people who have a strong sense of coherence had far lower mortality rates from cardiovascular disease and cancer over a 6-year period than people low on this trait (Surtees et al., 2003), and sense of mastery has similar beneficial effects over time (Surtees et al., 2006). Taken together, positive personality traits like optimism, mastery, and sense of coherence apparently protect health. Although the status of the concept and measurement of hardiness is uncertain at this time, research on related aspects of personality has provided clearer evidence of health benefits. Future research will need to clarify what these personality variables are and how they operate.

Personality Strengths and Health in Old Age

Old age is a time when very difficult life events often occur, particularly those that involve reduced income, failing health and disability, and the loss of one's spouse and close friends. Personality strengths like those described above can be important in meeting these difficulties. For example, older people with a strong sense of purpose in life seem to live longer, even when the possibly overlapping effects of negative emotions like depression are taken into account (Boyle et al., 2009). What other personality characteristics reflect resilience in old age?

Elizabeth Colerick (1985) studied 70- to 80-year-old men and women for the quality she called *stamina*, which is similar to hardiness. This research was undertaken to determine how people who do and do not have stamina in later life deal with setbacks, such as the loss of a loved one. She identified with questionnaires and interviews two groups: one with high stamina and one with low stamina. She found that stamina in old age is characterized by "a triumphant, positive outlook during periods of adversity," as illustrated by the following interview excerpts from two different high-stamina people:

The key to dealing with loss is not obvious. One must take the problem, the void, the loneliness, the sorrow and put it on the *back* of your neck and use it as a driving force. Don't let such problems sit out there in front of you, blocking your vision.... Use hardships in a positive way. (p. 999)

I realize that setbacks are a part of the game. I've had 'em, I have them now, and I've got plenty more ahead of me. Seeing this—the big picture—puts it all into perspective, no matter how bad things get. (p. 999)

In contrast, low-stamina people described a negative outlook and feelings of helplessness and hopelessness in facing life events in old age. One woman who had undergone surgery for colon cancer said:

I was certain that I would die on the table ... never wake up.... I felt sure it was the end. Then I woke up with a colostomy and figured I have to stay inside the house the rest of my life. Now I'm afraid to go back to the doctor's and keep putting off my checkups. (p. 999)

In summary, people with a high degree of optimism, mastery, coherence, or resilience—or some related personality traits—may have some protection against the harmful effects of stress on health. The fact that several different labels have been given to what seem to be very similar personality strengths with possibly overlapping associations with future health suggests that an organizing framework would be useful in understanding personality as a modifier of stress. A widely accepted framework from personality science has been useful in this way, especially because it helps to organize personality factors that are sources of resilience or sources of vulnerability.

The Five-Factor Model of Personality

A general consensus has emerged among personality researchers that five broad traits provide a reasonably thorough description of normal variations in human personality (Costa & McCrae, 1992; Digman, 1990). These traits, listed in Table 3.1, are useful in research on personality (Smith & Williams, 1992; Smith & MacKenzie, 2006). Researchers can examine correlations of personality concepts and measures proposed as influences on health with these basic dimensions and their more specific components. By doing this, researchers can create an organized and systematic *catalogue* of these modifiers of stress responses. The traits of the five-factor model also can be measured with well-established personality scales, and these scientifically validated instruments can be used directly

Table 3.1   *Traits of the Five-Factor Model of Personality*

Trait	Specific Characteristics
Neuroticism vs. Emotional Stability	Tendency to experience negative emotions, such as anxiety, tension, sadness, and irritability; feeling vulnerable and unable to cope well with stress vs. calm, even-tempered, relaxed, able to deal with stressful situations without undue distress.
Extraversion vs. Introversion	Outgoing, gregarious, cheerful, and talkative interpersonal style; excitement seeking; assertiveness; a tendency to experience positive emotions vs. reserved; enjoyment of and even preference for solitude and quiet; subdued.
Openness vs. Closed Mindedness	Drawn to new experience; intellectual curiosity; flexibility; readiness to examine and re-consider values and beliefs, and to try new things; "in touch" with feelings and aesthetic experiences vs. dislike of change; rigid; dogmatic; narrow.
Agreeableness vs. Antagonism	Altruistic, high empathy and concern for others; warm; forgiving helpful; trusting; cooperative; straightforward; modest vs. cold-hearted; cynical; guarded; disingenuous; mistrusting; argumentative; competitive; arrogant; critical.
Conscientiousness vs. Unreliability	High self-control; organized; purposeful; self-image of being capable, prepared, competent; preference for order; dependable; deliberate; self-disciplined; achievement striving vs. unorganized; low ambition; lackadaisical; procrastinating.

in studies of stress and health outcomes. In this way, some of the best ways of conceptualizing and measuring personality available to researchers can be used to answer questions about which general dimensions of personality modify stress and influence health. By thinking about the traits in Table 3.1, readers can get a general sense of how they might be described in the five-factor system.

The personality strengths discussed above seem to correlate consistently with *emotional stability*—the opposite of *neuroticism* (Smith & MacKenzie, 2006). Neuroticism and its components, such as anxiety, sadness or depressive symptoms, and irritability, predict earlier death and several other negative health outcomes (Grossardt et al., 2009; Kubzansky et al., 2006; Suls & Bunde, 2005). However, positive aspects of personality generally predict good future health even when the possibly overlapping effects of emotional stability versus neuroticism are taken into account (Chida & Steptoe, 2008). Measures of personality strengths like optimism, mastery, and sense of coherence also correlate with other five-factor traits, especially *extraversion*, *conscientiousness*, and *openness*. These five-factor model traits also predict longevity and other health outcomes (Kern & Friedman, 2008; Taylor et al., 2009; Terracciano et al., 2008).

How does the five-factor model of personality relate to health? The answer involves the stress responses described in Chapter 2. Personality traits associated with better health are generally associated with less exposure to stressors at work and in relationships, less physiological reactivity, better recovery, and better restoration (Williams et al., 2010). In contrast, personality traits linked to poor health are consistently related to greater exposure to stressors, greater reactivity, less recovery,

and less restoration, as reflected in better sleep and lower levels of physiological stress responses during sleep. What's more, traits included in the five-factor model are also linked to one of the best known psychosocial modifiers of stress, the Type A or B behavioral and emotional style.

TYPE A BEHAVIOR AND BEYOND

The history of science has many stories about researchers accidently coming upon an idea that changed their focus and led to major discoveries. Such was the case for bacteriologist Alexander Fleming, for instance: when bacteria cultures he was studying developed unwanted molds, he happened to notice some properties of the molds that led to the discovery of penicillin. Serendipity also led to the discovery of the "Type A" behavior pattern. Cardiologists Meyer Friedman and Ray Rosenman were studying the diets of male heart disease victims and their wives when one of the wives exclaimed: "If you really want to know what is giving our husbands heart attacks, I'll tell you. It's stress, the stress they receive in their work, that's what's doing it" (Friedman & Rosenman, 1974, p. 56). These researchers began to study this possibility and noticed that heart patients were more likely than nonpatients to display a pattern of behavior we now refer to as Type A.

Defining and Measuring Behavior Patterns

The **Type A behavior pattern** consists of four characteristics (Chesney, Frautschi, & Rosenman, 1985; Friedman & Rosenman, 1974):

1. *Competitive achievement orientation.* Type A individuals strive toward goals with a sense of being in competition—or even opposition—with others, and not feeling a sense of joy in their efforts or accomplishments.

2. *Time urgency.* Type A people seem to be in a constant struggle against the clock. Often, they quickly become impatient with delays and unproductive time, schedule commitments too tightly, and try to do more than one thing at a time, such as reading while eating or watching TV.

3. *Anger/hostility.* Type A individuals tend to be easily aroused to anger or hostility, which they may or may not express overtly.

4. *Vigorous Vocal Style.* Type A people speak loudly, rapidly, and emphatically, often "taking over" and generally controlling the conversation.

In contrast, the **Type B behavior pattern** consists of low levels of competitiveness, time urgency, and hostility. People with the Type B pattern tend to be more easygoing and "philosophical" about life—they are more likely to "stop and smell the roses." In conversations, their speech is slower, softer, and reflects a more relaxed "give and take."

Type A behavior is measured in several ways. The Structured Interview has been considered the "gold standard" of Type A assessments. It consists of a series of questions that require about 15 to 20 minutes, and it is intended to obtain not only self-reports of competitiveness, time urgency, and anger/hostility, but also to obtain an actual sample of Type A versus B behavior. The questions are asked in such a way that Type As will reveal their competitive, impatient, hostile, and vigorous style not simply in what they say, but in how they say it. In contrast, Type Bs display their more relaxed and easy-going style. The interview is time-consuming and expensive to use, but it measures all four Type A characteristics (competitiveness, time urgency, anger/hostility, vocal style) better than self-report, paper and pencil survey measures of Type A do, and its scores are more consistently associated with health, especially heart disease (Miller et al., 1991).

Behavior Patterns and Stress

Individuals who exhibit the Type A behavior pattern react differently to stressors from those with the Type B pattern. Type A individuals respond more quickly and strongly to stressors, often interpreting them as threats to their personal control (Glass, 1977). Type A individuals also often choose more demanding or pressured activities at work and in their leisure times, and they often evoke angry and competitive behavior from others (Smith & Anderson, 1986). Hence, they have greater exposure to stressors, too.

We saw in Chapter 2 that the response to a stressor—or strain—includes a physiological component called *reactivity*, such as increased blood pressure, catecholamine, or cortisol levels compared to baseline levels. Type As often show greater reactivity to stressors than Type Bs, especially during situations involving competition, debates and arguments, or other stressful social interactions (Contrada & Krantz, 1988; Glass et al., 1980).

Age and Developmental Differences in Type A Behavior

Longitudinal studies suggest that adult Type A behavior may have its roots in the person's early temperament, and although behavior patterns often change over time, many individuals exhibit the same pattern across many years (Bergman & Magnusson, 1986; Carmelli et al., 1991; Carmelli, Rosenman, & Chesney, 1987). Still, cross-sectional studies have found that the Type A behavior pattern among Americans becomes more prevalent with age from childhood through middle age or so and then declines (Amos et al., 1987; Moss et al., 1986). But some of the decline in prevalence in old age could be result of Type A individuals dying at earlier ages than Type Bs.

Heredity also affects the development of Type A and B behavior. Research with identical (monozygotic) and fraternal (dizygotic) twins has found a genetic role in the development of both temperament (Buss & Plomin, 1975, 1986) and Type A behavior (Carmelli, Rosenman, & Chesney, 1987; Rebollo & Boomsma, 2006). That is, identical twins are more similar to each other in temperament and behavior patterns than are fraternal twins. They are much more similar than fraternal twins in their reactivity to stressors, too (Ditto, 1993; Turner & Hewitt, 1992). Demographic and genetic variations in Type A behavior are important because of the relationships researchers have found between reactivity and health, such as in the development of heart disease.

If your course has you read the modules from the Appendix, The Body's Physical Systems, distributed to the chapters, read **Module 5** (The Cardiovascular System) now.

Type A Behavior and Health

How are people's health and behavior patterns related? Researchers have studied this issue in two ways. First, studies have examined whether Type A individuals are at greater risk than Type Bs for becoming sick with any of a variety of illnesses, such as asthma and indigestion, but the associations appear to be weak and inconsistent (Orfutt & Lacroix, 1988; Suls & Sanders, 1988).

Second, studies have focused on the Type A pattern as a risk factor for **coronary heart disease (CHD)**—illnesses involving the narrowing of the coronary arteries, which supply blood to the heart muscle. This narrowing is called atherosclerosis, and causes several manifestations of CHD. A*ngina* is chest pain that occurs when the supply of oxygen carried by blood to the heart muscle is not sufficient to meet the muscle's demand. When the demand exceeds the supply available through the narrowed coronary arteries and the heart is not getting enough oxygen, the heart muscle becomes *ischemic*. If the blood supply is blocked severely enough and for a long enough period of time, the ischemic portion of the heart muscle dies. This is called a *myocardial infarction*, or what is commonly called a "heart attack." A severely ischemic heart sometimes develops a lethal disturbance in rhythm, causing it stop pumping blood through the body. This is the usual cause of sudden cardiac death, where the victim dies within a few minutes or hours of first noticing symptoms.

Dozens of studies have been done to assess the link between Type A behavior and CHD. An example of research on this link comes from the Western Collaborative Group Study, a large-scale prospective study of 3,000 39- to 59-year-old initially healthy men who were tested for behavior patterns using the Structured Interview (Rosenman et al., 1976). A follow-up 8 1/2 years later showed that the Type A individuals were twice as likely as Type Bs to have developed CHD and to have died of CHD. Have other studies found similar results? Yes, but the answer depends on the way Type A behavior was measured: the link between Type A behavior and CHD is *clearest in studies using the Structured Interview* (Miller et al., 1991).

Type A's "Deadly Emotion"

Why would the link between Type A behavior and CHD depend on the way behavior patterns are measured? It could be that people are not completely honest and accurate in describing their own behavior on self-report surveys, whereas observational measures are less "filtered" in this way. However, it also could be the content of the measures. We saw earlier that the Structured Interview assesses all four components of Type A behavior well. This isn't so for available surveys, which assess competitive achievement and time urgency well but measure anger/hostility much less well and do not measure the vocal style at all. These discrepancies prompted researchers to examine the role of individual Type A components, which revealed that anger/hostility is the main aspect of Type A behavior in the link with CHD (Everson-Rose & Lewis, 2005; Smith & Gallo, 2001). Anger/hostility seems to be Type A's deadly emotion: people who are chronically hostile have an increased risk of developing CHD.

A study that supports this idea examined the records of 255 doctors who had taken a psychological test that included a scale for hostility while they were in medical school 25 years earlier (Barefoot, Dahlstrom, & Williams, 1983). For the doctor with high scores on the hostility scale, the rates of both CHD and overall mortality during the intervening years were several times higher than for those with low hostility scores. The researchers measured hostility with a widely used test, the *Cook-Medley Hostility Scale*, which has 50 true/false items, such as "It is safer to trust nobody" and "Some of my family have habits that bother and annoy me very much" (Cook & Medley, 1954). This scale measures anger, as well as cynicism, suspiciousness, and other negative traits (Friedman, Tucker, & Reise, 1995). In pursuing anger and hostility as the toxic element within the Type A pattern, a wide variety of self-report and behavioral measures of these traits have been used (Smith, 1992). A meta-analysis of the many studies of the topic found that anger and hostility are associated with an increased risk of CHD in initially healthy individuals (Chida & Steptoe, 2009). Further, among people who already have CHD, anger and hostility are associated with increased risk of poor medical outcomes, such as additional heart attacks or death from CHD.

What links anger and hostility to the development of CHD? Here again, the four stress processes of exposure, reactivity, recovery, and restoration seem important. Angry and hostile people experience more conflict with others at home and work (Smith et al., 2004), indicating greater stress exposure. The suspicious and mistrusting style of hostile persons is likely to make them cold and argumentative during interactions with others, sometimes even with friends and family members. The resulting conflict and reduced social support may, in turn, contribute to the maintenance or even worsening of their hostile behavior toward others in a vicious cycle or self-fulfilling prophecy (Smith et al., 2004). Further, in difficult interpersonal situations in general, and at work and with family members in particular, they show greater physiological reactivity or strain (Brondolo et al., 2009; Chida & Hamer, 2008; Smith & Gallo, 1999).

Further, unlike non-hostile people, hostile people do not respond to social support with reduced physiological reactivity during stressful situations (Holt-Lunstad et al., 2008; Vella et al., 2008), perhaps because they are too distrusting or worry that support providers will evaluate them negatively. After a stressful situation, hostile people show delayed or incomplete recovery of their physiological stress responses, perhaps because they are more likely to brood or ruminate about upsetting events (Neuman et al., 2004). Also, their sleep quality is more likely to suffer during stressful periods (Brissette & Cohen, 2002). Combined, these stress processes can produce a lot of wear and tear on the cardiovascular system. As we discuss further in a later section of this chapter, cardiovascular reactivity and other physiological stress responses can contribute to coronary atherosclerosis and the development of other indications of CHD.

However, these stress processes might not be the only link between anger/hostility and CHD. Anger and hostility are related to several unhealthy conditions and behaviors, such as heavier drinking, obesity, and cigarette smoking, that put people at risk for CHD (Bunde & Suls, 2006; Nabi et al., 2009; Patterson et al., 2008). Although anger and hostility generally are associated with CHD even when these health behaviors and conditions are taken into account, some evidence suggests that they are at least part of the link between these personality traits and health (Boyle et al., 2007; Everson et al., 1997).

Are There Other Dangerous Aspects of the Type A Pattern?

Anger might not be the only unhealthy Type A behavior (Houston et al., 1992, 1997). Social dominance—the tendency or motive to exert power, control, or influence over other people—is also associated with coronary atherosclerosis and CHD (Siegman et al., 2000; Smith et al., 2008). Further, this personality trait is associated with greater physiological reactivity or strain during challenging interpersonal tasks and situations, like arguments or debates, and efforts to influence other people also evoke larger increases in blood pressure and stress hormones (Newton, 2009; Smith et al., 2000).

As a summary of the role of psychosocial modifiers of stress, we have seen that social support, personal control, various personality strengths, and aspects of the Type A and B behavior patterns are factors that can modify the impact of stress on health. High levels of social support, personal control, and related personality traits, are generally associated with reduced stress and resulting illnesses; Type A behavior, especially the

anger/hostility component, is associated with increased stress and cardiovascular illness. The remainder of this chapter examines health problems that are affected by people's experience of stress. We begin by considering how stress leads to illness.

HOW STRESS AFFECTS HEALTH

Why does stress lead to illnesses in some individuals, but not others? One answer: other factors influence the effects of stress. This idea forms the basis of the *diathesis-stress model*, the view that people's vulnerability to a physical or psychological disorder depends on the interplay of their predisposition to the disorder (the diathesis) and the amount of stress they experience (Steptoe & Ayers, 2004). The predisposition can result from organic structure and functioning, often genetically determined, or from prior environmental conditions, such as living in a community that promotes tobacco use. For example, chronically high levels of stress are especially likely to lead to CHD if the person's body produces high levels of cholesterol. Or students are likely to catch cold around final exams week if their immune system functioning is impaired. This concept may explain why not all individuals in the following experiment caught cold.

Researchers conducted an interesting experiment: they gave people nasal drops that contained a "common cold" virus or a placebo solution and then quarantined them to check for infection and cold symptoms (Cohen, Tyrrell, & Smith, 1991). Before the nasal drops were administered, the subjects filled out questionnaires to assess their recent stress. Of these people, 47% of those with high stress and 27% of those with low stress developed colds. Other studies have produced three related findings. First, people under chronic, severe stress are more vulnerable to catching cold when exposed to the virus than people under less stress (Cohen et al., 1998). Second, people who experience a lot of *positive emotions*, such as feeling energetic or happy, are less likely to catch a cold or the flu when exposed to the viruses than people who have less of these emotions (Cohen et al., 2006). Third, people who have sleep problems prior to their exposure to the virus are more likely to develop colds (Cohen et al., 2009).

What is it about stress that leads to illness? The causal sequence can involve two routes: (1) a direct route, resulting from changes stress produces in the body's *physiology*, or (2) an indirect route, affecting health through the person's *behavior*. Figure 3-4 gives a summary of these routes. Let's look first at the behavioral route.

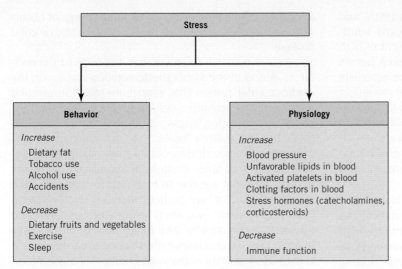

STRESS, BEHAVIOR, AND ILLNESS

Stress can affect behavior, which, in turn, can lead to illness or worsen an existing condition. We can see the behavioral links between stress and illness in many stressful situations, such as when a family undergoes a divorce. In many cases during the first year following the separation, the parent who has the children is less available and responsive to them than she or he was before, resulting in haphazard meals, less regular bedtimes, and delays in getting medical attention, for instance.

People who experience high levels of stress tend to behave in ways that increase their chances of becoming ill or injured (Weidner et al., 1996; Wiebe & McCallum, 1986). For instance, compared with people with low stress, those with high stress are more likely to eat higher fat diets with less fruit and vegetables, engage in less exercise, smoke cigarettes, and consume more alcohol (Baer et al., 1987; Cartwright et al., 2003; Ng & Jeffery, 2003). These behaviors are associated with the development of various illnesses. In addition, stress impairs sleep (Hall et al., 2004). And the resulting inattention and carelessness probably play a role in the relatively high accident rates of people under stress. Studies have found that children and adults who experience high levels of stress are more likely to suffer accidental injuries at home, in sports activities, on the job, and while driving a car than individuals under less stress (Johnson, 1986; Quick et al., 1997). Further, disrupted sleep can itself be stressful, and as described previously poor sleep interferes with a key way that the body is restored physiologically.

STRESS, PHYSIOLOGY, AND ILLNESS

Stress produces many physiological changes in the body that can affect health, especially when stress is chronic and severe. In Chapter 2, we discussed the concept of *allostatic load* in which the strain involved in reacting repeatedly to intense stressors produces wear and tear on body systems that accumulate over time and lead to illness (McEwen & Stellar, 1993). A study found that for elderly individuals whose allostatic load increased or decreased across a three-year period, those with increased loads had higher mortality rates during the next four years (Karlamangla, Singer, & Seeman, 2006). Connections have been found between illness and the degree of reactivity people show in their cardiovascular, endocrine, and immune systems when stressed.

Cardiovascular System Reactivity and Illness

Cardiovascular reactivity refers to physiological changes that occur in the heart, blood vessels, and blood in response to stressors. Before middle age, people's degree of cardiovascular reactivity is generally stable, showing little change when retested with the same stressors years later (Sherwood et al., 1997; Veit, Brody, & Rau, 1997). In later years, cardiovascular reactivity increases with age, which corresponds to increases in risk of cardiovascular illness (Uchino et al., 2005, 2006).

Research has discovered links between high cardiovascular reactivity and the development of CHD, hypertension, and stroke (Everson et al., 2001; Henderson & Baum, 2004; Manuck, 1994). For example, high levels of job stress are associated with high blood pressure and abnormally enlarged hearts (Schnall et al., 1990), and people's laboratory reactivity to stress in early adulthood is associated with their later development of high blood pressure (Menkes et al., 1989) and atherosclerosis (Matthews et al., 2006). The blood pressure reactivity that people display in laboratory tests appears to reflect their reactivity in daily life (Turner et al., 1994). A meta-analysis found that greater cardiovascular reactivity and poor cardiovascular recovery after stressors were associated with greater risk of cardiovascular disease, including higher blood pressure, diagnosed hypertension, and atherosclerosis (Chida & Steptoe, 2010).

Stress produces several cardiovascular changes that relate to the development of CHD. For instance, the blood of people who are under stress contains high concentrations of activated platelets (Everson-Rose & Lewis, 2005; Patterson et al., 1994) and clotting factors that thicken the blood, which can contribute to a heart attack (Wirtz et al., 2006). Stress also produces unfavorable levels of cholesterol (Patterson et al., 1995; Steptoe & Brydon, 2005) and inflammatory substances circulating in the blood (Steptoe et al., 2007). These changes in blood composition promote atherosclerosis—the growth of plaques (inflamed, fatty patches) within artery walls. These changes narrow and stiffen the arteries, thereby increasing blood pressure and the risk of a heart attack or stroke.

Stephen Manuck and his colleagues (1995) have demonstrated this link between stress and atherosclerosis in research with monkeys. In one study, over many months some of the subjects were relocated periodically to different living groups. This required stressful adjustments among the animals as they sought to re-establish the social hierarchies these animals naturally form, especially for higher-ranking or dominant animals to retain their status. The remaining subjects stayed in stable living groups. The stressed monkeys who tended to hold dominant status in their living groups developed greater atherosclerosis than the dominant animals in the low stress condition, and greater than the lower ranking or subordinate monkeys in either living condition. These effects were prevented when the animals were given a drug that blocked sympathetic nervous system excitation of the heart muscle, strongly implicating the role of chronic or recurring activation of the "fight or flight" response in development of atherosclerosis. Similar effects of experimentally manipulated stressful living conditions on atherosclerosis have been demonstrated in rabbits (McCabe et al., 2002). Although human stress and cardiovascular disease probably differs somewhat from what occurs in these animals, the ability to perform true experiments in which chronic stress is manipulated over long periods of time provides important converging evidence to the findings of observational studies of human stress and cardiovascular disease.

Recent research suggests that it is not just the excitatory effects of the sympathetic nervous system on the cardiovascular system that contribute to cardiovascular disease. If this activating system functions like the "gas pedal" in activating stress responses, the parasympathetic nervous system "brake" on such reactivity is also important. The functioning of this stress-dampening system can be measured though increases and decreases in heart rate that are due to respiration; changes in the activity of the parasympathetic nervous system cause heart rate to slow down when we breathe out and speed up when we breathe in. The magnitude of this change in heart rate—sometimes called "vagal tone" because it is caused by activity of the vagus nerve—is a good indicator of the strength of an individual's parasympathetic stress dampening system. Importantly, higher vagal tone is associated with lower risk of cardiovascular disease (Thayer & Lane, 2007). That is, good parasympathetic "brakes" on stress are protective.

Endocrine System Reactivity and Illness

Part of reactivity involves activation of the adrenal glands, both directly by sympathetic nervous system stimulation of these glands and by the *hypothalamus-pituitary-adrenal axis* as described previously. In this process, the adrenal glands release hormones—particularly catecholamines and corticosteroids—during stress (Henderson & Baum, 2004; Lundberg, 1999). The increased endocrine reactivity that people display in these tests appears to reflect their reactivity in daily life (Williams et al., 1991). One way in which high levels of these hormones can lead to illness involves their effects on the cardiovascular system. For example, an intense episode of stress with high levels of these hormones can cause the heart to beat erratically and may even lead to sudden cardiac death (Williams, 2008). In addition, chronically high levels of catecholamines and corticosteroids, such as cortisol, can contribute to the development and progression of atherosclerosis (Lundberg, 1999; Matthews et al., 2006). But social support may help: people with high levels of social support tend to exhibit lower endocrine reactivity than with those with lower levels (Seeman & McEwen, 1996).

Stress also seems to contribute to health through endocrine system pathways that involve fat stored in the abdominal cavity. The *metabolic syndrome* (Kyrou & Tsigos, 2009) is a set of risk factors including high levels of cholesterol and other blood fats; elevated blood pressure; high levels of insulin in the blood or impairments in the ability of insulin to facilitate transportation of glucose out of the blood stream; and larger fat deposits in the abdomen. The metabolic syndrome seems to be made worse by exposure to stressors and the related physiological stress responses, especially heightened neuroendocrine activity. The metabolic syndrome also promotes chronic inflammation in the blood stream and elsewhere, increasing the risk of cardiovascular disease and other serious conditions, such as diabetes (Goldbacher & Matthews, 2007; Rizvi, 2009).

If your course has you read the modules from the Appendix, The Body's Physical Systems, distributed to the chapters, read **Module 6** (The Immune System) now.

Immune System Reactivity and Illness

The release of catecholamines and corticosteroids during arousal affects health in another way: these stress responses alter the functioning of the immune system (Kemeny, 2007; Segerstrom & Miller, 2004). Brief stressors typically activate some components of the immune system, especially non-specific immunity, while suppressing specific immunity. Chronic stressors, in contrast, more generally suppress both non-specific and specific immune functions. Chronic stressors also increase *inflammation*, an important process that disrupts immune function when it occurs on a long-term basis (Kemeny, 2007; Segerstrom & Miller, 2004). So, rather than a simple "up or down" effect of stress on this vital system, stress dysregulates or disrupts it.

The effects of acute and chronic stress on the immune system can be measured in many ways, such as the extent to which immune system cells multiply or proliferate in response to antigens, or the ability of such cells to destroy foreign microorganisms or viruses. Immune system functioning can also be measured in others ways, such as whether or not an individual has a successful immune response to a flu vaccination. For example, increases in cortisol and adrenaline are associated with decreased activity of T cells and B cells against antigens. This decrease in lymphocyte activity appears to be important in the development and progression of a variety of infectious diseases and cancer (Kiecolt-Glaser & Glaser, 1995; Vedhara et al., 1999). Among people with cancer, those with high levels of killer-T-cell activity have a better prognosis than those with low levels of activity (Kemeny, 2007; Uchino et al., 2007).

Immune processes also protect the body against cancers that result from excessive exposure to harmful chemical or physical agents called *carcinogens*, which include radiation (nuclear, X-ray, and ultraviolet types), tobacco smoke, and asbestos (AMA, 2003). Carcinogens can damage the DNA in body cells, which may then develop into mutant cells and spread. Fortunately, people's exposure to carcinogens is generally at low levels and for short periods of time, and most DNA changes probably do not lead to cancer (Glaser et al., 1985). When mutant cells develop, the immune system attacks them with killer T cells. Actually, the body begins to defend itself against cancer even before a cell mutates by using enzymes to destroy chemical carcinogens or to repair damaged DNA.

But research has shown that high levels of stress reduce the production of these enzymes and the repair of damaged DNA (Glaser et al., 1985; Kiecolt-Glaser & Glaser, 1986). Given that the immune system has far-reaching protective effects, if stress disrupts the immune system it can affect a great variety of health conditions from the common cold to herpes virus infections (Chida & Mao, 2009) to cancer

PSYCHONEUROIMMUNOLOGY

We have seen in this and earlier chapters that psychological and biological systems are interrelated—as one system changes, the others are often affected. The recognition of this interdependence and its connection to health and illness led researchers to form a new field of study called **psychoneuroimmunology**. This field focuses on the relationships between psychosocial processes and the activities of the nervous, endocrine, and immune systems (Ader & Cohen, 1985; Byrne-Davis & Vedhara, 2004; Kemeny, 2007; Marsland et al., 2001). These systems form a *feedback loop*: the nervous and endocrine systems send chemical messages in the form of neurotransmitters and hormones that increase or decrease immune function, and cells of the immune system produce chemicals, such as cytokines and ACTH, that feed information back to the brain. The brain appears to serve as a control center to maintain a balance in immune function, since too little immune activity leaves the individual open to infection and too much activity may produce autoimmune diseases.

Emotions and Immune Function

People's emotions—both positive and negative—play a critical role in the balance of immune functions. Research has shown that pessimism, depression, and stress from major and minor events are related to impaired immune function (Byrne-Davis & Vedhara, 2004; Leonard, 1995; Marsland et al., 2001). For example, research compared immune variables of caregiver spouses of Alzheimer's disease patients with matched control subjects and found that the caregivers had lower immune function and reported more days of illness over the course of about a year (Kiecolt-Glaser et al., 1991). Another study compared individuals who received a flu vaccination and found that those who developed and maintained a high level of flu antibodies over 5 months had experienced less stress in the interim than those with fewer antibodies (Burns, Carroll, et al., 2003).

Positive emotions can also affect immune function, giving it a boost (Futterman et al., 1994; Stone et al., 1994). In the study by Arthur Stone and his coworkers, adult men kept daily logs of positive and negative events and gave saliva samples for analyses of antibody content. Negative events were associated with reduced antibodies only for the day the events occurred, but positive events enhanced antibody content for the day of occurrence and the next two.

Some stressful situations start with a crisis, and the ensuing emotional states tend to continue and suppress immune processes over an extended period of time. This was demonstrated with healthy elderly individuals who were taking part in a longitudinal study of the aging process (Willis et al., 1987). These people were asked to contact the researchers as soon as they were able if they experienced any major crisis, such as the diagnosis of a serious illness in or the death of a spouse or child; 15 of them did so. A month after the crisis, and again months later, the researchers assessed the people's cortisol and lymphocyte blood concentrations, recent diets, weights, and psychological distress. Because the subjects were already participating in the longitudinal study, comparable data were available from a time prior to the crisis. Analysis of these data revealed that lymphocyte concentrations, caloric intake, and body weight decreased, and cortisol concentrations and psychological distress increased, soon after the crisis. By the time of the last assessment several months later, however, all of these measures had returned almost to the precrisis levels. Similarly, a study found that people who become unemployed show impaired immune function that recovers after they get a new job (Cohen et al., 2007).

When people react to short-term, minor events, such as doing difficult math problems under time pressure,

changes in the number and activity of immune cells occur for fairly short periods of time—minutes or hours (Delahanty et al., 1996). The degree of change depends on which immune system component is measured and the event's characteristics—long-lasting and intense interpersonal events seem to produce especially large immune reductions (Herbert & Cohen, 1993). Of course, immune system reactivity varies from one person to the next, but a person's degree of response to a type of event seems to be much the same when tested weeks apart (Marsland et al., 1995). This suggests that an individual's reaction to specific stressors is fairly stable over time.

One key process of the immune system—inflammation—is receiving increased attention because it is implicated in a wide variety of serious medical conditions (Gouin et al., 2008; Libby et al., 2009; Steptoe et al., 2007). Stress can evoke increases in inflammatory substances in the blood, as can chronic levels of negative affect (Howren et al., 2009; Steptoe et al., 2007). Inflammation, in turn, can contribute to atherosclerosis, rheumatoid arthritis and other chronic conditions, and seems to generally accelerate age-related diseases. One puzzling question in this area is the fact that one stress response, the release of cortisol, generally decreases inflammation. But emerging perspectives suggest that under conditions of chronic stress the immune system becomes less sensitive to the normal anti-inflammatory effects of cortisol, so that inflammatory responses remain activated and can eventually damage health (Segerstrom & Miller, 2004).

Psychosocial Modifiers of Immune System Reactivity

As we've seen, psychosocial factors in people's lives may modify the stress they experience. Such factors seem to affect immune system responses, too. For instance, social support affects the immune function of people under long-term, intense stress. People who have strong social support have stronger immune systems and smaller immune impairments in response to stress than others with less support (Kennedy, Kiecolt-Glaser, & Glaser, 1990; Levy et al., 1990).

A related psychosocial modifier is disclosure—describing one's feelings about stressful events. An experiment with college students examined the effect of expressing such feelings on blood levels of antibodies against the Epstein-Barr virus, a widespread virus that causes mononucleosis in many of those who are infected (Esterling et al., 1994). The students were randomly assigned to three conditions that met in three weekly 20-minute sessions when they either described *verbally* or *in writing* a highly stressful event they had experienced or wrote about a trivial (non–stress-related) topic, such as the contents of their bedrooms. The students in each condition had the same level of immune control against the virus before the study. But blood samples taken a week after the last session revealed that immune control improved substantially in the verbal condition, moderately in the written condition, and declined slightly in the control (trivial topic) condition, as Figure 3-5 depicts. Other research has found that describing feelings about stressful events is more effective in enhancing immune function in cynically hostile people than in nonhostile individuals (Christensen et al., 1996).

The influence of optimism on immune function appears to depend on whether the stress is short-term or chronic (Segerstrom, 2005). Optimism is often associated with better immune functioning, but sometimes worse, perhaps because optimists persist in physiologically taxing efforts to influence or control stressful circumstances. Optimism has also been associated with lower levels of inflammation (Roy et al., 2010). (Go to 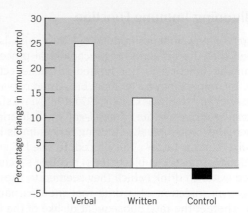.)

Lifestyles and Immune Function

Do people's lifestyles affect the functioning of their immune systems? Some evidence suggests that they do. People with generally healthful lifestyles—including

Figure 3-5   Percent change in immune control against the Epstein-Barr virus, as reflected in blood concentrations of specific antibodies, for subjects having sessions for verbal expression of stress feelings, written expression of stress feelings, or a control condition. (Based on data from Esterling et al., 1994, Figure 3.)

exercising, getting enough sleep, eating balanced meals, and not smoking—show stronger immune functioning than those with less healthful lifestyles (Kusaka, Kondou, & Morimoto, 1992). Other studies have found that sleeping poorly can impair immune function the next day (Irwin et al., 1994), and people who smoke are more susceptible than those who don't to catching colds (Cohen et al., 1993).

HIGHLIGHT

Stress and Wound Healing

We usually think of the central task of the immune systems as the detection and destruction of foreign invaders or antigens and the destruction of abnormal cells. But an equally important function of the immune system is wound healing. Whether wounds result from accidental injuries or are intentional as in surgery, the immune system plays the key role in repairing the injured tissue, as well as keeping the site from becoming infected. If stress can impair the immune system, can it also interfere with wound healing? A study by Janice Kiecolt-Glaser and her colleagues (2005) suggests it can. Married couples came to the hospital on two occasions. Both times, small blisters were created on participants' arm with a precise suction device. During one of the hospital admissions the couples engaged in a supportive marital interaction task, and during the other they discussed a marital disagreement or conflict.

Blister healing was measured over about two weeks after both admissions to the hospital. The blister wounds healed more slowly after marital conflicts than after more supportive marital interactions, and they healed more slowly for couples whose interactions included high level of hostile behavior toward each other. In other studies, tape is applied to the skin and then stripped off, creating an abrasion. A variety of stressors, including examinations and stressful interviews, and negative affect appear to delay healing of these experimental wounds (Bosch et al., 2007; Robles, 2007). Interventions that reduce stress, such as exercise or written disclosure about past traumas, can facilitate wound healing after such procedures (Emery et al., 2005; Weinman et al., 2008). These results may have important implications for patients undergoing surgery.

Conditioning Immune Function

Research on psychoneuroimmunology with animals has revealed that the influence of psychological processes on immune function is not limited to the effects of stress. The impact may be far more broad and pervasive. Robert Ader and Nicholas Cohen (1975, 1985) have shown that *immune suppression can be conditioned*. In their original research, they were actually studying how animals learn to dislike certain tastes. The procedure used a single conditioning trial: the subjects (rats) received saccharin-flavored water to drink (which they seemed to like) and then got an injection of a drug that induces nausea. To see whether the rats' subsequent dislike of the taste depended on its strength, some subjects received more saccharin flavoring than others in this conditioning trial. Over the next several weeks, the drug was *not* used, but the animals continued to receive saccharin- flavored water. During this time, the researchers noticed a curious thing: a number of rats had fallen ill and died—and these animals tended to be the ones that had consumed the greatest amount of saccharin in the conditioning trial.

How did these deaths relate to immune suppression? Since the nausea-inducing drug used in the conditioning trial was also known to suppress immune function temporarily, Ader and Cohen hypothesized that the continued intake of saccharin water served as a conditioned stimulus, suppressing the ability of the rats to fight infection. Subsequent experiments by these researchers and others confirmed this hypothesis and demonstrated that conditioning can raise or lower immune function and can influence both antibody-mediated and cell-mediated immune processes (Kusnecov, 2001). Similar conditioning effects have been demonstrated in humans, such as cancer patients who receive medications that impair immune function.

PSYCHOPHYSIOLOGICAL DISORDERS

The word *psychosomatic* has a long history, and was coined to refer to symptoms or illnesses that are caused or aggravated by psychological factors, mainly emotional stress (Sarafino, 2004b). Although many professionals and the general public still use this term, the concept has undergone some changes and now has a new name: **psychophysiological disorders**, which refers to physical symptoms or illnesses that result from the interplay of psychosocial and physiological processes. This definition clearly uses a biopsychosocial perspective. We will discuss several illnesses traditionally classified as psychosomatic. Some of these illnesses will be examined in greater detail in later chapters.

DIGESTIVE SYSTEM DISEASES

Several psychophysiological disorders can afflict the digestive system. **Ulcers** and **inflammatory bowel disease** are two illnesses that involve wounds in the digestive tract that may cause pain and bleeding (AMA, 2003). Ulcers are found in the stomach and the duodenum, or upper section of the small intestine. Inflammatory bowel disease, which includes *ulcerative colitis* and *Crohn disease*, can occur in the colon (large intestine) and the small intestine. Another illness, **irritable bowel syndrome**, produces abdominal pain, diarrhea, and constipation (AMA, 2003). Although these diseases afflict mainly adults, similar symptoms occur in childhood (Blanchard et al., 2008).

Most ulcers are produced by a combination of gastric juices eroding the lining of the stomach and duodenum that has been weakened by bacterial infection (AMA, 2003). But stress plays a role, too (Levenstein, 2002). In a classic study, a patient (called Tom) agreed to cooperate in a lengthy and detailed examination of gastric function (Wolf & Wolff, 1947). Tom was unique in that many years earlier, at the age of 9, he had had a stomach operation that left an opening to the outside of the body. This opening, which provided the only way he could feed himself, was literally a window through which the inside of his stomach could be observed. When Tom was subjected to stressful situations, his stomach-acid production greatly increased. When he was under emotional tension for several weeks, there was a pronounced reddening of the stomach lining. Another study reported similar effects with a 15-month-old girl who had a temporary stomach opening. Her highest levels of acid secretion occurred when she was angry (Engel, Reichsman, & Segal, 1956). The physical causes of inflammatory bowel disease and irritable bowel syndrome are not well known (AMA, 2003). Stress is related to flare-ups of these illnesses, but its specific role is currently unclear (Blanchard, 2008; Kiank et al., 2010).

ASTHMA

Asthma is a respiratory disorder in which inflammation, spasms, and mucous obstruct the bronchial tubes and lead to difficulty in breathing, with wheezing or coughing. This ailment is prevalent around the world—an estimated 300 million people worldwide suffer from asthma (AAAAI). Asthma attacks appear to result from some combination of three factors: allergies, respiratory infections, and biopsychosocial arousal, such as from stress or exercise (AAFA, 2010; Lehrer et al., 2002). In most cases, the cause of an attack is largely physical, but sometimes it may be largely psychosocial.

Professionals working with hospitalized children have noticed that the asthma symptoms of many children decrease shortly after admission to the hospital, but reappear when they return home (Purcell, Weiss, & Hahn, 1972). Are these children allergic to something in their own houses, such as dust, that isn't in the hospital? This question was tested with asthmatic children who were allergic to house dust (Long et al., 1958). Without the children knowing, the researchers vacuumed the children's homes and then sprayed the collected dust from each house into their individual hospital rooms. The result: *none* of the children had respiratory difficulty when exposed to their home dust, which suggests that psychosocial factors may be involved. Findings of other research indicate that stress can trigger asthma attacks (Lehrer et al., 2002; Miller & Wood, 1994; Sarafino, 1997). Several psychosocial factors have been implicated in the development of asthma, the occurrence of asthma attacks, and the inflammatory processes that worsen asthma, including adversity during childhood and family patterns that involve stress or low social support (Chen et al., 2010; Marin et al., 2009; Miller et al., 2009; Scott et al., 2008). A meta-analysis of this research indicated that the association between stress-related psychosocial factors and asthma is bi-directional; stress and negative emotions can contribute to the development and worsening of asthma, and having asthma can contribute to future stress and negative emotion (Chida, Hamer, & Steptoe, 2008).

RECURRENT HEADACHE

Many people suffer chronically from intense headaches. Although there are many types of recurrent headache, two of the most common are called tension-type and migraine headache. **Tension-type** (or *muscle contraction*) **headache** seems to be caused by a combination of a central nervous system dysfunction and persistent contraction of the head and neck muscles (AMA, 2003; Holroyd, 2002). The pain it produces is a dull and steady ache that often feels like a tight band of pressure around the head. Recurrent tension-type headaches occur twice a week or more, and may last for hours, days, or weeks (Dalessio, 1994).

Migraine headache seems to result from dilation of blood vessels surrounding the brain and a dysfunction in the brainstem and trigeminal nerve that extends throughout the front half of the head (AMA, 2003; Goadsby, 2005; Holroyd, 2002). The pain often begins on one side of the head near the temple, is sharp and throbbing, and lasts for hours or, sometimes, days (Dalessio, 1994). Sometimes migraines begin with or follow an *aura*, a set of symptoms that signal an impending headache episode. These symptoms usually include sensory phenomena, such as seeing lines or shimmering in the visual field. This may be accompanied by dizziness, nausea, and vomiting. Recurrent migraine is marked by periodic debilitating symptoms, which occur about once a month, with headache-free periods in between (Dalessio, 1994).

Most adults and children have headaches at least occasionally, and tension-type headaches are common (AMA, 2003). The prevalence of migraine varies widely across cultures, but is about 10% overall, is far greater in females than males, and increases with age from childhood to middle age, and then declines (Stewart, Shechter, & Rasmussen, 1994). Many children experience their first headaches in the preschool years, and chronic headaches have been reported in boys and girls as young as 6 years of age (Andrasik, Blake, & McCarran, 1986). Figure 3-6 presents a drawing by an 11-year-old girl named Meghan to describe her experience of migraine headache pain.

What triggers headaches? They often are brought on by hormonal changes, missing a meal, sunlight, sleeping poorly, and consuming certain substances, such as alcohol or chocolate. Research has also shown that stressors—particularly the hassles of everyday living—are common triggers of migraine and tension-type headaches (Köhler & Haimerl, 1990; Nash & Thebarge, 2006; Robbins, 1994). Yet some patients with chronic headache have attacks when they are not under great stress, and others fail to have headaches when they are under stress. Stress appears to be one of many factors that produce headaches, but the full nature of these causes is not yet known.

OTHER DISORDERS

There are several other psychophysiological disorders for which stress appears to be involved in triggering or aggravating episodes. One of these illnesses is *rheumatoid arthritis*—a chronic and very painful disease that produces inflammation and stiffness of the small joints, such as in the hands. It afflicts about 1% of the American population, and its victims are primarily women (AF, 2006), and stress seems to play a role in arthritis inflammation, pain, and limitations in physical activity (Parrish et al., 2008). Another disorder, called *dysmenorrhea*, affects millions of women. It is characterized by painful menstruation, which may be accompanied by nausea, headache, and dizziness (AMA, 2003; Calhoun & Burnette, 1983). A third stress-related problem involves skin disorders, such as *hives*, *eczema*, and *psoriasis*, in which the skin develops rashes or becomes dry and flakes or cracks (AMA, 2003). In many cases, specific allergies

Figure 3-6   Drawing by 11-year-old Meghan of her experience of migraine headache pain. The lower left-hand corner has a self-portrait with a dramatic facial expression. When a headache begins, Meghan typically retreats to her bedroom "to ride out the storm," lying down in a darkened room. (From Andrasik, Blake, & McCarran, 1986, Figure 18.1.)

are identified as contributing to episodes of these skin problems.

Although current evidence implicates both biological and psychosocial causes for each of the psychophysiological disorders we have considered, the evidence is sketchy and the nature of the interplay of these factors is unclear. The remainder of this chapter focuses on the role of stress in the development of cardiovascular disorders and cancer.

STRESS AND CARDIOVASCULAR DISORDERS

Earlier in this chapter, we saw that psychosocial modifiers of stress can affect health—for instance, the risk of developing CHD is greater for chronically angry and hostile people. Such findings suggest that stress may be a factor in the development of cardiovascular disorders, the number-one cause of death in many countries. We'll look more closely at the role of stress in hypertension and CHD.

HYPERTENSION

Hypertension—the condition of having high blood pressure consistently over several weeks or more—is a major risk factor for CHD, stroke, and kidney disease (AHA, 2010; NKF, 2006). In the United States, nearly 30%

of adults are classified as hypertensive, having blood pressures at or above 140 (systolic) over 90 (diastolic). By comparison, the hypertension rates elsewhere are (Hajjar, Kotchen, & Kotchen, 2006):

- Australia, 21%–32%
- Canada, 20%
- Europe, 44% (across several nations)
- Worldwide, 26%.

Because lesser elevations in blood pressure are now known to increase risk substantially, current guidelines designate less than 120/80 as "normal," or conveying little risk, as shown in Table 3.2. Prevalence rates for hypertension increase in adulthood, particularly after about 40 years of age (NCHS, 2009a). Some cases of hypertension are caused by, or are *secondary* to, disorders of other body systems or organs, such as the kidneys or endocrine system. Secondary hypertension can usually be cured by medical procedures. But the vast majority—over 90%—of hypertensive cases are classified

Table 3.2   *Blood Pressure Categories (values in mm Hg units)*

Category	Systolic		Diastolic
Normal (recommended)	Less than 120	*and*	Less than 80
Prehypertension	120–139	*or*	80–89
Hypertension: Stage 1	140–159	*or*	90–99
Hypertension: Stage 2	160 or higher	*or*	100 or higher

Source: AHA, 2010.

as *primary* or *essential hypertension*, in which the causes of the high blood pressure are unknown.

To say that the causes for essential hypertension are unknown is somewhat misleading. In cases of essential hypertension, doctors are unable to identify any biomedical causes, such as infectious agents or organ damage. But many risk factors are associated with the development of hypertension—and there is evidence implicating the following as some of the risk factors for hypertension (AHA, 2010; Hajjar, Kotchen, & Kotchen, 2006):

• Obesity
• Dietary elements, such as high salt, fats, and cholesterol
• Excessive alcohol use
• Physical inactivity
• Family history of hypertension
• Psychosocial factors, such as chronic stress, anger, and anxiety

Stress, Emotions, and Hypertension

People's occupations provide sources of stress that can have an impact on their blood pressure. Traffic controllers at airports provide an example. Sidney Cobb and Robert Rose (1973) compared the medical records of thousands of men employed as air traffic controllers or as second-class airmen, separating the data for different age groups, since blood pressure increases with age. Comparisons for each age group revealed prevalence rates of hypertension among traffic controllers that were several times higher than for airmen. The researchers also compared the records of traffic controllers who experienced high and low levels of stress, as measured by the traffic density at the air stations where they worked. Figure 3-7 depicts the results: for each age group, prevalence rates of hypertension were higher for traffic controllers working at high-stress locations than for those at low-stress sites.

Aspects of social environments, such as crowding and aggression, are also linked to stress and hypertension. Experiments with animals have shown that living in crowded, aggressive conditions induces chronic hypertension (Henry et al., 1993). Research with humans compared people living in crowded and uncrowded neighborhoods to see if these living conditions influence blood pressure (Fleming et al., 1987). The people from the two types of neighborhoods were similar in important characteristics, such as age, gender, and family income. While working on a stressful cognitive task, the subjects showed greater increases in heart rate and systolic and diastolic pressure if they lived in crowded neighborhoods. Other research has found that psychological stress and high cardiovascular reactivity to stress

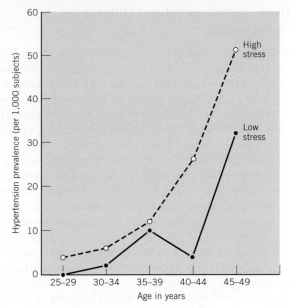

Figure 3-7   Prevalence of hypertension per 1,000 air traffic controllers as a function of stress and age. Hypertension rates increase with age and stress. (Data from Cobb & Rose, 1973, Table 3.)

may be a risk factor for, or even a cause of, hypertension (Chida & Steptoe, 2010; Sparrenberger et al., 2009; Tuomisto et al., 2005). Taken together, the evidence suggests that chronic stress plays a role in the development of hypertension.

Studies on pessimism, anger, and hostility have revealed important links to the development of hypertension; we'll consider three. First, blood pressure is higher in pessimistic than optimistic individuals (Räikkönen et al., 1999). Second, people who are hypertensive are more likely to be chronically hostile and resentful than are *normotensive* people, those with normal blood pressure (Diamond, 1982). Anger is also associated with higher nighttime blood pressure (Beatty & Matthews, 2009). Third, resting blood pressure is higher among individuals who ruminate or dwell on events that provoke anger than among people who don't ruminate (Hogan & Linden, 2004).

Interestingly, the effects of stress on blood pressure can complicate the medical diagnosis of hypertension. Some people become anxious when medical professionals measure their blood pressure, producing an elevated reading that actually is not representative of their usual blood pressure levels, leading to a false diagnosis of hypertension. If undetected, this "white coat hypertension" can lead to unnecessary medical treatment (McGrady & Higgins, 1990; Ogedegbe et al., 2008).

Stress and Sociocultural Differences in Hypertension

The impact of stress on hypertension may be particularly relevant for Black people in the United States, who have a much higher prevalence rate of high blood pressure than Whites do (NCHS, 2009a). In a study of Black and White people in Detroit, the highest blood pressure readings found were those of Blacks living in high-stress areas of the city—neighborhoods that were crowded and had high crime rates and low incomes (Harburg et al., 1973). But Blacks and Whites who lived in low-stress areas had similar blood pressures. Two other findings suggest that perceived racism is a stressor that plays a major role in the high rates of hypertension among African Americans. First, Black women's blood pressure reactivity to stressors is higher among those who feel that racial discrimination underlies the mistreatment they've experienced than those who do not (Guyll, Matthews, & Bromberger, 2001). Second, blood pressure in waking daily life is higher among Black men and women who perceive frequent racism in their lives than those who do not (Steffen et al., 2003).

Few cases of essential hypertension are likely to be caused by emotional factors alone (Schneiderman & Hammer, 1985). Most cases of high blood pressure probably involve several of the determinants listed earlier in this section. (Go to 💡.)

CORONARY HEART DISEASE

Epidemiologists have studied the distribution and frequency of CHD over many decades in many different cultures. The data they have collected suggest that CHD is, to some extent, a disease of modernized societies—that is, the incidence rate of heart disease is higher in technologically advanced countries than in other nations (Susser, Hopper, & Richman, 1983). In advanced societies, people live long enough to become victims of CHD, which afflicts mainly older individuals, and are more likely than those in less developed countries to have certain risk factors for CHD, such as obesity and low levels of physical activity. Last, the psychosocial stressors of advanced societies are different from those in other societies and may be more conducive to the development of heart disease. For instance, people in less advanced societies may have more social support to protect them from the effects of stress and perceive less reason for anger and hostility, which we've already seen can increase the risk of CHD.

The link between stress and CHD has considerable support (Williams, 2008). For example, job stress, conflict in close relationships, post-traumatic stress disorder, and stress-related personality factors such as anger and optimism predict the development of CHD, as indicated by myocardial infarctions or death from CHD (Chida & Steptoe, 2009; Dedert et al., 2010; De Vogli et al., 2007; Eller et al., 2009; Kubzansky et al., 2009; Tindle et al., 2009). Associations between stress and myocardial infarctions or death from CHD could occur across various phases of the disease. Stress could contribute to the initiation and progression of atherosclerosis, even years before the first symptoms and other outward indications of CHD occur. Later, in the presence of advanced atherosclerosis, stress could contribute to the occurrence of ischemia, myocardial infarction, or disturbances in the

HIGHLIGHT

Does Acculturation Increase Blood Pressure?

Does adapting to living in a new Western culture put people at risk for hypertension? To answer this question, Patrick Steffen and his colleagues (2006) performed a meta-analysis on blood pressure data from 125 studies that had compared people who were or were not living in a new Western culture. This analysis revealed several interesting findings. First, blood pressure was substantially higher among people adapting to a new culture. Second, the higher blood pressures were not the result of differences in body weight or cholesterol levels. Third, the impact of acculturation on blood pressure was greater for men than for women and greater for people who relocated from rural to urban areas than from urban to rural. Fourth, the impact of adapting to a new culture decreased with time: the effect of acculturation on blood pressure was far greater in the first months after relocating than after several years. Acculturation is stressful, but people adapt in time. The stress of acculturation has also been linked to risk for developing the metabolic syndrome (Peek et al., 2009), which combines high blood pressure with high cholesterol, abdominal fat, and impaired glucose metabolism. Hence, the health risks of acculturation may extend beyond hypertension to include other cardiovascular diseases and diabetes.

rhythm of the heart that reveal clinically apparent CHD. Still later, stress could contribute to worrisome health outcomes for people with established CHD, such as additional heart attacks or coronary death.

Research has supported each of these possibilities. For example, anger is associated with stiffness in arteries that indicate very early signs of atherosclerosis (Shimbo et al., 2007). Also, research has found higher levels of atherosclerosis in the arteries of African American women who perceived high levels of stress, unfair treatment, and racial discrimination in their lives than those who did not (Troxel et al., 2003). Also, experiences of high demand and low control in dealing with daily stressors is associated with greater progression of atherosclerosis over time (Kamarck et al., 2007). Later in the development of CHD, a variety of stressful events and negative emotions such as episodes of anger can precipitate heart attacks in people with advanced atherosclerosis (Bhattacharyya & Steptoe, 2007). Finally, anger, depression, and stressful aspects of neighbor-hoods have all been found to predict poor medical outcomes, including recurring heart attacks and death, in CHD patients (Chida & Steptoe, 2009; Nicholson, Kuper, & Hemingway, 2006; Scheffler et al., 2008).

What processes link stress and CHD? We've discussed three processes already (Kop, 2003; Williams, 2008). First, stress evokes increases in lipids and inflam-matory substances in the blood, cardiovascular reactiv-ity, and increases in catecholamine and corticosteroid release by the endocrine glands. These physiological responses, especially if they become chronic, can damage the arteries and heart, promote atherosclerosis, and lead to the development of hypertension. These same phys-iological processes can cause advanced and unstable coronary artery plaques to rupture, causing a blood clot that can close off an artery that otherwise brings blood and oxygen to the heart muscle. This is the most common cause of a myocardial infarction or heart attack. Second, stress can cause cardiac arrhythmia, especially if the heart is susceptible to ischemia. When severe, arrhyth-mias can cause a cardiac episode and sudden death. Third, stress is associated with cigarette smoking and high levels of alcohol use, for example, which are behav-ioral risk factors for CHD. In later chapters we will examine in greater detail various risk factors and issues relating to CHD and the next stress-related illness, cancer.

STRESS AND CANCER

The idea that stress and other psychosocial factors contribute to the development of cancer has a long history. The doctor Galen, who practiced in Rome during the second century A.D., believed that individuals who were sad and depressed, or "melancholy," were more likely to develop cancer than those who were happy, confident, and vigorous (Sklar & Anisman, 1981). Similar ideas have appeared in the writings of doctors in later eras. *Cancer* is a term that refers to a broad class of disease in which cells multiply and grow in an unrestrained manner. As such, cancer does not refer to a single illness, but to dozens of disease forms that share this characteristic (ACS, 2009). It includes, for instance, *leukemias*, in which the bone marrow produces excessive numbers of white blood cells, and *carcinomas*, in which tumors form in the tissue of the skin and internal organ linings. Some cancers take longer to develop or follow more irregular courses in their development than others do.

Does stress play a role in cancer? Early evidence linking stress and cancer came from research using retro-spective methods (Sklar & Anisman, 1981). This research generally had cancer patients fill out life events ques-tionnaires to assess the stress they experienced during the year or so preceding the diagnosis. Although some studies found that the appearance of cancer was associ-ated with self-reported high levels of prior stress, others did not (Steptoe & Ayers, 2004). And problems with retro-spective methods cloud the interpretation of the results of these studies. Because the cancer diagnoses were typically made years after the disease process started, the patients' cancers were probably present prior to and during the year for which they reported high lev-els of stress. Also, the patients' perceptions or rec-ollections of prior stress may have been distorted by their knowledge that they have cancer. More recent, better designed research using prospective or lon-gitudinal approaches has also produced inconsistent results, but a meta-analysis of the large number of available studies indicated that stress-related psychoso-cial factors predicted the initial occurrence of cancer, as well as the medical course of the disease, includ-ing survival and death from cancer (Chida et al., 2008).

The effects of stress on cancer are probably influ-enced by many factors. If stress plays a causal role in cancer development or progression, it may do so by impairing the immune system's ability to combat the disease and by increasing behavioral risk factors, such as smoking cigarettes. As in the case of CHD, cancer progresses in a complex manner. Cancer progression eventually involves the recruitment of a blood supply to permit growth of the tumor beyond early stages, called angiogenesis. Further, cancer can spread beyond the tissue where it originally occurred, a process called metastasis. Recent research has begun to identify ways in which physiological stress responses can influence angiogenesis and metastasis, as well as the health behavior and immune system mechanisms traditionally thought to link stress and cancer (Antoni et al., 2006).

SUMMARY

Researchers have identified several psychosocial factors that modify the impact of stress on the individual. One of these factors is social support—the comfort, caring, esteem, or help a person actually receives or simply perceives as available from others. There are four basic types of support: emotional or esteem, tangible or instrumental, informational, and companionship. Whether people receive social support depends on characteristics of the recipients and of the providers of support and on the composition and structure of the social network. Social support appears to reduce the stress people experience and to enhance their health. The greater people's social support, the lower their mortality rates and likelihood of becoming ill. These benefits seem to accrue in accordance with the buffering and direct effects hypotheses. That is, social support may buffer a person against the negative effects of high levels of stress and may enhance health regardless of the level of stress by simply providing encouragement for leading healthful lifestyles, for instance.

Another psychosocial modifier of stress is people's sense of personal control over events in their lives, such as through behavioral and cognitive control. Personal control includes beliefs about one's locus of control—that is, whether control is internal or external to the person—and self-efficacy. People acquire a sense of personal control from their successes and failures and through the process of social learning. Individuals who experience prolonged, high levels of stress and have a weak sense of personal control tend to feel helpless. The cognitive process of attribution seems to be important in the development of learned helplessness. A strong sense of personal control tends to benefit people's health and help them adjust to a serious illness if it occurs. Hardiness and similar personality traits are additional psychosocial modifiers of stress that may help people remain healthy when under stress, and the five-factor model of personality can help to organize the growing list of personality traits that modify stress.

One other psychosocial modifier of stress is people's tendency toward either the Type A or the Type B behavior pattern. The Type A behavior pattern consists of four characteristics: competitive achievement orientation, time urgency, anger or hostility, and a vigorous or controlling vocal style. Compared with Type Bs, Type A individuals respond more quickly and strongly to stressors both in their overt behaviors and in their physiological reactivity. Anger/hostility is the component of this pattern that is most closely associated with the development of coronary heart disease (CHD) and hypertension.

Chronic stress may affect health in two ways. First, it may increase health-compromising behaviors, such as alcohol and cigarette use. Second, it produces changes in the body's physical systems, as when the endocrine system releases catecholamines and corticosteroids, which can cause damage to the heart and blood vessels and impair immune system functioning. The physical effects of stress can even impair healing of wounds. Psychoneuroimmunology is the field of study that focuses on how psychosocial processes and the nervous, endocrine, and immune systems are interrelated. Stress also plays a role in many psychophysiological disorders, such as ulcers, inflammatory bowel disease, irritable bowel syndrome, asthma, and tension-type and migraine headache. In addition, stress is strongly implicated in the development of hypertension and CHD, and may also affect cancer.

KEY TERMS

social support	self-efficacy	psychoneuroimmunology	irritable bowel syndrome
buffering hypothesis	learned helplessness	psychophysiological	asthma
direct effects hypothesis	hardiness	disorders	tension-type headache
personal control	Type A behavior pattern	ulcers	migraine headache
behavioral control	Type B behavior pattern	inflammatory bowel	hypertension
cognitive control	coronary heart disease	disease	
locus of control	(CHD)		

> **Note:** If you read Modules 5 and 6 (from the Appendix) with the current chapter, you should include the key terms for those modules.

4

COPING WITH AND REDUCING STRESS

PROLOGUE

Adam was a carpenter in Poland, and he worked long hours for little pay. He wanted to get married to his fiancée, move out of his parents' house, and have children, but he could never make enough money in his hometown. His friend, Leon, was moving to England to find better wages, and had asked Adam to go with him. "This is sure to help me make more money," Adam thought.

Leon's parents were in poor health and Leon wanted to earn more money so he could get them better health care, maybe even afford a full-time carer. Adam wanted to save up enough to find a nice flat in the city, somewhere his future wife would be happy to call home. In England, they both found work as food packers and were earning almost triple what they did back home.

One morning before work, Leon's father called and told him his mother had been taken to hospital. Leon couldn't go back home—he'd lose wages for the month and his job would be given away immediately—but he couldn't stop worrying about his mother. He became increasingly moody, slept poorly, and developed headaches. He wouldn't leave the flat except to work in case he missed a call from his father. After several weeks of worrying, Leon became run-down and had a rough time keeping up with his quota at work.

Adam began to worry about Leon and tried to give him advice. He offered Leon some money that he had saved up, and even spoke to their manager to see if Leon could have a few days of compassionate leave. Adam knew that if Leon continued this way, he could get injured at work, or even lose his job. After several days of pestering, Adam convinced Leon to talk to the plant manager personally. To their surprise, the manager let Leon go home for five days and promised to keep his job.

People vary in the ways they deal with stress. Sometimes people confront a problem directly and rationally (as Adam did) and sometimes they do not. In this chapter we discuss the ways that people handle stress. Through this discussion, you will find answers to questions you may have about the different methods people use for managing stress. Are some methods for coping with stress more effective than others? How can people reduce the potential for stress in their lives? When people encounter a stressor, how can they reduce the strain it produces?

COPING WITH STRESS

Individuals of all ages experience stress and try to deal with it. During childhood years, people learn ways to manage feelings of stress that arise from the many fearful situations they experience (Sarafino, 1986). For instance, psychologist Lois Murphy (1974, p. 76) has described the progress and setbacks a 4-year-old named Molly had made in dealing with the terror she felt during thunderstorms. In her last steps at gaining control over her fear, she experienced two storms a few months apart. During the first storm, she awoke and didn't cry, "but I just snuggled in my bed," she said later. In the second storm, she showed no outward fear and comforted her frightened brother, saying, "I remember when I was a little baby and I was scared of thunder and I used to cry and cry every time it thundered." Like most children, Molly became better able to cope with the stress of storms as she grew older. What's more, in the last steps of her progress she showed pride in having mastered her fear.

WHAT IS COPING?

Because the emotional and physical strain that accompanies stress is uncomfortable, people are motivated to do things to reduce their stress. These "things" are what is involved in coping.

What is coping? Several definitions of coping exist (Lazarus & Folkman, 1984). We'll use a definition based on how we defined stress in Chapter 2, when we saw that stress involves a *perceived discrepancy* between the demands of the situation and the resources of the person. **Coping** is the process by which people try to *manage the perceived discrepancy* between the demands and resources they appraise in a stressful situation. Notice the word *manage* in this definition. It indicates that coping efforts can be quite varied and do not necessarily lead to a solution of the problem. Although coping efforts can be

aimed at correcting or mastering the problem, they may also simply help the person alter his or her perception of a discrepancy, tolerate or accept the harm or threat, or escape or avoid the situation (Lazarus & Folkman, 1984; Carver & Connor-Smith, 2010). For example, a child who faces a stressful exam in school might cope by feeling nauseated and staying home.

We cope with stress through our cognitive and behavioral transactions with the environment. Suppose you are overweight and smoke cigarettes, and your doctor has asked you to lose weight and stop smoking because several factors place you at very high risk for developing heart disease. This presents a threat—you may become disabled or die—and is stressful, especially if you don't think you can change your behavior. How might you cope with this? Some people would cope by seeking information about ways to improve their ability to change. Other people would simply find another doctor who is not so directive. Others would attribute their health to fate or "the will of God," and leave the problem "in His hands." Still others would try to deaden this and other worries with alcohol, which would add to the risk. People use many different methods to try to manage the appraised discrepancy between the demands of the situation and their resources.

The coping process is not a single event. Because coping involves continuous transactions with the environment, the process is best viewed as a dynamic series of appraisals and reappraisals that adjust to shifts in person–environment relationships. And so, in coping with the threat of serious illness, people who try to change their lifestyles may receive encouragement and better relationships with their doctor and family. But individuals who ignore the problem are likely to experience worse and worse health and relations with these people. Each shift in one direction or the other is affected by the transactions that preceded it and affects subsequent transactions (Lazarus & Folkman, 1984).

FUNCTIONS AND METHODS OF COPING

You have probably realized by now that people have many ways for coping with stress. Because of this, researchers have attempted to organize coping approaches on the basis of their functions and the methods they employ. (Go to 🍎.)

Functions of Coping

According to Richard Lazarus and his colleagues, coping can serve two main functions (Lazarus, 1999; Lazarus & Folkman, 1984). It can alter the *problem* causing the stress or it can regulate the *emotional* response to the problem.

ASSESS YOURSELF

Your Focuses in Coping

Think about a very stressful personal crisis or life event you experienced in the last year—the more recent and stressful the event, the better for this exercise. How did you handle this situation and your stress? Some of the ways people handle stressful experiences are listed below. Mark an "X" in the space preceding each one you used.

_____ Tried to see a positive side to it

_____ Tried to step back from the situation and be more objective

_____ Prayed for guidance or strength

_____ Sometimes took it out on other people when I felt angry or depressed

_____ Got busy with other things to keep my mind off the problem

_____ Decided not to worry about it because I figured everything would work out fine

_____ Took things one step at a time

_____ Read relevant material for solutions and considered several alternatives

_____ Drew on my knowledge because I had a similar experience before

_____ Talked to a friend or relative to get advice on handling the problem

_____ Talked with a professional person (e.g., doctor, clergy, lawyer, teacher, counselor) about ways to improve the situation

_____ Took some action to improve the situation

Of the first six ways listed, count how many you marked; these are examples of "emotion-focused" ways. How many of the second six—"problem-focused"—ways did you mark? When you read the upcoming text material entitled Functions of Coping, answer these questions: Did you use mostly emotion- or problem-focused methods? Why, and what functions did your methods serve? (Based on material in Billings & Moos, 1981.)

Emotion-focused coping is aimed at controlling the emotional response to the stressful situation. People can regulate their emotional responses through _behavioral_ and _cognitive_ approaches. Examples of _behavioral_ approaches include using alcohol or drugs, seeking emotional social support from friends or relatives, and engaging in activities, such as sports or watching TV, which distract attention from the problem. _Cognitive_ approaches involve how people think about the stressful situation. In one cognitive approach, people _redefine_ the situation to put a good face on it, such as by noting that things could be worse, making comparisons with individuals who are less well off, or seeing something good growing out of the problem. We can see this approach in two statements of women with breast cancer (Taylor, 1983):

> What you do is put things into perspective. You find out that things like relationships are really the most important things you have—the people you know and your family—everything else is just way down the line. It's very strange that it takes something so serious to make you realize that. (p. 1163)

> The people I really feel sorry for are these young gals. To lose a breast when you're so young must be awful. I'm 73; what do I need a breast for? (p. 1166)

People who want to redefine a stressful situation can generally find a way to do it since there is almost always _some_ aspect of one's life that can be viewed positively (Taylor, 1983).

Other emotion-focused cognitive processes include strategies Freud called "defense mechanisms," which involve distorting memory or reality in some way (Cramer, 2000). For instance, when something is too painful to face, the person may deny that it exists, as Beth did with the lump on her breast. This defense mechanism is called _denial_. In medical situations, individuals who are diagnosed with terminal diseases often use this strategy and refuse to believe they are really ill. This is one way by which people cope by using _avoidance_ strategies. But strategies that promote avoidance of the problem are helpful mainly in the short run, such as during an early stage of a prolonged stress experience (Suls & Fletcher, 1985). This is so for individuals who are diagnosed with a serious illness, for instance. As a rule of thumb, the effectiveness of avoidance-promoting methods seems to be limited to the first couple of weeks of a prolonged stress experience. Thereafter, coping is better served by giving the situation attention.

People tend to use emotion-focused approaches when they believe they can do little to change the stressful conditions (Lazarus & Folkman, 1984). An example of this is when a loved one dies—in this situation, people often seek emotional support and distract themselves with funeral arrangements and chores at home or at work. Other examples can be seen in situations in which individuals believe their resources are not and cannot be adequate to meet the demands of the stressor. A child who tries very hard to be the "straight A" student his or her parents seem to want, but never succeeds, may reappraise the situation and decide, "I don't need their love." Coping methods that focus on emotions are important because they sometimes interfere with getting medical treatment or involve unhealthful behaviors, such as using cigarettes, alcohol, and drugs to reduce tension. People often use these substances in their efforts toward emotion-focused coping (Wills, 1986).

Problem-focused coping is aimed at reducing the demands of a stressful situation or expanding the resources to deal with it. Everyday life provides many examples of problem-focused coping, including quitting a stressful job, negotiating an extension for paying some bills, devising a new schedule for studying (and sticking to it), choosing a different career to pursue, seeking medical or psychological treatment, and learning new skills. People tend to use problem-focused approaches when they believe their resources or the demands of the situation are changeable (Lazarus & Folkman, 1984). For example, caregivers of terminally ill patients use problem-focused coping more in the months prior to the death than during bereavement (Moskowitz et al., 1996).

To what extent do people use problem-focused and emotion-focused approaches in coping with stress in their lives? Andrew Billings and Rudolf Moos (1981) studied this issue by having nearly 200 married couples fill out a survey. The respondents described a recent personal crisis or negative life event that happened to them and then answered questions that were very similar to the ones you answered in the self-assessment exercise. The outcomes of this research revealed some interesting relationships. Both the husbands and the wives used more problem-focused than emotion-focused methods to cope with the stressful event. But the wives reported using more emotion-focused approaches than the husbands did. People with higher incomes and educational levels reported greater use of problem-focused coping than those with less income and education. Last, individuals used much less problem-focused coping when the stress involved a death in the family than when it involved other kinds of problems, such as illness or economic difficulties.

Can problem-focused and emotion-focused coping be used together? Yes, and they often are. For instance, a study had patients with painful arthritis keep track of their daily use of problem- and emotion-focused coping (Tennen et al., 2000). Most often, they used the two types of coping together; but when they used only one type, three-quarters of the time it was problem-focused coping. We can see an example of both types of coping in a man's experience when a coworker accused him of not sending out the appropriate letters for a job. In describing how he reacted to this stressful situation, he said he first confirmed that the coworker's accusation

> was not true, that everything [letters] had gone out. There's always a chance you might be wrong so I checked first. Then I told him. No, everything had gone out. My immediate reaction was to call him on the carpet first. He doesn't have any right to call me on something like this. Then I gave it a second thought and decided that that wouldn't help the situation. (Kahn et al., cited in Lazarus & Folkman, 1984, p. 155)

This example shows problem-focused coping in confirming that the letters had gone out, and emotion-focused coping in controlling his angry impulse "to call him on the carpet."

Coping Methods and Measurement

What specific methods—that is, skills and strategies—can people apply in stressful situations to alter the problem or regulate their emotional response? Researchers have described about 400 methods and incorporated sets of them into dozens of instruments to assess overall coping and categories of coping types (Skinner et al., 2003). Table 4.1 lists two dozen coping methods that are easy to conceptualize, without stating definitions, to give you a sense of the great variety of possible methods people can use.

Unfortunately, instruments to measure coping haven't been very useful so far. They were typically developed with the expectation that the scores would predict mental or physical health, but they don't (Coyne & Racioppo, 2000; Skinner et al., 2003). And they don't seem to be very accurate in measuring people's coping. Most measures of coping are retrospective, asking respondents about the methods used in the past week, month, or more. Do you remember exactly how you coped 2 weeks ago with a stressful event, such as a poor grade on a test or an argument with a close friend? A study tested the accuracy issue by having people report daily for a month on the coping strategies they used with the most negative event that occurred that day (Todd et al., 2004). The subjects used a list with descriptions of 16 strategies that comprise a widely used coping survey for the daily reports; at the end of the study they filled out the survey to report on the whole month. Comparisons of daily and full-month reports showed weak correspondence for about half of the coping methods, suggesting

Table 4.1   *Methods of Coping with Stressful Situations (listed alphabetically)*

Assistance seeking[p]	Hiding feelings[e]	Positive reappraisal[e]
Avoidance[e]	Humor[e]	Praying[e]
Confrontive assertion[p]	Increased activity[e]	Resigned acceptance[e]
Denial[e]	Information seeking[p]	Seeking meaning[e]
Direct action[p]	Intrusive thoughts[e]	Self-criticism[e]
Discharge (venting)[e]	Logical analysis[p]	Substance use[e]
Distraction (diverting attention)[e]	Physical exercise[e]	Wishful thinking[e]
Emotional approach[e]	Planful problem solving[p]	Worry[e]

Note: Superscripted letters refer to the method's most likely function, [p] = problem-focused and [e] = emotion-focused coping, but some methods may serve either function.
Source: Skinner et al., 2003, Table 3.

that assessments of coping pertaining to more than the past week or so are inaccurate for many methods.

Researchers are currently working to identify the coping methods that are most important—those that can be measured accurately and are related to psychological and health outcomes, such as people's development of and recovery from illnesses. Let's look at some directions that look promising (Folkman & Moskowitz, 2004; Carver & Connor-Smith, 2010).

1. *Engaging positive emotions.* One approach for coping with stress involves the use of positive emotions to soften or balance against feelings of distress. For instance, Susan Folkman (1997; Folkman & Moskowitz, 2004) has found that individuals who were caring for a dying spouse or partner and then lost that person report both positive and negative emotions occurring together during times of great stress. As an example, a gay man described the difficulty of tending for his partner during the extreme sweating episodes he, like many AIDS patients, had many times each day and noted that he feels "proud, pleased that I can comfort him .... We are still making our love for each other the focal point" (Folkman, 1997, p. 1213).

2. *Finding benefits or meaning.* People who are trying to cope with severe stress often search for benefits or meaning in the experience, using beliefs, values, and goals to give it a positive significance (Folkman, 1997; Sears, Stanton, & Danoff-Burg, 2003). They find benefits or meaning in many ways, such as

> when people whose loved ones have died from a disease become advocates for research on that disease; finding that new or closer bonds with others have been formed because of having experienced or survived a natural disaster together; or finding that the event has clarified which goals or priorities are important and which are not (Folkman, 1997, p. 1215).

A meta-analysis of over 80 studies found partial support for a role of benefit finding in coping: it was associated with less depression and greater feelings of well-being,

but was *not* related to anxiety and self-reports of physical health (Helgeson, Reynolds, & Tomich, 2006).

3. *Engaging in emotional approach.* In emotional approach, people cope with stress by actively processing and expressing their feelings (Stanton et al., 2000). To assess emotional approach, people rate how often they engage emotional *processing* (in such activities as, "I take time to figure out what I'm really feeling" and "I delve into my feelings to get a thorough understanding of them") and emotional *expression* ("I take time to express my emotions"). Emotional approach probably includes the method of disclosure of negative experiences and feelings we discussed in Chapter 3 as a way of reducing stress and enhancing health.

4. *Accommodating to a stressor.* Another way to cope is to adapt or adjust to the presence of the stressor and carry on with life (Carver & Connor-Smith, 2010, Morling & Evered, 2006). For instance, people with chronic pain conditions may come to accept that the pain is present and engage in everyday activities as best as they can.

Research has found psychological and health benefits for each of these coping methods (Folkman & Moskowitz, 2004). For example, researchers tested women with breast cancer for emotional approach soon after medical treatment and for psychological and health status 3 months later (Stanton et al., 2000). They found that high levels of emotional *expression* were associated with improved self-perceived health, increased vigor, fewer medical visits for cancer-related problems, and decreased distress. But high levels of emotional *processing* were linked with increased distress. It may be that emotional processing includes or leads to *rumination*, in which people have *intrusive thoughts* and images that perpetuate their stress (Baum, 1990). For example, people may think repeatedly about how they or others are to blame for their problems or have "flashbacks" of painful or angry events. People who often ruminate take longer for their blood pressure to decrease after starting to think about arousing events and report having poorer health habits and health than individuals who seldom have such thoughts (Gerin et al., 2006; Nowack, 1989).

Using and Developing Methods of Coping

No single method of coping is uniformly applied or effective with all stressful situations (Ilfeld, 1980; Pearlin & Schooler, 1978). Four issues about people's patterns in using different coping methods should be mentioned. First, people tend to be consistent in the way they cope with a particular type of stressor—that is, when faced with the same problem, they tend to use the same methods they used in the past (Stone & Neale, 1984). Second, people seldom use just one method to cope with a stressor. Their efforts typically involve a combination of problem- and emotion-focused strategies (Tennen et al., 2000). Third, the methods people use in coping with short-term stressors may be different from those they use under long-term stress, such as from a serious chronic illness (Aldwin & Brustrom, 1997). Fourth, although the methods people use to cope with stress develop from the transactions they have in their lives, a genetic influence is suggested by the finding that identical twins are more similar than fraternal twins in the coping styles they use (Busjahn et al., 1999).

Psychologists assume that coping processes change across the life span. But the nature of these changes is unclear because there is little research, especially longitudinal studies, charting these changes (Aldwin & Brustrom, 1997; Lazarus & Folkman, 1984). Some aspects of the changes in coping that occur in the early years are known. Infants and toddlers being examined by their pediatricians are likely to cope by trying to stop the examination (Hyson, 1983). We saw earlier in the case of Molly that young children develop coping skills that enable them to overcome many of their fears, making use of her expanding cognitive abilities. Over the next several years, children come to rely increasingly on cognitive strategies for coping (Brown et al., 1986; Miller & Green, 1984). So, for example, they learn to think about something else to distract themselves from stress. More and more, they regulate their feelings with emotion-focused methods, such as playing with toys or watching TV, especially when they can't do anything to solve the problem, such as a serious illness in their parents (Compas et al., 1996).

Few studies have examined changes in methods of coping from adolescence to old age. One study used interviews and questionnaires to compare the daily hassles and coping methods of middle-aged and elderly men and women (Folkman et al., 1987). The middle-aged individuals used more problem-focused coping, whereas the elderly people used more emotion-focused approaches. Why do adults use less problem-focused and more emotion-focused coping as they get older? These changes probably result at least in part from differences in what people must cope with as they age. The elderly individuals in this study were retired from full-time work and reported more stress relating to health than did the middle-aged people, who reported more stress relating to work, finances, and family and friends. The stressors encountered in middle age are more changeable than those in old age. But the age groups also differed in outlook: regardless of the source of stress, the elderly people appraised their problems as *less* changeable than the middle-aged individuals did. As we saw earlier, people tend to use problem-focused approaches when they believe the situation is changeable, and rely on emotion-focused coping when they do not.

Because most adults are married or partnered, adults' coping strategies usually operate and develop jointly as a system, with each member's coping processes being shared by and influencing the other's (Berg & Upchurch, 2007). This sharing and social influence in coping may be clearest when a couple copes with long-term major stressors, such as the diagnosis, treatment, and future course of a life-threatening or disabling illness in one or both of them. Their psychological adjustment to the stressors will depend on the type of illness, whether their joint coping strategies are effective, and the quality of their relationship.

Gender and Sociocultural Differences in Coping

Studies of gender differences in coping have generally found that men are more likely to report using problem-focused strategies and women are more likely to report using emotion-focused strategies in dealing with stressful events (Marco, 2004). But when the men and women are similar in occupation and education, no gender differences are found (Greenglass & Noguchi, 1996). These results suggest that societal sex roles play an important role in the coping patterns of men and women.

Billings and Moos (1981) found that people with higher incomes and educational levels report greater use of problem-focused coping than those with less income and education. This finding suggests that the social experiences of disadvantaged people lead many of them to believe they have little control over events in their lives. In general, disadvantaged individuals—a category that typically includes disproportionately more minority group members—are more likely to experience stressful events and less likely to cope with them effectively than other people are (Marco, 2004). Thus, people in Asian cultures and African- and Hispanic-Americans tend to use more emotion-focused and less problem-focused coping than White Americans do.

We have examined many ways people cope with stress. Each method can be effective and adaptive for the individual if it neutralizes the current stressor and does not increase the likelihood of future stressful situations. In the next section, we consider how people can reduce the potential for stress for themselves and for others.

REDUCING THE POTENTIAL FOR STRESS

Can people become "immune" to the impact of stress to some extent? Some aspects of people's lives can reduce the potential for stressors to develop and help individuals cope with problems when they occur. Efforts taken that prevent or minimize stress are called *proactive coping*, and they typically use problem-focused methods (Carver & Connor-Smith, 2010). We will look at several proactive coping methods. (Go to .)

ENHANCING SOCIAL SUPPORT

We have all turned to others for help and comfort when under stress at some time in our lives. If you have ever had to endure troubled times on your own, you know how important social support can be. But social support

is not only helpful after stressors appear, it also can help avert problems in the first place. Consider, for example, the tangible support newlyweds receive, such as items they will need to set up a household. Without these items, the couple would be saddled either with the financial burden of buying the items or with the hassles of not having them.

Although people in all walks of life can lack the social support they need, some segments of the population have less than others (Antonucci, 1985; Broadhead et al., 1983; Ratliff-Crain & Baum, 1990). For instance:

- Men tend to have larger social networks than women, but women seem to use theirs more effectively for support.
- Many elderly individuals live in isolated conditions and have few people on whom to rely.
- Network size is related to social prestige, income, and education—the lower these variables are for individuals, the smaller their social networks tend to be.

Furthermore, the networks of people from lower socioeconomic classes are usually less diverse than those of people from higher classes—that is, lower-class networks contain fewer nonkin members. In contemporary American society, the traditional sources of support have shifted to include greater reliance on individuals in social and helping organizations. This is partly because extended family members today have different functions and live farther apart than they did many decades ago (Pilisuk, 1982).

HIGHLIGHT

Does Religiousness Reduce Stress and Enhance Health?

Here's an intriguing finding: *religiousness*—that is, people's personal involvement in a religion—is associated with lower anxiety and depression, better physical health, and longer life (Chida, Steptoe, & Powell, 2009; Masters, 2004). Some reasons for this link have been proposed—for instance, some religions promote healthy lifestyles, such as by preaching against smoking, and religious meetings provide social contact and support. To the extent that these processes happen, they are likely to reduce stress and enhance health. But keep in mind three issues. First, some people are involved in a religion for utilitarian reasons, such as to promote status or political goals, and their stress reactions do not seem to benefit from their involvement (Masters et al., 2004). Second, social contact appears to play a strong role

in health benefits of religious involvement (Nicholson, Rose, & Bobak, 2010). Third, the link between religiousness and lower mortality applies to people who were initially healthy, not to individuals who were already sick (Chida, Steptoe, & Powell, 2009).

One other reason for the link between religiousness and health that some people have proposed is that religious people may receive direct help from their God, especially if others pray for their health. This idea has been disconfirmed. A meta-analysis on data from 14 studies on the role of people's praying to help another person found no impact of that prayer on the object person's health or life condition (Masters, Spielmans, & Goodson, 2006). The health or life conditions of people who are or are not the objects of prayer are not different.

Social support is a dynamic process. People's needs for, giving of, and receipt of support change over time. Unfortunately, people who experience high levels of chronic stress, such as when their health declines severely, often find that their social support resources deteriorate at the same time (Kaplan et al., 1997; Lepore, 1997; Wortman & Dunkel-Schetter, 1987). These results are disheartening because they suggest that people whose need for social support is greatest may be unlikely to receive it.

People can enhance their ability to give and receive social support by joining community organizations, such as social, religious, special interest, and self-help groups. These organizations have the advantage of bringing together individuals with similar problems and interests, which can become the basis for sharing, helping, and friendship. In the United States, there are many widely known self-help groups, including Alcoholics Anonymous and Parents without Partners, and special-interest groups, including the American Association of Retired People and support groups for people with specific illnesses, such as arthritis or AIDS. Although groups like these are helpful, we don't yet know which ones work best for specific problems (Hogan, Linden, & Najarian, 2002). People are most likely to join a support group for a serious illness if it is embarrassing or stigmatizing, such as AIDS or breast cancer (Davison, Pennebaker, & Dickerson, 2000). Isolated people of all ages—especially the elderly—with all types of difficulties should be encouraged to join suitable organizations.

Communities can play a valuable role in enhancing people's resources for social support by creating programs to help individuals develop social networks, such as in occupational and religious settings, and by providing facilities for recreation and fitness, arranging social events, and providing counseling services. But social support may not be effective if the recipient interprets it as a sign of inadequacy or believes his or her personal control is limited by it. Providing effective social support requires sensitivity and good judgment. (Go to 💡.)

IMPROVING ONE'S PERSONAL CONTROL

When life becomes stressful, people who lack a strong sense of personal control may stop trying, thinking, "Oh, what's the use." Instead of feeling they have power and control, they feel helpless. For instance, people with a painful and disabling chronic illness may stop doing physical therapy exercises. When seriously ill patients who feel little personal control face a new severe stressor, they show more emotional distress than others who feel more control (Benight et al., 1997). The main psychological help such people need is to bolster their self-efficacy and reduce their passiveness and helplessness (Smith & Wallston, 1992). A pessimistic outlook increases people's potential for stress and can have a negative effect on their health.

How can a person's sense of control be enhanced? The process can begin very early. Parents, teachers, and other caregivers can show a child their love and respect, provide a stimulating environment, encourage and praise the child's accomplishments, and set reasonable standards of conduct and performance that he or she can regard as challenges, rather than threats. At the other end of the life span, nursing homes and families can allow elderly people to do things for themselves and have responsibilities, such as in cleaning, cooking, and arranging social activities. One woman described the prospect of living with her children in the following way: "I couldn't stand to live with my children, as much as I love them, because they always want to take over my life" (Shupe, 1985). For people with serious illnesses, health psychologists can help patients with little control by training them in effective ways to cope with stress (Thompson & Kyle, 2000).

ORGANIZING ONE'S WORLD BETTER

"Where did I put my keys?" you have surely heard someone ask frantically while running late to make an appointment. People often feel stress because they are running late or believe they don't have enough time to do the tasks of the day. They need to organize their worlds to make things happen efficiently. This can take the form of keeping an appointment calendar, designating certain places for certain items, or putting materials in alphabetized file folders, for instance. Organizing one's world reduces frustration, wasted time, and the potential for stress.

Teachers can help enhance children's social support by having them work together.

HIGHLIGHT

The Amish Way of Social Support in Bereavement

The Amish people in North America form a conservative religious sect that settled in Pennsylvania in the 18th century. Amish families generally live in colonies that now exist in many states and Canada. These families have a strongly religious orientation and a serious work ethic that revolves around farming. Their way of life is quite distinctive: they wear uniquely simple and uniform clothing; speak mainly a Pennsylvania-German dialect; and reject modern devices, using horse-driven buggies instead of automobiles, for example. Their social lives require their adherence to strict rules of conduct and obedience to patriarchal authority.

One feature of Amish life is that community members give assistance to one another in all times of need. Their way of dealing with death provides a good example, as Kathleen Bryer (1986) has studied and described. Before death, a person who is seriously ill receives care from his or her family. This generally occurs at home, rather than in a hospital. The Amish not only expect to give this care, but see it as a positive opportunity. A married woman who was asked about caring for a dying relative replied, "Oh yes, we had the chance to take care of all four of our old parents before they died. We are both so thankful for this" (p. 251). Death typically occurs in the presence of the family.

Upon someone's death, the Amish community swings into action. Close neighbors notify other members of the colony, and the community makes most of the funeral arrangements. The family receives visits of sympathy and support from other Amish families, some of whom come from other colonies far away and may not even know the bereaved family. In contrast to the social support most Americans receive in bereavement, Amish supportive efforts do not end shortly after the funeral—they continue at a high level for at least a year. Supportive activities include evening and Sunday visiting, making items and scrapbooks for the family, and organized quilting projects that create fellowship around a common task. Moreover, Amish individuals often give extraordinary help to bereaved family members. For instance, the sister of one widower came to live with him and care for his four children until he remarried. The community encourages widowed individuals to remarry in time, and they often do so.

An Amish funeral procession. The Amish provide social support to one another in many ways, particularly after a member dies.

An important approach for organizing one's time is called **time management**. It consists of three elements (Lakein, 1973). The first element is to *set goals*. These goals should be reasonable or obtainable ones, and they should include long-term goals, such as graduating from college next year, and short-term ones, such as getting good grades. The second element involves making daily *To Do* lists with priorities indicated, keeping the goals in mind. These lists should be composed each morning or late in the preceding day. Each list must be written—trying to keep the list in your head is unreliable and makes setting priorities difficult. The third element is to set up a *schedule* for the day, allocating estimated time periods to each item in the list. If an urgent new task arises during the day, the list should be adjusted to include it.

EXERCISING: LINKS TO STRESS AND HEALTH

You have probably heard from TV, radio, magazine, and newspaper reports that exercise and physical fitness can protect people from stress and its harmful effects on health. These reports cite a wide range of benefits of exercising, from increased intellectual functioning and personal control to decreased anxiety, depression, hostility, and tension. Do exercise and fitness reduce the potential for stress and its effects on health?

Correlational and retrospective studies of this question have found that people who exercise or are physically fit often report less anxiety, depression, and tension in their lives than do people who do not exercise or are less fit (Dishman, 1986; Holmes, 1993). Although these results are consistent with the view that exercise and fitness reduce stress, there are two problems in interpreting them. First, the reduction in self-reported stress and emotion may have resulted partly from a placebo effect—that is, the subjects' expectations that psychological improvements would occur (Desharnais et al., 1993). Second, the results of correlational research do not tell us what causes what. Do exercise and fitness cause people to feel less stress? Or are people more likely to exercise and keep fit if they feel less stress and time pressures in their lives? Fortunately, there is stronger evidence for the beneficial effects of exercise and fitness on stress and health.

An experiment by Bram Goldwater and Martin Collis (1985) examined the effects of 6-week exercise programs on cardiovascular fitness and feelings of anxiety in healthy 19- to 30-year-old men who were randomly assigned to one of two groups. In one group, the men worked out 5 days a week in a vigorous fitness program, including swimming and active sports, such as soccer; the second group had a more moderate program with less demanding exercise activities. Compared with the men in the moderate program, those in the vigorous program showed greater gains in fitness and reductions in anxiety. Other experiments have shown similar beneficial effects of exercise on depression and anxiety with men and women, particularly if the programs last at least 2 or 3 months (Babyak et al., 2000; Phillips, Kiernan, & King, 2001).

Research has also assessed the role of exercise on stress and cardiovascular function. Although most studies were correlational, finding that people who exercise or are physically fit show less reactivity to stressors and are less likely to be hypertensive than individuals who do not exercise or are less fit, some used experimental methods (Blumenthal, Sherwood et al., 2002; Dimsdale, Alpert, & Schneiderman, 1986). We'll consider two experiments. First, healthy young adults who had sedentary jobs and had not regularly engaged in vigorous physical activity in the previous year were recruited (Jennings et al., 1986). During the next 4 months, these people spent 1 month at each of four levels of activity, ranging from below normal (which included 2 weeks of rest in a hospital) to much above-normal activity (daily vigorous exercise for 40 minutes). Heart rate and blood pressure were measured after each month. The much above-normal level of activity reduced heart rate by 12% and systolic and diastolic blood pressure by 8% and 10% compared with the normal sedentary activity level. Below-normal activity levels did not alter heart rate or blood pressure. Second, researchers had undergraduates experience a stress condition and then engage in moderate exercise or sit quietly for 3 minutes (Chafin, Christenfeld, & Gerin, 2008). Measures taken

soon after revealed that exercise enhanced recovery from stress: the individuals who exercised had lower blood pressure levels than those who sat.

Do exercise and fitness prevent people from developing stress-related illnesses? The results of several studies suggest they do (Phillips, Kiernan, & King, 2001). For example, one study used prospective methods by first assessing the subjects' recent life events and fitness, and then having them keep records concerning their health over the next 9 weeks (Roth & Holmes, 1985). The results revealed that individuals who reported high levels of stress had poorer subsequent health if they were not fit; stress had little impact on the health of fit subjects. Overall, the evidence is fairly strong that engaging in regular exercise can promote health by reducing stress.

PREPARING FOR STRESSFUL EVENTS

In this and previous chapters we have discussed many types of stressful events, ranging from being stuck in traffic, to starting day care or school, being overloaded with work, going through a divorce, and experiencing a disaster. Preparing for these events can reduce the potential for stress. For instance, parents can help prepare a child for starting day care by taking the child there in advance to see the place, meet the teacher, and play for a while (Sarafino, 1986).

Irving Janis (1958) pioneered the psychological study of the need to prepare people for stressful events, such as surgery. In general, research on preparing for surgery indicates that the higher the patients' *preoperative* fear, the worse their *postoperative* adjustment and recovery tend to be, as reflected in the following measures (Anderson & Masur, 1983; Johnson, 1983):

- The patient's self-reported pain
- The amount of medication taken to relieve pain
- Self-reported anxiety or depression
- The length of stay in the hospital after surgery
- Ratings by hospital staff of the patient's recovery or adjustment

These outcomes suggest that preparing patients to help them cope with their preoperative concerns should enhance later adjustment and recovery. The most effective methods for preparing people psychologically for the stress of surgery attempt to enhance the patients' feelings of *control* (Anderson & Masur, 1983; Mathews & Ridgeway, 1984). To promote *behavioral control*, for example, patients learn how to reduce discomfort or promote rehabilitation through specific actions they can take, such as by doing leg exercises to improve strength or deep breathing exercises to reduce pain. For *cognitive control*, patients learn ways to focus their thoughts on pleasant or beneficial aspects of the surgery, rather than the unpleasant aspects. And for *informational control*, patients receive information about the procedures and/or sensations they will experience.

Although receiving preparatory information is usually helpful, sometimes it can have the opposite effect—for instance:

> The Los Angeles City Council had placed cards in the city elevators assuring riders that they should stay calm, since "there is little danger of the car dropping uncontrollably or running out of air." … A year later the cards had to be removed because of complaints from elevator riders that the message made them anxious. (Thompson, 1981, p. 96)

Also, having too much information can be confusing and actually arouse fear. Young children often become more anxious when they receive a great deal of information about the medical procedures they will undergo (Miller & Green, 1984). With children in dental or medical settings, it is generally best not to give a lot of detail. Describing some sensory experiences to expect is especially helpful, such as the sounds of equipment or the tingly feeling from the dental anesthetic.

In summary, we have discussed several methods that are helpful in reducing the potential for stress and, thereby, benefiting health. These methods take advantage of the stress-moderating effects of social support, personal control, exercise, being well organized, and being prepared for an impending stressor. In the next section, we consider ways to reduce the reaction to stress once it has begun.

REDUCING STRESS REACTIONS: STRESS MANAGEMENT

People acquire coping skills through their experiences, which may involve strategies they have tried in the past or methods they have seen others use. But sometimes the skills they have learned are not adequate for a current stressor because it is so strong, novel, or unrelenting. When people cannot cope effectively, they need help in learning new and adaptive ways of managing stress. The term **stress management** refers to any program of behavioral and cognitive techniques that is designed to reduce psychological and physical reactions to stress. Sometimes people use *pharmacological* approaches under medical supervision to reduce emotions, such as anxiety, that accompany stress.

MEDICATION

Of the many types of drugs doctors prescribe to help patients manage stress, we will consider two: benzodiazepines and beta-blockers, both of which reduce physiological arousal and feelings of anxiety (AMA, 2003; Kring et al., 2010). *Benzodiazepines*, which include drugs with the trade names Valium and Xanax, activate a neurotransmitter that decreases neural transmission in the central nervous system. *Beta-blockers*, such as Inderal, are used to reduce anxiety and blood pressure. They block the activity stimulated by adrenaline and noradrenaline in the peripheral nervous system. Beta-blockers cause less drowsiness than benzodiazepines, probably because they act on the peripheral rather than central nervous system. Although many people use drugs for long-term control of stress and emotions, using drugs for stress should be a temporary measure. For instance, they might be used during an acute crisis, such as in the week or two following the death of a loved one, or while the patient learns new psychological methods for coping.

BEHAVIORAL AND COGNITIVE METHODS

Psychologists have developed methods they can train people to use in coping with stress. Some of these techniques focus mainly on the person's behavior, and some emphasize the person's thinking processes. People who use these methods usually find them helpful.

Relaxation

The opposite of arousal is relaxation—so relaxing should be a good way to reduce stress. "Perhaps so," you say, "but when stress occurs, relaxing is easier said than done." Actually, relaxing when under stress is not so hard to do when you know how. One way people can learn to control their feelings of tension is called **progressive muscle relaxation** (or just *progressive relaxation*), in which they focus their attention on specific muscle groups while alternately tightening and relaxing these muscles (Sarafino, 2001).

The idea of teaching people to relax their skeletal muscles to reduce psychological stress was introduced many years ago by Edmund Jacobson (1938). He found that muscle tension could be reduced much more if individuals were taught to pay attention to the sensations as they tense and relax individual groups of muscles. Although today there are various versions of the progressive muscle relaxation technique, they each outline a sequence of muscle groups for the person to follow. For example, the sequence might begin with the person relaxing the hands, then the forehead, followed by the lower face, the neck, the stomach, and, finally, the legs. For each muscle group, the person first tenses the muscles for 7–10 seconds, and then relaxes them for about 15 seconds, paying attention to how the muscles feel. This is usually repeated for the same muscle group two or three times in a relaxation session, which generally lasts 20 or 30 minutes. The tensing action is mainly important while the person is being trained, and can be eliminated after he or she has mastered the technique (Sarafino, 2001). Relaxation works best in a quiet, nondistracting setting with the person lying down or sitting on comfortable furniture.

Stress management is applied mainly with adults, but children also experience stress without being able to cope effectively. Fortunately, many behavioral and cognitive methods are easy to learn and can be adapted so that an adult can teach a young child to use them (Siegel & Peterson, 1980). Relaxation exercises provide a good example. An adult could start by showing the child what relaxing is like by lifting and then releasing the arms and legs of a rag doll, allowing them to fall down. Then, the adult would follow a *protocol*, or script, giving instructions like those in Table 4.2. When children and adults first learn progressive muscle relaxation, they sometimes don't relax their muscles when told to do so. Instead of letting their arms and legs *fall* down, they *move* them down. They may also tense more muscles than required—for example, tightening facial muscles when they are asked to tense hand muscles. These errors should be pointed out and corrected.

Often, after individuals have thoroughly mastered the relaxation procedure, they can gradually shorten the procedure so they can apply a very quick version in times of stress, such as when they are about to give a speech (Sarafino, 2001). This quick version might have the following steps: (1) taking a deep breath, and letting it out; (2) saying to oneself, "Relax, feel nice and calm"; and (3) thinking about a pleasant thought for a few seconds. In this way, relaxation methods can be directly applied to help people cope with everyday stressful events.

Research has demonstrated that progressive muscle relaxation is highly effective in reducing stress (Carlson & Hoyle, 1993; Jain et al., 2007; Lichstein, 1988). What's more, people who receive training in relaxation show less cardiovascular reactivity to stressors and stronger immune function (Lucini et al., 1997; Sherman et al., 1997).

Systematic Desensitization

Although relaxation is often successful by itself in helping people cope, it is frequently used in conjunction with **systematic desensitization**, a useful method for reducing fear and anxiety (Sarafino, 2001). This method is based on the view that fears are learned by *classical conditioning*—that is, by associating a situation or object with an unpleasant event. This can happen, for example, if a person associates visits to the dentist with pain, thereby becoming "sensitized" to dentists. Desensitization is

Table 4.2 *Progressive Muscle Relaxation Protocol for Children*

1. "OK. Let's raise our arms and put them out in front. Now make a fist with both your hands, really hard. Hold the fist tight and you will see how your muscles in your hands and arms feel when they are tight." (hold for 7–10 seconds)
   "That's very good. Now when I say relax, I want the muscles in your hands and arms to become floppy, like the rag doll, and your arms will drop to your sides. OK, relax." (about 15 seconds)
2. "Let's raise our legs out in front of us. Now tighten the muscles in your feet and legs, really hard. Make the muscles really tight, and hold it." (7–10 seconds)
   "Very good. Now relax the muscles in your feet and legs, and let them drop to the floor. They feel so good. So calm and relaxed." (15 seconds)
3. "Now let's do our tummy muscles. Tighten your tummy, really hard—and hold it." (7–10 seconds)
   "OK. Relax your tummy, and feel how good it feels. So comfortable." (15 seconds)
4. "Leave your arms at your side, but tighten the muscles in your shoulders and neck. You can do this by moving your shoulders up toward your head. Hold the muscles very tightly in your shoulders and neck." (7–10 seconds)
   "Now relax those muscles so they are floppy, and see how good that feels." (15 seconds)
5. "Let's tighten the muscles in our faces. Scrunch up your whole face so that all of the muscles are tight—the muscles in your cheeks, and your mouth, and your nose, and your forehead. Really scrunch up your face, and hold it." (7–10 seconds)
   "Now relax all the muscles in your face—your cheeks, mouth, nose, and forehead. Feel how nice that is." (15 seconds)
6. "Now I want us to take a very, very deep breath—so deep that there's no more room inside for more air. Hold the air in. (use a shorter time: 6–8 seconds)
   "That's good. Now slowly let the air out. Very slowly, until it's all out . . . . And now breathe as you usually do." (15 seconds)

Source: From Sarafino, 1986, pp. 112–113.

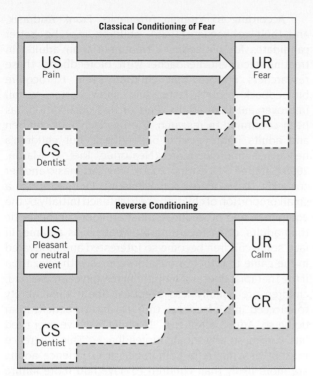

Figure 4-1 Classical conditioning in learning to fear dental visits and in reversing this learning. In conditioning the fear, the unconditioned stimulus (US) of pain elicits the unconditioned response (UR) of fear automatically. Learning occurs by pairing the dentist, the conditioned stimulus (CS), with the US so that the dentist begins to elicit fear. The reverse conditioning pairs the feared dentist with a US that elicits calm.

a classical conditioning procedure that *reverses* this learning by pairing the feared object or situation with either pleasant or neutral events, as Figure 4-1 outlines. According to Joseph Wolpe (1958, 1973), an originator of the desensitization method, the reversal comes about

through the process of *counterconditioning*, whereby the "calm" response gradually replaces the "fear" response. Desensitization has been used successfully in reducing a variety of children's and adults' fears, such as fear of dentists, animals, high places, public speaking, and taking tests (Lichstein, 1988; Sarafino, 2001).

An important feature of the systematic desensitization method is that it uses a *stimulus hierarchy*—a graded sequence of approximations to the conditioned stimulus, the feared situation. The purpose of these approximations is to bring the person gradually in contact with the source of fear in about 10 or 15 steps. To see how a stimulus hierarchy might be constructed, we will look at the one in Table 4.3 that deals with the fear of dentists. The person would follow the instructions in each of the 14 steps. As you can see, some of the steps involve real-life, or *in vivo*, contacts with the feared situation, and some do not. Two types of non–real-life contacts, of varying degrees, can be included. One type uses *imaginal* situations, such as having the person think about calling the dentist. The other involves *symbolic* contacts, such as by showing pictures, films, or models of the feared situation.

The systematic desensitization procedure starts by having the person do relaxation exercises. Then the steps in a hierarchy are presented individually, while the person is relaxed and comfortable (Sarafino, 2001). The steps follow a sequence from the least to the most fearful for the individual. Each step may elicit some wariness or fear behavior, but the person is encouraged to relax. Once the wariness at one step has passed and the person is calm, the next step in the hierarchy can be introduced. Completing an entire stimulus hierarchy and reducing a fairly strong fear can be achieved fairly quickly—it is likely to take several hours, divided into several separate sessions. In one study with dental-phobic adults who simply imagined each step in a hierarchy, the procedure

Table 4.3   *Example of a Stimulus Hierarchy for a Fear of Dentists*

1. Think about being in the dentist's waiting room, simply accompanying someone else who is there for an examination.
2. Look at a photograph of a smiling person seated in a dental chair.
3. Imagine this person calmly having a dental examination.
4. Think about calling the dentist for an appointment.
5. Actually call for the appointment.
6. Sit in a car outside the dentist's office without having an appointment.
7. Sit in the dentist's waiting room and hear the nurse say, "'The hygienist is ready for you."
8. Sit in the examination room and hear the hygienist say, "I see one tooth the dentist will need to look at."
9. Hear and watch the drill run, without its being brought near the face.
10. Have the dentist pick at the tooth with an instrument, saying, "That doesn't look good."
11. See the dentist lay out the instruments, including a syringe to administer an anesthetic.
12. Feel the needle touch the gums.
13. Imagine having the tooth drilled.
14. Imagine having the tooth pulled.

successfully reduced their fear in six 1 1/2-hour sessions (Gatchel, 1980). Individual sessions for reducing fears in children are usually much shorter than those used with adults, especially for a child who is very young and has a short attention span.

Biofeedback

Biofeedback is a technique in which an electromechanical device monitors the status of a person's physiological processes, such as heart rate or muscle tension, and immediately reports that information back to the individual. This information enables the person to gain voluntary control over these processes through operant conditioning. If, for instance, the person is trying to reduce neck-muscle tension and the device reports that the tension has just decreased, this information reinforces whatever efforts the individual made to accomplish this decrease.

Biofeedback has been used successfully in treating stress-related health problems. For example, an experiment found that patients suffering from chronic headaches who were given biofeedback regarding muscle tension in their foreheads later showed less tension in those muscles and reported having fewer headaches than subjects in control groups (Budzynski et al., 1973). What's more, these benefits continued at a follow-up after 3 months. Biofeedback and progressive muscle relaxation are effective for treating headache and many other stress-related disorders (Gatchel, 2001; Nestoriuc, Rief, & Martin, 2008). Both biofeedback and progressive muscle relaxation techniques can help reduce stress, but some individuals may benefit more from one method than the other.

According to Virginia Attanasio, Frank Andrasik, and their colleagues (1985), children may be better candidates for biofeedback treatment than adults. In treating recurrent headache with biofeedback, these researchers noticed that children seem to acquire biofeedback control faster and show better overall improvement than adults. Part of this observation has been confirmed in research: the headaches of children and adults improve with biofeedback, but children's headaches improve more (Nestoriuc, Rief, & Martin, 2008; Sarafino & Goehring, 2000). Why? Attanasio and her coworkers have offered some reasons. First, although a small proportion of children are frightened initially by the equipment and procedures, most are more enthusiastic than adults, often regarding biofeedback as a game. In fact, some children become so interested and motivated in the game that their arousal interferes with relaxation if the therapist does not help them remain calm. Second, children are usually less skeptical about their ability to succeed in biofeedback training and to benefit from doing so. Adults often say, "Nothing else I've ever tried has worked, so why should biofeedback?" This difference in skepticism may reflect differences in experience: adults are more likely than children to have had more failure experiences with other treatments. Third, children may be more likely than adults to practice their training at home, as they are instructed to do.

Although children have characteristics that make them well suited to biofeedback methods, they also have some special difficulties (Attanasio et al., 1985). For one thing, children—particularly those below the age of 8—have shorter attention spans than adults. If biofeedback sessions last more than 20 minutes or so, it may be necessary to divide each session into

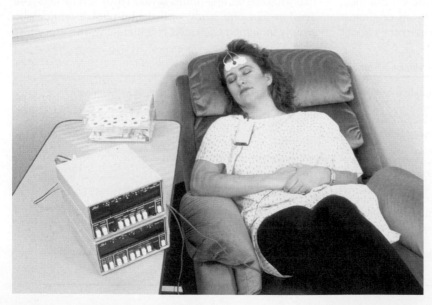

A biofeedback procedure for forehead muscle tension. One way to give feedback regarding the status of the muscles is with audio speakers, such as by sounding higher tones for higher levels of tension.

smaller units with brief breaks in between. A related problem is that children sometimes perform disruptive behaviors during a session, disturbing the electrodes and wires or interrupting to talk about tangential topics, for instance. The therapist can reduce the likelihood of these unwanted behaviors, such as by providing rewards for being cooperative. Clearly, the difficulties some children have in biofeedback training can usually be overcome.

Modeling

People learn not just by doing, but also by observing. They see what others do and the consequences of the behavior these models perform. As a result, this kind of learning is called **modeling**, and sometimes "observational" or "social" learning. People can learn fears and other stress-related behavior by observing fearful behavior in other individuals. In one study, children (with their parents' permission) learned to fear a Mickey Mouse figure by watching a short film showing a 5-year-old boy's fear reaction to plastic figures of Mickey Mouse and Donald Duck (Venn & Short, 1973). This learned fear reaction was pronounced initially—but declined a day or two later.

Since people can learn stressful reactions by observing these behaviors in others, modeling should be effective in reversing this learning and helping people cope with stressors, too. A large body of research has confirmed that it is effective (Sarafino, 2001; Thelen et al., 1979). The therapeutic use of modeling is similar to the method of desensitization: the person relaxes while watching a model calmly perform a series of activities arranged as a stimulus hierarchy—that is, from least to most stressful. The modeling procedure can be presented *symbolically*, using films or videotapes, or *in vivo*, with real-life models and events. Using symbolic presentations, for example, researchers have shown that modeling procedures can reduce the stress 4- to 17-year-old hospitalized children experience and improve their recovery from surgery (Melamed, Dearborn, & Hermecz, 1983; Melamed & Siegel, 1975). But the child's age and prior experience with surgery were also important factors in the results. Children under the age of 8 who had had previous surgery experienced increased anxiety rather than less. These children may benefit from other methods to reduce stress, such as activities that simply distract their attention.

Approaches Focusing on Cognitive Processes

Because stress results from cognitive appraisals that are frequently based on a lack of information, misperceptions, or irrational beliefs, some approaches to modify people's behavior and thought patterns have been developed to help them cope better with the stress they experience. These methods guide people toward a "restructuring" of their thought patterns (Lazarus, 1971). **Cognitive restructuring** is a process by which stress-provoking thoughts or beliefs are replaced with more constructive or realistic ones that reduce the person's appraisal of threat or harm.

What sorts of irrational beliefs do people have that increase stress? Two leading theorists have described a variety of erroneous thought patterns that some people use habitually and frequently that lead to stress; we'll consider two from each theorist. The beliefs described by Albert Ellis (1962, 1977, 1987) include:

- *Can't-stand-itis*—as in, "I *can't stand* not doing well on a test."
- *Musterbating*—for instance, "People *must* like me, or I'm worthless."

And the beliefs described by Aaron Beck (1976; Beck et al., 1990) include:

- *Arbitrary inference* (drawing a specific conclusion from insufficient, ambiguous, or contrary evidence). For example, a husband might interpret his wife's bad mood as meaning she is unhappy with something he did when she is actually just preoccupied with another matter.
- *Magnification* (greatly exaggerating the meaning or impact of an event). For instance, a recently retired person diagnosed with arthritis might describe it as a "catastrophe."

These ways of thinking affect stress appraisal processes, increasing the appraisal of threat or harm because the perspectives are so extreme. The circumstances that are the bases of these thoughts are not "good," but they're probably not as bad as the thoughts imply.

A widely used cognitive restructuring approach to change maladaptive thought patterns is called **cognitive therapy** (Beck, 1976; Beck et al., 1990). Although it was developed originally to treat psychological depression, it is also being applied today for anxiety. Cognitive therapy attempts to help clients see that they are not responsible for all of the problems they encounter, the negative events they experience are usually not catastrophes, and their maladaptive beliefs are not logically valid. For instance, the following dialogue shows how a therapist tried to counter the negative beliefs a woman named Sharon had.

THERAPIST: ... what evidence do you have that all this is true? That you are ugly, awkward? Or that it is not true? What data do you have?

SHARON: Comparing myself to people that I consider to be extremely attractive and finding myself lacking.

THERAPIST: So if you look at that beautiful person, you're less?

SHARON: Yeah.

THERAPIST: Or if I look at that *perfect* person, I'm less. Is that what you're saying? ...

SHARON: Yeah. I always pick out, of course, the most attractive person and probably a person who spends 3 hours a day on grooming and appearance.... I don't compare myself to the run-of-the-mill.... (Freeman, 1990, p. 83)

One technique cognitive therapy uses, called *hypothesis testing*, has the person treat an erroneous belief as a hypothesis and test it by looking for evidence for and against it in his or her everyday life. Research has shown that cognitive therapy is clearly effective in treating depression (Hollon, Shelton, & Davis, 1993; Robins & Hayes, 1993) and appears to be a very promising approach for treating anxieties (Chambless & Gillis, 1993).

Another cognitive approach is designed to help clients solve problems in their lives. By a "problem" we mean a life circumstance, such as being stuck in traffic or feeling a worrisome chest pain, that requires a response based on thinking and planning. People experience stress when they face a problem and don't know what to do or how to do it. In **problem-solving training**, clients learn a strategy for identifying, discovering, or inventing effective or adaptive ways to address problems in everyday life (D'Zurilla, 1988; Nezu, Nezu, & Perri, 1989). They learn to watch for problems that can arise, define a problem clearly and concretely, generate a variety of possible solutions, and decide on the best course of action. Evidence indicates that problem-solving training reduces anxiety and other negative emotions (D'Zurilla, 1988; Elliott, Berry, & Grant, 2009).

Stress-inoculation training is an approach that uses a variety of methods that are designed to teach people skills for alleviating stress (Meichenbaum & Cameron, 1983; Meichenbaum & Turk, 1982). The training involves three phases in which the person (1) learns about the nature of stress and how people react to it; (2) acquires behavioral and cognitive skills, such as relaxation and seeking social support; and (3) practices coping skills with actual or imagined stressors. The methods used in stress-inoculation training are well-thought-out, include a number of well-established techniques, and are useful for people who anticipate a stressful event, such as surgery (Dale, 2004). (Go to 🗣.)

Multidimensional Approaches

The coping difficulties individuals have are often multidimensional and multifaceted. As a result, one particular technique may not be sufficient in helping a client, and the most effective intervention usually draws upon many techniques. When designing a multidimensional approach, the program for helping an individual cope better with stress would be tailored to the person's specific problems (Sarafino, 2001). The program may make use of any of the methods we have considered, many methods that would take this discussion too far afield, and the methods we are about to examine.

MASSAGE, MEDITATION, AND HYPNOSIS

Three additional techniques have been used in stress management. The first two we will consider—massage and meditation—are often classified as relaxation methods. The third technique—hypnosis—seems to produce

---

CLINICAL METHODS AND ISSUES

Treating Insomnia

Insomnia often results from stress, as when people can't sleep because they worry about their jobs or health. People who show evidence of maladaptive behaviors or arousal that persistently interfere with sleep, thereby leading to daytime distress or impaired function, are candidates for cognitive–behavioral therapy for insomnia (Smith & Perlis, 2006). Many people with insomnia have a medical condition, such as cancer or arthritis, which is stressful because of its prognosis or the disability or symptoms it produces. A meta-analysis on data from 23 experiments found that cognitive–behavioral therapy is very effective in treating

insomnia (Irwin, Cole, & Nicassio, 2006). Using sleep medication for the first few weeks of treatment enhances the long-term success of this therapy (Morin et al., 2009).

What methods do cognitive–behavioral approaches use for insomnia? Behavioral methods include relaxation and sleep restriction, which involves setting a regular routine for sleeping and not using the bed as a place for reading or working. Cognitive methods include restructuring beliefs, such as that not sleeping will "wreck tomorrow," and using fantasies about being in a relaxing place, such as on a beach or in a forest.

an *altered state of consciousness* in which mental functioning differs from its usual pattern of wakefulness. Some people believe that meditation and massage are other ways by which we can alter consciousness.

Massage

Massage has several forms that vary in the degree of pressure applied. Some forms of massage use soothing strokes with light pressure, others involve a rubbing motion with moderate force, and others use a kneading or pounding action. *Deep tissue massage* uses enough pressure to penetrate deeply into muscles and joints. Infants seem to prefer light strokes, but adults tend to prefer more force (Field, 1996). When seeking a massage therapist, it is a good idea to ask about licensing and certification.

Massage therapy can reduce anxiety and depression (Moyer, Rounds, & Hannum, 2004). It also increases the body's production of a hormone called *oxytocin* that decreases blood pressure and stress hormone levels (Holt-Lunstad, Birmingham, & Light, 2008). And it helps reduce hypertension, some types of pain, and asthma symptoms; and some evidence indicates that it may bolster immune function (Field, 1996, 1998).

Meditation

Transcendental meditation is a method in the practice of yoga that was promoted by Maharishi Mahesh Yogi as a means of improving physical and mental health and reducing stress (Benson, 1984, 1991; Nystul, 2004). Individuals using this procedure are instructed to practice it twice a day, sitting upright but comfortably relaxed with eyes closed, and mentally repeating a word or sound (such as "om"), called a *mantra*, to prevent distracting thoughts from occurring.

Psychologists and psychiatrists have advocated similar meditation methods for reducing stress. For example, Herbert Benson has recommended that the person:

> Sit quietly in a comfortable position and close your eyes .... Deeply relax all your muscles .... Become aware of your breathing. As you breathe out, say the word *one* silently to yourself .... Maintain a passive attitude and permit relaxation to occur at its own pace. Expect other thoughts. When these distracting thoughts occur, ignore them by thinking, "Oh well," and continue repeating, "One." (1984, p. 332)

The purpose of this procedure is to increase the person's ability in the face of a stressor to make a "relaxation response," which includes reduced physiological activity, as an alternative to a stress response. According to Benson, the relaxation response enhances health, such as by reducing blood pressure, and may be achieved

in many different ways. For example, a religious person might find that a meditative prayer is the most effective method for bringing forth the relaxation response.

Although meditation helps people relax, it has a broader purpose: to develop a clear and *mindful awareness*, or "insight" regarding the essence of one's experiences, unencumbered by cognitive or emotional distortions (Hart, 1987; Solé-Leris, 1986). Jon Kabat-Zinn (1982; Kabat-Zinn, Lipworth, & Burney, 1985) has emphasized the mindful awareness component of meditation to help individuals who suffer from chronic pain to detach themselves from the cognitive and emotional distortions they have with their pain. He trains patients to pay close attention to their pain and other sensations without reacting toward them in any way, thereby enabling the people to be aware of the pain itself with no thoughts or feelings about it. Using this technique leads to a reduction in the patients' reports of physical and psychological discomfort.

Many people believe that meditation enables people to reach a state of profound rest, as is claimed by popular self-help books (for example, Forem, 1974). Some studies have found lower anxiety and blood pressure among meditators than nonmeditators, but the research was quasi-experimental (Jorgensen, 2004). Other research findings are more important here. First, Buddhist monks in Southeast Asia can dramatically alter their body metabolism and brain electrical activity through meditation (Benson et al., 1990). Second, people's blood pressure decreases while they meditate (Barnes et al., 1999). Third, stress management interventions using meditation alleviate stress effectively in people's daily lives (Chiesa & Serretti, 2009; Jain et al., 2007; Jorgensen, 2004; Williams, Kolar et al., 2001). Fourth, practicing meditation on a regular basis appears to reduce blood pressure and enhance immune function (Barnes, Treiber, & Johnson, 2004; Davidson et al., 2003). (Go to 💡.)

Hypnosis

The modern history of hypnosis began with its being called "animal magnetism" and "Mesmerism" in the 18th and 19th centuries. The Austrian doctor Franz Anton Mesmer popularized its use in treating patients who had symptoms of physical illness, such as paralysis, without a detectable underlying organic disorder. Today, *hypnosis* is considered to be an altered state of consciousness that is induced by special techniques of suggestion and leads to varying degrees of responsiveness to directions for changes in perception, memory, and behavior (Moran, 2004).

People differ in *suggestibility*, or the degree to which they can be hypnotized. Perhaps 15–30% of the general

HIGHLIGHT

Can Increasing Positive Emotions Enhance Health?

Did you know that, on average, winners of the Nobel Prize and Academy Award live longer than their colleagues who don't receive these honors? Maybe the reason for the winners' longer lives is that they experience more positive emotions because of the respect and prestige their work receives. People who have relatively high levels of positive affect experience less negative emotion when under stress (Ong et al., 2006) and better health: they have fewer illnesses and live longer than people who have low levels of positive emotions (Pressman & Cohen, 2005).

We've seen that stress management can reduce negative emotions, but can it increase positive emotions? Some evidence indicates that it can (Chesney et al., 2005). Interventions that include training in relaxation, meditation, and methods to enhance social support, stress-appraisal processes, and problem- and emotion-focused coping with stress reduce people's negative emotions and increase their positive affect, and the effects on positive emotions last for at least a year.

population is easily and deeply hypnotizable (Evans, 1987; Hilgard, 1967). Suggestibility appears to change with age, being particularly strong among children between the ages of about 7 and 14, and then declining in adolescence to a level that remains stable throughout adulthood (Hilgard, 1967; Place, 1984). People who are reasonably suggestible can often learn to induce a hypnotic state in themselves—a process called *self-hypnosis*. Usually they learn to do this after they have experienced hypnosis under the supervision of a skilled hypnotist.

Because individuals who have been hypnotized usually claim that it is a relaxing experience, researchers have examined whether it can reduce stress. These studies have generally found that hypnosis is helpful in stress management, but not necessarily more effective than other relaxation techniques (Moran, 2004; Wadden & Anderton, 1982). Other research has revealed that people who received training in and practiced regularly either hypnosis or relaxation showed enhanced immune function weeks later (Kiecolt-Glaser et al., 2001; McGrady et al., 1992).

In summary, we have seen that many different behavioral and cognitive methods, massage, meditation, and hypnosis offer useful therapeutic approaches for helping people cope with stress. Research is also revealing more and more clearly the important benefits of stress management in preventing illness.

USING STRESS MANAGEMENT TO REDUCE CORONARY RISK

Of the many risk factors that have been identified for CHD, a few of them—such as age and family history—are beyond the control of the individual.

But many risk factors for CHD are directly linked to the person's experiences and behavior, which should be modifiable. One of these risk factors is stress, and stress management interventions appear to produce cardiovascular improvements and prolong life in CHD patients (Orth-Gomér et al., 2009). Let's now consider how stress management methods can be applied to reduce the risk of developing CHD.

MODIFYING TYPE A BEHAVIOR

When the Type A behavior pattern was established as a risk factor for CHD, researchers began to study ways to modify Type A behavior to reduce coronary risk. One approach used a multidimensional program that included progressive muscle relaxation, cognitive restructuring, and stress-inoculation training (Roskies, 1983; Roskies et al., 1986). An experiment randomly assigned Type A men to the multidimensional program or to one of two physical exercise programs, aerobic training (mostly jogging) or weight-training, each lasting 10 weeks. Then the men were tested for Type A behavior and cardiovascular reactivity (blood pressure and heart rate) to stressors, such as doing mental arithmetic, to compare with measures taken earlier. One finding can be seen in Figure 4-2: the hostility component of Type A behavior decreased markedly in the multidimensional program but not in the exercise groups. These benefits can be quite durable: another study found that improvements in Type A behavior with a similar intervention were maintained at a 2-year follow-up (Karlberg, Krakau, & Undén, 1998).

Other research has demonstrated the usefulness of stress-inoculation training and relaxation in helping people control their anger (Novaco, 1975, 1978). The

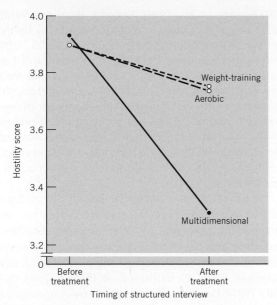

Figure 4-2 Hostility of Type A men measured by the Structured Interview method before and after a 10-week multidimensional, aerobic exercise, or weight-training treatment program. (Data from Roskies et al., 1986, Table 4.)

subjects first learned about the role of arousal and cognitive processes in feelings of anger. Then they learned muscle relaxation along with statements—like those in Table 4.4—they could say to themselves at different times in the course of angry episodes, such as at the point of "impact and confrontation." The program improved the subjects' ability to control their anger, as measured by self-reports and their blood pressure when provoked in the laboratory. Many studies have

confirmed the success of interventions using cognitive and behavioral methods in decreasing anger (Del Vecchio & O'Leary, 2004; DiGiuseppe & Tafrate, 2003), and research has shown that such interventions reduce both hostility and diastolic (resting) blood pressure in patients with CHD and mild hypertension (Gidron, Davidson, & Bata, 1999; Larkin & Zayfert, 1996).

Does decreasing Type A behavior with stress management techniques decrease the incidence of CHD? Researchers studied this issue with over 1,000 patients who had suffered a heart attack and who agreed to participate in the study for 5 years (Friedman et al., 1986; Powell & Friedman, 1986). The patients were *not* selected on the basis of their exhibiting Type A behavior, and they continued to be treated by their own doctors throughout the study. The subjects were randomly assigned to two intervention groups and a control group. One intervention, called *cardiac counseling*, presented information, such as about the causes of heart disease and the importance of altering standard coronary risk factors, such as cigarette smoking (Type A behavior was not discussed). The other intervention, called the *Type A/cardiac group*, included the same cardiac counseling plus a multidimensional program, including progressive muscle relaxation and cognitive restructuring techniques, to modify Type A behavior. The results revealed that the Type A/cardiac group showed a much larger decrease in Type A behavior (measured with Structured Interview and questionnaire methods) than those in the other groups and had substantially lower rates of cardiac morbidity and mortality (Friedman et al., 1986). For example, subsequent heart attacks occurred in about 13% of the Type A/cardiac subjects, 21% of the cardiac counseling subjects, and 28% of the control subjects during the 4 1/2-year follow-up.

Table 4.4   *Examples of Anger Management Self-Statements Rehearsed in Stress-Inoculation Training*

Preparing for Provocation

    This could be a rough situation; but I know how to deal with it. I can work out a plan to handle this. Easy does it. Remember, stick to the issues and don't take it personally. There won't be any need for an argument. I know what to do.

Impact and Confrontation

    As long as I keep my cool, I'm in control of the situation. You don't need to prove yourself. Don't make more out of this than you have to. There is no point in getting mad. Think of what you have to do. Look for the positives and don't jump to conclusions.

Coping with Arousal

    Muscles are getting tight. Relax and slow things down. Time to take a deep breath. Let's take the issue point by point. My anger is a signal of what I need to do. Time for problem solving. He probably wants me to get angry, but I'm going to deal with it constructively.

Subsequent Reflection

a. *Conflict unresolved.* Forget about the aggravation. Thinking about it only makes you upset. Try to shake it off. Don't let it interfere with your job. Remember relaxation. It's a lot better than anger. Don't take it personally. It's probably not so serious.

b. *Conflict resolved.* I handled that one pretty well. That's doing a good job. I could have gotten more upset than it was worth. My pride can get me into trouble, but I'm doing better at this all the time. I actually got through that without getting angry.

Source: From Novaco, 1978, p. 150.

Research has shown that pharmacological approaches can reduce hostility and Type A behavior (Kamarck et al., 2009; Schmieder et al., 1983). Although using drugs may not be the treatment of choice for most people with high levels of anger or Type A behavior, it may be appropriate for those who are at coronary risk who do not respond to behavioral and cognitive interventions (Chesney, Frautschi, & Rosenman, 1985).

TREATING HYPERTENSION

As we discussed in Chapter 3, essential hypertension is an important risk factor for CHD. Patients with diagnosed hypertension usually receive medical treatment that includes a prescription drug, such as a *diuretic*, and advice to control their body weight, exercise regularly, and reduce their intake of cholesterol, sodium, caffeine, and alcohol (AHA, 2010). Sometimes doctors and others urge hypertensive patients "to try to relax" when hassles occur, but untrained people who make an effort to relax often end up raising their blood pressure rather than lowering it (Suls, Sanders, & Labrecque, 1986).

Because the development of essential hypertension has been linked to the amount of stress people experience, researchers have examined the utility of stress management techniques in treating high blood pressure. The findings suggest three conclusions. First, using a single technique, such as relaxation, to lower blood pressure often provides only limited success; stress management methods are more effective when combined in multidimensional programs (Larkin, Knowlton, & D'Alessandri, 1990; Spence et al., 1999). Second, if an intervention uses a single technique, meditation seems to be more effective than other methods (Rainforth et al., 2007). Third, a meta-analysis by Wolfgang Linden and Laura Chambers (1994) of dozens of studies found that *multidimensional* programs consisting of behavioral and cognitive methods for stress management are highly effective—as effective as diuretic drugs—in reducing blood pressure. It is now clear that psychological approaches have considerable value in treating hypertension, making effective treatment possible without drugs or with lower doses for most patients.

In an effort to improve the health of employees, many large companies have introduced voluntary stress management programs for their workers. Studies of these programs have found that they produce improvements in workers' psychological and physiological stress (Alderman, 1984; Richardson & Rothstein, 2008; Sallis et al., 1987). Despite the success of stress management programs in reducing coronary risk by modifying Type A behavior and lowering blood pressure, they are not yet widely applied—partly because the evidence supporting the use of these programs is relatively new, and partly because they cost money to run. Also, many people who could benefit from stress management programs don't join one when it is available, drop out before completing the program, or don't adhere closely to its recommendations, such as to practice relaxation techniques at home (Alderman, 1984; Hoelscher, Lichstein, & Rosenthal, 1986).

SUMMARY

Coping is the process by which people try to manage the real or perceived discrepancy between the demands and resources they appraise in stressful situations. We cope with stress through transactions with the environment that do not necessarily lead to solutions to the problems causing the stress.

Coping serves two functions. (1) Emotion-focused coping regulates the person's emotional response to stress—for example, by using alcohol or seeking social support, and through cognitive strategies, such as denying unpleasant facts. (2) Problem-focused coping reduces the demands of a stressor or expands the resources to deal with it, such as by learning new skills. People tend to use emotion-focused coping when they believe they cannot change the stressful conditions; they use problem-focused coping when they believe they can change the situation.

Adults report using more problem-focused than emotion-focused coping approaches when dealing with stress. People tend to use a combination of methods in coping with a stressful situation.

Coping changes across the life span. Young children's coping is limited by their cognitive abilities, which improve throughout childhood. During adulthood, a shift in coping function occurs as people approach old age—they rely less on problem-focused and more on emotion-focused coping. Elderly people tend to view the stressors they experience as less changeable than middle-aged individuals do.

People can reduce the potential for stress in their lives and others' lives in several ways. First, they can increase the social support they give and receive by joining social, religious, and special-interest groups. Second, they can improve their own and others' sense of personal control and hardiness by giving and taking responsibility. Also, they can reduce frustration and waste less time by organizing their world better, such as through time management. And by exercising and keeping fit, they can reduce the experience of stress and the impact it has on their health. Last, they can prepare for stressful events, such as a medical procedure, by improving their behavioral, cognitive, and informational control.

Sometimes the coping skills individuals have learned are not adequate for dealing with a stressor that is very strong, novel, or unrelenting. A variety of techniques are available to help people who are having trouble coping effectively. One technique is pharmacological, that is, using prescribed drugs, such as beta-blockers. Stress management methods include progressive muscle relaxation, systematic desensitization, biofeedback, modeling, and several cognitive approaches. Cognitive therapy attempts to modify stress-producing, irrational thought patterns through the process of cognitive restructuring. Stress-inoculation training and problem-solving training are designed to teach people skills to alleviate stress and achieve personal goals. Beneficial effects on people's stress have been found for all of the behavioral and cognitive stress management methods, particularly relaxation. Massage, meditation, and hypnosis have shown promise for reducing stress, too. Stress management techniques can reduce coronary risk by modifying Type A behavior and by treating hypertension.

KEY TERMS

coping
emotion-focused coping
problem-focused coping
time management

stress management
progressive muscle
    relaxation
systematic desensitization

biofeedback
modeling
cognitive restructuring

cognitive therapy
problem-solving training
stress-inoculation training

5

HEALTH-RELATED BEHAVIOR AND HEALTH PROMOTION

PROLOGUE

"Is it just me, or has the government become our health care nanny? Everything good is bad for you all of a sudden," said Sam, while he smoked his cigarette.

It may not be all of a sudden, but governments, health departments, charity organisations, and even some religions are being more vocal about public health issues. Is everything good becoming bad for us, or are we simply more educated now about the dangers of smoking, excessive alcohol, and pollution, to name a few?

Almost every civilisation had public health laws, including the ancient Greeks and the Islamic Empire. By the mid-1800s some countries had public health laws covering sanitation and drainage, the building of hospitals, and new health budgets. Advocates of women's health taught family planning and cleanliness in the home. Because more children were going to school, central school boards employed nurses to examine children for communicable and preventable diseases. People's diets improved and many began to exercise in a effort to improve overall health.

To this day, governments look to improving the health of their citizens by implementing programmes that allow people to take control of their own health. The World Health Organization offers advice and assistance on health topics ranging from radiation, to HIV/AIDS, to malaria. Healthcare and medicine have become international topics for debate, yet some people choose not to take care of themselves. Who becomes responsible for these people?

This part of the book contains three chapters concerned with behaviours that can enhance or compromise health. In the present chapter, we will start with the health habits people practice and how their lifestyles affect their health. Then we turn to factors that influence the health-related behaviours that individuals adopt, and programmes that help people lead healthier lifestyles. As we study these topics, you will find answers to questions you may have about health-related behaviour and health promotion. Are people leading healthier lives today than they did in the past? Why do some people take better care of themselves than others? How effective are health promotion programmes that try to motivate healthy behaviour through fear?

HEALTH AND BEHAVIOR

The role of behavior in health has been receiving increased attention in countries around the world because people's *health habits*—that is, their usual health-related behaviors—influence their likelihood of developing chronic and fatal diseases, such as heart disease, cancer, and AIDS (WHO, 2009). Illness and early death could be substantially reduced if people would adopt lifestyles that promote wellness, such as by eating healthful diets and not smoking.

The percentage of deaths resulting from any specific cause changes over time. Figure 5-1 depicts the pattern of changes in the United States that occurred since the late 1960s. These changes resulted partly from the

modifications people made in behavioral risk factors for major chronic diseases. Cardiovascular disease (heart disease and stroke) is the most deadly illness worldwide. In virtually all developed nations, the first and second leading killers are cardiovascular diseases and cancer (WHO, 2009). Of course, we can't live forever, but we can extend our lives and be healthier in old age by making several lifestyle changes (Manton, 2008; Yates et al., 2008). If we made all these changes and researchers found cures for most major diseases, people's average life expectancy in technologically advanced countries would rise several years to about 85 years, its likely upper limit (Olshansky, Carnes, & Cassel, 1990).

LIFESTYLES, RISK FACTORS, AND HEALTH

The typical person's lifestyle includes many behaviors that are risk factors for illness and injury. For instance, millions of Americans smoke cigarettes, drink excessively, use drugs, eat high-fat and high-cholesterol diets, eat too much and become overweight, have too little physical activity, and behave in unsafe ways, such as by not using seat belts in automobiles. Many people realize these dangers and adjust their behavior to protect their health. Adults with healthful lifestyles that include exercising, eating diets with fruits and vegetables, not smoking, and not drinking too much, can expect to live 12 years longer than they would otherwise (Kvaavik et al., 2010). Each of these four behaviors raises the likelihood of a longer life. Table 5.1 shows that the chances of individuals in their 70s surviving to 90 years of age decrease substantially with each additional risk factor they have.

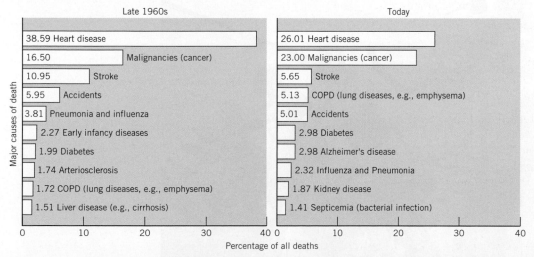

Figure 5-1   Percentage of all deaths caused by each of the 10 leading causes of death in the United States in the *late* 1960s (1968) and *today*. Notice that cancer and COPD deaths increased markedly since 1968 (partly due to cigarette smoking); heart disease and stroke deaths declined (partly due to recent lifestyle changes, such as in diet); deaths from diseases of early infancy declined markedly and are no longer in the top ten. (Data from USBC, 1971, Table 77; USBC, 2010, Table 116.)

Table 5.1 *Likelihood of 70-Year-Old Men with Certain Risk Factors Living to Age 90*

Risk factors present at age 70	Percent living to 90
None of the five risk factors examined	54
Having a sedentary lifestyle	44
Having high blood pressure	42
Being obese	32
Having diabetes	28
Smoking	25
Three of the five risk factors	14
All five of the risk factors	4

Source: Data from Yates et al., 2008.

Health Behavior

Health behavior is any activity people perform to maintain or improve their health, regardless of their perceived health status or whether the behavior actually achieves that goal. Researchers have noted that people's health status influences the type of health behavior they perform and their motivation to do it (Kasl & Cobb, 1966a, b; Parsons 1951). To illustrate these differences, we will consider examples of behaviors people perform when they are well, experience symptoms, and are clearly sick.

Well behavior is any activity people undertake to maintain or improve current good health and avoid illness. These activities can include healthy people's exercising, eating healthful diets, having regular dental checkups, and getting vaccinations against diseases. But when people are well, they may not feel inclined to devote the effort and sacrifice that healthful behavior entails. Thus, engaging in healthful behavior depends on motivational factors, particularly with regard to the individual's perception of a threat of disease, the value in the behavior in reducing this threat, and the attractiveness of the opposite behavior. Some unhealthful behaviors, such as drinking or smoking, are often seen as pleasurable or the "in" thing to do. As a result, many individuals do not resist beginning unhealthful behaviors and may reject efforts or advice to get them to quit.

Symptom-based behavior is any activity people who are ill undertake to determine the problem and find a remedy. These activities usually include complaining about symptoms, such as stomach pains, and seeking help or advice from relatives, friends, and medical practitioners. Some people are more likely than others to engage in symptom-based behavior when symptoms appear, and there are many reasons for these differences. For instance, some individuals may be more afraid than others of doctors, hospitals, or the serious illness a diagnosis may reveal. Some people are stoic or unconcerned about the aches and pains they experience, and others do not seek medical care because they simply do not have the money to pay for it. Chapter 8 will examine these and other reasons why people do and do not use health care services.

Sick-role behavior refers to any activity people undertake to get well after deciding that they are ill and what the illness is. This behavior is based on the idea that sick people take on a special "role," making them exempt from their normal obligations and life tasks, such as going to work or school. You'd be showing sick-role

People engage in health behaviors, such as using exercise bikes, to maintain or improve their health and avoid illness.

behaviors if you got a prescription filled, used it as the doctor directed, stayed home from work to recover, and had someone else do your household chores. Although this status ordinarily obligates patients to try to get well, many do not follow their recommended treatment, particularly if it is inconvenient or uncomfortable to do. Sometimes sick-role behaviors seem to serve emotional functions, as when patients moan or sigh and receive sympathy as a result.

How people behave when they are sick depends in large measure on what they have learned. As an example, a study of female college students assessed whether they had been encouraged during adolescence to adopt the sick role for menstruation or had observed their mothers exhibit menstrual distress. Compared with students who did not have these experiences, those who *did* reported more menstrual symptoms, disability, and clinic visits for these symptoms as adults (Whitehead et al., 1986). Other research has found that there are cultural differences in the way people respond to their symptoms and go about trying to get well (Korol & Craig, 2001). For example, studies in the United States have found differences among groups of immigrants in their willingness to tolerate pain, but these differences diminish in succeeding generations (Chapman & Brena, 1985). (Go to 💡.)

Practicing Health Behaviors

What health behaviors do people actually do? In the United States, national surveys of men and women for a limited set of health-related behaviors revealed the results given in Table 5.2. Although these data show important shortcomings in the health practices of American adults, some of these levels of health-related behaviors are improvements over the levels assessed in earlier surveys (McGinnis & Lee, 1995).

Who practices healthful behavior and why? We are far from a complete answer to this question, but there are gender, sociocultural, and age differences in practicing health behaviors (Schoenborn, 1993; NCHS, 2009a). For instance, an international survey of adults in European countries found that women perform more healthful behaviors than men (Steptoe et al., 1994). One reason for such differences is that people seem to perform behaviors that are salient to them. For example, a study compared the health behaviors of medical and nonmedical students and found that the medical students exercised more and were much less likely to smoke cigarettes, drink alcohol excessively, and use drugs (Golding & Cornish, 1987).

You probably know some individuals who are highly health-conscious and others who display little concern

HIGHLIGHT

Two Health Behaviors: Breast and Testicular Examinations

Breast cancer is a leading cause of women's deaths around the world and is the third-most-frequent type of cancer diagnosed in Europe (Boyle & Ferlay, 2004). In 2007 there were 45,972 new cases of breast cancer diagnosed in the UK alone (Cancer Research, 2007a). Compared with breast cancer, *testicular cancer* is much less prevalent: in 2007 1,990 in the UK were diagnosed with testicular cancer (Cancer Research, 2007b). Both cancers have very high cure rates if treated early.

Individuals can detect cancer of the breast or testicles in its early stages by self-examination. Breast and testicular self-examinations are done with the fingers, searching mainly for abnormal lumps. For breast self-examination (BSE), the woman lies on her back and uses the middle three fingertips of her opposite-side hand to press flatly against the breast tissue and moves them in a systematic pattern until she examines the entire breast. The method for testicular self-examination (TSE) is relatively simple: the man rotates the entire surface of each testicle between the fingers and thumbs

of both hands. Unfortunately, people don't perform BSEs and TSEs very often for such reasons as not knowing how important early detection can be, being afraid they will find a malignant lump, or just forgetting and having no reminders (Aiken, Gerend, & Jackson, 2001; Moore, Barling, & Hood, 1998; Solomon, 2004; Ullrich, 2004).

One way to encourage the practice of BSE and TSE is through the mass media, which can note the very high cure rates (over 90%) and less extensive and disfiguring treatments for these cancers when detected in early than in later stages. For example, breast cancer in its early stages can often be treated without removing the entire breast. Two other ways to encourage self-examinations involve health practitioners, such as nurses: they can provide information and training through individual and group contacts, such as at worksites and medical offices, and send reminders to do the examinations (Solomon, 2004). Individuals with family histories or other risk factors for cancer should devise effective BSE or TSE reminders, such as by writing them in a calendar.

Table 5.2   *Percentages of American Adults with Selected Health-Related Behaviors or Characteristics*

Behavior/characteristics	Men (%)	Women (%)
Eat breakfast almost every day[a]	54.6	58.0
Rarely snack[a]	25.6	25.4
Smoke at least occasionally[b]	23.6	18.1
Drink alcohol at least occasionally[b]	67.4	54.9
Had 5 or more drinks on at least 12 days past year	14.4	4.3
Get regular leisure time physical activity[b, c]	33.1	29.0
Overweight or obese (measured directly)[b]	72.6	61.2

Sources: [a]USBC, 1995, Table 215 and [b]NCHS, 2009, Tables 63, 68, 69, 74, and 75. [c]Vigorous activity for at least 20 min. three times a week or light-to-moderate activity for at least 30 min. five times a week.

about their health. To some extent individuals who practice certain behaviors that benefit their health also practice other healthful behaviors and continue to perform these behaviors over time (Schoenborn, 1993). But other people show little consistency in their health habits (Kaczynski et al., 2008; Mechanic, 1979). Research results suggest three conclusions. First, although people's health habits are fairly stable, they often change over time. Second, particular health behaviors are not strongly tied to each other—that is, if we know a person practices one specific health habit, such as using seat belts, we cannot accurately predict that he or she practices another specific habit, such as exercising. Third, health behaviors do not seem to be governed in each person by a single set of attitudes or response tendencies. Thus, a girl who uses seat belts to protect herself from injury may watch her weight to be attractive and not smoke because she is allergic to it.

Why are health behaviors not more stable and strongly linked to each other? Here are a few reasons (Leventhal, Prohaska, & Hirschman, 1985). First, various factors at any given time in people's lives may differentially affect different behaviors. For instance, a person may have lots of social encouragement to eat too much ("You don't like my cooking?"), and, at the same time, to limit drinking and smoking. Second, people change as a result of experience. For example, many people did not avoid smoking until they learned that it is harmful. Third, people's life circumstances change. Thus, factors, such as peer pressure, that may have been important in initiating and maintaining exercising or smoking at one time may no longer be present, thereby increasing the likelihood that the habit will change.

INTERDISCIPLINARY PERSPECTIVES ON PREVENTING ILLNESS

The advances in health that have occurred over the years have come about through two avenues: efforts to prevent

illness and improvements in medical diagnosis and treatment. Efforts to prevent illness can be of three types, which we'll illustrate with tooth decay as an example:

- *Behavioral influence.* In this approach, we might promote tooth brushing and flossing by providing information and demonstrating the techniques.

- *Environmental measures.* Public health officials might support fluoridating water supplies.

- *Preventive medical efforts.* Dental professionals can remove tartar from teeth and repair cavities.

In much of the world, behavioral influence approaches may have the greatest impact on health promotion, such as in reducing cigarette smoking and unhealthful dietary practices (Breslow, 1983).

We usually think of prevention as occurring before an illness takes hold. Actually, there are three levels of prevention, only one of which applies before a disease or injury occurs (Herndon & Wandersman, 2004; Runyan, 1985). These levels are called *primary*, *secondary*, and *tertiary* prevention. Each level of prevention can include the efforts of oneself in our well, symptom-based, and sick-role behaviors; one's social network; and health professionals.

Primary Prevention

Primary prevention consists of actions taken to avoid disease or injury. In avoiding automobile injuries, for example, primary prevention activities might include our well behavior of using seat belts, a friend reminding us to use them, and public health reminders on TV to buckle up. Primary prevention can be directed at almost any health behavior, including dietary practices, exercise, tooth brushing and flossing, and immunity against a contagious disease.

Primary prevention for an individual can begin before he or she is born, or even conceived. For example, *genetic counselors* can estimate the risk of a child's inheriting a genetic disorder and, in some cases, to diagnose genetic abnormalities in the unborn fetus (AMA, 2003). These estimates are based on the parents' family histories, biological tests for carriers of specific genes, and biological tests on the fetus. Prospective and expectant parents may use this information to help them make important family planning decisions. Doctors can help in selecting genetic counselors. Another way parents can exercise primary prevention is by having their children vaccinated against several diseases, including diphtheria, tetanus, whooping cough, measles, rubella, mumps, and polio. Although worldwide vaccination rates have increased in recent decades, they remain lower in poorer than richer societies (WHO, 2009). In the United States, the percentage of preschool children with full vaccination from controllable diseases has increased to nearly 80% across all major ethnic groups (USBC, 2010).

How else can medical professionals promote primary prevention? One way involves having them give health-promotion advice to patients. Because doctors find it hard to incorporate prevention advice in their practices, nurses or other medical staff might be better able to do it (Glasgow et al., 2001; Radecki & Brunton, 1992). A system of reminders to provide such advice with individual patients can improve these activities (Anderson, Janes, & Jenkins, 1998). Another approach involves constructing websites that give health promotion information (for example, http://www.hc-sc.gc.ca).

Secondary Prevention

In **secondary prevention**, actions are taken to identify and treat an illness or injury early with the aim of stopping or reversing the problem. In the case of someone who has developed an ulcer, for example, secondary prevention activities include the person's symptom-based behavior of seeking medical care for abdominal pain, the doctor's prescribing medication and dietary changes, and the patient's sick-role behavior of following the doctor's prescriptions. For other health problems, instances of secondary prevention might include examination of the mouth and jaw regions for early cancer detection during dental visits, free blood pressure measurements at shopping malls, and assessments of children's vision and hearing at school.

A common secondary prevention practice is the complete physical examination, often done each year. These checkups are costly in time and money because they include several imaging (such as X-ray) and laboratory tests. Because not all of these tests have proven useful in prevention, medical experts now recommend getting specific tests, each with recommended schedules ranging from 1 to 10 years, depending on the person's

age (CU, 1998). For instance, the American Cancer Society recommends regular schedules after specific ages for all women to have *mammograms* (breast X-ray) and for all adults to have colon inspections, such as a *colonoscopy* (ACS, 2009). The schedules depend on risk. Individuals who are not healthy or are considered to be at high risk—for example, because of age, past illnesses, family history, or hazardous work conditions—should be examined more often than other people.

These medical examinations are recommended because they detect the disease earlier and save lives. In the case of mammograms, women who follow the recommended schedules after age 50 reduce their mortality rates by 26% in follow-ups of 10 years or so after diagnosis (Kerlikowske et al., 1995). A national survey found that two-thirds of American women over 40 years of age had had a mammogram in the prior 2 years, but the rate was much lower for poor and less educated women (USBC, 2010). Explicitly describing to a woman her relatively high risk of breast cancer due to her family history increases the likelihood that she will increase her frequency of mammograms (Curry et al., 1993). Among elderly middle- and upper-middle-class women, the main reasons for not having mammograms are fears of pain and radiation (Fullerton et al., 1996).

Tertiary Prevention

When a serious injury occurs or a disease progresses beyond the early stages, the condition often leads to lasting or irreversible damage. **Tertiary prevention** involves actions to contain or retard this damage, prevent disability or recurrence, and rehabilitate the patient. For people with severe arthritis, for instance, tertiary prevention includes doing exercises for physical therapy and taking medication to control inflammation and pain. In the treatment of incurable forms of cancer, the goal may be simply to keep the patient reasonably comfortable and the disease in remission as long as possible. And people who suffer disabling injuries may undergo intensive long-term physical therapy to regain the use of their limbs or develop other means for independent functioning.

PROBLEMS IN PROMOTING WELLNESS

The process of preventing illness and injury can be thought of as operating as a *system*, in which the individual, his or her family, health professionals, and the community play a role. According to health psychologist Craig Ewart (1991), many interrelated factors and problems can impair the influence of each component in the system, and each component affects each other. Let's look at some of these factors, beginning with those within the individual.

Factors Within the Individual

People who consider ways to promote their own health often face an uphill battle with themselves. One problem is that many people perceive some healthful behaviors as less appealing or convenient than their unhealthful alternatives. Some people deal with this situation by maintaining a balance in their lives, setting reasonable limits on the unhealthful behaviors they perform. But other people do not, opting too frequently in favor of pleasure, sometimes vowing to change in the future: "I'll go on a diet next week," for example. They see little incentive to change immediately, especially if they think they are healthy. Even when individuals know they have health problems, many drop out of treatment or fail to follow some of the recommendations of their doctor.

Four other factors within the individual are also important. First, adopting wellness lifestyles may require individuals to change longstanding behaviors that have become habitual and may involve addictions, as in cigarette smoking. Habitual and addictive behaviors are very difficult to modify. Second, people need to have certain cognitive resources, such as the knowledge and skills, to know what health behaviors to adopt, to make plans for changing existing behavior, and to overcome obstacles to change, such as having little time or no place to exercise. Third, individuals need sufficient self-efficacy regarding their ability to carry out the change. Without self-efficacy, their motivation to change will be impaired. Last, being sick or taking certain drugs can affect people's moods and energy levels, which may affect their cognitive resources and motivation.

Interpersonal Factors

Many social factors influence people's likelihood to adopt health-related behaviors. For instance, one partner's exercising or eating unhealthfully before marriage can lead his or her partner to adopt the same behavior over time (Homish & Leonard, 2008). The social influence probably involves individuals giving social support and encouragement for the other person to change his or her lifestyle.

People living in a family system may encounter problems in their efforts to promote wellness. Some problems come about because the family is composed of individuals with their own motivations and habits. Suppose, for instance, that a member of a family wants to consume less cholesterol, but no one else is willing to stop eating high-cholesterol foods, such as

butter, eggs, and red meats. Or suppose the person has begun exercising three times a week, but this disrupts the daily routine of another family member. The interpersonal conflicts that circumstances like these can create in the family may undermine preventive efforts that the majority of family members support. Similar interpersonal conflicts can undermine prevention efforts among friends, classmates at school or college, and fellow employees at work.

Factors in the Community

People are more likely to adopt healthful behaviors if these behaviors are promoted or encouraged by community organizations, such as governmental agencies and the health care system. Health professionals don't usually have accurate information regarding their patients' health-related behavior, and they have traditionally focused their attention on treating, rather than preventing, illness and injury. But this focus began to change some years ago, and doctors became more interested in prevention (Radecki & Brunton, 1992).

The larger community faces an enormous array of problems in trying to prevent illness and injury. These problems include having insufficient funds for public health projects and research, needing to adjust to and communicate with individuals of very different ages and sociocultural backgrounds, and providing health care for those who need it most. In some communities, a lack of safe and convenient places to exercise and a high number of fast food restaurants can impair health promotion. Also, people's health insurance may not cover preventive medical services. Among the most difficult problems communities face is trying to balance public health and economic priorities. For example, suppose the surrounding community of an industry is subjected to potentially unhealthful conditions, such as toxic substances. But the community depends heavily on that industry for jobs and tax revenue, and the cost of reducing the potential for harm would force the company out of business. What should the community do? Many such dilemmas exist in most societies throughout the world.

WHAT DETERMINES PEOPLE'S HEALTH-RELATED BEHAVIOR?

If people were all like Mr. Spock of the *Star Trek* TV show and movies, the answer to the question of what determines people's health-related behavior would be simple: facts and logic, for the most part. These people would have no conflicting motivations in adopting wellness lifestyles to become as healthy as they can be. In this section we examine the complex factors that affect health-related behavior.

GENERAL FACTORS IN HEALTH-RELATED BEHAVIOR

The "average" person can describe healthful behaviors and generate a fairly complete list: "Don't smoke," "Don't drink too much, and don't drive if you do," "Eat balanced meals, and don't overeat," "Get regular exercise," and so on. But practicing these acts is another matter. Several processes affect people's health habits, and one factor is *heredity*. Genetic factors influence some health-related behaviors—excessive alcohol use provides a good example. As we'll see in Chapter 6, twin studies and adoption studies have confirmed that heredity plays a role in the development of alcoholism.

Learning

People also learn health-related behavior, particularly by way of *operant conditioning*, whereby behavior changes because of its consequences (Sarafino, 2001). Three types of consequences are important.

1.   **Reinforcement.** When we do something that brings a pleasant, wanted, or satisfying consequence, the tendency to repeat that behavior is increased or *reinforced*. A child who receives something she wants, such as a nickel, for brushing her teeth at bedtime is more likely to brush again the following night. The nickel in this example is a positive reinforcer because it was *added* to the situation (the word "positive" refers to the arithmetic term for addition). But reinforcement can also occur in another way. Suppose you have a headache, you take aspirin, and the headache goes away. In this case, your headache was unpleasant, and your behavior of taking aspirin *removed* it from the situation. The headache is called a "negative" reinforcer because it was *taken away* (subtracted) from the situation. In both cases of reinforcement, the end result is a desirable state of affairs from the person's point of view.

2.   **Extinction.** If the consequences that maintain a behavior are eliminated, the response tendency gradually weakens. The process or procedure of extinction exists only if no alternative maintaining stimuli (reinforcers) for the behavior have supplemented or taken the place of the original consequences. In the above example of toothbrushing behavior, if the money is no longer given, the child may continue brushing if another reinforcer exists, such as praise from her parents or her own satisfaction with the appearance of her teeth.

3.   **Punishment.** When we do something that brings an unwanted consequence, the behavior tends to be suppressed. A child who gets a scolding from his parents for playing with matches is less likely to repeat that behavior, especially if his parents might see him. The influence of punishment on future behavior depends on whether the person expects the behavior will lead to punishment again. Take, for example, people who injure themselves (punishment) jogging—those who think they could be injured again are less likely to resume jogging than those who do not.

People can also learn by observing the behavior of others—a process called *modeling* (Bandura, 1969, 1986). In this kind of learning, the consequences the model receives affect the behavior of the observer. If a teenager sees people enjoying and receiving social attention for smoking cigarettes, these people serve as powerful models and increase the likelihood that the teenager will begin smoking, too. But if models receive punishment for smoking, such as being avoided by classmates at school, the teenager may be less likely to smoke. In general, people are more likely to perform the behavior they observe if the model is *similar to themselves*—that is, of the same sex, age, or race—and is a *high-status person*, such as a physically attractive individual, movie star, or well-known athlete. Advertisers of products such as alcoholic beverages know these facts and use them in their commercials.

If a behavior becomes firmly established, it tends to be *habitual*; that is, the person often performs it automatically and without awareness, such as when a smoker catches a glimpse of a pack of cigarettes and absentmindedly reaches, takes a cigarette from the pack, and lights up. Even though the behavior may have been learned because it was reinforced by positive consequences, it is now less dependent on consequences and more dependent on antecedent cues (seeing a pack of cigarettes) with which it has been linked in the past (Sarafino, 2001). A*ntecedents* are internal or external stimuli that precede and set the occasion for a behavior. A smoker who says, "I must have a cigarette with my coffee after breakfast," is pointing out an antecedent. Behaviors that become habitual can be very difficult to change.

Because habitual behaviors are hard to change, people need to develop well behaviors as early as possible and eliminate unhealthful activities as soon as they appear. Families play a major role in children's learning of health-related behaviors (Baranowski & Nader, 1985). Children observe, for example, the dietary, exercise, and smoking habits of other family members and may be encouraged to behave in similar ways.

Table 5.3   *Associations of Conscientiousness with Health-Related Behaviors or Characteristics*

Higher Conscientiousness is Linked to Higher	Higher Conscientiousness is Linked to Lower
Fitness level[a]	Alcohol use[a]
Healthy food selection[a]	Drug use[a]
Mammogram testing[b]	Risky driving[a]
Medication taking, as prescribed[c]	Risky sex[a]
Self-reported health[d]	Tobacco use[a,d]

Sources: [a]Bogg & Roberts, 2004; [b]Siegler, Feaganes, & Rimer, 1995; [c]Christensen & Smith, 1995; [d]Hampson et al., 2006.

Children who observe and receive encouragement for healthful behavior at home are more likely than others to develop good health habits.

Social, Personality, and Emotional Factors

Many health-related behaviors are affected by *social* factors (Baranowski & Nader, 1985; Thirlaway & Upton, 2009). Friends and family can encourage or discourage children's practice of health-related behaviors, such as smoking and exercising, by providing consequences, such as praise or complaints, for a behavior; modeling it; and conveying a value for good health. These social processes may also lead to gender differences in health behavior, such as the greater physical activity of American boys than girls. Very different patterns of encouragement may lead boys more than girls toward healthful physical activity.

Two other factors that are linked to health-related behavior are the person's *personality* and *emotional state*, particularly stress. *Conscientiousness*— the tendency of a person to be dutiful, planful, organized, and industrious—is a personality characteristic that is associated with practicing many health behaviors, as Table 5.3 describes. And the role of emotions can be seen in two ways. First, among women who have a close relative with breast cancer and are low in conscientiousness, those who are very distressed about cancer are especially unlikely to have a mammogram (Schwartz et al., 1999). A brief cognitive intervention to enhance coping skills can reduce cancer distress among women who have a close relative with cancer and substantially improve their preventive behavior (Audrain et al., 1999). Second, we saw in Chapter 3 that people who experience high levels of stress engage in less exercise and consume poorer diets and more alcohol and cigarettes than those who experience less stress. If you ask people why they smoke, for example, they often will say, "To relieve tension." Many people cite coping with stress as an important reason for continuing to smoke (Gottlieb, 1983).

Perception and Cognition

The *symptoms* people experience can influence their health-related behaviors. The way they react varies from ignoring the problem to seeking immediate professional care. Certainly when the perceived symptoms are severe—as with excruciating pain, obvious bone fractures, profuse bleeding, or very high fever—almost everyone who has access to a health care system will try to use it (Rosenstock & Kirscht, 1979). When symptoms are not so severe, people often adjust their health habits, such as by limiting certain foods and drink, to meet the needs of the health problem as they see it (Harris & Guten, 1979).

Cognitive factors play an important role in the health behaviors people perform. As we saw earlier, people must have correct knowledge about the health issue and the ability to solve problems that arise when trying to implement healthful behavior, such as how to fit an exercise routine into their schedules. People also make many judgments that have an impact on their health. They assess the general condition of their health, such as whether it is good or bad, and make decisions about changing a health-related behavior: *If I begin an exercise program, will I stick to it?* But the judgments they make can be based on misconceptions, as when hypertensive patients overestimate their ability to sense when their blood pressure is high (Baumann & Leventhal, 1985; Brondolo et al., 1999; Pennebaker & Watson, 1988). Hypertensive patients often report that they can tell when their blood pressure is up, citing symptoms—headache, warmth or flushing face, dizziness, and nervousness—that are actually poor estimators of blood pressure. People's assessments of their blood pressure often correlate with their symptoms and moods, but not with their actual blood pressure. The potential harm in their erroneous beliefs is that patients often alter their medication-taking behavior or drop out of treatment on the basis of their subjective assessments of their blood pressure. Clearly, beliefs are important determinants of health behavior.

Another important belief that can impair health behavior is called *unrealistic optimism*. Neil Weinstein (1982) studied how optimistically people view their future health by asking them, "Compared to other people your age and sex, are your chances of getting lung cancer greater than, less than, or about the same as theirs?" He then had students fill out a questionnaire with a long list of health problems, rating each problem for their own likelihood of developing it, relative to other students of the same sex at the university. The results revealed that the students believed they were less likely than others to develop three-quarters of the health problems listed, including alcoholism, diabetes, heart attack, lung cancer, and venereal disease. They believed they were more susceptible than other students to only one of the health problems—ulcers. In a later study, Weinstein (1987) used similar questions in a mailed survey with 18- to 65-year-old adults in the general population. He found that these people were just as unrealistically optimistic as the students and that this optimism is based on illogical ideas—for instance, that they are at lower risk than other people if the health problem occurs rarely and has not happened to them yet. These factors do not affect one's risk relative to that of others.

Do people remain optimistic about their health when they are sick or when a threat of illness is clear? Evidently not. Using a procedure similar to Weinstein's, a study found that university students who were waiting for treatment at the student health center were less optimistic about their future health than were healthy students in a psychology course (Kulik & Mahler, 1987b). Another study was conducted with students in Poland, just after the radioactive cloud reached their community from the explosion of the atomic power plant at Chernobyl in the Soviet Union (Dolinski, Gromski, & Zawisza, 1987). Although these people believed they were less likely than others to have a heart attack or be injured in an accident, they believed they were equally likely to develop cancer and *more* likely than others to suffer illness effects of the radiation over the next several years. Thus, in the face of a real threat, they showed "unrealistic pessimism" regarding their health.

Studies of optimistic and pessimistic beliefs are important for three reasons. First, they have revealed that feelings of *invulnerability* are not a unique feature of adolescence (Cohn et al., 1995). Second, people who practice health behaviors tend to feel they would otherwise be at risk for associated health problems (Becker & Rosenstock, 1984). This means that people with unrealistically optimistic beliefs about their health are unlikely to take preventive action. Third, health professionals may be able to implement programs to address these beliefs in helping people see their risks

more realistically. The next section examines the role of people's health beliefs in more detail.

THE ROLE OF BELIEFS AND INTENTIONS

Suppose your friend believes in *reflexology*, a "healing" method that involves massaging specific areas of the feet to treat illnesses. The belief that underlies this method is that each area of the foot connects to a specific area of the body—the toes connect to the head, for instance, and the middle of the arch links to certain endocrine glands (Livermore, 1991). For a patient with recurrent headaches, a reflexologist's treatment might include massaging the toes. Your friend would probably try ways to prevent and treat illness that are different from those most other people would try. Psychologists are interested in the role of health beliefs in people's practice of health behaviors. A widely researched and accepted theory of why people do and do not practice these behaviors is called the health belief model (Becker, 1979; Becker & Rosenstock, 1984; Rosenstock, 1966). Let's see what this theory proposes.

The Health Belief Model

According to the **health belief model**, the likelihood that a person will take *preventive action*—that is, perform some health behavior—depends directly on the outcome of two assessments he or she makes. Figure 5-2 shows that one assessment pertains to the *threat* the person feels regarding a health problem, and the other weighs the *pros and cons* of taking the action.

Three factors influence people's *perceived threat*—that is, the degree to which they feel threatened or worried by the prospect of a particular health problem:

1. *Perceived seriousness* of the health problem. People consider how severe the organic and social consequences are likely to be if they develop the problem or leave it untreated. The more serious they believe its effects will be, the more likely they are to perceive it as a threat and take preventive action.

2. *Perceived susceptibility* to the health problem. People evaluate the likelihood of their developing the problem. The more risk they perceive for themselves, the more likely they are to perceive it as a threat and take action.

3. *Cues to action*. Being reminded or alerted about a potential health problem increases the likelihood of perceiving a threat and taking action. Cues to action can take many forms, such as a billboard about the dangers of unprotected sex, a friend or relative developing an illness, an episode about a specific illness and its symptoms on a TV medical drama, or a reminder phone call for an upcoming medical appointment.

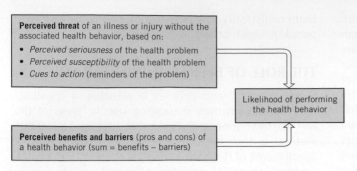

Figure 5-2 shows that in weighing the pros and cons of performing a health behavior, people assess the *benefits*—such as being healthier or reducing health risks—and the *barriers* or costs they *perceive* in taking action. What barriers might people see in preventive action? For the health behavior of getting a physical checkup, the barriers might include financial considerations ("Can I afford the bills?"), psychosocial consequences ("People will think I'm getting old if I start having checkups"), and physical considerations ("My doctor's office is across town, and I don't have a car"). The outcome of weighing the benefits against the barriers is an assessed *sum*: the extent to which taking the action is more beneficial for them than not taking the action. This assessed sum combines with the perceived threat of illness or injury to determine the likelihood of preventive action. Thus, for the health behavior of having a medical checkup, people who feel threatened by an illness and believe the benefits of having a checkup outweigh the barriers are likely to go ahead with it. But people who do not feel threatened or assess that the barriers are too strong are unlikely to have the checkup. According to the health belief model, these processes apply to primary, secondary, and tertiary prevention activities.

The theory also proposes that characteristics of individuals can influence their perceptions of benefits, barriers, and threat. These factors include the person's age, sex, race, ethnic background, social class, personality traits, and knowledge about or prior contact with the health problem. Thus, for example, people who are poor are likely to see strong barriers to getting medical treatment. Women, but not men, over 50 are likely to perceive a substantial risk of breast cancer. And elderly individuals whose close friends have developed severe cases of cancer or heart disease are more likely to perceive a personal threat of these illnesses than young adults whose friends are in good health.

Has research generally supported the health belief model's explanation of health-related behavior? The model has generated hundreds of studies, most of which have upheld its predictions for a variety of health

behaviors, including getting vaccinations, having regular dental visits, and taking part in exercise programs (Becker & Rosenstock, 1984; Conner & McMillan, 2004a; Kirscht, 1983). For instance, compared to people who do not take prescribed medication as directed or do not stick with dietary programs, those who *do* are more likely to believe they would be susceptible to the associated illness without the behavior and that the benefits of protective action exceed the barriers. Perceived risk (susceptibility) and perceived barriers appear to be critical elements for predicting health behavior, such as getting vaccinations and performing BSEs (Brewer et al., 2007; Conner & McMillan, 2004a), but strong barriers may have more influence than risk. Research has also supported the role of cues to action—for instance, individuals are more likely to perform BSEs or engage in brisk walking if they receive reminders (Craun & Deffenbacher, 1987; Prestwich, Perugini, & Hurling, 2010).

Despite the health belief model's success, it has some shortcomings. One shortcoming is that it does not account for health-related behaviors people perform habitually, such as tooth brushing—behaviors that probably originated and have continued without the person's considering health threats, benefits, and costs. Another problem is that there is no standard way of measuring its components, such as perceived susceptibility and seriousness. Different studies have used different questionnaires to measure the same factors, thereby making it difficult to compare the results across studies. These problems do not mean the theory is wrong, but that it is incomplete. We now turn to another theory that focuses on the role of people's beliefs on their practice of health-related behavior.

The Theory of Planned Behavior

Suppose you are having dinner at a restaurant with Dan, a friend who is overweight, and you wonder whether he will order dessert. How could you predict his behavior? That's simple—you could ask what he *intends* to do. According to the **theory of planned behavior** (Ajzen, 1985), an

Figure 5-2   The health belief model. People's likelihood of taking preventive action is determined by two assessments they make: their perceived threat of the health problem and the sum of pros and cons they perceive in taking action. Many factors contribute to these assessments. (Adapted from Becker & Rosenstock, 1984, Figure 2.)

expanded version of the *theory of reasoned action* (Ajzen & Fishbein, 1980), people decide their intention in advance of most voluntary behaviors, and intentions are the best predictors of what people will do.

What determines people's intentions? The theory indicates that three judgments determine a person's intention to perform a behavior, which we'll illustrate with a girl named Ellie who has decided to start exercising:

1. *Attitude regarding the behavior*, which is basically a judgment of whether or not the behavior is a good thing to do. Ellie has decided that exercising "would be a good thing for me to do." This judgment is based on two expectations: the likely *outcome* of the behavior (such as, "If I exercise, I will be healthier and more attractive") and whether the outcome would be *rewarding* (for example, "Being healthy and good looking will be satisfying and pleasant").

2. *Subjective norm*. This judgment reflects the impact of social pressure or influence on the behavior's acceptability or appropriateness. Ellie has decided that exercising "is a socially appropriate thing for me to do." This decision is based on her beliefs about *others' opinions* of the behavior (such as, "My family and friends think I should exercise") and her *motivation to comply* with those opinions (as in, "I want to do what they want").

3. *Perceived behavioral control*, or the person's expectation of success in performing the contemplated behavior (which is very similar to the concept of *self-efficacy*). Ellie thinks she can do the exercises and stick to the program.

The theory of planned behavior proposes that these judgments combine to produce an intention that leads to performance of the behavior. If Ellie had the opposite beliefs, such as, "Exercising is a waste of time," "I don't care about my family's opinion," and "I'll never find time to exercise," she probably wouldn't generate an intention to exercise, and thus would not do so. Self-efficacy is an important component. When deciding whether to practice a health behavior, people appraise their efficacy on the basis of the effort required, complexity of the task, and other aspects of the situation, such as whether they are likely to receive help from other people (Schunk & Carbonari, 1984).

The theory of planned behavior has generated many dozens of studies, including a meta-analysis showing that attitudes toward a behavior, subjective norms, and perceived behavioral control (self-efficacy) influence intentions and behavior (Conner & McMillan, 2004b). Table 5.4 gives a sample of studies on a variety of health-related behaviors that support the role of the three factors. Also, a meta-analysis of dozens of experiments revealed that interventions can change the factors, and these changes strongly influence intentions, which, to a much lesser extent, improve the targeted health behaviors (Webb & Sheeran, 2006).

What shortcomings does the theory of planned behavior have? One problem is that intentions and behavior are only moderately related—people do not always do what they plan (or *claim* they plan) to do. But the "gap" between intention and behavior can be reduced. Research has found that people are more likely to carry out their intentions if they make careful plans for doing so, keep track of their efforts, and recognize that they will need to continue the behavior on a long-term basis and are confident they can (Sniehotta, Scholz, & Schwarzer, 2005). Keep in mind that people's intentions to perform a

Table 5.4   A *Sample of Research Supporting the Theory of Planned Behavior*

The theory proposes that for each of three factors, the higher its level the more likely the intention will be made and the behavior will be performed. Each study referenced below found this relationship between the factor and the intention or behavior.

Factor	Intention/Behavior	Reference
Attitude regarding the behavior	Donating blood	Bagozzi, 1981
	Starting smoking	Van De Ven et al., 2007
	Quitting smoking	Norman, Conner, & Bell, 1999
	Exercising	Wurtele & Maddux, 1987
	Eating healthful diet	Conner, Norman, & Bell, 2002
	Testicular self-exam	Moore, Barling, & Hood, 1998
Subjective norm	Starting smoking	Van De Ven et al., 2007
	Cancer screening	Sieverding, Matterne, & Ciccarello, 2010
	Exercising	Latimer & Ginis, 2005
Perceived behavioral control (self-efficacy)	Starting smoking	Van De Ven et al., 2007
	Quitting smoking	DiClemente, Prochaska, & Gilbertini, 1985
	Exercising	Armitage, 2005
	Losing weight	Schifter & Ajzen, 1985
	Rehabilitation exercises	Jenkins & Gortner, 1998; Kaplan, Atkins, & Reinsch, 1984

health behavior, such as using condoms for safer sex, can change from one day to the next (Kiene, Tennen, & Armeli, 2008). But if individuals perform preparatory behaviors, such as buying and carrying condoms, after the intention is made, the chances of actually using condoms in sex increases greatly (Bryan, Fisher, & Fisher, 2002).

Another problem is that the theory is incomplete; it does not include, for example, the important role of people's prior experience with the behavior. In the blood donation study listed in Table 5.4, the subjects were asked about their past behavior in donating or not donating blood (Bagozzi, 1981). Of those subjects who said they intended to give blood, those who had given before were more likely actually to give than those who had not donated in the past. Similarly, studies have found that people's history of performing a health-related behavior, such as exercising or using alcohol or drugs, strongly predicts their future practice of that behavior (Bentler & Speckart, 1979; Godin, Valois et al., 1987). Thus, for example, compared to adults who have engaged in little exercise in the past, those who have exercised are much more likely to carry out their promises to exercise in the future.

The health belief model and the theory of planned behavior provide valid explanations for parts of the process that determines people's practice of health-related behavior. At their core, both theories assume people weigh perceived benefits and costs and behave according to the outcome of their analysis. But neither approach is sufficient, and both have limitations (Janis, 1984; Kirscht, 1983; Weinstein, 1988). One weakness in these theories is that they assume people think about risks in a detailed fashion, knowing what diseases are associated with different behaviors and estimating the likelihood of becoming seriously ill. In reality, people may modify their lifestyles, such as reducing coffee consumption, for very vague reasons, such as, "My doctor says coffee is bad for you." People appear to be especially inaccurate in estimating the degree of increased risk when the risks of illness, such as cancer, increase beyond moderate levels—for example, for individuals who smoke more than 15 cigarettes a day (Sastre, Mullet, & Sorum, 1999; Weinstein, 2000).

The Stages of Change Model

A wife's letter in a newspaper advice column once described her worry about her husband, who had suffered a heart attack but hadn't tried to lose weight or exercise as his doctor recommended. This situation is not uncommon. Although there are probably many reasons why this man hadn't changed his behavior, one may be that he wasn't "ready." Readiness to change is the main focus of a theory called the **stages of change**

model (also called the *transtheoretical model* because it includes factors described in other theories) (DiClemente et al., 1991; Prochaska & DiClemente, 1984; Prochaska, DiClemente, & Norcross, 1992). Figure 5-3 defines the model's five *stages* of intentional behavior change and shows how they spiral toward successful change.

According to the stages of change model, people who are currently in one stage show different psychosocial characteristics from people in other stages. For instance, people in the precontemplation stage regarding an unhealthy behavior, such as eating a high-cholesterol diet, are likely to have less self-efficacy and see more barriers than benefits for changing that behavior than people in the more advanced stages. Efforts to change the behavior are not likely to succeed until these individuals advance through the stages. But people's stages may regress, too: someone who reached the action stage and began to change may fail, drop back to a less advanced stage, and repeat the process of advancing toward change. People who justify continuing an unhealthy behavior, such as when smokers say, "I know heavy smokers who have lived long, healthy lives," tend to progress through the stages slowly (Kleinjan et al., 2006).

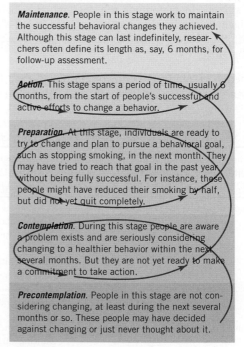

Maintenance. People in this stage work to maintain the successful behavioral changes they achieved. Although this stage can last indefinitely, researchers often define its length as, say, 6 months, for follow-up assessment.

Action. This stage spans a period of time, usually 6 months, from the start of people's successful and active efforts to change a behavior.

Preparation. At this stage, individuals are ready to try to change and plan to pursue a behavioral goal, such as stopping smoking, in the next month. They may have tried to reach that goal in the past year without being fully successful. For instance, these people might have reduced their smoking by half, but did not yet quit completely.

Contemplation. During this stage people are aware a problem exists and are seriously considering changing to a healthier behavior within the next several months. But they are not yet ready to make a commitment to take action.

Precontemplation. People in this stage are not considering changing, at least during the next several months or so. These people may have decided against changing or just never thought about it.

Figure 5-3 Five stages of change in the transtheoretical model advancing as a spiral from *precontemplation* (bottom), when the person is not considering change, to *maintenance*, when change is complete and stable.

Is it possible to help people advance through the stages? Two ways that help are having them:

- Describe in detail how they would carry out the behavior change, such as the exact foods they would eat to achieve a low-fat diet (Armitage, 2006).
- Plan for problems that may arise when trying to implement the behavior change, such as if they crave a cigarette after quitting smoking (Armitage, 2008).

Another way uses a unique feature of the stages of change model: it describes important characteristics of people at each stage, enabling an intervention to *match* strategies to the person's current needs in order to promote advancement to the next stage (Perz, DiClemente, & Carbonari, 1996; Prochaska, DiClemente, & Norcross, 1992). Let's consider an example of matching. Suppose you are a nurse providing care to an elderly woman with heart disease who doesn't exercise, even though her doctor advised her to do so. If she is at the precontemplation stage, you might talk with her about why exercise would help her and not exercising would harm her physically, for instance, and have her generate ways this would improve her general functioning. The goal at this point is just to get the person to consider changing the behavior. If she is at the contemplation stage, the goal might be to help her decide to change soon. Discussing the benefits and barriers she perceives in exercising, finding ways to overcome barriers, and showing her that she can do the physical activities would help.

The stages of change model is a very useful theory. Table 5.5 lists a sample of studies which have confirmed that people at higher stages are more likely than others to succeed at adopting healthful behaviors. Research has also confirmed the processes the model describes as leading to advancement or regression within the stages (Schumann et al., 2005) and the value of matching an intervention to people's stage of readiness to improve its success in changing unhealthful behaviors, such as smoking (Spencer et al., 2002). However, some evidence suggests that a smaller number of stages with somewhat different focuses may account better for behavior changes (Armitage, 2009).

In the preceding sections, we have examined many aspects of people's beliefs and intentions that appear to influence their health-related behavior. These aspects include people's perceived susceptibility to illness, perceived barriers and benefits to changing unhealthy behavior, ideas about what behaviors are socially acceptable and encouraged by family and friends, self-efficacy beliefs, and readiness to change. These factors seem sensible for individuals to consider, but the decisions they make are often *irrational* or *unwise*. The flawed decisions that people make about their health often result from motivational and emotional processes that are not addressed in the theories. For instance, these theories do

> not provide an adequate explanation for the widespread tendency of patients who have painful heart attacks to delay obtaining medical aid…. Typically, when the afflicted person thinks of the possibility that it might be a heart attack, he or she assumes that "it couldn't be happening to me." The patients' delay of treatment is not attributable to unavailability of medical aid or transportation delays; approximately 75% of the delay time elapses before a patient decides to contact a doctor. (Janis, 1984, pp. 331–332.)

Thus, theories that focus on rational thinking do not adequately consider the processes we're about to see that can override logical decision making.

THE ROLE OF LESS RATIONAL PROCESSES

Although body builders generally know that using anabolic steroids can harm their health, some may try to justify using these substances to build muscles with statements like, "Experts have been wrong before." Why do people make decisions regarding health-related behavior that are not more rational? We'll look first at motivational factors that influence people's decisions.

Motivational Factors

People's desires and preferences influence the judgments they make of the validity and utility of new information through a process called **motivated reasoning** (Kunda, 1990). In one form of motivated reasoning, individuals who prefer to reach a particular conclusion, such as to continue to eat fatty foods or smoke cigarettes, tend to use biased cognitive processes: they search for reasons to accept supportive information and

Table 5.5 *Sample of Research Supporting the Stages of Change Model*

Health Behaviors	Reference
Quit cigarette smoking	Spencer et al., 2002
Breast cancer screening	Spencer, Pagell, & Adams, 2005
Vegetable and fruit consumption	Lippke et al., 2009
Using safer sex practices	Bowen & Trotter, 1995
Exercising	Hellsten et al., 2008; Lippke et al., 2009; Marshall & Biddle, 2001

discount disconfirming information. The reasons they choose seem "reasonable" to them, even if the logic is actually faulty.

Studies have demonstrated nonrational thought processes in several types of health-related decisions. First, of people with a chronic illness, such as diabetes, those who tend to use illogical thought patterns in health-related situations tend not to follow medical advice for managing their illness (Christensen, Moran, & Weibe, 1999). Second, people who use defense mechanisms a lot to cope with stressful information are more likely than other individuals to deny that they are at risk for AIDS, especially if their risk of infection is high (Gladis et al., 1992). Perhaps their high feeling of threat motivates their use of denial. Similarly, individuals seem to use irrelevant information, such as a sexual partner's attractiveness, to judge the risks in having sex with that person (Blanton & Gerrard, 1997; Gold & Skinner, 1996). Third, people who smoke cigarettes give lower ratings of risk than nonsmokers do when asked to rate their own risk of developing smoking-related diseases, such as lung cancer (Lee, 1989; McCoy et al., 1992). Beliefs like these appear very resistant to change (Kreuter & Strecher, 1995; Weinstein & Klein, 1995).

False Hope and Willingness

Here are two features of health-related behaviors the theories we've considered don't account for well. First, most people who lose weight gain it back within a year or so, yet they try again at a later time. Similar patterns occur for quitting smoking or starting to exercise. Second, many risky behaviors occur spontaneously, without the individuals having thought it through.

It's encouraging to know that people who don't maintain a healthier behavior try again, but why do they decide to retry if they've failed previously and are likely to fail again? The reason may be that they develop **false hopes**, believing without rational basis that they will succeed (Polivy & Herman, 2002). They form false hopes because they did succeed for a while, which provides reinforcement for the efforts they made to that point, and they misinterpret their failures. Probably most changed behaviors are not maintained because people expect too large a change in their behavior, too great an effect it would have for them, and too quick and easy a process of change. But they often decide instead that they just didn't try hard enough for enough time—after all, they succeeded initially.

What risky behaviors occur without careful thought? Lots, maybe most. People often find themselves in situations they didn't expect to happen in which they have the opportunity to perform an attractive behavior,

such as drinking a bit too much or having sex, but there's some risk. In this type of situation, the critical issue may not be whether they "intend" to engage in a risky behavior, but whether they are *willing* to do it. High **willingness** to engage in a risky behavior depends on four factors (Gibbons et al., 1998). Two factors are positive subjective norms and attitudes toward the behavior, which we considered as part of the theory of planned behavior. The other two factors that heighten willingness are having engaged in the behavior previously and having a favorable social image of the type of person who would perform the behavior.

Emotional Factors

Stress also affects the cognitive processes people use in making decisions. For example, when given health promotion information, people under high stress pay less attention to it and remember less of it than people under low stress (Millar, 2005). **Conflict theory** presents a model to account for both rational and irrational decision making, and stress is an important factor in this model (Janis, 1984; Janis & Mann, 1977). According to conflict theory, the cognitive sequence people use in making important decisions starts when an event challenges their current course of action or lifestyle. The challenge can be either a *threat*, such as a symptom of illness or a news story on the dangers of smoking, or an *opportunity*, such as the chance to join a free program at work to quit smoking. This produces an appraisal of risk: if the person sees no risk, the behavior stays the same, and the decision-making process ends; but if a risk is seen, the process continues—for instance, with a survey of alternatives for dealing with the challenge.

Conflict theory proposes that people experience stress with all major decisions, particularly those relating to health, because of the importance of and conflicts about what to do. People's coping with decisional conflict depends on their perceptions of the presence or absence of three factors: *risk*, *hope*, and *adequate time*. These three factors produce different coping patterns, two of which are:

- *Hypervigilance.* People sometimes see serious risks in their current behaviour *and* those alternatives they have considered. If they believe they may still find a better solution *but* think they are fast running out of time, they experience high stress. These people tend to search frantically for a solution—and may choose an alternative hastily, especially if it promises immediate relief.

- *Vigilance.* When people perceive serious risks in all possibilities they have considered *but* believe they may find a better alternative and have time to search, they experience only moderate levels of stress. Under these conditions, people tend to search carefully and make rational choices.

When the challenge is very serious, such as a doctor's warning or obvious symptoms of illness, vigilance is the most adaptive coping pattern. Although the conflict theory has not been tested sufficiently to know its strengths and weaknesses, there is little question that the impact of stress is an important determinant of preventive action, particularly in people's symptom-based and sick-role behavior.

We have examined how each of many different psychological and social factors can affect people's health behavior. But we have not yet considered the influence of age, sex, and sociocultural background, which we examine next.

DEVELOPMENTAL, GENDER, AND SOCIOCULTURAL FACTORS IN HEALTH

It comes as no surprise that people's health changes across the life span, that women and men have some differences in health risks and needs, and that variations in preventive behavior occur between individuals of different social classes and ethnic backgrounds.

What are some of these changes and differences, and why do they exist? Let's examine these health issues, starting with the role of development.

DEVELOPMENT AND HEALTH

The biological, psychological, and social factors that affect people's health change throughout the life span, causing individuals to face different health risks and problems as they develop. For instance, adolescents and young adults are at relatively high risk for injury from automobile accidents, but older adults are at relatively high risk for hypertension and heart disease. As a result, people's preventive needs and goals change with age. Table 5.6 presents main preventive goals for each period in the life span. Other individuals, such as parents, may assume responsibility for prevention, especially early and very late in the life span.

During Gestation and Infancy

Each year millions of babies around the world are born with birth defects—in the United States alone,

Table 5.6   *Prevention Goals over the Life Span*

Health Goals of Gestation and Infancy

- To provide the mother a healthy, full-term pregnancy and rapid recovery after a normal delivery.
- To facilitate the live birth of a normal baby, free of congenital or developmental damage.
- To help both mother and father achieve the knowledge and capacity to provide for the physical, emotional, and social needs of the baby.
- To establish immunity against specified infectious diseases.
- To detect and prevent certain other diseases and problems before irreparable damage occurs.

Health Goals of Childhood and Adolescence

- To facilitate the child's optimal physical, emotional, and social growth and development.
- To establish healthy behavioral patterns (in children) for nutrition, exercise, study, recreation, and family life, as a foundation for a healthy lifetime lifestyle.
- To reinforce healthy behavior patterns (in adolescents), and discourage negative ones, in physical fitness, nutrition, exercise, study, work, recreation, sex, individual relations, driving, smoking, alcohol, and drugs.

Health Goals of Adulthood

- To prolong the period of maximum physical energy and to develop full mental, emotional, and social potential.
- To anticipate and guard against the onset of chronic disease through good health habits and early detection and treatment where effective.
- To detect as early as possible any of the major chronic diseases, including hypertension, heart disease, diabetes, and cancer, as well as vision, hearing, and dental impairments.

Health Goals in Old Age

- To minimize handicapping and discomfort from the onset of chronic conditions.
- To prepare in advance for retirement.
- To prolong the period of effective activity and ability to live independently, and avoid institutionalization so far as possible.
- When illness is terminal, to assure as little physical and mental stress as possible and to provide emotional support to patient and family.

Source: Based on Breslow & Somers, 1977.

there are over 120,000 cases, or 3 out of every 100 births annually (MD, 2010). These defects range from relatively minor physical or mental abnormalities to gross deformities; some are not apparent until months or years later, and some are fatal. Birth defects result from genetic abnormalities and harmful factors in the fetal environment.

A mother can control much of the fetal environment through her behavior. Early in gestation, a *placenta* and *umbilical cord* develop and begin to transmit substances to the fetus from the mother's bloodstream. These substances typically consist mostly of nourishment, but they can also include hazardous microorganisms and chemicals that happen to be in her blood. Many babies are at risk of low birth weight, which can result from three prenatal hazards. First, the mother may be malnourished due to inadequate food supplies or knowledge of nutritional needs. In addition to low weights, babies born to malnourished mothers tend to have poorly developed immune and central nervous systems and a high risk of mortality in the first weeks after birth (Chandra, 1991; Huffman & del Carmen, 1990; Smart, 1991). Second, certain infections the mother may contract during pregnancy can also attack her gestating baby, sometimes causing permanent injury or death (LaBarba, 1984; Tortora & Derrickson, 2009). Vaccinations can prevent most of these infections.

Third, various substances the mother uses may enter her bloodstream and harm the baby (LaBarba, 1984; Tortora & Derrickson, 2009). Babies exposed prenatally to addictive drugs, such as cocaine, are far more likely than others to die in infancy or be born with very low weights or malformations, such as of the heart (Lindenberg et al., 1991). Also, cigarette smoke exposure

from the mother's smoking or from her environment—for instance, if the father smokes—is associated with low birth weight and other health problems in babies (DiFranza & Lew, 1995; Martinez et al., 1994; Tortora & Derrickson, 2009). And the mother's drinking alcohol, especially heavy drinking, can cause *fetal alcohol syndrome*, which has several symptoms: (1) slow growth before and after birth, (2) subnormal intelligence, and (3) certain facial characteristics, such as small eye openings (NIAAA, 1993; Tortora & Derrickson, 2009). Ideally, expectant mothers should use *none* of these substances. Health education for pregnant women can help, such as by getting those who drink or smoke to abstain or reduce their use (Stade et al., 2009; Windsor et al., 1993).

Table 5.7 gives the percentages of newborns with low birth weight and the rates of infant mortality for selected nations around the world. The rate of infant mortality in some developing countries is extremely high, greater than 100 per 1,000 live births for the first year of life (WHO, 2009). In early infancy, the baby's immunity to disease depends largely on the white blood cells and antibodies passed on by the mother prenatally and in her milk if she breast-feeds (Tortora & Derrickson, 2009). Because of the immunity it gives to the baby, breast milk is sometimes called "nature's vaccine." Parents should arrange for the baby to begin a vaccination program early in infancy for such diseases as diphtheria, whooping cough, and polio.

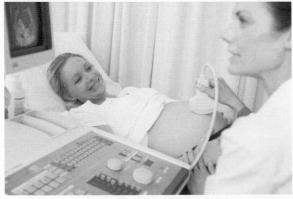

A pregnant woman receives an ultrasound procedure in prenatal care to check the development of her baby. Following medical advice during pregnancy can enhance the healthfulness of the baby's prenatal environment.

Table 5.7 *Percentage of Newborns with Low Birth Weight and Infant Mortality Rate (Number per 1,000 Live Births Who Die in the First Year of Life) in Selected Countries*

Country	Percent Low Birth Weight	Infant Mortality (per 1,000 births)
Australia	7	5
Brazil	8	20
Canada	6	5
China	2	19
Germany	7[a]	4
India	30[a]	54
Italy	6[a]	3
Netherlands	NA	4
Singapore	8	2
South Africa	15[a]	46
Sweden	4[a]	2
Turkey	16[a]	21
United Kingdom	8	5
United States	8	6

Note: NA = data not available.
Sources: WHO, 2009, except [a] = newest data available from WHO, 2006.

Childhood and Adolescence

In the second year of life, toddlers are walking and beginning to "get into everything," with the risk for injury, such as while swimming or from sharp objects and chemicals around the house. In the United States, accidental injury is the leading cause of death during childhood and adolescence (USBC, 2010). Parents, teachers, and other caregivers can reduce the likelihood of injury by teaching children safety behaviors, supervising them when possible, and decreasing their access to dangerous situations, such as by keeping chemicals out of reach. The role of cognitive processes in the practice of health-related behavior has important implications here, since cognitive abilities are immature in early childhood and become more sophisticated as children get older (Burbach & Peterson, 1986; Murphy & Bennett, 2004). With these advances, children are more able to make decisions and assume responsibility for promoting their own health and safety.

Adolescence is a very critical time in the development of preventive behavior. Although teenagers have the cognitive ability to make the logical decisions leading to healthful behavior, they face many temptations and forces—especially peer pressure—that lead them in other directions (La Greca & Stone, 1985; Leffert & Petersen, 1998). This is the time when they stand the greatest chance of starting to smoke, drink, use drugs, and have sexual relations. These risky behaviors are interrelated: teens who smoke and drink are more likely to use marijuana and have unsafe sex (Duncan, Strycker, & Duncan, 1999). Teens also learn to drive, and too often combine this new skill with drinking and using drugs. Most teenage deaths in developed countries result from accidents. In the United States, death rates for accidents rise sharply during the teenage years and are several times as high for 15- to 24-year-olds as for younger age groups (USBC, 2010). All these newly acquired behaviors involve substantial health risks, which teenagers are highly susceptible to taking.

Adulthood and Aging

When people reach adulthood, they become less likely than they were in adolescence to adopt new behavioral risks to their health. In general, older adults are more likely than younger ones to practice various health behaviors, such as eating healthful diets and getting medical checkups, even though they have similar beliefs about the value of these behaviors in preventing serious illnesses, such as heart attack and cancer (Belloc & Breslow, 1972; Leventhal, Prohaska, & Hirschman, 1985). One likely reason for this age difference is that older adults perceive themselves as more vulnerable to these

illnesses than younger adults, and engage in preventive acts for that reason.

Old age is not what it used to be. Older people in industrialized countries live longer and are in better financial and physical condition than in the past (Horn & Meer, 1987). One health behavior that generally declines as adults get older is regular vigorous exercise (Leventhal, Prohaska, & Hirschman, 1985). Many elderly people avoid physical exercise because they tend to exaggerate the danger that exertion poses to their health, underestimate their physical capabilities, and feel embarrassed by their performance of these activities (Woods & Birren, 1984).

GENDER AND HEALTH

In almost all countries of the world, an average female's expected life span at birth is at least a few years longer than a male's (WHO, 2009). The gap in life expectancy is about 4 to 6 years in Europe, 5 years in the United States, and usually somewhat smaller in developing countries. For people in the United States who survive to 65 years of age, the remaining life expectancy of women is about 3 years longer than men's (USBC, 2010). Why do women live longer? The answer involves both biological and behavioral factors (Murphy & Bennett, 2004; Reddy, Fleming, & Adesso, 1992; Williams, 2003). Some of these factors are:

- Physiological reactivity, such as blood pressure and stress hormones, when under stress is greater in men than women, which may make men more likely to develop cardiovascular disease.

- The female sex hormone estrogen appears to delay heart disease by reducing blood cholesterol levels and platelet clotting.

- Men smoke and drink more than women do, thereby making men more susceptible to cardiovascular and respiratory diseases, some forms of cancer, and cirrhosis of the liver.

- Males have higher levels of drug use, unhealthy diets, and risky driving and sexual activity.

- Males are less likely than females to consult a doctor when they feel ill.

- Work environments of males are more hazardous than those of females; men account for the large majority of fatalities on the job.

One of the few behavioral advantages men have is that they get more strenuous exercise than women do. The practice of many other health-related behaviors is similar for men and women.

Women's longer lives do not mean that they have fewer health problems than men. Actually, the opposite may be true (USBC, 2010; Reddy, Fleming, & Adesso, 1992; Williams, 2003). For example, American women have much higher rates than men of acute illnesses, such as respiratory and digestive ailments, and nonfatal chronic diseases, such as varicose veins, arthritis, anemia, and headache. They also use medical drugs and services much more than men, even when pregnancy and other reproductive conditions are not counted.

SOCIOCULTURAL FACTORS AND HEALTH

"Did a doctor ever tell you that you had [medical condition]?" Researchers asked this question of thousands of late-middle-age American and British people, inserting eight serious medical conditions (Banks et al., 2006). The surveys for this age group revealed that Americans had far higher prevalence rates for all of the illnesses—for example, the respective rates for Americans and British were 12.5% and 6.1% for diabetes, 15.1% and 9.6% for heart disease, and 9.5% and 5.5% for cancer. Do differences in health behaviors account for these results? Probably not: the British people smoked somewhat more and drank heavily much more than the Americans, but the Americans had much higher rates of obesity—and when obesity was equated statistically, the British were still healthier. These results point out that health differs across nations.

Another aspect of the study on American and British health is that the researchers surveyed only non-Hispanic White people. Why? Cultural differences also exist within nations, and the United States has larger percentages of Hispanic and Black people. A national survey of American adults of all ages and backgrounds found that fewer than 13% claimed to be in only "fair" to "poor" health (NCHS, 2009b). But this was not uniform across segments of the population. Compared with the population as a whole, people were much more likely to rate their health as "fair" or "poor" if they were over 45 years of age, or from the lower social classes, or of African American or American Indian background. As it turns out, these lower assessments reflect real health problems of the individuals these groups comprise.

Social Class and Minority Group Background

Did you know that when the *Titanic* sank, passengers did not all have an equal chance of surviving? Mortality was far higher for passengers who were from third class cabins than from first class (Rugulies, Aust, & Syme, 2004). Similarly, the devastation of hurricane Katrina was greater for poor than for richer people. Social class and health are linked.

The concept of *social class*, or *socioeconomic status*, describes differences in people's resources, prestige, and power within a society (Adler, 2004; Elo, 2009). These differences are reflected in three main characteristics: income, occupational prestige, and education. The lowest social classes in industrialized societies contain people who live in poverty or are homeless. By almost any gauge of wellness, health correlates with social class (Adler, 2004; Anderson & Armstead, 1995; Banks et al, 2006; Gruenewald et al., 2009; Lantz et al., 2005; Lemelin et al., 2009). For example, individuals from lower classes are more likely than those from higher classes to:

- Be born with very low birth weight.
- Die in infancy or in childhood.
- Develop early signs of cardiovascular disease, such as atherosclerosis.
- Have poorer overall health and develop a longstanding illness in adulthood.
- Experience major stressors, followed in later years by poorer health and greater limitations in everyday functioning.

Not coincidentally, individuals from the lower classes have poorer health habits and attitudes than those from higher classes. For instance, they smoke more, participate less in vigorous exercise and have poorer diets and less knowledge about risk factors for disease (Adler, 2004; Murphy & Bennett, 2004; Myers, 2009). And they are less likely than individuals from upper classes to get health information from the mass media (Ribisl et al., 1998). You probably realize that members of minority groups usually are disproportionately represented in the lower social classes.

Minority group background is an important risk factor for poor health. Today a baby born in Cuba stands a better chance of reaching the age of one than the average African American newborn in the United States (USBC, 2010; WHO, 2009). The rate of infant mortality in America is twice as high for Blacks as it is for Whites. Among babies who survive the first year, the life expectancy for an African American baby is about 4 1/2 years shorter than that for a White baby in America (USBC, 2010). Moreover, the death rates in the United States for the three most deadly diseases are far higher for Blacks than Whites, as Figure 5-4 shows. Although American racial differences in health were much larger decades ago, they are still substantial and remain a national disgrace.

Three minority groups in the United States have high levels of health problems: in a national survey of adults, self-ratings of fair or poor health were given by 21.6% of Native Americans, 18.4% of Blacks, and 17.4% of Hispanics (compared with 12.2% of Whites, NCHS,

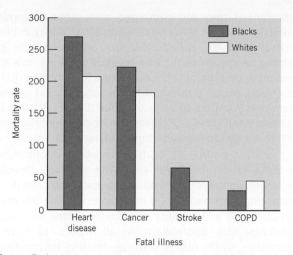

Figure 5-4   Death rates (per 100,000 individuals in the population) for Whites and Blacks in the United States, resulting from four leading chronic diseases (COPD is chronic obstructive lung disease). The rates are averaged for males and females and age-adjusted to take into account that mortality rates increase with age and that the average age of Blacks is less than that of Whites. (Data from NCHS, 2009a, Table 28.)

2009b). Many individuals in these minority groups live in environments that do not encourage the practice of health behavior (Johnson et al., 1995; Whitfield et al., 2002). African Americans and Hispanics also share a vulnerability to four health-related problems: stress from discrimination, substance abuse, AIDS, and injury or death from violence (Myers, 2009; Whitfield et al., 2002). These individuals are more likely than whites to smoke, use drugs, and practice unsafe sex. And African Americans and Hispanics—especially young males—are several times more likely than their White counterparts to become victims of homicide. These problems are disturbing, and correcting them will take a great deal of time, effort, and social change.

Promoting Health with Diverse Populations

Immigrants tend to adopt the health behaviors of their new culture through the process of acculturation (Corral & Landrine, 2008). How can societies help their diverse populations lead healthful lives? Long-term approaches involve reducing poverty, increasing literacy, and providing illness prevention services. A more immediate approach would be to present health information at low literacy levels (Pignone et al., 2005). And because communities contain people of different ages, genders, and sociocultural backgrounds, professionals who are trying to prevent and treat illness need to take a biopsychosocial perspective (Flack et al., 1995; Johnson et al., 1995; Landrine & Klonoff, 2001). You can see what this means in Table 5.8, which presents three factors professionals can address to make health-promotion services culturally sensitive. Ideally, programs to promote minority health would use a grassroot, culturally relevant approach with trained health leaders from the community (Castro, Cota, & Vega, 1999). An example program, called *Por La Vita*, increased breast and cervical cancer testing in Hispanic women by identifying and training respected women of their community to provide weekly educational sessions on cancer prevention (Navarro et al., 1998). The remainder of this chapter focuses on techniques and program designs for enhancing health and preventing illness.

PROGRAMS FOR HEALTH PROMOTION

Hoping to save money on the costs of health care and lost productivity, some employers have begun offering incentives for healthy behavior—for example, for meeting weight loss goals, workers can earn a cash bonus, or days off work, or even a tropical vacation. Other creative approaches to promote health have been used to change other behaviors in other situations. Often programs

Table 5.8   *Cultural Diversity Issues for Professionals in Promoting Health*

- *Biological factors.* Sociocultural groups can differ in their physiological processes, as reflected in African Americans' high risk of developing the genetic blood disease of sickle-cell anemia. For instance, we saw in Chapter 3 that Black people show relatively high reactivity to stress, which may result from heredity or environmental factors, such as living under relatively high stress.
- *Cognitive and linguistic factors.* People of different sociocultural groups seem to have different ideas about the causes of illness, give different degrees of attention to their body sensations, such as pain, and interpret symptoms differently. For example, Hispanic Americans often believe in using "folk healing" practices, such as actions to drive away evil spirits. Professionals who try to refute these beliefs may drive their patients away. Language differences between professionals and the people they serve impair their ability to communicate with each other.
- *Social and emotional factors.* Sociocultural groups differ in the amount of stress they experience, their physiological reactivity to it, and the ways they cope with it. They also differ in their amount and use of social support.

for health promotion address several behaviors, which is efficient: people achieve more changes when more behaviors are addressed (Young et al., 2009). Let's look at some methods these efforts can use.

METHODS FOR PROMOTING HEALTH

Interventions to promote health can encourage the practice of healthful behavior with dozens of methods (Abraham & Michie, 2008; Sarafino, 2011). These interventions usually start by teaching individuals what these behaviors are and how to perform them, and by persuading people to change unhealthful habits. An important step in this effort is motivating individuals to *want* to change, and this often requires modifying their health beliefs and attitudes. What methods do these programs use to encourage health behavior?

Providing Information

People who want to lead healthful lives need information—they need to know what to do and when, where, and how to do it. In reducing dietary cholesterol, people need to know what cholesterol is and that it can clog blood vessels, leading to heart disease. They also need to know where they can have their blood tested for cholesterol level, what levels are high, how much cholesterol is in the foods they currently eat, which foods might be good substitutes for ones they should eliminate from their diets, and how best to prepare these foods. There are several sources for information to promote health.

One source for health information is the *mass media*: TV, radio, newspapers, and magazines can promote health by presenting warnings and information, such as advice to help people avoid or stop smoking. For instance, the mass media sometimes presents in public service advertisements information about the *negative consequences* of an activity, such as smoking. This approach has had limited success in changing behavior (Flay, 1987; Maes & Boersma, 2004). One reason for the limited success may be that many people just don't want to change the behavior at issue: a noted newspaper columnist who did not want to change his diet railed against warnings, writing,

> Cholesterol, shmolesterol! ... Almost everything [experts] say is good for you will turn out bad for you if you hang around long enough, and almost everything they say is bad for you will turn out not to matter. (Baker, 1989, p. A31; note that this quote is a good example of motivated reasoning!)

But when people already want to change an unhealthful habit, programs conducted on TV can be more effective,

especially if they are combined with other methods (Freels et al., 1999; Maes & Boersma, 2004). For example, a program on TV, called *Cable Quit*, was successful in helping people stop smoking by showing them how to prepare to quit, helping them through the day they quit, describing ways to maintain their success, and giving them opportunities to call for advice (Valois, Adams, & Kammermann, 1996). Of those who started the program, 17% continued to abstain from smoking a year later.

Another source of health promotion information is the *computer*, particularly via the Internet. People anywhere in the world who are already interested in promoting their health and have access to the Internet can contact a wide variety of websites. Some are huge databases with information on all aspects of health promotion, while others provide detailed information on specific illnesses, such as cancer and arthritis, or support groups for health problems. People can learn how to avoid health problems and, if they become ill, what the illness is and how it can be treated.

A third source of health promotion information is *medical settings*, particularly doctors' offices, which offer some advantages and disadvantages. Two advantages are that many individuals visit a doctor at least once a year, and they respect health care workers as experts. Three disadvantages are that medical personnel have tight schedules, feel a lack of expertise to help, and worry that they may be intruding in patients' personal lives (Schroeder, 2005). For reasons like these, medical staff don't provide enough health promotion advice. A study found that American doctors checked the smoking status in a bit more than two-thirds of adult patients and counseled only about one-fifth of smokers on ways to quit (Thorndike, Regan, & Rigotti, 2007). Because of the problem of tight schedules, researchers have developed 5- to 10-minute counseling programs that medical staff can be trained to give in person or by telephone; having a system that cues the staff to give the program increases its delivery (Adams et al., 1998). These programs enhance many types of health behaviors, such as eating low-fat diets, curbing alcohol intake, and getting cancer screening (Ockene et al., 1999; Ockene, Reed, & Reiff-Hekking, 2009; Rimer, 1998). Just asking patients if they smoke, advising them to quit, and suggesting that they contact a telephone "quit line" takes less than a minute and can help (Schroeder, 2005).

Medical professionals now have another avenue for providing health promotion information. They can offer individuals who are at risk for inherited illnesses, such as some forms of cancer, estimates of their chances of getting the disease and opportunities to undergo tests, such as periodic examinations and genetic testing. But even when genetic testing is offered at no cost, less than half of individuals request the testing and results (Lerman et al., 1996; Lerman, Hughes et al., 1999). Are there psychological risks for people who receive this advice and undergo the tests? Making the decision to have genetic testing can be agonizing because of the possibility that it will reveal a genetic risk and conflicts that arise among family members who do and do not want the information. In breast and ovarian cancer testing, for example, women who learn that they are carriers of the gene experience some distress in the subsequent weeks that declines markedly in the next few months (Hamilton, Lobel, & Moyer, 2009). (Go to 👤.)

Features of Information to Enhance Motivation

Individuals do not necessarily follow advice and warnings on ways to promote their health. How can the information they receive enhance their motivation to adopt health behaviors?

One approach to enhance people's motivation to follow health promotion advice is to use *tailored content*—that is, the advice delivered in person, in print, or on the telephone is designed for a specific individual, based on characteristics of that person. For example, the message would refer to the person by name and might include personal or behavioral details, such as the person's age or smoking history, and a message geared to the person's readiness to adopt the proposed health behavior, such as stopping smoking, scheduling a mammogram, or losing weight. Tailoring the content appears to enhance the success of health promotion information (Noar, Benac, & Harris, 2007; Skinner et al., 1999).

Another approach to enhance motivation is based on a concept called *message framing*, which refers to whether the information emphasizes the benefits (gains) or costs (losses) associated with a behavior or decision. For a health behavior, a gain-framed message would focus on attaining desirable consequences or avoiding negative ones; it might state, for example, "If you exercise, you will become more fit and less likely to develop heart disease." A loss-framed message would focus on getting undesirable consequences and avoiding positive ones; for instance, "If you do not get your blood pressure checked, you could increase your chances of having a heart attack or stroke, and you will not know that your blood pressure is good." A large body of evidence indicates that the best type of framing to use depends on

---

CLINICAL METHODS AND ISSUES
Dialogues to Help People Stop Smoking

Patients who smoke tend to express many common rationalizations for not quitting that their medical or psychological practitioner can discuss with them. Each of the following rationalizations has a reply the practitioner can give (Adapted from USDHHS, 1986a).

PATIENT: *I am under a lot of stress, and smoking relaxes me.*

STAFF (Practitioner): Your body has become accustomed to nicotine, so you naturally feel more relaxed when you get the nicotine you have come to depend on. But nicotine is actually a stimulant that temporarily raises heart rate, blood pressure, and adrenaline level. After a few weeks of not smoking, most ex-smokers feel less nervous.

PATIENT: *Smoking stimulates me and helps me to be more effective in my work.*

STAFF: Difficulty in concentrating can be a symptom of nicotine withdrawal, but it is a short-term effect. Over time, the body and brain function more efficiently when you don't smoke, because carbon monoxide from cigarettes is displaced by oxygen in the bloodstream.

PATIENT: *I have already cut down to a safe level.*

STAFF: Cutting down is a good step toward quitting. But smoking at any level increases the risk of illness. And some smokers who cut back inhale more often and more deeply, thus maintaining nicotine dependence. It is best to quit smoking completely.

PATIENT: *I only smoke safe, low-tar/low-nicotine cigarettes.*

STAFF: Low-tar cigarettes still contain harmful substances. Many smokers inhale more often or more deeply and thus maintain their nicotine levels. Carbon monoxide intake often increases with a switch to low-tar cigarettes.

PATIENT: *I don't have the willpower to give up smoking.*

STAFF: It can be hard for some people to give up smoking, but for others it is much easier than they expect. Millions of people quit every year. It may take more than one attempt for you to succeed, and you may need to try different methods of quitting. I will give you all the support I can.

Similar dialogues can help people change other health-related behaviors, too.

the type of health behavior (Rothman & Salovey, 1997, 2004). Gain-framed messages work best for motivating behaviors that serve to prevent or recover from illness or injury; two such behaviors are using condoms and performing physical therapy. Loss-framed messages work best for behaviors that occur infrequently and serve to detect a health problem early, as getting a mammogram can do (Gerend, Shepherd, & Monday, 2008).

A special case of loss-framed messages is when information is a *fear appeal*—it arouses fear. According to the health belief model, people are likely to practice healthful behavior if they believe that by not doing so they are susceptible to serious health problems. In other words, they are motivated by fear to protect their health. Studies have found that fear appeals can motivate people to adopt a variety of more healthful attitudes and behavior (Diefenbach, 2004). But the effects tend to be transient, sometimes not lasting long enough to carry a changed intention into a behavior. What can be done to make fear appeals more effective? Fear messages for changing unhealthful behavior are most persuasive if they:

- Emphasize the organic and social consequences—that is, the perceived seriousness—of developing the health problem (Banks et al., 1995; Kalichman & Coley, 1995).

- Are presented as a personal testimonial, rather than statistical chances (de Wit, Das, & Vet, 2008).

- Provide specific instructions or training for performing the behavior (Albarracín et al., 2003; Diefenbach, 2004).

- Help bolster people's self-confidence, or self-efficacy, for performing the behavior before urging them to begin the plan (Self & Rogers, 1990).

Motivational Interviewing

A one-on-one technique called **motivational interviewing**, a counseling style designed to help individuals explore and resolve their ambivalence in changing a behavior, was originally developed to help people overcome addictions, such as to alcohol and drugs (Miller & Rollnick, 1991; Miller & Rose, 2009). The counselor uses a style that leads the client, rather than the counselor, to voice arguments for behavior change. Two important features of the process are *decisional balance* and personalized *feedback*. In decisional balance, clients list their reasons for and against changing their behavior so that these can be discussed and weighed. In personalized feedback, clients receive information on their pattern of the problem behavior, comparisons to national norms for the behavior, and risk factors and other consequences of the behavior.

Motivational interviewing has been extended for use in health care settings to promote healthful behavior,

such as to help a girl named Latisha to get her boyfriend to use condoms when they had sex. The following exchange ensued after she pointed out that he had used condoms in the past "when he got 'em."

INTERVIEWER: So if you had them around, would you be able to use them with him?

LATISHA: If I really wanted him to. He'd probably use it.

INTERVIEWER: All you'd have to do is ask him to use a condom, and he'd do it?

LATISHA: Well, I'd have to be nice about it, so he don't think I'm sayin' he's dirty or go around anymore. I'd have to be nice.

INTERVIEWER: It sounds like you know what he would be sensitive about. What could you say to make it sound nice? (Brown & Lourie, 2001, P. 262)

An interview like this one would then discuss the things she could say, the problems that could arise, and how she would deal with them.

The course of motivational interviewing can take one session or several and typically leads the client to identify many of the elements of theories we've previously discussed, such as the benefits and barriers (decisional balance) to the behavior change. They then work through identified problems that have made the behavior hard to change in the past. Research has revealed promising outcomes of motivational interviewing, such as in helping patients follow the medication directions their doctor prescribed and getting sexually active people to use condoms (Resnicow et al., 2002). Decisional balance and feedback are critical components of the process, particularly in helping college students reduce heavy drinking (LaBrie et al., 2006; Walters et al., 2009).

Behavioral and Cognitive Methods

Behavioral methods focus directly on enhancing people's performance of the preventive act by managing its antecedents and consequences. The antecedents for health-related behavior can be managed in many ways, such as by using calendars to indicate when to perform infrequent preventive actions and reminders not to eat high-calorie foods or drink too much.

The consequences for health-related behavior can be managed by providing reinforcers when the person practices healthful behaviors, such as flossing teeth or not smoking. But the effectiveness of reinforcement depends on the types of reward used and the age of the individual (Sarafino, 2001). People differ in their reward preferences; one person might like to receive a CD of rock music, but someone else might prefer classical. The consequences need to be matched to the person, which can be done by having the person fill out a questionnaire (Sarafino & Graham, 2006). Some evidence suggests that reward preferences change with age: kindergarten children tend to prefer material rewards (a charm, money, candy) over social rewards such as praise, but this preference seems to reverse by third grade (Witryol, 1971). For adults, monetary rewards seem to be very effective in encouraging health behaviors, such as stopping smoking in pregnancy and breast self-examination (Lumley et al., 2009; Solomon et al., 1998).

Cognitive methods can be applied to change people's thought processes, such as to enhance their self-efficacy for quitting smoking. Therapists often teach behavioral and cognitive methods to clients so they can apply them themselves—an approach called **self-management** (Sarafino, 2011). Although each behavioral and cognitive method helps in changing a behavior, such as eating more healthfully, they appear to be most effective when combined and used together, particularly when the individuals monitor their own behavior and keep records of it (Michie et al., 2009).

Maintaining Healthy Behaviors

When people change a long-standing behavior, their success usually has some setbacks, or lapses (Sarafino, 2001). A *lapse* is an instance of backsliding—for instance, a person who quits smoking might have an occasional cigarette. Lapses should be expected; they do not indicate failure. A more serious setback is a **relapse**, or falling back to one's original pattern of the undesirable behavior. Relapses are very common when people try to change long-term habits, such as their eating and smoking behaviors.

Psychologists G. Alan Marlatt and Judith Gordon (1980) have proposed that for many individuals who quit a behavior, such as smoking, experiencing a lapse can destroy their confidence in remaining abstinent and precipitate a full relapse. This is called the **abstinence-violation effect**. Because these people are committed to total abstinence, they tend to see a lapse as a sign of a personal failure. They might think, for instance, "I don't have any willpower at all and I cannot change." Programs to change behavior can reduce relapses by training individuals to cope with lapses and maintain self-efficacy about the behavior and by providing "booster" sessions or contacts (Curry & McBride, 1994; Irvin et al., 1999). Contacts, even by phone, can reduce relapses substantially by providing counseling on dealing with difficult situations that could lead to lapses (Zhu et al., 1996).

Interventions to promote health have been carried out in many settings and with a variety of goals, methods, and populations. We will examine different types of programs, beginning with health education efforts in schools and religious organizations.

PROMOTING HEALTH IN SCHOOLS AND RELIGIOUS ORGANIZATIONS

Schools and religious organizations have unique opportunities to promote health for two reasons. First, they have access to virtually all children and adolescents in developed nations during the years that are probably most critical in the development of health-related behaviors. Second, they can reach many minority and immigrant adults who are at high risk of serious illnesses, such as heart disease and cancer.

Are health promotion programs in schools and religious organizations effective? Many have been (Campbell et al., 2007; Katz, 2009). Some programs in schools have been designed to promote a broad range of health behaviors—for example, nutrition, exercise, tobacco and alcohol use, and sexual activity—which improved the children's health behavior and physical condition (Katz, 2009; Maes & Boersma, 2004). The most effective programs for promoting health in schools are comprehensive and involve the children's family and community over a long period.

Schools can encourage fitness by providing exercise equipment and showing children how to use it, as in this Project Fit America program.

WORKSITE AND COMMUNITY–BASED WELLNESS PROGRAMS

Wellness programs are spreading rapidly in workplaces in industrialized countries. A national survey of American worksites with 50 or more employees found that over 90% offered some form of health promotion activity, such as for fitness or diet (USDHHS, 2004). One-third of small worksites and 50% of large worksites offered comprehensive programs, which focus on lifestyle change and screen employees for health promotion needs. Workers with poor health habits in the United States cost employers substantially more in health benefits and other costs of absenteeism than those with good habits. These savings offset and often exceed the expense of running a wellness program (Goetzel & Ozminkowski, 2008). Psychologists who study or administer such programs are called *occupational health psychologists* (Quick, 1999).

Worksite wellness programs vary in their aims, but often apply self-management methods and address some or all of several risk factors: hypertension, cigarette smoking, unhealthful diets and overweight, poor physical fitness, alcohol abuse, and high levels of stress. These risk factors do not seem to be equally changeable. For example, although self-management can be sufficient for dietary and exercise behaviors, smoking often requires counseling and pharmacological treatment to overcome nicotine dependence, too (Cahill, Moher, & Lancaster, 2008; Emmons et al., 1999). Housing these interventions in workplaces has several advantages. Worksite programs are convenient to attend, are fairly inexpensive for employees, can provide participants with reinforcement from the employer and coworkers, and can structure the environment to encourage healthful behavior, such as by making healthy food available in the cafeteria (Cohen, 1985). Although the number of employees who participate in worksite programs is not as high as one would hope, over 60% of American workers do (USDHHS, 2004). And the number of workers who participate and stick with the programs increases markedly if the employer actively recruits them (Linnan et al., 2002).

Let's look at a model worksite intervention. Johnson & Johnson, America's largest producer of health care products, began the *Live for Life* program in 1978. The program covers thousands of employees and is highly effective (Maes & Boersma, 2004; Nathan, 1984). The program is designed to improve employees' health knowledge, stress management, and efforts to exercise, stop smoking, and control their weight. For each participating employee, Live for Life provides a *health screen*—a detailed assessment of the person's current health and health-related behavior, which is shared with the person later—and professionally led *action groups*

for specific areas of improvement, such as quitting smoking or controlling weight, focusing on how people can alter their lifestyle and maintain improvements permanently. Follow-up contacts are made with each participant during the subsequent year. The company also provides a work environment that supports and encourages healthful behavior: it has designated no-smoking areas, established exercise facilities, and made nutritious foods available in the cafeteria, for example.

Community-based programs for health promotion are designed to reach large numbers of people and improve their knowledge and performance of preventive behavior (Thompson et al., 2003). These interventions may address a set of behaviors or just one and use any of the methods we have considered. They may, for instance, use the media and social organizations to provide information and advice regarding the risks factors for cancer, the dangers of drinking and driving, or the availability of free blood pressure testing or vaccinations. Community-based programs may also provide incentives for performing a health behavior or reaching a goal, such as losing a certain amount of weight. An early example of a community-based program is the *Three Community Study*, which was carried out in California to spur people to change their behavior and reduce their risk of cardiovascular disease (Farquhar et al., 1977; Meyer et al., 1980). The program delivered an extensive 2-year mass-media campaign, consisting of warnings and information concerning diet, exercise, and smoking. Research has revealed that the long-term success of the program was greatest with older people and least with individuals who were much younger, had little education, and were from the lower socioeconomic classes (Winkleby, Flora, & Kraemer, 1994). Although the success of this program and similar ones was modest—for instance, reducing blood pressure by a few points—small changes across thousands of people can affect disease greatly (Thompson et al., 2003).

ELECTRONIC INTERVENTIONS FOR HEALTH PROMOTION

Electronically delivered psychosocial interventions are being developed to promote health. *Internet-based programs* use the World Wide Web to deliver interventions, and *computer-based programs* use software that is loaded on individual computers (Tate, 2008). Table 5.9 presents some examples of electronic interventions with evidence of success in changing several health-related behaviors. Internet-based programs are particularly useful because they are easily accessed by enormous numbers of people around the world, but nearly 50% of people who begin using them drop out (Bennett & Glasgow,

Table 5.9   *Examples of Electronic Health Promotion Interventions with Research Evidence of Success*

Purpose	Population and Program Description (Reference)	Related Evidence
Decrease drinking	Heavy drinkers. Motivational interview methods to help them commit to change; and if they do, negotiate goals and plan for change (Squires & Hester, 2004).	Carey et al., 2009
Decrease smoking	Smokers who purchased a nicotine patch. Cognitive-behavioral program, including methods to manage antecedents and enhance self-efficacy and coping (Strecher, Shiffman, & West, 2005).	Myung et al., 2009; Seidman et al., 2010; Shahab & McEwen, 2009
Decrease chronic pain	Headache sufferers. Stress management, including relaxation training and some biofeedback (Devineni & Blanchard, 2005).	Bennett & Glasgow, 2009
Decrease insomnia	Adults with insomnia. Cognitive-behavioral methods, such as going to bed only when sleepy and changing counterproductive beliefs (Ritterband et al., 2009).	
Reduce risk of eating disorder	Females at high risk of eating disorders. Cognitive-behavioral program to change beliefs about their bodies and societal standards that put them at risk (Taylor et al., 2006).	
Reduce risk of substance use	Girls, 11 to 13 years old, and their mothers. Each pair worked together on a computerized program, which taught them ways to manage their moods and stress, to reduce the girls' risk of using tobacco, alcohol, and illicit drugs (Schinke, Fang, & Cole, 2009).	Hustad et al., 2010; Norman et al., 2008
Reduce dietary fat; increase exercise	Adults in general population. An Internet intervention had participants provide information about their fat intake and physical activity. Tailored feedback and suggestions were given on the healthfulness of their behaviors and ways to improve them (Oenema et al., 2008).	Winett et al., 2007

2009). Providing personal contact and incentives and reminders to use the programs can reduce drop out rates. (Go to 🍎.)

PREVENTION WITH SPECIFIC TARGETS: FOCUSING ON AIDS

Sometimes prevention programs focus on reducing people's risk of developing a specific health problem and center these efforts on specific segments of the population. One example of this approach is the Multiple Risk Factor Intervention Trial (MRFIT), a project that recruited and provided health promotion programs for thousands of men across the United States who were at substantial risk for heart disease (Caggiula et al., 1981). Another example involves efforts to reduce the spread of infection with the *human immunodeficiency virus* (HIV), which causes *acquired immune deficiency syndrome* (AIDS). We'll focus on efforts to reduce HIV infection.

HIV Infection

The magnitude of the AIDS threat is astounding (UNAIDS, 2009): tens of millions of its victims have died around the world, over 33 million people are currently infected with HIV, and millions are newly infected each year. Over 160 countries have reported cases of AIDS, but the infection is unevenly distributed worldwide. The largest concentration of infections continues to be in sub-Saharan Africa, which has two-thirds of all people currently living with HIV/AIDS. Although the incidence of infection is high in Asian and Latin American regions, it has declined worldwide since the mid-1990s. New medical treatments can extend the lives of victims, are widely used in industrialized nations, and are being used increasingly in developing nations (UNAIDS, 2009). There is no vaccine against HIV, and complications from AIDS kill most people who develop it.

HIV spreads to an uninfected person only through contact of his or her body fluids with those of an infected person, generally either through sexual practices or when intravenous drug users share needles. The likelihood of infection increases if the person has wounds or inflammation from other sexually transmitted diseases, such as syphilis or herpes, and from rough sex (Klimas, Koneru, & Fletcher, 2008). Infected mothers sometimes transmit the virus to their babies during gestation, delivery, and later during breast-feeding (Carey & Vanable, 2004; Klimas, Koneru, & Fletcher, 2008).

ASSESS YOURSELF

Your Knowledge about AIDS

Answer the following true-false items by circling the T or F for each one.

T F 1.   Most people who develop AIDS die from its complications.

T F 2.   Blood tests can usually tell within a week after infection whether someone has received the AIDS virus.

T F 3.   People do not get AIDS from using swimming pools or rest rooms after someone with AIDS does.

T F 4.   Some people have contracted AIDS from insects, such as mosquitoes, that have previously bitten someone with AIDS.

T F 5.   AIDS can now be prevented with a vaccine and cured if treated early.

T F 6.   People who have the AIDS virus can look and feel well.

T F 7.   Gay women (lesbians) get AIDS much more often than heterosexual women, but not as often as gay men.

T F 8.   Health workers have a high risk of getting AIDS from or spreading the virus to their patients.

T F 9.   Kissing or touching someone who has AIDS can give you the disease.

T F 10.   AIDS is less contagious than measles.

Check your answers against the key below that is printed upside down—a score of **8** items correct is good, **9** is very good, and **10** is excellent. (Carey, Morrison-Beedy, & Johnson, 1998; DiClemente, Zorn, & Temoshok, 1987; Vener & Krupka, 1990).

Answers:

1. T, 2. F, 3. T, 4. F, 5. F, 6. T, 7. F, 8. F, 9. F, 10. T

Who is at high risk of HIV infection? Table 5.10 shows that the modes of exposure to HIV for people newly infected vary greatly across areas of the world. In the United States, unprotected male-to-male anal intercourse is still a major mode of exposure, but the rate of infection from male-to-male sex was much higher in the early 1980s and declined sharply in the next several years (Catania et al., 1991; Coates, 1990). And the risk of infection has increased among American low-income and minority groups over the years. In other parts of the world, the main exposure modes are injection drug use (sharing needles) and unprotected heterosexual vaginal intercourse, often with paid sex workers. And the percentage of people living with HIV who are female has increased worldwide—today 50% are female (UNAIDS, 2009). Men who are circumcised have a much lower risk of infection from vaginal sex than uncircumcised men (Klimas, Koneru, & Fletcher, 2008). But unsafe behavior is still the main risk, and global prevention efforts have concentrated on using fear arousing warnings and providing information to promote safer-sex behavior.

These efforts also try to correct misconceptions about HIV transmission—for instance, that AIDS can only happen to homosexuals and drug users, that all gay men are infected, that mosquitoes can spread the virus, or that the virus can be transmitted through casual contact, such as by touching or hugging infected individuals or by sharing office equipment they have used (DiClemente, Zorn, & Temoshok, 1987). Many people also believe that health care personnel are usually at high risk of becoming infected when working with AIDS patients, but research has disconfirmed this. It is rare for health care workers to become infected, even when they are accidentally stuck with a needle that had been used on an AIDS patient (Clever & LeGuyader, 1995; Klimas, Koneru, & Fletcher, 2008).

Why do people continue to engage in unsafe sex? Although ignorance and a lack of availability of protection are the main reasons in many developing countries, other factors are more influential in other cultures. Let's look at some of these factors:

- People are much more likely to have unsafe sex if they are promiscuous or have sex while under the influence of alcohol or drugs (Lowry et al., 1994; Norris et al., 2009; O'Hare, 2005). In men, intoxication seems to increase negative attitudes and decrease self-efficacy about using condoms and to increase the willingness to have unsafe sex when they are sexually aroused (Gordon & Carey, 1996; MacDonald et al., 2000). Women are less likely to request condom use when they've been drinking (Norris et al., 2009).

- Young adults are much more likely to engage in risky sex if their parents reject them for their sexual orientation (Ryan et al., 2009).

Table 5.10 *Percent of New HIV Infections by Exposure Mode for the United States and Some Regions of the World Where the Incidence Is High*

Exposure Mode[a]	Country or Region (annual number of new cases)			
	United States (56,300)	Eastern Europe and Central Asia (110,000)	Latin America (170,000)	South[b] and South-East Asia (280,000)
Male-to-male sex	41.7%	4%	26%	5%
Injection drug use	21.6%	67%	19%	22%
Heterosexual sex	30.9%	NA	NA	NA
Sex workers/clients	NA	5%/7%	4%/13%	8%/41%
Other (see note)	5.9%	17%	38%	24%

[a]Data on exposure modes were available from the sources (below) only in 2006 reports and only for the country and regions included in the table. Regions for which exposure data were not available include sub-Saharan Africa, which at 1.9 million new cases has the highest incidence, but exposure there is mainly via heterosexual sex.

[b]Data for India were included in the number of new cases, but *not* exposure mode, which is mainly heterosexual sex, including with commercial sex workers.

Notes: NA = data not available; cases for this mode are included in one or more other exposure categories; "other" includes cases with more than one mode, making the actual exposure unclear, and cases of exposure at or soon after birth and via blood transfusion.

Sources: New cases data from CDC, 2009; UNAIDS, 2009. Exposure mode data from CDC, 2006; UNAIDS, 2006.

- Unmarried partners are less likely to use condoms if they perceive their relationship to be close or serious (Cooper & Orcutt, 2000; Misovich, Fisher, & Fisher, 1997).

- Decision making in sexual situations is often subject to nonrational processes, such as denial or wishful thinking (Blanton & Gerrard, 1997; Gold, Skinner, & Hinchy, 1999; Thompson et al., 1999). Sexual arousal and having an attractive partner decrease rationality in sexual decisions (Shuper & Fisher, 2008).

- Many individuals have maladaptive beliefs about their own low self-efficacy to use condoms and the effect that doing so would have on sexual pleasure and spontaneity (Kelly et al., 1991, 1995; Wulfert, Wan, & Backus, 1996).

- Many people, especially young women, are embarrassed to buy condoms and make errors putting them on a penis, such as not leaving a space at the tip and squeezing air out (Brackett, 2004; Grimley et al., 2005).

- The advent of medical treatments that lower viral load and prolong life has led to over-optimism in many individuals, leading them to think that protection is not so necessary anymore (Kalichman et al., 2007; Lightfoot et al., 2005).

People's maladaptive beliefs are often clear when they recognize their behavior contradicts what experts say, so they add qualifiers, such as, "I know that's what they say but …" or, "but in my case …" (Maticka-Tyndale, 1991).

Basic Messages to Prevent HIV Infection

Major efforts have been introduced in most countries around the world to prevent HIV infection by having the mass media and health organizations provide information about several basic behaviors (Carey, 1999; Kalichman, 1998). First, people should avoid or reduce having sex outside of long-term monogamous relationships or, otherwise, to use "safer sex" practices with new partners. Safer sex involves selecting partners carefully, avoiding practices that may injure body tissues, and using condoms in vaginal and anal intercourse. Second, not all people who have the virus know they do, and not all of those who know they do tell their sexual partners (Ciccarone et al., 2003; Simoni et al., 1995). Third, drug users should not share a needle or syringe; if they do, they should be sure it is sterile. Fourth, women who could have been exposed to the virus should have their blood tested for the HIV antibody before becoming pregnant and, if the test is positive, avoid pregnancy. Much of this information has been designed to arouse fear, and it has in many people.

Do informational efforts change people's HIV knowledge and behavior? In the United States, public health programs have been directed toward adolescents and young adults in the general population, intravenous drug users and their sexual partners, and gays and bisexuals. Although providing information to youth in the general population increases their knowledge about HIV (Yankah & Aggleton, 2008), most sexually experienced teenagers and young adults do not seem to follow recommended precautions (Leigh et al., 1994). Other approaches try to convince teenagers to abstain from sex until marriage—often having them take "virginity pledges"—or just reduce sexual risk, but these approaches are not effective in reducing sexual activity or risk (Rosenbaum, 2009; Underhill, Montgomery, & Operario, 2008). Although programs that focus on getting adolescents to abstain from or reduce their sexual activity can help for some people, efforts to promote condom use are more effective for teens who are sexually experienced (Jemmott, Jemmott, & Fong, 1999). A study found that men who had received school-based condom education in adolescence were less likely to contract sexually transmitted diseases (Dodge, Reece, & Herbenick, 2009).

Providing information about HIV has been more effective in reducing risky behaviors of intravenous drug users and gay men. Drug users have learned that sharing needles can transmit HIV and that there are ways to protect themselves (Des Jarlais & Semaan, 2008). In the United States, most of these people have begun to use sterile needles, reduce their drug use, or use drugs in other ways, such as by inhaling. The risk of HIV infection among drug users decreases if they can buy needles legally or exchange used needles for new ones (Des Jarlais & Semaan, 2008; Ksobiech, 2003). Although drug users' caution may not extend readily to their sexual behavior, interventions that have addressed both issues have reduced their injection and sexual risk behaviors (Meader et al., 2010). Most drug users are heterosexual men, and their sexual partners often are women who know about the risks but feel powerless and are willing to go along with having unprotected sex (Logan, Cole, & Leukefeld, 2002).

Perhaps the best-organized efforts to change sexual practices have been directed at gay men, particularly in gay communities in large cities. This is partly because many gay social, political, and religious organizations existed before the AIDS epidemic began, and these groups became actively involved in public health campaigns to prevent the spread of the disease. These efforts have had a substantial impact: AIDS education and prevention campaigns with gay and bisexual men have reduced their sexual risk behavior markedly (Johnson et al., 2008), producing "the most profound modifications of personal health-related behaviors ever recorded" (Stall, Coates, & Hoff, 1988, p. 878).

Focusing on Sociocultural Groups and Women

Although more needs to be done to reduce HIV risk in urban gay men and intravenous drug users around the world, efforts must be intensified among heterosexual women and disadvantaged sociocultural groups (Alvarez et al., 2009; Logan, Cole, & Leukefeld, 2002; Raj, Amaro, & Reed, 2001). For minority groups in the United States, particularly African Americans and Hispanics, there can be added problems of lesser knowledge about risky behavior and suspicions concerning information from health care systems they believe have treated them badly (Boulware et al., 2003; Raj, Amaro, & Reed, 2001). Women are often vulnerable to HIV infection when they are with a male partner who resists using condoms, are socially or economically dependent on the man, and have less power in their relationships (Sikkema, 1998). A woman's ability to protect herself from infection by asking for condom use under these circumstances is especially difficult if she lacks self-efficacy and the man interprets such requests negatively—for example, that she doesn't care about him or thinks he's been unfaithful (Neighbors, O'Leary, & Labouvie, 1999; O'Leary, Jemmott, & Jemmott, 2008).

Interventions have been tested with large numbers of Hispanic and African American women who met in small group sessions to enhance their motivation and interpersonal skills for adopting safer sex practices. Comparisons with women in control groups were made during subsequent months. Women who received the

Efforts to prevent the spread of AIDS include using billboards to reach teenagers.

interventions were more likely to report using safer sex practices and to use coupons to redeem free condoms (Carey et al., 2000; Sikkema, Kelly et al., 2000); they were also less likely to develop STDs (chlamydia or gonorrhea) over the next year (Shain et al., 1999).

Making HIV Prevention More Effective

Many interventions provide individual counseling, such as motivational interviewing, to prevent HIV infection (Carey, 1999; Kelly & Kalichman, 2002). Although these methods are moderately effective in decreasing risky behavior, their success is mainly with men and women who are already infected (Weinhardt et al., 1999). Uninfected people who should reduce their risky sexual behavior often do not, and the reasons they don't seem to be similar for homosexual and heterosexual individuals. We need to keep in mind that the vast majority of today's new infections worldwide are in individuals who are neither gay nor intravenous drug users (UNAIDS, 2009).

How can programs to reduce the spread of HIV infection be made more effective? Prevention programs must provide information about HIV transmission and prevention, use techniques to increase people's motivation to avoid unsafe sex, and teach behavioral and cognitive skills needed to perform preventive acts (Albarracín et al., 2005; Carey & Vanable, 2004). Some ways to enhance these features include:

- Tailoring the program to meet the needs of the sociocultural group being addressed (Raj, Amaro, & Reed, 2001).

- Involving the person's family in the intervention (Dilorio et al., 2007; Prado et al., 2007).

- Giving strong emphasis to training in the actual skills individuals will need to resist having unsafe sex (Fisher et al., 1996; Kalichman, Rompa, & Coley, 1996; St. Lawrence et al., 2002).

- Using methods to reduce behaviors, such as alcohol and drug use, that increase the risk of unsafe sex (Morgenstern et al., 2009; Naar-King et al., 2006; Patrick & Maggs, 2009).

- Making sure the training is geared toward bolstering self-efficacy and advancing the individuals through the stages of change (Galavotti et al., 1995).

- Making use of experts who are like the program recipients—such as in ethnicity and gender—and respected or popular individuals as leaders to endorse the program and promote its acceptance by the recipients (Durantini et al., 2006; Kelly et al., 1997).

- Encouraging infected individuals to disclose their HIV status to prospective sexual partners (Kalichman & Nachimson, 1999).

- Using techniques to reduce nonrational influences in sexual decisions. For example, having people give advice publicly that contradicts their own behavior can reduce their future use of denial (Eitel & Friend, 1999).

SUMMARY

People's behavior has an important impact on their health. Mortality from today's leading causes of death could be markedly reduced if people would adopt a few health behaviors, such as not smoking, not drinking excessively, eating healthful diets, and exercising regularly. Although some individuals are fairly consistent in their practice of health-related behaviors, these behaviors can be quite changeable over time. Health-related behaviors that become well established often become habitual.

Health problems can be averted through three levels of prevention and can involve efforts by the individual and by his or her social network, doctor, and other health professionals. Primary prevention consists of actions taken to avoid illness or injury. It can include public service announcements, genetic counseling, and a variety of health behaviors, such as using seat belts and performing breast or testicular self-examinations. Secondary prevention involves actions taken to identify and stop or reverse

a health problem. It includes tests and treatments health professionals may conduct, as well as people's visiting a doctor when ill and taking medication as prescribed. Tertiary prevention consists of actions taken to contain or retard damage from a serious injury or advanced disease, prevent disability, and rehabilitate the patient.

People acquire health-related behaviors through modeling and through operant conditioning, whereby behavior changes because of its consequences: reinforcement, extinction, and punishment. Other determinants of these behaviors include genetic, social, emotional, and cognitive factors. Errors in symptom perception and ideas people have about illnesses can lead to health problems. People's thinking about health and illness is not always logical—it often includes motivated reasoning, unrealistic optimism, and false hopes about their health. Unhealthful behaviors are not always planned and often depend on the person's willingness to be drawn into an attractive situation.

Some theories focus on the role of health beliefs to account for people's health-related behavior. The health belief model proposes that people take preventive action on the basis of their assessments of the threat of a health problem and the pros and cons of taking the action. Threat perceptions are based mainly on the person's perceived seriousness of and susceptibility to the health problem. Assessing the pros and cons of the action involves weighing its perceived benefits and barriers. These assessments combine to determine the likelihood of preventive action. The theory of planned behavior proposes that health-related behaviors are determined by people's intentions, which are a function of their attitudes regarding the behaviors, subjective norms, and self-efficacy. The stages of change model focuses on people's readiness to modify their behavior; conflict theory focuses on the role of stress in decisions.

People's age, sex, and sociocultural background also affect health-related behavior and need to be considered in programs for health promotion. Efforts to promote healthy behavior use information, fear appeals, motivational interviewing, and behavioral and cognitive methods, which can be applied with self-management procedures. But changes in behavior can be temporary; relapses can occur, partly via the abstinence-violation effect. Programs for health promotion can be effective in the schools and in worksites. Community-based wellness programs are designed to reach large numbers of people and improve their knowledge and practice of preventive behavior. The Three Community Study demonstrated that media campaigns can promote health, and subsequent research has also integrated extensive efforts by community organizations toward improving people's preventive actions, such as in stemming the spread of AIDS.

KEY TERMS

health behavior	extinction	motivated reasoning	self-management
primary prevention	punishment	false hopes	relapse
secondary prevention	health belief model	willingness	abstinence-violation effect
tertiary prevention	theory of planned behavior	conflict theory	
reinforcement	stages of change model	motivational interviewing	

6

SUBSTANCE USE AND ABUSE

PROLOGUE

The odds of quitting smoking for good had been slight for Bill. He had tried to do it several times over the years, but this time he knew that he had to make the effort as his health was suffering—he recently had a minor heart attack scare, but had managed to pull through. He also lost his father to lung cancer that same year. Like his father, Bill was a heavy smoker; he smoked a pack of cigarettes a day for the last 25 years.

Bill had seen the television commercials on the effects of smoking on the lungs and arteries, but until now these had not had any impact on him. Friends at work had told him that there were nicotine patches and nicotine gum that he could purchase from the local pharmacy to help with his cravings while quitting. He had called the Quitline to obtain information on how to quit, and his wife had persuaded him to see the community health psychologist.

It had not been easy, but with the help of the health psychologist, Bill has been a non-smoker for six months. He learnt to recognise situations that prompted him to smoke, and how to control his cravings around friends who still smoked. Since quitting, Bill has also become more physically active and feels much happier than he did before, such that he wonders why it had taken so long to decide to quit for good.

People voluntarily use many different substances that can harm their health. This chapter focuses on people's use of three of the most common of these substances: tobacco, alcohol, and drugs. For each substance, we examine who uses it and why, how the substance can affect their health, and what can be done to prevent people from using it and abusing it once they start. We also address questions of concern to people who want to enhance their own and other people's health. Do people smoke tobacco, drink alcohol, or use drugs more heavily now than in the past? Why do people start to smoke, drink excessively, or use drugs? Why is it so difficult to quit these behaviours? If individuals succeed in their efforts to stop smoking, will they gain weight?

SUBSTANCE ABUSE

"I just can't get started in the morning without a cup of coffee and a cigarette—I must be addicted," you may have heard someone say. The term *addicted* used to have a very limited meaning, referring mainly to the excessive use of alcohol and drugs. It was common knowledge that these chemical substances have *psychoactive effects*: they alter the person's mood, cognition, or behavior. We now know that other substances, such as nicotine and caffeine, have psychoactive effects, too—but people are commonly said to be "addicted" also to eating, gambling, buying, and many other things. How shall we define addiction?

ADDICTION AND DEPENDENCE

Addiction is a condition, produced by repeated consumption of a natural or synthetic psychoactive substance, in which the person has become physically and psychologically dependent on the substance (Baker et al., 2004). **Physical dependence** exists when the body has adjusted to a substance and incorporated it into the "normal" functioning of the body's tissues. For instance, the structure and function of brain cells and chemistry change (Torres & Horowitz, 1999). This state has two characteristics:

1. **Tolerance** is the process by which the body increasingly adapts to a substance and requires larger and larger doses of it to achieve the same effect. At some point, these increases reach a plateau.
2. **Withdrawal** refers to unpleasant physical and psychological symptoms people experience when they discontinue or markedly reduce using a substance on which they have become dependent. The symptoms experienced depend on the particular substance used, and can include anxiety, irritability, intense cravings for the substance, hallucinations, nausea, headache, and tremors.

Substances differ in their *potential* for producing physical dependence: the potential is very high for heroin but

appears to be lower for other substances, such as LSD (Baker et al., 2004; NCADI, 2000; Schuster & Kilbey, 1992).

Psychological dependence is a state in which individuals feel compelled to use a substance for the effect it produces, without necessarily being physically dependent on it. Despite knowing that the substance can impair psychological and physical health, they rely heavily on it—often to help them adjust to life and feel good—and spend much time obtaining and using it. Dependence develops through repeated use (Cunningham, 1998). Users who are not physically dependent on a substance experience less tolerance and withdrawal (Schuckit et al., 1999). Being without the substance can elicit *craving*, a motivational state that involves a strong desire for it. Users who become addicted usually become psychologically dependent on the substance first; later they become physically dependent as their bodies develop a tolerance for it. Substances differ in the potential for producing psychological dependence: the potential is high for heroin and cocaine, moderate for marijuana, and lower for LSD (NCADI, 2000; Schuster & Kilbey, 1992).

The terms and definitions used in describing addiction and dependence vary somewhat (Baker et al., 2004). But diagnosing substance dependence and abuse depends on the extent and impact of clear and ongoing use (Kring et al., 2010). Psychiatrists and clinical psychologists diagnose **substance abuse** when dependence is accompanied by at least one of the following:

- Failing to fulfill important obligations, such as in repeatedly neglecting a child or being absent from work.
- Putting oneself or others at repeated risk for physical injury, for instance, by driving while intoxicated.
- Having substance-related legal difficulties, such as being arrested for disorderly conduct.

Psychiatric classifications of disorders now include the pathological use of tobacco, alcohol, and drugs—the substances we'll focus on in this chapter.

PROCESSES LEADING TO DEPENDENCE

Researchers have identified many factors associated with substance use and abuse. In this section, we'll discuss factors that apply to all addictive substances, are described in the main theories of substance dependence, and have been clearly shown to have a role in developing and maintaining dependence.

Reinforcement

We saw in Chapter 5 that reinforcement is a process whereby a consequence strengthens the behavior on which it is contingent. There are two types of reinforcement: positive and negative (Sarafino, 2001). In **positive reinforcement**, the consequence is an event or item the individual finds pleasant or wants that is introduced or *added* after the behavior occurs. For example, many cigarette smokers report that smoking produces a "buzz" or "rush" and feelings of elation, and drinking alcohol increases this effect (Baker, Brandon, & Chassin, 2004; Piasecki et al., 2008). People who experience a buzz from smoking, smoke more than those who don't (Pomerleau et al., 2005). Alcohol and drugs often produce a buzz or rush and other effects. In **negative reinforcement**, the consequence involves *reducing* or *removing* an aversive circumstance, such as pain or unpleasant feelings. For instance, tobacco, alcohol, and drugs relieve stress and other negative emotions at least temporarily (Baker et al., 2004). Positive and negative reinforcement both produce a wanted state of affairs; with substance use, it occurs very soon after the behavior. Thus, dependence and abuse develop partly because users rely increasingly on the substance to regulate their cognitive and emotional states (Holahan et al., 2001; Pomerleau & Pomerleau, 1989).

Avoiding Withdrawal

Because withdrawal symptoms are very unpleasant, people want to avoid them (Baker, Brandon, & Chassin, 2004). People who have used a substance long enough to develop a dependence on it are likely to keep on using it to prevent withdrawal, especially if they have experienced the symptoms. As an example of the symptoms, for people addicted to alcohol, the withdrawal syndrome (called *delirium tremens*, "the DTs") often includes intense anxiety, tremors, and frightening hallucinations when their blood alcohol levels drop (Kring et al., 2010). Each substance has its own set of withdrawal symptoms.

Substance-Related Cues

When people use substances, they associate with that activity the specific internal and environmental stimuli that are regularly present. These stimuli are called *cues*, and they can include the sight and smell of cigarette smoke, the bottle and taste of beer, and the mental images of and equipment involved in taking cocaine. These associations occur by way of **classical conditioning**: a conditioned stimulus—say, the smell of cigarette smoke—comes to elicit a response through association with an unconditioned stimulus, the substance's effect, such as the "buzz" feeling. There may be more than one response, but an important one is craving: for people who are alcohol or nicotine dependent, words related

to the substance or thinking about using it can elicit cravings for a drink or smoke (Erblich, Montgomery, & Bovbjerg, 2009; Tapert et al., 2004).

Evidence now indicates that the role of cues in substance dependence involves physiological mechanisms. Let's look at two lines of evidence. First, learning the cues enables the body to anticipate and compensate for a substance's effects (McDonald & Siegel, 2004). For instance, for a frequent user of alcohol, an initial drink gets the body to prepare for more, which may lead to tolerance; and if an expected amount does not come for a user who is addicted, withdrawal symptoms occur. Second, studies have supported the *incentive-sensitization theory* of addiction, which proposes that a neurotransmitter called *dopamine* enhances the salience of stimuli associated with substance use so that they become increasingly powerful in directing behavior (Robinson & Berridge, 2001, 2003). These powerful cues grab the substance user's attention, arouse the anticipation of the reward gained from using the substance, and compel the person to get and use more of it.

Expectancies

People develop *expectancies*, or ideas about the outcomes of behavior, from their own experiences and from watching other people. Some expectancies are positive; that is, the expected outcome is desirable. For example, we may decide by watching others that drinking alcohol is "fun"—people who are drinking are often boisterous, laughing, and, perhaps celebrating. These people may be family members, friends, and celebrities in movies—all of whom are powerful models. Even before tasting alcohol, children acquire expectancies about the positive effects of alcohol via social learning processes, such as by watching TV shows and advertisements (Dunn & Goldman, 1998; Grube & Wallack, 1994; Scheier & Botvin, 1997). Teenagers also perceive that drinking is "sociable" and "grown up," two things they generally want very much to be. As a result, when teens are offered a drink by their parents or friends, they usually see this as a positive opportunity. Other expectancies are negative—for instance, drinking can lead to a hangover. Similar processes operate for other substances, such as tobacco (Cohen et al., 2002).

Genetics

Heredity influences addiction (Agrawal & Lynskey, 2008). For example, twin studies have shown that identical twins are more similar in cigarette smoking behavior and becoming dependent on tobacco than fraternal twins, and researchers have identified specific genes that are involved in this addictive process (Chen et al., 2009; Lerman & Berrettini, 2003). Also dozens of twin and adoption studies, as well as research with animals, have clearly demonstrated a genetic influence in the development of alcohol problems (Campbell & Oei, 2009; NIAAA, 1993; Saraceno et al., 2009). For instance, twin studies in general have found that if one member of a same-sex twin pair is alcoholic, the risk of the other member being alcoholic is twice as great if the twins are identical rather than fraternal. And specific genes have been identified for this substance, too.

Three other findings on the role of genetics are important. First, the genes that affect smoking are not the same ones that affect drinking (Bierut et al., 2004). Second, although both genetics and social factors, such as peer and family relations, influence substance use, their importance changes with development: substance use is strongly influenced by social factors during adolescence and genetic factors during adulthood (Kendler et al., 2008). Third, high levels of parental involvement with and monitoring of their child can counteract a child's high genetic risk of substance use (Brody et al., 2009; Chen et al., 2009).

If your course has you read the modules from the Appendix, The Body's Physical Systems, distributed to the chapters, read **Module 4** (The Respiratory System) now.

SMOKING TOBACCO

When Columbus explored the Western Hemisphere, he recorded in his journal that the inhabitants would set fire to leaves—rolled up or in pipes—and draw in the smoke through their mouths (Ashton & Stepney, 1982). The leaves these people used were tobacco, of course. Other early explorers tried smoking and, probably because they liked it, took tobacco leaves back to Europe in the early 1500s, where tobacco was used mainly for "medicinal purposes." Smoking for pleasure spread among American colonists and in Europe later in that century. In the 1600s, pipe smoking became popular, and the French introduced *snuff*, powdered tobacco that people consumed chiefly by inserting it in the nose and sniffing strongly. After inventors made a machine for mass-producing cigarettes and growers developed mellower tobacco in the early 1900s for easier inhaling, the popularity of smoking grew rapidly over the next 50 years.

Today there are about 1.25 billion smokers in the world (Shafey et al., 2009). In the United States, cigarette smoking reached its greatest popularity in the mid-1960s, when about 53% of adult males and 34% of adult females smoked regularly (Shopland & Brown, 1985). Before that time, people generally didn't know about the serious health effects of smoking. But in 1964 the Surgeon General issued a report describing these health effects, and warnings against smoking began to appear in the American media and on cigarette packages. Since that time, the prevalence of adult smokers has dropped steadily, and today about 24% of the men and 18% of the women in the United States smoke (NCHS, 2009a).

Teen smoking has also declined: today about 11% of high-school seniors smoke daily (Johnston et al., 2009).

Do these trends mean cigarette manufacturers are on the verge of bankruptcy? Not at all—their profits are still quite high! At the same time that smoking has declined in many industrialized countries, it has increased in developing nations, such as in Asia and Africa (Shafey et al., 2009).

WHO SMOKES AND HOW MUCH?

Although huge numbers of people in the world smoke, most do not. In the United States, the adolescent and adult populations have five times as many nonsmokers as smokers. Are some people more likely to smoke than others?

Age and Gender Differences in Smoking

Smoking varies with age. For example, few Americans begin to smoke regularly before 12 years of age (Johnston et al., 2009), and few people who will ever become regular smokers begin the habit after their early 20s (Thirlaway & Upton, 2009). The habit generally develops gradually over several years. Figure 6-1 shows three patterns about the habit's development. First, many people in a given month smoke infrequently—at less than a daily level. Many of them are trying out the habit, and some will progress to daily and then half a pack or more. Second, this pattern starts in eighth grade (about 13 years) for an alarming number of children and involves more and more teens in later grades. Third, teens in every grade who do not plan to complete 4 years of college are at high risk of trying smoking and progressing to heavy smoking. The percentage of Americans who smoke levels off in

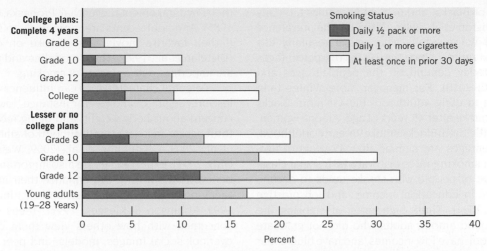

Figure 6-1 Percent of individuals in the United States at different grades or ages with different cigarette smoking statuses, depending on their college plans: either to complete 4 years or to complete less or no college. The survey assessed whether they had smoked in the last 30 days *at least once* or *daily* either at least 1 cigarette or at least half a pack (10 cigarettes). The graph does not separate data for males and females because they are very similar. (Data from Johnston et al., 2009, Tables D–89 through D–97.)

early adulthood and declines after about 35 years of age (USBC, 2010). Many adults are *former* smokers.

Gender differences in smoking are quite large in some parts of the world: about 1 billion men and 250 million women smoke worldwide (Shafey et al., 2009). Among Americans, the prevalence of smoking had always been far greater among males than females before the 1970s (McGinnis, Shopland, & Brown, 1987). But this gender gap has narrowed greatly—for instance, the percentage of high school seniors today who smoke is similar for girls and boys (Johnston et al., 2009). Cigarette advertising targeted at one gender or the other, such as by creating clever brand names and slogans, played a major part in these gender-related shifts in smoking (Pierce & Gilpin, 1995). A slogan designed to induce young females to smoke is:

> "You've come a long way, baby," with its strong but still subtle appeal to the women's liberation movement. The "Virginia Slims" brand name artfully takes advantage of the increasingly well-documented research finding that, for many female (and male) smokers, quitting the habit is associated with gaining weight. (Matarazzo, 1982, p. 6)

Although cigarette advertising still has a strong influence on teens starting to smoke, antismoking advertisements appear to counteract this influence (Gilpin et al., 2007; Murphy-Hoefer, Hyland, & Higbee, 2008). There is an important and hopeful point to keep in mind about the changes that have occurred in smoking behavior: they show that people can be persuaded to avoid or quit smoking.

Sociocultural Differences in Smoking

Large variations in smoking occur across cultures, with far higher rates in developing than in industrialized countries (Shafey et al., 2009). Over 80% of the world's smokers live in developing countries, where it's not unusual for 50% of men to smoke. Table 6.1 gives the percentages of adults who smoke in selected countries around the world.

In the United States, smoking prevalence differs across ethnic groups. Of high school seniors, 14.3% of

Table 6.1 *Prevalence of Adult Cigarette Smoking in Selected Countries: Percentages by Gender and Overall*

Country	Males	Females	Overall
Australia	27.7	21.8	24.8
Brazil[a]	20.3	12.8	na
Canada	24.3	18.9	21.6
China	59.5	3.7	31.8
Germany	37.4	25.8	31.6
India	33.1	3.8	18.6
Italy	32.8	19.2	26.1
Netherlands	38.3	30.3	34.3
Singapore	24.2	3.5	13.7
South Africa	27.5	9.1	18.4
Sweden	19.6	24.5	22.0
Turkey	51.6	19.2	35.5
United Kingdom	36.7	34.7	35.7

Notes: adult = age 15 and older; na = data not available; data from different countries and sources may vary somewhat, reflecting different definitions or survey years.

Sources: WHO, 2009, except [a] Shafey et al., 2009.

Whites, 5.8% of Blacks, and 6.7% of Hispanics are daily smokers (Johnston et al., 2009). Although the prevalence of Black and White adults who smoke regularly has declined substantially since the 1960s, the percentages who smoke today depend on the people's ages and gender (USBC, 2010). For men, far more Whites than Blacks smoke in early adulthood, but far more Blacks than Whites smoke after 45 years of age. Among women, far more Whites than Blacks smoke in early adulthood, but the percentages are similar after 45 years of age. Differences in smoking rates also vary with social class: the percentage of people who smoke tends to decline with increases in education, income, and job prestige class (Adler, 2004). Thus, high rates of smoking are likely to be found among adults who did not graduate from high school, have low incomes, and have blue-collar occupations, such as maintenance work and truck driving.

Although the percentage of Americans who smoke has decreased by about half in the years since the mid-1960s, the effect of these changes on the total number of smokers and cigarettes consumed has been offset by rises in the number of adults in the population and the proportion of smokers who smoke *heavily*, more than a pack a day (McGinnis, Shopland, & Brown, 1987). The people who continued to smoke after the 1960s were the ones who needed to quit the most.

WHY PEOPLE SMOKE

Cigarette smoking is a strange phenomenon in some respects. If you ever tried to smoke, chances are you coughed the first time or two, found the taste unpleasant, and, perhaps, even experienced nausea. This is not the kind of outcome that usually makes people want to try something again. But many teenagers do, even though most teens say that smoking is unhealthy (Johnston et al., 2009). Given these circumstances, we might wonder why people start to smoke and why they continue.

Starting to Smoke

Psychosocial factors provide the primary forces that lead adolescents to begin smoking. For instance, teens who perceive low risk and high benefits in smoking are likely to start the habit (Song et al., 2009). Also, teenagers' social environment is influential in shaping their attitudes, beliefs, and intentions about smoking—for example, they are more likely to begin smoking if their parents and friends smoke (Bricker et al., 2006; O'Loughlin et al., 2009; Robinson & Klesges, 1997; Simons-Morton et al., 2004). Teens who try their first cigarette often do so in the company of peers and with

their encouragement (Leventhal, Prohaska, & Hirschman, 1985). And adolescents are more likely to start smoking if their favorite movie stars smoke on or off screen (Distefan et al., 1999). Thus, modeling and peer pressure are important determinants of smoking.

Personal characteristics can influence whether adolescents begin to smoke—for instance, low self-esteem, concern about body weight, and being rebellious and a thrill-seeker increase the likelihood of smoking (Bricker et al., 2009; O'Loughlin et al., 2009; Weiss, Merrill, & Gritz, 2007). Expectancies are also important. Many teens believe that smoking can enhance their image, making them look mature, glamorous, and exciting (Dinh et al., 1995; Robinson & Klesges, 1997). Teens who are very concerned with how others view them do not easily overlook social images, models, and peer pressure. Do the psychosocial factors we've considered have similar effects with all teens? No, the effects seem to depend on the person's gender and sociocultural background. For example, smoking by peers and family members in America is more closely linked to smoking in girls than boys and in White than Black teens (Flay, Hu, & Richardson, 1998; Robinson & Klesges, 1997). (Go to 💡.)

Becoming a Regular Smoker

There is a rule of thumb about beginning to smoke that seems to have some validity: individuals who smoke their *fourth* cigarette are very likely to become regular smokers (Leventhal & Cleary, 1980). Although the vast majority of youngsters try at least one cigarette, most of them never get to the fourth one and don't go on to smoke regularly. Becoming a habitual smoker usually takes a few years, and the faster the habit develops, the more likely the person will smoke heavily and have trouble quitting (Chassin et al., 2000; Dierker et al., 2008).

Why is it that some people continue smoking after the first tries, and others don't? Part of the answer lies in the types of psychosocial influences that got them to start in the first place. Studies that tested thousands of adolescents in at least two different years have examined whether the teens' social environments and beliefs about smoking were related to changes in their smoking behavior (Bricker et al., 2006, 2009; Chassin et al., 1991; Choi et al., 2002). Smoking tended to continue or increase if the teens:

- Had at least one parent who smoked.
- Perceived their parents as unconcerned or even encouraging about their smoking.
- Had siblings or friends who smoked and socialized with friends very often.

HIGHLIGHT

Do Curiosity and Susceptibility "Kill the Cat?"

Whether or not you've tried smoking, did you at some earlier time feel curious about what smoking is like or make a commitment never to smoke? These two factors affect the likelihood of starting to smoke: the likelihood rises as the teen's curiosity increases and in the absence of a commitment (Pierce et al., 2005). The absence of a commitment never to smoke is called *susceptibility* to smoking. Researchers have examined how susceptibility combines with stages of change—that is, readiness to start smoking—to

affect teenagers' likelihood of becoming smokers in the future (Huang et al., 2005). Figure 6-2 presents the findings: susceptible teenagers are more and more likely to become smokers as their stages advance from precontemplation (not considering smoking) to contemplation (considering smoking) to preparation (intending to smoke). A susceptible teenager at the preparation stage is nearly 10 times more likely to start smoking within a couple of years than a nonsusceptible teen at the precontemplation stage.

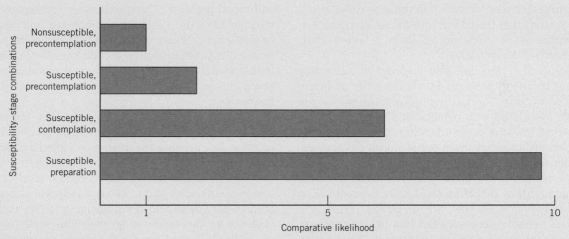

Figure 6-2   Comparative likelihood of nonsmoking teenagers becoming smokers within 2 years, depending on the teens' combination of susceptibility and stage of change. Note that the nonsusceptible, precontemplation combination arbitrarily = 1 in the graph. (Data from Huang et al., 2005, Table 2.)

- Were rebellious, thrill-seekers, and low in school motivation.

- Were receptive to tobacco advertisements, such as by naming a favorite one.

- Felt peer pressure to smoke, for example, reporting, "Others make fun of you if you don't smoke," and, "You have to smoke when you're with friends who smoke."

- Held positive attitudes about smoking, such as, "Smoking is very enjoyable," and, "Smoking can help people when they feel nervous or embarrassed."

- Did not believe smoking would harm their health, for instance, feeling, "Smoking is dangerous only to older people," and, "Smoking is only bad for you if you have been smoking for many years."

- Believed they'd be able to quit smoking if they wanted.

Three other findings are important. First, part of the way smoking by family and friends promotes teenagers' smoking is that it reduces the belief that smoking might harm the teens' own health (Rodriguez, Romer, & Audrain-McGovern, 2007). Second, teenagers usually smoke in the presence of other people, especially peers, and smokers consume more cigarettes when in the company of someone who smokes at a high rate rather than a low rate (Antonuccio & Lichtenstein, 1980; Biglan et al., 1984). Third, feeling negative emotions, such as depression, increases people's smoking (Fucito & Juliano, 2009; McCaffery et al., 2008).

Reinforcement is another important factor in continuing to smoke. For many smokers, the taste of a cigarette provides positive reinforcement for smoking. Research has found that people who feel that the taste of a cigarette is the main reason for smoking smoke less than other smokers when their cigarettes are altered to taste less pleasant (Leventhal & Cleary, 1980). Negative reinforcement maintains smoking when people use the behavior as a means of coping with stress or other unpleasant emotional states (Baker et al., 2004). Smoking is also related to stress: the greater the stress, the more smokers smoke (Wills, 1986). And smokers report less anxiety and greater ability to express their opinions if they smoke during stressful social interactions than if they do not smoke (Gilbert & Spielberger, 1987). But even if smokers perform better and feel more relaxed in stressful situations when they are allowed to smoke than when they are not, they do not necessarily perform better or feel more relaxed than nonsmokers do (Schachter, 1980). Some findings suggest that smoking may reduce stress temporarily, but may increase it in the long run (Parrott, 1999). A study that tested this idea found support for it, but another did not (Orlando, Ellickson, & Jinnett, 2001; Wills, Sandy, & Yeager, 2002).

Biological factors are also involved in sustaining smoking behavior, probably by affecting the addictive effects of nicotine. The fact that adolescent smoking is strongly associated with parental and sibling smoking shows that smoking runs in families. Certainly part of this relationship results from social learning processes. But there are at least three biological routes. First, nicotine passed on by a smoking mother to her baby in pregnancy may make the child more susceptible to nicotine addiction (Kandel, Wu, & Davies, 1994). The second is heredity: genetics affect how likely people are to become smokers, how easily and strongly they become physically dependent on tobacco, and how able they are to quit (Lerman, Caporaso et al., 1999; Pomerleau et al., 1993). Third, researchers have found that an area of the brain, the *insula*, may control the desire to smoke: smokers who suffer a stroke with damage to that area instantly lose their desire to smoke (Naqvi et al., 2007).

The Role of Nicotine

People become physically dependent on tobacco because of the chemical substances their bodies take in when they use it. A person who smokes a pack a day takes more than 50,000 puffs a year, with each puff delivering chemicals into the lungs and bloodstream (Pechacek et al., 1984; USDHHS, 1986b). These chemicals include carbon monoxide, tars, and nicotine. Cigarette smoke has high concentrations of **carbon monoxide**, a gas that is readily absorbed by the bloodstream and rapidly affects the person's physiological functioning, such as by reducing the oxygen-carrying capacity of the blood. **Tars** exist as minute particles, suspended in smoke. Although tars

have important health effects, there is no evidence that they affect the desire to smoke. **Nicotine** is the *addictive chemical* in cigarette smoke and produces rapid and powerful physiological effects. Nicotine dependence does not necessarily take months or years to develop: a study found that some beginning smokers who had smoked infrequently experienced symptoms of dependence, such as craving (O'Loughlin et al., 2003).

Nicotine is a substance that occurs only in tobacco. When people smoke, alveoli in the lungs quickly absorb the nicotine and transmit it to the blood (Pechacek et al., 1984; Baker, Brandon, & Chassin, 2004). In a matter of seconds the blood carries the nicotine to the brain, where it leads to the release of various chemicals that activate both the central and sympathetic nervous systems, which arouse the body, increasing alertness, heart rate, and blood pressure. These and other consequences of nicotine form the basis for the positive and negative reinforcement effects of smoking. Then, while people smoke a cigarette, nicotine accumulates very rapidly in the blood. But it soon decreases through metabolism—in about 2 hours, half of the nicotine inhaled from a cigarette has decayed.

Biological explanations of people's continued cigarette smoking have focused chiefly on the role of nicotine. One prominent explanation, called the **nicotine regulation model**, proposes that established smokers continue to smoke to maintain a certain level of nicotine in their bodies and to avoid withdrawal symptoms. Stanley Schachter and his associates (1977) provided evidence for this model in an ingenious series of studies with adult smokers. In one study, the researchers had subjects smoke low-nicotine cigarettes during one week and high-nicotine cigarettes during another week. As the model predicts, the subjects smoked more low- than high-nicotine cigarettes. This effect was especially strong for heavy smokers, who smoked 25% more of the low- than high-nicotine cigarettes. Consistent with these results, other researchers have found that people who regularly smoke ultralow-nicotine cigarettes do not consume less nicotine than those who smoke other cigarettes—ultralow smokers simply smoke more cigarettes (Maron & Fortmann, 1987).

Although the nicotine regulation model has received research support, there are reasons to think it provides only part of the explanation for people's smoking behavior (Leventhal & Cleary, 1980). One reason is that most people who quit smoking continue to crave it, and many return to smoking, long after all the nicotine is gone from their bodies. Another reason is that some people smoke a few cigarettes a day for years and don't increase their use—that is, they don't show tolerance. These people usually don't experience withdrawal symptoms but absorb as much nicotine from a cigarette as heavier smokers do (Shiffman et al., 1990; Shiffman et al., 1995). Why do these people continue to smoke? Each of the processes of addiction we considered earlier provides a cogent explanation. For instance, nicotine provides powerful reinforcement of smoking behavior soon after the first puff of a cigarette (Baker, Brandon, & Chassin, 2004; McGehee et al., 1995; Ray, Schnoll, & Lerman, 2009).

Researchers today generally recognize that a full explanation of the development and maintenance of smoking behavior involves the interplay of biological, psychological, and social factors (Shadel et al., 2000). An example of this interplay is seen in the finding that among depressed smokers, those with a specific gene rely more on smoking to cope than those without that gene (Lerman et al., 1998).

SMOKING AND HEALTH

"Warning: The Surgeon General has determined that cigarette smoking is dangerous to your health," states a cigarette pack sold in the United States. Current projections for deaths annually from smoking-related illnesses are 6 million in 2010 rising to 8 million by 2030 (Shafey et al., 2009). Smoking reduces people's life expectancy by several years and impairs their quality of life in old age, and these effects worsen with heavier smoking (Strandberg et al., 2008). No other single behavior takes such a toll. To what extent do your odds of dying of lung cancer or heart disease increase if you smoke? Figure 6-3 shows that the odds increase greatly, especially for lung cancer. The more you smoke, the worse your odds become—and if you quit, your odds improve steadily, in about 15 years becoming similar to those of people who never smoked (Godtfredsen et al., 2002; LaCroix et al., 1991). Smoking and, specifically, nicotine also impair immune function (McAllister-Sistilli et al., 1998).

 WEB ANIMATION: The Case of the Worried Smoker

Access: www.wiley.com/go/global/sarafino. This interactive animation describes the symptoms and medical test results of a woman with a smoking-related illness.

Cancer

In the late 1930s, two important studies were done that clearly linked smoking and cancer for the first time (Ashton & Stepney, 1982). One study presented

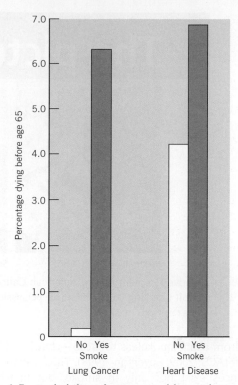

Figure 6–3 Probability of a 35-year-old man dying of lung cancer or heart disease before age 65 as a function of smoking heavily or not smoking. Data for women were less complete, but probably would reveal similar risk increases. (Data from Mattson, Pollack, & Cullen, 1987, p. 427.)

statistics showing that nonsmokers live longer than smokers. In the other study, researchers produced cancer in laboratory animals by administering cigarette tar. By producing cancer with experimental methods, these researchers demonstrated a causal link between cancer and a chemical in tobacco smoke and identified tar as a likely *carcinogen*, a substance that causes cancer. A few decades later the evidence was clear that tobacco tars and probably other byproducts of tobacco smoke cause cancer (Denissenko et al., 1996; USDHHS, 1986b).

Prospective research provides fairly strong evidence for a causal relationship because smokers and nonsmokers are identified and then followed over a long period of time to see if they develop cancer. Many large-scale prospective studies have linked smoking with cancers of various body sites, including the lung, mouth, esophagus, prostate, bladder, and kidney (Huncharek et al., 2010; Levy, 1985; Shopland & Burns, 1993). The last two may result because carcinogenic chemicals in tobacco smoke are absorbed into the blood and conveyed to the urine. Cancers of the mouth and esophagus can also

The pictures say it all.

| Healthy lung | Smoker's lung (cancerous tumor) | Smoker's lung (emphysema) |

An advertisement by the American Cancer Society that may motivate people to avoid starting or to quit smoking. Reprinted by the permission of the American Cancer Society, Inc. from www.cancer.org. All rights reserved.

result from using smokeless tobacco—chewing tobacco or snuff (ACS, 2009; Severson, 1993). Thus, carcinogenic substances exist not only in smoke, but in tobacco itself.

In the 1930s, lung cancer in America was quite uncommon and much less prevalent than many other forms of cancer, such as cancer of the breast, stomach, and prostate (ACS, 2009). Deaths from lung cancer at that time occurred at an annual rate of about 5 per 100,000 people in the population, whereas mortality rates for breast and stomach cancer were more than five times that high. Over the years, the mortality rates for most forms of cancer have either declined or remained fairly constant, but not for lung cancer. The annual death rate for lung cancer rose sharply in the second half of the 20th century per 100,000 Americans—it is now about 54 (USBC, 2010); the corresponding rate in the European Union is nearly 38 (WHO/Europe, 2010). In the UK, the deadliest form of cancer is of the lung, claiming about 35,260 lives in 2008 and being responsible for over three times more deaths than cancer of the rectum, the second-most-deadly form (Cancer Research, 2008).

The correspondence between the rises in lung cancer deaths and in smoking prevalence since the 1930s is quite striking (McGinnis, Shopland, & Brown, 1987; Shopland & Burns, 1993). The rate of mortality from lung cancer began to rise about 15 or 20 years after the rate of smoking started to rise, and these rates have paralleled each other ever since. During this time, the rates of smoking and of lung cancer were higher for males than for females, but since the mid-1960s, important gender-related changes have occurred. Smoking has decreased among men and increased among women, thus narrowing the gender gap—and corresponding changes in incidence rates of lung cancer are now evident: since the mid-1980s, the rates declined steadily for men but rose and leveled off for women (ACS, 2009).

How does smoking harm the lungs? When smoke recurrently passes through the bronchial tubes, the lining of the tubes begins to react to the irritation by increasing the number of cells just below the surface. Then,

> the fine, hairlike growths, or cilia, along the surface of the lining, whose function is to clear the lungs of foreign particles, begin to slow or stop their movement. In time, the cilia may disappear altogether, and as a consequence carcinogenic substances remain in contact with sensitive cells in the lining of the bronchi instead of being removed in the mucus .... At this stage, a *smoker's cough* may develop. It is a feeble attempt by the body to clear the lungs of foreign particles in the absence of functioning cilia. (La Place, 1984, p. 326)

Lung cancer usually originates in the bronchial tubes. In most cases, it probably develops because of the extensive contact of carcinogens with the bronchial lining.

Smoking is a major risk factor for all forms of cancer, but its role is more direct and powerful in lung cancer than in other cancers. People's environments contain many other carcinogens, and smoking is not the only cause of these diseases. (Go to 💡.)

HIGHLIGHT

Does Someone Else's Smoking Affect Your Health?

"What do you mean I can't smoke in this bar! It isn't your business what I do to my body," a patron said indignantly to a bartender. Some smokers have reacted strongly to smoking bans in public places. Why were these regulations introduced?

Excess tobacco smoke goes into the environment, either as *sidestream smoke* from the burning tip of the tobacco item or as exhaled smoke from smokers' bodies. This excess smoke constitutes *secondhand smoke* that others consume (Eriksen, LeMaistre, & Newell, 1988). Breathing secondhand smoke is called **passive smoking**. In the mid-1980s, the United States Surgeon General issued a report on the effects of passive smoking that included three conclusions (USDHHS, 1986b, p.7):

1. Involuntary smoking is a cause of disease, including lung cancer, in nonsmokers.

2. Compared with the children of nonsmoking parents, children of parents who smoke have a higher frequency of respiratory infections, increased respiratory symptoms, and slightly smaller rates of increase in lung function as the lungs mature.

3. The simple separation of smokers and nonsmokers within the same air space may reduce, but does not eliminate, the exposure of nonsmokers to environmental tobacco smoke.

Public places, such as worksites, have high levels of secondhand smoke when smoking is permitted (Hammond et al., 1995). Levels of secondhand smoke can be so high as to produce high nicotine levels in the blood of nonsmokers (Okoli, Kelly, & Hahn, 2007).

Evidence of the harmful effects of secondhand smoke is quite substantial. Studies of nonsmokers whose spouses smoked have generally found that passive smokers' risk of lung cancer increases, sometimes doubling or tripling (Eriksen, LeMaistre, & Newell, 1988; USDHHS, 1986b). Studies have also found a higher risk of cardiovascular disease in nonsmoking spouses of smokers than nonsmokers (Humble et al., 1990), and exposure to secondhand smoke increases atherosclerosis (Howard et al., 1998; Penn & Snyder, 1993). What's more, for people with existing cardiovascular conditions, such as angina, and respiratory problems, such as asthma and hay fever, environmental tobacco smoke can bring on attacks or aggravate acute symptoms (Eriksen, LeMaistre, & Newell, 1988). Increasingly, people are becoming aware of the health effects of secondhand smoke and making efforts to have smoke-free environments.

Cardiovascular Disease

Cardiovascular disease—including coronary heart disease (CHD) and stroke—is the leading cause of death worldwide (WHO, 2009). In the United States, it is responsible for over 34% of all deaths each year and claims more lives than cancer, accidents, and several other causes combined (USBC, 2010). When you point out these facts to smokers, some say, "Well you have to die of *something*." Of course, that's true—but *when* you will die and how disabled you will be before are the real issues. Cardiovascular disease takes many lives early: for instance, one in six Americans it kills are under 65 years of age.

Many millions of Americans suffer from CHD and stroke. The risk of developing CHD is two to four times as high for smokers as for nonsmokers (AHA, 2010). And the more cigarettes people smoke, the greater the risk: a prospective study of smoking and CHD across $8\frac{1}{2}$ years found that the risk of developing heart disease was far higher for individuals who smoked more than a pack a day than those who smoked less (Rosenman et al., 1976). Two other points are important in the

link between smoking and CHD. First, the greater risks smoking conveys for CHD may be aggravated by stress. An experiment tested smokers in a stressful task and found that their stress-hormone and cardiovascular reactivity were higher if they had smoked recently (that is, they had *not* been deprived of smoking) than if they had not smoked for many hours (Robinson & Cinciripini, 2006). Since smoking usually increases when people are under stress, the resulting heightened reactivity raises their CHD risk. Second, smokers tend to have lifestyles that include other risk factors for CHD, such as being physically inactive (Castro et al., 1989).

How does smoking cause cardiovascular disease? The disease process appears to involve several effects that the nicotine and carbon monoxide in cigarette smoke have on cardiovascular functioning (USDHHS, 1986a). Nicotine constricts blood vessels and increases heart rate, cardiac output, and both systolic and diastolic blood pressure. Carbon monoxide reduces the availability of oxygen to the heart, which may cause damage and lead to atherosclerosis. Studies have found that the more cigarettes people smoke per day, the greater their level of serum cholesterol and size of plaques on artery walls (Muscat et al., 1991; Tell et al., 1994). After stopping smoking, cardiovascular risk factors, such as cholesterol levels, improve markedly within 2 months (Eliasson et al., 2001), and the risk of heart attack or stroke declines greatly in the next few years (Kawachi et al., 1993; Negri et al., 1994).

Other Illnesses

Smoking can lead to a variety of other illnesses—particularly emphysema and chronic bronchitis—which are classified together as *chronic obstructive pulmonary disease* (COPD) (ALA, 2010; Haas & Haas, 1990). People with COPD experience permanently reduced airflow, which is especially evident when they try to exhale with force. Over 80% of cases of COPD in the United States are related to smoking (ALA, 2010). As we saw earlier, recurrent smoking irritates and damages respiratory organs. Research has shown that more damage occurs from smoking high-tar than low-tar cigarettes and that regularly smoking nontobacco (marijuana) cigarettes also damages the respiratory system (Bloom et al., 1987; Paoletti et al., 1985). COPD can incapacitate its victims, often forcing relatively young individuals to retire from work. It causes 3 million deaths each year worldwide, particularly among its victims who smoke (WHO, 2010).

Smoking may also increase acute respiratory infections. This has been shown in two ways. First, studies have found that children of smokers are more likely to develop pneumonia than are children of nonsmokers (USDHHS, 1986b). Second, when exposed to common cold viruses, smokers are much more likely to catch cold than nonsmokers, probably because their immune functions are impaired (Cohen et al., 1993).

ALCOHOL USE AND ABUSE

People's use of alcoholic beverages has a very long history, beginning before the eras of ancient Egypt, Greece, and Rome, when using wine and beer was very common. Its popularity continued through the centuries and around the world—except in cultures that strongly prohibited its use, as in Islamic nations—and eventually reached America in the colonial period. Colonial Americans arrived with

> the drinking habits and attitudes of the places they left behind. Liquor was viewed as a panacea; even the Puritan minister Cotton Mather called it "the good creature of God." By all accounts, these people drank, and drank hard. (Critchlow, 1986, p. 752)

But the Puritans also realized that excessive drinking led to problems for society, so they condemned drunkenness as sinful and enforced laws against it.

Over the next two centuries, attitudes about alcohol changed in many cultures. In the United States, the *temperance* movement began in the 18th century and pressed for total abstinence from alcohol. By the mid-1800s, the use of alcohol had diminished sharply and so had its reputation: many Americans at that time believed alcohol destroyed morals and created crime and degenerate behavior (Critchlow, 1986). These attitudes persisted and helped bring about Prohibition, beginning in 1920, when the production, transport, and sale of alcohol became unlawful. After the repeal of Prohibition,

Women in the temperance movement were very assertive, and some went to saloons to keep records of who bought drinks.

the use of alcohol increased, of course, and attitudes about alcohol softened. Americans today believe alcohol has both good and bad effects. (Go to 🍎.)

WHO DRINKS, AND HOW MUCH?

People's attitudes about alcohol and its use are tied to their own characteristics and backgrounds, such as their age, gender, and sociocultural experiences.

Age, Gender, and Alcohol Use

Age and gender affect people's experience with drinking alcoholic beverages in most societies. One reason for gender differences in drinking is that females on average experience more intoxication than males from the same amount of alcohol. This is because, even when body size is the same, females metabolize alcohol less quickly than males (Tortora & Derrickson, 2009).

Drinking typically begins in adolescence, and sometimes in childhood. In a survey of thousands of students across the United States, high school seniors' answers indicated that 72% had consumed an alcoholic drink at some time in their lives, 43% had a drink in the last month, 46% had been drunk in the past year, and 25% had drunk five or more drinks in a row in the preceding 2 weeks (Johnston et al., 2009). Males reported more drinking than females. About 32% of eighth graders claimed they'd had a drink in the past year. Although young people sometimes have alcohol at home with the

parents present, such as at special occasions, most teenage drinking occurs in different circumstances. Even when it is illegal for high school and college students to purchase alcohol and to drink without parental supervision, many do anyway. In adulthood, more males than females continue to drink (NCHS, 2009a). Although most young adult and middle-aged Americans drink, the prevalence is much lower in older groups.

Sociocultural Differences in Using Alcohol

Alcohol use varies widely across cultures around the world. Per capita, Americans each year consume 2.3 gallons (9.77 liters) of ethanol—the alcohol in beer, wine, and spirits (NIAAA, 2009). Table 6.2 compares several countries on the amount of alcohol consumed per person and alcohol-related traffic accidents. Traditionally, countries were classified into two types of alcohol use: those that integrate alcohol into daily life, as in serving it with meals in Italy and France, and those that restrict its use, such as the United States and Scandinavian nations (Bloomfield et al., 2005). Daily drinking occurred more in the former, and intoxication in the latter. But these distinctions are disappearing.

In the United States, drinking patterns differ among its many ethnic groups. The percentage of adults who drink is higher for Whites than for other ethnic groups: Black, Hispanic, Asian, and Native Americans (NCHS, 2009b). And the percentage of adults who sometimes drink several drinks in a day is much higher for White,

---

ASSESS YOURSELF

What's True about Drinking?

Put a check mark in the space preceding each of the following statements you think is true.

_____ Alcohol is a stimulant that energizes the body.

_____ Having a few drinks enhances people's performance during sex.

_____ After drinking heavily, people usually sober up a lot when they need to, such as to drive home.

_____ Most people drive better after having a few beers to relax them.

_____ Drinking coffee, taking a cold shower, and getting fresh air help someone who is drunk to sober up.

_____ People are more likely to get drunk if they switch drinks, such as from wine to beer, during an

evening rather than sticking with the same kind of drink.

_____ 1.5 litres of beer won't make someone as tipsy as four mixed drinks, such as highballs.

_____ People seldom get drunk if they have a full meal before drinking heavily.

_____ People can cure a hangover by any of several methods.

_____ Most people with drinking problems are either "skid row bums" or over 50 years of age.

Which statements did you think were true? They are wrong—all of the statements are false. (Based on *Drinking Myths* distributed by the U.S. Jaycees.)

Table 6.2 *Per Capita Pure Alcohol (Ethanol) Consumption Annually and Alcohol-Related Traffic Accident Rate (per 100,000 Accidents) in Selected Countries*

Country	Consumption in Liters per Capita Ages 15 and Over[a]	Alcohol-Related Traffic Accident Rate[b]
Australia	9.02	na
Brazil	5.76	na
Canada	7.80	na
China	5.20	na
Germany	11.99	29.4
India	0.29	na
Italy	8.02	5.1
Netherlands	9.68	12.8
Singapore	2.17	na
South Africa	6.72	na
Sweden	5.96	11.7
Turkey	1.37	28.2
United Kingdom	11.75	18.8

Note: The amount of pure alcohol per liter varies with the beverage: beer, wine, or spirits; na = data not available.
Sources:[a] WHO, 2009, [b] WHO/Europe, 2010.

Hispanic, and Native Americans than for Black and Asian Americans. Some years ago, the percentage of adults who drank several drinks in a day was far higher for Native Americans than for all other groups, but their drinking has moderated.

Problem Drinking

Figure 6-4 shows that nearly 64% of Americans age 18 and older drink alcohol at least occasionally. Most of these people are light-to-moderate drinkers, consuming fewer than, say, 60 drinks a month. Many people drink much more heavily, but not all of them meet the criteria for substance abuse we described earlier. One definition of *heavy drinking* is engaging in **binge drinking**—that is, consuming five or more drinks on a single occasion at least once in a 30-day period. Using this definition, the percentage of American current drinkers who drink heavily at least occasionally is about 10% for teenagers, 42% for 18- to 25-year-olds, and 22% for adults over 25 (USBC, 2010). In comparison, of European 15- and 16-year-olds, 43% reported having engaged in binge drinking in the past month, and 39% said they had been drunk in the past year (ESPAD, 2009). The next step toward alcohol abuse, called *heavy use drinking*, involves binge drinking five or more times in a month (Kring et al., 2010). Binge and heavy use drinking occur at very high levels on college campuses, especially among fraternity and sorority members (Courtney & Polich, 2009; SAMHSA, 2008). Of individuals who develop problems associated with drinking, most—but not all—do so within about 5 years of starting to drink regularly (Sarason & Sarason, 1984).

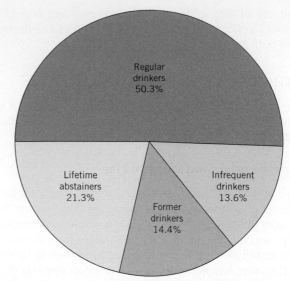

Figure 6–4 Proportions of American adults with four drinking statuses: regular drinkers (12 or more drinks in the past year), infrequent drinkers (more than 1, but fewer than 12 drinks, past year), former drinkers (no drinks, past year), and lifetime abstainers (fewer than 12 drinks ever). (Data from NCHS, 2009b, Table 27.)

How many drinkers meet the criteria for substance abuse? Estimates have been made on the basis of the proportion of individuals at a given time who had ever displayed the problem. This statistic, called the *lifetime prevalence rate*, indicates that over 17% of adults in the United States become alcohol abusers (Kring et al., 2010). People who abuse alcohol—or **problem drinkers**—drink heavily on a regular basis and suffer social and occupational impairments from it. Many of them frequently get drunk, drink alone or during the day, and drive under the influence. Although alcohol abuse is more common in males than females, it is most likely to develop between the ages of 18 and 25 for both sexes (McCrady, 1988; NIAAA, 2006). More than half of those who abuse alcohol are physically dependent on it, or addicted to it, and are classified as **alcoholics**. These people have developed a very high tolerance for alcohol and often have blackout periods or substantial memory losses; many experience delirium tremens when they stop drinking. Although alcoholics often drink the equivalent of a fifth of whiskey (about 0.7 litres) a day, 0.2 litres can sometimes be sufficient to produce addiction in humans (Davidson, 1985).

Who abuses alcohol? Many people have an image of the "typical" alcoholic as a scruffy looking, unemployed male derelict with no family or friends. But this image is valid for only a small minority of people who abuse alcohol (Mayer, 1983; McCrady, 1988; NIAAA, 2006).

Drinking and celebrating often occur together, and this association conveys the message that drinking is fun.

Most problem drinkers are married, living with their families, and employed—and many are women. Although individuals from the lower social classes, especially homeless people, are at greater risk than those from higher classes for abusing alcohol, large numbers of problem drinkers come from the higher classes and hold high-status jobs. Problem drinking is very rare in childhood; its prevalence increases in adolescence, rises sharply in early adulthood, and gradually declines across ages thereafter (NIAAA, 2006). Alcohol abuse is a major social problem that affects substantial numbers of people from almost all segments of many societies around the world. (Go to 🍎.)

WHY PEOPLE USE AND ABUSE ALCOHOL

In examining why people use and abuse alcohol, we need to consider why individuals start to drink in the first place.

The chief reasons for starting to drink involve social and cultural factors, particularly the expectancies that form from watching other individuals enjoying themselves while drinking (Thirlaway & Upton, 2009; Wood, Vinson, & Sher, 2001). For example, the more teens see alcohol scenes in movies and ads on TV, the more they are likely to drink in the future (Dal Cin et al., 2009; Stacy et al., 2004). Underage drinking is more likely among teens who have high feelings of depression, believe their friends drink a lot, have low school grades, and have parents who drink and provide little monitoring or rules against drinking (Fang, Schinke, & Cole, 2009). Children who are depressed, abused, or neglected are at risk for drinking heavily in adolescence and adulthood (Crum et al., 2008; Shin, Edwards, & Heeren, 2009).

Adolescents continue drinking partly for the same reasons they started, but these factors intensify, and new ones come into play. For one thing, the role of peers increases. Although teenagers often begin occasional drinking under their parents' supervision, such as at celebrations, drinking increases with peers at parties or in cars. Figure 6-5 shows that the percentage of American adolescents who claim to have been drunk in the past month increases with year in school, and is higher for teens who do not plan to complete 4 years of college than for those who do. Individuals who start to drink on a regular basis in early adolescence are at heightened risk of drinking heavily in adulthood (Pitkänen, Lyyra, & Pulkkinen, 2005). In late adolescence and early adulthood, drinkers drink frequently and almost always socially, with friends at parties or in bars. The social aspect is important in two ways (McCarty, 1985; Thirlaway & Upton, 2009). First, in social drinking, modeling processes affect behavior—for

---

ASSESS YOURSELF

Do You Abuse Alcohol?

Ask yourself the following questions about your drinking:

- Do you usually have more than 14 drinks a week (assume a drink is one mixed drink with 35 ml of alcohol, 0.3 litres of beer, or the equivalent)?
- Do you often think about how or when you are going to drink again?
- Is your job or academic performance suffering from your drinking?
- Has your health declined since you started drinking a lot?

- Do family or friends mention your drinking to you?
- Do you sometimes stop and start drinking to "test" yourself?
- Have you been stopped for drunk driving in the past year?

If you answered "yes" to the first question, consider changing your drinking pattern. If you answered "yes" to any additional questions, consult your college's counseling office for their advice or help. (Based on TSC, 1992, and USDHHS, 1995.)

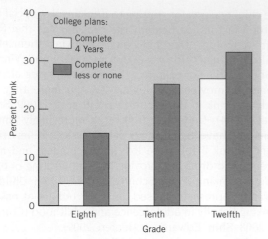

Figure 6-5 Percent of American adolescents at different grades in school who claimed to have been drunk at least once in the past month, depending on their college plans: either to complete 4 years or to complete less or no college. The graph does not separate data for males and females because they are fairly similar. (Data from Johnston et al., 2009, Tables D–68 to D–70.)

example, people tend to adjust their drinking rates to match those of their companions. Second, drinking socially creates a subjective norm in individuals that the behavior is appropriate and desirable.

With continued drinking, the strength of the behavior increases through positive and negative reinforcement, and substance-related cues develop (Baker, Brandon, & Chassin, 2004; Cunningham, 1998; Thirlaway & Upton, 2009). Individuals may receive *positive* reinforcement for drinking if they like the taste of a drink or the feeling they get from it, or if they think they succeeded in business deals or social relationships as a consequence of drinking. Having reinforcing experiences with drinking increases their expectancies for desirable consequences when deciding to drink in the future (Adesso, 1985; Stacy, 1997). In the case of *negative* reinforcement—that is, the reduction of an unpleasant situation—we've seen that people often use alcohol to reduce stress and unpleasant emotions. They may, for instance, drink to suppress their negative thoughts or feelings of anxiety in social situations (Gilles, Turk, & Fresco, 2006; Zack et al., 2006). But the effects of alcohol on negative emotions are not so simple. Although drinkers report that alcohol reduces tension and improves their mood, it seems to do so only with the first few drinks they consume in a series. After people consume many drinks, their anxiety and depression levels usually increase (Adesso, 1985; Davidson, 1985; Hull & Bond, 1986). In cases of severe trauma, such as witnessing terrorism, alcohol use may be heightened for a couple of years (DiMaggio, Galea, & Li, 2009).

Why can most people drink in moderation, but others become problem drinkers? We'll consider four psychosocial differences between these people. First, compared to individuals who do not abuse alcohol, those who do are more likely to perceive fewer negative consequences for drinking (Hansen, Raynor, & Wolkenstein, 1991). Second, heavy drinkers tend to experience high levels of stress and live in environments that encourage drinking. For instance, adolescents who abuse alcohol are more likely to have experienced a major trauma, such as physical assault, and have family members who drink heavily (Kilpatrick et al., 2000). Third, heavy drinkers may form particularly strong substance-related cues: they develop heightened physiological reactions and positive feelings to alcohol-related stimuli, such as seeing or smelling liquor, especially when alcohol is available (Turkkan, McCaul, & Stitzer, 1989). Fourth, people who drink in moderation are more likely to use alcohol control strategies, such as avoiding situations where heavy drinking is likely (Sugarman & Carey, 2007).

But a complete answer to why people become problem drinkers also includes developmental and biological factors. For instance,

- Heredity plays a much stronger role when the abuse begins before age 25 than after (Kranzler & Anton, 1994).
- People with a family history of alcoholism appear to develop a tolerance to alcohol, drinking increasing amounts to feel the same effects, more readily than other people (Morzorati et al., 2002).
- People with a specific gene pattern experience stronger cravings for alcohol after having a drink than other individuals do (Hutchinson et al., 2002).
- Some evidence suggests that people at high genetic risk for alcohol dependence find alcohol more rewarding each time they drink, but low-risk people do not (Newlin & Thompson, 1991).

Genetic factors seem to combine with psychosocial processes, especially conditioning, in the development of drinking problems. (Go to 💡.)

DRINKING AND HEALTH

Drinking too much is linked to a wide range of health hazards for the drinker and for people he or she may harm. Drinkers can harm others in several ways. Pregnant women who drink more than two drinks a day place their babies at substantial risk for health problems, such as being born with low birth weight or *fetal alcohol syndrome*, which involves impaired nervous system development and cognitive and physical defects (Gray, Mukherjee, & Rutter, 2009; Wood, Vinson, & Sher, 2001). Drinking

HIGHLIGHT

Drinking—Games People Play

"Hey, let's play *Kings, Queens*," said Julie, holding up a deck of playing cards at a party. She was referring to one of many *drinking games*; in this one, the players assign rules for the amount and type of alcoholic beverage they will drink when specific cards are played. The beverage can be hard liquor or soft, such as beer. Some drinking games involve team competition or chugging (drinking a full container without pausing). Drinking games are very popular at university and college campuses and lead some students to consume seven or more drinks and become quite intoxicated while playing (Zamboanga et al., 2006). Some students play these games weekly and drink at levels that suggest substance abuse.

lesser amounts during pregnancy has been associated with impaired learning ability in the child. The safest advice to pregnant women is *not to drink at all*.

Drinking also increases the chance that individuals will harm themselves and others through accidents of various types, such as from unintentionally firing a gun to having a mishap while boating or skiing (Taylor et al., 2008; Wood, Vinson, & Sher, 2001). Drink driving is a major cause of death in the United States: over 17,600 traffic deaths each year are associated with alcohol use (NHTSA, 2008). Consuming alcohol impairs cognitive, perceptual, and motor performance for several hours, particularly the first 2 or 3 hours after drinks are consumed. The degree of impairment people experience can vary widely from one person to the next and depends on the rate of drinking and the person's weight. Figure 6-6 gives the *average* impairment for driving—but for some individuals, one or two drinks may be too many to drive safely.

People's judging how many drinks they can have before engaging in a dangerous activity can be difficult for a couple of reasons. First, many people have misconceptions about the effects of alcohol, such as believing that drinking on a full stomach prevents drunkenness, or thinking, "I'll be OK as soon as I get behind the wheel." A study found that students underestimated the impact that alcohol has 2 or 3 hours after drinking, thought that later drinks in a series have less impact than the first couple, and downplayed the effects of beer and wine relative to mixed drinks (Jaccard & Turrisi, 1987). Second, people tend to "super-size" a drink they make for themselves, and still count it as "a single drink," especially if the glass is large (White et al., 2003). So if we try to gauge how intoxicated we're becoming by counting drinks, we may underestimate the effect.

Long-term, heavy drinkers are at risk for developing several health problems (Thirlaway & Upton, 2009; Wood, Vinson, & Sher, 2001). One of the main risks is for a disease of the liver called *cirrhosis*. Heavy drinking over a long period can cause liver cells to die off and be replaced by permanent, nonfunctional scar tissue. When this scar tissue becomes extensive, the liver is less able to cleanse the blood and regulate its composition. Heavy drinking also presents other health risks: it has been linked to the development of some forms of *cancer, high blood pressure,*

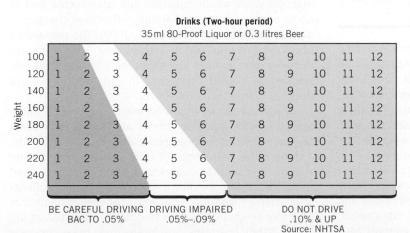

Figure 6-6 Chart developed by the National Highway Traffic Safety Administration (NHTSA) showing the *average* effects of blood alcohol concentration (BAC) on driving. Although alcohol impairment varies from one person to the next, three drinks (the equivalent of about one litre of beer) in a 2-hour period will make most adults' driving unsafe.

and *heart* and *brain damage*. Let's look at two of these. First, the more alcohol people consume over years, the higher their blood pressure becomes (Taylor et al., 2009). Second, the brain damage in heavy drinkers occurs in several structures of the central nervous system and can impair their perceptual and memory functions (Anstey et al., 2006; Parsons, 1986). These functions may recover gradually after the person stops drinking, but some impairments may persist for years or never disappear. As you might expect, long-term heavy drinkers have higher death rates than do other people (Schutte et al., 2003; Thun et al., 1997). But if they quit, their mortality risk declines greatly in several years.

Some people believe that drinking in moderation—having, say, a drink or two each day—is *good* for their health, and they may be right. Long-term prospective studies of many thousands of people have found that individuals who drink light or moderate amounts of alcohol, especially wine, each month have lower morbidity and mortality rates than those who drink heavily or who do not drink at all (Grønbæk et al., 2000; Sacco et al., 1999; Thun et al., 1997). Does moderate drinking *cause* better health? It appears that it does, largely by yielding substantial improvements in cardiovascular risk factors, such as blood cholesterol levels (Mukamal & Rimm, 2001). Although all types of alcohol, consumed as one or two drinks a day, can improve health, wine appears to have the strongest effects because of substances it contains (Corder et al., 2001; Klatsky et al., 2003; Stein et al., 1999). Another reason for the health benefits of moderate drinking is that alcohol affects the body's response to stress, reducing cardiovascular and endocrine (for example, catecholamine production) reactions (Levenson, 1986). But as we've seen, larger amounts of alcohol can impair health.

DRUG USE AND ABUSE

The word "drug" can refer to many substances, including illegal chemicals and prescription and nonprescription medicine, that people may take into their bodies. We will limit the term *drug* to mean psychoactive substances other than nicotine and alcohol that can cause physical or psychological dependence. Like smoking and drinking, the use of drugs has a long history—for example, the Chinese evidently used marijuana 27 centuries B.C. In the United States, addiction to narcotics was widespread among people of all ages in the 19th century. Many "patent medicines" in those days contained opium and were sold without government regulation. As a result, large numbers of people became addicted at early ages

(Kett, 1977). Laws were enacted in the early 1900s against the use of narcotics in America. (Go to 💡.)

WHO USES DRUGS, AND WHY?

Drug use has become a serious problem in many countries of the world, especially in North America and Europe, but its worldwide prevalence is very low (Thirlaway & Upton, 2009). In societies where drugs are a problem, certain individuals and segments are more likely than others to use drugs.

Age, Gender, and Sociocultural Differences in Drug Use

We have seen that smoking and drinking are more likely to begin in adolescence than at any other time in the life span. This developmental pattern is true for using most drugs, too. Three types of drugs that are exceptions to this pattern are tranquilizers, barbiturates, and painkillers (such as OxyContin): use commonly begins in adulthood, often with prescriptions from doctors (AMA, 2003; Kring et al., 2010).

One of the most popular drugs in the world is marijuana. In the United States, the percentages of people aged 12 and older who have used it in their lifetimes and abused it in a given year are about three times as high as for any other drug (NCADI, 2006). Using marijuana often begins by the eighth grade, and nearly 43% of American teenagers try it before they graduate from high school (Johnston et al., 2009). Teenagers' use of most other drugs tends to begin somewhat later and is much less prevalent—for instance, about 7% try cocaine before graduation. In comparison, of European 15- and 16-year-olds, 19% had tried marijuana and 7% had tried some other drug (ESPAD, 2009). Drug use in the United States has fluctuated over time and has been decreasing in recent years, which coincides with adolescents' beliefs about whether drugs are harmful, rather than changes in drug availability (Johnston et al., 2009). The prevalence of adolescent drug use in a given month is far greater in males than females and increases with age. Drug use reaches its highest prevalence in early adulthood and declines thereafter (USBC, 2010).

Table 6.3 shows that drug use in the United States increases with grade in school and varies depending on the students' college plans and race or ethnicity. Although the prevalence of drug use is lower among seniors who plan to complete 4 years of college than those who do not, the drug use of college-bound students after leaving high school catches up or even exceeds that of students who do not go to college (Johnston et al., 2009). Ethnic patterns are interesting: marijuana use

HIGHLIGHT

Types and Effects of Drugs

"Oh, I feel so light, like a feather," said Dolores, after taking several hits from a "joint." That lightness of feeling is a common effect people get from smoking a marijuana cigarette. Each drug has its own set of general psychological and physiological effects (Kring et al., 2010; NCADI, 2000; Schuster & Kilbey, 1992). Some drugs are highly addictive, and others have little potential for producing physical dependence. Drugs are usually classified into four categories: stimulants, depressants, hallucinogens, and narcotics.

Stimulants are chemicals that produce physiological and psychological arousal, keeping the user awake and making the world seem to race by. This category of drugs includes *amphetamines*, *caffeine*, and *cocaine*, which can be inhaled, injected, or smoked ("crack"). Chronic use of stimulants can produce mental confusion, exhaustion, and weight loss; it can lead to psychological and physical dependence. Withdrawal symptoms for stimulants are often subtle, but are still very influential on behavior.

Depressants decrease arousal and increase relaxation. People use these drugs to reduce anxiety and induce sleep. Depressants include various *tranquilizers* (such as Valium) and *barbiturates*, which are commonly called "downers." Chronic, heavy use of depressants interferes with motor and emotional stability and produces psychological dependence. Addiction can develop with long-term use of depressants and can occur rapidly for barbiturates.

Hallucinogens produce perceptual distortions, such as when the body or mind feels light. The most commonly used drug of this type is *marijuana*, which people use for the relaxation and intoxication it causes. Other hallucinogens, such as *mescaline*, LSD (lysergic acid diethylamide), and PCP (phencyclidine), often produce a feeling of exhilaration. Hallucinogens have a relatively low potential for causing physical dependence, but chronic use of these drugs can lead to psychological dependence.

Narcotics or *opiates* are sedatives that relieve pain. In many people, but not all, they produce a euphoric and relaxed feeling. The narcotics include *morphine*, *codeine*, and *heroin*. These drugs, especially heroin, generally cause intense physical *and* psychological dependence when used in large doses continually.

The effects of drugs can vary. The same dose of a drug from the same batch may produce quite different reactions in different people and in the same person on different occasions (Bardo & Risner, 1985). Why? Physiological processes, such as metabolism and absorption by tissues, vary from one person to the next and within each individual over time. People with low metabolism rates, such as the elderly, tend to experience relatively strong reactions to drugs. Stress can also influence a drug's effects, causing physiological changes that may increase its impact.

is similar for White, Black, and Hispanic students, but Black teens report less use of other drugs. Black- and Hispanic-American drug use appears to depend on two factors (Szapocznik et al., 2007). First, minority teens are less likely to use drugs if they have a strong racial or ethnic identity. Second, Hispanic teens become more likely to use drugs after they have lived in the United States a long time and become acculturated.

Many individuals engage in *polysubstance use*—that is, using more than one substance. Does using one substance affect the use of another? The likelihood that individuals will progress from a less serious drug, such as marijuana, to a more serious drug, such as cocaine, is related to how heavily the earlier drug was used (Kandel & Faust, 1975; Newcomb & Bentler, 1986). Heavy users of a less serious drug are more likely to begin using more serious drugs than light users are. Similarly, smoking cigarettes and using alcohol have been linked to subsequent drug use (Pérez et al., 2010; Petraitis et al.,

1998). What's more, for people who use marijuana and alcohol at least twice a week, the more they drink, the greater their risk of becoming dependent on marijuana (Smucker-Barnwell, Earleywine, & Gordis, 2006).

Why Adolescents Use Drugs

Why do teens use marijuana and other drugs? They do so for many of the same reasons they drink or smoke cigarettes (Hansen et al., 1987; Stein, Newcomb, & Bentler, 1987). Genetic, psychosocial, and environmental factors are involved (Gillespie et al., 2009). If drugs are available, drug use is linked to social factors and certain personality traits, such as high levels of thrill seeking (Newcomb, Maddahian, & Bentler, 1986). Many teens see peers and important adults, such as parents and celebrities, model behaviors and positive attitudes for drug use, which encourages them to try drugs. Studies have shown that adolescents are more likely to use

Table 6.3 *Percentage of American Students Using Illicit Drugs in a Given Month by Grade in School, College Plans, and Race or Ethnicity*

Student characteristic	Any Drug Except Marijuana		Marijuana	
	Grade 8	Grade	Grade 8	Grade 12
College plans				
Complete 4 years	3.1	8.1	4.5	17.7
Under 4 years or none	11.4	13.1	19.1	24.9
Race or ethnicity				
White	3.7	11.0	5.0	20.1
Black	1.8	3.4	6.1	16.3
Hispanic	4.5	6.7	7.1	15.3

Note: These data come from the annual *Monitoring the Future* survey, which tested about 16,800 eighth-graders and 14,700 twelfth-graders; the data do not reflect individuals who dropped out of school.

Source: Johnston et al., 2009, Table 4.7.

marijuana and other drugs if their family and friends use mood-altering substances, such as alcohol and marijuana (Petraitis et al., 1998; Gillespie et al., 2009). Teenagers' marijuana use seems to be affected more by their friends' than their parents' substance use, and the first introduction of most youths to marijuana is through a friend (Kandel, 1974).

After people try using a drug, they tend to continue if they like the experience—that is, if the drug makes them "feel good" or helps them feel *better* than they felt before taking it (Barrett, 1985). Many people claim that taking drugs reduces their anxiety and tension. In other words, drugs have reinforcing effects. Then, with continued use, drug-related cues become conditioned to the drug, can elicit effects like those the drug itself produces, and compel the user to use it again (Childress, 1996; Robinson & Berridge, 2003). Because people often use drugs in the presence of friends and other peers, social pressure and encouragement also tend to maintain and increase drug use.

Why do some individuals progress from drug use to drug *abuse*? One factor is personality. Compared to individuals who use drugs occasionally, those who go on to abuse drugs tend to be *more* rebellious, impulsive, accepting of illegal behavior, and oriented toward thrill seeking; and they tend to be *less* socially conforming and less committed to a religion (Brook et al., 1986; Cox, 1985; Newcomb, Maddahian, & Bentler, 1986; Stein, Newcomb, & Bentler, 1987). Social factors are also important: heavy users of a drug, such as marijuana, report having friends and relatives who use substances (Scherrer et al., 2008).

DRUG USE AND HEALTH

The effects of drug use and abuse on people's health are not as well documented as those of drinking and cigarette smoking. This is because drug use did not become widespread until the 1960s, it is still much less prevalent than drinking and smoking, and many drug users are unwilling to admit to researchers that they use drugs—a criminal offense—for fear of being prosecuted. Nevertheless, some health effects are known. For example, drugs taken by women during pregnancy cross the placenta and may harm the fetus; and babies born to addicted mothers are likely to be addicted, too (Cook, Petersen, & Moore, 1990). Also, each year millions of teens and young adults drive under the influence of drugs (SAMHSA, 2008; Terry & Wright, 2005). What's more, long-term marijuana smoking is linked to damage to the user's lungs that is similar to that caused by tobacco smoking (Bloom et al., 1987; Moore et al., 2005).

The harmful effects of cocaine and methamphetamine on the cardiovascular system are becoming clear (AMA, 2003; Kaye et al., 2007; Mittleman et al., 1999). Using these drugs can cause the person's blood vessels to constrict, heart rate to speed up, and blood pressure to increase suddenly. They can also trigger cardiac arrhythmia. These events can lead to a stroke or myocardial infarction and can cause death. Cocaine also produces many other health problems. For example, the more people use it in their mid-20s, the more likely they will have neurological symptoms and poor general health 10 years later (Chen, Scheier, & Kandel, 1996). Also, poor health leads to continued cocaine use.

REDUCING SUBSTANCE USE AND ABUSE

How can we help prevent people from using or abusing substances and help them stop using tobacco, alcohol, and drugs if they start?

PREVENTING SUBSTANCE USE

The focus for prevention is on helping people avoid beginning to use specific substances in the first place. To do this effectively, prevention programs must consider two factors: *when* and *why* individuals start to use the substances, and the information we've already discussed on these issues can be applied. The first factor is straightforward and easily addressed. Because tobacco, alcohol, and drug use often begins during the junior high school years and increases sharply in the high school years, prevention programs should begin early, usually before children reach the age of 12 or so (Evans, 1984). To address

A demonstration against the use of drugs.

Interventions years ago to prevent substance use usually focused on only one substance, but programs today recognize that beginning to use tobacco, alcohol, and drugs happens mainly during adolescence and for similar reasons. As a result, many programs now try to address all three substances. A program of this type that does *not* seem to work is the widely publicized Project DARE, in which police officers lead sessions in school to prevent substance use (Lynam et al., 1999). The most common and effective prevention approaches have had three focuses: public policy and legal issues, health promotion and education, and family involvement; the last two are implemented by professionals trained in preventing substance use.

Public Policy and Legal Approaches

Governments apply public policy and legal approaches to reduce per-capita consumption of tobacco, alcohol, and drugs by creating barriers to buying and using them. For tobacco, effective approaches include increasing the price of cigarettes through taxation and restricting the advertisement and purchase of cigarettes, such as by underage adolescents (Altman et al., 1999; Cummings, Fong, & Borland, 2009). For alcohol, two methods are effective: increasing the price of alcoholic beverages through taxation and prohibiting underage persons from buying or consuming alcohol (Ashley & Rankin, 1988; Thirlaway & Upton, 2009). These methods reduce alcohol consumption and related automobile accidents among individuals in the late adolescent and early adulthood years. Another approach has not been very effective in reducing drinking: limiting the number of outlets where alcoholic beverages can be bought and restricting the times when they are on sale. For preventing drug use, the main approaches have been to outlaw possessing, selling, and consuming drugs.

Health Promotion and Education

Programs to prevent substance use focused originally on giving fear-arousing warnings of the health consequences of smoking, drinking, and using drugs (Evans, 1984). These programs did not take into account the past social experiences and current psychosocial forces that have a strong influence on teenage behavior. Although knowing the health consequences can change children's beliefs and attitudes about a substance, such as tobacco, it is usually not sufficient to stop them from starting to use it (Bruvold, 1993; Larimer & Cronce, 2007). This failure points out the need for prevention programs to address *why* youth begin to use substances.

As we saw earlier, researchers have identified several psychosocial reasons why young people start using

why people start using substances, programs usually try to combat psychosocial factors that encourage use.

Another risky time for youth to start or increase substance use is at college, particularly if they join a fraternity or sorority. A 3-year longitudinal study monitored the substance use of nearly 5,900 American high school seniors who went to college, with 17% joining a fraternity or sorority (McCabe et al., 2005). Before entering college, the prevalence of using tobacco, alcohol, and marijuana and of engaging in binge drinking was far higher among students who later joined a fraternity or sorority than those that did not. After entering college, substance use increased for those that did and did not join a fraternity or sorority, but the increase was much greater for those who joined. Binge drinking in a given 2-week period was reported by about 70% of fraternity members and 42% of male nonmembers, and about 50% of sorority members and 29% of female nonmembers. These findings suggest that colleges need to increase prevention efforts for all students, with particular focus on those who want to join or are already members of a fraternity or sorority.

tobacco, alcohol, and drugs. Personality and social influences appear to have stronger effects on adolescents' substance use than long-range health consequences that seem remote, both in time and in likelihood. Researchers recognized this and implemented school-based programs to curb teenage substance use by addressing psychosocial factors. Let's consider two types of interventions to prevent smoking for examples of useful methods:

- *Social influence approaches* focus on training skills to help individuals resist social pressures to smoke. They include (1) discussions and films regarding how peers, family members, and the media influence smoking; (2) modeling and role-playing of specific refusal skills, such as saying, "No thank you, I don't smoke"; and (3) having each student decide his or her intention regarding whether to smoke and announce that decision publicly to classmates (Flay et al., 1985).

- *Life skills training approaches* address general social, cognitive, and coping skills. Because many teens who begin smoking seem to lack these skills, this approach focuses on improving (1) personal skills, including critical thinking for making decisions, techniques for coping with anxiety, and basic principles for changing their own behavior; and (2) general social skills, including methods for being assertive and making conversation (Botvin & Wills, 1985).

Studies have tested these approaches for smoking prevention, usually with children in sixth or seventh grade (about age 12) and with follow-up assessments spanning 2 years or longer. The students' self-reports of smoking were usually verified, using biochemical analyses of saliva or breath samples.

Were these approaches successful? Compared with the control subjects, children who received each type of program were far less likely to begin to smoke during the next couple of years or so (Botvin & Wills, 1985; Bruvold, 1993; Flay et al., 1985; Murray et al., 1988; Sussman & Skara, 2004). Longer-term studies have found that although the programs' beneficial effects diminish greatly by 4 years or so (Flay et al., 1989; Murray et al., 1989), about 10% to 15% fewer individuals begin smoking in the next 15 years if they received the programs than if they did not (Sussman & Skara, 2004).

The success of these approaches may be enhanced in several ways, such as by adding periodic "booster" sessions, starting at earlier ages and focusing on attitudes about smoking, and involving the parents. By the time children enter fifth grade many already have positive attitudes about smoking, and having these attitudes at that time is linked with beginning to smoke by the ninth grade (Dinh et al., 1995). Involving the

parents is important: if they smoke and quit in the program, their child is much less likely to start smoking, especially if the parents' quitting occurs before the child is 9 years old (Farkas et al., 1999). One other strategy may help: using an Internet program, such as *Smoking Zine*, to assist smoking prevention and quitting interventions in schools (Norman et al., 2008). This program is available at http://www.smokingzine.org and includes interactive self-assessments with tailored feedback to prevent teens from starting to smoke, advance the person's readiness to change, and help smokers design a plan for quitting.

Because of the successes psychosocial programs have had with smoking, they have been extended for preventing alcohol and drug use. Programs like these effectively reduce teenage and college drinking (Carey et al., 2007; Fromme & Corbin, 2004; Kivlahan et al., 1990) and marijuana use (Chou et al., 1998). A psychosocial program that addressed and followed tobacco, alcohol, and marijuana use over 18 months prevented seventh and eighth graders from starting to use substances they hadn't begun using and reduced the use of substances the students were already using (Ellickson et al., 2003).

Family Involvement Approaches

Parents can be involved in preventing or reducing teens' substance use by participating in an intervention and supervising their children more actively (Szapocznik et al., 2007). Family involvement makes sense, and the need for it is supported by three findings from research. First, children of parents who provide little monitoring, rules, and supervision are four times more likely to try drugs in the future than children with actively involved parents (Chilcoat, Dishion, & Anthony, 1995). Second, children are far less likely to use a substance if they know their parents would disapprove of it and would punish that behavior (Komro et al., 2003; SAMHSA, 2008). Third, most parents of teenagers who use a substance are not aware of it: the percentages of parental awareness for each substance are 39% for tobacco use, 34% for alcohol use, and 11% for drugs (Williams et al., 2003).

An intervention using family involvement to prevent tobacco, alcohol, and marijuana use was applied with sixth grade students, whose substance use was followed for 4 years (Spoth, Redmond, & Shin, 2001). The families were recruited from the general population—that is, they were not selected on the basis of the children's using or not using a substance. The programs were presented in several weekly sessions and were designed to teach parenting skills that should help the children delay starting to use the substances or reduce their current use of them. For example, the parents learned how to monitor the child's behavior and use appropriate discipline, teach the child ways to resist peer pressure to use substances, and reduce family conflict. Comparisons in tenth grade with a control group revealed that the children in the family program were far less likely to have begun smoking, drinking, or using marijuana; and for those who used substances, they used much less.

QUITTING A SUBSTANCE WITHOUT THERAPY

Alcohol and drug abuse have been viewed in most societies as deviant behaviors for centuries, and today cigarette smoking is viewed more and more like a deviant behavior. Many nonsmokers resent people smoking in their presence, and many smokers feel guilty when smoking because they know it offends others and believe it is unhealthy, irrational behavior. Smokers often have negative thoughts about their smoking and claim they'd like to quit (Köblitz et al., 2009; Solberg et al., 2007). Still, most teenage and young adult smokers think they're at least as healthy as nonsmokers their age, and many are not concerned about potential health problems, even if they've already developed a smoker's cough (Prokhorov, 2003). And only about half of smokers who have an asthma attack quit (King et al., 2007). Few substance abusers seek therapy to stop—for example, less than 29% of Americans who think they need treatment for drug or alcohol use seek it (SAMHSA, 2008). Let's look at the process of quitting substances without therapy.

Stopping Smoking on One's Own

You probably know people who were smokers—perhaps heavy smokers—who have quit. Chances are they quit on their own, without any sort of professional help, like millions of people do around the world. What motivates smokers to quit? The main motivation is to protect their health (Falba, 2005; McCaul et al., 2006). But only a small percentage of individuals who begin smoking in adolescence quit in the next 20 years (Chassin et al., 2000). Smokers are more likely to try to quit and succeed when others in their social networks do so (Christakis & Fowler, 2008). Are people usually effective at stopping on their own, and does it take enormous effort?

Stanley Schachter (1982) interviewed adults with histories of having smoked regularly and found that over 60% of those that tried to quit eventually succeeded—virtually all had not smoked in the last 3 months, and the average length of abstinence was more than 7 years. Was it harder for heavy smokers (smoking at least three-quarters of a pack a day) to quit than light smokers? Yes, much harder. Nearly half of the heavy smokers who quit reported severe withdrawal symptoms, such as intense cravings, irritability, sleeplessness, and cold sweats; less than 30% reported having no difficulties. In contrast, almost all of the light smokers said quitting had been easy, even if they had failed! A similar study conducted by researchers at another university found very similar results (Rzewnicki & Forgays, 1987).

The results of these studies suggest that most people can stop smoking on their own, even if they smoke heavily. Other studies have clarified the process of quitting on one's own (Carey et al., 1993; Cohen et al., 1989; Curry, Wagner, & Grothaus, 1990; DiClemente et al., 1991; Gritz, Carr, & Marcus, 1991; Pallonen et al., 1990; Rose et al., 1996). Most people do not succeed in one attempt, but eventually succeed after several tries, and certain factors differentiate those people who do and don't succeed. Compared to smokers who do not succeed in quitting, those who do are likely to:

- Have decided that they want and are ready to quit.
- Feel confident that they can succeed.
- Have smoked less than a pack a day.
- Experience less stress.
- Feel less nicotine dependence and experience less craving for tobacco and fewer and less-severe withdrawal symptoms, such as restlessness and tension.
- Be highly motivated, especially by *intrinsic* factors, such as a feeling of self-control or a concern about their health.
- Be willing to try again if they don't succeed. Many people fail the first few times they try, but learn from their mistakes.

People often decide to quit smoking when rules restricting smoking are introduced at work, especially if the worksite offers a program to help them stop; the above factors seem to affect their success, too (Bauer et al., 2005; Fielding, 1991; Klesges et al., 1999).

What methods do smokers use when trying to quit? To answer this question, researchers interviewed participants in a month-long communitywide stop-smoking contest that had a grand prize of a trip to Disney World (Glasgow et al., 1985). These interviews revealed that:

- The vast majority of the men and women attempted to quit cold turkey rather than trying to reduce their smoking gradually before the contest began.
- Most participants used oral substitutes, such as candy or mints, in place of cigarettes.

- Most tried to go it alone, without involving other people, but many others used a buddy system or made bets with others.

- Most used cognitive strategies, such as telling themselves, "I don't need a cigarette," or reminding themselves of the health risks in smoking, the commitment they made to quit, or the possibility of winning a prize.

- A minority of individuals provided themselves with material rewards for sticking with quitting or punishment for backsliding.

Fifty-five participants—about 40%—remained abstinent throughout the month (which was verified through biochemical saliva or breath analyses). Quitting cold turkey rather than gradually and providing rewards for abstaining were more strongly related to successful quitting than some other methods the smokers used.

Several factors other than how heavily a person smokes can make quitting relatively difficult. One of these factors is invalid beliefs. For example, some smokers have low rates of quitting because they switched to "light" cigarettes with the incorrect notion that doing so will reduce their health risks (Tindle et al., 2006). Other smokers don't try to quit because they generate illogical thoughts ("I don't need to stop because some smokers live to 90 years") to justify continuing to smoke (Kleinjan et al., 2006). Smokers are also likely to have a difficult time quitting if they are having emotional problems, such as depression; drink heavily; or use smoking to manage their stress (Agrawal et al., 2008; Dollar et al., 2009; Yong & Borland, 2008).

Stopping Alcohol and Drug Use on One's Own

Most of the little we know about quitting alcohol and drug use on one's own deals with problem drinkers' reducing their alcohol intake without treatment. How many people who abuse alcohol recover without treatment? Researchers have estimated that about 20% markedly reduce or stop drinking on their own (Miller & Hester, 1980; Moyer & Finney, 2002). This estimate is based on data from studies of treatment effectiveness in which some problem drinkers were randomly assigned to control groups and stopped drinking with no treatment. How do drinkers who quit on their own differ from those who do not? Those who quit have higher self-esteem, fewer past experiences of intoxication, and social networks with members who drink less (Russell et al., 2001). And they have social support from a spouse and changed the way they weighed the pros and cons of drinking—for example, realizing "I was sick and tired of it, really weary of it" (Sobell et al., 1993).

Early Intervention

Efforts for *early intervention* try to identify people at high risk for substance abuse and then provide information to reduce that risk (Ashley & Rankin, 1988). Although early intervention can be used for smoking and drug use, we'll focus on alcohol use. Most high-risk drinkers are identified on the basis of current drinking patterns or problems, such as being charged with drink driving. Although interventions for them have been successful *only* with people who are relatively *light* drinkers—heavy drinkers often get *worse* after an intervention (McGuire, 1982)—the picture is brighter for interventions with most other people who are at high risk for abusing alcohol. If drinking problems are detected early, successful interventions can simply involve giving information and advice, and the individuals may be able to reduce their drinking to a moderate level (Ashley & Rankin, 1988; NIAAA, 1993; Sobell et al., 2002).

Early interventions have been successful with high-risk drinkers identified at colleges, in medical settings, and at worksites; these people are often identified by having them fill out a survey that includes questions on drinking. In medical settings, identified high-risk drinkers who received an intervention of information and advice on reducing drinking incurred lower expenses for health care and for legal and motor vehicle events over the next year than did drinkers who did not get the intervention (Fleming et al., 2000). In worksites, many employers and unions provide *employee assistance programs* (EAPs) to help individuals who have personal problems, such as with drinking or stress (USDHHS, 1990). EAPs can be helpful, but workers with addictions seek help far less often than workers with other problems (Chan, Neighbors, & Marlatt, 2004). This may be because EAPs usually don't identify high-risk drinkers until the problem is severe, and workers may worry that counselors will leak information to their bosses. A worksite should be a good place for preventing alcohol abuse because most individuals who abuse alcohol have jobs, and drinking is often related to stress on the job (Mayer, 1983).

TREATMENT METHODS TO STOP SUBSTANCE USE AND ABUSE

Of the substance users who are willing to try to quit or reduce their use, the ones who seek professional help are likely to be psychologically and physically dependent on the substance, making it hard for the effort to succeed. Therapies can vary in their structure and methods—some, such as stop smoking *quitlines*, simply offer telephone counseling that helps people quit a substance (Lichtenstein, Zhu, & Tedeschi, 2010).

Therapists can design programs that use a variety of methods to help. (Go to .)

Psychosocial Methods for Stopping Substance Abuse

Substance abuse involves entrenched behaviors that are difficult to stop, particularly if physical dependence has developed. In many cases, chemical approaches are useful to decrease craving and other withdrawal symptoms, as we'll see later. For now, we'll focus on psychosocial methods. Because the psychosocial processes leading to and maintaining substance abuse

are similar for using tobacco, alcohol, and drugs, the approaches health psychologists apply to help people stop or reduce using them are basically the same for all three substances. We'll concentrate on methods for which there is good evidence for their success. Other methods, such as *hypnosis* and *acupuncture*, for stopping substance use have received much media hype, but research has not yielded clear evidence of success (Nash, 2001; White, Rampes, & Campbell, 2006).

An initial issue in treating substance abuse is the person's desire and readiness to change. Although most people who seek treatment to stop or reduce their substance use want to change, not all do—some were coerced or required to enter therapy by their family,

---

HIGHLIGHT

Where Should Treatment Occur, and What Should Be the Goals and Criteria for Success?

Because of the physical dependence when alcohol and drug abusers enter treatment, the first step in their recovery is **detoxification**—the drying out process to get an addicted person safely through the period of withdrawal from a substance. This is an essential step before treatment can proceed. Because withdrawal symptoms can be severe enough to cause death, detoxification often occurs in hospitals under medical supervision, using medication to control the symptoms (Digiusto et al., 2005; Miller & Hester, 1986). Improved assessment procedures and detoxification methods today enable many addicted people to undergo detoxification at home if they receive careful assistance and support from trained individuals. After that, the question becomes: should treatment be carried out in a residential setting or on an outpatient basis? Most problem drinkers and drug users can be treated as outpatients. But with alcoholics, for example, those who are strongly addicted appear to benefit more from inpatient than outpatient care (Finney & Moos, 1997; NIAAA, 1993; Rychtarik et al., 2000). In the United States, most substance users who receive treatment do so as outpatients (USBC, 2010).

Ideally, treatment should "cure" the person's substance problem forever, but at what point can therapists expect that their treatment will have durable effects? On this issue, there is considerable agreement among researchers: They generally recommend and use a minimum follow-up interval of 12 to 18 months to determine the success of treatment (Emrick & Hansen, 1983; Nathan, 1986). Many programs today also attempt to verify self-reports of substance use through other sources—reports by the ex-abuser's spouse or through

blood or breath tests, for instance—and measure other outcomes of treatment, such as physical health, employment status, and legal problems encountered.

Because of legal and medical considerations, the treatment goal for tobacco and drug users is to quit completely. But what about alcohol use—should treatment aim to have drinkers become *permanently abstinent*, or can some return gradually to *controlled drinking*? This distinction generated a bitter controversy in the 1980s (Marlatt, 1983; Peele, 1984). Although the controversy is not completely resolved, it does appear that *some* problem drinkers can learn through treatment to drink in moderation (Maisto, 2004; Walitzer & Connors, 2007). Problem drinkers who have the best prospects for controlled drinking:

- Are relatively young.
- Are socially stable, such as married or employed.
- Have had a relatively brief history of alcohol abuse.
- Have *not* suffered severe withdrawal symptoms while becoming abstinent.
- Prefer trying to drink in moderation.

In other words, the less severe the drinking problem, the better the chances of succeeding in controlled drinking. What's more, long-term alcoholics who choose abstinence as their goal have fewer drinking problems at 1-year follow-up than those who choose controlled drinking (Hodgins et al., 1997). For long-term alcoholics to pursue a goal of controlled drinking is unrealistic and probably not in their best interests (Nathan, 1986; Sandberg & Marlatt, 1991).

employer, or the justice system. And clients who do want to change vary in their degree of commitment. We saw in Chapter 5 that professionals can use the *stages of change model* to describe people's readiness to modify health-related behaviors. A critical transition occurs when the person's stage of readiness moves from *contemplation*, or thinking about changing, to *preparation* and *action*. According to psychologist William Miller (1989), this transition is like a door that opens for a period of time and closes if the substance abuser doesn't use it in that time. Family, friends, coworkers, doctors, or therapists can encourage the transition in several ways, such as:

- Giving the person clear advice about why and how to change.

- Removing important barriers for change.

- Introducing external consequences, such as rewards for changing or real threats (for example, of being fired) if no change occurs.

- Offering help and showing a helping attitude.

Bolstering the person's self-efficacy is critical for initiating his or her efforts to change (Baldwin et al., 2006). Family members who receive training in motivational methods can be very successful in helping substance users decide to start therapy (Meyers et al., 2002; Miller, Meyers, & Tonigan, 1999). These methods are based on the technique of *motivational interviewing* we discussed in Chapter 5. Therapists also use motivational interviewing methods during treatment to enhance its success; although these methods can help smokers quit, they appear to be more effective with drinking and drug use (Burke, Arkowitz, & Menchola, 2003; Lai et al., 2010).

Another effective psychosocial method for treating substance use is to provide the user with *positive reinforcement* for stopping or reducing use. Compared to treatments that don't include reinforcement, treatments that do use it are more successful in reducing the use of tobacco, alcohol, and a variety of drugs, including marijuana, cocaine, and opiates (Higgins, Heil, & Lussier, 2004). The reinforcers are mainly monetary based—for instance, vouchers that can be exchanged for desirable items—and programs usually spend several times more per client to treat opiate abuse than to treat smoking (about $150). Some researchers have designed and tested programs with reinforcers that cost less, as one study did with cocaine abusers who were randomly assigned to either a standard treatment or the same treatment with reinforcement (Petry & Martin, 2002). The clients in both conditions submitted urine samples two or three times a week, which was analyzed for opioids and cocaine. If they were abstinent—the sample was negative—they could participate in a lottery that determined whether they would win a prize and what it

would be. Most prizes were small, such as a choice of a $1 coupon for fast food or some toiletries, and some were larger (worth $20); each drawing also offered a slim chance of winning a much larger prize, such as a small TV or a boombox. Compared to the clients with the standard treatment, those in the reinforcement condition were far more abstinent during the 12-week program and for the following 3 months. The reinforcement program cost $137 per client.

Therapists sometimes use **aversion strategies**, which pair unpleasant stimuli with substance use, making the behavior less pleasant. One way to make smoking unpleasant is called *satiation*: the person doubles or triples his or her usual smoking rate at home for some period of time (Lichtenstein & Mermelstein, 1984). For some smokers, satiation may be useful as a first step in a program for quitting. Aversion strategies have also been applied to treat alcohol abuse: an injection of an **emetic drug**, such as *emetine*, is given that induces nausea when alcohol is consumed. In each half-hour session, the person receives emetine and then repeatedly drinks an alcoholic beverage, each time quickly becoming nauseated and vomiting (Miller & Hester, 1980). The person undergoes several of these sessions, typically as an inpatient in a hospital, and then receives booster sessions periodically after discharge. A study of hundreds of problem drinkers who received emetine therapy revealed that 63% of the men and women remained abstinent during the 12 months after treatment, and half of these individuals remained abstinent for the next 2 years (Wiens & Menustik, 1983).

Because of the role of substance-related cues in maintaining smoking, drinking, and drug use, therapists use a method called **cue exposure** to counteract the classical conditioning that occurs with long-term substance use. Let's use drinking as an example. The cues, such as seeing a liquor bottle, had been paired with substance use, drinking, to gain the ability through conditioning to produce internal responses like those that happen with alcohol use. In using cue exposure to reduce these internal reactions to conditioned stimuli, therapists expose problem drinkers repeatedly to substance-related cues, such as holding a beer can, while not allowing them to drink. Cue exposure has had some success in treating substance abuse, particularly drinking (Brandon, Vidrine, & Litvin, 2007; Drummond & Glautier, 1994; Rohsenow et al., 2001).

We saw earlier that one reason people use a substance is that they gain negative reinforcement from it: they use it to regulate emotional states—that is, to cope—and need to learn ways to deal with stress that are more adaptive. As a result, therapists often help substance abusers learn to manage their stress with behavioral and cognitive methods for *stress management* that we described in Chapter 4. These methods include:

- Progressive muscle relaxation, in which people alternately tighten and relax individual muscle groups.
- Meditation, an alternative relaxation method.
- Cognitive restructuring, in which people learn to replace stress-provoking thoughts with more constructive and realistic ones.

Cognitive–behavioral methods are among the most effective approaches in treating problem drinking (Finney & Moos, 1997; Stockwell & Town, 1989) and drug use (Maude-Griffin et al., 1998; Tims, Fletcher, & Hubbard,

1991). They are also useful in helping people stop smoking. (Go to ☻.)

Self-Help Groups

Alcoholics Anonymous (AA) is a widely known self-help program that was founded in the 1930s by people with drinking problems (Dolan, 2004; McCrady & Irvine, 1989). The program now has thousands of chapters around the world and has set up organizations to help alcoholics' families, such as *Alateen* for their adolescent children and *Al-Anon* for adults in the family. The AA philosophy includes two basic views. First, people who abuse alcohol are alcoholics and remain alcoholics for life, even if they never take another drink. Second, alcoholics must

---

CLINICAL METHODS AND ISSUES

Behavioral Methods for Treating Substance Abuse

Psychologists apply behavioral methods to gain control over environmental conditions that sustain an undesirable behavior, such as smoking or drinking (Sarafino, 2001). These methods are based on the recognition that modifying behavior requires changing the *behavior itself* and its *antecedents* and *consequences*. For example, the consequences can be changed by introducing rewards for not using a substance and penalties for using it. These techniques are often taught to clients to use in *self-management* procedures, which we discussed in Chapter 5. Let's look at some behavioral methods that can help clients stop or reduce substance use.

- *Self-monitoring* is a procedure in which people record information pertaining to their problem behavior, such as how often they smoked or drank and the circumstances, place, and time of each instance. Although this technique is used mainly in gathering data, it is a very important method for making self-management procedures effective (Michie et al., 2009).
- *Stimulus control* procedures address the antecedents by altering elements of the environment that serve as cues and lead a person to perform the problem behavior. For example, many smokers report that they regularly have (and "*need* to have") a cigarette in certain situations, such as after meals, or with alcohol, or when talking on the phone. And many problem drinkers are unable to resist having a drink when friends are drinking. These environments can be altered in many ways—for example, by making the substance less available, removing cues such as ashtrays, or restricting the time spent in situations where the behavior occurs,

such as watching TV or sitting at the table after meals. Stimulus control procedures can help a great deal: a study on quitting smoking found that getting rid of cigarettes is a critical factor in remaining abstinent on the first day (O'Connell et al., 2002).

- *Competing response* substitution involves performing and rewarding a behavior that is incompatible with or not likely to be performed at the same time as the problem behavior. For instance, a smoker who "has to have a cigarette with coffee after breakfast" would receive a reward for skipping coffee and taking a shower right after breakfast. People are not likely to smoke in the shower (but some smokers do!).
- *Scheduled reduction* is a method in which the person uses the substance only at specified regular intervals, and these intervals get longer and longer across days. So far, scheduled reduction has been used mainly with smoking and is effective (Catley & Grobe, 2008; Cincirpini et al., 1995).
- *Behavioral contracting* is a technique for spelling out conditions and consequences regarding the problem behavior in writing. Behavioral contracts usually indicate the conditions under which the behavior may or may not occur and specify reinforcing and punishing consequences that will be applied, and when. Contracts for quitting substance use often have the person deposit a substantial sum of money, which is then meted out if he or she meets certain goals.

Although each of these methods is useful in changing behavior, such as smoking or drinking, they are most effective when combined and used together.

commit to the goal of permanent and total abstinence, and their approach is aimed at helping their members resist even one drink. A critical feature of the AA approach is the person's developing a social network that does not support drinking (Litt et al., 2009). A similar organization for drug users is called Narcotics Anonymous.

Because the AA philosophy has its roots in evangelical Protestantism, the program emphasizes the individual's needs for spiritual awakening, public confession, and contrition (McCrady & Irvine, 1989; Peele, 1984). This philosophy can be seen in the Twelve Steps AA uses to help drinkers quit—for example, one step is, "Admitted to God, to ourselves, and to another human being the exact nature of our wrongs." Members attend frequent AA meetings, which use the Twelve Steps to promote frank discussions about the members' experiences with alcohol and difficulties resisting drinking. An important feature of the AA approach is that its members develop friendships with other ex-drinkers and get encouragement from each other and from knowing individuals who have succeeded.

Does AA work, and is it more effective than other approaches for helping drinkers quit? Until the late 1990s, AA's effectiveness was unknown because its membership is anonymous and the organization does not keep systematic information about people who attend. Today, there are two lines of evidence for its success. First, studies compared different methods conducted by professional therapists and found that treatments using the AA approach produced as much improvement as other treatments (Ouimette, Finney, & Moos, 1997; PMRG, 1998). Second, research has shown that the greater the duration and frequency of alcoholics' involvement in AA, the less their binge drinking and the better their social functioning in the following years (McKellar, Stewart, & Humphreys, 2003; Moos & Moos, 2004). But AA may not be appropriate for problem drinkers who reject aspects of the AA approach, such as the belief in God, and other social networks may be substituted (Litt et al., 2009; Tonigan, Miller, & Schermer, 2002. AA is often used as an approach to prevent relapse after other forms of treatment (NIAAA, 1993).

Chemical Methods for Treating Substance Abuse

Treatments for substance abuse often use prescribed drugs that the person is required to take regularly to combat the conditions that maintain the behavior. Some of these drugs interact with the abused substance, such as alcohol, producing unpleasant reactions, such as nausea and vomiting. The chemical methods we are discussing here are different from the use of emetine

that we described earlier, which is not taken on a regular basis but is used in conditioning sessions as an aversion strategy.

Different chemicals are used in treatments for different substances. In stopping tobacco use, the main chemical used is *nicotine*, which the person can administer as a gum, a lozenge, a patch placed on the skin, an inhaler, or a nasal spray. Using nicotine decreases craving and withdrawal symptoms, such as sleeplessness, and helps toward short-term and long-term quitting success (Cummings & Hyland, 2005; Ferguson, Shiffman, & Gwaltney, 2006; Stead et al., 2008). And if an abstinent smoker uses a fast-acting version, such as the lozenge, when exposed to smoking cues, it reduces the resulting craving (Shiffman et al., 2003). Two other useful chemicals for reducing smoking are *bupropion hydrochloride*, an antidepressant drug, and *varenicline* (Hughes, 2009). Using a nicotine lozenge with any of the other chemicals enhances success in quitting (Smith et al., 2009). Because genetic processes influence the effects of specific anti-smoking chemicals (Uhl et al., 2008), medical tests may help select the best chemical for each person.

Two types of chemicals are used in treating alcohol abuse. One chemical is an emetic drug called *disulfiram* (brand name Antabuse) that the person needs to take each day orally (Maisto, 2004; Schuckit 1996). In addition to producing nausea if the person drinks, it has some important side effects that can preclude its use—it causes drowsiness, raises blood pressure, and has physiological effects that make it inappropriate for people with heart and liver diseases. For those who can use it, disulfiram can be an effective therapy, but getting them to take the drug consistently is often a problem. The second chemical is *naltrexone*, a drug that blocks the "high" feeling that alcohol and narcotics produce (AMA, 2003). Alcohol-dependent individuals treated with naltrexone experience fewer days of heavy drinking and fewer drinks on days when they drink than those in control groups that receive a placebo (Garbutt et al., 2005; Monti et al., 2001).

Several chemical agents can be used for treating narcotic addiction. The most widely used of these agents is *methadone*, a chemical that has physiological effects that are similar to those of opiates. However, methadone does not produce euphoria and, when taken regularly, it prevents euphoria from occurring if the person then takes an opiate (Mattick et al., 2003; Sindelar & Fiellin, 2001). Methadone is usually taken orally. Having a narcotics addict take methadone—or a similar agent, *levoalpha acetylmethadyl* (LAAM)—regularly to reduce opiate use is called *methadone maintenance*. Another chemical agent that blocks the euphoria from opiates taken after it is *buprenorphine*, which has advantages over methadone, such as its staying active longer, but seems to be less effective (Mattick et al., 2003; Sindelar & Fiellin, 2001). Naltrexone, which we just discussed for treating alcohol abuse, blocks opiate euphoria but isn't used often for narcotic abuse.

Multidimensional Programs

You may know someone who tried to quit smoking just by using a nicotine patch, and failed. Research has shown that the psychosocial and chemical methods we've discussed are useful in stopping or reducing substance use, but none is highly effective *alone*—as a result, the methods are usually combined in a *multidimensional program* to improve their success. For instance, studies of treatments to stop smoking have found that combining cognitive–behavioral methods with the nicotine patch is far more effective than using either approach alone (Alterman, Gariti, & Mulvaney, 2001; Cinciripini et al., 1996). For drug abuse, treating narcotic addiction with methadone and psychosocial methods is far more effective than methadone alone (McClellan et al., 1993). And treating marijuana dependence with motivational interviewing and rewards for providing marijuana-free urine samples is more effective than either approach alone (Carroll et al., 2006).

Five other features should be considered in designing multidimensional programs to curb substance use. First, using biochemical analyses to verify self-reports of use and demonstrating these verification procedures at the *beginning* of treatment enhances the success of a program (Glynn, Gruder, & Jegerski, 1986). Second, a brief daily phone call to the clients improves their performance of certain procedures, such as keeping records of smoking (McConnell, Biglan, & Severson, 1984). Third, involving the client's family or significant person in the program improves the outcome (Carlson et al., 2002; Fals-Stewart & O'Farrell, 2003). Fourth, doctor involvement helps. For example, people are more likely to try to quit smoking and stick with it if they are advised to stop by their doctor, receive a prescription for nicotine, are shown on an apparatus how impaired their respiratory system is, and have been diagnosed with a serious smoking-related disease (Fiore, Jorenby, & Baker, 1997; Ockene et al., 1991, 1994; Risser & Belcher, 1990; USD-HHS, 1986a). Fifth, supplementing standard treatment with a computer-based intervention improves abstinence and helps it last (Carroll et al., 2009).

DEALING WITH THE RELAPSE PROBLEM

Quitting substance use is one thing—staying quit is another. As Mark Twain noted, "To cease smoking is the easiest thing I ever did; I ought to know because I've done it a thousand times" (Grunberg & Bowen, 1985). The methods we have considered work well in helping people stop or reduce substance use, but preventing backsliding is a major problem.

The Relapse Problem

Regardless of how smokers quit, their likelihood of *relapse*—that is, returning to the full-blown pattern of behavior—is very high in the first weeks and months after stopping. Most people who quit smoking start again within a year, and most relapses occur in the first 3 months (Ockene et al., 2000). Estimates of relapse rates vary from 50 to 80%, depending on many factors, including the methods used in quitting, how heavily the person smoked, and characteristics of the individual and his or her environment (Curry & McBride, 1994; Ossip-Klein et al., 1986).

The problem of relapse is at least as severe in efforts to stop drinking and using drugs as it is in quitting smoking. Many of the more successful treatment approaches for alcohol abuse produce very high rates of success initially, but these rates decline sharply by the end of the first year and again during the next 2 years (Nathan, 1986). For drug use relapse, researchers have estimated that 60% or more of individuals return to using drugs after quitting (Donovan, 2003).

Why People Relapse

Withdrawal symptoms probably contribute strongly to immediate relapses. But these symptoms decline over time. For instance, nicotine withdrawal declines sharply in the first week or so after stopping (Gritz, Carr, & Marcus, 1991; Killen & Fortmann, 1994; Piasecki et al., 1997). Smokers who are trying to quit need reassurance that their cravings and negative feelings will diminish greatly in less than a month. Another factor that can affect relapse is satisfaction: the more satisfied people are with the results of having quit the less likely they are to relapse (Baldwin et al., 2006).

What other factors lead people to return to using a substance they quit? Table 6.4 describes several, and research has clarified the role of the first two. First, self-efficacy during quitting is dynamic—when quitting smoking, for instance, it remains fairly high before a lapse and drops after the lapse; the sharper the drop, the more likely a relapse will occur (Shiffman et al., 2000). Second, the role of emotion is particularly important: for example, people who experience high levels of stress are more likely to start smoking again than those who experience less stress (Cohen & Lichtenstein, 1990; Lichtenstein et al., 1986; Shiffman et al., 1996). Ex-smokers who go back

Table 6.4 *Several Factors That Can Lead to a Relapse of a Changed Behavior*

Factors	Description of Factor's Influence
Low self-efficacy	Maintaining self-efficacy for staying abstinent is not always easy: people who quit a behavior and experience a lapse may lose their confidence in remaining abstinent and see their violation as a sign of a personal failure. As we saw in Chapter 5, these events can lead to a full relapse through the process called the *abstinence violation effect*.
Negative emotions and poor coping	Because people often use substances to regulate their emotional states, they tend to lack good coping skills to take the place of the substance when difficulties arise.
High craving	The greater the craving, the more likely a relapse.
Expectation of reinforcement	People tend to relapse if they think that using the substance again would be rewarding, such as "Having a drink would taste great and make me feel so relaxed."
Low motivation	People at lower levels of readiness to change when they try to quit are more likely to relapse than people at higher readiness levels.
Interpersonal issues	Substance users who quit, but lack constructive social support or have social networks that promote substance use, are more likely to relapse than others who have strong, helpful support.

Source: Witkiewitz & Marlatt, 2004.

to smoking often report that acute episodes of anxiety or frustration at work or at home led to their relapse (Shiffman, 1986).

Two other factors in relapse relate mainly to smoking. First, an interesting thing happens to smokers' beliefs when they relapse: they tend to lower their perceptions of the health risks of smoking. A study of people who relapsed after completing a treatment program to stop smoking found that they reported strong beliefs that smoking could harm their health when they entered the program, but after the relapse these beliefs decreased (Gibbons, McGovern, & Lando, 1991). Why? They probably used cognitive processes, such as motivated reasoning or denial, to cope with the fact that their attempt to quit smoking failed. This finding is important because it means people who relapse may not be ready to retry quitting until their beliefs change back again. Many smokers deny or minimize the health risks of smoking, thereby decreasing the likelihood that they will try to quit (Lee, 1989; Strecher, Kreuter, & Kobrin, 1995).

Second, some people who go back to smoking claim they did so because they were *gaining weight* (Jeffery et al., 2000). Smokers tend to weigh less than nonsmokers, and this difference is greater among middle-aged than younger individuals (Klesges et al., 1998). When people stop smoking, most—but not all—do, in fact, tend to gain several pounds over the next few years (Klesges et al., 1997; Parsons et al., 2009). There are two reasons why this is so (Klesges, Benowitz, & Meyers, 1991). First, ex-smokers often increase their caloric intake, sometimes by eating more fats and sweet-tasting foods. Second, the amount of energy they expend in metabolism declines, for at least a short time, after quitting. To prevent weight gain, many ex-smokers may need to control their diets, get more exercise, and perhaps use a nicotine supplement. Ex-smokers who use nicotine gum or patches during the weeks after quitting gain much less weight than controls with a placebo (Allen et al., 2005; Doherty et al., 1996). Some programs for quitting smoking are now incorporating methods to prevent weight gain (Parsons et al., 2009).

Can Relapses Be Prevented?

One approach for reducing relapse uses a process called the **relapse prevention method**, which is based on G. Alan Marlatt's view that relapses develop through the cognitive events of the abstinence violation effect that follow a lapse (Marlatt & Gordon, 1980; Witkiewitz & Marlatt, 2004). The cognitive events involve mainly guilt and reduced self-efficacy. The relapse prevention method is basically a therapist-supervised self-management program in which clients take the following steps:

1. *Learn to identify high-risk situations* by generating a list and descriptions of antecedent conditions in which lapses are most likely to occur.

2. *Acquire competent and specific coping skills* through training in specific behaviors and thought patterns that will enable the person to deal with high-risk situations and avoid lapses. For example, people who get treatment for stopping smoking need to receive training in ways to cope with stress without relying on smoking as a coping strategy (Shadel & Mermelstein, 1993).

3. *Practice effective coping skills in high-risk situations* under a therapist's supervision. For example, a problem drinker might go with the therapist to a bar and practice ways to avoid drinking.

This method provides an important component of relapse prevention, but its success in helping individuals stay abstinent for a substance after quitting has been modest when used by itself (Brandon, Vidrine, & Litvin, 2007; Hajek et al., 2009).

Three additional approaches may enhance relapse prevention. First, interventions can provide *booster sessions*—extra sessions periodically to shore up or refresh the treatment's effects. Providing booster sessions or contacts with training on ways to cope with lapses and maintain self-efficacy reduces relapses (Brandon et al., 2000; Irvin et al., 1999; McKay et al., 2004). Second, clients can *continue using a chemical method* after formal treatment ends: for example, they'd continue to use nicotine if they quit smoking or methadone if they quit a narcotic (Klesges, Benowitz, & Meyers, 1991; Mattick et al., 2003). Third, clients can be helped to develop social networks that provide constructive support for abstinence and minimize negative support, such as friends expressing doubt that they will stay quit (Lawhon et al., 2009; Litt et al., 2009). AA attendance is one way to develop social networks that can help ex-drinkers remain abstinent.

SUMMARY

People's use of tobacco, alcohol, or drugs can affect their health. Addiction is a condition that involves a physical and psychological dependence on a substance. People who are physically dependent on a substance have developed a tolerance for it and suffer withdrawal symptoms when they abruptly stop using it. Substance abuse exists when a person shows a clear pattern of pathological use with resulting problems in social and occupational functioning. Processes leading to dependence include positive and negative reinforcement, classical conditioning of substance-related cues, expectancies, and heredity.

Smoking tobacco is a worldwide problem. In the United States, it reached its greatest popularity in the mid-1960s and then declined after its harmful health effects were publicized. Most people who become cigarette smokers begin the habit in adolescence. Although a larger percentage of men than women smoke, this gap has decreased in recent years. Americans are more likely to smoke if they are from the lower rather than the higher social classes. Psychosocial factors influence whether individuals start to smoke; going on to smoke on a regular basis is determined by biopsychosocial factors. The likelihood of individuals becoming regular smokers increases if they have peer and adult models of smoking, experience peer pressure to smoke, and find that smoking helps them relax and have less tension.

Cigarette smoke contains tars, carbon monoxide, and nicotine, a chemical that appears to produce physical dependence. One theory that describes why established smokers continue to smoke is the nicotine regulation model, which proposes that they smoke to maintain a certain level of nicotine in their bodies and avoid withdrawal. Smoking reduces the person's life expectancy and increases the risk of lung cancer, other cancers, cardiovascular disease, and chronic obstructive pulmonary disease. Breathing secondhand smoke is called passive smoking and is also harmful to one's health.

Alcohol use varies widely across cultures and time periods. Most American adults drink at least occasionally, and many adolescents and adults engage in binge drinking. Many individuals who drink abuse alcohol and are classified as problem drinkers; those who are physically dependent on alcohol are classified as alcoholics. People who are addicted to alcohol suffer withdrawal symptoms when they quit drinking. Psychosocial factors—such as modeling, social pressure, and reinforcement—have a very powerful influence on drinking. Heredity plays an important role in the development of alcohol abuse. Heavy drinking is related to a variety of health problems, including fetal alcohol syndrome in babies of drinking mothers, injuries from accidents, and such diseases as cirrhosis of the liver and brain damage.

Drugs can be classified as stimulants, depressants, hallucinogens, and narcotics; they differ in their potential for producing physical and psychological dependence. Drug abuse is related to a number of psychosocial factors, such as modeling, social pressure, reinforcement, and personality traits. The health effects of drug use and abuse are becoming increasingly clear. For example, using cocaine produces cardiovascular reactions that can cause a potentially fatal myocardial infarction.

Programs to prevent smoking and alcohol and drug abuse attempt to address relevant psychosocial factors by providing information and teaching important social skills. These programs teach children and adolescents about the immediate and long-term consequences of the substances, the ways modeling and peer pressure influence their tendency to use substances, and the ways they can resist these forces. Some programs also teach general social, cognitive, and coping skills. Once people become regular users of tobacco, alcohol, or drugs, many are able to quit on their own, but many others are not, especially if they use the substances heavily. Alcoholics Anonymous and Narcotics Anonymous are self-help groups that help substance users to quit.

People who can't stop or reduce their substance use on their own or through a self-help group can receive professional treatment. Alcohol or drug abusers typically undergo detoxification. Effective psychosocial treatment approaches for substance use include reinforcing abstinence, aversion strategies (which can involve using an emetic drug for alcoholics), substance-related cue exposure, and behavioral and cognitive methods. Chemical treatments are also effective and include administering nicotine for smokers and methadone for narcotics users. Combining effective methods in a multidimensional approach improves treatment success. Many people who quit eventually return to smoking. Although the relapse prevention method helps reduce relapse rates, its effects can be enhanced by providing booster sessions, continuing chemical methods after treatment ends, and developing constructive social networks.

KEY TERMS

addiction	negative reinforcement	binge drinking	detoxification
physical dependence	classical conditioning	problem drinkers	aversion strategies
tolerance	carbon monoxide	alcoholics	emetic drug
withdrawal	tars	stimulants	cue exposure
psychological dependence	nicotine	depressants	relapse prevention
substance abuse	nicotine regulation model	hallucinogens	method
positive reinforcement	passive smoking	narcotics	

Note: If you read **Module 4** (from the Appendix) with the current chapter, you should include the key terms for that module.

7

NUTRITION, WEIGHT CONTROL AND DIET, EXERCISE, AND SAFETY

Nutrition
Components of Food
What People Eat
Nutrition and Health

Weight Control and Diet
Desirable and Undesirable Weights
Becoming Overly Fat
Dieting and Treatments to
    Lose Weight
Anorexia and Bulimia

Exercise
The Health Effects of Physical Activity
Who Gets Enough Exercise, Who Does
    Not—and Why?
Promoting Exercise Behavior

Safety
Accidents
Environmental Hazards

PROLOGUE

Every year, the teachers in a lagere (primary) school in Maastricht, the Netherlands, invite parents to come to class and talk to the students about their professions. In the past, the teachers noted an abundance of manual labourers, factory workers, as well as lawyers and bankers. This time, there was a nutritionist, an aerobics instructor,

and a community physician, in addition to the "regular" occupations.

During the course of the talks, the guests would ask questions of the children. When the nutritionist asked what a balanced meal meant, the students were able to suggest fruit, vegetables, bread, and cheese. When the doctor asked for some examples of being safe, the children's responses included looking both ways before crossing the road, not playing with things that are dangerous, and wearing a helmet when bicycling. But when the fitness instructor asked if they or their parents exercised regularly, most said, "No," or "They used to, but are too busy now."

Parents pass down their feelings about exercise, diet, and safety to their children. People give many reasons for not leading more healthy lifestyles. Some of the obstacles they face can be overcome fairly easily, but others are more difficult. In most cases, people could find ways to overcome obstacles to healthy and positive behaviour if they believed it was important and were motivated to do so.

In this chapter we discuss how nutrition, weight control, exercise, and safety habits are important to people's health. We also examine what people do, or do not do, in these areas of their lives, as well as why they behave as they do and how they can change unhealthy behaviours. As we study these topics, we will consider important questions and problems people have in leading healthy lives. Which foods are healthy and which are not? What determines people's preferences for different foods, such as sweets? Why do overweight individuals have such a hard time losing weight and keeping it off? What kinds of exercises, foods, and behaviours benefit health? What hazards exist in our environments, and how can we protect ourselves from them?

NUTRITION

"You are what you eat," as the saying goes. This saying has at least two meanings. Most commonly, it means that the quality of your diet can determine how you look, act, and feel. Another meaning is that the same five types of chemicals—water, carbohydrates, fats, proteins, vitamins, and minerals—that make up food also make up the human body and contribute to the cells' metabolic processes (Holum, 1994; Peckenpaugh, 2007). In this section, we will examine both meanings, beginning with the components of food and their importance in metabolic processes.

COMPONENTS OF FOOD

Healthful diets provide optimal amounts of all essential nutrients for the body's metabolic needs. Let's consider the five types of chemical components, besides water, of food that provide specific nutrients for body functioning.

1.   *Carbohydrates* include simple and complex sugars that are major sources of energy for the body. Simple sugars include *glucose*, which is found in foods made of animal products, and *fructose*, which is found in fruits and honey. Diets may also provide more complex sugars,

such as *sucrose* (table sugar), *lactose* in milk products, and *starch* in many plants.

2.   *Lipids* or "fats" also provide energy for the body. Lipids include saturated and polyunsaturated fats, as well as cholesterol. Nutritionists recommend that diets contain not more than 30% of calories (nor less than 10%) from fat. To calculate food's percent of calories from fat, you need to know its number of calories and grams of fat. Multiply the grams of fat by 9 (because a gram of fat has 9 calories), and divide that value by the number of calories in the food.

3.   *Proteins* are important mainly in the body's synthesis of new cell material. They are composed of organic molecules called *amino acids*; about half of the 20 or so known amino acids are essential for body development and functioning, and must be provided by our diet.

4.   *Vitamins* are organic chemicals that regulate metabolism and functions of the body. They are used in converting nutrients to energy, producing hormones, and breaking down waste products and toxins. Some vitamins (A, D, E, and K) are *fat-soluble*—they dissolve in fats and are stored in the body's fatty tissue. The remaining vitamins (B and C) are *water-soluble*—the body stores very little of these vitamins and excretes excess quantities as waste.

5.   *Minerals* are inorganic substances, such as calcium, phosphorus, potassium, sodium, iron, iodine, and zinc, each of which is important in body development and functioning. For example, calcium and phosphorus are components of bones and teeth, potassium and sodium are involved in nerve transmission, and iron helps transport oxygen in the blood.

Reading labels informs the consumer of the food's content. Guidelines adopted in the 1990s for labeling packaged foods in the United States make nutritious choices easier for consumers.

Food also contains *fiber*, which is not considered a nutrient because it is not used in metabolism but is still needed in the process of digestion. People can get all the nutrients and fiber they need by eating diets that consist of a variety of foods from several basic groups, and you can see the relative amounts of foods from these groups to make a healthful diet in Figure 7-1. The way food is prepared is also important. Consider the potato: A baked or boiled potato by itself has few calories and almost no fat, but when french-fried or made into potato chips, its calorie and fat content skyrockets. People's increased use of processed and fast foods has made their diets less healthful.

Most people who eat healthfully do not need to supplement their diets with vitamins and other nutrients—one carrot, for instance, provides enough vitamin A to last 4 days. A class of vitamins called *antioxidants*—including vitamins A (carotene), C, and E—reduce damage to cells from a process in metabolism called oxidation. Early evidence suggested that antioxidants may reduce the risk of several diseases, such as cancers and cardiovascular and eye diseases (Johnson, Meacham, & Kruskall, 2003). Newer research has found that taking vitamins C and E does not prevent cardiovascular disease (Sesso et al., 2008; Vivekananthan et al., 2003).

Some people who take supplements have an attitude of "the more the better." But one can overdo taking some nutrients, leading to a "poisoning" if they accumulate in the body. For example, although vitamin D seems to protect against cancer (Garland et al., 2006), too much of vitamins A and D can pose serious health hazards to the liver and kidneys, respectively. Women who are pregnant have greater needs of all nutrients; although most of their extra nutrients can come from dietary adjustments, they should also take recommended supplements, such as of iron (Insel & Roth, 1998; Peckenpaugh, 2007). Pregnant women with a specific, detectable gene may need to take folic acid, a B vitamin, to prevent a severe birth defect called *spina bifida*, in which the baby's spinal column doesn't close and may protrude through the back (AMA, 2003).

Unprocessed foods are generally more healthful than processed foods, which often contain additives that benefit the food industry more than the consumer. Some additives lengthen the shelf life of the food, improve or maintain the texture of foods, or enhance the taste of foods, for example (Insel & Roth, 1998). Although most additives are not harmful, some cause allergic reactions or may be carcinogenic. For instance, some people are sensitive to monosodium glutamate (MSG, a flavor enhancer), experiencing heightened blood pressure and sweating when they consume it. Children may be very vulnerable to the effects of additives because their body systems are still forming and maturing rapidly and, pound-for-pound, they eat more than adults. Many people buy foods labeled "organic," believing that they have less of harmful chemicals, which may be true, but organic foods do not appear to be more nutritious than conventional foods (Dangour et al., 2009).

WHAT PEOPLE EAT

Diets vary by gender and culture. A survey of nearly 20,000 university students in 23 countries showed that women report eating healthier diets—less fat and more fruit and fiber—than men in almost all countries, but there are marked national differences in dietary practices (Wardle et al., 2004). Table 7.1 lists countries with the most and least healthful practices. For most of the 20th century, American diets had a fairly consistent trend: people consumed more and more sugar, animal fats, and animal proteins, while consuming less and less fiber (Winikoff, 1983). Since the mid-1980s, dietary trends in

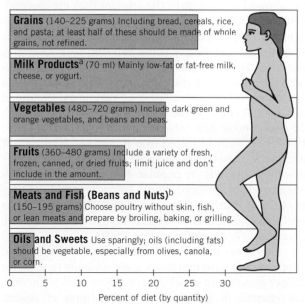

[a]People who cannot consume milk products, or prefer not to, may choose other calcium sources, such as lactose-free products made from rice or soy beans.

[b]People who eat little or no animal products substitute beans and nuts.

Figure 7-1 Proportions of six food groups in a healthful diet. The colored bars reflect the portions of the diet recommended for each food group for adults; ranges in daily amounts in parentheses reflect that males and younger adults need higher quantities. The shaded jogger represents the importance of physical activity. Diagram based mainly on the latest food-guide pyramid of the United States Department of Agriculture, which can be accessed online (www.mypyramid.gov) for detailed information.

Table 7.1 *Two Countries among the Highest and the Lowest in Percentage of Individuals with Healthful Practices for Each of Three Dietary Components (Fat, Fruit, and Fiber)**

Healthful Practices	Countries with High Practice (% of males, females)	Countries with Low Practice (% of males, females)
Dietary fat, avoid eating	Colombia (36.3, 55.7)	France (16.6, 38.2)
	Thailand (34.5, 59.2)	Korea (11.3, 13.2)
Dietary fruit, eat daily	Italy (57.9, 63.8)	Japan (11.9, 12.1)
	Spain (57.1, 64.0)	Korea (16.0, 33.3)
Dietary fiber, eat daily	Korea (38.7, 58.8)	Bulgaria (12.5, 25.4)
	Thailand (64.6, 78.6)	France (10.9, 28.7)

*The percentages were intermediate for the United States (33.1, 50.4 for fat; 31.7, 35.5 for fruit; 21.2, 20.4 for fiber) and England (29.8, 49.5 for fat; 35.8, 44.1 for fruit; 26.0, 38.7 for fiber).
Source: Wardle et al., 2004, abstracted from Table 2.

the United States have shown some good news and bad news (USBC, 2010):

- *Healthful changes.* Consumption of red meat and whole milk has decreased, and poultry, rice, skim milk, and vegetables increased.
- *Unhealthful changes.* Intake of sugars, soft drinks, cheese, cream, and fats and oils has increased.

Table 7.2 compares the diets available for consumption in the United States and several countries in Europe and suggests that Americans consume much more calories and fats than Europeans do.

Why do people eat what they eat? The answer involves biopsychosocial factors (Peckenpaugh, 2007). One factor is *inborn processes*: for instance, newborn babies like sweet tastes and avoid bitter tastes. Brain chemicals can bias people to eat fatty foods and activate their brain pleasure centers when they do (Azar, 1994). Another factor is the person's *skills*—for example, the ability to regulate or manage one's food buying or eating (Anderson, Winett, & Wojcik, 2007). The more able people are in setting goals, planning, and monitoring the foods they consume, the healthier their diets are likely to be. Another factor is one's *environment or experience* with foods; we'll look at five environmental influences. First,

Table 7.2 *Average Quantities of Calories, Fat, and Protein Available for Consumption per Person per Day in the United States and Several European Countries*

Country	Calories (in kilocalories)	Fat (in grams)	Protein (in grams)
United States	3900	178	111
Germany	3484	142	100
Italy	3675	156	113
Netherlands	3495	140	105
Sweden	3208	127	108
Turkey	3328	91	96
United Kingdom	3450	135	105

Sources: USBC, 2010, Table 211; WHO/Europe, 2010.

newborns can learn to like foods they might otherwise avoid: a study tested newborns' liking of pureed green beans, then had their breastfeeding mothers eat green beans daily for 8 days, and retested the babies' liking of pureed green beans (Forestell & Mennella, 2007). At retesting, the infants ate more of the beans than they had originally, but infants in a control group that was formula fed showed no change in the amount they ate. Second, some foods are more available than others at home, work, or school, depending on cultural and economic conditions—and simply being exposed to a food may increase one's liking of it (Hearn et al., 1998; Larson & Story, 2009). Third, the more fast-food restaurants in a neighborhood, the more fast-food people eat (Moore et al., 2009). Fourth, people observe in person and through TV commercials how others respond to a food and tend to become more attracted to it if they see others eat it and like it. Sweet, high-fat snack and convenience foods dominate the ads in popular American children's TV shows and are available almost everywhere we go (Farley et al., 2010; Harrison & Marske, 2005). Fifth, portion sizes are often "supersized"—the larger the portions, the more people eat (Rolls, Morris, & Roe, 2002).

Enormous numbers of children around the world simply do not have nutritious diets available to them for proper growth and development. About half of children are stunted in growth from malnutrition in several countries, such as Ethiopia, Guatemala, and Angola (WHO, 2009). Children are much shorter if they live in very impoverished areas than in wealthier regions, even in the same countries (Meredith, 1978). Regional and social class differences in bodily growth result from many factors, including genetics, nutrition, and disease.

NUTRITION AND HEALTH

The mass media announce almost daily that many individuals eat diets that are not as healthful as they should be. Some people react by using foods and substances sold at health food stores. Although some of these products—such as whole grains—are clearly beneficial, many supplements and other products are of dubious worth (Peckenpaugh, 2007). Some people attempt to improve their diets by becoming *vegetarians*. There are degrees of vegetarianism, ranging from simply avoiding red meats to strictly using only plant foods and no animal products whatsoever. When people avoid all animal products, they must plan very carefully to assure that their diets, and especially their children's, contain a balance of proteins and a sufficient amount of essential vitamins and minerals (Peckenpaugh, 2007). In many nations of the world, dietary excesses are the main nutritional problem, especially in developing atherosclerosis, hypertension, and cancer.

Diet and Atherosclerosis

Cholesterol is the main dietary culprit in atherosclerosis, the deposit of fatty plaques in our blood vessels, illustrated in Figure 7-2. Cholesterol is a fatty substance. Our bodies produce most of the cholesterol in blood, and our diets provide the remainder. Whether cholesterol forms plaques in our blood vessels depends on the presence of different types of **lipoproteins**, which consist of fat and proteins. There are several types of lipoproteins, but two are most important: **low-density lipoprotein** (LDL) is related to *increased* plaque deposits; **high-density lipoprotein** (HDL) is linked to *decreased* likelihood of plaque buildup (AHA, 2010; AMA, 2003).

Cholesterol carried by LDL is called "bad cholesterol" because it mixes with other substances to form plaques, whereas cholesterol carried by HDL is called "good cholesterol" because it seems to carry LDL away to be processed or removed by the liver. There are many other types of dietary fat, three of which are clearly linked

to health. *Triglycerides* are in most fats people consume and increase the risk of heart disease; *omega-3 fatty acids*, which occur at high levels in fish, reduce serum triglycerides and raise HDL; and *trans-fatty acids*, which are in certain oils, such as margarine, increase LDL and lower HDL (Mozaffarian et al., 2006; Peckenpaugh, 2007). Because of the role of dietary fats in cardiovascular disease, communities have begun passing laws against the use of certain fats in preparing foods sold commercially.

How much cholesterol in the blood is too much? Normal levels of cholesterol increase with age in adulthood; they are measured in milligrams of cholesterol per 100 milliliters of blood serum. Experts once thought that long-term *total* serum cholesterol levels above 240 mg put people at high risk for heart disease or stroke, but they have refined this view (EPDET, 2001). "Bad" cholesterol (LDL) *is the real culprit*, and its risk depends on five other risk factors:

- *Age* (over 45 years for men, 55 for women)
- *Cigarette smoking*
- *High blood pressure*
- *Low "good" cholesterol* (HDL less than 40 mg)
- *Family history* of early cardiovascular disease

To determine one's heart attack or stroke risk, count up the person's risk factors and subtract 1 if his or her HDL is high (60 mg or higher). People with scores of 0 or 1 are at *low risk* and should keep LDL levels below 160 mg. People with higher scores should maintain much lower LDL levels, and those who already have heart disease should strive to keep LDL levels below 100 mg (AHA, 2010).

People's cholesterol levels are determined partly by heredity and partly by their lifestyles (AHA, 2010; McCaffery et al., 2001). For instance, smoking cigarettes appears to increase LDL and decrease HDL levels (Muscat et al., 1991). Diet is an important factor: some

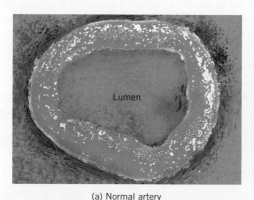

(a) Normal artery

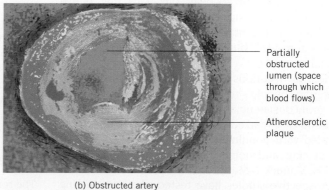

Partially obstructed lumen (space through which blood flows)

Atherosclerotic plaque

(b) Obstructed artery

Figure 7–2 Magnified cross-sectional views of two arteries, (a) normal and (b) obstructed from atherosclerosis. As the plaque (shaded in color) builds up, the lumen becomes smaller, limiting blood flow.

foods, such as eggs, many milk products, and fatty meats, contain very high concentrations of cholesterol. Daily intake of cholesterol should not exceed 300 mg (Peckenpaugh, 2007); it should be much lower for people at moderate or high risk for cardiovascular disease. Children older than 5 years should follow diets like those recommended for adults; those whose parents or grandparents had heart disease at early ages should have their cholesterol levels and diets assessed because atherosclerosis can begin in childhood (DISC, 1995). If dietary changes do not lower adults' cholesterol levels enough, doctors may prescribe medication. *Statin* drugs (some brand names: Crestor, Lipitor, Zocor) greatly reduce LDL and raise HDL levels (AMA, 2003; Nissen et al., 2006).

Does lowering LDL reduce cardiovascular illness? Yes. Studies have shown that large reductions in LDL, produced with combined dietary and drug treatment, retard and slowly *reverse* atherosclerosis and reduce the risk of heart attacks (Karnik, 2001; Nissen et al., 2006). Dietary patterns, such as the "Mediterranean diet," that conform to the recommendations in Figure 7-1 appear to reduce the risk of heart disease and metabolic syndrome (Buckland et al., 2009; Salas-Salvado et al., 2008). Most people can lower their cholesterol intake markedly if they will modify their eating habits, sometimes by making very simple changes, such as by substituting low-cholesterol foods, such as cereals, for just four eggs per week—an egg contains over 200 mg of cholesterol. Most cereals, breads, fruits, nuts, and vegetables contain little or no cholesterol. Other ways include switching to fish or poultry in place of red meats, broiling or baking foods instead of frying, using low-fat dairy products, and using low-cholesterol vegetable fats for cooking. But people should be wary of processed foods that don't specify the type of vegetable oil they use—these products often contain *saturated* fats (coconut or palm oils) instead of the more expensive polyunsaturated fats, such as corn or soybean oils. Oils that derive from certain plants, such as olives, consist of *monounsaturated* fats that contain no cholesterol and appear to *lower* serum LDL, but not HDL (Insel & Roth, 1998; Peckenpaugh, 2007).

There is a curious caution on the health effects of lowering people's cholesterol: although the evidence is inconsistent and inconclusive, some studies have found that markedly reduced serum cholesterol is associated with nonillness deaths, such as from accidents, suicide, and violence (Muldoon & Manuck, 1992; Muldoon, Manuck, & Matthews, 1990). But we don't know why. Prospective studies have tested whether lowering cholesterol might, perhaps, increase people's negative moods in the following months or years and found

that it does not (Bovbjerg et al., 1999; Coutu, Dupuis, & D'Antono, 2001).

Diet and Hypertension

People with blood pressures exceeding 140 systolic/90 diastolic are classified as hypertensive. About one billion people around the world and 30% of American adults are hypertensive (Hajjar, Kochen, & Kochen, 2006; NCHS, 2009a). Although medication can lower blood pressure, the first methods doctors advise usually involve lifestyle changes, especially losing weight and restricting certain foods in the patient's diet. People who are at risk for developing hypertension can effectively reduce their risk by making such changes (Blumenthal, Sherwood et al., 2002).

Of all the substances in people's diets that could affect blood pressure, *sodium*—such as in salt (sodium chloride)—may play the strongest role. Consuming high levels of sodium can increase people's blood pressure and reactivity when stressed (Blumenthal, Sherwood et al., 2002; Falkner & Light, 1986). The body needs about 500 mg of sodium a day, and health experts recommend consuming less than 2,300 mg, the amount in 1 teaspoon of salt (Peckenpaugh, 2007). Individuals who frequently eat processed meats, snacks, and other convenience foods probably consume more than the recommended amount. Because sodium can elevate blood pressure, doctors often place hypertensive patients on low-sodium diets. Although some people are more sensitive to the effects of sodium than others, the evidence is now clear that reducing dietary sodium lowers blood pressure in hypertensive people. Salt-sensitive individuals can lower their blood pressure by reducing sodium intake and by increasing potassium intake, which counteracts sodium effects (Blumenthal, Sherwood et al., 2002; West et al., 1999). Reducing dietary salt also decreases the risk of developing heart disease (Bibbins-Domingo et al., 2010).

Caffeine is another dietary substance that can affect blood pressure. Most of the caffeine people consume comes from drinking caffeinated coffee, tea, and cola. Caffeine increases people's reactivity to stress and raises their blood pressure during the days that it is consumed (James, 2004; Lane et al., 2002). Does consuming caffeine lead to high blood pressure and coronary heart disease? Reviews of research have revealed no link between caffeine consumption and hypertension and heart disease (Riksen, Rongen, & Smits, 2009; Wu et al., 2009).

Diet and Cancer

The role of diet in cancer is becoming clear: diets high in saturated fat and low in fiber and fish are associated with the development of cancer, particularly of the colon and prostate gland (ACS, 2009; Norat et al., 2005). Cancer experts advise people to maintain a healthy weight, consume little of fatty meats, and eat much fish, vegetables, fruits, and high-fiber breads and cereals to reduce their risk of cancer.

Do vitamins protect people from cancer? Many fruits and vegetables are rich in *beta-carotene*, which the body converts to vitamin A; these foods are also good sources of vitamin C. Early studies yielded results suggesting that these vitamins may protect people from cancers, but the current evidence is not definitive (Johnson, Meacham, & Kruskall, 2003). On the basis of the early findings, some people began to take high doses of vitamin A and C supplements. Nutritionists recommend against this, especially with vitamin A because it builds up in the body, and it is easy to overdose.

Interventions to Improve Diet

Dietary interventions take many forms. They can focus on a single nutritional component, such as cholesterol, or promote a healthy overall diet of low fat and high vegetable and fruit content. And they can be provided as counseling sessions with individuals who have a known dietary or health problem and as large-scale programs for members of a group or community, such as employees or school students, using written or computer materials and group meetings. The most effective dietary interventions today incorporate or address elements of the theories of health-related behavior we considered in Chapter 5—for example, the person's perceived barriers and benefits of change (health belief model), self-efficacy (social-cognitive theory), and readiness to change (stages of change model) (Glanz, 2001). To maximize success, interventions can use behavioral and educational methods for the person, training and cooperation by members of the person's household, support groups, and a long-term follow-up program (Carmody et al., 1982). They should also address the person's strong preferences for high-fat, low-fiber foods and difficulties having healthful foods when not eating at home (Terry, Oakland, & Ankeny, 1991).

Let's look at a couple of examples of dietary interventions, one that focused on reducing cholesterol and another that addressed the overall diet. The program to reduce cholesterol was part of the Multiple Risk Factor Intervention Trial (MRFIT) and was designed to modify

the diets of thousands of men over a period of 6 years (Caggiula et al., 1981; Dolecek et al., 1986). The men were at risk of coronary heart disease because of high serum cholesterol levels, high blood pressure, and cigarette smoking. The intervention provided counseling and information each year about the benefits of and methods for modifying diets when the men and "their homemakers" attended group meetings. Compared with a control group with "usual care" from their doctors, the MRFIT program markedly modified the men's diets and lowered their serum cholesterol levels. The men who most needed to modify their diets tended to do so and achieved the greatest gains. A meta-analysis of many similar interventions found that programs to reduce high serum cholesterol help people improve their diets and reduce cardiovascular risk (Brunner et al., 1997).

The intervention to modify overall diets recruited over 600 adult females from a large medical practice who were not already eating a low-fat diet and assigned them randomly to an intervention or control condition (Stevens et al., 2002). The intervention applied elements of the stages of change model, motivational interviewing, and social-cognitive theory to decrease fat and increase vegetable and fruit consumption. The women in the intervention received two individual counseling sessions that included a 20-minute computer program to assess and give feedback on their dietary habits. They also received two counseling phone calls and healthful recipes and hints on shopping, snacking, and eating in restaurants. Assessments after a few months revealed that the diets had improved—that is, contained much less fat and more vegetables and fruit—for women in the intervention but had gotten a little worse for those in the control condition.

What people include in their diets is clearly related to their risk of developing several major chronic diseases. Do people who receive an intervention and improve their intake of fat, vegetables, and fruit dislike their new diets? No, and across years they report greater life satisfaction and confidence that they can promote their health than similar people without the intervention (Corle et al., 2001). Other dietary problems that affect health arise from consuming too many calories. Research with animals has shown that reducing calorie intake by 30% from standard nutritious diets decreases metabolism, slows the aging process, and increases longevity (Lane et al., 1996). Eating too much food can be unhealthful, as we are about to see.

If your course has you read the modules from the Appendix, The Body's Physical Systems, distributed to the chapters, read **Module 3** (The Digestive System) now.

WEIGHT CONTROL AND DIET

People in many cultures around the world are "weight conscious." In the United States, individuals often start being concerned about their weight in childhood and adolescence, particularly if they are overweight and are teased and excluded from social groups (Rosen, 2002; Zeller & Modi, 2008). Many teens become greatly preoccupied with their physical appearance and would like to change how they look. They frequently express concerns about skin problems and wanting to have a better figure or more athletic body, to be taller or shorter, and to be the "right" weight. People with less-than-ideal bodies are often thought of as lazy and self-indulgent, and many of them wish or strive for bodies they are biologically unable to achieve (Brownell, 1991). Being very overweight puts teens—especially girls—at risk for developing depression and anxiety disorders (Anderson et al., 2007; Petry et al., 2008).

DESIRABLE AND UNDESIRABLE WEIGHTS

We judge the desirability of our weight with two criteria. One is attractiveness. Being the "wrong" weight often affects people's self-esteem, and American females provide a clear example. A study of overweight 10- to 16-year-old Caucasians found that girls' self-esteem declined sharply and consistently through those years, but boys' self-esteem declined only during the early

years (Mendelson & White, 1985). Perhaps as overweight boys get older, some degree of bulk is considered "manly." And a survey of teenagers found that most of the girls and few boys were trying to *lose* weight, and many boys were trying to *gain* weight (Rosen & Gross, 1987). The greater concern among females than males about their weight—especially about being overweight—continues in adulthood (Forman et al., 1986). But cultural differences exist. Among overweight women in the United States, African Americans are more satisfied with their bodies than Whites are (Flynn & Fitzgibbon, 1998).

The other criterion for judging weight is healthfulness, based on data from studies of morbidity and mortality rates of men and women. Individuals who stay within certain weight ranges for their height have far lower rates of chronic illness and longer life spans than others do. *Whether* individuals do anything about their weight and *what* they do can have important implications for their health.

Overweight and Obesity

No matter how fit we are, our bodies have some fat—and they should. Having fat is a problem only when we have too much. The question is, how much is too much? Determining how much fat a person's body has is not as easy as it may seem. Bulk or stockiness alone can be misleading since some stocky people simply have larger skeletal frames than others, or their bodies are more

Table 7.3   *Values of the Body Mass Index Calculated from Height and Weight, with Shading for Health-Related Categories: Underweight, Healthy Weight, Overweight, and Obese*

Height in cm	Weight in Kilograms											
	58.5	63	67.5	72	76.5	81	85.5	90	94.5	99	103.5	108
135	31	34	36	39	41	43	46	48	51	53	56	58
140	29	31	34	36	38	40	43	45	47	49	52	54
145	27	29	31	34	36	38	40	42	44	46	48	50
150	25	27	29	31	33	35	37	39	41	43	45	47
155	24	26	27	29	31	33	35	37	38	40	42	44
160	22	24	26	28	29	31	33	34	36	38	40	41
165	21	23	24	26	27	29	31	32	34	36	37	39
170	20	21	23	24	26	27	29	30	32	34	35	37
175	19	20	22	23	24	26	27	29	30	32	33	35
180	18	19	20	22	23	24	26	27	28	30	31	33
185	17	18	19	21	22	23	24	26	27	28	30	31
190	16	17	18	20	21	22	23	24	26	27	28	29
195	15	16	17	19	20	21	22	23	24	25	27	28

Under-weight	Healthy-weight	Over-weight	Obese*
BMI = below 18.5	BMI = below 18.5–24.9	BMI = 25.0–29.9	BMI = 30 or more

*People with BMIs of 40 or more are described as extremely or morbidly obese.

muscular. Until the mid-1990s, overweight was evaluated by the degree of excess over ideal weights given in tables. Today, these judgments are based on the **body mass index** (BMI): people are classified as **overweight** if their BMI is 25 or higher, and **obese** if their BMI equals or exceeds 30 (NCHS, 2009a). You can find your approximate BMI in Table 7.3 or calculate it exactly: simply divide your weight in kilograms twice by your height in meters. Although the BMI doesn't measure the amount of body fat an individual has, professionals can use complex methods that do (Perri, Nezu, & Viegener, 1992).

Sociocultural, Gender, and Age Differences in Weight Control

The prevalence of overly fat people varies with nationality, sociocultural factors, gender, and age. Some national differences can be seen in Table 7.4, which gives the percentages of men and women who are obese in a variety of countries—obesity rates are high in the United States and low in Asian nations. And in most countries, obesity rates are higher among women than men.

Research has revealed a disturbing trend: among children and the population as a whole in the United States and other developed nations, the percentage who are overly fat has increased substantially during the last few decades (NCHS, 2009a; Wadden, Brownell, & Foster, 2002). As Table 7.5 shows, the prevalence rates of overweight for Americans has increased dramatically for men and women and more than quadrupled for children since the early 1970s. The reason is simple: people are consuming more calories and engaging in

Table 7.4 *Percentages of Adult[a] Men and Women Who Are Obese (BMI = 30 or Higher) in Various Nations Around the World*

Country	Men	Women
Australia	20.5	25.5
Brazil	8.9	13.1
Canada	22.9	23.2
China	2.4	3.4
Germany	20.5	21.1
Italy	7.4	8.9
India	1.3	2.8
Netherlands	10.2	11.9
Singapore	6.4	7.3
South Africa	8.8	27.4
Sweden	11.0	14.0
Turkey	na	22.7
United Kingdom	22.3	23.0
United States	33.1	35.2

[a]Adults were usually defined as 15 and older; some countries used different lower age limits or applied upper limits. Although the data were collected recently, some are a few years older than others; na = data not available.
Sources: NCHS, 2009a, Table 75 (for the United States); WHO, 2009.

Table 7.5 *Percentages of American Adult and Child Population Who Were Overweight (BMI = 25 or higher) in the Early 1970s and Today*

Years	Ages 6 to 11 Years Both Sexes	Ages 20 to 74 Years Men	Ages 20 to 74 Years Women
1971–1974	4.0	54.7	41.1
2003–2006	17.0	72.6	61.2

Source: NCHS, 2009a, Tables 75 and 76.

Table 7.6 *Percentage of White, Black, and Mexican American Men and Women Age 20 and Over Who Are Overweight (BMI = 25 or more) and Obese (BMI = 30 or more)*

Weight Status	White Male	White Female	Black Male	Black Female	Mexican Male	Mexican Female
Overweight	72.1	57.4	72.0	80.5	77.3	74.4
Obese	33.0	32.5	36.3	54.3	30.4	42.6

Source: NCHS, 2009a, Table 75.

less physical activity than in the past. For instance, in the three decades preceding 2000, Americans' daily consumption increased by 168 calories (7%) for men and 335 (22%) for women (CDC, 2004). Americans get heavier throughout the early- and middle-adulthood years, with the prevalence of overweight reaching and staying at their highest levels from 50 to 75 years of age (NCHS, 2009a).

Table 7.6 illustrates two important points about the body weights of American adults. First, the rates of overweight and obesity are extremely high across the three largest ethnic groups. Second, ethnic differences in overweight and obesity are clear and vary with gender. African American women have the highest rates of overweight and obesity; Mexican American women have the second-highest rate of obesity. The rates of obesity are similar for White men and women, Black men, and Mexican American men; White women have the lowest rates of overweight.

BECOMING OVERLY FAT

People add fat to their bodies by consuming more calories than they burn up through metabolism. Children who put on a lot of weight also eat much more fatty foods than others do (Robertson et al., 1999). The body stores excess calories as fat in *adipose tissue*, which consists of cells that vary in number and size (Logue, 1991). According to researcher Margaret Straw, the

> growth of adipose tissue throughout childhood and adolescence involves both an increase in cell size and in cell number. Thereafter, it appears that growth in adipose tissue is initially associated with an increase in cell size; if cell size becomes excessive, new adipose tissue is generated through an increase in the number of cells. (1983, p. 223)

A good way to control weight and promote health is to eat foods that are low in calories and fat, such as salads with low fat dressings.

There are two main reasons why adults tend to gain weight as they get older. First, people often put on weight at certain times, such as during pregnancy or around holidays, without taking it all off; the balance accumulates across years (Amorim Adegboye, Linne, & Lourenco, 2008; Phelan et al., 2008). Second, physical activity and metabolism decline with age (Smith, 1984). To maintain earlier weight levels, people need to take in fewer calories and exercise more after weight gains and as they get older. Both biological and psychosocial factors affect weight control.

Biological Factors in Weight Control

Because the metabolic rates of individuals can differ greatly, some thin people consume many more calories than some heavy people do and still stay slim. Fat tissue is less metabolically active than lean tissue, "so fatness itself can directly lower metabolic rate if fat tissue begins to replace lean tissue" (Rodin, 1981, p. 362). This means that people who are obese may continue to gain weight even if they don't increase caloric intake. Do heavy people eat more than normal-weight people? Yes, on average they do, and their diets contain more fats (Wing & Polley, 2001). Keep in mind that people's self-reports of dietary intake without corroboration can be misleading. Underreporting dietary intake is very common and occurs more among heavy

than normal-weight individuals, females than males, and people with little education (Klesges, Eck, & Ray, 1995; Lichtman et al., 1992).

Is heredity important in the development of obesity? Yes—for one thing, fatness of parents and their offspring are related (Whitaker et al., 1997). The chances of normal-weight children becoming obese by 30 years of age are low if their parents are of normal weight rather than obese. For obese children, the risk of being obese in adulthood is high even if they have normal-weight parents, and that risk doubles if their parents are obese. Of course, parent–child similarities may not be the result only of genetic factors: children learn many of their eating habits and physical activity patterns from their parents. But there is clearer evidence for the role of genetics:

- Twin and adoption studies have consistently found a genetic link in obesity (Wardle & Carnell, 2009; Wing & Polley, 2001).

- Evidence is mounting for a role of epigenetic processes in obesity (Waterland & Michels, 2007). Recall from Chapter 1 that environmental factors at critical times in the lifespan can produce chemical structures at DNA that can suppress a gene's usual activity and be transmitted to one's offspring.

- Researchers have identified specific genes in humans and animals that are linked to obesity (de Krom et al., 2009; Frayling et al., 2007; Wardle & Carnell, 2009). Two such genes are FTO, which affects the feeling of satiation and is linked to developing adipose tissue, and MC4R, which is associated with preferring and consuming high amounts of dietary fat.

But keep in mind three points about genetics and obesity. First, heredity is not destiny: a study found that people with the FTO gene who were very physically active were no heavier than others who did not have the gene (Rampersaud et al., 2008). This suggests that being physically active may overcome a genetic predisposition to be overweight. Second, we don't know how many people have genes that promote weight gain or how much of their excess weight results from these genes. Third, the recent surge in obesity around the world could not have resulted only from changes in genes—environmental factors are important, too.

Part of the way heredity affects our weight seems to be described in **set-point theory**, which proposes that each person's body has a certain or "set" weight that it strives to maintain (Keesey, 1986; Wonderlich & Freiburger, 2004). The body tries to maintain its weight near the set-point by means of a thermostat-like mechanism that involves the hypothalamus. When a person's weight departs from the set-point, the body takes corrective measures, increasing or decreasing eating and metabolism. According to the theory, people whose caloric intake is either drastically reduced or increased for a few months should show rapid corresponding weight changes initially, but the weight should then show slower changes and reach a limit. Studies have found that these predictions are correct and that people soon return to their original weight when they can eat what they want again (Leibel, Rosenbaum, & Hirsch, 1995; Sims, 1976; Wonderlich & Freiburger, 2004). But set-point theory is incomplete: it doesn't explain, for instance, why some people who lose a lot of weight manage to keep it off.

How is the hypothalamus involved in regulating body weight? One way is by monitoring the blood for levels of two hormones, leptin and insulin, that increase or decrease in proportion to the amount of body fat the person has (Tortora & Derrickson, 2009). **Leptin** regulates circuits in the hypothalamus that stimulate and inhibit eating and metabolism. **Insulin** is produced by the pancreas and has a similar, smaller effect on the hypothalamus, but it also regulates the amount of sugar (glucose) in the blood, glucose's conversion to fat, and the storage of fat in adipose tissue (Rodin, 1981, 1985). Obese people tend to have high serum levels of insulin—a condition called *hyperinsulinemia*—which increase one's sensations of hunger, perceived pleasantness of sweet tastes, and food consumption. Taken together, these findings indicate that weight gain results from a biopsychosocial process in which physiological factors interact with psychological and environmental factors (Rodin, 1985).

It seems likely that the setting and function of the set-point in regulating weight depend on the number and size of fat cells in the body. Because the number of fat cells increases mainly in childhood and adolescence, the diets of individuals during that time in the life span are likely to be very important. Obese children have fat cells that are as large as those of adults (Knittle et al., 1981). As these children gain weight, they do so mainly by adding fat cells, which normal-weight children don't do. Also, it appears that the number of fat cells can increase, but *not* decrease (Brownell, 1982). Individuals who develop too many fat cells—a condition called *fat-cell hyperplasia*—may be doomed to struggle against a high set-point for the rest of their lives. When fat-cell-hyperplastic adults try to lose weight, their fat cells shrink and

> send out metabolic signals similar to those during food deprivation. As a result, bodily mechanisms respond as though the person were starving, resulting in, among other things, an increase in hunger and a decrease in basal metabolism so that energy stores (i.e., fat) are maintained more efficiently. (Buck, 1988, p. 467)

This suggests that children's dietary and exercise patterns may be critical in determining whether they become overly fat. Once a person's set-point becomes established, changing it appears to be difficult. (Go to 💡.)

Psychosocial Factors in Weight Control

Psychosocial factors are also involved in weight control. For one thing, negative emotion affects eating and weight gain. Many people claim to eat more when they are anxious or upset, and evidence indicates that stress can induce eating (Logue, 1991). What's more, the foods people and animals eat when stressed tend to be sweet and high in fat—that is, "comfort foods" (Dallman et al., 2003; Oliver, Wardle, & Gibson, 2000). Prospective

HIGHLIGHT

Do "Fat-Bugs" Lead to Overweight?

Obese people's intestines are teeming with a type of bacteria, called Firmicutes, that lean people have in much smaller numbers (Bajzer & Seeley, 2006). Laboratory mice have the same pattern: obese mice have more of these bacteria than lean mice do. These bacteria are extremely efficient at drawing calories out of food, allowing the calories to be absorbed into the bloodstream. What happens to obese people's Firmicute levels when they lose weight? Researchers tested this and found that the levels decline. What would happen if researchers were to transfer large numbers of bacteria from the guts of obese mice to normal-weight mice that have none of these bacteria? Researchers tested this, too, and found that the mice that received bacteria from obese mice gained more weight than a control group that received bacteria from lean mice.

These findings are intriguing, but there's a lot we don't know yet about the role of these "fat-bugs" in overweight. How much of one's weight gain results from high levels of Firmicutes? Do set-point mechanisms, especially the role of leptin, influence the levels or functioning of these bacteria? Would removing or disabling Firmicutes in obese people help them lose weight?

research found that experiencing chronic stress and negative emotion, such as depression, puts people at risk for binge eating and becoming obese (Block et al., 2009; Stice, Presnell, & Spangler, 2002; Vogelzangs et al., 2008). **Binge eating** refers to episodes in which the person eats far more than most people would in a fairly short period, such as a couple of hours, and feels unable to control that behavior during that time (Garfinkel, 2002). Frequent binge eating is a common feature of individuals who seek treatment for obesity (Stice et al., 1999).

Another factor is the person's social network. A study found that individuals with a spouse or a same-sex sibling or friend who is obese are more likely in the next few years to become obese themselves than people without close social ties to obese people (Christakis & Fowler, 2007). And people with a close person in their social network who *lost* weight tended to lose weight. These links do not seem to result simply from people with shared eating and exercise patterns gravitating toward one another. Other research found that youths ate more at a meal if their eating partner ate a lot and was a friend rather than an unfamiliar peer, and those who were overweight ate more if the partner was overweight (Salvy et al., 2009). Perhaps models in our social network affect our concept of desirable body size, and we tend to adopt their eating patterns. If this is so, we're generally unaware of these influences (Vartanian, Herman, & Wansink, 2008).

Other lifestyle factors are also important. For example, regularly drinking a lot of alcohol adds calories to the diet and reduces the body's disposal of fat (Suter, Schutz, & Jequier, 1992; Tremblay et al., 1995). Being physically inactive lowers the rate at which the body burns calories. In adulthood, having a sedentary job may lead to overweight (Mummery et al., 2005). At all ages, watching TV can lead to weight gain by decreasing physical activity and by presenting mainly low-nutrient, sweet foods in shows and ads (Andersen, Crespo et al., 1998; Harris, Bargh, & Brownell, 2009; Story et al, 2008). In fact, watching some TV shows can reduce metabolic rates to *below* the person's resting rate: a study compared obese and normal-weight children while they simply rested and while they watched a show (*The Wonder Years*). During the show, their metabolic rates dropped to 12% below resting rates for the normal-weight and 16% below for the obese children (Klesges et al., 1992).

Another psychosocial factor in weight control is the person's sensitivity to food-related cues in the environment: obese people are more sensitive than nonobese people to certain cues (Schachter, 1971). For example, compared with the amount normal-weight people eat, obese individuals eat more when food tastes good, but eat less when it tastes bad. This stronger responsiveness to food cues may explain why obese restaurant diners are more susceptible than nonobese diners to the influence of a waitress's description or display of desserts (Herman, Olmstead, & Polivy, 1983). Because of this susceptibility to food-related cues, obese children may have difficulty controlling their eating at home. Studies examining family behaviors at mealtimes have shown that parents give more encouragement for eating and offer food more often to heavier children than to slimmer ones (Baranowski & Nader, 1985). Another food-related cue that affects eating is the size of the dish and serving utensil the person uses: people serve themselves larger portions if the dish or utensil is larger (Wansink, van Ittersum, & Painter, 2006).

Immigrants to a new land encounter many changes in their lifestyles and food availability. How does this affect their weight? Researchers studied this issue in the United States longitudinally with about 4,500 immigrants. When these people arrived in the country, their rate of obesity was very low. But their weights increased over time, and after about 15 years, their prevalence of obesity almost equaled the high levels of people born and raised in America (Goel et al., 2004). Surely, a major reason for their increase in obesity is that they adopted their new culture's unhealthy dietary and activity patterns.

Overweight and Health

In a study of overweight and normal-weight men and women, people were asked to rate their own health on a 10-point scale, where 1 equaled the "worst health" and 10 equaled the "best health" they could imagine (Laffrey, 1986). The ratings of the overweight and normal-weight

Given what we know about the development of obesity, this boy is likely to become an overweight adult and be at heightened risk of developing heart disease and diabetes. And the treat he is eating won't help matters.

individuals were about the same, averaging in the mid-7s. Are overweight and normal-weight people equally healthy?

To answer this question, we need to consider three factors, one of which is the *degree of overweight*. Research has clearly demonstrated that obesity is associated with high cholesterol levels and developing hypertension, heart disease, stroke, diabetes, and cancer (AHA, 2010; Bjørge et al., 2008; Calle et al., 2003; Kurth et al., 2003). This risk even applies to obese adolescents dying by the time they reach middle age. In general, the more severe the obesity, the greater the person's risk of developing and dying from one of these diseases. Thus, a person whose BMI is over 32 has a much greater risk of morbidity and mortality from, say, heart disease than someone whose BMI is 26, whose risk may not be elevated very much. What's more, the greater the BMI of overweight people, the more years they lose from their life span, as shown in Figure 7-3 (Fontaine et al., 2003). And adults' medical costs are related to BMI: compared with costs for healthy-weight individuals, annual costs are 69% higher for severely obese and 43% higher for underweight people (Wang et al., 2003). Add to all of this the role of smoking: obese smokers have many times the risk of dying of cardiovascular disease before age 65 than normal-weight nonsmokers (Freedman et al., 2006).

The two other factors in the health risks of being heavy are people's *fitness* and *distribution of fat* on the body. Among heavy people, those who are physically active and fit have much lower rates of death and of heart disease and diabetes than those who are sedentary (Blair & Brodney, 1999; Sui et al., 2007). Regarding body fat distribution, men's fat tends to collect in the abdominal region, but heavy women have more of their fat on the thighs, hips, and buttocks. Research has found higher rates of hypertension, diabetes, coronary heart disease, and mortality among people with higher, rather than lower, ratios of *waist to hip girth*—that is, their waist measurements compared to their hip measurements

(Wing & Polley, 2001). The heightened health risks when bodies are "rounded in the middle" may result from the unfavorable lipid levels and cardiovascular reactivity to stress these people show (Daniels et al., 1999; Goldbacher, Matthews, & Salomon, 2005).

Preventing Overweight

Each weekday morning, Amy and her son ride bikes to his school instead of taking a bus as part of a program to improve children's fitness and weight control. Becoming obese presents disadvantages to health and social relationships in childhood and adulthood (Wadden, Brownell, & Foster, 2002). Is it true, as many people believe, that children tend to outgrow weight problems, or that they will find it easy to lose weight when they are interested in dating? Probably neither belief is true for most children (Brownell, 1986; Jeffery, 1998). Losing weight after becoming obese is not easy at any age, and this is one reason why it is important to try to prevent overweight.

Preventing overweight should begin early. Infant obesity and unusually fast weight increases are related to obesity in later childhood, adolescence, and adulthood (Baird et al., 2005). And obesity in childhood is likely to continue into adult life (Serdula et al., 1993). As Figure 7-4 depicts, the risk depends on the child's age: the relationship to adult obesity is much stronger for obese 10- to 13-year-olds than infants. Normal-weight children don't usually become obese adults. Another reason to begin early is to prevent the excess development of fat cells, which occurs in childhood and adolescence. Obese adults who were fat in childhood have the double burden of dealing with bigger fat cells and more of them. Parents who exercise control over the feeding process do in fact prevent weight gain in infants (Farrow & Blissett, 2006). Still, there's a problem in preventing obesity in childhood: over one-third of parents of overweight

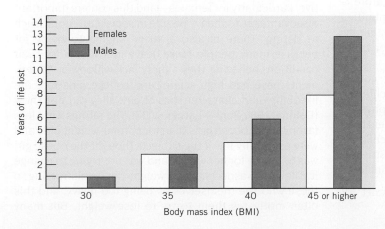

Figure 7-3 Years of life lost for obese Caucasian men and women in the United States as a function of their BMI in early adulthood. The number of years lost is the difference between the death ages for each BMI category and the life expectancies for same-age normal-weight people. Similar trends were found for African Americans, but the impact of BMI was less for the women and far greater for the men—for instance, among Blacks with BMIs at or above 45, the women lost about 5 years of life, and the men lost 20. (Abstracted from Fontaine et al., 2003, Figure 1.)

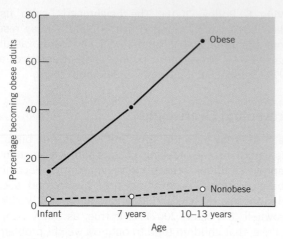

Figure 7-4 Percentage of obese and nonobese children who eventually become obese adults, as a function of age when weight status is assessed. (Data of Epstein, reported in Brownell, 1986, p. 313.)

children claim their child is "at about the right weight" (Jeffery et al., 2005; Maynard et al., 2003).

Most school nutrition programs have not been very successful at reducing future obesity, and those that have been tended to focus their efforts on females and students who volunteered to participate (Stice, Shaw, & Marti, 2006). Schools that simply provide menus with healthy alternative foods do not reduce the percentage of their students who are overweight (Veugelers & Fitzgerald, 2005). Children who are likely to need special preventive efforts to control their weight have a family history of obesity or have become overweight already (Jeffery, 1998). Efforts to help children control their weight need to focus on improving their diets and physical activity, involve cafeteria and educational facilities and staff, and enlist the cooperation of the parents (Baranowski & Hearn, 1997; Jeffery, 1998; Striegel-Moore & Rodin, 1985). Some researchers propose that societal law and policies should prevent obesity (Fabricatore & Wadden, 2006). For instance, laws in some communities now require labeling calories for foods in restaurant menus; when calories are labeled, patrons order fewer calories (Roberto et al., 2010).

Parents provide almost all the food that comes into the house and most of the food their children eat. They also model and encourage eating and physical activity patterns. Nutritionists and other researchers have identified several ways parents can help their children avoid becoming overly fat (Peckenpaugh, 2007; Striegel-Moore & Rodin, 1985). These recommendations include:

- Encourage regular physical activity and restrict TV watching.

- Don't use unhealthful food rewards for eating a nonpreferred food (e.g., "You may have dessert if you eat your peas"); use praise as the reward instead.

- Decrease buying high-cholesterol and sugary foods of all kinds, including soft drinks, for use in the home or elsewhere; avoid fast food restaurants.

- Use fruits, nuts, and other healthful foods as regular desserts, and reserve rich cakes and other less healthful desserts for special occasions or once-a-week treats.

- Make sure the child eats a healthful breakfast (with few eggs) each day and does not have high-calorie snacks at night. Metabolism generally decreases later in the day, so calories consumed at night tend to become fat.

- Monitor the child's BMI on a regular basis.

Childhood is probably the ideal time to establish activity and dietary habits to prevent individuals from becoming overly fat. A potentially useful survey has been developed to assess modifiable nutrition and physical activity practices in families and predict a child's risk for obesity (Ihmels et al., 2009). Nurses at schools or pediatric clinics may be able to administer the survey and counsel parents on ways to lower the risk. (Go to 💡.)

DIETING AND TREATMENTS TO LOSE WEIGHT

Many millions of people around the world are dieting on any given day of the year, especially in the spring when they are getting ready to bare their bodies in the summer. In the United States alone, about 48% of the women and 34% of the men try to lose weight in a given year (Weiss et al., 2006). Some individuals try to lose weight because they are concerned about the health risks of being overly fat: losing weight does in fact improve blood pressure and levels of lipids and lipoproteins (Reinehr et al., 2006; Linden & Chambers, 1994). But attractiveness motivates many people.

By American tastes, fatness is considered unattractive, particularly for females—and this confers important disadvantages for heavy people in social situations, such as dating. There is also a social stigma to being fat because many people *blame* heavy individuals for their condition, believing they simply lack willpower. Experiments have had high school and college girls rate the likeability and characteristics of girls they did not know (DeJong, 1980; Puhl & Latner, 2007). The ratings were less favorable for obese girls than for normal-weight girls and were especially low if the subjects thought the obese girl was to blame for her weight and was not trying to change it. The social aspects of overweight can be distressing to those who see themselves as being too heavy, and this often motivates them to try to lose weight. But many

HIGHLIGHT

Which "Carbs" to Avoid

The turn of the century brought a diet craze: avoid carbohydrates ("carbs"). In the process of digestion, carbs increase *glycemia*, or level of sugar in the blood. Avoiding carbs as a general diet strategy ignores the fact that carbohydrates differ in the speed and intensity of conversion to sugar. The physical effect on the body of an amount of carbs in a serving combined with the speed and intensity of conversion can be expressed with a measure called the **glycemic load** (Brand-Miller et al., 2003). Foods that contain a lot of carbs per serving and raise blood sugar quickly and markedly have high glycemic loads; these foods require strong insulin responses and are digested quickly. In contrast, foods with low glycemic loads make lower insulin demands and spread them out, are digested slowly, and delay feelings of hunger. A study randomly assigned children to receive low or high glycemic-load breakfasts and found that those in the former condition ate less at lunch, where they could choose their diets freely (Warren, Henry, & Simonite, 2003).

Thus, not all carbs are equal in their effects, and we should try to avoid foods with high glycemic loads. Foods with low glycemic loads include most fruits, vegetables, nuts, and whole grains; foods with high glycemic loads include candies, russet potatoes (not new potatoes), and items containing refined grains, such as instant rice, corn flakes, and most cakes and pasta. Meats and most dairy products have low glycemic loads, but often contain high levels of cholesterol and saturated fats. Eating high-glycemic-load diets has been linked to the development of coronary heart disease, diabetes, and cancer (Mente et al., 2009; Miller & Gutschall, 2009; Peckenpaugh, 2007).

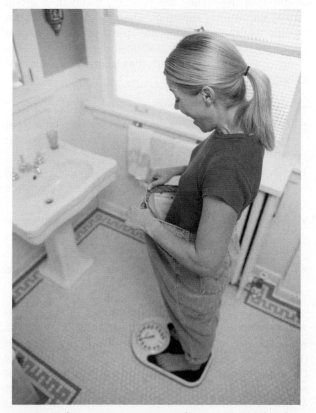

Losing weight is an important goal in many people's lives that brings great joy when it is clear that the effort worked.

overweight individuals adopt these weight biases—and when they do, they are less likely to carry out self-management acts in a treatment program that could reduce their weight (Carels et al., 2009).

Most people try to reduce their weight on their own by "going on a diet." In the United States, only about one-third of people who try to lose weight follow minimum guidelines to reduce calories and get 2½ hours of exercise a week; many use poor dieting strategies, such as skipping meals and taking nonprescription supplements (Weiss et al., 2006). Using ineffective methods may account for a paradoxical finding: the more that teenage girls and boys try control their weight, the greater their increases in weight in the long run (Field et al., 2003; Stice et al., 1999). Losing weight and keeping it off are difficult. The best approach for losing weight is to do it gradually and make lifestyle changes that the dieter and his or her family can accept and maintain permanently. People are more likely to succeed at losing weight if they have constructive social support from their families and others in their social network and if they have a high degree of self-efficacy or confidence that they can do it (Edell et al., 1987; Wing & Polley, 2001).

Although many overweight people succeed in making and sticking with the lifestyle changes needed to lose weight on their own, most do not (Rzewnicki & Forgays, 1987; Schachter, 1982). Many who do not succeed on their own feel they need help, and probably all people who seek help to lose weight have failed numerous times either to reduce or to maintain the new weight. What kinds of help do people seek, and what works?

Crash "Fad Diet" Plans

One kind of help millions of people try is the latest "crash" *fad diet*, which is often "guaranteed" to work in a short time. Some fad diets prescribe a strict dietary regimen with virtually no deviations permitted, and others have people eat certain types of food, such as only fruit, as in the "Beverly Hills diet," or foods that are high in protein and fat and low in carbohydrates and sugar, as in the "Atkins Diet." Some plans sell low-calorie liquid or solid replacements for part or all of the person's diet, but provide little or no help in maintaining weight loss. To the extent that people stick to these diets, they lose similar amounts of weight with each diet across several months because they consume fewer calories (Dansinger et al., 2005; Sacks et al., 2009). No crash diet is a substitute for adopting a healthful lifestyle of exercise and moderately sized, balanced meals.

Exercise

Physical activity is an important component in controlling weight. One of its benefits is that it increases metabolism, thereby helping the body to burn calories. Unfortunately, dieters often fail to exercise as part of reducing because they notice that it takes a lot of exercise to use up a few hundred calories—for instance, they would have to jog about half an hour to burn off the 400 or so calories in a milkshake. But studies of dieting obese individuals have revealed a variety of benefits of exercise in weight control. One benefit of exercise occurs in the first few months: it focuses weight reduction mostly on body fat, while preserving lean tissue (Andersen et al., 1999). When overweight people combine exercise with reduced caloric intake, they lose more weight than with dieting alone; and the greater the exercise intensity, the greater the loss (Goldberg & King, 2007). After losing weight, continued physical activity helps maintain the reduced weight, especially if the activity is vigorous.

Lifestyle Interventions Using Behavioral and Cognitive Methods

People who try to lose weight usually find that changing their eating patterns is very hard to do. Why? A major reason is that they don't know how to control antecedents and consequences in their environments that maintain their eating patterns. Behavioral methods have been developed to help dieters gain the control they need. Richard Stuart (1967) conducted a pioneering study of the utility of behavioral techniques, such as self-monitoring

and stimulus control, in helping several obese women lose weight over a 12-month period. The results were impressive: each of the eight women who stayed with the program lost weight fairly consistently throughout the year, losing from 12 to 20 kilograms.

The dramatic success of Stuart's program led to the incorporation of behavioral methods in programs called *lifestyle interventions*, which are designed to modify diet and exercise in overweight people (Fabricatore & Wadden, 2006). Meta-analyses have shown that lifestyle interventions are very effective in helping overweight and obese adolescents lose weight (Epstein et al., 2007; Kitzmann et al., 2010). Research findings suggest three conclusions about lifestyle interventions (Fabricatore & Wadden, 2006). First, these programs decrease initial body weight by 7% to 10% in 4 to 6 months. Second, lifestyle interventions are most effective in lowering weight and maintaining the loss when they provide meal replacements or structured meal plans, such as with menus and shopping lists. Third, although on average obese people who complete a behavioral program for weight control gain much of it back in the first year, many maintain their lower weight.

What techniques do lifestyle interventions for weight loss use? They are typically given in a group format with weekly meetings when participants submit records of their eating, are weighed, and receive information and feedback (Fabricatore & Wadden, 2006; Wing & Polley, 2001). And they usually include the following components:

- *Nutrition* and *exercise counseling*.
- *Self-monitoring* by having the person keep careful records of the foods eaten, when, where, with whom, and under what circumstances.
- *Stimulus control* techniques, such as shopping for food with a list, storing food out of sight, and eating at home in only one room.
- *Altering the act of eating*, for example, by chewing the food very thoroughly before swallowing and putting utensils down on the table between mouthfuls.
- *Behavioral contracting*, or setting up a system of rewards for sticking to the diet.

Two other features are important in lifestyle interventions for weight loss. First, having family or friends working as a team in the program enhances its success (Kitzmann et al., 2010; Wing & Jeffery, 1999). Having these people as weight-loss support partners is most successful if the partners lose weight, too (Gorin et al., 2005). Second, rewarding overweight individuals for *not engaging in sedentary activities*, such as watching TV or playing computer games, and unplugging the TV and computer are very helpful in promoting weight loss (Epstein et al., 2004).

Cognitive methods have also been used in weight loss programs. *Motivational interviewing*, which we've discussed in earlier chapters, is applied to increase the person's commitment to and self-efficacy for change; it is helpful in promoting weight loss (Burke, Arkowitz, & Menchola, 2003). Another method, called *problem-solving training*, is designed to teach people strategies to help them deal with everyday difficulties they encounter in sticking to their diets (Perri, Nezu, & Viegener, 1992). Individuals often have difficulty sticking to a diet at family celebrations, when eating at restaurants, and when under stress, for instance. The skills learned in problem-solving training enable people to find solutions to these difficulties. Overweight people who can generate these kinds of solutions tend to lose more weight and have fewer lapses than do others (Drapkin, Wing, & Shiffman, 1995. (Go to 👤.)

Self-Help and Worksite Weight-Loss Programs

There are dozens of commercial self-help organizations for weight control, and most of the largest ones provide group or individual support sessions; some of them, such as *Jenny Craig* and *Optifast*, require members to buy their meal replacement products (Tsai & Wadden, 2005). Different self-help organizations have their own mix of

methods to help people lose weight. *Weight Watchers* has members use behavioral methods, prepare their own meals, and attend group meetings for information and social support. Although little research has been done on the success of self-help groups, the evidence for *Weight Watchers* is the strongest so far, showing that this program produces moderate weight losses for those who complete them (Heshka et al., 2003; Tsai & Wadden, 2005). But dropout rates for self-help groups may be high, sometimes over 50% in the first 6 weeks alone (Stunkard, 1987).

Worksite weight-loss programs have been introduced and evaluated in a variety of businesses and industries. These programs generally used behavioral techniques, but were not very successful (Foreyt & Leavesley, 1991). High dropout rates and small weight losses have been common, suggesting that inadequate motivation is a major flaw. These problems can be reduced in two ways: gearing the program to the workers' stages of readiness to change and providing incentives for participation (Gomel et al., 1993). Using teams in *weight-loss competitions* at worksites provides incentives and increases the amount of weight lost (Brownell et al., 1984; Wing & Polley, 2001). Also, a company might offer a prize for the team achieving the greatest percentage of a weight loss goal. To help the teams do well, the company could provide information about nutrition, exercise, and behavioral methods, such as self-monitoring, stimulus control, and rewards.

CLINICAL METHODS AND ISSUES

Problem-Solving Training to Control Weight

The cognitive method called problem-solving training can help people deal with a variety of behavioral and emotional difficulties by teaching them how to generate solutions to specific problems in their lives (Sarafino, 2001). For example, when people try to follow a low calorie diet, they often have trouble eating healthfully when they eat outside their own households, such as at restaurants, work, or sporting events. Here are some common problems these dieters face and examples of solutions they might produce.

PROBLEM: *I eat vending machine and restaurant food too much. How can I curb this?*

SOLUTIONS: Prepare lunch and take it to work; eat with others who do the same. Take low calorie snacks with you to work, movies, sporting events, shopping malls, etc.

PROBLEM: *When I know I will be eating out, how can I choose a restaurant that will make it easier to stick to my diet?*

SOLUTIONS: Identify restaurants in advance that have healthy selections. Avoid going to all-you-can-eat buffet restaurants that have tempting high calorie selections.

PROBLEM: *When faced with a restaurant menu that includes high calorie foods, how can I restrict the calories I eat?*

SOLUTIONS: Learn about high and low calorie ingredients and preparation methods, such as frying versus grilling, and ask the waiter questions. Skim the menu to reject high calorie selections; read only low calorie options. If ordering a salad, ask for the dressing on the side; use only a little. If others are having dessert, either share one with another person or order fruit or sherbet. Ask about portion size; if too large, ask for smaller.

Medically Supervised Approaches

Some approaches for losing weight involve medical procedures or require supervision by a doctor. Because of the risks and side effects, these methods are recommended only for people who are *obese* and have failed to control their weight with diet and exercise. One medical approach uses prescribed drugs, two of which are *sibutramine*, which suppresses appetite, and *orlistat*, which decreases intestinal absorption of ingested fat. Each of these drugs produces moderate weight loss, and combining pharmacological and behavioral treatments is more effective than either alone (Han & Yanovski, 2008; Phelan & Wadden, 2002; Snow et al., 2005). Another medical approach for losing weight involves placing the patient on a *protein-sparing modified fast* regimen that contains fewer than 800 calories per day (Han & Yanovski, 2008). Although this approach is safe, it requires vigilant medical supervision and promotes only short-term weight loss.

The most drastic medical approaches for losing weight involve *bariatric surgery*, procedures that change the structure of the stomach or intestines (AMA, 2003). The two most common forms of bariatric surgery alter the stomach. One form simply installs a band around the upper part of the stomach to create a little chamber with a small opening to the rest of the stomach. Because the chamber holds only 25–50 g the person feels full after ingesting a small amount. The second form reduces the size of the stomach by literally stapling part of it up. Although bariatric surgery markedly reduces weight, it entails some surgical risk and possible side effects (Han & Yanovski, 2008; Snow et al., 2005). As a result, these methods are recommended only for patients who are extremely obese (BMI of 40 or more). Most bariatric surgery programs require psychological screening, and they may reject the procedure for patients with certain characteristics, such as current mental illness or heavy drinking (Bauchowitz et al., 2005). Another surgical procedure called *liposuction* sucks adipose tissue from the body with a tube, but is not a weight reduction method—its function is strictly cosmetic, "body sculpting." It is used for removing fat from specific regions of the body, such as the thighs or abdomen. Although the procedure is usually safe, complications can include blood clots or even death (AMA, 2003).

We have considered methods for losing weight that range from adjusting one's diet and exercising to using surgical procedures. When overweight people decide which approaches to use, they should first try to alter their diets and exercise conscientiously on their own, perhaps with behavioral methods and a support partner.

If that doesn't work, the next steps might be to join a reputable self-help group and then to get psychological or medical help.

Relapse after Weight Loss

The problem of relapse after completing treatment to lose weight is similar to that which many people experience after quitting smoking, drinking, or using drugs. The situations in which people who have lost weight overeat usually involve *food cues*, such as being at a restaurant or having a special meal, *negative emotions*, such as stress or depression, and *boredom* (Wing & Polley, 2001). Individuals who maintain their reduced weight for a few years stand a very good chance of maintaining that weight in subsequent years (McGuire et al., 1999). When considering weight gain in the years after losing weight, keep in mind that people generally gain weight as they get older. A fair assessment of weight loss success should also take into account *the weight dieters didn't gain* that other people do (Perri, Nezu, & Viegener, 1992).

Can we prevent relapse after weight loss? Michael Perri and his colleagues (1988) demonstrated that follow-up treatment programs can diminish the relapse problem after people lose weight, allowing them to maintain most of their loss. The treatment had two critical components: frequent therapist meetings to deal with problems individuals were having in maintaining their weight and social influences of other members who met as a group. Most lifestyle interventions today continue contact after people lose weight (Fabricatore & Wadden, 2006). Perri and colleagues (2001) later found that problem-solving training after weight loss with behavioral methods was also effective in helping clients maintain the loss.

Most people who lose weight do not use effective ways to maintain the loss. If you wanted to lose weight and keep it off, what methods could you use? Here are some:

- When losing the weight, use behavioral techniques—such as self-monitoring and stimulus control—to help you diet and increase exercise. Choose a reasonable final weight goal, and plan to lose weight *gradually*, such as a pound a week or less.

- After reaching your weight goal, permanently eat a low-calorie-and-fat diet. Pay attention to calories and use structured meal plans (Fabricatore & Wadden, 2006; Phelan et al., 2009). For carbohydrates, choose ones that have low glycemic loads. Stick to this diet fairly consistently throughout the week, including weekends (Gorin et al., 2004).

- Continue to exercise—it's a strong predictor of long-term weight maintenance (Phelan et al., 2009; Wing & Polley, 2001). Weigh yourself each time you exercise.

- Avoid situations that prompt lapses, and reward good behavior. Occasional lapses are not a problem as long as you get back on track as soon as possible.

- Get social support from family and friends for maintaining your weight loss. Join a self-help or support group if you find that you have too many lapses.

(Go to 🍎.)

ANOREXIA AND BULIMIA

Although gaining weight by overeating is a very common problem with psychosocial impacts, it is not a psychiatric disorder. In contrast, two less common eating problems—*anorexia nervosa* and *bulimia nervosa*—are included as psychiatric disorders in the *Diagnostic and Statistical Manual of Mental Disorders* (DSM-IV) of the American Psychiatric Association (2000). People with these disorders use extreme ways to keep their weight down. Anorexia is illustrated in the following case study of a 19-year-old, 158cm tall coed named Frances who had been 9 kilograms overweight 6 years earlier. She

> weighed 37.5 kg upon admission [to therapy]. She reported eating very little food each day (estimated to be less than 500 kcal). She exercised for at least 3 hours each day by attending aerobics classes and running. When she did consume a normal meal, she purged it via self-induced vomiting…. She never binged (i.e., ate large quantities of food). She was

obsessed with fears of weight gain. (Williamson, Cubic, & Fuller, 1992, p. 367)

When she was younger, she had been teased by peers and repeatedly criticized by her mother for being overweight. As Frances's case shows, **anorexia nervosa** is an eating disorder that involves a drastic reduction in food intake and an unhealthy loss of weight. People with this disorder are characterized by a weight at least 15% below normal (BMI at or less than 17.5), an intense fear of gaining weight, and a distorted idea of their body shape (Keel, 2010; Kring et al., 2010). The starvation in anorexia may be so extreme as to cause or contribute to the person's death—for instance, by causing kidney failure, cardiac arrest, extremely low blood pressure, or cardiac arrhythmias (due to low levels of electrolytes, such as potassium) (Kring et al., 2010).

Bulimia nervosa is characterized by recurrent episodes of *binge eating*, generally followed by *purging* by self-induced vomiting, laxative use, or other means to prevent gaining weight, such as excessive exercise (Becker, 2010; Kring et al., 2010). These episodes often occur when feelings of positive affect are low and stress and negative emotions are high (Smyth et al., 2007). People with bulimia nervosa appear to experience chronic high stress levels (Ludescher et al., 2009). This disorder can cause a wide range of medical problems, including inflammation of the digestive tract and cardiac problems, such as arrhythmias. Bulimic individuals are

---

ASSESS YOURSELF

Your Weight Control Patterns

For each of the following questions, put a check mark in the preceding space if your answer is "yes."

_____ Do you watch your calorie intake more carefully than anyone else you know?

_____ Is your BMI less than 19?

_____ Do you think gaining a few pounds during a holiday season would be a terrible thing?

_____ Have you ever eaten so much so quickly that you felt as though you had lost control of your eating?

_____ If yes, has this happened more than about 10 times in the past year?

_____ Have you ever eaten a lot and then tried to "purge" the food by using laxatives, diuretics, or self-induced vomiting?

_____ If yes, has this happened more than about 10 times in the past year?

_____ Have you felt a lot of emotional distress in recent months?

_____ Do you often eat fewer than two meals a day?

_____ Do you regularly exercise more than 10 hours a week to lose weight?

How many "yes" answers did you give? A high number suggests that you may have an eating disorder. If your number is: from 3 to 5, you may want to consider getting professional help, especially if your situation seems to be getting worse; 6 or more, you should seek help right away. You can find help through your college's counseling office or by contacting professional organizations, such as the American Psychological Association and the American Psychiatric Association, which are in Washington, DC. (Based on material in Brownell, 1989; Kring et al., 2010; Logue, 1991.)

aware that their eating pattern is abnormal, are fearful of having lost control of their eating, and tend to be depressed and self-critical after a bulimic episode. Many people exhibit some bulimic behaviors, such as purging, but are not classified as bulimic because they engage in these behaviors infrequently.

It is difficult to know how prevalent eating disorders are. A study that compared women's medical records with returned surveys on eating disorders to the researchers found that many of those who did not return the survey did in fact have eating disorders (Beglin & Fairburn, 1992). Thus, existing data are likely to be underestimates. Estimates of prevalence for the general population in Western cultures are 0.5–1.0% for anorexia and 1–2% for bulimia, with more than 90% of diagnosed cases being females, and these disorders are becoming increasingly common in other cultures (Becker, 2010; Keel, 2010; Kring et al., 2010). Anorexia is especially common among dance students, models, and athletes who feel pressured to control their weight (French & Jeffery, 1994).

Why People Become Anorexic and Bulimic

What causes the eccentric eating habits of anorexia and bulimia? The answer is still unclear, and researchers have suggested biological, psychological, and cultural factors that may be involved. There is evidence for genetic and physiological links to these disorders (Becker, 2010; Keel, 2010; Kring et al., 2010). For example, studies have examined the occurrence of anorexia and bulimia in twins and found that these disorders are far more likely to appear in *both* twin members if they are identical twins rather than fraternal twins. Other research findings indicate that the functioning of neuroendocrine and neurotransmitter processes may be abnormal in eating-disordered individuals.

Cultural factors may provide the answer to two obvious questions about these eating disorders: Why is the prevalence of anorexia and bulimia particularly high among White females, and why has it increased in recent years? In the United States, Black girls have lower prevalence rates of eating disorders than White girls, partly because they tend to be less concerned about their weight even when they are heavy (Abrams, Allen, & Gray, 1993). Beauty plays a central role in the sex-role stereotype of women in many cultures, and Western cultures have witnessed recent changes in their ideals about female beauty (Striegel-Moore, 1997). Years ago, the "ideally beautiful woman" had a figure that was more rounded, with larger bust and hip measurements. After 1960 or so, the ideal figure of a woman became much thinner, and the social pressures on women to be slender increased. Caucasian females are more likely than males to wish they were thinner and to diet, and these gender

This anorexic girl probably sees herself as "too fat" despite her thinness.

differences begin to show up by age 11 or so (Cohen, Brownell, & Felix, 1990). In social interactions with other children, parents, and teachers, girls more than boys are given the message: thin is better (Attie & Brooks-Gunn, 1987). And once the message is clear, they reach puberty, when girls add an average of over 9 kilograms of fat to their bodies while boys add muscle. This is a no-win situation for adolescent girls. How do they deal with it?

When adolescents—especially females—start trying to control their weight, they typically adjust their diets in a normal manner, but for many teens the methods they use become more extreme, involving occasional fasting or purging. A study found that about 13% of 15-year-olds engaged in some form of purging behavior, mainly on a monthly basis or less, with the rate for females being twice as high as that for males (Killen et al., 1986). Prospective evidence indicates that individuals who become anorexic and bulimic typically start out dieting normally but have relatively strong concerns about their weight, and then begin using more extreme methods (French & Jeffery, 1994; Killen et al., 1994). Dieters with strong weight concerns may come to rely more and more on fasting and purging because these methods keep weight off, and this pattern becomes entrenched in those who become bulimic, especially if they were overweight in childhood (Fairburn et al., 2003). The development of eating disorders has been linked to the prior experience of chronic stress and other psychiatric difficulties, often with a major life event in the weeks before the disorder's onset (Rojo et al., 2006).

Why does disordered eating become so compulsive? People who are extremely concerned about their weight tend to see themselves as round-faced and pudgy, even when others do not. Studies using ingenious apparatuses, such as special projectors, have shown that the great majority of women overestimate their size and generally perceive themselves to be one-fourth larger than they really are (Thompson, 1986). Although men make similar errors, they do so to a much lesser degree—and, unlike women, many of these men may *want* to be larger. Body size overestimation is very pronounced among anorexic individuals, and the idea that they are overweight persists long after they have become slim. When they are reduced to skin and bones, anorexic individuals still claim to be "too fat" and greatly overestimate their size (Askevold, 1975; Crisp & Kalucy, 1974). Another factor that ties in here is the relatively high levels of the personality trait of perfectionism that people with anorexia and bulimia tend to have (Becker, 2010; Keel, 2010). That is, no matter how hard these individuals strive to achieve their "perfect" body, they are never satisfied. Interventions delivered on computers or in person can reduce the risk of developing eating disorders in people who are very dissatisfied with their body shapes (Franko et al., 2005; Stice, Shaw, & Marti, 2007).

Treatments for Anorexia and Bulimia

Because anorexia nervosa involves a severe and health-threatening underweight condition, the first priority in treating this disorder is to restore the person's body weight and nutrition to as near normal as possible. This is often done in a hospital setting. Treatment with behavioral techniques is effective for putting weight on (Kring et al., 2010). But keeping the weight on is difficult; about half of previously treated anorexics continue to have eating problems and often show other social and emotional difficulties, such as depression. The main form of psychological therapy for anorexia involves the patient's family and often focuses on the dynamics of mealtime interactions; drugs to treat depression or other disorders are also used (Keel, 2010; Kring et al., 2010).

Psychotherapy is more effective for bulimia than anorexia, particularly when it includes behavioral and cognitive methods (Becker, 2010; Hay et al., 2009; Kring et al., 2010). These methods—such as self-monitoring, reinforcement, and cognitive restructuring—focus on reducing bingeing and purging behaviors; sometimes drugs are added to these approaches to decrease depression. Treatment is less effective for clients with bulimia who have very high initial rates of bingeing and purging and a history of substance abuse (Wilson, Loeb et al., 1999).

We have discussed the problems people have in controlling their weight through adjustments in their diets. We have also seen that exercise can play an important role in reducing body fat and, thereby, can enhance people's health. The next section examines exercise as a means of becoming fit and keeping well.

EXERCISE

Sometimes it seems like a fitness boom has occurred in many nations. For instance, the proportion of Americans who exercise doubled in the 20 years after the early 1960s (Serfass & Gerberich, 1984). Joggers and bicyclists today can be seen on roads and paths in cities and out in the country, and fitness clubs have sprung up everywhere. But in the United States and most other industrialized countries, adults' lifestyles still include very little or irregular physical activity (Brownson, Boehmer, & Luke, 2005; Sallis & Owen, 1999). We've all heard that exercise is healthy. We'll see why in this section. (Go to 💡.)

HIGHLIGHT

Types and Amounts of Healthful Exercise

All physical activities—even just fidgeting—use energy and burn calories. *Exercise* is a special class of physical activity in which people exert their bodies in a structured and repetitive way for the sake of health or body development. There are several types of exercise, each with its own form of activity, physical goals, and effects.

Isotonics, Isometrics, and Isokinetics

Isotonic exercise builds strength *and* endurance by the person's moving a heavy object, exerting most of the muscle force in one direction. This type of exercise includes weight lifting and many calisthenics. In doing push-ups, for example, most of the exertion occurs in raising the body.

(continued)

HIGHLIGHT *(Continued)*

Isometric exercise builds mainly strength rather than endurance—the person exerts muscle force against an *immovable* object. For example, in the "chair lift" the person sits in a standard unupholstered chair, grasps the sides of the seat with both hands, and pulls upward, straining the arm muscles. The seat doesn't move. **Isokinetic exercise** builds strength *and* endurance—the person exerts muscle force to move an object in more than one direction, such as forward and back. Isokinetic exercise usually requires special equipment, such as Nautilus machines.

Aerobics

The word *aerobic* literally means "with oxygen." What does oxygen have to do with exercise? When we exert ourselves physically, the energy for it comes from the metabolic process of burning fatty acids and glucose in the presence of oxygen. Continuous exertion at high intensity over many minutes requires a great deal of oxygen. Being "fit" means the person consumes a high *volume of oxygen* (VO_2) per heartbeat during exertion.

The term **aerobic exercise** refers to energetic physical activity that requires high levels of oxygen over an extended time, say, 20 minutes. Aerobic activities generally involve rhythmical actions that move the body over a distance or against gravity—as occurs in fast dancing, jogging, bicycling, swimming, or certain calisthenics. Performing aerobic activity with sufficient intensity and duration on a regular basis increases the body's ability to extract oxygen from the blood and burn fatty acids and glucose.

An Ideal Exercise Program for Health

How much and what kinds of exercise are best for fitness? The answer depends on the individual's age, current health and physical capacity, goals, interests, and opportunities, such as whether facilities or partners are available (Insel & Roth, 1998). Almost all individuals need to begin with a moderate *starter program* and progress in a gradual manner toward fitness; people who are elderly or less fit should progress more slowly than others. Starting gradually avoids muscle soreness and injury and allows the body to adapt to increasing physical demands.

Americans spend an average of 6 hours a day performing physical activities (Matthews et al., 2008). An ideal exercise program would add the equivalent of 30 minutes a day of moderate-intensity physical activity, such as walking briskly (USDA, 2005). This translates to about 3 hours of exercise a week, which can be divided into three to six sessions, each having three phases (Blair et al., 1992; Insel & Roth, 1998):

1. *Warmup.* Each session should include two types of warmup activities: (1) stretching and flexibility exercises, for various major muscle groups, such as of the neck, back, shoulders, abdomen, and legs; and (2) strength and endurance exercises, such as push-ups, pull-ups, and lifting.

2. *Aerobics.* The next 20 minutes or more involves rhythmical exercise of large muscle groups, performed vigorously, raising the heart (pulse) rate to a moderately high target range. One way to estimate the target range for an adult is to use a formula based on the person's age: the *minimum* heart rate equals 160 pulse beats per minute minus the person's age; the *maximum* is 200 minus age (La Place, 1984). Thus, 30-year-olds would maintain their heart rate between 130 and 170 beats per minute during aerobics.

3. *Cool-down.* The last few minutes of exercise should taper off in intensity to return the body to its normal state. These exercises can include calisthenics or walking.

Although this ideal seems fairly rigid, there is room for variation. For instance, individuals who exercise at the upper end of their target range can use fewer or shorter exercise periods each week. People can also tailor the program to their goals and interests by varying the exercises they perform during each phase and across sessions, such as by varying the aerobics they do: jogging on one day, skipping rope on another, swimming on another, and so on. If they want to firm their abdomens, they can focus on appropriate activities during the warmup and cool-down phases.

Is the Ideal Necessary to Benefit Health?

Not all people can or will get the ideal amount and type of physical activity. Can they benefit from less? Absolutely, and the activity needn't be "exercise"—it can be riding a bike or gardening, for instance—and it can occur in, say, 10-minute periods rather than all at once (Phillips, Kiernan, & King, 2001). Although the greatest health benefits accrue with vigorous activity, avoiding an almost completely sedentary lifestyle is critical.

THE HEALTH EFFECTS OF PHYSICAL ACTIVITY

If you asked fitness-conscious people why they exercise, they'd probably give a variety of reasons: "Exercising helps me keep my weight down," "I like it when I'm in shape—and so does my boyfriend," "It helps me unwind and relieves my tension," "Being in shape keeps me sharp on my job," "I don't get sick as often when I'm fit," and "It makes people's hearts stronger, so they live longer." These answers describe psychosocial and physical health benefits of exercising and are, for the most part, correct.

Psychosocial Benefits of Exercise

Three psychosocial benefits of exercise have been shown in many studies. First, engaging in regular vigorous exercise is associated with lower feelings of *stress* and anxiety, as we discussed in Chapter 4. Second, people who engage in a fitness program with aerobic exercise show improved cognitive processes, such as in making fewer errors and having better memory (Quick et al., 1997; Smith et al., 2010). Third, participating in regular exercise is linked to enhanced *self-concepts* of individuals, especially children (Dishman, 1986; Sallis & Owen, 1999). Self-concept enhancements may occur because these people are able to maintain an attractive appearance and engage successfully in sports activities; as a result, they receive many social advantages that accrue with being fit.

But keep in mind two issues about psychosocial benefits from exercise. First, most studies on stress and self-concept used correlational or retrospective methods, making it difficult to determine cause-effect relationships. Some evidence suggests that part of the self-reported benefits may have resulted from a placebo effect of the subjects' expecting that psychosocial benefits would occur (Desharnais et al., 1993). Second, the extent to which individuals experience these benefits appears to depend on their genetic makeup (Mata, Thompson, & Gotlib, 2010).

Physical Benefits of Exercise

Of the many physiological effects that physical activity produces, one effect is especially intriguing: vigorous exercise seems to increase the body's production of *endorphins*, which are morphinelike chemical substances. Studies have shown that endorphin levels in the blood are higher after exercise than before (Carr et al., 1981). Some researchers claim that the euphoric "runner's high" that many individuals feel after a very vigorous aerobic workout results from high levels of endorphins reaching the brain, which then decreases stress and sensations of pain. But evidence for these possibilities is unclear (Phillips, Kiernan, & King, 2001).

Exercise can enhance many aspects of people's physical fitness throughout the life span. In childhood, aerobic exercise improves agility and cardiovascular function (Alpert et al., 1990). What about much later in the life span, when people generally show a gradual decline in their flexibility, strength, and endurance? This decline occurs partly because many individuals get less exercise as they get older. Compared with people who are sedentary in mid-life, individuals who have physically active lifestyles have higher physical function years later (Hillsdon et al., 2005). And an 18-year longitudinal study of men who were over 50 years of age at the start of the study and who engaged in aerobic exercise regularly found that their work capacity decreased only slightly across the 18 years, whereas men in the general population tend to show a 1–2% decrease per year (Kasch, Wallace, & Van Camp, 1985). Also, the resting blood pressure and percentage of body fat of these men did not show the increases that usually occur during these years. The evidence clearly indicates that engaging in aerobic exercise curbs the usual decline in fitness that people experience as they get older (Buchner et al., 1992).

The physical benefits from regular exercise are reflected also in people's health and longevity, even if they are overweight (Carlsson et al., 2007; Koster et al., 2009; Leitzmann et al., 2007). Vigorous exercise produces the greatest gains, but even taking brisk walks or expending energy in everyday activities, such as climbing stairs, can benefit longevity (Kujala et al., 1998, Manini et al., 2006). The main health benefits of exercise relate to preventing cardiovascular problems and some forms of cancer (Phillips, Kiernan, & King, 2001; Sallis & Owen, 1999). Many studies have found that people who regularly engage in vigorous physical activity are less likely to develop and die from coronary heart disease (CHD) than those who lead relatively sedentary lives (Powell et al., 1987; Weinstein et al., 2008). Although no experimental research has been done in which humans were randomly assigned to exercise and nonexercise conditions, research with animals and prospective studies with humans indicate that the link between physical activity and reduced risk of CHD is probably causal. Table 7.7 describes ways by which fitness and physical activity protect individuals against cardiovascular disease.

The risk of developing cancer has been linked to low physical activity; the evidence is fairly strong for colon cancer and more modest for other cancers, such as of the breast and prostate (Sallis & Owen, 1999). Although the reason for this link is unclear, part of it may involve the beneficial effect of both immediate and long-term exercise on the immune system. One study tested healthy, physically active adults and found that

Table 7.7   *How Physical Activity/Fitness Protects Cardiovascular Health*

Benefit	Description
Blood pressure	People who are active and fit have lower systolic and diastolic blood pressure than those who are not, and they are less likely to develop hypertension (Blair et al., 1992; Haskell, 1984). Exercise lowers blood pressure in people with and without hypertension (Braith et al., 1994; Kokkinos et al., 1995; Martinez-Gomez et al., 2009).
Lipids	Physical activity improves serum lipid levels—it raises HDL and lowers LDL and triglycerides (Szapary, Bloedon, & Foster, 2003).
Reactivity to stress	Fit individuals show lower heart rate and blood pressure reactivity to stress than unfit people do (Forcier et al., 2006).

vigorous exercise sessions increased their natural killer cell number and function (Fiatarone et al., 1989).

Are There Health Liabilities to Exercise?

Not all effects of exercise are beneficial—there can be hazards as well. One hazard occurs when people jog or bicycle in traffic, of course, risking a collision. But the most common problems that arise involve injury to bones or muscles from other kinds of accidents and from overstraining the body (Sallis & Owen, 1999). For instance, high impact exercises, such as jogging and tennis, can injure joints and lead to arthritis. Many injuries happen to people who do not exercise regularly or are beginners, mainly from overtaxing their bodies and from unsafe exercise conditions, such as having improper shoes. Exercising too long in very hot weather can lead to heat exhaustion—with symptoms of dizziness, rapid and weak pulse, and headache—or a more severe condition called heat stroke, which can be fatal.

Sudden cardiac death can occur when exercising. Autopsy reports for individuals who had died in association with exercising typically reveal that the cause was cardiac arrest, and most of them had cardiovascular problems that existed prior to the attack (Northcote, Flannigan, & Ballantyne, 1986). Most of these problems could have been detected by medical screening, which does in fact reduce the risk of sudden death (Corrado et al., 2006). Cardiac arrest from exercising is unlikely—one case per 1.5 million sessions of physical exertion—and occurs much less frequently in people who exercise five times rather than once a week (Albert et al., 2004).

Doctors and physical therapists can prescribe exercise programs for people with specific health problems, such as diabetes and CHD.

Another health hazard that relates to exercise is people's use of *anabolic steroids*—male hormones that build tissue—to increase muscle size and strength. Many more males than females use steroids, and most users are athletes (AMA, 2003; Strauss & Yesalis, 1991). Using steroids for an extended period has several negative health effects. It raises LDL and lowers HDL serum cholesterol and is related to liver and kidney tumors and to heart attacks and strokes. It also has a permanent masculinizing effect in women, increasing facial hair and lowering the voice, for instance. In males, it increases acne and balding and decreases the size and firmness of testes, at least temporarily. Some who use steroids share needles with others, putting each other at risk for HIV infection (DuRant et al., 1993).

Conclusions regarding the health effects of exercise are fairly clear. Frequent physical activity, especially vigorous exercise, is psychologically and physically healthful, particularly for preventing heart disease. People who begin exercise programs should guard against overtaxing their bodies, exercise under safe conditions with proper skills, and have periodic medical examinations to determine whether any underlying risks exist. Although more people exercise today than was the case decades ago, most adults in industrialized countries do not get enough regular and energetic physical activity.

WHO GETS ENOUGH EXERCISE, WHO DOES NOT—AND WHY?

Most people in many developed nations do not get enough exercise. Many individuals who could be physically active in their normal lifestyles choose not to be—they may take rest breaks rather than sustaining an activity or opt to use a machine instead of doing a task manually. The high physical activity of early childhood declines sharply during adolescence: for instance, only half of American teenagers are vigorously active on a regular basis (Duncan et al., 2007; Marcus et al., 2000). Teens with high levels of physical activity tend to have high activity levels in adulthood, too (Telama et al., 2005). Because little is known about people's everyday physical activities, we will emphasize factors associated with doing and not doing exercises.

Gender, Age, and Sociocultural Differences in Exercise

Physical activity varies across cultures. Probably most people around the world have lifestyles that provide regular, vigorous, and sustained activity naturally, without actually doing exercises. They commute to work by bicycle, for instance, or have jobs that involve energetic work, as farmers, laborers, and homemakers often do.

Demographic patterns give a portrait of who exercises in the United States. Adults who exercise tend to have more income and education than those who don't exercise and are more likely to be men than women and White than Black or Hispanic (NCHS, 2009a). Also, adults who exercise tend to have exercised regularly in the past (Dishman, 1991). Similar patterns exist in other industrialized countries, such as Australia (Sallis & Owen, 1999). Another factor is age—as adults get older, most tend to engage less and less in physical activity, not so much because of declining physical functioning but because of changes in their beliefs and attitudes (Sarkasian et al., 2005; Vertinsky & Auman, 1988). They often have exaggerated expectations of decreased physical ability, risk of injury, fear of failure, and others' disapproval regarding exercise in old age, and these ideas are particularly strong among many of today's elderly women.

Women seem to learn from past sex-role experiences that men are more socially and physically suited to vigorous activity than females. Although both male and female older people tend to underrate their physical capabilities and exaggerate their health risks in performing energetic exercise after middle age, women are especially prone to these beliefs (Vertinsky & Auman, 1988; Woods & Birren, 1984). Health care workers and organizations for the elderly have many opportunities to dispel incorrect beliefs about health risks, change sex-role stereotypes regarding exercise, and encourage active lifestyles.

Reasons for Not Exercising

When individuals are asked why they don't exercise, the most common reason they give is that they cannot find the time (Dishman, 1991; Godin et al., 1992). Actually, of course, most people could have the time but choose to use it in other ways. People also report not exercising because they have no convenient place to do it or because the weather or other environmental conditions make it unpleasant or impossible.

Whether people exercise is also related to the amount of stress in their lives, social influences, and their beliefs. People who exercise regularly tend to skip sessions when they experience high levels of stress (Stetson et al., 1997). Social influences on exercise involve modeling, encouragement, and reinforcement by peers and family. Adults who exercise tend to have spouses who encourage them to do so, and children and adolescents who exercise or engage in sports tend to have friends

or family who also do so (Dishman, Sallis, & Orenstein, 1985; Gottlieb & Baker, 1986; Sallis et al., 1988). People's beliefs can influence exercising in at least four ways:

- People with high self-efficacy for their ability to perform and maintain exercise are more likely to do it and stick with it than those with low self-efficacy (Anderson et al., 2006; Armitage, 2005; Sniehotta, Scholz, & Schwarzer, 2005).

- Perceived susceptibility to illness can spur people to exercise. People who received information describing their level of fitness or indicating they might be susceptible to health problems that could be prevented through exercise were more likely to start exercising than others who did not get such information (Godin, Desharnais et al., 1987; Wurtele & Maddux, 1987).

- Perceived barriers reduce exercise; enjoying exercise increases it (Rhodes, Fiala, & Conner, 2009; Sallis et al., 2007; Salmon et al., 2003). The barriers can be *personal*, such as feeling tired or having work commitments, or *environmental*, such as cost, weather, or safety. But keep in mind that people who are overweight and sedentary tend to perceive barriers to physical activity when there are none (Gebel, Bauman, & Owen, 2009).

- Compared to people who believe they failed to stick with an exercise program, those who believe they succeeded are more likely to resume exercising in the future, even if they had dropped out of the program (Shields, Brawley, & Lindover, 2005).

A study found evidence of a biopsychosocial sequence that influences whether people will continue to exercise after starting: genetic factors influence the amount of exertion individuals perceive as they exercise, which affects the mood they feel after exercising, which influences their intention to exercise in the future (Bryan et al., 2007). Individuals who experience positive moods after exercising tend to stick with it.

People who do *not* exercise tend to have other risk factors for developing serious illnesses, such as by being overweight or smoking cigarettes. From the standpoint of performing health-protective behavior, people whose health would benefit most from physical activity seem to be the most resistant to starting or maintaining an exercise program. Quitting smoking may help: a study of smokers found that those who quit were more likely to start exercising than those who didn't (Perkins et al., 1993).

PROMOTING EXERCISE BEHAVIOR

A person who spends time watching youngsters play is likely to have the impression that children are innately very active—running, jumping, and climbing—and that they do not need to be encouraged to exercise, as older individuals do. Some children seem to find physical activity naturally reinforcing (Epstein et al., 1999). Although most children and adolescents are more active than adults, many children are not active enough (Marcus et al., 2000). School-based programs are effective at increasing the amount of time children spend in physical activity and fitness, but are less successful in increasing the percentage of children who are active in leisure time (Dobbins et al., 2009). People of all ages could benefit from school, park, and worksite recreation programs and facilities, such as parks and trails, to promote exercise (Giles-Corti et al., 2005; Sallis et al., 2006).

To obtain the full health benefits of physical activity, people need to exercise or be very active as a permanent part of their normal lifestyles. Few people in industrialized societies achieve this ideal. Of individuals who are already exercising regularly at any given time, about half will quit in the coming year (Dishman, Sallis, & Orenstein, 1985). Table 7.8 presents several strategies that help people start and continue exercising. These strategies can be applied by individuals who decide on their own to start or by organized interventions to promote exercise in target populations, such as school children, workers, or the elderly.

Note five additional points. First, we can promote physical activity by giving rewards for increased exercising *and* for decreased sedentary behavior (Epstein, Saelens, & O'Brien, 1995). Second, doctors can increase physical activity in sedentary patients by giving verbal advice and written plans for specific behaviors and goals (Grandes et al., 2009). Third, sedentary people who are willing to increase their activity are more likely to stick with an exercise routine that requires a high frequency (5 or more days per week) than a high intensity (Perri et al., 2002). Fourth, individuals in an exercise program who are more likely than others to reach and maintain moderately high exercise levels have higher incomes and exercise self-efficacy, are more fit, and are more likely to see neighbors being physically active (King et al., 2006). Fifth, people are more likely to stick with an exercise program if they can deal with lapses or setbacks constructively, such as by expecting them and attributing them to temporary factors (Schwarzer et al., 2008)

Interventions can promote exercise with various populations, particularly if they include behavioral methods to modify the antecedents and consequences of physical activity (Sallis & Owen, 1999). Interventions since the late 1980s that have included strategies like those in Table 7.8 have reported higher rates of exercise adherence and fewer dropouts than earlier programs (Marcus et al., 2000). Two other strategies appear to increase success. First, providing contact by telephone to assess progress and give advice when there are problems improves interventions' success (Marcus et al., 2000). Second, an important factor in people's starting and sticking with an exercise routine is their *readiness* to do so, in terms of the stages of change model (see Chapter 5). People who are at the contemplation stage—that is, they're already considering the change—are more likely to start exercising, and to exercise vigorously once they do, than are people at the precontemplation stage (Armstrong et al., 1992). Interventions that provide telephone and print information tailored to the motivational readiness of individuals to exercise are more effective than nontailored programs (Marcus et al., 1998).

People of all ages can benefit from exercise programs. These children are in a physical education class.

Table 7.8   *Strategies to Promote Exercising*

- *Preassessment.* Before people begin an exercise program, they need to determine their purposes for exercising and the benefits they can expect. They should also assess their health status, preferably through a medical checkup.
- *Exercise selection.* The exercises included in the program should be tailored to meet the health needs of the individual and his or her interests and purposes, such as firming up certain parts of the body. People are more likely to stick with the program if it includes exercises that they enjoy doing.
- *Exercise conditions.* Before people start an exercise program, they should determine when and where they will exercise and arrange to get any equipment they will need. Some people seem to adhere to a program if they pick a fixed time for exercising and refuse to schedule anything else at that time; others can be more flexible and still make sure to exercise about every other day. The exercise conditions should be safe and convenient.
- *Goals.* Most people adhere to a program more closely if they write out a specific sequence of goals and consequences for exercise behavior in a behavioral contract. The goals should be graduated, beginning at a modest level. They should also be measurable—as body weight or number of push-ups would be—rather than vague, such as "to feel good."
- *Consequences.* Exercise should lead to reinforcement. Some individuals may need tangible reinforcers to maintain their exercise behavior in the early stages of the program. After these people get in shape, many will find that the enjoyment of exercise and the physical benefits are sufficient rewards.
- *Social influence.* People are more likely to start and stick with an exercise program if these efforts have the support and encouragement of family and friends. Exercising with a partner or in groups sometimes enhances people's motivation to continue in a program.
- *Record keeping.* People can enhance their motivation to exercise by keeping records of their weight and performance. Seeing on paper how far they have progressed can be very reinforcing.

Sources: Dishman, Sallis, & Orenstein, 1985; Oldridge, 1984; Sallis & Owen, 1999; Serfass & Gerberich, 1984.

SAFETY

Unsafe conditions threaten people's health in virtually all environments—in traffic, at home, on the job, and at the beach—producing huge numbers of illnesses, injuries, and deaths each year. In most cases, these health problems could have been avoided if the victim or other people had used reasonable safety precautions. Sometimes people don't know how to prevent injury, as is often the case for elderly individuals who become injured when they fall, but safety training can reduce these injuries (Tinetti et al., 1994). Let's see what is known about the hazards people face and how to help people live safer lives.

ACCIDENTS

Each year in the United States, over 34 million injuries or poisonings occur that require medical attention (USBC, 2010). Some of these events are serious enough to cause long-term disability or death. More than 121,000 Americans die each year from unintentional injuries in accidents (USBC, 2010). By far the most frequent of these accidental fatalities involve traffic mishaps. Nearly 5,800 people die in accidents at their jobs each year, and thousands of other workers are seriously injured (NCHS, 2009a). The industries with the highest mortality and injury rates include transportation and warehousing,

manufacturing, construction, and mining. Government data reveal that accidental injury is:

- The fifth most frequent cause of death in the American population as a whole.
- The leading cause of death of individuals under age 45.
- Responsible for over 30% of all deaths of children 1 to 14 years of age (USBC, 2010).

Accidents are a global health problem: for instance, thousands of people die in traffic accidents in the European Union each year (WHO/Europe, 2010).

Another way to see the relative impact of injury versus disease is to estimate the years of life lost by the victims of these causes of death. Using age 65 as a standard, we'd subtract the age of death of each person who dies earlier and then sum the years lost for injuries and disease separately. Calculations like these reveal that the total number of years lost from unintentional and intentional (that is, homicide or suicide) injuries in the United States is about the same as from the total of the three most frequent causes of death in America: heart disease, cancer, and stroke (USDHHS, 1995). Over 60% of all injury deaths are unintentional.

How can accidental injuries be prevented? We will focus on injuries in traffic mishaps because they account for about half of all accidental deaths and researchers have done many studies on methods to prevent traffic injuries. One approach to reduce traffic accidents capitalizes on perception research on reducing drivers' errors and reaction time: mounting an extra brake light above the trunk of vehicles reduced rear-end collisions by 50% (Robertson, 1986). Another approach addresses the role of cell phones in accidents: the risk of traffic mishaps is four times as likely during or shortly after the driver uses a phone, even a hands-free phone (McEvoy et al., 2005). As a result, laws against drivers using cell phones are being enacted. Other ways to reduce traffic accidents focus on the driver's age: traffic-accident death rates in the United States increase dramatically during adolescence, as depicted in Figure 7-5. Safe-driving programs have been used for teens learning to drive, but they seem to have little effect on accidents (Robertson, 1986). Two other approaches that effectively promote safe driving and reduce traffic deaths are not very popular with teenagers; one involves raising the legal driving age, and the other has parents restrict their teenager's driving (Robertson, 1986; Simons-Morton et al., 2005).

Traffic injuries and deaths can also be prevented if drivers and passengers will use protective equipment, such as seat belts in cars and helmets when riding motorcycles or bicycles (Lee et al., 2010; Macpherson & Spinks, 2009; NHTSA, 2006). After seat belts were installed as standard equipment in cars, few Americans opted to use them; today over 80% use them

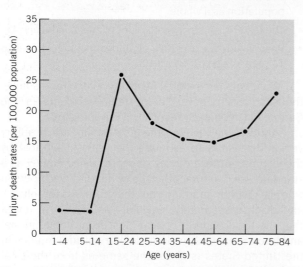

Figure 7-5 The relationship between age and motor-vehicle-injury death rates in the United States. (Data from NCHS, 2009a, Table 43.) Note, however, that the dramatic increase during adolescence primarily reflects the deaths of individuals who are *occupants* of motor vehicles; much of the upswing in old age reflects deaths of individuals who are *pedestrians*. (Cataldo et al., 1986.)

(NHTSA, 2006). Safety programs have targeted parents and children, and laws requiring seat belt use have been enacted. A successful educational program provided computer-assisted video instruction on using an infant safety seat to mothers before leaving the hospital after giving birth (Hletko et al., 1987). Observation by a parking lot attendant at the hospital 4 months later when mothers brought their babies for a checkup revealed that many more trained than untrained mothers had their infants correctly restrained. As you might expect, parents often fail to follow the safety rules they convey to their children (Morrongiello, Corbett, & Bellisimo, 2008). These children tend to follow the stated rules, but they also plan not to do so when they become adults.

A program to increase seat belt use was presented to children in preschools, using a theme character called "Bucklebear" (Chang et al., 1985). The children in several other preschools served as a control group who were matched to the experimental subjects for their prior seat belt use. Observations in the preschool parking lots 3 weeks after the program ended found that over 44% of the "Bucklebear" children and only about 22% of the control children were using seat belts. Other programs have addressed the use of bicycle helmets or car safety restraints; some included incentives for the parents, such as discounts to buy helmets (Tremblay & Peterson, 1999). After one of these programs, children in the community increased helmet use markedly and had fewer head injuries over the next several years.

ENVIRONMENTAL HAZARDS

A 1987 newspaper poll in New Jersey asked people, "Do you use sunscreen in the summer?" One young man answered, "No. I don't use anything—never have, never will," and a young woman said, "Never, because the sun's not too hot in New Jersey." Another young woman said she uses only the weakest sunscreen because, "I want to have a gorgeous tan." Ever since the French fashion designer Coco Chanel made tanning fashionable, people in many parts of the world have come to believe tans are attractive and healthful. This belief develops by early adolescence (Broadstock, Borland, & Gason, 1992).

Today we know that excessive exposure to the sun's ultraviolet rays makes the skin age and can cause skin cancers, particularly in people who are fair skinned and burn easily (AMA, 2003; Harrison et al., 1994). Keep in mind that sunlamps and sunbeds have the same effect,

Parents can teach their children to use sunscreen.

and the more exposure to them, the greater the chance of getting cancer (Westerdahl et al., 1994). Although most cases of skin cancer can be easily treated and cured, others cannot, especially if they are discovered late (ACS, 2009). Dermatologists and other health care practitioners recommend that most people use sunscreens (SPF of 15 or more) when exposed to the sun for more than, say, an hour or so. But only about a third of American children and adolescents use sunscreen, and over 80% report having had a sunburn in the past year (Geller et al., 2002). Girls use sunscreen more than boys do, but they also use tanning beds more. Because skin appearance is a main motivator for tanning, researchers have tested interventions with appearance information to promote sunscreen use. One approach used message framing and found that information has a greater influence on the likelihood of sunscreen use if it has gain-framed messages ("Using sunscreen increases your chances of maintaining healthy, young looking skin") than loss-framed messages, which might state that not using sunscreen can cause cancer and prematurely aged skin (Detweiler et al., 1999). Another approach showed college students ultraviolet photographs of their skin, which reveal normally invisible damage from sun radiation, and found that these students later used tanning beds less than others who did not see such photographs (Gibbons et al., 2005).

Ultraviolet radiation is only one of many environmental hazards people need to guard against. Many harmful chemicals and gases exist in households, worksites, and general communities. Some of these hazards and their effects are (AMA, 2003):

- *Lead* poisoning, which can damage children's nervous system and impair intelligence if they ingest it, such as by mouthing objects painted with lead-based paints, drinking water from a plumbing system with poorly soldered lead joints, or drinking acidic beverages from lead-glazed ceramics.

- *Radon*, a radioactive odorless gas that can cause lung cancer with long-term exposure, enters dwellings from the ground; ventilating a basement can reduce radon pollution.

- *Asbestos* is a substance that was used in buildings and equipment as a fire retardant. People who have regular contact with it risk developing lung cancer.

- *Radiation* poisoning, which can occur with one very high-level exposure or long-term lower exposure, causes cancer. It can be released into the environment from many sources, such as nuclear testing sites and power plants, hospitals, and military facilities. A massive radiation release occurred in 1986 at the Soviet nuclear power plant in Chernobyl.

People who work with hazardous materials need to know what the substances are, what dangers they pose, and how to use them safely. Some states in America have enacted "Right to Know" laws that require (1) employers to notify and train employees regarding the safe use of hazardous materials and (2) community agencies to provide information about the exposure of residents to hazardous materials. If people know a danger exists, they can try to take protective action (for example, by drinking bottled water), become involved in community change, and notify their doctor so that appropriate tests can be done (Winett, King, & Altman, 1989).

People are becoming increasingly concerned about the chemicals and gases that pervade our lives. They should be vigilant—but they should also be aware of three things. First, not every chemical or gas is harmful. Second, exposure to toxic or carcinogenic substances poses little risk when the contact is infrequent and the dosage is small (Ames & Gold, 1990; Cohen & Ellwein, 1990). Third, some harmful substances may have benefits that outweigh their dangers. For example, chlorinating water has all but erased many of the waterborne infections that once threatened enormous numbers of lives. But chlorinated water often has very small amounts of the carcinogen *chloroform* in it. Given these circumstances, the benefits of chlorinating appear to outweigh the risks.

SUMMARY

In addition to water, food contains five types of chemical components: carbohydrates, lipids or "fats," proteins, vitamins, and minerals. People can get all the nutrients and fiber they need from diets that include grains, fruits, vegetables, milk products, and meats and fish. People's food preferences are determined by biological and psychosocial factors.

Diet is associated with the development of atherosclerosis, hypertension, and cancer. Cholesterol leads to atherosclerosis. Whether plaques form in our blood vessels depends on the presence of two types of cholesterol-carrying proteins: low-density lipoprotein and high-density lipoprotein. Low-density lipoprotein is often called "bad cholesterol" because it is the main culprit in plaque buildup. Genetic factors and the foods people eat determine serum cholesterol levels. Interventions can be effective in helping people reduce dietary cholesterol substantially. High blood pressure can result from consuming too much sodium.

Many people are very conscious of and concerned about their weight. Most concerns among Americans are with being too fat, rather than too thin, particularly among females. If people's body mass index (BMI) is 25 or more, they are overweight; if their BMI is 30 or more, they are considered obese. People become fat because they consume more calories than they burn up through metabolism. Heredity plays a role in weight control, probably by affecting the set-point for body weight. The set-point mechanism involves the hypothalamus and serum leptin and insulin levels. Psychosocial factors also affect weight control, especially in the role of emotions in binge eating.

Obesity is associated with the development of many illnesses, such as hypertension, coronary heart disease, and diabetes. These health risks decrease with fitness and increase as the degree of obesity increases and when fat is concentrated in the abdominal region. Prevention of overweight should begin in childhood to avoid fat-cell hyperplasia. People can control their weight by exercising and eating diets that are low in calories, fat, and carbohydrates with high glycemic loads.

Most heavy people try to reduce their weight on their own by going on a diet. Those who are not able to lose weight on their own often seek help, such as through self-help groups and weight-loss programs. Behavioral and cognitive methods are more effective than other approaches. Relatively extreme cases may warrant drastic procedures with medical supervision, including placing the patient on a very-low-calorie diet, using appetite-suppressing drugs, or performing surgery. Although many people who lose weight keep most of that weight off, others do not; relapse can be reduced with follow-up programs.

Anorexia nervosa is an eating disorder that results in an unhealthy and extreme loss of weight. Bulimia nervosa is an eating disorder that involves recurrent episodes of binge eating and purging. Both of these disorders occur mainly in adolescence and early adulthood, and are much more prevalent in females than in males. Treatment is more difficult and less successful for anorexia than for bulimia.

Isotonic, isometric, and isokinetic exercises have different procedures and effects. Aerobic exercise refers to energetic physical activity that involves rhythmical movement of large muscle groups and requires high levels of oxygen over a period of half an hour or so. Engaging regularly in vigorous exercise increases people's life span and protects them against coronary heart disease, by improving lipid levels and reducing blood pressure and stress reactivity.

Tens of thousands of Americans die each year in accidents, especially traffic mishaps. Death rates for traffic accidents increase dramatically during adolescence. People also need to guard against many environmental hazards, including excessive exposure to sunlight and harmful chemicals and gases.

KEY TERMS

lipoproteins	obese	glycemic load	isokinetic exercise
low-density lipoprotein	set-point theory	anorexia nervosa	aerobic exercise
high-density lipoprotein	leptin	bulimia nervosa	
body mass index	insulin	isotonic exercise	
overweight	binge eating	isometric exercise	

Note: If you read **Module 3** (from the Appendix) with the current chapter, you should include the key terms for those modules.

8

USING HEALTH
SERVICES

PROLOGUE

Amelia's life had just undergone major changes—she had been promoted by her employer and relocated to a new town with her two children. A year ago, she was diagnosed with high blood pressure and began taking a prescribed medication, which she supplements with sassafras and herbal tea that an assistant at a natural food store recommended. Now that she was settled, she decided to find a new general practitioner soon. A colleague suggested she try Dr. Davis and, when asked, said that he was not like Jo's last GP, who would sweep into the room, hurriedly ask very specific short-answer questions, dominate the conversation, and rush on to the next patient.

The colleague was right: Dr. Davis was competent and caring. After chatting with Amelia to learn more about her and to establish a friendly relationship, he asked about her health, did some physical tests, and discussed with her a few alternatives for treating her hypertension. She felt comfortable enough with him to tell him about the supplements she was using, and he replied that she could continue them if she'd like, but the evidence for their benefit was not yet very solid. He gave her a pamphlet about hypertension and the URL for the Blood Pressure Association website so she could get more information if she wanted it. Amelia left the office relieved and feeling secure in having found a GP whom she and her children could talk to easily and trust.

With this chapter, our main focus in this book begins to *shift from primary to secondary prevention* efforts. Most health care systems engage chiefly in secondary and tertiary care, providing treatment to stop or reverse a problem or to retard damage it might cause and rehabilitate the person. In this chapter, we will see that the relationship formed between the patient and the health care *practitioner*, or health professional, can influence the actions they take in preventing and managing illness. The importance of this relationship will become clear as we discuss the kinds of health services available and the factors that affect when and how effectively people use these services. As we examine these topics, you'll find answers to questions you may have about people's use of health services. How do people decide they are sick and may need medical attention? How can patients influence their health care? Do people follow medical advice—and if not, why?

TYPES OF HEALTH SERVICES

Systems of medical care are complex in most societies, particularly in industrialized nations where the medical systems consist of an enormous variety of health services. To see the complex nature of health care systems, we will consider the specialized functions of health care workers, compare office-based and inpatient treatment, and contrast universal health care systems found in the UK, Australia, Canada and parts of Europe and Asia with systems in other countries such as the United States, which are only partially funded.

SPECIALIZED FUNCTIONS OF PRACTITIONERS

Medical care systems have staffs of health care workers who differ greatly in their roles and specialties. The UK National Health Service (NHS), for instance, employs over a million professionals, including doctors of many types—general practitioners (GPs), pediatricians, cardiologists, neurosurgeons, dermatologists, gynecologists, psychiatrists, and so on—as well as nurses, dentists, optometrists, respiratory therapists, physical therapists, medical social workers, and dietitians, to name only a small number. Each type of practitioner provides a different type of health service, using specialized knowledge and skills.

Because each of these services involves an enormous amount of knowledge and skill that grows and changes very rapidly, individual practitioners cannot perform with a high degree of skill the services of several specialties simultaneously. The advantage in organizing the health care system into specialties is that patients can receive the greatest expertise available for each aspect of the treatment of each health problem. But this great advantage has drawbacks. For instance, the many professionals who provide care for a particular individual do not always communicate with each other effectively, so that the doctor in charge of the treatment may not have a full picture of the person's condition or progress (Weiner et al., 2005). Also, because many practitioners work with a patient very briefly—spending just a few minutes together, for example—the contact these practitioners have with patients is often impersonal.

OFFICE-BASED AND INPATIENT TREATMENT

When we get sick and seek professional treatment, the first place we usually go is to our GP at his or her surgery. This practitioner can treat the illness, refer us to a specialist for treatment, or arrange for hospitalization.

People with serious illnesses who require medical attention either on a continuous basis or with complex equipment or procedures generally receive treatment as inpatients in hospitals and nursing homes. *Hospitals* are the most complex medical facilities in medical care systems, employing highly sophisticated equipment and skilled practitioners from almost all specialty areas (AMA, 2003). As a result, they can provide a wide variety of services, ranging from emergency care, to diagnostic testing, to curative treatment, to rehabilitation and social services. Many hospitals also offer health promotion facilities, such as wellness centers and weight loss programs. Some hospitals have specialized missions, such as in providing care for children or for certain health problems—cancer, eye diseases, or orthopedic problems, for instance.

Nursing homes provide care for individuals who need relatively long-term medical and personal care, particularly if the patients or their families cannot provide this care (AMA, 2003; USBC, 2010). The large majority of patients in nursing homes are disabled or frail, elderly individuals who often need help in day-to-day activities such as dressing and bathing themselves. The average nursing home in the United Kingdom is a moderately sized facility, having about 50 beds (Netten et al., 2001). Nursing homes vary in the degree of skilled nursing and rehabilitative services they are prepared to provide. Although most nursing homes provide high-quality care, many others do not; for example, quality ratings can be obtained online via the Quality Care Commission's website for England at www.cqc.org.uk.

People with serious health problems in many nations have been relying less and less on inpatient

Most patients in nursing homes are elderly individuals who need long-term medical and personal care.

services in recent years, using *outpatient* or *home health care* instead (AMA, 2003; NCHS, 2009a). The shift away from inpatient care has occurred because of the fast-rising costs of hospital and nursing home services and because technological advances have made it possible to maintain medical treatment with outpatients. Two examples of technological devices that provide outpatient treatment are *pacemakers*, which are installed in the body to send electrical pulses to regulate heartbeat, and *insulin pumps*, which inject insulin into the body on a specific schedule. Clients who use home care usually begin their treatment on an inpatient basis, but are then discharged in the care of a home health care service.

Outpatient care offers some advantages over inpatient care. For one thing, home care is less expensive. Also, people usually prefer being at home, and can often return to work or school while receiving outpatient treatment. But for some patients—particularly the elderly—home health care can present problems if they lack needed help from family or friends and do not have transportation to make periodic visits to their doctors.

UNIVERSAL HEALTH CARE SYSTEMS

Many countries have *universal health care* systems—they provide medical coverage for virtually all of their citizens—usually funded by taxes and payroll deductions (PNHP, 2006; WHO, 2005). These nations include Australia, Canada, Germany, Italy, the Netherlands, Sweden, and the United Kingdom. The health care they provide is excellent and usually less complicated to use than non-universal systems. Under non-universal systems, people in poorer countries generally have little or no coverage, and the ability to pay for service or private insurance restricts medical care even in richer nations (WHO, 1999).

How are universal health care systems structured, and what do they cover? Each one is different—for instance:

- Many systems cover prescription drugs, sometimes only for certain age or income groups, or those with certain medical conditions.

- Most, but not all, systems encourage the use of supplemental private insurance, especially for types of care the system does not cover, such as dental.

- Some systems are partly funded with medical savings accounts, such as Singapore's *Medisave*, which requires all employees and self-employed individuals to put part of their pay into an account that the contributor and relatives can use to pay for treatments (Drechsler & Jütting, 2005).

- In some systems, such as in Italy and the United Kingdom, most doctors are employed by the government, but in others most doctors are privately employed.

- Some systems, such as in Australia and the Netherlands, have the primary care doctor serve as a "gatekeeper" for receiving care by a specialist or hospital.

In the Canadian system, each province pays its citizens' medical bills and determines its own policies, such as what types of care will be covered. Most Canadian doctors are employed privately, and patients may choose any doctor they wish. The fees doctors charge are set by the province in negotiation with a medical association.

Compared with other systems, universal health care systems are far less expensive in terms of costs per citizen and the percentage of each nation's gross domestic product spent on health care (WHO, 2009). However, because of steadily increasing costs in most countries, efforts are being made around the world to slow these increases in universal health care systems. Sometimes funding problems in some nations, such as Canada and the United Kingdom, have led to long waits for diagnostic tests and elective surgery (CU, 2007).

A NON-UNIVERSAL HEALTH CARE SYSTEM: THE CASE OF THE US

For most Americans, when they get sick and seek treatment, a large part of the costs is covered by their health insurance. Employers provide insurance for most of their employees, who usually have to pay for at least part of the coverage. Other people buy private insurance or may be covered under governmental insurance programs, such as *Medicare* (which covers all elderly people) or *Medicaid* (which covers low-income people). But over 15% of Americans—46 million people—have no health insurance, and the percent uninsured is much higher for Hispanics and Blacks than for Whites (USBC, 2010). These uninsured people cannot afford to get sick, and they have higher mortality rates than insured individuals (Wilper et al., 2009). The US government enacted a law in 2010 that would phase in insurance coverage so that 95% of Americans would have health insurance coverage within a few years, but the structure of the health care system would remain much the same.

Up until several decades ago, private-practice doctors provided all office-based medical treatment in the US, and a fee was charged for each service. American health insurance now structures medical care within two broad options: *fee-for-service* (also called "traditional") and *managed-care* programs. Most of these programs charge the members, or their employers, annual fees. The fees are lower for managed-care plans.

People in the fee-for-service programs can choose their doctors, and the insurance pays most (often 80%) of the incurred charges. Practitioners who treat fee-for-service patients generally must accept the amount of payment the insurance plans specify. This amount is often lower than the practitioner requests. (*Medicaid* plans usually pay very low amounts, thus members may have difficulty finding a practitioner who will provide treatment.) Managed-care programs, on the other hand, place restrictions on their members' choice of services. Over 70% of employed Americans are in managed-care plans; and *Medicare* now offers managed-care programs (Luft, 1998; CU, 2001). Some managed-care programs provide financial incentives to their doctors for cost-saving behaviors, such as sending fewer patients to hospitals as this may foster suboptimal care.

One type of managed-care plan is the *Health Maintenance Organization* (HMO). Members are entitled to use the services of any affiliated doctor or hospital with little or no additional charges (CU, 2001; Miller & Luft, 1994). Visits to specialists or for nonemergency hospital treatment must be preapproved and referred by the primary care doctor. The HMO pays for treatments it arranges, or recommends, and negotiates with specific hospitals and doctors for discounted rates.

Another type of managed-care plan, the *Preferred Provider Organization* (PPO), is similar to some HMOs. Each PPO consists of a network of affiliated doctors and hospitals that discount their fees, and patients usually may go to any affiliated specialist without preapproval. Although the overall care of patients in HMOs, PPOs, and fee-for-service plans is similar, HMO patients tend to use more preventive services but are less likely to see a doctor quickly or to be admitted to a hospital when seriously ill (CU, 1999, 2001; Miller & Luft, 1994). Ratings

Table 8.1 *Overall Health System Performance (OHSP) Rankings and Number of Doctors and Nurses per 10,000 People in Selected Nations*

Country	OHSP[a]	Doctors[b]	Nurses[b]
Australia	32	25	97
Brazil	125	12	38
Canada	30	19	101
China	144	14	10
Germany	25	34	80
India	112	6	13
Italy	2	37	72
Netherlands	17	37	146
Singapore	6	15	44
South Africa	175	8	41
Sweden	23	33	109
Turkey	70	16	29
United Kingdom	18	23	128
United States	37	26	94

[a]The latest rankings available are from WHO, 2000 and include 191 countries.
[b]Data from WHO, 2009.

of managed-care plans are available, but are not very useful (Schauffler & Mordavsky, 2001).

What is the quality of health care in different countries around the world? We can gauge the quality using the World Health Organization's ranking of the overall health system's performance and the number of doctors and nurses a country has for its population. Table 8.1 gives these comparisons.

In any health care system, a critical step in seeking medical attention is finding a regular doctor to contact when we fall sick. He or she can either cure our illness, or help us find other help within the system.

Now, suppose someone who has a regular doctor develops some symptoms, say, nausea and a moderately high fever—will the person go to the doctor? An important step in using health services involves deciding when we are sick enough to require medical attention in the first place. This is the topic of the next section.

PERCEIVING AND INTERPRETING SYMPTOMS

If you came down with a case of strep throat as a child, chances are the symptoms you experienced were obvious to you and your parents. You had a very sore throat, fever, and headache, for instance, and your doctor prescribed a curative course of action. From experiences of this type, you learned that symptoms accompany illness, certain symptoms reliably signal certain illnesses, some symptoms are more serious than others, and when they go away, you're well again. As an adult, you decide whether to visit your doctor on the basis of the symptoms you perceive and what they mean to you.

PERCEIVING SYMPTOMS

Perceiving symptoms of illness is more complicated than it may seem. It's true that we perceive internal states on the basis of physical sensations, and we're more likely to notice strong sensations than weak ones. But we do not assess our internal states very accurately. For example, people's estimates of their own heart rate, breathing function, and degree of nasal congestion correlate poorly with physiological measures of these states (Pennebaker, 1983; Rietveld & Brosschot, 1999). Individuals also have trouble perceiving external symptoms, such as whether a mole-like spot is melanoma, a skin cancer (Miles & Meehan, 1995). Partly because of people's low degree of accuracy in assessing signs of illness, the point at which people recognize a symptom can differ from one individual to the next and within the same person from one time to the next. Furthermore, people do not always notice a symptom—even a strong one—when it is there, and sometimes they may perceive a symptom that has no actual physical basis. Let's see what factors affect our perception of symptoms.

Individual Differences

"He's such a big baby; he notices every little ache and pain," you may have heard someone say. Why do some individuals report more symptoms than others do? One reason is that some people simply *have* more symptoms than others, of course. Although people could differ in the sensations they experience from the same symptom, such as a specific painful stimulus, studies testing large numbers of normal individuals with stimuli of different temperatures have cast doubt on this possibility. They found that people seem to have a uniform threshold at which heat becomes painful—"almost all persons begin to feel pain when the tissue temperature rises to a level between 44°C and 46°C" (Guyton, 1985, p. 302). But individuals differ in the degree of pain they will tolerate before doing something about it, such as taking medication (Karoly, 1985; Melzack & Wall, 1982).

Some individuals seem to pay more attention to their internal states than others do (Pennebaker, 1983). They show a heightened awareness of or sensitivity to their body sensations. As a result, these people notice changes more quickly than individuals who tend to focus their attention on external happenings. This doesn't mean internally focused individuals' perceptions of internal changes are more *accurate*—indeed, research has found that they are more likely than externally focused people

to overestimate their bodily changes, such as in heart rate (Pennebaker, 1983). Among patients who seek medical treatment, those who are internally focused tend to have less severe illness and perceive their recovery as slower than those who pay less attention to their internal states (Miller, Brody, & Summerton, 1987). Many internally focused individuals may pay *too much* attention to their internal states and, in so doing, magnify departures from normal bodily sensations.

Competing Environmental Stimuli

You may have heard anecdotes about athletes who were unaware of a major injury they had suffered during a competition until after the sporting event was over—*then* it hurt! The extent to which people pay attention to internal stimuli at any given time depends partly on the nature or degree of environmental stimuli present at that time.

When the environment contains a great deal of sensory information or is exciting, people become less likely to notice internal sensations. People are far more likely to report sensations or physical symptoms when the external environment is boring or lacks information than when the environment captures their attention (Pennebaker, 1983). For instance, when watching a movie, they are more likely to notice an itch or a tickle in their throats during boring parts. Also, people who hold boring jobs or live alone tend to report more physical symptoms and use more aspirin and sleeping pills than those who hold interesting jobs or live with other people.

Psychosocial Influences

Because people are not very accurate in assessing their actual internal physical states, their perception of body sensations can be heavily influenced by cognitive, social, and emotional factors (Petrie & Pennebaker, 2004; Rietveld & Brosschot, 1999). One way researchers have demonstrated the role of cognitive factors in symptom perception is in the effects of *placebos*, which are inert substances or sham treatments (Rehm & Nyak, 2004; Roberts, 1995). For example, people who receive a placebo "drug" to reduce their pain, not knowing the drug is inert, often report that it relieves their symptoms or sensations.

Expectations can also increase the symptoms people perceive. For instance, patients who are taking an active medication sometimes show a *nocebo* phenomenon: they perceive side effects, such as dizziness or fatigue, that could not be the direct result of the drug (Barsky et al., 2002). They may have "manufactured" sensations based on their expectations. In another example, researchers recruited residents of neighborhoods that were scheduled to receive a spraying of an insecticide by aircraft

(Petrie et al., 2005). A questionnaire was used to separate these people into three groups: high, medium, and low in health worries relating to aspects of modern life, such as genetically modified food and fluoridation of water. After the spraying, these people reported on the symptoms they experienced that they attributed to exposure to the spray. The people with the high health worries reported three times the number of symptoms, such as headache and dizziness, than did those with low health worries. These findings suggest that the symptoms people perceive can result not only from actual physiological changes that occur in their bodies but from their beliefs, too. Keep in mind, though, that worry can also make people more vigilant, such as when individuals who worry a lot about their asthma are more accurate in noticing symptoms and attributing them to their asthma condition (Mora et al., 2007).

The combined roles of cognitive, social, and emotional factors in symptom perception can be seen in two interesting phenomena. The first is called *medical student's disease*. As medical students learn about the symptoms of various diseases, more than two-thirds of them come to believe incorrectly that they have contracted one of these illnesses at one time or another (Mechanic, 1972). The second phenomenon, called *mass psychogenic illness*, involves widespread symptom perception across individuals, even though tests indicate that their symptoms have no medical basis in their bodies or in the environment, such as from toxic substances (Petrie & Pennebaker, 2004). Usually it begins with an event, such as an unusual odor or someone fainting—then a chain reaction occurs with person after person feeling symptoms, and some may even be taken to the hospital.

Why do such phenomena occur? Researchers have described several conditions that heighten the perception of symptoms (Colligan et al., 1979; Mechanic, 1972; Petrie & Pennebaker, 2004). First, the people are already feeling negative emotions, such as high stress—that is, medical student's disease, and mass psychogenic illness tend to occur when people have been experiencing high levels of anxiety, interpersonal conflict, or heavy workloads. Second, the symptoms involve common physical sensations, such as headache or dizziness, that are vague and very subjective in nature. Third, expectations and other cognitive factors exaggerate the sensations, attaching to them more importance than they warrant. Fourth, modeling of the symptoms occurs. (Go to 💡.)

Gender and Sociocultural Differences

Women in research on pain report feeling discomfort at lower stimulus intensities than men and request sooner that a painful stimulus be terminated (Fillingim,

2000). Why? There is evidence for several factors, such as differences in sex hormones and sex role beliefs.

People of different cultural backgrounds seem to differ in their perceptions of and reactions to illness symptoms—for instance, displaying much more distress and disability to pain in some cultures than in others (Young & Zane, 1995). These differences may result from cultural norms for reinforcing stoical versus distressed and disabled behaviors when in pain. Let's consider three examples of cultural differences. First, people of Asian cultures report more physical symptoms with psychological bases than people of other cultures (Chun, Enomoto, & Sue, 1996). Second, a study compared disability in patients with long-term low back pain conditions of similar severity and duration in six different countries (Sanders et al., 1992). American patients reported the most overall impairment, such as in work and social activities. Italians and New Zealanders reported the second-largest impairments, followed by Japanese, Colombian, and Mexican patients. Third, of heart attack patients in the United States, Black individuals experience symptoms that are less typical than those of Whites and delay getting treatment longer (Lee et al., 1999).

In summary, people's perception of a symptom depends on the strength of the underlying physical sensation, their tendency to pay attention to their internal states, the degree to which external stimuli compete for their attention, and a variety of cognitive, social, and emotional processes. What individuals *do* when they perceive symptoms is the topic of the next section.

INTERPRETING AND RESPONDING TO SYMPTOMS

Psychiatrist George Engel (1980) described the case of a 55-year-old man whom he called Mr. Glover, who suffered his second heart attack 6 months after his first. He was at work, alone at his desk, when he experienced general discomfort, pressure over his chest, and pain down his left arm.

> The similarity of those symptoms to those of his heart attack six months earlier immediately came to mind ... but he dismissed this in favor of "fatigue," "gas," "muscle strain," and, finally, "emotional tension." But the negation itself, "*not another heart attack*," leaves no doubt that the idea "heart attack" was very much in his mind despite his apparent denial. Behaviorally, he alternated between sitting quietly to "let it pass," pacing about the office "to work it off," and taking Alka-Seltzer. (p. 539)

When Mr. Glover's boss noticed his strange behavior and sick appearance, she convinced him to let her take him to the hospital.

HIGHLIGHT

Symptoms by Suggestion?

Researchers studied the role of expectation and modeling in symptom perception in an experiment (Lorber, Mazzoni, & Kirsch, 2007). They recruited students as participants who were tested in pairs (but one member was actually a confederate of the researchers). Each pair was told that the study was testing the effects of a substance that reportedly produces in some people four "known" symptoms—itchy skin, drowsiness, headache, and nausea—that are mild and usually last for less than an hour. And the pair was told that one or both of them would inhale the substance as a spray and that the study was also testing to see if a few other symptoms might occur. The spray was actually inert.

The participants were randomly assigned either to receive the spray or not, and these conditions were subdivided: seeing the confederate either receive or not receive the spray. Then the pair sat for an hour, free to read magazines or do homework. During this time, the confederate displayed behaviors, such as scratching and yawning, that were consistent with the known symptoms. Every 10 minutes, the pair rated their experience of the four known symptoms and four others; each of eight symptoms had been reported in prior research on mass psychogenic illness. A videotape of the sessions was used to confirm the occurrence of two symptoms, itchy skin and drowsiness, which would be reflected in the students' behavior. Figure 8-1 shows the outcome: ratings of the known symptoms were far greater for students who received the spray, especially if they also saw the confederate receive the spray. A similar,

subsequent experiment confirmed that modeling is a critical factor in this effect (Mazzoni et al., 2010).

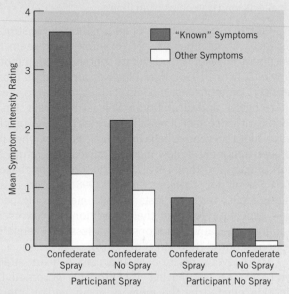

Figure 8-1 Participants' ratings of the "known" symptoms and other symptoms, depending on whether they had received the inhaled spray and whether they had seen the confederate receive the spray. These ratings were taken 40 minutes after the spray condition was implemented; scale: 0 = not at all, 6 = extreme. (Data from Lorber, Mazzoni, & Kirsch, 2007, Table 1.)

The role of people's prior experiences in their decision of what the symptoms they feel reflect and whether they warrant attention can be complex. Most often, past experience probably helps people make correct judgments. For instance, one of the strongest factors in mothers' correct decisions to seek medical care for their children is prior experience—that is, whether the child or a relative had a similar problem in the past (Turk et al., 1985). But sometimes people's prior experiences and expectations can lead them to incorrect interpretations of their symptoms. For example, many elderly people assume that feeling weak is a symptom of old age rather than a sign of illness (Leventhal & Prohaska, 1986). And people who notice symptoms while under long-term, intense stress may see the symptoms as a stress reaction (Cameron, Leventhal, & Leventhal,

1995). Although these interpretations may sometimes be correct, they may also lead people to ignore symptoms that do, in fact, need treatment.

From direct experience and the things we read and hear, we develop ideas and expectations about illnesses—some are correct, some are not—and use this information to construct *cognitive representations* or **commonsense models** of those illnesses (Lau & Hartman, 1983; Leventhal, Leventhal, & Contrada, 1998; Petrie & Pennebaker, 2004). These models can affect our health-related behavior and seem to involve four basic components of how people think about disease:

- *Illness identity,* which consists of the name and symptoms of the disease.
- *Causes and underlying pathology,* which are ideas concerning how one gets the disease ("I got a cold because a girl

sneezed her germs in my face") and what physiological events occur with it.

- *Time line*, or prognosis ideas, such as how long the disease takes to appear and lasts. For instance, symptoms of salmonella take many hours to appear after eating tainted food; some people know this, and others think the symptoms occur immediately.

- *Consequence*, which involves ideas about the seriousness, effects, and outcomes of an illness.

People use many types of information in constructing ideas about illnesses—for example, they seem to use illness *prevalence* in judging its seriousness (Jemmott, Croyle, & Ditto, 1988). Rare illnesses are seen as more serious. Commonsense models of illness appear to affect future health and disability in at least two ways. First, people with incorrect illness ideas are less likely than others to adopt preventive behaviors and less likely, when ill, to seek treatment, follow medical advice, and return to work quickly (Frostholm et al., 2005; Petrie & Pennebaker, 2004; Schiaffino, Shawaryn, & Blum, 1998). Second, as an illness, such as arthritis, lasts and becomes chronic, people's expectations about their condition often worsen, leading to negative emotions and a lessened sense of personal control (Kaptein et al., 2010).

Mr. Glover's reaction to the classic heart attack symptoms he was having was probably governed by emotion elicited by the memory of his earlier attack. Although fear can motivate a person toward health behavior, it can also motivate maladaptive avoidance behavior. He finally decided to go to the hospital after his boss persuaded him that his symptoms needed treatment. Before people decide to seek medical attention for their symptoms, they typically get advice from friends, relatives, or coworkers (Rothrock, 2004; Suls, Martin, & Leventhal, 1997). These advisers form a **lay referral network** of nonpractitioners who provide their own information and interpretations regarding the person's symptoms (Freidson, 1961). These people may respond to a request for help or just the ill person's appearance and might:

- Help interpret a symptom—such as, "Jim and his sister Lynn both had rashes like that. They were just allergic to a new soap their mother had bought."

- Give advice about seeking medical attention—as in, "MaryLou had a dizzy spell like the one you just had, and it was a mild stroke. You'd better call your doctor."

- Recommend a remedy—such as, "A little chicken soup, some aspirin, and bed rest, and you'll be fine in no time."

- Recommend consulting another lay referral person—as in, "Pat had the same problem. You should give him a call."

Although the lay referral system often provides good advice, laypersons are, of course, far more likely than practitioners to recommend actions that worsen the condition or delay the person's use of appropriate and needed treatment.

USING AND MISUSING HEALTH SERVICES

A pharmacist is often the first health professional that people consult when they have a health problem. A customer might ask, "My hands get these red patches that peel, and hand creams don't do any good. Do you have anything that'll help?" When pharmacists suggest an over-the-counter remedy, they usually recommend that the person see a doctor if it doesn't work.

In countries where healthcare is non-universal, many prospective patients try hard to avoid visiting doctors and even when there is universal healthcare, people can be unwilling for other reasons. Americans visit their doctors as outpatients over 990 million times a year—3.36 visits per person (USBC, 2010), and people in the European Union visit their doctors 6.86 times per person per year (WHO/Europe, 2010). What conditions do patients commonly discuss with doctors? The conditions include ear and respiratory infections, pregnancy-related issues, and a variety of chronic illnesses, such as hypertension, diabetes, and cancer (USBC, 2010). Of course, these conditions are not evenly distributed across all segments of the population.

WHO USES HEALTH SERVICES?

People with health risks, such as obesity and high stress, use health care substantially more than others do (Tucker

People with health problems often consult pharmacists for over-the-counter remedies before seeing their doctor.

& Clegg, 2002). Demographic and sociocultural factors are also related to how people use health services in any country.

Age and Gender

One factor in using health services is *age* (USBC, 2010). In general, young children and the elderly have contact with doctors more often each year than adolescents and young adults. Young children visit doctors for general checkups and vaccinations, and they develop a variety of infectious diseases. Doctor contacts are less frequent from late childhood through early adulthood, but increase in the middle-age and elderly years as the prevalence of chronic diseases rises.

Figure 8-2 depicts how doctor contacts vary with age and with another important factor, the patient's *gender*. Through the life span, females have higher rates of doctor visits than males do (NCHS, 2009a). Although much of women's higher visit rates in early adulthood results from pregnancy-related care, the difference remains even when doctor visits for pregnancy and childbirth are not counted (Reddy, Fleming, & Adesso, 1992; Verbrugge, 1985). The reasons for gender differences in using medical care are unclear, but there are several possible explanations. One obvious explanation is that women may simply

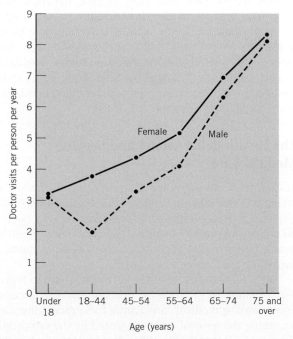

Figure 8-2 Average number of doctor visits in the United States per person per year as a function of age and gender. (Data from NCHS, 2009a, Table 94.)

develop more illnesses that require medical attention: they show higher rates of medical drug use and illness from acute conditions, such as respiratory infections, and from nonfatal chronic diseases, such as arthritis and migraine headache. Another reason is that men are more hesitant to admit having symptoms and to seek medical care for the symptoms they experience. In a study that asked men and women about recent experiences of various symptoms, women reported more of almost all symptoms, including ones that had no medical confirmation (Kroenke & Spitzer, 1998). Gender differences in reporting and, perhaps, perceiving symptoms probably reflects sex-role stereotypes—that is, societies often encourage men more than women to ignore pain and to be tough and independent.

Sociocultural Factors in Using Health Services

Data on health service usage by different segments of a country's population show sociocultural differences in usage rates (NCHS, 2009a). These differences lead to two important conclusions. First, the percentage of people who fail to get prescriptions filled or seek medical care at a doctor's office decreases with family income. Second, individuals with low family incomes are more likely than those with middle and higher incomes to use the NHS in the United Kingdom (Dixon et al., 2003). This is probably because those on lower incomes are more likely to have higher travel costs, lower car ownership and lower literacy skills. In America the gap in usage of health services between social classes has narrowed since the mid-1960s, when the government introduced Medicare and Medicaid insurance programs for the elderly and poor, respectively. These programs account for much of the 25% increase in doctor visits that occurred between 1968 and 1972 (USDHHS, 1985).

Despite the help these programs provide, the costs American patients must bear for medical treatment can still be substantial because public and private insurance programs generally do not cover all the expenses. Some kinds of treatment are excluded, and patients typically must pay part of the costs for those treatments that are covered, which is especially difficult for individuals with low incomes. People on Medicaid who have a heart attack are more likely than others to delay seeking treatment that could stop damage to the heart (Foraker et al., 2008). Worldwide, a lack of knowledge about prevention and poor access to health counseling and preventive services contributes to the high illness rates of low-income people (WHO, 1999).

Although medical insurance can help many low income people get the treatment they need, there are reasons besides the expense of medical care for the gap between social classes and cultural groups in using health services in any country (Flack et al., 1995; Penn et al., 1995; Rundall & Wheeler, 1979; Young & Zane, 1995). For one thing, individuals from the lower classes tend to perceive themselves as being less susceptible to illness than those from the higher classes do. As a result, low-income people are less likely to seek out preventive care. Second, people with low incomes and from minority groups (in some countries) are less likely to have regular access to sources of health care than others are. Often this situation develops because low-income regions are less able to attract doctors to provide health services there, even if the health service is government-run. In addition, people in the lower classes and from minority groups may feel less welcomed by and trustful of the health care system than other individuals. Third, in many countries language can be a barrier to health care for immigrants if they do not speak the dominant language and no translators are available. These and many other factors tend to reduce the likelihood that low-income individuals will use health services for preventive care and when they are ill. Public health informational programs need to combat cultural barriers that impede the use of health care and prevention services.

The title of this section is Who Uses Health Services? We've seen that the most frequent users of health services are young children, women, and elderly individuals, and they also tend to be from the higher social classes. Nonusers are likely to be males, particularly in adolescence and early adulthood, and from disadvantaged groups. But almost all people use health services at some time, and many upper-class individuals fail to get medical treatment when they should. These portraits give us an image of *who* uses health services, but they do not explain *why*.

WHY PEOPLE USE, DON'T USE, AND DELAY USING HEALTH SERVICES

Health psychologists and others who study health care have discovered many factors that influence whether and when individuals are likely to seek medical care. Some of these factors involve people's ideas and beliefs about treating illness.

Ideas, Beliefs, and Using Health Services

An ailing man who was considering whether to seek treatment thought, "Remember how the medicine Steve's doctor gave him made him sicker? I don't trust doctors." Patients sometimes develop health problems as a *result* of medical treatment, and these problems are called

iatrogenic conditions. The condition can result from a practitioner's error, such as giving the wrong type or dose of medication, or as a normal side effect or risk of a treatment, as when people undergo surgery or begin to take a new medication. Some errors can be prevented with technology, such as scanning bar-codes on drug packages (Poon et al., 2006). Tens of thousands of people are killed each year as a result of medical errors in the hospital and adverse effects of drugs, either from prescription or filling errors (Gerlin, 1999; Phillips & Bredder, 2002). The stories we hear about the treatment patients received may influence our decisions to use medical services.

Not trusting practitioners can stop people from seeking the care they need; we will consider two issues of trust. First, individuals may avoid getting care because they worry that their practitioners will not keep information confidential. For instance, a study found that most American adolescents have health concerns they want to keep private from their parents, and one-fourth said they would forgo treatment if their parents could find out about it (Cheng et al., 1993). Many gay men and women avoid medical care because of concerns about confidentiality or doctor reaction to their sexual orientation (Mann, 1996). Second, minority group members have heard stories, some of which are true, of discriminatory practices and atrocities carried out by medical personnel against them (Landrine & Klonoff, 2001). One true story is that between 1932 and 1972, doctors in the United States falsely told a group of Black men with syphilis that they were being treated for their illness and that the disease was "bad blood." This unethical action was done so that a research project, called the Tuskegee Syphilis Study, could chart the effects of untreated syphilis, which include blindness, brain damage, and death (CDC, 2010).

The Health Belief Model and Seeking Medical Care

In Chapter 5, we examined the role of health beliefs in taking preventive action, and saw that the *health belief model* provides a useful framework for explaining why people do and do not practice healthful behaviors. How does the health belief model apply to people's seeking medical care when they notice symptoms?

According to the health belief model (refer to Figure 5-2), symptoms initiate a decision-making process about seeking medical care. Part of this process involves assessing the *perceived threat* suggested by the symptoms (Becker & Rosenstock, 1984; Rosenstock & Kirscht, 1979). How much threat individuals perceive depends mainly on three factors. One factor is *cues to action*, which can include the symptoms themselves, advice sick people receive in lay referral, and information from the mass media, such as descriptions of cancer symptoms. Two other factors, *perceived susceptibility* and *perceived seriousness*, modify the concern the cues arouse: the threat individuals feel intensifies with increases in the perceived susceptibility to the particular illness and the perceived seriousness of the physical and social consequences of contracting the disease.

The health belief model also proposes that people assess whether the *perceived benefits* of getting treatment outweigh the *perceived barriers* to doing so. People who believe treatment can cure the symptoms or arrest the progression of the illness are more likely to seek medical care than those who believe otherwise. In assessing the barriers to medical care, people consider whether the treatment will have unpleasant side effects and will be costly, painful, and difficult to obtain. Individuals who feel threatened by their symptoms and believe the benefits of receiving treatment outweigh the barriers are likely to visit a practitioner. But people who do not feel threatened or assess that the barriers are too strong are likely to decide to delay treatment or avoid it altogether.

The results of research suggest that the factors described by the health belief model do influence people's decisions of whether and how soon to use health services (Becker & Rosenstock, 1984; Rosenstock & Kirscht, 1979). For example, many elderly people report that medical bills, transportation difficulties, and other barriers have hindered their ability to get medical care (Fitzpatrick et al., 2004). Many Americans believe erroneously that cancer cannot be cured and that treatment can cause cancer to spread (Gansler et al., 2005). Still, some studies have found only a weak relationship between factors in the health belief model and people's likelihood of using health services, which suggests that other variables are also important in decisions to seek treatment (Harris & Guten, 1979; Langlie, 1977).

Social and Emotional Factors and Seeking Medical Care

Earlier, we considered the case of Mr. Glover, who delayed medical treatment for clear symptoms of a heart attack, and we saw that social and emotional factors can play important roles in people's decisions about seeking treatment for their symptoms.

The role of strong emotions when symptoms appear can vary. People who are already very depressed tend to delay getting medical care for symptoms, such as of a heart attack, perhaps because they can't mobilize the energy to seek it (Bunde & Martin, 2006). Fear may have different effects. People who are frightened by their cancer symptoms are more likely to seek care quickly,

within several days, than are people with little fear (Petrie & Pennebaker, 2004). But if they expect and fear pain from the disease or its treatment, they may delay care (Levin, Cleeland, & Dar, 1985). Expectations of pain affect dental care, too—about 5% of Americans are so fearful that they avoid all kinds of dental treatment (Gatchel, 1980) and as many as 10% of Britons have a true phobia of dentists. Concerns of possible embarrassment may also lead individuals to avoid medical care. For instance, people with heart symptoms may worry that if "it turns out to be nothing," they'll be embarrassed that they created a crisis and rushed to the hospital (Dracup, 2004). Sometimes the symptoms are themselves embarrassing, such as when adults have problems of bladder control.

Social factors influence people's tendencies to seek medical care for their symptoms. For example, many men believe getting medical care is a sign of weakness, violating their social role for being strong. But social factors can also encourage people to seek care, such as through the process of lay referral, which can serve as a "social trigger" to seek treatment (Zola, 1973). One social trigger is called *sanctioning*, in which someone asks or insists that an ill person have his or her symptoms treated. For instance, a man who had been having problems with his vision for a while finally went to a doctor after his wife prodded him to do so. Some sick individuals seek medical care if they simply believe significant others want them to do that (Timko, 1987).

Stages in Delaying Medical Care

When symptoms of a potentially serious illness develop, seeking treatment promptly is imperative. **Treatment delay** refers to the time that elapses between when a person first notices a symptom and when he or she enters medical care. In medical emergencies, such as severe injury or a heart attack, people often seek help in a matter of minutes or hours, as Mr. Glover did. What determines how long people wait?

On the basis of interviews with patients at a clinic, researchers discovered that treatment delay occurs as a sequence of three stages (Safer et al., 1979). As the diagram in Figure 8-3 illustrates, the three stages are:

1. *Appraisal delay*—the time a person takes to interpret a symptom as an indication of illness.
2. *Illness delay*—the time taken between recognizing one is ill and deciding to seek medical attention.
3. *Utilization delay*—the time after deciding to seek medical care until actually going in to use that health service.

The people's reasons for delaying treatment revealed that different factors were important in different stages of delay. During *appraisal delay*, the sensory experience of a symptom had the greatest impact on taking action—for

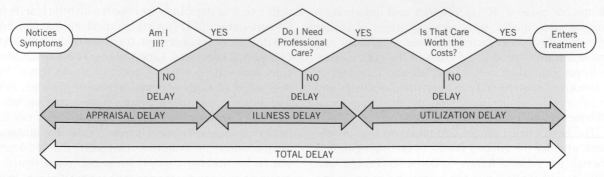

Figure 8-3 Treatment delay is conceptualized as having three stages: appraisal delay, illness delay, and utilization delay. (From Safer et al., 1979, Figure 1.)

instance, patients recognized a symptom as an indication of illness more quickly if they experienced severe pain or bleeding than if they did not.

In the *illness delay* stage, thoughts about the symptom had the greatest impact. Thus, individuals decided to seek medical attention more quickly if the symptom was new rather than very familiar and if they didn't think much about the symptom and its implications. During *utilization delay*, perceptions of benefits and barriers were important—delay was shortest for those people who were less concerned about the cost of treatment, had severe pain, and felt that their symptoms could be cured. In addition, the researchers found that having a major nonillness problem or life event, such as a marriage or divorce, was an important factor that increased the *total* treatment delay.

Some people delay getting care for a long time, sometimes weeks or months, because they are not experiencing pain. This factor is potentially very important

because pain is *not* a major symptom of many very serious diseases, such as hypertension. Pain is also not one of the main warning signs of cancer. Most people who notice a warning sign of cancer, such as a skin blemish or lump, wait a few weeks before seeing a doctor for it, and perhaps a third delay more than 3 months (Antonovsky & Hartman, 1974; Bish et al., 2005). A heart attack often involves pain and requires treatment quickly: *thrombolytic drugs* can prevent myocardial damage if administered within 3 hours after the attack begins (AHA, 2010). Do heart attack victims seek treatment quickly? More than a third of them delay the decision for more than 3 hours, and those who seek treatment early are more likely to be men than women and have relatively high levels of problem-focused coping (Martin et al., 2004; O'Carroll et al., 2001; Walsh et al., 2004). People who lack health insurance or have financial concerns about being sick are more likely than others to delay (Smolderen et al., 2010). (Go to 💡.)

HIGHLIGHT

A New Meaning for "Diehard" Sports Fan

The 2004 baseball World Series play-offs for the American League championship were in progress—and for fans, it was a big deal! The Boston Red Sox had come from behind and tied the series with their archrival, the New York Yankees, each having won three games. During the seventh and deciding game, the volume of patients at the emergency rooms of six Boston-area hospitals was about 15% *below* the normal or expected number (Reis, Brownstein, & Mandl, 2005). A few days earlier, when it looked like the Red Sox would not win the championship, the volume at the hospitals was about 15% *above* the expected number.

Deciding to go to an emergency room involves the person's discretion, and failing to go for medical care is not unusual for diehard fans when critical games with popular teams are in progress. But we don't know for sure why they don't go. Do they simply not notice their symptoms? Do they notice the symptoms but appraise them as innocuous? Do they assess the barriers and benefits of going right away and decide that delaying a few hours won't matter? As we've seen, delaying can matter a lot, depending on the health problem.

USING COMPLEMENTARY AND ALTERNATIVE MEDICINE

When Elena feels a cold coming on, she takes echinacea, an herb that is extracted from a plant. Many people in various parts of the world, including industrialized nations, try to prevent or treat illnesses with practices or products, such as massage or herbal methods, not currently considered part of conventional medicine. As a group, these methods are called **complementary and alternative medicine** (CAM)—a method is *complementary* if used along with conventional treatments, and *alternative* if used in place of them. Although CAM methods are quite diverse, they can be classified into five types (NCCAM, 2006):

- *Manipulative and body-based methods* maneuver or move parts of the body, as occurs in chiropractic and massage procedures.
- *Biologically based methods* apply materials found in nature, such as herbal products and dietary supplements.
- *Mind-body interventions* use techniques for enhancing the mind's ability to manage body function and symptoms, as in progressive muscle relaxation and meditation.
- *Energy therapies* employ hypothesized or known physical energy fields, such as "biofields" believed to exist and surround the body and electric or magnetic fields.
- *Alternative medical systems*, such as traditional Chinese medicine and homeopathy, are complex theoretical approaches for treating illness that differ from and often preceded the development of the system of medicine practiced by professionals with MD degrees. These alternative systems often use one or more of the preceding four methods.

Although these treatments are viewed as unconventional by medical societies in developed nations, many are widely used, traditional methods in other countries—such as China, Puerto Rico, and Haiti—and emigrants take these methods to their new lands (Ahn et al., 2006; Belluck, 1996; Bezkor & Lee, 1999). Some CAM procedures require the services of a practitioner, and others do not. Patients rarely tell their doctors that they use CAM treatments.

Who uses CAM? Probably most people around the world who use CAM learned to do so through their religious or cultural backgrounds. Individuals in the United States who use CAM tend to be well educated, have beliefs and values that are consistent with the method's rationale, and have troublesome symptoms, such as pain or stress, that have not improved with standard medical care (Astin, 1998; CU, 2000; NCCAM, 2006). Over one-third of American adults use CAM; mind-body and biologically based methods are the most frequently used types (USBC, 2010). A survey of thousands of North Americans regarding illness treatments in the prior 2 years found that most were satisfied with the medical care they received and, if they had tried CAM methods, had gotten better results from medical treatment for almost all illnesses (CU, 2000). Most CAM methods were not very successful, having helped the people "feel much better" in only 10–30% of cases, depending on the illness and method used. (Although there was no control group, a placebo would probably have gotten similar ratings.) Two alternative treatments, chiropractic and deep-tissue massage, were particularly successful for back pain.

A main issue for CAM methods is that they have little or no scientific evidence of their safety and effectiveness for treating specific disorders. Once sufficient evidence is found, they are adopted into conventional health care, as has occurred for the dietary supplements glucosamine sulfate to prevent and treat arthritis and folic acid to prevent birth defects (AMA, 2003; NCCAM, 2006). Some CAM treatments have been tested in careful experiments. At various points in this book, you will find evidence for the utility of relaxation techniques, deep-tissue massage, and biofeedback in treating pain and other chronic conditions, such as asthma and diabetes. Although spinal manipulation appears useful for treating back pain, it is not effective with tension headache (Bove & Nilsson, 1998). Many dietary supplements and herbal remedies are not very effective, and some have serious side effects (CU, 2004; Hurley, 2007), but a few have good evidence of success, such as in treating irritable bowel syndrome (Bensoussan et al., 1998). Smelling a lavender aroma does not reduce stress or pain (Kiecolt-Glaser et al., 2008). Some CAM methods have value, but others clearly do not. People who want to use a CAM treatment should look for independent information on its effectiveness and side effects and discuss it with their doctors.

PROBLEMATIC HEALTH SERVICE USAGE

Sometimes health care usage becomes problematic, such as overusing it when there is no medical need because of the patients' emotional distress. People in the general population commonly refer to these patients as "hypochondriacs" and think these people are either malingering or imagining symptoms, so that the illness is "all in their heads."

But this common view is inaccurate. Although some individuals do imagine symptoms and some malinger to get various benefits of the sick role, *hypochondriacs* tend to interpret real but benign bodily sensations as symptoms of illness (Williams, 2004). They may think, for example, that their gastric pains are signs of a serious disease rather than the results of eating spicy foods or amplify minor sensations, such as muscle soreness or twinges, and perceive them as very painful. **Hypochondriasis** is the tendency of individuals to worry excessively about their health, monitor their bodily sensations closely, make frequent unfounded medical complaints, and believe they are ill despite reassurances by doctors that they are not (AMA, 2003; Costa & McCrae, 1985; Kring et al., 2010). It is considered a psychiatric disorder when it lasts at least 6 months and causes significant emotional distress or functional impairments. Psychotherapy with cognitive and behavioral methods can markedly reduce hypochondriasis (Kring et al., 2010; Thomson & Page, 2009).

Paul Costa and Robert McCrae (1980, 1985) have demonstrated an important link between hypochondriasis and emotional maladjustment, or *neuroticism*, which involves a high degree of self-consciousness and "vulnerability to stress as well as the tendency to experience anxiety, hostility, and depression" (1985, p. 21). Their analysis of people's survey responses showed that somatic complaints increase with neuroticism and that the proportion of people who are hypochondriacs is not higher in old age than in earlier adult periods. Although these findings suggest that neuroticism leads to more unfounded health complaints (Costa & McCrae, 1985; Feldman et al, 1999), neuroticism has been linked also to the future development of a variety of diagnosed illnesses, such as cardiovascular disease, arthritis, and irritable bowel syndrome (Turk-Charles et al., 2008; Lahey, 2009).

One other issue should be discussed: sometimes people may have real health problems that medical technology cannot yet confirm. A clear example is a condition called *chronic fatigue syndrome* (CFS). The main symptom of CFS is unexplained, persistent severe fatigue for at least 6 months, but other symptoms can include sore throat and headaches (Hurwitz, 2004). Doctors had incorrectly thought this condition was an extended form of mononucleosis, which is caused by the Epstein-Barr virus, but it isn't, and the cause remains a mystery. Although CFS has been linked with high allostatic load and low blood pressure (Maloney et al., 2009; Newton et al., 2009), there are no medical tests to detect CFS; diagnosis is based on ruling out all other diseases. Studies attempting to link CFS with psychological disorders have produced inconclusive results (Hurwitz, 2004).

To summarize, there are many reasons why people use, don't use, overuse, and delay using health services. These reasons include the nature of the symptoms people perceive, the health beliefs they hold, and social and emotional factors. Another factor that affects people's decisions to use health services is the quality of the relationships they have with their doctors, as we are about to see.

THE PATIENT–PRACTITIONER RELATIONSHIP

A woman who had been receiving treatment for cancer at a clinic on a regular basis began to procrastinate about going in for periodic examinations and care. When her family asked why she had not gone in on schedule, she replied, "They gave me a new doctor, and he's not very nice. He treats me like a number, and I feel uncomfortable talking to him—he talks down to me when I ask him questions." Many patients have stories about negative experiences with practitioners, and these experiences can lead people to delay or stop getting the medical attention they need. These stories often involve the practitioner's hurried manner, insensitivity, lack of responsiveness, failure to explain the medical problem or the treatment, or unwillingness to involve the client in planning the treatment. Problems like these are likely to be aggravated if the client and practitioner have very different cultural backgrounds (Young & Zane, 1995).

PATIENT PREFERENCES FOR PARTICIPATION IN MEDICAL CARE

When people visit doctors about health problems, do they just want to be "cured," or do they also want to know about the illnesses and how to treat them? How involved do they want to be in decisions and activities in their treatment? Doctors often misjudge the involvement patients want (Kindelan & Kent, 1987). Correctly judging the amount and type of participation they prefer can be important—patient–practitioner relationships depend to some extent on the compatibility between what the patient wants and what the practitioner provides.

People differ in the participation they want—although almost all want to know what their illnesses are and how to treat them, some want more details about the illnesses, self-administration of treatment, and involvement in decisions than others do. But most patients with a serious condition want substantial information and involvement (Stewart et al., 2004). Research has revealed important associations with clients' participation preferences. First, gender, age, and sociocultural differences exist. In terms of the amount of information and involvement in medical decisions that people want, women want more than men do, younger adults want more than older adults do, and White people want more than people from certain other ethnic groups do (Levinson et al., 2005; Stewart et al., 2004; Turk-Charles, Meyerowitz, & Gatz, 1997). Second, receiving the desired amount and type of participation enhances individuals' adjustment to and satisfaction with medical treatment (Auerbach, Martelli, & Mercuri, 1983; Stewart et al., 2004). Third, patients who report that they usually want or take an active role in their treatment tend to adjust to their recovery periods better and recover faster than those who prefer an inactive role (Auerbach, 2000; Mahler & Kulik, 1991).

Just as people differ in the information and involvement they want regarding their health, practitioners differ in the participation they are inclined to provide. Some doctors are less inclined than others to share their authority and decision making, often with the incorrect belief that clients are not able to understand medical information and make good decisions (Auerbach, 2000). What happens in the patient–practitioner relationship

when the person wants a different level of participation from what the practitioner gives? The mismatch has at least three important outcomes. First, the patients experience more stress during unpleasant medical procedures (Auerbach, Martelli, & Mercuri, 1983; Miller & Mangan, 1983). Second, clients are less likely to follow the practitioner's advice, such as for dietary changes, outside the medical setting and improve their medical conditions (Cvengros et al., 2009). Third, dissatisfaction and interpersonal discomfort can lead to a switch in doctors (Haug & Lavin, 1981; Keating et al., 2002). In deciding how much information and involvement to provide each client, practitioners clearly need to assess and consider how much the person wants. (Go to 💡.)

THE PRACTITIONER'S BEHAVIOR AND STYLE

Imagine this test: you recently completed medical training and have just started a position in a clinic as a general practitioner. Your next patient this morning

HIGHLIGHT

Fighting for Your Life

Not all victims of serious diseases who are getting medical care receive the most effective treatments available. Some doctors have difficulty keeping up with rapid advances in medical knowledge or are reluctant to switch from a procedure that works reasonably well to one that may work better. What can people do to get the best possible treatment?

Patients and people close to them can join the fight for their lives by taking an active interest in their health care (CU, 2007; Gipson, Liskevych, & Swillinger, 1996). Let's use a hypothetical case of a man named Mark who has a serious illness, such as heart disease or cancer. After learning the diagnosis, he and his family or friends can swing into action. They can:

- Get information about the disease and the usual courses of treatment. Information is readily available on the Internet and in books they can purchase in bookstores or use through public, college, and medical school libraries.
- Make a list of questions to ask at each meeting with doctors working on his case. Mark should have a companion accompany him and take notes in doctor visits. They should ask to know all possible treatment options, what each involves, what the risks are, and

the likelihood of success. Be sure all uncertainties are cleared up before leaving each meeting.

- Broaden the sources of information. Organizations—such as the British Heart Foundation and Cancer Research UK—have websites with information about support groups and treatment methods (most of these websites are included in the reference list for this book). At least one of the doctors Mark consults for treatment options should be a consultant in the specialty and, preferably, on staff at a major university hospital. Many people consult only the original doctor on their case, and this is a mistake.
- Use reputable information sources to find out about very new medical procedures (and even some risky experimental ones). Even though many newer approaches may provide the most effective treatment, not all doctors know about them or feel comfortable about recommending them.

When patients and people close to them take an active interest in their health care, they can play an informed role in discussions and negotiations with their doctors toward making decisions. Patients who do this can be satisfied that they are getting the best treatment available and feel a sense of efficacy in themselves and in their doctors.

is waiting in an examination room, which you are preparing to enter. Your task will be to decide which one of the more than 1,300 disease entities known to medicine this person has (Mentzer & Snyder, 1982). Or maybe the person has no physical problem at all. You have less than 20 minutes.

Diagnosing and treating health problems are difficult tasks, which different doctors undertake with their own behaviors and styles of interacting with patients. Patrick Byrne and Barrie Long (1976) identified different styles of interacting by analyzing about 2,500 tape-recorded medical consultations with doctors in several countries, including England, Ireland, Australia, and the Netherlands. Each doctor tended to use a consistent style for all clients treated. Most of the styles were classified as **doctor-centered** (sometimes called **paternalistic**), in which the doctor asked questions that required only brief answers—generally "yes" or "no"—and focused mainly on the first problem the person mentioned. These doctors tended to ignore attempts by patients to discuss other problems. Doctor-centered doctors seemed to be intent on establishing a link between the initial problem and some organic disorder, without being sidetracked. In contrast, doctors who used a **patient-centered** style took less controlling roles. They tended to ask open-ended questions, such as, "Can you describe the situations when the pain occurs?" that allow a patient to relate more information and introduce new facts that may be pertinent. They also tended to avoid using medical jargon and to allow clients to participate in some of the decision making. On average, doctor visits take about 20 minutes, and longer visits tend to be of higher quality (Chen,

Farwell, & Jha, 2009). Female doctors tend to use a more patient-centered style and spend 10% more time with patients than male doctors do (Krupat, 2004).

The patient–practitioner relationship depends on the ability of the two participants to communicate with each other. But doctors sometimes impede communication by using *medical jargon* or technical terms. For example, telling hypertensive patients to "reduce sodium intake" is an accurate recommendation, but will they know what it means? Some people will know exactly what sodium is, others won't have any idea, and others will think it only means table salt, not realizing that there are other sources of dietary sodium. Studies have found that most patients, particularly those from lower-class backgrounds, fail to understand many of the terms their doctors use—such terms as "mucus," "sutures," and "glucose," for instance (DiMatteo & DiNicola, 1982; IOM, 2004; McKinlay, 1975). Although jargon is useful for accuracy and for communicating among medical professionals, practitioners who use technical terms in talking with clients without explaining the terms or checking comprehension can create confusion, incorrect ideas, and dissatisfaction in them.

John McKinlay (1975) assessed lower-class women's understanding of 13 terms their doctors used with them in a maternity ward. Although over two-thirds of the women understood the terms "breech" and "navel," almost none understood "protein" and "umbilicus"— and on the average, each of the 13 words was understood by only about 39% of the patients. McKinlay also had the doctors indicate for each word whether they thought "average lower-working-class women" would

Patients tend to prefer a doctor who gives clear explanations about illnesses and treatments, encourages them to ask questions, and conveys a feeling of concern for them.

understand the term. The doctors expected even *less* comprehension than the clients showed, yet they used these terms often with these women.

Why would doctors use terms with a patient when they do not expect the person to understand? Sometimes they may do this "out of habit," that is, the terms are so familiar to them that they forget the client is less medically sophisticated. Or they may feel—perhaps in a patronizing way—that the person "doesn't need to know." Other reasons for using jargon may involve their perceptions of what would benefit the patient or the medical staff (DiMatteo & DiNicola, 1982; McKinlay, 1975). What might these benefits be? Sometimes the person's knowing exactly what the disease or its treatment is may produce too much stress or interfere with treatment. And there can be another issue: using "big words" the client does not understand elevates the status of practitioners.

First and foremost, people prefer to have a practitioner they think is competent. But there are other important factors in the patient–practitioner relationship, too—especially the *sensitivity*, *warmth*, and *concern* the person perceives in the practitioner's behavior. People prefer, evaluate highly, and express greater satisfaction for dentists and doctors who seem friendly and interested in them as persons, show empathy for their feelings, project a sense of reassurance, and present a calm and competent image (CU, 2007; van Dulmen & Bensing, 2002; Weiner et al., 2005). In contrast, practitioners who seem emotionally neutral are often evaluated less positively, perhaps because they appear unconcerned. People assess these characteristics not just by the practitioner's words, but by his or her facial expressions, eye contact, and body positions (DiMatteo, 1985; Krupat, 2004). The practitioner's style can have important implications: greater satisfaction with the practitioner translates into a higher likelihood that patients will follow medical advice and keep medical appointments (DiMatteo, Hays, & Prince, 1986; Krupat, 2004).

Perhaps the most important implication of doctors' styles relates to the diagnostic information they receive from their patients. Doctors vary greatly in their ability to elicit significant diagnostic information from their clients (Marvel et al., 1999; Roter & Hall, 1987). Doctors who ask more open- and closed-ended questions, allow clients to give a full answer, give more information about the cause and prognosis of the illness, and discuss more details about prevention and treatment, receive more diagnostic facts from their clients than doctors who do less of these things. The additional facts doctors receive are not trivial ones, but ones other physicians judge to be important in diagnosing the person's illness. The first complaint or detail the client gives is often not the most significant one, and getting a full statement of the client's concerns takes only several additional seconds: at the start of a visit, the practitioner can elicit a list of the person's concerns and then set an agenda together (Mauksch et al., 2008). Findings like these have led medical schools to introduce programs to educate future physicians regarding interviewing skills and psychosocial factors in treating patients (Krupat, 2004; Weiner et al., 2005). (Go to 🍎.)

THE PATIENT'S BEHAVIOR AND STYLE

It takes two to tango, as the saying goes. Although the practitioner's behavior plays an important role in the relationship he or she forms with a patient, the client's behavior and style are important, too. Doctors reported in surveys, for instance, that some patients do things that can be unsettling for a doctor (CU, 2007; Smith & Zimny, 1988). Some of these behaviors include:

- Not following the prescribed treatment.
- Waiting too long with symptoms before contacting the doctor.
- Insisting on laboratory tests, medications, or procedures the doctor thinks are unnecessary.
- Requesting that the doctor certify something, such as a disability, the doctor thinks is untrue.
- Making sexually suggestive remarks or behaviors toward the doctor.

If behaviors such as these lead to a breakdown in the relationship between the patient and practitioner, the quality of the medical care may suffer.

Do patients do things that impair patient–practitioner communication? Yes. For one thing, people who are high in neuroticism may convey too much concern about their conditions and seem less credible and less in need of medical care (Ellington & Wiebe, 1999). Also, some clients describe their symptoms in unclear or misleading ways. Let's consider two examples. First, a patient simply said, "I can't see to thread a needle or read the paper," and didn't clarify what the problem was—it was far-sightedness—even when asked (Zola, 1973). Second, a woman with chest pain and dizziness for a month finally went to a doctor, who had tried unsuccessfully to identify what symptoms had gotten worse. He tried one more time, and then became exasperated by her repeated ambiguity (Seaburn et al., 2005, p. 525):

DOCTOR: What's been worse over the last month?

PATIENT: The sharpness mostly and the dullness gets a little bit …

ASSESS YOURSELF

Do You Know Medical Terms' Meanings?

The following 10 medical terms were used in McKinlay's (1975) study of patients' understanding of medical jargon, which is described in the text. Match the terms with the definitions given below: in the space preceding each term, place the number for the corresponding definition.

_____ antibiotic   _____ mucus

_____ breech   _____ protein

_____ enamel   _____ purgative

_____ glucose   _____ suture

_____ membrane   _____ umbilicus

1. The rump or back part.
2. A small scar on the abdomen; the navel.
3. A substance that makes up plant and animal tissue.
4. A simple sugar that the body manufactures from ingested food.
5. A joining together of separated tissue or bone, or a device to achieve this joining.
6. A sheet of tissue that covers or lines a body organ.
7. An agent that works against bacterial infections.
8. A hard, glossy coating or surface.
9. A substance or procedure that causes a cleansing of a body organ, as occurs in a bowel movement.
10. A secretion of body tissues.

Check your answers against the key below. Did you get them all correct? Would you have known as many of the definitions if they weren't given? Would your friends—especially ones who have not gone to college—know the terms?

Answers, in order:

7, 1, 8, 4, 6, 10, 3, 9, 5, 2.

DOCTOR: And you didn't think it would be a good idea to see a doctor sooner than today for something that has been going on for a month? It didn't cross your mind?

PATIENT: Do you think this could be serious?

DOCTOR: If it was serious, you'd be dead by now.

Her symptoms were ones that people with heart conditions often report, and her doctor was upset by her ambiguity and delay in seeking medical care. The patient–practitioner relationship was clearly strained.

Why do patients give unclear descriptions of their symptoms? Let's look at a few reasons. One reason may lie in the way they perceive or interpret different symptoms. As we saw earlier, people differ in the attention they pay to internal states and the degree to which they associate different sensations with health problems. Second, individuals form different commonsense models of illness. When reporting symptoms to a doctor, people may describe only or mainly those problems they think are important, based on their own notions (Bishop & Converse, 1986). Third, clients may try either to emphasize or to downplay a symptom they believe may reflect a serious illness. For example, people high in hypochondriasis may try to maximize the doctor's attention to a sensation they are worried about, and other patients may describe a worrisome symptom very casually or offhandedly in the hope that the doctor will agree that "it's nothing." Last, the clients may be very young or immigrants and lack a good command of the practitioner's primary language, making their symptom descriptions unclear and incomplete (Giachello & Arrom, 1997). These patients are also unlikely to understand fully what their illnesses are or what they need to do to treat them.

What can be done to improve communication between patients and practitioners? Doctors' interviewing skills can be enhanced with training programs that teach how and when to summarize information, ask questions, and check for comprehension (Roter & Hall, 1989; Weiner et al., 2005). Researchers have also found that a simple approach can improve clients' communication: while patients wait for their visits, they can fill out a form that has them list any symptoms and questions they have and encourages them to ask questions when they see the doctor (Thompson, Nanni, & Schwankovsky, 1990).

One thing to keep in mind about patient–practitioner communication is that often practitioners lack feedback for their work. For example, although a patient may visit the doctor again if symptoms persist or if the illness is serious or long term, doctors cannot be certain that *not* hearing from a person means a diagnosis was correct or the treatment was effective. And as we are about to see, practitioners usually cannot be sure to what extent a client is following the medical *regimen*—the treatment program or lifestyle change—they recommended.

COMPLIANCE: ADHERING TO MEDICAL ADVICE

"Now don't tell the doctor, but I don't always take my medicine when I'm supposed to," Amy whispered to a friend in her doctor's waiting room. People don't always *adhere to*, or *comply with*, their practitioner's advice. **Adherence** and **compliance** are terms that refer to the degree to which patients carry out the behaviors and treatments their practitioners recommend. Most researchers have used these terms interchangeably, and we will, too. But *adherence* is a better term because it suggests a collaborative nature of treatment, and the dictionary definition of the word *compliance*—"giving in to a request or demand" or "acquiescence"—suggests that the person obeys reluctantly (DiMatteo & DiNicola, 1982; Wiebe, 2004). The remainder of this chapter examines the extent of clients' failure to follow medical advice, why they do and do not comply, and what can be done to increase their adherence.

EXTENT OF THE NONADHERENCE PROBLEM

How widespread is the problem of noncompliance? Answering this question is actually more difficult than it may seem (Dunbar-Jacob & Schlenk, 2001; Marteau & Weinman, 2004). First of all, failures to adhere may occur for many different types of medical advice. For instance, patients may fail to take medication as directed, not show up for appointments, skip or stop doing rehabilitation exercises, or "cheat a little" in following specific diet or other lifestyle changes advised by practitioners. Second, people can violate each of these types of advice in many different ways. In failing to take medication as directed, for example, they might omit some doses, use a drug for the wrong reasons, take medication in the wrong amount or at the wrong time, or discontinue the drug before the prescribed course of therapy ends. Finally, there is a problem in determining whether a person has or has not complied: What is the most accurate and practical way to assess compliance?

Researchers assess patient adherence to medical recommendations in several ways, and each has advantages and disadvantages (Dunbar-Jacob & Schlenk, 2001; Rand & Weeks, 1998; Wiebe, 2004). One of the easiest approaches for measuring compliance is to *ask a practitioner* who works with the client to estimate it. As it turns out, however, practitioners do not really know; they generally overestimate their patients' compliance and are poor at estimating which clients adhere better than others. Another simple approach is to *ask the patient*. But people tend to overreport their adherence, perhaps because they know they should "follow the doctor's orders." These two methods are very subjective and open to various forms of bias, including lying and wishful thinking. As a result, researchers who use these approaches today often supplement them with reports of family members or medical personnel and with other methods that are more objective. Table 8.2 describes three relatively objective approaches for assessing adherence to using medication.

Despite the complexities in assessing adherence, we can provide some general answers to the question we started with: How widespread is noncompliance? Speaking in very broad terms, the average rate of nonadherence to medical advice is about 40%—that is, *two of every five patients fail to adhere* fairly closely to their regimens (DiMatteo, 1985; Rand & Weeks, 1998). Conversely, the overall rate of *adherence* is about 60%. Adherence varies considerably, depending on the type

Table 8.2   *Objective Methods for Assessing Adherence to Using Medication*

- *Pill or quantity accounting*, in which the remaining medication is measured, such as by counting the number of pills left. This is compared against the quantity that should be left at that point in treatment if the patient has been following the directions correctly. Of course, this method does not reveal whether the person used the medication at the right times, and patients who expect an accounting and want to conceal their noncompliance can discard some of the contents.
- *Medication-recording dispensers* contain mechanical or electromechanical recording devices that can count and record the time when the dispenser is used. Although this approach is expensive to implement, it assesses compliance accurately as long as the patient does not deliberately create a ruse. If patients know about the device and want to avoid taking the medicine, they can operate the dispenser at the right time and discard the drug.
- *Biochemical tests*, such as of the patient's blood or urine. This approach can assess whether medication was used recently, but usually cannot determine how much or when, and it can be very time-consuming and expensive to implement.

of medical advice, the duration of the recommended regimen, and whether its purpose is to prevent an illness from occurring or to treat or cure an illness that has developed. An overview of the findings of research on compliance indicates the following conclusions (Dunbar-Jacob & Schlenk, 2001; Shearer & Evans, 2001; Stilley et al., 2010):

- The average adherence rate for taking medicine to treat acute illnesses with short-term treatment regimens is about 67%; for chronic illnesses with long-term regimens, the rate drops to 50–55%.
- Adherence to taking medicine is higher in the days before and after visiting a doctor than at other times.
- Adherence to recommended changes in lifestyle, such as stopping smoking or altering one's diet, is generally quite variable and often very low.

Keep in mind three things about these conclusions. First, the percentages stated may *overestimate* adherence because most studies have included in their samples only people who agreed to participate (Cluss & Epstein, 1985). It's likely that people who do not participate differ from those who do, such as by having lower health motivation. Second, the adherence rates cited do not reflect the *range* of noncompliance: some patients adhere exactly to a medical regimen, others do not comply at all, and probably most adhere to some degree. Third, nonadherence can have serious health effects: CHD patients with low adherence to taking their prescribed medication or making lifestyle changes are far more likely than those with high adherence to have or die from a stroke or heart attack in subsequent months or years (Chow et al., 2010; Gehi et al., 2007).

WHY PATIENTS DO AND DO NOT ADHERE TO MEDICAL ADVICE

Given that practitioners don't generally know how well their clients adhere to medical advice, what do they think when they learn their patients have not followed their advice? They are concerned about the effects of noncompliance on the person's health, of course, and they tend to place most of the "blame" on the patients' "uncooperative" personalities, inability to understand the advice, or difficult life situations (Davis, 1966). But as we'll see, both the practitioners and patients impact adherence, and an individual's adherence depends on characteristics of (1) the *illness or regimen*, (2) the *person*, and (3) the *interactions* between the practitioner and patient.

Medical Regimens and Illness Characteristics

The medical regimens practitioners advise can differ in many ways, such as in their complexity, duration, cost,

side effects, and the degree to which they require changes in the patient's habits. Let's see how each of these factors relates to compliance.

Some regimens require clients to *change longstanding habits*—for example, to begin and maintain exercising regularly, reduce the calories or certain components in their diets, stop smoking cigarettes, or cut down on drinking alcoholic beverages. We have seen in previous chapters that these changes can be very difficult for people to make. Recommendations by doctors can induce many patients to make changes in such habits, particularly if the individuals are at high risk for serious illness (Dolecek et al., 1986; Pederson, 1982). But studies have consistently found that people are much less likely to adhere to medical advice for changes in personal habits than to advice for taking medication (Dunbar-Jacobs & Schlenk, 2001; Haynes, 1976).

Some treatment regimens are more *complex* than others—such as by requiring the person to take two or more drugs, each with its own special instructions: "Take one of these pills after meals, and two of these other pills at bedtime, and one of these other pills every 8 hours." As you might expect, the greater the number of drugs and the more complex the medication schedule and dosage, the greater the likelihood the person will make an error, thereby failing to adhere to the regimen (Ingersoll & Cohen, 2008; Wiebe, 2004). Regimens also become difficult if they require a variety of complicated tasks, as, for example, individuals suffering from chronic *kidney disease* must do (NKF, 2010; Swigonski, 1987). Many of these patients must:

- Undergo *hemodialysis*, in which the blood is shunted from an artery to a filtering apparatus and returned to a vein. This procedure generally takes about 4 hours three times a week, during which complications may occur, such as an extreme drop in blood pressure.
- Take large quantities of medication and vitamins—sometimes involving dozens of pills a day—while also strictly limiting fluid intake.
- Severely restrict their dietary intake of *sodium*, mainly salt; *potassium* and *phosphorus*, which are found in many fruits and vegetables; and *protein*, especially meats and dairy products.

In general, the more a client is required to do, the more likely compliance will suffer.

The duration, expense, and side effects of a medical regimen are also factors in people's adherence to their practitioner's advice. Studies have confirmed the role of *duration*—compliance tends to decline over time (Parrish, 1986; Wiebe, 2004). Short-term regimens are usually prescribed for acute illnesses and show clear beneficial effects fairly quickly, but long-term regimens usually apply to chronic health problems and have slower and less obvious benefits. The *expense* and *side effects* of treatment play a role, too. Most people will adhere to treatment because they have sufficient incomes or insurance to pay for it or feel the benefits of the treatment are essential despite the cost, and most drugs don't have noticeable or worrisome side effects. But what happens, for instance, when individuals cannot afford their medicine or its side effects do become a problem? Some patients may reduce the dosage of the drug or discontinue using it entirely. The expense and side effects of treatment can impair adherence for many people (Murdaugh, 1998; NCHS, 2009a; Piette, Heisler, & Wagner, 2004).

We might expect that individuals who have health problems that could disable them or threaten their lives would be more likely to adhere to their treatment regimens than people with less serious illnesses. Whether this idea is correct seems to depend on whose perspective of the severity of the health problem we consider—the practitioner's or the patient's. When comparisons are based on illness severity judged by *doctors*, clients with serious illnesses are no more likely to adhere than those with milder health problems (Becker & Rosenstock, 1984; Haynes, 1976). Perhaps this is because many very serious health problems, such as hypertension and atherosclerosis, have no symptoms that worry people greatly or interfere with their functioning; on the other hand, many less serious illnesses do have such symptoms. In contrast, when comparisons are based on illness severity judged by *patients* who have the health problem, clients who rate their illness as relatively serious generally show better adherence to their treatment regimens than those who perceive their illness to be less severe (Becker & Rosenstock, 1984; Stafford, Jackson, & Berk, 2008).

Age, Gender, and Sociocultural Factors

Research has found little or no association between compliance in general and clients' specific personal and demographic characteristics, such as their age, gender, social class, race, and religion (Cluss & Epstein, 1985; Wiebe, 2004). Does this mean these factors never affect compliance? Probably not. For one thing, although each of these factors is not *by itself* strongly related to adherence, when they are *joined*—for example, gender plus age plus social class—their combination shows a stronger association to compliance (Korsch, Fine, & Negrete, 1978). What's more, some of these factors may be related to adherence in some circumstances but not others.

Consider the factor of *age*, which seems to affect adherence in different ways, depending on the illness. For example, research found that:

- For childhood cancer patients, problems in adherence to specific care procedures, such as using antibiotics

correctly, were greater for younger than for older children (Manne et al., 1993). Although the parents mainly controlled these procedures, the child's age made a difference.

- Among child and adolescent diabetics, adolescents were less adherent to their special diets than children (Johnson et al., 1992).

- For adult arthritis patients, 47% of 55- to 84-year-olds and only 28% of 34- to 54-year-olds made no medication errors in several weeks of monitoring; middle-aged people with very busy lives made the most errors (Park et al., 1999).

Children become increasingly responsible for their own medical treatment as they get older (La Greca & Stone, 1985). Adolescents may be less likely than individuals from other age groups to comply with long-term treatments that single them out or make them different from peers. And the elderly are more likely than other age groups to suffer from visual, hearing, and cognitive impairments that may lead to noncompliance (Murdaugh, 1998).

Gender and *sociocultural* influences on adherence may also depend on specific circumstances. For instance, women's concern about controlling their weight appears to interfere with using medication to control their blood sugar (Polonsky et al., 1994). Two sociocultural factors are important. First, some cultural groups may have beliefs or customs that undermine adherence. As an example, among Native American Indians, the idea "of taking something all the time, like an antihypertensive drug, is foreign to some cultures where 'cure' is inherent to the healing process, thus making medications that must be taken continuously appear ineffective" (Baines, 1992). Second, minority groups often have low literacy rates (in terms of health literacy and reading ability) and high health risks; special efforts are needed to enhance regimen adherence in these patient groups (Marteau & Weinman, 2004; Pignone et al., 2005).

Psychosocial Aspects of the Patient

We saw earlier that the seriousness of an illness and the costs of its treatment can affect compliance, depending on the point of view of the patient. Perceived seriousness and perceived costs and benefits are two psychosocial factors that should have a familiar ring by now—we have examined them more than once before as components in the *health belief model*. The health belief model components are as important in explaining why people do and do not adhere to medical advice as they are in explaining other health-related behaviors, such as whether people are likely to adopt health behaviors or use health services (Becker, 1979; Becker & Rosenstock, 1984). Thus, a patient who feels threatened by an illness and believes the benefits of the recommended regimen outweigh the barriers is likely to adhere to his or her practitioner's advice. But individuals who do not feel threatened by the health problem or assess that the barriers of the regimen outweigh the benefits are unlikely to comply.

Sometimes not adhering to a treatment regimen may be *deliberate* and based on *valid reasons*, regardless of whether they are medically sound (Kaplan & Simon, 1990; Turk & Meichenbaum, 1991). This is called **rational nonadherence**. How can not adhering to medical advice be rational? Patients may be acting rationally when they fail to take medication as directed because they:

- Have reason to believe the medication isn't helping.
- Feel that its side effects are very unpleasant, worrisome, or seriously reducing the quality of their lives.
- Are confused about when to take it, or how much.
- Don't have the money to buy the next refill.
- Want to "see if the illness is still there" when they withdraw the medication.

These are not unreasonable reasons—and sometimes the clients may be medically correct in not adhering, such as when they experience symptoms they think may be serious side effects. Very common *intentional* reasons for not taking medication are its side effects and cost, and a preference to take as little medicine as possible (Lorish, Richards, & Brown, 1989; Pound et al., 2005). But most nonadherence in taking medication occurs unintentionally: by forgetting (Dunbar-Jacob & Schlenk, 2001).

Adherence to medical advice is often affected by *cognitive and emotional* factors, and Table 8.3 describes the impact on patients' memory when these factors operate at the time that clients receive instructions. For people to comply with a treatment regimen, they must be cognitively and emotionally able to understand and remember what they are to do. The directions patients receive are often complex and given at a time when they may not be listening as carefully as they should. Even when health information is given in writing, most adult patients may not understand it if it is written much above the fifth-grade reading level (Estey, Musseau, & Keehn,

1994). The role of cognitive function and emotions on adherence can also be important outside of medical settings. People who have difficulty paying attention, remembering, or planning adhere less well than others to taking medications at the correct time and dosage (Stilley et al., 2010). And negative affect, especially depression, has been linked to low levels of adherence (Marteau & Weinman, 2004; Trivedi et al., 2008).

Two other psychosocial factors that are associated with adherence are *self-efficacy* and *social support*. Generally speaking, people who feel they can carry out the regimen and receive the comfort, caring, and help they need from family, friends, or support groups are more likely to follow medical advice than clients who have less social support (DiMatteo, 2004; Dunbar-Jacob & Schlenk, 2001). Self-efficacy can include the person's confidence in being able to perform the activities or recover from lapses or other setbacks (Schwarzer et al., 2008). Social support is most effective when a cohesive family gives tangible or instrumental support in caring for the medical regimen. But for some people, such as kidney disease patients who must restrict fluid intake, social relationships can sometimes lead to nonadherence (Swigonski, 1987). This may happen because social gatherings often occur with food and beverages present—in meetings for lunch, dinner, drinks, or just a cup of coffee, for instance. Some evidence indicates that individuals who are low in conscientiousness are more likely to be led astray by social support than people who are high in conscientiousness (Moran, Christensen, & Lawton, 1997).

PATIENT–PRACTITIONER INTERACTIONS

The word "doctor" comes from the Latin *docere*, which means "to teach." Two features of good teaching involve explaining information in a clear and organized fashion and assessing whether the learner has learned or understands. Some medical practitioners are good teachers, and others are not:

> for example, there are documented cases of men consuming contraceptive drugs intended for their wives. The idea may be amusing, but the fact of an unwanted child was not. (Hunt & MacLeod, 1979, p. 315)

Table 8.3   *Cognitive and Emotional Factors in Patients' Recall of Information from Doctors*

1. Patients forget much of what the doctor tells them.
2. Instructions and advice are more likely to be forgotten than other information.
3. The more a patient is told, the greater the proportion he or she will forget.
4. Patients will remember: (a) what they are told first and (b) what they consider most important.
5. More intelligent patients do not remember more than less intelligent patients.
6. Older patients remember just as much as younger ones.
7. Moderately anxious patients recall more of what they are told than highly anxious patients or patients who are not anxious.
8. The more medical knowledge a patient has, the more he or she will recall.

Source: Cassata, cited in DiMatteo & DiNicola, 1982, p. 45.

This example illustrates that doctors do not always make sure the patient understands what they have said. Successful communication in patient–practitioner interactions is essential if the client is to adhere to the advice.

Communicating with Patients

If your doctor told you to "take one pill every 6 hours," does that mean you should wake up in the middle of each night to take one? Or would it be OK simply to take four pills a day, equally spaced during your waking hours? Would you ask? Sometimes the information people get from practitioners is not very clear. You might argue that the advice *was* clear: every 6 hours, on the dot. But practitioners need to anticipate unspoken questions—saying, for instance, "You'll need to wake up to take one because the infection may recur if the medicine wears off." If practitioners don't do this, patients usually answer these questions themselves, often incorrectly.

Many people leave their doctors' offices not knowing how to follow their treatment regimens. Bonnie Svarstad (1976) conducted a study in which she interviewed patients at a community health center, recorded their actual verbal interactions with their doctors, and checked their medication containers a week later. This study revealed four findings. First, the patients' knowledge about their treatment was deficient—for example, half did not know how long to continue the medication, and about one-fifth did not know the purpose of or how often to take the prescribed drugs. Second, the patients' poor knowledge often resulted from the doctors not providing the needed information. Third, the clients asked very few questions during the visits. Fourth, the more explicit the doctors' directions, the more the people complied, which was measured by pill counts at the patients' homes about a week later. Today, many pharmacies provide instructions.

Doctors spend very little time giving information to patients during a visit. The average visit lasts about 20 minutes in the United States (Chen, Farwell, & Jha, 2009; Krupat, 2004) and 8-10 minutes in the United Kingdom, according to the NHS Choices website, www.nhs.uk. Studies assessing hundreds of visits have examined the amount of time doctors spend giving information to clients about their illnesses and treatment: averaging across the studies, it appears that doctors spend perhaps 10% of the time, or 2 minutes, giving patients information (DiMatteo, 1985). But the doctors themselves reported a very different picture: when asked how much time they spent giving information, they gave estimates that were several times higher than the research records showed (Waitzkin & Stoeckle, 1976). A person's adherence to medical advice depends on the practitioner's communicating information. Good communication takes time and

is much more likely to occur when the practitioner's style is more patient-centered than doctor-centered.

Adherence and the Patient–Practitioner Relationship

As we have seen, people generally prefer medical care that involves a patient-centered style. Research has shown that individuals who have good relationships with their doctors are more likely to adhere to the medical advice they give (DiMatteo, 1985; Garrity, 1981; Krupat, 2004). For example, researchers found that mothers who were very satisfied with the warmth, concern, and communication of information of their child's doctor were three times more likely to adhere closely to the regimens than mothers who were dissatisfied (Francis, Korsch, & Morris, 1969). It may be that doctors who succeed in fostering compliance are those who use patient-centered styles.

To summarize, the reasons why patients do and do not adhere to medical advice include characteristics of the illness and regimen, the clients and practitioners, and the way these people interrelate or communicate. While reading this material, you may have thought, "Couldn't many of the circumstances that lead to nonadherence be changed to enhance compliance?" The next section examines this question.

INCREASING PATIENT ADHERENCE

Implicit in our interest in enhancing adherence is the assumption that doing so would benefit the person's health. How important is adherence to the patient's health? If it is very important, should health care workers aim for each client to comply perfectly to his or her regimen, or would a lesser degree of adherence be acceptable? We will address these questions briefly before considering ways to increase compliance.

Noncompliance and Health Outcomes

By not adhering to regimens recommended by their doctors, people increase their risk of developing health problems they don't already have or of prolonging or worsening their current illnesses. Hospital admissions are substantially higher for people who fail to follow medication regimens for serious conditions, such as hypertension (Dunbar-Jacobs & Schlenk, 2001). And prospective studies of people with serious illnesses have shown that individuals who adhered poorly to their medical regimens were much more likely to die during 1- or 2-year follow-up periods than people who adhered well. For example, two studies found higher mortality rates in heart disease patients who adhered poorly to taking drugs to prevent heart attacks (Ho et al., 2006;

Irvine et al., 1999); another study found higher death rates among kidney disease patients who adhered poorly to dialysis treatments (Kimmel et al., 1998). For HIV drug treatment, strict adherence to the regimen is necessary to prevent the virus from rebounding and developing drug resistance (Catz et al., 2000; Ingersoll & Cohen, 2008).

But failing to follow a practitioner's orders exactly is not always detrimental to the client's health. One reason is that the effect of nonadherence is greater for serious and chronic illnesses than for less serious conditions (DiMatteo et al., 2002). Another reason may be that doctors sometimes prescribe drugs or other procedures with nonmedical goals in mind, such as to avoid risking malpractice suits. But even when medically sound regimens are given—as in the great majority of cases—some people who follow their doctors' orders closely show little benefit from the treatment, whereas others who are much less compliant show substantial improvements in their health (Cluss & Epstein, 1985; Hayes et al., 1994). The importance of following medical advice closely seems to depend on the particular health problem and the treatment prescribed: for some illnesses, 80% adherence for the medication may be the minimum level of compliance needed; for other health problems a 50% rate may be sufficient. Unhealthful noncompliance might be defined as "the point below which the desired preventive or therapeutic result is unlikely to be achieved with the medication prescribed" (Parrish, 1986, p. 456). Unfortunately, compliance cutoff points still need to be established for specific illnesses and treatments.

Although research is needed to determine compliance cutoff points, two things should be clear. First, *perfect* adherence may not be necessary in many cases. Second, the current adherence levels of clients are very far from perfect.

Improving Doctors' Communication Skills

Probably most doctors in the past who have dealt with the compliance problem at all did so after the fact. Rather than trying to prevent noncompliance, they tried to correct it if and when they learned about it. How did they try to correct it? A study examined this question and found that the first step doctors used when a client failed to adhere was to give a "thorough explanation of the regimen and repeat it so that the patient understands" (Davis, 1966). As we have seen, explaining the regimen and making sure the person understands can prevent noncompliance in the first place.

Getting practitioners to improve their style of communicating with patients is not necessarily difficult to accomplish. One study presented a brief program to instruct doctors at a hospital clinic about the kinds of reasons hypertensive people have for not adhering to their regimens and about ways to detect and improve low compliance (Inui, Yourtee, & Williamson, 1976). Compared to doctors in a control group, the doctors who received the program subsequently spent more time giving information during patient visits—and, more important, their clients showed more knowledge about their regimens and illnesses, greater adherence in taking medications, and better blood pressure control. Oftentimes such changes in doctor behavior last indefinitely (Roter & Hall, 1989). (Go to 🔲 .)

CLINICAL METHODS AND ISSUES

How to Present Medical Information

Because patients often misunderstand or forget medical recommendations, practitioners are also learning specific techniques for presenting medical information. Several methods are particularly effective (Parrish, 1986; Schraa & Dirks, 1982; Shearer & Evans, 2001). These methods include:

- Orienting patients to the disease process and reason for the treatment in terms they can understand.
- Simplifying verbal instructions by using clear and straightforward language and sentences, without condescending.
- Using specific and concrete statements—such as, "You should walk a mile a day for the first week, and 2 miles after that," instead of, "You should get daily exercise."

- Breaking down a complicated or long-term regimen into smaller segments. The patient might begin the regimen by doing only part of it and then adding to it later. Or the regimen might involve a series of smaller goals that the client believes he or she can achieve.
- Emphasizing key information by stating why it is important and offering it early in the presentation.
- Using simple, written instructions.
- Having the patient repeat instructions or state them in his or her own words.
- Assessing the person's self-efficacy, motivation, and opportunities for social support in the regimen.

Interventions Directed at Patients

Other approaches to promote adherence focus on the patient. One method that seems to help at least for short-term regimens is to have the person state explicitly that he or she will comply. In an experiment with parents of children suffering from acute infections, parents who were asked to promise (all agreed) to give all of the medication doses had higher compliance rates than those who were not asked to promise to comply (Kulik & Carlino, 1987). And the children of the parents who promised showed greater recovery later from their illnesses. For long-term regimens, a useful simple approach is to have the doctor's office send follow-up letters explaining why the treatment is important and the risks if the regimen isn't followed (Smith et al., 2008). Although follow-ups and other simple methods help, they improve adherence only modestly (Haynes et al., 2008).

Social and motivational forces in a patient's life can have important effects on adherence, particularly when the regimen is long term or requires lifestyle changes. One helpful approach that we discussed in Chapter 5 is for practitioners to use *motivational interviewing* methods to identify the benefits and problems of adherence and to reduce resistance to implement the regimen (Resnicow et al., 2002; Shearer & Evans, 2001). Another approach is for the practitioner or client to recruit constructive sources of *social support* (Jenkins, 1979; Shearer & Evans, 2001). Family and friends who are committed to the regimen can promote compliance by having positive attitudes about the treatment activities and making sure they occur. Effective social support can also come from self-help and support groups established to give information and assistance with specific health problems. Practitioners can help clients make contact with appropriate groups.

Several *behavioral methods* are also useful in enhancing patients' motivation to adhere to their treatment regimens (Burke, Dunbar-Jacob, & Hill, 1997; Haynes et al., 2008; Roter et al., 1998; Wiebe, 2004). These methods include:

- *Tailoring the regimen*, in which activities in the treatment are designed to be compatible with the patient's habits and rituals. For example, taking a pill at home at breakfast or while preparing for bed is easier to do and remember for most people than taking it in the middle of the day.
- *Providing prompts and reminders*, which serve as cues to perform recommended activities. These cues can include reminder phone calls for appointments or notes posted at home that remind the client to exercise. Innovative drug packaging can also help—for instance, some drugs today come in dispensers with dated compartments or built-in reminder alarms.
- *Self-monitoring*, in which the patient keeps a written record of regimen activities, such as the foods eaten each day.
- *Behavioral contracting*, whereby the practitioner, the client, and a family member negotiate a series of treatment activities and goals in writing and specify rewards the patient will receive for succeeding.

A major advantage of these methods is that the client can become actively involved in their design and execution (Turk & Meichenbaum, 1991). Furthermore, the patient can carry them out alone or with the aid of the practitioner, family, or friends.

The procedures we have examined for increasing patient compliance are often combined into a complex program, particularly to enhance medication adherence for people with chronic illnesses, such as hypertension or heart disease. But these programs have been only moderately effective so far, and new methods are needed (Haynes et al., 2008). Some current methods are easy for practitioners to incorporate into existing ways of working with clients, but others are time-consuming to apply and involve skills that are outside the expertise of most medical workers.

FOCUSING ON PREVENTION

Health-care systems have focused mainly on secondary and tertiary prevention—that is, treating an illness to reverse the condition or to contain or slow its progress—and have developed processes for managing chronic diseases. This approach is called the *chronic care model*. Can the chronic care model be applied to promote primary prevention and help people avoid health problems? Researchers have proposed that it can if efforts for primary prevention in a health care organization incorporate six features of the chronic care model (Glasgow et al., 2001):

1. *Organization of care*. The administrators of the health care system give explicit and obvious priority to primary prevention, such as identifying smokers and helping them quit, and provide incentives for staff to engage in these efforts.

2. *Clinical information systems*. The organization requires regularly updated, easily accessed data in clients' files regarding the need for and status of preventive services so that clients and staff can receive performance feedback and reminders.

3. *Delivery-system design*. Doctors initiate preventive interventions, such as mailings and counseling for stopping smoking, which non-doctors carry out.

4. *Decision support*. The organization provides its staff with guidelines, training, and reminders to identify clients who need intervention and to carry it out.

5. *Self-management support*. The health care system provides information and referrals to clients and their families to help them recognize the need for preventive services and for change in unhealthful behaviors.

6. *Community resources*. The health care system extends its prevention efforts into the community by making use of self-help organizations, such as for quitting smoking and losing weight, and supporting public health programs and laws.

The chronic care model provides a blueprint for designing prevention programs in health care organizations, some of which have already begun to use it and improve prevention.

SUMMARY

Health care systems for the delivery and management of medical care are complex, involving professionals with a variety of specialized functions. Inpatient treatment for people with serious illnesses occurs in hospitals; nursing homes provide care mainly for elderly individuals who need long-term medical and personal care. Health care systems in many countries provide universal health care or insurance for all citizens. The United States didn't have a system of universal health coverage before 2010, but a law was passed so that almost all citizens will be insured within a few years.

People decide they are sick and in need of medical attention chiefly on the basis of the symptoms they perceive. They often consult a lay referral network before going to a doctor. Some people seem to notice changes in physical sensations more than others do and to perceive these sensations as symptoms. Stimuli in the environment can interfere with or mask people's attention to internal sensations. Because people generally do not assess their internal states very accurately, psychosocial factors can influence perceptions of symptoms, which may account for the phenomena of medical student's disease and mass psychogenic illness. Commonsense models and other knowledge people extract from their experience generally help them to make appropriate decisions about seeking medical attention. But sometimes people's knowledge of iatrogenic conditions and their emotions, such as intense fear or anxiety, can lead them to interpret their symptoms incorrectly and lead to treatment delay.

Young children and the elderly use health services more than adolescents and young adults do, and women use more medical services and drugs than men do. Many people use complementary and alternative medicine methods to supplement or take the place of medical care. The health belief model has been useful in helping to explain why people use, don't use, and delay using health services. Many individuals wait months before seeking attention for symptoms of serious illnesses, such as cancer. In contrast, some people overuse health services. Hypochondriasis involves the tendency for a person to interpret real but benign bodily sensations as symptoms of illness despite reassurances by a doctor that they are harmless. This tendency is linked to emotional maladjustment.

People generally express high levels of satisfaction with the care they receive from doctors who communicate with a patient-centered rather than a doctor-centered style. Patient-centered doctors tend to ask open-ended questions, avoid using medical jargon or technical terms, and allow clients to participate in some of the decision making regarding the treatment of their illness. These doctors are also likely to project feelings of concern and reassurance and to give clear explanations about illnesses and treatments. Of course, patients vary in their behaviors and styles, too, and may impair communication with their doctors because of the way they describe their symptoms.

Patient compliance with or adherence to medical advice varies greatly, and poor adherence is very common. Individuals tend to be less compliant for long-term regimens to treat chronic diseases than for short-term regimens to treat acute illnesses, and they are particularly unlikely to adhere to recommendations to change long-standing habits. Also, the more complicated the regimen, the more likely adherence will suffer. Adherence is affected by various psychosocial factors, including rational nonadherence decisions and the patient's health beliefs, social support, and cognitive and emotional factors. Patients are more likely to adhere closely to a regimen when their practitioners are patient-centered and explain their illnesses and treatments clearly. Behavioral methods and communication enhancement can improve people's adherence to medical advice.

KEY TERMS

commonsense models	treatment delay	hypochondriasis	adherence
lay referral network	complementary and	doctor-centered	compliance
iatrogenic conditions	alternative medicine	patient-centered	rational nonadherence

9

IN THE HOSPITAL: THE SETTING, PROCEDURES, AND EFFECTS ON PATIENTS

PROLOGUE

"I had a fast-growing conviction that a hospital was no place for a person who was seriously ill," a patient once wrote. This patient was Norman Cousins, former editor of *Saturday Review*, who had developed and recovered from a typically incurable and painful crippling disease. His symptoms began with a fever and general achiness—the kinds of sensations we usually associate with minor illnesses. Within a week, however, his condition worsened, and he began to have difficulty moving his neck, legs, arms, and hands. He was soon hospitalized for the diagnostic tests that pinpointed his disease: ankylosis spondylitis.

What experiences did Cousins have that led to his negative view of hospitals? One example he described is (1985, pp. 55–56):

> I was astounded when four technicians from four different departments took four separate and substantial blood samples on the same day. That the hospital didn't take the trouble to coordinate the tests, using one blood specimen, seemed to me inexplicable and irresponsible.

He reacted by stating he would not give more than one sample every 3 days and that he expected different departments to draw from it. He also criticized other hospital practices, such as awakening patients from

221

sleep to carry out regular routines. In his view, sleep in the hospital is an "uncommon blessing" that should not be interrupted casually.

Few people enjoy being hospitalized, even under the best of circumstances. Although many people probably have more positive feelings about their hospital experiences than those Cousins had, some have even worse impressions. We have all heard stories of mistakes being made or other situations that produced more serious health problems than those with which the patient was admitted to the hospital. This chapter focuses on the experience of being hospitalized. First we examine the hospital—its history, setting, and procedures—as well as the roles and points of view of the hospital staff. Then we consider what being hospitalized is like from the perspective of patients, and what can be done to assess and provide help for their psychological needs. As we study these topics, we will consider important questions that are of great concern to patients, their families, and practitioners. For instance, hospital personnel have difficult jobs—what impact does this have on them? How do people adjust to being hospitalized? What special needs do children have as patients, and how can hospitals and parents help? How can practitioners reduce the difficulty people experience with unpleasant, painful, and surgical procedures and with having a terminal illness?

THE HOSPITAL—ITS HISTORY, SETTING, AND PROCEDURES

Hospitals in industrialized countries around the world are typically large institutions with separate wards or buildings for different kinds of health problems and treatment procedures. These institutions have changed in their long history, and so have people's attitudes about them. People in the United States today are more likely than people years ago to view hospitals as places to go to get well rather than to die, even though most Americans are in hospitals when they die (Easterbrook, 1987). Let's see how hospitals began and evolved.

HOW THE HOSPITAL EVOLVED

Special places to care for the ill did not always exist. One of the earliest roots of this approach can be seen in the ancient Greeks' establishment of temples where sick people would pray and receive cures or advice from the god Aesculapius (Anderson & Gevitz, 1983). But the idea of having special facilities to house and treat

the sick probably began with the Roman military, who established separate barracks for their ill and disabled soldiers.

The first institutions established to care for the sick were associated with Christian monasteries and had a broad charitable purpose: to help the less fortunate members of society. As a result, these facilities housed not only sick people, but also orphans, the poor, and even travelers who needed lodging. One of the earliest of these hospitals, the Hôtel-Dieu of Lyons in present-day France, was established in A.D. 542 (Anderson & Gevitz, 1983). In the 18th and 19th centuries, these institutions became more specialized in two ways. First, they began to restrict admissions to people who were both sick and judged to be members of the "worthy poor"—that is, those who could make contributions to society. The aged, handicapped, and mentally deficient did not meet this criterion and were placed in poorhouses, whether or not they needed medical care. Second,

> hospitals became more medically specialized. Wards were established for different illness categories. …By keeping patients with the same or seemingly related ailments together, one could readily make far more detailed comparisons and thus advance learning. (Anderson & Gevitz, 1983, p. 307)

The American colonies used similar approaches to those used in Europe for the care of the sick. In 1751, Pennsylvania Hospital opened in Philadelphia as the first institution in the colonies devoted exclusively to treating disease. It was built as a result of a citizens' campaign led by Benjamin Franklin.

Until the 20th century, hospitals had always had a well-deserved bad reputation as places that gave miserable care and ministered exclusively to poor people, who often died from infections they did not have when they entered. Sick people from the upper and middle classes were treated at home. But this situation quickly changed with advances in medical knowledge and technology in the late 1800s (Anderson & Gevitz, 1983). By the early 20th century, hospitals had gained a much more positive reputation and were attracting patients from all social classes. Nowadays, the number of inpatients admitted to hospitals for acute care each year is huge—for example, over 35 million in the United States and 70 million in the European Union (USBC, 2010; WHO/Europe, 2010).

Hospitals today involve a wider variety of functions than ever before. They provide services to inpatients and outpatients to cure disease and repair injury, prevent illness, conduct diagnostic tests, and aid people's rehabilitation and life situations after being discharged. They are also involved in conducting research and

Typical of hospitals prior to the 20th century, this women's ward had many beds close together in a huge room.

teaching current and future medical personnel. To carry out these complex and varied functions, hospitals require organized hierarchies of personnel with specific roles and lines of authority.

THE ORGANIZATION AND FUNCTIONING OF HOSPITALS

Although the organizational structures of hospitals vary across nations, most share many aspects of the organization used in the United States. At the top of the structure is a board of trustees, whose members are generally upper-level business and professional people from the community (Anderson & Gevitz, 1983; APA, 1998). Most boards limit their role mainly to long-range planning and fund-raising. At the next level of authority, the chain of command splits into two parallel lines of responsibility. The hospital *administrators* are mainly in charge of the day-to-day business of the institution, such as in purchasing equipment and supplies, keeping records, and providing food and maintenance services. These functions often affect the medical care patients receive. The *medical staff* are responsible for patient care. Each of these two lines has its own hierarchy of authority. We will focus on the medical staff.

The head of the medical staff is a doctor who usually has the title "Medical Director" or "Chief of Staff." The next level of authority consists of the staff (or "attending") physicians. In the majority of American hospitals, most staff physicians are not actually employed or paid

by the institution. They are employed in private practice or affiliated with a private clinic or group health plan, and they provide services at the hospital for their clients from these sources (Anderson & Gevitz, 1983; APA, 1998). To become a staff physician, a doctor must receive *admission privileges*, typically from a committee of doctors at the hospital, and agree to do certain tasks, such as teaching or providing emergency or clinic service. The main exception to this system of staff physicians occurs at "teaching hospitals," which are affiliated with medical schools. Although teaching hospitals grant admission privileges, they also have large staffs of doctors whom they employ; these doctors include (1) *residents*, who are recent medical school graduates, and (2) full-fledged physicians, whose duties include supervising the residents.

Nurses form the next rung in the hierarchy of medical staff in hospitals. They are salaried hospital employees who have two functions: caring for patients and managing the wards. Nurses are as important as doctors to a patient's recovery, and they spend more time with the person, often explaining medical regimens and procedures when doctors do not. The medical staff also includes a great variety of allied health workers, such as physical therapists, respiratory therapists, laboratory technicians, pharmacists' assistants, and dietitians (Ginzberg, 1983). These workers often have less authority than nurses. Farther down the medical staff hierarchy are orderlies and other workers whose roles require less advanced skills than those of the allied health workers. (Go to 🍎.)

ASSESS YOURSELF

Who's Who in Physician Care

The medical staffs in hospitals contain a great variety of specialized personnel. If you were hospitalized, chances are you'd receive care from at least two of the ten types of medical specialists listed below. Do you know what their specialty areas of illness or treatment are? For this matching task, write the number for each specialty area in the space preceding the corresponding type of specialist. Then use the answer key to find out how many you matched correctly.

_____ Neurologist   _____ Otolaryngologist
_____ Orthopedist   _____ Proctologist
_____ Oncologist   _____ Radiologist

Specialty areas: **1**. Cancer; **2**. Blood; **3**. Nervous system; **4**. Colon and rectum; **5**. Painkilling drugs; **6**. Ear, nose, and throat; **7**. Bones and joints; **8**. X rays; **9**. Heart; **10**. Digestive system.

Answers, in order:

_____ Anesthesiologist   _____ Gastroenterologist
_____ Cardiologist   _____ Hematologist

8, 4, 6, 1, 7, 3, 2, 10, 9, 5

ROLES, GOALS, AND COMMUNICATION

Picture this scene: as the ambulance crew wheels the victim of an automobile accident into the emergency room, the medical staff swings into action. Their specific actions and roles are dictated by the presenting health problems of the patient and would be different if the person had suffered serious burns in a fire or experienced symptoms of a heart attack, for instance. Nurses and orderlies know the usual procedures for patients with the presenting problems and begin to perform their roles without specific instruction—for example, a nurse may prepare to take a blood sample and an orderly may wheel a piece of equipment into place. The physician is, of course, in charge and either conducts needed actions directly or orders others to do them.

Coordinating Patient Care

Years ago, the typical hospital patient received services from a small team of doctors and nurses who worked side by side in close communication throughout the person's stay (Benoliel, 1977). This situation rarely exists today. Instead, assessment and treatment procedures for a hospitalized person involve a wide array of personnel who have different specialties and carry out their roles separately, often with little contact with each other and with the patient. The danger in the current approach is that the patient's care can become *fragmented*, or uncoordinated. Hospitals attempt to minimize this danger by giving a particular staff position, usually a nurse, responsibility for coordinating the care of each patient in a ward (Aiken, 1983). But all major decisions about patient care should be made with the primary care doctor's participation and

coordination, lessening the chances of errors (Weiner et al., 2005).

Health Hazards in Hospitals

Several health hazards exist in hospitals. For one thing, hospitals use many chemicals for treatment and other hospital procedures that can create hazards for personnel and patients (Clever & Omenn, 1988). Good channels of communication can protect workers and patients from excessive exposure to harmful chemicals and substances. Other hazards arise from errors, such as in performing surgery on the wrong patient or body part. These errors can be greatly reduced by using a safety checklist that has medical staff ask the patient's name and mark the body area to receive surgery before anesthesia is applied and check that all instruments and sponges are accounted for at the end of the procedure (Haynes et al., 2009).

Another hazard in hospitals is the potential exposure of personnel and patients to disease-causing microorganisms (AMA, 2003). As we saw earlier, hospitals prior to the 20th century were places where infection spread quickly and widely, and patients often died of diseases they did not have when they entered. Although the spreading of infection in hospitals has been reduced, it still occurs often. Each year, about 5% of patients in American hospitals—1.7 million people—acquire a **nosocomial infection**, an infection a person contracts while in the hospital setting, and tens of thousands of them die from these infections (CU, 2010). Nosocomial infection rates are especially high in intensive care units and vary widely across hospitals. A particularly difficult infection is MRSA (pronounced MERsa), which resists antibiotic treatment. To combat

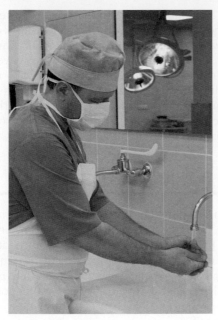

Hospitals try to reduce the spread of infection by establishing rules about medical staff wearing clean masks, clothing, and gloves.

hospital infections, guidelines for infection control have been developed and widely adopted. Guidelines in the United States, for instance, state that each hospital should have an Infection Control Committee headed by an epidemiologist to establish policies to control the spread of disease, and the medical staff should include an Infection Control Nurse (ICN). The ICN has the most direct role in curbing the spread of disease, being responsible for detecting and recording instances of nosocomial infections and taking measures to prevent them.

To reduce nosocomial infections, hospitals have established regulations regarding such issues as when medical workers must wash their hands or wear masks. But hospital personnel often fail to follow these rules (CU, 2010). Although all levels of medical staff violate the rules, ICNs are more likely to correct a nurse or laboratory technician than a doctor (Raven & Haley, 1982). Safety checklists and interventions with behavioral methods can increase infection control actions (CU, 2010; DeVries, Burnette, & Redmon, 1991), but these programs should be repeated periodically because their effects may fade over time (Vincent, 2003). Hospitals also need to find constructive ways to enable a staff member at a lower level of the medical staff hierarchy to give feedback to individuals at higher levels regarding their nonadherence to infection control regulations.

THE IMPACT OF THE "BOTTOM LINE"

The costs of hospital services are very high, but health care systems around the world are trying to contain them. In the United States, the Medicare system helps contain costs, but it didn't when it was first introduced because its procedures encouraged overcharging, keeping patients in the hospital, and performing many tests and procedures. In those days, maintaining a hospital's financial solvency was a relatively easy job for administrators.

This situation in America soon changed when Medicare adopted a payment method called the *prospective-payment system* (PPS) (APA, 1998; Lave, 1989). With the PPS approach, health problems are classified into "diagnostic-related groups," and the fee a hospital receives for treating a person with a particular health problem is predetermined. This fee reflects the average cost of treating individuals in the corresponding diagnostic-related group, based on past recovery rates for similar people. If the patient's condition does not respond to the treatment as readily as expected and requires extra care, the hospital usually bears the cost beyond the PPS allowance. But if the patient's condition responds better than expected, the hospital keeps the excess payment. The ever-increasing costs of medical care and concern by hospital administrators for the "bottom line" have led to changes in hospital procedures.

How have hospital procedures changed? Although some hospitals focus on treating patients who require long-term care, the great majority were established to treat people quickly and discharge them in good health (Lawrence & Gaus, 1983; USDHHS, 1985). Most hospitals keep patients for an average of less than 30 days, and are classified as *short-stay* (or acute care) *hospitals*. As Figure 9-1 shows, the rate at which American short-stay hospitals discharge (and admit) patients increased from 1970 to 1980, when the average length of stay was about a week. After 1980, both discharges and lengths of stay declined sharply. For European hospitals, available data show that lengths of stay have declined there, too. These decreases reflect three important changes. First, people are having more procedures done on an outpatient basis. Second, medical procedures are becoming increasingly efficient. For example, new surgical methods for correcting orthopedic injuries entail little or no cutting of healthy tissue, so that recovery time and pain are greatly diminished. And emergency room diagnoses are made more quickly with the aid of new, accurate tests, such as for heart attacks (Puleo et al., 1994). Third, patients are being released at earlier stages of recovery, so that a larger part of their recovery time is spent at home while receiving care as outpatients. Evidence indicates that being released quickly from

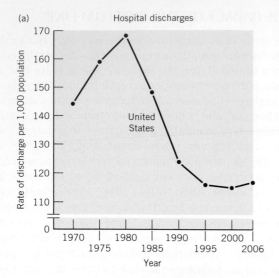

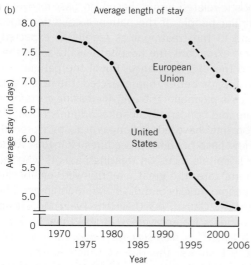

Figure 9-1 Hospital utilization from 1970 to present. (*a*) Patient discharge rates in the United States. (*b*) Average length of stay in "short-stay" acute care hospitals in the United States (U.S., solid line) and the European Union (E.U., dashed line). *Notes:* Not all relevant E.U. data were available, and changes in U.S. research methods beginning in 1988 may be responsible for part of any differences seen between earlier and later data. (E.U. data from WHO/Europe, 2010. U.S. pre-1980 data from USDHHS, 1985, Figure 30; later data from NCHS, 2009a, Table 102.)

hospitals, and even receiving hospital-level care at home entirely, does not harm patients (Ashton et al., 2003; Kahn et al., 1990; Leff et al., 2005).

People typically prefer being released from the hospital as early as possible. Being hospitalized is in many ways a negative experience—financially, physically,

socially, and emotionally. Some hospitals in the United States and other countries are changing the look and feel of their wards, using recommendations of an organization called Program Planetree (CU, 1995). Wards have rooms with homelike furnishings and libraries with medical and health information, and the staff work as a team with a nurse-coordinator for each patient. The next section considers the impact on the patient of being hospitalized.

BEING HOSPITALIZED

Although being sick is unpleasant and being seriously ill is worse, being hospitalized adds many other negative aspects to a person's sick-role experience: it limits privacy, restricts the individual's activity, requires a high degree of dependency on others, and presents events that can be very distressing, some of which may involve interactions between the patient and the hospital staff.

RELATIONS WITH THE HOSPITAL STAFF

Imagine that you have just been admitted to a hospital. How should you behave toward the staff if you don't get the care or information you want? Hospital patients have a clear social role: they are typically strangers in the hospital community, unfamiliar with its structure and procedures, and dependent for their very lives on the medical staff, who have most of the knowledge, authority, and power in their relationship (CU, 1995; Rodin & Janis, 1979; Taylor, 1979). These conditions often make the person feel uneasy in an already worrisome situation.

Psychosocial Issues of Patients

Anxiety is probably the most common and pervasive emotion of hospitalized people (Newman, 1984a). If their health problems have not yet been identified, they worry about what the problems are, what the outcomes will be, and how the illnesses will influence their lives. If the diagnoses have been made, they worry about many other matters, such as what the treatment will be like and the degree to which it will be successful. Many of the worries patients have stem from uncertainties that result from a lack of information, which may occur because tests have not yet been completed or because no one has taken the time to inform the person (CU, 1995). One hospital patient, for example, gave the following description of experiences with a doctor who would:

> talk fast, he out-talks you—and rushes out of the room and then when he's out of the room you think, well, I

was supposed to ask him what he's going to do about my medicine … you run in the hall and he has disappeared that fast. (Tagliacozzo & Mauksch, 1972, p. 177)

Hospitals are busy places, and the limited time of medical personnel accounts in part for their failure to provide the information patients may need. But, not providing information may lead to misunderstandings that may impair the person's adherence to the advice of the medical staff or lead to unnecessary emotional suffering.

Another common characteristic of the way practitioners interact with patients is called **depersonalization**, or treating the person as if he or she were either not present or not a person. Sociologist Erving Goffman referred to this characteristic as "nonperson treatment"—the patient is treated like "a possession someone has left behind" (1961, pp. 341–342). A psychologist has described a personal example of depersonalization as a patient for an eye injury. The doctor

abruptly terminated his conversation with me as soon as I lay down on the operating table. Although I had no sedative, or anesthesia, he acted as if I were no longer conscious, directing all his questions to a friend of mine—questions such as, What's his name?, What occupation is he in? … As I lay there, these two men were speaking about me as if I were not there at all. The moment I got off the table and was no longer a cut to be stitched, the surgeon resumed his conversation with me, and existence was conferred upon me again. (Zimbardo, 1970, p. 298)

Practitioners may treat patients as nonpersons to distance themselves from the fact that the body they are treating belongs to a thinking and worried person who can observe what is going on, ask questions, and behave in ways that can interfere with their work (Goffman, 1961). Medical workers may try to save themselves and the patient trouble, awkwardness, and anxiety by acting as if the person had dropped off the defective body at the hospital for repair and would pick it up when it was ready.

There are also many emotional factors that lead hospital workers to treat patients in a depersonalized manner. Hospital jobs entail heavy responsibilities and can be very hectic, particularly when many emergencies punctuate the day. These features can create high levels of stress, which may lead workers to give less personalized care. Practitioners need ways to protect themselves emotionally when a patient takes a turn for the worse or dies, which can be a crushing experience (Benoliel, 1977). Depersonalization probably helps practitioners feel less attached and emotionally affected when these events occur.

Burnout Among Health Care Professionals

Hour after hour, day after day, people who work with people who are suffering and distressed must cope with the stress these encounters produce. All jobs have stressful conditions of some kind, such as heavy workloads, deadlines, and interpersonal conflicts. But workers in certain professions—for example, police work, social work, and health care—have the added emotional burden of working continuously in emotionally charged situations that involve feelings of anxiety, fear, embarrassment, and hostility. This burden makes the risk of "burnout" greater in these professions than in most others. **Burnout** is a state of psychosocial and physical exhaustion that results from chronic exposure to high levels of stress and little personal control (Maslach & Jackson, 1982; Maslach, Schaufeli, & Leiter, 2001). Workers who experience burnout tend to have low levels of job satisfaction and high levels of absenteeism, job turnover, and alcohol and drug abuse.

What are the psychological characteristics of burnout in workers? There are three psychosocial components of burnout:

* *Emotional exhaustion*—feeling drained of emotional resources and unable to help others on a psychological level.
* *Depersonalization*—a lack of personal regard for others, as shown by treating people as objects, having little concern for and sensitivity to their needs, and developing callous attitudes toward them.
* *Perceived inadequacy of professional accomplishment*—feeling low in self-efficacy and of falling short of personal expectations for work performance.

Maslach and Jackson (1982) studied burnout in a large sample of workers in a variety of helping professions and in separate samples of nurses and doctors. Let's consider three findings from this research. First, the nurses, doctors, and workers in various helping professions reported fairly similar, high levels of emotional exhaustion. Second, differences were found among occupations for the two other components of burnout: the nurses showed the lowest degree of depersonalization, and the doctors reported the least dissatisfaction with their sense of accomplishment in their work. The low degree of depersonalization among nurses may reflect a sex difference in empathy toward people: almost all the nurses but few of the doctors were females. The relatively high sense of accomplishment among doctors may be the result of such factors as their high pay and status in the medical staff hierarchy. Third, the more time health care workers spent in direct care of patients, the greater was their risk of emotional exhaustion. For instance, doctors who spent almost all their time in direct care reported greater emotional exhaustion than those who spent some of their time in teaching or administrative duties.

How can hospitals help health care workers avoid or cope with burnout? Here are two ways. First, hospitals can provide opportunities for workers to mix direct care for patients and other tasks in their daily activities whenever possible. Second, hospitals can help establish support groups for their health care workers. Meetings of these groups can provide training in stress-management and coping methods, like those we discussed in Chapter 4. Health care workers who receive such training and periodic booster sessions experience much less burnout than individuals without such training (Rowe, 1999).

SICK-ROLE BEHAVIOR IN THE HOSPITAL

Relations between patients and practitioners in the hospital are affected not only by the behavior of the medical staff, but by the patient's behavior, too. A hospital presents an unfamiliar and strange environment that requires psychological and social adjustments that most patients have difficulty making, which complicates their transition to the sick role (Kasl & Cobb, 1966b). How are patients supposed to behave in the hospital?

When patients enter the hospital, they have ideas about how they should behave. Judith Lorber (1975) studied new patients who thought they should be *active* or *passive* ("conforming") and found that people with passive beliefs were less likely than those with active beliefs to argue with the staff and complain about minor discomforts. Another purpose of this study was to examine the reactions of the medical staff to the patients' sick-role behaviors. At the end of each patient's stay, the medical staff rated the individual as a "good patient," "average patient," or "problem patient." They were also asked to provide verbal descriptions of the person's behavior and their reactions when the behavior occurred. In general, individuals rated as *good patients* were those who behaved passively, being cooperative, uncomplaining, and stoical; those rated as *problem patients* were seen as uncooperative, constantly complaining, overemotional, and dependent. Medical staff described one "problem" patient who had psychological and medical complications after gallbladder surgery: he would lie, call people names, and was so uncooperative that it was difficult for staff to carry out routine procedures.

Severe medical conditions can make patients' difficult behavior understandable, and so the staff in Lorber's study distinguished between two types of problem patients. One type consists of individuals who are very seriously ill, having severe complications or poor prognoses. Although these patients show problem behaviors and require a lot of attention, the staff often forgives their behavior because of their medical conditions. The second type consists of people who are not seriously ill but take up more staff time than is warranted by their conditions, and they complain or fail to cooperate a lot. Hospital patients' loss of control and freedoms may be involved: problem patients who are not seriously ill may be engaging in **reactance**—people's angry responses when they feel controlled or that their freedom is threatened (Brehm, 1966). Although hospital staff try to deal with problem patients pleasantly, they sometimes respond by giving sedatives and, for highly problematic cases, even arranging a premature discharge (Lorber, 1975).

Fortunately, the large majority of patients are not problem patients (Lorber, 1975). Most hospitalized people try to be considerate, recognizing that medical workers have difficult jobs. Other individuals behave as "good patients" because they are wary of the consequences of being disliked by the staff. These people do not want to appear to be "troublemakers," by being too demanding or too dependent. They may think an angered staff may "refuse to answer your bell" or "refuse to make your bed," for instance. As a result, these patients may anxiously watch the clock when their medication does not arrive on time, rather than reminding the nurse (Tagliacozzo & Mauksch, 1972). We've discussed several factors that determine how people react to being hospitalized,

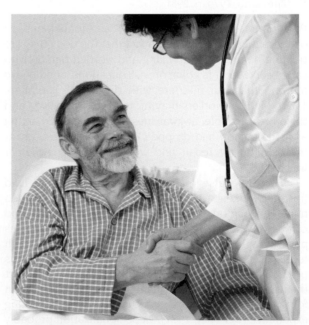

"Good patients" are cooperative, calm, and attentive in discussions with the medical staff.

and we turn now to the role of their emotional adjustment with their medical conditions and the medical treatment procedures they experience in the hospital.

EMOTIONAL ADJUSTMENT IN THE HOSPITAL

Imagine you are in your 30s, waiting in your hospital room for surgery to remove the large tumor you have seen in X-rays that is growing in your lung. Then imagine that the operation goes badly, not all of the tumor could be removed, and the radiation and chemotherapy treatments over the next several weeks leave you weak and nauseated for days at a time. This was the real experience of Fitzhugh Mullan, which he described in his 1983 book called *Vital Signs*. Being hospitalized with a serious illness or injury produces enormous stress and anxiety.

Hospitalized people must cope with their emotions, and they tend to adjust gradually. For example, most surgical patients experience anxiety levels that are especially high when they are admitted, remain quite high prior to the operation, and then decline steadily during the week or two after surgery (Newman, 1984a). But sometimes the anxiety levels of patients increase with time, as happened with a 25-year-old man who had suffered serious burns over 30% of his body. After 3 weeks of hospitalization, he became increasingly difficult and demanding. Interviews revealed the reason: he had

> a very exaggerated view of the nature of his injury, expecting it would render him a cripple for life and unable to support himself or his family. He feared discharge and the subsequent demands of his family. (Steiner & Clark, 1977, p. 138)

How a patient adjusts to his or her health problem and treatment in the hospital depends on many factors, such as the person's age, gender, and perceived characteristics of the illness or injury (Moos, 1982). For instance, young adults often have more difficulty coping with serious illnesses than older individuals do. Also, men tend to be more distressed than women by illnesses that reduce their vigor and physical abilities, but women often have an especially difficult time adjusting to disfigurement, such as facial injuries or losing one of their breasts.

COPING PROCESSES IN HOSPITAL PATIENTS

Two broad ways of coping with stress, such as of being hospitalized, were discussed in Chapter 4: *problem-focused coping* to alter the cause of the stress, and *emotion-focused coping* to regulate the emotional response to the situation. Some stressful situations in the hospital can be altered by the patient taking action in problem-focused coping, such as by asking for medication to reduce pain or by reading information about his or her health problem. These actions can reduce the demands of the stressor or expand the person's resources for dealing with it.

Hospital patients experience many stressors they believe they cannot change. In some cases these beliefs are correct, as when a person whose spinal cord was severed in an accident must cope with not being able to walk. But in other cases the beliefs are not correct, as when a patient does not realize it may be possible to use another medication if the current one produces discomfort or other side effects. People who believe they can do nothing to change a stressor usually try to use emotion-focused coping methods. Patients may try to regulate their emotions by denying unpleasant facts, performing distracting activities, or seeking social support, for example. Research has consistently shown that social support aids people's recovery from and adjustment to illness (Krohne & Slangen, 2005; Kulik & Mahler, 1989; Wills & Fegan, 2001).

Cognitive Processes in Coping

One cognitive process many patients engage in after becoming ill or injured is attributing *blame*—trying to answer the question, "Who's at fault for my condition?" They often grapple with this issue while in the hospital, and they may blame mainly themselves, someone else, or even luck or God's will. Does the way people attribute blame affect their success in coping with their conditions?

We might expect that people who blame themselves would have intense feelings of guilt and self-recrimination and, therefore, have more difficulty adjusting to their conditions than those who blame someone else. On the other hand, blaming someone else may induce intense feelings of anger and bitterness, which would impair adjustment. In fact, both types of blame are related to poor adjustment (Downey, Silver, &Wortman, 1990). But poor adjustment seems to be more strongly related to blaming others than to self-blame (Bulman & Wortman, 1977; Kiecolt-Glaser & Williams, 1987). Although it is unclear why adjustment is so difficult when patients blame someone else, the reason may be that these people feel an added sense of injustice if the person they blame did not suffer severe consequences, too. These feelings are reflected in such statements as, "I'm paralyzed, but the driver only broke his leg," or, "I can't walk now, but the guy who shot me is now walking free" (Bulman & Wortman, 1977, p. 360).

One thing to keep in mind about the cognitive processes used in ascribing blame is that they can be quite convoluted or disturbed: a young man set himself on fire and blamed his act on his father-in-law's saying bad things about him (Kiecolt-Glaser & Williams, 1987).

Another cognitive process that patients engage in involves the assessment of their personal control. Patients enter the hospital with the expectation of losing some degree of control, either from the effects of the illness itself or from being dependent on the actions of the medical staff. Hospital environments induce patients to believe their involvement in the treatment process is irrelevant—that they are *helpless*. Some patients enter the hospital feeling quite helpless right from the start, but others try to exert control and fail. Through repeated failures in exerting control, many people learn to be helpless in the hospital, eventually making no effort to initiate changes when control is actually possible. One study of patients found, for instance, that feelings of helplessness and depression increased with time in the hospital, even as their health improved (Raps et al., 1982).

Connections among "good patient" behavior, helplessness, and depression can be seen in the case of a 50-year-old divorced man who had suffered burns over 40% of his body. When he returned to the hospital 6 months later for a follow-up visit, his hands were still stiff, and he was having many psychological problems. He had moved in with his very supportive daughter and son-in-law

> in hopes that he would be able to take care of repair work that needed doing around the house. When it became clear that he was not able to do any of these things to his satisfaction, he became increasingly depressed.... On reviewing his case it turned out that he had indeed been a very "good" patient, quiet and cooperative. He never asked any questions about the details or the implications of his illness. (Steiner & Clark, 1977, p. 139)

Being a "good patient" and feeling helpless may have made him vulnerable to depression. Patients' emotional adjustment has serious links to health: regardless of the severity of people's illness, they are more likely to die in the hospital if they are depressed than if they are not (Cavanaugh et al., 2001).

Helping Patients Cope

Suppose you were having surgery with *full anesthesia*. Would it make any difference to your recovery if *during surgery* someone said to you, "How quickly you recover from your operation depends on you," and gave suggestions of things you should do to speed recovery? Perhaps.

An experiment found that anesthetized patients who received this kind of information recovered more quickly and had fewer complications than control patients who got no suggestions during their operations (Evans & Richardson, 1988). These results and those of other studies indicate that people hear and understand at least broad meanings while anesthetized, especially emotionally negative information, even though they cannot say what they heard (Bennett, 1989; Gidron et al., 2002). This is important for two reasons: (1) medical staff often make negative remarks during surgery, and (2) it may be possible to help surgical patients cope by giving them constructive suggestions while they are anesthetized.

An effective way to help hospitalized people cope is to provide psychological counseling during their stays. Walter Gruen (1975) gave brief counseling sessions to heart attack patients almost every day during the 3 weeks or so that they were in the hospital. Compared with a control group, the subjects who received the counseling spent fewer days in intensive care and in the hospital, had fewer heart complications and less psychological depression during their stays, and showed fewer signs of anxiety problems when contacted about 4 months after discharge.

A circumstance in the hospital that may help a patient adjust to his or her illness and impending treatment is sharing a room with a person who is recovering after having a similar medical procedure. James Kulik and Heike Mahler (1987a) did an experiment with male patients who were scheduled for coronary bypass surgery. Upon admission, each man was assigned a roommate, based on room availability, for the 2 days prior to surgery. About half of them shared rooms with men who were also awaiting operations, and the remaining patients shared rooms with men who had already had operations and were recovering. Assessments showed that compared to the men who had preoperative roommates, those with roommates who had already undergone surgery were far less anxious before their operation, engaged in much more physical activity after surgery, and were able to leave the hospital an average of 1.4 days sooner.

Why did the type of roommate affect patients' adjustment? The findings of two studies may provide an answer. First, when patients have multiple roommates, they spend more time talking to roommates with a similar surgery status and health problem than to other roommates (Moore, Kulik, & Mahler, 1998). Second, having presurgery patients share a room may increase the anxiety of both individuals by some form of "emotional contagion" (Kulik, Moore, & Mahler, 1993). Perhaps presurgery patients try to alleviate their anxiety by talking to a similar roommate, but the information they share makes things worse for both.

PREPARING PATIENTS FOR STRESSFUL MEDICAL PROCEDURES

Preparing people psychologically for surgery has important implications for their recovery: among patients with similar medical conditions, the more anxiety they feel before surgery, the more difficult their adjustment and recovery are likely to be after surgery. People with high preoperative anxiety tend to report more pain, use more medication for pain, stay in the hospital longer, and report more anxiety and depression during their recovery than patients with less preoperative fear (Anderson & Masur, 1983; Marteau & Weinman, 2004). What can psychologists do to reduce the stress people experience in conjunction with medical procedures?

Psychological Preparation for Surgery

Although several methods seem to be useful in helping people cope with impending surgery, the most effective of these approaches are those that enhance patients' sense of *control* over the situation or the recovery process (Anderson & Masur, 1983; Marteau & Weinman, 2004; Thompson, 1981). These approaches are generally designed to give the person one or more of the following types of control:

- *Behavioral control*—being able to reduce discomfort or promote recovery during or after the medical procedure by performing certain actions, such as special breathing or coughing exercises.
- *Cognitive control*—knowing how to focus on the benefits of the medical procedure and not its unpleasant aspects.
- *Informational control*—gaining knowledge about the events and/or sensations to expect during or after the medical procedure.

Patients can acquire the knowledge for these types of control in many ways, such as through discussion with practitioners, reading, listening to tape recordings, or watching film or video recordings.

An experiment demonstrated the utility of *cognitive control* with individuals in the hospital to undergo major *elective* surgeries who were assigned to groups on a random basis (Langer, Janis, & Wolfer, 1975). One of the groups received training in cognitive control that pointed out how paying attention to negative aspects of an experience increases stress and taught them to focus on the positive aspects of their impending surgery when feeling distressed by the surgical experience. A comparison group spent an equal amount of time with a psychologist, talking only about the general hospital experience. The records and nurses' ratings on the surgical ward revealed important benefits of training

in cognitive control: the patients who received this training showed greater reductions in preoperative stress behavior, less postoperative stress, and fewer requests for medication after surgery than the comparison subjects.

Other studies have demonstrated beneficial effects of enhancing surgical patients' *informational* and *behavioral control* (Johnston & Vögele, 1993; Marteau & Weinman, 2004). In an experiment, Erling Anderson (1987) randomly assigned to three groups 60 adult male cardiac patients who were scheduled for coronary bypass surgery. One group had a general conversation with the researcher and received the *standard preparation* of the hospital, in which the patient and a nurse discussed two pamphlets that outlined the procedures related to the upcoming surgery. A second group received the standard preparation plus training in *informational control* that gave procedural and sensory information in two ways. These men (1) watched a videotape of former bypass patients in interviews going through preoperative tests and exercises, preparation for surgery, recovery, and discharge; and (2) were given an audiotape, describing sensations they might experience, that they could play in their rooms. The third group received training in both *informational and behavioral control*. They had the same preoperative training as the informational control group, but were also taught how to perform various behaviors, such as coughing exercises and ways to turn in bed, that they would need to do after the operation.

Anderson had the patients fill out a questionnaire to measure their distress at three times: when they were admitted, the evening before surgery, and 1 week later. As Figure 9-2 depicts, anxiety levels in the three groups were almost identical on admission, but then diverged after the different preparation methods were conducted. Both types of psychological preparation reduced the patients' anxiety substantially before and after the operation. Although medical records showed no difference between groups on their use of pain medication and length of stay in the hospital, they did differ on a potential blood pressure complication: dangerous levels of acute hypertension are very common during the first 12 hours after bypass surgery. For this critical issue, psychological preparation had a very beneficial effect. Of the patients who received the standard preparation, 75% developed acute hypertension and required medication to dilate their blood vessels. In contrast, only 45% of subjects in the informational control group and 40% of those in the informational and behavioral control group had episodes of acute hypertension.

Similar benefits accrue with videotapes showing the hospital experiences of patients with comparable

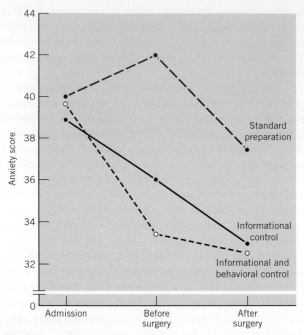

Figure 9-2 Anxiety levels of cardiac surgery patients as a function of the psychological preparation they received. Anxiety was measured by the State-Trait Anxiety Inventory at three times: on admission, the evening before surgery, and 1 week after the operation. (Adapted from Anderson, 1987, Figure 1.)

surgeries. For instance, men and women awaiting hip replacement who saw a videotape of a prior hip surgery patient subsequently showed less anxiety, lower serum cortisol levels, fewer instances of acute hypertension during the surgery, and less pain medication use than comparable patients without the videotape (Doering et al., 2000). Although psychological preparations that increase patients' sense of control when awaiting operations have obvious value, the materials and instructions must be clear and straightforward. Unclear information can lead to misconceptions and anxiety, producing more harm than good (Wallace, 1986). Patients may need to discuss the information with medical and psychological staff. Of course, surgery is only one of many types of stressful medical procedures that may occur in the hospital, and patients often dread experiencing each of them.

Psychological Preparations for Nonsurgical Procedures

How would you like to be awake while a doctor inserts a thin, hollow tube called a *catheter* into one of your blood vessels, gently threads it toward your heart, and then injects dye through the catheter? This is a procedure called *cardiac catheterization*, which is used with people who show signs of cardiovascular disorders, such as damage to a major blood vessel or heart valve. The dye enables practitioners to see the damage with the aid of X-ray or other radiological devices. By using this procedure, doctors can determine whether to recommend other medical procedures, such as bypass or open-heart surgery. A patient undergoing cardiac catheterization receives tranquilizing medication and a local anesthetic for the area where the tube enters the body. This procedure is not painful, but can be unpleasant and produce strange and frightening sensations, such as "hot flashes" when dye is injected into the heart.

Preparing patients for unpleasant medical procedures helps reduce their anxiety and disruptive behavior during the procedures. Philip Kendall and his associates (1979) examined the effects of psychological preparation for cardiac catheterization on the anxiety experienced by male patients, about two-thirds of whom had undergone the procedure at least a year earlier. The men were randomly assigned to four groups. One group received training in *cognitive control* methods from a therapist, learning how to recognize signs of their own anxiety and ways to cope when these signs occur. Another group received preparation to enhance their *informational control*, learning about the procedures and sensations to expect through printed materials and discussions with therapists. Two other groups served as comparison (control) conditions. Analyses of the patients' self-reports and of hospital staff ratings showed that individuals who received the cognitive and the informational control preparations experienced less anxiety than those in the two comparison groups before and during catheterization.

As you may have surmised, the catheterization procedure requires that the patient be inactive. There are no actions the person can take to make the process occur more smoothly or pleasantly—that is, the patient has little or no behavioral control. This is true of many but not all aversive medical procedures. One medical procedure in which patients can perform useful actions is called an *endoscopy*, which is used in diagnosing ulcers and other disorders of the digestive tract. The procedure's most aversive aspect is that a long, flexible, fiberoptic tube, almost over 1 cm in diameter, must be passed through the patient's mouth and down to the stomach and intestine. This tube remains in the digestive tract, transmitting images of the lining, for about 15 to 30 minutes. During this procedure, the person is awake, but has received tranquilizing medication, and the throat has been swabbed with a local anesthetic. Using methods of informational control (describing endoscopy and sensations to expect) and behavioral control (teaching how to breathe and swallow during the procedure) reduces patients' emotional behavior and gagging during an endoscopy (Johnson & Leventhal, 1974).

In summary, psychological preparation benefits patients in surgical and nonsurgical medical procedures. Generally speaking, when these procedures offer little opportunity for the person to take helpful action, psychological preparation to promote informational and cognitive control may be especially effective. But when patients will undergo procedures in which they can take direct action to facilitate the process and reduce their own discomfort, preparation should usually include approaches to enhance behavioral control. (Go to 💡.)

Coping Styles and Psychological Preparation

People use many different styles in coping with stress, as we discussed in Chapter 4. When faced with stressful medical procedures, for instance, some individuals tend to cope by using *avoidance* strategies to minimize the impact of the situation. They may deny that a threat exists; suppress unpleasant thoughts; or refuse to seek or attend to threatening information, perhaps saying, "I don't want to know." In contrast, other individuals tend to use *attention* or "vigilant" strategies, seeking detailed information about the situation (Newman, 1984a). Studies have found that some patients who use avoidance strategies show better emotional adjustment to medical procedures, such as blood donation or dental surgery, than those who use attention strategies (Kaloupek, White, & Wong, 1984; Kiyak, Vitaliano, & Crinean, 1988). If this is so, how do people who use avoidance strategies react to psychological preparations to enhance their control?

Researchers have examined this question by using approaches to enhance informational control with

HIGHLIGHT

Lamaze Training as a Method of Psychological Preparation for a Medical Procedure

Some people believe that a mother in childbirth will experience intense and prolonged pain unless she is given pain-reducing drugs and that the use of drugs is best for the mother and her baby. But these beliefs are questioned for two reasons. First, drugs given to the mother during childbirth pass through the placenta and can have unwanted effects, such as reducing oxygen flow to the fetus and impairing breastfeeding in the newborn's first days (Feldman, 2000; LI, 2010). Second, anthropologists have reported that women in cultures where childbirth is regarded as an easy and open process have shorter and less complicated labors than women in cultures where birth is regarded as fearful and private (Mead & Newton, 1967). Could it be that part of the difficulty many mothers have in childbirth is the result of the inadequate psychological preparation they receive?

Because of these considerations, many prospective parents opt for preparation involving "natural childbirth" methods, such as **Lamaze training**, in which the mother learns how to participate in childbirth and receives minimal medication (LI, 2010). Birth is essentially a process in which the muscles of the uterus contract in a rhythmical pattern to push the baby out. Natural childbirth methods prepare the woman to be more relaxed and better able to manage her body positions, muscular activity, and breathing to help in the process at each stage. Lamaze methods enhance the mother's social support during childbirth and three types of personal control (LI, 2010; Wideman & Singer, 1984):

- *Informational control*, such as with descriptions of the physiological processes in birth and the procedures and sensations to expect during labor and delivery.

- *Behavioral control*, for example, via instruction and practice in breathing patterns and body positions and movements.

- *Cognitive control*, such as by teaching the woman to stare at an object in the room or to concentrate on images or phrases during the childbirth process.

Hospitals generally cooperate with the procedures the method describes.

Is Lamaze preparation beneficial? Findings from studies suggest that it is: women who receive Lamaze training use less painkilling medication during delivery and are less anxious about the birth procedure than those who do not (LI, 2010). But these studies have used quasi-experimental designs and self-report methods (Feldman, 2000; Wideman & Singer, 1984). A difficulty in interpreting these findings is that women who choose natural childbirth are different from those who do not—for example, they tend to be from higher social classes and report lower anxiety levels even before receiving the training.

patients who were classified as using avoidance or attention styles. Suzanne Miller and Charles Mangan (1983) conducted one of these studies with women who were scheduled to undergo an unpleasant but painless diagnostic test for gynecological cancer. By random assignment, half of the avoidance subjects (called "blunters") and the attention subjects ("monitors") received extensive information regarding the procedures and sensations they would experience during the examination; the remaining women got very little information about the examination. Measures of the patients' distress were taken at three times: before receiving the information, after getting the information but before the examination, and after the examination. Figure 9-3 presents the results of this research, using the women's pulse rates as the measure of distress. These findings indicate that monitors who receive very little information and blunters who receive extensive information react negatively to the amount of information they receive, as shown by their continued high pulse rates after the examination.

Other research has confirmed these findings and shown that preparation for medical procedures is most effective when its content is matched to the coping needs of the person (Litt, Nye, & Shafer, 1995; Ludwick-Rosenthal & Neufeld, 1993; Williams-Piehota et al., 2005). In addition, the number of times patients see the information seems to affect the stress they experience during a procedure. In one study, people filled out a questionnaire that assessed their coping styles and then watched a videotape that showed the procedures and sensations they could expect during an upcoming endoscopy (Shipley et al., 1978). Some subjects watched the informational tape only once, and others viewed it three times. A comparison group watched an irrelevant tape. Measures of the patients' anxiety during their endoscopies included heart rate and questionnaire assessments by the patients and practitioners after the examinations. The study found that *avoidance copers* who saw the informational tape only once experienced more anxiety than those who saw it three times and those who watched the irrelevant tape. Of the *attention copers*, those who watched the irrelevant tape experienced the most anxiety, and those who viewed the informational tape three times had the least anxiety.

The benefits of psychological preparations for medical procedures seem to depend on the patients' coping styles, and it may be that different preparations are more helpful for people using avoidance strategies than for those using attention strategies. Although being exposed to information about impending medical procedures more than once appears to help all patients, it may be particularly beneficial to those who tend to cope by using avoidance strategies.

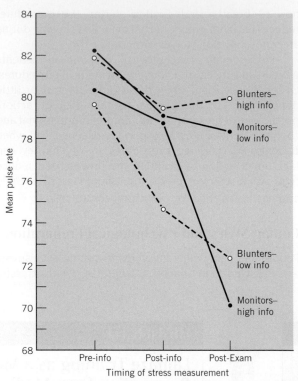

Figure 9-3   Effects of extensive information versus little information regarding an impending medical examination on the stress experienced by patients who use avoidance coping strategies (the "blunters") or attention strategies (the "monitors"). Pulse rate, the measure of stress, was taken for each subject at three times: before receiving the information, after the information, and after the examination. High pulse rate indicates more distress. (From Miller & Mangan, 1983, Figure 7.)

WHEN THE HOSPITALIZED PATIENT IS A CHILD

Nearly 2.3 million individuals who are admitted to short-stay hospitals in the United States each year are under 15 years of age, and most of these children are under 5 (USBC, 2010). We have seen that adults become distressed by pain and illness, think hospitals are big and scary places, and become anxious when undergoing unpleasant or painful medical procedures. So do children, but their level of psychosocial development may make some aspects of the hospital experience particularly difficult for them. For one thing, children are less able than adults to influence and understand what is happening to them. Children at young ages may also feel abandoned or unloved by being without their families, and some may even believe that they were put in the hospital as punishment for misbehavior. What special adjustments do hospitalized children need to make, and how well do they cope? Answers to these questions depend partly on the child's age.

Hospitalization in the Early Years of Childhood

The experience of being hospitalized is distressing for children of all ages, but the reasons for their distress tend to change as they get older (La Greca & Stone, 1985; Sarafino, 1986). For children in toddlerhood and the preschool years—who are rarely inactive when healthy—a hospital stay that involves being vaccinated can be very stressful. These children may protest loudly and struggle against medically necessary devices that restrain their movement (Smith & Autman, 1985). But the most salient source of stress of young children in the hospital is being separated from their parents.

Separation distress is young children's normal reaction of being upset and crying when they are separated from their parents, particularly in unfamiliar surroundings (Ainsworth, 1973, 1979). Late in the first year of life, most infants begin showing this reaction, even in everyday short separations of a few minutes or hours. As Figure 9-4 illustrates, the tendency of children to show distress in situations of short-term separation peaks at roughly 15 months of age. This is true of children from a wide variety of cultures around the world. After

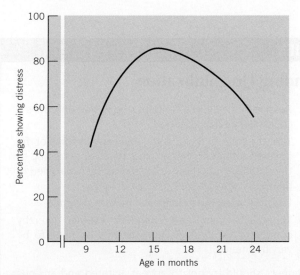

Figure 9-4 Illustration of children's tendency to exhibit separation distress when tested with short-term separations at different ages. (From Sarafino & Armstrong, 1986, Figure 5-3.) The graph represents approximate percentages at each age, averaged across cultures—for example, the reaction occurs in about 90% of American working-class infants and 70–80% of Guatemalan babies at 15 months. (Super, 1981.)

that age, the percentage of children showing distress with short-term separations declines universally (Super, 1981). Being hospitalized can involve prolonged periods of separation, with little parent–child contact for days, weeks, or longer. How well do toddlers and preschool-age children cope with long-term separation? Prolonged separation produces dramatic and, perhaps, long-lasting reactions in young children: it may begin with intense crying, calling, and searching for his or her parents, typically the mother; eventually the child shows behaviors suggesting *despair*—reduced activity, withdrawal, and apparent hopelessness (Bowlby, 1969, 1973).

After a prolonged or difficult stay in the hospital, young children often display anxious behavior at home. They may begin having nightmares or become very clinging and unwilling to let their mothers out of their sight. One child named Sara, for instance, had attended nursery school and was becoming quite independent for her age before having a difficult hospital experience that included receiving 22 injections in just 2 days. After she returned home, she was highly anxious. Her mother reported:

> She follows me everywhere! I can't even go to the bathroom alone. She wakes up screaming five or six times at night, shaking and crying, "The nurses are giving me shots! I can't run away! They're tying me down" … and when I approach her, she backs away and shakes like a hurt puppy! (Ramsey, 1982, p. 332)

Sara's hospital experience was very traumatic. Subsequently, she seemed to be afraid that if she were separated from her mother, she would again be left alone and unprotected.

Preschoolers do not yet think very logically and, as a result, may have many misconceptions about their health problems and why things happen in the hospital (Eiser, 1985; Ramsey, 1982; Smith & Autman, 1985). They may, for example, believe their illnesses or the treatments they receive are punishments for having been bad. Perhaps these ideas come from adults saying, for instance, "You'll catch cold if you don't wear your coat" or "You'll get an upset stomach if you eat too much candy." Some adults even threaten children with going to the doctor or having an operation if they continue to disobey (Eiser, 1985). In the hospital, young children may become worried when they see other patients with disfigurements, such as an amputation or extensive scars, and think one of these conditions may happen to themselves in the hospital.

Hospitalized School-Age Children

Advances in school-age children's psychosocial development enable them to cope with some aspects of hospitalization better than younger patients can. For instance, although prolonged separation from their parents can be difficult for older children, they usually tolerate it more easily than preschoolers can. The cognitive ability of school-age children progresses rapidly, but they sometimes retain earlier misconceptions about their illnesses or develop new ones. An older child's incorrect ideas can be seen in a nursing student's report about a 10-year-old hemophiliac patient:

> When I asked him what happened when he bled, he said, "Oh … there's a hemophiliac bug eating his way in and out of my blood vessels, and that's what makes me bleed." And when asked what caused his disease, he answered, "Well, it's 'cause I ate too much candy after my mom told me not to." (Ramsey, 1982, pp. 335–336)

Clearly, the idea that illness is a punishment can continue long after early childhood.

Four aspects of hospitalization seem to become increasingly difficult for children as they get older (Ramsey, 1982; Smith & Autman, 1985). One aspect involves feelings of personal control. As children get older and their greater cognitive and social abilities strengthen their sense of control, the limited independence and influence they experience in the hospital may become very irritating and distressing. Second, school-age children's increased cognitive abilities allow them to think about and worry about the outcomes of their illness or treatment, such as whether they will be physically harmed or even die. Third, being away from friends and schoolmates can lead to feelings of loneliness, boredom, and concern about losing friends or status in their social groups. Fourth, as children get older—particularly when they are entering puberty—they tend to become more embarrassed by exposing their bodies to strangers or needing help with "private" activities, such as toileting.

Studies conducted in industrialized nations in the 1950s revealed that most children who were hospitalized were very poorly prepared for the experience (Eiser, 1985). Most children were either told nothing about why they were there, or received only vague reasons, or learned why by overhearing others' conversations. This situation has changed since then, and children today are much better prepared for stays in the hospital. A survey in the United States, for example, found that the great majority of hospitals in the late 1990s provided the kinds of preparation we have described for children who will undergo surgery or other major procedures (O'Byrne, Peterson, & Saldana, 1997). (Go to 🧒.)

Helping Children Cope with Being Hospitalized

Many children suffer long-term fears from being hospitalized, particularly if they were relatively young, more severely ill, and endured a high number of invasive procedures (Rennick et al., 2002). How can hospitals help?

CLINICAL METHODS AND ISSUES
Preparing Children for Impending Hospitalization

Ideally, psychological preparation should begin before the child enters the hospital, if at all possible. Children cope better with medical procedures if their parents give them information about their illnesses and treatment and try to allay their fears (Melamed & Bush, 1985). Hospitals can initiate this process by discussing it with the parents and providing materials and services. Medical and psychological staff can inform parents about several ways to help their child cope with an impending hospital stay (Sarafino, 1986). Parents can:

• Explain the reason for the stay and what it will be like.

• Give the child opportunities to ask questions, answering them carefully and in a way he or she can understand.

• Read with the child a children's book that describes a child's hospital experience.

• Take the child to the hospital and explain some of the hospital routines, such as what to do about going to the bathroom and how he or she will be awakened in the morning and have breakfast in bed.

• Describe when the parents will be with the child.

• Maintain a calm and confident manner, thereby conveying the message that there is no need to be very frightened.

Parents should try not to appear agitated and anxious about the child's medical treatment because they can transmit their fear. Children of outwardly anxious parents do not cope as well with medical procedures as those with parents who are relatively calm (Bush et al., 1986; Melamed & Bush, 1985).

Medical procedures and equipment are often very frightening to young children.

When a child is admitted to the hospital, one or both parents (or another very familiar adult) should accompany and remain with the child at least until he or she is settled into the room. Many parents stay much longer, taking advantage of opportunities hospitals provide today for a parent to "room-in" with the child, especially when the patient is very young or very seriously ill (Olivet, 1982). American pediatric hospitals typically have rooming-in options (Melamed & Bush, 1985).

What kinds of psychological preparation can hospitals provide for children? American hospitals use several approaches (O'Byrne, Peterson, & Saldana, 1997). Printed leaflets, narrative presentations, and tours describing hospital routines and medical procedures are among the most commonly used methods. Another method involves using puppets in a play activity to demonstrate medical procedures, such as inducing anesthesia or taking an X-ray. This approach may be especially appropriate for preschoolers and younger school age children. Two other commonly used approaches involve training in coping skills and relaxation, using methods like those we examined in Chapter 4.

Another approach hospitals often use with children involves a video or film presentation. This method was evaluated in an experiment by Barbara Melamed and Lawrence Siegel (1975) with 4- to 12-year-old children who were in the hospital for elective surgery, such as for hernias or tonsillectomies. The children were assigned to two groups, matching for age, sex, race, and type of operation. One group saw a film that was relevant to having surgery, and the other group saw a film about a boy who goes on a nature trip in the country. The relevant film, entitled "Ethan Has an Operation," portrays the hospital experience of a 7-year-old boy,

> showing various events that most children encounter when hospitalized for elective surgery from the time

of admission to time of discharge including the child's orientation to the hospital ward and medical personnel such as the surgeon and anesthesiologist; having a blood test and exposure to standard hospital equipment; separation from the mother, and scenes in the operating and recovery rooms. In addition to explanations of the hospital procedures provided by the medical staff, various scenes are narrated by the child, who describes his feelings and concerns. (Melamed & Siegel, 1975, p. 514)

Although Ethan exhibits visible apprehension initially, he overcomes his fear and has the operation without serious distress.

The researchers assessed the emotional adjustment of the children in the two groups the evening before surgery and at a follow-up visit about 3 weeks after the operation with three types of measures: the children's hand sweating, questionnaire self-reports of fear, and ratings of their emotional behavior by trained observers. The results with all three measures revealed that the children who saw the film about Ethan's operation experienced less anxiety before and after surgery than those who saw the irrelevant film. Several studies have found similar benefits in reducing children's medical fears with video presentations (Eiser, 1985; Miller & Green, 1984). What's more, video preparations for surgery are cost-effective: a study of children in the hospital for elective surgery found that those who received video preparation recovered more quickly than those who did not. The savings from being released from the hospital sooner amounted to several times the cost of providing the preparation (Pinto & Hollandsworth, 1989).

Information about impending medical procedures presented with any of the methods we have considered benefits most, but not all, children—and some are actually made *more* anxious by it. The effects of the preparation depend on its timing and on the child's age, previous medical experience, and coping style (Dahlquist et al., 1986; Melamed & Bush, 1985; Melamed, Dearborn, & Hermecz, 1983; Miller & Green, 1984). More specifically,

- *Age.* Children younger than age 7 or so seem to profit from information presented shortly before the medical procedure; older children are more likely to benefit from information presented several days before.

- *Experience.* For children who have had prior difficult experiences with medical procedures, information is more likely to make younger more so than older ones more anxious.

- *Coping.* Children who tend to use avoidance strategies to cope with stressful events probably derive less benefit from information about medical procedures than those who use attention strategies.

Hospitals and medical workers usually try to make a child's stay as pleasant as they can. Pediatric nurses, for instance, receive training in the special needs of children and ways to introduce tests and equipment in a nonthreatening manner (Ramsey, 1982). When preparing to take the child's blood pressure with a sphygmomanometer, for example, the nurse might demonstrate its use on someone else and say, "When I squeeze this ball, the thing on the arm just becomes tight, like a belt. It doesn't hurt—it just gets tight…. Now when I'm done, I make it get loose and take it off."

Often when a young child undergoes stressful procedures, such as drawing blood, a parent is present. Although most techniques parents use to help reduce the child's distress don't work very well, one that does involves distracting attention from the procedure—for instance, by saying, "Look at this nice picture" (Manne et al., 1992, 1994). Hospital pediatric wards also arrange for children to play together when possible and try to have entertainment, such as a clown show, for their patients. For most hospitalized children who have positive health outcomes today, the stress of their hospital experience tends to be temporary and does not seem to produce serious long-term emotional problems (La Greca & Stone, 1985).

People of all ages can have difficulty coping with hospitalization and medical procedures. Psychological interventions can help promote positive emotional adjustment among patients and reduce the psychological problems that may be associated with their medical conditions.

HOW HEALTH PSYCHOLOGISTS ASSIST HOSPITALIZED PATIENTS

Some patients in hospitals have illnesses that result partly from psychosocial factors, such as Type A behavior or alcohol abuse, and some people develop psychosocial problems because of their illnesses, hospitalizations, or treatment regimens. In the former case, health psychologists are interested in correcting the factors that produced the disease to help these patients recover and prevent recurrences of their illnesses. In the latter case, health psychologists try to help clients cope with their illnesses, treatment regimens, possible disabilities or deformities, and, for terminal conditions, with impending death.

The potential importance of the help psychologists can provide is clear in research findings on psychological characteristics among people with cardiovascular disease. Two of these characteristics are *depression* and

pessimism. Compared with people who are not depressed, those who are very depressed show slower recovery and are much more likely to develop subsequent cardiac problems (Carney et al., 1988; Tennen, Eberhardt, & Affleck, 1999). And compared with optimistic people, coronary bypass patients who have a very pessimistic outlook are more likely to be hospitalized again for coronary problems in subsequent months (Scheier et al., 1999). Two other characteristics are *anxiety* and *personal control*: heart attack patients with high anxiety combined with low personal control are at high risk of complications, such as arrhythmia, while in the hospital (Moser et al., 2007).

The number of psychologists working in hospitals in the United States expanded greatly after the 1970s, as did their role in treatment programs for patients (APA, 1998; Enright et al., 1990; Sweet, 1991). Psychologists

- Consult with patients' specialists, such as cardiologists, neurologists, and pediatricians, to provide diagnostic and counseling services.

- Assess clients' needs for and provide psychological preparation to cope with surgery and other stressful procedures.

- Help patients adhere to medication and treatment regimens in the hospital.

- Provide behavioral programs for improving clients' self-care skills and compliance with medical and lifestyle regimens after discharge.

- Assist in rehabilitation processes, such as by promoting adherence to physical therapy, helping family members adjust to a patient's condition, and helping clients decide on new careers, if needed.

Let's look at how health psychologists assist patients, beginning with determining who needs and wants help.

INITIAL STEPS IN HELPING

Patients who need psychological help generally don't request it themselves—the request usually comes from a doctor or nurse who has noticed signs of a psychological, social, or intellectual problem (Huszti & Walker, 1991). This is not an ideal situation: studies have found that doctors and nurses are not good at recognizing emotional problems in their clients—they tend to judge that such problems exist if they think the patient has a severe medical illness and is dissatisfied with the present treatment (Jones, Mabe, & Riley, 1989; Ziegelstein et al., 2005). A brief training seminar does not improve their judgments (Deshields et al., 1995).

After the psychologist receives the request to see a patient, he or she then consults the person who made the request and reviews the client's medical record. The next step is to interview the patient and/or relevant family members to arrive at an impression of what the problem is and its history and status (Sweet, 1991). Sometimes the resulting impression is sufficient for the psychologist to decide how to help, but frequently more information is needed and can be obtained by administering psychological tests.

TESTS FOR PSYCHOLOGICAL ASSESSMENT OF MEDICAL PATIENTS

Psychologists have developed hundreds of instruments to assess a wide variety of psychological characteristics of people. The tests the psychologist administers depend on the type of illness or problem the client seems to have (Derogatis et al., 1995; Sweet, 1991). For example, patients with serious head injuries and behavioral signs of neurological problems are especially likely to be assessed with tests of intelligence, academic skills, and specific perceptual and motor functions. Clients who will need to change existing or planned careers may be tested for vocational interests and abilities. Some of the most widely used instruments with hospital patients assess their psychosocial needs and problems (Piotrowski & Lubin, 1990). We will describe a few of these instruments.

The Minnesota Multiphasic Personality Inventory

One approach psychological tests use for assessing the needs and problems of individuals is to ask them questions about themselves to reveal aspects of their personalities. The most widely used personality test is the **Minnesota Multiphasic Personality Inventory** (MMPI), which was developed in the 1930s and updated in the 1980s as the MMPI.2 (Butcher et al., 1989; Kring et al., 2010). This test has the person respond in a true-false format to over 500 statements, such as, "I would rather win than lose a game" and "I am worried about sex matters." The items in the test cover a great variety of topics.

Although the MMPI was developed to characterize the personalities that underlie or correspond with specific psychiatric disorders, portions of the test can supply important information about the emotional adjustment of medical patients. The instrument contains ten scales, each of which assesses features of psychiatric conditions and personality traits. Three of these scales are especially relevant toward providing psychological help for medical patients. These scales are:

- *Hypochondriasis*, which assesses people's preoccupation with and complaints about their physical health.

- *Depression*, which measures people's feelings of unhappiness, pessimism, and hopelessness.

- *Hysteria*, which assesses people's tendency to cope with problems by using avoidance strategies and developing physical symptoms.

The scores individuals obtain on these scales can suggest significant issues for the therapist to explore further. For one thing, individuals who score high on these three scales are prone to developing psychophysiological disorders, such as ulcers and chronic headaches (Gilberstadt & Duker, 1965). Also, patients with serious illnesses, such as cancer or heart disease, may fail to comply with their treatment regimens because of intense feelings of depression, which might be revealed by their scores on the depression scale of the MMPI (Green, 1985).

The MMPI can be usefully applied in psychological treatment in medical settings, but it has two important drawbacks: it takes about $1\frac{1}{2}$ hours to complete, and it measures many traits that are not pertinent to the treatment of most medical patients.

Specialized Tests for Medical Patients

Psychologists have developed tests that are specifically designed to assess psychological characteristics associated with physical illness. These tests include measures of people's stress and Type A and Type B behavior patterns—two characteristics that are associated with heart disease, for instance. As we saw in Chapter 4, psychological methods can be applied effectively to reduce people's stress and modify their Type A behavior, thereby lowering their risk of heart attack. We turn now to a discussion of other psychological tests that were designed specifically for medical populations.

The **Millon Behavioral Medicine Diagnostic** (MBMD) is a self-report test that was developed to assess specific psychosocial factors and decision-making issues that are known to be relevant for medical patients (Pearson Assessments, 2009). It consists of 165 items that provide information regarding several factors, such as the client's coping style, negative health habits, and stress moderators. The MBMD also attempts to assess the client's reaction to his or her illness and predict difficulties with the treatment regimen. Although the MBMD is being used in medical settings, such as in pain treatment centers and cancer units, and it should prove to be a valuable tool, more research is needed to establish its utility.

The **Psychosocial Adjustment to Illness Scale** (PAIS) is another psychological test designed specifically for use with medical patients (Derogatis, 1977, 1986). The PAIS consists of just 46 items, and the person responds to each item on a 4-point scale, such as "not at all," "mildly," "moderately," or "markedly." This test

Table 9.1   *Patients' Psychosocial Characteristics Assessed by the Psychosocial Adjustment to Illness Scale (PAIS)*

- *Health care orientation*—the nature of the patient's attitudes about health care in general, views regarding health care professionals, and expectancies about his or her health problem and its treatment.
- *Vocational environment*—the impact of the health problem on such issues as the person's vocational performance and satisfaction.
- *Domestic environment*—difficulties the health problem will present for the client and his or her family in the home environment.
- *Sexual relationships*—modifications in sexual activity as a result of the health problem.
- *Extended family relationships*—disruptions in relationships between the patient and family members outside of his or her immediate family.
- *Social environment*—the impact of the health problem on the client's socializing and leisure time activities.
- *Psychological distress*—the effect of the health problem on such factors as the patient's self-esteem and feelings of depression, anxiety, and hostility.

is available in two forms—one that patients can fill out on their own and one that is administered by an interviewer. It was designed to assess seven psychosocial characteristics of the client's life, each of which has been associated with adjustment to medical illness. Table 9.1 outlines these characteristics. The results of several studies appear to confirm the ability of the PAIS to measure adjustment problems accurately in patients with a variety of serious illnesses, such as kidney disease, hypertension, and cancer (Derogatis, 1986).

In summary, psychologists have developed instruments specifically for the purpose of assessing the psychological needs and problems of medical patients. These tests offer considerable promise for aiding health psychologists and other health care workers in promoting the health and adjustment of their patients.

PROMOTING PATIENTS' HEALTH AND ADJUSTMENT

Once health psychologists determine the nature and extent of the client's difficulty, they decide which specific therapeutic techniques should be applied to address it. As we have seen in previous chapters and will see ahead, behavioral and cognitive methods have been applied with some success—sometimes with great success—in many primary, secondary, and tertiary prevention efforts. These techniques are useful in helping people improve their eating and exercise habits, stop smoking and curb their drinking, and reduce the stress and other negative emotional states they experience (Parker, 1995; Sarafino, 2001; Turk & Salovey, 1995).

Many hospitalized people develop severe psychosocial problems, particularly if their illnesses or injuries continue to be life threatening or leave them disfigured or handicapped. These individuals and their families often need help to overcome feelings of depression and counseling to anticipate and plan for the difficulties they are likely to experience. Spouses and partners have a great burden, especially if the patient's condition is

disabling, and they are much more likely than spouses of healthy individuals to die themselves in the next several years (Christakis & Allison, 2006). Several psychological approaches can relieve psychosocial difficulties of patients and their families. These approaches often involve group-discussion and cognitive-behavioral therapy to identify, examine, and replace negative thought patterns with more constructive ones (Kring et al., 2010; Turk & Salovey, 1995).

Health psychologists are working to enhance their effectiveness in helping clients and to develop stronger relationships with medical professionals, such as by expanding their knowledge of the language and rules of hospital settings (Huszti & Walker, 1991). More and more, medical and psychological staff are working together to improve these relationships for the benefit of their patients.

WHEN THE ILLNESS IS TERMINAL

When people talk about the hypothetical prospects of dying, you will often hear them say, "I hope I go quickly and without pain." Some people might argue that there are no good ways to die, but almost everyone would agree that a slow and painful death is the worst way. By definition, a *terminal illness* entails a slow death. The patient typically suffers a progressive deterioration in the feeling of well-being and ability to function and may also experience chronic pain. Although dying from a terminal illness generally takes several weeks, it sometimes takes as little as a few days or as long as several months (Hinton, 1984). Much of this time is spent in a hospital. One factor that affects how people adapt to a terminal illness is the age of the victim.

THE PATIENT'S AGE

"Tragic" and "untimely" are words people use to describe a young person's terminal illness or death. Death is more "appropriate" at 80 years of age than at 10.

A Terminally Ill Child

What does "dying" mean? Death is a very abstract concept and, as such, it is not well understood by young children (Lonetto, 1980; Speece & Brent, 1984). Prior to about 5 years of age, children think death is like living in another place and the person can come back. They may also believe people can avoid death. For instance, a child might conceive of death as a monster and argue that "you won't die if you run faster than the monster or trick it." By about 8 years of age, most children understand that death happens to everyone, is final, and involves the absence of bodily functions.

Most children at early ages have some experience with dying—for instance, in the death of a close person, such as a grandparent or neighbor, or of a pet. Dying is not an easy topic for many adults to discuss, and they may try to spare children the realities of death, saying that the dead person "has gone away," or "is in heaven, with Jesus," or "is only sleeping" (Koch, 1977; Sarafino, 1986). Although parents of a child with a terminal illness sometimes decide not to tell him or her, dying school-age children seem to realize their illnesses are extremely serious even when they are not told, and they exhibit far more anxiety than seriously ill children who are not dying (Spinetta, 1974). Child specialists today generally believe children should know as much about their illnesses as they can comprehend and should be told in an open, honest, and sensitive manner (La Greca & Stone, 1985).

A Terminally Ill Adolescent or Young Adult

Adolescents and young adults who develop terminal illnesses realize how unlikely dying at their ages is and feel angry about the "senselessness" and "injustice" of it and about not having a chance to develop their lives. As one dying college student put it, "Now a perfectly good person with an awful lot to give is going to die" (Shneidman, 1977, p. 77). He was having a very difficult time coping with his impending death, and a therapist was called in to help him because of his shouting and quarrelsome behavior in the hospital.

Having a terminal illness seems especially untimely when victims have young children. This condition is a threat to the family unit, and the patients feel guilty at not being able to care for their children and cheated out of the joys of seeing them develop. Because death at this point is so untimely, young adults seem to experience more anger and emotional distress when they have life-threatening illnesses than older individuals do (Leventhal, Leventhal, & Van Nguyen, 1985).

Terminal Illness in Middle-Aged and Older Adults

As people develop beyond the early adulthood years, the likelihood of contracting a high-mortality chronic illness—especially heart disease, cancer, or stroke—increases sharply. Although dying may not be easy at any point in the life span, it seems to become less difficult as people progress from middle age to old age. Studies have found, for instance, that adults become less and less afraid of death as they get older (Bengston, Cuellar, & Ragan, 1977; Kalish & Reynolds, 1976). Why is this?

Researcher Richard Kalish (1985) has outlined several reasons why the elderly have an easier time than younger individuals in facing impending death. As people get older, developing a terminal illness becomes less unexpected, less of a shock. The elderly know their remaining years are few, they realize that they will probably die of a chronic illness, and they think and talk more about poor health and death than most younger people do. Most of their peers and many relatives are suffering from declining health or have died. They often have made financial preparations, and some have even made plans or given instructions regarding the terminal care they would prefer and their funeral arrangements. In addition, older individuals have had longer pasts than younger people, which have allowed them the time to achieve more. People who review their pasts and believe they have accomplished important things and lived good lives tend to have less difficulty adapting to terminal illnesses than others do (Mages & Mendelsohn, 1979).

PSYCHOSOCIAL ADJUSTMENTS TO TERMINAL ILLNESS

Most people with life-threatening illnesses adapt reasonably well to their conditions over time, and so do the closest people in their lives. But when their conditions worsen and progress to a terminal phase, new crises emerge that require intense coping efforts.

How People Cope with Terminal Illness

How do terminally ill people and their families cope, and what types of stress do they experience? The principal coping mechanism people use during the phase of terminal illness is denial (Hackett & Weisman, 1985; Hinton, 1984). As we saw in Chapter 4, emotion-focused coping is especially useful when the individuals cannot do anything to change their situations. Unfortunately, when people mutually avoid facing the imminent death, they may not discuss with each other how they feel or have any way to "say their good-byes."

Psychiatrist John Hinton (1984) has described three types of stress terminal patients experience. First, they must cope with the physical effects of their worsening conditions, such as pain, difficulty breathing, sleeplessness, or loss of bowel control. Second, their conditions severely alter their styles of living, restricting their activity and making them highly dependent on others. Most terminally ill people are restricted in their activities during the last 3 months of their lives, and many of them are confined to bed. Third, they typically realize that the end of their lives is near, even when they are not told so. If they are in a hospital, they may think about never going home again or no longer being able to experience the intimacy they used to have with those they love.

Thinking about someone who is dying typically arouses feelings of sadness in people, but these people may not realize how well many terminally ill people come to face and accept dying. Hinton (1984) has noted similarities between people who are dying and those with diminished lives—such as the frail, disabled, or bereaved: they can still get pleasure from their lives despite earlier thoughts that such circumstances would be unbearable. The quality of life for such persons can be fairly good if they have a sense of fulfillment, such as from the family they'll leave behind or their career. Most people adapt to dying with little anger or depression if they are in little pain, receive sensitive and caring social support, feel satisfied with their lives, and have a history of coping well with life's problems and crises (Carey, 1975; Hinton, 1984; Kalish, 1985). Often, patients adapt better than their loved ones. For instance, spouses of dying people often experience increased

health problems, depression, and memory difficulties (Howell, 1986). Support groups and family therapy can be of great help to dying individuals and their families.

Does Adapting to Dying Happen in "Stages"?

Because "time changes things," we might expect that the way patients come to terms with their impending deaths would change with time. Do these changes occur in a predictable pattern, as a series of stages? On the basis of interviews with over 200 terminally ill people, Elisabeth Kübler-Ross (1969) proposed that people's adjustment to dying usually follows a pattern, passing through a sequence of *five stages*. Table 9.2 outlines these stages. Not all the patients she interviewed showed this pattern—a few, for example, continued to deny that they were dying to the very last. But the pattern of adjustments seemed sufficiently regular for Kübler-Ross to propose that coping in most dying people begins with denial and advances through the stages in order.

Do Kübler-Ross's stages correctly reflect the emotional reactions most dying patients experience as they cope with terminal illnesses? Available evidence does not support the idea that most individuals adjust to dying with a predictable and orderly sequence of coping reactions (Hinton, 1984; Kalish, 1985; Silver & Wortman, 1980; Zisook et al., 1995). An overview of this evidence indicates that some terminal patients do follow an orderly and predictable sequence of adjustment, but most people's emotions and coping patterns fluctuate. Some people may go through a specific stage, such as anger, more than once during their adjustment; others have more than one emotional reaction simultaneously; and some seem to skip stages. And some evidence indicates that people who achieve an "acceptance" of their impending

Table 9.2 *Kübler-Ross's Stages of Adjustment to Dying*

1. *Denial.* The first reaction to the prognosis of death involves refusing to believe it is true. Terminally ill patients say, "No, it can't be true," or "There must be some mistake," or "The lab reports must have gotten mixed up." Denial can be a valuable first reaction by giving patients time to mobilize other coping strategies and motivation to get second opinions. According to Kübler-Ross, denial soon fades in most patients and is replaced by anger.
2. *Anger.* The patients now realize, "Oh, yes, it is me, it was not a mistake," and are outraged and irate, asking, "Why me?" or, "Why couldn't it have been that miserable no-good guy down the street?" They resent others who are healthy and may show their anger in outbursts toward almost anyone—nurses, doctors, and family.
3. *Bargaining.* At this point, patients try to change their circumstances by offering to "make a deal." Most of the bargains they try to negotiate are with God, for example, thinking, "Oh, God, I promise to be a better person if you'll just make me well."
4. *Depression.* When bargaining no longer helps and patients feel their time is running out, hopelessness and depression set in. They grieve for things they had in the past and for things they will miss in the future. According to Kübler-Ross, even though depression is painful and may last for a prolonged period, it is helpful because part of the grieving process involves becoming detached from the things in the patient's world. Being detached enables the last stage—acceptance—to occur.
5. *Acceptance.* Patients who live long enough may reach the last stage in which they are no longer depressed, but feel a quiet calm and readiness for death.

Source: Kübler-Ross, 1969.

death die much sooner than those who do not reach this stage (Reed et al., 1994).

Despite these shortcomings, Kübler-Ross's work has had many positive effects. For one thing, it has been influential in stimulating people's awareness and discussion of the dying process and the needs of terminal patients. It has also led to important and very beneficial changes in the care and treatment of dying people, thereby improving the quality of the last weeks and days of their lives. A principal issue in people's judgments about terminal care is the patient's preferences and quality of life in death. (Go to 🍎.)

MEDICAL AND PSYCHOLOGICAL CARE OF DYING PATIENTS

The medical community and patients' families face one dilemma after another in trying to do what's best for a dying person. Medical technology has made it possible to keep some patients alive only in a legal sense, such

---

ASSESS YOURSELF

Your Living Will Choices

Fill out the *Health Care Living Will and Proxy* below, indicating what your wishes would be if you were unable to make decisions about your medical treatment, such as if you were in a coma. What specific treatments would you *want* or *not want* to receive? Whom would you choose as your agent or "proxy" in making decisions if you were unable to make them? This person should be an adult who is familiar with your personal and health care views—someone you would trust to make the decisions you would make.

If this were a legal document, you and two witnesses would need to sign it. Some living wills are much more complicated than this one, having the person make dozens of choices regarding many different medical procedures that might be considered in very different scenarios. Being so specific can present problems if the person's preferences or the evidence on a treatment's value changes between the time a patient rejects it in the will and the scenario actually occurs. Another problem with living wills is that a person who serves as a proxy may have difficulty interpreting what a particular instruction means. Although people must complete living wills if they want to influence the care they receive when they're unable to communicate directly, few individuals do so (Ditto & Hawkins, 2005; Klinkenberg et al., 2004). It's important to put these decisions in writing because people often misremember the directives they made (Sharman et al., 2008).

Health Care Living Will and Proxy

To my Family, Doctors, and Other Concerned Parties:

I, _____ (the *principal*), being of sound mind, make the following advance directives to be carried out if I become unable to make or communicate decisions about my medical treatment.

Living Will

I request the withdrawal or withholding of life-sustaining procedures, consistent with my desire that I be permitted to die naturally if the situation occurs that I am either (1) near death with no reasonable likelihood of recovery or (2) in a coma or vegetative state and my doctors believe that there is no significant possibility of my ever regaining consciousness or higher functions of my brain. Under these circumstances, I specifically:

1. DO NOT want the following treatments I have *initialed*.

   - Cardiac resuscitation _____
   - Artificial respiration _____
   - Artificial feeding or fluids _____
   - Other (specify) _____

2. DO want the following conditions I have *initialed*.

   - Medication to relieve pain _____
   - To die at home, if possible _____
   - Other (specify) _____

I designate here:

1. A *first proxy*, _____ (name), to make decisions in accordance with the wishes and conditions specified above, or as he or she otherwise knows, and

2. A *second proxy*, _____ (name), as a substitute if the first proxy is unable, unwilling, or unavailable to act as my health care proxy.

as in a coma with virtually no chance of recovery, and societies are questioning whether these people are alive in a humane sense. Most doctors in the United States and many European nations favor withdrawing life-support systems from hopelessly ill or irreversibly comatose individuals if the patients request it, personally or in a written statement, such as a living will (Miccinesi et al., 2005; Shogren, 1988).

The terminal phase of care begins when medical judgment indicates that the patient's condition is worsening and no treatment is available to reverse or arrest the progress toward death (AMA, 2003; Benoliel, 1977). At this point, medical treatment is mainly *palliative*, that is, it focuses on reducing pain and discomfort. This phase of treatment can be very distressing not only to the patients and their families, but to medical personnel, who entered the medical field to save lives. Terminally ill people in the United States can request that the specific instruction, "Do Not Resuscitate," be entered on their hospital charts. If they begin to die—for instance, if the person's heart stops beating—the medical staff is not to interfere. Should terminally ill adults be told they are dying? The great majority of dying patients want to know so they can be prepared psychologically and legally (Abrahm, 2003). Because some patients would prefer not to know, doctors can probe sensitively to assess the person's wishes. Those who prefer not to know may be given the option of having their families handle all decisions (Blackhall et al., 1995).

Individuals who work with dying people on a daily basis must come to grips with feelings of failure and loss they experience when patients die (Benoliel, 1977; Maguire, 1985). To protect themselves from this pain and to perform efficiently in their heavy workloads, medical staff may distance themselves psychologically from terminally ill people. By doing this, doctors and nurses avoid dealing with the psychological problems these patients are having. How do staff members distance themselves? They may simply not ask about the person's feelings or adjustment, or they may provide false reassurance, saying, "I'm sure you'll feel better soon," when they believe otherwise. But discussing the prognosis and end-of-life care has important benefits: compared to terminally ill people who don't have such talks with their doctors, those that do are more likely to accept their condition, have a higher quality of life, and incur less health care costs as they approach death (Wright et al., 2008; Zhang et al., 2009).

Although many people are able to approach death with a feeling of acceptance and peacefulness, others become very troubled, often depressed. What can be done to help dying patients cope? Practitioners can try to assess depression in a preliminary way, such as by asking patients sensitively whether they have "felt depressed a lot recently" and what they "think is ahead with the illness." Answers that affirm emotional difficulty can be confirmed in more extensive evaluations (Abrahm, 2003). Depressed patients can receive antidepressant drugs and psychotherapy to provide emotional support and help them use positive reappraisal strategies. Health care workers may also be able to provide information about support groups that have developed specifically to improve the quality of life for people with terminal illnesses. And professionally led group therapy can help terminally ill patients face their impending deaths with less anxiety and depression and a greater sense of control over their remaining periods of life (Levy, 1983). (Go to 🌳.)

A PLACE TO DIE—HOSPITAL, HOME, OR HOSPICE?

Most people in developed nations die in hospitals or nursing homes (Hays et al., 1999). Although hospitals can provide a great deal of expertise, technical equipment, and efficient caregiving, they are usually not "psychologically comfortable" places for people. The environment there is unfamiliar, and patients have little control over their daily routine and activities and lack access to such things as photo albums or musical recordings, for example, that they have relied on in the past for enjoyment and to enrich their experiences. Moreover, most of the people there are strangers, not family or friends. As a result, many terminally ill people would rather die at home. Is this a reasonable alternative?

Home Care for the Dying Patient

Whether home care is a reasonable alternative for a dying person depends on his or her condition and the quality of care available at home. Terminally ill people receive very good care at home if they have regular contact with a medical team and if family members are trained (Malkin, 1976; Zimmer, Juncker, & McCusker, 1985). Many dying patients may not have the option of home care because they lack family members who are able to provide the care they need or financial resources that may be required.

Caring for a terminally ill person at home can be very physically and emotionally exhausting (Hinton, 1984). There may be only one individual at home who can provide the care, and all of the burden falls on that person's shoulders. If the patient requires continuous attention, the life of that one caretaker may become limited to coping with the dying person's needs. This may go on for weeks or, sometimes, months. Even when

CLINICAL METHODS AND ISSUES

Saying Goodbye

When someone we care about is dying, we want to let that person know how much he or she has meant to us, but we often have trouble finding the "right time" or "right words," and the goodbyes are not said. Because this happens for medical personnel as well, some professionals have written a guide for doctors to say goodbye to a dying patient (Back et al., 2005; all quotes below are from pages 683 and 684 of that article). As you read the five steps, think about how they could be adapted if you wanted to say your goodbyes to someone you care about.

1. *Choosing the time and place*
   When it is clear that the patient has only a short time remaining, pick a time and place that offer privacy for at least several minutes.

2. *Broaching the topic and checking for acceptance*
   Start by acknowledging uncertainty about future contacts, perhaps saying, "You know, I'm not sure if we will see each other again in person, so while we are with each other now I want to say something about our relationship." To determine whether the patient wants the discussion, ask something like, "Would that be okay?"

3. *Frame goodbye as an appreciation of the relationship*
   A good way to say the goodbye is to express appreciation for something of value in the relationship, allowing the person to see that he or she had an impact. For example, "I just wanted to say how much I've enjoyed you and how much I've appreciated your flexibility [or cooperation, good spirits, courage, honesty, directness, collaboration] and your good humor [or your insights, thoughtfulness, love for your family]." Make this appreciation personal, perhaps with a specific example or two.

4. *Address the possible awkwardness and emotion*
   Because this conversation can make the person anxious and emotional, say, "I realize this might seem awkward, but I wanted to make sure that you knew how I felt, rather than risk not having a chance to tell you." If the person begins to cry, stay silent for a while to allow him or her to regain composure; often the person will explain the tears. If he or she offers a compliment, reply with a sincere thank you.

5. *Ongoing commitment*
   Make sure the person does not feel abandoned, saying, "Of course, you know I remain available to you ... I will be here if you need me, and I'll be thinking about you."

there is more than one person available to help, their lives are restricted by the patient's needs. Some terminally ill people are bedridden and need to be fed and bathed, for instance. Despite these hardships, many people who have cared for dying persons at home claim it is extremely rewarding to know they have done everything they could to make the last days or weeks as pleasant as possible for someone they love.

Hospice Care for the Dying Patient

Is it possible to combine the strengths of a professional support system with the warm and loving care one can get at home, thereby helping terminal patients die comfortably and with dignity? This question led to the development of the concept of **hospice care**, which involves a medical and social support system to provide an enriched quality of life—through physical, psychosocial, and spiritual care—for terminally ill people and their families (Abrahm, 2003; Cioppa, 1984; HFA, 2010). In hospice care, the staff consists of a medically

supervised team of professionals and volunteers. Much of the physical care the staff provides is designed to reduce discomfort and pain, often with the use of drugs.

The hospice care approach originated in Great Britain, largely through the efforts of doctor Cicely Saunders, who was originally trained as a nurse and social worker (HFA, 2006; Torrens, 1985). At first, hospices were designed as separate institutions for the purpose of caring for dying patients on an inpatient basis. But as the philosophy of hospice care spread to the United States and Canada, the organizational structure for delivering this care began to broaden. Hospice services in North America are available today both at *home* and at hundreds of *inpatient facilities*, many of which are housed in hospitals or nursing homes. Inpatient facilities generally try to make the environment as much like home as possible, often including a kitchen and family room area. When home hospice care is used, services are provided on a part-time, regularly scheduled basis and staff are available on-call 24 hours a day, 7 days a week (Cioppa, 1984).

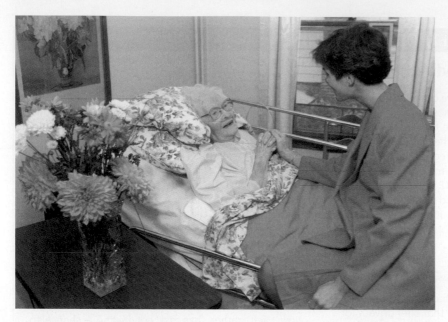

A hospice nurse attends a terminally ill patient. Hospice care can be given at home or in inpatient facilities that look more like a home than a hospital.

Cicely Saunders (1986) has outlined several "essential elements" in the hospice approach. First, people who are dying should be in a *place of choice* as they end their lives. They and their families should decide whether that place should be at home or in an inpatient setting. Most people prefer to be at home (Hays et al., 1999). Second, the care given during the terminal phase should enable patients to *maximize their potential*, so that they perform to the limits of their physical, cognitive, and social potential, particularly as active members of their families. Third, the care should *address all family members' needs*, which may involve resolving interpersonal discord and feelings of anxiety, guilt, and depression. Fourth, *follow-up care* is available for family members to receive help through and after the period of bereavement.

Does hospice care help patients and their families cope better with the dying process than conventional care does? Testimonials from patients and family members are massive and glowing, describing the programs as enormously supportive and enriching. And studies have found that the quality of life is better with inpatient hospice care than standard hospital care (Viney et al., 1994). Evidence from a small number of carefully controlled studies of inpatient hospice and conventional care suggests that both provide similar pain control and daily activities, but hospice patients show less anxiety, and their families report greater satisfaction with their care (Casarett et al., 2005; Torrens, 1985).

SUMMARY

The huge hospitals of today evolved from institutions in Europe that were established to give help to people with various needs—the sick, the poor, orphans, and even travelers who needed lodging. Well-to-do individuals received better care at home. In the early 20th century, hospitals gained a much better reputation and began to attract patients from all social classes.

The hospital medical staff has a typical hierarchy of authority with doctors at the top, followed by nurses and various allied health workers. The specialization and variety of hospital personnel can lead to fragmented health care. Good communication among hospital personnel not only improves the treatment patients receive but can help protect patients from potential hazards in the hospital, such as from nosocomial infection. Hospital admissions and the length of time patients stay there have declined.

Being hospitalized is unpleasant to patients because of the disruptions it produces in their lifestyles, the high degree of dependency they have on others, the experience of aversive medical procedures, and the many worries they have about their conditions, treatment, and futures. Sometimes the treatment people receive is characterized by depersonalization. Working in emotionally charged situations with heavy workloads can lead to burnout among health care professionals, especially those who spend almost all of their time providing direct care to clients.

Some patients are described by hospital staff as "good patients," being relatively cooperative, uncomplaining, and stoical. Other clients believe they should be more active in their sick role, and some of them are described as "problem patients," showing little cooperation, voicing many complaints, and being very dependent and emotional. When problem patients are very seriously ill, their difficult behavior is usually understandable to the medical staff. But other problem patients take up more time and attention than their conditions seem to warrant, and may display angry reactance behavior in response to having their freedoms or control curtailed.

Patients engage in problem-focused and emotion-focused coping techniques to adjust to the stress and anxiety that they experience in the hospital. Some of their anxiety stems from their impending surgery and other medical procedures, such as cardiac catheterization and endoscopy. High levels of anxiety before surgery impair people's physical recovery after the operation. Reducing the anxiety about medical procedures can be accomplished through methods of psychological preparation that provide clients with behavioral, cognitive, and informational control. Lamaze training for childbirth seems to provide these kinds of preparation.

Although most patients benefit from methods of psychological preparation that enhance control, one factor that seems to affect the success of these methods is whether the patient's coping style tends toward avoidance rather than attention. Children's separation distress in the hospital can be reduced if parents visit often or room in. Children can also benefit from psychological preparation for medical procedures, but the success of providing children with information depends on its timing and on their ages, coping styles, and previous medical experience.

The role of psychologists in the overall treatment effort for hospitalized people has increased in recent years, particularly in preparing clients for medical procedures, helping them adjust to their medical conditions, and enhancing their adherence to treatment regimens after discharge. To identify the needs and problems of patients, psychologists administer tests, such as the Minnesota Multiphasic Personality Inventory, and instruments developed specifically for use with medical clients, such as the Millon Behavioral Medicine Diagnostic and the Psychosocial Adjustment to Illness Scale.

If and when health deteriorates and no cure is likely, the illness is considered terminal. Young children have little understanding of the meaning of death; by about 8 years of age, their understanding is fairly complete. Adolescents and young adults react to their impending deaths with strong feelings of anger and emotional distress. As adults get older, they become less fearful of death. Dying people may react to their conditions with denial, anger, bargaining, depression, and acceptance. The hospice care approach provides physical, psychosocial, and spiritual care for dying patients and their families.

KEY TERMS

nosocomial infection
depersonalization
burnout
reactance

Lamaze training
separation distress
Minnesota Multiphasic
  Personality Inventory

Millon Behavioral
  Medicine Diagnostic
Psychosocial Adjustment
  to Illness Scale

hospice care

10

THE NATURE AND SYMPTOMS OF PAIN

PROLOGUE

Most people are averse to pain, whether the pain is felt by them or by people they care about. When we were younger, our mothers would sometimes kiss a scratch or cut, telling us that, "The kiss will make it all better." How many times did that work? Enough times that you will probably do the same thing to your children. But why did it work at all? It might all come down to perception. To a child, a cut can be very painful because it may be the first time he or she felt that particular pain. After several scraped knees, the intensity reduces as we realise the cut will heal, or that the broken arm we had last month caused much worse pain.

The perception of pain is different for each person, so each person's reaction to pain will vary. Some people can go to work with a migraine, while others are unable to even open their eyes. There is even pain where there is no body—phantom limb pain is as real to those suffering from it as a kidney stone would be to a kidney stone patient. Do we really know what pain is and why it happens?

Studies are now showing that it may indeed be true that women can take more pain (have a higher pain threshold) than men. Women experience more chronic pain than men and will focus on the emotional aspects of pain, according to some research. Increasing knowledge of hormones, psychology, and gender differences may mean that doctors will have to change the way they treat pain to be more individual.

We may not want to feel pain and we take pain relievers to help, but if we didn't feel pain we may end up with dangerous third-degree burns, or we may step on broken glass and not notice it. People with a condition called *congenital insensitivity to pain*, which is present from birth, may report only a 'tingling' or 'itching' sensation when seriously injured. Unfortunately these people often die young because they do not notice injuries or illnesses, such as acute appendicitis.

Health psychologists study pain because it influences whether individuals seek and comply with medical treatment, and because being in pain can be very distressing, particularly when it is intense or enduring. In this chapter we examine the nature and symptoms of pain, and the effects it has on its victims when it is severe. As we consider these topics, you will find answers to questions you may have about pain. What is pain, and what is the physical basis for it? Can people feel pain when there is no underlying physical disorder? Do psychosocial factors affect our experience of pain? Since pain is a subjective experience, how do psychologists assess how much pain a person feels?

WHAT IS PAIN?

Pain is the sensory and emotional experience of discomfort, which is usually associated with actual or threatened tissue damage or irritation (AMA, 2003). Virtually all people experience pain and at all ages—from the pains of birth for mother and baby, to those of colic and teething in infancy, to those of injury and illness in childhood and adulthood. Some pain becomes chronic, as with arthritis, problems of the lower back, migraine headache, or cancer.

People's experience with pain is important for several reasons. For one thing, no medical complaint is more common than pain—it accounts for more than 80% of all visits to doctors (Gatchel et al., 2007). As we saw in Chapter 8, people are more likely to seek medical treatment without delay if they feel pain. Also, severe and prolonged pain can come to dominate the lives of its victims, impairing their general functioning, ability to work, social relationships, and emotional adjustment. Last, pain has enormous social and economic effects on all societies of the world. In the United States in any given year, a third or more people suffer from one or more continuous or recurrent painful conditions that require medical care, and millions of these people are disabled by their conditions (Turk, 2001). One condition, low back pain, is the most common cause of work disability and a major reason for missed work (NCHS, 2006). Americans spend billions of dollars each year on pain-related expenses, such as for treatment, disability payments, and loss of income.

THE QUALITIES AND DIMENSIONS OF PAIN

Our sensations of pain can be quite varied and have many different qualities. We might describe some pains as "sharp" and others as "dull," for example—and sharp pains can have either a stabbing or pricking feel. Some pains involve a burning sensation, and others have a cramping, itching, or aching feel. And some pains are throbbing, or constant, or shooting, or pervasive, or localized. Often the feelings we experience depend on the kinds of irritation or damage that has occurred and the location. For instance, when damage occurs deep within the body, people usually report feeling a "dull," "aching," or "throbbing" pain; but damage produced by a brief noxious event to the skin is often described as "sharp" (Schiffman, 1996; Tortora & Derrickson, 2009).

The painful conditions people experience also differ in how the pain originates and how long it lasts. We will consider two dimensions that describe these differences, beginning with the degree to which the origin of the pain can be traced to tissue damage.

Organic Versus Psychogenic Pain

The pain we experience that is clearly linked to tissue pressure or damage is described as *organic pain*. For example, damage can arise from a burn or sprain; pressure can develop when the opening in a disc of the spine narrows and squeezes the spinal cord. Narrowing in the spine can occur when discs degenerate—a condition that is affected by genetics (Battié et al., 2007). For other pains, no tissue damage appears to exist—at least, medical examinations fail to find an organic basis. The discomfort involved in these pains seems to result primarily from psychological processes. For this reason, this type of discomfort is described as *psychogenic pain*. I once witnessed an extreme example of psychogenic pain in a schizophrenic man: he claimed—and *really* looked like—he was "feeling" stings from being "shot by enemy agents with ray guns."

Not long ago, researchers considered organic and psychogenic pain to be separate entities, with psychogenic pain not involving "real" sensations. As pain researcher Donald Bakal has noted, a practitioner's reference to pain as "psychogenic"

> was taken to mean "due to psychological causes," which implied that the patient was "imagining" his pain or that it was not really pain simply because an organic basis could not be found. Psychogenic pain is not experienced differently, however, from that arising from physical disease or injury. Psychogenic and organic pain both hurt. (1979, p. 167)

Researchers now recognize that virtually all pain experiences involve an interplay of both physiological and psychosocial factors, and the dimension of pain involving organic and psychogenic causes is viewed as a continuum rather than a dichotomy.

Different pain experiences simply involve different mixtures of organic and psychogenic factors. A mixture of these factors seems clear in the findings that many people with tissue damage experience little or no pain, others without damage report severe pain, and the role of psychological factors in people's pain increases when the condition is long-lasting (Turk, 2001). When people experience severe long-term pain with no detectable physical basis, psychiatrists diagnose the condition as a *pain disorder* (classified within *somatoform disorders*) and often assume the origin is mainly psychogenic (Kring et al., 2010). Keep in mind, however, that failing to find a physical basis for someone's pain does not necessarily mean there is none. Unfortunately, many health care workers still think pain that has no demonstrated physical basis is purely psychogenic, and their patients struggle to prove that "the pain isn't just in my head, Doc" (Karoly, 1985).

Acute Versus Chronic Pain

Experiencing pain either continuously or frequently over a period of many months or years is different from having occasional and isolated short-term bouts with pain. The length of experience an individual has had with a painful condition is an important dimension in describing his or her pain.

Most of the painful conditions people experience are temporary—the pain arrives and then subsides in a matter of minutes, days, or even weeks, often with the aid of painkillers or other treatments prescribed by a doctor. If a similar painful condition occurs in the future, it is not connected in a direct way to the earlier experience. This is the case for most everyday headaches, for instance, and for the pain typically produced by such conditions as toothaches, muscle strains, accidental wounds, and surgeries.

Acute pain refers to the discomfort people experience with temporary painful conditions that last less than a few months (Mann & Carr, 2006; Turk, Meichenbaum, & Genest, 1983). Patients with acute pain often have higher than normal levels of anxiety while the pain exists, but their distress subsides as their conditions improve and their pain decreases (Fordyce & Steger, 1979).

When a painful condition lasts longer than its expected course or for more than a few months, it is called *chronic*. People with chronic pain continue to have high levels of anxiety and tend to develop feelings of

hopelessness and helplessness because various medical treatments have not helped. Pain interferes with their daily activities, goals, and sleep (Affleck et al., 1998), and it can come to dominate their lives. These effects can be seen in the following passage:

> Pain patients frequently say that they could stand their pain much better if they could only get a good night's sleep . . . . They feel worn down, worn out, exhausted. They find themselves getting more and more irritable with their families, they have fewer and fewer friends, and fewer and fewer interests. Gradually, as time goes by, the boundaries of their world seem to shrink. They become more and more preoccupied with their pain, less and less interested in the world around them. Their world begins to center around home, doctor's office, and pharmacy. (Sternbach, quoted in Bakal, 1979, p. 165)

Several findings about sleep and pain are important: First, although pain itself can impair sleep, intrusive thoughts and worry do, too (Smith et al., 2000). Second, long-term sleep deprivation increases people's negative affect, sensitivity to pain, and amount of pain experienced in future weeks (Hamilton et al., 2008; Kundermann et al., 2004; Quartana et al., 2010). Many people with chronic pain leave their jobs for emotional and physical reasons and must live on reduced incomes at the same time that their medical bills are piling up. The experience of pain is very different when the condition is chronic than when it is acute.

The effects of chronic pain also depend on whether the underlying condition is *benign* (harmless) or is *malignant* (injurious) and worsening, and whether the discomfort exists *continuously* or occurs in frequent and intense *episodes*. These factors define three types of chronic pain (Turk, Meichenbaum, & Genest, 1983):

1. **Chronic-recurrent pain** stems from benign causes and involves repeated and intense episodes of pain separated by periods without pain. Two examples of chronic-recurrent pain are migraine headaches and tension-type (muscle-contraction) headaches; another example is *myofascial pain*, a syndrome that typically involves shooting or radiating, but dull, pain in the jaw and muscles of the head and neck, and sometimes the back (AMA, 2003; Hare & Milano, 1985).

2. **Chronic-intractable-benign pain** refers to discomfort that is typically present all of the time, with varying levels of intensity, and is not related to an underlying malignant condition. Sometimes chronic low back pain has this pattern.

3. **Chronic-progressive pain** is characterized by continuous discomfort, is associated with a malignant condition, and becomes increasingly intense as the

underlying condition worsens. Two of the most prominent malignant conditions that frequently produce chronic-progressive pain are rheumatoid arthritis and cancer.

As we shall see later in this chapter and in the next one, the type of pain people experience influences their psychosocial adjustment and the treatment they receive to control their discomfort. (Go to 💡.)

PERCEIVING PAIN

Of the several perceptual senses the human body uses, the sense of pain has three unique properties (Chapman, 1984; Melzack & Wall, 1982). First, although nerve fibers in the body sense and send signals of tissue damage, the receptor cells for pain are different from those of other perceptual systems, such as vision, which contain specific receptor cells that transmit only messages about a particular type of stimulation—light, for the visual system. The body has no *specific* receptor cells that transmit *only* information about pain. Second, the body senses pain in response to many types of noxious stimuli, such as physical pressure, lacerations, and intense heat or cold. Third, the perception of pain almost always includes a strong emotional component. As we are about to see, perceiving pain involves a complex interplay of physiological and psychological processes.

The Physiology of Pain Perception

To describe the physiology of perceiving pain, we will trace the bodily reaction to tissue damage, as when the body receives a cut or burn. The noxious stimulation instantly triggers chemical activity at the site of injury, releasing chemicals—which include *serotonin*, *histamine*, and *bradykinin*—that promote immune system activity, cause inflammation at the injured site, and activate endings of nerve fibers in the damaged region, signaling injury. Afferent neurons of the peripheral nervous system carry the signal of injury to the spinal cord, which carries the signal to the brain. The afferent nerve endings that respond to pain stimuli and signal injury are called **nociceptors** (Mann & Carr, 2006; Tortora & Derrickson, 2009). These fibers exist in every body tissue except the brain.

Pain signals are carried by afferent peripheral fibers of two types: A-delta and C fibers. A-*delta fibers* are coated with myelin, a fatty substance that enables neurons to transmit impulses very quickly. These fibers are associated with sharp, well-localized, and distinct pain experiences. C *fibers* transmit impulses more slowly—because they are not coated with myelin—and seem to be involved in experiences of diffuse dull, burning, or aching pain sensations (Mann & Carr, 2006; Tortora & Derrickson, 2009). Signals from A-delta and C fibers follow different paths when they reach the brain (Bloom, Lazerson, & Hofstadter, 1985; Guyton, 1985). The brain regions we'll mention are shown in Figures A-3 and A-4 in the Appendix. A-delta signals, which reflect sharp pain, go to motor and sensory areas, which suggests that these signals receive special attention in our sensory awareness, probably so that we can respond to them quickly. C fiber signals, which reflect burning or aching pain, terminate mainly in the brainstem and forebrain, with their remaining impulses connecting with a diffuse network of neurons. Signals of dull pain are less likely to command our immediate attention than those of sharp pain, but are more likely to affect our mood, general emotional state, and motivation.

So far, the description we have given of physiological reactions to tissue damage makes it seem as though the process of perceiving pain is rather straightforward. But it actually isn't. One phenomenon that complicates the picture is that pains originating from internal organs are often perceived as coming from other parts of the body, usually near the surface of the skin. This is called **referred pain** (AMA, 2003; Tortora & Derrickson, 2009). The pain people often feel in a heart attack provides a widely known example of this phenomenon: the pain is referred to the shoulders, pectoral area of the chest, and arms. Other examples of referred pain include:

- Pain perceived in the right shoulder resulting from a problem in the liver or gallbladder.
- Pain in the upper back originating in the stomach.
- Pain in the neck and left shoulder that results from a problem in the diaphragm.

Referred pain results when sensory impulses from an internal organ and the skin use the same pathway in the spinal cord (AMA, 2003; Tortora & Derrickson, 2009). Because people are more familiar with sensations from the skin than from internal organs, they tend to perceive the spinal cord impulses as coming from the skin. Another issue that complicates our understanding of pain perception is that people feel pains that have no detectable physical basis, as the next section discusses.

Pain with No Detectable Current Cause

Some pains people experience are curious because medical exams find no current cause for them—for instance, no noxious stimulus is present. These pains are usually classified as *neuropathic pain* which result from current or past disease or damage in peripheral nerves (AMA, 2003; Mann & Carr, 2006). Three common neuropathic pain syndromes are neuralgia, causalgia, and phantom limb

HIGHLIGHT

Acute Pain in Burn Patients

We often hear or read about people being seriously burned, such as in a fire or through scalding. About 300,000 burn injuries each year in the United States are serious (AMA, 2003). People with serious burns suffer acute pain both from their injuries and from the treatment procedures that must be performed.

Medical workers describe the severity of a burn on the basis of its location and with two measures of its damage (AMA, 2003). One measure estimates the amount of skin *area* affected in terms of the percentage of the body surface burned; the other assesses the *depth* of the burn, expressed in three "degrees":

1. *First-degree burns* involve damage restricted to the epidermis, or outermost layer of skin. The skin turns red, but does not blister—as, for example, in most cases of sunburn.

2. *Second-degree burns* are those that include damage to the dermis, the layer below the epidermis. These burns are quite painful, often form blisters, and can result from scalding and fire.

3. *Third-degree burns* destroy the epidermis and dermis down to the underlying layer of fat, and may extend to the muscle and bone. These burns usually result from fire. When third-degree burns damage nerve endings, there is generally no pain sensation in these regions initially.

Practitioners assess the depth of a burn by its appearance and the sensitivity of the region to pain.

Hospital treatment for patients with severe burns progresses through three phases (AMA, 2003; Wernick, 1983). The first few days after the burn is called the *emergency phase*, during which medical staff assess the severity of the burn and work to maintain the patient's body functions and defenses, such as in preventing infection and balancing fluids and electrolytes (substances that conduct electrical messages). The *acute phase* extends from the end of the emergency phase until the burned area is covered with new skin. This process can take from several days to several months, depending on the severity of the burn. The pain is constant during most or all of this phase, particularly when nerve endings begin to regenerate in third-degree burns. Suffering is generally

> greatest during "tankings," in which the patient is lowered on a stretcher into a large tub. The old dressings are removed and the patient is gently scrubbed to remove encrusted medication. Debridement, which is usually necessary during the early weeks of hospitalization, involves the vigorous cutting away of dead tissue in burned areas. The process, which may last for more than an hour and involve several people working on different parts of the body simultaneously, ends when fresh medication and new dressings are applied. (Wernick, 1983, p. 196)

These and many other painful medical procedures occur very frequently, and burn patients must also do exercises for physical or occupational therapy. The *rehabilitation phase* begins at about the time of discharge from the hospital and continues until the scar tissue has matured. Although the pain has now subsided, itching in the healed area (which should not be scratched) can be a source of discomfort, as can using devices and doing exercises to prevent scarring and contractures (skin shrinkage that can restrict the person's range of motion).

Analgesic medication is the main approach for controlling acute pain in the hospital (AMA, 2003). But psychological approaches can also help burn patients cope with their pain so that they need less medication. Robert Wernick (1983) used a program of psychological preparation with adult severe-burn patients to enhance the patients' sense of informational, behavioral, and cognitive control over their discomfort, especially with regard to the tanking and debridement procedures. Although these patients were not specifically asked to reduce their use of drugs, they subsequently requested much less medication than patients in a comparison (control) group who received the standard hospital preparation. Similar preparation methods have also been successful with children (Tarnowski, Rasnake, & Drabman, 1987). Also, because burn patients with high levels of depression and anxiety tend to experience more pain and disability in the future, they would probably benefit from psychosocial therapy before leaving the hospital (Edwards, Smith et al., 2007).

pain. These syndromes often begin with tissue damage, such as from disease or injury, but the pain persists long after healing is complete, may spread and increase in intensity, and may become stronger than the pain experienced with the initial damage (AMA, 2003; Melzack & Wall, 1982).

Neuralgia is an extremely painful syndrome in which the patient experiences recurrent episodes of intense shooting or stabbing pain along the course of a nerve (AMA, 2003; Melzack & Wall, 1982; Tortora & Derrickson, 2009). Sometimes neuralgia begins after an infection, such as of shingles (herpes zoster), in the nerve. In one form of this syndrome, called *trigeminal neuralgia*, excruciating spasms of pain occur along the trigeminal nerve that projects throughout the face. Episodes of neuralgia occur very suddenly and without any apparent cause, and attacks can often be provoked more readily by innocuous stimuli than by noxious ones. For instance, drawing a cotton ball across the skin can trigger an attack, but a pin prick does not.

Causalgia, renamed "complex regional pain syndrome," typically involves recurrent episodes of severe burning pain that often can be triggered by minor stimuli, such as clothing resting on the area or a puff of air (AMA, 2003; Harden & Bruehl, 2006; Melzack & Wall, 1982). A patient with causalgia might report, for instance, that the pain feels "like my arm is pressed against a hot stove." In this syndrome, the pain feels as though it originates in a region of the body where the patient had at some earlier time been seriously wounded, such as by a gunshot or stabbing, but only a small minority of severely wounded patients develop causalgia—and for those who do, the pain persists long after the wound has healed and damaged nerves have regenerated. Episodes of causalgia can be unpredictable and often occur spontaneously.

Phantom limb pain is an especially puzzling phenomenon because the patient—an amputee or someone whose peripheral nervous system is irreparably damaged—feels pain in a limb that either is no longer there or has no functioning nerves (AMA, 2003; Melzack & Katz, 2004). After an amputation, for instance, most patients claim to have sensations of their limb still being there—such as by feeling it "move"—and most of these individuals report feeling pain, too. Phantom limb pain generally persists for months or years, can be quite severe, and sometimes resembles the pain produced by the injury that required the amputation. Individuals with phantom limb pain may experience either recurrent or continuous pain and may describe it as shooting, burning, or cramping. For example, many patients who feel pain in a phantom hand report sensing that the hand is tightly clenched and its fingernails are digging into the palm.

Why do people feel pain when no noxious stimulation is present? Although the answer probably relates to neural damage that preceded the neuropathic condition, it is unclear why most patients who suffer obvious neural damage do not develop these pain syndromes. This puzzle is far from solved, but the explanation will almost surely involve both physiological and psychological factors.

The Role of the "Meaning" of Pain

Some people evidently like pain—at least under some, usually sexual, circumstances—and are described as *masochists*. For them, the meaning of pain seems to be different from what it is for most people. Some psychologists believe individuals may come to like pain through classical conditioning, that is, by participating in or viewing activities that associate pain with pleasure in a sexual context (Wincze, 1977). Evidence for a role of classical conditioning in the meaning of pain comes mainly from research with animals. For example, Pavlov (1927) found that dogs' negative reaction to aversive stimuli, such as electric shocks or skin pricks, changed if the stimuli repeatedly preceded presentation of food. Eventually, the dogs would try to approach the aversive stimuli, which now signaled that food, not danger, was coming.

Doctor Henry Beecher (1956) described a dramatic example of how the meaning of pain affects people's experience of it. During World War II, he had examined soldiers who had recently been very seriously wounded and were in a field hospital for treatment. Of these men, only 49% claimed to be in "moderate" or "severe" pain and only 32% requested medication when asked if they "wanted something to relieve it." Some years later, Beecher conducted a similar examination—this time with civilian men who had just undergone surgery. Although the surgical wounds were in the same body regions as those of the soldiers, the soldiers' wounds had been more extensive. Nevertheless, 75% of the civilians claimed to be in "moderate" or "severe" pain and 83% requested medication. (The painkillers used for the soldiers and civilians were narcotics.)

Why did the soldiers—who had more extensive wounds—perceive less pain than the civilians? Beecher described the meaning the injuries had for the soldiers, who

> had been subjected to almost uninterrupted fire for weeks. Notable in this group of soldiers was their optimistic, even cheerful, state of mind.... They thought the war was over for them and that they would soon be well enough to be sent home. It is not difficult

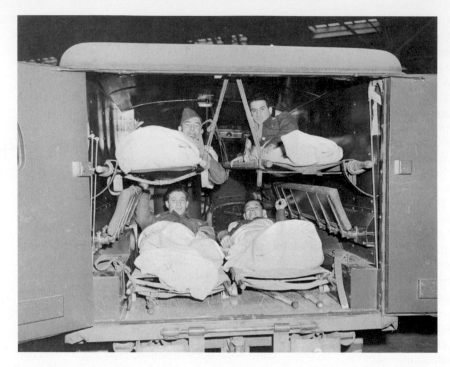

For many wounded soldiers, their pain seemed to be reduced by the knowledge that they were going home.

to understand their relief on being delivered from this area of danger. The battlefield wound marked the end of disaster for them. (1956, p. 1069)

For the civilian surgical patients, however, the wound marked the *start* of a personal problem, and their condition represented a major disruption in their lives.

We discussed in Chapter 8 how people's perceptions of body sensations are influenced by cognitive, social, and emotional factors—for instance, that they are less likely to notice pain when they are distracted by competing environmental stimuli, such as while participating in competitive sports. Psychological factors play an important role in perceiving pain, and theories of pain need to take these factors into account.

THEORIES OF PAIN

You have probably seen demonstrations in which hypnotized people were instructed that they would not feel pain—they were then stuck by a pin and did not react. When people under hypnosis do not react to noxious stimulation, do they still perceive the pain—only "it doesn't matter" to them? Similarly, do patients who seem relaxed while under the influence of painkillers actually perceive their pain? Some theories of pain would answer "yes" to these questions (Karoly, 1985). Let's look at two of these theories as we begin to examine how to explain pain perception.

EARLY THEORIES OF PAIN

In the early 1900s, the dominant theories of pain took a very mechanistic view of pain perception. They proposed that if an appropriate stimulus activates a receptor, the signal travels to the spinal cord and then the brain, and sensation results (Fletcher & Macdonald, 2005; Gatchel et al., 2007; Melzack & Wall, 1982). *Specificity theory* argued that the body has a separate sensory system for perceiving pain—just as it does for hearing and vision. This system was thought to contain its own special receptors for detecting pain stimuli, its own peripheral nerves and pathway to the brain, and its own area of the brain for processing pain signals. But this structure is not correct.

Another view of pain, called *pattern theory*, proposed that there is no separate system for perceiving pain, and the receptors for pain are shared with other senses, such as of touch. According to this view, people feel pain when certain patterns of neural activity occur, such as when appropriate types of activity reach excessively high levels in the brain. These patterns occur only with intense stimulation. Because strong and mild stimuli of the same sense modality produce different patterns of neural activity, being hit hard feels painful, but being caressed does not.

These early theories did not adequately explain pain perception (Gatchel et al., 2007; Melzack & Wall, 1982). Pattern theory has been criticized because it requires that the stimuli triggering pain must be intense. Thus, it cannot account for the fact that innocuous stimuli can trigger episodes of causalgia and neuralgia. Perhaps the most serious problem with the early theories is that they do not attempt to explain why the experience of pain is affected by psychological factors, such as the person's ideas about the meaning of pain, beliefs about the likelihood of pain, and attention to (or distraction from) noxious events. Partly because these theories overlook the role of psychological factors, they incorrectly predict that a person must feel just as much pain when hypnotized as when not hypnotized, even though he or she does not show it. Research findings indicate that people who are instructed not to feel pain actually do feel less pain when deeply hypnotized than when in the normal waking state (Hilgard & Hilgard, 1983). (Go to 💡.)

THE GATE-CONTROL THEORY OF PAIN

In the 1960s, Ronald Melzack and Patrick Wall (1965, 1982) introduced the **gate-control theory** of pain perception. This theory integrated useful ideas from earlier theories and improved on them in several ways, particularly by describing a physiological mechanism by which psychological factors can affect people's experience of pain. As a result, the gate-control theory can account for many phenomena in pain perception that have vexed earlier theories. For instance, it does not have to predict that hypnotized people must feel noxious stimulation (Karoly, 1985).

The Gating Mechanism

At the heart of the gate-control theory is a neural "gate" that can be opened or closed in varying degrees, thereby modulating incoming pain signals before they reach the brain. The theory proposes that the *gating mechanism* is located in the spinal cord—more specifically, in the *substantia gelatinosa* of the *dorsal horns*, which are part of the *gray matter* that runs the length of the core of the spinal cord. Figure 10-2 depicts how the gate-control process works. You can see in both diagrams of the figure that signals of noxious stimulation enter the gating mechanism (substantia gelatinosa) of the spinal cord from *pain fibers* (A-delta and C fibers). After these signals pass through the gating mechanism, they activate *transmission cells*, which send impulses to the brain. When the output of signals from the transmission cells reaches a critical level, the person perceives pain; the greater the output beyond this level, the greater the pain intensity.

HIGHLIGHT

Inducing Pain in Laboratory Research

To conduct an experiment dealing with pain, researchers sometimes need to create a physically painful situation for human participants. How can they accomplish this in a standard way without harming the people? Several approaches have been used safely; two common methods are the *cold-pressor* and *muscle-ischemia* procedures (Turk, Meichenbaum, & Genest, 1983).

The Cold-Pressor Procedure

The cold-pressor procedure basically involves immersing the person's hand and forearm in ice water for a few minutes. A special apparatus is used, like the one illustrated in Figure 10-1, so that the researcher can maintain a standard procedure across all people they test. The apparatus consists of an armrest mounted on an ice chest filled with water, which is maintained at a temperature of 2°C (35.6°F). Water at this temperature produces a continuous pain that subjects describe as "aching" or "crushing." A pump circulates the water to prevent it from warming in local areas around the arm.

Before using the apparatus, the person's arm is immersed in a bucket of room-temperature water for 1 minute. The researcher also explains the cold-pressor procedure, solicits questions, and indicates that some temporary discoloration of the arm is common. When the procedure is over and the person's arm is removed from the apparatus, the researcher notes that the discomfort will decrease rapidly but that it sometimes increases first for a short while (Turk, Meichenbaum, & Genest, 1983). When using this procedure, the person's pain may be assessed in several ways, such as by self-ratings or by the length of time he or she is willing to endure the discomfort.

An experiment had people experience the cold-pressor procedure twice to test the role of coping methods on pain perception (Girodo & Wood, 1979). Before the second procedure, subjects in different groups received different types of training for coping with pain.

(continued)

HIGHLIGHT *(Continued)*

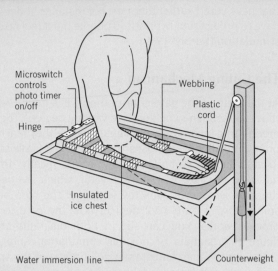

Microswitch controls photo timer on/off

Webbing

Plastic cord

Hinge

Insulated ice chest

Water immersion line

Counterweight

Figure 10-1 Apparatus for the cold-pressor procedure.

We will focus on two groups. One group was trained to cope by making positive *self-statements*; they were taught a list of 20 statements, such as, "No matter how cold it gets, I can handle it," and "It's not the worst thing that can happen." For the other group, training involved the same self-statements, but they also received an *explanation* of how using these statements can enhance their personal control and help them cope with the pain. Immediately after each cold-pressor procedure, the people rated their experience of pain on a scale. Pain ratings *decreased* from the first to the second test for subjects who received the explanation for making the statements and *increased* for those who did not receive the explanation. These results suggest that people's beliefs about the purpose of using self-statements may affect their experience of pain.

The Muscle-Ischemia Procedure

The condition of *ischemia*—or insufficient blood flow—is an important stimulus for the experience of pain when circulation is blocked in internal organs (AMA, 2003). The pain people experience in a heart attack, for instance, results from poor blood flow in the blood vessels to the heart muscle.

The muscle-ischemia procedure typically involves reducing blood flow to the muscles of the arm. This is accomplished by wrapping the cuff of a sphygmomanometer (blood pressure testing device) around the arm, inflating it, and maintaining the pressure at a high level—240 mm Hg (Turk, Meichenbaum, & Genest, 1983).

This pressure produces pain without causing damage and can be applied safely for up to 50 minutes or so. Before the procedure begins, the arm is raised over the subject's head for 1 minute to drain excess venous blood. The researcher also informs the person that the procedure is safe and harmless, but that it is uncomfortable and may produce temporary numbness, throbbing, changes in arm temperature, and discoloration of the arm and hand. When the cuff is removed, the person raises the arm over his or her head for a few minutes to allow blood flow to return gradually and comfortably. As with the cold-pressor procedure, measures of muscle-ischemia pain can include self-ratings and endurance.

Another way to measure muscle-ischemia pain uses a variation of the procedure we described; that is, the cuff is inflated only to the point when the subject first reports discomfort. This approach assesses the individual's pain *threshold*. Using this method, researchers found that people's pain thresholds, or cuff pressures at which they reported discomfort, were much (50%) higher for individuals who were listening to a comedy recording (by Lily Tomlin) or practicing relaxation than for people in control groups (Cogan et al., 1987). Thus, listening to comedy and practicing relaxation reduces the experience of pain. Other researchers have assessed pain thresholds and found almost no correlation for different types of pain *within* individuals (Janal et al., 1994). This suggests that most people cannot be characterized as "stoical" or "sensitive" to pain in general.

Pain Research and Ethical Standards

When conducting any kind of research with human participants, psychologists are obliged to follow the ethical standards set forth by the American Psychological Association (separate guidelines apply for animal studies). Some of the standards are especially pertinent for research with aversive stimuli. First of all, researchers should make certain that any aversive stimulus they use is not actually harmful. In addition, all participants should:

- Be informed of any features of the study that might affect their willingness to participate.
- Receive clear answers to their questions.
- Be allowed to choose freely, and without undue influence, whether to participate and whether to quit at any point.

If a participant is a child, researchers should also obtain consent from an appropriate guardian, usually a parent.

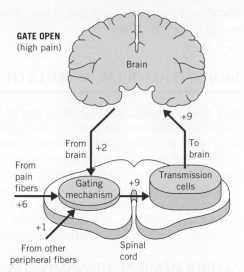 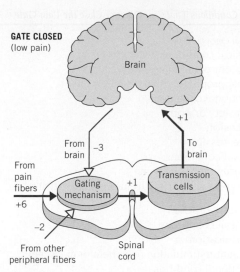

Figure 10-2 Two diagrams to illustrate gate-control theory predictions when strong pain signals arrive from *pain fibers* (A-delta and C) at the spinal cord, along with signals from other *peripheral fibers* (A-beta) and the *brain*. The diagram on the left depicts what conditions might exist when the gate is *open*, and the person feels strong pain; the one on the right shows a scenario when the gate is *closed*, and the person feels little pain. The thick arrows indicate "stimulation" conditions that tend to open the gate and send pain signals through, and the thin ones indicate the opposite, "inhibition," effect. The numbers that accompany each arrow represent hypothetical values for the degrees of pain *stimulation* (positive numbers) or *inhibition* (negative numbers). Pain signals enter the spinal cord and pass through a gating mechanism before activating transmission cells, which send impulses to the brain. (From information in Melzack & Wall, 1965, 1982.)

The two diagrams in the figure outline how the gating mechanism controls the output of impulses by the transmission cells. When pain signals enter the spinal cord and the gate is open, the transmission cells send impulses freely; but to the extent that the gate is closed, the output of the transmission cells is inhibited. What controls the opening and closing of the gate? The gate-control theory proposes that three factors are involved:

- *The amount of activity in the pain fibers*. Activity in these fibers tends to open the gate. The stronger the noxious stimulation, the more active the pain fibers.

- *The amount of activity in other peripheral fibers*. Some peripheral fibers, called A-*beta fibers*, carry information about harmless stimuli or mild irritation, such as touching, rubbing, or lightly scratching the skin. Activity in A-beta fibers tends to close the gate, inhibiting the perception of pain when noxious stimulation exists. This would explain why gently massaging or applying heat to sore muscles decreases the pain.

- *Messages that descend from the brain*. Neurons in the brainstem and cortex have efferent pathways to the spinal cord, and the impulses they send can open or close the gate. The effects of some brain processes, such as those in anxiety or excitement, probably have a general impact, opening or closing the gate for *all* inputs from *any* areas of the body. But the impact of other brain

processes may be very specific, applying to only some inputs from certain parts of the body.

The idea that brain impulses influence the gating mechanism helps to explain why people who are hypnotized or distracted by competing environmental stimuli may not notice the pain of an injury.

The theory proposes that the gating mechanism responds to the combined effects of these three factors. Table 10.1 presents a variety of conditions in people's lives that seem to open or close the gate. For instance, anxiety and boredom tend to open the gate, and positive emotions and distraction tend to close it. Melzack later proposed the idea of a *neuromatrix*, a neural network in the brain that integrates information from the senses, cognitive and emotional areas of the brain, and stress-regulation systems (Melzack & Katz, 2004). In phantom limb pain, the neuromatrix creates the perception of pain from the pattern of impulses in the network, without the presence of a noxious stimulus.

Evidence on the Gate-Control Theory

The gate-control theory has stimulated a great deal of research and has received strong support from the findings of many, but not all, of these studies (Melzack & Katz, 2004; Winters, 1985). One study, for instance, confirmed the theory's prediction that impulses from the brain can inhibit the perception of pain. David Reynolds

Table 10.1 *Conditions That Can Open or Close the Pain Gate*

Conditions That Open the Gate
- Physical conditions
  Extent of the injury
  Inappropriate activity level
- Emotional conditions
  Anxiety or worry
  Tension
  Depression
- Mental conditions
  Focusing on the pain
  Boredom; little involvement in life activities

Conditions That Close the Gate
- Physical conditions
  Medication
  Counterstimulation (e.g., heat or massage)
- Emotional conditions
  Positive emotions (e.g., happiness or optimism)
  Relaxation
  Rest
- Mental conditions
  Intense concentration or distraction
  Involvement and interest in life activities

Source: Based on material by Karol et al., cited in Turk, Meichenbaum, & Genest, 1983.

(1969) conducted this study with rats as subjects. He first implanted an electrode in the midbrain portion of each rat's brainstem (see Figure A-3), varying the exact location from one rat to the next. Then he made sure they could feel pain by applying a clamp to their tails—and all reacted. Several days later, he provided continuous, mild electrical current through the electrode and again applied the clamp to test whether the current would block pain. Although most of the subjects did show a pain reaction, those with electrodes in a particular region of the midbrain—the **periaqueductal gray** area—did not. The electrical stimulation had produced a state of not being able to feel pain, or *analgesia*, in these rats. Then Reynolds used these few rats for a dramatic demonstration: he performed abdominal surgery on them while they were awake and with only the analgesia produced through electrode stimulation. Subsequent studies by other researchers have confirmed that stimulation to the periaqueductal gray area can induce analgesia in animals and in humans. Moreover, they have determined that morphine works as a painkiller by activating the brainstem to send impulses down the spinal cord (Chapman, 1984; Melzack & Wall, 1982; Winters, 1985).

The gate-control theory clearly takes a biopsychosocial perspective in explaining how people perceive pain.

You'll see many features of this theory as you read the material in the next section.

BIOPSYCHOSOCIAL ASPECTS OF PAIN

Why does electrical stimulation to the periaqueductal gray area of the brainstem produce analgesia? The search for an answer to this question played an important part in major discoveries about the neurochemical bases of pain. We will begin this section by examining some of these discoveries and seeing that the neurochemical substances that underlie acute pain are linked to psychosocial processes. Then we will consider how psychosocial factors are related to the experience of chronic pain.

NEUROCHEMICAL TRANSMISSION AND INHIBITION OF PAIN

The phenomenon whereby stimulation to the brainstem produces insensitivity to pain has been given the name **stimulation-produced analgesia** (SPA). To understand how SPA occurs, we need to see how transmission cells are activated to send pain signals to the brain. This activation is triggered by a neurotransmitter called *substance P* that is secreted by pain fibers and crosses the synapse to the transmission cells (Mann & Carr, 2006; Tortora & Derrickson, 2009). SPA occurs when another chemical blocks the pain fibers' release of substance P. Let's see how this happens and what this other chemical is.

What Stimulating the Periaqueductal Gray Area Does

Stimulation to the periaqueductal gray area starts a neurochemical chain reaction that seems to take the course shown in Figure 10-3. The impulse travels down the brainstem to the spinal cord, where the neurotransmitter *serotonin* activates nerve cells called "inhibitory interneurons." Impulses in these interneurons then cause the release of the neurotransmitter *endorphin* at the pain fibers; endorphin inhibits these fibers from releasing substance P (Mann & Carr, 2006; Tortora & Derrickson, 2009).

Endorphin is a chemical belonging to a class of opiatelike substances called **endogenous opioids** that the body produces naturally; *enkephalin* is another of these chemicals. (*Endogenous* means "developing from within," and *oid* is a suffix meaning "resembling.") Endogenous opioids and opiates (morphine and heroin) appear to function in much the same way in reducing pain (Snyder, 1977; Winters, 1985). Many neurons in the central nervous system have receptors that are sensitive to both opiates

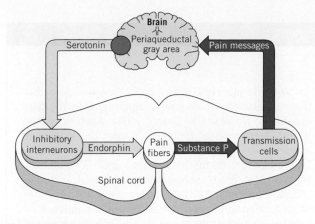

Figure 10-3 Illustration of the chain of activity involved in SPA. Stimulation to the periaqueductal gray area of the brain starts a sequence of electrochemical reactions, eventually leading to inhibition (shown by shaded arrows) of the pain fibers' release of substance P, thereby reducing pain messages from the transmission cells to the brain.

and opioids, and allow these chemicals to bind to them. Evidence now indicates that people with chronic pain have impaired endogenous opioid systems, which may partly explain why their pain gets worse and why they are highly sensitive to acute pain (Bruehl, McCubbin, & Harden, 1999). This impairment is especially strong if their parents also suffered from chronic pain (Bruehl & Chung, 2006).

How Opiates and Opioids Work

Researchers have studied the action of opiates and endogenous opioids by using the drug *naloxone*, which acts in opposition to opiates and opioids and prevents them from working as painkillers (Schiffman, 1996; Winters, 1985). In fact, doctors administer naloxone to counteract the effects of heroin in addicts who have taken an overdose of the narcotic. In studying the action of opioids, researchers have examined whether these chemicals are involved in the phenomenon of SPA and found that naloxone blocks the analgesic effects of electrical stimulation to the periaqueductal gray area: animals with naloxone react strongly to the pain, but those without naloxone do not (Akil, Mayer, & Liebeskind, 1976). Furthermore, research with humans found that injecting naloxone in patients who have undergone tooth extractions increases their pain (Levine, Gordon, & Fields, 1978). These findings indicate that endogenous opioids are involved in producing SPA.

The body clearly contains its own natural painkilling substances, but the ways by which they reduce pain are more complicated than they once appeared (Cannon

et al., 1982; Melzack & Wall, 1982). Three issues are relevant. First, studies have found that naloxone does not always block SPA. Second, some research findings suggest that neurotransmitters may have different effects for momentary pain than for pain lasting for an hour or more; most research has been with pain that lasts only seconds or minutes. Third, when morphine is given to control pain, tolerance to the drug occurs quickly for momentary pain but does *not* seem to occur for longer-lasting acute pain and for chronic severe pain, such as that experienced by some cancer patients. These patients generally don't increase their doses, even across months or years of use (Melzack & Wall, 1982). Just why these differences in tolerance occur is unclear.

Having internal pain-relieving chemicals in the body serves an adaptive function. It enables people to regulate the pain they experience to some extent so that they can attend to other matters, such as taking immediate action to survive serious injuries. Pain activates this analgesic system (Winters, 1985). But most of the time, high levels of endogenous opioid activity are not needed and would be maladaptive since chronic analgesia would undermine the value of pain as a warning signal. Perhaps because pain and emotions are closely linked, studies have found that psychological stress can trigger endogenous opioid activity (Bloom, Lazerson, & Hofstadter, 1985; Winters, 1985). The release of endogenous opioids in times of stress may help to explain how injured athletes in competition and soldiers on the battlefield continue to function with little or no perception of pain. The connection between stress, coping, and opioid activity points up the interplay between biological and psychosocial factors in people's experience of pain. (Go to 💡.)

PERSONAL AND SOCIAL EXPERIENCES AND PAIN

Imagine this scene: little Stevie is a year old and is in the pediatrician's office to receive a standard vaccination injection, as he has done before. As the doctor approaches with the needle, Stevie starts to cry and tries to kick the doctor. He is reacting in anticipation of pain—something he learned through *classical conditioning* when he had received vaccinations before.

Learning and Pain

We learn to associate pain with antecedent cues and its consequences, especially if the pain is severe and repeated, as it usually is with chronic pain (Martin, Milech, & Nathan, 1993). Many individuals who suffer from migraine headaches, for example, often can tell

HIGHLIGHT

Placebos and Pain

You have probably heard of doctors prescribing a medicine that actually consisted of "sugar pills" when they could not find a physical cause for a patient's complaints or did not know of any medication that would help. You may also have heard that this treatment sometimes works—the patient claims the symptoms are reduced. An inert substance or procedure that produces an effect is called a *placebo*. Studies have shown that placebos are often effective in treating a variety of ailments, including asthma, nausea, and pain (Hróbjartsson & Gøtzsche, 2010; Sauro & Greenberg, 2005). And an effective placebo need not be a substance: an experiment found that of patients who got sham surgery for arthritis of the knee or real surgery, nearly 40% of each group claimed to have less pain and better movement (Moseley et al., 2002).

Placebos do not always work in treating pain, but they produce substantial relief in about half as many patients as do real drugs, such as aspirin or morphine (Melzack & Wall, 1982; Rehm & Nayak, 2004). The effect of placebos depends on the patient's belief that they will work—for instance, they are more effective:

- With large doses—such as more capsules or larger ones—than with smaller doses.
- When injected than when taken orally.
- When the practitioner indicates explicitly and strongly that they will work.

Unfortunately, however, the effectiveness of placebos in treating pain tends to decline with repeated use.

Why do placebos reduce pain? One reason is that they sometimes reduce stress, which reduces the pain experience (Aslaksen & Flaten, 2008). Another reason is that psychological processes trigger the release of endogenous opioids in the person's body, thereby inhibiting the transmission of pain signals. Two of these triggering processes are *expectancies* and *classical conditioning* (Stewart-Williams, 2004). These are the same processes we discussed in Chapter 6 that lead to dependence on substances, such as drugs and alcohol. In both processes, people acquire from past experience a connection between active treatments and their effects, such as reduced pain, so that something resembling an active treatment—the placebo—can lead to the effect. Earlier in the current chapter, we saw the role of endogenous opioids in stimulation-produced analgesia (SPA); this role is important in placebos, too. Research with double blind procedures has shown that placebos do, in fact, elicit the body's production of endogenous opioids and that people who receive naloxone to block the transmission of pain signals report more discomfort than those who do not get naloxone with pain from muscle-ischemia and actual tooth extractions (Benedetti et al., 2003; Fields & Levine, 1984; Johansen, Brox, & Flaten, 2003).

The effects of placebos are fascinating and important, but they also present major ethical dilemmas for practitioners. Is it appropriate to use placebo drugs or procedures to treat symptoms and illnesses—and if so, when and under what circumstances?

---

when headaches are on the way because they experience symptoms, such as dizziness, that precede the pain. These symptoms become conditioned stimuli that tend to produce distress, a conditioned response, and may heighten the perception of pain when it arrives.

Words or stimuli that relate to the pain we have experienced can also become conditioned stimuli and produce conditioned responses. A study of people who do and do not have migraine headaches measured their physiological arousal in response to pain-related words, such as "throbbing" and "stabbing" (Jamner & Tursky, 1987). Migraine sufferers displayed much stronger physiological reactions to these words—especially the words that described their own experience with pain—than those without migraines did. Similarly, people without chronic pain who were asked to imagine situations associated with pain-related words, such as

"excruciating" and "squeezing," showed brain activation in pain regions to those words but not others (Richter et al., 2010). Other research found that people can learn via classical conditioning to make specific muscular responses to stimuli that had been presented with pain repeatedly, and that this association may contribute to low back pain becoming chronic in everyday life (Schneider, Palomba, & Flor, 2004).

Learning also influences the way people behave when they are in pain. People in pain behave in characteristic ways—they may moan, grimace, or limp, for instance. These actions are called **pain behaviors**, and they can be classified into four types (Turk, Wack, & Kerns, 1985):

- *Facial or audible expression of distress*, as when people clench their teeth, moan, or grimace.

- *Distorted ambulation or posture*, such as moving in a guarded or protective fashion, stooping while walking, or rubbing or holding the painful area.
- *Negative affect*, such as being irritable.
- *Avoidance of activity*, as when people lie down frequently during the day, stay home from work, or refrain from motor or strenuous behavior.

Pain behaviors are a part of the sick role, and people in pain may begin to exaggerate these behaviors because, they think, "No one believes me" (Hendler, 1984). Regardless of why the behaviors start, they are often strengthened or maintained by reinforcement in *operant conditioning*, without the person's awareness (Hölzl, Kleinböhl, & Huse, 2005; Turk, 2001). When pain persists and becomes chronic, these behaviors often become part of the person's habits and lifestyle. People with entrenched patterns of pain behavior usually feel powerless to change.

How are pain behaviors reinforced? Although being sick or in pain is unpleasant, it sometimes has benefits, or "secondary gains." Someone who is in pain may be relieved of certain chores around the house or of going to work, for instance. Also, when a person has a painful condition that flares up in certain circumstances, such as when lifting heavy objects, he or she may begin to avoid these activities. In both of these situations, pain behavior is reinforced if the person does not like doing these activities in the first place: getting out of doing them is rewarding. Another way pain behavior and other sick-role behaviors may be reinforced is if the person receives disability payments. Studies of injured or ill patients who differ in the financial compensation they receive have found that those with greater compensation tend to remain hospitalized and miss work longer, report more chronic pain, and show less success from pain treatments (Chapman, 1991; Ciccone, Just, & Bandilla, 1999; Rohling, Binder, & Langhinrichsen-Rohling, 1995). In some cases, people who take longer to recover are probably *malingering*, but others may just be willing to take more time and prevent a relapse. Still, many pain patients who receive disability compensation show substantial emotional and behavioral improvements from pain rehabilitation programs (Trabin, Rader, & Cummings, 1987).

Social Processes and Pain

People who suffer with pain generally receive attention, care, and affection from family and friends, which can provide social reinforcement for pain behavior. Researchers have demonstrated this relationship with both child and adult patients. Karen Gil and her colleagues (1988) videotaped parents' reactions to the pain behavior of their children who had a chronic skin disorder with severe itching that should not be scratched since it can cause peeling and infection. An analysis revealed that the children's scratching *increased*, rather than decreased, when parents paid attention to scratching, and paying attention to the children when they were *not* scratching seemed to reduce their scratching behavior. Parents of children with pain conditions who distract their children from the symptoms decrease pain behavior, and their children report feeling better than others who receive attention for their symptoms (Walker et al., 2006). Children whose parents are critical or overly protective of their pain tend to become increasingly disabled, particularly if they have high levels of emotional distress (Claar, Simons, & Logan, 2008).

Studies have assessed how patients' pain behaviors relate to their receiving social rewards, such as being able to avoid disliked social activities or getting solicitous care from a spouse—that is, high levels of help and attention (Ciccone, Just, & Bandilla, 1999; Newton-John, 2002). Receiving higher levels of social reward is associated with patients reporting more pain and showing more disability and less activity, such as in visiting friends or going shopping. In one study, patients with chronic pain were interviewed about their spouses' solicitousness regarding their pain behavior (Block, Kremer, & Gaylor, 1980). The interviews occurred in meetings in which the patients were aware of being observed through a one-way mirror and of who was observing: their spouse or a hospital employee. The degree of pain the patients described depended on whether the spouse or the employee was observing and whether the patient thought the spouse was solicitous. Patients who felt their spouses were solicitous reported *more* pain when their spouses watched than when the employee did, but those who felt their spouses were not solicitous reported *less* pain when their spouses watched than when the employee did. Spouses very often overestimate the pain that patients feel, and those who do are less supportive of patients' engaging in everyday activities (Martire et al., 2006).

Findings on parents' and spouses' reactions to chronic pain behavior and the social climate within the family system illustrate how each family member's behavior impacts on the behavior of the others (Kerns & Weiss, 1994; Romano, Turner, & Jensen, 1997; Turk, 2001). When families lack cohesion or the members are highly solicitous to pain behavior without encouraging the patient to become active, they tend to promote sick-role behavior. These conditions can lead to a vicious circle: solicitousness may elicit more pain behavior, which leads to more solicitousness, and so on. Showing care and concern when people are in pain is, of course, important and constructive. But social processes in the family system of pain patients can gradually and insidiously increase the patients' dependency and physical deterioration, such as through muscle atrophy, and decrease their self-efficacy and self-esteem. Self-efficacy is important because people who believe they cannot control their pain very well experience more pain and use more medication than those who believe they can control it (Gatchel et al., 2007; Turk, 1996).

Gender, Sociocultural Factors, and Pain

Studies have found gender and sociocultural differences in the experience of pain. Men and women differ in the types of pain they experience and reactions to pain. In cold-pressor tests, women have lower thresholds and give higher ratings for pain, and some evidence suggests this may result in part from different effects of endogenous opioids (al' Absi et al., 2004; Rollman, 2004). Women also have higher incidence rates of pain from arthritis, migraine headache, myofacial neuralgia, and causalgia, but men have a greater incidence of back pain and cardiac pain (Bodnar, 1998). Women report more than men that pain interfered with their daily activities (Lester, Lefebvre, & Keefe, 1994).

Research has compared pain in people from different socioeconomic and ethnic groups. People in a variety of nations in lower socioeconomic classes experience more pain than those in higher classes (Poleshuck & Green, 2008). Surveys of adults in different countries who suffer from chronic low back pain revealed greater work and social impairments among Americans, followed by Italians and New Zealanders, and then by Japanese, Colombian, and Mexican individuals (Sanders et al., 1992). In the United States, African-Americans showed less tolerance for muscle-ischemia pain and reported higher levels of chronic pain than Whites (Edwards et al., 2001). Also, Blacks reported more pain after dental surgery than people of European, Asian, or Hispanic backgrounds, and women in each group reported more pain than men (Faucett, Gordon, & Levine, 1994). But other studies have found no ethnic pain differences, and knowing of actual differences is of little value for a practitioner treating individual people (Korol & Craig, 2001).

EMOTIONS, COPING PROCESSES, AND PAIN

Pain and emotion are intimately linked, and cognitive processes mediate this link. In a study of these relationships, dental patients filled out a brief dental anxiety scale while waiting for their appointments (Kent, 1985). Then they rated the pain they expected in their visits. After the appointment, the patients rated the pain

they actually experienced, and rated it again by mail 3 months later. The results revealed that anxiety played a role in their expectations of pain and in their memories of it 3 months later. The patients with high dental anxiety expected *and* later remembered four times as much pain as they experienced. In contrast, the low-anxiety patients expected and remembered less than twice as much pain as they experienced. These and similar findings of other researchers (Gedney & Logan, 2006) suggest that high-anxiety patients' memories of pain are determined more by what they expect than by what they feel.

Does Emotion Affect Pain?

Most people with chronic pain experience high levels of depression, anxiety, or anger (Gatchel et al., 2007). Do emotions affect pain? In the case of headache, investigations using self-report methods have found a sequence: migraine and muscle-contraction headaches tend to occur after periods of heightened stress and that this link is pronounced for depressed individuals (Janke, Holroyd, & Romanek, 2004; Köhler & Haimerl, 1990; Wittrock & Myers, 1998). Has research shown that emotion can cause headaches?

Convincing evidence that stress can cause headaches comes from a study with adults who suffered from either chronic headache or only occasional

Pain is an important factor in dentistry: it motivates patients to seek treatment, but the discomfort during visits makes them feel uneasy about going in the future.

headaches (Gannon et al., 1987). Before testing a subject, a researcher attached sensors to the person's body to take physiological measurements, such as of heart rate. Soon, the subjects were given a stressful task—calculating arithmetic problems, such as 349 + 229, for an hour—and told that a buzzer would sound if their performance fell below a norm. Actually, the buzzer sounded periodically regardless of their performance. What effect did these conditions have? More than two-thirds of the chronic headache sufferers and only one-fourth of the occasional sufferers reported developing headaches during the stress task. Ratings of headache pain increased throughout the stress condition, and decreased later while they sat quietly. The headaches tended to resemble tension-type headaches and be preceded by sustained physiological arousal. These and similar findings of other researchers (Martin, Todd, & Reece, 2005) indicate that stress can cause headaches.

Emotions are also related to other kinds of pain, but the degree to which emotions cause the pain is still in question (Gatchel et al., 2007). Stress and negative mood appear to lead to and result from chronic pain and disability in people with sickle-cell disease and recurrent low back pain, but happy moods seem to reduce their pain (Gil et al., 2004; Tang et al., 2008; Truchon et al., 2008). Pain is itself very stressful, and many people with chronic pain consider their discomfort—the actual pain and the physical limitations it produces—to be the most prominent stressor in their lives (Gatchel et al., 2007; Turner, Clancy, & Vitaliano, 1987). Health psychologists who work with pain patients often try to assess how well they cope with their pain. (Go to 🔳.)

Coping with Pain

Part of the stress that chronic pain patients experience stems from their common belief that they have little personal control over their pain, aside from avoiding activities they believe can trigger an attack or make it worse. As a result, they tend to deal with their stress by using emotion-focused coping strategies. That is, rather than trying to alter the problem itself, they try to regulate their emotional responses to it. Some of the more common coping methods adults and children with chronic pain use include hoping or praying the pain will get better someday and diverting their attention, such as by counting numbers or running a song through their heads (Gil, Wilson, & Edens, 1997; Keefe & Dolan, 1986). These approaches are not very effective in reducing chronic pain.

How effectively do people cope with pain? Studies that tested pain patients with the MMPI have found some fairly consistent outcomes (Cox, Chapman, & Black, 1978; Rappaport et al., 1987; Rosen et al., 1987). These outcomes lead to three conclusions. First, individuals who suffer from various types of chronic pain, such as severe headache and low back pain, often show a characteristic MMPI profile with extremely high scores on hypochondriasis, depression, and hysteria—the neurotic triad scales, as Figure 10-4 illustrates. But their scores on the seven other MMPI scales tend to be well within the normal range. Second, this pattern appears to hold regardless of whether their pain has a known organic source. In other words, people whose pain might be classified as psychogenic by a doctor tend to show similar problems of

CLINICAL METHODS AND ISSUES
Assessing Difficulty Coping with Pain

One way a psychologist can evaluate coping difficulties of pain patients is to assess their emotional adjustment with psychological tests, particularly the Minnesota Multiphasic Personality Inventory (MMPI). As we saw in Chapter 9, this test contains several scales, three of which are especially relevant for medical patients. These three scales assess: *hypochondriasis*, the tendency toward being preoccupied with physical symptoms and health; *depression*, feelings of unhappiness, pessimism, and hopelessness; and *hysteria*, the tendency to cope with problems by developing physical symptoms and using avoidance methods, such as denial. Because the MMPI is given and scored in a standardized manner and has been administered to large samples of

people, norms exist that allow psychologists to compare an individual's scores on the different scales with those of the general population. For instance, a score of 70 or above on any scale occurs in less than 5% of the population and is considered extreme and clinically significant (Anastasi, 1982). Psychologists generally refer to hypochondriasis, depression, and hysteria as the *neurotic triad* because clients with neurotic disorders often have high scores on these three scales. By combining information from psychological tests and other sources, such as interviews, psychologists can identify and help patients who are having difficulty coping with the stress of pain conditions.

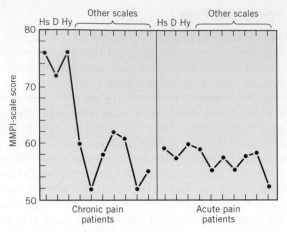

Figure 10-4 Illustration of MMPI profiles comparing chronic pain and acute pain patients: chronic pain patients typically show abnormally high scores (70 or above) on the "neurotic triad" scales (Hs = hypochondriasis, D = depression, Hy = hysteria), but not on the seven other MMPI scales. These data were averaged across mean scores presented in two studies. (Cox, Chapman, & Black, 1978; Rosen et al., 1987.)

adjustment on the MMPI as those whose pain has a clear organic basis. Third, individuals with acute pain, such as patients recovering from injuries, sometimes have moderately elevated scores on the neurotic triad scales, but these scores and those for the remaining MMPI scales are generally well within the normal range. These findings make sense and reflect the differential psychological impact of pain that patients expect will end soon versus pain they fear will never end. Keep in mind also that people with chronic-recurrent pain conditions show worse psychological symptoms during pain episodes than during pain-free periods (Holroyd et al., 1993).

It is clear that being in frequent, severe discomfort is related to having high scores on the MMPI neurotic triad scales, but does chronic pain cause maladjustment? Yes, it can: people whose pain has ended show substantial reductions in various measures of psychological disturbance (Melzack & Wall, 1982). Depression is especially common, and two factors are involved. One factor is the stress these people experience without being able to change their situations (Anderson et al., 1985; Turk & Holzman, 1986). They develop a sense of helplessness, which leads to depression. The other factor is that they may begin to *catastrophize*, or have frequent, magnified negative thoughts about their plight, which women do more than men (Edwards et al., 2004; Holtzman & DeLongis, 2007; Turk, 2001). Catastrophizing is associated with the patient's perception of poor spousal support (Cano et al., 2009). However, maladjustment can

also lead to pain: people who are depressed are somewhat more likely than others to develop a chronic pain condition in the future (Magni et al., 1994). Pain affects and is affected by maladjustment, but chronic pain is more likely to lead to maladjustment than the other way around.

Keep in mind that not all patients with severe chronic pain become maladjusted—many adapt to their conditions much better than others do (Klapow et al., 1993; Linton et al., 1994). Coping well with chronic pain is a struggle that unfolds over time, as this arthritis patient noted:

> Over time I've figured out that I can do things to bring on the pain and things that could limit it. I also figured out that my flares won't last forever, although while they're happening it seems like forever. It took quite a while to figure that out. (Tennen & Affleck, 1997, p. 274)

A characteristic of people who cope well with chronic pain is called *pain acceptance*, which involves being inclined to engage in activities despite the pain and disinclined to control or avoid the pain. People with high levels of pain acceptance pay less attention to their pain, have greater self-efficacy for performing daily tasks, function better, and use less pain medication than those with low pain acceptance (McCracken & Eccleston, 2005; Viane et al., 2004).

To summarize, the process by which people perceive pain involves a complex chain of physiological and neurochemical events that psychosocial processes can affect. Pain affects and can be influenced by people's learning, cognition, social experiences, and emotion. Although people can indicate through their behavior that they are feeling pain, the pain they perceive is actually a private and subjective experience. How can researchers and clinicians who work with pain patients assess the level and type of pain these individuals perceive? We turn now to answering this question.

ASSESSING PEOPLE'S PAIN

Researchers and clinicians have developed a variety of techniques for assessing people's pain. Although virtually all these methods can be applied both in research and in treating pain patients, some techniques are used more often in research, whereas others are used mostly to supplement a detailed medical history in clinical practice. In either setting, it's a good idea to use two or more different measurement techniques to enhance the accuracy of the assessment (Bradley, 1994). We'll organize our discussion by classifying ways to measure pain into three groups: self-report methods, behavioral assessment approaches, and psychophysiological measures.

SELF-REPORT METHODS

An obvious approach to measure people's pain is to ask them to describe the discomfort, either in their own words or by filling out a rating scale or questionnaire. In treating a patient's acute pain, health care workers ask where the pain is, what it feels like, how strong it is, and when it tends to occur. With chronic pain patients, medical and psychological professionals often incorporate this kind of questioning within the structure of a clinical interview.

Interview Methods in Assessing Pain

To treat chronic pain effectively, professionals need more information than a description of the pain. Interviews with the patient and key others, such as family members and coworkers, provide a rich source of background information in the early phases of treatment (Chapman, 1991; Karoly, 1985; Turk, Monarch, & Williams, 2004). These discussions ordinarily focus on such issues as:

- The history of the pain problem, including when it started, how it progressed, and what approaches have been used for controlling it.
- The patient's emotional adjustment, currently and before the pain syndrome began.
- The patient's lifestyle before the pain condition began: recreational interests, exercise patterns, diet, and so on.
- The pain syndrome's impact on the patient's current lifestyle, interpersonal relations, and work.
- The social context of pain episodes, such as happenings in the family before an attack and how family members respond when the pain occurs.
- Factors that seem to trigger attacks or make them worse.
- How the patient typically tries to cope with the pain.

The information obtained in these interviews can also be supplemented by having the patient and key others fill out questionnaires.

Pain Rating Scales and Diaries

A direct, simple, and commonly used way to assess pain is to have individuals rate some aspect of their discomfort on a scale (Jensen & Karoly, 2001; Mann & Carr, 2006). This approach is used very often to measure how strong the pain is, and three different types of scales for rating pain intensity are illustrated in Figure 10-5. One type is

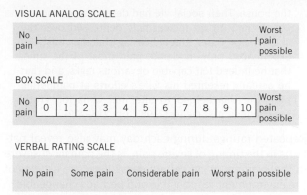

Figure 10-5 Illustrations of the visual analog, box, and verbal rating scales. Example instructions are as follows: *visual analog scale*—"Mark a point on the line to show how strong your pain is"; *box scale*—"Rate the level of your pain by circling one number on the scale, where 0 means 'no pain' and 10 means 'worst pain possible'"; *verbal rating scale*—"Circle the one phrase that best describes your pain." The labels and number of choices on a scale can be different from those shown here.

the *visual analog scale*, which has people rate their pain by marking a point on a line that has labels only at each end. This type of scale is very easy for people to use and can be used with children as young as 5 years of age (Karoly, 1985). The *box scale* has individuals choose one number from a series of numbers that represent levels of pain within a specified range. The *verbal rating scale* has people describe their pain by choosing a word or phrase from several that are given.

Because rating scales are so easy and quick to use, people can rate their pain frequently. Averaging these ratings across time gives a more accurate picture of the pain the person generally experiences than individual ratings do (Jensen & McFarland, 1993). Repeated ratings can also reveal pain changes over time, such as during everyday activities or during the course of an experiment. Patients could rate their pain each waking hour of each day for, say, 2 weeks, also indicating whenever they take pain medication. Before starting this procedure, they would learn what to say if someone sees them doing the rating, ways to remind themselves to do each hourly rating, and what to do if they forget (Turk, Meichenbaum, & Genest, 1983). One use of repeated ratings is in showing the ebbs and flows of pain intensity that patients often experience. For instance, one patient's wife

believed that her husband was experiencing incapacitating and severe pain every waking hour of his life. This belief contributed to her preventing him from participating in any but the simplest chores around the house. Their social life had deteriorated, and the couple had grown increasingly depressed over the course of 4 years. Upon hearing that her husband experienced only moderate pain most of the time, that he indeed felt capable of various tasks, and that he actually resented his wife's efforts at pampering him, she was helped to alter her behavior. (Turk, Meichenbaum, & Genest, 1983, pp. 218–219)

Repeated ratings during each day may also reveal patterns in the timing of severe pain. Is the pain most severe in the evening, or on certain days? If so, are aspects of the environment responsible and perhaps changeable?

Pain ratings can also be used in a *pain diary*, which is a detailed record of a person's pain experiences. As Figure 10-6 illustrates, the pain diary a patient keeps would include pain ratings and information about the time and circumstances of pain episodes, any medications taken, and comments about each episode. (Go to 🍎.)

Pain Questionnaires

Pain is only partly described by the intensity of the discomfort people feel—the experience of pain has many qualities and dimensions. Melzack began to recognize the multidimensional nature of pain through his interactions with pain patients. He described in an interview how this realization emerged from talks he had with a woman who suffered from phantom limb pain. She

would describe burning pains that were like a red-hot poker being shoved through her toes and her

ankle. She would cry out from the pain in her legs. Of course, there were no legs. Well, that made me realize the utter subjectivity of pain—no objective physical measure is very likely to capture that…. I began to write down the words she used to describe her pain. I realized that the words describing the *emotional-motivational* component of her pain—"exhausting, sickening, terrifying, punishing"—were very different from those for the *sensory* component—"shooting, scalding, splitting, cramping." Later I came to see there was also an *evaluative* component, such as "it's unbearable" or "it's annoying." I wrote down the words other patients used, too, but I didn't know what to do with them. (Warga, 1987, p. 53; italics added)

Melzack determined that pain involves three broad dimensions—*affective* (emotional-motivational), *sensory*, and *evaluative*—by conducting a study in which subjects sorted over 100 pain-related words into separate groups of their own making (Melzack & Torgerson, 1971).

Melzack's research also indicated that each of the three dimensions consisted of subclasses. For instance, the sensory dimension included a subclass with the words "hot," "burning," "scalding," and "searing"—words relating to temperature. Notice that these four words connote increasingly hot temperatures, with searing being the hottest. Similarly, the affective dimension included a subclass of three words relating to fear: "fearful," "frightful," "terrifying." Then, by determining the degree of pain reflected by each word, Melzack (1975)—a professor at McGill University—was able to construct an instrument to measure pain. This test is called the

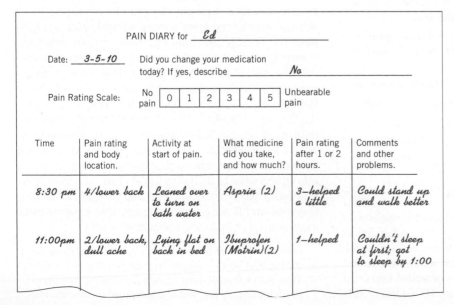

Time	Pain rating and body location.	Activity at start of pain.	What medicine did you take, and how much?	Pain rating after 1 or 2 hours.	Comments and other problems.
8:30 pm	4/lower back	Leaned over to turn on bath water	Asprin (2)	3—helped a little	Could stand up and walk better
11:00pm	2/lower back, dull ache	Lying flat on back in bed	Ibuprofen (Motrin)(2)	1—helped	Couldn't sleep at first; got to sleep by 1:00

PAIN DIARY for *Ed*

Date: *3-5-10*   Did you change your medication today? If yes, describe *No*

Pain Rating Scale: No pain | 0 | 1 | 2 | 3 | 4 | 5 | Unbearable pain

Figure 10-6 A pain diary. The chronic pain patient keeps a daily record of important information about pain episodes.

ASSESS YOURSELF

Describing Your Pain

Use the questionnaire in Figure 10-7 to assess an acute or chronic pain you have experienced. Try to choose a painful condition that you currently have, had recently, or remember vividly from the past. If the pain you assess is not current, answer the questions as if it is. Do this now.

Ronald Melzack (1975) developed this questionnaire and described its scoring system, which is too complex to do here. You can get a sense of the pain you assessed in two ways: (1) Review the answers you chose—for instance, questions 2 and 3 of Part 4 tell you its range of intensity. (2) Refer to your answers as you read the description of the McGill Pain Questionnaire in the text.

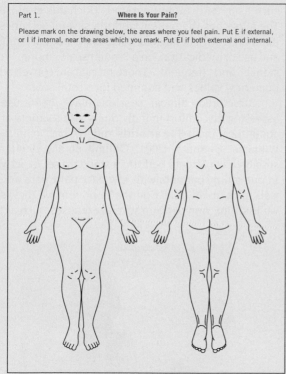

Part 1.   Where Is Your Pain?

Please mark on the drawing below, the areas where you feel pain. Put E if external, or I if internal, near the areas which you mark. Put EI if both external and internal.

Part 2.   What Does Your Pain Feel Like?

Some of the words below describe your present pain. Circle ONLY those words that best describe it. Leave out any category that is not suitable. Use only a single word in each appropriate category—the one that applies best.

1	2	3	4
Flickering Quivering Pulsing Throbbing Beating Pounding	Jumping Flashing Shooting	Pricking Boring Drilling Stabbing Lancinating	Sharp Cutting Lacerating

5	6	7	8
Pinching Pressing Gnawing Cramping Crushing	Tugging Pulling Wrenching	Hot Burning Scalding Searing	Tingling Itchy Smarting Stinging

9	10	11	12
Dull Sore Hurting Aching Heavy	Tender Taut Rasping Splitting	Tiring Exhausting	Sickening Suffocating

13	14	15	16
Fearful Frightful Terrifying	Punishing Grueling Cruel Vicious Killing	Wretched Blinding	Annoying Troublesome Miserable Intense Unbearable

17	18	19	20
Spreading Radiating Penetrating Piercing	Tight Numb Drawing Squeezing Tearing	Cool Cold Freezing	Nagging Nauseating Agonizing Dreadful Torturing

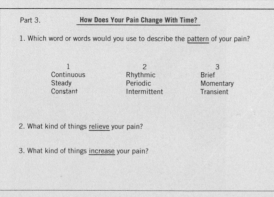

Part 3.   How Does Your Pain Change With Time?

1. Which word or words would you use to describe the pattern of your pain?

1	2	3
Continuous Steady Constant	Rhythmic Periodic Intermittent	Brief Momentary Transient

2. What kind of things relieve your pain?

3. What kind of things increase your pain?

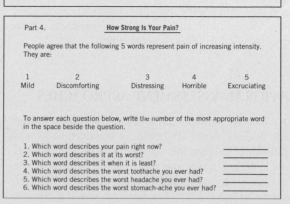

Part 4.   How Strong Is Your Pain?

People agree that the following 5 words represent pain of increasing intensity. They are:

1	2	3	4	5
Mild	Discomforting	Distressing	Horrible	Excruciating

To answer each question below, write the number of the most appropriate word in the space beside the question.

1. Which word describes your pain right now?
2. Which word describes it at its worst?
3. Which word describes it when it is least?
4. Which word describes the worst toothache you ever had?
5. Which word describes the worst headache you ever had?
6. Which word describes the worst stomach-ache you ever had?

Figure 10-7   The McGill Pain Questionnaire. (Melzack, 1975.)

McGill Pain Questionnaire (MPQ), which you filled out in the Assess Yourself exercise.

Part 2 of the MPQ presents a list of descriptive words, separated into a total of 20 subclasses. The test instructs the person to select from each subclass the best word to describe his or her pain. Each word in each class has an assigned value based on the degree of pain it reflects. Let's look, for instance, at subclass 7, which ranges from "hot" to "searing." Selecting "searing" would contribute the highest number of points from this subclass to the person's pain score ("hot" would contribute the lowest number). The sum of these points across the 20 subclasses is called the *pain rating index.* Part 4 of the MPQ contains a series of verbal rating scales; the one that rates "your pain right now" yields a separate score called the *present pain intensity.*

The MPQ appears to have many strengths as an instrument for assessing chronic pain, both for research and for clinical purposes (Melzack & Katz, 2001). For one thing, research has confirmed that the experience of pain is multidimensional. Also, individuals with similar pain syndromes tend to choose the same patterns of words to describe their pain. But people suffering from very different types of pain—for example, toothache, arthritis, cancer, and phantom limb pain—choose different patterns of words in the MPQ to describe their different pain experiences. The main limitation of the MPQ is that it requires a fairly strong English vocabulary (Chapman et al., 1985; Karoly, 1985). For instance, it includes a few words, such as "taut" and "lancinating," that many people may not know. Moreover, sometimes respondents must make very fine distinctions between words, as with "throbbing," "beating," and "pounding." Even if an interviewer is present to define the words, the MPQ may be of limited use with people who have poor English skills and with children under about 12 years of age.

The MPQ is the best-known and most widely used pain questionnaire, but others are available. One of these, the *Multidimensional Pain Inventory,* accurately assesses people's pain and its psychosocial effects (Jacob & Kerns, 2001; Kerns, Turk, & Rudy, 1985).

BEHAVIORAL ASSESSMENT APPROACHES

Because people tend to exhibit pain behaviors when they are in discomfort, it should be possible to assess their pain by observing their behavior. A person is likely to show different types and patterns of behavior if the pain is intense as compared to moderate, if it involves a headache as opposed to low back pain, and if chronic pain is recurrent than if it is intractable. Psychologists have developed procedures for assessing pain behavior

in two types of situations: in *everyday activities* and in *structured clinical sessions.*

Assessing Pain Behavior in Structured Clinical Sessions

Procedures are available whereby health care workers can assess the pain behavior of patients in structured sessions that are usually conducted in hospital settings. They are structured by the specific pain behaviors to be assessed and the tasks the patient is asked to perform. One approach of this kind has been developed into a pain assessment instrument—the UAB *Pain Behavior Scale*—for use by nurses during their standard routines, such as in early morning rounds (Richards et al., 1982). The nurse has the patient perform several activities and rates each of 10 behaviors, such as the patient's mobility and use of medication, on a 3-point scale: "none," "occasional," and "frequent." These ratings are converted into numerical values and summed for a total score.

Structured clinical sessions have been used in assessing discomfort in individuals with a variety of pain conditions, including arthritis and low back pain (Keefe, Williams, & Smith, 2001; Öhlund et al., 1994). Each session has patients perform a standard set of activities. In one study, patients with low back pain were asked to walk, pick up an object on the floor, remove their shoes while sitting, and perform several exercises, such as trunk

This woman's pain behavior can be used in assessing her discomfort.

rotations, toe touching, and sit-ups (Kleinke & Spangler, 1988). The patients were videotaped, and trained assessors rated their performance for several pain behaviors, such as guarded movement, rubbing the pain area, grimacing, and sighing. Pain behaviors can be assessed in this manner easily and reliably, and these assessments correlate well with patients' self-ratings of pain.

Assessing Pain Behavior in Everyday Activities

How does the pain patient behave in everyday activities, especially at home? Does the person spend much time in bed, complain of discomfort a lot, seek help frequently in moving, or walk with a limp most of the time? How much of these behaviors does the person exhibit? Behavioral assessments of everyday activities like these can be made.

Family members or key others in the patient's life are usually the best people to make these everyday assessments of pain behavior. These people must, of course, be willing to help and be trained to make careful observations and keep accurate records. Researcher Wilbert Fordyce (1976) designed a procedure whereby the assessor—say, the client's spouse—compiles a list of five to ten behaviors that generally signal when the patient is in pain. Then the spouse is trained to watch for these behaviors, to keep track of the amount of time the patient exhibits them, and to monitor how people, including the assessor, react to the client's pain behavior. This procedure is useful not only in assessing the patient's pain experiences but in determining their impact on his or her life and the social context that may maintain pain behaviors. As a supplement to this procedure, the assessor can keep a pain diary about the patient's severe pain episodes, recording the date and time, as well as where the episode occurred, such as in the car or at home in bed (Turk, Meichenbaum, & Genest, 1983). The assessor can also describe what he or she:

- Noticed as behaviors that suggested the patient was in pain.
- Thought and felt during the episode.
- Did in order to help, along with a rating of the action's effectiveness, ranging on a scale from "did not help at all" to "seemed to stop the pain completely."

These supplemental procedures provide additional data that can be of value in dealing with interpersonal issues that influence the pain experience.

PSYCHOPHYSIOLOGICAL MEASURES

Another approach for assessing pain involves taking measurements of physiological activity, since pain has both sensory and emotional components that can produce changes in bodily functions. *Psychophysiology* is the study of mental or emotional processes as reflected by changes they produce in physiological activity (Lykken, 2004).

One psychophysiological measure researchers have used for assessing pain uses an apparatus called an *electromyograph* (EMG) to measure the electrical activity in muscles, which reflects their tension. Because *muscle tension* is associated with various pain states, such as headaches and low back pain, we might expect EMG recordings of tension in affected muscles when physically or psychologically stressed to be greater for pain patients than pain-free controls, and they are (Flor, 2001). But when the muscles are inactive, no consistent difference is found. Does EMG level reflect pain intensity? Yes, but only when assessments are taken over an extended period of time (Flor, 2001). When EMG and pain levels are measured for a brief period, the correlation between the two is not reliable.

Researchers have also attempted to assess people's pain with measures of *autonomic activity*, such as of heart rate and skin conductance, but these measures do not seem to be very useful (Chapman et al., 1985; Flor, 2001). This is because changes in autonomic activity are more strongly related to people's ratings of pain than to the strength of the pain stimulus, are inconsistently associated with chronic pain, and readily occur in the absence of the sensation of pain, such as when people feel stressed. As a result, interpreting variations in autonomic activity as reflecting pain is often difficult.

The last psychophysiological measure of pain we will consider involves the electrical activity of the brain, as measured by an *electroencephalograph* (EEG). When a person's sensory system detects a stimulus, such as a clicking sound from earphones, the signal to the brain produces a change in EEG voltage. Electrical changes produced by stimuli are called *evoked potentials* and show up in EEG recordings as sharp surges or peaks in the graph. Pain stimuli produce evoked potentials that vary in magnitude—the amplitudes of the surges increase with the intensity of the stimuli, decrease when subjects take analgesics, and correlate with people's subjective reports of pain (Chapman et al., 1985; Flor, 2001).

Even though psychophysiological measures provide objective assessments of bodily changes that occur in response to pain, these changes may also be affected by other factors, such as attention, diet, and stress. In clinical situations, measures of muscle tension, autonomic activity, and evoked potential are probably best used as supplements to self-report and behavioral assessment approaches (Chapman et al., 1985).

PAIN IN CHILDREN

We have focused in this chapter mainly on the experience of pain by adults, but children experience almost all of the types of discomfort and pain syndromes that adults have (Gibson & Chambers, 2004; McGrath & Hillier, 1996). And many children suffer from an arthritislike condition in their arms and legs that is called *widespread pain* or "growing pains" (AMA, 2003; Mikkelsson et al., 2008). The prevalence of widespread pain appears to increase from childhood to adolescence, but children typically outgrow the condition.

Although less is known about the pain people experience in childhood than at other times in their lives, much research since the early 1980s has focused on children's pain (Jeans, 1983; McGrath & Hillier, 1996). Before then, some practitioners believed that babies feel relatively little pain because their nervous systems are immaturely developed and their reactions to pain often differ from those of older individuals. As a result, minor surgery, such as circumcision, was commonly done on infants with little or no anesthesia. But this situation changed rapidly as a result of new research. Let's see what is known today about pain in children.

PAIN AND CHILDREN'S SENSORY AND COGNITIVE DEVELOPMENT

Although the issue of whether babies are as sensitive as adults to pain is not yet resolved, one thing is clear: newborn babies feel pain. The fact that they typically cry when slapped on the rump if they do not start to breathe after birth certainly suggests that they feel pain. Is clearer evidence available?

Better evidence that babies perceive pain comes from studies with newborns as they underwent medical procedures, such as when the foot is pierced to draw a blood sample. One of these studies found that babies' reactions to the noxious stimulus included a "pain" facial expression: they had their eyes squeezed, brows contracted, tongue taut, and mouth open (Grunau & Craig, 1987). This pattern is comparable to the expression adults display when in pain. Another study found that newborns' crying varied with the intensity of the noxious procedure (Porter, Miller, & Marshall, 1986). Highly noxious procedures elicited cries with certain characteristics, such as relatively high-pitched peak tones, that adults judged as indicating "urgency."

One difficulty young children have in expressing their experience of pain is that their language abilities are very limited. Toddlers may know the words "hurt," "ouch," and "ow," but they do not usually have many other words to describe their pain (McGrath & Hillier, 1996; Stanford, Chambers, & Craig, 2005). Instead of telling adults of their pain, they may display other pain behaviors, such as crying, rubbing the affected area, or clenching their jaws. By 13 years of age, children use about 26 words to describe their pain (Jeans, 1983).

ASSESSING PAIN IN CHILDREN

When a patient has symptoms that include pain, the doctor usually needs to know its location, intensity, quality, duration, and temporal patterning. This

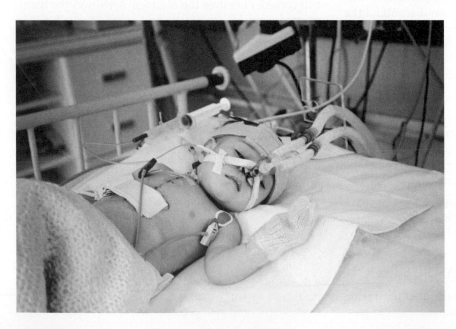

Very young children in acute pain do not have sufficient language to express what they are feeling and need special efforts to reduce their distress.

information helps in making an accurate diagnosis. Although children's ability to provide this information is limited, especially if they are young, researchers have developed age-specific measures that use self-report, behavioral, and physiological methods (Gibson & Chambers, 2004; Mann & Carr, 2006). Interviewing children requires skill in developing rapport with them, asking the right questions in ways they can understand, and knowing what their answers mean.

What kinds of self-report methods are available to assess children's pain? One approach uses rating scales to describe the intensity of their pain (McGrath & Gillespie, 2001). With children under about 5 years of age, pain assessments are usually made on the basis of pain behavior, such as vocalizations and facial expressions. Older children can understand and use visual analog scales and verbal rating scales if the choices are labeled in ways they can understand, such as with faces indicating graded degrees of distress. Other approaches are designed to measure multiple dimensions of child and adolescent pain experiences, two of which are the Pediatric Pain Questionnaire (Varni & Thompson, 1986) and the Children's Comprehensive

Pain Questionnaire (McGrath & Hillier, 1996). These instruments assess the pain itself and its psychosocial effects, such as how the child and family reacted to the pain. Adults may help the children fill out portions of the questionnaires when they lack needed language skills.

Behavioral and physiological assessment approaches also provide valuable ways to measure children's pain, especially in early childhood (Gibson & Chambers, 2004; McGrath & Gillespie, 2001). The most obvious behavioral approach simply involves having the child or parents report the child's pain behaviors in pain diaries. Other behavioral assessments can use structured clinical sessions in which health care workers rate or record the occurrence of pain behavior. Methods for physiological assessment are like those we considered earlier.

Children's pain experiences are affected by a variety of psychosocial factors, particularly the social environment in which pain occurs (Gibson & Chambers, 2004). But little is known about the personality and family characteristics of children that may contribute to the intensity and frequency of their pain.

SUMMARY

Although pain is typically unpleasant, it is a critical sense for survival because it warns us of actual or threatened tissue damage. It is the most frequent medical complaint and the most commonly stated reason for disability. Pain includes both sensory and emotional components, and it has many different qualities. It can feel sharp and localized or dull and pervasive; sometimes it has a burning sensation, and other times it has a cramping or aching feeling.

Pain experiences also vary from those that are mostly organic in origin to those that are mostly psychogenic. Virtually all pain experiences involve both physiological and psychological processes. Acute pain may last just a moment or as long as a few months and eventually disappears; chronic pain conditions last longer and can be classified as chronic-recurrent, chronic-intractable-benign, and chronic-progressive pain.

The body's tissues contain chemical substances that are released at the site where an injury occurs, thereby activating afferent nociceptors, which are free nerve endings. Pain signals are carried toward the central nervous system by A-delta fibers, which carry signals of sharp and well-localized pain rapidly to motor and sensory areas of the cortex, and C fibers, which carry information about dull and diffuse pain to the forebrain.

The process of pain perception involves three curious phenomena. The first is called referred pain, whereby pain

originating from internal organs is perceived as coming from other parts of the body. Second, pain can occur with no detectable physical basis: neuralgia, causalgia, and phantom limb pain are syndromes that involve intense pain even though no noxious stimulus is present. Third, people's experience of pain depends on its meaning: individuals for whom pain means a personal disaster is almost over and better things are coming seem to perceive less pain than do people with similar wounds who believe the personal disaster is just beginning.

The gate-control theory of pain proposes that neural signals of pain pass through a gate that can modulate the signals before they reach the brain. The degree to which the gate is open or closed depends on three factors: the amount of activity in the pain fibers, the amount of activity in other peripheral fibers, and messages that descend from the brain. This theory allows for the influence of psychological factors in pain perception. The phenomenon of stimulation-produced analgesia supports this theory, demonstrating that stimulation to the periaqueductal gray area of the brainstem can block the sensation of noxious stimulation elsewhere in the body. The findings of research with a drug called naloxone indicate that this phenomenon depends on the action of endogenous opioids—a class of neurochemicals that includes endorphin and enkephalin. The effect of placebos in reducing pain also depends on opioids.

Psychological processes play an important role in the experience of pain. People in pain generally display pain behaviors, such as moaning or guarded movement, which are often reinforced—for instance, when they result in the person being relieved of doing disliked activities or receiving special attention. Pain and stress are intimately linked: pain is stressful, and stress can produce pain—at least headache pain. People often have difficult times coping with chronic pain, which can lead to psychological maladjustment.

A person's pain can be measured in several ways. Self-report methods include interviews, rating scales, and pain questionnaires. The McGill Pain Questionnaire assesses three dimensions of pain: affective, sensory, and evaluative. Behavioral assessment approaches can measure pain in the person's everyday activities and in structured clinical sessions. Psychophysiological measures of pain assess muscle tension, autonomic activity, and evoked potentials of the brain. Children can perceive pain when they are born. Methods to assess pain and its psychosocial effects in children have been developed.

KEY TERMS

pain	chronic-progressive pain	periaqueductal gray	pain behaviors
acute pain	nociceptors	stimulation-produced	McGill Pain Questionnaire
chronic-recurrent pain	referred pain	analgesia	
chronic-intractable-benign pain	gate-control theory	endogenous opioids	

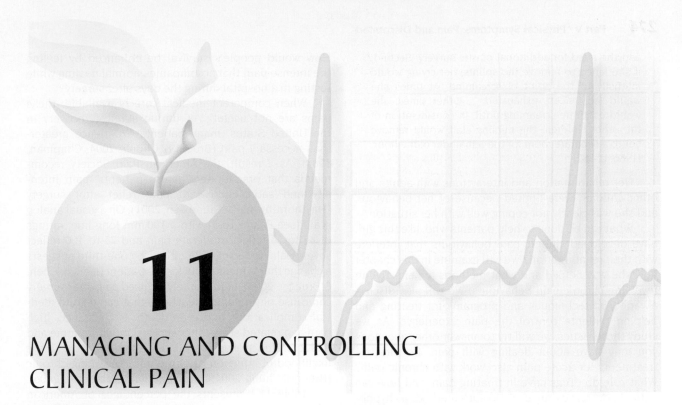

11

MANAGING AND CONTROLLING CLINICAL PAIN

Clinical Pain
Acute Clinical Pain
Chronic Clinical Pain

Medical Treatments for Pain
Surgical Methods for Treating Pain
Chemical Methods for Treating Pain

Behavioral and Cognitive Methods for Treating Pain
The Operant Approach
Fear Reduction, Relaxation, and Biofeedback
Cognitive Methods

Hypnosis and Interpersonal Therapy
Hypnosis as a Treatment for Pain
Interpersonal Therapy for Pain

Physical and Stimulation Therapies for Pain
Stimulation Therapies
Physical Therapy

Pain Clinics
Multidisciplinary Programs
Evaluating the Success
  of Pain Clinics

PROLOGUE

"Ouch! My foot hurts," the little girl cried as she tried to walk. The nurse responded quickly, saying, "I'm sorry it hurts. Show me where it hurts…. Let's get some exercise some other time." This 3-year-old girl was a patient who had had a difficult life. She was in her tenth month of hospitalisation after receiving second- and third-degree burns to her legs and buttocks from having been immersed in scaldingly hot water. Some evidence indicated that the burn had been deliberately inflicted, and that she was a victim of child abuse.

After all these months this little girl's discomfort was not over. She still needed physical therapy and plastic surgery and still had to wear uncomfortable knee-extension splints to prevent contractures. But her therapy was not going well, and the hospital staff was inadvertently reinforcing her pain behaviour by comforting her and allowing her to avoid disliked activities. James Varni and Karen Thompson have described how this situation was not in the child's long-term best interests, having disrupted her physical, social, and emotional rehabilitation:

> Physical therapy was essentially terminated because of the patient's interfering pain behaviours. Two patterns emerged when the patient was placed in her bedroom in the crib with knee extension splints on. First, the child would struggle until she had removed the splints, resulting in further contractures

273

and the need for additional plastic surgery. Second, if she failed to remove the splints, her crying would intensify to the point of screaming. At times she would fall asleep, exhausted…. Other times, she would continue screaming until, in consideration of the other children, the nursing staff would remove her to a separate room for the remainder of the hour. (1986, p. 382)

Her rehabilitation and interactions with adults and other children were limited because of her behaviour, and she was clearly not coping well with her situation.

What can be done to help patients who, like this girl, have developed chronic pain behaviours that interfere with their rehabilitation? We will examine in this chapter how she was helped and what methods are effective in reversing chronic pain behaviours. We will also discuss a variety of techniques and programs for treating and helping patients control the pain experience. As we study these issues, we will try to answer other questions you may have about dealing with pain. Do effective treatments for acute pain also work with chronic pain? What role do drugs have in treating pain, and how can patients decrease drug use? Do such methods as hypnosis and acupuncture really work in reducing pain? What are pain clinics, and are they effective in treating pain?

CLINICAL PAIN

Not all of our pain experiences receive professional treatment, and not all of them require it. The term **clinical pain** refers to any pain that receives or requires professional care. The pain may be either acute or chronic and may result from known or unknown causes (Sanders, 1985). Clinical pain calls for treatment in and of itself, and not only because it may be a symptom of a progressive disease, such as arthritis or cancer. Relieving pain is important for humanitarian reasons, of course—and doing so also produces medical and psychosocial benefits for the patient. Let's look at medical and psychosocial issues that are associated with controlling clinical pain, beginning with acute pain.

ACUTE CLINICAL PAIN

By preventing or relieving acute pain, practitioners make medical procedures go more smoothly, reduce patients' stress and anxiety, and help them recover more quickly. Much of the acute pain people experience in today's world has little survival value (Chapman, 1984). What survival value would there be in feeling the pain as a dentist drills a tooth or a surgeon removes an appendix?

How would people's survival be enhanced by feeling the intense pain that accompanies normal healing while resting in a hospital during the days after surgery?

When competent medical care is available, these pains are not useful. Yet during surgical recovery in the United States, many patients experience greater-than-necessary pain (Bruehl & Chung, 2004; Chapman, 1984). As a result, the American Pain Society recommends that practitioners assess patients' pain intensity and satisfaction with pain relief after surgery (Haythornthwaite & Fauerbach, 2001). On a visual analog scale (see Figure 10-5) with a 100 mm long line, ratings of 45 to 74 reflect moderate pain and 75 to 100 reflect severe pain; reducing pain ratings by one-third suggests a change that is meaningful for the patient (Jensen, Chen, & Brugger, 2003). Inadequately reduced pain after surgery can cause physiological reactions that can lead to medical complications and even death. For instance, high pain and related stress after surgery impair immune and endocrine function, slow wound healing, and increase the likelihood of infection or of the pain becoming chronic (Bruehl & Chung, 2004; Chapman, 1984; Glaser et al., 2006).

Table 11.1 presents the percentages of American adults at different ages with pain conditions of different durations and body locations. Notice that the prevalence of acute pain lasting less than a month is greatest for the youngest age group, chronic pain lasting more than a year is greatest for the oldest group, and joint pain increases and headache decreases with age. The ratings of joint pain intensity were in the severe range for 27% of the people. Also, keep in mind that some of the pain conditions in the shorter durations were on the way to becoming chronic. Acute pain conditions are at risk of transitioning to chronic pain if the individuals have experienced many traumatic life events and have high levels of depression and early beliefs that the condition may be permanent (Casey et al., 2008).

CHRONIC CLINICAL PAIN

When pain persists and becomes chronic, patients begin to perceive its nature differently. Although in the acute phase the pain was very aversive, they expected it to end and did not see it as a permanent part of their lives. As the pain persists, they tend to become discouraged and angry. Some seek care from other doctors, which can be constructive. But when this is not successful, and as patients come to see less and less likelihood that medical care will effectively treat their disorder, increasing hopelessness and despair may lead them to consult quacks (Chapman, 1984).

The transition from acute to chronic pain is a critical time when many of these people become increasingly

Table 11.1   *Percentages of American Adults with Pain Lasting More than 24 Hours, Separated by Age, Pain Duration, and Pain Location*

Age in years	Duration of pain				Location of pain[a,b]			
	Less than 1 month	1 to 3 months	3 to 12 months	Over 1 year	Low back	Severe headache	Neck	Joint
18/20 to 44	39.1	11.9	12.5	36.5	23.9	18.4	12.4	20.5
45 to 64	27.2	13.6	15.5	43.7	30.8	15.0	18.7	39.9
65 and over	18.9	10.4	13.4	57.3	30.4	6.2	14.4	49.9

[a]For low back, headache, and neck pain, the survey instructed respondents to report on pain that lasted a whole day and were not minor. The questions were: "During the past 3 months, did you have neck pain? Or low back pain? Or severe headache or migraine?"
[b]For joint pain, the survey asked, "During the past 30 days, have you had any symptoms of pain, aching, or stiffness in or around a joint?" and had the respondents rate the pain on a 0 to 10 scale, where 10 was labeled "as bad as it can be."
Source: NCHS, 2006, data tables for Figures 29, 30, and 32.

disabled, especially if they experience a loss of self-efficacy for performing activities and a fear that certain behaviors will cause painful episodes or worsen their condition (Boersma & Linton, 2005; Denison, Åsenlöf, & Lindberg, 2004). As this happens, they may develop feelings of helplessness and psychological disorders, such as depression, especially if the disability advances (Epping-Jordan et al., 1998; Gatchel, 1996). The neurotic triad—hypochondriasis, depression, and hysteria—often becomes a dominant aspect of their personalities (Gatchel, 1996; Rosen et al., 1987).

These changes typically parallel alterations in the patients' lifestyles, employment status, and family lives —as the following letter from a wife to her husband's therapist reflects:

perhaps if I could explain my husband's attitudes it might help you understand his problems.... The questionnaire you gave him to complete and send back became a tremendous ordeal for him. Why, I'll never know, because the questions were simple, but in the state of mind he is in, everything gets to be a chore.... Since his back operation five years ago he has become increasingly impatient and progressively slower with no ambition at all to even try to help himself. He had made himself an invalid and it has become very difficult for me or my family to tolerate his constant complaining. He blames me, blames our two sons, who he says don't help him around the house when in fact he does little or nothing to help himself. He does exactly the same things day after day with projects he starts and never completes and always because of his health .... To dwell on his illness is what he wants and only that he will do, believe me. He needs psychiatry of some kind. (Flor & Turk, 1985, p. 268)

A study of people who had suffered for years with severe chronic-recurrent and chronic-intractable-benign pain

found that about half had considered suicide because of their conditions (Hitchcock, Ferrell, & McCaffery, 1994). Chronic pain often creates an array of long-term psychosocial problems and impaired interrelationships, which distinguish its victims from those of acute pain (Weir et al., 1994). In addition to these personality and lifestyle alterations, chronic pain patients often use drugs excessively and experience frequent sleep disturbance (Sanders, 1985; Schofield, 2005).

Because of the differences between acute pain and chronic pain in their duration and the effects they have on their victims, these conditions usually require different treatment methods. Health care professionals need to distinguish between acute and chronic pain conditions and provide the most appropriate pain relief techniques for the patient's needs (Gatchel, 1996). Failing to do so can make the condition worse. Keeping this caution in mind, we'll turn our attention for the remainder of this chapter to the many medical, psychological, and physical techniques available to help control patients' pain.

MEDICAL TREATMENTS FOR PAIN

A few centuries ago, peasants in Western cultures commonly treated pain by piercing the affected area of the body with a "vigorous" twig of a tree, believing that the twig would absorb the pain from the body (Turk, Meichenbaum, & Genest, 1983). Then, to prevent anyone from getting the pain from that twig, they buried it deep in the ground. Other early practices for controlling pain were not so farfetched, but they were crudely applied, even by doctors. In 19th century America, alcoholic beverages and "medicines" laced with opium were readily available (Critchlow, 1986; Kett, 1977). Many people used these substances to alleviate pain, and doctors commonly employed them as anesthetics for surgery before ether was introduced. Many people today still use alcohol

Readily available elixirs in 19th-century America often contained such substances as opium and cocaine.
Collection of the New-York Historical Society (negative #5707).

to manage pain, especially if they were already heavy drinkers before the pain condition began (Brennan, Schutte, & Moos, 2005). But doctors now try to reduce pain in two ways—chemically and surgically.

SURGICAL METHODS FOR TREATING PAIN

Treating clinical pain with surgical methods is a relatively radical approach and is likely to be more effective for acute pain than chronic pain (Turk & Winters, 2006). In some methods, the surgery removes or disconnects portions of the peripheral nervous system or the spinal cord, thereby preventing pain signals from reaching the brain (Hare & Milano, 1985; Melzack & Wall, 1982). Because these extreme procedures seldom provide long-term relief and often have side effects, such as producing numbness or paralysis in the affected region of the body, they are rarely used today.

Other surgical procedures for relieving pain do not remove or disconnect nerve fibers and are much more successful. One example is the *synovectomy*, a technique whereby a surgeon removes membranes that become inflamed in arthritic joints (AMA, 2003; Anderson et al., 1985). Another example is *spinal fusion*, a procedure that joins two or more adjacent vertebrae to treat severe back pain (AMA, 2003). Surgery is often used in the United States to treat back pain, but there is little evidence that it produces better long-term pain reduction than nonsurgical methods, and it is used at a far lower rate in other developed countries, such as Denmark and England (Cherkin et al., 1994; Turk, 2002). Surgery for chronic skeletal pain conditions is most appropriate when the person is severely disabled and nonsurgical treatment

methods have failed. Doctors and patients usually prefer other medical approaches, such as chemical methods.

CHEMICAL METHODS FOR TREATING PAIN

Although medical research has led to many advances in treating pain since the 1800s, this progress has been slow. The field of medicine has focused much more on developing methods for curing disease than on reducing pain (Melzack & Wall, 1982). Let's look at the use of chemical methods for treating acute and chronic pain. (Go to 💡.)

Using Chemicals for Acute Pain

Many pharmaceuticals are very effective for relieving acute pain, such as after surgery. Doctors choose the specific drug and dosage by considering many factors, such as how intense the pain is and its location and cause. Their effective use of these chemicals, giving as much pain relief as they safely can, depends on characteristics of the drug, the patients, and sociocultural factors. In some countries, such as in Latin America, using narcotics for pain relief is extremely rare (DePalma, 1996). Other cultures have become much more accepting of narcotic pain control.

Many hospital patients in pain are *undermedicated*, and those who receive too little pain relief tend to be children and minority group members, even when compared against other patients with the same medical condition (Hadjistavropoulos, 2004; Ng et al., 1996). Practitioners may administer a painkiller less frequently, use a dosage below the recommended level, and discontinue it earlier, especially if the drug is a narcotic. The reasons for these age and sociocultural differences are unclear. In the case of children, it may be that practitioners believe children feel less pain than adults or are more likely to become addicted to a drug (Bush, Holmbeck, & Cockrell, 1989). Or children may simply request less medication, perhaps because they dislike injections or taking pills more than adults do. Similar reasons may explain the ethnic differences.

The conventional ways for administering painkilling chemicals involve giving injections or pills, and these are given under one of two arrangements: a prescribed schedule or "as needed" (called PRN for the Latin *pro re nata*) by the patient. But two other methods are available today (AMA, 2003; Mann & Carr, 2006). In one of these methods—called an *epidural block*—practitioners inject narcotics or local anesthetics epidurally, that is, near the membrane that surrounds the spinal cord. These chemicals then prevent pain signals from being

HIGHLIGHT

Types of Pain–Relieving Chemicals

The most common medical approaches for treating pain today involve the use of various chemicals, some of which are used mainly in hospitals. Four types of chemicals are commonly used in treating pain (Mann & Carr, 2006; Winters, 1985).

1. *Peripherally active analgesics* make up one class of pain-relieving chemical. As the name implies, these drugs reduce pain by their action in the peripheral nervous system, such as by inhibiting the synthesis of neurochemicals that sensitize nociceptors to algogenic substances released at the site of tissue damage. These analgesics include *acetaminophen* or *paracetamol* (brand names Tylenol, Calpol, Pamol and Panadol) and *nonsteroidal anti-inflammatory drugs* (NSAIDs), such as *aspirin, ibuprofen* (Advil, Anadin and Nurofen), and *naproxen* (Aleve and Feminax). NSAIDs reduce inflammation and relieve joint pain and stiffness, but most irritate the stomach lining with heavy use (AMA, 2003). Aspirin was first manufactured in the late 1800s and is by far the best-known and most widely used drug in this class; Worldwide, people take many billions each year. Peripherally acting analgesics provide substantial pain relief for many pain conditions, especially arthritis and other conditions that involve inflammation.

2. *Centrally acting analgesics* are narcotics (opioids) that bind to opiate receptors in the central nervous system and inhibit nociceptor transmission or alter the perception of pain stimuli. These drugs are derived either directly from the opium poppy—as are *codeine* and *morphine*—or synthetically, such as *heroin, methadone*, and the brand name drugs Percodan and Demerol. Narcotics are very effective in reducing severe acute pain, but patients who use them on a long-term basis report only about a one-third reduction in pain (Turk, 2002). Doctors and patients often worry about the potential these drugs have for producing tolerance, in which the individual requires increasingly large doses, and for causing addiction with long-term use. But the risk of addiction to opioids used in low doses to relieve pain is not as great as many people believe, and practitioners are obliged to monitor use carefully (DEA, 2004).

3. *Local anesthetics*, such as *novocaine, lidocaine*, and *bupivacaine*, make up the third category of chemicals for relieving pain. Although local anesthetics can be applied topically, they are much more potent when injected at the site where the pain originates, as a dentist does before drilling or pulling a tooth. These chemicals block nerve cells in the region from generating impulses—and they often continue to relieve pain for hours or days after the chemical action has worn off (AMA, 2003; Hare & Milano, 1985). Long-term use of currently available local anesthetics is not recommended because they have serious side effects (Melzack & Wall, 1982).

4. *Indirectly acting drugs* affect nonpain conditions, such as emotions, that produce or contribute to pain. These drugs include depressants (tranquilizers and sedatives) and antidepressants. Although *depressants* reduce anxiety and help patients sleep, they do not relieve pain and can produce psychological and physical dependence with long-term use. Drugs classed as *antidepressants* not only reduce psychological depression, they markedly relieve chronic pain in about one-third of individuals (Turk, 2002).

transmitted to the brain. The second technique is called *patient-controlled analgesia*. This procedure allows the patient to determine how much painkiller, such as morphine, he or she needs, and get it without delay. The patient simply pushes a button to activate a computerized pump that dispenses a preset dose of the chemical through a needle that remains inserted continuously. Practitioners monitor the patient's use of the drug and set limits on the rate and amount of its use.

Do people who use patient-controlled analgesia get sufficient pain relief, and do they abuse the opportunity to control their use of narcotics? A meta-analysis with over 50 studies found that patients in the days after surgery used somewhat more medication but got better pain relief with patient-controlled than conventional methods (Hudcova et al., 2006). Other adverse effects of using opioids, such as nausea and urinary retention, were similar for the two methods. Because patients with acute pain use narcotic drugs for only a short time, the risk of abuse is low. In a study with hospitalized men with severe cancer pain who used patient-controlled analgesia for about 2 days, the rate of morphine use actually *declined* over time rather than increased, being used far more heavily in the first few hours than it was later (Citron et al., 1986). Similar results have been found with male and female adolescent patients following surgery (Tyler, 1990). Because research has revealed few problems with patient-controlled analgesia for acute pain, it is becoming standard in hospitals throughout the Western world (Hudcova et al., 2006).

Using Chemicals for Chronic Pain

Chronic pain occurs most commonly with disorders that are not life threatening, such as arthritis, but it can also occur with cancer, which practitioners generally view differently for pain relief. Using opioids for managing moderate to severe cancer pain is widely accepted today (DEA, 2004). But some cancer patients still receive inadequate analgesic drugs, perhaps because they fear they will become addicted if the drug is a narcotic and believe that "good" patients don't complain (Ward et al., 1993). Practitioners need to discuss these issues with their patients and correct misconceptions.

Should narcotics be used in treating chronic non-cancer pain? Practitioners first consider other treatment methods—other chemicals or methods discussed later in this chapter—but if those don't provide enough relief, they can consider long-term opioid treatment with careful monitoring (DEA, 2004). The results of many studies show that narcotics provide effective pain relief for patients with several noncancer chronic pain conditions, such as arthritis, neuralgia, and phantom limb pain (Eisenberg, McNicol, & Carr, 2005; Kalso et al., 2004). The extent to which narcotic treatments for chronic pain lead to addiction is unresolved because few studies have included long-term follow-ups. But a study tested men and women with severe phantom limb pain, using methadone and an antidepressant, over a 2-year period (Urban et al., 1986). These people began drug therapy as hospital patients after having been in almost constant pain and having tried a variety of treatments in the past. They reported at discharge that their pain had been reduced by about two-thirds and maintained this level of pain reduction throughout the next 2 years with very low daily doses of each drug. However, for chronic back pain patients, opioids do not reduce pain and are associated with substance abuse (Martell et al., 2007).

These findings are very important and indicate that narcotics in low doses can provide safe and effective relief for some, but not all, noncancer chronic pain conditions. Because of a growing body of similar findings, practitioners are using narcotics more than in the past for pain patients who are severely disabled by their conditions, such as rheumatoid arthritis (Turk, Brody, & Okifuji, 1994). But increases in using narcotics for chronic pain are occurring cautiously for at least three reasons. First, some patients do become addicted to narcotics used to treat chronic pain (Dunham, 2005),

and those with depressive or anxiety disorders are at higher risk for addiction than others are (Sullivan et al., 2005). Second, studies need to determine specifically how taking daily doses of narcotics alters patients' lives and functioning. Third, researchers need to find out why tolerance and addiction to narcotics are less likely when taken to relieve pain, at least for some conditions. Is it because the doses are so small, for instance, or that the practitioners monitor and set limits on the drug use? Or is it that the patients believe they may lose their painkillers if they use them too much?

Chemical methods alone are usually not sufficient for controlling pain. The need for other approaches in helping pain patients is suggested in research findings on three psychosocial factors. First, chronic headache patients tend to use maladaptive ways of coping with everyday stressors more than people without chronic headaches (Mosley et al., 1990). Second, arthritis patients with high feelings of helplessness before starting drug treatment report poorer treatment success in reducing pain and disability than do comparable low-helplessness patients (Nicassio et al., 1993). Third, many patients who receive *placebo* drugs in research with double-blind procedures report substantial pain relief (Andrasik, Blake, & McCarran, 1986; Feuerstein & Gainer, 1982). Because placebo effects result from psychological processes, we might expect that psychological methods might also relieve pain. As we saw in the gate-control theory in Chapter 10, separating physiological and psychosocial aspects of a person's pain experience is artificial.

To summarize, medical treatments of pain focus mainly on using chemical approaches to reduce discomfort. For chronic pain patients, these approaches can be enhanced when combined with pain control methods that other health care professions provide.

Collaborating with Other Professionals

Because psychosocial factors, particularly anxiety and depression, have a major impact on people's likelihood of transitioning from acute to chronic pain and their experience of chronic pain, it may be important to detect and treat psychosocial problems early to curb difficulties with chronic pain (Casey et al., 2008; Edwards, Klick et al., 2007; Sullivan et al., 2009). Toward this end, many medical practitioners today treat pain patients by joining forces with other professionals—psychologists, social workers, and physical and occupational therapists. When introducing a team approach to chronic pain patients, doctors need to describe the rationale for it and the functions each professional can provide. For instance, because pain conditions generally have a physical basis, a patient may balk and not see why a doctor advises them to consult a psychologist. Thus,

> the patient may infer that the doctor making the referral believes the problem to be somehow less than real, or believes the patient to be seriously maladjusted psychologically. Patients who interpret the referral this way are likely to be guarded with the psychologist. (Cameron & Shepel, 1986, p. 242)

The doctor should state clearly that (1) he or she realizes the patient is "obviously living in a great deal of pain," (2) patients can help themselves control their pain by working with these other professionals, and (3) the doctor will be an active part of the team.

Psychologists conduct therapy with patients individually and in groups. Table 11.2 describes some advantages of a group format in helping patients cope with their pain and disability. The pain group provides a forum for talking about their worst fears and conflicts to people who share these concerns and understand. Patients often say, "I'm afraid the pain will get worse," "I was beginning to believe I was imagining the pain," and "I can't do things because of the pain, and I feel guilty, helpless, frustrated, and angry" (Hendler, 1984). Patients in the group may answer, for instance, "You hurt whether you go shopping or not; so the choice isn't between having pain or not, it's between whether you go shopping or stay home!" (Gentry & Owens, 1986). These people can say things to each other that others could not, without seeming cruel. Group members can also disconfirm each other's misconceptions, share their own ways for managing pain on a day-to-day basis, give each other hope and social support, and detect and confront each others' pain games, such as when patients engage in pain behaviors that bring them attention and sympathy.

The goals of psychological treatments for pain include helping clients reduce their frequency and intensity of pain, improve their emotional adjustment to the pain they have, increase their social and physical activity, and reduce their use of analgesic drugs. Doctors usually want to minimize their patients' use of medication, especially when drugs would be taken on a long-term basis.

BEHAVIORAL AND COGNITIVE METHODS FOR TREATING PAIN

Gate-control theory changed the way many health care workers conceptualize pain by proposing that pain can be controlled not only by biochemical methods that alter sensory input directly, but by modifying motivational and cognitive processes, too. This more complex view of pain provided the rationale for psychologists to develop techniques to help patients *cope more effectively* with the pain and other stressors they experience and *reduce their reliance on drugs* for pain control. Some of these techniques use behavioral and cognitive methods, such as by changing patients' pain behavior through techniques of operant conditioning.

THE OPERANT APPROACH

At the start of this chapter, we considered the case of a 3-year-old girl whose pain behaviors hampered her rehabilitation after she suffered severe burns months earlier. The therapists used an *operant approach*—applying operant conditioning methods to modify patients' behavior—and it was successful.

Table 11.2   *Advantages of Group Psychotherapy Over Individual Therapy in Treating Pain*

1. *Efficiency.* Although each patient has unique problems, chronic pain sufferers also face common difficulties, such as depression and addiction to medication. As a result, they often need similar types of advice and information. Group meetings use the therapist's time more efficiently.
2. *Reduced isolation.* Chronic pain sufferers are typically isolated from extended social contact. This situation can lead to a sense of alienation, which involves feelings of being different from others and of anger and suspicion toward them. Group meetings can help to overcome these feelings.
3. *Credible feedback for patients.* Pain patients often resist feedback or advice from therapists, saying such things as, "You don't know what it's like to live with pain 24 hours a day!" In their eyes, the type of feedback other patients can give may be more believable.
4. *A new reference group for patients.* Patients in a pain group develop new social networks of individuals who are comparable to themselves and who can provide social pressure to conform to the realities and constructive "rules" of living with pain and physical limitations.
5. *A different perspective for the therapist.* Watching a patient relate to other individuals in a group provides the therapist with certain kinds of information that may aid in identifying specific problems therapy should address, such as maladaptive coping styles.

Source: Based on Gentry & Owens, 1986.

The approach the therapists used with this girl involved extinction procedures for her pain behavior and reinforcement for appropriate, or "well," behavior (Varni et al., 1986; Varni & Thompson, 1986). Observations revealed that the hospital staff had been reinforcing her pain behaviors—crying, complaining of pain, resisting the nurse's efforts to put her splints on, and so forth—by giving attention to those behaviors and allowing her to avoid uncomfortable or disliked activities, such as physical therapy. To change this situation, the therapists instructed the hospital staff to:

- Ignore the pain behaviors they paid attention to in the past; this method is extinction.
- Provide rewards for compliant behavior—telling her, for instance, "If you don't cry while I put your splints on, you can have some cookies when I'm finished," or, "If you do this exercise, we can play a game."
- Praise her if she helps in putting on the splints, sleeps through naptime, goes for a period of time without complaining, or does an exercise.

Changing the consequences of her behavior in these ways had a dramatic effect: her pain behaviors decreased sharply, and she began to comply with requests to do exercises, make positive comments about her accomplishments, and assist in putting on her splints.

The operant approach to treating pain can be adapted for use with individuals of all ages, in hospitals and at home—and elements of the operant approach can be introduced before pain behavior becomes chronic. But treatment programs using this approach are usually applied with patients whose chronic pain has already produced serious difficulties in their lives. These programs typically have two main goals: the first is to reduce the patient's reliance on medication. This can be achieved, with the patient's approval, by mixing the painkiller with a flavored syrup, called a "pain cocktail," and giving it on a fixed schedule, such as every 4 hours, rather than whenever the patient requests it (Fordyce, 1976). Because receiving the painkiller is not tied to requesting it, any reinforcing effect the drug may have on that pain behavior is eliminated. Then, over a period of several weeks, the dosage of medication in the cocktail is gradually reduced until the syrup contains little or no drugs.

The second goal of the operant approach is to reduce the disability that generally accompanies chronic pain conditions. This is accomplished by altering the consequences for behavior so that they promote "well" behavior and discourage pain behavior, as we just saw in the program with the young burn patient. The chief feature of this approach is that the therapist trains people in the patient's social environment to monitor and keep a record of pain behaviors, try not to reinforce them, and

systematically reward physical activity. The reinforcers may be of any kind—attention, praise and smiles, candy, money, or the opportunity to watch TV, for example—and may be formalized within a behavioral contract (Fordyce, 1976). The therapist periodically reviews the record of pain behavior to determine whether changes in the program are needed.

Is the operant approach effective? Studies have shown that operant techniques can successfully decrease patients' pain reports and medication use and increase their activity levels (Morley, Eccleston, & Williams, 1999; Roelofs et al., 2002). Although these findings are promising, some limitations should be mentioned. First, after the operant intervention ends and rewards are discontinued, some patients revert to their old pattern of inactivity and pain behavior. Second, not all chronic pain patients are likely to benefit from operant methods. For one thing, the goals of this approach seem more appropriate for patients with chronic-recurrent or chronic-intractable-benign pain than for those with chronic-progressive pain, such as in cancer patients. Also, patients are less likely to show behavioral improvements if they or people in their social environment are unwilling to participate and if they receive disability compensation (Fordyce, 1976). Despite these limitations, it seems clear that the operant approach can be a very useful component in treatment programs for many acute and chronic pain patients.

FEAR REDUCTION, RELAXATION, AND BIOFEEDBACK

Many people experience chronic episodes of pain resulting from underlying physiological processes that can be exacerbated by fears and stress. If these patients could control their physiological processes that cause pain or their fears or stress, they should be able to decrease the frequency or intensity of discomfort they experience.

Fear Reduction

An example of fear exacerbating a pain condition comes from people with low back pain: many of these patients come to fear moving "the wrong way" and bringing on an episode of pain (Gatchel et al., 2007; Vlaeyen et al., 1995). These fears lead them to avoid certain activities, and each time they avoid an activity they receive negative reinforcement—they don't experience the pain they feared would occur. This negative reinforcement makes the fear persist and leads them to engage in less and less activity, weakening their back muscles and worsening their condition.

Chapter 4 described the systematic desensitization procedure for reducing fears and anxieties that involves arranging feared stimuli in a stimulus hierarchy and presenting them in a structured manner from the weakest to the strongest while the person engages in relaxation. In *vivo exposure* is a similar procedure that omits the relaxation component (Kring et al., 2010). When in vivo exposure is used in treating pain fears, a hierarchy of feared activities is developed, and the pain patient engages in each activity repeatedly. This approach has successfully reduced pain fears and catastrophizing and increased activity levels in people with chronic low back pain (Leeuw et al., 2008; Woods & Asmundson, 2008).

Relaxation and Biofeedback

Chapter 3 described that stress is one of many factors that can cause episodes of migraine and tension-type headache. A prominent view is that stress triggers migraine headache by dilating arteries surrounding the brain and triggers tension-type headache by persistently contracting muscles of the scalp, neck, and shoulders (Andrasik, 1986). Migraine and tension headaches do involve dilating arteries and muscle contractions, but it is now clear that they also involve nervous system dysfunctions, such as sensitization or inflammation of nerves in the face and arteries around the brain (AMA, 2003; Holroyd, 2002).

Although the exact role of stress in these processes is not yet known, researchers have applied relaxation and biofeedback methods to reduce stress and physiological processes that lead to headache and other pain conditions. These treatments are usually conducted in weekly sessions that span about 2 or 3 months (see, for example, Blanchard et al., 1986). Chapter 4 presented three methods for relaxation and biofeedback.

- *Progressive muscle relaxation*. The person focuses attention on specific muscle groups while alternately tightening and relaxing these muscles.
- *Meditation*. The individual focuses attention on a meditation stimulus, such as an object, event, or sound; in mindfulness meditation for pain, the person attends to the pain and tries to become detached from thoughts and feelings about it.
- *Biofeedback*. The person learns to exert voluntary control over a bodily function, such as heart rate, by monitoring its status with information from electronic devices.

Of the many physiological processes people can learn to control through biofeedback, we'll consider one: to treat tension-type headaches, patients learn to control the tension of specific muscle groups, such as those in the forehead or neck. They learn by receiving biofeedback

from an electromyograph (EMG) device, which measures electrical activity in those muscles. Therapists urge patients to practice these skills at home and use them when they feel pain episodes beginning—doing so improves treatment success (Gauthier, Côté, & French, 1994).

Do Relaxation and Biofeedback Help Relieve Pain?

Relaxation and biofeedback methods relieve pain. This broad conclusion comes from reviews and meta-analyses of studies that examined the effectiveness of these procedures (Hoffman et al., 2007; Morley, Eccleston, & Williams, 1999; Nestoriuc, Rief, & Martin, 2008; Palermo et al., 2010; Penzien, Rains, & Andrasik, 2002). But several points need to be made about this conclusion. First, although studies have demonstrated that relaxation and biofeedback treatments can help alleviate many types of pain, including arthritic and phantom limb pain, most studies testing these treatments have focused on headache and low back pain. For migraine and tension-type headaches, treatment with relaxation or biofeedback reduces their frequency by about 40 to 50% (Holroyd, 2002).

Second, although progressive muscle relaxation and EMG biofeedback treatments are very effective in relieving headache pain, biofeedback is somewhat more effective (Holroyd, 2002). Studies have examined the success of these procedures by assessing whether the patients' daily records at the end of treatment showed decreases in the headache pain (its frequency, intensity, and duration) and by comparing the headache pain of patients who received these treatments with those who were in control groups. In one type of control group, the subjects receive no training but monitor their headache pain with daily records. In another type of control condition, subjects keep records and receive a placebo treatment, such as by taking sham medication or by having biofeedback sessions that give false feedback about changes in their bodily functions. Generally speaking, treatment with relaxation or biofeedback is about twice as effective in relieving pain as placebo conditions, which are more effective than just monitoring headache pain (Holroyd & Penzien, 1986). Figure 11-1 depicts these effects for tension-type (muscle-contraction) headache sufferers, averaged across subjects in many studies.

Third, the graph in Figure 11-1 suggests that headache sufferers get more pain relief when biofeedback and progressive muscle relaxation are combined, but these differences are not reliable because patients vary greatly in the amount of benefit they get from

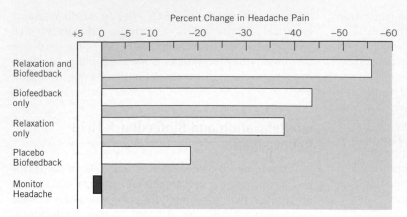

Figure 11-1 Percentage of change in headache pain, pretreatment to post-treatment, across many studies with patients suffering from chronic *muscle-contraction* (tension-type) headaches. Treatments consisted of EMG biofeedback, or relaxation, or EMG biofeedback and relaxation combined. Control conditions consisted of placebo biofeedback or simply monitoring headache pain. (Data from Holroyd & Penzien, 1986, Table IV.)

these treatments. For instance, among individuals who received relaxation treatment only, the percentage by which their pain improved ranged from 17 to 94%; among those who had the combined treatment, improvements ranged from 29 to 88% (Holroyd & Penzien, 1986). This variability is important: it reflects that many patients—especially middle-aged and elderly ones—seem to gain relatively little relief with these treatments (Blanchard & Andrasik, 1985; Holroyd & Penzien, 1986). Being able to predict who will benefit from them most would be useful. Some evidence suggests, for example, that most children and those individuals of all ages who show certain psychophysiological patterns, such as a high correlation between their pain and EMG levels, may be better candidates for biofeedback treatment than other people (Keefe & Gil, 1985; Sarafino & Goehring, 2000).

Fourth, although the pain relief patients experience with progressive muscle relaxation or biofeedback treatment may result from the specific skills they have learned for controlling physiological processes, other psychological factors also seem to play a role. Consider, for instance, two findings. One is that placebo conditions often produce more relief than simply monitoring headache pain (Andrasik, 1986). The other is that massage therapy over a period of time can reduce people's chronic pain and improve their sleep (Lawler & Cameron, 2006; Moyer, Rounds, & Hannum, 2004). Why? Patients' thoughts, beliefs, and spontaneous cognitive strategies probably account for these findings and contribute to part of the success of relaxation and biofeedback treatments in controlling pain (Turk, Meichenbaum, & Genest, 1983).

Are the Improvements from Relaxation and Biofeedback Durable?

After a patient completes the treatment for chronic pain, how long do the effects of the treatment last? Do the effects wear off in a few weeks or months? This is an issue of great importance in health psychology. As we saw in earlier chapters, interventions do not always last, such as in cases of alcohol abuse, and relapse often occurs. Pain researchers have addressed this issue by conducting a 5-year follow-up investigation on chronic headache patients who completed training for either progressive muscle relaxation or for both relaxation and biofeedback (Blanchard et al., 1986; Blanchard, Andrasik et al., 1987; Blanchard, Appelbaum et al., 1987).

The patients in this research were adults who had suffered many years either from muscle-contraction (tension-type) headache or from "vascular" headache, which includes both migraine and combined (migraine plus tension-type) headache. All patients received relaxation training in 10 sessions, spanning 8 weeks. Those people whose headache pain had not improved by at least 60% were offered additional treatment with biofeedback. All subjects had an audiotape to guide their practice of relaxation at home, and the vascular patients who received temperature biofeedback were given a temperature-monitoring device. The patients kept daily "headache diaries" with four ratings each day of their headache pain. Psychological assessment before and after the treatment revealed that their feelings of depression and anxiety decreased substantially (Blanchard et al., 1986). For 6 months after completing the treatment, the patients received treatment booster sessions if they desired them.

A difficulty in doing longitudinal research is that the number of original subjects who are available and willing to participate declines over time. At the time of the last annual follow-up, a little more than half of the patients could be located and agreed to participate. Figure 11-2 presents the people's ratings of headache pain during each of seven 4-week periods: pretreatment, post-treatment, and years 1 through 5 in the follow-up. As you can see, the treatment effects were quite durable for these

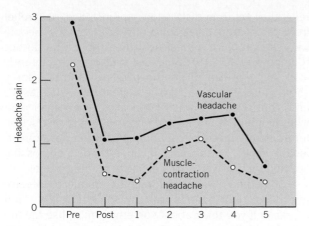

Figure 11–2 Averaged ratings of headache pain for muscle-contraction (tension-type) and vascular (migraine and combined) headache patients who successfully completed treatment and continued to participate in the follow-up. The graphs depict these ratings at pretreatment, posttreatment, and follow-up years 1 through 5. (Data from Blanchard, Appelbaum, et al., 1987, Table 1.)

patients. What about the patients who did not continue through the 5-year follow-up? Although there is no way of knowing for sure, the researchers presented evidence to suggest the treatments were durable for them, too (Blanchard, Andrasik et al., 1987; Blanchard, Appelbaum et al., 1987). And findings of other follow-up studies confirm that completing relaxation training or both relaxation and biofeedback training provides durable headache relief for at least 2 years (Blanchard, 1987).

Relaxation and biofeedback methods are very helpful in reducing the discomfort many chronic pain patients experience, but these treatments do not provide all the pain relief most patients need. Because chronic pain involves a complex interplay of sensory and psychosocial factors, therapists generally use these techniques along with several other approaches, especially cognitive therapies that address the thought patterns that occur when people experience pain.

COGNITIVE METHODS

What do people think about when they experience pain? In an acute pain situation, some people focus on the ordeal and how uncomfortable and miserable they are, but others do not (Turk & Rudy, 1986). For example, researchers asked children and adolescents what they think about when getting an injection at their dentist's office (Brown et al., 1986). Over 80% of the subjects reported thoughts that focused on negative emotions and pain, such as, "This hurts, I hate injections," "I'm

scared," and "My heart is pounding and I feel shaky." One-fourth of the subjects had thoughts of escaping or avoiding the situation, as in, "I want to run away." Thoughts like these focus the person's attention on unpleasant aspects of the experience and make the pain worse (Keefe et al., 1994; Turk & Rudy, 1986).

Not all people in pain focus on the ordeal and discomfort; many use cognitive strategies to modify their experience. For instance, by 10 years of age, many children report that they try to cope with pain in a dental situation by thinking about something else or by saying to themselves such things as, "It's not so bad" or "Be brave" (Brown et al., 1986). But even when children know ways to cope with pain and recommend them for others to use, they don't necessarily use those skills themselves (Peterson et al., 1999). Although coping skills tend to improve as children get older, many patients in adulthood still exaggerate the fearful aspects of the painful medical procedures they experience (Chaves & Brown, 1987). When these people experience acute or chronic pain, they may use *passive coping*, such as taking to bed or curtailing social activities, which puts them at risk for disability (Mercado et al., 2005). For them, a vicious circle can develop with chronic pain in which passive coping leads to feelings of helplessness and depression, which leads to more passive coping, and so on (Smith & Wallston, 1992). Other people in pain use *active coping*: they try to keep functioning by ignoring the pain or keeping busy with an interesting activity. Family and friends influence these coping patterns by reinforcing some behaviors, but not others (McCracken, 2005; Menefee et al., 1996). To help people cope effectively with pain, medical and psychological practitioners need to assess and address their patients' pain coping techniques and beliefs.

Active Coping Techniques

Cognitive techniques for treating pain include active coping strategies, and many of these methods are, in fact, quite effective in helping people cope with pain. These techniques can be classified into three basic types: *distraction*, *imagery*, and *redefinition* (Fernandez, 1986; McCaul & Malott, 1984). We will examine these methods and consider their usefulness for people with acute and chronic pain.

At your dentist's office, do the examination rooms have colorful pictures or large windows with nice views on all the walls that a patient can see while in the dental chair? My dentist's rooms do, and I use the pictures and windows to distract my attention when I feel the need. **Distraction** is the technique of focusing on a nonpainful stimulus in the immediate environment to divert one's attention from discomfort (Fernandez, 1986). We can be distracted from pain in many ways, such as by looking at a picture, listening to someone's voice, singing a song, counting ceiling tiles, playing a video game, or doing mathematics problems.

Not all distraction attempts are likely to work in relieving pain. Research on acute pain has shown that distraction is more effective if the pain is mild or moderate than if it is strong (McCaul & Malott, 1984). Three aspects of the distraction task seem to affect how well it works:

- The *amount of attention* the task requires: the greater the attention required, the lower the pain ratings (Christenfeld, 1997; Dahlquist et al., 2007; McCaul, Monson, & Maki, 1992). Distraction tasks are more effective when the person must be an active participant than when they are passive onlookers.

- The extent to which the task is *interesting or engrossing*, such as watching a movie or engaging in an activity that the person has chosen (Cohen, 2002; Cohen et al., 1999; Dahlquist et al., 2002).

- The task's *credibility* to the person—for example, if you were asked to listen to a sound that isn't there, the task would lose its credibility quickly and not relieve pain (Melzack, Weisz, & Sprague, 1963).

Because of the role of credibility in using distraction methods, therapists may need to help patients understand how the technique works. One therapist described the following approach for doing this:

> First, I ask the patient to be aware of the sensations in his thighs as he sits in his chair. I note that those sensations are real, and they have a physical basis, but they are not normally experienced because other things occupy his attention. Then I suggest that he think of a TV set: he could block out the channel 9 signal by tuning in channel 11; the channel 9 signal is still there, but not being tuned in. I suggest that while his pain signals are real, he can learn to "tune them out." … A number of pain patients have reported that they frequently think of the TV metaphor when experiencing pain and take appropriate action to "tune out." (Cameron, quoted in Turk, Meichenbaum, & Genest, 1983, p. 284)

By providing plausible explanations for a recommended technique, therapists can increase its effectiveness and the likelihood that the patient will use it.

Distraction strategies are useful for reducing acute pain, such as that experienced in some medical or dental procedures, and they can also provide relief for chronic pain patients in some circumstances (McCaul & Malott, 1984). However, individuals vary in the pain relief they get from distraction—for instance, pain relief from distraction takes longer to start among people who catastrophize a great deal than those who do not (Campbell et al., 2010). Singing a song or staring intently at a stimulus can divert the person's attention for a short while—and this may be a great help, such as for an arthritis sufferer who experiences heightened pain when climbing stairs. People who want to use distraction for moderate levels of continuous pain may get longer-lasting relief by engaging in an extended engrossing activity, such as watching a movie or reading a book.

Sometimes when children are about to receive injections, their parents will say something like, "It'll be easier if you think about something nice, like the fun things we did at the park." **Nonpain imagery**—also called *guided imagery*—is a strategy whereby the person tries to alleviate discomfort by conjuring up a mental scene that is unrelated to or incompatible with the pain (Fernandez, 1986). The most common type of imagery people use involves scenes that are pleasant to them—they think of "something nice." This scene might involve being at the beach or in the country, for instance. Therapists usually encourage, or "guide," the person to include aspects of different senses: vision, hearing, taste, smell, and touch. As an example, the scene at the beach could include the sight and smell of the ocean water, the sound of the waves, and the warm, grainy feel of the sand. The person generally tries to keep the imagined event in mind as long as possible.

The imagery technique is in many ways like distraction. The main difference is that imagery is based on the person's imagination rather than on real objects or events in the environment. As a result, individuals who use imagery do not have to depend on the environment to provide a suitably distracting stimulus. They can develop one or more scenes that work reliably, which they "carry" around in their heads. They can then call one of these scenes up for pain relief whenever they need it. Imagery seems to work best when it attracts high levels of the person's attention or involvement, and it is likely to work better with mild or moderate pain than with strong pain (McCaul & Malott, 1984; Turk, Meichenbaum, & Genest, 1983). Although imagery clearly helps in reducing acute pain, the extent of this technique's usefulness with longer-lasting pain episodes is unclear. One limitation with using imagery in pain control is that some individuals are less adept in imagining scenes than others (Melzack & Wall, 1982).

The third cognitive strategy for reducing discomfort is **pain redefinition**, in which the person substitutes constructive or realistic thoughts about the pain experience for ones that arouse feelings of threat or harm (Fernandez, 1986; McCaul & Malott, 1984). Therapists can help people redefine their pain experiences in several ways. One approach involves teaching clients to engage in an internal dialogue, using positive self-statements that take basically two forms (Fernandez, 1986):

- *Coping statements* emphasize the person's ability to tolerate the discomfort, as when people say to themselves, "It hurts, but you're in control," or, "Be brave—you can take it."
- *Reinterpretative statements* are designed to negate the unpleasant aspects of the discomfort, as when people think, "It's not so bad," "It's not the worst thing that could happen," or, "It hurts, but think of the benefits of this experience."

This last statement can be particularly appropriate when undergoing painful medical procedures.

Two other methods can help people redefine their pain experiences. First, for patients about to undergo potentially uncomfortable medical procedures, a therapist can provide information about the sensations to expect, thereby reducing discomfort during the procedures (Anderson & Masur, 1983). Because many patients misremember past pain experiences in medical procedures, a therapist can also help clients remember more accurately the amount of pain they experienced in these procedures in the past and how well they coped (Chen et al., 1999). Providing realistic information helps them redefine the experiences in advance. Second, therapists can help chronic pain patients see that some of their beliefs are illogical and are making the discomfort worse. (Go to 🖐.)

Promoting Pain Acceptance

We saw in Chapter 10 that people's inclination to keep active despite feeling pain is part of *pain acceptance*, which is linked to subsequently better functioning. The impact of chronic pain also depends on they way patients view their conditions (Jensen et al., 1999; Williams & Keefe, 1991). Those who believe their pain will last a very long time, is a sign of a disabling injury, and has unknown causes tend to show more pain behaviors, cope poorly, and feel that active coping strategies will not work. In contrast, patients who believe that they understand the nature of their pain and that their conditions will improve tend to use active coping strategies. Those who cope well with their pain are more likely to return to work despite their discomfort (Linton & Buer, 1995).

Pain therapists can promote active coping and pain acceptance with a cognitive–behavioral approach called *Acceptance and Commitment Therapy* (ACT), which is designed to teach clients to experience their condition and emotions directly, without the negative implications that

have usually accompanied them (Blackledge & Hayes, 2001; Hayes & Wilson, 1995). ACT teaches pain patients coping skills and has them perform activities to see that they can enjoy activity even when some pain is present, helping them redefine these situations, increase their self-efficacy, and reduce their pain fears. ACT methods have incorporated mindfulness meditation, discussion about thoughts and feelings related to experiencing pain, in vivo exposure for feared activities, and assessments of life values to generate a commitment to achieving daily activity goals, such as going shopping despite the pain (McCracken, Vowles, & Eccleston, 2005; Wicksell et al., 2009). The ACT approach improves pain patients' social, emotional, and physical functioning and quality of life.

The Value of Cognitive Strategies in Treating Pain

Studies have found that active coping strategies effectively reduce *acute* pain (Fernandez & Turk, 1989; Manne et al., 1994). Distraction and imagery are particularly useful with mild or moderate pain, and redefinition is more effective with strong pain (McCaul & Malott, 1984). How helpful are these methods with *chronic* pain? Redefinition may be more effective in relieving chronic pain than distraction is. A study with patients with chronic pain from several medical problems, including arthritis and amputation, found that those who received redefinition training reported less pain and exhibited less pain behavior than those who were trained in distraction (Rybstein-Blinchik, 1979).

Because each behavioral and cognitive strategy we've considered can be helpful in treating clinical pain, programs for chronic pain sufferers generally combine different methods. A study with chronic low back pain patients, for instance, gave one group a program that combined imagery, redefinition, and progressive muscle relaxation training (Turner, 1982). Patients in another group received a program of only relaxation training; a third group served as controls. Compared with the control subjects, the patients with the two other programs reported much less pain, depression, and disability by the end of treatment. A follow-up on the people in the two programs more than 1 1/2 years later revealed that the benefits of the treatments were maintained, as measured by the people's ratings of pain and reports of health care use. But the patients who received the program combining cognitive strategies and relaxation also showed marked improvements in their employment, working 60% more hours per week than those who had relaxation only.

Reviews and meta-analyses of research have revealed that cognitive–behavioral programs are effective

CLINICAL METHODS AND ISSUES

Guiding a Client to Pain Redefinition

The following dialogue illustrates how a clinical health psychologist can guide a client with illogical beliefs toward pain redefinition. "Mrs. D," a 56-year-old patient, worried that her chronic-recurrent head pain was actually caused by a tumor, which repeated neurological tests had failed to reveal. The therapist suggested that they examine those thoughts, and she replied:

MRS. D: Yes, I know they're not true but I cannot help it.

THERAPIST: You don't think you have control over your thoughts?

MRS. D: Yes, they just come to me.

T: Well, let's come back to the idea that your thoughts are automatic. First, let's break down your flood of negative thoughts and look at each part separately. Do you really think that you have a tumor?

MRS. D: I don't know. I guess not (pause) but it's hard not to worry about it. My head hurts so bad.

T: Yes, I know. So how do you convince yourself that you don't have a tumor or something else seriously wrong?

MRS. D: Well, as you know I've been examined many times by the best neurologists around. They say I'm OK. Also, my pain always goes away and I've never had any other neurological problems. My only problem is the pain. But, it's hard to remember these facts when my pain is so awful.

T: It's much easier to be positive about your condition when you're not suffering. Nevertheless, rationally, you really are convinced that there's nothing seriously wrong.

MRS. D: I guess so. If only I could remember that when my pain starts coming on.

T: So the goal of our work today could be to figure out a strategy to increase the likelihood that you'll remember the positive thoughts during a pain episode.

MRS. D: Yes, that sounds good.

T: Let's start by generating a list of accurate statements about your pain. Then we can talk about ways you can cue yourself to remember the list when you begin to feel pain. You already mentioned a couple of beliefs about your pain; that is, that there's nothing seriously wrong, that the pain always goes away, and that, other than the pain, you feel pretty healthy. Can you think of other accurate and positive thoughts? (Holzman, Turk, & Kerns, 1986, pp. 45–46)

In this example, the therapist helped the client examine the logic of her thought patterns and generate a list of ideas she believed that were incompatible with her irrational fears. They later rehearsed these beliefs so that she could use them as self-statements when pain episodes occurred.

in treating chronic pain conditions, such as headache, arthritis, and low back pain (Hoffman et al., 2007; Morley, Eccleston, & Williams, 1999; Palermo et al., 2010). These programs are at least as effective as chemical methods in reducing chronic tension-type headache (Holroyd, 2002) and are also effective when delivered via the Internet (Cuijpers, van Straten, & Andersson, 2008; Palermo et al., 2009). They are most effective when patients follow their therapist's requests to practice the program skills, such as relaxation, at home and when the programs are given before the client has had chronic pain for several months or more (Heapy et al., 2005; Sullivan et al., 2008). Although cognitive–behavioral therapy is often very durable, relapse to pain behavior can occur and can be prevented with an automated telephone intervention (Naylor et al., 2008). (Go to 🍎.)

HYPNOSIS AND INTERPERSONAL THERAPY

You may have noticed that the behavioral and cognitive methods we just described for relieving pain sound familiar—and they should. Many involve psychological procedures derived from the stress reduction techniques we considered in Chapter 4. Because people's experiences of pain include an emotional component and are stressful, and because behavioral and cognitive methods are effective in reducing stress, psychologists have adapted these techniques to help people control their pain. Other psychological approaches, such as hypnosis and interpersonal therapy, have also been applied to relieve pain.

Would Behavioral or Cognitive Methods Help *Your* Pain?

For each of the following questions about your recent experiences relating to pain, put a check mark in the preceding space if your answer is "yes."

_____ Have you been experiencing strong pain three or more days a week for more than a month?

_____ Do you take painkillers four or more days a week?

_____ Do you often take painkillers to prevent pain before it begins?

_____ Has your pain been getting worse?

_____ Have you cancelled or avoided making social plans in the past month because you thought your pain would interfere with them?

_____ Do you ever drink alcohol to relieve your pain or the stress it produces?

_____ Have you seen more than three doctors about your pain?

_____ Are you afraid of performing physical activities, feeling they could elicit or aggravate your pain condition?

_____ Has your pain caused you to feel depressed and helpless for more than a couple of weeks or so?

_____ Do family or friends either seem annoyed by your pain or often ask how your pain is doing?

If you have been suffering from pain but have not yet seen a doctor about it, see one soon. If you have seen your doctor about the pain repeatedly but the treatments have not worked, consider supplementing your medical therapy with behavioral and cognitive approaches, especially if you answered "yes" to three or more of the above questions. If you answered "yes" to five or more questions, consider contacting a *multidisciplinary pain clinic*, as described toward the end of this chapter. (Based on material in Tunks and Bellissimo, 1991.)

HYPNOSIS AS A TREATMENT FOR PAIN

In the mid-1800s, before ether was discovered, dramatic reports began to appear of doctors performing major surgery on individuals, using hypnosis as the sole method of analgesia (Bakal, 1979; Barber, 1986). In one such case, a surgeon made an incision halfway across the chest of a woman with breast cancer and removed the tumor as well as several enlarged glands in her armpit. During the procedure, the woman conversed with the surgeon and showed no signs of feeling pain. Another doctor reported having done hundreds of surgeries with hypnosis as the only analgesic and argued that the patients experienced no pain.

Can Hypnosis Eliminate Acute Pain?

Were all of these operations painless? Probably not—although many patients *claimed* to feel no pain, some showed other pain behaviors, such as facial expressions, suggesting they were suppressing their agony (Bakal, 1979). Nevertheless, hypnosis can reduce the intensity of acute pain, but it is not highly effective for all people (Accardi & Milling, 2009; Hilgard & Hilgard, 1983;

Patterson & Jensen, 2003). People vary in their ability to be hypnotized, and those who can be hypnotized very easily and deeply seem to gain more pain relief from hypnosis than those who are less hypnotically susceptible (De Pascalis, Cacace, & Massicolle, 2004; Liossi, White, & Hatira, 2006; Milling et al., 2007; Milling, Reardon, & Carosella, 2006).

How does hypnosis reduce pain? Although the mechanisms underlying pain relief from hypnosis are not clear, part of the answer seems to involve physiological changes that occur in the brain and spinal cord of people who are highly suggestible when they are hypnotized (Patterson & Jensen, 2003). Other factors may involve the deep relaxation people experience when hypnotized—as we saw earlier, relaxation can relieve pain—and cognitive factors, such as expectancies for pain relief (Barber, 1986; Milling et al., 2007; Milling, Reardon, & Carosella, 2006). Studies have shown that hypnosis and cognitive-behavioral methods produce similar pain relief and that combining these methods does not enhance their effects (Liossi & Hatira, 1999; Milling, Reardon, & Carosella, 2006). Contrary to myths about hypnosis, people usually show as much pain reduction using cognitive strategies, such as imagery and redefinition, as they do under hypnosis (Barber, 1982).

Can Hypnosis Relieve Chronic Pain?

Hypnosis can reduce chronic pain. Although most relevant studies have tested patients with recurrent headache, some have shown that hypnosis helps also with other pain conditions, such as low back pain and cancer pain (Patterson & Jensen, 2003; Jensen, 2009). In general, hypnosis is about as effective as relaxation therapy, and, interestingly, regardless of which of these therapies people receive, their pain relief is greatest if they are high in hypnotic suggestibility. These findings lead to an important question: What is it about being highly suggestible that helps people apply psychological methods to control their pain?

INTERPERSONAL THERAPY FOR PAIN

Interpersonal therapy uses psychoanalytic and cognitive-behavioral perspectives to help people deal with emotional difficulties, such as adjusting to chronic pain, by changing the way they interact with and perceive their social environments (Kring et al., 2010). The underlying theory is that people's emotional difficulties arise from the way they relate to others, particularly family members. Therapy sessions involve discussions to help clients gain insights into their own motivations and how their behavior toward other people affects their own emotional adjustment. In the case of chronic pain patients, the insights often relate to feelings they and their families have about the pain condition, how they deal with pain behavior, and relationship changes that have developed among these people.

An example of this approach involves showing patients how their pain behavior is part of "pain games" they play with other people (Szasz, cited in Bakal, 1979). In these games, individuals with chronic pain seem to take on roles in which they continually seek to confirm their identities as suffering persons, maintain their dependent lifestyles, and receive various secondary gains, such as attention and sympathy. These patients are probably not aware of what is actually happening in these games, and the purpose of this psychotherapeutic approach is to make them aware so that they can give up the games if they want to and are shown how.

Therapies leading to insight can also help chronic pain patients and their families understand the problems they experience in their relationships within the family system (Flor & Turk, 1985; Kerns & Payne, 1996). For instance, when a spouse suffers from chronic pain, both spouses experience feelings of frustration,

anger, helplessness, and guilt that they often do not communicate openly to each other. These feelings can result from changes in their roles, general style of communication, and sexual relationship. The following excerpt shows how a therapist was able to help a pain patient, John Cox, and his wife gain insights about their feelings and behavior. The three of them were discussing a pain episode John had had while he watched TV with his wife, and the therapist (T) asked the wife how she reacted when she realized he was in pain:

MRS. COX: I really felt sorry for John, but I didn't know what to do. I just tried to watch the show and not say anything to him. At those times I feel … so helpless.

T: Mr. Cox, it sounds as if your wife tried to avoid talking about your pain. She sounds sort of helpless and frustrated . . . . How did you feel about her response?

MR. COX: I think I got kind of mad at her because she seemed to be ignoring me, not really caring how I was feeling.

T: Mr. Cox, what do you think she should have done at that time?

MR. COX: I don't really know.

T: Mr. Cox, do you think there was anything she could have done to make you feel better?

MR. COX: Not really.

T: … Perhaps at such times ignoring your pain may be the most she can do… .

MR. COX: Perhaps.

T: Perhaps?

MR. COX: Well maybe she did know how I was feeling, but I felt upset that she didn't tell me. (Turk, Meichenbaum, & Genest, 1983, pp. 244–245)

Insights such as these help family members understand each others' feelings and points of view, and this understanding can help to break down the longstanding confusion and conflicts that have developed over time. Improvements in family relationships can enable the therapist to enhance the cooperation of each member in the treatment process (Kerns & Payne, 1996). Also, interpersonal therapy appears to be useful in treating depression, a common problem among pain patients (Kring et al., 2010).

In summary, hypnosis and interpersonal therapy offer promising techniques in the treatment of chronic pain. Thus far in our discussion of methods for reducing pain we have considered a variety of medical and psychological techniques. In the next section, we will see how physical therapy and certain skin stimulation methods can also play important roles in controlling pain.

PHYSICAL AND STIMULATION THERAPIES FOR PAIN

Anthropologists and medical historians have noted that most, if not all, cultures in recorded history have learned that people can "fight pain with pain" (Melzack & Wall, 1982). One pain can cancel another—a brief or moderate pain can cancel a longer-lasting or stronger one. For example, you might reduce the pain of an injection by pressing your thumbnail into your forefinger as the injection is given. Reducing one pain by creating another is called **counter-irritation**. People in ancient cultures developed a counter-irritation procedure called *cupping* to relieve headaches, backaches, and arthritic pain. In this procedure, one or more heated glass cups are inverted and pressed on the skin. As the air in the cup cools, it creates a vacuum, causing the skin to be bruised as it is drawn up into the cup. This method is still used in some parts of the world today (Melzack & Wall, 1982).

The principle of counter-irritation is the basis for present-day stimulation therapies for reducing pain. After examining these pain control methods, we will discuss the important role other physical approaches can play in reducing pain.

STIMULATION THERAPIES

Why does counter-irritation relieve pain? One reason is that people actively distract their attention from the stronger pain to the milder one. Another explanation comes from gate-control theory. Recall that activity in the peripheral fibers that carry signals about mildly irritating stimuli tends to close the gate, thereby inhibiting the transmission cells from sending pain signals to the brain. Counter-irritation, such as massaging a sore muscle, activates these peripheral fibers, and this may close the gate and soothe the pain.

This gate-control view of how counter-irritation works led to the development of a pain control technique called **transcutaneous electrical nerve stimulation** (TENS). This technique involves placing electrodes on the skin near where the patient feels pain and stimulating that area with mild electric current, which is supplied by a small portable device. Anecdotal reports suggest that TENS can reduce postoperative pain (Chapman, 1984; Mann & Carr, 2006). For example, a 9-year-old boy began receiving TENS while still unconscious after kidney surgery and then awoke, not feeling any pain. He thought the surgery had not occurred and that the hospital staff was not telling the truth when they said it did. When asked why it couldn't be true, he asserted confidently, "Because I haven't got any bandages." We asked

him to feel his belly, since his hands were outside of the bedclothes. When he did, an expression of astonishment came over his face. (Chapman, 1984, p. 1265)

Now he claimed to feel pain and began to cry. Despite this dramatic anecdote, evidence today indicates that TENS is not effective in reducing acute pain (Johnson, 2001). And its success in treating chronic pain is unclear and may just result from a placebo effect (Mann & Carr, 2006). When TENS does relieve discomfort for some chronic conditions, such as phantom limb pain, its effects are often short-lived (Hare & Milano, 1985).

Another stimulation therapy that is used today for reducing pain is **acupuncture**, a technique in which fine metal needles are inserted under the skin at special locations and then twirled or electrically charged to create stimulation. Acupuncture has been used in China for at least the past 2,000 years and was originally based on the idea that pain occurs when the life forces of yin and yang are out of balance (AMA, 2003; Bakal, 1979; CU, 1994). Although acupuncturists do not necessarily believe this rationale any longer, many, but not all, still determine the placement of the needles on the basis of charts that show hundreds of insertion points on the body that link to pain relief in associated parts of the body. On the nose and ear, for example, certain points are associated with the small intestine, whereas other points are associated with the kidney, or heart, or abdomen.

Does acupuncture work? Despite anecdotes of surgeons having performed major surgery on patients with only acupuncture anesthesia, research findings currently do not support its use for surgical anesthesia (Lee & Ernst, 2005). Other evidence points to a few

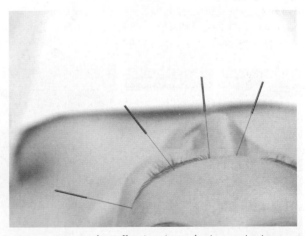

Acupuncture can be effective in reducing pain in some individuals.

conclusions about its effects and its limitations (Bakal, 1979; Chapman, 1984; Melzack & Wall, 1982):

- In China, doctors perform only a small percentage (less than 10%) of surgeries with acupuncture analgesia, patients must volunteer for the procedure, and doctors select candidates very carefully and make sure these patients are well indoctrinated.

- Laboratory studies have shown that acupuncture produces only mild analgesia in most people.

- The degree of analgesia acupuncture produces depends on the intensity of the stimulation, and not on its being applied at the exact points described on acupuncture charts.

- Pain patients who benefit most from acupuncture tend to be those who are also easily and deeply hypnotizable.

Does acupuncture provide long-term relief for chronic pain? Not for most pain patients. Although it is far more effective than conventional therapy in treating low back pain, so is *sham* acupuncture where needles are placed at nonacupuncture points (Haake et al., 2007; Manheimer et al., 2005); it is not effective for migraine and tension-type headache (Linde et al., 2005; Melchart et al., 2005). Gate-control theory provides two plausible reasons for any effects of acupuncture: stimulation from the needles may close the gate by activating peripheral fibers or the release of opioids, such as endorphins (Bakal, 1979).

PHYSICAL THERAPY

Physical therapy is an important rehabilitation component for many medical conditions—for instance, after injury or surgery, patients perform exercises to enhance muscular strength and tissue flexibility to restore their range of motion. Physical therapists have a variety of techniques they can incorporate into individualized treatment programs to help patients who suffer from acute and chronic pain conditions. Exercise is a common feature in these programs (AMA, 2003; Mann & Carr, 2006).

The therapist and patient generally plan the program together, setting daily or weekly goals that promote very gradual but steady progress. The progress is tailored to the patient's needs, being fast enough to promote a feeling of accomplishment but slow enough to prevent overexertion, reinjury, or failure. In cases of acute injury, such as serious damage to the knee joint, the exercise program might span a year or two. The rationale for using exercise to control pain depends on the type of health problem the patient has—with arthritis, for instance, exercise helps by maintaining the flexibility of the joints and preventing them from becoming deformed (Minor & Sanford, 1993). Other approaches in physical therapy, such as massage, traction, and applying heat or cold to the painful area of the body, seem to provide temporary pain relief (Tunks & Bellissimo, 1991). The spinal manipulation treatment people get from *chiroproactic* and *osteopathic* specialists for low back pain is not generally considered to be physical therapy, but it

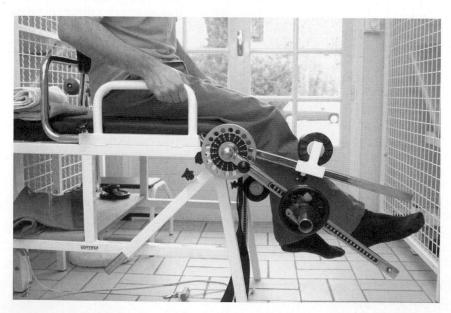

Physical therapy not only promotes rehabilitation for this patient suffering from a leg injury but may also help in reducing his pain.

is effective for many patients—and the best candidates can be identified by features of their condition, such as symptom durations of less than 16 days and low scores on a test of fear and avoidance of pain (Andersson et al., 1999; Childs et al., 2004).

Physical therapy is widely used in treating two highly prevalent chronic pain conditions, arthritis and low back pain (Minor & Sanford, 1993; Moffet et al., 1999). For low back pain physical therapy, graded stretching and strengthening exercises produce substantial improvements in self-reports of pain and ability to perform physical activities (Hayden, van Tulder, & Tomlinson, 2005; Moffet et al., 1999). Sometimes physical therapy is combined with cognitive and behavioral methods in treating chronic pain to gain the benefits of each approach: physical therapy should improve physical functioning, and cognitive–behavioral methods should enhance psychosocial adjustment (Heinrich et al., 1985). When these methods have been combined in treating low back pain, research has found that patients show less pain behavior, disability, and self-reported pain than with either approach alone (Turner et al., 1990).

In this chapter we have described many different types of treatment, including medical, psychological, and physical therapies, and we have seen that each method can help to alleviate clinical pain. Some methods seem to be more effective than others, especially for particular pain conditions. Typically, no single approach is sufficient by itself. Therefore, specialists who provide treatment in pain clinics often apply several methods in combination. (Go to 💡.)

PAIN CLINICS

Years ago, if a person's pain lingered, and doctors could not determine its cause or find a remedy, that patient was left with virtually no reasonable treatment alternatives. In desperation, such people often tried extreme medical approaches that could lead to drug addiction or irreversible nerve damage, or they may have turned to charlatans. Although many people with chronic pain still use ill-conceived, desperate measures to gain relief from their discomfort, helpful alternatives are available, as we have seen. Today people with chronic pain can receive effective pain control through **pain clinics** (or *pain centers*), which are institutions or organizations that have been developed specifically for treating pain conditions.

The first pain clinic was founded in the 1970s at the University of Washington Medical School (Fordyce, 1976; Melzack & Wall, 1982). By the late 1990s there were

perhaps a thousand pain clinics in the United States alone (Turk & Stacey, 2000). The structure, methods, and quality of pain clinics vary widely. Many pain clinics are private organizations, whereas others are affiliated with medical schools, university departments of behavioral medicine, and hospitals. Many provide inpatient treatment, and others focus on outpatient care; many incorporate a variety of treatment methods, and others provide basically one approach, such as acupuncture, hypnosis, or biofeedback (Follick et al., 1985; Kanner, 1986; Turk & Stacey, 2000). Pain centers in the United States, Canada, and some European nations that offer high-quality treatment can receive accreditation by the Commission on Accreditation of Rehabilitation Facilities (online at http://www.carf.org).

MULTIDISCIPLINARY PROGRAMS

A theme that has appeared more than once in this chapter is that treating chronic pain with just one method is less likely to succeed than a combined program. In fact, one doctor has advised avoiding clinics that focus on applying a single approach, such as biofeedback or nerve block methods (Kanner, 1986). *Multidisciplinary pain clinics* (or *centers*)—those that combine and integrate several effective approaches—are likely to succeed for the largest percentage of patients and provide the greatest pain relief for each individual. Clinics that use multidisciplinary programs generally use assessment and treatment methods for each patient that involve medical, psychosocial, physical therapy, occupational therapy, and vocational factors and approaches (Fletcher & Macdonald, 2005; Turk & Stacey, 2000).

Assessment procedures are used in determining the factors that are contributing to the patient's condition, identifying the specific problems to address in the program, and customizing the program to match the needs of the patient (Chapman, 1991; Turk & Stacey, 2000). Although the goals and objectives of different multidisciplinary programs vary, they typically include:

- Reducing the patient's experience of pain.
- Improving physical and lifestyle functioning.
- Decreasing or eliminating drug intake.
- Enhancing social support and family life.
- Reducing the patient's use of medical services.

Multidisciplinary programs generally integrate specific treatment components to achieve each goal (Follick et al., 1985). These programs include, for example, procedures to decrease the patient's reliance on medication and physical exercises to increase the person's strength, endurance, flexibility, and range of motion. They provide

HIGHLIGHT

Physical Activity and Back Pain

The spine has an intricate structure, with each of its many sections of bone, called *vertebrae*, being cushioned from adjacent sections by rubbery *disks* of connective tissue. Each vertebra is connected to adjacent ones by antler-shaped *facet joints* that enable the vertebrae to pivot against one another (Tortora & Derrickson, 2009). But the spine depends on the muscles of the back and abdomen for support, without which it would just topple over. When all these muscles are strong and in good working order, they balance each other's action and keep the body's weight centered on the spine. But when these muscles are weak or the back muscles are under excessive or prolonged tension—sometimes due to emotional stress—back problems tend to occur.

A 10-year longitudinal study of men and women found evidence suggesting that low back pain progresses over time through a vicious circle: poor muscle function may lead to low back disorders, which lead to poorer muscle function, and so on (Leino, Aro, & Hasan, 1987). Although back pain can arise from such conditions as arthritis and ruptured disks, this is not typical—medical examinations fail to find underlying physical causes in the large majority of back cases (Chapman, 1984; Deyo et al., 1991). Most backaches seem to arise from muscle or ligament strains, lack of proper exercise, and normal wear and tear on facet joints. These problems tend to increase with age for many reasons—for instance, people's muscular conditioning usually declines as they get older, the effects of wear and tear accumulate, and the disks gradually dry out and provide less cushioning for the vertebrae. People whose jobs require

frequent heavy lifting are more likely than other workers to develop low back pain (Kelsey & Hochberg, 1988). Exercise can help protect people from back problems, but it needs to consist of *proper* activities. People who do the wrong kinds of exercises do not get this protection, and those who overexert themselves can precipitate back pain.

What kinds of physical activity can help protect against back problems? Proper exercise involves a program of back-strengthening and stretching activities, along with abdominal exercises. When people have backaches, exercises are helpful, and Figure 11-3 presents a few easy ones. Brisk walking a few hours a week also helps (Hurwitz, Morgenstern, & Chiao, 2005). Although medical advice for backaches in the past called for getting lots of bed rest and taking aspirin, this advice has changed (Deyo et al., 1991; Mann & Carr, 2006). Most backaches resolve themselves in a few days or weeks with or without medical attention. Doctors today recommend that the person *become active as soon as possible*—walking and exercising cautiously—even if it hurts a little. People with back pain should consult their doctor when the pain is:

- Linked to a known injury, such as from a fall.
- Severe enough to disable the sufferer and awaken him or her at night.
- Not relieved by changing position or lying down.
- Accompanied by nausea, fever, difficulty or pain in urinating, loss of bladder or bowel control, numbness or weakness in a leg or foot, or pain that shoots down the leg.

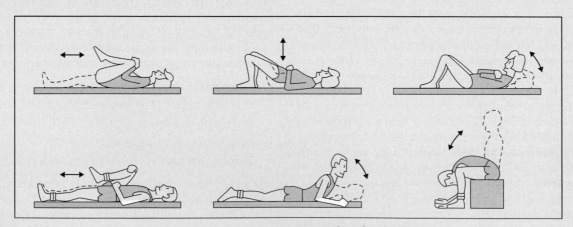

Figure 11-3 Six stretching and strengthening exercises to protect from low back pain.

counseling to improve family relationships and to enable the patient to find full-time employment when possible. And they offer a range of psychological services to reduce the experience of pain, decrease pain behavior, and improve the patient's psychological adjustment to the pain condition.

EVALUATING THE SUCCESS OF PAIN CLINICS

How effective are multidisciplinary pain clinics? To answer this question, we'll start by examining the procedures and results of two pain programs. Each program (1) was conducted by a hospital-affiliated pain clinic, (2) provided treatment on an inpatient basis for 4 weeks with weekends off, (3) treated several patients at a time with a variety of treatment techniques, and (4) had staff to provide medical, psychological, physical, and occupational therapy. Each program also used a medication reduction procedure, physical therapy, relaxation and biofeedback training, cognitive-behavioral group therapy, family involvement and training, and other methods.

In the first of these programs, the patients were men and women who had suffered intractable pain from known injuries or diseases, such as arthritis, for at least a year and were unemployed because of their pain conditions (Cinciripini & Floreen, 1982). All subjects received the full program. The researchers assessed the patients' behavior and functioning at the start and at the end of the program, and in follow-ups 6 and 12 months after. By the end of this program, the patients' activity levels had increased, and their pain experiences, pain behaviors, and drug use had decreased sharply—indeed, 90% of the patients were now free of analgesic medication. The subjects who participated in the follow-up assessments reported that they continued to be active, and about half were employed. Moreover, their pain continued to diminish: before treatment their average pain rating was 4.6 on a 10-point scale; by the end of the program it was 2.2, and after a year it was 1.2.

The second program compared a *treatment group* that completed the program with a *control group* that met all the criteria for acceptance into the program but declined to participate solely because they lacked insurance coverage (Guck et al., 1985). Follow-up assessments comparing the treatment and control subjects 1 to 5 years later revealed impressive outcomes: the treatment group reported experiencing far less pain, less evidence of depression, and less interference from pain in various activities, such as household chores, socializing, sexual relations, exercise, and sleep. Almost two-thirds of the treatment group and only one-fifth of the controls were employed, and far fewer treatment subjects used painkilling drugs.

Meta-analyses of dozens of studies have shown that people suffering with chronic pain who receive treatment at multidisciplinary pain centers report much less subsequent pain and are far more likely to return to work than individuals who have standard pain treatment (Cutler et al., 1994; Flor, Fydrich, & Turk, 1992). What's more, the cost of the treatment is only a small fraction of the medical and disability payments patients would receive for a year (Stieg & Turk, 1988). Two other research findings on multidisciplinary treatment are important. First, reductions in pain helplessness and catastrophizing during treatment lead to later decreases in pain severity and anxiety (Burns, Glenn et al., 2003). Second, pain patients who receive this treatment and benefit from it continue to have lower pain in the next year, but some show regression in their catastrophizing and disability and may benefit from booster interventions (Jensen, Turner, & Romano, 2007).

SUMMARY

Pain that receives or requires professional attention is called clinical pain. Practitioners try to reduce acute clinical pain for humanitarian reasons and for practical reasons, such as to enable medical procedures to be carried out smoothly, reduce patients' stress, and help patients recover quickly and without complications. Although medical care for pain may involve surgery if all other methods have failed, it usually involves pharmaceuticals selected from four types: peripherally acting analgesics; centrally acting analgesics; local anesthetics; and indirectly acting drugs, such as tranquilizers and antidepressants. These chemical methods are used extensively for relieving acute pain; they can be administered in several ways, such as by epidural block or patient-controlled analgesia. Drugs can also be used in treating chronic pain.

One of the main goals of behavioral and cognitive methods for treating chronic pain is to reduce the patient's drug consumption. The operant approach focuses on reducing pain behaviors through extinction procedures and increasing other behavior through reinforcement. Therapists apply progressive muscle relaxation and biofeedback to reduce the stress and muscle tension that can cause or aggravate patients' pain; this treatment produces effective and long-lasting relief for many chronic pain patients. Cognitive techniques focus on changing thought patterns that increase the intensity or frequency of pain experiences. Distraction and nonpain imagery methods appear to be effective chiefly for mild or moderate acute pain or for brief episodes of heightened chronic pain. Pain redefinition can involve clarifying what a pain experience will be like, using positive self-statements, and correcting faulty beliefs and logic. Redefinition can help reduce strong pain and chronic pain.

Hypnosis seems to relieve pain, particularly for individuals who can be deeply hypnotized. In general, people can reduce their pain as effectively with cognitive strategies in the waking state as with hypnosis. Interpersonal therapy strives to help people achieve insight into the social and motivational factors underlying their emotional difficulties.

For pain patients, this may involve making them aware of what is happening in the pain games they play or of how others feel about their pain conditions.

In counter-irritation procedures, a brief or moderate pain cancels a longer-lasting or stronger one. A pain control technique based on this procedure, called transcutaneous electrical nerve stimulation, is not as effective as researchers had thought. Acupuncture is an ancient Asian procedure for reducing pain; it produces analgesia for acute pain in some patients, but not in most. Although it does not provide long-term relief for most chronic pain patients, it may be useful in treating low back pain. Physical therapy includes such approaches as exercise, massage, traction, and the application of heat and cold to painful regions. Spinal manipulation techniques and proper exercise can reduce low back pain and protect individuals from back problems.

Pain clinics are institutions developed specifically for treating chronic pain. Multidisciplinary pain clinics use a variety of methods to provide highly effective and long-lasting pain relief, while also rehabilitating patients physically, psychologically, socially, and vocationally.

KEY TERMS

clinical pain	pain redefinition	transcutaneous electrical	pain clinics
distraction	counter-irritation	nerve stimulation	
nonpain imagery		acupuncture	

12

SERIOUS AND DISABLING CHRONIC ILLNESSES: CAUSES, MANAGEMENT, AND COPING

PROLOGUE

"Shirin, please sit down. If you have another one, you could really hurt yourself."

Shirin's mother is worried that there will be another seizure. But since she lacks knowledge of what epilepsy is and how seizures come about, she almost always forces Shirin to sit or lie on the floor. Whenever Shirin has a seizure, her parents and siblings know to put pillows around her, and the clinic staff has told them all what to do if she begins to choke or has trouble breathing. The closest hospital is many miles away, and even the clinic doctor only comes to the village once a week, so the family has learned to cope on their own.

Medication can help as many as 70% of sufferers, but it is expensive and the correct medication requires ongoing medical care, which is nearly impossible for Shirin's family. Epilepsy is a worldwide concern, but it is particularly prevalent in developing countries. It also happens that in many of these countries, health care is expensive and difficult to find, especially in remote areas.

Epilepsy is a tendency to have recurrent seizures (what used to be called "fits"). A seizure is caused by a sudden burst of electrical activity in the brain, causing a temporary disturbance in the normal activity of brain cells. This disturbance results in the brain's messages becoming frozen or confused.

The brain is responsible for every function in your body, so your experiences during a seizure will depend on where in your brain the electrical activity is. This means there are many different types of seizures, and each sufferer may experience epilepsy in a unique way.

Individuals react differently to a developing chronic illness. Their reactions depend on many factors, such as their coping skills and personalities, the social support they receive, access to medical care, the nature and consequences of their illnesses, and the impact of the illnesses on their daily functioning. At the very least, a chronic condition can mean a burden for patients and their families, who are often the only caregivers.

Chronically ill people may suffer episodes of illnesses and need to have regular medical checkups, restrict their diets, or take daily medication, for instance. Many chronic conditions produce frequent pain or lead to disability, or even death. Not surprisingly, they often cause serious emotional distress, including depression and feelings of helplessness. Many of us will develop at least one of these illnesses in our lifetimes, and one of them, such as cancer or cardiovascular disease, will probably take our lives.

This chapter and the next focus mainly on *tertiary prevention* for chronic illness—to retard its progression, prevent disability, and rehabilitate the person, physically and psychologically. We examine how people react to and cope with chronic health problems, and what can be done to help them cope effectively. In contrast to the next chapter, which deals with illnesses that have higher rates of mortality, the present chapter concentrates on health problems that are usually less likely to result in death but often lead to disability. This chapter begins by discussing people's reactions to having a chronic condition, and then examines the experiences of, and psychosocial interventions for, individuals living with various health problems. These discussions address many questions that are of great concern to the patients, to their families and friends, and probably to you. How do individuals react after learning that they have a chronic illness? What kinds of health problems usually involve the most difficult adjustments for people? How do patients' chronic conditions affect their families? What can families, friends, and therapists do to help chronically ill people adapt effectively to their conditions?

ADJUSTING TO A CHRONIC ILLNESS

"I felt like I'd been hit in the stomach by a sledge-hammer"—this is how many patients describe their first reaction upon learning that they have a disabling or life-threatening illness. Questions without immediate answers flash through their minds: Is the diagnosis right and, if so, what can we do about it? Will I be disabled, disfigured, or in pain? Will I die? How soon will these consequences happen? Will medical costs burden my family?

INITIAL REACTIONS TO HAVING A CHRONIC CONDITION

The first reaction most individuals experience when a doctor diagnoses a serious health problem is *shock*—being stunned or bewildered and behaving in an automatic and detached fashion (Shontz, 1975). The shock may last only a short while or may continue for weeks, occurs to some degree in any crisis people experience, and is likely to be most pronounced when the crisis comes without warning. Then, after a period of using emotion-focused strategies, such as denial, reality begins to intrude: the symptoms remain or get worse, additional diagnoses confirm the original one, and it becomes clear that adjustments need to be made. Patients tend to contact reality a little at a time until they reach some form of adjustment to the problem and its implications. Not all people react this way; some may be "cool and collected," while others may be "paralyzed" with anxiety or may become "hysterical" (Silver & Wortman, 1980).

People who use denial and other avoidance strategies do so to control their emotional responses to a stressor, especially when they believe they can do nothing to change the situation (Croyle & Ditto, 1990; Lazarus & Folkman, 1984). But this approach has limits, and excessive avoidance can soon become maladaptive to patients' physical and psychological well-being (Roesch & Weiner, 2001; Suls & Fletcher, 1985). For example, when hospitalized people receive information about their conditions and future risk factors, those who heavily use avoidance strategies gain less information about their conditions than those who use these strategies to a lesser degree (Shaw et al., 1985). How can they make decisions about their treatment rationally if they fail to take in the information practitioners present? What factors influence how people cope with their health problems? The next section provides some answers to this question.

INFLUENCES ON COPING WITH A HEALTH CRISIS

Healthy people tend to take their health for granted. When a serious illness or injury occurs, their daily activities and social roles are disrupted. Regardless of whether the condition is temporary or chronic, the first phases in coping with it are similar. But there is an important difference: chronic health problems usually require that patients and their families make permanent behavioral, social, and emotional adjustments. Learning of a serious chronic illness quickly changes the way they view themselves and their lives, and some plans they had made for the near or distant future may evaporate after

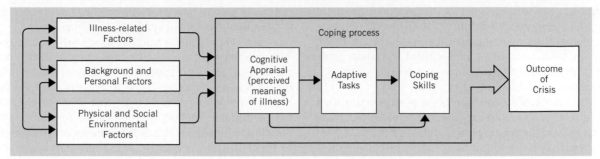

Figure 12-1   A diagram of crisis theory's description of factors and the coping process patients use in the first phases of adjusting psychologically to a serious illness. Arrows denote the flow of effects. (Adapted from Moos, 1982, Figure 1.)

the diagnosis. Adjustment to life-threatening or potentially disabling illness or injury may require major coping efforts (Cohen & Lazarus, 1979). And often no one can tell for certain exactly what the course of the illness will be.

Why do some individuals cope differently from others after learning they have a chronic health problem? **Crisis theory** describes factors that influence how people adjust (Moos, 1982; Moos & Schaefer, 1986). Figure 12-1 presents a diagram of the theory, showing that the outcome of the crisis—or the adjustment the person makes—depends on the coping process, which depends on three contributing influences: *illness-related* factors, *background and personal* factors, and *physical and social environmental* factors. We will look at each of these factors, and then see how they affect the patient's coping.

Illness-Related Factors

Some health problems present a greater threat to the person than others do—they may be more disabling, disfiguring, painful, or life-threatening, for example. The greater the threat patients perceive for any of these circumstances, the more difficulty they're likely to have coping with their conditions (Cohen & Lazarus, 1979; Moos, 1982). For example, adjusting to being disfigured can be extremely difficult. Many individuals whose faces are badly scarred withdraw from social encounters, particularly if they lack self-efficacy for controlling others' social reactions (Hagedoorn & Molleman, 2006).

Patients also have difficulty coping with illness-related factors that involve annoying or embarrassing changes in bodily functioning or that draw attention to their conditions (Bekkers et al., 1995). People with some illnesses may need artificial devices for excreting fecal or urinary wastes that are noticeable either visibly or by their odors. In other illnesses, people must treat their conditions with ointments that may have odors or with equipment that is visible or makes noise. Still others may experience periodic seizures or muscle spasms that can be embarrassing. Many people with

chronic illnesses feel self-conscious about their health problems—or even stigmatized by them—and want to hide them from others (Scambler, 1984).

Various aspects of treatment regimens can make adjustment very difficult, too. For instance, some treatments are painful or involve medications that produce serious side effects—either by leading to additional health problems or by interfering with the patient's daily functioning, such as by causing fatigue. Other regimens may have schedules and time commitments that require patients and their families to make substantial changes in their lifestyles and make it difficult for the person to find or hold a job. Each of these factors can impair people's adjustment to chronic health problems.

Background and Personal Factors

People who cope well with chronic health problems tend to have hardy or resilient personalities that allow them to see a good side or find meaning in difficult situations (Pollock, Christian, & Sands, 1991). As an example, a 16-year-old boy named Ralfie, whose body had wasted away to 22 kilograms from a rare spinal-muscular disease, stated:

> When I take a bath and look at myself naked, I think, "God Jesus." I'm disappointed when it comes to my body, but when it comes to my inside, my personality, my sense of humor, I'm proud of the way I am. I think I'm a nicer person. The girls always tell me, "You're very special. You're different than the other guys." (Hurley, 1987, p. 34)

People with chronic diseases who are like Ralfie can often find purpose and quality in their lives, maintain their self-esteem, and resist feeling helpless and hopeless.

The ways individuals cope with chronic health problems also depend on many other background and personal factors, such as their age, gender, social class, philosophical or religious commitments, emotional maturity, and self-esteem (Moos & Schaefer, 1986). With respect to gender differences, for instance, men are more likely than women to have difficulty with health problems that restrict their vigor or physical abilities (Moos, 1982). For men, having to take on a dependent and passive role can be especially difficult since it is inconsistent with their assertive and independent roles.

The timing of a health problem in the person's life span also affects the impact. Young children are not likely to understand the nature of their illnesses, the treatment regimens they must follow, and the long-term implications of their conditions (Burbach & Peterson, 1986). Their concerns are likely to focus on restrictions that are imposed on their activities, the frightening medical procedures, and possible separations from their parents. Adolescents can understand information about their illnesses and treatment, but their need to be like their peers and to feel accepted by them can lead to difficulties in coping with their health problems (La Greca & Stone, 1985). To avoid appearing different from their friends and risking rejection, adolescents may deny important aspects of their conditions and neglect their medical care.

In adulthood, too, the difficulties individuals have in coping with chronic health problems change with age (Mages & Mendelsohn, 1979; Moos, 1982). When people develop disabling or life-threatening illnesses or injuries in early adulthood, they tend to resent not having had the chance to develop their lives in the direction they planned—to get married, to have children, or to enter a particular career. In contrast, middle-aged patients may have problems adjusting to the disruption of established roles and lifestyles, and to being unable to finish tasks they have started, such as building up a business. In old age, people who develop chronic illnesses may resent not being able to enjoy the leisure they feel they earned in their lifetimes of work and self-sacrifice.

Another personal factor that affects how people cope with health problems is self-blame. People who believe they are personally responsible for developing a chronic illness and its symptoms tend to cope poorly, showing higher levels of depression over time than patients with less self-blame (Schiaffino, Shawaryn, & Blum, 1998). People's beliefs about the causes, effects, and treatments of their illnesses are often wrong and can affect their adjustment. Facing a serious disease and an uncertain future, some people worry excessively and imagine the worst when they consider their condition. Over time, this *rumination* and *catastrophizing* is associated with poor emotional adjustment, and worsening pain and other symptoms (Edwards et al., 2006; Soo, Burney, & Basten, 2009). Because chronic illness often limits what people can accomplish, self-esteem often fluctuates. This personal factor also influences the emotional and physical impact of chronic illness (Juth, Smyth, & Santuzzi, 2008).

Physical and Social Environmental Factors

Many physical and social features of our environments can affect the way we adjust to chronic health problems (Moos, 1982). The physical aspects of a hospital environment, for instance, are usually very dull and confining for patients, thereby depressing their general morale and mood. For some individuals, the home environment may not be much better. Many patients have difficulty getting around their houses or performing self-help tasks, such as buttoning clothes or opening food containers, and lack special equipment or tools that can

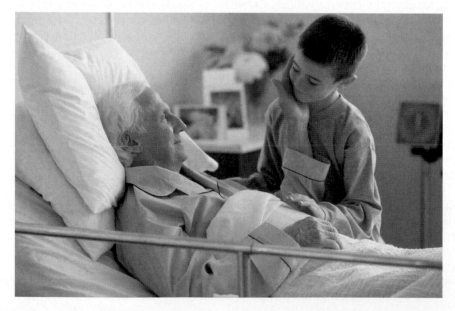

Sources of social support for patients usually involve their families, but also include friends and people from support groups and religious organizations.

help them do these tasks and be more self-sufficient. These people's adjustment to their health problems can be impaired as long as these situations persist.

The patient's social environment functions as a system, with the behavior of each person affecting the others (Cutrona & Gardner, 2004; Kerns & Weiss, 1994). The presence of social support, for example, generally helps patients and their families and friends cope with the illnesses. People who live alone and have few friends or who have poor relationships with the people they live with tend to adjust poorly to chronic ill health (Cutrona & Gardner, 2004; Stanton, Revenson, & Tennen, 2007). People in a patient's social network may sometimes undermine effective coping by providing criticism, bad examples, or poor advice (Suls, 1982). The degree to which each member of the social system adjusts in constructive ways to the illness affects the adjustment of the others. The primary source of social support for most people who are ill typically comes from their immediate families (Berg & Upchurch, 2007; Miller & Cafasso, 1992). But friends and neighbors also help, and patients may join *support groups* for people with specific medical problems. These groups can provide informational and emotional support.

Figure 12-1 shows that the three contributing influences in crisis theory are interrelated. The patient's social class or cultural background, for instance, may affect his or her self-consciousness about or access to special devices and equipment to promote self-sufficiency. These contributing factors combine to influence the coping process.

THE COPING PROCESS

Crisis theory proposes that coping begins with the patient's *cognitive appraisal* of the meaning or significance of the health problem to his or her life. The outcome of this appraisal leads the individual to formulate an array of *adaptive tasks* and to apply various *coping skills* to deal with these tasks. Let's see what these tasks and skills are.

The Tasks and Skills of Coping

According to Moos (1982), people who are ill need to address two types of adaptive tasks in the coping process:

1. *Tasks related to the illness or treatment*, which involve learning to (1) cope with the symptoms or disability the health problem causes, (2) adjust to the hospital environment and medical procedures or regimens needed to treat the problem, and (3) develop and maintain good relationships with their practitioners.

2. *Tasks related to general psychosocial functioning*, which involve striving to (1) control negative feelings and retain a positive outlook for the future, (2) maintain a satisfactory self-image and sense of competence, (3) preserve good relationships with family and friends, and (4) prepare for an uncertain future.

These tasks can be very difficult for patients, particularly when their health problems may lead to disability, disfigurement, or death. Still, many people with poor prognoses for their health manage to adapt successfully and make the most of their new circumstances. Patients are likely to adapt well to a chronic condition if their family members participate actively in their treatment regimens, encourage them to be self-sufficient, and respond to their needs in a caring and sensitive manner.

What coping skills do patients and their families employ to deal with these adaptive tasks? Table 12.1 describes several useful strategies that they commonly use, and each can help in achieving the goals of adaptive tasks and in leading to a positive outcome of the crisis. Is one approach best? Some coping skills may be more appropriate for dealing with some tasks than with others (Moos, 1982). As a result, people generally use these skills selectively, often in combination. For instance, seeking information may help patients deal with the symptoms, and setting reasonable goals may help them do exercises and reduce their incapacitation. Individuals who have adjusted successfully to each phase of their crises are ready to deal with longer-term aspects of their conditions.

Long-Term Adaptation to Chronic Health Problems

Facing chronic disorders often lasting many years, patients and their families need to adapt to the illness and whether it worsens, stays the same, or improves over time. The term **adaptation** refers to the process of making changes in order to adjust constructively to life's circumstances. As the focus of coping moves from a crisis or recent change in health to dealing with more permanent changes, successful adjustment for people with chronic medical conditions involves several major adaptive tasks that continue indefinitely: mastery of demands directly related to on-going management of the disease, such as adherence to medical regimens and the self-care portions of required medical treatments; minimizing physical limitations and disability; preserving as much positive functioning as possible in important domains, like work, relationships, and recreation; avoiding significant emotional distress; and maintaining an overall positive quality of life (Stanton, Revenson, & Tennen, 2007). What does "quality of life" mean? **Quality**

Table 12.1   *Coping Strategies for Chronic Health Problems*

- *Denying or minimizing* the seriousness of the situation. As we have seen, this approach can be beneficial in the early phases of adjusting to a health problem. Patients may benefit from this approach by using it selectively to put aside their emotions temporarily, thereby saving them from feeling overwhelmed and giving them time to organize other personal coping resources.
- *Seeking information* about the health problem and treatment procedures.
- *Learning to provide one's own medical care* such as self-administering insulin shots. With this approach, patients gain a sense of control and personal effectiveness with respect to their conditions.
- *Setting concrete, limited goals* such as in exercising or in going to shows or social gatherings, and maintaining regular routines as well as possible. By doing this, patients and their families have things to look forward to and opportunities to achieve goals they consider meaningful.
- *Recruiting instrumental and emotional support* from family, friends, and practitioners by expressing needs and feelings.
- *Considering possible future events* and stressful circumstances in order to know what lies ahead and to be prepared for unexpected difficulties.
- *Gaining a manageable perspective* on the health problem and its treatment by finding a long-term "purpose" or "meaning" for the experience. Patients often do this by applying religious beliefs or by recognizing how they have been changed in positive ways by the experience.

Source: Based on Moos, 1982.

of life refers to the degree of excellence people appraise their lives to contain. People around the world appraise excellence with similar criteria, such as performing daily activities, energy or discomfort, positive and negative feelings, personal control, interpersonal relations, pleasant activities, personal and intellectual growth, and material possessions (Gill & Feinstein, 1994; Power et al., 1999). For health care providers, the medical management of chronic illness broadens from a narrow focus on treating the underlying condition that is typical in acute illnesses to also include the patient's quality of life.

A common threat to the quality of life for people with chronic medical conditions is serious emotional distress, mostly in the form of depression and anxiety. These emotional problems are two or three times more common among people with chronic medical conditions than in the general population (Katon, Lin, & Kroenke, 2007; Smith, 2010). Depression and anxiety are common understandable consequences of the loss of functioning, burdens of physical discomfort and medical treatments, and uncertainly about the future that come from chronic medical conditions. But when it occurs, significant emotional distress can also worsen the course or outcome of the condition itself. As a result, for most of the chronic medical conditions we discuss in this chapter and the next, complete patient care often requires psychological components in addition to traditional medical and surgical aspects.

To summarize, most people tend to react to becoming seriously ill with shock, but they eventually deal with critical adaptive tasks they identify through the process of cognitive appraisal. The importance of each adaptive task depends on the person's personality, the physical and social environment, and the specific health problem to which he or she must adjust. In chronic medical conditions, these elements of the crisis become more permanent, on-going challenges in the process of adaptation.

IMPACTS OF DIFFERENT CHRONIC CONDITIONS

More than 130 million Americans—nearly one in two adults—are living with a chronic medical illness or disorder, and these conditions account for about 75% of the annual health care costs in the United States (CDC, 2009). Chronic diseases are similarly common in most industrialized nations around the world (WHO, 2010). What this common challenge of living with a chronic health problem is like depends on the illness. Beginning with this section, we consider the impact of specific chronic medical conditions on patients and their families. The particular health problems we will examine were selected to illustrate disorders of different body systems and widely different adjustment difficulties. Some of the health problems tend to develop at much earlier ages than others; some require much more complex treatment regimens than others; and some produce more pain and disability than others. People who are disabled by illness are more likely than others to adjust poorly to their condition and become seriously depressed (Leventhal et al., 2004). At the end of the chapter, we will consider psychosocial approaches to help chronically ill people adapt to their condition.

Although the medical problems we will discuss here include some that can be life-threatening, none of these chronic conditions is among the most deadly illnesses people around the world develop—particularly heart disease, cancer, stroke, and AIDS, which we will examine in the next chapter. We will use a *life-span perspective* to order the health problems in this chapter: illnesses that generally begin in childhood will be presented first, and illnesses that usually begin in old age will be considered last. As we have seen, the impact of a health problem and the way people cope with it depend partly on the patient's age. We will start by considering the impact of asthma, a chronic respiratory disorder that generally begins in the early childhood years.

ASTHMA

We all experience respiratory disorders. Fortunately, for most of us these disorders are limited to common colds or the flu. But many people around the world suffer from chronic respiratory problems. Some problems involve constant breathing impairments that vary in intensity from one day to the next. In others, the victims breathe normally most of the time but suffer episodes of impaired breathing. Some chronic respiratory illnesses, such as *emphysema*, result largely from environmental causes, such as cigarette smoking. Others do not. Some chronic respiratory disorders become severe enough to disable their victims and may even claim their lives. This can happen with *asthma*.

What is Asthma?

Imagine being at home reading one evening and noticing that a slight whistling, wheezing sound starts to accompany each breath you take. Soon the sound becomes louder, and your breathing becomes labored. You try opening your mouth to breathe, but very little air goes in or out. When your chest begins to contract from the effort and your heart pounds rapidly, you are quite frightened and worry, "Will my next gasp for air be my last?" This is what a major asthma attack is like. Victims of extreme attacks may begin to turn blue and look as if they are about to die, and some do die.

Asthma is a respiratory disorder involving episodes of impaired breathing when the airways become inflamed and obstructed. This disease afflicts 300 million people around the world, and more than 250,000 die from its attacks each year (WHO, 2007). Although the disorder may emerge at any age, prevalence rates are much higher for children than adults. Fortunately, most childhood cases of asthma become less severe over time (Burg & Ingall, 1985), and one-fourth of children who develop asthma no longer have symptoms by the time they reach adulthood (ALA, 2006). The death rates for American children are several times higher for Blacks than Whites (Akinbami & Schoendorf, 2002). Because African Americans have lower incomes than Whites and are less likely to have regular doctors, they tend to use hospital emergency rooms as their main source of treatment for asthma and seek help mainly when attacks are severe.

Asthma is a leading cause of short-term disability in the United States, resulting in millions of restricted-activity days in which patients either remain in bed or are unable to carry out their usual major activities, such as going to work or school. Each year, asthma results in:

- 15 million lost work days and 14 million lost school days.
- 2 million emergency room visits.
- 500,000 hospitalizations (AAFA, 2010).

Asthma is clearly a major health problem. Let's see what causes asthma attacks.

The Physiology, Causes, and Effects of Asthma

Asthma episodes typically begin when the immune system is activated to react in an allergic manner, producing antibodies that cause the bronchial tubes and other affected body tissues to release a chemical called *histamine*. This chemical causes irritation to those tissues. In an asthma attack, these events cause the bronchial tubes to become obstructed as their smooth muscles become inflamed, develop spasms, and produce mucus (AAFA, 2010; Evans, 1990). These events last, perhaps, an hour or two and can lead to tissue damage, thereby increasing the likelihood of more frequent and severe future attacks. For some asthmatics, airway inflammation becomes constant.

What causes asthma attacks to happen? We do not have a full answer to this question, but we do know that attacks usually occur in the presence of certain conditions, called *triggers* (Evans, 1990). Asthma triggers can include *personal factors*, such as having a respiratory infection or feelings of anger or anxiety; *environmental conditions*, such as air pollution, pollen, or cold temperature; and *physical activities*, such as strenuous exercise (ALA, 2006; Sarafino & Goldfedder, 1995). The triggers that lead to attacks are different for different asthmatics, and some individuals have attacks only when two or more triggers occur at the same time (Evans, 1990). The main triggers for many asthmatics are allergens—substances, such as pollens or molds, that are known to cause allergic reactions. But other asthmatics do not have any known allergies, and other factors, such as physical exercise or cold air, are the main triggers for them. Tests for allergic reactions usually involve injecting a small amount of the allergen under the skin and checking to see if the skin in that area becomes inflamed.

Researchers demonstrated the important role of immune processes in the development of allergic reactions with a study involving transplanted bone marrow, the tissue that produces white blood cells (Agosti et al., 1988). The subjects were cancer patients who needed the transplants as part of their treatment. Each subject and donor was given skin tests with 17 allergen extracts—including house dust, cat hair, mites, and ragweed—before the transplant and one year after. In some of the pretransplant tests, the donor showed a positive allergic reaction but the subject did not. When tested again a year later, the subjects now showed reactions in 44.5% of the tests. In other pretransplant tests, neither the donor nor the patient showed an allergic reaction. This situation served as a control condition—and a year later the subjects showed reactions in only 3% of these tests. These findings indicate that bone marrow contains allergen-specific antibodies and that the donors' allergies were passed on to the patients. This research also found cases of asthma being transmitted from donors to people with no history of the disease.

What causes the condition of asthma to develop? Twin studies and other genetic research have shown that heredity clearly plays a role (Sarafino, 2004a). Research has also found evidence linking genetic factors to the severity of the condition and some of the specific triggers that are involved (Sarafino & Goldfedder, 1995). Other important factors include the person's history of respiratory infection and exposure to cigarette smoke. Individuals who contract serious viral infections in infancy or early childhood are more likely to develop asthma than individuals who do not (Li & O'Connell, 1987; Sarafino & Dillon, 1998). Children are more likely to develop asthma if their parents smoke (Hu et al., 1997). It may be that infections and smoke damage the respiratory system, making it highly sensitive to certain triggering conditions.

Medical Regimens for Asthma

Medical approaches provide the cornerstone of treatment for asthma (ALA, 2006; Evans, 1990). Asthma regimens consist of three components, the first being to *avoid known triggers* of attacks. The second component involves medication. To treat an acute attack, patients mainly use *bronchodilators*, which open constricted airways. To prevent attacks, patients can use *anti-inflammatories*, such as inhaled corticosteroids, which, when used regularly, reduce the sensitivity and inflammation of the airways when a trigger occurs.

The third component of asthma regimens is *exercise*. In the past, doctors advised many asthmatics to avoid exercise because it could induce an attack (Stockton, 1988). But it now appears that the less these people exercise, the worse their conditions get. Many doctors today recommend treatment regimens that carefully combine fitness training and the use of medication. Asthma's potential for producing disability and, sometimes, death makes it important that patients take their medications as directed, but large numbers of them fail to do so (Leventhal et al., 2004).

Psychosocial Factors in Asthma

We saw in Chapter 3 that psychosocial factors such as stress and negative emotions contribute to the development and worsening course of asthma, and once developed asthma can be a significant source of emotional distress (Chida, Hamer, & Steptoe, 2008). Stress can also produce or aggravate individual asthmatic attacks or episodes. Research with asthmatic children has clarified the role of emotional factors in two ways. First, excitement by watching an exciting movie can trigger attacks in some children (Miller & Wood, 1994). Second, anxiety increases symptom perception, especially at the start of an asthma episode (Chen et al., 2006; Janssens et al., 2009). Catastrophizing or appraising vague respiratory symptoms as an impending and potentially severe asthma attack can increase anxiety and symptoms of respiratory distress (DePeuter et al., 2008). Anxiety and catastrophizing can also worsen the impact of more severe episodes. In some severe instances, asthma co-occurs with severe anxiety disorders such as panic, and these anxiety symptoms worsen the severity and impact of asthma (Feldman et al., 2009).

Studies have also found that *suggestion* can induce asthma symptoms. In one study, researchers had asthmatics inhale several doses of a placebo solution, with each succeeding dose labeled as containing an increasingly strong level of an allergen (Luparello et al., 1968). Nearly half of the subjects developed symptoms, either as full asthma attacks or as spasms of the bronchial muscles. Other studies have confirmed that suggestion can affect attacks and also showed that people can learn through classical conditioning to make respiratory reactions to harmless stimuli and can become breathless if given false feedback indicating that the airways are becoming obstructed (Butler & Steptoe, 1986; De Peuter et al., 2005; Rietveld & Brosschot, 1999). Over time, asthmatics who utilize adaptive coping strategies like acceptance, reappraisal, and distraction tend to have improved lung function (Schreier & Chen, 2008). Although there is little question that psychosocial factors can influence asthma attacks, we do not know how precisely these factors work and which asthmatics are more affected by them.

Frequent asthma episodes are costly, disruptive, and stressful for asthmatics and their families. Levels and rates of maladjustment, especially anxiety disorders, are higher among people with than without asthma (Lehrer et al., 2002). This probably involves two causal directions: living with asthma may lead to emotional problems, and maladjustment increases the frequency and severity of asthmatic episodes (Chida et al., 2008). Some asthmatics are chronically short of breath and have frequent attacks, and others have long attack-free periods. The psychosocial impact of asthma depends on many factors, such as how severe and disabling the condition is, and these factors probably play a role in asthmatics' low levels of adherence to taking medication and avoiding triggers, such as cigarette smoke (Cabana et al., 2004; Lehrer et al., 2002). Family factors are clearly important, too. Children with asthma whose families have more structured daily routines show decreasing asthma-related inflammation over time (Schreier & Chen, 2010), and when parents quit smoking their children's asthma improves (Borrelli et al., 2010).

EPILEPSY

Epilepsy is a condition marked by recurrent, sudden seizures that result from electrical disturbances of the cerebral cortex (AMA, 2003; EFA, 2006; Fraser, 1999). Although the form of seizures can vary greatly, a common and very severe form is the *tonic-clonic*, or *grand mal*, which has two phases. It begins with a very brief "tonic" phase, in which the person loses consciousness and body is rigid. It then progresses to a longer "clonic" phase that lasts 2 or 3 minutes and includes muscle spasms and twitching. The body may then relax until the person awakens soon. Sometimes before tonic-clonic seizures epileptics experience an *aura*, which consists of unexplained sounds, smells, or other sensations. In mild forms of seizures, the person may just stare blankly for a few seconds and show slight facial twitching.

Epilepsy afflicts 50 million people worldwide (WHO, 2007). An estimated 2.4 million new cases occur each year globally, at least 50% of cases begin in childhood or adolescence (WHO, 2010). But many people with epilepsy are undiagnosed and untreated. What causes epilepsy? Although we don't know why the neurological disorder develops, risk factors for epilepsy include a strong family history of the condition, severe head injury, and other brain disorders, such as cerebral palsy, stroke, and Alzheimer's disease (EFA, 2006; Hauser & Hesdorffer, 1990). Most people with epilepsy eventually become seizure-free for at least 5 years. (Go to 💡.)

Medical Regimens for Epilepsy

Anticonvulsant drugs provide the main medical treatment for epilepsy (AMA, 2003; EFA, 2006; Fraser, 1999). These medications must be taken regularly to maintain the most effective serum concentrations throughout the day. In cases when medication does not control the seizures, doctors consider other methods, such as implanting a device that stimulates the vagal nerve or surgery if the seizures result from clear neurological

---

HIGHLIGHT

What to Do for a Seizure

People react negatively to seeing a grand mal attack for many reasons, one of which may be that they don't know what to do to help. There is little one *can* do other than to remain calm and try to protect the epileptic from injury as he or she falls or flails about. But the following five actions are recommended (Eichenwald, 1987; EFA, 2006):

1. Prevent injury from falls or flailing. Break the fall if possible and provide a cushion, such as a coat, between the person's head and the ground.

2. Do *not* put anything in the person's mouth. Many people believe they must put a spoon or other object in the mouth to prevent the epileptic from swallowing his or her tongue, which actually cannot happen. Loosen tight clothing around the neck. Turn the person on his or her side so that saliva does not obstruct breathing.

3. Do *not* restrain the person. If you believe the epileptic could be injured while flailing near a hard object, try to move the object.

4. If the person does not come out of the attack in about 5 minutes, call an ambulance.

5. After the person wakes up, describe what happened and see if he or she needs any help. Epileptics are often disoriented after an attack.

For the most part, bystanders should remain calm and composed, and use common sense.

defects. Neuropsychologists conduct tests to pinpoint the affected area of the brain and minimize cognitive and motor impairments the surgery might produce (DeAngelis, 1990). After surgery, as many as 80% of patients become seizure-free in the next few years (Noachtar & Borggraefe, 2009). But undergoing surgery without becoming seizure-free may lead to subsequent psychosocial difficulties, such as heightened anxiety and depression (Jacoby & Baker, 2008).

Psychosocial Factors in Epilepsy

Because people having epileptic episodes lose control of their behavior and "act strange," their condition stigmatizes them among people who do not understand it (Jacoby & Baker, 2008). This is clear in the experience of a college freshman named Kurt when he witnessed an epileptic attack for the first time: a young worker in the college dining hall

> had collapsed in a convulsion. Four students quickly piled on top of him. His arms and legs jerked violently and, in the process of trying to hold him down, the students seemed to be smothering him. The young man's face, twisted and red, made him appear to be in great pain and, somehow, inhuman. Yet I could see myself in his place—I had just found out that I had epilepsy.
>
> I did not want to say anything, but I thought the four students, in their panic, might kill the young man. So I told the largest of them, who by then had a headlock on the kitchen worker, to let go. The student brushed off my concern and seemed irritated that I should bother him at such a time. I paused, then repeated my statement in louder tones. The student was angry. "Look, kid, I'm a pre-med. I know what I'm doing. What makes you think you know so much?" I opened my mouth, but no words came out. Instead, I walked to a corner and leaned against a wall. As the young man's convulsions grew more violent, I whispered an apology to him and began to cry. (Eichenwald, 1987, p. 30)

Kurt had been advised to keep his own epilepsy a secret, or people would fear and discriminate against him. Long ago, many people believed that individuals with epilepsy were possessed by the devil. Although few people in advanced societies today shun victims of epilepsy, witnessing an attack may still arouse feelings of fear and aversion.

Aside from the reactions their attacks produce in others, what other problems do epileptics face as a result of their illness? Having strong seizures, especially with a loss of consciousness, is sometimes associated with cognitive and motor impairments that can limit eligibility for certain activities and jobs, such

as those with high memory loads or danger from heights or machinery (Smeets et al., 2007). The case of Kurt, the freshman we just discussed, provides an example of the discrimination epileptics have experienced. Because of his condition, he was dismissed from the prestigious college he attended. As it turned out, however, he was reinstated after the United States Department of Health and Human Services ruled that dismissal was discriminatory. He graduated in 1983.

Epilepsy seems to be related to psychosocial processes in two ways. First, some evidence suggests that emotional arousal, such as of anxiety, may increase the likelihood or severity of epileptic episodes (Goldstein, 1990). Second, epileptics and their families sometimes adjust poorly to the disorder, especially if episodes are frequent and severe (Ekinci et al., 2009). Some epileptics drop out of rehabilitation programs because of emotional difficulties. Many of the adjustment problems that epileptics face can be reduced through counseling when the diagnosis is made and through the work of support groups. A major determinant of the emotional, social, and vocational impact of epilepsy is the level of success of medical or surgical management; the better the control over seizures that is achieved and the less extensive the treatment required to achieve it, the better the patient's adaption. Beyond those factors, stigma is associated with worse adjustment, whereas optimism, social support, and a sense of control of the condition and its impact are associated with better adjustment (Jacoby & Baker, 2008).

NERVOUS SYSTEM INJURIES

A woman named Leslie who suffered a *brain injury* in a car accident awoke very disoriented after 17 days in a coma; in her words,

> I didn't know who I was, what happened to me. All of a sudden you wake up in this bed one day and these people are hurting you, bending your leg and such. And you think it's a dream or a nightmare of some kind. (Leonard, 1990, p. 49)

This was the start of her long recovery. Thousands of people suffer injuries to the brain or spinal cord each year, leaving them debilitated for life. Neuropsychologists and health psychologists play important roles in assessing these patients' impairments and helping them adapt to their conditions (Bleiberg, Ciulla, & Katz, 1991), a general field that is called *rehabilitation psychology*. In this section, we will focus on spinal cord injury.

Prior to the 1940s, medical practitioners knew little about treating people with severe spinal cord injuries (Hendrick, 1985). In World War I, 80% of soldiers with such injuries died within 2 weeks, and little attempt was made to rehabilitate those who survived. But in World War II, England established special medical units to develop and provide comprehensive care and rehabilitation for people with spinal cord injuries. These medical units served as a model for others to be developed in countries around the world.

The Prevalence, Causes, and Physical Effects of Spinal Cord Injuries

The term **spinal cord injury** refers to neurological damage in the spine that results in the loss of motor control, sensation, and reflexes in associated body areas. The damage may be caused by disease or an injury that compresses, tears, or severs the cord (AMA, 2003; NSCIA, 2006). When the cord is badly torn or severed, the damage is permanent because little or no nerve tissue will regenerate. If the cord is compressed or has an abrasion, some function may be recovered when pressure is removed or healing occurs. The extent to which the person's function is impaired depends on the amount and location of damage. If the cord is severed in the neck region, *quadriplegia* results—the body is paralyzed from the neck down. If a lower portion is severed, *paraplegia* results. If the cord is not completely severed, partial function remains.

Millions of people around the world are living with spinal cord injuries; in the United States, there are over 250,000 people with this affliction, and about 7,800 new cases occur each year (NSCIA, 2006). About half of these people are quadriplegics. The great majority of Americans who receive spinal cord injuries are males, and most of them are under 30 years of age at the time. The most common cause is motor vehicle accidents, and the remainder result mainly from falls, sporting activities, and wounds, such as from a gunshot or stabbing. During war, many veterans are affected.

The physical effects patients experience after spinal cord injuries change over time, and the full extent of damage may not be clear for some time. Long-term prognoses are difficult to make during the first 6 months or so (Hendrick, 1985). If the cord is not severed, considerable functional recovery may occur over a long period of time. If the cord is severed, some autonomic functions will recover, but other functions will not. People who survive severe damage to higher regions of the cord are usually fully paralyzed and unable to breathe without a respirator. Once the patient's condition has stabilized, the process of rehabilitation begins. Most of these patients enter rehabilitation expecting to regain total function and are not prepared to cope with the reality of permanent functional losses. A major goal for psychologists at this time is to help these people adjust to the demands and limitations of rehabilitation (Richards et al., 2010).

Physical Rehabilitation

The process of physical rehabilitation for people with spinal cord injuries is geared toward helping them regain as much physical function as the neurological damage will allow and become as independent in their functioning as possible. This process focuses initially on training the patients to develop bladder and bowel control and on assisting them in moving paralyzed limbs to maintain their range of motion (Hendrick, 1985). Although many of these people will eventually be able to control their bladder functions, others will not and will need to use catheters or other devices. Hygienic bladder care is extremely important because a common cause of death in these patients is kidney failure from repeated infections (Richards et al., 2010; NSCIA, 2006).

The next phase of rehabilitation extends the focus of physical therapy toward maintaining and improving the function of muscles over which the person has some control (Hendrick, 1985). For example, quadriplegics receive special attention toward improving respiration; paraplegics do exercises to strengthen the upper body. When some neural connection to affected parts of the body remains, therapy with biofeedback to "reeducate" the muscles in those areas appears to help some, but not all, patients (Klose et al., 1993). The last phase of physical rehabilitation extends the therapy as

Actor Christopher Reeve resumed an active life for several years after a horse-riding accident rendered him quadriplegic, but he died in 2004 of complications from his condition.

much as possible to include activities of daily living: performing self-care activities independently and to using devices to compensate for permanent physical losses. Some devices today are highly sophisticated and use computers, allowing paralyzed individuals to turn on lights, answer the telephone, and operate computer keyboards with voice commands.

Psychosocial Aspects of Spinal Cord Injury

People with spinal cord injuries who survive the first 24 hours have a long life ahead: 10 years later, 85% are still alive, and many live another 30 years or more (NSCIA, 2006). Most victims who were employed prior to the injury are working again within a year or so. However, returning to work is more difficult with more severe injuries and related physical limitations, communities with poor access to workplaces, discrimination by employers and co-workers, limited social support from friends and family, depression, or low levels of self-reliance (Burns et al., 2010). The victims' main challenges after spinal cord injury are to make the most of their remaining abilities and lead as full a life as possible. Many aspects of quality of life are challenged after spinal cord injury, including overall health, career concerns, finances, living circumstances, relationships, and emotional adjustment (Krause & Reed, 2009). For some patients, these challenges are particularly difficult because they often suffer from chronic pain and poor sleep, and lack the resources to help them live and function independently (Jensen et al., 2009; Mariano, 1992; Tate, Maynard, & Forchheimer, 1993). The circumstances of the initial injury also shape the course of recovery. For example, veterans whose wounds result in spinal cord injuries are at increased risk of post-traumatic stress disorder, as well as depression (Goldman, Radnitz, & McGrath, 2008).

What can health care workers, family, and friends do to help? A lot depends on the way they respond to the person's condition. John Adams and Erich Lindemann (1974) contrasted the cases of two young men, 17 and 18 years of age, who had suffered spinal cord injuries that rendered them quadriplegic. One adapted well: he was able to accept the injury and cope with no longer being a fine athlete. He turned his energies toward academic pursuits and eventually became a history teacher and coached a local basketball team from his wheelchair. The other patient provides a striking contrast. He was never able to accept the injury or the permanence of his condition. He became withdrawn and depressed—at one point he was spending "much time in bed with the curtains drawn and frequently with the sheet over his head." Years later, he was readmitted to the hospital after taking an overdose of medication and was still clinging to the

hope that he would walk again. Why did these young men adapt so differently to similar physical conditions? Part of the answer may be in their strikingly different social environments. The patient who adapted well had family and friends who could accept his paralysis and help him redefine his self-concept. For instance, his parents installed ramps in their home and widened doorways to accommodate a wheelchair. The other patient's family and friends were not able to accept his condition or provide the support he needed to help him adapt.

Family and friends can also help by providing social support without being overprotective and "taking over" when patients have difficulty helping themselves. Having a disabled individual in the household increases stress for all family members. They need to make many adjustments in daily living and, while doing so, try not to make the person feel like a burden. If the patient is a husband or wife, the spouse faces difficult adjustments; partners of spinal cord injury patients are also at greater risk of emotional difficulties (Chandler, Kennedy, & Sandhu, 2007). Role changes occur immediately—at least for a while, and perhaps permanently, the healthy spouse must provide the family's income, do the household chores, and care for the children and disabled spouse.

Sexual problems brought on by the patient's injury may become a major source of stress in the marital relationship. Although many people believe that all individuals who become paralyzed below the waist lose all sexual function and interest, this is not correct (Richards et al., 2010; NSCIA, 2006). Males usually lose their fertility. But although they initially lose the ability to have an erection, they often regain it to some degree. Females generally retain their fertility after paralysis, and about half become able to achieve orgasm. The most serious barriers to sexual function in people with spinal cord injuries appear to be psychosocial rather than physical. These patients and their partners can overcome many of these barriers through counseling and education, such as in ways to position themselves during sex and to heighten the degree of stimulation they achieve.

Disabled people also experience unpleasant thoughts about themselves, their future, their relations with other people, and physical barriers in society (Eisenberg, 1984). They find that many places they once liked to go to are inaccessible by wheelchair, for example. Further, people in general may act strangely toward them—staring, or averting their eyes, or behaving awkwardly in their presence. These experiences can reduce self-esteem in disabled people, many of whom have heightened levels of depression and drug and alcohol use (Richards et al., 2010). Adapting to disability takes time, and a couple of years may pass before many individuals with spinal cord injuries report improvements in their adjustment and quality of life (Krause & Crewe, 1991). Despite these challenges, many—if not most—patients display resilience in response to their condition and the demanding process of rehabilitation; others struggle initially but show steady improvements over time (Quale & Schanke, 2010). Acceptance of their changed circumstances, tolerance of frustration and negative affect, perceived competence, perseverance, and the ability to find meaning in their new circumstances contribute to resilience, whereas a more severe and continuing sense of loss contributes to poor adjustment (deRoon-Cassini et al., 2009; White, Driver, & Warren, 2010).

DIABETES

"Too much of a good thing is wonderful," the late actress Mae West once said. Although her rule might possibly apply for some good things, glucose in the blood is not one of them. The body needs glucose to fuel metabolic processes, but too much of it in the blood over a long period of time—a condition called *hyperglycemia*—is the mark of *diabetes mellitus*. The body normally controls blood sugar levels with the hormone *insulin*, which the pancreas produces. In the disorder of diabetes, however, abnormal levels of glucose accumulate in the blood because the pancreas either does not produce sufficient insulin or the body no longer responds normally to insulin (ADA, 2006; AMA, 2003).

Diabetes is a prevalent illness—about 180 million people around the world have been diagnosed with it (WHO, 2007); in the United States, there are currently 15.6 million diagnosed diabetics, 1.5 million cases diagnosed each year, and over 6 million people who are unaware that they have the disorder (ADA, 2006). Prevalence rates for diagnosed diabetes in American adults increase greatly with age and vary across ethnic groups, as Table 12.2 shows. Women from Hispanic, African, and Native American groups are at especially high risk of dying from diabetes (USDHHS, 1995).

The Types and Causes of Diabetes

Diabetes is not a single disease—it occurs in two major forms that require different kinds of treatment and may have somewhat different causes. The two patterns of diabetes are:

1. **Type 1 diabetes** (formerly called *insulin-dependent diabetes*) typically develops in childhood or adolescence and accounts for 5 to 10% of cases. In Type 1, autoimmune processes have destroyed cells of the pancreas that normally produce insulin, a hormone that enables body cells to use glucose. Type 1 diabetics require insulin injections to prevent acute and very serious complications (ADA, 2006; AMA, 2003). One such acute complication in type 1 diabetes is *ketoacidosis*, in which high levels of fatty acids in the blood lead to kidney malfunctions, thereby causing wastes to accumulate and poison the body. Symptoms of ketoacidosis are subtle at first, but advance to nausea, vomiting, abdominal pain, and labored breathing. If untreated, ketoacidosis can lead to coma and death in a matter of days or weeks.

2. **Type 2 diabetes** is very prevalent, accounting for the vast majority of diabetes cases. In this form, the pancreas produces at least some insulin, and treatment may not require insulin injections. Most, but not all, people with type 2 diabetes can manage their glucose levels with diet and medication (AMA, 2003). Although type 2 diabetes can develop at any age, it usually appears after age 40. Most type 2 patients are very overweight, and many produce substantial amounts of insulin—sometimes more than normal—but their bodies seem to "resist" the glucose-controlling action of insulin. Some "pre-diabetic" individuals have moderately high levels of blood glucose and evidence of insulin insensitivity, before later reaching the levels required for the Type 2 diagnosis (ADA, 2006; Kohrt et al., 1993). Normal-weight type 2 patients seem to produce reduced levels of insulin. In either case, hyperglycemia results.

What causes the pancreas to reduce insulin production? Heredity plays a role: a gene that many people carry has been found that confers a high risk of diabetes (Ræder et al., 2006). Most diabetics probably inherit a susceptibility to the effects of environmental conditions that affect insulin production (ADA, 2006; AMA, 2003). In type 1, one such condition seems to involve a viral infection that stimulates the immune system to attack pancreas cells (Conrad et al., 1994). For type 2, evidence exists for three possible conditions: diets high in fat and

Table 12.2 *Percent of the American Adult Population with Diagnosed Diabetes by Age and Ethnic Group*

Age and Ethnic Group[a]	Percent
Years of age	
20 to 39	1.7
40 to 59	8.3
60 and over	16.9
Ethnic group	
White	6.9
African American	11.8
Mexican American	7.9

[a]Data for ethnic groups are age adjusted to eliminate differences in observed rates that result from age differences in population composition, thereby allowing risk comparisons for two or more populations at one point in time.
Source: NCHS, 2009a, Table 54.

sugar, stress, and an overproduction of a protein that impairs the metabolism of sugars and carbohydrates (Maddux et al., 1995; Surwit, 1993). Some evidence suggests that chronic stress, negative emotions, and other psychosocial vulnerabilities increase risk for developing diabetes (Knol et al., 2006; Golden et al., 2008; Mezuk et al., 2008), although other evidence suggests that these factors can lead to poor medical outcomes in established diabetes but not the initial development of diabetes (Chida & Hamer, 2008). Smoking may also contribute to the development of diabetes (Willi et al., 2007). The importance of diet, exercise, and weight as causes of type 2 diabetes is demonstrated by the success of related lifestyle interventions involving diet and exercise in treating "pre-diabetic" conditions and preventing their progression to diabetes (Davidson et al., 2009; Magkos et al., 2009; Orozco et al., 2008). (Go to 🍎.)

Health Implications of Diabetes

Diabetes can be a direct cause of death: each year it claims over 1,000,000 lives worldwide (WHO, 2007). Many of these deaths result from acute complications that can be prevented by appropriate medical care. Few diabetics die of acute complications if they follow the recommended medical regimens for controlling glucose levels (Santiago, 1984).

But the deaths that are caused directly by diabetes constitute only part of the toll of this disease (ADA, 2006; AMA, 2003). For instance, diabetes can lead to *neuropathy*, or nerve disease. High blood glucose levels appear to cause chemical reactions that can destroy the myelin sheath that insulates nerve fibers. When this occurs in peripheral fibers, such as in the feet, the person may lose sensation in the affected area or have abnormal sensations, such as chronic pain. Other health problems caused by diabetes include blindness, kidney disease, gangrene (and as a result, amputation), heart disease, and stroke. Diabetes contributes to these health problems through its effects on the vascular system (AMA, 2003). High levels of glucose in the blood lead to a thickening of arterial walls as a result of atherosclerosis: in large blood vessels, it can cause gangrene in a limb or heart disease; in small blood vessels and capillaries, it can cause blindness and stroke. We saw in Chapter 3 that a cluster of conditions called *metabolic syndrome* that includes poor control of glucose and abnormal insulin sensitivity raises the risk of diabetes and coronary heart disease. The long-term health risks of diabetes are quite serious, and patients and their families worry about them greatly (Wilkinson, 1987).

Medical Regimens for Diabetes

Ideally, the treatment for diabetes would enable the body to perform or simulate the normal biochemical activities for processing and maintaining healthy levels of glucose. Normal and diabetic serum glucose levels in the hours after eating are shown in Figure 12-2. Medical regimens today compensate for these differences, but they do not enable the body to function exactly as it normally does, such as in continuously monitoring the need for insulin and secreting this hormone in precisely needed bursts.

The main approach for treating diabetes entails a balancing act with medication, diet, and regular exercise. Can diabetics reduce their long-term health risks? Yes, these risks can be markedly reduced—with complications occurring much later and far less often—if diabetics control their blood glucose levels, keeping them within the normal range, by carefully following prescribed treatment regimens and lifestyle changes (ADA, 2006; Magkos et al., 2009; Nathan et al., 2005). But the *full extent* of the reduced risk is unclear because long-term complications of diabetes take many years or decades to

---

ASSESS YOURSELF

Do You Have Diabetes?

Nearly one-third of the people who have diabetes don't know it. To tell if you might have this disorder, put a check mark in the space preceding each of the following warning signs that are true for you.

____ Very frequent urination.
____ Frequent excessive thirst.
____ Often hungry, even after eating.
____ Unexplained large weight loss.

____ Increased chronic fatigue.
____ Blurry vision.
____ Higher than usual irritability.

If you check one or more of these signs, see your doctor—one or two signs alone may not mean anything is wrong. But the more signs you checked, the greater the chance that you have diabetes. (ADA, 2006.)

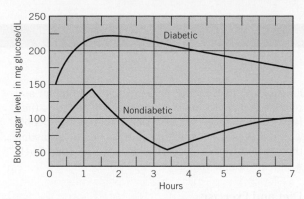

Figure 12-2 Serum levels of glucose for nondiabetics and unmedicated diabetics in the hours after consuming glucose. The data come from a standardized procedure in which subjects consume a specified amount of glucose per kilogram of body weight. (From Holum, 1994, Figure 26.4.)

develop, and many diabetics with good blood glucose control are not always able to keep their glucose levels consistently in the normal range. Today's treatments for diabetes allow patients to have better control over their blood sugar than in the past, but these new methods are still not perfect, and many diabetics do not adhere to them closely.

Do Diabetics Adhere to their Regimens?

Following the medical regimen in diabetes clearly improves control over blood glucose, though not perfectly (Hood et al., 2009). Noncompliance with these otherwise effective treatment regimens is a major problem in managing diabetes. Years ago, reviews of studies on this issue found most people with diabetes tested their glucose levels incorrectly, administered wrong doses of insulin, and failed to follow the recommended diets carefully (Wing et al., 1986). And the situation may be worse today, as blood sugar control among type 2 diabetics decreased from 1988 to 2000 (Koro et al., 2004). People with diabetes generally *try* to adhere to their regimens, but they do not always succeed. In some cases, poor literacy limits understanding of the disease and regimen (Rothman et al., 2004). In other cases, diabetics rely on symptoms they perceive, such as dizziness or emotional states, to assess their glucose levels (Cox et al., 1993; Meltzer et al., 2003). Although many diabetics can make crude estimates of their actual glucose levels on the basis of perceived symptoms, these judgments are usually not very accurate.

Some research has found that people with diabetes have more difficulty following dietary and exercise advice than the more "medical" aspects of their

regimens—testing their glucose levels and taking their insulin on time (Glasgow, McCaul, & Schafer, 1987). The patients' self-reports indicated they had complied fairly closely with their insulin and testing regimens. However, self-report data can be misleading. In two studies, for instance, researchers secretly inserted memory chips in blood glucose testing devices of adult and adolescent diabetics but also had the subjects keep records of their testing (Mazze et al., 1984; Wilson & Endres, 1986). The results showed that many subjects' records were inaccurate—at least according to the memory chips' records. The records did *not* contain data for some tests the subjects had done and *did* contain data for tests that they did not actually perform. (Go to 💡.)

Psychosocial Factors in Diabetes Care

A 60-year-old diabetic named Beth had not been able to get her glucose levels under control (Holt, 1995). Part of the problem was that she had mental retardation and didn't understand how to plan her diet at home. A home-care nurse discovered an approach to help: they made up recipe cards for each meal, with pictures of its foods and a shopping list—and it worked! Not understanding the regimen and how to adjust it on the basis of glucose test results is a common problem even among people with normal cognitive abilities (Patrick et al., 1994; Trief, 2004).

We saw in Chapter 8 that compliance with medical recommendations tends to be low when the regimen is complex, must be followed for a long time, requires changes in the person's lifestyle, and is designed to prevent rather than cure illness. Regimens for diabetes have all of these characteristics, and they must be dealt with many times every day—diabetes has no vacation (Trief, 2004). In addition, psychosocial factors in patients' lives are related to compliance. Two of these factors are social support and self-efficacy. A study found that diabetics' self-reports of adherence to dietary, exercise, and glucose testing aspects of their regimens increased with their perceived social support (Wilson et al., 1986). But the role of social support is unclear because it was not related to actual glucose control measured by analysis of blood samples. Research on diabetics' self-efficacy has shown that the greater their self-efficacy for following the diabetes regimen, the higher their subsequent self-reports of adherence and the better their actual glucose control (Johnston-Brooks, Lewis, & Garg, 2002; Skelly et al., 1995).

Coping processes are also important in diabetes care. Stress impairs blood sugar control in many diabetics (Kramer et al., 2000), especially those who have sedentary lifestyles (Aikens et al., 1997). The effects of stress may occur in two ways. First, when people are under stress, the adrenal glands release epinephrine

HIGHLIGHT

Self-Managing Diabetes

Managing diabetes requires self-care activities that focus mainly on four components: self-monitoring of blood glucose, taking insulin or other medication, diet, and exercise.

Monitoring Blood Glucose and Taking Insulin or Medication

Patients typically test their blood sugar by pricking a finger to get a drop of blood that a blood-glucose meter analyzes (ADA, 2006). The treatment regimen may require patients to do these tests just once a day or several times, often before meals and at bedtime, and adjust medications, food intake, and activity levels accordingly (Trief, 2004).

Many diabetics can use medication to help control their blood glucose levels. Different medications work in different ways—for instance, some drugs increase insulin production in the pancreas whereas others reduce the liver's glucose release to the blood (AMA, 2003). Other patients must use *insulin*, usually by injection. In the early 1920s, a doctor named Frederick Banting devised a method that made it possible to extract insulin from the pancreas glands of slaughtered pigs and cattle. The insulin used today can be from these sources, or it can be synthetic. The doctor's decision on the frequency and dosage of insulin depends on many factors, such as the person's size, age, food intake, and activity level (AMA, 2003). Some diabetics are able to use a device called an insulin pump that can be implanted in the body and delivers small amounts of insulin continuously, with extra doses at mealtimes.

One of the difficulties in using insulin is knowing how much to inject—taking too much may be as dangerous as taking too little. Using too much insulin can produce *hypoglycemia*, the condition of having too little sugar in blood; if it is severe, it can cause the person to lose consciousness (AMA, 2003). When hypoglycemia is less severe, it can impair cognitive and emotional functioning, making the person excited, irritable, and confused. Diabetics dread these episodes, and so do their families (Wilkinson, 1987). With careful training, people with diabetes can reduce these episodes by adjusting their insulin doses accurately to keep glucose levels within the normal range.

Diet and Exercise

The diets recommended for diabetics are designed to help them maintain normal blood glucose levels, achieve or maintain a healthful weight, and limit foods that may raise their already high risk of developing heart disease (AMA, 2003). To maintain normal glucose levels, patients usually need to reduce their intake of foods that contain sugar and some other carbohydrates. People who take insulin must also maintain consistency in timing their meals and, usually, in their calorie intake. Once they take their insulin, they usually need to eat within a range of time thereafter to prevent an episode of hypoglycemia.

Because physical activity burns up glucose as fuel, exercise is another important part of the treatment of diabetes. Physical activity inhibits the liver's glucose production, increases glucose use by the muscles, and complements dietary efforts to reduce body weight and maintain overall fitness (AMA, 2003; Zinman, 1984). Regular exercise also enhances glucose control in people with diabetes (Snowling & Hopkins, 2006). But unplanned vigorous activity can cause an episode of hypoglycemia in diabetics; they need to plan activities and eat a sufficient number of calories to last through the event or carry packets of medication to adjust their blood sugar quickly.

Following a regimen to treat diabetes is difficult, but the risks of not doing so are very serious. It takes a good deal of planning, strong efforts to maintain the routine with few departures, and the confidence of patients and their families that they can do it.

and cortisol into the bloodstream (Surwit, Feinglos, & Scovern, 1983). *Epinephrine* causes the pancreas to decrease insulin production; *cortisol* causes the liver to increase glucose production and body tissues to decrease their use of glucose. These biological stress responses can worsen the glucose regulation problems of diabetics. Second, stress can affect blood glucose levels indirectly by reducing adherence to diabetes regimens (Goldston et al., 1995). Many diabetics do not cope well with their condition and suffer from emotional distress and even depression (Musselman et al., 2007). Negative mood, reduced feelings of control or efficacy in managing diabetes, and disruption of daily activities can all interfere with adherence and control of blood sugar, and worsen mood still further (Fortenberry et al., 2009; Sacco et al., 2005). And the more distressed and depressed the patients feel, the worse their adherence and glucose control (Fisher et al., 2010; Gonzalez et al., 2008) and the greater their risk of health complications from diabetes (de Groot et al., 2001; Van Tilburg et al., 2001). Emotional distress specifically related to difficulties with diabetes, rather than broader and more serious levels of depression, can contribute to these problems with adherence and blood sugar control (Fisher et al., 2010). Problem-focused coping is generally associated with better emotional adjustment in diabetes (Duangdao & Roesch, 2008), perhaps resulting in improved adherence.

People's everyday lives present many circumstances that make it difficult to adhere to diabetes regimens (Glasgow, McCaul, & Schafer, 1986). Diabetics may feel that testing their glucose levels at work or school is embarrassing, or forget to take their testing materials with them, or have difficulty getting up on weekend mornings to take their injections on time, or make mistakes in judgments about what they can eat, for example. Four other issues can be important. First, because some temporary weight gain tends to occur when diabetics get their glucose under control, many female patients, in an effort to control their weight, fail to take their insulin (Polonsky et al., 1994). Second, a regimen's dietary recommendations may be incompatible with the food habits of patients in certain ethnic groups (Raymond & D'Eramo-Melkus, 1993). Third, diabetics often feel frustrated when they "didn't cheat," but their glucose control is off target for some other reason, such as being under stress. Fourth, because diabetes is not painful, patients may not feel that following the regimen closely is critical (Kilo & Williamson, 1987).

Another situation that can lead to noncompliance is when the patient and the doctor have different treatment goals. A study demonstrated this by having doctors and parents of diabetic children serve as subjects, and asked them to assess hypothetical glucose test profiles (Marteau et al., 1987). The doctors were asked to pick the profile they would be "happiest to see" for a child at their clinic; the parents were asked to pick the one they would be "happiest to see" for *their* own child. The vast majority of doctors, but only about half of the parents, chose a profile reflecting a normal glucose level. More than a third of the parents chose either a mild or a moderate *hyperglycemic* profile. This suggests that doctors focus on preventing long-term complications, and parents may be more interested in preventing *hypoglycemic* episodes and promoting the day-to-day well-being and activity of their children. Not surprisingly, the children's actual glucose levels more closely matched the goals of their parents than those of doctors. Because much smaller deviations

from normal blood sugar levels result in symptoms of hypoglycemia than in those of hyperglycemia, parents and diabetics may choose to err on the side of higher glucose levels (Varni & Babani, 1986).

When the Diabetic is a Child or Adolescent

Most parents of diabetic children cope well with the disease (Eiser, 1985). But the stress parents feel is especially great if the child is under 2 years of age, partly because they may find having to take a drop of the child's blood for testing emotionally and physically difficult (Anderson & Bracket, 2005). But even with older children, family stressors remain and stem from having to deal with occasional diabetic crises, taking the child in for medical examinations, giving glucose tests and injections, and making and monitoring dietary adjustments. Parents of diabetics also worry about their child's future health.

Diabetic children younger than, say, 8 or 10 years of age have little understanding about their conditions and tend to dislike most the aspects of their regimen that set them apart from other children—for example, the glucose monitoring and rigid eating patterns and restrictions (Anderson & Bracket, 2005; Eiser, 1985). Maintaining the treatment regimen during childhood is essentially the parents' responsibility, but children can learn to select appropriate foods by 8 years of age, give themselves injections by 9 or 10, and perform glucose testing by 12 (Eiser, 1985). As adolescence approaches, parents allow children more responsibility for managing the regimen, but too much responsibility without parental monitoring can lead to lower adherence and poorer glucose control (Gonder-Frederick, Cox, & Ritterband, 2002). Normal adolescent development involves a growing sense of autonomy and independence from parents, but this otherwise healthy change can lead to less cooperation between teens and parents in managing diabetes and to less control over blood sugar (Beveridge et al., 2006; Butner et al., 2009). Adherence to glucose monitoring and diet declines with age in adolescence, and blood sugar control also decreases (Anderson et al., 1990; Johnson et al., 1990). Adolescent diabetics can generate solutions that would enable them to adhere, but they often succumb to peer pressure, such as in drinking (Thomas, Peterson, & Goldstein, 1997). Noncompliance is probably not the only reason for decreased glucose control in adolescence, as hormonal changes may make controlling blood glucose more difficult (Eiser, 1985).

Teenagers' adherence to their diabetes regimens is relatively high among those who have high levels of self-esteem and social competence and have good relations with their parents (Berg et al., 2009; Jacobson et al., 1994; Miller-Johnson et al., 1994). Teens who feel less sure of themselves may neglect their self-care activities partly because they may feel a greater need to avoid appearing different from their peers.

ARTHRITIS

Before developing a severe case of arthritis, Ron had been active in athletics for most of his 50 years of life, having played and coached college football and become an avid golfer and tennis player (McIlwain et al., 1991). Playing sports became increasingly difficult over a period of 5 years because of pain in his knee and hip, and he eventually stopped playing completely. After 2 months of treatment with medication and exercise, he was able to resume these activities without severe pain.

Musculoskeletal disorders affecting the body's muscles, joints, and connective tissues near the joints are classified as **arthritis** (also called *rheumatic diseases*), which includes over 100 conditions that cause pain, stiffness, or inflammation (AF, 2006; Danoff-Burg, 2004). Disorders of the bones and joints have probably always plagued humans and other animals—paleontologists have found evidence of arthritis in the fossil bones of dinosaurs and prehistoric bears, for instance (Achterberg-Lawlis, 1988).

The Types and Causes of Rheumatic Diseases

Osteoarthritis is a disease in which the joints degenerate, mainly as a result of wear and tear (AF, 2006; AMA, 2003). It afflicts over 20 million Americans and is by far the most common rheumatic condition. People's risk of developing this condition increases with age and body weight and is associated with certain occupations in which particular joints are subjected to repeated heavy use (Kelsey & Hochberg, 1988). Athletes often have affected knees and hips, whereas weavers and cotton pickers often develop osteoarthritis of the hands, and ballet dancers often have the condition in their feet.

Fibromyalgia produces pain and stiffness mainly in the muscles and other soft tissue (AF, 2006; AMA, 2003). *Gout* can affect any of the body's joints, but is most common in the big toe. In this disease, the body produces more uric acid than the kidneys can process, and the excess acid circulates in the blood and leaves crystalline deposits at the joints (AF, 2006; AMA, 2003). *Rheumatoid arthritis* is a disease that involves extreme inflammation of joint tissues and also affects the heart, blood vessels, and lungs when it reaches advanced stages (AF, 2006; AMA, 2003). It is potentially the most serious arthritic condition, being the most crippling and painful type. It can spread to all of the body's joints. Rheumatoid arthritis is typically marked by waxing and waning episodes of painful inflammation, which over time causes progressive and eventually severe deterioration of the joints. Although the mechanisms that lead to rheumatoid arthritis are unclear, they seem to involve an autoimmune response that attacks the tissues and bones of the joints (Coico & Sunshine, 2009; Danoff-Burg, 2004).

Each rheumatic disease appears to have its own pattern of causes, including genetic factors and viral infections (McIlwain et al., 1991). Although arthritis can appear at any age, it becomes far more prevalent as people get older, as Figure 12-3 depicts. In the United States, it afflicts over half of people over 75 years of age and is more prevalent in females than males and in Whites and Blacks than Hispanic and Asian Americans. But the data in the figure should be clarified in three ways. First, they probably underestimate the actual prevalence of people who have the disorder because mild cases often are not reported to health agencies (Kelsey & Hochberg, 1988). Second, the figure does not show that, whereas females are much more likely than males to develop most forms of arthritis, males are more likely to develop gout (AF, 2006). Third, many children have arthritis, such as *juvenile rheumatoid arthritis*. An encouraging point about juvenile rheumatoid arthritis is that most patients do *not* suffer serious disability in their adult lives; for many, the

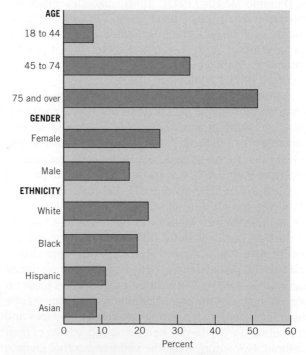

Figure 12-3   Percent of American adults, 18 years and over, of different age, gender, and ethnic groups with diagnosed arthritis of any type. (Based on data in USBC, 2006, Table 184.)

disorder disappears in several years (AMA, 2003; Burg & Ingall, 1985).

The Effects and Treatment of Arthritis

Arthritis is a major cause of disability around the world. Of the major chronic diseases in the United States, arthritis is the leading cause of disability in people over age 15 and is second, behind heart disease, in causing work disability (AF, 2006). Elderly people have more functional limitations from osteoarthritis of the knee than from most other chronic illnesses (Guccione et al., 1994). In the case of rheumatoid arthritis, some patients experience only mild episodes of inflammation and pain in a few joints, but others suffer intense pain in many joints, often showing the following progression:

- The lubricating fluid leaks out of the joints, usually in the knees, ankles, shoulders, elbows, and wrists.
- Cartilage is destroyed, and joint function is reduced.
- The conversion of organic matter into minerals for bones decreases near the joints.
- Bone erosions take place near the joints.
- Joints become dislocated and sometimes fused, producing deformities (Anderson et al., 1985).

Some of the people whose rheumatoid arthritis progresses to the later stages show associated damage to other organs, including vascular or heart valve diseases.

What treatments can be used in managing the pain and functional impairment of arthritis? People with arthritis typically take some form of pain-relieving medication, especially aspirin and other NSAIDs that reduce inflammation (AF, 2006; AMA, 2003; Danoff-Burg, 2004). Other drugs may be used for more severe cases. If pain and joint deterioration are severe enough, surgeons may replace affected joints with artificial ones. People can also reduce arthritic pain and impairment by maintaining proper body weight—for each kilogram of weight lost, the knee has 4 kilograms less load with each step—and, especially for people with gout, limiting certain foods and alcohol (AF, 2006). Regular exercise involving aerobic activity and strength training can improve fitness, and reduce disability and pain (Hurkman et al., 2009). Physical therapy is very important in treating arthritis, and can combine exercise with application of heat or cold, and use of devices to prevent joint damage and assist patients in performing daily activities (Danoff-Burg, 2004; Minor & Sanford, 1993). For example, a woman with rheumatoid arthritis whose hand pain and weakness made doing household tasks difficult received physical therapy with three components (Philips, 1989). First, she did *exercises* to increase hand strength and range of motion. Second, she wore *splints* at night to reduce pain and swelling. Third, she received *advice on devices* that make daily activities easier, such as a cart to transport things, purses that hang from the shoulder instead of the hand, and handles with large diameters. Many arthritis sufferers use complementary and alternative medicine methods, such as acupuncture and herbal therapy, especially if they are dissatisfied with medical procedures (Vecchio, 1994).

Physical therapy for a patient with arthritic hands can involve enjoyable activities that exercise the affected joints.

In studies of compliance with medical treatment regimens, people with arthritis adhere closely to recommendations for more powerful drugs, but not for milder ones, such as aspirin. They also adhere less closely with physical therapy than with taking medication (Anderson et al., 1985). Many patients dislike physical therapy, seeing its negative aspects rather than its positive ones (Jensen & Lorish, 1994). They feel, for instance, that exercising is boring, and its often considerable future value is not obvious.

Psychosocial Factors in Arthritis

Any chronic pain condition is distressing for the patients and their families, and more so if the pain is severe and frequent. If the pain is disabling, the condition can produce a great deal of stress for patients and their families. People with arthritis experience more anxiety and depression than healthy individuals. These emotional conditions do not predict the initial occurrence of arthritis, but having arthritis clearly increases one's risk of emotional distress (Land et al., 2010). Once the disease develops, a vicious circle occurs for many patients: arthritis symptoms increase the person's stress, which, in turn, increases symptoms (Dougall & Baum, 2001). Some distress is caused by concerns over physical appearance that are common in more severe arthritis (Mahaghan et al., 2007). Also, most people with arthritis have at least one other chronic illness, such as diabetes, asthma, or another pain condition, which increases their disability (Stang et al., 2006).

People with severe rheumatoid arthritis experience at least some pain virtually every day, and on many days it is intense (Affleck et al., 1991). This pain can interfere in many everyday activities: as one patient stated,

> There are times when I'm downright miserable, like when I can't even pick up a pot off the stove. Every once in a while, I have to miss work for a week or two because I simply can't keep my knee in a position to drive a car. (Tennen & Affleck, 1997, p. 264)

People with severe arthritis are more likely to feel helpless and depressed than those with milder conditions. One study, for instance, examined over 200 arthritis patients' disability and feelings of helplessness about their conditions over a 1-year period (Nicassio et al., 1985). Feelings of helplessness correlated with changes in their ability to perform daily activities, such as dressing, turning faucets on and off, and getting in and out of a car. Some arthritis patients engage in catastrophic or exaggerated negative thinking about the condition and its future implications, and as in the case of helplessness, catastrophizing predicts greater pain and depression (Edwards et al., 2006; Smith et al., 1994). Other studies have confirmed that arthritis severity, helplessness, and other forms of maladaptive thinking or appraisals are related, and have found that these beliefs and appraisals lead to maladjustment and depression (Nicassio et al., 1993; Somers et al., 2009; Zautra et al., 1995). And people with a prior history of depression who develop arthritis tend to cope poorly with their pain (Conner et al., 2006; Tennen, Affleck, & Zautra, 2006). Depression and other forms of emotional distress obviously detract from the quality of life in arthritis and other rheumatic diseases, but depression in this population has also been found to predict earlier mortality (Ang et al., 2005). Sleep problems are common in this population, and are increasingly recognized as a potentially important influence on emotional adjustment and physical symptoms (Hamilton et al., 2008). Given the daily demands of coping with chronically painful and limiting rheumatic disease, a good night's sleep is almost always welcome, but unfortunately infrequent for many patients.

Of course, not all individuals with severe arthritis experience serious emotional difficulties. Even with severe pain, some people with arthritis feel a greater sense of personal control over their conditions than others do, and this may benefit their emotional adjustment. Researchers examined this relationship by interviewing adults with rheumatoid arthritis, which revealed three main findings (Affleck et al., 1987). First, the subjects generally thought their practitioners had greater control over the *course* of the disease than they did themselves. Second, of the patients who had relatively active symptoms, those who believed they could control their *daily symptoms* reported less mood disturbance than those who did not. Third, the people who saw themselves as *active partners* in decisions about their medical care and treatment showed better adjustment to their illness. These findings are also important because people with arthritis who understand their treatment and believe it can help are more likely to adhere closely to their medical regimens than those individuals who do not (Jette, 1984).

What impact does the arthritis condition have on the psychological status of the patient's family? The severity of the disease by itself seems to have little impact. For spouses of arthritis patients, their levels of distress or depression relate mainly to their perceptions of the quality of the marriage and of social support (Manne & Zautra, 1990). Social processes affect the spouse and patient in several ways. First, as arthritis severity increases, spouses who perceive little social support in their lives report *more* depression, while spouses with high levels of social support report *less* depression (Revenson & Majerovitz, 1991). Second, arthritis patients who cope by expressing negative emotions a lot and perceive their spouses as reacting negatively to their pain show poorer adjustment and disease status over time than others (Griffin et al., 2001). Also, when patients and their spouses hold similar or congruent perceptions of control over arthritis, they report better emotional adjustment; couples holding discrepant views of the disease report more distress (Sterba et al., 2008). Finally, if the patient is willing to express emotions like compassion or guilt to a spouse who is in the role of caregiver, the spouse reports less stress—especially when the husband is the patient (Morin et al., 2009). The quality of interpersonal experiences in general can affect adjustment. Arthritis patients who experience more positive interpersonal contacts during daily activities have more positive moods and less fatigue, whereas negative social contacts increase negative emotions and lead to more fatigue over time (Parris, Zautra, & Davis, 2008; Smith et al., 2008).

WEB ANIMATION: The Case of the Forgetful Father

Access: www.wiley.com/go/global/sarafino. This interactive animation describes the symptoms and medical test results of a man with a brain disorder.

ALZHEIMER'S DISEASE

For a long time, Martha, the wife of 75-year-old Alfred, denied her husband was sick, making excuses for his forgetful and odd behavior. Then

one evening, they were out dining with friends. During the meal, Alfred refused to remove his overcoat and wouldn't talk to anyone. Instead, he clanged his fork on his plate, put his napkin in his soup, and tried to eat his salad with his knife. When Martha whispered to him to put down his silverware, he yelled at her. She burst into tears. Finally, one of the male dinner guests led Alfred from the table, leaving a humiliated, mortified wife to confront a reality that could no longer be ignored: Alfred had Alzheimer's disease. (McCahon, 1991, p. 44)

Dementia is a term that refers to a progressive loss of cognitive functions that often occurs in old age. By far, the most common form of dementia is **Alzheimer's disease**, a brain disorder characterized by a deterioration of attention, memory, and personality. Figure 12-4 illustrates the cognitive deficits of an Alzheimer victim. An estimated 4.6 million Americans have Alzheimer's disease, and the prevalence doubles with each 5-year increase in age after 65: whereas probably 3% of individuals ages 65 to 74 have the disease, nearly half of those 85 and older have it (NIA, 2006; Sliwinski, 2004). Some individuals show symptoms of the disease in their 40s (Gruetzner, 1992).

The cognitive functions of people with Alzheimer's disease do not disappear all at once, and the first ones to go are attention and memory (Vitaliano et al., 1986). The first memory losses are generally for recent events and new learning, and later progresses to include distant events and information that had been well learned (Sliwinski, 2004). As the disease advances over several years, its effects become broader and more pronounced (Haley, 1998). Personality changes often emerge, with

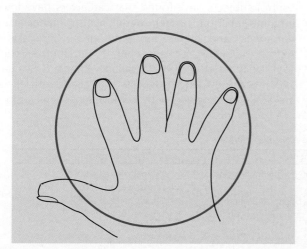
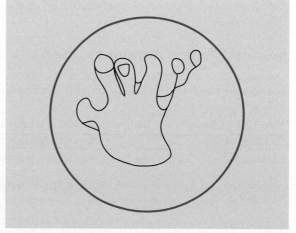

Figure 12-4 Illustration of cognitive deficits in Alzheimer's disease. A graphic artist with this disorder was asked to copy the drawing of a hand shown on the left. The hand he drew was much smaller and had distortions in spatial relationships, misplaced fingernails, and an incorrect number of fingers.

the victims becoming apathetic and withdrawn. Self-care deteriorates, and behavior problems appear, as when these individuals wander and become lost, and many become disoriented with regard to time, their location, and their identity. These declines develop faster if the patients suffer a severe loss of language or have a history of alcohol abuse or of neurological disorders, such as stroke or Parkinson's disease (Bracco et al., 1994; Teri, Hughes, & Larson, 1990).

The Causes and Treatment of Alzheimer's Disease

What causes Alzheimer's disease? A promising answer seems to involve a characteristic that differentiates the brains of Alzheimer victims from those of other elderly individuals: Alzheimer brains contain extensive *lesions*, consisting of gnarled and tangled nerve and protein fibers (AMA, 2003; Querfurth & LaFerla, 2010). Evidence now indicates that genetic defects may cause these large deposits to occur. For instance, one study examined stored tissue samples from many members of a family across three generations (Murrell et al., 1991). All members with the genetic defect also had Alzheimer's disease, and no member who did not have the defect had the disease. A likely gene involved in early onset of the disease has been identified (Levy-Lahad et al., 1995). Table 12.3 presents several health and lifestyle characteristics that appear to increase the risk of Alzheimer's disease, and they are mainly ones that are also risk factors for cardiovascular disease (Sabia et al., 2009; Scarmeas et al., 2009).

Diagnosis of Alzheimer's disease should be made at specialized centers, based mainly on tests of mental ability and physiological signs. No preventive treatment exists for the disease, but some medications can slow its progression and improve symptoms (NIA, 2006; Sliwinski, 2004).

Psychosocial Effects of Alzheimer's Disease

Most victims of Alzheimer's disease live at home and receive care from their spouses or adult children (Gruetzner, 1992; Haley, 1998). In the early stages of the disease, family members and others may be able to help maximize the person's functioning, such as by marking objects clearly and giving social support. But many families either don't know or deny that the person has Alzheimer's disease. As patients lose more and more of their cognitive function, their inability to do simple tasks and remember everyday things becomes very frustrating and often leads to feelings of helplessness, which may account for their high rates of depression (Migliorelli et al., 1995).

Alzheimer patients' behavior becomes increasingly problematic as the disease progresses, producing great stress in the family. People with this disease may, for instance, accuse a family member of hiding things they cannot find, develop sleep disturbances and stay awake most of the night, get lost after wandering out of the house, lose control of their bowels and bladder, or become bedridden (Gruetzner, 1992; Haley, 1998). The burden and stress of caring for Alzheimer patients is similar to caring for cancer patients, and greater than caring for someone with diabetes or advanced frailty (Kim & Schulz, 2008). Caregiving burden and the related symptoms of depression can be significant, and they usually decrease when the patient is eventually placed in a nursing home or other assisted living arrangements (Gangler et al., 2009).

The burden of caring for someone with Alzheimer's at home can become physically and emotionally overwhelming, particularly when the caregivers are elderly spouses in failing health or grown children who have many career and family pressures of their own. The stress these caregivers experience is likely to affect their own health. Studies comparing caregivers with control subjects have found that caregivers have lower immune function, poorer overall health, higher stress hormones, and higher mortality rates (Christakis & Allison, 2006; Kiecolt-Glaser et al., 1991; Schulz & Beach, 1999; Vedhara et al., 1999; Vitaliano, Zhang, & Scanlan, 2003). Some evidence suggests that the health effects are worse in caregivers with low levels of social support

Table 12.3   *Characteristics That Increase the Risk of Developing Alzheimer's Disease*

Characteristic	Description or Comment	References
Low education	Less (fewer years) education is associated with higher risk of Alzheimer's disease.	Kivipelto et al., 2006; Lindsay et al., 2002
Prior strokes	Having strokes, even mild ones, increases the risk of Alzheimer's.	Snowdon et al., 1997
No alcohol use	Moderate use decreases Alzheimer risk compared to little or no alcohol use.	Lindsay et al., 2002; Ruitenberg et al., 2003
Sedentary lifestyle	Regular physical activity is related to lower risk of Alzheimer's.	Lindsay et al., 2002
High body weight	Obesity is associated with increased risk of Alzheimer's.	Kivipelto et al., 2006
Hypertension	High blood pressure is related to higher Alzheimer risk.	Kivipelto et al., 2006
High cholesterol	High levels of serum cholesterol are linked to higher Alzheimer risk.	Kivipelto et al., 2006

and high distress from dementia-related behaviors. The emotional and physical effects on Alzheimer caregivers appear similar in different cultures, such as in America and China (Patterson et al., 1998).

Some evidence suggests that the everyday burdens of caregiving might not be unhealthy; helping others who are disabled may actually reduce our mortality (Brown et al., 2009). Only when caregiving is combined with frequent exposure to suffering—especially the suffering of a loved one—does it become highly stressful and unhealthy (Morin & Schulz, 2009). In other words, helping and taking care of those with chronic illness can be difficult but also deeply rewarding; watching loved ones suffer and deteriorate, however, is always painful and exhausting. In the case of Alzheimer's disease, these two aspects of caregiving typically occur together.

In the Alzheimer's case we saw earlier, Martha provided care for Alfred at home for a few years until his condition became too difficult for her to handle (McCahon, 1991). When she placed Alfred in a nursing home, she felt "defeated, inadequate, and guilty" for doing so. She visited him almost daily and eventually developed psychological problems because watching him deteriorate and realizing that he had, in effect, died years ago was so stressful. Alzheimer's patients usually need care for 5 to 10 years of decline (Haley, 1998). The slow decline, severe dementia-related behavior problems, and knowledge that it will only end when the patient dies generally makes Alzheimer's disease more difficult for families to adapt to than the other chronic illnesses we have considered. The families often feel that watching the process is like watching an endless funeral.

We have examined in this chapter what it is like to live with each of a variety of chronic health problems. Some of these disorders begin earlier in the life span than others, some are more visible to people than are others, some involve more difficult treatment regimens than others, and some are more painful, disabling, or life-threatening than others. Each of these differences is important in determining patients' and their families' adaptation to the health problems and the psychosocial help they may need from professionals.

PSYCHOSOCIAL INTERVENTIONS FOR PEOPLE WITH CHRONIC CONDITIONS

Before people actually experience specific chronic illnesses in their families, they usually have some ideas about how serious the health problems are. How do they feel about an illness after someone in the family develops it? Is it worse than they expected, or not as bad, or about the same? The answers to these questions should have a bearing on how well the family adjusts to health problems. One study had parents whose children had either diabetes, asthma, epilepsy, or no chronic illness rate how serious each of the three health problems would be if their children were to develop it or had it now (Marteau & Johnston, 1986). The ratings revealed two interesting findings: (1) the lowest ratings of seriousness the parents gave were for the health problems their own children had and (2) parents whose children did not have chronic illnesses rated each of the health problems as being very serious. These findings indicate that parents who live with chronic illnesses in their children tend to have less negative views of the health problems than parents whose children do not have those illnesses. The prospect of a health problem is frightening, but most families adjust fairly well if a child develops a chronic illness (Cadman et al., 1991).

But, as we have seen, many people do not adjust well to chronic health conditions. The types of adjustment problems that commonly develop with chronic conditions are outlined in Table 12.4. The problems patients and their families experience depend on many factors, such as how visible, painful, disabling, or life-threatening the illness is. Another factor is the patient's age (O'Dougherty & Brown, 1990). In the early childhood years, victims of chronic illness may become excessively dependent if the parents are overprotective, such as by not allowing an epileptic child to play in a wading pool with careful supervision. In later childhood and adolescence, chronically ill individuals may experience academic and social difficulties that impair their friendships, self-confidence, and self-esteem. Adults who develop a chronic condition may have difficulties if their illness leads them to stop working or change jobs, alter their parenting role, or change or stop their sexual relations.

Ideally, interventions to help individuals with chronic health problems involve interdisciplinary teams of professionals—doctors, nurses, psychologists, physical and occupational therapists, vocational counselors,

Table 12.4 *Types of Adjustment Problems in Chronic Illness*

- *Physical*—Being unable to cope with disability or pain.
- *Vocational*—Having difficulty revising educational and career plans or finding a new job.
- *Self-concept*—Being unable to accept one's changed body image, self-esteem, and level of achievement or competence.
- *Social*—Having difficulty with losing enjoyable activities or finding new ones and coping with changed relationships with family, friends, and sexual partners.
- *Emotional*—Experiencing high levels of denial, anxiety, or depression.
- *Compliance*—Failing to adhere to the rehabilitation regimen.

and social workers—working in an integrated manner toward the overall goals of rehabilitation (Bleiberg, Ciulla, & Katz, 1991). Psychologists contribute to this process by advising other team members on psychological and behavioral issues, and helping each client and his or her family to cope with the psychosocial implications of the medical condition and by using psychosocial principles to enhance the person's participation in and adherence to the therapeutic regimen. Involving family members in this process benefits them and the patient, such as in reducing their feelings of depression and of burden from caregiving (Martire et al., 2004). We'll consider many useful psychosocial approaches, most of which can be used either with individuals or in groups and for a variety of illnesses.

EDUCATIONAL, SOCIAL SUPPORT, AND BEHAVIORAL METHODS

The first thing chronically ill people and their families need to help them adapt to a health problem is correct *information* about the disease and its prognosis and treatment. Part of the problem Martha had dealing with Alfred's Alzheimer's disease is that she was led to believe initially that he would "be a vegetable" in a matter of months. But Alfred's deterioration went on for years, as it does for most Alzheimer victims. She needed better information and might also have benefited from community services for Alzheimer families: many American communities have *respite centers* where Alzheimer patients can get occasional day care and temporary overnight care, giving the family a break from the caregiving burden (Gruetzner, 1992; NIA, 2006).

Effective systems of social support are also important for patients' and their families' adaptation to chronic health problems. People with chronic medical conditions usually receive this support from family or friends, but it can also come from *support groups* that offer patients and family information and opportunities to meet with people who are in the same boat. These groups give sensitive emotional support and share their own experiences and ways of dealing with everyday problems and difficult decisions, such as whether to place the patient in a nursing home (Gruetzner, 1992; NIA, 2006). People are more likely to join health-related support groups for potentially stigmatizing conditions than for equally serious but less stigmatizing ones (Davison, Pennebaker, & Dickerson, 2000), but individuals who do not want to participate in person can utilize more anonymous internet-based support groups instead (Tanis, 2008). Internet-based groups can increase patients' self-esteem and quality of life and decrease symptoms of emotional distress (Ranis & Young, 2009). Contact

information for support groups in specific geographical areas can be obtained through doctors, local community service agencies, or organizations for any particular illness. All major illness-related organizations now have websites that provide information about support groups and about the disease and its treatment. (The website for this book gives links to many of these websites.)

In Chapter 8, we discussed how adherence to medical regimens is often a problem for people with chronic conditions. One way to enhance adherence involves improving practitioners' communication of information about the procedures and the importance of following the treatment. Other approaches use *behavioral methods*, such as tailoring the regimen to make it as compatible as possible with the person's habits, using prompts and reminders, having patients keep records of their self-care activities, and providing a system of rewards through the method of behavioral contracting. These methods can help improve compliance, such as with different aspects of diabetes regimens (Goodall & Halford, 1991; Wing et al., 1986). As an example, a program used self-monitoring and behavioral contracting methods for 8 weeks to improve regimen adherence in three noncompliant 16- to 18-year-old type 1 diabetes patients: Kathy, Tom, and Kim (Schafer, Glasgow, & McCaul, 1982). Adherence and glucose control improved greatly in both Kathy and Tom. Kim's self-care did not improve, probably because she came from a family with severe marital and family problems, and therapy had failed to resolve their conflicts. Family problems can have an overriding influence and undermine efforts to improve compliance with medical recommendations.

Another example of using behavioral methods to enhance compliance with medical regimens involves the physical rehabilitation process for individuals with spinal cord injuries. Reinforcement techniques are very effective in improving these patients' performance of beneficial behaviors (Brucker, 1983), such as:

- Increasing daily fluid intake to prevent urinary tract infections.
- Changing one's sitting or lying position frequently to reduce the occurrence of bedsores.
- Using orthopedic devices to improve limb functioning.
- Performing exercises to increase strength and endurance.

Reinforcement can be given, for instance, by praising the client for each measurable improvement, such as in arm strength, and periodically updating the person's graph that charts these improvements.

The goal of most training and education programs is to enable patients and their families to self-manage the condition effectively, and this is best achieved by combining information with behavioral and cognitive methods. **Self-management** programs provide information and train patients in behavioral and cognitive skills to enhance their ability to carry out their regimens, create and adapt to the new behaviors or life roles the health condition requires, and cope with their emotions (Lorig & Holman, 2003). An important feature of self-management approaches is that they teach problem-solving skills so that the individuals can deal effectively with day-to-day circumstances and decisions, such as what to do when their ride to a doctor's office is cancelled. Self-management programs can be provided by professionals in medical settings or by trained laypersons, such as in support groups. For example, the Arthritis Self-Management Program (Lorig et al., 1998) was designed to help arthritis sufferers cope with their illness and comply with their treatment. It is now offered in several countries by the Arthritis Foundation. The program involves six weekly group meetings in which individuals with arthritis receive training in:

- Exercising, including which exercises to do and exactly how to do them.
- Protecting their joints, such as through changing the way they lift heavy objects.
- Relaxation techniques to control stress.
- Appropriate diets for their illness.
- Self-monitoring and behavioral contracting to promote their complying with regimen activities.

The program is often conducted by a layperson who has arthritis. Programs like this one help arthritis patients to reduce pain and enhance their health status (Lorig & Holman, 2003; Lorig et al., 1998). What's more, in the first year alone, the savings in health care costs is more than seven times the cost of providing such programs for arthritis patients (Cronan, Groessl, & Kaplan, 1997).

Similar programs have been developed for other illnesses, such as asthma and heart disease (Lorig & Holman, 2003), and cultural tailoring of these programs can improve their effectiveness with ethnic minorities (Bailey et al., 2009). Support and self-management interventions are also effective in helping caregivers of spinal cord injury patients and Alzheimer's patients feel less burden and distress, and improve their health and overall quality of life (Elliott, Bugion, & DeCoster, 2010; Schulz et al., 2009).

RELAXATION AND BIOFEEDBACK

We have seen that stress and anxiety can aggravate some chronic conditions, such as by decreasing diabetics' ability to metabolize glucose and by triggering or worsening asthma attacks. Psychologists use stress management techniques—especially *progressive muscle relaxation* and *biofeedback*—to help patients control these psychosocial factors and the underlying body processes (Parker, 1995).

These approaches are useful for several chronic conditions—for instance, they help diabetic patients manage their stress and blood glucose levels (Surwit, Feinglos, & Scovern, 1983; Wing et al., 1986; Soo & Lam, 2009). Biofeedback can also be used to increase muscle function after paralysis (Montgomery, 2004). And people with epilepsy can benefit from relaxation, stress management, and biofeedback training (Mittan, 2009). In using relaxation, epileptics are taught to recognize sensations and events that precede attacks and to apply relaxation techniques when those situations occur. In biofeedback, they receive training with feedback from an electroencephalograph (EEG) device, which measures electrical brain activity (Goldstein, 1990). Although not all patients benefit from this approach, many do, but there is no good way to determine in advance who will benefit from biofeedback to reduce seizures and who will not. (Go to ✿.)

COGNITIVE METHODS

Cognitive processes affect a person's management of chronic health problems in at least two ways: they guide the individual's medical decisions and behaviors, and they affect the emotional adjustment to the condition. Therapists use *cognitive methods* to help clients change their thought processes and feelings (Sarafino, 2001). The coping skills methods we discussed in Chapter 11, such as guided imagery and distraction, are helpful and are often included in treating pain conditions, such as arthritis (Keefe, Abernathy, & Campbell, 2005). Here, we'll discuss problem-solving training and cognitive restructuring, which can be used with individual clients or in groups.

In Chapter 4, we discussed *problem-solving training* as a method to help clients reduce the anxiety and other negative emotions they experience when they don't know how to solve many of their everyday difficulties. This approach also helps them manage their medical condition by teaching them new strategies for thinking through medical problem situations that arise and making good decisions, such as in managing diabetes (Hill-Briggs, 2003). As an example, diabetes patients often need to deal with situations in which appropriate foods may not be available. In problem-solving training, they would learn how to watch for or predict these situations, identify what form the problem is likely to take (for instance, most foods may be sweet), generate

CLINICAL METHODS AND ISSUES

Treating Asthma with Biofeedback and Relaxation

Asthma provides a good example of how biofeedback and relaxation can help manage a chronic condition. In using *biofeedback* with asthmatics, an apparatus gives feedback regarding airflow in breathing so that the asthma patient can learn to control the diameter of the bronchial airways (Sarafino, 1997). One way to measure airflow has the person breathe through a device that varies the air pressure and assesses airway resistance to these variations: the greater the resistance, the poorer the airflow. The feedback tells the person when changes occur; it can be presented as corresponding numbers on a gauge or as different levels of (1) brightness of a light or (2) pitch or loudness of tones. Although airflow improvements are slight initially, feedback over several training sessions helps the person make them stronger, eventually enabling the person to increase airflow when an attack begins. Training in *progressive muscle relaxation* is used to help the person reduce the role of tension in either initiating an asthma attack or making it worse if one occurs. Studies have generally found that these methods provide useful supplements to medical treatments for asthma (Nickel et al., 2005; Sarafino, 1997).

a variety of possible solutions, and decide on the best course of action. The solutions may involve actions to take before the situation, such as packing their own food, or while there, such as asking which foods have sugar in them and choosing from the others.

In *cognitive restructuring*, clients discuss incorrect thoughts and beliefs and learn ways to cope better by thinking more constructively or realistically. We have seen that many chronically ill people and their families experience strong feelings of helplessness, hopelessness, and depression. In the case of caregivers, such as for Alzheimer's disease or cancer patients, they are far more likely to suffer severe levels of depression than are similar individuals who are not caregivers, particularly if they are women and elderly (Pinquart & Sörensen, 2003). Their depression is related to the degree of stress or burden they perceive in their caregiving role, such as from the patient's memory and behavioral problems. Many people who are disabled or have chronic pain also become severely depressed, often because of their restricted daily activities (Talbot et al., 1999). Cognitive approaches can help people identify distorted thoughts ("I never get to do anything I like anymore"), replace those thoughts with more accurate ones, and learn how to increase their ability to perform activities, such as by scheduling them in reasonable amounts. Cognitive methods are very effective in treating depression (Sarafino, 2001).

Interventions that include these cognitive techniques have been found to be useful in managing a variety of chronic conditions, including symptoms of irritable bowel syndrome (Hunt, Moshier, & Milonova, 2009), pain and depression in rheumatoid arthritis (Pradhan et al., 2007; Zautra et al., 2008), and depression and fatigue in multiple sclerosis (Mohr, Hart, & Vella, 2007; Van Kessel et al., 2008). These approaches can be adapted for delivery over the telephone, providing useful flexibility when chronically ill patients have limited mobility (Mohr et al, 2007).

As with all aspects of illness management, the success of the approach depends on how carefully and conscientiously the patient carries out the methods. For example, one study used a cognitive–behavioral program that consisted of training in relaxation, pain redefinition, and distraction techniques; they also met periodically in groups to discuss their pain behavior and family dynamics (Parker et al., 1988). Although no difference in reports of pain and helplessness 6 and 12 months after treatment was found between the group that received this program and two control groups, the program subjects who reported a high degree of adherence to the cognitive–behavioral methods reported much less pain and helplessness than the other subjects. Another study found that the more patients follow their therapist's requests to practice the program skills, such as relaxation, at home, the more they achieve the goals they set for therapy (Heapy et al., 2005). These results suggest that *adherence* to practicing cognitive–behavioral skills may be critical for chronically ill people to benefit from these programs.

INTERPERSONAL AND FAMILY THERAPY

We saw in Chapter 11 that *interpersonal therapies* are designed to help people change the way they interact with and perceive their social environments by gaining insights about their feelings and behavior toward other people. This approach is especially useful in helping patients deal with their anxieties and changed self-concepts or relationships with family and friends (Bleiberg, Ciulla, & Katz, 1991). As an example, one hospitalized quadriplegic man who became difficult to deal with each night revealed in group therapy that he felt very vulnerable and helpless at nighttime, which frightened him. By learning that other patients had similar feelings, he began to cope better with his disability and the day-to-day social problems it created (Eisenberg, 1984). Similar approaches have been used in helping chronically ill people deal with sexual difficulties and understand the thoughts, needs, and problems their friends and family members face.

Family therapy typically has the family meet as a group and draws on cognitive, behavioral, and interpersonal methods to examine and change interaction patterns among family members (Kerns, 1995; Kring et al., 2010; Patterson & Garwick, 1994). A family with a chronically ill member might meet to review household and medical-regimen responsibilities, discuss grievances, and plan ways to alter daily routines. If the patient is a child, they may discuss, for instance:

- Jealousies siblings may feel if the patient seems to be getting more or special attention.
- Activities the chronically ill person can engage in successfully to build his or her feelings of competence and self-esteem.
- How to tell friends and relatives about the illness so they will understand what it is, the limitations it imposes on the patient, and what to do if an episode occurs.
- How and when the ill person could take responsibility for or improve self-care.

Parents and their ill children often do not communicate about sharing responsibilities for the patients' care (Anderson et al., 1990). As a result, each person incorrectly assumes someone else is taking care of a task. Family therapy also can help to uncover and resolve anxieties that develop when the family dynamics and modes of interaction change.

COLLABORATIVE OR INTEGRATED CARE APPROACHES

In the chronic illnesses we have discussed so far, and those in the next chapter, patients face multiple challenges and difficulties, often with the co-occurrence of their medical condition and potentially serious levels of depression or other types of emotional distress. Because these various problems are best addressed by different types of professionals, newer models of health care delivery have been proposed. Rather than assigning separate parts of the patient's care to different professionals who might not interact, integrated or collaborative care combines the perspectives of multiple professionals and providers. For example, in one approach health care providers—often nurses—receive special training in the integration of multiple perspectives and approaches (such as, internal medicine, psychology, physical therapy, nursing), and have regular consultation with an interdisciplinary team. This approach is effective in managing chronic illness and its multiple impacts, and has the added benefit of lowering medical costs (Hunkeler et al., 2006; Simon et al., 2007).

In summary, psychosocial intervention can apply many approaches to address many different adjustment problems that chronically ill people and their families face. In most cases, using more than one approach provides the optimal help these people need.

SUMMARY

The initial reaction of individuals when diagnosed with serious illnesses is usually shock, in which they are bewildered and behave in an automatic fashion. Avoidance coping is likely if people believe they can do nothing to change the situation.

Crisis theory provides a model that describes how patients adjust to learning they have chronic health problems. According to this model, their adjustment depends on the coping processes they use, which, in turn, depend on three types of factors: illness-related, background and personal, and physical and social environmental. Patients begin the coping process with a cognitive appraisal of the meaning or significance of the health problem to their lives. This appraisal leads to their formulating adaptive tasks, such as adjusting to their symptoms or maintaining pos-

itive relations with family or friends, and applying coping skills to deal with these tasks, such as by denying the implications of the illness, learning how to provide their own treatment, maintaining regular routines as well as possible, and discussing the future. Long-term adaptation to chronic health problems occurs when the patient and his or her family make adjustments that enhance the patient's quality of life by promoting effective physical, psychological, and social functioning.

Some chronic conditions usually begin early in the life span, and asthma is one of them. Asthma is a respiratory disorder that produces periodic attacks of extremely labored breathing. Episodes are generally triggered by certain circumstances, such as allergens, respiratory infections, weather conditions, air pollution, and emotions, such as stress and anger. Although asthma is treated mainly with medication to prevent and combat attacks, exercise can be useful. Psychosocial factors are also important.

Epilepsy is a disorder in which electrical disturbances in the brain produce seizures that vary in intensity. In tonic-clonic attacks, the epileptic loses consciousness and exhibits muscle spasms. Sometimes specific neurological defects are identified as causing the disorder. Drugs provide the main form of treatment, but sometimes surgery is useful. Psychosocial processes are important because emotions may trigger episodes and lead to clients dropping out of rehabilitation. Spinal cord injuries occur most often in adolescence or early adulthood, are generally caused by accidents, and render the person paraplegic or quadriplegic. Rehabilitation programs are geared toward helping these individuals regain as much physical function and independence as possible.

Other chronic health problems are more likely to begin in middle adulthood and old age than at other times in the life span. One of those chronic diseases is diabetes, in which the blood contains high levels of glucose. Some people with this disorder have type 1 diabetes and must inject insulin daily because the pancreas produces insufficient insulin; this type usually begins in childhood or adolescence. But the vast majority of diabetics have type 2 diabetes; most of them can use medication and diet to control their blood sugar.

Both types can lead to very serious acute and long-term health complications.

Disorders that affect the joints and connective tissues are classified as arthritis, or rheumatic diseases. Some rheumatic diseases produce painful inflammation and stiffness of the joints. Four common rheumatic diseases are osteoarthritis, fibromyalgia, gout, and rheumatoid arthritis, usually the most crippling and painful of the four. Treatment is mainly through drugs, but also includes physical therapy and maintaining proper body weight. Alzheimer's disease involves a progressive deterioration of the person's cognitive functions, beginning with attention and memory. Since there is no effective treatment for this disorder, therapy focuses on maximizing the patient's functioning and helping the family cope.

Many chronically ill people and their families have difficulty adjusting to the health problem and its medical regimen. They can be helped with psychosocial interventions that involve education, support services, behavioral methods, relaxation and biofeedback, cognitive methods, and interpersonal and family therapy. Self-management programs combine these techniques to help patients adhere to their regimens, adapt to their new roles, and cope with their emotions. Many patients with chronic illness benefit from approaches to medical care that combine multiple professions and perspectives.

KEY TERMS

crisis theory	asthma	type 1 diabetes	Alzheimer's disease
adaptation	epilepsy	type 2 diabetes	self-management
quality of life	spinal cord injury	arthritis	

13

HEART DISEASE, STROKE, CANCER, AND AIDS: CAUSES, MANAGEMENT, AND COPING

PROLOGUE

For Baruti, a young man growing up in a poor township in South Africa, death was always close by. He had seen violent deaths, and deaths from unknown illnesses, but the one disease he knew very well was AIDS. He watched as friends and family members became ill and, unable to afford the anti-retroviral therapy, eventually die. He had always thought that since he was exposed to the pain and anguish caused by AIDS, he'd never put himself in a position where he would become infected. The teachers in his school had taught the students how HIV was transmitted, the myths surrounding HIV/AIDS, and how to protect themselves.

One afternoon while walking home from university, Baruti was hit by a speeding car. He was taken to the hospital and treated for a compound femur fracture, which required a blood transfusion. In many African countries, including South Africa, most donated blood comes from the patient's family members. In this case, a cousin and uncle offered to donate blood for Baruti's operation. The doctors and nurses took the blood and transferred it directly to Baruti. Several days later, he was sent home to recuperate. After a few months, the uncle who donated the blood was diagnosed with HIV. Baruti was tested and was told he also had HIV. Baruti and his family were devastated.

Many countries around the world do not test for HIV/AIDS in donated blood. The World Health Organization (WHO) in 2000 estimated that 25% of the blood transfused in Africa was not tested for HIV. And unfortunately, about 5–10% of HIV infections in Africa in that year were transmitted through blood transfusions.

AIDS emerged in the 1980s as a major killer, and public attention has focused on how it is spread and the huge numbers of people who are infected with the virus and die each year around the world. The WHO estimated the number of deaths from AIDS in Africa in 2004 was over 1.6 million. In the world, the number of deaths was just over 2 million for the same year.

In developed nations, on the other hand, the majority of deaths result from chronic diseases: mainly heart disease, cancer, and stroke (WHO, 2009). People know these are the leading causes of death—and for many patients and their families, being diagnosed with one of these diseases *means* death.

These four very different, high-mortality illnesses are the focus of this chapter. Although many people deal with having high-mortality chronic illnesses in positive and constructive ways, not all do. In this chapter we will examine how patients and their families react to and cope with health problems that have a high likelihood of taking their lives. As we study these circumstances, we'll provide answers to questions you may have. What is it like to live with heart disease, stroke, cancer, or AIDS? How do these illnesses affect the patients' functioning, and what treatment regimens are used? What psychosocial interventions can help these patients and their families?

COPING WITH AND ADAPTING TO HIGH-MORTALITY ILLNESS

Many healthy individuals who wonder how much longer they are likely to live look up the statistical life expectancy for people their age and gender and probably adjust that figure on the basis of the longevity of other people in their families. But estimates of a person's life expectancy

are very imprecise, and this is true even for people with health conditions that threaten their lives. Public opinion aside, having a high-mortality disease does not usually mean a person will die in a few weeks or months. Many cancer patients, for instance, survive for 10 or 20 years before the disease takes their lives, and some are totally cured. Still, no one can tell for sure what the course of the disease will be, and these individuals and their families must adapt to this uncertainty.

ADAPTING WHILE THE PROSPECTS SEEM GOOD

Since none of us knows for sure what lies ahead for us, we all live with some degree of uncertainty. But for patients with high-mortality illnesses, the uncertainty for them and their families is more real and urgent. Even though they may have good prospects for the future, either in the short run or more permanently, the diagnosis changes them.

Mortality is the main issue of concern to patients in the first few months of convalescence with a seriously life-threatening illness. During this time, patients often show optimistic attitudes, hope they will be cured, but begin to view their plans for the future more tentatively (Moos, 1982). They also tend to switch from using avoidance coping to active problem-focused approaches. Lifestyle changes are typically part of the rehabilitation programs people with heart disease, stroke, cancer, and AIDS are asked to follow. Self-help and support groups can provide for patients a sense of community, information about treatments for their illness, and greater empowerment and sense of control in dealing with others, especially practitioners (Ussher et al., 2006). Groups can interact in meetings or online to discuss and get advice about problems and stressors in their daily lives (Davison, Pennebaker, & Dickerson, 2000). As a patient's recovery progresses, he or she is able to return more and more to a regular routine, often gaining great satisfaction by once again being able to do simple household or self-help activities.

Having activities to occupy the day is important to convalescing people with high-mortality health problems. These activities give them some respite from thinking about their conditions. Patients often try to isolate the diseases from the rest of their lives by focusing on other things, such as preparing to do projects around the house or to return to work, but they sometimes overestimate what they can do. For example, a man named Clay who had suffered a serious stroke described making plans the "glorious day" he left the hospital—projects to do, museums and galleries to visit, friends I had wanted to meet for lunch. It was not until several days later that I realized I simply couldn't do them. I didn't have the mental or physical strength, and I sank into depression. (Dahlberg, 1977, p. 124)

Patients need to be encouraged to develop reasonable plans and carry them out, especially with regard to going back to work or getting training to enter a new job, if necessary.

Sometimes the helplessness that chronically ill people feel and the nurturance their families give lead to a cycle of continued dependence that persists when the patients are able to begin doing things for themselves. This was starting to happen with Clay after his stroke, and his wife realized it. So she gradually began to leave things undone that he had previously taken care of, ask him to do things she thought he could do, and act in indecisive ways so he would take over. Gentle nudges by family members, like those from Clay's wife, can help patients become more self-sufficient, thereby making them feel useful and bolstering their self-esteem.

In the process of adapting to high-mortality illnesses over a long period of time, some individuals make helpful cognitive adjustments, such as positive reappraisals of their life situations. For instance, the champion cyclist Lance Armstrong said of his cancer experience the day he went for the diagnosis, he left home

> as one person and came home another . . . . The truth is that cancer was the best thing that ever happened to me. I don't know why I got the illness, but it did wonders for me, and I wouldn't want to walk away from it. (Sears, Stanton, & Danoff-Burg, 2003, p. 487)

Women with breast cancer have described similar reappraisals, often centering on three themes (Taylor, 1983; Taylor, Lichtman, & Wood, 1984). First, many find *meaning* in their illness experiences, either by determining a purpose of the illness or by rethinking their attitudes and priorities. One woman said, for instance,

> I have much more enjoyment each day, each moment. I am not so worried about what is or isn't or what I wish I had. All those things you get entangled with don't seem to be part of my life right now. (Taylor, 1983, p. 1163)

Second, some individuals gain a *sense of control* over their illnesses, such as by engaging in activities that reduce their risk of their conditions getting worse or increase their knowledge about their care. A spouse said of his wife:

> She got books, she got pamphlets, she studied, she talked to cancer patients, she found out everything

that was happening to her, and she fought it. She went to war with it. She calls it taking in her covered wagons and surrounding it. (1983, p. 1164)

Third, some patients *restore their self-esteem*, often by comparing themselves with less fortunate people. For example, a married woman compared herself with others who may be dating and having to tell the man about the cancer.

These cognitive adjustments seem to promote adaptation: the greater the degree of patients' positive reappraisals after cancer diagnosis, the better their perceived health and psychosocial functioning months later (Sears, Stanton, & Danoff-Burg, 2003). But many individuals do not achieve high adjustment levels, particularly if they perceive low levels of social support in the months after diagnosis (Helgeson, Snyder, & Seltman, 2004).

ADAPTING IN A RECURRENCE OR RELAPSE

One thing that makes some diseases more likely than others to kill their victims is that the medical conditions they produce often recur or relapse. Patients correctly recognize their heightened vulnerability and worry about it, and so do their families. Convalescing individuals tend to be very watchful for symptoms and changes in their conditions even if they are optimistic about their health. When a recurrence or relapse occurs, patients and their families rightly perceive this event as a bad sign—it typically indicates that the prognosis is now worse than before. Patients focus again on the illness, trying to forestall deterioration in their general functioning and quality of life. They undergo a new round of hospitalization, medical procedures, and, perhaps, surgery. Patients and their families go through the kinds of coping processes they experienced in the original bout, but they are likely to be less hopeful than they were before (Moos, 1982).

Living with any high-mortality disease can be quite stressful, but each disease creates a pattern of stress that is unique. We turn now to consider how people adapt to living with specific high-mortality health problems, starting with heart disease.

 WEB ANIMATION: The Case of the Man with a Pain in His Jaw

Access: www.wiley.com/go/global/sarafino. This interactive animation describes the symptoms and medical test results of a man with a cardiovascular problem.

HEART DISEASE

Coronary heart disease refers to illnesses that result from the narrowing and blocking of the coronary arteries, which supply the heart with oxygen-rich blood. As we've seen in earlier chapters, blood vessels become narrowed as plaque builds up in the condition called *atherosclerosis*, reducing blood flow to the heart and increasing the risk of blockage. Brief reductions of oxygenated blood to the heart can produce pain, called **angina pectoris**, in the chest and arm, back, or neck (AMA, 2003). This results from ischemia—or lack of sufficient oxygen available to the muscular portion of the heart. Some ischemia is "silent" in that it occurs without pain. Ischemia and angina are most likely during physical exertion or stress, when the heart muscle's demand for oxygen outstrips the limited supply. Little or no permanent damage to the heart occurs if the ischemia ends quickly. But if the reduced blood supply is severe or prolonged, part of the muscle tissue of the heart (myocardium) may be destroyed—a condition called **myocardial infarction**, or "heart attack." Table 13.1 describes common symptoms of a heart attack. Many people die suddenly from coronary disease, with little if any prior warning of trouble. Some people believe that sudden coronary death is caused by a massive myocardial infarction, but this is not actually the case. It is most commonly caused by a catastrophic disturbance in the rhythm of the heart—ventricular fibrillation—where the myocardium twitches chaotically rather than contracting in its normal forceful pumping action. Many elderly cardiac patients—especially those with previous heart attacks—develop *congestive heart failure*, a condition in which the heart's capacity to pump can no longer meet the body's needs, and the individuals become short of breath with little exertion. In this often disabling condition, their hearts may become enlarged from being overworked, and lungs often become congested with fluid (AMA, 2003).

Heart disease is prevalent in developed countries. Table 13.2 gives data on hospital discharges for heart disease in several nations, which may reflect the relative prevalence of the condition. In the United Kingdom, each year over 1.4 million heart attacks occur, and more than

Table 13.1   *Symptoms of a Heart Attack*

Many victims delay going to the hospital for hours because they don't know the symptoms of a heart attack, which are:

- Uncomfortable pressure, fullness, squeezing, or pain in the center of the chest that lasts for more than a few minutes
- Pain or discomfort spreading to the shoulders, neck, jaw, or arms
- Shortness of breath
- Lightheadedness, fainting, sweating, or nausea may occur

Not all of these symptoms always happen in a heart attack—if some start to occur, the person should get medical care immediately. Prompt treatment can often prevent serious myocardial damage.

Source: AHA, 2010.

a third of the victims die; heart disease is the number one killer of men and women (BHF, 2010). Many heart attack victims die before they reach a hospital because they delay getting help, and the heart damage increases with each hour up to about 6 hours (AMA, 2003). More than a third of heart attack victims delay deciding to get help for more than 3 hours (Martin et al., 2004; Walsh et al., 2004). The greater the damage the worse the person's condition and prognosis. The declining death rate from heart disease seems to reflect two important factors: improved medical care of people with the disease and reductions in rates of coronary risk factors, especially smoking (Capewell et al., 2009; Wijeysundera et al., 2010). However, the welcome decline in coronary deaths has slowed in recent years, apparently offset somewhat by a rising tide of obesity and diabetes (Nemetz et al., 2008). (Go to 💡.)

WHO IS AT RISK OF HEART DISEASE, AND WHY?

Several demographic, lifestyle, and physiological characteristics are associated with developing heart disease.

Table 13.2   *Hospital Discharges for Ischemic Heart Disease per 100,000 Population in Selected Nations*

Country	Discharges	Country	Discharges	Country	Discharges
Australia	798.8	Italy	606.4	Turkey	276.6
Canada	565.7	Netherlands	555.2	United Kingdom	532.5
Germany	959.8	Sweden	818.1	United States	662.0

Sources: ABS, 2006, for Australia; NCHS, 2006, for the United States; PHAC, 2006, for Canada; WHO/Europe, 2006, for European Union countries.

HIGHLIGHT

Anatomy of a Heart Attack

Plaque begins to develop when the lining of inside wall of an artery becomes damaged—such as from infection, high blood pressure, or stress hormones. This weakened lining permits fatty substances in the blood—LDL cholesterol—to penetrate into the artery wall, especially when blood levels of LDL are high. This event activates inflammatory chemical signals that attract immune system cells. These cells consume LDL particles, becoming foam cells and initiating progressively greater *inflammation* at the site (Libby, Ridker, & Hansson, 2009), and forming a microscopic fatty streak in the artery wall. Over many years, continuing inflammation and accumulation of LDL cholesterol

deposits cause the initial fatty streak to become a progressively enlarging plaque, eventually covered by a fibrous cap. In some artery sections, the plaque forms a bulge, reducing the lumen (opening) and blood flow, as shown in Figure 13-1. Later, inflammation and chemicals that the foam cells secrete weaken small areas of the cap. When one of these weak areas ruptures, some of the plaque contents seeps out, joins with blood platelets, and forms a clot. If the clot is large enough, it lodges in the artery and sharply decreases or stops blood flow, resulting in an infarction (death) of the heart tissue served by the blocked artery. This is a heart attack.

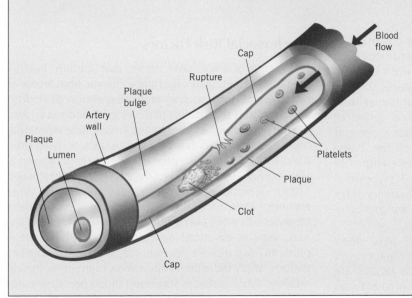

Figure 13-1 Lengthwise cross-section view of an artery with a ruptured plaque bulge and a resulting clot blocking the blood flow, causing a heart attack.

Age, Gender, and Sociocultural Risk Factors

The prevalence rates for heart disease increase as people get older, particularly after about 45 years of age, and American death rates from heart disease are higher in men than women at all ages (NCHS, 2009a). The link between heart disease and sociocultural factors can be seen in the death rate data for different ethnic groups in the United States. Among both men and women, heart disease death rates are two to three times higher for Blacks than for Asian Americans, with the rates for Whites, Native Americans, and Hispanics being intermediate (NCHS, 2009a).

Interestingly, a study of death rates in New York City around 1990 revealed that Blacks who were born in

the Southern United States had far higher mortality rates from cardiovascular disease than those born in the North, whose death rates were similar to those of Whites (Fang, Madhavan, & Alderman, 1996). And a cross-cultural study found that men and women in Russia have extremely high death rates from cardiovascular disease, while the French and Japanese have very low rates (AHA, 1995). These findings suggest an important role of lifestyle in heart disease. (Go to 🍎.)

Lifestyle and Biological Risk Factors

Part of the reason for age, sex, and sociocultural differences in risk of heart disease lies in biological and lifestyle variations in the risk factors you just assessed

ASSESS YOURSELF

Are You at Risk for Heart Disease?

Put a check mark in the space before each item that describes your situation:

_____ I have a *family history* of heart disease: a biological parent, sibling, grandparent, aunt, or uncle was diagnosed with or died of it, especially if before age 55.

_____ I *smoke* regularly, at least a few cigarettes a day.

_____ I do *not* engage in regular *physical activity*.

_____ I am very *overweight* (BMI over, say, 27) or *obese* (see Table 7.3).

_____ I experience more *stress* than most people do.

_____ My doctor told me I have *high* LDL *or low* HDL cholesterol levels.

_____ My doctor told me I have *high blood pressure*.

_____ My doctor told me I have *diabetes*.

These items describe known risk factors for heart disease (AHA, 2006). The more items you checked and the greater the level of each risk, such as smoking a few cigarettes a day versus two packs, the greater your risk.

---

in yourself. For example, *hypertension*—the condition of having high blood pressure consistently over an extended period of time—is a major risk factor for heart disease. High blood pressure has no overt symptoms, but its presence means that the heart is working harder than normal. When this continues over a long period of time, the heart becomes enlarged and has more and more difficulty meeting the demands of the body. High blood pressure also increases the development of atherosclerosis, increasing the risk of myocardial infarction and sudden coronary death. Prevalence rates for hypertension increase with age and are higher in Black than White Americans (NCHS, 2009a).

The great majority of people who have heart attacks have at least one of the risk factors you assessed (Greenland et al., 2003). Which factors are most important? A study examined all of the listed factors except family history across 52 countries and about 30,000 people, half of whom had a heart attack, and found that high LDL with low HDL was the strongest risk factor, and smoking was second (Yusuf et al., 2004). The next most important factors were stress, obesity, diabetes, and hypertension. These risks are modifiable: people who stop smoking and reduce their cholesterol intake and blood pressure halve their risk of dying of heart disease, and for people with heart disease, each risk behavior they change lowers their chance of heart attack further (Daubenmier et al., 2007; Jousilahti et al., 1995). When combined, three modifiable aspects of a healthy lifestyle—being physically fit, being normal weight, and not smoking—can reduce your chances of heart disease by over 50% (Lee, Sui, & Blair, 2009).

Psychosocial Risk Factors

Prospective studies have shown that initially healthy men and women who experience chronic high levels of negative emotions, such as anger, depression, or anxiety, are more likely than others to develop heart disease. And among people with heart disease, these same emotional traits increase risk of having a heart attack or dying from the disease (Chida & Steptoe, 2009; Nicholson, Kuper, & Hemingway, 2006; Suls & Bunde, 2005). The link between negative emotions and heart disease may involve three avenues. First, people tend to have less healthful lifestyles when they experience negative emotions. Second, negative emotions have physiological effects that promote heart disease: for example, when in stressful situations, angry individuals often show high physiological *reactivity*, which includes increased blood pressure, catecholamine, and corticosteroid levels (Smith et al., 2004). Third, shared genetic factors might increase vulnerability to both heart disease and negative emotions (McCaffery et al., 2006). In contrast, people with positive traits such as optimism are less likely to suffer from coronary disease (Kubzansky & Thurston, 2007; Tindle et al., 2009).

Social relationships also influence the risk of coronary disease. People with high levels of social support are less likely to develop coronary disease and less likely to die from it if they already have it (Lett et al., 2005). Conflict and disruption, such as divorce or separation, in close relationships have the opposite effects on the initial development and outcome of coronary disease, raising risk (De Vogli, Chandola, & Marmot, 2007; Matthews & Gump, 2002; Rohrbaugh,

Shoham, & Coyne, 2006). Job stress also increases the chances of developing heart disease, and for having a second and possibly fatal heart attack (Eller et al., 2009). As in the case of negative emotions, stress in close relationships and at work can increase risk through physiological or behavioral avenues. Marital conflicts evoke substantial increases in blood pressure, for example (Smith et al., 2009), and positive relationships tend to dampen our stress responses (Uchino, 2006).

As we discussed in Chapter 3, episodes of stress and strong emotions like anger can be the "straw that breaks the camel's back" by precipitating a heart attack or potentially fatal heart rhythm disturbance in people with advanced atherosclerosis (Bhattacharyya & Steptoe, 2007). Even positive events that arouse strong emotions—like watching important sporting events—can provoke heart attacks in people at high risk (Wilbert-Lampen et al., 2008). Other psychosocial risk factors may delay seeking medical care during the early minutes of an unfolding heart attack. For example, patients who deny or minimize the importance of their early symptoms are slower to get essential medical attention during a heart attack, as are people who lack health insurance or worry about the potential cost of their medical care (Smolderen et al., 2010). Because prompt treatment can minimize or even prevent heart damage at such critical times, these psychological factors can have life-changing—or life-ending—consequences. The fact that stress, negative emotions, and other psychological factors increase a heart patient's risk of further trouble with their heart has important implications for their medical care.

MEDICAL TREATMENT AND REHABILITATION OF CARDIAC PATIENTS

Many cardiac patients have not had a heart attack, but tests and symptoms indicate that they have heart disease, such as significant blockage in one or more coronary arteries. These individuals usually receive long-term pharmacological therapy to protect against a heart attack and stop or reverse atherosclerosis; they may also receive one of two invasive procedures (AMA, 2003). One procedure is called *balloon angioplasty*, in which a tiny balloon is inserted in the blocked artery and inflated to open the blood vessel. A metal mesh *stent* is then placed permanently at the site to keep the vessel open. The other procedure—called *bypass surgery*—directs blood flow around the diseased section of artery with a healthy vessel taken from another part of the person's body. People who suffer a heart attack are likely to eventually get similar treatments, but their

condition is an emergency: because little heart damage typically occurs in the first hour or two after an attack starts, immediate treatment is critical (AMA, 2003). Their treatment starts with emergency care and continues with a program of rehabilitation.

Initial Treatment for Heart Attack

When heart attack victims enter the hospital, medical treatment focuses on preventing or limiting damage to the myocardium. Part of this treatment generally involves using clot-dissolving *thrombolytic drugs*, which can prevent myocardial damage if administered within 2 hours or so after the attack begins (AHA, 2006). Most patients are then placed in *coronary care units*, where medical staff can monitor their physiological functioning closely. The risk of another attack is high during the first few days. These people often require other procedures, such as angioplasty or bypass surgery, too.

As you might expect, most heart attack patients experience extremely high levels of anxiety in the first day or two of coronary care. Many of these people cope with this crisis through *denial*, and those who use denial tend to be less anxious in the first few days than those who do not (Froese et al., 1974). Regardless of whether the patients use denial, their anxiety levels soon start to decline. After a few days, the anxiety levels of those who do and do not use denial are similar, but still higher than normal. These fairly high anxiety levels tend to persist for the remainder of their hospital stays (Cay, Vetter, Philip, & Dugard, 1972; Froese et al., 1974). The heart attack patients with the greatest difficulty coping are not necessarily the ones who are the most seriously ill—instead, they tend to be those who were experiencing distress and social problems before the heart attack.

Excessive anxiety, depression, or denial can impair recovery, and psychological intervention may be needed (Erdman, 1990). For example, some patients may deny they had a heart attack and insist on leaving the hospital too early. Many patients anticipate psychosocial problems ahead, particularly in relation to their work. A rehabilitation program generally begins when cardiac patients are transferred to a general ward.

Rehabilitation of Cardiac Patients

Rehabilitation programs for heart attack patients are designed to promote recovery and reduce risk factors for having another attack (Lounsbury, 2004). These programs provide patients with information on such topics as lifestyle changes and restrictions they should follow, medications to take, and symptoms to expect. Many patients will experience recurrent angina pectoris pain for many months or even years after discharge (AMA, 2003; Rey, 1999). These episodes can be very frightening. Sometimes the pain requires medical attention, but the patients often can simply take medication to control it. For some patients, the pain can be quite severe and even disabling (Rey, 1999; Wielgosz et al., 1984). In some cases, tests reveal no substantial artery blockage or ventricle impairment, but the pain persists (Ketterer et al., 1996).

To reduce the likelihood of another infarction, most cardiac patients receive advice on lifestyle changes, such as to:

- Quit smoking
- Lose weight
- Exercise
- Reduce dietary fat and cholesterol
- Reduce high alcohol consumption

Heart disease patients who participate in prevention programs consisting of education and counseling for lifestyle changes and supervised exercise and stress management do in fact experience better health outcomes, better functioning, and lower emotional distress than others who receive standard medical care (Blumenthal et al., 2005; Clark et al., 2005). As you might expect, many people fail to adhere to regimens for cardiac rehabilitation, particularly for lifestyle changes, such as stopping smoking, but also for medication use (Rozanski, 2005). Patients who fail to take their heart medications are at much higher risk of dying in the first year than are those who comply (Ho et al., 2006).

Exercise is an important part of rehabilitation programs for heart attack patients, and it needs to be introduced gradually and tailored to each person's physical condition. It often begins in the hospital with supervised short-distance walking. In the next weeks, the activities become more and more vigorous and long-lasting, and are likely to include long-distance walking, calisthenics, and often jogging, bicycling, or swimming. Exercise-based rehabilitation programs for heart patients have well-documented benefits for health and emotional well-being; most importantly, these programs reduce the likelihood of additional and potentially fatal heart attacks (Taylor et al., 2004). This is especially the case for patients who adhere to their exercise programs (Miller, Balady, & Fletcher, 1997). They reduce their risk of dying in the next few years by 20 to 25%, their risk of another heart attack, and their symptoms, such as of angina. But many cardiac patients never begin an exercise program and more than half of those who do discontinue it in the first 6 months (Dishman, 1982; Moore et al., 2006).

Depression increases the likelihood that heart patients will drop out of exercise-based rehabilitation (Casey et al., 2008). A cognitive–behavioral program to enhance their self-efficacy and skills in problem solving and relapse prevention can improve greatly their likelihood of continuing to exercise through the first year (Moore et al., 2006). After consultation with their doctors, patients can pursue exercise-based rehabilitation programs at home, and these programs are as effective as those based in a rehabilitation center for preventing further heart attacks (Dalal et al., 2010). Flexibility and convenience of home-based programs may help patients achieve better adherence.

Cardiac patients may also have a difficult time making other lifestyle changes, particularly in their diets and in stopping smoking. Dietary changes to reduce fat and cholesterol are often hard to make because they have an impact on family life (Croog, 1983). With respect to stopping smoking, studies have found that only perhaps 30 to 40% of people who suffer myocardial infarctions quit or substantially reduce their smoking (Falba, 2005; Rigotti et al., 1991). Depression complicates this important change, as it is associated with lower likelihood of smoking cessation among heart patients and greater risk of relapse after quitting initially (Thorndike et al., 2008). A variety of approaches to smoking cessation are effective for heart patients, especially more intensive approaches that include behavior therapy and follow-up support (Barth, Critchley, & Bengel, 2008). Although difficult, these lifestyle changes are important. Adherence to these exercise, smoking, and diet recommendations is associated with significant reductions in risk of additional heart attacks (Chow et al., 2010; Gehi et al., 2007). Cardiac patients' beliefs influence their adherence. A study found that men were more likely than women to attribute their heart attacks to their dietary and exercise patterns and to improve those behaviors (Martin et al., 2005). Two other important factors are social support and self-efficacy: cardiac patients who perceive little social support in their lives or have low self-efficacy for carrying out their regimens show less adherence (Bastone & Kerns, 1995; Evon & Burns, 2004; Wills & Fegan, 2001).

THE PSYCHOSOCIAL IMPACT OF HEART DISEASE

"Is it OK for me to drive a car, do chores around the house, or lift heavy things?" heart attack patients often ask their doctors, fearing that overexertion could bring on another attack (Erdman, 1990). The extent of patients' disability is likely to affect how well they and their families adjust to their conditions.

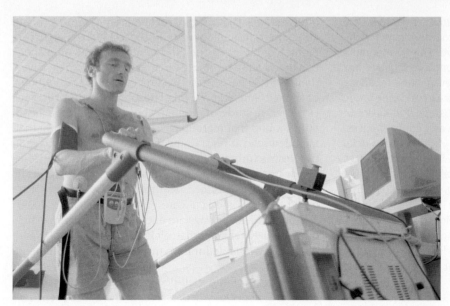

The treadmill test is used in assessing the ability of heart patients to engage in strenuous exercise.

Being able to work has a special meaning to individuals who suffer from chronic health problems, and heart attack victims often view going back to work as an important sign that they are recovering (Croog, 1983). Advice about returning to work depends on how severe the heart condition is and the physical requirements of the job (Rey, 1999). In part because jobs in industrialized countries are less physically demanding than they used to be, most heart attack patients can resume working now in a few weeks without risking another cardiac episode (Dennis et al., 1988). Doctors often advise people with heart disease to cut back on the amount of physical effort and stress they experience on the job. Following this advice may mean finding a new job, which may be difficult to do, retiring if possible, or lead to interpersonal problems with coworkers. Nevertheless, most cardiac patients—roughly 80%—do go back to work within the year following the heart attack, often with jobs requiring less productivity or shorter hours than previously (Doehrman, 1977; Shanfield, 1990). Compared to individuals who do not return to work, those who do return tend to be younger, in better physical condition, better educated, and employed in white-collar jobs. Delaying or failing to go back to work is more likely among patients who are depressed and those who describe their jobs as stressful (Fukuoka et al., 2009).

Cardiac illness and family relationships are closely interrelated: as noted previously, cardiac patients with strong social support recover faster and survive longer than those with less support (Lett et al., 2005; Wills & Fegan, 2001). For many heart patients, family difficulties—such as quarreling over financial or sexual problems—existed prior to the infarction, and these difficulties often become worse (Croog & Fitzgerald, 1978; Swan, Carmelli, & Rosenman, 1986). But even when harmonious relations exist before the attack, the illness adds to the stress of all members of the family. One marital difficulty that may arise after a heart attack relates to sexual activity, which often never returns to the level that existed prior to the attack (Krantz & Deckel, 1983; Michela, 1987). Either or both spouses may fear that having sex could precipitate another attack, even though this risk is very low, especially if the patient exercises regularly (Muller et al., 1996). The marital satisfaction of both partners generally benefits by having little or no sex initially and then increasing its frequency gradually, with the advice of the patient's doctor (Michela, 1987).

Families have an enormous impact on the process of cardiac rehabilitation: patients adjust better, adhere more closely to their regimens, and recover sooner if their efforts receive family encouragement (Kaplan & Toshima, 1990; Krantz & Deckel, 1983). But the danger exists that families will promote *cardiac invalidism*, in which people with heart disease become increasingly dependent and helpless. The beliefs a spouse has about the patient's physical capabilities can aid or retard rehabilitation (Joekes, Maes, & Warrens, 2007). Two research findings about their beliefs are important. First, family members increase their estimates of the physical ability of cardiac patients by seeing and personally experiencing the level of exertion the patients can perform safely on a treadmill testing (Taylor et al., 1985), a standard technique in evaluating heart disease. These family members are likely to provide more effective encouragement for the person to become increasingly active. Family members who do not have this experience continue to have low estimates of the patient's ability, even after receiving medical counseling to the contrary. Second, the more similar the patient's and spouse's positive beliefs about heart disease, such as of its timeline and consequences, the better the patient's physical and psychosocial functioning months later (Figueiras & Weinman, 2003). The patient's and spouse's emotional adjustment affect each other's quality of life (Chung et al., 2009), and the spouse's distress can interfere with the patient's adherence to medical regimens (Molloy et al., 2008). Fortunately, the spouse's anxiety and distress can be lowered even by simply providing additional information about the disease and its treatment (Broadbent et al., 2009).

What are the long-term emotional consequences of heart disease? During the first weeks or months after having a heart attack, most patients have higher-than-normal levels of anxiety and depression, but their distress tends to decline during the next year or two (Carney et al., 1995; Doehrman, 1977). Most eventually adjust fairly well, especially if they have high levels of social support (Holahan et al., 1997). But if very high levels of anxiety and depression continue beyond a few months, these emotions become signs of poor adaptation and tend to be linked to decreased compliance with the cardiac regimen, low quality of life, deterioration in the person's physical condition, and increased risk of recurrent cardiac events (Nicholson et al., 2006). Similarly, patients who, after undergoing a successful angioplasty, feel optimistic about the future and have a strong sense of personal control and self-esteem are less likely than others to suffer a heart attack or require bypass surgery or another angioplasty in the next several months (Helgeson & Fritz, 1999).

PSYCHOSOCIAL INTERVENTIONS FOR HEART DISEASE

Interventions to enhance people's recovery from and long-term adaptation to having heart disease have used health and regimen education, psychosocial counseling, stress management, or combinations of these approaches, in order to improve their compliance with the cardiac regimen, enhance their adjustment to the illness, and reduce their risk of future cardiac problems. A meta-analysis of studies evaluating the effects of these interventions indicated that they reduce mortality in heart patients by over 25% during the first two years after treatment (Linden, Phillips, & LeClerc, 2007).

Interventions that began immediately after the heart attack were less effective than those initiated after two months or more. Further, these interventions were effective in reducing mortality for men but not women. Given that heart disease is the leading cause of death among both men and women, this latter finding is worrisome. However, a study of women who had suffered a heart attack found that a group psychosocial intervention that included relaxation training, self-monitoring and cognitive restructuring concerning stress at home and work, risk factor education, and efforts to improve self-care and adherence reduced death rates by over 50% compared to usual medical care (Orth-Gomer et al., 2009). Although these findings are encouraging, more research is needed to ensure that effective psychosocial treatments are available for both men and women with heart disease.

Because of the well-documented role of negative emotions, especially depression, in the subsequent cardiac problems and mortality of heart disease patients, research has assessed the impact of treating these emotional difficulties. Does psychotherapy improve depressed cardiac patients' health and survival? Standard psychological treatments for depression such as cognitive-behavioral therapy are effective in reducing depression in heart patients (Freedland et al., 2009). Collaborative or integrative care approaches described in Chapter 12 have been adapted for delivery over the telephone, with success in reducing depressive symptoms in heart patients (Rollman et al., 2009). However, the results of a very large, multi-site trial—Enhancing Recovery in Coronary Heart Disease, or ENRICHD—were disappointing in this regard. It demonstrated modest benefits of cognitive-behavioral therapy in improving depression and social isolation, but no overall effects on mortality or recurrent cardiac events (Berkman et al., 2003). Although depression in and of itself is a major and common threat to quality of life among heart patients and should be treated for that reason alone, it is difficult to justify aggressive treatment of depression on the basis of physical health benefits (Thombs et al., 2008). Few studies have examined the benefits of treatment for anger and hostility in heart patients, but some preliminary evidence suggests that they are effective in reducing anger and risk of future cardiac events (Davidson et al., 2007).

In a now-famous intervention, Dean Ornish and his colleagues (1990) tested a multi-component program of dietary, exercise, and stress management approaches for cardiac rehabilitation. The patients volunteered and were randomly assigned to receive either the program or standard medical care. The program had the people eat a mainly vegetarian diet, eliminate caffeine and restrict alcohol intake, stop smoking, get moderate exercise regularly, meet regularly as support groups, and use stress management methods, including relaxation and meditation. Medical assessments were made at the start of the study and at the end of a year. Comparisons of the groups showed that atherosclerosis and reports of chest pain worsened for the people who received standard medical care but improved for those in the intervention program. Although the results don't indicate which features of the program worked, they show that changes in lifestyle can halt and possibly reverse the progression of atherosclerosis. Other studies have confirmed these findings and found that this intensive lifestyle modification reduces subsequent cardiac problems and hospitalizations (Haskell et al., 1994; Lisspers et al., 2005; Ornish et al., 1998).

To summarize, recovery after a heart attack presents difficult physical and psychosocial challenges for patients and their families. Effective cardiac rehabilitation programs have individuals adhere to regimens of exercise, diet, medication, and stress management. These programs can improve the medical course of the disease. The long-term impact of heart disease often involves emotional, vocational, and marital problems that may require therapeutic interventions to enhance adaptation.

 WEB ANIMATION: The Case of the Man with the Tingling Arm

Access: www.wiley.com/go/global/sarafino. This interactive animation describes the symptoms and medical test results of a man with a cardiovascular disorder.

STROKE

Sitting at the breakfast table, Neil began to feel faint and weak, his vision dimmed, and the right side of his body became numb and tingly. As he realized he was having a stroke, he tried to say so, but the words would not come out. Soon he lost consciousness. Table 13.3 states that these are common symptoms of a **stroke**—a condition in which damage occurs in an area of the brain when the blood supply to that area is disrupted, depriving it of oxygen. Stroke is a prevalent disorder around the world. Table 13.4 gives data on hospital discharges for stroke in several nations, which suggest the relative prevalence of the condition. Worldwide, 15 million people suffer a stroke annually. Of these, 5 million die and 5 million are left permanently disabled (WHO 2004).

Table 13.3   *Symptoms of Stroke*

Individuals who experience any of the following warning signs of a stroke should see a doctor immediately.
- Sudden numbness or weakness of the face, arm, or leg, especially on one side of the body
- Sudden confusion, trouble speaking or understanding
- Sudden trouble seeing in one or both eyes
- Sudden trouble walking, dizziness, loss of balance or coordination
- Sudden, severe headache with no known cause

Source: AHA, 2010.

CAUSES, EFFECTS, AND REHABILITATION OF STROKE

The disruption in blood supply that causes strokes occurs in two ways (AHA, 2006; AMA, 2003). In an *ischemic stroke*, damage results when the blood supply in a cerebral artery is sharply reduced or cut off, similar to atherosclerosis and myocardial infarction in coronary disease, except it damages the brain rather than the heart. In a *hemorrhagic stroke*, a blood vessel ruptures and bleeds into the brain. A stroke caused by a hemorrhage generally occurs rapidly and causes the person to lose consciousness; most of the damage it produces happens in a few minutes. In contrast, an ischemic stroke tends to occur more slowly, and the person is less likely to lose consciousness. Strokes from hemorrhages occur much less frequently but are much more likely to cause extensive damage and death than those from ischemia (AHA, 2006; AMA, 2003).

Age, Gender, and Sociocultural Risk Factors for Stroke

The incidence of stroke is very low prior to the middle-age years; from then on, its death rates in America triple in each successive decade (NCHS, 2006). Men are more likely than women to develop a stroke and die from it. We can see a role of sociocultural factors in death rate data for different ethnic groups in the United States: among both men and women, stroke death rates are far higher for Blacks than for Whites and Asians, Hispanics, and Native Americans (NCHS, 2006).

As in heart disease, part of the reason for age, sex, and sociocultural differences in the risk of stroke lies in biological and lifestyle variations. For example, high blood pressure is a risk factor for stroke, and the prevalence rates for hypertension increase with age and are much higher in Black than White Americans (NCHS, 2006).

Table 13.4 *Hospital Discharges for Stroke per 100,000 Population in Selected Nations*

Country	Discharges	Country	Discharges	Country	Discharges
Australia	151.1	Italy	502.8	Turkey	183.7
Canada	206.7	Netherlands	213.2	United Kingdom	224.9
Germany	453.2	Sweden	418.4	United States	290.2

Sources: ABS, 2006, for Australia; NCHS, 2006, for the United States; PHAC, 2006, for Canada; WHO/Europe, 2006, for European Union countries.

Lifestyle and Biological Risk Factors for Stroke

Several lifestyle and biological factors can increase the risk of a person having a stroke, and some of them can be changed or treated (AHA, 2006). In addition to age, gender, and race, these risk factors are:

- High blood pressure
- Cigarette smoking
- Cardiovascular disease, diabetes, and their risk factors, such as high cholesterol, obesity, and physical inactivity
- Family history of stroke
- Atrial fibrillation, a form of heart arrhythmia
- Drug or alcohol abuse
- "Mini-strokes" called *transient ischemic attacks* that may occur one or more times before a full stroke

Negative emotions and stress also appear to be involved: prospective studies have found that people who are depressed are more likely than others to develop a stroke and die from one in the next two decades (Everson et al., 1998; Jonas & Mussolino, 2000). Job stress also has been found to predict risk of stroke (Tsutsumi et al., 2009). Many of the risk factors for a stroke are the same as those for heart disease (Fung et al., 2008). As a result, people who have had strokes are usually asked to make similar lifestyle changes to those of people who have had heart attacks: lose weight, stop smoking, exercise, and reduce dietary fat and cholesterol.

Stroke Effects and Rehabilitation

Strokes vary in severity. People who survive moderate or severe strokes generally suffer some degree of motor, sensory, cognitive, or speech impairment as a result of the brain damage. If enough cells are affected, the functions controlled by the damaged area of the brain can be severely disrupted. The extent and type of impairment stroke patients suffer and their medical treatment—drugs and surgery—can vary greatly, depending on the amount and location of damage (AHA, 2006; AMA, 2003). Getting immediate treatment is critical because clot-dissolving drugs can limit the damage from

an ischemic stroke. The following discussion applies to strokes that cause at least moderately severe damage.

Although the initial deficits stroke victims experience can be permanent, these people often show considerable improvement over time. Medical treatment and physical, occupational, and speech therapy can help patients regain some of the functions they lost (AHA, 2006; Dobkin, 2005). Functional impairments are usually more easily overcome in hemorrhagic than ischemic strokes. Hemorrhages often impair functioning partly by creating pressure on neurons. If that pressure is relieved, such as if the body reabsorbs the pool of blood, the person may gradually recover some of the lost functioning.

Stroke is one of the most disabling chronic illnesses (AHA, 2006; Guccione et al., 1994). The most common deficits stroke patients experience involve motor action (Diller, 1999; Newman, 1984b). For these patients, some degree of paralysis occurs immediately, and the person usually cannot move the arm and leg on one side of the body. Which side is paralyzed depends on which side of the brain is damaged: the left hemisphere of the brain controls movement of the right side of the body; the right hemisphere controls the left side. As a result, paralysis occurs on the side of the body opposite to the hemisphere that sustained damage in the stroke. Because of the paralysis, these patients often cannot walk, dress themselves, or perform many usual self-help activities. Most of the gains these people show in the first month appear to happen spontaneously (AHA, 2006). Although most patients will be able to get around on their own and perform self-care, such as bathing and dressing, after 6 months without formal rehabilitation, engaging in rehabilitation activities reduces their disability (Diller, 1999). Biofeedback and intensive physical therapy can markedly improve motor function in stroke victims (Dobkin, 2004, 2005; Moreland & Thompson, 1994). For complex sequences of behavior, many patients benefit from using verbal instructions (O'Callaghan & Couvadelli, 1998). For instance, to transfer from a wheelchair to a bed, the person might say, "I position the wheelchair facing the bed; perpendicular to it," "Next, I put on the brakes," and so on.

Other deficits many stroke patients face involve cognitive functions—language, learning, memory, and perception. The specific type of impairment they have depends on which side of the brain was damaged. In most people, the left hemisphere contains the areas for language processes, including speech and writing (Tortora & Derrickson, 2009). Thus, damage on the left side often causes language and learning deficits. A common language disorder in stroke patients is *aphasia*, which is marked by difficulty in understanding or using words. There are two kinds of aphasia: *receptive aphasia* refers to a difficulty in understanding verbal information; *expressive aphasia* involves a problem in producing language, even though the person can make the component sounds. For example, the individual may not be able to differentiate between two verbalized words, such as "coal" and "cold." Or the patient may have difficulty remembering a sequence of things he or she is told to do—such as, "Touch your right ear with your left hand, and touch your left eyebrow with your right hand."

What deficits are associated with damage on the right side of the brain? The right hemisphere usually processes visual imagery, emotions, and the perception of patterns, such as melodies (Tortora & Derrickson, 2009). As a result, visual disorders are common with right-brain damage (Diller, 1999). In the disorder called *visual neglect*, patients fail to process information on the left side of the normal visual field. For example, they may not notice food on the left side of a tray, items on the left side of a menu, or a minus sign in an arithmetic task (see Figure 13-2). This problem also impairs their ability to perceive distances correctly and causes them to bump into objects or doorframes on the left side of the visual field, making them accident-prone. Sometimes patients with this disorder feel they are "going crazy" when they hear someone speaking but cannot see the person because he or she is standing in the left side of the visual field. The discrepancy between what they hear and what they see makes them wonder if they are hallucinating.

The specific location of damage in the brain also can determine emotional disorders that stroke patients may show. Some studies have found associations between (1) specific left-hemisphere damage and patients' degree of depression and (2) specific right-hemisphere damage and patients' ability to interpret and express affect (Bleiberg, 1986; Newman, 1984b). An example of an emotional disorder some stroke patients have is called *emotional lability*, which can occur in varying degrees (AHA, 2006; Bleiberg, 1986). Some people with this disorder may laugh or cry with little or no provocation, realizing and being surprised by the discrepancy; others with milder disorders may display an appropriate emotion,

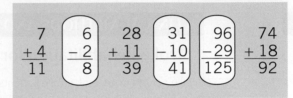

Figure 13-2 An illustration of arithmetic errors (circled items) a stroke patient with a visual disorder might make at the start of rehabilitation. In this case, the patient fails to scan to the left and assumes all of the problems involve addition. Rehabilitation can help patients overcome this deficit.

but at excessive levels, such as sobbing when thinking mildly sad thoughts. In other emotional disorders, stroke patients may be unable to interpret other people's emotions correctly and may react oddly to them. (Go to 👤.)

PSYCHOSOCIAL ASPECTS OF STROKE

Recovery from a severe stroke is a long and arduous process. The initial physical and cognitive deficits are extremely frightening, but many patients are heartened by early gains in their functioning. Although patients with all chronic illnesses often rely on avoidance strategies to cope during the early phases of convalescence, denial seems to be more common among patients who have had strokes than those with heart disease or cancer (Krantz & Deckel, 1983). Stroke patients who continue to deny their current or possible future limitations often retard their progress in rehabilitation. Instead, they need a balance of reality and hope: stroke patients who feel a sense of control over their condition at the end of the first month show better recovery months later than others do (Johnston et al., 1999).

When a stroke produces physical or cognitive deficits, the emotional adjustments can be very difficult. Stroke patients are very prone to depression (Bleiberg, 1986; Krantz & Deckel, 1983; Newman, 1984b). Those who are depressed in the first weeks remain in the hospital much longer and show less improvement from the rehabilitation program before they leave (Tennen, Eberhardt, & Affleck, 1999). As patients see the gains in recovery slowing down and begin to realize the extent of their impairment, they may feel hopeless and helpless. At this point, the more severe their condition, the stronger the depression they develop (Diller, 1999). Intervention with cognitive-behavioral therapy is effective in preventing and treating depression (Hackett et al. 2008; Sarafino, 2001).

CLINICAL METHODS AND ISSUES

Stroke Rehabilitation for Visual Neglect

Like people in general, stroke patients with visual neglect initially take for granted that what they see reflects the full size of their normal visual field. Because they think they see the whole field, they first need to have their visual deficits clearly demonstrated. One way psychologists can do this involves placing paper money on a

> table in front of the patient. The large bills are purposely put on the impaired side. The patient is asked to pick up all of the money on the table. Naturally, a large sum of money remains on the table after the patient says that he or she has

completed the task. Having the patient turn his or her head to see all the money that was left on the table is one way to begin to teach the patient that … this difficulty can be overcome by turning the head. (Gordon & Diller, 1983, p. 119)

Rehabilitation then proceeds from very simple tasks, such as turning the head to track squares in a ceiling, to more difficult ones, such as tracking objects that move from the right to the left side of the visual field, so that the patient turns the head automatically (Diller, 1999). The therapist can provide cues before the response and reinforcement when it occurs.

Although stroke usually afflicts individuals who are beyond retirement age, many of its victims are employed when the illness occurs and suffer impairments that prevent them from returning to work. The results of follow-up studies suggest that less than half of patients who were working prior to the stroke return to work within 6 months, often at reduced hours (Diller, 1999). Some stroke victims who do not return to work are old enough to retire early with pensions, but others must leave the work force under less favorable circumstances, which can be financially and emotionally trying.

The impairments produced by stroke have important social effects on patients and their families, particularly when the patients are severely paralyzed or have aphasia (Evans et al., 1992; Newman, 1984b). Some families adjust to the patient's condition reasonably well, as in the following case:

> Mrs. M. had always taken charge of bookkeeping and running the family. When her husband had a stroke, she adapted very well to his aphasia, inventing ways to communicate with him. When he developed cancer five years later, she helped him keep track of his medications by putting them in little cups at the beginning of the day, with coded instructions on how many to take and when to take them. In this way, Mr. M., who worried that he hadn't taken his medication, could keep track of it when she wasn't there. (Gervasio, 1986, p. 115)

But other families do not adjust well to the changing role relationships, and marital harmony often declines. In addition, social contacts and leisure activities with friends also drop off for both the stroke patient and his or her spouse (Newman, 1984b). Although the decrease in social and leisure activities worsens with the extent of the victim's disability, it is often substantial even when the person has made a good recovery. Family therapy and support groups can help stroke patients and their families adapt, but these approaches often need to address practical problems, such as not having transportation, before trying to resolve interpersonal problems (Evans et al., 1992; Krantz & Deckel, 1983).

In summary, stroke is a high-mortality illness that involves neurological damage as a result of disrupted blood flow to the brain. Survivors of stroke often suffer substantial physical and cognitive impairments, but medical treatment and physical, occupational, and speech therapy can help these people regain many of their lost abilities (Hackett et al., 2008). The more severe the remaining deficits after rehabilitation, the more likely patients are to experience psychosocial problems.

CANCER

Cancer is probably the disease most people fear most—the word "cancer" itself scares many people, and they often overestimate the deaths that cancer causes (Burish et al., 1987). Receiving mammogram results indicating possible breast cancer can leave some women with high levels of anxiety months after further tests disconfirm the suspicion (Lerman et al., 1991). But most women's distress from false-positive cancer tests is not very severe or long-lasting (Wardle et al., 1993). Although most practitioners recognize how people feel about cancer and are reluctant to discuss the disease and its effects with their patients, they are more likely today than in the past to share details about serious medical conditions with their patients (Andersen, Golden-Kreutz, & DiLillo, 2001; Laszlo, 1987).

THE PREVALENCE AND TYPES OF CANCER

A basic characteristic of life and growth is that body cells reproduce in an orderly and controlled fashion. Scientists know what the normal pattern of tissue growth looks like. Irregularities in this process can cause unrestricted cell growth, usually forming a tumor called a *neoplasm* (AMA, 2003; Tortora & Derrickson, 2009). *Oncogenes* regulate cell division, but genetic processes and carcinogens can damage them, causing unrestricted growth. Some neoplasms are harmless, or benign, but others are malignant.

Cancer is a disease of the cells characterized by uncontrolled cell proliferation that usually forms a malignant neoplasm. There are many forms of cancer, and the large majority can be classified into five types based on the kind of tissue in which it develops (Tortora & Derrickson, 2009; Williams, 1990):

1. *Carcinomas*, which are malignant neoplasms in cells of the skin and the lining of body organs, such as the digestive, respiratory, and reproductive tracts. About 85% of human cancers are carcinomas.

2. *Melanomas*, or neoplasms of a special type of skin cell that produces the skin pigment called melanin.

3. *Lymphomas*, or cancers of the lymphatic system.

4. *Sarcomas*, which are malignant neoplasms of the muscle, bone, or connective tissue.

5. *Leukemias*, or cancers of the blood-forming organs, such as the bone marrow, that lead to an extreme proliferation of white blood cells.

An important characteristic of cancer cells is that they do not adhere to each other as strongly as normal cells do (AMA, 2003; Williams, 1990). As a result, they may separate and spread to other parts of the body through the blood or lymph systems. This migration is called *metastasis*, as is the new neoplasm (plural is *metastases*). As the neoplasm or tumor grows, it must eventually recruit its own blood supply for nutrients, a process called angiogenesis.

Cancer is a leading cause of death worldwide (WHO, 2006). In the United States, it is the second most frequent cause of death; its death rates increased in the second half of the 20th century, and then began to decline (NCHS, 2006). The data on American cancer mortality and morbidity are sobering: each year cancer takes more than 550,000 lives, and about 1.4 million new cases are diagnosed (ACS, 2006). About 60% of these newly diagnosed people can expect to live at least 5

years—most of these people will be *cured* having virtually the same life expectancy as someone who never had the disease. Although cancer can strike any area of the body, as Figure 13-3 shows, almost all of the increase in cancer death rates after 1950 was from neoplasms in one body site: the lung.

THE SITES, EFFECTS, AND CAUSES OF CANCER

What are the physical effects of cancer, and how does it kill? Cancer progresses by enlarging and spreading to different sites; its growth at each site interferes with normal development and functioning. As the disease progresses, it can produce pain, often because the tumor creates pressure on normal tissue and nerves or blocks the flow of body fluids (Melzack & Wall, 1982). Substantial pain afflicts 40% of cancer victims in intermediate stages of the disease and 70 to 90% of those with advanced cancer (Greenwald, Bonica, & Bergner, 1987; Ward et al., 1993). The disease leads to death in direct and indirect ways. In the direct route, the cancer spreads over time to a vital organ, such as the brain, liver, or lungs; it then competes for and takes most of the nutrients the organ tissues need to survive, thereby causing the organ to fail. Cancer kills indirectly in two ways: the disease itself weakens the victims, and both the disease and the treatment can impair the patient's appetite and ability to fight infection (Laszlo, 1987).

Prognosis and Causes of Cancer

The prognosis for cancer depends on how early it is detected and its location (ACS, 2006; Williams, 1990). Table 13.5 describes cancers of common sites worldwide.

We have seen in earlier chapters that cancer is caused by the interplay of genetic, environmental, and behavioral and psychosocial factors (Foulkes, 2008). Environmental factors include ultraviolet radiation, and household and worksite chemical hazards. Behavioral or lifestyle factors include smoking, diet, obesity, and physical activity. As discussed in Chapter 3, stress and related psychosocial factors seem to play a role in the development and course of cancer (Chida et al., 2008), probably through the effects of stress on the immune system and the process of metastasis and angiogenesis (Antoni et al., 2006). Some research has also found a link between certain viral infections and the development of some cancers, such as in the cervix and in the liver (Tortora & Derrickson, 2009; Williams, 1990). In cervical cancer, viral transmission probably occurs during intercourse. Because not all women who are exposed to the viruses develop cancer, it seems likely that the effects

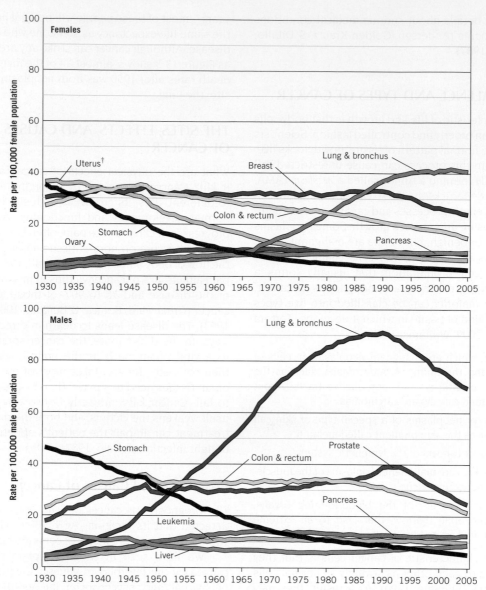

Figure 13-3 Age-adjusted death rates for selected cancer sites per 100,000 females and males in the United States between 1930 and 2005 (from ACS, 2010). Notice three things: First, mortality rates for most forms of cancer have either declined or remained fairly constant; lung cancer is the dramatic exception. Second, the increases in lung cancer deaths for males and females correspond to gender differences in the prevalence of cigarette smoking. Third, corresponding to declines in smoking rates, the death rates now for lung cancer are declining for males and have leveled off for females. (American Cancer Society. *Cancer Facts and Figures* 2010. Atlanta: American Cancer Society, Inc.)

of the infections depend on or combine with genetic and environmental factors to produce the disease.

Age, Gender, and Sociocultural Factors in Cancer

The risk of developing cancer typically increases with age, especially from the middle-age years onward: over 75% of all cancers are diagnosed in people 55 years of age and older (ACS, 2006). Taking age into account, the incidence rates of cancer are higher for males than females in many countries, as Table 13.6 shows. In the United States, the risk of developing cancer in one's lifetime is 1 in 2 for males and 1 in 3 for females (ACS, 2006). Two of the most common newly diagnosed malignancies are prostate cancer for men and breast cancer for women.

Table 13.5 *Prevalent Cancer Sites and Facts Worldwide*

- *Skin cancer.* With over 3 million cases diagnosed in the skin each year, one in every three cancers diagnosed is a skin cancer (WHO, 2010c). The vast majority of these cancers are *basal cell* and *squamous cell carcinomas*, and cure is almost assured with early detection (for this reason, these cases are often not included in incidence data). But about 5% of skin cancers are *melanomas*, which are more serious because they metastasize quickly. Still, 92% of melanoma patients survive at least 5 years.
- *Lung cancer.* Worldwide 1.2 million new cases of lung cancer are diagnosed annually, and the incidence is far greater among males than females, probably because of men's higher smoking rates in the past. The 5-year survival rate is only 16% overall and 50% if the disease is discovered while still localized. In lung cancer, neoplasms tend to metastasize while still small, and, for this reason, they generally have already spread by the time they are discovered.
- *Breast cancer.* The incidence of breast cancer worldwide is about 1.38 million cases a year. Early detection permits about 89% of breast cancer patients to survive at least 5 years, but this rate drops to 81% if the cancer has begun to spread. Across all stages of the disease, 80% survive at least 10 years.
- *Prostate cancer.* Worldwide, an estimated 913,000 diagnoses were made of neoplasms of the prostate gland in male reproductive systems (Ferlay et al., 2008). The 5- and 10-year survival rates for prostate cancer are nearly 99% and 93%, respectively; 90% are detected early.
- *Colorectal cancer.* Neoplasms of the colon or rectum account for over 1.23 million cancer diagnoses and 639,000 deaths per year worldwide. The 5-year survival rates are about 66% overall and 90% when detected early (less than 40% of cases) in recommended tests.

Links for gender and cultural factors in cancer can be seen in the data for different ethnic groups in the United States: cancer incidence and death rates are higher for males than females in each ethnic group and far higher for Blacks than for each of the other groups, as Figure 13-4 shows. And although the incidence rates are fairly high for Whites, death rates are much higher in Blacks partly because their diagnoses occur later (Meyerowitz et al., 1998). Evidence indicates that environmental factors may play a role in cultural differences in cancer development. A study compared cancer rates for Japanese people who either stayed in Japan or moved to Hawaii and adopted Western habits but did not intermarry (Williams, 1990). For almost all cancer types, the incidence for those in Hawaii was more similar to that of local Caucasians than to people in Japan.

Table 13.6 *Annual Incidence of All Types of Cancer per 100,000 Males and Females in Selected Nations*

Country	Males	Females
Australia	468.5	415.5
Canada	500.4	429.2
Germany	498.6	462.7
Italy	547.9	420.0
Netherlands	466.9	435.5
Sweden	577.2	510.2
Turkey	80.6	59.7
United Kingdom	470.5	446.4
United States	525.7	393.3

Sources: ABS, 2006, for Australia; NCHS, 2006, for the United States; PHAC, 2006, for Canada; WHO/Europe, 2006, for European Union countries.

DIAGNOSING AND TREATING CANCER

People can increase the likelihood of early rather than late detection of certain cancers by knowing the warning signs of cancer and having or doing regular examinations, which are listed in Table 13.7.

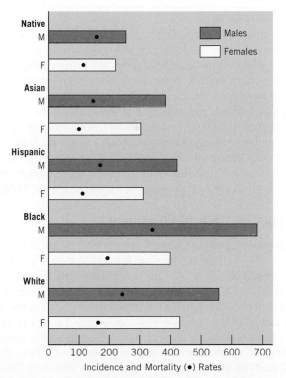

Figure 13-4 Age-adjusted annual incidence and mortality (solid dots) rates of all types of cancer per 100,000 males and females of five ethnic groups—White, Black, Hispanic, Asian (and Pacific Islander), and Native (American Indian and Alaskan)—in the United States. (Data from ACS, 2006, p. 32.)

Table 13.7   *Early Cancer Detection: Examinations and Warning Signs*

Examinations
Doctor or self-administered examinations are available for early detection of the following cancer sites: • Breast • Skin • Colon or rectum • Testes • Prostate • Uterus or cervix *Warning Signs of Cancer:* "CAUTION" If you have any of the following signs, see your doctor soon. Notice that the first letters spell "caution." • **C**hange in bowel or bladder habits • **A** sore that does not heal • **U**nusual bleeding or discharge • **T**hickening or lump in the breast or elsewhere • **I**ndigestion or difficulty swallowing • **O**bvious change in a wart or mole • **N**agging cough or hoarseness

Sources: ACS, 1989, 2009.

Diagnosing cancer can involve three medical procedures (AMA, 2003; Laszlo, 1987; Nguyen et al., 1994). First, *blood* or *urine tests* can suggest the presence of cancer by revealing telltale signs, such as unusual levels of certain hormones or enzymes. Second, *radiological imaging*, such as with X-ray and MRI, allows doctors to see the structure of internal organs and whether a tumor exists. Third, in a *biopsy* a doctor takes out a small piece of suspicious tissue and has it analyzed. Even when the tissue is deep within the abdomen, it can generally be removed with minor surgical procedures and a local anesthetic.

Types of Medical Treatment

The ideal goal of cancer treatment is to cure the disease—to free the person from it forever. This ideal is possible when all the neoplasms are found and eliminated (Laszlo, 1987). If not all of the cancer was eliminated, the patient's symptoms may disappear for a time—or "go into remission"—only to return at a later date. Sometimes doctors can be reasonably certain that all of the cancer was removed, but often they cannot be sure. This is why they use the individual's survival for at least 5 years as a gauge of a treatment's success. There are basically three types of treatment for cancer—surgery, radiation, and chemotherapy—that may be used singly or in combination. When choosing the treatment components, patients and practitioners consider many factors, such as the size and site of

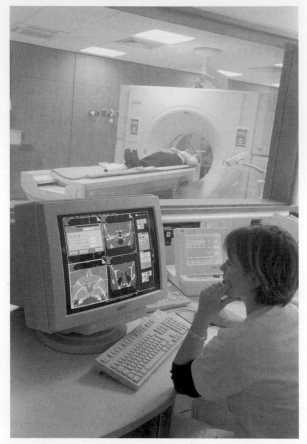

While the patient lies on a table in a large apparatus in the background, a radiological image of his brain appears on the monitor.

the neoplasm, whether it has metastasized, and how the treatment will affect the patient's quality of life. Widespread misconceptions about cancer treatment, such as that surgery for cancer can cause it to spread, may lead some people to delay or adhere poorly to their treatments (Gansler et al., 2005).

From a medical standpoint, *surgery* is frequently the preferred treatment for eliminating a neoplasm, such as in breast or colorectal cancer (AMA, 2003; Williams, 1990). If the cancer is localized, surgery often can be completely effective by itself; if the cancer has spread, surgery may be useful in removing large clusters of cancerous cells, leaving the remainder for radiation or chemotherapy treatment. Sometimes the surgeon removes large portions of tissue near the neoplasm because of the possibility that the cancer has spread to those areas, too. In patients with colorectal cancer, for example, the surgeon may remove a long section of the colon even though the neoplasm seems to be restricted to a small area. But the practice of removing large amounts of nearby tissue is changing, particularly in the treatment of breast cancer: a *mastectomy*—the removal of the entire breast—is not necessary in many, if not most, cases (ACS, 2006; Jacobson et al., 1995). Instead, a woman may choose to have a *lumpectomy*, in which just the tumor is removed, followed by radiation treatment.

Radiation in high doses damages the DNA of cells, and malignant cells are much less able than normal cells to repair the damage. In treating cancer, radiation is used in two ways (AMA, 2003; Laszlo, 1987). One approach, *external beam therapy*, involves directing a beam of intense radiation at the malignant tissue for a period of seconds or minutes. This is the most commonly used method and the one most people picture when the term "radiation therapy" is used. External beam therapy is usually given several times in a week, and may be continued for up to several weeks. The second approach is called *internal radiation therapy* and involves applying radiation inside the body, near or into the tumor, such as by injection. Although radiation is painless, it can have problematic side effects, depending on the area of the body radiated and the dose. Because radiation affects both healthy and malignant cells, the affected area may suffer irritation, burns, or hair loss, for example. The person may experience nausea, vomiting, loss of appetite, sterility, and reduced bone marrow function, particularly if the radiated area is large or is in the abdomen. In the days preceding radiation treatment, individuals often worry about these side effects and report heightened anxiety (Andersen, Golden-Kreutz, & DiLillo, 2001).

In *chemotherapy*, patients receive powerful drugs, usually orally or by injection, that circulate through the body to kill cells that divide very rapidly (AMA, 2003; Williams, 1990). The intended targets, of course, are cancerous cells, most of which reproduce rapidly. Different forms of cancer respond more readily to some types of drugs than to others. One problem with chemotherapy is that the drugs also kill many normal cells that divide rapidly, which can produce adverse side effects, including reduced immunity to infection, sores in the mouth, hair loss, nausea and vomiting, and damage to internal organs (ACS, 2006, AMA, 2003; Williams, 1990). Most of these effects are temporary—for instance, lost hair typically grows back.

Side Effects of Treatment

For many patients, two side effects of cancer treatment are especially difficult. First, most people who undergo repeated radiation or chemotherapy experience severe and long-lasting *fatigue* that often gets worse after the treatment ends (Cella et al., 1998; Jacobsen & Thors,

2003). This fatigue can be treated effectively with exercise and various cognitive-behavioral therapies (Cramp & Daniel, 2008; Kangas, Bovbjerg, & Montgomery, 2008). Second, chemotherapy and radiation often produce periods of *nausea and vomiting* during and soon after each treatment. Drugs to reduce nausea are effective for only some patients (Jordan, Schmoll, & Aapro, 2007). The nausea and vomiting can have serious effects. For example, they can be so aversive that patients have discontinued treatment, knowing that doing so could shorten their lives (Carey & Burish, 1988). And many patients develop anticipatory nausea and learned food aversion.

In *anticipatory nausea*, patients who have received a few treatments and are about to receive the drug again begin vomiting before it is given. Some even become nauseated and throw up when they arrive at the hospital or while thinking about the upcoming treatment at home the night before. Anticipatory nausea appears to develop in about 25 to 50% of chemotherapy patients who have received repeated treatments (Andrykowski, 1990; Carey & Burish, 1988). Part of this reaction develops by classical conditioning: the drug is the unconditioned stimulus that reflexively produces the unconditioned response of nausea. By association, other related events, such as seeing the hospital or thinking about the procedure, become conditioned stimuli and can elicit nausea in the absence of the drug (Bovbjerg et al., 1992; Jacobsen et al., 1995). A similar process appears to occur in the fatigue chemotherapy patients develop (Bovbjerg, Montgomery, & Raptis, 2005). Anticipatory nausea is more likely to develop in people who, before treatments start, expect they will become nauseated than in those who do not expect nausea (Montgomery & Bovbjerg, 2003). Using behavioral methods, such as relaxation techniques, can help to reduce the nausea (Redd & Jacobsen, 2001).

Cancer patients who receive chemotherapy or radiation therapy often report that they develop a distaste for some foods they once liked, which is called a *learned food aversion*. The food becomes distasteful because the person associates it with symptoms of nausea and vomiting. Learned food aversion is a medical problem because cancer patients often experience a loss of appetite, which can lead to excessive weight loss. Research with chemotherapy patients has revealed several interesting findings (Mattes, Arnold, & Boraas, 1987a, 1987b). First, 55% of the patients developed aversions to foods consumed within the 24 hours preceding and following treatments. Second, many of these aversions formed after only one treatment, and subsequent treatments produced fewer and fewer new dislikes. Third, the amount of time (up to 24 hours) between eating the food and receiving the treatment did not affect whether an aversion would develop. Fourth, compared with individuals whose side effects did not include vomiting, subjects who vomited developed more learned food aversions, but receiving drugs to prevent vomiting did not help prevent aversions from forming. Fifth, the aversions generally lasted less than a month and included many of the foods the patients previously ate frequently and liked a great deal.

Can something be done to prevent cancer patients from learning to dislike foods they normally eat? One approach involves having a patient consume a strongly flavored, unfamiliar food between his or her last meal and the chemotherapy treatment. Why? The purpose is to create a scapegoat—that is, to direct the learning process to this new food and allow *it* to become disliked, instead of foods in the patient's normal diet. Research has shown that this approach works for many adult and child cancer patients (Broberg & Bernstein, 1987; Mattes, Arnold, & Boraas, 1987b). Individuals who form aversions to the scapegoat foods are much less likely to develop dislikes to foods in normal diets.

Cancer treatment not only can be unpleasant, it can be complex and demanding. Most cancer patients must also take medications at home, and many must return to their clinics frequently for laboratory tests, keep diaries of their food intake, or adhere to dietary and other changes in living habits. Do these conditions lead cancer patients to show poor compliance with their treatment regimens? Most adults seem to adhere well to cancer regimens, but adolescents and minority group individuals from the lower classes do not (Nehemkis & Gerber, 1986; Tebbi et al., 1986). Adherence to medical regimens depends on and affects psychosocial factors in patients' lives.

THE PSYCHOSOCIAL IMPACT OF CANCER

Like all chronic illnesses, cancer involves a series of threats and difficulties that change, often getting worse over time. Cancer creates unique stressors for patients and their families. These patients have a disease they recognize as a "real killer," and one that can lead to intense pain, disability, and disfigurement. The treatment decisions they make are complex—having to balance health benefits against distressing side effects, such as toxic reactions or disfigurement—and can lead to adjustment problems if the outcomes are not as expected (Stanton et al., 1998).

Even among patients who go into remission and adapt well in the first months or years, the threat of a recurrence looms. Fear of the future is a common and severe stressor reported by cancer patients (Lebel et al., 2007). If the disease does flare up, the distress is worse than with the initial illness (Andersen, Golden-Kreutz, & DiLillo, 2001). What's more, some patients experience medical procedures that, for them, can be more aversive than the disease itself. Some evidence suggests that how well patients adapt to having cancer can affect the progression of the disease. Those who have high levels of hopelessness, depression, and other psychosocial vulnerabilities have been found to survive for shorter periods after diagnosis than others do (Brown et al., 2003; Chida et al., 2008; Watson et al., 1999), perhaps because of the effects of stress and negative emotion on immunity and other processes described earlier (Antoni et al., 2006).

Despite all of the stress associated with having cancer, most patients show a remarkable amount of resilience and adapt fairly well (van't Spijker, Trijsburg, & Duivenvoorden, 1997). Even among hospitalized cancer patients, studies have generally found that less than half show significant emotional difficulties, and most of these involve relatively transient problems—chiefly anxiety and depressed mood—that are usually responsive to psychological therapy (Burish et al., 1987). This incidence of emotional problems may seem high, but keep in mind that hospitalization itself elevates emotional difficulties and the patients may have been highly anxious or depressed before the illness. Psychologists often consider it "normal" for cancer patients to have some elevations in depression and anxiety. Given the life circumstances of these patients, our deciding when these reactions are appropriate and when they are dysfunctional is likely to be difficult and based on arbitrary criteria.

Although adaptation to cancer can be very difficult for patients during the first several months and if their conditions worsen, their ability to adjust to their illnesses appears to improve with time during remission or after a cure (Burish et al., 1987; Glanz & Lerman, 1992). By 2 years or so, their psychosocial functioning stabilizes at levels similar to those they had prior to the diagnosis. Studies have compared the psychosocial adjustment of cancer patients who had been diagnosed and treated months or years earlier and other adults from the general population (Cordova et al., 2001; Schroevers, Ranchor, & Sanderman, 2006). The patients and the other adults showed similar levels of self-esteem, depression, happiness, optimism for the future, and perceived health. However, other large-scale studies have suggested that long-term cancer survivors have increased rates of emotional distress, especially low SES survivors and those who are unmarried and disabled (Hoffman et al., 2009). People with cancer who cope by using active, problem-focused strategies show better adjustment after treatment ends than do those who use avoidance coping

The social support of the young cancer patient in the foreground (wearing shirt) is evident from his family having shaved their heads to help him feel more comfortable about losing his hair from chemotherapy.

(Bellizzi & Blank, 2006; Roesch et al., 2005). In contrast, those who blame themselves for their illness have more distress and lower quality of life (Friedman et al., 2007).

The adaptation of people with cancer depends on many aspects of their illnesses and psychosocial situations. For example, the emotional adjustment cancer victims achieve depends on their ages and physical conditions—adults who are middle-aged or physically impaired seem to fare worse than those who are older or less impaired (Costanzo, Ryff, & Singer, 2009; Vinokur et al., 1990). Patients who become most severely depressed tend to be those who are physically disabled by the disease or in pain (Burish et al., 1987; Spiegel, Sands, & Koopman, 1994). Patients who were more involved in decisions about treatment and follow-up care and those who had higher levels of perceived control report less distress and a higher quality of life (Andersen et al., 2009; Barez et al., 2009). Finding meaning in the difficulties they faced from the disease and its treatment also predicts better patient adjustment (Park et al., 2008; Yanez et al., 2009). Patients who were depressed at the time of diagnosis often have a lower quality of life among cancer survivors (Howren et al., 2010).

The site of the cancer is also important, and its impact often depends on the patient's age and gender. Some cancers relate to sexual function, physically and psychologically, particularly for prostate and testicular cancer in men and for breast and gynecological cancer in women. Men with prostate cancer often become impotent and experience urinary incontinence. Before 1990, treatments for testicular cancer rendered men sterile, which generally distressed its younger victims. Newer treatments preserve fertility, and about three-quarters of men succeed in having children if they try after treatment for testicular cancer (Brydøy et al., 2005).

For women, sex-related cancer sites that produce great distress are the breast, cervix, and uterus, especially before old age (Andersen, Woods, & Copeland, 1997; Glanz & Lerman, 1992; Spencer et al., 1999). Their difficulties may be compounded if cancer or its treatment disfigures their bodies or alters their physical ability to function sexually, but breast-conserving surgery reduces disfigurement and adjustment problems (Moyer, 1997). Keep in mind, however, that sexual problems do not occur only among patients with cancers in sex-related organs. Many patients with cancers in other sites may also experience sexual problems as a result of their medical regimens, such as when chemotherapy causes fatigue (Burish et al., 1987; Redd et al., 1991).

Many cancer patients experience psychosocial problems that stem from changes in their relationships with family members and friends. Patients who perceive little social support and negative behaviors from significant people tend to have adjustment problems in part because they do not feel others want to talk about the cancer experience (Lepore & Helgeson, 1998; Manne, 1999). Although patients may withdraw from social contact because they feel socially awkward or embarrassed by their conditions, two other reasons are probably more common (Bloom, Kang, & Romano, 1991). First, patients' physical conditions and treatment may interfere with their seeing friends and family. Second, people may begin to avoid the patient—for instance, because they may feel personally vulnerable in his or her presence (Wortman & Dunkel-Schetter, 1979). They may also worry that they will "break down," or "say the wrong thing" in front of the patient. When these people and the patient do get together, everyone may behave awkwardly. What's more, receiving social support may lead some patients to feel like a burden, lowering their self-esteem (Lepore, Glaser, & Roberts, 2008).

For couples in which one partner has cancer, the partners often "share" distress. That is, for better or worse, the patient's and spouse's level of emotional adjustment affects their partner's level (Dorros et al., 2010; Hagedoorn et al., 2008; Kim et al., 2008). Couples with cancer who engage in active efforts to maintain their relationship can avoid the conflict and distance that often develop under the strain of cancer (Badr & Carmack Taylor, 2008). Some of the distress couples face is likely due to the fact that cancer survivors have a greater risk of unemployment, especially in the case of breast cancer, female reproductive cancers, and cancers of the digestive system (de Boer et al., 2009). In contrast, prostate and testicular cancer and cancers of the blood are not associated with unemployment.

PSYCHOSOCIAL INTERVENTIONS FOR CANCER

Psychosocial approaches for helping individuals cope with their cancers can begin in the diagnostic interview with the doctor (Roberts et al., 1994). The doctor can promote positive adaptation to the illness by discussing the diagnosis while the patient is alert with a spouse or other significant person present, expressing concern and giving the people an opportunity to react emotionally and compose themselves, and then presenting information about the prognosis and treatment options. Medical personnel can also help by providing information on ways to manage the disease and difficult aspects of treatment and advice on improving the patient's diet and physical activity (Helgeson et al., 1999; Pinto, Eakin, & Maruyama, 2000). Exercise, such as brisk walking several hours a week, enhances the physical function of cancer patients and may improve their survival (Markes, Brockow, & Resch, 2006).

Psychosocial interventions have been applied to deal with several difficulties of cancer patients, and we'll focus on ones to reduce patients' nausea from chemotherapy, reduce their physical pain, and improve their emotional adjustment and quality of life. Two successful approaches to reduce nausea are relaxation and systematic desensitization (Redd & Jacobsen, 2001). For example, one study found that training patients to use progressive muscle relaxation and imagery before and during chemotherapy sessions sharply reduced the development of nausea after the first session (Burish & Jenkins, 1992). Another study showed that systematic desensitization can help people who have already developed anticipatory nausea (Morrow et al., 1992). Patients used relaxation techniques while they imagined increasingly difficult scenes relating to chemotherapy, such as driving to the clinic or entering the waiting room. These individuals reported much less nausea and vomiting in subsequent chemotherapy sessions. Not all patients benefit from these techniques, partly because they don't believe psychosocial approaches will help (Carey & Burish, 1988).

Cancer pain is a serious problem when the illness is in advanced stages, especially in the last months before death (Butler et al., 2003). Although treatment with narcotic drugs is very useful, psychosocial interventions can also help (Keefe, Abernathy, & Campbell, 2005). For example, researchers compared cancer pain patients who were randomly assigned to three groups (Dalton et al., 2003). A control group received usual medical care and two experimental groups received cognitive–behavioral treatment; one used a standard approach, and other was tailored to address specific difficulties assessed with psychological tests. The cognitive–behavioral treatments used a variety of methods, such as relaxation and problem-solving training. The patients in both of these groups, especially the tailored treatment group, reported having less pain and engaging in more daily activities than the usual care group.

Other interventions have been applied successfully to improve cancer patients' adjustment to their illnesses and quality of life (Meyer & Mark, 1995). For example, a cognitive–behavioral stress management program had breast cancer patients meet for 2 hours weekly in groups to discuss their difficulties and learn methods, such as relaxation and coping strategies, to apply at home (Antoni et al., 2001; McGregor et al., 2004). The program improved their adjustment in two ways: it reduced the prevalence of depression and increased their use of positive reappraisal strategies, such as seeing benefits to their condition; these effects were strongest among women whose optimism was low at the start. And the program enhanced the women's immune function. This program also has been found to reduce women's cancer-related anxiety, general anxiety symptoms, cortisol levels, and levels of inflammation (Antoni et al., 2009). The main factor in the success of this stress management program is the patients' learning skills that allow them to relax at will (Antoni, Lechner et al., 2006).

Mindfulness-based stress reduction has been found to reduce depressive symptoms and other indications of emotional distress in cancer patients (Ledesma & Kumano, 2009; Lengacher et al., 2009). Various types of supportive therapies and coping skills training also help manage cancer patient's depressive reactions (Akechi et al., 2008; Manne et al., 2007). When these therapies are delivered in group settings, higher levels of group cohesion are associated with treatment outcomes (Andersen et al., 2007; Schnur & Montgomery, 2010). Because of the social problems cancer patients face, they and their families may benefit from family therapy and attending support groups that include education, group discussion, and coping skills training (Helgeson & Cohen, 1996; Scott, Halford, & Ward, 2004). Couples-focused treatments can be effective in treating distress in women with breast cancer, especially for women whose coping style involves approach rather than avoidance (Manne, Ostroff, & Winkell, 2007). For men with prostate cancer, cognitive-behavioral stress management can improve sexual functioning (Molton et al., 2008). (Go to ⬤.)

CHILDHOOD CANCER

Cancer strikes tens of thousands of children around the world each year, including 1,500 cases in the United Kingdom, which has one of the lowest incidence rates for cancer in children in Europe, whilst Northern Europe countries have some of the highest incidence rates (Cancer Research, 2010). *Leukemia* accounts for around a third of these cases and is by far the most common form of cancer in childhood. The 5-year survival rate for childhood leukemia is 80%; the main form of treatment is chemotherapy, which produces much the same side effects in children as in adults, including chronic nausea and vomiting. Losing their hair can be a very traumatic and embarrassing experience to most children and teenagers even though it does grow back (Spinetta, 1982). If a child receives treatment and a relapse does not occur

in the first 5 years after diagnosis, the chances are very high that the leukemia will never recur (Laszlo, 1987).

The treatment program for leukemia is grueling. It begins on an inpatient basis with an "induction" phase, in which the patients receive combinations of drugs in high doses to produce a full remission, and radiation may be used to prevent the disease from developing in the brain (AMA, 2003; Williams, 1990). Chemotherapy then continues at regular intervals on an outpatient basis for the next 2 or 3 years in a "maintenance" phase. Many leukemia patients require a *bone marrow transplant*, an extremely painful process in which a large needle is inserted into the child's hip bone to remove the marrow and replace it with a donor's marrow. Although painkilling drugs help somewhat, the patients still feel intense pain. Children's pain and distress in this procedure can be reduced with psychological methods, such as showing them a film of a child coping realistically and teaching them to use techniques to distract their attention from the pain (Jay et al., 1987; Reeb & Bush, 1996).

What are the psychosocial effects of having cancer on children and their families? In an overall sense, the effects are like those with adult patients: the initial trauma is extremely difficult, but adjustment tends to improve over time (Eiser, 1985; Koocher et al., 1980). Cognitive–behavioral intervention can reduce parents' emotional distress and help them cope with day-to-day problems (Sahler et al., 2005). Two factors that

HIGHLIGHT

Can Psychosocial Interventions Improve Cancer Survival?

Around 1990, some very exciting research findings were published, indicating that psychosocial interventions can improve cancer survival. In one of the studies, patients attended weekly group meetings for a year where they could discuss their feelings and coping strategies and learn self-hypnosis to manage pain (Spiegel et al., 1989). A 10-year follow-up revealed that the patients who received the intervention lived nearly 18 months longer than others in a control group. Other similar interventions also produced positive results (Fawzy, Cousins et al., 1990; Fawzy, Kemeny et al., 1990). Assessments made 6 months after intervention revealed that the subjects had better immune function and reported more vigor, better coping behavior, and less depression than control subjects. A follow-up 6 years later revealed that 29% of the controls and only 9% of the intervention subjects had died (Fawzy et al., 1993).

These outcomes were very encouraging, but some years later similar efforts were not successful (Cunningham et al., 1998; Edelman et al., 1999), and another one was (Andersen et al., 2008). Although we don't yet know why the results conflict, meta-analyses and reviews have concluded that at this time psychosocial interventions do not appear to prolong cancer patients' survival (Coyne, Stefanek, & Palmer, 2007; Edwards, Hulbert-Williams, & Neal, 2008). These interventions can help cancer patients cope with their difficult circumstance and emotional distress, but patients should not pursue these treatments in an effort to extend their lives. Enhancing the quality of life in the face of serious illness is reason enough to seek help when needed.

are important in children's psychosocial adaptation to cancer are the age at the onset and the time since the diagnosis. The earlier the diagnoses and treatment occurred in their lives and the longer they survive in remission, the better their long-term adjustment tends to be. Another psychosocial issue in childhood cancer is that these patients often lag behind other children in academic skills, particularly during the first few years of school (Allen & Zigler, 1986; Eiser, 1985). These deficits probably result from their missing many school days and the psychosocial and physical effects of their medical treatment.

AIDS

Acquired immune deficiency syndrome—AIDS—is a very different high-mortality chronic illness from the others we have discussed in at least three ways. First, AIDS is a new disease and was virtually unknown before 1980. Second, it is an infectious disease that is caused by a virus (HIV) and is spread through the shared contact of blood and semen. Third, although the death rate from AIDS is fairly low in developed countries, it is a worldwide epidemic with 2.7 million new infections and 2 million deaths annually (UNAIDS, 2009). Worldwide, most newly infected people are heterosexuals with high rates of unsafe sex in developing nations, and they will probably die of AIDS.

RISK FACTORS, EFFECTS, AND TREATMENT OF AIDS

The risk factors for AIDS involve ways by which an infected person's blood or semen contacts the body fluid of an uninfected person. This contact almost always occurs in one of three main ways: sexual activity that exposes each person's body fluids to the other's, sharing contaminated syringes in drug use, and birth by an infected mother. We saw in Chapter 5 that public health efforts have reduced these risks, especially among gay men and drug users in technologically advanced countries. But many people around the world still engage in risky behavior.

Age, Gender, and Sociocultural Factors in AIDS

The likelihood of becoming infected and developing AIDS depends on the person's age, gender, and sociocultural background. Worldwide, there are over 33 million people living with HIV/AIDS, and over 16% of newly infected individuals per year are children (UNAIDS,

Table 13.8 *Percentages of Adults Living with HIV and of All Childhood (0 to 5 years) Deaths That are Attributed to AIDS in Selected Nations*

Country	Percent of Adults with HIV	Percent Childhood Deaths from AIDS
Australia	0.1	0.0
Brazil	0.5	0.2
Canada	0.3	0.0
China	0.1	0.2
Germany	0.1	0.0
India	0.3	0.5
Italy	0.3	0.1
Netherlands	0.1	0.0
Singapore	0.1	2.0
South Africa	16.3	44.9
Sweden	0.1	0.0
United Kingdom	0.2	0.0
United States	0.5	0.0

Source: WHO, 2009; adults defined as over 14 years of age.

2009). Table 13.8 gives the percentage of individuals 14 to 49 years old living with HIV and the percentage of all childhood deaths that result from AIDS in selected nations.

In the United States, the number of new HIV diagnoses annually is much higher among 25- to 55-year-old adults than other age groups and about three times higher in men than women; males have constituted over 80% of all AIDS cases since the epidemic began (CDC, 2006b). New HIV infections remain concentrated in men who have sex with men, and among African Americans. After declining for many years since its peak in the mid 1980s, the rate of new infections has been stable for about ten years (Hall et al., 2008). The mortality rates among persons with HIV have declined steadily, to the point that the death rate over five years is similar to the general population (Bhaskaran et al., 2008), although longer-term rates are difficult to determine. American death rate data reveal sociocultural differences: for males and females, AIDS death rates are far higher for Blacks and Hispanics than for Whites and Native Americans, whose rates are higher than for Asian Americans (NCHS, 2006). Hispanic AIDS data reflect infections mainly among those of Puerto Rican descent (Flack et al., 1995). By far, the largest concentrations of HIV infection in the world today are in sub-Saharan Africa (UNAIDS, 2009).

From HIV Infection to AIDS

When HIV infection occurs, several years may pass before the person's immune function is impaired—mainly from reduced numbers of helper T cells—and symptoms appear (Coico, Sunshine, & Benjamini, 2003). During the period before symptoms emerge, the virus appears to hide in the person's lymph tissue, multiplying there and battling the immune system (Carey & Vanable, 2004; Cole & Kemeny, 1997).

The diagnosis of AIDS is made only once the victim's condition has reached a certain criterion. The original criterion required that the person have contracted one of several opportunistic diseases associated with the loss of immune function. These illnesses include P*neumocystis carinii pneumonia* and K*aposi's sarcoma*, a previously rare form of cancer. In 1993, the criterion became a low level of helper T cells (also called CD4 cells) in the person's blood. Years before reaching either of these criteria, however, the victim may have learned from a blood test that he or she was infected with HIV. There is now an accurate method to test a person's "viral load," an assessment of the number of viral particles in a blood sample, reflecting the amount of HIV in the body.

Several years after the infection, an untreated victim's immune system falters, usually producing a variety of recurrent symptoms, such as spiking fever, night sweats, diarrhea, fatigue, and swollen lymph glands (Carey & Vanable, 2004). If the diagnosis comes after symptoms appear, the immune system is already weakened and struggling to fight opportunistic diseases, which often can be treated with medication (AMA, 2003).

Medical Treatment for People with HIV/AIDS

For untreated AIDS patients whose immune systems continue to falter, the prognosis is poor. Their bodies become severely weakened and gradually waste away. Many of them develop a brain disorder when the HIV invades the central nervous system and causes it to deteriorate—a condition called *encephalopathy* in which patients gradually lose their cognitive functions, become disoriented and confused, and eventually lapse into comas.

The main treatment for AIDS today uses drugs called *antiretroviral agents*, which suppress HIV reproduction and reduce viral load. When two or more of these agents are combined, the treatment is extremely effective and called *highly active antiretroviral therapy* (HAART). Treatment with HAART has had dramatic effects: the incidence of opportunistic diseases is much lower in patients after using HAART than before (Gona et al., 2006). And in some patients, HIV is no longer detected in their blood tests. But there are several problems with this treatment. First, it is very expensive. Second, although its use in treating HIV is widespread in high-income nations, only about 42% of people who need HAART in low and middle-income countries are getting it (UNAIDS, 2009). Third, the HAART regimen is complex and rigorous (Carey & Vanable, 2004): it often has the person take

medication several times a day and requires strict adherence—some experts claim that 95% compliance is needed or its value in suppressing the virus diminishes (Ironson et al., 2005). Fourth, many people who use HAART do not adhere to the regimen well enough because of its complexity and side effects and because of emotional difficulties, drug abuse, poor social support, or cognitive difficulties that sometimes result from HIV infection (Catz et al., 2000; Gonzalez et al., 2004; Lovejoy & Suhr, 2009; Mellins et al., 2002). A study found greater adherence in older than younger adult HIV patients, with two-thirds of the individuals age 50 and over achieving 95% adherence (Barclay et al., 2007). Educational interventions that focus on skills or social support for medication management can improve HAART adherence (Koenig et al., 2008; Rueda et al., 2006).

AIDS is still fatal to most of its victims; if untreated, most die within 3 years of the AIDS diagnosis (Cole & Kemeny, 1997). HIV victims with high stress reactivity, depression, and avoidance coping show poorer immune function and faster progression of the disease than others do (Chida & Vedhara, 2009; Cole & Kemeny, 1997; Ironson et al., 2005). Personality traits also seem to be associated with HIV progression: patients with higher levels of conscientiousness show slower progression (Ironson et al., 2008; O'Cleirigh et al., 2007). The effects of stress and negative emotions on various aspects of the immune system and other physiological mechanisms may underlie these associations between psychosocial characteristics and HIV progression (Cole, 2008). Because AIDS is a new disease, most of the current knowledge about treatment and long-term survival is tentative.

THE PSYCHOSOCIAL IMPACT OF AIDS

Every epidemic arouses fear—but when little is known about the disease except that it is so deadly, people tend to react in extreme ways to protect themselves and the people they love. The American news media in the1980s had frequent stories of AIDS patients being fired from their jobs, children with AIDS not being allowed to attend school, families with an AIDS patient being driven from their homes, and health care workers refusing to treat AIDS patients. Although stories like these are less common, HIV/AIDS still arouses fear and discrimination in many people around the world (Herek, 1999; Lee et al., 2005). Many Americans still believe AIDS patients are being punished by God for their misbehavior, and in some developing nations, people with HIV are shunned by neighbors and medical workers, and a woman was beaten to death for revealing her illness.

Because of the fears about AIDS, and because the disease is often associated with homosexuality and drug

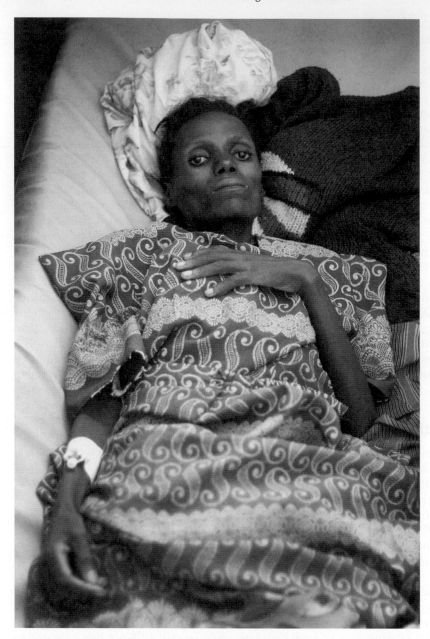

Most AIDS victims in sub-Saharan Africa do not receive effective drug treatment and waste away to skin and bones, as has happened to this woman who then was probably nearing death.

abuse in industrialized countries, AIDS patients and their families—which includes lovers—often feel stigmatized (Flaskerud, 1988; Herek, 1999). One of the first questions they consider is, ''Should I tell anyone—and if so, who?'' Some with HIV infections don't even tell their immediate family (Simoni et al., 1995). They worry that family, friends, neighbors, and coworkers will reject them. This may lead to their being secretive and withdrawn, thereby curbing social support. For some families, the AIDS diagnosis comes at the same time they first learn that the patient—their child or spouse—is gay, or bisexual,

or a drug user. Spouses or lovers fear that the patient has already infected them, too. All these factors fuel the stigma associated with the disease, which has three health effects. First, some societies have resisted acknowledging the disease, thereby allowing it to spread. Second, the stigma leads some people to delay being tested for HIV and getting care and to avoid telling partners if they are infected (Chesney & Smith, 1999). Third, the progression of people's HIV disease appears to slow after they disclose their illness to others (Sherman et al., 2000).

Adapting to HIV and AIDS depends on access to effective treatment. Using antiretroviral agents after many months of less effective care reduces patients' distress, and these reductions seem to result mainly from decreases in physical symptoms and limitations (Rabkin et al., 2000). Many people without access to effective treatment still manage to adapt well to their conditions eventually, but others don't (Rotheram-Borus et al., 1996). Some fear they will be abandoned by those they love and suffer pain, debilitation, and disfigurement (Flaskerud, 1988). And cycles of AIDS-related diseases can arouse feelings of hopelessness and helplessness. Depression may become severe, especially among those patients who try to cope mainly with avoidance strategies, believe their illness is punishment for past wrongdoings, and have been rejected by people they care about (Ciesla & Roberts, 2001; Maj, 1990). Generally, coping through direct action or positive reappraisal is associated with better emotional adjustment, health behavior, and physical health among people with HIV, whereas coping through disengagement or using drugs and alcohol is associated with lower levels of these outcomes (Moskowitz et al., 2009). Depressed HIV patients subsequently show faster disease progression than those who are not depressed (Chida & Vedhara, 2009; Ironson et al., 1994; Patterson et al., 1996). The effects of negative emotion on disease progression may be particularly important for individuals with HIV who don't adhere strictly to their regimens. Increases in spirituality and finding benefits in the difficult circumstances faced by people coping with HIV have also been linked to better adjustment (Ironson & Kremer, 2009; Littlewood et al., 2008).

PSYCHOSOCIAL INTERVENTIONS FOR AIDS

Psychosocial efforts for AIDS need to begin when patients are tested for HIV (Sheridan, 1991). These individuals usually decide to get tested because they believe they could have the virus. They need carefully presented information to help reduce anxiety during the time before getting the results. Those who test HIV-positive will need counseling regarding the illness, treatment, and the many organizations and support groups available today to help AIDS patients and their families cope. Interventions for individuals with access to HAART need to focus on enhancing their emotional adaptation, social support, and knowledge and self-efficacy for treatment adherence (Carrico et al., 2006; Ekstrand & Chesney, 2002; Simoni, Frick, & Huang, 2006).

Many people with HIV and AIDS need psychosocial interventions for other problems, including emotional distress, pain management, and sleep disorders (Sikkema & Kelly, 1996). Research before the advent of antiretroviral drugs focused on reducing anxiety and depression in patients in the absence of effective treatment. For example, Michael Antoni and his colleagues (1990, 1991) recruited gay men who didn't know their HIV status and randomly assigned them to stress management and control groups. The stress management intervention began weeks before HIV testing and consisted of aerobic exercise, relaxation training, and group meetings that included cognitive restructuring methods to modify maladaptive beliefs. For individuals who tested positive, those who received the intervention showed substantially less anxiety and depression and much stronger immune function, and these benefits increased with the amount of relaxation practice they did. Other studies have found that similar interventions also enhance immune function and reduce anxiety and depression for people with advanced HIV or AIDS (Antoni et al., 2000; Lutgendorf et al., 1997; Maj, 1990).

Can psychosocial methods also help individuals who use HAART? Yes. In one approach, patients who received a stress management intervention like the one we just described had markedly lower viral loads in the next months than those in a control group (Antoni, Carrico et al., 2006). In another approach, cognitive-behavioral therapy reduced depression and improved medication adherence (Safren et al., 2009). Although positive effects of various forms of stress management on immune functioning in HIV have been replicated (McCain et al., 2008), the bulk of the available evidence suggests that these interventions improve emotional adjustment and other aspects of quality of life, but have less consistent effects on immune functioning (Brown & Vanable, 2008; Scott-Sheldon et al., 2008).

An emerging area of needed intervention research on people coping with HIV involves smoking. Most people with HIV in the United States smoke cigarettes, which is at least twice the rate as the general population (Nahvi & Cooperman, 2009). Further, among people with HIV, smoking is also associated with greater depression and lower adherence to medical regimens (Webb et al., 2009). Some smoking-related illnesses can be worse in the presence of HIV. The psychosocial interventions that are useful in helping people cope with HIV perhaps could be expanded to address smoking as an additional important health behavior change.

In this chapter, we have examined what it is like to live with and adapt to four very different high-mortality health problems. Whether the patient dies suddenly and unexpectedly or with warning over a long time, there are survivors who must then come to terms with the death and eventually pick up the pieces of their lives.

THE SURVIVORS: AND LIFE GOES ON

Suffering a loss through death is called *bereavement*. Feelings of *grief* and the expression of these feelings in *mourning* characterize this state. People adapt to their bereavement in their own individual ways. This process takes time, usually at least a year, but it does not seem to follow a particular pattern, and there is no rule of thumb that predicts how long it will take (Maciejewski et al., 2007; Silver & Wortman, 1980; Zisook et al., 1995).

PHYSICAL AND PSYCHOSOCIAL IMPACT

Bereavement is, of course, very stressful, and we've seen in earlier chapters that prolonged stress can impair people's health. For example, in the months after a major crisis, such as the death of a loved one, people often have reduced immune function, lower calorie intake and body weight, and higher stress-related hormones in the blood (Willis et al.,1987). Bereavement also predicts an increased risk of death in the months after the loss (Stroebe, Schut, & Stoebe, 2007). Even just the hospitalization of a spouse is linked to increased subsequent mortality rates for the partner (Christakis & Allison, 2006). In the AIDS epidemic, many people have experienced a series of bereavements within a few years—often losing long-term partners and most of their friends—without completing their mourning between deaths. Coping repeatedly with illness and death takes a severe emotional toll, and each death adds to the toll with increased demoralization, sleep problems, and stress (Martin, 1988; Martin & Dean, 1993).

Each grieving person needs to adjust at his or her own pace, and urgings early in the adjustment process to "start living again" may be insensitive and unproductive. A longitudinal study of individuals whose spouses succumbed to serious illnesses revealed that their psychological distress was similar before and soon after the death, remained high for about a year, and was greater for middle-aged than elderly individuals (Hays, Kasl, & Jacobs, 1994). Other findings indicate that adjustment is very difficult when the death is sudden, such as from an accident or violence, and that the amount of stress people with heavy caregiving strain experience after the death stays about the same as it was before (CFAH, 2003). Some survivors try to cope with avoidance strategies, such as by deliberately not thinking or expressing feelings about the deceased person—does

that help? Probably not, but its role appears to differ across cultures. In the United States and the Netherlands, avoidance coping in bereavement impairs adjustment, but in China it has little or no impact (Boelen, van den Bout, & van den Hout, 2006; Bonanno et al., 2005).

People in or after bereavement often cite social support from family and friends as being especially helpful in coping with the loss (Stylianos & Vachon, 1993). But not all grieving people get the support they need, and we'll consider two examples. First, gay individuals who have lost their lovers receive less social support from others, such as bosses and coworkers, than heterosexuals do. For instance, a man who was troubled by his partner's death and performing below par at work reported that his getting little understanding from his boss "makes me feel depressed, angry, and used.... I really loved him and I do miss him" (Moskowitz et al., 1996, p. 49). Most people in the larger society probably do not realize that gay couples' relationships can be strong and loving. Second, elderly people often have less social support than they once had because they live far from or have lost to death their children and closest friends.

Some people think coming to terms with the loss of someone we love means we forget that person—he or she no longer means anything to us. This is not so. People who eventually adapt to the loss may feel recurrent moments or periods of sadness years later, especially on anniversaries or other significant dates (Joyce, 1984). A mother who lost her infant child years ago wrote:

> My mind does not mourn yesterday
>
> It mourns today
>
> The images that pass before my eyes
>
> Do not recall the infant son
>
> But see you running through my house
>
> A teenage child in search of food and gym shoes and maybe me.
>
> I do not mourn you for what you were,
>
> But for what can't be ... (Anonymous, cited in Silver & Wortman, 1980, p. 337)

The death of a child is one of the most tragic events that can happen to a family, and parents often experience grief for many years after the loss (CFAH, 2003). When a parent dies, the children need special attention and understanding: if they are young, they may not understand fully what death is, and older children may be so confused and shocked by the tragedy that they are simply numbed emotionally (Koch, 1977; Sarafino, 1986).

PSYCHOSOCIAL INTERVENTIONS FOR BEREAVEMENT

Some bereaved individuals have a great deal of difficulty adapting to their loss and may suffer from a disorder called *complicated grief*, which resembles posttraumatic stress disorder (Shear et al., 2005). Symptoms of complicated grief include intense yearning for the deceased person and persistent disbelief, bitterness, depression, and intrusive thoughts about the death. Bereaved individuals who still have these symptoms at high levels after 6 months following the loss may benefit from psychosocial evaluation and intervention (Maciejewski et al., 2007), although people with normal grief reactions do not (Stroebe, Schut, & Strobe, 2005).

Several types of psychosocial intervention, such as individual therapy and support groups, can help people who are having difficulty adjusting to loss (CFAH, 2003; Zisook et al., 1995). We'll describe briefly two interventions that have had some success. One intervention used group discussion and role-playing to teach clients how to reduce distress by applying the coping methods, such as problem-focused coping, that we discussed in Chapter 4 (Sikkema et al., 2006). The second intervention used a variety of approaches, including systematic desensitization (see Chapter 4) to confront the death in gradual exercises and discussions of what the clients would like their futures to include, and how to achieve those goals, if their grief was lessened (Shear et al., 2005). Compared to control groups, both of these interventions successfully reduced their clients' grief. A meta-analysis of psychological interventions for bereavement found evidence suggesting that most people adjust well and fairly quickly to bereavement, but interventions provide greater benefits for people suffering from more pronounced distress (Currier, Neimeyer, & Berman, 2008).

REACHING A POSITIVE ADAPTATION

Most bereaved people are resilient and adapt to their loss in time (Bonanno, 2004). In the first weeks after the death of a spouse, the surviving husband or wife usually receives a great deal of attention from friends and relatives. But soon this changes, and the bereaved person must become involved again in work and leisure activities, in maintaining old friendships and developing new ones, and, perhaps, in finding a new mate. One man described his experience as a widower in the following way:

> Having to "date" in the early 40s, or older, and after long years of marriage is, for many, an unnerving experience. I suggest there is something even worse—not getting out and having companionship.
>
> How the widower chooses to begin his new social and sex life depends, of course, on his personality, his philosophy, and the sort of companionship he wants.... I had friends and relatives who put forward suggestions and invited me to dinner parties. I found most of these either tedious or painful. One night ... however I did meet a beautiful woman. She was a widow, with one child.... We are a complete household again and throughout the home there once again is the sound of laughter, of music and, best of all, the rich sound of meaningful conversation between children and their parents. (Lindeman, 1976, pp. 285–286)

Of course, not all stories of people's coping with the loss of someone they love have happy endings. Some bereaved individuals never adjust to the loss. But with the help and support of others and a determined drive on their own part, most people can build a new and once-again enriching life.

SUMMARY

People with a high-mortality illness realize their lives are threatened, and they and their families must adapt to living with uncertainty and watching for symptoms and changes in their conditions. Families can help patients adapt by encouraging them to be active, rather than encouraging helplessness and dependence. In adapting to illness over a long period of time, patients make cognitive adjustments by making positive reappraisals, such as finding meaning in their illness experiences, and gaining a sense of control over their illnesses. A recurrence or relapse of the condition creates a new and difficult crisis.

Three of the leading causes of death worldwide are heart disease, cancer, and stroke. Coronary heart disease may appear as an episode of angina pectoris or a myocardial infarction. The prevalence of heart disease increases with age, and the death rate is greater in men than women. Cardiac rehabilitation involves the use of medication, a program of exercise, stress management, and changes in diet and other aspects of lifestyle, especially if the person smokes, drinks too much, or is overweight. Many heart patients fail to comply with the exercise programs and lifestyle changes. Most cardiac patients who were employed before the illness eventually return to work, often in less demanding jobs. Some people with heart disease need special interventions to enhance adaptation.

A stroke can cause damage to the brain and can occur by cutting off the blood supply or by a hemorrhage. Depending on the amount and location of neurological damage, patients may suffer motor and cognitive deficits, such as in language and perception, and emotional disorders. Some impairments recover with time and rehabilitation, but others are permanent. Stroke patients are very prone to depression.

Although there are many varieties of cancer, most can be classified into five types: carcinomas, melanomas, lymphomas, sarcomas, and leukemias. Untreated neoplasms eventually metastasize and spread to other parts of the body. Medical treatment consists of surgery, radiation, and chemotherapy, each of which has important drawbacks. Chemotherapy, in particular, causes nausea and vomiting that can lead to anticipatory nausea and learned food aversions. Despite the great stress cancer victims experience, most show a remarkable ability to adapt in remission or after a cure. Some, however, become very depressed and withdraw from social contact, but usually benefit from psychosocial interventions. Leukemia is the most common form of cancer in childhood.

Acquired immune deficiency syndrome is caused by HIV infection, which impairs the immune system, leaving the victims subject to opportunistic diseases. Most people with AIDS die within 3 years of that diagnosis if they do not receive effective antiretroviral treatment. Because AIDS is an infectious disease, many people have reacted to its outbreak with alarm and discrimination, making adaptation all the more difficult. Psychosocial intervention can reduce anxiety and depression and enhance immune function. Interventions can also help bereaved survivors who have difficulty adapting to the loss of a loved one.

KEY TERMS

angina pectoris	stroke	acquired immune
myocardial infarction	cancer	deficiency syndrome

14

WHAT'S AHEAD FOR HEALTH PSYCHOLOGY?

PROLOGUE

"Oh, this looks very good," the palm reader said as she studied Marty's hand. She explained: "Your life line is very long, which usually means you will have a long and prosperous life. At first I thought this break here in the line meant you might have a serious health problem in your 50s, but these lines here at your wrist suggest otherwise. You'll have a long and healthy life!" Marty was relieved. He had come to have his fortune told rather than being tested for HIV. He knew that his past behaviour put him at risk for HIV infection, but he couldn't bring himself to reveal this to the palm reader. Unreasoned behaviour is not uncommon when people are very anxious.

Predicting the future is always a chancy enterprise. Still, because the field of health psychology is at an early stage in its development, many people wonder what the field and its goals will be like in the future. This chapter will try to predict what's ahead for health psychology, and our crystal ball will involve the views of noted researchers and trends that seem clear in recent research. As we consider what the crystal ball suggests, we will try to answer questions you may have about the field's prospects. What role will future health psychologists play in medical care? Will career opportunities and training programs for health psychologists flourish? How will the field's goals, issues, and perspectives change? What factors will affect the success and direction of health psychology in the coming years?

GOALS FOR HEALTH PSYCHOLOGY

Health and health care systems around the world have changed dramatically over the last several decades. People in most parts of the world today are living longer and are more likely to develop chronic illnesses than ever before. Many current health problems result from or are aggravated by people's long-standing habits, such as smoking cigarettes and coping poorly with stress, that medical professionals lack sufficient skills and time to change. The field of health psychology has made enormous advances, generating new knowledge and applying information gained from many disciplines to supplement medical efforts in promoting health. Let's look at some major goals that lie ahead for health psychology.

ENHANCING ILLNESS PREVENTION AND TREATMENT

A major issue driving the need for illness prevention around the world is the escalating costs of health care and the need to contain them. The burden of health costs to different nations can be seen in Figure 14-1, which presents health spending as a percent of the gross domestic product for selected countries. As you can see, this burden has risen sharply in the United States since 1980, where health spending is higher and rising faster than in other industrialized nations. We have seen that efforts to prevent health problems should try to reduce unhealthful behaviors. These efforts can be directed toward health-protective activity while the person is well, when symptoms appear, or once an illness is identified and treatment starts.

Health-related behaviors that become features of people's lifestyles have received a great deal of attention in health psychology. Efforts have been directed toward preventing unhealthful behaviors from developing and changing behaviors that already exist. Unhealthful lifestyles seem to be harder to change than to prevent (Wright & Friedman, 1991). We have seen that psychologists' efforts to change lifestyle behaviors, such as smoking, exercising, and eating habits, have focused mainly on cognitive and behavioral approaches. Although these approaches are often very effective in producing initial changes, the behaviors frequently revert back to unhealthful patterns later. Relapse is a critical problem that researchers are working to reduce, and it will certainly be an important focus for health psychology in the future.

Once people notice symptoms or are diagnosed with serious health conditions, they often—but by no means always—engage in symptom-based and sick-role behaviors to protect their health. For instance, they may

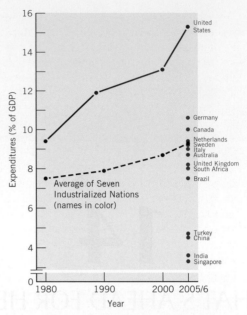

Figure 14-1 Total health expenditures as a percent of the gross domestic product for the specified years. The isolated data points (color) for 2005/6 reflect the most recent available data on expenditures for 13 non-U.S. selected nations. The two line graphs present expenditures for 1980, 1990, 2000, and 2005/6 for the United States (solid line) and the average (dashed line) of the seven industrialized countries of the 13 selected nations. This figure depicts the relative current expenditures across 14 nations and a comparison of the increases in expenditures for the United States and other industrialized countries. (Data for 1980–2000 from NCHS, 2006, Table 119; data for 2005/6 from WHO, 2009, Table 7.)

go to doctors, take medication, or even follow medical advice that involves changing their lifestyles. Researchers have identified many psychosocial factors that influence whether people will seek health care and adhere to medical regimens. We know, for example, that individuals often decide to reject or delay seeking medical attention because they don't know the symptoms of serious diseases, such as cancer or diabetes. And people are less likely to adhere to medical advice if the regimens involve complex or long-term behavioral changes and if their doctors do not seem caring or explain the illnesses and treatment clearly. Although we know some methods to reduce these problems, these methods often require extra time or effort that medical professionals are just beginning to incorporate into their practices.

Advances in Research and Theory

Health psychologists in the future will continue their search for ways to improve people's health behaviors before illness develops, use of health care services, and disease management after illness develops. New research methods and theories we've discussed in this book will promote these efforts. For example, the method called *ecological momentary assessment* has enabled researchers to examine people's behavior and feelings in daily life. And theories have appeared that attempt to explain why people do or do not change unhealthful behaviors, building on knowledge gained from earlier theories, especially the health belief model. The *stages of change model*, which outlines a series of stages in people's readiness to change health-related behaviors, is an example. This and other theories have generated important research that will contribute to our understanding of ways to promote healthier lifestyles. Research and theory of the future need to expand their focus in at least two ways (Smith, Orleans, & Jenkins, 2004). First, they need to incorporate more levels of factors to represent the biological, psychological, and social systems that work together in affecting health. Second, they need to give more attention to life-span changes in the nature of health threats.

Advances in Technology

Technological advances will play an increasing role in preventing and managing illness (Saab et al., 2004). For example, Internet sites have been developed to provide medical information and two-way video and audio communication to individuals in numerous countries and inaccessible areas. This process, called *telehealth* or *telemedicine*, provides diagnostic and treatment services and advice on lifestyle changes (Celler, Lovell, & Basilakis, 2003). For instance, a parent can use a device to scan a child's injured leg and send the image electronically to the hospital where the child had been treated so they can monitor recovery. Because Internet sites for health information vary in quality, they need to be selected carefully (Kalichman et al., 2006). As we saw in Chapter 5, the Internet can also provide software versions of effective psychosocial interventions to improve health.

IMPROVING EFFORTS FOR HELPING PATIENTS COPE

Major advances have been made in using psychosocial methods to help people cope with various difficulties in their lives. Stress management programs are being applied widely with nonpatient populations, such as in worksite wellness programs, to help prevent illness.

People with serious medical conditions often must cope with pain, anxiety and fear, and depression. Psychosocial interventions are being applied more and more widely with patients in pain clinics, hospitals, and other medical settings. Years ago, the main function of psychologists in medical settings involved administering and interpreting tests of patients' emotional and cognitive functioning (Wright & Friedman, 1991). But this situation has changed, and psychologists are focusing much more on a broader array of activities, such as training medical students and interns and applying interventions to help patients cope with illnesses and medical treatment. Health psychologists' role is likely to continue to expand in hospitals and outpatient rehabilitation programs for people with chronic health problems, such as heart disease and arthritis (Nicassio, Meyerowitz, & Kerns, 2004).

IDENTIFYING EVIDENCE-BASED INTERVENTIONS AND COST–BENEFIT RATIOS

Should health care organizations and employers provide psychosocial interventions to prevent illness and help patients cope? Perhaps most people would answer, "Yes, because it's the humane thing to do." But with today's spiraling medical costs, the answer is more commonly based on two factors: the intervention's *efficacy*, or degree to which it has the needed effect, and **cost–benefit ratio**, or the extent to which it saves more money in the long run than it costs (Graham et al., 1998; Kaplan & Groessl, 2002). Bottom-line issues are often weighed heavily in deciding whether to offer wellness or psychosocial programs at work and in medical settings.

Health care professionals recognize the importance of documenting the efficacy of approaches they use, and they do careful research to compare different approaches against each other and control groups. This research is now being used by professionals in medicine and health psychology to identify **evidence-based treatments**—techniques or interventions with strong efficacy that have clear support across many high-quality studies, particularly randomized controlled trials (Glasgow et al., 2006; Kazdin, 2008). Ideally, the research would have:

- Been carefully evaluated in a meta-analysis or systematic review.
- Assessed the treatment effect's *clinical significance*, or meaningfulness for the person's life and functioning (Sarafino, 2001). The effect is meaningful if the person's health or behavior has improved greatly or is now at or near the normal or desired level. For example, a treatment that reduces pain intensity by one-third would be meaningful from the patient's point of view (Jensen, Chen, & Brugger, 2003).
- Conducted follow-up assessments to determine whether the effect is durable.

After evidence-based treatments have been identified for specific conditions or behaviors, professionals need to be apprised of that status and encouraged to adopt and implement those treatments (McHugh & Barlow, 2010). Major efforts are currently underway to accomplish these goals.

Psychologists seldom calculate the financial costs and benefits of interventions. Often the costs of providing an intervention are easily assessed, but the full benefits are not. At a worksite, for instance, what benefits of a wellness program could you assess in monetary value to compare with the costs of running it? You might assess worker absenteeism or medical insurance claims, but these variables would reflect only part of the benefits; they wouldn't reflect other important financial gains, such as increases in workers' job satisfaction and resulting productivity. In medical settings, measuring the benefits of interventions can be easier—for example, you could assign monetary values to the reduced time intervention patients spend recovering in the hospital and compare these data against the cost of the program.

Many psychosocial interventions for promoting health and helping patients cope have the potential for producing far more financial benefits than costs. More and more evidence is becoming available to document these effects (Aldana, 2001; Kaplan & Groessl, 2002). We considered research in Chapter 9 showing, for example, that hospital patients who receive help in coping with medical procedures recover more quickly and use less medication than those who don't receive such help. Table 14.1 lists some specific behavioral or and health problems with studies showing that psychosocial–educational interventions produced financial savings that were far greater than their costs. Other research has shown that the benefits of worksite wellness programs outweigh their costs (Golaszewski, 2001; Matson-Koffman et al., 2005). Although most psychosocial methods with documented efficacy have not yet been subjected to cost–benefit analyses, health psychologists in the future will probably give much more attention to these analyses than they have in the past. They will also need to develop more effective methods to help people change unhealthful lifestyles—such as for eating healthful diets and exercising—and demonstrate that the benefits of these methods outweigh the costs.

ENHANCING PSYCHOLOGISTS' ACCEPTANCE IN MEDICAL SETTINGS

A woman wrote an article in the late 1980s and described her experience when she developed breast cancer. Her doctors advised her to get treatment from a variety of medical professionals but

> at no point did anyone in the medical fraternity recommend that I see a mental health professional to help me cope with the emotional impact of breast cancer. Perhaps they didn't realize that breast cancer had an emotional impact. But I did. So, I went to see a psychologist, ironically the one specialist not covered by my insurance. It was worth the cash out of pocket. (Kaufman, cited in Cummings, 1991, p. 119)

Although gaining acceptance by the medical profession has progressed steadily since the 1980s, it continues to be a challenge for health psychology (Belar & McIntyre, 2004).

Part of the difficulty health psychologists have faced in gaining acceptance in medical settings stems from their past role and training. Before 1970, psychological services were usually seen as tangential to the medical needs of most patients, and psychologists had little or no training in physiological systems, medical illnesses and treatments, and the organization and protocols of

Table 14.1 *Psychosocial–Educational Interventions with Very Favorable Cost–Benefit Ratios for Reducing Specific Behavioral and Health Problems*

Problem	Population	Studies
Behavior		
Drinking	Men and women, general	Cobiac et al., 2009; Fleming et al., 2000
Drug abuse	Clients in residential treatment	French, Salome, & Carney, 2002
HIV transmission	HIV-positive youth	Lee, Leibowitz, & Rotheram-Borus, 2005
Smoking	Men and women, general	Alterman, Gariti, & Mulvaney, 2001; Curry et al., 1998
Smoking	Pregnant women	Windsor et al., 1993
Health		
Arthritis	Elderly men and women patients	Cronan, Groessl, & Kaplan, 1997
Asthma	Children and adult patients	Liljas & Lahdensuo, 1997
Back pain	Employee patients	Jensen et al., 2005; Turk, 2002
Heart disease	Men patients	Blumenthal, Babyak et al., 2002; Davidson et al., 2007

hospitals. But these conditions have changed. Today, health psychologists are receiving the training they need to work effectively in medical settings. And more and more doctors are coming to recognize the importance of psychosocial factors in their patients' health, adherence to treatment regimens, and rehabilitation. They also realize that they do not have the skills or time to address many of these factors.

Initial relations between medical staff and health psychologists still tend to be strained in some settings, particularly when one function of the psychologist may be to teach doctors and interns the "people skills" that are important for interviewing patients and communicating with them effectively. This kind of training may get a mixed reception, especially from some medical staff who feel that these skills are not part of medicine (Christensen & Levinson, 1991). Even after medical and psychological staff have collaborated for a long time and seen that a biopsychosocial approach to health care can benefit patients, be intellectually stimulating, and lead to developing new techniques, their different styles and points of view can lead to conflicts (McDaniel & Campbell, 1986). For example, psychologists generally want to talk directly with the attending doctor to describe subtle and complex issues relating to a patient's treatment plan, but medical specialists typically communicate with each other in writing, such as with notes in a hospital chart. Differences like these can be resolved. Medical education guidelines now promote the training of doctors to include skills in teamwork and partnering with professionals in nonmedical fields (Belar & McIntyre, 2004; Daw, 2001).

What about patients—how do they feel about receiving psychological services? Their view is likely to depend on the way the doctor and psychologist introduce these services. If a patient thinks the services are offered because his or her doctor thinks he or she is "crazy" or that the problem "is all in your head," the patient is likely to have negative attitudes and fail to cooperate. People are more likely to view psychosocial interventions positively if the services are introduced as part of a standard "team approach" with a biopsychosocial orientation. (Go to 🔲.)

CAREERS AND TRAINING IN HEALTH PSYCHOLOGY

Most health psychologists follow one of two career categories: working mainly in clinical capacities with patients or working mainly in academic or research capacities (Belar & McIntyre, 2004; Sweet, Rozensky, & Tovian, 1991). Many health psychologists have careers that combine these areas, being involved in both clinical and academic or research activities, and some do administrative work, such as in governmental agencies or programs to promote health.

CAREER OPPORTUNITIES

The opportunities for careers in health psychology in the United States have been good, especially in health care settings. In the early years, the number of psychologists working in health care more than doubled from about 20,000 in 1974 to over 45,000 in 1985 (Enright et al., 1990). Career opportunities have continued to grow since then. States have passed laws enabling psychologists to obtain full staff status in hospitals, giving them the same privileges as doctors. The current outlook for the next decade is for strong job growth for psychologists, particularly those with a doctoral degree in fields related to health (USDL, 2010).

Besides hospitals, where else do health psychologists work? Some of the more prominent sites are:

- Colleges and universities
- Medical schools
- Health maintenance organizations
- Rehabilitation centers
- Pain clinics
- Private practice and consultancy offices

CLINICAL METHODS AND ISSUES

Psychologists in the Primary Care Team

In the late 1990s, some American managed-care programs, such as HMOs, began to include psychologists as members of the medical care team (D. Bruns, personal communication, September 1, 1998). Why? Program administrators came to realize that psychological factors, such as stress and emotional problems, play a pivotal role in the symptoms most patients present in their health care visits. Primary care psychologists evaluate these patients' needs and provide help, such as with brief counseling or training to improve adherence to treatment recommendations or manage stress or pain (McDaniel & Fogarty, 2009).

Sometimes job descriptions for these settings are broad, making eligible professionals from nonpsychology fields, such as nursing, public health, or social work. Although this can increase the competition for those jobs, broad job descriptions can increase the number of opportunities for psychologists, too.

TRAINING PROGRAMS

What kind of training is available and necessary in health psychology? Training is offered at three educational levels: *undergraduate* courses in health psychology or behavioral medicine, *graduate* programs, and *postdoctoral* programs. Because health psychologists typically hold doctoral degrees, dozens of graduate programs now exist in the United States and other countries specifically for that training. Postdoctoral programs are available in health psychology or behavioral medicine, particularly for people with doctoral degrees that did not focus on the relationship between health and psychology.

Graduate training programs in health psychology are diverse (Belar & McIntyre, 2004; HP, 2010). Some are highly interdisciplinary programs that are designed solely for this field. They often specialize in training students either for research careers or for direct clinical service to patients. Other programs provide graduate training in traditional psychology areas, such as clinical or social psychology, and contain special tracks or emphases relating to health. Common to all these programs is a solid grounding in psychology, along with training in research methods, biopsychosocial processes in health and disease, and health care terminology and organization. Programs that educate students for direct clinical service to patients generally include medical courses, such as in physiology and pharmacology. The future may see greater standardization of health psychology training programs in the United States and around the world, based on the identification of specific core competencies that clinical health psychologists should have when they enter the profession (France et al., 2008).

Information about graduate and postdoctoral training programs in health psychology can be obtained by contacting the following professional organizations:

- American Psychological Association, Division of Health Psychology, 750 First Street N.E., Washington, DC 20002-4242
  Web Page: http://www.health-psych.org (the Education and Training page has a Find Training Programs database)
- Society of Behavioral Medicine, 555 East Wells Street, Suite 1100, Milwaukee, WI 53202-3823
  Web Page: http://www.sbm.org

The European Health Psychology Society (http://www.ehps.net) is a professional group for researchers and practitioners; the delegates they list may be able to suggest training programs in their specific countries.

ISSUES AND CONTROVERSIES FOR THE FUTURE

Findings from research and clinical experience will enable health psychologists to help societies resolve important issues and controversies in the future. We will look at several examples, beginning with the impact of environmental conditions on health and psychology.

ENVIRONMENT, HEALTH, AND PSYCHOLOGY

Each of the environments in which people live around the world contains conditions that have the potential to harm or benefit the health and psychological status of its inhabitants. For example, some communities contain barriers to physical activity; they can encourage activity by changing land-use and residential density policies (Sallis et al., 2006; Salmon et al., 2003). We also read and hear in the news media that the environment is becoming increasingly polluted with toxic substances, released accidentally or deliberately into the air, ground, or bodies of water. The environments in which people live are also becoming more crowded and noisy. What effects do these conditions have? How can we reduce harmful environmental conditions? Some answers use a public health approach: because cigarette smoke pollutes the air and can lead to illnesses in those who breathe it, some psychologists have called for governmental control of tobacco products (Cummings, Fong, & Borland, 2009; Kaplan et al., 1995).

Many toxic environmental pollutants are produced as byproducts either of manufacturing or of generating energy. For instance, some manufacturing industries produce highly toxic cyanide or mercury as byproducts, which have made their ways into the environment. What direct effects on health does long-term exposure to low levels of pollutants have? How stressful is it to live or work in contaminated environments, and how much does this stress affect health? How much does the stress of crowding and noise affect health? Health psychologists can help in efforts to answer these questions and find ways to change behaviors that produce these problems (Weinman, 1990). Although we have some information on these questions, much more research will be needed in the future before we can provide accurate answers.

QUALITY OF LIFE

People's *quality of life* has become a significant issue in medical care because (1) it is reduced by becoming sick and by staying sick, and (2) it is an important consideration in prevention efforts before and after an illness occurs. Efforts to maintain people's good health also maintain their quality of life, and efforts to help patients recover quickly and fully lessen the negative impact of the illness on their lives. For people who are ill, their quality of life enters into decisions about the medical and psychological treatment they will receive. Are they in pain? If so, what type of painkilling medication should they get, and how much? If they're distressed, what psychosocial methods are likely to improve their emotional status?

Life-or-death medical decisions are often heavily influenced by appraisals of patients' current and future quality of life. Current quality of life is especially important if there is virtually no hope of the patient's recovery. In such cases, the views of the patient, family, and medical staff are likely to come down to a judgment of whether living in the current state is better than not living at all. Future quality of life is important in medical decisions that can enable the patient to survive, but will leave him or her with seriously impaired physical, psychological, and social capacities. For example, the family of an elderly man with a disabling cardiovascular condition felt he would be better off not living

> if he was just going to be a vegetable. They said his whole life revolved around working in his yard and playing bridge; these were the things in life that gave him joy. Now the doctors were not giving any hope that he would ever get back to what he was before; the best that could be hoped for was that he would be able to sit in a wheelchair. They said they didn't want that for him, and … he wouldn't want that for himself either. (Degner & Beaton, 1987, p. 64)

Decisions to withhold heroic medical efforts clearly involve humane concerns, but financial considerations are important, too (Spurgeon et al., 1990). Heroic medical efforts and aftercare are extremely expensive. With the enormous pressures to contain the cost of health care, are these expenses always justified even when the resulting quality of life will be poor?

Making medical and psychological decisions based on a patient's current or future quality of life is difficult, partly because researchers need to determine the best ways to measure it. One approach that some people favor to help make these decisions uses a scale called *quality-adjusted life years* (QALYs, pronounced "KWAL-eez"). To calculate the QALYs for a medical treatment, we would assess how long a person is likely to live after receiving the treatment, multiply each year by its quality of life, and total these data (Bradley, 1993; Kaplan, 2004). Using QALYs, we could rank the value of different treatments for a particular person or in general, perhaps even taking the cost per QALY into account, and decide whether to provide the treatment. At the heart of this approach is the measurement of quality of life. Although there are dozens of questionnaires to assess quality of life, the qualities they measure vary widely (Gill & Feinstein, 1994; Kaplan, 2004). Which should we use? Health psychologists will play an important role in resolving how best to use quality of life assessments in making treatment decisions.

ETHICAL DECISIONS IN MEDICAL CARE

Suppose you were an obstetrician delivering a baby when you realized that complications you see developing will surely kill the baby and, maybe, the mother, too. Suppose also that the mother flatly refuses a Caesarean delivery for religious reasons. What do you do? One medical response might be to seek an immediate court order to override her decision. The decisions made in this case and the quality of life decisions we just considered all involve ethical issues. Many hospitals today have *bioethics committees* to discuss ethical issues in health care, make policy, and recommend action regarding specific cases. The ethical issues these committees consider often involve the patient's right to choose treatments, to withhold or withdraw treatment, or to die (Bouton, 1990). We will examine two other important issues: the role of technology in medical decisions and the role of doctors in helping patients die.

Technology and Medical Decisions

The technological advances we have seen in our lives over the past few decades have been quite remarkable. Many of these advances have been in medical technology, and they have sometimes raised important ethical questions.

One of these technological advances is a computer program that calculates the odds that individual patients will die in intensive care or after they leave it (Seligmann & Sulavik, 1992). Why might this be a problem? Decisions about whether intensive care treatment will help the patient survive are made every day, based on doctors' broad estimates, such as, "Her chances look bleak." With the computer program, doctors can get precise estimates of the person's odds of dying if he or she continues in intensive care, say 42%, versus if he or she is transferred, say 78%. In this example, transferring the patient would greatly increase the odds that he or she would die. The comparison helps in making the decision. The ethical problems relate to how these numbers will be used. Should doctors tell families these numbers? Will doctors and families weigh these data too heavily in their decisions? Will hospitals release these data to insurance companies, which could then decide to limit coverage when scores drop below some level? Health psychologists can play a role in some of these decisions, especially those relating to families having and using these data (Weinman, 1990).

Other ethical dilemmas arise in deciding whether to provide an organ transplant for patients. Nearly 28,000 transplants are done each year in the United States (USBC, 2010). Health psychologists help medical practitioners to select candidates who are best able to benefit from the surgery and the scarce organs because these people are able to cope with the stress and behave appropriately to maintain their health with the new organ. To help make these decisions, psychologists screen potential candidates—some patients will be clearly up to the task, and some will not, such as candidates for liver transplant who have not been able to control their drinking. Others will be in between and may benefit from interventions of behavioral contracting and therapy to help them cope better (Dew et al., 2004; Olbrisch et al., 2002).

Advances in genetics technology may also present ethical problems. For instance, geneticists can identify individuals who are likely to develop serious diseases, such as cystic fibrosis and some forms of cancer, and may soon be able to identify individuals who are vulnerable to environmental causes of cancer and heart disease (Detjen, 1991; Lerman, Audrain, & Croyle, 1994). Who should be tested for these risks, and who should have access to the results? Insurance companies would like this information, and some are already turning down applicants for insurance on the basis of known family histories of certain diseases.

Assisted Dying: Suicide and Euthanasia

Some people with serious illnesses come to the decision that they want to end their lives. Should doctors help them in their wishes? This is a very controversial issue for society in general and in the medical community (Miccinesi et al., 2005). Among doctors, some feel they should not help because of certain beliefs they hold, such as that life is sacred or that medical workers should only save lives and not take them. Other doctors feel they should participate in this act if the patient is actually beyond all help and the decision was not made because

of psychological depression that could be reduced (Sears & Stanton, 2001). Most terminally ill people who are interested in ending their lives are mainly worried about future pain and loss of autonomy and function (Ganzini, Goy, & Dobscha, 2009). Others who want to end their lives are depressed and may change their minds if the depression is relieved (Ransom et al., 2006; Zisook et al., 1995).

Some doctors have helped patients end their lives in two ways (Rosenfeld, 2004; Sears & Stanton, 2001). In *assisted suicide* the patient takes the final act, but the doctor knowingly prescribes the needed drugs or describes the methods and doses required. Because of the legal consequences for doctors who help people take their lives, a book called *Final Exit* was published in 1991 describing procedures doctors would recommend. In *euthanasia* the doctor (or someone else) takes the final act, usually by administering a drug that ends the life. Laws permit euthanasia in the Netherlands, Luxembourg and Albania. Physician-assisted suicide can be administered in Switzerland, Belgium, and the states of Oregon, Washington, and Montana under carefully specified and monitored circumstances. When societies decide that it is acceptable for doctors to help a patient end his or her life, laws can require psychological assessment of the person's emotional status, ability to make sound decisions, and likelihood of benefiting from psychosocial intervention (Sears & Stanton, 2001). (Go to 🍎.)

FUTURE FOCUSES IN HEALTH PSYCHOLOGY

The research that contributes to our knowledge in health psychology comes from many different fields. But early studies gave a relatively narrow view of the biopsychosocial processes involved in health and illness because of the people researchers tended to recruit as subjects: in studies of Type A behavior, for example, they often were 18- to 60-year-old White American males. Two reasons for this focus are that these people were readily available and some researchers incorrectly believed that the findings would easily generalize to other populations. In the 1980s, studies began to focus on including subjects representing a wider range of people. This trend will surely continue in the future.

LIFE-SPAN HEALTH AND ILLNESS

We've seen that the health problems people have and the extent to which they use health services change with age. Very young and elderly individuals use health

ASSESS YOURSELF

Some Ethical Dilemmas: What Do You Think?

Each of the following cases describes a decision involving an ethical dilemma that is related to health. Circle the Y for "yes" or the N for "no" preceding each case to indicate whether you agree with the decision.

Y N   A 47-year-old woman developed cirrhosis of the liver as a result of long-term alcoholism. She promised to stop drinking if she could receive a liver transplant. Her request was denied because of likely future drinking.

Y N   An overweight, chain-smoking, sedentary 51-year-old man with high blood pressure had his first heart attack 7 years ago. His request for a heart transplant was denied because of continuing risk factors.

Y N   A 28-year-old married woman with a hereditary crippling disease that is eventually fatal decided to become pregnant, knowing that there was a 50% chance that she would pass on the disease to her baby and she would not consider having an abortion.

Y N   A 37-year-old executive was told by his boss that he would have to pay half of the costs of his employer-provided health insurance

if he did not quit smoking and lower his cholesterol.

Y N   An obese 20-year-old woman who refused to try to lose weight was expelled from nursing school, despite having good grades and clinical evaluations, because it was said she would "set a poor example for patients."

Y N   State workers are assessed an extra health insurance fee each month if they smoke cigarettes or are overweight because people with these statuses generate far higher medical expenses than other employees do.

Y N   A 30-year-old woman was denied a promotion to a job that involved working in an area with gases that could harm an embryo if she were to become pregnant.

Y N   A year after a boy developed leukemia, the company that provided his family's health insurance quadrupled their premium.

These dilemmas are all based on real examples from the news media. Because they all involve controversies, there is no key to the "right" answers. But you might want to ask friends or classmates what they think.

services more than others do. Populations are aging rapidly around the world, which will lead to health care challenges in the future.

From Conception to Adolescence

Children's prenatal environments have a major effect on their health. Enormous numbers of babies are born each year with illnesses or defects that develop because of prenatal exposure to harmful conditions or chemicals, particularly when mothers use alcohol, drugs, or tobacco during pregnancy. The health problems these babies develop can last for years or for life. Health psychologists study ways to improve babies' prenatal environments, such as by educating and counseling prospective parents (Weinman, 1990). Although these approaches help, we need to find more effective ways to prevent these health problems from developing.

Childhood and adolescence are important periods in the life span because many health beliefs and habits form during these years (Smith, Orleans, & Jenkins, 2004). But very little research has examined how these beliefs

and habits develop. We do know that efforts to promote health should be introduced early, before unhealthful beliefs and habits develop. Early childhood is clearly the time to intervene for some behaviors, such as for proper diets, exercise, dental care, and seat belt use. In later childhood, interventions should focus on preventing accidents, cigarette and drug use, and unsafe sex. We saw in Chapter 6, for example, that programs to prevent children from starting to smoke cigarettes have had some success. We have also seen that behaviors that put people at high risk for AIDS can be changed substantially, thereby reducing their risk. Efforts to prevent the spread of HIV need to be intensified and applied worldwide. To design more effective health promotion programs, we will need to focus more research—especially longitudinal studies—on how health behaviors form and change in childhood and adolescence.

Adulthood and Old Age

By the time people reach adulthood, most health-related values and behaviors are ingrained and difficult to change. People's lifestyles during the early adulthood and middle-age years tend to continue and affect whether or when they will develop major chronic illnesses, particularly heart disease and cancer. The earlier people change unhealthful behaviors, the lower their health risks are likely to be. In addition, prolonged emotional difficulties, particularly depression, are linked to future illness, such as heart disease. Among elderly people equated for initial physical health, those who are depressed show sharper physical declines, such as in walking speed, over the next few years than nondepressed elders do (Penninx et al., 1998).

As the world population ages, the proportion of individuals with disabling or life-threatening illnesses will surely grow, requiring more health services and psychosocial interventions. This will be compounded if life expectancy increases (Sierra et al., 2009). In the United States, an unusually high birth rate after World War II created a very large generation of people called "baby boomers," who are starting to swell the ranks of the elderly. Figure 14-2 shows the aging trend in America: the elderly are becoming an increasingly large portion of population. This trend means that health care costs will increase sharply in the future. How will health care systems around the world respond to the added loads? This potential makes it even more crucial that we find ways to prevent or change risky lifestyles, particularly with regard to diet, exercise, and substance use. We will also need to improve ways to help families cope with the difficulties of caring for elderly relatives. The number of studies dealing with health issues in old age published each year has increased since 1980 and will continue to be a major focus of health psychologists in the future.

SOCIOCULTURAL FACTORS IN HEALTH

Sociocultural differences around the world are related to health and health behavior. For instance, people from the lower social classes and from minority groups tend to have poorer health and health habits than Whites and those from higher classes. These differences have been clear for a long time. Although researchers have begun to investigate why these differences exist and what can be done to reduce them, our knowledge on these issues is not very specific. For example, we don't know how cultural customs and socioeconomic factors shape the everyday lives of different ethnic groups (Anderson & Armstead, 1995; Yali & Revenson, 2004). And so we tend to make broad conclusions, as when we say people in a minority group "live in environments that do not encourage the practice of health-protective behavior." Health psychology must give greater emphasis

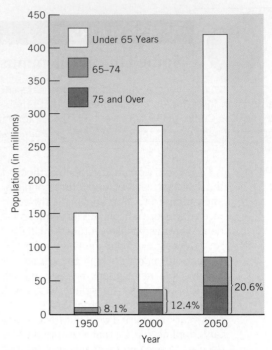

Figure 14-2   United States population at 1950, 2000, and 2050 (projection), with portions consisting of elderly age groups designated and percent of people 65 and older specified. (Data from NCHS, 2009a, p. 111.)

to sociocultural issues so that we can provide specific and useful solutions in the future.

Cross-cultural research also needs more emphasis. We have spotty information about cultural differences in lifestyles, perceiving symptoms of illness, and using health services, and most research on these differences is old and very incomplete. Although some books and journal articles address ethnic differences within countries, especially the United States, few examine differences across countries (Kazarian & Evans, 2001). In the poorer nations of the world, such as in African and Eastern Mediterranean regions where infectious diseases and malnutrition are often rampant, it is not unusual for 10–15% of children under the age of five to die each year (WHO, 2009). The number of people infected with HIV in Africa and other developing areas of the world is astounding and growing rapidly. The countries with the most urgent need to change behavioral risk factors have not yet recognized that principles of health psychology can help promote public health. In addition, health psychologists need to conduct research to determine how to adapt the principles that work in the United States and other industrialized countries to the needs of other cultures.

GENDER DIFFERENCES AND WOMEN'S HEALTH ISSUES

Health issues relating to women and gender differences were also neglected in health psychology research until the 1980s. Since that time, studies have examined women's health behaviors, such as diet, smoking, and exercise; cardiovascular and pain disorders; and issues that are specific to women, such as screening for cervical and breast cancer (Revenson & Jeltova, 2004; Rimer, McBride, & Crump, 2001). Research has also studied differences between males and females in a wide variety of characteristics, such as reactions to stress, Type A and B behavior patterns, risk of AIDS and of heart disease, weight regulation, and tobacco and alcohol use. Gender-related research has become a main focus of health psychology today and for the future. This research is making clearer the uniqueness of women and men in their health and health-protective behaviors and the special interventions they are likely to need to promote their health.

FACTORS AFFECTING HEALTH PSYCHOLOGY'S FUTURE

The picture of health psychology's future that we have considered is based on trends and needs that can change in the future. The prospects for our discipline will depend on forces and events in society, medical fields, and psychology. What factors are likely to affect the role and direction of health psychology in the future?

Some factors can have a broad impact on health psychology, affecting the amount and type of research, clinical intervention, and health promotion activities that we do. One of these factors is monetary (Tovian, 2004): how much financial support will there be for these activities? During hard economic times, cutbacks in governmental and private funding may reduce this support. But there is another side to this coin—health care costs around the world are increasing, and many health experts believe that two of the best ways to decrease these costs involve improving people's health behaviors and helping those individuals who become ill to recover quickly. We've seen that health psychologists can help reduce costs in both of these ways. Funding will also depend on how health insurance and services are structured. Health care systems are changing rapidly in many countries. The changes that emerge will probably continue or strengthen support for psychosocial interventions with favorable research evidence regarding their cost–benefit ratios.

Another factor that can have a broad impact on health psychology's future is education and training in this discipline (Weinman, 1990). Undergraduate courses in health psychology can reach students from various nonpsychology fields, such as nursing, premed, and sociology. Students who have a positive view of the role and success of health psychology are likely to promote its research, application, and interdisciplinary contacts in the future. If these students go into medical fields, they are likely to be receptive to learning about psychosocial methods by which they and health psychologists can promote the health of their patients. These circumstances can enhance acceptance of health psychologists in medical settings.

Developments in medicine will also influence the future of health psychology (Weinman, 1990). New and growing health problems generally require psychosocial interventions to reduce people's risk factors for these illnesses and help patients and their families cope. This can be seen clearly in the role of health psychology in addressing these kinds of issues in AIDS and Alzheimer's disease, for instance. Health psychologists often have an important role to play when new medical treatments are found, particularly if these treatments are unpleasant or if they may impair the patient's quality of life.

As you can see, many factors can affect the future of health psychology. The field has made dramatic and rapid advances in its short history, but we still have much to learn. Although we sometimes head in the wrong direction, we can take heart and humor from the following perspective:

> Life is a test,
> It is only a test.
> If this were your actual life,
> You would have been given better instructions!
> (Anonymous, cited in Pattishall, 1989, p. 47)

SUMMARY

Major changes have occurred in health and health care systems around the world in the past several decades. People are living longer today and are more likely to develop chronic illnesses that result from or are aggravated by their longstanding health habits. Health psychology has made major advances in helping to prevent or change these behaviors. The field has also developed effective psychosocial methods to help patients and their families cope with chronic illnesses, and some of these methods have been identified as evidence-based treatments. For many interventions health psychologists use, research has also demonstrated favorable cost–benefit ratios. These successes have helped to promote the acceptance of health psychologists in medical settings.

Career opportunities for health psychologists have expanded rapidly, and the employment outlook for the future continues to look good. The availability of training in health psychology has grown at the undergraduate, graduate, and postgraduate levels. This training is solidly based in psychology and includes a substantial amount of information on biopsychosocial processes in health and illness and on medical terminology and procedures.

Health psychology has begun to address important health issues and controversies that societies will need to resolve in the future. These issues and controversies include the impact of environmental factors on people's health and psychological status, patients' quality of life, and ethical decisions in medical care. Some ethical questions relate to the use of technological advances in health care and whether doctors should participate in helping hopelessly ill patients end their lives. Health psychology has also begun to focus its attention on life-span, sociocultural, and gender issues in health. Forces and events in society, medicine, and psychology will affect the future role and direction of health psychology.

KEY TERMS

cost–benefit ratio   evidence-based treatments

Appendix

THE BODY'S PHYSICAL SYSTEMS

PROLOGUE

When Tom was born 20 years ago, his parents were thrilled. Here was their first child—a delightful baby with such promise for the future. He looked healthy, and his parents were pleased that he was consuming large amounts of milk, often without becoming satiated. They took this as a good sign. But, in this case, it wasn't.

As the weeks went by, Tom's parents noticed that he wasn't gaining as much weight as he should, especially since he was still consuming lots of milk. He started to cough and wheeze often and developed one respiratory infection after another. They became concerned, and so did his pediatrician. After a series of tests, the devastating diagnosis was clear: Tom had *cystic fibrosis*, a chronic, progressive, and eventually fatal disease. Cystic fibrosis is an inherited disease of the respiratory system for which there is no cure and no effective treatment.

Tom has had a difficult life, and so has his family. The respiratory infections he had in infancy were just the beginning. His disease causes thick, sticky secretions that constantly block airways, trap air in the lungs, and help bacteria to thrive. Other body systems also become affected, causing additional problems, such as insufficient absorption of food and vitamins. As a result, he was sick often and remained short, underweight, and weak compared with other children. His social relationships have always been limited and strained, and the burden of his illness has taken its toll on his parents.

When Tom was younger and people asked him, "What do you want to be when you grow up?" he would answer, "I'm going to be an angel when I grow up." What other plans could he have had, realistically? At 20, he has reached the age by which half of the victims of cystic fibrosis die. Physical complications, such as heart damage, that generally afflict several body systems in the last stages of this disease have begun to appear.

We can see in Tom's story that biological factors, such as heredity, can affect health; illness can alter social relationships; and all interrelated physiological systems of the body can be affected. In this appendix we outline the major physical systems of the body. Our discussion focuses on the normal functions of these systems, but we consider some important problems, too. What determines the degree of paralysis a person suffers after injury to the spine? How does stress affect our body systems? What is a heart attack, and what causes it?

This appendix is organized into six *modules* that can be covered *all at once* or *distributed* to the chapters in the book, depending on the approach the instructor prefers. You will find notices at appropriate points in the chapters, each telling students using the distributed approach who've not yet read a specific module to "read it now." As an example, the notice for **Module 4** on the respiratory system appears in Chapter 6, as the students prepare to read the material on cigarette smoking.

MODULE 1: THE NERVOUS SYSTEM

We all know that the nervous system, particularly the brain, in human beings and other animals controls the way we initiate behavior and respond to events in our world. The nervous system receives information about changes in the environment from sensory organs, including the eyes, ears, and nose, and it transmits directions that tell our muscles and other internal organs how to react. The brain also stores information—being a repository for our memory of past events—and provides our capability for thinking, reasoning, and creating.

HOW THE NERVOUS SYSTEM WORKS

The nervous system constantly integrates the actions of our internal organs—although we are not generally aware of it. Many of these organs, such as the heart and digestive tract, are made of muscle tissues that respond to commands. The nervous system provides these commands through an intricate network of billions of specialized nerve cells, called *neurons*.

Although neurons in different parts of the nervous system have a variety of shapes and sizes, the diagram in Figure A-1 shows their general features. Projecting from the *cell body* are clusters of branches called *dendrites*, which generally function as receivers for messages from adjacent neurons. These messages then travel through an *axon*, which splits into branches at the far end. The tips of these branches have small swellings called *synaptic knobs* that connect to the dendrites of other neurons, usually through a fluid-filled gap. This junction

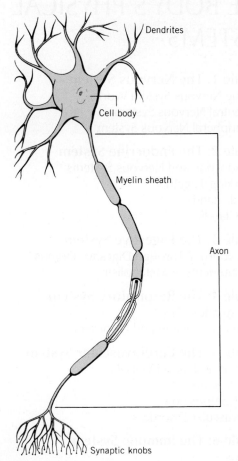

Figure A-1 An idealized diagram of a neuron and some of its major parts. Electrochemical messages received by the dendrites are transmitted to the synaptic knobs. The myelin sheath covers the axon of most neurons.

is called a *synapse*. Messages from the knobs cross the gap to adjacent neurons, and in this way eventually reach their destination. These messages consist of *electrochemical* activity. If the chemical activity at a dendrite produces a sufficient concentration of electrically charged particles, called *ions*, an impulse of electrical potential is triggered. Normally this process occurs in a controlled pattern. But in the disorder of *epilepsy*, large clusters of neurons fire at several times the normal rate, causing victims to have seizures that can involve convulsions and losing consciousness (AMA, 2003). The severity of the seizure depends on the amount of the brain and the specific areas that are activated.

Impulses in a neuron travel through the axon and stimulate the synaptic knobs to release a chemical called a **neurotransmitter**, which travels to the dendrites of an adjacent neuron. There are dozens of different neurotransmitters. Some tend to *excite* the receiving neuron, increasing the likelihood that an electrical impulse will be generated; others tend to *inhibit* the neuron, making an impulse less likely; and others can have either effect, depending on characteristics of the receiving neuron.

What changes occur in the nervous system as a person develops? By the time the typical baby is born, a basic structure has been formed for almost all the neurons this person will have. But the nervous system is still quite immature—for instance, the brain weighs only about 25% of the weight it will have when the child reaches adulthood (Sarafino & Armstrong, 1986). Most of the growth in brain size after birth results from an increase in the number of *glial cells* and the presence of a white fatty substance called *myelin*. The glial cells are thought to service and maintain the neurons. A myelin sheath surrounds the axons of most, but not all, neurons. This sheath is responsible for increasing the speed of nerve impulses and preventing them from being interfered with by adjacent nerve impulses, much the way insulation is used on electrical wiring. The importance of myelin can be seen in the disease called *multiple sclerosis*, which results when the myelin sheath degenerates and nerves become severed (Trapp et al., 1998). People afflicted with this disease have weak muscles that lack coordination and move spastically (AMA, 2003).

As the infant grows, the network of dendrites and synaptic knobs to carry messages to and from other neurons expands dramatically, as Figure A-2 shows. The myelin sheath covering the neurons is better developed initially in the upper regions of the body than in the lower regions. During the first years of life, the progress in myelin growth spreads down the body—from the head to shoulders, to the arms and hands, to the upper chest and abdomen, and then the legs and feet. This sequence is reflected in the individual's motor development: the upper parts of the body are brought under control at earlier ages than the lower parts. Studies with animals have found that chronic poor nutrition early in life impairs brain growth by retarding the development of myelin, glial cells, and dendrites. Such impairment can produce long-lasting deficits in a child's motor and intellectual performance (Reinis & Goldman, 1980). The brain appears to form few, if any, new neurons after birth, and their development is limited to certain areas of the brain (Kornack & Rakic, 2001).

Beginning in early adulthood, the brain slowly loses weight with age (Tortora & Derrickson, 2009). Although the number of brain cells does not change very much, the synapses do, leading to a decline in ability to send nerve impulses. These alterations in the brain are associated with the declines people often notice in their mental and physical functions after they reach 50 or 60 years of age.

The nervous system is enormously complex and has two major divisions—the central nervous system and the peripheral nervous system—that connect to each other. The **central nervous system** consists of the brain and spinal cord. The *peripheral nervous system* is composed of the remaining network of neurons throughout the body. Each of these divisions consists of interconnected lower-order divisions or structures. We will examine the nervous system, beginning at the top and working our way down.

THE CENTRAL NERVOUS SYSTEM

People's brain and spinal cord race toward maturity early in life. For example, the brain weighs 75% of its adult weight at about 2 years of age, 90% at 5 years, and 95% at 10 years (Tanner, 1970, 1978). The brain may be divided into three parts: the *forebrain*, the *cerebellum*, and the *brainstem*. Each of these parts has special functions.

WEB ANIMATION: The Nervous System

Access Web animations via the Student Companion Website (www.wiley.com/go/global/sarafino) for this book. This interactive animation describes the structure and functioning of the nervous system. The *To the Student* section at the front of this book gives instructions for using the animations.

At birth

At 1 month

At 6 months

At 2 years

Figure A-2 Drawings showing the neural structure of a section of the human cortex at four different ages. Notice that the number of cell bodies (dark spots) does not change much, while the network of dendrites expands with age. (Drawings from Lenneberg, 1967, Figure 4-6, based on photographs from Conel, 1939–1963.)

The Forebrain

The forebrain is the uppermost part of the brain. As Figure A-3 shows, the forebrain has two main subdivisions: the *telencephalon*, which consists of the cerebrum and the limbic system, and the *diencephalon*, which

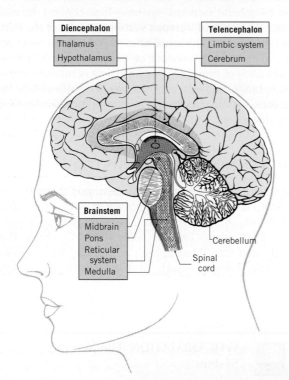

Diencephalon
Thalamus
Hypothalamus

Telencephalon
Limbic system
Cerebrum

Brainstem
Midbrain
Pons
Reticular
system
Medulla

Cerebellum

Spinal
cord

Figure A-3 A side view of the human brain in cross section, sliced through the middle from front to back. The forebrain, shown shaded in color, consists of the telencephalon (cerebrum and limbic system) and the diencephalon (thalamus and hypothalamus). The remaining divisions of the central nervous system—the cerebellum, the brainstem (shaded gray), and the spinal cord—are also labeled.

includes the thalamus and hypothalamus. As a general rule, areas toward the top and outer regions of the brain are involved in our perceptual, motor, learning, and conceptual activities. Regions toward the center and bottom of the brain are involved mainly in controlling internal and automatic body functions and in transmitting information to and from the telencephalon.

The **cerebrum** is the largest portion of the human brain and includes the *cerebral cortex*, its outermost layer. It controls complex motor and mental activity. The cerebrum has two halves—the *left hemisphere* and the *right hemisphere*—each of which looks like the drawing in Figure A-4. Although the left and right hemispheres are physically alike, they control different types of processes. For one thing, the motor cortex (shown in the figure) of each hemisphere controls motor movements on the opposite side of the body. This is why damage to the motor cortex on, say, the right side of the brain may leave part of the left side of the body paralyzed. The two hemispheres also control different aspects of cognitive and language processes. In most people, the left hemisphere contains the areas that handle reasoning, spoken and written language, and numerical skills. The right hemisphere usually processes such things as visual imagery, emotions, and the perception of patterns, such as melodies (Tortora & Derrickson, 2009).

Figure A-4 also shows that each hemisphere is divided into a front part, called the frontal lobe, and three back parts: the temporal, occipital, and parietal lobes. The *frontal lobe* is involved in many functions—for instance, the back region of the frontal lobe contains the motor cortex, which controls the skeletal muscles of the body. If a patient who is undergoing brain surgery receives stimulation to the motor cortex, some part of the body will move. The frontal lobe is also involved in important mental activities, such as the association of ideas, planning, self-awareness, and emotion. As a result, injury to areas of this lobe can produce personality and

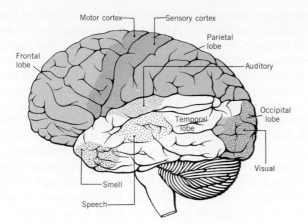

Figure A-4 The surface of the left hemisphere of the cerebrum. The shaded sections show the four parts of the hemisphere, and the areas associated with specific functions are identified. The right hemisphere has the same four parts and functional areas.

emotional reactions, like those described by the doctor of Phineas P. Gage:

> He is fitful, irreverent, indulging in the grossest profanity (which was not previously his custom), manifesting but little deference to his fellows, impatient of restraint or advice when it conflicts with his desires, at times … obstinate, capricious, and vacillating …. His mind was radically changed, so that his friends said he was no longer Gage. (Cited in McClintic, 1985, p. 93)

Phineas had survived a workplace accident in which a tamping iron was blown through the front of his head.

The *temporal lobe* is chiefly involved in hearing, but also in vision and memory. Damage to this region can impair the person's comprehension of speech and ability to determine the direction from which a sound is coming. Because the *occipital lobe* houses the principal visual area of the brain, damage there can produce blindness or the inability to recognize an object by sight. The *parietal lobe* is involved mainly in body sensations, such as of pain, cold, heat, touch, and body movement.

The second part of the telencephalon—called the **limbic system**—lies along the innermost edge of the cerebrum, and adjacent to the diencephalon (refer to Figure A-3). The limbic system is not well understood yet. It consists of several structures that seem to be important in the expression of emotions, such as fear, anger, and excitement. To the extent that heredity affects a person's emotions, it may do so by determining the structure and function of the limbic system (McClintic, 1985).

The diencephalon includes two structures—the thalamus and hypothalamus—that lie below and are partially encircled by the limbic system. The **thalamus** is a truly pivotal structure in the flow of information in the nervous system. It functions as the chief relay station for directing sensory messages, such as of pain or visual images, to appropriate points in the cerebrum, such as the occipital or parietal lobe. The thalamus also relays commands going out to the skeletal muscles from the motor cortex of the cerebrum.

The **hypothalamus**, a small structure just below the thalamus, plays an important role in people's emotions and motivation. Its function affects eating, drinking, and sexual activity, for instance (Tortora & Derrickson, 2009). For example, when the body lacks water or nutrients, the hypothalamus detects this and arouses the sensation of thirst or hunger, which is relieved when we consume water or food. Research with animals has shown that stimulation of specific areas of this structure can cause them to eat when they are full and to stop eating when they are hungry. A rare disease that affects this structure can cause people to become overweight. Another important function of the hypothalamus is to maintain *homeostasis*—a state of balance or normal function among our body systems. Our normal body temperature and heart rate, which are characteristic of healthy individuals, are examples of homeostasis. When our bodies are cold, for instance, we shiver, thus producing heat. When we are very warm, we perspire, thus cooling the body. The hypothalamus controls these adjustments (AMA, 2003). We will see later that the hypothalamus also plays an important role in our reaction to stress.

 WEB ANIMATION: Communication, Regulation and Homeostasis

Access: www.wiley.com/go/global/sarafino. This interactive animation describes homeostasis and how the nervous and endocrine systems regulate it.

The Cerebellum

The **cerebellum** lies at the back of the brain, below the cerebrum; its main function is in coordinating our movements and maintaining body balance. The cerebellum has nerve connections to the motor cortex of the cerebrum and most sense organs of the body. When areas of the cerebrum initiate specific movements, the cerebellum makes our actions precise and well coordinated.

How does the cerebellum do this? One way is by continuously comparing our intent with our performance, ensuring that a movement goes in the right direction, at the proper rate, and with appropriate force. Another way is by smoothing our movements. Because of the forces involved in movement, there is an underlying tendency for our motions to go quickly back and forth, like a tremor. The cerebellum damps this tendency (McClintic, 1985). When injury occurs to the cerebellum, the person's actions become jerky and uncoordinated—a condition called *ataxia*. Simple movements, such as walking or touching an object, become difficult and unsteady.

Look back to Figure A-3 to locate the cerebellum relative to the brainstem, which is the next section of the brain we will discuss.

The Brainstem

The lowest portion of the brain—called the **brainstem**—has the form of an oddly shaped knob at the top of the spinal cord. The brainstem consists of four parts: midbrain, pons, reticular system, and medulla.

The *midbrain* lies at the top of the brainstem. It connects directly to the thalamus above it, which relays messages to various parts of the forebrain. The midbrain receives information from the visual and auditory systems and is especially important in muscle movement. The disorder called *Parkinson's disease* results from degeneration of areas in or linked to the midbrain (Tortora & Derrickson, 2009). People severely afflicted with this disease have noticeable motor tremors, and their neck and trunk postures become rigid, so that they walk in a crouch. Sometimes the tremors are so continuous and vigorous that the victim becomes crippled.

The *reticular system* is a network of neurons that extends from the bottom to the top of the brainstem and into the thalamus. The reticular system plays an important role in controlling our states of sleep, arousal, and attention. When people suffer a coma, often it is this system that is injured or disordered (McClintic, 1985). The *pons* forms a large bulge at the front of the brainstem and is involved in eye movements, facial expressions, and chewing. The *medulla* contains vital centers that control breathing, heartbeat rate, and the diameter of blood vessels (which affects blood pressure). Because of the many vital functions it controls, damage to the medulla can be life threatening. *Polio*, a crippling disease that was once epidemic, sometimes damaged the center that controls breathing. Patients suffering such damage needed constant artificial respiration to breathe (McClintic, 1985).

The Spinal Cord

Extending down the spine from the brainstem is the **spinal cord**, a major neural pathway that transmits messages between the brain and various parts of the body. It contains neurons that carry impulses away from (the *efferent* direction) and toward (*afferent*) the brain. Efferent commands travel down the cord on their way to produce muscle action; afferent impulses come to the spinal cord from sense organs in all parts of the body.

The organization of the spinal cord parallels that of the body—that is, the higher the region of the cord, the higher the parts of the body to which it connects. Damage to the spinal cord results in impaired motor function or paralysis; the duration and extent of the impairment depends on the amount and location of damage. If the damage does not sever the cord, the impairment is less severe, and may be temporary. If the lower portion of the cord is severed, the lower areas of the body are paralyzed—a condition called *paraplegia*. If the upper portion of the spinal cord is severed, paralysis is more extensive. Paralysis of the legs and arms is called *quadriplegia*.

Figure A-5 depicts the spinal cord and its relation to the brain and the branching network of afferent and efferent neurons throughout the body—the peripheral nervous system. (Go to 🌳.)

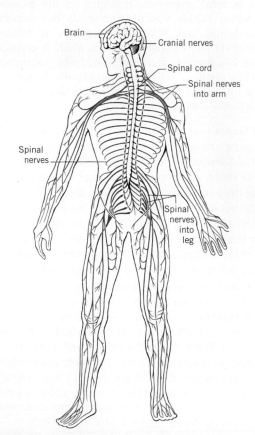

Brain — — Cranial nerves

— Spinal cord

— Spinal nerves into arm

Spinal nerves

Spinal nerves into leg

Figure A-5 Diagram showing the branching network between the spinal cord and the peripheral nervous system.

CLINICAL METHODS AND ISSUES

Biofeedback Treatment for Paralysis

Neuromuscular disorders, which impair the muscles and nerves that control movement, often involve paralysis resulting from a spinal cord injury or a stroke that damages the brain. Biofeedback, the operant conditioning method we describe in Chapter 1, is a treatment that psychologists and physical therapists can apply successfully to improve muscle control (Montgomery, 2004). The procedure involves attaching sensors to the skin to detect tiny changes in the activity of an affected muscle, immediately reporting back to the person when the muscle has tensed a bit, and encouraging him or her to tense it more and more. One study found that two biofeedback sessions a week for 6 weeks improved muscle function substantially in patients who had suffered strokes years earlier (Burnside, Tobias, & Bursill, 1982). Biofeedback can also help people gain control over other body processes, enabling them to reduce their blood pressure, for example (Sarafino, 2001).

THE PERIPHERAL NERVOUS SYSTEM

The **peripheral nervous system** has two parts: the somatic nervous system and the autonomic nervous system. The **somatic nervous system** is involved in both sensory and motor functions, serving mainly the skin and skeletal muscles. The **autonomic nervous system** activates internal organs, such as the lungs and intestines, and reports to the brain the current state of activity of these organs.

In the somatic nervous system, afferent neurons carry messages from sense organs to the spinal cord, as Figure A-6 diagrams. Efferent neurons carry messages to, and activate, *striated* (grooved) skeletal muscles, such as those in the face, arms, and legs, that we can move voluntarily. A disorder called *myasthenia gravis* can develop at the junction of these muscles and neurons, weakening muscle function of the head and neck. This produces characteristic symptoms—such as drooping eyelids, blurred vision, and difficulty swallowing and breathing—and can lead to paralysis. Medical treatment can improve muscle function, and reducing stress can alleviate symptoms (AMA, 2003).

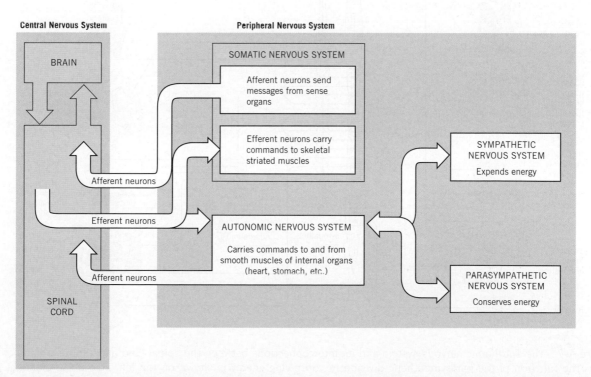

Figure A-6 Illustration of the flow and function of nerve impulses among the major parts of the nervous system.

Figure A-7 diagrams two other features of the autonomic nervous system. First, neurons carry messages between the spinal cord and the *smooth* muscles of the internal organs, such as the heart, stomach, lungs, blood vessels, and glands. Second, this system itself has two divisions, the sympathetic and parasympathetic, which often act in opposite ways. The **sympathetic nervous system** helps us mobilize and expend energy in responding to emergencies, expressing strong emotions, and performing strenuous activity. For instance, suppose you are crossing a street, notice a speeding car barreling toward you, and hear its brakes start to squeal. The sympathetic nervous system instantly moves into action, producing several simultaneous changes—for example, it speeds up the heart, dilates certain arteries to increase blood flow to the heart and skeletal muscles, constricts other arteries to decrease blood flow to the skin and digestive organs, decreases salivation, and increases perspiration. These changes, in general, enable you to mobilize energy, and you leap to safety out of the car's path. This system is called "sympathetic" because it acts in agreement with your current emotional state.

What does the parasympathetic division do? The prefix *para* means "alongside of"—this division acts alongside of, and often in opposition to, the sympathetic division. The **parasympathetic nervous system** regulates "quiet" or calming processes, helping our individual organ systems conserve and store energy. One example of parasympathetic activity can be seen in the digestion of food. When you eat a meal, the parasympathetic nervous system carries messages to regulate each step in the digestive process, such as by increasing salivation and stomach contractions. Another example can be seen in the course of emotional or emergency

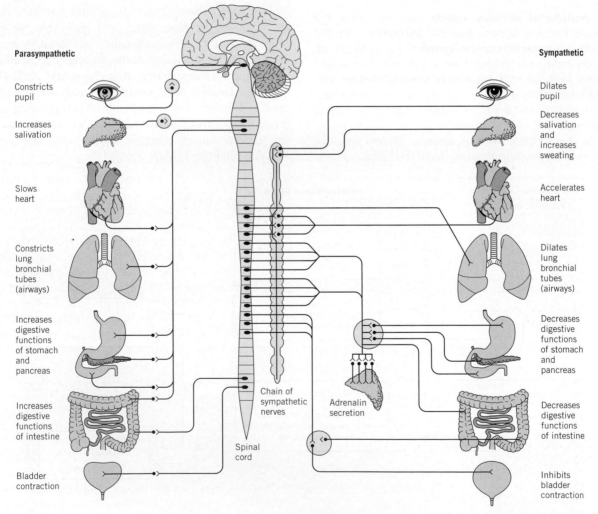

Figure A-7   The autonomic nervous system and its interconnections between the spinal cord and various organs of the body. The function of the parasympathetic division in conserving energy is shown on the left side of the diagram. The function of the sympathetic division in expending energy is shown on the right side. Notice that each organ connects to both divisions.

reactions—when an emergency has passed, the parasympathetic division helps restore your normal body state.

Communication within the peripheral nervous system is handled by 12 sets of *cranial nerves*, most of which originate in the brainstem. The *vagus nerve* extends from there to muscles of most major body organs, such as the airways, lungs, heart, and intestines, and is directly involved in the regulation of sympathetic and parasympathetic activity (Porges, 1995; Tortora & Derrickson, 2009). Efferent messages from the brain can target specific organs to increase or decrease their function.

SUMMARY

The central nervous system consists of the brain and spinal cord and is the control center, sending and receiving electrochemical messages, such as with neurotransmitters, through neurons throughout the body. The brain is divided into the forebrain (which includes the cerebrum, limbic system, thalamus, and hypothalamus), the cerebellum, and the brainstem. The uppermost regions of the brain are involved in perceptual, motor, learning, and conceptual activities. Areas toward the center and bottom of the brain are important in controlling internal and automatic body functions and the flow of information to and from the brain. The spinal cord is the major neural pathway that connects the brain to the peripheral nervous system.

The peripheral nervous system is a branching network of afferent and efferent neurons throughout the body. It has two divisions: the somatic nervous system is involved in sensory and motor functions; the autonomic nervous system carries messages between the spinal cord and various internal organs, and this system has two parts, sympathetic and parasympathetic. The sympathetic nervous system acts in agreement with our current emotional state and helps us mobilize and expend energy. The parasympathetic nervous system is involved in processes to conserve and store energy and in calming the body following sympathetic arousal. The nervous system is connected to and regulates all of our other body systems, and the brain is the control center.

MODULE 2: THE ENDOCRINE SYSTEM

The **endocrine system** consists of a set of glands that often work in close association with the autonomic nervous system. These systems share the function of communicating with various parts of the body, but they do this in somewhat different ways. Whereas the nervous system uses both electrical and chemical messages, the endocrine system communicates only with chemical substances, which are called **hormones**. Each endocrine gland secretes specific hormones directly into the bloodstream, which carries these chemicals to various parts of the body. Figure A-8 shows where several important endocrine glands are located. Certain chemicals are produced by both the endocrine and nervous systems and function as both hormones and neurotransmitters.

THE ENDOCRINE AND NERVOUS SYSTEMS WORKING TOGETHER

How are the endocrine and nervous systems associated? The nervous system is linked to the endocrine system by connections between the hypothalamus (in the forebrain) and a gland that lies just below it—the **pituitary gland**. The hypothalamus sends chemical messages directly to the pituitary gland, causing it to release pituitary hormones into the blood. In turn, most of these hormones selectively stimulate the other endocrine glands to secrete chemicals. Because the pituitary gland controls the secretion of other endocrine glands, it is called the "master gland."

Researchers have identified dozens of different hormones that course through our veins and arteries. Each hormone has its own specific effects on cells and organs of the body, thereby directly or indirectly affecting psychological and physical functions. Some hormones, such as estrogens and testosterone, are produced mainly in females' *ovaries* (where egg cells develop) and males' *testes* (where sperm develop). These hormones are especially important in the development and functioning of female and male reproductive systems. Other hormones affect blood pressure, general body growth, and the balance of various chemicals, such as calcium, in the body. Still other hormones help us react to specific situations we encounter in our lives.

We saw earlier that the autonomic nervous system plays an important role in our reaction to an emergency. So does the endocrine system through a process called the *hypothalamus–pituitary–adrenal axis* (Henderson & Baum, 2004). Let's see how by returning to the incident in which you leaped out of the path of a speeding car. When the sympathetic nervous system reacts to your emergency, the hypothalamus immediately sends a hormone called

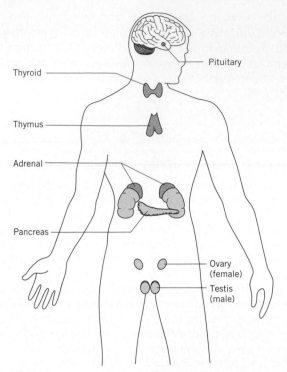

Figure A-8 Some of the endocrine glands and their locations in the body.

corticotropin-releasing factor to the pituitary gland. This causes the pituitary to release ACTH (adrenocorticotropic hormone) into the blood. The ACTH then travels throughout the body and stimulates the release of a variety of hormones—especially those of the adrenal glands—that affect your reaction to the emergency.

 WEB ANIMATION: The Endocrine System

Access: www.wiley.com/go/global/sarafino. This interactive animation shows the structure and functioning of different parts of the endocrine system.

ADRENAL GLANDS

The **adrenal glands** are located on top of the kidneys (see Figure A-8). These glands release several important hormones in response to emergencies and stress (AMA, 2003). One of these hormones, *cortisol*, helps control swelling when we are injured. If when you leaped to avoid being hit by the car you sprained your ankle, this hormone would help reduce swelling. But continued high levels of cortisol and similar hormones over a long time can be harmful to the body. They can lead to high blood pressure and the formation of ulcers, for example.

Two other important adrenal hormones are *adrenaline* and *noradrenaline* (also called epinephrine and norepinephrine). These hormones work in conjunction with the sympathetic nervous system to produce such bodily reactions as speeding up heart and respiration rates and increasing the liver's sugar output for quick energy. After the emergency has passed and sympathetic activity has subsided, some impact of the hormones may continue for a while because they are still in the bloodstream.

The impact of the nervous and endocrine systems' activities in emergency situations differs in the speed and persistence of their effect. The nervous system responds by sending messages that move instantly to specific locations; once they reach their destination, they become deactivated or dissipated. For example, the nervous system also produces and uses adrenaline and noradrenaline, but these chemicals function as neurotransmitters, relaying their commands from neuron to neuron and having a localized effect. The impact of the message stops quickly, and persists only if additional messages are sent. Hormones from the endocrine system move more slowly and broadly through the bloodstream, and their effects can be delayed and long-lasting.

OTHER GLANDS

Several other endocrine glands are also important. The *thymus gland*, which is located in the chest, is quite large in infancy and childhood but diminishes in size and efficiency after puberty (AMA, 2003). The thymus plays an important role early in life in the development of antibodies and immunities against diseases.

The *thyroid gland*, located in the neck, produces hormones, such as thyroxine, that regulate the body's general activity level and growth. Disorders in thyroid production are of two types: *hypothyroidism*, or insufficient secretion of thyroid hormones, and *hyperthyroidism*, or excessive thyroid secretion (AMA, 2003). Hypothyroidism leads to low activity levels and to weight gain. If the condition is congenital and untreated, dwarfism and mental retardation often result. The condition can be treated medically by having the person take hormone supplements orally. Hyperthyroidism leads to high activity levels, short attention spans, tremors, insomnia, and weight loss. Untreated people with a common form of this condition, called *Graves' disease*, act in a highly restless, irritable, and confused manner.

Another endocrine gland is the *pancreas*, which is located below the stomach. Its main function is to regulate the level of blood sugar, or glucose. The pancreas does this by producing two hormones, *glucagon* and *insulin*, that act in opposition. Glucagon

HIGHLIGHT

Our Physiological Individuality

Think about some differences between two people you know. Probably the first things that come to mind are their physical and behavioral characteristics. One person is tall and has blond hair, blue eyes, and an outgoing personality; the other is short and has dark hair, dark eyes, and is shy. But what about their internal physiological structure and functions?

We don't usually think about internal physiological differences between people. This is partly because all pictures of any internal organ we see in books are virtually the same. As a result, we get the impression that if you've seen one heart, brain, or stomach, you've seen them all. This impression is wrong. Our individuality exists not only in our external features, but in our internal organs and bodily chemistry as well. For example, the aorta is a major blood vessel that arches, or curves, over and attaches to the heart, and drawings of some of its structural variations are given in Figure A-9. The drawing on the left depicts the usual branching that forms at the arch of the aorta, and the other drawings show variations that occur, sometimes quite frequently. Major structural variations occur in virtually all internal organs,

and the usual structure occurs in only about two-thirds of cases (Wikipedia, 2010).

Our physiological individuality can have major implications for health and behavior. How? One way is that people's reactions to medicines differ, sometimes quite substantially. Some people may require many times the normal dose of certain drugs before the desired effect occurs. A person's age, weight, and heredity contribute to this variability (Bennett, 1987; USDHHS, 1981). Heavy people usually require larger doses of a drug than other people do. Infants and the elderly seem to be particularly sensitive to the effects of drugs, and overdoses are a danger for them. Blood pressure medication in the elderly may overshoot and lower the pressure too far, for example.

There are gender differences in many organ systems, too. Males generally have larger hearts and lungs, and higher blood pressure, than females do. Their body systems also react to stress differently. We saw earlier that the adrenal glands respond to stress by secreting hormones—two of which are adrenaline and cortisol. When under stress, males secrete more of these hormones than females do (Collins & Frankenhaeuser, 1978).

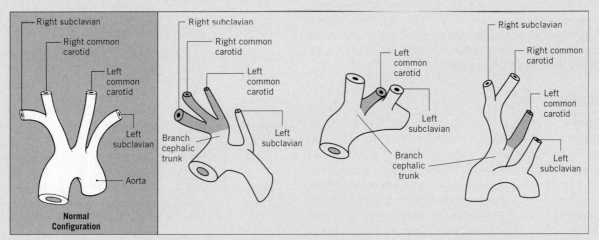

Figure A-9 Common variations from the normal configuration in arterial branching of the aortic arch. The dark coloring highlights regions of variation. (Drawings of variations are from Nayak et al., 2006, Figures 2,3, and 4.)

raises the concentration of glucose in the blood, and insulin lowers it (AMA, 2003). The disorder called *diabetes mellitus* results when the pancreas does not produce sufficient insulin to balance the action of glucagon. This imbalance produces excess blood sugar

levels—a condition called *hyperglycemia*. If this condition persists and is untreated, it may cause coma and death. Diabetes can be medically controlled, generally through diet and either medication or daily insulin injections (AMA, 2003; Trief, 2004) (Go to 💡.)

SUMMARY

Like the nervous system, the endocrine system also communicates with various parts of the body, but does so by sending chemical messages through the bloodstream. This system consists of several glands that secrete hormones. As the "master gland" in this system, the pituitary gland releases hormones that stimulate other glands to secrete.

The adrenal glands secrete hormones, such as cortisol and adrenaline (epinephrine), that the body uses in response to emergencies and stress. Other glands are important in regulating such factors as general body growth and the level of blood sugar.

MODULE 3: THE DIGESTIVE SYSTEM

Whether we eat an apple, drink some milk, or swallow a pill, our bodies respond in the same general way. The **digestive system** breaks down what we have ingested, converts much of it to chemicals the body can use, and excretes the rest. The chemicals the body uses are absorbed into the bloodstream, which transports them to all of our body cells. Chemical nutrients in the foods we eat provide energy to fuel our activity, body growth, and repair.

FOOD'S JOURNEY THROUGH DIGESTIVE ORGANS

Think of the digestive system as a long hose—about 20 feet long—with stations along the way. The journey of food through this hose begins in the *mouth* and ends at the *rectum*. The digestive organs and major organs in between are shown in Figure A-10.

Digesting Food

How does this system break down food? One way is mechanical: for example, we grind food up when we chew it. Another way is chemical: by the action of **enzymes**, substances that act as catalysts in speeding up chemical reactions in cells. How do enzymes work? You can see the effect of an enzyme by doing the following experiment (Holum, 1994). Place a bit of liver in some hydrogen peroxide and watch what happens: An enzyme in liver called *catalase* causes the peroxide to decompose, frothing as oxygen is given off as a gas. This is the same reaction you see when you use peroxide to disinfect a wound.

   In most cases, the names for enzymes end in the letters *-ase*, and the remainder of each name reflects the substance on which it acts. Here are some examples:

- *Carbohydrase* acts on carbohydrates.
- *Lactase* acts on lactose (milk).

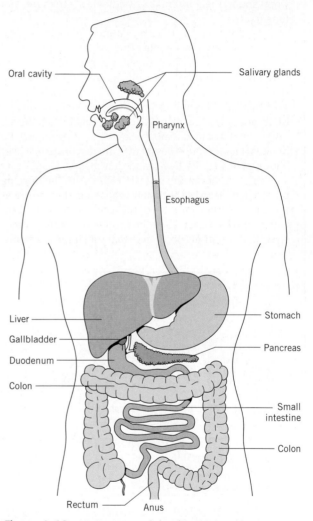

Figure A-10   Major parts of the digestive system.

- *Phosphatase* acts on phosphate compounds.
- *Sucrase* acts on sucrose (sugar).

   As food is broken down into smaller and smaller units in the digestive tract, water molecules become attached to these units (Rhoades & Pflanzer, 1996).

When food is in the mouth, there is more digestive action going on than just chewing. Saliva moistens food and contains an enzyme that starts the process of breaking down starches. The salivary glands release saliva in response to commands from the brainstem, which responds primarily to sensory information from taste buds. Simply seeing, smelling, or even thinking about food can produce neural impulses that cause the mouth to water (Rhoades & Pflanzer, 1996).

The journey of food advances to the *esophagus*, a tube that is normally flattened when food is not passing through it. The esophagus pushes the food down to the stomach by wavelike muscle contractions called *peristalsis*. By the time food enters the esophagus, the stomach has already begun digestive activities by releasing small amounts of gastric juice even before food reaches it. Tasting, smelling, seeing, or thinking about food can initiate this process (Feldman & Richardson, 1986). Once food reaches the stomach, this organ amasses large amounts of gastric juices, including *hydrochloric acid* and *pepsin*, an enzyme that breaks down proteins. (This enzyme name is one of the few that does not end in -*ase*.) The stomach also produces a sticky mucus substance to protect its lining from the highly acidic gastric juices. The muscular stomach walls produce a churning motion—that we are generally not aware of—which mixes the food particles with the gastric juices. This mixing continues for 3 or 4 hours, producing a semiliquid mixture.

Peristalsis in the stomach then moves this mixture on, a little at a time, to the initial section of the small intestine called the *duodenum*. Important digestive processes occur in the small intestine (Rhoades & Pflanzer, 1996; Tortora & Derrickson, 2009). First, the highly acidic food mixture becomes chemically alkaline from substances added from various organs—an important process because the linings of the small intestine and remainder of the digestive tract are not protected from high acidity, as the stomach is. Second, enzymes secreted by the pancreas into the duodenum break down carbohydrates, proteins, and fats further. Third, *absorption* increases. Because the stomach lining can absorb only a few substances, such as alcohol and aspirin, most materials we ingest are absorbed into the bloodstream through the lining of the small intestine (Tortora & Derrickson, 2009). If alcohol is consumed along with fatty foods, very little alcohol is absorbed until it reaches the small intestine. When food is ready to be absorbed through the intestine wall, nutrients have been broken down into molecules—carbohydrates are broken down into *simple sugars*, fats into *glycerol* and *fatty acids*, and proteins into *amino acids*.

How does absorption occur? The inside of the small intestine is made of a membrane that will allow molecules to pass through. To increase the absorbing surface, the intestine wall has many folds that contain projections, as pictured in Figure A-11. Each of the many thousands of projections contains a network of structures

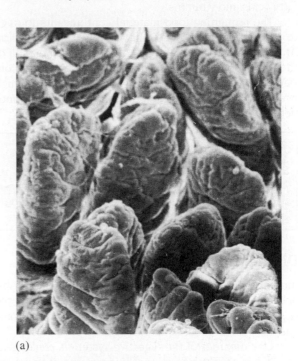

(a)

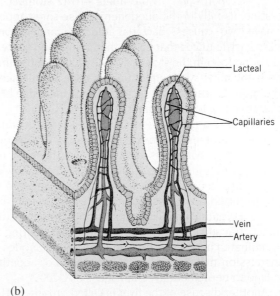

Lacteal

Capillaries

Vein

Artery

(b)

Figure A-11   The interior wall of the small intestine. (a) The wall has many tiny projections, shown greatly magnified in the photograph (b) The cross-sectional drawing shows the capillaries and lacteal of each projection.

that will accept the molecules and transport them away to other parts of the body. These structures include tiny blood vessels called *capillaries* and a tube called a *lacteal*. Capillaries absorb amino acids, simple sugars, and water; they also absorb some fatty acids, vitamins, and minerals. Lacteals accept glycerol and the remaining fatty acids and vitamins.

The remaining food material continues its journey to the large intestine, most of which is called the *colon*. Absorption, mainly of water, continues in the first half of the colon, and the remaining material is transported on. Bacterial action converts the material into feces, which eventually reach the rectum, where they are stored until defecation occurs.

WEB ANIMATION: The Digestive System

Access: www.wiley.com/go/global/sarafino. This interactive animation describes the structure and functioning of the digestive system.

Disorders of the Digestive System

Judging from the many media advertisements for stomach and "irregularity" remedies, it seems that people have a good deal of trouble with their digestive processes. We will consider a few digestive problems.

One disorder of the digestive system is *peptic ulcers*, which are open sores in the lining of the stomach or intestine, usually in the duodenum. These sores appear to have two causes: bacterial infection and chronic excess gastric juices that erode the lining when there is little or no food in the stomach (AMA, 2003). Abdominal pain is the chief symptom of the disorder. People seem to be more susceptible to ulcers if they experience high rather than low levels of stress.

Hepatitis is a class of several viral diseases in which the liver becomes inflamed and unable to function well. The first symptoms often are like those of flu. But the symptoms persist, and jaundice, a yellowing of the skin, generally follows. *Hepatitis* A appears to be transmitted through contaminated food, water, and utensils. *Hepatitis* B and C infections occur through sexual contact, transfusion of infected blood, and sharing of contaminated needles by drug addicts, but the modes of transmission may be broader. Some forms of hepatitis can lead to permanent liver damage (AMA, 2003).

Another disease of the liver is called *cirrhosis*. In this disease, liver cells die off and are replaced by nonfunctional fibrous scar tissue. The scar tissue is permanent, and when it becomes extensive, the liver's normal functions are greatly impaired. As we will see later, the liver is not only important in the digestive process; it also cleanses and regulates the composition of the blood. Cirrhosis can result from several causes, including hepatitis infection and, particularly, alcohol abuse (AMA, 2003).

Cancer may occur in any part of the digestive tract, especially in the colon and rectum (ACS, 2006; AMA, 2003). People over 40 years of age have a higher prevalence for cancers of the digestive tract than do younger individuals. Early detection for many of these cancers is possible and greatly improves the person's chances of recovery.

USING NUTRIENTS IN METABOLISM

The term **metabolism** refers to all chemical reactions that occur in the body's cells (Holum, 1994). Three principal outcomes of metabolism are:

- *Synthesis* of new cell material from proteins and minerals to build and repair the body.
- *Regulation* of body processes—by producing enzymes and hormones, for example—through the use of proteins, minerals, and vitamins.
- *Energy* to heat the body and fuel its activities.

We will focus on the third outcome, energy production.

Metabolism takes place constantly in the cells of all living organisms. Without the energy it produces, all of our body systems would cease to function. The energy to fuel our internal functions and our physical actions comes mainly from the metabolism of carbohydrates and fats (Tortora & Derrickson, 2009). The amount of energy a food contains is measured in *calories*. One calorie is the amount of heat needed to raise one gram of water one degree Celsius. Nutrition researchers measure the calories contained in a given quantity of a food by burning it in a special apparatus.

How much energy do we use to support our basic bodily functions? The number of calories we burn up when our bodies are at rest—an index called the *basal metabolic rate*—depends on the size of the body (Tortora & Derrickson, 2009). For this reason, the basal metabolic rate is expressed in terms of calories per area of body surface (in square meters) per hour. A person who is 170 cm tall and weighs 60 kilograms has a body surface area of about 1.7 square meters, for example. The basal metabolic rate also varies with the person's age and gender: the average rate is higher in males than in females and higher in younger people than in older people, as Figure A-12 indicates.

What other factors affect the basal metabolic rate? People who are under stress, who live in cold climates, or whose hormone secretion by the thyroid gland is greater

ASSESS YOURSELF

How Many Calories Do You Burn While Resting?

To figure out the number of calories your body probably burns while you are just resting, we need to estimate two factors:

1. *Your basal metabolic rate* (BMR). Although we cannot assess your BMR directly, we can use Figure A-12 to estimate it by finding the average BMR for people of your age and gender. Do this by: (a) finding on the horizontal axis where your age would be, (b) drawing a vertical line from that point to the graph for your gender, and (c) drawing a horizontal line to the vertical axis. The value at this intersect is our estimate of your BMR, which you should enter in the formula (below, right column).

2. *Your body surface area* (BSA). Estimates of BSA in square meters are usually made by plotting the person's height and weight on complex graphs. We have used one of these graphs (Hafen, 1981, Figure 16-5) to develop an alternative two-step method. First, start with a BSA score of 1.540 and adjust it based on your height by adding (or subtracting) .035 for 2.5 cm by

which you are taller (or shorter) than 152 cm. Thus, if you are 168 cm tall, your score at this point would be 1.750. Second, take your weight into account by adjusting your score in *one* of four ways: (a) If your body has a small frame and you are very slim, subtract .08 to get your BSA. (b) If you have a medium frame and an average weight, do nothing; your current score is your BSA. (c) If your frame is large and/or you are moderately heavy, add .08 to get your BSA. (d) If you are overweight by 9 kilograms or more, add .15 to get your BSA.

Enter your BSA in the formula below and multiply it by your BMR to estimate the number of calories you burn per hour while sleeping or lying down.

_____ BMR × _____ BSA = _____ cal/hr

When engaged in light activities, such as shopping or golfing, you burn 2 to 4 times that much, and when doing moderate or heavy activities, such as scrubbing floors or jogging, you burn 4 to 10 times that much.

than normal tend to have high basal metabolic rates (McClintic, 1985; Tortora & Derrickson, 2009). Factors such as these account in part for the variation in metabolic rates among different people of the same size, age, and gender.

Activity raises metabolism above the basal rate. Food materials that are not used up by metabolic processes are stored as body fat. This means that people become overweight generally because they regularly consume more calories than their body uses to fuel their internal functions and physical actions. To maintain normal body weight, people who do not metabolize all the calories they consume need to eat less, exercise more, or both. (Go to 🍎.)

SUMMARY

The digestive system provides the body with essential nutrients and other substances for energy, body growth, and repair. It also removes wastes from the body. Enzymes break down foods by speeding up chemical reactions in the body's cells. The outcomes of chemical reactions called metabolism that occur in our body cells include the synthesis of new cells, the regulation of body processes, and the production of energy to heat the body and fuel its activity.

MODULE 4: THE RESPIRATORY SYSTEM

Breathing supplies the body with oxygen—but why do we need oxygen? The chemical reactions in metabolism require oxygen, some of which joins with carbon atoms from food to form *carbon dioxide* (CO_2) as a waste product. So breathing has another function—it lets us get rid of this waste product. We will begin our examination of the **respiratory system** by looking at its structures.

THE RESPIRATORY TRACT

After air enters the body through the nose or mouth, it travels past the *larynx*, down the *trachea* and *bronchial*

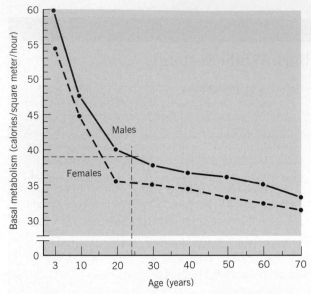

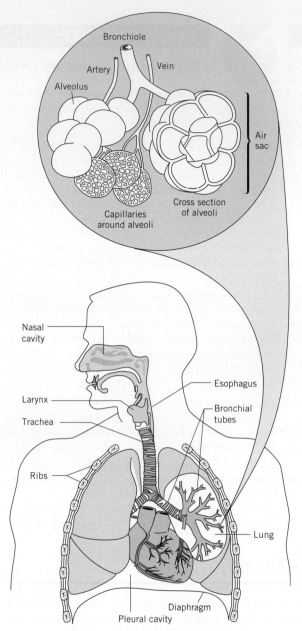

Figure A-12 Normal basal metabolic rate for males and females at different ages in the life span. The dashed vertical and horizontal lines give an illustration: an average 24-year-old male's basic metabolism is 38.7 calories per square meter per hour. (Data from Hafen, 1981, Table 16.6.)

tubes, and into the *lungs*. These organs are depicted in Figure A-13. The bronchial tubes divide into smaller and smaller branches called *bronchioles* inside the lungs. These branches finally end in millions of tiny air sacs called *alveoli*. Each alveolus looks like a minute bubble made of a membrane that is thin enough to allow oxygen, CO_2, and other gases to pass through. Alveoli are enmeshed in beds of capillaries so that gases can be transferred to and from the bloodstream quickly and efficiently.

When we breathe, what makes the air go in and out? When we inhale, the rib muscles draw the ribs up and outward and the diaphragm—a horizontal sheet of muscle below the lungs (see Figure A-13)—contracts, pulling downward on the bottom of the lungs. These actions pull air in and enlarge the lung chambers (Rhoades & Pflanzer, 1996). When we exhale, these muscles relax, and the elasticity of the lungs forces the air out, like a balloon.

Figure A-13 Major organs of the respiratory (also called pulmonary) system and closeup of alveoli. The organ shown between the lungs and the pleural cavity is the heart.

 WEB ANIMATION: The Respiratory System

Access: www.wiley.com/go/global/sarafino. This interactive animation shows the structure and functioning of the respiratory system.

RESPIRATORY FUNCTION AND DISORDERS

How do the muscles ''know'' when it's time to inhale and exhale? Our blood vessels contain sensors that monitor blood gases and send this information to the medulla of the brain, which directs actions of the muscles to cause us to inhale and exhale. When the CO_2 level is high, the medulla increases the breathing rate; when the level is low, breathing rate is decreased (Rhoades & Pflanzer, 1996).

Foreign matter, such as airborne particles and microorganisms, can readily enter the respiratory tract. The respiratory system therefore needs protective mechanisms to prevent foreign matter from reaching the lungs and entering the bloodstream. Two protective mechanisms are *reflexes*: (1) sneezing in response to irritation in nasal passages and (2) coughing in response to irritation in lower portions of the system. Another protective mechanism is the *mucociliary escalator*. How does this mechanism work? Most of the lining of the respiratory system is coated with a sticky mucus that traps foreign matter. And the air passages leading from the mouth to the lungs are lined with tiny hairlike structures called *cilia* that move in such a way as to force the mucus coating up toward the mouth. Hence the name "mucociliary escalator." When the mucus reaches the back of the mouth, it is usually swallowed (McClintic, 1985). In this way, the respiratory system cleanses itself and protects the body from harmful matter that we inhale.

The opening story of this appendix is about a young man named Tom who is a victim of cystic fibrosis, a fatal disease of the respiratory system. We will look at several of the many other disorders that attack this system. Some of these disorders mainly affect the alveoli of the lungs, thereby impairing the normal exchange of CO_2 and oxygen. For instance, there are several types of *pneumonia*, which can be caused by either bacterial or viral infection (AMA, 2003). Although this disease often affects the bronchial tubes, the most serious types of pneumonia cause the alveoli to become inflamed and filled with fluid. In another respiratory disease called *emphysema* the walls between alveoli are destroyed. This decreases the lungs'

surface area for exchanging gases and their elasticity for exhaling CO_2 (Haas & Haas, 1990; Tortora & Derrickson, 2009). *Pneumoconiosis* is a disease that afflicts people who chronically inhale air containing high concentrations of dust—generally at their workplaces. The black lung disease of coal miners provides an example. Dust that is not removed by protective mechanisms accumulates as thick sheets around the alveoli and bronchioles, damaging these structures and blocking air exchange.

Other disorders of the respiratory system primarily affect the bronchial tubes, usually by narrowing the tubes and reducing airflow. *Asthma* is a disorder in which the bronchial airways narrow, because they become inflamed, develop spasms, and secrete too much mucus (AAFA, 2010; Sarafino, 2004a). Attacks usually are temporary and occur in response to an irritant, such as an infection or something to which the victim is allergic. Breathing becomes difficult and, in very serious attacks, portions of the lungs may collapse temporarily. In *chronic bronchitis*, inflammation and excess mucus occur in the bronchial tubes for an extended period. This condition may be permanent or occur several times a year, lasting 2 weeks or more each episode (Haas & Hass, 1990).

Lung cancer involves an unrestrained growth of cells that crowd out cells that aid respiration. This process usually begins in the bronchial tubes and spreads to the lungs (Tortora & Derrickson, 2009). In its final stages, the diseased cells enter the bloodstream through the capillaries and spread throughout the body. At this point death is almost always near. Many of the respiratory diseases we have discussed can be caused or worsened by smoking cigarettes. This risk factor is also important in diseases of the cardiovascular system.

SUMMARY

The respiratory system provides the body cells with oxygen for energy in metabolism, body growth, and repair. Air enters the body through the nose or mouth and travels to the lungs via bronchial tubes. Oxygen is transferred through alveoli to the bloodstream. The respiratory system also removes carbon dioxide wastes from the body.

MODULE 5: THE CARDIOVASCULAR SYSTEM

The physical design of every complex organism has to deal with a basic problem: How can the body service its cells—supplying the substances they need to function properly and removing the wastes that metabolism produces? In humans and many other animals, this problem is solved by having a **cardiovascular system** to transport these materials. The blood circulates through blood vessels—capillaries, arteries, and veins—within a closed system, one in which the blood does not directly contact the cells and tissues it services. All transfers of oxygen, nutrients, waste products, and other substances occur through membranes that are separated by fluid-filled spaces. The heart is the center of the cardiovascular system.

WEB ANIMATION: The Cardiovascular System

Access: www.wiley.com/go/global/sarafino. This interactive animation shows the structure and functioning of the cardiovascular system.

THE HEART AND BLOOD VESSELS

The *heart* is a fist-sized pump made of muscle that circulates the blood throughout the body. It "beats," or pumps, about 100,000 times a day. The muscular portion of the heart wall is called the *myocardium*. Figure A-14 gives two drawings of a heart: (a) an exterior view and (b) an interior view, showing that the heart has four chambers. The two upper chambers are called atriums, and the two lower ones are called ventricles; the left and right sides are labeled from the body's perspective, not from ours.

Looking at the drawings, we see *coronary arteries* and veins that service the myocardium, bringing oxygen and nutrients to it and taking CO_2 away, and several large blood vessels that carry blood to and from the chambers of the heart. How are arteries and veins different? *Arteries* carry blood *from* the heart, and *veins* carry blood *to* it. You will also notice in the drawings that the shading of some blood vessels of the heart is gray, and in others the shading is in color. The vessels with gray shading carry blood that is laden with CO_2 toward the lungs; the vessels with color shading carry blood from the lungs after it has expelled CO_2 and received oxygen.

Now, let's follow the route of blood shown in Figure A-14b. The blood that enters the *right atrium* of the heart is laden with waste products, such as CO_2, from our cells and is deficient in oxygen, which makes the blood bluish in color. After the atrium is filled, the blood passes through a valve to the *right ventricle*. The ventricles provide the main pumping force for circulation as the heart muscle contracts, and their valves prevent the blood from going back up to the atriums. From the right ventricle, the blood enters pulmonary circulation to the lungs, where it becomes oxygenated and, consequently, red in color. The oxygenated blood travels to the *left atrium* of the heart and is passed to the *left ventricle*, which pumps it out through the *aorta* into general circulation. It then goes to various parts of the body before returning to the heart and beginning the cycle again. The complete cycle takes about 1 minute in the resting person.

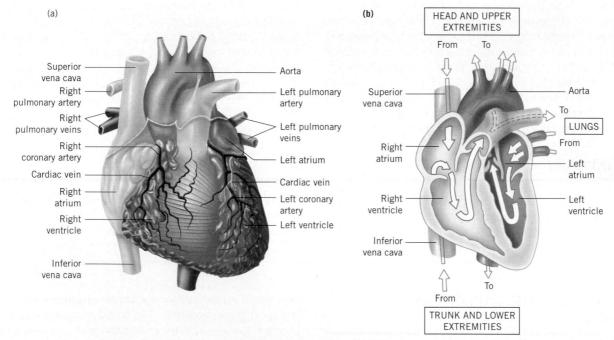

Figure A-14   Drawings of the heart. (a) An exterior view from the front, showing major blood vessels. The left and right *coronary arteries* and cardiac veins service the myocardium; larger arteries and veins carry blood to and from the heart's chambers. (b) An interior view of the heart's chambers, showing that blood comes from general circulation—that is, the rest of the body—to the *right atrium* via the superior and inferior vena cava. The blood then travels to the *right ventricle* and then to the lungs, where it exchanges CO_2 for oxygen. The oxygenated blood enters the *left atrium* via pulmonary veins and goes to the *left ventricle*, which pumps it via the aorta to the rest of the body.

Portions of each quantity of blood pumped by the heart travel through the liver and kidneys, where important functions take place before the blood returns to the heart. The *kidneys* cleanse the blood of waste products and pass the wastes on to be eliminated in the urine. The *liver* receives blood laden with nutrients, such as simple sugars, from the intestinal tract, and the remainder comes from general circulation. What does the liver do to the blood? First, it cleanses the blood of harmful debris, such as bacteria. Second, the liver removes nutrients and stores them. Large portions of these nutrients are retained in the liver until the body needs them. In this way, the ebbs and flows of nutrients in the blood are kept relatively even over time.

BLOOD PRESSURE

Imagine you are holding a long balloon that is filled with air. Its end is tied off. If you squeeze it in the middle, the rest of it expands. This is what happens when pressure is applied to a closed system. The cardiovascular system is also closed, and the myocardium does the squeezing when it pumps blood from the heart. Like the inflated balloon, the cardiovascular system always has some pressure in it. The squeezing increases the pressure.

Our arteries are elastic—they expand when pressure is applied. **Blood pressure** is the force exerted by blood on the artery walls. The heart is at rest between myocardial contractions, while it fills with blood. The resting force in the arteries that occurs at this time is called *diastolic pressure*. When the heart pumps, each contraction produces a maximum force in the arteries, which is called *systolic pressure*. A person's blood pressure is expressed with two numbers: a larger number, representing systolic pressure, followed by a smaller number, representing diastolic pressure. Your doctor might tell you that your blood pressure is "120 over 80," for example. Blood pressure readings are standardized in units of *mm Hg* to reflect the number of millimeters (mm) the pressure can raise a column of mercury (Hg).

Blood pressure varies. It changes from one moment to the next, it is higher in one part of the body than in another, and different people have different blood pressures. What determines blood pressure? We can answer this question in two ways—one involves the laws of fluid dynamics and the other involves factors in people's lives that affect these dynamics. We will start with the first approach and examine five aspects of fluid dynamics that affect blood pressure (McClintic, 1985).

1. *Cardiac output* is the volume of fluid being pumped per minute. Blood pressure increases as cardiac output rises.

2. *Blood volume* refers to the total amount of blood circulating in the system. The greater the volume, the higher the blood pressure needed to move it.

3. *Peripheral resistance* refers to the difficulty fluid encounters in passing through narrow tubes or openings. When you put a nozzle on a hose and turn on the water, the pressure is greater at the nozzle than in the hose. Arteries vary in diameter; resistance is generally greater in small-diameter arteries than in larger ones.

4. *Elasticity*, as we have seen, describes the ease in expanding and contracting. When blood vessels become less elastic, blood pressure—especially systolic pressure—rises.

5. *Viscosity* refers to the thickness of the fluid. The viscosity of blood depends on its composition, such as whether it contains high levels of red blood cells. Thicker blood flows less easily than thinner blood and requires more blood pressure for it to circulate through the cardiovascular system.

What factors in people's lives affect these dynamics? A variety of states affect our blood pressure in everyday life. The *temperature* of our environment defines one of these states. When the temperature is high, the blood vessels in our skin enlarge and our cardiac output and diastolic pressure fall, which makes us feel drowsy. Low temperatures have the opposite effect. Another factor is *activity*. For example, exercise increases blood pressure during and for a while after the activity. Simply changing posture can also affect blood pressure. When we go from a lying position to standing, blood flow in the veins that feed the heart slows down because of gravity. This causes a drop in cardiac output and blood pressure. As a result, blood flow to the brain drops and can make us feel dizzy (McClintic, 1985). A third factor is *emotional experience*. When we experience stress, anger, or anxiety, the sympathetic nervous system is activated. This causes cardiovascular reactions, such as increased cardiac output. Both systolic and diastolic pressures increase when people are emotionally aroused (James et al., 1986).

High blood pressure strains and damages the heart and arteries. Some people have high blood pressure consistently over a period of several weeks or more. This condition is called *hypertension*. How high is "high" blood pressure? People whose pressure is at or above 140 (systolic) over 90 (diastolic) are classified as hypertensive, and those at or above 120/80 are "prehypertensive" (AHA, 2010). Optimal blood pressure levels are below 120/80. High blood pressure is a major risk factor for heart disease and stroke. For instance, when the pressure is very high—such as exceeding 200—the danger is high that a rupture may occur in a blood vessel, particularly in the brain. This is one way by which strokes occur.

There are several known risk factors for hypertension. One risk factor is being overweight (AHA, 2010). Heavy people have more body mass to move when they are active than lighter people do, and they have a larger volume of blood for the heart to pump. Another factor is age—blood pressure generally rises with age. For example, the percentage of Americans who are hypertensive is many times higher among the elderly than among young adults (NCHS, 2009a). But aging per se may not be the reason for this relationship. Why? As adults get older, for instance, they tend to get heavier, at least in industrialized countries. In primitive societies where adults do not show an increase in body weight as they get older, blood pressure does not seem to increase with age (Herd & Weiss, 1984).

Other risk factors for hypertension among Americans relate to gender, race, and family history (AHA, 2010; NCHS, 2009a). Until recently, men were more likely than women to have hypertension, but now the prevalence rate for hypertension is higher for women than for men, particularly after about 50 years of age. Black adults develop hypertension at a much higher rate than White and Mexican Americans do. The reasons for these gender and racial differences in hypertension are unclear. Family history is important, too. People are more likely to become hypertensive if their parents had high blood pressure. Evidence from twin studies suggests that genetics plays a role in blood pressure (Rose, 1986; Smith et al., 1987).

 WEB ANIMATION: Negative Feedback Control of Blood Pressure

Access: www.wiley.com/go/global/sarafino. This interactive animation describes the importance of blood pressure and how the body regulates it.

BLOOD COMPOSITION

Blood is sometimes thought of as a "liquid tissue" because it consists of cells that are suspended in a liquid. The average adult's body contains about 10 pints of blood (AMA, 2003). Because our bodies can replace blood quickly, we can donate a pint of blood with no ill effects. Blood composition can affect blood pressure. As we saw earlier, the thicker the blood, the more pressure is needed to circulate it. What is blood made of, and how does its composition change its thickness? Blood has two components, formed elements and plasma (Holum, 1994; Tortora & Derrickson, 2009). We'll look at formed elements first.

Formed Elements

Formed elements are the cells and cell-like structures in the blood that constitute about 45% of our blood volume. There are three types of formed elements:

1. *Red blood cells* are the most abundant cells in the blood—there are about 5 million of them per cubic millimeter of blood. They are formed in the bone marrow and have a lifetime of about 3 months. Red blood cells are important mainly because they contain *hemoglobin*, a protein substance that attaches to oxygen and transports this element to body cells and tissues. *Anemia* is a condition in which the level of red blood cells or hemoglobin is below normal (AMA, 2003).

2. *Leukocytes* are white blood cells. Each of several types of leukocytes serves a special protective function—for example, some engulf or destroy bacteria. White blood cells are produced in the bone marrow and various organs in the body. Although there normally are several thousand leukocytes per cubic millimeter of an adult's blood, they are the least abundant type of formed element. *Leukemia* is a malignant disease in which abnormal white blood cells are produced in extremely high quantities, crowding out normal leukocytes, which fight infection, and red blood cells, which prevent anemia (ACS, 2009; AMA, 2003).

3. *Platelets* are granular fragments, produced by the bone marrow, that enable the body to prevent blood loss. They do this by plugging tiny wounds or helping the blood to clot when the wound is larger. *Hemophilia* is a disease in which the platelets do not function properly, thereby impairing clotting, because the blood lacks a critical protein (AMA, 2003).

How do formed elements affect the viscosity of blood? The higher the concentration of formed elements suspended in the plasma, the thicker the blood.

Plasma

Plasma is a liquid substance that comprises about 55% of our blood. About 90% of plasma is water, and the remainder consists of proteins and other organic and inorganic elements (Holum, 1994; Tortora & Derrickson, 2009). Plasma proteins increase blood thickness. Although the remaining elements in plasma constitute only a small percentage of its volume, they are very important substances. They include hormones, enzymes, and waste products. They also include the nutrients we derive from digestion—vitamins, minerals, simple sugars, amino acids, and fatty materials.

Fatty materials make up the broad class of substances in the blood called **lipids**. Two of these fatty materials are triglycerides and cholesterol (Holum, 1994;

Rhoades & Pflanzer, 1996). T*riglycerides* are the material we commonly think of as fat. Made of glycerol and fatty acids, they are the most abundant lipid in the body. Some of the fatty acids in triglycerides are fully hydrogenated—they cannot take up any more hydrogen—and are called *saturated* for that reason. They are usually solid at room temperature and are mostly derived from animal fat. Other fatty acids are *unsaturated* or *polyunsaturated*. They can take up more hydrogen, are usually liquid at room temperature, and are derived from plants.

Cholesterol is a fatty substance that builds up in patches in artery walls over time and narrows the artery (AMA, 2003). Although the body manufactures most of the cholesterol in the blood, the rest comes from the foods we eat. Eating fats that are highly saturated tends to increase blood cholesterol levels. Let's see why this is a problem.

CARDIOVASCULAR DISORDERS

The accumulation of fatty patches, or plaques, in artery walls is called **atherosclerosis**. These plaques tend to harden. This is a common process by which the diameter and elasticity of arteries is reduced—a condition called **arteriosclerosis** (AMA, 2003). The narrowing and hardening of arteries increase blood pressure. Although arteriosclerosis becomes an increasing problem as adults get older, plaque begins to form early in life. Autopsies on thousands of 15- to 34-year-old American males and females who died of other causes showed that atherosclerosis had begun in all subjects and worsened with age (Strong et al., 1999).

Of the many diseases of the heart and blood vessels, we will describe just a few. One of them is *myocardial infarction*, or "heart attack." Infarction refers to the death of tissue caused by an obstruction in the supply of blood to it. Thus, a myocardial infarction is the death of heart muscle (myocardium) tissue as a result of arterial blockage, usually resulting from a clot in an artery with atherosclerosis (AMA, 2003). Another form of heart disease is *congestive heart failure*, a condition in which an underlying problem, such as severe arteriosclerosis, has reduced the heart's pumping capacity permanently. This condition occurs most frequently in old age. Although its victims can live for years, they are quite disabled. A third form of heart disorder is *angina pectoris*, in which the victim feels strong pain and tightness in the chest because of a brief obstruction in an artery, but little or no damage occurs. Physical exertion or stress often brings an episode of angina.

One disorder of the blood vessels is an *aneurysm*, a bulge in a weakened section of an artery or vein. If the bulge is in a major blood vessel and it ruptures, the person may die (AMA, 2003). Another disorder of the blood vessels—a *stroke*—occurs when the blood supply to a portion of the brain is disrupted by an event in a cerebral blood vessel. This event can be a rupture of an artery, causing a hemorrhage in the brain, or a blockage from a blood clot, called a *thrombosis*. In either case, damage occurs to the brain. The effects of this damage depend on where it occurs and how extensive it is. It may cause paralysis or sensory impairments, for instance, or even death (AHA, 2010). Aneurysms and strokes can result from atherosclerosis and hypertension.

SUMMARY

The cardiovascular system uses the heart to pump blood through an intricate network of blood vessels. The blood's circulation takes it to body cells, where it supplies oxygen and nutrients for metabolism and takes CO_2 and other waste materials away. Cardiac output, blood volume, peripheral resistance, elasticity, and viscosity affect systolic and diastolic blood pressure. Blood consists of plasma and formed elements. Lipids in the blood can lead to atherosclerosis, the deposit of fatty plaque in arteries, and arteriosclerosis, the thickening and hardening of artery walls.

MODULE 6: THE IMMUNE SYSTEM

You may not realize it, but wars are raging inside your body. They happen continuously, every day. Most of the time they are minor skirmishes, and you are unaware of them. When they become major battles, however, you are usually aware something's going on. The "good guys" are the organs and cells that make up your **immune system**.

This system fights to defend the body against "foreign" invaders, such as bacteria and viruses.

The immune system is quite remarkable. Scientists knew little about this intricate and enormously important system until the 1970s. But it is now a major topic of research that has produced new information rapidly about how the immune system functions. We know, for instance, that this system is highly sensitive to invasions by foreign matter and is able to distinguish between "self," or normal body constituents, and "not self"—friend and foe.

ANTIGENS

When the body recognizes something as a "not self" invader, the immune system mobilizes body resources and attacks. Any substance that can trigger an immune response is called an **antigen**. Bacteria and viruses are recognized as invaders by telltale aspects of their protein coats and DNA (Krieg et al., 1995).

What triggers an immune response? Some of the first antigens that come to mind are bacteria, fungi, protozoa, and viruses. *Bacteria* are microorganisms that exist in vast numbers throughout the environment—in rivers and oceans, in the air, on and in plants and animals, and in decaying organic matter. Billions of them may populate just one kilogram of rotting garbage. Because they help in breaking down organic matter into simpler units, their activities are essential to the life and growth of all living things. Some bacteria cause illnesses, such as tuberculosis, scarlet fever, and food poisoning. They do this by growing rapidly and competing with our cells for nutrients and by excreting *toxic*, or poisonous, substances that destroy our cells or impair their metabolic processes (AMA, 2003; Jaret, 1986). Although treatment with antibiotics kills bacteria, these drugs are becoming less effective because they have been overused and bacteria are developing drug-resistant strains.

Fungi are organisms, such as molds and yeasts, that attach to an organic host and absorb nutrients from it. Some of them can cause skin diseases through direct contact, as occurs in ringworm and athlete's foot, and internal diseases by inhaling contaminated air. Other fungi are very beneficial—for example, penicillin is derived from molds. *Protozoa* are one-celled animals that live primarily in water and insects. Drinking water contaminated with protozoa can cause amoebic dysentery, an intestinal illness, and being bitten by an infected mosquito can cause malaria (AMA, 2003; Jaret, 1986).

The tiniest antigens are *viruses*, particles of protein and nucleic acid that are smaller than cells and, strictly speaking, may not even be alive. They consist of genetic information that allows them to reproduce. A virus functions by attaching to a cell, slipping inside, and taking over by issuing its own genetic instructions. The invaded cell abandons its own metabolic activities and becomes a "factory" for making viruses. In short order, enough viruses can be produced to rupture the cell and spread to infect other cells. Viruses can be quite devious, too, developing new strains and lying dormant in the body for periods of time before becoming infectious.

They are responsible for a variety of diseases, including flu, herpes, measles, and polio (AMA, 2003).

The immune system also tends to recognize the tissue of an organ transplant as "not self" and treat it as an antigen. This is what doctors mean when they say that the body "rejected" a transplant. There are two basic ways to encourage transplant acceptance. The first is to select the transplant carefully so that the tissues of the donor and the recipient are closely matched. The closer the genetic relationship between the two people, the better the match is likely to be. Identical twins provide the best match, of course. The second approach uses drugs to suppress parts of the immune system so it won't mobilize and reject the organ. A drawback to this approach is that suppressing immune function can leave the patient susceptible to disease.

For many people, the immune system mounts an attack against normally harmless substances, such as pollen, tree molds, poison ivy, animal dander, and particular foods. These people suffer from *allergies*; the specific substances that trigger their allergic reactions, such as sneezing and skin rashes, are called *allergens*. Most allergic people react to some, but not all, of the known allergens—someone with hay fever may not be allergic to poison ivy, for instance. Being allergic is partly determined by heredity (Hershey et al., 1997; Sarafino, 2000). Some allergies can be reduced by administering regular, small doses of the allergen, usually by injection (Coico & Sunshine, 2009).

 WEB ANIMATION: The Lymphatic and Immune Systems

Access: www.wiley.com/go/global/sarafino. This interactive animation describes the structure and functioning of different parts of the immune system.

THE ORGANS OF THE IMMUNE SYSTEM

The organs of the immune system are located throughout the body (Coico & Sunshine, 2009; Tortora & Derrickson, 2009). These organs are generally referred to as *lymphatic* or *lymphoid* organs because they have a primary role in the development and deployment of **lymphocytes**, specific white blood cells that are the key functionaries or "soldiers" in our body's defense against invasion by foreign matter. The main lymphatic organs include the bone marrow, thymus, lymph nodes and vessels, and spleen.

Lymphocytes originate in *bone marrow*, the soft tissue in the core of all bones in the body. Some of these cells migrate to one of two organs where they mature. One of these organs is the *thymus*, which is an endocrine gland that lies in the chest. The other organ is not known for certain, but it is thought to have the same function in maturing human lymphocytes that a structure called the "bursa" has in birds (Coico & Sunshine, 2009). Most of this processing of lymphocytes occurs before birth and in infancy.

The *lymph nodes* are bean-shaped masses of spongy tissue that are distributed throughout the body. Large clusters of them are found in the neck, armpits, abdomen, and groin. What do they do? Each lymph node contains filters that capture antigens and compartments that provide a home base for lymphocytes and other white blood cells. A network of *lymph vessels* that contains a clear fluid called *lymph* connects the lymph nodes. These vessels ultimately empty into the bloodstream. Although the lymph nodes and vessels play an important role in cleansing body cells of antigens, they can become a liability in some forms of cancer either by becoming infected with cancer or by distributing cancer cells to other parts of the body through the lymph and blood.

Lymphocytes and antigens that enter the blood are carried to the *spleen*, an organ in the upper left side of the person's abdomen. The spleen functions like an enormous lymph node except that blood, rather than lymph, travels through it. The spleen filters out antigens and serves as a home base for white blood cells. It also removes ineffective or worn-out red blood cells from the body.

SOLDIERS OF THE IMMUNE SYSTEM

White blood cells play a key role in the immune system—they serve as soldiers in our counterattack against invading substances in the body. There are two types of white blood cells. Lymphocytes, as we have seen, are one type; phagocytes are the other.

> **Phagocytes** are scavengers that patrol the body and engulf and ingest antigens. They are not choosy. They will eat anything suspicious that they find in the bloodstream, tissues, or lymphatic system. In the lungs, for instance, they consume particles of dust and other pollutants that enter with each breath. They can cleanse lungs that have been blackened with the contaminants of cigarette smoke, provided the smoking stops. Too much cigarette smoking, over too long a time, destroys phagocytes faster than they can be replenished. (Jaret, 1986, p.715)

There are two main types of phagocytes: *macrophages* become attached to tissues and remain there, and *neutrophils* circulate in the blood (Coico & Sunshine, 2009; Tortora & Derrickson, 2009). The fact that phagocytes "are

not choosy" means that they are involved in *nonspecific immunity*—they respond to any kind of antigen.

Lymphocytes react in a more discriminating way, being tailored for attacks against specific antigens. The diagram in Figure A-15 shows that, in addition to the process of nonspecific immunity, there are two types of *specific* immune processes: cell-mediated immunity and antibody-mediated "humoral" immunity. Let's examine these two specific immune processes and how they interrelate.

Cell-mediated immunity operates at the level of the cell. The soldiers in this process are lymphocytes called **T cells**—the name of these white blood cells reflects their having matured in the thymus. T cells are divided into several groups, each with its own important function:

- *Killer T cells* (also called CD8 cells) directly attack and destroy three main targets: transplanted tissue that is recognized as foreign, cancerous cells, and cells of the body that have already been invaded by antigens, such as viruses.

- *Memory T cells* "remember" previous invaders. At the time of an initial infection, such as with mumps, some T cells are imprinted with information for recognizing that specific kind of invader—the virus that causes mumps—in the future. Memory T cells and their offspring circulate in the blood or lymph for long periods of time—sometimes for decades—and enable the body to defend against subsequent invasions more quickly.

- *Delayed-hypersensitivity T cells* have two functions. They are involved in delayed immune reactions, particularly in allergies such as of poison ivy, in which tissue becomes inflamed. They also produce protein substances called *lymphokines* that stimulate other T cells to grow, reproduce, and attack an invader.

- *Helper T cells* (also called CD4 cells) receive reports of invasions from other white blood cells that patrol the body, rush to the spleen and lymph nodes, and stimulate lymphocytes to reproduce and attack. The lymphocytes they stimulate are from both the cell-mediated and the antibody-mediated immunity (also called "humoral" immunity) processes.

- *Suppressor T cells* operate in slowing down or stopping cell-mediated and antibody-mediated immunity processes as an infection diminishes or is conquered. Suppressor and helper T cells serve to regulate cell-mediated and antibody-mediated immune processes.

What is antibody-mediated immunity, and how is it different from the cell-mediated process? **Antibody-mediated immunity** attacks bacteria, fungi, protozoa, and viruses while they are still in body fluids and before they have invaded body cells. Unlike the cell-mediated process of attacking infected cells of the body, the

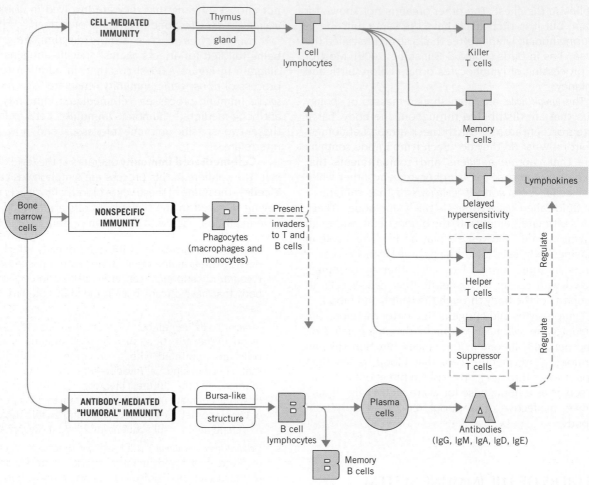

Figure A-15 Components and interrelationships of the immune system. The bone marrow produces two types of white blood cells (leukocytes): *phagocytes* and *lymphocytes*. There are two kinds of lymphocytes: T *cells*, which are processed by the *thymus* gland; and B *cells*, which are processed by an as-yet-unknown *bursa*-like structure (B cells were first discovered in the "bursa of Fabricius" structure of birds). See text for description. (Borysenko, 1984; Braveman, 1987; Coico & Sunshine, 2009; Jaret, 1986; Rhoades & Pflanzer, 1996; Tortora & Derrickson, 2009.)

antibody-mediated approach focuses on the antigens directly. The soldiers in this approach are lymphocytes called **B cells**. Figure A-15 shows that B cells give rise to *plasma cells* that produce antibodies. This process is often induced by helper T cells or inhibited by suppressor T cells.

How are antibodies involved? **Antibodies** are protein molecules called *immunoglobulins* (Ig) that attach to the surface of invaders and accomplish three results. First, they slow down the invader, making it an easier and more attractive target for phagocytes to destroy. Second, they recruit other protein substances that puncture the membrane of an invading microorganism, causing it to burst. Third, they find new invaders and form *memory B cells* that operate in the future like memory T cells. As

you can see, antibodies are like sophisticated weapons in immune system wars. Researchers have identified five classes of antibodies—IgG, IgM, IgA, IgD, and IgE—each with a special function and "territory" in the body. For example, IgA guards the entrances of the body in fluids, such as saliva, tears, and secretions of the respiratory tract. (Go to 💡.)

DEFENDING THE BODY WITH AN IMMUNE RESPONSE

Now that we have seen the soldiers and weaponry of the immune system, let's see how all of this is orchestrated in defending your body. Protection from disease actually

HIGHLIGHT

When Immune Functions are Absent

I can remember reading for the first time many years ago about a child who had to live in a large plastic "bubble" because he was born with virtually no major immune defenses. The condition he had is very rare and is called *severe combined immunodeficiency disease*. He lived in the bubble because it was germ-free—exposure to microorganisms in the general environment would have been fatal. Transplants of healthy bone marrow tissue early in the child's life can cure this disorder now (Coico & Sunshine, 2009). More common inborn immune deficiencies involve the absence of only part of the system and can sometimes be treated with injections.

Having little or no immune defense was almost unheard of prior to the 1970s, and people were not very concerned about immune processes. All that changed in the 1980s as people became aware of the disorder called *acquired immune deficiency syndrome* (AIDS). This disorder is not inborn—it results from an infection when a virus (*human immunodeficiency virus*, or HIV) from an infected person's body fluid, such as blood or semen, contacts the body fluid of an uninfected person. This occurs in three major ways: through sexual activity if the body fluids become exposed to each other, in intravenous drug use if syringes are shared, and from an infected mother to her baby (Tortora & Derrickson, 2009). Receiving contaminated blood in a transfusion was once a major source of the virus, but in many countries close monitoring of hospital blood supplies has sharply reduced this risk.

Although AIDS is a deadly disease, it does not kill directly. It disables or destroys important components of the immune system—such as *helper* T *cells*—and leaves the victim vulnerable to a variety of diseases, such as pneumonia (Tortora & Derrickson, 2009). One of these diseases becomes the actual cause of death. Researchers have made great progress in finding ways to prevent and treat, but not cure, AIDS.

AIDS is a global epidemic: health agencies estimate that in the two decades after the epidemic began in the early 1980s, over 20 million AIDS victims had died (UNAIDS, 2004). Today, over 33 million people are infected with HIV worldwide, and 2 million victims die each year (UNAIDS, 2009). Developing countries have had the vast majority of HIV/AIDS cases, mostly becoming infected through heterosexual contact. But in North America and Europe, infection has occurred mainly through sharing needles when injecting illicit drugs and practicing certain sexual acts, particularly homosexual anal intercourse. Prevention by changing high-risk behavior is essential.

---

involves a series of defenses (Coico & Sunshine, 2009; Jaret, 1986; Tortora & Derrickson, 2009). We will start at the beginning, as the invader tries to enter the body.

Your body's first line of defense is the skin and the mucous membranes that line the respiratory and digestive tracts. The skin serves as a barrier to entry, and mucous membranes are coated with fluids that contain antibodies and other antimicrobial substances. Even though these defenses are highly effective, large numbers of antigens get through, either by eluding the antibodies or by entering a wound in the skin or the mucous membrane. Once an antigen penetrates this barrier, it encounters the second line of defense, which includes nonspecific and specific immune processes. Phagocytes in your blood and tissues attack and consume invading substances of all types. They also have another important function: They present the antigen to B cells and helper T cells, as if to say, "Here's the enemy. Go get 'em!" The B cells respond to this message and to stimulation from helper T cells by giving rise to plasma cells that produce the needed antibodies. The role of the phagocytes is especially important if the antigen is new and the body has no memory B cells for this substance. Antibodies in body fluids attach to microorganisms, thereby aiding the phagocytes and other protein substances that can kill the invaders.

Antigens that manage to get through and invade body cells encounter the third line of defense in which killer T cells destroy the invaded cells. Phagocytes often initiate this process by presenting antigens to T cells, as we have seen. Once again, this is especially important if the antigen is new to the cell-mediated system and the body has no memory T cells for the substance. As the invasion subsides, suppressor T cells slow down the cell-mediated and antibody-mediated immune responses. Memory B and T cells are left in the blood and lymph, ready to initiate the immune response if the same antigen invades the body again.

You may be thinking, "This is a wonderful and complex system that responds when there are antigens in the body, but don't killer T cells also attack cancer cells? Aren't cancer cells basically normal cells that multiply out of control?" Cancer cells have antigens on their surface, and the immune system attacks some but not all of these cells (Coico & Sunshine 2009). One reason why some cancers escape destruction is that they can release substances that suppress the immune response (Acevedo, Tong, & Hartsock, 1995; Mizoguchi et al., 1992). Another possibility is that the antigen is simply not easy for the immune system to recognize. As a result, the immune response may not be strong enough to stop the cells from multiplying wildly. Some researchers are studying ways to treat cancer that are designed to strengthen the patient's own immune processes. In one of these approaches, for example, researchers manufacture antibodies that are sensitive to and seek out a specific type of cancer cell. These approaches are not yet perfected, but they are very promising.

LESS-THAN-OPTIMAL DEFENSES

If our immune systems always functioned optimally, we would become sick much less often. Why and in what ways do our defenses function less than optimally?

Developmental Changes

Immune system functioning changes over the life span, becoming increasingly effective throughout childhood and declining in old age (Coico & Sunshine, 2009; Tortora & Derrickson, 2009). Newborns come into the world with relatively little immune defense. They have only one type of antibody (IgG), for example, which they receive prior to birth from their mothers through the placenta (the filterlike organ that permits the exchange of nutrients and certain other substances between the bloodstreams of the mother and baby). Infants who are breast fed receive antibodies, particularly IgA, in their mother's milk (Ashburn, 1986; Tortora & Derrickson, 2009).

In early infancy, children in technological societies generally begin a regular schedule of inoculation through the use of vaccines. Most vaccines contain dead or disabled disease microorganisms that get the body to initiate an immune response and produce memory lymphocytes, but do not produce the full-blown disease (AMA, 2003). The efficiency and complexity of the immune system develop very rapidly in childhood. As a result, the incidence of illness serious enough to keep children home from school declines with age (Ashburn, 1986).

Throughout adolescence and much of adulthood, the immune system generally functions at a high level. Then, as people approach old age, the effectiveness of the system tends to decline (Braveman, 1987; Tortora & Derrickson, 2009). Although the overall numbers of T cells, B cells, and antibodies circulating in the blood do not decrease, their potency diminishes in old age. Compared with the T cells and B cells of younger adults, those of elderly people respond weakly to antigens and are less likely to generate the needed supply of lymphocytes and antibodies to fight an invasion.

Lifestyles, Stress, and Immune Function

Unhealthful lifestyles, such as smoking cigarettes and being sedentary, have been associated with impaired immune function (Kusaka, Kondou, & Morimoto, 1992). Poor nutrition can also lead to less-than-optimal immune function (Coico & Sunshine, 2009; Braveman, 1987). Diets deficient in vitamins seem to diminish the production of lymphocytes and antibodies, for example.

Many people believe stress and illness often are related—and they are right. Research has confirmed this belief, showing, for instance, that people who experience high levels of stress contract more infectious diseases (Henderson & Baum, 2004). Is there a direct link between stress and immune function? Yes. Kiecolt-Glaser and her colleagues from a variety of disciplines have done research to examine this link. One study of first-year medical students who were scheduled to take a series of highly stressful final examinations assessed important variables in two sessions, 1 month before the finals and 1 month after their last major exam (Kiecolt-Glaser et al., 1984). In the first session, the researchers took a sample of blood from the students and had them fill out questionnaires that assessed their experience of loneliness and stress during the past year. In the second session, only a blood sample was taken. Analyses of the samples revealed that killer-T-cell activity was considerably lower in the second (high stress) blood sample than in the first and among students who scored high on the loneliness and stress questionnaires than for those who scored low. Another study analyzed blood samples of married and separated or divorced women (Kiecolt-Glaser et al., 1987). This study found weaker immune function among married women who reported less marital satisfaction than those who reported greater satisfaction and among the separated or divorced women who refused to accept the fact of the separation or thought excessively about their ex-spouse than those who did not. Studies by other researchers support these results, finding, for example, weaker immune function during bereavement and after experiencing natural disasters (Henderson & Baum, 2004).

Autoimmune Diseases

When your immune system functions optimally, it attacks foreign matter and protects the body. Sometimes this process goes awry, and the immune response is directed at parts of the body it should protect. Several disorders result from this condition—they are called *autoimmune diseases* (AMA, 2003; Coico & Sunshine, 2009). One of these diseases is *rheumatoid arthritis*, in which the immune response is directed against tissues and bones at the joints. This causes swelling and pain and can leave the bones pitted. In *rheumatic fever*, the muscles of the heart are the target, often leaving the heart valves permanently damaged. *Multiple sclerosis* results when the immune system attacks the myelin sheath of neurons. Another autoimmune disease is *systemic lupus erythematosus*, which affects various parts of the body, such as the skin and heart. What causes autoimmune diseases to develop? Evidence indicates that heredity and immune responses to prior infections play important roles.

SUMMARY

The immune system responds to antigens by attacking and eliminating invading substances and microorganisms to protect us from infection and disease. It does this by using white blood cells, including phagocytes and two types of lymphocytes: B cells, which produce antibodies, and T cells. These cells operate in different immune processes: antibody-mediated immunity uses B cells, cell-mediated immunity involves T cells, and nonspecific immunity uses phagocytes. Stress, poor nutrition, and HIV infection impair the effectiveness of the immune system.

KEY TERMS (SEPARATED BY MODULES)

MODULE 1
neurotransmitter
central nervous system
cerebrum
limbic system
thalamus
hypothalamus
cerebellum
brainstem
spinal cord
peripheral nervous system
somatic nervous system

autonomic nervous system
sympathetic nervous system
parasympathetic nervous system

MODULE 2
endocrine system
hormones
pituitary gland
adrenal glands

MODULE 3
digestive system
enzymes
metabolism

MODULE 4
respiratory system

MODULE 5
cardiovascular system
blood pressure
lipids
atherosclerosis
arteriosclerosis

MODULE 6
immune system
antigen
lymphocytes
phagocytes
cell-mediated immunity
T cells
antibody-mediated immunity
B cells
antibodies

GLOSSARY

abstinence-violation effect   A cognitive process whereby a relapse occurs when people feel guilt and reduced self-efficacy if they experience a lapse in efforts to change their behavior.

acquired immune deficiency syndrome (AIDS)   An infectious disease that disables the immune system. Individuals with AIDS are susceptible to a variety of life-threatening diseases.

acupuncture   A pain-control technique in which fine metal needles are inserted under the skin at certain locations and then activated.

acute pain   The discomfort patients experience with temporary medical conditions, lasting less than about 6 months.

adaptation   The changes people undergo in making positive adjustments to circumstances in their lives.

addiction   The condition of physical and psychological dependence on using a substance.

adherence   The degree to which patients follow the medical recommendations of practitioners. Also called *compliance*.

adoption studies   Research with subjects adopted at very early ages, comparing their characteristics with corresponding traits of their adoptive and natural parents to assess the influence of heredity.

adrenal glands   Endocrine glands that secrete several hormones, such as cortisol, adrenaline, and noradrenaline, that are involved in stress reactions.

aerobic exercise   (air-OH-bik) Sustained and energetic physical activity in which the body uses high volumes of oxygen over many minutes.

alarm reaction   The first stage in the general adaptation syndrome when the body's resources are mobilized.

alcoholics   People who drink alcohol heavily and are addicted to it.

allostatic load   (al-o-STAT-ic) The cumulative physiological effect of chronic stress.

Alzheimer's disease   A chronic and progressive brain disorder marked by a loss of cognitive functions, such as memory.

angina pectoris   (an-JEYE-nah, or AN-ji-nah, PEK-to-ris) A condition marked by chest pain that generally results from a brief or incomplete blockage of the blood supply to heart tissue.

anorexia nervosa   (an-or-EX-ee-ah ner-VOE-sah) An eating disorder marked by self-starvation and an extreme and unhealthy loss of weight.

antibodies   Protein molecules created to protect against specific antigens in body fluids.

antibody-mediated immunity   The immune process that employs antibodies to attack antigens while they are still in body fluids and before they have invaded the cells.

antigen   Any substance that can trigger the immune system to respond.

arteriosclerosis   (ar-TEER-ee-o-skleh-ROE-sis) A condition in which fatty patches have accumulated to and hardened on artery walls, thereby reducing the elasticity of these walls.

arthritis   A category of painful and potentially disabling chronic conditions that involve inflammation of the joints.

asthma   A psychophysiological disorder of the respiratory system in which bronchial inflammation and spasms lead to episodes of difficult breathing.

atherosclerosis   (ATH-eh-roe-skleh-ROE-sis) The condition in which fatty patches (plaques) form on artery walls.

autonomic nervous system   A division of the peripheral nervous system that carries messages between the central nervous system and the internal organs. It has two parts: the sympathetic and parasympathetic nervous systems.

aversion strategies   Methods that use unpleasant stimuli to discourage undesirable behaviors.

B cells   Lymphocytes that lead to the formation of antibodies.

behavioral control   A form of personal control involving the ability to reduce the impact of a stressor by taking concrete action.

behavioral medicine   An interdisciplinary field introduced in the early 1970s to study the relationships between behavior and health.

behavioral methods   Psychological techniques that use mainly operant and classical conditioning principles to change behavior.

binge drinking   Consuming five or more alcoholic drinks in a single drinking session, such as during a party.

binge eating   An episode of consuming much more food than most people would in a short period of time.

biofeedback   A process by which individuals can acquire voluntary control over a physiological function by monitoring its status.

biomedical model   The view that illness results from physical causes, such as infection or injury; psychosocial processes are not viewed as causal factors.

biopsychosocial model   The view that health and illness involve the interplay of biological, psychological, and social factors in people's lives.

blood pressure   The force of the blood against the inner walls of the arteries.

body mass index (BMI)   A calculated measure of the ratio of weight to height; people with a BMI of 30 or more are considered obese.

brainstem   The lowest portion of the brain, located at the top of the spinal cord, consisting of the midbrain, reticular system, pons, and medulla.

buffering hypothesis   The view that the health benefits of social support come from its reducing the negative health effects of high stress levels.

bulimia nervosa   (buh-LIM-ee-ah ner-VOE-sah) An eating disorder marked by repeated binge eating, usually followed by purging.

burnout   An emotional and behavioral impairment resulting from exposure to high levels of occupational stress.

cancer   A class of malignant diseases in which cells proliferate in an unrestricted manner, usually forming a tumor.

carbon monoxide   A gas that is a constituent of cigarette smoke.

cardiovascular system   A network of organs that circulates blood to supply oxygen and nutrients to the body's cells and removes wastes and other substances.

catecholamines   (kat-eh-KOL-a-meenz) A class of hormones, including adrenaline and noradrenaline, secreted by the adrenal glands.

cell-mediated immunity   The immune process that operates at the cellular level, using T cells to attack infected cells.

central nervous system   That part of the nervous system consisting of the brain and spinal cord.

cerebellum   (ser-uh-BEL-um) A large portion of the brain that coordinates motor activities and maintains body balance.

cerebrum   (ser-EE-brum) The upper and largest portion of the human brain. It has primary control over motor and mental activity.

chronic diseases   Illnesses that persist and generally get worse over a long period of time.

chronic-intractable-benign pain   Long-term continuous, but variable, discomfort stemming from benign causes.

chronic-progressive pain   Long-term continuous discomfort that worsens as the underlying malignant condition progresses.

chronic-recurrent pain   Long-term repeated and intense episodes of discomfort stemming from benign causes.

classical conditioning   A learning process in which a stimulus gains the ability to elicit a particular response by its repeated pairing with an unconditioned stimulus that already elicits that response.

clinical pain   Any pain symptoms that receive or require professional treatment.

cognitive appraisal   The mental process people use in assessing whether a demand is threatening and what resources are available to meet the demand.

cognitive control   A form of personal control involving the ability to reduce the impact of a stressor by using thought processes.

cognitive methods   Psychological techniques that focus on changing people's feelings and thought processes.

cognitive restructuring   A therapeutic process for replacing thoughts that provoke stress with ones that do not.

cognitive therapy   A cognitive restructuring approach that has clients test hypotheses about maladaptive beliefs they hold about events in their lives.

commonsense models   Cognitive representations people develop regarding specific illnesses.

complementary and alternative medicine   Methods not included in conventional medicine to prevent or treat illnesses: they are complementary if used along with conventional methods and alternative if used instead of them.

compliance   See *adherence*.

conflict theory   An explanation of health-related behavior that includes both rational and emotional factors.

coping   The process by which people try to manage the stress they experience.

coronary heart disease (CHD)   A class of illnesses that result when a narrowing or blockage of the coronary arteries restricts the blood supply to the heart muscle (myocardium).

correlation coefficient   A statistic that reflects the degree and direction of relationship between two variables; it can range from +1.00, through .00, to −1.00.

correlational studies   Nonexperimental research conducted to determine the degree and direction of relationship between variables.

corticosteroids   (cor-ti-koe-STEH-royds) A class of hormones, including cortisol, secreted by the adrenal glands.

cost–benefit ratio   The degree to which an intervention or technique saves more money over time than it costs.

counter-irritation   A technique whereby one pain is reduced by creating another one.

crisis theory   A model describing the factors that affect people's adjustment to having serious illnesses. The theory proposes that coping processes are influenced by three types of factors: illness-related, background and personal, and physical and social environmental.

cross-sectional approach   Method of studying developmental trends by observing different groups of subjects of different ages within a relatively short period of time.

cue exposure   A method to counteract the ability of stimuli linked to substance use to elicit use.

daily hassles   Everyday annoyances or unpleasant events.

depersonalization   A behavioral style of some practitioners that involves treating a patient as if he or she were not there or not a person.

depressants   Drugs that induce relaxation and sleep.

detoxification   The process of getting an addicted individual safely through withdrawal after discontinuing the use of a substance.

digestive system The network of organs that processes ingested food by breaking it down for the body's use and excreting the remains.

direct effects hypothesis The view that the health benefits of social support accrue regardless of whether people experience high or low levels of stress.

distraction A pain management technique in which people divert their focus to nonpain stimuli in the environment.

doctor-centered The behavioral style of some physicians in which interactions with patients are highly controlled by the practitioner and focus on the symptoms or treatment rather than the person.

double blind An experimental procedure whereby neither the subject nor the researcher knows which research treatment the subject is receiving.

emetic drug (eh-MEH-tik) A chemical that induces nausea, for example, when a person drinks alcohol.

emotion-focused coping Approaches people use for managing stress that are aimed at regulating their emotional responses.

endocrine system An array of glands that secrete hormones into the bloodstream.

endogenous opioids (en-DAH-je-nus OH-pee-oydz) Opiate like substances the body produces naturally that reduce the sensation of pain.

enzymes (EN-zymz) Substances that increase the speed of chemical reactions in cells.

epidemic The situation in which the occurrence of a health problem has increased rapidly.

epigenetics The process in which chemicals at DNA affect gene action.

epilepsy A chronic condition of the nervous system that produces recurrent seizures.

evidence-based treatments Interventions or techniques with clear support for efficacy from high-quality research.

experiment A controlled study in which variables are manipulated and observed to assess cause–effect relationships.

extinction In operant conditioning, a process by which a previously reinforced behavior no longer receives reinforcement, making it less likely to occur in the future.

false hopes Nonrational beliefs that positive outcomes of a behavior change are likely.

gate-control theory An explanation of pain perception that proposes that a neural gate in the spinal cord can modulate incoming pain signals. The opening and closing of the gate is influenced by messages that descend from the brain and by the amount of activity in pain fibers and in other peripheral fibers.

general adaptation syndrome (GAS) The sequence of physiological reactions to prolonged and intense stress. The sequence consists of the alarm reaction, the stage of resistance, and the stage of exhaustion.

glycemic load (gleye-SEE-mik) A measure of the speed and intensity of carbohydrate conversion to sugar in the blood.

hallucinogens (ha-LOO-sin-a-jins) Drugs that can produce perceptual and cognitive distortions.

hardiness An array of personality characteristics that enables individuals to withstand stress and not succumb to its negative health effects.

health A positive state of physical, mental, and social well-being that changes in degree over time.

health behavior Any behavior people perform with the intention of promoting or maintaining well-being regardless of the state of their health.

health belief model An explanation of people's health-related behavior based on their perception of the threat of illness or injury and the pros and cons of taking action.

health psychology A field of psychology introduced in the late 1970s to examine the causes of illnesses and to study ways to promote and maintain health, prevent and treat illness, and improve the health care system.

high-density lipoprotein (HDL) A cholesterol-carrying protein that is associated with decreased cholesterol deposits in blood vessels.

hormones Chemical substances secreted by endocrine glands that affect body functions and behavior.

hospice care A philosophy and procedure for enriching the quality of life of terminally ill patients and their families.

hypertension The condition of persistent high blood pressure.

hypochondriasis (hy-poe-kon-DRY-uhsis) The tendency of some individuals to be excessively concerned and vigilant regarding their health and body sensations.

hypothalamus A part of the forebrain that contains control centers for many body functions, such as eating, drinking, and sexual activity.

iatrogenic conditions (eye-a-tro-JEN-ik) Health problems that develop as a result of medical treatment.

illness/wellness continuum A model that describes health and sickness as overlapping concepts that vary in degree, rather than being separate categories.

immune system The organs and structures that protect the body against harmful substances or agents, such as bacteria and viruses.

incidence The number of *new* cases reported during a given period of time, such as the previous year.

infectious diseases Illnesses caused by the body being invaded by microorganisms, such as bacteria or viruses.

inflammatory bowel disease A psychophysiological disorder involving wounds in the large or small intestine.

insulin A hormone secreted by the pancreas that speeds the conversion of blood sugar to fat.

irritable bowel syndrome A digestive system disease with symptoms of pain, diarrhea, and constipation but no evidence of organic disorder.

isokinetic exercise (eye-so-kin-EH-tic) A type of activity that involves exerting muscle force in more than one direction while moving an object.

isometric exercise (eye-so-MET-rik) A type of activity that involves exerting muscle force against an object that does not move.

isotonic exercise (eye-so-TAH-nik) A type of activity that involves exerting most of the muscle force in one direction.

Lamaze training An educational and procedural program for natural childbirth that involves preparation, participation, and minimal medication.

lay referral network An informal system of individuals who provide advice or information regarding a person's symptoms and health.

learned helplessness A condition of apathy or inactivity that results from repeated experiences with unavoidable stress.

leptin A hormone that influences eating and metabolism through its action in the hypothalamus of the brain.

life events Major occurrences in people's lives that require some degree of psychological adjustment.

limbic system A set of structures in the forebrain that seems to play a role in emotional expression.

lipids (LIH-pidz) Fatty materials, such as the cholesterol found in blood.

lipoproteins (LIP-oh-pro-teenz, or LY-po-pro-teenz) Proteins that transport cholesterol in the blood.

locus of control A generalized belief people have about the causes of events in their lives—whether the causes are within or outside their control.

longitudinal approach Method of studying developmental changes in the same subjects by making repeated observations over a long period of time.

low-density lipoprotein (LDL) A cholesterol-carrying protein that is associated with increased cholesterol deposits in blood vessels.

lymphocytes (LIM-foe-sites) Various types of white blood cells that have several important functions in the body's immune response.

McGill Pain Questionnaire (MPQ) A self-report instrument for assessing people's pain.

meta-analysis A statistical technique that combines the results from earlier studies to generate an overview of those findings.

metabolism The chemical reactions of the body's cells that synthesize new cell material, regulate body processes, and create energy.

migraine headache Recurrent head pain that results from the constriction and dilation of blood vessels in the head.

Millon Behavioral Medicine Diagnostic (MBMD) A test that assesses several relevant characteristics of medical patients, such as their basic coping styles and hypochondriacal tendencies.

mind/body problem The issue in psychology and philosophy regarding the relationship between processes and functions of the mind and those of the body.

Minnesota Multiphasic Personality Inventory (MMPI) A lengthy test that assesses a variety of psychological problems, such as hypochondriasis, depression, and hysteria.

modeling Learning by watching the behavior of other people.

morbidity The condition of illness, injury, or disability.

mortality Death, usually with reference to large populations.

motivated reasoning Cognitive process whereby people's desires or preferences influence their decisions about the validity and utility of new information.

motivational interviewing A client-centered counseling style of leading a person to recognizing the need to change a behavior and to become committed to the change.

myocardial infarction (my-oh-KAR-dee-al in-FARK-shun) Damage to the heart muscle (myocardium) that results from severe or prolonged blockage of blood supply to the tissue. Commonly called a *heart attack*.

narcotics Drugs that relieve pain, act as sedatives, and may produce euphoria. These substances are also called *opiates* and usually lead to addiction with continued use.

negative reinforcement A process in which reducing or stopping an undesired stimulus as a consequence of performing a behavior strengthens that behavior.

neurotransmitter A chemical involved in the transmission of impulses across the synapse from one neuron to another.

nicotine A chemical in cigarette smoke that appears to produce physical dependence.

nicotine regulation model An explanation of continued cigarette smoking based on the body's dependence on nicotine.

nociceptors (noe-see-SEP-torz) Afferent nerve endings that respond to pain stimuli in the damaged region of the body.

nonpain imagery A pain management method that involves picturing a mental scene that is unrelated to or incompatible with feeling discomfort.

nosocomial infection (noe-soe-KOE-mee-al) An infection a patient acquires while in the hospital.

obese The weight classification of individuals whose *body mass index* exceeds a value of 30 as a result of excess fat (formerly based on weight more than 20% over the desirable range).

overweight The weight classification of individuals whose *body mass index* exceeds a value of 25 as a result of excess fat (formerly based on weight 10–20% over the desirable range).

pain Sensory and emotional discomfort, usually related to actual or threatened tissue damage.

pain behaviors Characteristic ways people behave when they are in pain.

pain clinics Centers specializing in the treatment of chronic pain.

pain redefinition A pain management technique in which thoughts about pain that arouse a sense of threat are replaced with other thoughts that are more constructive or realistic.

parasympathetic nervous system A division of the autonomic nervous system that helps the body conserve energy and restore the normal body state after arousal.

passive smoking Breathing the smoke in the environment from someone else's cigarette or other smoking product.

patient-centered The behavioral style of some physicians in which their interactions encourage patients to share information and participate in medical decisions.

periaqueductal gray (per-ee-ak-weh-DUK-tal) A region of the midbrain that plays a major role in the perception of and reaction to pain stimuli.

peripheral nervous system The network of nerve fibers that carry messages between the central nervous system and the skin, skeletal muscles, and internal organs. This network has two parts: the somatic and autonomic nervous systems.

personal control The feeling people have that they can make decisions and take action to produce favorable events and avoid unfavorable ones.

personality Cognitive, affective, or behavioral predispositions of people in different situations and over time.

phagocytes (FAG-oh-sites) Certain types of white blood cells that engulf and ingest any kind of invading particles.

physical dependence A state in which the body has become accustomed to the presence of a substance in its physiological functioning.

pituitary gland An endocrine gland that has connections to the brain and secretes hormones that stimulate other endocrine glands to secrete.

placebo An inactive substance or procedure that may cause a change in an individual's behavior or health.

polygraph An electromechanical device that assesses the body's arousal by measuring and recording several physiological indexes, such as blood pressure and respiration rate, simultaneously.

positive reinforcement A process in which adding or introducing a consequence for a behavior strengthens that behavior.

prevalence The total number of cases existing at a given moment in time.

primary appraisal The cognitive process people use in assessing the meaning of an event or situation for their well-being.

primary prevention Actions undertaken to avoid health problems before they occur.

problem drinkers People who are psychologically dependent on alcohol and drink heavily.

problem-focused coping Approaches people use for managing stress aimed at reducing the discrepancy between their resources and the demands of the situation.

problem-solving training A cognitive approach in stress reduction that teaches clients strategies to address life problems.

progressive muscle relaxation A stress reduction technique in which people are trained to alternate between tightening and relaxing specific muscle groups.

prospective approach A research strategy whereby characteristics of subjects are measured and later examined for their relationships to future conditions, such as health problems.

psychological dependence A state in which a person feels compelled to use a substance for the pleasant effect it produces.

psychoneuroimmunology (psy-ko-noo-roe-ih-myu-NOL-oh-jee) A field of study focusing on relationships between psychosocial processes and nervous, endocrine, and immune system functioning.

psychophysiological disorders Physical symptoms or illnesses resulting from some combination of psychosocial and physiological processes.

Psychosocial Adjustment to Illness Scale (PAIS) A test of several psychosocial aspects of a patient's life that are related to adjustment to medical illness.

psychosomatic medicine A field introduced in the 1930s to study the relationships between people's symptoms of illness and their emotions.

punishment A process by which a consequence of an operant behavior suppresses that response.

quality of life Individuals' appraisals of the degree to which their lives contain features that they find satisfying or meaningful.

quasi-experimental studies Nonexperimental research in which subjects are categorized or separated into two or more groups on the basis of existing characteristics and then compared regarding other variables.

rational nonadherence Noncompliance with medical regimens for valid, but not necessarily medically beneficial, reasons.

reactance People's angry responses to restrictions on their freedom of action or choice.

reactivity The physiological component of the response to stress.

referred pain The experience of discomfort as coming from an area of the body other than where the injury exists.

reinforcement A process whereby a consequence of an operant response strengthens or maintains that behavior.

relapse Regressing to the full-blown pattern of an unwanted behavior after beginning to change it.

relapse prevention method A self-management program to help maintain improved behavior by teaching the person how to identify and deal effectively with situations that tend to lead to relapses.

respiratory system A network of organs that supply oxygen for metabolism and expel carbon dioxide.

retrospective approach A research strategy whereby the histories of subjects are examined for their relationships to recent conditions, such as health problems.

risk factors   Characteristics or conditions that occur more often among individuals who develop particular diseases or injuries than among those who do not.

secondary appraisal   The cognitive process people use in assessing the resources they have to meet demands.

secondary prevention   Actions undertaken to identify or treat a health problem early with the aim of arresting or reversing the condition.

self-efficacy   People's belief that they can succeed at something they want to do.

self-management   Methods used in helping people gain control over the conditions in their environment that encourage undesirable behaviors.

separation distress   Emotional upset often shown by infants and young children when separated from their primary caretakers, typically their parents.

set-point theory   An explanation of weight regulation that proposes that each person has a "set" physiologically based weight level that the body strives to maintain.

social support   The perceived comfort, caring, esteem, or help an individual receives from other people or groups.

sociocultural   Relating to or involving social and cultural features or processes.

somatic nervous system   A division of the peripheral nervous system that transmits sensory and motor impulses.

spinal cord   The major neural pathway that carries impulses between the brain and the peripheral nervous system.

spinal cord injury   Neurological damage in the spine that impairs motor and sensory function.

stage of exhaustion   The third stage in the general adaptation syndrome, when the body's energy reserves are severely depleted.

stage of resistance   The second stage in the general adaptation syndrome, when the body tries to adapt to the stressor.

stages of change model   A theory of intentional behavior that describes people's readiness to change with five potential stages: precontemplation, contemplation, preparation, action, and maintenance.

stimulants   Drugs that activate the nervous system, producing physiological and psychological arousal.

stimulation-produced analgesia (SPA)   A phenomenon whereby stimulation to the brainstem causes insensitivity to pain.

strain   The psychological and physiological response to a stressor.

stress   The condition that results when person-environment transactions lead the individual to perceive a discrepancy between the demands of a situation and his or her resources.

stress-inoculation training   A cognitive-behavioral approach for stress management that teaches people a variety of skills for alleviating stress and achieving personal goals.

stress management   Program of behavioral and cognitive methods to reduce psychological and physical strain from stress.

stressors   Events or circumstances a person perceives as threatening or harmful.

stroke   A condition involving brain damage that results from a disruption in the blood supply to that area of the brain.

substance abuse   The prolonged overuse of a substance, involving a clear pattern of pathological use and heightened social and occupational problems.

sympathetic nervous system   A division of the autonomic nervous system that enables the body to mobilize and expend energy during physical and emotional arousal.

system   A continuously changing entity that consists of constantly interrelated components.

systematic desensitization   A classical conditioning technique for reducing fear or anxiety by replacing it with a calm response.

tars   Tiny particles in cigarette smoke.

T cells   A class of lymphocytes; some attack antigens directly, and some work to regulate other immune functions.

temperaments   Basic personality characteristics or dispositions that individuals show right from birth, allowing many of them to be classified broadly as "easy" or "difficult."

tension-type headache   Recurrent head pain that results from persistent muscle tension in the head and neck. Also called *muscle-contraction* headache.

tertiary prevention   Actions undertaken to contain or slow the progress of damage from a serious or established health problem.

thalamus   A structure in the forebrain that serves as a relay station for sensory impulses to and commands from the cerebrum.

theory   A tentative explanation of phenomena.

theory of planned behavior   An explanation of people's health-related behavior. Their behavior depends on their intention, which is based on their attitudes regarding the behavior and beliefs about the subjective norm and behavioral control.

time management   Methods for managing stress that involve organizing one's time.

tolerance   A gradual decrease in the body's response to a drug, thereby requiring larger and larger doses to achieve the same effect.

transactions   The continuous interplay and adjustments of the person and environment.

transcutaneous electrical nerve stimulation (TENS)   (tranz-kyu-TAIN-ee-us) A counter-irritation pain control technique that involves electrically stimulating an area near where the patient feels pain.

treatment delay   The elapsed time between noticing a symptom and getting medical care.

twin studies   Research to assess the influence of heredity in determining a characteristic by focusing on differences between identical and fraternal twins.

type 1 diabetes   The health problem of having chronically elevated blood sugar levels because the pancreas produces little or no insulin. People with type 1 diabetes typically require daily insulin supplements. Formerly called *insulin-dependent diabetes mellitus* (IDDM).

type 2 diabetes   The health problem of having chronically elevated blood sugar levels even though the pancreas does produce at least some insulin. Most people with type 2 diabetes can manage their conditions without insulin supplements. Formerly called *non-insulin-dependent diabetes mellitus* (NIDDM).

Type A behavior pattern   A behavioral or emotional style characterized by high levels of competitiveness, time urgency, and anger or hostility.

Type B behavior pattern   A behavioral or emotional style characterized by low levels of competitiveness, time urgency, and anger or hostility.

ulcers   A psychophysiological disorder involving wounds to the stomach or upper section of the small intestine.

variable   A measurable characteristic of people, objects, or events that may change in quantity or quality.

willingness   A factor that affects health-related behavior: the more disposed or open people are toward engaging in a specific unplanned risky behavior, the more likely they are to do so when the opportunity arises.

withdrawal   Physical and psychological symptoms that occur when people stop taking a substance on which they have become dependent.

REFERENCES*

AAFA (Asthma and Allergy Foundation of America) (2010). *Asthma facts and figures*. Retrieved (1-10-2010) from http://www.aafa.org.

ABOA-EBOULÉ, C., BRISSON, C., MAUNSELL, E., MÂSSE, B., BOURBONNAIS, R., et al. (2007). Job strain and risk of acute recurrent coronary heart disease events. *Journal of the American Medical Association, 298,* 1652–1660.

ABRAHAM, C., & MICHIE, S. (2008). A taxonomy of behavior change techniques used in interventions. *Health Psychology, 27,* 379–397.

ABRAHM, J. L. (2003). Update in palliative medicine and end-of-life care. *Annual Review of Medicine, 54,* 53–72.

ABRAMS, K. K., ALLEN, L., GRAY, J. J. (1993). Disordered eating attitudes and behaviors, psychological adjustment, and ethnic identity: A comparison of black and white female college students. *International Journal of Eating Disorders, 14,* 49–57.

ABRAMSON, L. Y., SELIGMAN, M. E. P., & TEASDALE, J. D. (1978). Learned helplessness in humans: Critique and reformulation. *Journal of Abnormal Psychology, 87,* 49–74.

ABS (Australian Bureau of Statistics) (2006). *National Health Survey,* 2004–05. Retrieved (2-9-2007) from http://www.abs.gov.au/ausstats.

ACCARDI, M. C., & MILLING, L. S. (2009). The effectiveness for reducing procedure-related pain in children and adolescents: A comprehensive methodological review. *Journal of Behavioral Medicine, 32,* 328–339.

ACEVEDO, H. F., TONG, J. Y., & HARTSOCK, R. J. (1995). Human chorionic gonadotropin-beta subunit gene expression in cultured human fetal cells of different types and origins. *Cancer, 76,* 1467–1475.

ACHTERBERG-LAWLIS, J. (1988). Musculoskeletal disorders. In E. A. BLECHMAN & K. D. BROWNELL (Eds.), *Handbook of behavioral medicine for women* (pp. 222–235). New York: Pergamon.

ACS (American Cancer Society) (1989). *Cancer facts and figures—1989.* Atlanta: Author.

ACS (American Cancer Society) (2006). *Cancer facts and figures—2006.* Retrieved (12-3-2006) from http://www.cancer.org.

ACS (American Cancer Society) (2009). *Cancer facts and figures—2009.* Retrieved (1-5-2009) from http://www.cancer.org.

ADA (American Diabetes Association) (2006). *All about diabetes; Complications of diabetes in the United States; Diabetes symptoms; Total prevalence of diabetes and pre-diabetes.* Retrieved (12-6-2006) from http://www.diabetes.org.

ADAMS, A., OCKENE, J. K., WHEELER, E. V., & HURLEY, T. G. (1998). Alcohol counseling: Physicians will do it. *Journal of General Internal Medicine, 13,* 692–698.

ADAMS, J. E., & LINDEMANN, E. (1974). Coping with long-term disability. In G. V. COELHO, D. A. HAMBURG, & J. E. ADAMS (Eds.), *Coping and adaptation* (pp. 127–138). New York: Basic Books.

ADER, R. (1997). The role of conditioning in pharmacotherapy. In A. HARRINGTON (Ed.), *The placebo effect* (pp. 138–165). Cambridge: Harvard University Press.

ADER, R., & COHEN, N. (1975). Behaviorally conditioned immunosuppression. *Psychosomatic Medicine, 37,* 333–340.

ADER, R., & COHEN, N. (1985). CNS-immune system interactions: Conditioning phenomena. *Behavioral and Brain Sciences, 8,* 379–395.

ADESSO, V. J. (1985). Cognitive factors in alcohol and drug use. In M. GALIZIO & S. A. MAISTO (Eds.), *Determinants of substance abuse: Biological, psychological, and environmental factors* (pp. 179–208). New York: Plenum.

ADLER, N. E. (2004). Socioeconomic status and health. In A. J. CHRISTENSEN, R. MARTIN, & J. M. SMYTH (Eds.), *Encyclopedia of health psychology* (pp. 287–289). New York: Kluwer.

ADLER, N. E. & REHKOPF, D. H. (2008). U.S. disparities in health: Descriptions, causes, and mechanisms. *Annual Review of Public Health, 29,* 235–52.

ADLER, N. E., & STONE, G. C. (1979). Social science perspectives on the health system. In G. C. STONE, F. COHEN, & N. E. ADLER (Eds.), *Health psychology—A handbook* (pp. 19–46). San Francisco: Jossey-Bass.

AF (Arthritis Foundation) (2006). *Disease center: Facts about arthritis, rheumatoid arthritis, osteoarthritis, fibromyalgia, and gout.* Retrieved (12-6-2006) from http://www.arthritis.org.

AFFLECK, G., TENNEN, H., PFEIFFER, C., & FIFIELD, J. (1987). Appraisals of control and predictability in adapting to a chronic disease. *Journal of Personality and Social Psychology, 53,* 273–279.

AFFLECK, G., TENNEN, H., URROWS, S., & HIGGINS, P. (1991). Individual differences in the day-to-day experience of chronic pain: A prospective daily study of rheumatoid arthritis patients. *Health Psychology, 10,* 419–426.

AFFLECK, G., TENNEN, H., URROWS, S., HIGGINS, P., ABELES, M., et al. (1998). Fibromyalgia and women's pursuit of personal goals: A daily process analysis. *Health Psychology, 17,* 40–47.

AGOSTI, J. M., SPRENGER, J. D., LUM, L. G., WITHERSPOON, R. P., FISHER, L. D., et al. (1988). Transfer of allergen-specific IgE-mediated hypersensitivity with allogenic bone marrow

---

*Authorship for references with more than six authors is cited with the format: first five authors et al.

transplantation. *New England Journal of Medicine*, 319, 1623–1628.

AGRAWAL, A., & LYNSKEY, M. T. (2008). Are there genetic influences on addiction: Evidence from family, adoption and twin studies. *Addiction*, 103, 1069–1081.

AGRAWAL, A., SARTOR, C., PERGADIA, M. L., HUIZINK, A. C., & LYNSKEY, M. T. (2008). Correlates of smoking cessation in a nationally representative sample of U.S. adults. *Addictive Behaviors*, 33, 1223–1226.

AHA (American Heart Association) (1995). *Heart and stroke facts: 1996 statistical supplement*. Dallas, TX: Author.

AHA (American Heart Association) (2006). *Heart and stroke encyclopedia*. Retrieved (12-6-2006) from http://www.americanheart.org.

AHA (American Heart Association) (2010). *Heart and stroke encyclopedia*. Retrieved (1-4-2010) from http://www.americanheart.org.

AHN, A. C., NGO-METZGER, Q., LEGEDZA, A. T. R., MASSAGLI, M. P., CLARRIDGE, B. R., & PHILLIPS, R. S. (2006). Complementary and alternative medical therapy use among Chinese and Vietnamese Americans: Prevalence, associated factors, and effects of patient-clinician communication. *American Journal of Public Health*, 96, 647–653.

AIKEN, L. H. (1983). Nurses. In D. MECHANIC (Ed.), *Handbook of health, health care, and the health professions* (pp. 407–431). New York: Free Press.

AIKEN, L. S., GEREND, M. A., & JACKSON, K. M. (2001). Subjective risk and health protective behavior: Cancer screening and cancer prevention. In A. BAUM, T. A. REVENSON, & J. E. SINGER (Eds.), *Handbook of health psychology* (pp. 727–746). Mahwah, NJ: Erlbaum.

AIKENS, K. S., AIKENS, J. E., WALLANDER, J. L., & HUNT, S. (1997). Daily activity level buffers stress-glycemia associations in older sedentary NIDDM patients. *Journal of Behavioral Medicine*, 20, 379–390.

AINSWORTH, M. D. S. (1973). The development of infant-mother attachment. In B. M. CALDWELL & H. N. RICCIUTI (Eds.), *Review of child development research* (Vol. 3, pp. 1–94). Chicago: University of Chicago Press.

AINSWORTH, M. D. S. (1979). Infant-mother attachment. *American Psychologist*, 34, 932–937.

AJZEN, I. (1985). From intentions to actions: A theory of planned behavior. In J. KUHL & J. BECKMAN (Eds.), *Action control: From cognition to behavior* (pp. 11–39). New York: Springer Verlag.

AJZEN, I., & FISHBEIN, M. (1980). *Understanding attitudes and predicting social behavior*. Englewood Cliffs, NJ: Prentice Hall.

AKECHI, T., OKUYAMA, T., ONISHI, J., MORITA, T., & FURUKAWA, T. A. (2008). Psychotherapy for depression among incurable cancer patients. *Cochrane Database of Systematic Reviews*, Issue 2. Retrieved (1-30-2010) from http://www.the cochranelibrary.com. DOI:10.1002/14651858.CD005537.pub2.

AKIL, H., MAYER, D. J., & LIEBESKIND, J. C. (1976). Antagonism of stimulation-produced analgesia by naloxone, a narcotic antagonist. *Science*, 191, 961–962.

AKINBAMI, L. J., & SCHOENDORF, K. C. (2002). Trends in childhood asthma: Prevalence, health care utilization, and mortality. *Pediatrics*, 110, 315–322.

ALA (American Lung Association) (2006). *Fact sheets: Asthma in adults, Asthma & children, and Chronic obstructive pulmonary disease* (COPD). Retrieved (5-11-2004) from http://www.lungusa.org.

ALA (American Lung Association) (2010). *Understanding COPD*. Retrieved (3-29-2010) from http://www.lungusa.org.

AL'ABSI, M., WITTMERS, L. E., ELLESTAD, D., NORDEHN, G., KIM, S. W., et al. (2004). Sex differences in pain and hypothalamic-pituitary-adrenocortical responses to opioid blockade. *Psychosomatic Medicine*, 66, 198–206.

ALBARRACÍN, D., GILLETTE, J. C., EARL, A. N., GLASMAN, L. R., DURANTINI, M. R., & HO, M.-H. (2005). A test of major assumptions about behavior change: A comprehensive look at the effects of passive and active HIV-prevention interventions since the beginning of the epidemic. *Psychological Bulletin*, 131, 856–897.

ALBARRACÍN, D., MCNATT, P. S., KLEIN, C. T. F., HO, R. M., MITCHELL, A. L., & KUMKALE, G. T. (2003). Persuasive communications to change actions: An analysis of behavioral and cognitive impact in HIV prevention. *Health Psychology*, 22, 166–177.

ALBERT, C. M., MITTLEMAN, M. A., CHAE, C. U., LEE, I.-M., HENNEKENS, C. H., & MANSON, J. E. (2004). Triggering of sudden death from cardiac causes by vigorous exertion. *New England Journal of Medicine*, 343, 1355–1361.

ALDANA, S. G. (2001). Financial impact of health promotion programs: A comprehensive review of the literature. *American Journal of Health Promotion*, 15, 296–320.

ALDERMAN, M. H. (1984). Worksite treatment of hypertension. In J. D. MATARAZZO, S. M. WEISS, J. A. HERD, N. E. MILLER, & S. M. WEISS (Eds.), *Behavioral health: A handbook of health enhancement and disease prevention* (pp. 862–869). New York: Wiley.

ALDWIN, C. M., & BRUSTROM, J. (1997). Theories of coping with chronic stress: Illustrations from the health psychology and aging literatures. In B. H. GOTTLIEB (Ed.), *Coping with chronic stress* (pp. 75–103). New York: Plenum.

ALEXANDER, F. (1950). *Psychosomatic medicine: Its principles and applications*. New York: Norton.

ALLEN, K., BLASCOVICH, J., MENDES, W. B. (2002). Cardiovascular reactivity and the presence of pets, friends, and spouses: The truth about cats and dogs. *Psychosomatic Medicine*, 64, 727–739.

ALLEN, L., & ZIGLER, E. (1986). Psychosocial adjustment of seriously ill children. *Journal of the American Academy of Child Psychiatry*, 25, 708–712.

ALLEN, S. S., HATSUKAMI, D., BRINTNELL, D. M., & BADE, T. (2005). Effect of nicotine replacement therapy on post-cessation weight gain and nutrient intake: A randomized controlled trial of postmenopausal female smokers. *Addictive Behaviors*, 30, 1273–1280.

ALPERT, B., FIELD, T., GOLDSTEIN, S., & PERRY, S. (1990). Aerobics enhances cardiovascular fitness and agility in preschoolers. *Health Psychology*, 9, 48–56.

ALTERMAN, A. I., GARITI, P., & MULVANEY, F. (2001). Short- and long-term smoking cessation for three levels of intensity of behavioral treatment. *Psychology of Addictive Behaviors*, 15, 261–264.

ALTMAN, D. G., WHEELIS, A. Y., MCFARLANE, M., LEE, H., & FORTMANN, S. P. (1999). The relationship between tobacco access and use among adolescents: A four community study. *Social Science & Medicine*, 48, 759–775.

ALVAREZ, M. E., JAKHMOLA, P., PAINTER, T., TAILLEPIERRE, J. D., ROMAGUERA, R. A., et al. (2009). Summary of comments and recommendation from the CDC consultation on the HIF/AID epidemic and prevention in the Hispanic/Latino community. *AIDS Education and Prevention*, 21(Suppl. B), 7–18.

AMA (American Medical Association) (2003). *American Medical Association complete medical encyclopedia*. New York: Random House.

American Psychiatric Association (2000). *Diagnostic and statistical manual of mental disorders* (4th ed., revised). Washington, DC: Author.

AMES, B. N., & GOLD, L. S. (1990). Too many rodent carcinogens: Mitogenesis increases mutogenesis. *Science*, 249, 970–971.

AMORIM ADEGBOYE, A. R., LINNE, Y. M., & LOURENCO, P. M. (2008). Diet or exercise, or both, for weight reduction in women after childbirth. *Cochrane Database of Systematic Reviews*, Issue 3. Retrieved (1-30-2010) from http://www.thecochranelibrary.com. DOI:10.1002/14651858.CD005627.pub2

AMOS, C. I., HUNTER, S. M., ZINKGRAF, S. A., MINER, M. H., & BERENSON, G. S. (1987). Characterization of a comprehensive Type A measure for children in a biracial community: The Bogalusa Heart Study. *Journal of Behavioral Medicine*, 10, 425–439.

ANASTASI, A. (1982). *Psychological testing* (5th ed.). New York: Macmillan.

ANDERSEN, B. L., FARRAR, W. B., GOLDEN-KREUTZ, D., KUTZ, L. A., MACCALLUM, R., et al. (1998). Stress and immune responses after surgical treatment for regional breast cancer. *Journal of the American Cancer Institute*, 90, 30–36.

ANDERSEN, B. L., GOLDEN-KREUTZ, D. M., & DILILLO, V. (2001). Cancer. In A. BAUM, T. A. REVENSON, & J. E. SINGER (Eds.), *Handbook of health psychology* (pp. 709–725). Mahwah, NJ: Erlbaum.

ANDERSEN, B. L., SHELBY, R. A., & GOLDEN-KREUTZ, D. M. (2007). RCT of a psychological intervention for patients with cancer: I. Mechanisms of change. *Journal of Consulting and Clinical Psychology*, 75, 927–938.

ANDERSEN, B. L., WOODS, X. A., & COPELAND, L. J. (1997). Sexual self-schema and sexual morbidity among gynecological cancer survivors. *Journal of Consulting and Clinical Psychology*, 65, 221–229.

ANDERSEN, B. L., YANG, H., FARRAR, W., GOLDEN-KREUTZ, D., EMERY, C., et al. (2008). Psychologic intervention improves survival for breast cancer patients: A randomized clinical trial. *Cancer*, 113, 3450–3458.

ANDERSEN, M. R., BOWEN, D. J., MOREA, J., STEIN, K. D., & BAKER, F. (2009). Involvement in decision-making and breast cancer survivor quality of life. *Health Psychology*, 28, 29–37.

ANDERSEN, R. E., CRESPO, C. J., BARTLETT, S. J., CHESKIN, L. J., & PRATT, M. (1998). Relationship of physical activity and television watching with body weight and level of fatness among children: Results from the Third National Health and Nutrition Survey. *Journal of the American Medical Association*, 279, 938–942.

ANDERSEN, R. E., WADDEN, T. A., BARTLETT, S. J., ZEMEL, B., VERDE, T. J., & FRANCKOWIAK, S. C. (1999). Effects of lifestyle activity vs. structured aerobic exercise in obese women: A randomized trial. *Journal of the American Medical Association*, 281, 335–340.

ANDERSON, B. J., AUSLANDER, W. F., JUNG, K. C., MILLER, J. P., & SANTIAGO, J. V. (1990). Assessing family sharing of diabetes responsibilities. *Journal of Pediatric Psychology*, 15, 477–492.

ANDERSON, B. J., & BRACKETT, J. (2005). Diabetes in children. In F. J. SNOEK & T. C. SKINNER (Eds.), *Psychology in diabetes care* (2nd ed., pp. 1–25). Chichester: Wiley.

ANDERSON, E. A. (1987). Preoperative preparation for cardiac surgery facilitates recovery, reduces psychological distress, and reduces the incidence of acute postoperative hypertension. *Journal of Consulting and Clinical Psychology*, 55, 513–520.

ANDERSON, E. S., WINETT, R. A., & WOJCIK, J. R. (2007). Self-regulation, self-efficacy, outcome expectations, and social support: Social cognitive theory and nutrition behavior. *Annals of Behavioral Medicine*, 34, 304–312.

ANDERSON, E. S., WOJCIK, J. R., WINETT, R. A., & WILLIAMS, D. M. (2006). Social–cognitive determinants of physical activity: The influence of social support, self-efficacy, outcome expectations, and self-regulation among participants in a church-based health promotion study. *Health Psychology*, 25, 510–520.

ANDERSON, K. O., BRADLEY, L. A., YOUNG, L. D., MCDANIEL, L. K., & WISE, C. M. (1985). Rheumatoid arthritis: Review of psychological factors related to etiology, effects, and treatment. *Psychological Bulletin*, 98, 358–387.

ANDERSON, K. O., & MASUR, F. T. (1983). Psychological preparation for invasive medical and dental procedures. *Journal of Behavioral Medicine*, 6, 1–40.

ANDERSON, L. A., JANES, G. R., & JENKINS, C. (1998). Implementing preventive services: To what extent can we change provider performance in ambulatory care? A review of the screening, immunization, and counseling literature. *Annals of Behavioral Medicine*, 20, 161–167.

ANDERSON, N. B., & ARMSTEAD, C. A. (1995). Toward understanding the association of socioeconomic status and health: A new challenge for the biopsychosocial approach. *Psychosomatic Medicine*, 57, 213–225.

ANDERSON, O. W., & GEVITZ, N. (1983). The general hospital: A social and historical perspective. In D. MECHANIC (Ed.), *Handbook of health, health care, and the health professions* (pp. 305–317). New York: Free Press.

ANDERSON, S. E., COHEN, P., NAUMOVA, E. N., JAQUES, P. F., & MUST, A. (2007). Adolescent obesity and risk for subsequent major depressive disorder: Prospective evidence. *Psychosomatic Medicine, 69,* 740–747.

ANDERSSON, G. B. J., LUCENTE, T., DAVIS, A. M., KAPPLER, R. E., LIPTON, J. A., & LEURGANS, S. (1999). A comparison of osteopathic spinal manipulation with standard care for patients with low back pain. *New England Journal of Medicine, 341,* 1426–1431.

ANDRASIK, F. (1986). Relaxation and biofeedback for chronic headaches. In A. D. HOLZMAN & D. C. TURK (Eds.), *Pain management: A handbook of psychological treatment approaches* (pp. 213–239). New York: Pergamon.

ANDRASIK, F., BLAKE, D. D., & MCCARRAN, M. S. (1986). A biobehavioral analysis of pediatric headache. In N. A. KRASNEGOR, J. D. ARASTEH, & M. F. CATALDO (Eds.), *Child health behavior: A behavioral pediatrics perspective* (pp. 394–434). New York: Wiley.

ANDRYKOWSKI, M. A. (1990). The role of anxiety in the development of anticipatory nausea in cancer chemotherapy: A review and synthesis. *Psychosomatic Medicine, 52,* 458–475.

ANG, D. D., CHOI, H, KROENKE, K., & WOLFE, F. (2005). Comorbid depression is an independent risk factor for mortality in patients with rheumatoid arthritis. *Journal of Rheumatology, 32,* 1013–1019.

ANSTEY, K. J., JORM, A. F., RÉGLADE-MESLIN, D., MALLER, J., KUMAR, R., et al. (2006). Weekly alcohol consumption, brain atrophy, and white matter hyperintensities in a community-based sample aged 60 to 64 years. *Psychosomatic Medicine, 68,* 778–785.

ANTONI, M. H., BAGGETT, L., IRONSON, G., LAPERRIERE, A., AUGUST, S., et al. (1991). Cognitive-behavioral stress management intervention buffers distress responses and immunologic changes following notification of HIV-1 seropositivity. *Journal of Consulting and Clinical Psychology, 59,* 906–915.

ANTONI, M. H., CARRICO, A. W., DURÁN, R. E., SPITZER, S., PENEDO, P., et al. (2006). Randomized clinical trial of cognitive behavioral stress management on human immunodeficiency virus viral load in gay men treated with highly active antiretroviral therapy. *Psychosomatic Medicine, 68,* 143–151.

ANTONI, M. H., CRUESS, D. G., CRUESS, S., LUTGENDORF, S., KUMAR, M., et al. (2000). Cognitive-behavioral stress management intervention effects on anxiety, 24-hr urinary norepinephrine output, and T-cytotoxic/suppressor cells over time among symptomatic HIV-infected gay men. *Journal of Consulting and Clinical Psychology, 68,* 31–45.

ANTONI, M. H., LECHNER, S., DIAZ, A., VARGAS, S., HOLLEY, H., et al. (2009). Cognitive behavioral stress management effects on psychosocial and physiological adaptation in women undergoing treatment for breast cancer. *Brain, Behavior, and Immunity, 23,* 580–591.

ANTONI, M. H., LECHNER, S. C., KAZI, A., WIMBERLY, S. R., SIFRE, T., et al. (2006). How stress management improves quality of life after treatment for breast cancer. *Journal of Consulting and Clinical Psychology, 74,* 1143–1152.

ANTONI, M. H., LEHMAN, J. M., KILBOURN, K. M., BOYERS, A. E., CULVER, J. L., et al. (2001). Cognitive-behavioral stress management intervention decreases the prevalence of depression and enhances benefit finding among women under treatment for early-stage breast cancer. *Health Psychology, 20,* 20–32.

ANTONI, M. H., LUTGENDORF, S., COLE, S., DHABHAR, F., SEPHTON, S., et al. (2006). The influence of biobehavioral factors on tumor biology: Pathways and mechanisms. *Nature Reviews Cancer, 6,* 240–248.

ANTONI, M. H., SCHNEIDERMAN, N., FLETCHER, M. A., GOLDSTEIN, D. A., IRONSON, G., & LAPERRIERE, A. (1990). Psychoneuroimmunology and HIV-1. *Journal of Consulting and Clinical Psychology, 58,* 38–49.

ANTONOVSKY, A. (1979). *Health, stress, and coping.* San Francisco: Jossey-Bass.

ANTONOVSKY, A. (1987). *Unraveling the mystery of health: How people manage stress and stay well.* San Francisco: Jossey-Bass.

ANTONOVSKY, A., & HARTMAN, H. (1974). Delay in the detection of cancer: A review of the literature. *Health Education Monographs, 2,* 98–128.

ANTONUCCI, T. C. (1985). Personal characteristics, social support, and social behavior. In R. H. BINSTOCK & E. SHANAS (Eds.), *Handbook of aging and the social sciences* (2nd ed., pp. 94–128). New York: Van Nostrand-Reinhold.

ANTONUCCIO, D. O., & LICHTENSTEIN, E. (1980). Peer modeling influences on smoking behavior of heavy and light smokers. *Addictive Behaviors, 5,* 299–306.

APA (American Psychological Association: Practice Directorate) (1998). *Practicing psychology in hospitals and other health care facilities.* Washington, DC: Author.

ARMITAGE, C. J. (2005). Can the theory of planned behavior predict the maintenance of physical activity? *Health Psychology, 24,* 235–245.

ARMITAGE, C. J. (2006). Evidence that implementation intentions promote transitions between the stages of change. *Journal of Consulting and Clinical Psychology, 74,* 141–151.

ARMITAGE, C. J. (2008). A volitional help sheet to encourage smoking cessation: A randomized exploratory trial. *Health Psychology, 27,* 557–566.

ARMITAGE, C. J. (2009). Is there utility in the transtheoretical model? *British Journal of Health Psychology, 14,* 195–210.

ARMSTRONG, C. A., SALLIS, J. F., HOVELL, M. F., & HOFSTETTER, C. R. (1992, March). *Predicting exercise adoption: A stages of change analysis.* Paper presented at the meeting of the Society of Behavioral Medicine, New York.

ASHBURN, S. S. (1986). Biophysical development of the toddler and the preschooler. In C. S. SCHUSTER & S. S. ASHBURN (Eds.), *The process of human development: A holistic life-span approach* (2nd ed., pp. 195–214). Boston: Little, Brown.

ASHLEY, M. J., & RANKIN, J. G. (1988). A public health approach to the prevention of alcohol-related health problems. *Annual Review of Public Health, 9,* 233–271.

ASHTON, C. M., SOUCHEK, J., PETERSON, N., J., MENKE, T. J., COLLINS, T. C., et al. (2003). Hospital use and survival among Veterans Affairs beneficiaries. *New England Journal of Medicine, 349,* 1637–1646.

ASHTON, H., & STEPNEY, R. (1982). *Smoking: Psychology and pharmacology.* London: Tavistock.

ASKEVOLD, F. (1975). Measuring body image. *Psychotherapy and Psychosomatics, 26,* 71–77.

ASLAKSEN, P. M., & FLATEN, M. A. (2008). The roles of physiological and subjective stress in the effectiveness of a placebo on experimentally induced pain. *Psychosomatic Medicine, 70,* 811–818.

ASTIN, J. A. (1998). Why patients use alternative medicine: Results of a national study. *Journal of the American Medical Association, 279,* 1548–1553.

ATTANASIO, V., ANDRASIK, F., BURKE, E. J., BLAKE, D. D., KABELA, E., & MCCARRAN, M. S. (1985). Clinical issues in utilizing biofeedback with children. *Clinical Biofeedback and Health, 8,* 134–141.

ATTIE, I., & BROOKS-GUNN, J. (1987). Weight concerns as chronic stressors in women. In R. C. BARNETT, L. BIENER, & G. K. BARUCH (Eds.), *Gender and stress* (pp. 218–254). New York: Free Press.

AUDRAIN, J., RIMER, B., CELLA, D., STEFANEK, M., GARBER, J., et al. (1999). The impact of a brief coping skills intervention on adherence to breast self-examination among first-degree relatives of newly diagnosed breast cancer patients. *Psycho-Oncology, 8,* 220–229.

AUERBACH, S. M. (2000). Should patients have control over their own health care?: Empirical evidence and research issues. *Annals of Behavioral Medicine, 22,* 246–259.

AUERBACH, S. M., MARTELLI, M. F., & MERCURI, L. G. (1983). Anxiety, information, interpersonal impacts, and adjustment to a stressful health care situation. *Journal of Personality and Social Psychology, 44,* 1284–1296.

AZAR, B. (1994, November). Eating fat: Why does the brain say, "Ahhh"? *American Psychological Association Monitor,* p. 20.

BABYAK, M., BLUMENTHAL, J. A., HERMAN, S., KHATRI, P., DORAISWAMY, M., et al. (2000). Exercise treatment for major depression: Maintenance of therapeutic benefit at 10 months. *Psychosomatic Medicine, 62,* 633–638.

BADR, H., & CARMACK TAYLOR, C. L. (2008). Effects of relationship maintenance on psychological distress and dyadic adjustment among couples coping with lung cancer. *Health Psychology, 27,* 616–627.

BAER, P. E., GARMEZY, L. B., MCLAUGHLIN, R. J., POKORNY, A. D., & WERNICK, M. J. (1987). Stress, coping, family conflict, and adolescent alcohol use. *Journal of Behavioral Medicine, 10,* 449–466.

BACK, A. L., ARNOLD, R. M., TULSKY, J. A., BAILE, W. F., & FRYER-EDWARDS, K. A. (2005). On saying goodbye: Acknowledging the end of the patient–physician relationship with patients who are near death. *Annals of Internal Medicine, 142,* 682–686.

BAGOZZI, R. P. (1981). Attitudes, intentions, and behavior: A test of some key hypotheses. *Journal of Personality and Social Psychology, 41,* 606–627.

BAILEY, E. J., CATES, C. J., KRUSKE, S. G., MORRIS, P. S., BROWN, N., & CHANG, A. B. (2009). Culture-specific programs for children and adults from minority groups who have asthma. *Cochrane Database of Systematic Reviews, 2.* Retrieved (1-30-2010) from http://www.thecochranelibrary.com.

BAINES, D. R. (1992). Issues in cultural sensitivity: Examples from the Indian peoples. In D. M. BECKER, D. R. HILL, J. S. JACKSON, D. M. LEVINE, F. A. STILLMAN, & S. M. WEISS (Eds.), *Health behavior research in minority populations: Access, design, and implementation* (pp. 230–232). Bethesda, MD: National Heart, Lung, and Blood Institute.

BAIRD, J., FISHER, D., LUCAS, P., KLEIJNEN, J., ROBERTS, H., & LAW, D. (2005). Being big or growing fast: Systematic review of size and growth in infancy and later obesity. *British Medical Journal.* Retrieved (11-16-2006) from http://www.bmj.com. DOI:10.1136/bmj.38586.411273.EO.

BAJZER, M., & SEELEY, R. J. (2006). Physiology: Obesity and gut flora. *Nature, 444,* 1009–1010.

BAKAL, D. A. (1979). *Psychology and medicine: Psychological dimensions of health and illness.* New York: Springer.

BAKER, R. (1989). The cholesterol thing. *New York Times,* p. A31.

BAKER, T. B., BRANDON, T. H., & CHASSIN, L. (2004). Motivational influences on cigarette smoking. *Annual Review of Psychology, 55,* 463–491.

BAKER, T. B., PIPER, M. E., MCCARTHY, D. E., MAJESKIE, M. R., & FIORE, M. C. (2004). Addiction motivation reformulated: An affective processing model of negative reinforcement. *Psychological Review, 111,* 33–51.

BAKKER, A. B., DEMEROUTI, E. & BURKE, R. (2009). Workaholism and relationship quality: A spillover–crossover perspective. *Journal of Occupational Health Psychology, 14,* 23–33.

BALDWIN, A. S., ROTHMAN, A. J., HERTEL, A. W., LINDE, J. A., JEFFERY, R. W., et al. (2006). Specifying the determinants of the initiation and maintenance of behavior change: An examination of self-efficacy, satisfaction, and smoking cessation. *Health Psychology, 25,* 626–634.

BANDURA, A. (1969). *Principles of behavior modification.* New York: Holt, Rinehart & Winston.

BANDURA, A. (1986). *Social foundations of thought and action: A social cognitive theory.* Englewood Cliffs, NJ: Prentice Hall.

BANDURA, A. (2004). Self-efficacy. In W. E. CRAIGHEAD & C. B. NEMEROFF (Eds.), *The concise Corsini encyclopedia of psychology and behavioral science* (3rd ed., pp. 860–862). Hoboken, NJ: Wiley.

BANDURA, A., REESE, L., & ADAMS, N. E. (1982). Microanalysis of action and fear arousal as a function of differential levels of perceived self-efficacy. *Journal of Personality and Social Psychology, 43,* 5–21.

BANDURA, A., TAYLOR, C. B., WILLIAMS, S. L., MEFFORD, I. N., & BARCHAS, J. D. (1985). Catecholamine secretion as a function of perceived coping self-efficacy. *Journal of Consulting and Clinical Psychology, 53,* 406–414.

BANKS, J., MARMOT, M., OLDFIELD, Z., & SMITH, J. P. (2006). Disease and disadvantage in the United States and in England. *Journal of the American Medical Association, 295,* 2037–2045.

BANKS, S. M., SALOVEY, P., GREENER, S., ROTHMAN, A. J., MOYER, A., et al. (1995). The effects of message framing on mammography utilization. *Health Psychology, 14,* 178–184.

BARANOWSKI, T., & HEARN, M. D. (1997). Health behavior interventions with families. In D. S. GOCHMAN (Ed.), *Handbook of health behavior research IV: Relevance for professionals and issues for the future* (pp. 303–323). New York: Plenum.

BARANOWSKI, T., & NADER, P. R. (1985). Family health behavior. In D. C. TURK & R. D. KERNS (Eds.), *Health, illness, and families: A life-span perspective* (pp. 51–80). New York: Wiley.

BARBER, J. (1986). Hypnotic analgesia. In A. D. HOLZMAN & D. C. TURK (Eds.), *Pain management: A handbook of psychological treatment approaches* (pp. 151–167). New York: Pergamon.

BARBER, T. X. (1982). Hypnosuggestive procedures in the treatment of clinical pain: Implications for theories of hypnosis and suggestive therapy. In T. MILLON, C. J. GREEN, & R. B. MEAGHER (Eds.), *Handbook of clinical health psychology* (pp. 521–560). New York: Plenum.

BARCLAY, T. R., HINKIN, C. H., CASTELLON, S. A., MASON, K. I., REINHARD, M. J., et al. (2007). Age-associated predictors of medication adherence in HIV-positive adults: Health beliefs, self-efficacy, and neurocognitive status. *Health Psychology, 26,* 40–49.

BARDO, M. T., & RISNER, M. E. (1985). Biochemical substrates of drug abuse. In M. GALIZIO & S. A. MAISTO (Eds.), *Determinants of substance abuse: Biological, psychological, and environmental factors* (pp. 65–99). New York: Plenum.

BAREFOOT, J. C., DAHLSTROM, W. G., & WILLIAMS, R. B. (1983). Hostility, CHD incidence and total mortality: A 25-year follow-up study of 255 physicians. *Psychosomatic Medicine, 45,* 559–563.

BÁREZ, M., BLASCO, T., FERNÁNDEZ-CASTRO, J., & VILADRICH, C. (2009). Perceived control and psychological distress in women with breast cancer: A longitudinal study. *Journal of Behavioral Medicine, 32,* 187–196.

BARNES, L. L., MENDES DE LEON, C. F., LEWIS, T. T., BIENIAS, J. L., WILSON, R. S., & EVANS, D. A. (2008). Perceived discrimination and mortality in a population-based study of older adults. *American Journal of Public Health, 98,* 1241–1247.

BARNES, V. A., TREIBER, F. A., & JOHNSON, M. H. (2004). Impact of transcendental meditation on ambulatory blood pressure in African-American adolescents. *American Journal of Hypertension, 17,* 366–369.

BARNES, V. A., TREIBER, F. A., TURNER, R., DAVIS, H., & STRONG, W. B. (1999). Acute effects of transcendental meditation on hemodynamic functioning in middle-aged adults. *Psychosomatic Medicine, 61,* 525–531.

BARRETT, R. J. (1985). Behavioral approaches to individual differences in substance abuse. In M. GALIZIO & S. A. MAISTO (Eds.), *Determinants of substance abuse: Biological, psychological, and environmental factors* (pp. 125–175). New York: Plenum.

BARSKY, A. J., SAINTFORT, R., ROGERS, M. P., & BORUS, J. F. (2002). Nonspecific medication side effects and the nocebo phenomenon. *Journal of the American Medical Association, 287,* 622–627.

BARTH, J., CRITCHLEY, J., & BENGEL, J. (2008). Psychosocial interventions for smoking cessation in patients with coronary heart disease. *Cochrane Database of Systematic Reviews,* Issue 1. Retrieved (1-30-2010) from http://www.thecochranelibrary.com.

BASTONE, E. C., & KERNS, R. D. (1995). Effects of self-efficacy and perceived social support on recovery-related behaviors after coronary artery bypass graft surgery. *Annals of Behavioral Medicine, 17,* 324–330.

BATTIÉ, M. C., VIDEMAN, T., LEVALAHTI, E., GILL, K., & KAPRIO, J. (2007). Heretability of low back pain and the role of disc degeneration. *Pain, 131,* 272–280.

BAUCHOWITZ, A. U., GONDER-FREDERICK, L. A., OLBRISCH, M. E., AZARBAD, L., RYEE, M.-Y., et al. (2005). Psychosocial evaluation of bariatric surgery candidates: A survey of present practices. *Psychosomatic Medicine, 67,* 825–832.

BAUER, J. E., HYLAND, A., LI, Q., STEGER, C., & CUMMINGS, K. M. (2005). A longitudinal assessment of the impact of smoke-free worksite policies on tobacco use. *American Journal of Public Health, 95,* 1024–1029.

BAUM, A. (1988, April). Disasters, natural & otherwise. *Psychology Today,* pp. 56–60.

BAUM, A. (1990). Stress, intrusive imagery, and chronic distress. *Health Psychology, 9,* 653–675.

BAUM, A., AIELLO, J. R., & CALESNICK, L. E. (1978). Crowding and personal control: Social density and the development of learned helplessness. *Journal of Personality and Social Psychology, 36,* 1000–1011.

BAUMANN, L. J., & LEVENTHAL, H. (1985). "I can tell when my blood pressure is up, can't I?" *Health Psychology, 4,* 203–218.

BAUMEISTER, R. F., & LEARY, M. (1995). The need to belong: Desire for human attachments as a fundamental human motivation. *Psychological Bulletin, 117,* 497–529.

BEATTY, D. L., & MATTHEWS, K. A. (2009). Unfair treatment and trait anger in relation to nighttime ambulatory blood pressure in African American and white adolescents. *Psychosomatic Medicine, 71,* 813–820.

BECK, A. T. (1976). *Cognitive therapy and the emotional disorders.* New York: International Universities Press.

BECK, A. T., Freeman, A., & Associates. (1990). *Cognitive therapy of personality disorders.* New York: Guilford.

BECKER, C. B. (2010). Bulimia nervosa. In I. B. WEINER & W. E. CRAIGHEAD (Eds.), *The Corsini encyclopedia of psychology* (4th ed., Vol., 1, pp. 260–262). Hoboken, NJ: Wiley.

BECKER, M. H. (1979). Understanding patient compliance: The contributions of attitudes and other psychosocial factors. In S. J. COHEN (Ed.), *New directions in patient compliance* (pp. 1–31). Lexington, MA: Heath.

BECKER, M. H., & ROSENSTOCK, I. M. (1984). Compliance with medical advice. In A. STEPTOE & A. MATHEWS (Eds.), *Health care and human behaviour* (pp. 175–208). London: Academic Press.

BEECHER, H. K. (1956). Relationship of significance of wound to pain experienced. *Journal of the American Medical Association, 161,* 1609–1613.

BEGLIN, S. J., & FAIRBURN, C. G. (1992). Women who choose not to participate in surveys on eating disorders. *International Journal of Eating Disorders, 12,* 113–116.

BEKKERS, M. J. T. M., VAN KNIPPENBERG, F. C. E., VAN DEN BORNE, H. W., POEN, H., BERGSMA, J., & VAN BERGE HENEGOUWEN, G. P. (1995). Psychosocial adaptation to stoma surgery: A review. *Journal of Behavioral Medicine, 18,* 1–31.

BELAR, C. D., & MCINTYRE, T. (2004). Professional issues in health psychology. In S. SUTTON, A. BAUM, & M. JOHNSTON (Eds.), *The Sage handbook of health psychology* (pp. 402–419). London: Sage.

BELLIZZI, K. M., & BLANK, T. O. (2006). Predicting posttraumatic growth in breast cancer survivors. *Health Psychology, 25,* 47–56.

BELLOC, N. B., & BRESLOW, L. (1972). Relationship of physical health status and health practices. *Preventive Medicine, 1,* 409–421.

BELLUCK, P. (1996, May). Mingling two worlds of medicine. *New York Times,* pp. B1, 4.

BENEDETTI, F., POLLO, A., LOPIANO, L., LANOTTE, M., VIGHETTI, S., & RAINERO, I. (2003). Conscious expectation and unconscious conditioning in analgesic, motor, and hormonal placebo/nocebo responses. *Journal of Neuroscience, 23,* 4315–4323.

BENGSTON, V. L., CUELLAR, J. B., & RAGAN, P. K. (1977). Stratum contrasts and similarities in attitudes toward death. *Journal of Gerontology, 32,* 76–88.

BENIGHT, C. C., ANTONI, M. H., KILBOURN, K., IRONSON, G., KUMAR, M. A., et al. (1997). Coping self-efficacy buffers psychological and physiological disturbances in HIV-infected men following a natural disaster. *Health Psychology, 16,* 248–255.

BENNETT, G. G., & GLASGOW, R. E. (2009). The delivery of public health interventions via the Internet: Actualizing their potential. *Annual Review of Public Health, 30,* 273–292.

BENNETT, H. L. (1989, Fall/Winter). Report of the First International Symposium on Memory and Awareness in Anaesthesia. *Health Psychologist,* pp. 3–4.

BENNETT, W. I. (1987, December 13). Monitoring drugs for the aged. *New York Times Magazine,* pp. 73–74.

BENOLIEL, J. Q. (1977). Nurses and the human experience of dying. In H. FEIFEL (Ed.), *New meanings of death* (pp. 123–142). New York: McGraw-Hill.

BENSON, H. (1984). The relaxation response and stress. In J. D. MATARAZZO, S. M. WEISS, J. A. HERD, N. E. MILLER, & S. M. WEISS (Eds.), *Behavioral health: A handbook of health enhancement and disease prevention* (pp. 326–337). New York: Wiley.

BENSON, H. (1991). Mind/body interactions including Tibetan studies. In THE DALAI LAMA, H. BENSON, R. A. F. THURMAN, H. E. GARDNER, & D. GOLEMAN (Eds.), *Mindscience: An East-West dialogue* (pp. 37–48). Boston: Wisdom.

BENSON, H., MALHOTRA, M. S., GOLDMAN, R. F., JACOBS, G. D., & HOPKINS, P. J. (1990). Three case reports of the metabolic and electroencephalographic changes during advanced Buddhist meditation techniques. *Behavioral Medicine, 16,* 90–94.

BENSOUSSAN, A., TALLEY, N. J., HING, M., MENZIES, R., GUO, A., & NGU, M. (1998). Treatment of irritable bowel syndrome with Chinese herbal medicine: A randomized controlled trial. *Journal of the American Medical Association, 280,* 1585–1589.

BENTLER, P. M., & SPECKART, G. (1979). Models of attitude–behavior relations. *Psychological Review, 86,* 452–464.

BERG, C. A., SKINNER, M., KO, K., BUTLER, J. M., PALMER, D. L., et al. (2009). The fit between stress appraisal and dyadic coping in understanding perceived coping effectiveness for adolescents with type 1 diabetes. *Journal of Family Psychology, 23,* 521–530.

BERG, C. A., & UPCHURCH, R. (2007). A developmental-contextual model of couples coping with chronic illness across the adult life span. *Psychological Bulletin, 133,* 920–954.

BERGMAN, L. R., & MAGNUSSON, D. (1986). Type A behavior: A longitudinal study from childhood to adulthood. *Psychosomatic Medicine, 48,* 134–142.

BERKMAN, L. F., BLUMENTHAL, J., BURG, M., CARNEY, R. M., CATELLIER, D., et al. (2003). Effects of treating depression and low perceived social support on clinical events after myocardial infarction: The Enhancing Recovery in Coronary Heart Disease Patients (ENRICHD) Randomized Trial. *Journal of the American Medical Association, 289,* 3106–3116.

BERKMAN, L. F., & SYME, S. L. (1979). Social networks, host resistance, and mortality: A nine-year follow-up study of Alameda County residents. *American Journal of Epidemiology, 109,* 186–204.

BEVERIDGE, R. M., BERG, C. A., WIEBE, D. J., & PALMER, D. L. (2006). Mother and adolescent representations of illness ownership and stressful events surrounding diabetes. *Journal of Pediatric Psychology, 31,* 818–827.

BEZKOR, M. F., & LEE, M. H. M. (1999). Alternative medicine and its relationship to rehabilitation. In M. G. EISENBERG, R. L. GLUECKAUF, & H. H. ZARETSKY (Eds.), *Medical aspects of disability: A handbook for the rehabilitation professional* (2nd ed., pp. 587–597). New York: Springer.

BHASKARAN, K., HAMOUDA, O., SANNES, M., BOUFASSA, F., JOHNSON, A. M., et al. (2008). Changes in the risk of death after HIV seroconversion compared with mortality in the general population. *Journal of the American Medical Association*, 300, 51–59.

BHATTACHARYYA, M. R., & STEPTOE, A. (2007). Emotional triggers of acute coronary syndromes: Strength of evidence, biological processes, and clinical implications. *Progress in Cardiovascular Disease*, 49, 353–365.

BHF (British Heart Foundation) (2010) *Heart and circulatory disease is the UK's biggest killer*. Retrieved (11-19-2010) from www.heartstats.org.

BIBBINS-DOMINGO, K., CHERTOW, G. M., COXSON, P. G., MORAN, A., LIGHTWOOD, J. M., et al. (2010). Projected effect of dietary salt reductions on future cardiovascular disease. *New England Journal of Medicine*, 362, 590–599.

BIERUT, L. J., RICE, J. P., GOATE, A., HINRICHS, A. L., SACCONE, N. L., et al. (2004). A genomic scan for habitual smoking in families of alcoholics: Common and specific genetic factors in substance dependence. *American Journal of Medical Genetics*, 124A, 19–27.

BIGLAN, A., MCCONNELL, S., SEVERSON, H. H., BAVRY, J., & ARY, D. (1984). A situational analysis of adolescent smoking. *Journal of Behavioral Medicine*, 7, 109–114.

BILLINGS, A. G., & MOOS, R. H. (1981). The role of coping responses and social resources in attenuating the stress of life events. *Journal of Behavioral Medicine*, 4, 139–157.

BISH, A., RAMIREZ, A., BURGESS, C., & HUNTER, M. (2005). Understanding why women delay in seeking help for breast cancer symptoms. *Journal of Psychosomatic Research*, 58, 321–326.

BISHOP, G. D., & CONVERSE, S. A. (1986). Illness representations: A prototype approach. *Health Psychology*, 5, 95–114.

BJØRGE, T., ENGELAND, A., TVERDAL, A., & SMITH, G. D. (2008). Body mass index in adolescence in relation to cause-specific mortality: A follow-up of 230,000 Norwegian adolescents. *American Journal of Epidemiology*, 168, 30–37.

BLACK, F. L. (1992). Why did they die? *Science*, 258, 1739–1740.

BLACKHALL, L. J., MURPHY, S. T., FRANK, G., MICHEL, V., & AZEN, S. (1995). Ethnicity and attitudes toward patient autonomy. *Journal of the American Medical Association*, 274, 820–825.

BLACKLEDGE, J. T., & HAYES, S. C. (2001). Emotion regulation in Acceptance and Commitment Therapy. *Journal of Clinical Psychology*, 57, 243–255.

BLAIR, S. N., & BRODNEY, S. (1999). Effects of physical inactivity and obesity on morbidity and mortality: Current evidence and research issues. *Medicine and Science in Sports and Exercise*, 31(Suppl.), S646–S662.

BLAIR, S. N., KOHL, H. W., GORDON, N. F., & PAFFENBARGER, R. S. (1992). How much physical activity is good for health? *Annual Review of Public Health*, 13, 99–126.

BLANCHARD, E. B. (1987). Long-term effects of behavioral treatment of chronic headache. *Behavior Therapy*, 18, 375–385.

BLANCHARD, E. B., & ANDRASIK, F. (1985). *Management of chronic headaches: A psychological approach*. New York: Pergamon.

BLANCHARD, E. B., ANDRASIK, F., APPELBAUM, K. A., EVANS, D. D., MYERS, P., & BARRON, K. D. (1986). Three studies of the psychologic changes in chronic headache patients associated with biofeedback and relaxation therapies. *Psychosomatic Medicine*, 48, 73–83.

BLANCHARD, E. B., ANDRASIK, F., GUARNIERI, P., NEFF, D. F., & RODICHOK, L. D. (1987). Two-, three-, and four-year follow-up on the self-regulatory treatment of chronic headache. *Journal of Consulting and Clinical Psychology*, 55, 257–259.

BLANCHARD, E. B., APPELBAUM, K. A., GUARNIERI, P., MORRILL, B., & DENTINGER, M. P. (1987). Five year prospective follow-up on the treatment of chronic headache with biofeedback and/or relaxation. *Headache*, 27, 580–583.

BLANCHARD, E. B., LACKNER, J. M., JACCARD, J., ROWELL, D., CAROSELLA, A. M., et al. (2008). The role of stress in symptom exacerbation among IBS patients. *Journal of Psychosomatic Research*, 64, 119–128.

BLAND, S. H., O'LEARY, E. S., FARINARO, E., JOSSA, F., KROGH, V., et al. (1997). Social network disturbances and psychological distress following earthquake evacuations. *Journal of Nervous and Mental Disease*, 185, 188–194.

BLAND, S. H., O'LEARY, E. S., FARINARO, E., JOSSA, F., & TREVISAN, M. (1996). Long-term psychological effects of natural disasters. *Psychosomatic Medicine*, 58, 18–24.

BLANTON, H., & GERRARD, M. (1997). Effect of sexual motivation on men's risk perception for sexually transmitted disease: There must be 50 ways to justify a lover. *Health Psychology*, 16, 374–379.

BLEIBERG, J. (1986). Psychological and neuropsychological factors in stroke management. In P. E. KAPLAN & L. J. CERULLO (Eds.), *Stroke rehabilitation* (pp. 197–232). Boston: Butterworth.

BLEIBERG, J., CIULLA, R., & KATZ, B. I. (1991). Psychological components of rehabilitation programs for brain-injured and spinal-cord-injured patients. In J. J. SWEET, R. H. ROZENSKY, & S. M. TOVIAN (Eds.), *Handbook of clinical psychology in medical settings* (pp. 375–400). New York: Plenum.

BLOCK, A. R., KREMER, E., & GAYLOR, M. (1980). Behavioral treatment of chronic pain: The spouse as a discriminative cue for pain behavior. *Pain*, 9, 243–252.

BLOCK, J. P., HE, Y., ZASLAVSKY, A. M., DING, L., & AYANIAN, J. Z. (2009). Psychosocial stress and change in weight among US adults. *American Journal of Epidemiology*, 170, 181–192.

BLOOM, F. E., LAZERSON, A., & HOFSTADTER, L. (1985). *Brain, mind, and behavior*. New York: Freeman.

BLOOM, J. R., KANG, S. H., & ROMANO, P. (1991). Cancer and stress: The effect of social support as a resource. In C. L. COOPER & M. WATSON (Eds.), *Cancer and stress: Psychological, biological and coping studies* (pp. 95–124). Chichester: Wiley.

BLOOM, J. W., KALTENBORN, W. T., PAOLETTI, P., CAMILLI, A., & LEBOWITZ, M. D. (1987). Respiratory effects of non-tobacco cigarettes. *British Medical Journal*, 295, 1516–1518.

BLOOMFIELD, K., STOCKWELL, T., GMEL, G., & REHN, N. (2005). *International comparisons of alcohol consumption*. National Institute on Alcohol Abuse and Alcoholism. Retrieved (2-9-2007, cached 9-26-2005) from http://niaaa.nih.gov.

BLUMENTHAL, J. A., BABYAK, M., WEI, J., O'CONNOR, C., WAUGH, R., et al. (2002). Usefulness of psychosocial treatment of mental stress-induced myocardial ischemia in men. *American Journal of Cardiology, 89,* 164–168.

BLUMENTHAL, J. A., SHERWOOD, A., BABYAK, M. A., WATKINS, L. L., WAUGH, R., et al. (2005). Effects of exercise and stress management training on markers of cardiovascular risk in patients with ischemic heart disease: A randomized controlled trial. *Journal of the American Medical Association, 293,* 1626–1634.

BLUMENTHAL, J. A., SHERWOOD, A., GULLETTE, E. C. D., GEORGIADES, A., & TWEEDY, D. (2002). Biobehavioral approaches to the treatment of essential hypertension. *Journal of Consulting and Clinical Psychology, 70,* 569–589.

BODMER, W. F., BAILEY, C. J., BODMER, J., BUSSEY, H. J. R., ELLIS, A., et al. (1987). Localization of the gene for familial adenomatous polyposis on chromosome 5. *Nature, 328,* 614–616.

BODNAR, R. J. (1998). Pain. In E. A. BLECHMAN & K. D. BROWNELL (Eds.), *Behavioral medicine and women: A comprehensive handbook* (pp. 695–699). New York: Guilford.

BOELEN, P. A., VAN DEN BOUT, J., VAN DEN HOUT, M. (2006). Negative cognitions and avoidance in emotional problems after bereavement: A prospective study. *Behaviour Research and Therapy, 44,* 1657–1672.

BOERSMA, K., & LINTON, S. J. (2005). How does persistent pain develop? An analysis of the relationship between psychological variables, pain and function across stages of chronicity. *Behaviour Research and Therapy, 43,* 1495–1507.

BOFFEY, P. M. (1987). Gains against cancer since 1950 are overstated, Congress is told. *New York Times,* pp. A1, B10.

BOGG, T., & ROBERTS, B. W. (2004). Conscientiousness and health-related behaviors: A meta-analysis of the leading contributors to mortality. *Psychological Bulletin, 130,* 887–919.

BOHM, L. C., & RODIN, J. (1985). Aging and the family. In D. C. TURK & R. D. KERNS (Eds.), *Health, illness, and families: A life-span perspective* (pp. 279–310). New York: Wiley.

BOLGER, N., & AMAREL, D. (2007). Effects of social support visibility on adjustment to stress: Experimental evidence. *Journal of Personality and Social Psychology, 92,* 458–475.

BOLGER, N., ZUCKERMAN, A., & KESSLER, R. C. (2000). Invisible support and adjustment to stress. *Journal of Personality and Social Psychology, 79,* 953–961.

BONANNO, G. A. (2004). Loss, trauma, and human resilience: Have we underestimated the human capacity to thrive after extremely aversive events? *American Psychologist, 59,* 20–28.

BONANNO, G. A., PAPA, A., LALANDE, K., ZHANG, N., & NOLL, J. G. (2005). Grief processing and deliberate grief avoidance: A prospective comparison of bereaved spouses and parents in the United States and the People's Republic of China. *Journal of Consulting and Clinical Psychology, 73,* 86–98.

BORRELLI, B., MCQUAID, E. L., NOVAK, S. P., HAMMOND, S. K., & BECKER, B. (2010). Motivating Latino caregivers of children with asthma to quit smoking: A randomized trial. *Journal of Consulting and Clinical Psychology, 78,* 34–43.

BORYSENKO, J. (1984). Stress, coping, and the immune system. In J. D. MATARAZZO, S. M. WEISS, J. A. HERD, N. E. MILLER, & S. M. WEISS (Eds.), *Behavioral health: A handbook of health enhancement and disease prevention* (pp. 248–260). New York: Wiley.

BOSCH, J. A., DE GEUS, E. J. C., CARROLL, D., GOEDHART, A. D., ANANE, L. A., et al. (2009). A general enhancement of autonomic and cortisol responses during social evaluative threat. *Psychosomatic Medicine, 71,* 877–885.

BOSCH, J. A., ENGELAND, C., CACIOPPO, J., & MARUCHA, P. (2006). Depressive symptoms and mucosal wound healing. *Psychosomatic Medicine, 69,* 597–605.

BOTVIN, G. J., & WILLS, T. A. (1985). Personal and social skills training: Cognitive-behavioral approaches to substance abuse prevention. In C. S. BELL & R. BATTJES (Eds.), *Prevention research: Deterring drug abuse among children and adolescents* (NIDA Research Monograph 63). Washington, DC: U.S. Government Printing Office.

BOULWARE, L. E., COOPER, L. A., RATNER, L. E., LAVEIST, T. A., & POWE, N. R. (2003). Race and trust in the health care system. *Public Health Reports, 118,* 358–365.

BOUTON, K. (1990). Painful decisions: The role of the medical ethicist. *New York Times Magazine,* pp. 22–25, 53, 65.

BOVBJERG, D. H., MONTGOMERY, G. H., & RAPTIS, G. (2005). Evidence for classically conditioned fatigue responses in patients receiving chemotherapy treatment for breast cancer. *Journal of Behavioral Medicine, 28,* 231–237.

BOVBJERG, D. H., REDD, W. H., JACOBSEN, P. B., MANNE, S. L., TAYLOR, K. L., et al. (1992). An experimental analysis of classically conditioned nausea during cancer chemotherapy. *Psychosomatic Medicine, 54,* 623–637.

BOVBJERG, V. E., MCCANN, B. S., RETZLAFF, B. M., WALDEN, C. E., & KNOPP, R. H. (1999). Effect of cholesterol-lowering diets on indices of depression and hostility. *Annals of Behavioral Medicine, 21,* 98–101.

BOVE, G. & NILSSON, N. (1998). Spinal manipulation in the treatment of episodic tension-type headache. *Journal of the American Medical Association, 280,* 1576–1579.

BOWEN, A. M., & TROTTER, R. (1995). HIV risk in intravenous drug users and crack cocaine smokers: Predicting stage of change for condom use. *Journal of Consulting and Clinical Psychology, 63,* 238–248.

BOWLBY, J. (1969). *Attachment and loss. Vol. 1: Attachment.* New York: Basic Books.

BOWLBY, J. (1973). *Attachment and loss. Vol. 2: Separation.* New York: Basic Books.

BOYLE, P. & FERLAY, J. (2004). Cancer Incidence in Mortality in Europe, 2004. *Annals of Oncology, 16,* 481–488.

BOYLE, P. A., BARNES, L. L., BUCHMAN, A. S., & BENNETT, D. A. (2009). Purpose in life is associated with mortality among community-dwelling older persons. *Psychosomatic Medicine, 71,* 574–579.

BOYLE, S. H., MORTENSEN, L., GRONBAEK, M, & BAREFOOT, J. C. (2007). Hostility, drinking patterns and mortality. *Addiction*, 103, 54–59.

BRACCO, L., GALLATO, R., GRIGOLETTO, F., LIPPI, A., LEPORE, V., et al. (1994). Factors affecting the course and survival in Alzheimer's disease. *Archives of Neurology*, 51, 1213–1219.

BRACKETT, K. P. (2004). College students' condom purchase strategies. *Social Science Journal*, 41, 459–464.

BRADFORD, L. P. (1986). Can you survive retirement? In R. H. MOOS (Ed.), *Coping with life crises: An integrated approach* (pp. 211–219). New York: Plenum.

BRADLEY, G. W. (1993). *Disease, diagnosis, & decisions*. New York: Wiley.

BRADLEY, L. A. (1994). Pain measurement in arthritis. *Arthritis Care and Research*, 6, 178–186.

BRAITH, R. W., POLLOCK, M. L., LOWENTHAL, D. T., GRAVES, J. E., & LIMACHER, M. C. (1994). Moderate- and high-intensity exercise lowers blood pressure in normotensive subjects 60 to 79 years of age. *American Journal of Cardiology*, 73, 1124–1128.

BRAND-MILLER, J., WOLEVER, T. M. S., FOSTER-POWELL, K., & COLAGIURI, S. (2003). *The new glucose revolution*. New York: Marlow.

BRANDON, T. H., COLLINS, B. N., JULIANO, L. M., & LAZEV, A. B. (2000). Preventing relapse among former smokers: A comparison of minimal interventions through telephone and mail. *Journal of Consulting and Clinical Psychology*, 68, 103–113.

BRANDON, T., H., VIDRINE, J. I., & LITVIN, E. B. (2007). Relapse and relapse prevention. *Annual Review of Clinical Pychology*, 3, 257–284.

BRAVEMAN, N. S. (1987). Immunity and aging: Immunologic and behavioral perspectives. In M. W. RILEY, J. D. MATARAZZO, & A. BAUM (Eds.), *Perspectives in behavioral medicine: The aging dimension* (pp. 93–124). Hillsdale, NJ: Erlbaum.

BREHM, J. W. (1966). *A theory of psychological reactance*. New York: Academic Press.

BRENNAN, P. L., SCHUTTE, K. K., & MOOS, R. H. (2005). Pain and use of alcohol to manage pain: Prevalence and 3-year outcomes among older problem and non-problem drinkers. *Addiction*, 100, 777–786.

BRESLOW, L. (1983). The potential of health promotion. In D. MECHANIC (Ed.), *Handbook of health, health care, and the health professions* (pp. 50–66). New York: Free Press.

BRESLOW, L., & SOMERS, A. R. (1977). The lifetime health-monitoring program. *New England Journal of Medicine*, 296, 601–608.

BREWER, N. T., CHAPMAN, G. B., GIBBONS, F. X., GERRARD, M., MCCAUL, K. D., & WEINSTEIN, N. D. (2007). Meta-analysis of the relationship between risk perception and health behavior: The example of vaccination. *Health Psychology*, 26, 136–145.

BRICKER, J. B., PETERSON, A. V., ANDERSEN, M. R., RAJAN, K. B., LEROUX, B. G., & SARASON, I. G. (2006). Childhood friends who smoke: Do they influence adolescents to make smoking transitions? *Addictive Behaviors*, 31, 889–900.

BRICKER, J. B., RAJAN, K. B., ZALEWSKI, M., ANDERSEN, M. R., RAMEY, M., & PETERSON, A. V. (2009). Psychological and social risk factors in adolescent smoking transitions: A population-based longitudinal study. *Health Psychology*, 28, 439–447.

BRISSETTE, I., & COHEN, S. (2002). The contribution of individual differences in hostility to the association between daily interpersonal conflict, affect, and sleep. *Personality and Social Psychology Bulletin*, 28, 1265–1274.

BROADBENT, E., ELLIS, C. J., THOMAS, J., GAMBLE, G., & PETRIE, K. J. (2009). Can an illness perception intervention reduce illness anxiety in spouses of myocardial infarction patients? A randomized controlled trial. *Journal of Psychosomatic Research*, 67, 11–15.

BROADHEAD, W. E., KAPLAN, B. H., JAMES, S. A., WAGNER, E. H., SCHOENBACH, V. J., et al. (1983). The epidemiologic evidence for a relationship between social support and health. *American Journal of Epidemiology*, 117, 521–537.

BROADSTOCK, M., BORLAND, R., & GASON, R. (1992). Effects of suntan on judgements of healthiness and attractiveness by adolescents. *Journal of Applied Social Psychology*, 22, 157–172.

BROBERG, D. J., & BERNSTEIN, I. L. (1987). Candy as a scapegoat in the prevention of food aversions in children receiving chemotherapy. *Cancer*, 60, 2344–2347.

BRODY, G. H., BEACH, S. R. H., PHILIBERT, R. A., CHEN, Y.-F., LEI, M.-K., et al., (2009). Parenting moderates a genetic vulnerability factor in longitudinal increase in youths' substance use. *Journal of Consulting and Clinical Pychology*, 77, 1–11.

BROMAN, C. L. (1993). Social relationships and health-related behavior. *Journal of Behavioral Medicine*, 16, 335–350.

BRONDOLO, E., GRANTHAM, K. I., KARLIN, W., TARAVELLA, J., MENCÍA-RIPLEY, A., et al. (2009). Trait hostility and ambulatory blood pressure among traffic enforcement agents: The effects of stressful social interactions. *Journal of Occupational Health Psychology*, 14, 110–121.

BRONDOLO, E., LIBBY, D. J., DENTON, E.-G., THOMPSON, S., BEATTY, D. L., et al. (2008). Racism and ambulatory blood pressure in a community sample. *Psychosomatic Medicine* 70, 49–56.

BRONDOLO, E., ROSEN, R. C., KOSTIS, J. B., & SCHWARTZ, J. E. (1999). Relationship of physical symptoms and mood to perceived and actual blood pressure in hypertensive men: A repeated-measures design. *Psychosomatic Medicine*, 61, 311–318.

BROOK, J. S., WHITEMAN, M., GORDON, A. S., & COHEN, P. (1986). Dynamics of childhood and adolescent personality traits and adolescent drug use. *Developmental Psychology*, 22, 403–414.

BROSSCHOT, J. F. (2010). Markers of chronic stress: Prolonged physiological activation and (un)conscious perseverative cognition. *Neuroscience and Biobehavioral Reviews*. DOI:10.1016/j.neubiorev.2010.01.004.

BROWN, J. L., & VANABLE, P. A. (2008). Cognitive–behavioral stress management interventions for persons living with HIV: A review and critique of the literature. *Annals of Behavioral Medicine, 35,* 26–40.

BROWN, J. M., O'KEEFFE, J., SANDERS, S. H., & BAKER, B. (1986). Developmental changes in children's cognition to stressful and painful situations. *Journal of Pediatric Psychology, 11,* 343–357.

BROWN, K. W., LEVY, A. R., ROSBERGER, Z., & EDGAR, L. (2003). Psychological distress and cancer survival: A follow-up 10 years after diagnosis. *Psychosomatic Medicine, 65,* 636–643.

BROWN, L. K., & LOURIE, K. J. (2001). Motivational interviewing and the prevention of HIV among adolescents. In P. M. MONTI, S. M. COLBY, & T. A. O'LEARY (Eds.), *Adolescents, alcohol, and substance abuse: Reaching teens through brief interventions* (pp. 244–274). New York: Guilford.

BROWN, S. L., SMITH, D. M., SCHULZ, R., KABETO, M. U., UBEL, P. A., et al. (2009). Caregiving behavior is associated with decreased mortality risk. *Psychological Science, 20,* 488–494.

BROWNELL, K. D. (1982). Obesity: Understanding and treating a serious, prevalent, and refractory disorder. *Journal of Consulting and Clinical Psychology, 50,* 820–840.

BROWNELL, K. D. (1986). Social and behavioral aspects of obesity in children. In N. A. KRASNEGOR, J. D. ARASTEH, & M. F. CATALDO (Eds.), *Child health behavior: A behavioral pediatrics perspective* (pp. 310–324). New York: Wiley.

BROWNELL, K. D. (1989, June). When and how to diet. *Psychology Today,* pp. 40–46.

BROWNELL, K. D. (1991). Personal responsibility and control over our bodies: When expectation exceeds reality. *Health Psychology, 10,* 303–310.

BROWNELL, K. D., COHEN, R. Y., STUNKARD, A. J., FELIX, M. R. J., & COOLEY, N. B. (1984). Weight loss competitions at the work site: Impact on weight, morale and cost-effectiveness. *American Journal of Public Health, 74,* 1283–1285.

BROWNSON, R. C., BOEHMER, T. K., & LUKE, D. A. (2005). Declining rates of physical activity in the United States: What are the contributors? *Annual Review of Public Health, 26,* 421–443.

BRUCKER, B. S. (1983). Spinal cord injuries. In T. G. BURISH & L. A. BRADLEY (Eds.), *Coping with chronic disease: Research and applications* (pp. 285–311). New York: Academic Press.

BRUEHL, S., & CHUNG, O. Y. (2004). Psychological interventions for acute pain. In T. HADJISTAVROPOULOS & K. D. CRAIG (Eds.), *Pain: Psychological perspectives* (pp. 245–269). Mahwah, NJ: Earlbaum.

BRUEHL, S., & CHUNG, O. Y. (2006). Parental history of chronic pain may be associated with impairments in endogenous opioid analgesic systems. *Pain, 124,* 287–294.

BRUEHL, S., MCCUBBIN, J. A., & HARDEN, R. N. (1999). Theoretical review: Altered pain regulatory systems in chronic pain. *Neuroscience and Biobehavioral Reviews, 23,* 877–890.

BRUNNER, E., WHITE, I., THOROGOOD, M., BRISTOW, A., CURLE, D., & MARMOT, M. (1997). Can dietary interventions change diet and cardiovascular risk factors? A meta-analysis of randomized controlled trials. *American Journal of Public Health, 87,* 1415–1422.

BRUVOLD, W. H. (1993). A meta-analysis of adolescent smoking prevention programs. *American Journal of Public Health, 83,* 872–880.

BRYAN, A., FISHER, J. D., & FISHER, W. A. (2002). Tests of the mediational role of preparatory safer sex behavior in the context of the theory of planned behavior. *Health Psychology, 21,* 71–80.

BRYAN, A., HUTCHISON, K. E., SEALS, D. R., & ALLEN, D. L. (2007). A transdisciplinary model integrating genetic, physiological, and psychological correlates of voluntary exercise. *Health Psychology, 26,* 30–39.

BRYDØY, M., FOSSÅ, S. D., KLEPP, O., BREMNES, R. M., WIST, E. A., et al. (2005). Paternity following treatment for testicular cancer. *Journal of the National Cancer Institute, 97,* 1580–1588.

BRYER, K. B. (1986). The Amish way of death: A study of family support systems. In R. H. MOOS (Ed.), *Coping with life crises: An integrated approach* (pp. 245–256). New York: Plenum.

BUCHNER, D. M., BERESFORD, S. A. A., LARSON, E. B., LACROIX, A. Z., & WAGNER, E. H. (1992). Effects of physical activity on health status in older adults II: Intervention studies. *Annual Review of Public Health, 13,* 469–488.

BUCK, R. (1988). *Human motivation and emotion* (2nd ed.). New York: Wiley.

BUCKLAND, G., GONZÁLEZ, C. A., AGUDO, A., VILARDELL, M., BERENGUER, A., et al. (2009). Adherence to the Mediterranean diet and risk of coronary heart disease in the Spanish EPIC cohort study. *Archives of Internal Medicine, 170,* 1518–1529.

BUDZYNSKI, T. H., STOYVA, J. M., ADLER, C. S., & MULLANEY, D. J. (1973). EMG biofeedback and tension headache: A controlled outcome study. *Psychosomatic Medicine, 35,* 484–496.

BULMAN, R. J., & WORTMAN, C. B. (1977). Attributions of blame and coping in the "real world": Severe accident victims react to their lot. *Journal of Personality and Social Psychology, 35,* 351–363.

BUNDE, J., & MARTIN, R. (2006). Depression and prehospital delay in the context of myocardial infarction. *Psychosomatic Medicine, 68,* 51–57.

BUNDE, J., & SULS, J. (2006). A quantitative analysis of the relationship between the Cook-Medley Hostility Scale and traditional coronary artery disease risk factors. *Health Psychology, 25,* 493–500.

BURBACH, D. J., & PETERSON, L. (1986). Children's concepts of physical illness: A review and critique of the cognitive-developmental literature. *Health Psychology, 5,* 307–325.

BURG, I. N., & INGALL, C. G. (1985). The immune system. In L. L. HAYMAN & E. M. SPORING (Eds.), *Handbook of pediatric nursing* (pp. 424–477). New York: Wiley.

BURG, M. M., & SEEMAN, T. E. (1994). Families and health: The negative side of social ties. *Annals of Behavioral Medicine, 16,* 109–115.

Burgard, S. A., & Ailshire, J. A. (2009). Putting work to bed: Stressful experiences on the job and sleep quality. *Journal of Health and Social Behavior, 50,* 476–492.

Burgard, S. A., Brand, J. E., & House, J. S. (2007). Toward a better estimation of the effect of job loss on health. *Journal of Health and Social Behavior, 48,* 369–384.

Burish, T. G., & Jenkins, R. A. (1992). Effectiveness of biofeedback and relaxation training in reducing the side effects of cancer chemotherapy. *Health Psychology, 11,* 17–23.

Burish, T. G., Meyerowitz, B. E., Carey, M. P., & Morrow, G. R. (1987). The stressful effects of cancer in adults. In A. Baum & J. E. Singer (Eds.), *Handbook of psychology and health* (Vol. 5, pp. 137–173). New York: Erlbaum.

Burke, B. L., Arkowitz, H., & Menchola, M. (2003). The efficacy of motivational interviewing: A meta-analysis of controlled clinical trials. *Journal of Consulting and Clinical Psychology, 71,* 843–861.

Burke, L. E., Dunbar-Jacob, J. M., & Hill, M. N. (1997). Compliance with cardiovascular disease prevention strategies: A review of the research. *Annals of Behavioral Medicine, 19,* 239–263.

Burns, J. W., Glenn, B., Bruehl, S., Harden, R. N., & Lofland, K. (2003). Cognitive factors influence outcome following multidisciplinary chronic pain treatment: A replication and extension of a cross-lagged panel analysis. *Behaviour Research and Therapy, 41,* 1163–1182.

Burns, S. M., Boyd, B. L., Hill, J., & Hough, S. (2010). Psychosocial predictors of employment status among men living with spinal cord injury. *Rehabilitation Psychology, 55,* 81–90.

Burns, V. E., Carroll, D., Drayson, M., Whitham, M., & Ring, C. (2003). Life events, perceived stress and antibody responses to influenza vaccination in young, healthy adults. *Journal of Psychosomatic Research, 55,* 569–572.

Burnside, I. G., Tobias, H. S., & Bursill, D. (1982). Electromyographic feedback in the remobilization of stroke patients: A controlled trial. *Archives of Physical Medicine and Rehabilitation, 63,* 217–222.

Bush, J. P., Holmbeck, G. N., & Cockrell, J. L. (1989). Patterns of PRN analgesic drug administration in children following elective surgery. *Journal of Pediatric Psychology, 14,* 433–448.

Bush, J. P., Melamed, B. G., Sheras, P. L., & Greenbaum, P. E. (1986). Mother-child patterns of coping with anticipatory medical stress. *Health Psychology, 5,* 137–157.

Busjahn, A., Faulhaber, H.-D., Freier, K., & Luft, F. C. (1999). Genetic and environmental influences on coping styles: A twin study. *Psychosomatic Medicine, 61,* 469–475.

Buss, A. H., & Plomin, R. (1975). *A temperamental theory of personality development.* New York: Wiley.

Buss, A. H., & Plomin, R. (1986). The EAS approach to temperament. In R. Plomin & J. Dunn (Eds.), *The study of temperament: Changes, continuities and challenges* (pp. 67–79). Hillsdale, NJ: Erlbaum.

Butcher, J. N., Dahlstrom, W. G., Graham, J. R., Tellegen, A., & Kraemer, B. (1989). *Minnesota Multiphasic Personality Inventory–2: Manual for administration and scoring.* Minneapolis: University Minnesota Press.

Butler, C., & Steptoe, A. (1986). Placebo responses: An experimental study of psychophysiological processes in asthmatic volunteers. *British Journal of Clinical Psychology, 25,* 173–183.

Butler, L. D., Koopman, C., Cordova, M. J., Garlan, R. W., Dimiceli, S., & Spiegel, D. (2003). Psychosocial distress and pain significantly increase before death in metastatic breast cancer patients. *Psychosomatic Medicine, 65,* 416–426.

Butner, J., Berg, C. A., Osborn, P., Butler, J. M., Godri, C., et al. (2009). Parent–adolescent discrepancies in adolescents' competence and the balance of adolescent autonomy and adolescent and parent well-being in the context of Type 1 diabetes. *Developmental Psychology, 45,* 835–849.

Bygren, L. O., Weissglas, G., Wikström, B-M., Konlaan, B. B., Grjibovski, A., et al. (2009). Cultural participation and health: A randomized controlled trial among medical care staff. *Psychosomatic Medicine, 71,* 469–473.

Byrne, P. S., & Long, B. E. L. (1976). *Doctors talking to patients.* London: Her Majesty's Stationery Office.

Byrne-Davis, L. M., & Vedhara, K. (2004). Psychoneuroimmunology. In A. J. Christensen, R. Martin, & J. M. Smyth (Eds.), *Encyclopedia of health psychology* (pp. 221–227). New York: Kluwer.

Cabana, M. D., Slish, K. K., Lewis, T. C., Brown, R. W., Nan, B., et al. (2004). Parental management of asthma triggers within a child's environment. *Journal of Allergy and Clinical Immunology, 114,* 352–357.

Cabizuca, M., Marques-Portella, C., Mendlowicz, M. V., Coutinho, E. S. F., Figueira, I. (2009). Posttraumatic stress disorder in parents of children with chronic illnesses: A meta-analysis. *Health Psychology, 28,* 379–388.

Cadman, D., Rosenbaum, P., Boyle, M., & Offord, D. R. (1991). Children with chronic illness: Family and parent demographic characteristics and psychosocial adjustment. *Pediatrics, 87,* 884–889.

Caggiula, A. W., Christakis, G., Farrand, M., Hulley, S. B., Johnson, R., et al. (1981). The Multiple Risk Intervention Trial (MRFIT): IV. Intervention on blood lipids. *Preventive Medicine, 10,* 443–475.

Cahill, K., Moher, M., & Lancaster, T. (2008). Workplace interventions for smoking cessation. *Cochrane Database of Systematic Reviews,* Issue 4. Retrieved (1-30-2010) from http://www.thecochranelibrary.com. DOI:10.1002/14651858.CD003440.pub3.

Calhoun, K. S., & Burnette, M. M. (1983). Etiology and treatment of menstrual disorders. *Behavioral Medicine Update, 5*(4), 21–26.

Calle, E. E., Rodriguez, C., Walker-Thurmond, K., & Thun, M. J. (2003). Overweight, obesity, and mortality from cancer in a prospectively studied cohort of U.S. adults. *New England Journal of Medicine, 348,* 1625–1638.

CAMERON, L., LEVENTHAL, E. A., & LEVENTHAL, H. (1995). Seeking medical care in response to symptoms and life stress. *Psychosomatic Medicine*, 57, 1–11.

CAMERON, R., & SHEPEL, L. F. (1986). The process of psychological consultation in pain management. In A. D. HOLZMAN & D. C. TURK (Eds.), *Pain management: A handbook of psychological treatment approaches* (pp. 240–256). New York: Pergamon.

CAMPBELL, C. M., WITMER, K., SIMANGO, M., CARTERET, A., LOGGIA, M. L., et al. (2010). Catastrophizing delays the analgesic effect of distraction. *Pain*, 149, 202–207.

CAMPBELL, J. M., & OEI, T. P. (2009). A cognitive model for the intergenerational transference of alcohol cue behavior. *Addictive Behaviors*, 35, 73–83.

CAMPBELL, M., HUDSON, M. A., RESNICOW, K., BLAKENEY, N., PAXTON, A., & BASKIN, M. (2007). Church-based health promotion interventions: Evidence and lessons learned. *Annual Review of Public Health*, 28, 213–234.

CAMPBELL, T., & CHANG, B. (1981). Health care of the Chinese in America. In G. HENDERSON & M. PRIMEAUX (Eds.), *Transcultural health care* (pp. 163–172). Menlo Park, CA: Addison-Wesley.

CANCER RESEARCH UK (2007a). *Breast Cancer - UK Incidence Statistics*. Retrieved (11-18-2010) from www.info.cancerresearchuk.org.

CANCER RESEARCH UK (2007b). *Testicular Cancer Statistics - UK*. Retrieved (11-18-2010) from www.info.cancerresearchuk.org.

CANCER RESEARCH UK (2008). *Prostate Cancer Statistics - UK*. Retrieved (11-18-2010) from www.info.cancerresearchuk.org.

CANKAYA, B., CHAPMAN, B. P., TALBOT, N. L., MOYNIHAN, J., DUBERSTEIN, P. R. (2009). History of sudden unexpected loss is associated with elevated interleukin-6 and decreased insulin-like growth factor-1 in women in an urban primary care setting. *Psychosomatic Medicine*, 71, 914–919.

CANNON, J. T., PRIETO, G. J., LEE, A., & LIEBESKIND, J. C. (1982). Evidence for opioid and non-opioid forms of stimulation-produced analgesia in the rat. *Brain Research*, 243, 315–321.

CANNON, W. B. (1929). *Bodily changes in pain, hunger, fear and rage* (2nd ed.). New York: Appleton.

CANO, A., LEONG, L., HELLER, J. B., & LUTZ, J. R. (2009). Perceived entitlement to pain-related supoort and pain catastrophizing: Associations with perceived and observed support. *Pain*, 147, 249–254.

CAPEWELL, S., HAYES, D. K., FORD, E. S., CRITCHLEY, J. A., CROFT, J. B., et al. (2009). Life-years gained among US adults from modern treatments and changes in the prevalence of 6 coronary heart disease risk factors between 1980 and 2000. *American Journal of Epidemiology*. 170, 229–236.

CAREK, V., NORMAN, P., & BARTON, J. (2010). Cognitive appraisals and posttraumatic stress disorder symptoms in informal caregivers of stroke survivors. *Rehabilitation Psychology*, 55, 91–96.

CARELS, R. A., BLUMENTHAL, J. A., & SHERWOOD, A. (1998). Effect of satisfaction with social support on blood pressure in normotensive and borderline hypertensive men and women. *International Journal of Behavioral Medicine*, 5, 76–85.

CARELS, R. A., YOUNG, K. M., WOTT, C. B., HARPER, J., GUMBLE, A., et al. (2009). Weight bias and weight loss treatment outcomes in treatment-seeking adults. *Annals of Behavioral Medicine*, 37, 350–355.

CAREY, K. B., SCOTT-SHELDON, L. A. J., CAREY, M. P., & DEMARTINI, K. S. (2007). Individual-level interventions to reduce college student drinking: A meta-analytic review. *Addictive Behaviors*, 32, 2469–2494.

CAREY, K. B., SCOTT-SHELDON, L. A. J., ELLIOTT, J. C., BOLLES, J. R., & CAREY, M. P. (2009). Computer-delivered interventions to reduce college student drinking: A meta-analyis. *Addiction*, 104, 1807–1819.

CAREY, M. P. (1999). Prevention of HIV infection through sexual behavior change: Progress report focusing on downstream, midstream, and upstream strategies. *American Journal of Health Promotion*, 14, 104–111.

CAREY, M. P., BRAATEN, L. S., MAISTO, S. A., GLEASON, J. R., FORSYTH, A. D., et al. (2000). Using information, motivational enhancement, and skills training to reduce risk of HIV infection for low-income urban women: A second randomized clinical trial. *Health Psychology*, 19, 3–11.

CAREY, M. P., & BURISH, T. G. (1988). Etiology and treatment of the psychological side effects associated with cancer chemotherapy: A critical review and discussion. *Psychological Bulletin*, 104, 307–325.

CAREY, M. P., KALRA, D. L., CAREY, K. B., HALPERIN, S., & RICHARDS, C. S. (1993). Stress and unaided smoking cessation: A prospective investigation. *Journal of Consulting and Clinical Psychology*, 61, 831–838.

CAREY, M. P., MORRISON-BEEDY, D., & JOHNSON, B. T. (1998). The HIV-Knowledge Questionnaire. In C. M. DAVIS, W. L. YARBER, R. BAUSERMAN, G. SCHREER, & S. L. DAVIS (Eds.), *Handbook of sexually related measures* (pp. 313–315). Thousand Oaks, CA: Sage.

CAREY, M. P., & VANABLE, P. A. (2004). HIV/AIDS. In A. J. CHRISTENSEN, R. MARTIN, & J. M. SMYTH (Eds.), *Encyclopedia of health psychology* (pp. 135–140). New York: Kluwer.

CAREY, R. G. (1975). Living until death: A program of service and research for the terminally ill. In E. KÜBLER-ROSS (Ed.), *Death: The final stage of growth* (pp. 75–86). Englewood Cliffs, NJ: Prentice Hall.

CAREY, W. B., & MCDEVITT, S. C. (1978). Stability and change in individual temperament diagnoses from infancy to early childhood. *Journal of the American Academy of Child Psychiatry*, 17, 331–337.

CARLSON, C. R., & HOYLE, R. H. (1993). Efficacy of abbreviated muscle relaxation training: A quantitative review of behavioral medicine research. *Journal of Consulting and Clinical Psychology*, 61, 1059–1067.

CARLSON, L. E., GOODEY, E., BENNETT, M. H., TAENZER, P., & KOOPMANS, J. (2002). The addition of social support to a community-based large-group behavioral smoking cessation intervention: Improved cessation rates and gender differences. *Addictive Behaviors, 27,* 547–559.

CARLSSON, S., ANDERSSON, T., LICHTENSTEIN, P., MICHAËLSSON, K., & AHLBOM, A. (2007). Physical activity and mortality: Is the association explained by genetic selection? *American Journal of Epidemiology, 166,* 255–259.

CARMELLI, D., DAME, A., SWAN, G., & ROSENMAN, R. (1991). Long-term changes in Type A behavior: A 27-year follow-up of the Western Collaborative Group Study. *Journal of Behavioral Medicine, 14,* 593–606.

CARMELLI, D., ROSENMAN, R. H., & CHESNEY, M. A. (1987). Stability of the Type A Structured Interview and related questionnaires in a 10-year follow-up of an adult cohort of twins. *Journal of Behavioral Medicine, 10,* 513–525.

CARMODY, T. P., FEY, S. G., PIERCE, D. K., CONNOR, W. E., & MATARAZZO, J. D. (1982). Behavioral treatment of hyperlipidemia: Techniques, results, and future directions. *Journal of Behavioral Medicine, 5,* 91–116.

CARNEY, R. M., FREEDLAND, K. E., RICH, M. W., & JAFFE, A. S. (1995). Depression as a risk factor for cardiac events in established coronary heart disease: A review of possible mechanisms. *Annals of Behavioral Medicine, 17,* 142–149.

CARNEY, R. M., RICH, M. W., FREEDLAND, K. E., SAINI, J., TEVELDE, A., et al. (1988). Major depressive disorder predicts cardiac events in patients with coronary artery disease. *Psychosomatic Medicine, 50,* 627–633.

CARR, D. B., BULLEN, B. A., SKRINAR, G. S., ARNOLD, M. A., ROSENBLATT, M., et al. (1981). Physical conditioning facilitates the exercise-induced secretion of beta-endorphin and beta-lipotropin in women. *New England Journal of Medicine, 305,* 560–563.

CARRICO, A. W., ANTONI, M. H., DURÁN, R. E., IRONSON, G., PENEDO, F., et al. (2006). Reductions in depressed mood and denial coping during cognitive behavioral stress management with HIV-positive gay men treated with HAART. *Annals of Behavioral Medicine, 31,* 155–164.

CARROLL, K. M., BALL, A., MARTINO, S., NICH, C., BABUSCIO, T. A., & ROUNSAVILLE, B. J. (2009). Enduring effects of a computer-assisted training program for cognitive behavioral therapy: A 6-month follow-up of CBT4CBT. *Drug and Alcohol Dependence, 100,* 178–181.

CARROLL, K. M., EASTON, C. J., NICH, C., HUNKELE, K. A., NEAVINS, T. M., et al. (2006). The use of contingency management and motivational/skills-building therapy to treat young adults with marijuana dependence. *Journal of Consulting and Clinical Psychology, 74,* 955–966.

CARTWRIGHT, M., WARDLE, J., STEGGLES, N., SIMON, A. E., CROKER, H., & JARVIS, M. J. (2003). Stress and dietary practices in adolescents. *Health Psychology, 22,* 362–369.

CARVER, C. S., & CONNOR-SMITH, J. (2010). Personality and coping. *Annual Review of Psychology, 61,* 679–704.

CASARETT, D., KARLAWISH, J., MORALES, K., CROWLEY, R., MIRSCH, T., & ASCH, D. A. (2005). Improving the use of hospice services in nursing homes: A randomized controlled trial. *Journal of the American Medical Association, 294,* 211–217.

CASEY, C. Y., GREENBERG, M. A., NICASSIO, P. M., HARPIN, R. E., & HUBBARD, D. (2008). Transition from acute to chronic pain and disability: A model including cognitive, affective, and trauma factors. *Pain, 134,* 69–79.

CASEY, E., HUGHES, J. W., WAECHTER, D., JOSEPHSON, R., & ROSNECK, J. (2008). Depression predicts failure to complete phase-II cardiac rehabilitation. *Journal of Behavioral Medicine, 31,* 421–431.

CASTRO, F. G., COTA, M. K., & VEGA, S. C. (1999). Health promotion in Latino populations: A sociocultural model for program planning, development, and evaluation. In R. M. HUFF & M. V. KLINE (Eds.), *Promoting health in multicultural populations: A handbook for practitioners* (pp. 137–168). Thousand Oaks, CA: Sage.

CASTRO, F. G., NEWCOMB, M. D., MCCREARY, C., & BAEZCONDE-GARBANATI, L. (1989). Cigarette smokers do more than just smoke cigarettes. *Health Psychology, 8,* 107–129.

CATALDO, M. F., DERSHEWITZ, R. A., WILSON, M., CHRISTOPHERSEN, E. R., FINNEY, J. W., et al. (1986). Childhood injury control. In N. A. KRASNEGOR, J. D. ARASTEH, & M. F. CATALDO (Eds.), *Child health behavior: A behavioral pediatrics perspective* (pp. 217–253). New York: Wiley.

CATANIA, J. A., COATES, T. J., STALL, R., BYE, L., KEGELES, S. M., et al. (1991). Changes in condom use among homosexual men in San Francisco. *Health Psychology, 10,* 190–199.

CATLEY, D., & GROBE, J. E. (2008). Using basic laboratory research to understand scheduled smoking: A field investigation of the effects of manipulating controllability on subjective responses to smoking. *Health Psychology, 27,* S189–S196.

CATZ, S. L., KELLY, J. A., BOGART, L. M., BENOTSCH, E. G., & MCAULIFFE, T. L. (2000). Patterns, correlates, and barriers to medication adherence among persons prescribed new treatments for HIV disease. *Health Psychology, 19,* 124–133.

CAVANAUGH, S. V. A., FURLANETTO, L. M., CREECH, S. D., & POWELL, L. H. (2001). Medical illness, past depression, and present depression: A predictive triad for in-hospital mortality. *American Journal of Psychiatry, 158,* 43–48.

CAY, E. L., VETTER, N., PHILIP, A. E., & DUGARD, P. (1972). Psychosocial status during recovery from an acute heart attack. *Journal of Psychosomatic Research, 16,* 425–435.

CDC (Centers for Disease Control and Prevention, U.S. Public Health Service) (2004). *Trends in intake of energy and micronutrients—United States, 1971–2000.* Retrieved (8-18-2004) from http://www.cdc.gov.

CDC (Centers for Disease Control and Prevention, U.S. Public Health Service) (2006). *HIV/AIDS prevention—Basic statistics.* Retrieved (12-8-2006) from http://www.cdc.gov.

CDC (Centers for Disease Control and Prevention, U.S. Public Health Service) (2009). *HIV/AIDS surveillance report* (Vol. 19). Retrieved (1-11-2010) from http://www.cdc.gov.

CELLA, D., PETERMAN, A., PASSIK, S., JACOBSEN, P., & BREITBART, W. (1998). Progress toward guidelines for the management of fatigue. *Oncology, 12,* 369–377.

CELLER, B. G., LOVELL, N. H., & BASILAKIS, J. (2003). Using information technology to improve the management of chronic disease. *Medical Journal of Australia, 179,* 242–246.

CFAH (Center for the Advancement of Health) (2003). *Report on bereavement and grief research.* Retrieved (5-18-2004) from http://www.cfah.org.

CHAFIN, S., CHRISTENFELD, N., & GERIN, W. (2008). Improving cardiovascular recovery from stress with brief poststress exercise. *Health Psychology, 27* (Suppl. 1), S64–S72.

CHAIX, B. (2009). Geographic life environments and coronary heart disease: a literature review, theoretical contributions, methodological updates, and a research agenda. *Annual Review of Public Health, 30,* 81–105.

CHAMBLESS, D. L., & GILLIS, M. M. (1993). Cognitive therapy of anxiety disorders. *Journal of Consulting and Clinical Psychology, 61,* 248–260.

CHAN, K. K., NEIGHBORS, C., & MARLATT, G. A. (2004). Treating addictive behaviors in the employee assistance program: Implications for brief interventions. *Addictive Behaviors, 29,* 1883–1887.

CHANDLER, M., KENNEDY, P. & SANDHU, N. (2007). The association between threat appraisals and psychological adjustment in partners of people with spinal cord injuries. *Rehabilitation Psychology, 52,* 470–477.

CHANDRA, R. K. (1991). Interactions between early nutrition and the immune system. In D. J. P. BARKER (Chair, Ciba Foundation Symposium, No. 156), *The childhood environment and adult disease.* New York: Wiley.

CHANG, A., DILLMAN, A. S., LEONARD, E., & ENGLISH, P. (1985). Teaching car passenger safety to preschool children. *Pediatrics, 76,* 425–428.

CHAPMAN, C. R. (1984). New directions in the understanding and management of pain. *Social Science and Medicine, 19,* 1261–1277.

CHAPMAN, C. R., CASEY, K. L., DUBNER, R., FOLEY, K. M., GRACELY, R. H., & READING, A. E. (1985). Pain measurement: An overview. *Pain, 22,* 1–31.

CHAPMAN, S. L. (1991). Chronic pain: Psychological assessment and treatment. In J. J. SWEET, R. H. ROZENSKY, & S. M. TOVIAN (Eds.), *Handbook of clinical psychology in medical settings.* New York: Plenum.

CHAPMAN, S. L., & BRENA, S. F. (1985). Pain and society. *Annals of Behavioral Medicine, 7*(3), 21–24.

CHASSIN, L., PRESSON, C. C., PITTS, S. C., & SHERMAN, S. J. (2000). The natural history of cigarette smoking from adolescence to adulthood in a Midwestern community sample: Multiple trajectories and their psychosocial correlates. *Health Psychology, 19,* 223–231.

CHASSIN, L., PRESSON, C. C., SHERMAN, S. J., & EDWARDS, D. A. (1991). Four pathways to young-adult smoking status: Adolescent social-psychological antecedents in a Midwestern community sample. *Health Psychology, 10,* 409–418.

CHAVES, J. F., & BROWN, J. M. (1987). Spontaneous cognitive strategies for the control of clinical pain and stress. *Journal of Behavioral Medicine, 10,* 263–276.

CHEN, E., HERMANN, C., RODGERS, D., OLIVER-WELKER, T., & STRUNK, R. C. (2006). Symptom perception in childhood asthma: The role of anxiety and asthma severity. *Health Psychology, 25,* 389–395.

CHEN, E., STRUNK, R., BACHARIER, L., CHAN, M., & MILLER, G. E. (2010). Socioeconomic status associated with exhaled nitric oxide responses to acute stress in children with asthma. *Brain, Behavior, and Immunity, 24,* 444–450.

CHEN, E., ZELTZER, L. K., CRASKE, M. G., & KATZ, E. R. (1999). Alteration of memory in the reduction of children's distress during repeated aversive medical procedures. *Journal of Consulting and Clinical Psychology, 67,* 481–490.

CHEN, K., SCHEIER, L. M., & KANDEL, D. B. (1996). Effects of chronic cocaine use on physical health: A prospective study in a general population sample. *Drug and Alcohol Dependence, 43,* 23–37.

CHEN, L. M., FARWELL, W. R., & JHA, A. K. (2009) Primary care visit duration and quality: Does good care take longer? *Archives of Internal Medicine, 169,* 1866–1872.

CHEN, L.-S., JOHNSON, E. O., BRESLAU, N., HATSUKAMI, D., SACCONE, N. L., et al. (2009). Interplay of genetic risk factor and parent monitoring in risk for nicotine dependence. *Addiction, 104,* 1731–1740.

CHEN, Y., CHEN, C-F., RILEY, D. J., ALLRED, D. C., CHEN, P-H., et al. (1995). Aberrant subcellular localization of BRCA1 in breast cancer. *Science, 270,* 789–791.

CHENG, T. L., SAVAGEAU, J. A., SATTLER, A. L., & DEWITT, T. G. (1993). Confidentiality in health care: A survey of knowledge, perceptions, and attitudes among high school students. *Journal of the American Medical Association, 269,* 1404–1407.

CHERKIN, D. C., DEYO, R. A., LOESER, J. D., BUSH, T., & WADDELL, G. (1994). An international comparison of back surgery rates. *Spine, 19,* 1201–1206.

CHESNEY, M. A., DARBES, L. A., HOERSTER, K., TAYLOR, J. M., CHAMBERS, D. B., & ANDERSON, D. E. (2005). Positive emotions: Exploring the other hemisphere in behavioral medicine. *International Journal of Behavioral Medicine, 12,* 50–58.

CHESNEY, M. A., FRAUTSCHI, N. M., & ROSENMAN, R. H. (1985). Modifying Type A behavior. In J. C. ROSEN & L. J. SOLOMON (Eds.), *Prevention in health psychology* (pp. 130–142). Hanover, NH: University Press of New England.

CHESNEY, M. A., & SMITH, A. W. (1999). Critical delays in HIV testing and care. *American Behavioral Scientist, 42,* 1162–1174.

CHIDA, Y. & HAMER, M. (2008a). An association of adverse psychosocial factors with diabetes mellitus: A meta-analytic review of longitudinal cohort studies. *Diabetologia, 51,* 2168–2178.

CHIDA, Y., & HAMER, M. (2008b). Chronic psychosocial factors and acute physiological responses to laboratory-induced stress in healthy populations: A quantitative review of 30 years of investigations. *Psychological Bulletin, 134,* 829–885.

CHIDA, Y., HAMER, M., & STEPTOE, A. (2008). A bidirectional relationship between psychosocial factors and atopic disorders: A systematic review and meta-analysis. *Psychosomatic Medicine*, 70, 102–116.

CHIDA, Y., HAMER, M., WARDLE, J., & STEPTOE, A. (2008). Do stress-related psychosocial factors contribute to cancer incidence and survival? *Nature Clinical Practice: Oncology*, 5, 466–475.

CHIDA, Y., & MAO, X. (2009). Does psychosocial stress predict symptomatic herpes simplex virus recurrence? A meta-analytic investigation on prospective studies. *Brain, Behavior, and Immunity*, 23, 917–925.

CHIDA, Y., & STEPTOE, A. (2008). Positive psychological well-being and mortality: A quantitative review of prospective observational studies. *Psychosomatic Medicine*, 70, 741–756.

CHIDA, Y., & STEPTOE, A. (2009). The association of anger and hostility with future coronary heart disease: A meta-analytic review of prospective evidence. *Journal of the American College of Cardiology*, 53, 936–946.

CHIDA, Y., & STEPTOE, A. (2010). Greater cardiovascular responses to laboratory mental stress are associated with poor subsequent cardiovascular risk status. A meta-analysis of prospective evidence. *Hypertension*, 55, 1026–1032.

CHIDA, Y., STEPTOE, A., & POWELL, L. H. (2009). Religiosity/spirituality and mortality: A systematic quantitative review. *Psychotherapy and Psychosomatics*, 78, 81–90.

CHIDA, Y., & VEDHARA, K. (2009). Adverse psychosocial factors predict poorer prognosis in HIV disease: A meta-analytic review of prospective investigations. *Brain, Behavior, and Immunity*, 23, 434–445.

CHIESA, A., & SERRETTI, A. (2009). Mindfulness-based stress reduction for stress management in healthy people: A review and meta-analysis. *Journal of Alternative and Complementary Medicine*, 15, 593–600.

CHILCOAT, H. D., DISHION, T. J., & ANTHONY, J. C. (1995). Parent monitoring and the incidence of drug sampling in urban elementary school children. *American Journal of Epidemiology*, 141, 25–31.

CHILDRESS, A. R. (1996). *Cue reactivity and drug craving*. Paper presented at the meeting of the Society of Behavioral Medicine, Washington, DC.

CHILDS, J. D., FRITZ, J. M., FLYNN, T. W., IRRGANG, J. J., JOHNSON, K. K., et al. (2004). A clinical prediction rule to identify patients with low back pain most likely to benefit from spinal manipulation: A validation study. *Annals of Internal Medicine*, 141, 920–928.

CHOI, W. S., AHLUWALIA, J. S., HARRIS, K. J., & OKUYEMI, K. (2002). Progression to established smoking: The influence of tobacco marketing. *American Journal of Preventive Medicine*, 22, 228–233.

CHOU, C.-P., MONTGOMERY, S., PENTZ, M. A., ROHRBACH, L. A., JOHNSON, C. A., et al. (1998). Effects of a community-based prevention program on decreasing drug use in high-risk adolescents. *American Journal of Public Health*, 88, 944–948.

CHOW, C. K., HOLLY, S., RAO-MELACINI, P., FOX, K. A. A., ANAND, S. S., & YUSUF, S. (2010). Association of diet, exercise, and smoking modification with risk of early cardiovascular events after acute coronary syndromes. *Circulation*, 121, 750–758.

CHOW, E., TSAO, M. N., & HARTH, T. (2004). Does psychosocial intervention improve survival in cancer? A meta-analysis. *Palliative Medicine*, 18, 25–31.

CHRISTAKIS, N. A., & ALLISON, P. D. (2006). Mortality after the hospitalization of a spouse. *New England Journal of Medicine*, 354, 719–730.

CHRISTAKIS, N. A., & FOWLER, J. H. (2007). The spread of obesity in a large social network over 32 years. *New England Journal of Medicine*, 357, 370–379.

CHRISTAKIS, N. A., & FOWLER, J. H. (2008). The collective dynamics of smoking in a large social network. *New England Journal of Medicine*, 358, 2284–2286.

CHRISTENFELD, N. (1997). Memory for pain and the delayed effects of distraction. *Health Psychology*, 16, 327–330.

CHRISTENFELD, N., GERIN, W., LINDEN, W., SANDERS, M., MATHUR, J., et al. (1997). Social support effects on cardiovascular reactivity: Is a stranger as effective as a friend? *Psychosomatic Medicine*, 59, 388–398.

CHRISTENSEN, A. J., EDWARDS, D. L., WIEBE, J. S., BENOTSCH, E. G., MCKELVEY, L., et al. (1996). Effect of verbal self-disclosure on natural killer cell activity: Moderating influence of cynical hostility. *Psychosomatic Medicine*, 58, 150–155.

CHRISTENSEN, A. J., MORAN, P. J., & WEIBE, J. S. (1999). Assessment of irrational health beliefs: Relation to health practices and medical regimen adherence. *Health Psychology*, 18, 169–176.

CHRISTENSEN, A. J., & SMITH, T. W. (1995). Personality and patient adherence: Correlates of the five-factor model in renal dialysis. *Journal of Behavioral Medicine*, 18, 305–313.

CHRISTENSEN, J., & LEVINSON, W. (1991). Implementing a behavioral medicine program in an internal medicine residency: A description of curriculum content, resources and barriers encountered. In M. A. JANSEN & J. WEINMAN (Eds.), *The international development of health psychology* (pp. 145–155). Chur, Switzerland: Harwood.

CHUN, C.-A., ENOMOTO, K., & SUE, S. (1996). Health care issues among Asian Americans: Implications of somatization. In P. M. KATO & T. MANN (Eds.), *Handbook of diversity issues in health psychology* (pp. 347–365). New York: Plenum.

CHUNG, M. L., MOSER, D. K., LENNIE, T. A., & RAYENS, M. K. (2009). The effects of depressive symptoms and anxiety on quality of life in patients with heart failure and their spouses: Testing dyadic dynamics using Actor–Partner Interdependence Model. *Journal of Psychosomatic Research*, 67, 29–35.

CICCARONE, D. H., KANOUSE, D. E., COLLINS, R. L., MIE, A., CHEN, J. L., et al. (2003). Sex without disclosure of positive HIV serostatus in a US probability sample of persons receiving medical care for HIV infection. *American Journal of Public Health*, 93, 949–954.

CICCONE, D., JUST, N., & BANDILLA, E. B. (1999). A comparison of economic and social reward in patients with chronic nonmalignant back pain. *Psychosomatic Medicine*, 61, 552–563.

CIESLA, J. A., & ROBERTS, J. E. (2001). Meta-analysis of the relationship between HIV infection and risk for depressive disorders. *American Journal of Psychiatry*, 158, 725–730.

CINCIRIPINI, P. M., CINCIRIPINI, L. G., WALLFISCH, A., HAQUE, W., & VAN VUNAKIS, H. (1996). Behavior therapy and the transdermal nicotine patch: Effects on cessation outcome, affect, and coping. *Journal of Consulting and Clinical Psychology*, 64, 314–323.

CINCIRIPINI, P. M., & FLOREEN, A. (1982). An evaluation of a behavioral program for chronic pain. *Journal of Behavioral Medicine*, 5, 375–389.

CINCIRIPINI, P. M., LAPITSKY, L., DEAY, S., WALLFISCH, A., KITCHENS, K., & VAN VUNAKIS, H. (1995). The effects pf smoking schedules on cessation outcome: Can we improve on common methods of gradual and abrupt nicotine withdrawal? *Journal of Consulting and Clinical Psychology*, 63, 388–399.

CIOPPA, A. L. (1984). Hospice care. In S. N. MCINTIRE & A. L. CIOPPA (Eds.), *Cancer nursing: A developmental approach* (pp. 595–601). New York: Wiley.

CITRON, M. L., JOHNSTON-EARLY, A., BOYER, M., KRASNOW, S. H., HOOD, M., & COHEN, M. H. (1986). Patient-controlled analgesia for severe cancer pain. *Archives of Internal Medicine*, 146, 734–736.

CLAAR, R. L., SIMONS, L. E., & LOGAN, D. E. (2008). Parental response to children's pain: The moderating impact of children's emotional distress on symptoms and disability. *Pain*, 138, 172–179.

CLARK, A. M., HARTLING, L., VANDERMEER, B., & MCALISTER, F. A. (2005). Meta-analysis: Secondary prevention programs for patients with coronary artery disease. *Annals of Internal Medicine*, 143, 659–672.

CLEVER, L. H., & LEGUYADER, Y. (1995). Infectious health risks for health care workers. *Annual Review of Public Health*, 16, 141–164.

CLEVER, L. H., & OMENN, G. S. (1988). Hazards for health care workers. *Annual Review of Public Health*, 9, 273–303.

CLUSS, P. A., & EPSTEIN, L. H. (1985). The measurement of medical compliance in the treatment of disease. In P. KAROLY (Ed.), *Measurement strategies in health psychology* (pp. 403–432). New York: Wiley.

COATES, T. J. (1990). Strategies for modifying sexual behavior for primary and secondary prevention of HIV disease. *Journal of Consulting and Clinical Psychology*, 58, 57–69.

COBB, S., & ROSE, R. M. (1973). Hypertension, peptic ulcer, and diabetes in air traffic controllers. *Journal of the American Medical Association*, 224, 489–492.

COBIAC, L., VOS, T., CORAN, C., & WALLACE, A. (2009). Cost-effectiveness of interventions to prevent alcohol-related disease and injury in Australia. *Addiction*, 104, 1646–1655.

CODDINGTON, R. D. (1972). The significance of life events as etiological factors in the diseases of children—II: A study

of a normal population. *Journal of Psychosomatic Research*, 16, 205–213.

COGAN, R., COGAN, D., WALTZ, W., & MCCUE, M. (1987). Effects of laughter and relaxation on discomfort thresholds. *Journal of Behavioral Medicine*, 10, 139–144.

COHEN, F., KEMENY, M. E., ZEGANS, L. S., JOHNSON, P., KEARNEY, K. A., & STITES, D. P. (2007). Immune function declines with unemployment and recovers after stressor termination. *Psychosomatic Medicine*, 69, 225–234.

COHEN, F., & LAZARUS, R. S. (1979). Coping with the stresses of illness. In G. C. STONE, F. COHEN, & N. E. ADLER (Eds.), *Health psychology—A handbook* (pp. 217–254). San Francisco: Jossey-Bass.

COHEN, L. L. (2002). Reducing infant immunization distress through distraction. *Health Psychology*, 21, 207–211.

COHEN, L. L., BLOUNT, R. L., COHEN, R. J., SCHAEN, E. R., & ZAFF, J. F. (1999). Comparative study of distraction versus topical anesthesia for pediatric pain management during immunizations. *Health Psychology*, 18, 591–598.

COHEN, L. M., MCCARTHY, D. M., BROWN, S. A., & MYERS, M. G. (2002). Negative affect combines with smoking outcome expectancies to predict smoking behavior over time. *Psychology of Addictive Behaviors*, 16, 91–97.

COHEN, R. Y., BROWNELL, K. D., & FELIX, M. R. J. (1990). Age and sex differences in health habits and beliefs of schoolchildren. *Health Psychology*, 9, 208–224.

COHEN, S., ALPER, C. M., DOYLE, W. J., ADLER, N., TREANOR, J. J., & TURNER, R. B. (2008). Objective and subjective socioeconomic status and susceptibility to the common cold. *Health Psychology* 27, 268–274.

COHEN, S., ALPER, C. M., DOYLE, W. J., TREANOR, J. J., & TURNER, R. B. (2006). Positive emotional style predicts resistance to illness after experimental exposure to rhinovirus or influenza A virus. *Psychosomatic Medicine*, 68, 809–815.

COHEN, S., DOYLE, W. J., ALPER, C. M., JANICKI-DEVERTS, D., TURNER, R. B. (2009). Sleep habits and susceptibility to the common cold. *Archives of Internal Medicine*, 169, 62–67.

COHEN, S., DOYLE, W. J., & BAUM, A. (2006). Socioeconomic status is associated with stress hormones. *Psychosomatic Medicine*, 68, 414–420.

COHEN, S., EVANS, G. W., STOKOLS, D., & KRANTZ, D. S. (1986). *Behavior, health, and environmental stress.* New York: Plenum.

COHEN, S., FRANK, E., DOYLE, W. J., SKONER, D. P., RABIN, B. S., & GWALTNEY, J. M. (1998). Types of stressors that increase susceptibility to the common cold in healthy adults. *Health Psychology*, 17, 214–223.

COHEN, S., KAMARCK, T., & MERMELSTEIN, R. (1983). A global measure of perceived stress. *Journal of Health and Social Behavior*, 24, 385–396.

COHEN, S., & LICHTENSTEIN, E. (1990). Perceived stress, quitting smoking, and smoking relapse. *Health Psychology*, 9, 466–478.

COHEN, S., LICHTENSTEIN, E., PROCHASKA, J. O., ROSSI, J. S., GRITZ, E. R., et al. (1989). Debunking myths about self-quitting: Evidence from 10 prospective studies of persons who attempt to quit smoking by themselves. *American Psychologist*, 44, 1355–1365.

COHEN, S., & RODRIGUEZ, M. S. (1995). Pathways linking affective disturbances and physical disorders. *Health Psychology*, 14, 374–380.

COHEN, S., & SPACAPAN, S. (1978). The aftereffects of stress: An attentional interpretation. *Environmental Psychology and Nonverbal Behavior*, 3, 43–57.

COHEN, S., TYRELL, D. A. J., RUSSELL, M. A. H., JARVIS, M. J., & SMITH, A. P. (1993). Smoking, alcohol consumption, and susceptibility to the common cold. *American Journal of Public Health*, 83, 1277–1283.

COHEN, S., TYRRELL, D. A. J., & SMITH, A. P. (1991). Psychological stress and susceptibility to the common cold. *New England Journal of Medicine*, 325, 606–612.

COHEN, S. M., & ELLWEIN, L. B. (1990). Cell proliferation in carcinogenesis. *Science*, 249, 1007–1011.

COHEN, W. S. (1985). Health promotion in the workplace: A prescription for good health. *American Psychologist*, 40, 213–216.

COHN, L. D., MACFARLANE, S., YANEZ, C., & IMAI, W. K. (1995). Risk-perception: Differences between adolescents and adults. *Health Psychology*, 14, 217–222.

COICO, R., & SUNSHINE, G. (2009). *Immunology: A short course* (6th ed.). Hoboken, NJ: Wiley.

COICO, R., SUNSHINE, G., & BENJAMINI, E. (2003). *Immunology: A short course* (5th ed.). Hoboken, NJ: Wiley.

COLE, S. W. (2008). Psychosocial influences on HIV-1 disease progression: Neural, endocrine, and virologic mechanisms. *Psychosomatic Medicine*, 70, 562–568.

COLE, S. W., & KEMENY, M. E. (1997). Psychobiology of HIV infection. *Critical Reviews in Neurobiology*, 11, 289–321.

COLERICK, E. J. (1985). Stamina in later life. *Social Science and Medicine*, 21, 997–1006.

COLLIGAN, M. J., URTES, M., WISSEMAN, C., ROSENSTEEL, R. E., ANANIA, T. L., & HORNUNG, R. W. (1979). An investigation of apparent mass psychogenic illness in an electronics plant. *Journal of Behavioral Medicine*, 2, 297–309.

COLLINS, A., & FRANKENHAEUSER, M. (1978). Stress responses in male and female engineering students. *Journal of Human Stress*, 4, 43–48.

COLLINS, G. (1987, April 29). Keeping fit wasn't easy in 1837, either. *New York Times*, pp. C1, 12.

COMPAS, B. E., WORSHAM, N. L., EY, S., & HOWELL, D. C. (1996). When mom or dad has cancer: II. Coping, cognitive appraisals, and psychological distress in children of cancer patients. *Health Psychology*, 15, 167–175.

CONEL, J. L. (1939). *The postnatal development of the human cerebral cortex* (Vols. 1–7). Cambridge, MA: Harvard University Press.

CONNER, M., & MCMILLAN, B. (2004a). Health belief model. In A. J. CHRISTENSEN, R. MARTIN, & J. M. SMYTH (Eds.), *Encyclopedia of health psychology* (pp. 126–128). New York: Kluwer.

CONNER, M., & MCMILLAN, B. (2004b). Theory of reasoned action and theory of planned behavior. In A. J. CHRISTENSEN,

R. MARTIN, & J. M. SMYTH (Eds.), *Encyclopedia of health psychology* (pp. 316–319). New York: Kluwer.

CONNER, M., NORMAN, P., & BELL, R. (2002). The theory of planned behavior and healthy eating. *Health Psychology*, 21, 194–201.

CONNER, T. S., TENNEN, H, ZAUTRA, A. J., AFFLECK, G., ARMELI, S, & FIFIELD, J. (2006). Coping with rheumatoid arthritis pain in daily life: within-person analyses reveal hidden vulnerability for the formerly depressed. *Pain*, 126, 198–208.

CONRAD, B., WEIDMANN, E., TRUCCO, G., RUDERT, W. A., BEHBOO, R., et al. (1994). Evidence for superantigen involvement in insulin-dependent diabetes mellitus aetiology. *Nature*, 371, 351–355.

CONTRADA, R. J., & GOYAL, T. M. (2004). Individual differences, health, and illness: The role of emotional traits and generalized expectancies. In S. SUTTON, A. BAUM, & M. JOHNSTON (Eds.), *The Sage handbook of health psychology* (pp. 143–168). London: Sage.

CONTRADA, R. J., & KRANTZ, D. S. (1988). Stress, reactivity, and Type A behavior: Current status and future directions. *Annals of Behavioral Medicine*, 10, 64–70.

COOK, P. S., PETERSEN, R. C., & MOORE, D. T. (1990). *Alcohol, tobacco, and other drugs may harm the unborn*. Rockville, MD: U. S. Department of Health and Human Services.

COOK, W. W., & MEDLEY, D. M. (1954). Proposed hostility and pharisaic-virtue scores for the MMPI. *Journal of Applied Psychology*, 38, 414–418.

COOPER, C. E., MCLANAHAN, S. S., MEADOWS, S. O., & BROOKS-GUNN, J. (2009). Family structure transitions and maternal parenting stress. *Journal of Marriage and Family*, 71, 558–574.

COOPER, M. L., & ORCUTT, H. K. (2000). Alcohol use, condom use, and partner type among heterosexual adolescents and young adults. *Journal of Studies on Alcohol*, 61, 413–419.

CORDER, R., DOUTHWAITE, J. A., LEES, D. M., KHAN, N. Q., VISEU DOS SANTOS, A. C., et al. (2001). Endothelin-1 synthesis reduced by red wine. *Nature*, 414, 863–864.

CORDOVA, M. J., CUNNINGHAM, L. L. C., CARLSON, C. R., & ANDRYKOWSKI, M. A. (2001). Posttraumatic growth following breast cancer: A controlled comparison study. *Health Psychology*, 20, 176–185.

CORDOVA, M. J., & RUZEK, J. I. (2004). Posttraumatic stress disorder (PTSD). In A. J. CHRISTENSEN, R. MARTIN, & J. M. SMYTH (Eds.), *Encyclopedia of health psychology* (pp. 215–218). New York: Kluwer.

CORLE, D. K., SHARBAUGH, C., MATESKI, D. J., COYNE, T., PASKETT, E. D., et al. (2001). Self-rated quality of life measures: Effects of change to a low-fat, high-fiber, fruit and vegetable enriched diet. *Annals of Behavioral Medicine*, 23, 198–207.

CORRADO, D., BASSO, C., PAVESI, A., MICHIELI, P., SCHIAVON, M., & THIENE, G. (2006). Trends in sudden cardiovascular death in young competitive athletes after implementation of a preparticipation screening program. *Journal of the American Medical Association*, 296, 1593–1601.

CORRAL, I., & LANDRINE, H. (2008). Acculturation and ethnic-minority health behavior: A test of the Operant Model. *Health Psychology*, 27, 737–745.

COSTA, P. T., & MCCRAE, R. R. (1980). Somatic complaints in males as a function of age and neuroticism: A longitudinal analysis. *Journal of Behavioral Medicine*, 3, 245–257.

COSTA, P. T., & MCCRAE, R. R. (1985). Hypochondriasis, neuroticism, and aging. *American Psychologist*, 40, 19–28.

COSTA, P. T. & MCCRAE, R. R. (1992). *Professional manual: Revised NEO Personality Inventory (NEO-PI-R) and the NEO Five-Factor Inventory (NEO-FFI)*. Odessa, FL: Psychological Assessment Resources.

COSTANZO, E. S., RYFF, C. D., & SINGER, B. H. (2009). Psychosocial adjustment among cancer survivors: Findings from a national survey of health and well-being. *Health Psychology*, 28, 147–156.

COTTINGTON, E. M., & HOUSE, J. S. (1987). Occupational stress and health: A multivariate relationship. In A. BAUM & J. E. SINGER (Eds.), *Handbook of psychology and health* (Vol. 5, pp. 41–62). Hillsdale, NJ: Erlbaum.

COURTNEY, K. E., & POLICH, J. (2009). Binge drinking in young adult: Data, definitions, and determinants. *Psychological Bulletin*, 135, 142–156.

COUSINS, N. (1985). Anatomy of an illness (as perceived by the patient). In A. MONAT & R. S. LAZARUS (Eds.), *Stress and coping: An anthology* (2nd ed, pp. 55–66). New York: Columbia University Press.

COUTU, M.-F., DUPUIS, G., & D'ANTONO, B. (2001). The impact of cholesterol lowering on patients' moods. *Journal of Behavioral Medicine*, 24, 517–536.

COX, D. J., GONDER-FREDERICK, L., ANTOUN, B., CRYER, P. E., & CLARKE, W. L. (1993). Perceived symptoms in the recognition of hypoglycemia. *Diabetes Care*, 16, 519–527.

COX, G. B., CHAPMAN, C. R., & BLACK, R. G. (1978). The MMPI and chronic pain: The diagnosis of psychogenic pain. *Journal of Behavioral Medicine*, 1, 437–443.

COX, W. M. (1985). Personality correlates of substance abuse. In M. GALIZIO & S. A. MAISTO (Eds.), *Determinants of substance abuse: Biological, psychological, and environmental factors* (pp. 209–246). New York: Plenum.

COYNE, J. C., & RACIOPPO, M. W. (2000). Never the twain shall meet?: Closing the gap between coping research and clinical intervention research. *American Psychologist*, 55, 655–664.

COYNE, J. C., STEFANEK, M., & PALMER, S. C. (2007). Psychotherapy and survival in cancer: The conflict between hope and evidence. *Psychological Bulletin*, 133, 367–394.

CRAMER, P. (2000). Defense mechanisms in psychology today: Further processes for adaptation. *American Psychologist*, 55, 637–646.

CRAMP, F., & DANIEL, J. (2008). Exercise for the management of cancer-related fatigue in adults. *Cochrane Database of Systematic Reviews*, Issue 2. Retrieved (1-30-2010) from http://www.thecochranelibrary.com.

CRAUN, A. M., & DEFFENBACHER, J. L. (1987). The effects of information, behavioral rehearsal, and prompting on breast self-exams. *Journal of Behavioral Medicine*, 10, 351–365.

CRISP, A. H., & KALUCY, R. S. (1974). Aspects of the perceptual disorder in anorexia nervosa. *British Journal of Medical Psychology*, 47, 349–361.

CRITCHLOW, B. (1986). The powers of John Barleycorn: Beliefs about the effects of alcohol on social behavior. *American Psychologist*, 41, 751–764.

CRONAN, T. A., GROESSL, E., & KAPLAN, R. M. (1997). The effects of social support and education interventions on health care costs. *Arthritis Care and Research*, 10, 99–110.

CROOG, S. H. (1983). Recovery and rehabilitation of heart patients: Psychosocial aspects. In D. S. KRANTZ, A. BAUM, & J. E. SINGER (Eds.), *Handbook of psychology and health* (Vol. 3, pp. 295–334). Hillsdale, NJ: Erlbaum.

CROOG, S. H., & FITZGERALD, E. F. (1978). Subjective stress and serious illness of a spouse: Wives of heart patients. *Journal of Health and Social Behavior*, 19, 166–178.

CROYLE, R. T., & DITTO, P. H. (1990). Illness cognition and behavior: An experimental approach. *Journal of Behavioral Medicine*, 13, 31–52.

CRUESS, D. G., ANTONI, M. H., MCGREGOR, B. A., KILBOURN, K. M., BOYERS, A. E., et al. (2000). Cognitive-behavioral stress management reduces serum cortisol by enhancing benefit finding among women being treated for early stage breast cancer. *Psychosomatic Medicine*, 62, 304–308.

CRUM, R. M., GREEN, K. M., STORR, C. L., CHAN, Y.-F., IALONGO, N., et al. (2008). Depressed mood in childhood and subsequent alcohol use through adolescence and young adulthood. *Archives of General Psychiatry*, 65, 702–712,

CU (Consumers Union) (1994, January). Acupuncture. *Consumer Reports*, pp. 54–59.

CU (Consumers Union) (1995, February). How is your doctor treating you? *Consumer Reports*, pp. 81–88.

CU (Consumers Union). (1998, August). Checkups: Are you getting what you need? *Consumer Reports*, pp. 17–19.

CU (Consumers Union). (1999, August). How does your HMO stack up? *Consumer Reports*, pp. 23–29.

CU (Consumers Union). (2000, May). The mainstreaming of alternative medicine. *Consumer Reports*, pp. 17–25.

CU (Consumers Union) (2001, October). Are you in the right plan? *Consumer Reports*, pp. 27–31.

CU (Consumers Union) (2004, May) Dangerous supplements still at large. *Consumer Reports*, pp. 12–17.

CU (Consumers Union) (2007, February). Get better care from your doctor. *Consumer Reports*, pp. 32–36.

CU (Consumers Union) (2010, March). Deadly infections. *Consumer Reports*, pp. 16–21.

CUIJPERS, P., VAN STRATEN, A., & ANDERSSON, G. (2008). Internet-administered cognitive behavior therapy for health problems: A systematic review. *Journal of Behavioral Medicine*, 31, 169–177.

CUMMINGS, K. M., FONG, G. T., & BORLAND, R. (2009). Environmental influences on tobacco use: Evidence from societal and community influence on tobacco use and dependence. *Annual Review of Clinical Psychology*, 5, 433–458.

CUMMINGS, K. M., & HYLAND, A. (2005). Impact of nicotine replacement therapy on smoking behavior. *Annual Review of Public Health*, 26, 583–599.

CUMMINGS, N. A. (1991). Arguments for the financial efficacy of psychological services in health care settings. In J. J. SWEET, R. H. ROZENSKY, & S. M. TOVIAN (Eds.), *Handbook of clinical psychology in medical settings* (pp. 113–126). New York: Plenum.

CUNNINGHAM, A. J., EDMONDS, C. V. I., JENKINS, G. P., POLLACK, H., LOCKWOOD, G. A., & WARR, D. (1998). A randomized controlled trial of the effects of group psychological therapy on survival in women with metastatic breast cancer. *Psycho-Oncology*, 7, 508–517.

CUNNINGHAM, C. L. (1998). Drug conditioning and drug-seeking behavior. In W. O'DONAHUE (Ed.), *Learning and behavior therapy* (pp. 518–544). Boston: Allyn & Bacon.

CURRIER, J. M., NEIMEYER, R. A., & BERMAN, J. S. (2008). The effectiveness of psychotherapeutic interventions for bereaved persons: A comprehensive quantitative review. *Psychological Bulletin*, 134, 648–661.

CURRY, S. J., GROTHAUS, L. C., MCAFEE, T., & PABINIAK, C. (1998). Use and cost effectiveness of smoking-cessation services under four insurance plans in a health maintenance organization. *New England Journal of Medicine*, 339, 673–679.

CURRY, S. J., & MCBRIDE, C. M. (1994). Relapse prevention for smoking cessation: Review and evaluation of concepts and interventions. *Annual Review of Public Health*, 15, 345–366.

CURRY, S. J., TAPLIN, S. H., ANDERMAN, C., BARLOW, W. E., & MCBRIDE, C. (1993). A randomized trial of the impact of risk assessment and feedback on participation in mammography screening. *Preventive Medicine*, 22, 350–360.

CURRY, S., WAGNER, E. H., & GROTHAUS, L. C. (1990). Intrinsic and extrinsic motivation for smoking cessation. *Journal of Consulting and Clinical Psychology*, 58, 310–316.

CUTLER, R. B., FISHBAIN, D. A., ROSOMOFF, H. L., ABDEL-MOTY, E., KHALIL, T. M., & ROSOMOFF, R. S. (1994). Does nonsurgical pain center treatment of chronic pain return patients to work?: A review and meta-analysis of the literature. *Spine*, 19, 643–652.

CUTRONA, C. E. (1986). Behavioral manifestations of social support: A microanalytic investigation. *Journal of Personality and Social Psychology*, 51, 201–208.

CUTRONA, C. E., & GARDNER, K. A. (2004). Social support. In A. J. CHRISTENSEN, R. MARTIN, & J. M. SMYTH (Eds.), *Encyclopedia of health psychology* (pp. 280–284). New York: Kluwer.

CVENGROS, J. A., CHRISTENSEN, A. J., CUNNINGHAM, C., HILLIS, S. L., & KABOLI, P. J. (2009). Patient preference for and reports of provider behavior: Impact of symmetry on patient outcomes. *Health Psychology*, 28, 660–667.

DAHLBERG, C. C. (1977, June). Stroke. *Psychology Today*, pp. 121–128.

DAHLQUIST, L. M., GIL, K. M., ARMSTRONG, F. D., DELAWYER, D. D., GREENE, P., & WUORI, D. (1986). Preparing children for medical examinations: The importance of previous medical experience. *Health Psychology*, 5, 249–259.

DAHLQUIST, L. M., MCKENNA, K. D., JONES, K. K., DILLINGER, L., WEISS, K. E., & ACKERMAN, C. S. (2007). Active and passive distraction using a head-mounted display helmet: Effects on cold pressor pain in children. *Health Psychology*, 26, 794–801.

DAHLQUIST, L. M., PENDLEY, J. S., LANDTHRIP, D. S., JONES, C. L., & STEUBER, C. P. (2002). Distraction intervention for preschoolers undergoing intramuscular injections and subcutaneous port access. *Health Psychology*, 21, 94–99.

DALAL, H. M., ZAWADA, A., JOLLY, K., MOXHAM, T., & TAYLOR, R. S. (2010). Home based versus centre based cardiac rehabilitation: Cochrane systematic review and meta-analysis. *British Medical Journal*, 340, b5631.

DAL CIN, S., WORTH, K. A., GERRARD, M., GIBBONS, F. X., STOOLMILLER, M., et al. (2009). Watching and drinking: Expectancies, prototypes, and friends' alcohol use mediate the effect of exposure to alcohol use in movies on adolescent drinking. *Health Psychology*, 28, 473–483.

DALE, J. A. (2004). Stress management. In A. J. CHRISTENSEN, R. MARTIN, & J. M. SMYTH (Eds.), *Encyclopedia of health psychology* (pp. 298–301). New York: Kluwer.

DALESSIO, D. J. (1994). Diagnosing the severe headache. *Neurology*, 44 (Suppl. 3), S6–S12.

DALLMAN, M. F., PECORARO, N., AKANA, S. F., LA FLEUR, S. E., GOMEZ, F., et al. (2003). Chronic stress and obesity: A new view of "comfort food." *Proceedings of the National Academy of Sciences*, 100, 11696–11701.

DALTON, J. A., KEEFE, F. J., CARLSON, J., & YOUNGBLOOD, R. (2003). Tailoring cognitive-behavioral treatment for cancer pain. *Pain Management Nursing*, 5, 3–18.

DANGOUR, A. D., DODHIA, S. K., HAYTER, A., ALLEN, E., LOCK, K., UAUY, R. (2009). Nutritional quality of organic foods: A systematic review. *American Journal of Clinical Nutrition*, 90, 680–685.

DANIELS, S. R., MORRISON, J. A., SPRECHER, D. L., KHOURY, P., & KIMBALL, T. R. (1999). Association of body fat distribution and cardiovascular risk factors in children and adolescents. *Circulation*, 99, 541–545.

DANOFF-BURG, S. (2004). Arthritis. In A. J. CHRISTENSEN, R. MARTIN, & J. M. SMYTH (Eds.), *Encyclopedia of health psychology* (pp. 17–19). New York: Kluwer.

DANSINGER, M. I., GLEASON, J. A., GRIFFITH, J. L., SELKER, H. P., & SCHAEFER, E. J. (2005). Comparison of the Atkins, Ornish, Weight Watchers, and Zone diets for weight loss and heart disease risk reduction: A randomized trial. *Journal of the American Medical Association*, 293, 43–53.

DAUBENMIER, J. J., WEIDNER, G., SUMNER, M. D., MENDELL, N., MERRITT-WORDEN, T., et al. (2007). The contribution of changes in diet, exercise, and stress management to changes in coronary risk in women and men in the Multisite Cardiac Lifestyle Intervention Program. *Annals of Behavioral Medicine*, 33, 57–68.

DAVIDSON, K. W., GIDRON, Y., MOSTOFSKY, E., & TRUDEAU, K. J. (2007). Hospitalization cost offset of a hostility intervention for coronary heart disease patients. *Journal of Consulting and Clinical Psychology, 75,* 657–662.

DAVIDSON, L. E., HUDSON, R., KILPATRICK, K., KUK, J. L., MCMILLAN, K., et al. (2009). Effects of exercise modality on insulin resistance and functional limitation in older adults: A randomized controlled trial. *Archives of Internal Medicine, 169,* 122–131.

DAVIDSON, R. J., KABAT-ZINN, J., SCHUMACHER, J., ROSENKRANZ, M., MULLER, D., et al. (2003). Alterations in brain and immune function produced by mindfulness meditation. *Psychosomatic Medicine, 65,* 564–570.

DAVIDSON, R. S. (1985). Behavioral medicine and alcoholism. In N. SCHNEIDERMAN & J. T. TAPP (Eds.), *Behavioral medicine: The biopsychosocial approach* (pp. 379–404). Hillsdale, NJ: Erlbaum.

DAVIS, M. C., MATTHEWS, K. A., & TWAMLEY, E. W. (1999). Is life more difficult on Mars or Venus? A meta-analytic review of sex differences in major and minor life events. *Annals of Behavioral Medicine, 21,* 83–97.

DAVIS, M. S. (1966). Variations in patients' compliance with doctors' orders: Analysis of congruence between survey responses and results of empirical investigations. *Journal of Medical Education, 41,* 1037–1048.

DAVISON, K. P., PENNEBAKER, J. W., & DICKERSON, S. S. (2000). Who talks? The social psychology of illness suport groups. *American Psychologist, 55,* 205–217.

DAW, J. (2001). New rule will change the psychologist–physician relationship. *Monitor on Psychology, 32,* pp. 66–69.

DEA (Drug Enforcement Administration of United States Department of Justice) (2004). *Frequently asked questions and answers for health care professionals and law enforcement personnel.* Retrieved (9-16-2004) from http://www.dea.gov.

DEANGELIS, T. (1990, October). Psychologists involved with epilepsy treatment. *American Psychological Association Monitor,* p. 24.

DE BOER, A. G., TASKILA, T., OJAJÄRVI, A., VAN DIJK, F. J., & VERBEEK, J. H. (2009). Cancer survivors and unemployment: A meta-analysis and meta-regression. *Journal of the American Medical Association, 301,* 753–762.

DEDERT, E. A., CALHOUN, P. S., WATKINS, L. L., SHERWOOD, A., & BECKHAM, J. C. (2010). Posttraumatic stress disorder, cardiovascular, and metabolic disease: A review of the evidence. *Annals of Behavioral Medicine, 39,* 61–78.

DEGNER, L. F., & BEATON, J. I. (1987). *Life-death decisions in health care.* New York: Hemisphere.

DE GROOT, M., ANDERSON, R., FREEDLAND, K. E., CLOUSE, R. E., & LUSTMAN, P. J. (2001). Association of depression and diabetes complications: A meta-analysis. *Psychosomatic Medicine, 63,* 619–630.

DEJONG, W. (1980). The stigma of obesity: The consequences of naive assumptions concerning the causes of physical deviance. *Journal of Health and Social Behavior, 21,* 75–87.

DE KROM, M., BAUER, F., COLLIER, D., ADAN, R. A. H., & LA FLEUR, S. E. (2009). Genetic variation and effects on human eating behavior. *Annual Review of Nutrition, 29,* 283–304.

DELAHANTY, D. L., DOUGALL, A. L., HAWKEN, L., TRAKOWSKI, J. H., SCHMITZ, J. B., et al. (1996). Time course of natural killer cell activity and lymphocyte proliferation in response to two acute stressors in healthy men. *Health Psychology, 15,* 48–55.

DELONGIS, A., COYNE, J. C., DAKOF, G., FOLKMAN, S., & LAZARUS, R. S. (1982). Relationship of daily hassles, uplifts, and major life events to health status. *Health Psychology, 1,* 119–136.

DEL VECCHIO, T., & O'LEARY, K. D. (2004). Effectiveness of anger treatments for specific anger problems: A meta-analytic review. *Clinical Psychology Review, 24,* 15–34.

DENISON, E., ÅSENLÖF, P., & LINDBERG, P. (2004). Self-efficacy, fear avoidance, and pain intensity as predictors of disability in subacute and chronic musculoskeletal pain patients in primary health care. *Pain, 111,* 245–252.

DENISSENKO, M. F., PAO, A., TANG, M.-S., & PFEIFER, G. P. (1996). Preferential formation of benzo[a]pyrene adducts at lung cancer mutational hotspots in P53. *Science, 274,* 430–432.

DENNIS, C., HOUSTON-MILLER, N., SCHWARTZ, R. G., AHN, D. K., KRAEMER, H. C., et al. (1988). Early return to work after uncomplicated myocardial infarction: Results of a randomized trial. *Journal of the American Medical Association, 260,* 214–220.

DENSON, T. F., SPANOVIC, M., & MILLER, N. (2009). Cognitive appraisals and emotions predict cortisol and immune responses: A meta-analysis of acute laboratory social stressors and emotion inductions. *Psychological Bulletin, 135,* 823–853.

DEPALMA, A. (1996). In Mexico, pain relief is a medical and political issue. *New York Times,* p. A6.

DE PASCALIS, V., CACACE, I., & MASSICOLLE, F. (2004). Perception and modulation of pain in waking and hypnosis: Functional significance of phase-ordered gamma oscillations. *Pain, 112,* 27–36.

DE PEUTER, S., LEMAIGRE, V., VAN DIEST, I., & VAN DEN BERGH, O. (2008). Illness-specific catastrophic thinking and overperception in asthma. *Health Psychology, 27,* 93–99.

DE PEUTER, S., VAN DIEST, I., LEMAIGRE, V., LI, W., VERLEDEN, G., et al. (2005). Can subjective asthma symptoms be learned? *Psychosomatic Medicine, 67,* 454–461.

DEROGATIS, L. R. (1977). *Psychological Adjustment to Illness Scale.* Baltimore: Clinical Psychometric Research.

DEROGATIS, L. R. (1986). The Psychological Adjustment to Illness Scale (PAIS). *Journal of Psychosomatic Research, 30,* 77–91.

DEROGATIS, L. R., FLEMING, M. P., SUDLER, N. C., & DELLAPIETRA, L. (1995). Psychological assessment. In P. M. NICASSIO & T. W. SMITH (Eds.), *Managing chronic illness: A biopsychosocial perspective* (pp. 59–116). Washington, DC: American Psychological Association.

DEROON-CASSINI, T. A., DE ST. AUBIN, E., VALVANO, A., HASTINGS, J., & HORN, P. (2009). Psychological well-being after spinal cord injury: Perception of loss and meaning making. *Rehabilitation Psychology, 54,* 306–314.

DESCARTES, R. (1664). *Traite de l'Homme*. Paris: Angot.

DESHARNAIS, R., JOBIN, J., CÔTÉ, C., LÉVESQUE, L., & GODIN, G. (1993). Aerobic exercise and the placebo effect: A controlled study. *Psychosomatic Medicine, 55,* 149–154.

DESHIELDS, T., CARMIN, C., ROSS, L., & MANNEN, K. (1995). *Diagnosis of psychological disorders in primary care patients by medicine residents*. Paper presented at the meeting of the Society of Behavioral Medicine, San Diego.

DES JARLAIS, D. C., & SEMAAN, S. (2008). HIV prevention for injecting drug users: The first 25 years and counting. *Psychosomatic Medicine, 70,* 606–611.

DETJEN, J. (1991). Will genetics revolution mark some as victims? *Philadelphia Inquirer*, pp. A1, 18.

DETWEILER, J. B., BEDEL, B. T., SALOVEY, P., PRONIN, E., & ROTHMAN, A. J. (1999). Message framing and sunscreen use: Gain-framed messages motivate beach goers. *Health Psychology, 18,* 189–196.

DEVELLIS, B. M., & DEVELLIS, R. F. (2001). Self-efficacy and health. In A. BAUM, T. A. REVENSON, & J. E. SINGER (Eds.), *Handbook of health psychology* (pp. 235–247). Mahwah, NJ: Erlbaum.

DEVINENI, T., & BLANCHARD, E. B. (2005). A randomized controlled trial of an internet-based treatment for chronic headache. *Behaviour Research and Therapy, 43,* 277–292.

DEVINS, G. M., BINIK, Y. M., HOLLOMBY, D. J., BARRÉ, P. E., & GUTTMANN, R. D. (1981). Helplessness and depression in end-stage renal disease. *Journal of Abnormal Psychology, 90,* 531–545.

DE VOGLI, R., CHANDOLA, T., & MARMOT, M. G. (2007). Negative aspects of close relationships and heart disease. *Archives of Internal Medicine, 167,* 1951–1957.

DEVRIES, J. E., BURNETTE, M. M., & REDMON, W. K. (1991). AIDS prevention: Improving nurses' compliance with glove wearing through performance feedback. *Journal of Applied Behavior Analysis, 24,* 705–711.

DEW, M. A., MYASKOVSKY, L., SWITZER, G. E., & DIMARTINI, A. F. (2004). Organ transplantation. In A. J. CHRISTENSEN, R. MARTIN, & J. M. SMYTH (Eds.), *Encyclopedia of health psychology* (pp. 189–192). New York: Kluwer.

DEWALL, C. N., BAUMEISTER, R. F., STILLMAN, T. F., & GAILLIOT, M. T. (2007). Violence restrained: Effects of self-regulation and its depletion on aggression. *Journal of Experimental Social Psychology, 43,* 62–76.

DE WIT, J. B. F., DAS, E., & VET, R. (2008). What works best: Objective statistics or a personal testimonial? An assessment of the persuasive effects of different types of message evidence on risk perception. *Health Psychology, 27,* 110–115.

DEYO, R. A., CHERKIN, D., CONRAD, D., & VOLINN, E. (1991). Cost, controversy, crisis: Low back pain and the health of the public. *Annual Review of Public Health, 12,* 141–156.

DIAMOND, E. L. (1982). The role of anger and hostility in essential hypertension and coronary heart disease. *Psychological Bulletin, 92,* 410–433.

DICKERSON, S. S., MYCEK, P. J., & ZALDIVAR, F. (2008). Negative social evaluation, but not mere social presence, elicits cortisol responses to a laboratory stressor task. *Health Psychology 27,* 116–121.

DICLEMENTE, C. C., PROCHASKA, J. O., FAIRHURST, S. K., VELICER, W. F., VELASQUEZ, M. M., & ROSSI, J. S. (1991). The process of smoking cessation: An analysis of precontemplation, contemplation, and preparation stages of change. *Journal of Consulting and Clinical Psychology, 59,* 295–304.

DICLEMENTE, C. C., PROCHASKA, J. O., & GILBERTINI, M. (1985). Self-efficacy and the stages of self-change of smoking. *Cognitive Therapy and Research, 9,* 181–200.

DICLEMENTE, R. J., ZORN, J., & TEMOSHOK, L. (1987). The association of gender, ethnicity, and length of residence in the Bay Area to adolescents' knowledge and attitudes about acquired immune deficiency syndrome. *Journal of Applied Social Psychology, 17,* 216–230.

DIEFENBACH, M. (2004). Fear appeals. In A. J. CHRISTENSEN, R. MARTIN, & J. M. SMYTH (Eds.), *Encyclopedia of health psychology* (pp. 107–108). New York: Kluwer.

DIEHR, P., KOEPSELL, T., CHEADLE, A., PSATY, B. M., WAGNER, E., & CURRY, S. (1993). Do communities differ in health behaviors? *Journal of Clinical Epidemiology, 46,* 1141–1149.

DIERKER, L., JIANPING, H., KALAYDJIAN, A., SWENDSEN, J., DEGENHARDT, L., et al. (2008). The importance of timing of transitions for risk of regular smoking and nicotine dependence. *Annals of Behavioral Medicine, 36,* 87–92.

DIFRANZA, J. R., & LEW, R. A. (1995). Effect of maternal cigarette smoking on pregnancy complications and sudden infant death syndrome. *Journal of Family Practice, 40,* 385–394.

DIGIUSEPPE, R., & TAFRATE, R. C. (2003). Anger treatment for adults: A meta-analytic review. *Clinical Psychology: Science and Practice, 10,* 70–84.

DIGIUSTO, E., LINTZERIS, N., BREEN, C., KIMBER, J., MATTICK, R. P., et al. (2005). Short-term ourcomes of five heroin detoxification methods in the Australian NEPOD Project. *Addictive Behaviors, 30,* 443–456.

DIGMAN, J. M. (1990). Personality structure: Emergence of the five-factor model. *Annual Review of Psychology, 41,* 417–440.

DILLER, L. (1999). Hemiplegia. In M. G. EISENBERG, R. L. GLUECKAUF, & H. H. ZARETSKY (Eds.), *Medical aspects of disability: A handbook for the rehabilitation professional* (2nd ed., pp. 528–547). New York: Springer.

DILORIO, C., MCCARTY, F., RESNICOW, K., LEHR, S., & DENZMORE, P. (2007). REAL Men: A group-randomized trial of an HIV prevention intervention for adolescent boys. *American Journal of Public Health, 97,* 1084–1089.

DIMAGGIO, C., GALEA, S., & LI, G. (2009). Substance use and misuse in the aftermath of terrorism: A Bayesian meta-analysis. *Addiction, 104,* 894–904.

DIMATTEO, M. R. (1985). Physician-patient communication: Promoting a positive health care setting. In J. C. ROSEN & L. J. SOLOMON (Eds.), *Prevention in health psychology* (pp. 328–365). Hanover, NH: University Press of New England.

DIMATTEO, M. R. (2004). Social support and patient adherence to medical treatment: A meta-analysis. *Health Psychology, 23,* 207–218.

DiMatteo, M. R., & Dinicola, D. D. (1982). *Achieving patient compliance: The psychology of the medical practitioner's role.* New York: Pergamon.

DiMatteo, M. R., Giordani, P. J., Lepper, H. S., & Croghan, T. W. (2002). Patient adherence and medical treatment outcomes: A meta-analysis. *Medical Care, 40,* 791–811.

DiMatteo, M. R., Hays, R. D., & Prince, L. M. (1986). Relationship of physicians' nonverbal communication skill to patient satisfaction, appointment noncompliance, and physician workload. *Health Psychology, 5,* 581–594.

Dimsdale, J. E., Alpert, B. S., & Schneiderman, N. (1986). Exercise as a modulator of cardiovascular reactivity. In K. A. Matthews, S. M. Weiss, T. Detre, T. M. Dembroski, B. Falkner, S. B. Manuck, & R. B. Williams (Eds.), *Handbook of stress, reactivity, and cardiovascular disease* (pp. 365–384). New York: Wiley.

Dinh, K. T., Sarason, I. G., Peterson, A. V., & Onstad, L. E. (1995). Children's perception of smokers and nonsmokers: A longitudinal study. *Health Psychology, 14,* 32–40.

DISC (Writing group for the DISC Collaborative Research Group) (1995). Efficacy and safety of lowering dietary intake of fat and cholesterol in children with elevated low-density lipoprotein cholesterol: The Dietary Intervention Study in Children (DISC). *Journal of the American Medical Association, 273,* 1429–1435.

Dishman, R. K. (1982). Compliance/adherence in health-related exercise. *Health Psychology, 1,* 237–267.

Dishman, R. K. (1986). Mental health. In V. Seefeldt (Ed.), *Physical activity and well-being* (pp. 304–341). Reston, VA: American Alliance for Health, Physical Education, Recreation, and Dance.

Dishman, R. K. (1991). Increasing and maintaining exercise and physical activity. *Behavior Therapy, 22,* 345–378.

Dishman, R. K., Sallis, J. F., & Orenstein, D. R. (1985). The determinants of physical activity and exercise. *Public Health Reports, 100,* 158–171.

Distefan, J. M., Gilpin, E. A., Sargent, J. D., & Pierce, J. P. (1999). Do movie stars encourage adolescents to start smoking? Evidence from California. *Preventive Medicine, 28,* 1–11.

Ditto, B. (1993). Familial influences on heart rate, blood pressure, and self-report anxiety responses to stress: Results from 100 twin pairs. *Psychophysiology, 30,* 635–645.

Ditto, P. H., & Hawkins, N. A. (2005). Advance directives and cancer decision making near the end of life. *Health Psychology, 24*(Suppl.), S63–S70.

Ditzen, B., Hoppmann, C., & Klumb, P. (2008). Positive couple interactions and daily cortisol: On the stress-protecting role of intimacy. *Psychosomatic Medicine, 70,* 883–889.

Dixon, A., Le Grand, J., Henderson, J., Murray, P., & Poteliakhoff, E. (2003) *Is the NHS Equitable? A Review of the Evidence.* Retrieved (11-23-10) from http://www2.lse.ac.uk/intranet/LSEServices/divisionsAnd Departments/ERD/pressAndInformationOffice/PDF/DP11_2003_Is_the_NHS_equitable.pdf.

Dobbins, M., Decorby, K., Robeson, P., Husson, H., & Tirilis, D. (2009). School-based physical activity programs for promoting physical activity and fitness in children and adolescents aged 6–18. *Cochrane Database of Systematic Reviews,* Issue 1. Retrieved (1-30-2010) from http://www.thecochranelibrary.com. DOI:10.1002/14651858.CD007651.

Dobkin, B. H. (2004). Strategies for stroke rehabilitation. *Lancet Neurology, 3,* 528–536.

Dobkin, B. H. (2005). Rehabilitation after stroke. *New England Journal of Medicine, 352,* 1677–1684.

Dodge, B., Reece, M., & Herbenick, D. (2009). School-based condom education and its relations with diagnoses of and testing for sexually transmitted infections among men in the United States. *American Journal of Public Health, 99,* 2180–2182.

Doehrman, S. R. (1977). Psycho-social aspects of recovery from coronary heart disease: A review. *Social Science and Medicine, 11,* 199–218.

Doering, S., Katzlberger, F., Rumpold, G., Roessler, S. Hofstoetter, M. S., et al. (2000). Videotape preparation of patients before hip replacement surgery reduces stress. *Psychosomatic Medicine, 62,* 365–373.

Doherty, K., Militello, F. S., Kinnunen, T., & Garvey, A. J. (1996). Nicotine gum dose and weight gain after smoking cessation. *Journal of Consulting and Clinical Psychology, 64,* 799–807.

Dohrenwend, B. S., & Dohrenwend, B. P. (1984). Life stress and illness: Formulation of the issues. In B. S. Dohrenwend & B. P. Dohrenwend (Eds.), *Stressful life events and their contexts* (pp. 1–27). New Brunswick, NJ: Rutgers University Press.

Dohrenwend, B. S., Krasnoff, L., Askenasy, A. R., & Dohrenwend, B. P. (1978). Exemplification of a method for scaling life events: The PERI Life Events Scale. *Journal of Health and Social Behavior, 19,* 205–229.

Dolan, S. L. (2004). Alcoholics Anonymous. In A. J. Christensen, R. Martin, & J. M. Smyth (Eds.), *Encyclopedia of health psychology* (pp. 8–9). New York: Kluwer.

Dolecek, T. A., Milas, N. C., Van Horn, L. V., Farrand, M. E., Gorder, D. D., et al. (1986). A long-term nutrition experience: Lipid responses and dietary adherence patterns in the Multiple Risk Factor Intervention Trial. *Journal of the American Dietetic Association, 86,* 752–758.

Dolinski, D., Gromski, W., & Zawisza, E. (1987). Unrealistic pessimism. *Journal of Social Psychology, 127,* 511–516.

Dollar, K. M., Homish, G. G., Kozlowski, L. T., & Leonard, K. E. (2009). Spousal and alcohol-related predictors of smoking cessation: A longitudinal study in a community sample of married couples. *American Journal of Public Health, 99,* 231–233.

Dominguez, T. P., Dunkel-Schetter, C., Glynn, L. M., Hobel, C., & Sandman, C. A. (2008). Racial differences in birth outcomes: The role of general, pregnancy, and racism stress. *Health Psychology, 27,* 194–203.

DONOVAN, D. M. (2003). Relapse prevention in substance abuse treatment. In J. L. SORENSEN, R. A. RAWSON, J. GUYDISH, & J. E. ZWEBEN (Eds.), *Drug abuse treatment through collaboration: Practice and research partnerships that work* (pp. 121–137). Washington, DC: American Psychological Association.

DORROS, S. M., CARD, N. A., SEGRIN, C., & BADGER, T. A. (2010). Interdependence in women with breast cancer and their partners: An interindividual model of distress. *Journal of Consulting and Clinical Psychology, 78*, 121–125.

DOUGALL, A. L., & BAUM, A. (2001). Stress, health, and illness. In A. BAUM, T. A. REVENSON, & J. E. SINGER (Eds.), *Handbook of health psychology* (pp. 321–337). Mahwah, NJ: Erlbaum.

DOWNEY, G., SILVER, R. C., & WORTMAN, C. B. (1990). Reconsidering the attribution-adjustment relation following a major negative event: Coping with the loss of a child. *Journal of Personality and Social Psychology, 59*, 925–940.

DRACUP, K. (2004). Treatment delay. In A. J. CHRISTENSEN, R. MARTIN, & J. M. SMYTH (Eds.), *Encyclopedia of health psychology* (pp. 321–323). New York: Kluwer.

DRAPKIN, R. G., WING, R. R., & SHIFFMAN, S. (1995). Responses to hypothetical high risk situations: Do they predict weight loss in a behavioral treatment program or the context of dietary lapses? *Health Psychology, 14*, 427–434.

DRECHSLER, D., & JÜTTING, J. P. (2005). *Private health insurance in low- and middle-income countries.* Retrieved (2-19-2007) from http://hc.wharton.upenn.edu/impactconference/drechsler 031005.pdf.

DRUMMOND, D. C., & GLAUTIER, S. (1994). A controlled trial of cue exposure treatment in alcohol dependence. *Journal of Consulting and Clinical Psychology, 62*, 809–817.

DUANGDAO, K. M., ROESCH, S. C. (2008). Coping with diabetes in adulthood: A meta-analysis. *Journal of Behavioral Medicine, 31*, 291–300.

DUBERSTEIN, P. R. (2004). Psychsomatic medicine. In A. J. CHRISTENSEN, R. MARTIN, & J. M. SMYTH (Eds.), *Encyclopedia of health psychology* (pp. 229–230). New York: Kluwer.

DUNBAR-JACOB, J., & SCHLENK, E. (2001). Patient adherence to treatment regimen. In A. BAUM, T. A. REVENSON, & J. E. SINGER (Eds.), *Handbook of health psychology* (pp. 571–580). Mahwah, NJ: Erlbaum.

DUNCAN, S. C., DUNCAN, T. E., STRYCKER, L. A., & CHAUMETON, N. R. (2007). A cohort-sequential latent growth model of physical activity from ages 12 to 17 years. *Annals of Behavioral Medicine, 33*, 80–89.

DUNCAN, S. C., STRYCKER, L. A., & DUNCAN, T. E. (1999). Exploring associations in developmental trends of adolescent substance use and risky sexual behavior in a high-risk population. *Journal of Behavioral Medicine, 22*, 21–34.

DUNHAM, M. (2005). Chronic pain pharmacology. In P. SCHOFIELD (Ed.), *Beyond pain* (pp. 181–195). London: Whurr.

DUNKEL-SCHETTER, C., & BENNETT, T. L. (1990). Differentiating the cognitive and behavioral aspects of social support. In B. R. SARASON, I. G. SARASON, & G. R. PIERCE (Eds.), *Social support: An interactional view* (pp. 267–296). New York: Wiley.

DUNN, M. E., & GOLDMAN, M. S. (1998). Age and drinking-related differences in the memory organization of alcohol expectancies in 3rd-, 6th-, 9th-, and 12th-grade children. *Journal of Consulting and Clinical Psychology, 66*, 579–585.

DURANT, R. H., RICKERT, V. I., ASHWORTH, C. S., NEWMAN, C., & SLAVENS, G. (1993). Use of multiple drugs among adolescents who use anabolic steroids. *New England Journal of Medicine, 328*, 922–926.

DURANTINI, M. R., ALBARRACÍN, D., MITCHELL, A. L., EARL, A. N., & GILLETTE, J. C. (2006). Conceptualizing the influence of social agents of behavior change: A meta-analysis of the effectiveness of HIV-prevention interventionists for different groups. *Psychological Bulletin, 132*, 212–248.

DWECK, C. S., & ELLIOTT, E. S. (1983). Achievement motivation. In P. H. MUSSEN (Ed.), *Handbook of child psychology* (4th ed., Vol. 4, pp. 643–692). New York: Wiley.

DWECK, C. S., & REPUCCI, N. D. (1973). Learned helplessness and reinforcement responsibility in children. *Journal of Personality and Social Psychology, 25*, 109–116.

D'ZURILLA, T. J. (1988). Problem-solving therapies. In K. S. DOBSON (Ed.), *Handbook of cognitive-behavioral therapies* (pp. 85–135). New York: Guilford.

EARLE, T. L., LINDEN, W., & WEINBERG, J. (1999). Differential effects of harassment on cardiovascular and salivary cortisol stress reactivity and recovery in women and men. *Journal of Psychosomatic Research, 46*, 124–141.

EASTERBROOK, G. (1987). The revolution. *Newsweek*, pp. 40–74.

EBY, L. T., MAHER, C. P., & BUTTS, M. M. (2010). The intersection of work and family life: The role of affect. *Annual Review of Psychology, 61*, 599–622.

EDELL, B. H., EDINGTON, S., HERD, B., O'BRIEN, R. M., & WITKIN, G. (1987). Self-efficacy and self-motivation as predictors of weight loss. *Addictive Behaviors, 12*, 63–66.

EDELMAN, S., LEMON, J., BELL, D. R., & KIDMAN, A. D. (1999). Effects of group CBT on the survival time of patients with metastatic breast cancer. *Psycho-Oncology, 8*, 474–481.

EDELSTEIN, L. (1984). *Maternal bereavement: Coping with the unexpected death of a child.* New York: Praeger.

EDWARDS, A. G. K., HULBERT-WILLIAMS, N., NEAL, R. D. (2008). Psychological interventions for women with metastatic breast cancer. *Cochrane Database of Systematic Reviews,* Issue 3. Retrieved (1-30-2010) from http://www .thecochranelibrary.com.

EDWARDS, R. R., BINGHAM, C. O., BATHON, J., & HAYTHORNTHWAITE, J. A. (2006). Catastrophizing and pain in arthritis, fibromyalgia, and other rheumatic diseases. *Arthritis & Rheumatism, 55*, 325–332.

EDWARDS, R. R., DOLEYS, D. M., FILLINGIM, R. B., & LOWREY, D. (2001). Ethnic differences in pain tolerance: Clinical implications in a chronic pain population. *Psychosomatic Medicine, 63*, 316–323.

EDWARDS, R. R., HAYTHORNTHWAITE, J. A., SULLIVAN, M. J., & FILLINGIM, R. B. (2004). Catastrophizing as a mediator of sex differences in pain: Differential effects for daily pain versus laboratory-induced pain. *Pain, 111*, 335–341.

EDWARDS, R. R., KLICK, B., BUENAVER, L., MAX, M. B., HAYTHORNTHWAITE, J. A., et al. (2007). Symptoms of distress as prospective predictors of pain-related sciatica treatment outcomes. *Pain*, 130, 47–55.

EDWARDS, R. R., SMITH, M. T., KLICK, B., MAGYAR-RUSSELL, G., HAYTHORNTHWAITE, J. A., et al. (2007). Symptoms of depression and anxiety as unique predictors of pain-related outcomes following burn injury. *Annals of Behavioral Medicine*, 34, 313–322.

EFA (Epilepsy Foundation of America) (2006). *Answer place: Epilepsy and seizure statistics; Medical aspects—First aid*. Retrieved (12-6-2006) from http://www.efa.org.

EICHENWALD, K. (1987, January 11). Braving epilepsy's storm. *The New York Times Magazine*, pp. 30–36.

EISENBERG, E., MCNICOL, E. D., & CARR, D. B. (2005). Efficacy and safety of opioid agonists in the treatment of neuropathic pain of nonmalignant origin: Systematic review and meta-analysis of randomized controlled trials. *Journal of the American Medical Association*, 293, 3043–3052.

EISENBERG, M. G. (1984). Spinal cord injuries. In H. B. ROBACK (Ed.), *Helping patients and their families cope with medical problems* (pp. 107–129). San Francisco: Jossey-Bass.

EISER, C. (1985). *The psychology of childhood illness*. New York: Springer-Verlag.

EITEL, P., K, & FRIEND, R. (1999). Reducing denial and sexual risk behaviors in college students: A comparison of a cognitive and a motivational approach. *Annals of Behavioral Medicine*, 21, 12–19.

EKINCI, O., TITUS, J. B., RODOPMAN, A. A., BERKEM, M., & TREVATHAN, E. (2009). Depression and anxiety in children and adolescents with epilepsy: Prevalence, risk factors, and treatment. *Epilepsy & Behavior*, 14, 8–18.

EKSTRAND, M. L., & CHESNEY, M. A. (2002). Adhering to complex medication regimens. In M. A. CHESNEY & M. H. ANTONI (Eds.), *Innovative approaches to health psychology: Prevention and treatment lessons from AIDS* (pp. 283–306). Washington, DC: American Psychological Association.

ELIASSON, B., HJALMARSON, A., KRUSE, E., LANDFELDT, B., & WESTIN, Å. (2001). Effect of smoking reduction and cessation on cardiovascular risk factors. *Nicotine and Tobacco Research*, 3, 249–255.

ELLER, N. H., NETTERSTROM, B., GYNTELBERG, F., KRISTENSEN, T., NIELSEN, F., et al. (2009). Work-related psychosocial factors and the development of ischemic heart disease: A systematic review. *Cardiology Reviews*, 17, 83–97.

ELLICKSON, P. L., MCCAFFREY, D. F., GHOSH-DASTIDAR, B., & LONGSHORE, D. L. (2003). New inroads in preventing adolescent drug use: Results from a large-scale trial of Project ALERT in middle schools. *American Journal of Public Health*, 93, 1830–1836.

ELLINGTON, L., & WIEBE, D. J. (1999). Neuroticism, symptom presentation, and medical decision making. *Health Psychology*, 18, 634–643.

ELLIOTT, A. F., BURGIO, L. D., & DECOSTER, J. (2010). Enhancing caregiver health: Findings from the Resources for Enhancing Alzheimer's Caregiver Health II Intervention. *Journal of the American Geriatrics Society*, 58, 30–37.

ELLIOTT, T. R., BERRY, J. W., & GRANT, J. S. (2009). Problem-solving training for family caregivers of women with disabilities: A randomized clinical trial. *Behaviour Research and Therapy*, 47, 548–558.

ELLIS, A. (1962). *Reason and emotion in psychotherapy*. New York: Lyle Stuart.

ELLIS, A. (1977). The basic clinical theory of rational-emotive therapy. In A. ELLIS & R. GRIEGER (Eds.), *Handbook of rational-emotive therapy* (pp. 3–34). New York: Springer.

ELLIS, A. (1987). The impossibility of achieving consistently good mental health. *American Psychologist*, 42, 364–375.

ELO, I. T. (2009). Social class differentials in health and mortality: Patterns and explanations in comparative perspective. *Annual Review of Sociology*, 35, 553–572.

ELWERT, F., & CHRISTAKIS, N. A. (2008). The effect of widowhood on mortality by the causes of death of both spouses. *American Journal of Public Health*, 98, 2092–2098.

EMERY, C. F., KIECOLT-GLASER, J. K., GLASER, R., MALARKEY, W. B. & FRID, D. J. (2005). Exercise accelerates wound healing among healthy older adults: A preliminary investigation. *Journal of Gerontology: Medical Sciences*, 60A, 432–436.

EMMONS, K., LINNAN, L. A., SHADEL, W. G., MARCUS, B., & ABRAMS, D. B. (1999). The Working Healthy Project: A worksite health-promotion trial targeting physical activity, diet, and smoking. *Journal of Occupational and Environmental Medicine*, 41, 545–555.

EMRICK, C. D., & HANSEN, J. (1983). Assertions regarding effectiveness of treatment for alcoholism. *American Psychologist*, 38, 1078–1088.

ENGEL, G. L. (1977). The need for a new medical model: A challenge for biomedicine. *Science*, 196, 129–136.

ENGEL, G. L. (1980). The clinical application of the biopsychosocial model. *American Journal of Psychiatry*, 137, 535–544.

ENGEL, G. L., REICHSMAN, R., & SEGAL, H. L. (1956). A study of an infant with a gastric fistula: I. Behavior and the rate of total hydrochloric acid secretion. *Psychosomatic Medicine*, 18, 374–398.

ENRIGHT, M. F., RESNICK, R., DELEON, P. H., SCIARA, A. D., & TANNEY, F. (1990). The practice of psychology in hospital settings. *American Psychologist*, 45, 1059–1065.

EPDET (Expert Panel on Detection, Evaluation, and Treatment of High Blood Cholesterol in Adults) (2001). Executive summary of the Third Report of the National Cholesterol Education Program (NCEP) Expert Panel on Detection, Evaluation, and Treatment of High Blood Cholesterol in Adults (Adult Treatment Panel III). *Journal of the American Medical Association*, 285, 2486–2497.

EPPING-JORDAN, J. E., WAHLGREN, D. R., WILLIAMS, R. A., PRUITT, S. D., SLATER, M. A., et al. (1998). Transition to chronic pain in men with low back pain: Predictive relationships among pain intensity, disability, and depressive symptoms. *Health Psychology*, 17, 421–427.

EPSTEIN, L. H., KILANOWSKI, C. K., CONSALVI, A. R., & PALUCH, R. A. (1999). Reinforcing value of physical activity as a determinant of child activity level. *Health Psychology*, 18, 599–603.

EPSTEIN, L. H., PALUCH, R. A., KILANOWSKI, C. K., & RAYNOR, H. A. (2004). The effect of reinforcement or stimulus control to reduce sedentary behavior in the treatment of pediatric obesity. *Health Psychology*, 23, 371–380.

EPSTEIN, L. H., PALUCH, R. A., ROEMMICH, J. N., & BEECHER, M. D. (2007). Family-baed obesity treatment, then and now: Twenty-five years of pediatric obesity treatment. *Health Psychology*, 26, 381–391.

EPSTEIN, L. H., SAELENS, B. E., & O'BRIEN, J. G. (1995). Effects of reinforcing increases in active behavior versus decreases in sedentary behavior for obese children. *International Journal of Behavioral Medicine*, 2, 41–50.

ERBLICH, J., MONTGOMERY, G. H., & BOVBJERG, D. H. (2009). Script-guided imagery of social drinking induce both alcohol and cigarette craving in a sample of nicotine-dependent smokers. *Addictive Behaviors*, 34, 164–170.

ERDMAN, R. A. M. (1990). Myocardial infarction and cardiac rehabilitation. In A. A. KAPTEIN, H. M. VAN DER PLOEG, B. GARSSEN, P. J. G. SCHREURS, & R. BEUNDERMAN (Eds.), *Behavioural medicine: Psychological treatment of somatic disorders* (pp. 127–146). Chichester: Wiley.

ERICKSON, R. J. (2005). Why emotion work matters: Sex, gender, and the division of household labor. *Journal of Marriage and Family*, 67, 337–351.

ERIKSEN, M. P., LEMAISTRE, C. A., & NEWELL, G. R. (1988). Health hazards of passive smoking. *Annual Review of Public Health*, 9, 47–70.

ESPAD (European School Survey Project on Alcohol and Other Drugs) (2009). *The 2007 ESPAD Report: Substance use among students in 35 European countries—Summary*. Retrieved (4-1-2010) from www.espad.org/espad-reports.

ESTERLING, B. A., ANTONI, M. H., FLETCHER, M. A., MARGULIES, S., & SCHNEIDERMAN, N. (1994). Emotional disclosure through writing or speaking modulates latent Epstein-Barr virus antibody titers. *Journal of Consulting and Clinical Psychology*, 62, 130–140.

ESTEY, A., MUSSEAU, A., & KEEHN, L. (1994). Patient's understanding of health information: A multihospital comparison. *Patient Education and Counseling*, 24, 73–78.

EVANS, C., & RICHARDSON, P. H. (1988). Improved recovery and reduced postoperative stay after therapeutic suggestions during general anaesthesia. *Lancet*, 332, 491–493.

EVANS, F. J. (1987). Hypnosis. In R. J. CORSINI (Ed.), *Concise encyclopedia of psychology* (pp. 554–555). New York: Wiley.

EVANS, G. W. (2001). Evironmental stress and health. In A. BAUM, T. A. REVENSON, & J. E. SINGER (Eds.), *Handbook of health psychology* (pp. 365–385). Mahwah, NJ: Erlbaum.

EVANS, R. (1990). What you should know about childhood asthma. *Asthma and Allergy Advance* (reprint), pp. 1–4.

EVANS, R. I. (1984). A social inoculation strategy to deter smoking in adolescents. In J. D. MATARAZZO, S. M. WEISS, J. A. HERD, N. E. MILLER, & S. M. WEISS (Eds.), *Behavioral health: A handbook of health enhancement and disease prevention* (pp. 765–774). New York: Wiley.

EVANS, R. L., HENDRICKS, R. D., HASELKORN, J. K., BISHOP, D. S., & BALDWIN, D. (1992). The family's role in stroke rehabilitation: A review of the literature. *American Journal of Physical Medicine & Rehabilitation*, 71, 135–139.

EVERSON, S. A., KAUHANEN, J., KAPLAN, G. A., GOLDBERG, D., JULKUNEN, J., et al. (1997). Hostility and increased risk of mortality and acute myocardial infarction: The mediating role of behavioral risk factors. *American Journal of Epidemiology*, 146, 142–152

EVERSON, S. A., LYNCH, J. W., CHESNEY, M. A., KAPLAN, G. A., GOLDBERG, D. E., et al. (1997). Interaction of workplace demands and cardiovascular reactivity in progression of carotid atherosclerosis: Population based study. *British Medical Journal*, 314, 553–558.

EVERSON, S. A., LYNCH, J. W., KAPLAN, G. A., LAKKA, T. A., SIVENIUS, J., & SALONEN, J. T. (2001). Stress-induced blood pressure reactivity and incident stroke in middle-aged men. *Stroke*, 32, 1263–1270.

EVERSON, S. A., ROBERTS, R. E., GOLDBERG, D. E., & KAPLAN, G. A. (1998). Depressive symptoms and increased risk of stroke mortality over a 29-year period. *Archives of Internal Medicine*, 158, 1133–1138.

EVERSON-ROSE, S. A., & LEWIS, T. T. (2005). Psychosocial factors and cardiovascular diseases. *Annual Review of Public Health*, 26, 469–500.

EVON, D. M., & BURNS, J. W. (2004). Process and outcome in cardiac rehabilitation: An examination of cross-lagged effects. *Journal of Consulting and Clinical Psychology*, 72, 605–616.

EWART, C. K. (1991). Social action theory for a public health psychology. *American Psychologist*, 46, 931–946.

FABRICATORE, A. N., & WADDEN, T. A. (2006). Obesity. *Annual Review of Clinical Psychology*, 2, 357–377.

FAIRBURN, C. G., STICE, E., COOPER, Z., DOLL, H. A., NORMAN, P. A., & O'CONNOR, M. E. (2003). Understanding persistence in bulimia nervosa: A 5-year naturalistic study. *Journal of Consulting and Clinical Psychology*, 71, 103–109.

FALBA, T. (2005). Health events and the smoking cessation of middle aged Americans. *Journal of Behavioral Medicine*, 28, 21–33.

FALKNER, B., & LIGHT, K. C. (1986). The interactive effects of stress and dietary sodium on cardiovascular reactivity. In K. A. MATTHEWS, S. M. WEISS, T. DETRE, T. M. DEMBROSKI, B. FALKNER, S. B. MANUCK, & R. B. WILLIAMS (Eds.), *Handbook of stress, reactivity, and cardiovascular disease* (pp. 329–341). New York: Wiley.

FALS-STEWART, W., & O'FARRELL, T. J. (2003). Behavioral family counseling and naltrexone for male opioid-dependent patients. *Journal of Consulting and Clinical Psychology*, 71, 432–442.

FANG, J., MADHAVAN, S., & ALDERMAN, M. H. (1996). The association between birthplace and mortality from cardiovascular causes among black and white residents of New York City. *New England Journal of Medicine, 335*, 1545–1551.

FANG, L., SCHINKE, S. P., & COLE, K. C. (2009). Underage drinking among young adolescent girls: The role of family processes. *Psychology of Addictive Behaviors, 23*, 708–714.

FARKAS, A. J., DISTEFAN, J. M., CHOI, W. S., GILPIN, E. A., & PIERCE, J. P. (1999). Does parental smoking cessation discourage adolescent smoking? *Preventive Medicine, 28*, 213–218.

FARLEY, T. A., BAKER, E. T., FUTRELL, L., & RICE, J. C. (2010). The ubiquity of energy-dense snack food: A national multicity study. *American Journal of Public Health, 100*, 306–311.

FARQUHAR, J. W., MACCOBY, N., WOOD, P. D. ALEXANDER, J. K., BREITROSE, H., et al. (1977). Community education for cardiovascular health. *Lancet*, 1192–1195.

FARROW, C., & BLISSETT, J. (2006). Does maternal control during feeding moderate early infant weight gain? *Pediatrics, 118*, e293–e298.

FAUCETT, J., GORDON, N., & LEVINE, J. (1994). Differences in postoperative pain severity among four ethnic groups. *Journal of Pain and Symptom Management, 9*, 383–389.

FAWZY, F. I., COUSINS, N. FAWZY, N. W., KEMENY, M. E., ELASHOFF, R., & MORTON, D. (1990). A structured psychiatric intervention for cancer patients: I. Changes over time in methods of coping and affective disturbance. *Archives of General Psychiatry, 47*, 720–725.

FAWZY, F. I., FAWZY, N. W., HYUN, C. S., ELASHOFF, R., GUTHRIE, D., et al. (1993). Malignant melanoma: Effects of an early structured psychiatric intervention, coping, and affective state on recurrence and survival 6 years later. *Archives of General Psychiatry, 50*, 681–689.

FAWZY, F. I., KEMENY, M. E., FAWZY, N. W., ELASHOFF, R., MORTON, D., et al. (1990). A structured psychiatric intervention for cancer patients: II. Changes over time in immunological measures. *Archives of General Psychiatry, 47*, 729–735.

FELDMAN, J. M., SIDDIQUE, M. I., THOMPSON, N. S., & LEHRER, P. M. (2009). The role of panic-fear in comorbid asthma and panic disorder. *Journal of Anxiety Disorders, 23*, 178–184.

FELDMAN, M., & RICHARDSON, C. T. (1986). Role of thought, sight, smell, and taste of food in the cephalic phase of gastric acid secretion in humans. *Gastroenterology, 90*, 428–433.

FELDMAN, P. J., COHEN, S., DOYLE, E. J., SKONER, D. P., & GWALTNEY, J. M. (1999). The impact of personality on the reporting of unfounded symptoms and illness. *Journal of Personality and Social Psychology, 77*, 370–378.

FELDMAN, R. S. (2000). *Development across the life span* (2nd ed.). Upper Saddle River, NJ: Prentice Hall.

FERGUSON, S. G., SHIFFMAN, S., & GWALTNEY, C. J. (2006). Does reducing withdrawal severity mediate nicotine patch efficacy? A randomized clinical trial. *Journal of Consulting and Clinical Psychology, 74*, 1153–1161.

FERNANDEZ, E. (1986). A classification system of cognitive coping strategies for pain. *Pain, 26*, 141–151.

FERNANDEZ, E., & TURK, D. C. (1989). The utility of cognitive coping strategies for altering pain perception: A meta-analysis. *Pain, 38*, 123–135.

FEUERSTEIN, M., & GAINER, J. (1982). Chronic headache: Etiology and management. In D. M. DOLEYS, R. L. MEREDITH, & A. R. CIMINERO (Eds.), *Behavioral medicine: Assessment and treatment strategies* (pp. 199–249). New York: Plenum.

FIATARONE, M. A., MORLEY, J. E., BLOOM, E. T., BENTON, D., SOLOMON, G. F., & MAKINODAN, T. (1989). The effect of exercise on natural killer cell activity in young and old subjects. *Journal of Gerontology: Medical Sciences, 44*, M37–45.

FIELD, A. E., AUSTIN, S. B., TAYLOR, C. B., MALSPEIS, S., ROSNER, B., et al. (2003). Relation between dieting and weight change among preadolescents and adolescents. *Pediatrics, 112*, 900–906.

FIELD, T. M. (1996). Touch therapies across the life span. In P. M. KATO & T. MANN (Eds.), *Handbook of diversity issues in health psychology* (pp. 49–67). New York: Plenum.

FIELD, T. M. (1998). Massage therapy effects. *American Psychologist, 53*, 1270–1281.

FIELDING, J. E. (1991). Smoking control at the workplace. *Annual Review of Public Health, 12*, 209–234.

FIELDS, H. L., & LEVINE, J. D. (1984). Placebo analgesia—A role for endorphins? *Trends in Neurosciences, 7*, 271–273.

FIGUEIRAS, M. J., & WEINMAN, J. (2003). Do similar patient and spouse perceptions of myocardial infarction predict recovery? *Psychology and Health, 18*, 201–216.

FILLINGIM, R. B. (2000). Sex, gender, and pain: Women and men really are different. *Current Review of Pain, 4*, 24–30.

FINNEY, J. W., & MOOS, R. H. (1997). Psychosocial treatments for alcohol use disorders. In P. E. NATHAN & J. M. GORMAN (Eds.), *A guide to treatments that work* (pp. 156–166). New York: Oxford University Press.

FIORE, M. C., JORENBY, D. E., & BAKER, T. B. (1997). Smoking cessation: Principles and practice based upon the AHCPR Guideline, 1996. *Annals of Behavioral Medicine, 19*, 213–219.

FISHER, J. D., FISHER, W. A., MISOVICH, S. H., KIMBLE, D. L., & MALLOY, T. E. (1996). Changing AIDS risk behavior: Effects of an intervention emphasizing AIDS risk reduction information, motivation, and behavioral skills in a college student population. *Health Psychology, 15*, 114–123.

FISHER, L., MULLAN, J. T., AREAN, P., GLASGOW, R. E., HESSLER, D., & MASHARANI, U. (2010). Diabetes distress but not clinical depression or depressive symptoms is associated with glycemic control in both cross-sectional and longitudinal analyses. *Diabetes Care, 33*, 23–28.

FISKE, D. W., & MADDI, S. R. (1961). A conceptual framework. In D. W. FISKE & S. R. MADDI (Eds.), *Functions of varied experience.* Homewood, IL: Dorsey.

FITZGERALD, S. T., HAYTHORNTHWAITE, J. A., SUCHDAY, S., & EWART, C. K. (2003). Anger in young Black and White workers: Effects of job control, dissatisfaction, and support. *Journal of Behavioral Medicine, 26*, 283–296.

FITZPATRICK, A. L., POWE, N. R., COOPER, L. S., IVES, D. G., & ROBBINS, J. A. (2004). Barriers to health care access among the elderly and who perceives them. *American Journal of Public Health, 94,* 1788–1794.

FLACK, J. M., AMARO, H., JENKINS, W., KUNITZ, S., LEVY, J., et al. (1995). Panel I: Epidemiology of minority health. *Health Psychology, 14,* 592–600.

FLASKERUD, J. H. (1988). AIDS: Psychosocial aspects. *Health Values, 12*(4), 44–52.

FLAY, B. R. (1985). Psychosocial approaches to smoking prevention: A review of findings. *Health Psychology, 4,* 449–488.

FLAY, B. R. (1987). Mass media and smoking cessation: A critical review. *American Journal of Public Health, 77,* 153–160.

FLAY, B. R., HU, F. B., & RICHARDSON, J. (1998). Psychosocial predictors of different stages of cigarette smoking among high school students. *Preventive Medicine, 27,* A9–A18.

FLAY, B. R., KOEPKE, D., THOMSON, S. J., SANTI, S., BEST, A., & BROWN, K. S. (1989). Six-year follow-up of the first Waterloo school smoking prevention trial. *American Journal of Public Health, 79,* 1371–1376.

FLAY, B. R., RYAN, K. B., BEST, J. A., BROWN, K. S., KERSELL, M. W., et al. (1985). Are social-psychological smoking prevention programs effective? The Waterloo Study. *Journal of Behavioral Medicine, 8,* 37–59.

FLEMING, I., BAUM, A., DAVIDSON, L. M., RECTANUS, E., & MCARDLE, S. (1987). Chronic stress as a factor in physiologic reactivity to challenge. *Health Psychology, 6,* 221–237.

FLEMING, M. F., MUNDT, M. P., FRENCH, M. T., MANWELL, L. B., STAUFFACHER, E. A., & BARRY, K. L. (2000). Benefit-cost analysis of brief physician advice with problem drinkers in primary care settings. *Medical Care, 38,* 7–18.

FLEMING, R., BAUM, A., GISRIEL, M. M., & GATCHEL, R. J. (1982). Mediating influences of social support on stress at Three Mile Island. *Journal of Human Stress, 8,* 14–22.

FLETCHER, L., & MACDONALD, H. (2005). The multidisciplinary team. In P. SCHOFIELD (Ed.), *Beyond pain* (pp. 37–59). London: Whurr.

FLOR, H. (2001). Psychophysiological assessment of the patient with chronic pain. In D. C. TURK & R. MELZACK (Eds.), *Handbook of pain assessment* (2nd ed., pp. 76–96). New York: Guilford.

FLOR, H., FYDRICH, T., & TURK, D. C. (1992). Efficacy of multidisciplinary pain treatment centers: A meta-analytic review. *Pain, 49,* 221–230.

FLOR, H., & TURK, D. C. (1985). Chronic illness in an adult family member: Pain as a prototype. In D. C. TURK & R. D. KERNS (Eds.), *Health, illness, and families: A life-span perspective* (pp. 255–278). New York: Wiley.

FLYNN, K. J., & FITZGIBBON, M. (1998). Body images and obesity risk among black females: A review of the literature. *Annals of Behavioral Medicine, 20,* 13–24.

FOLEY, D. L., CRAIG, J. M., MORLEY, R., OLSSON, C. J., DWYER, T., et al. (2009). Prospects for epigenetic epidemiology. *American Journal of Epidemiology, 169,* 389–400.

FOLKMAN, S. (1997). Positive psychological states and coping with severe stress. *Social Science and Medicine, 45,* 1207–1221.

FOLKMAN, S., LAZARUS, R. S., PIMLEY, S., & NOVACEK, J. (1987). Age differences in stress and coping processes. *Psychology and Aging, 2,* 171–184.

FOLKMAN, S., & MOSKOWITZ, J. T. (2004). Coping: Pitfalls and promise. *Annual Review of Psychology, 55,* 745–774.

FOLLICK, M. J., AHERN, D. K., ATTANASIO, V., & RILEY, J. F. (1985). Chronic pain programs: Current aims, strategies, and needs. *Annals of Behavioral Medicine, 7*(3), 17–20.

FONTAINE, K. R., REDDEN, D. T., WANG, C., WESTFALL, A. O., & ALLISON, D. B. (2003). Years of life lost due to obesity. *Journal of the American Medical Association, 289,* 187–193.

FORAKER, R. E., ROSE, K. M., MCGINN, A. P., SUCHINDRAN, CH. M., GOFF, D. C., et al. (2008). Neighborhood income, health insurance, and prehospital delay for myocardial infarction. *Annals of Internal Medicine, 168,* 1874–1879.

FORCIER, K., STROUD, L. R., PAPANDONATOS, G. D., HITSMAN, B., REICHES, M., et al. (2006). Links between physical fitness and cardiovascular reactivity and recovery to psychological stressors: A meta-analysis. *Health Psychology, 25,* 723–739.

FORDYCE, W. E. (1976). *Behavioral methods for chronic pain and illness.* St. Louis: Mosby.

FORDYCE, W. E., & STEGER, J. C. (1979). Behavioral management of chronic pain. In O. F. POMERLEAU & J. P. BRADY (Eds.), *Behavioral medicine: Theory and practice.* Baltimore: Williams & Wilkins.

FOREM, J. (1974). *Transcendental meditation.* New York: Dutton.

FORESTELL, C. A., & MENNELLA, J. A. (2007). Early determinants of fruit and vegetable acceptance. *Pediatrics, 120,* 1247–1254.

FOREYT, J. P., & LEAVESLEY, G. (1991). Behavioral treatment of obesity at the work site. In S. M. WEISS, J. E. FIELDING, & A. BAUM (Eds.), *Perspectives in behavioral medicine: Health at work* (pp. 99–115). Hillsdale, NJ: Earlbaum.

FORMAN, M. R., TROWBRIDGE, F. L., GENTRY, E. M., MARKS, J. S., & HOGELIN, G. C. (1986). Overweight adults in the United States: The behavioral risk factor surveys. *American Journal of Clinical Nutrition, 44,* 410–416.

FORTENBERRY, K. T., BUTLER, J. M., BUTNER, J., BERG, C. A., UPCHURCH, R., & WIEBE, D. J. (2009). Perceived diabetes task competence mediates the relationship of both negative and positive affect with blood glucose in adolescents with type 1 diabetes. *Annals of Behavioral Medicine, 37,* 1–9.

FOULKES, W. D. (2008). Inherited susceptibility to common cancers. *New England Journal of Medicine, 359,* 2143–2153.

FOX, D. K., HOPKINS, B. L., & ANGER, W. K. (1987). The long-term effects of a token economy on safety performance in open-pit mining. *Journal of Applied Behavior Analysis, 20,* 215–224.

FRANCE, D. R., MASTERS, K. S., BELAR, C. D., KERNS, R. D., KLONOFF, E. A., et al. (2008). Application of the competency model to clinical health psychology. *Professional Psychology, 29,* 573–580.

FRANCIS, V., KORSCH, B. M., & MORRIS, M. J. (1969). Gaps in doctor-patient communication. *New England Journal of Medicine, 280,* 535–540.

FRANKENHAEUSER, M. (1986). A psychobiological framework for research on human stress and coping. In M. H. APPLEY & R. TRUMBULL (Eds.), *Dynamics of stress: Physiological, psychological, and social perspectives* (pp. 101–116). New York: Plenum.

FRANKO, D. L., MINTZ, L. B., VILLAPIANO, M., GREEN, T. C., MAINELLI, D., et al. (2005). Food, mood, and attitude: Reducing risk for eating disorders in college women. *Health Psychology, 24*, 567–578.

FRASER, R. T. 1999). Epilepsy. In M. G. EISENBERG, R. L. GLUECKAUF, & H. H. ZARETSKY (Eds.), *Medical aspects of disability: A handbook for the rehabilitation professional* (2nd ed., pp. 225–244). New York: Springer.

FRATTAROLI, J. (2006). Experimental disclosure and its moderators: A meta-analysis. *Psychological Bulletin, 132*, 823–865.

FRAYLING, T. M., TIMPSON, N. J., WEEDON, M. N., ZEGGINI, E., FREATHY, R. M., et al. (2007). A common variant of the FTO gene is associated with body mass index and predisposes to childhood and adult obesity. *Science, 316*, 889–894.

FREEDLAND, K. E., SKALA, J. A., CARNEY, R. M., RUBIN, E. H., LUSTMAN, P. J., et al. (2009). Treatment of depression after coronary artery bypass surgery: A randomized controlled trial. *Archives of General Psychiatry, 66*, 387–396.

FREEDMAN, D. M., SIGURDSON, A. J., RAJARAMAN, P., DOODY, M. M., LINET, M. S., & RON, E. (2006). The mortality risk of smoking and obesity combined. *American Journal of Preventive Medicine, 31*, 355–362.

FREELS, S. A., WARNECKE, R. B., PARSONS, J. A., JOHNSON, T. P., FLAY, B. R., & MORENA, O. F. (1999). Characteristics associated with exposure to and participation in a televised smoking cessation intervention program for women with high school or less education. *Preventive Medicine, 28*, 579–588.

FREEMAN, A. (1990). Cognitive therapy. In A. S. BELLACK & M. HERSEN (Eds.), *Handbook of comparative treatments for adult disorders* (pp. 64–87). New York: Wiley.

FREIDSON, E. (1961). *Patients' views of medical practice.* New York: Russell Sage Foundation.

FRENCH, M. T., SALOME, H. J., & CARNEY, M. (2002). Using the DATCAP and ASI to estimate the costs and benefits of residential addiction treatment in the State of Washington. *Social Science & Medicine, 55*, 2267–2282.

FRENCH, S. A., & JEFFERY, R. W. (1994). Consequences of dieting to lose weight: Effects on physical and mental health. *Health Psychology, 13*, 195–212.

FRIEDMAN, H. S., TUCKER, J. S., & REISE, S. P. (1995). Personality dimensions and measures potentially relevant to health: A focus on hostility. *Annals of Behavioral Medicine, 17*, 245–253.

FRIEDMAN, L. C., ROMERO, C., ELLEDGE, R., CHANG, J., KALIDAS, M., et al. (2007). Attribution of blame, self-forgiving attitude and psychological adjustment in women with breast cancer. *Journal of Behavioral Medicine, 30*, 351–357.

FRIEDMAN, M., & ROSENMAN, R. H. (1974). *Type A behavior and your heart.* New York: Knopf.

FRIEDMAN, M., THORESEN, C. E., GILL, J. J., ULMER, D., POWELL, L. H., et al. (1986). Alteration of Type A behavior and its effect on cardiac recurrences in post myocardial infarction patients: Summary results of the Recurrent Coronary Prevention Project. *American Heart Journal, 112*, 653–665.

FROESE, A., HACKETT, T. P., CASSEM, N. H., & SILVERBERG, E. L. (1974). Trajectories of anxiety and depression in denying and nondenying acute myocardial infarction patients during hospitalization. *Journal of Psychosomatic Research, 18*, 413–420.

FROMME, K., & CORBIN, W. (2004). Prevention of heavy drinking and associated negative consequences among mandated and voluntary college students. *Journal of Consulting and Clinical Psychology, 72*, 1038–1049.

FROSTHOLM, L., FINK, P., CHRISTENSEN, K. S., TOFT, T., OERNBOEL, E., et al. (2005). The patients' illness perceptions and the use of primary health care. *Psychosomatic Medicine, 67*, 997–1005.

FRY, P. S. & DEBATS, D. L. (2009). Perfectionism and the five-factor personality traits as predictors of mortality in older adults. *Journal of Health Psychology, 14*, 513–524.

FUCITO, L. M., & JULIANO, L. M. (2009). Depression moderates smoking behavior in response to sad mood induction. *Psychology of Addictive Behaviors, 23*, 546–551.

FUKUOKA, Y., DRACUP, K., TAKESHIMA, M., ISHII, N., MAKAYA, M., et al. (2009). Effect of job strain and depressive symptoms upon returning to work after acute coronary syndrome. *Social Science & Medicine, 68*, 1875–1881.

FULLERTON, J. T., KRITZ-SILVERSTEIN, D., SADLER, G. R., & BARRETT-CONNOR, E. (1996). Mammography usage in a community-based sample of older women. *Annals of Behavioral Medicine, 18*, 67–72.

FUNG, T. T., CHIUVE, S. E., MCCULLOUGH, M. L., REXRODE, K. M., LOGROSCINO, G., HU, F. B. (2008). Adherence to a DASH-style diet and risk of coronary heart disease and stroke in women. *Archives of Internal Medicine, 168*, 713–720.

FUNK, S. C. (1992). Hardiness: A review of theory and research. *Health Psychology, 11*, 335–345.

FUTTERMAN, A. D., KEMENY, M. E., SHAPIRO, D., & FAHEY, J. L. (1994). Immunological and physiological changes associated with induced positive and negative mood. *Psychosomatic Medicine, 56*, 499–511.

GALAVOTTI, C., CABRAL, R. J., LANSKY, A., GRIMLEY, D. M., RILEY, G. E., & PROCHASKA, J. O. (1995). Validation of measures of condom and other contraceptive use among women at high risk for HIV infection and unintended pregnancy. *Health Psychology, 14*, 570–578.

GALLO, L. C., & MATTHEWS, K. A. (2003). Understanding the association between socioeconomic status and physical health: Do negative emotions play a role? *Psychological Bulletin, 129*, 10–51.

GALLO, L. C., TROXEL, W. M., MATTHEWS, K. A., & KULLER, L. H. (2003). Marital status and quality in middle-aged women: Associations with levels and trajectories of cardiovascular risk factors. *Health Psychology, 22*, 453–463.

GALLO, W. T., TENG, H. M., FALBA, T. A., KASL, S. V., KRUMHOLZ, H. M., & BRADLEY, E. H. (2006). The impact of late career job loss on myocardial infarction and stroke: A 10 year follow up using the health and retirement survey. *Occupational and Environmental Medicine*, 63, 683–687.

GANNON, L. R., HAYNES, S. N., CUEVAS, J., & CHAVEZ, R. (1987). Psychophysiological correlates of induced headaches. *Journal of Behavioral Medicine*, 10, 411–423.

GANSLER, T., HENLEY, S. J., STEIN, K., NEHL, E. J., SMIGAL, C., & SLAUGHTER, E. (2005). Sociodemographic determinants of cancer treatment health literacy. *Cancer*, 104, 653–660.

GANZINI, L., GOY, E. R., & DOBSCHA, S. K. (2009). Oregonians' reasons for requesting physician aid in dying. *Archives of Internal Medicine*, 169, 489–492.

GARBUTT, J. C., KRANZLER, H. R., O'MALLEY, S. S., GASTFRIEND, D. R., PETTINATI, H. M., et al. (2005). Efficacy and tolerability of long-acting injectable naltrexone for alcohol dependence: A randomized controlled trial. *Journal of the American Medical Association*, 293, 1617–1625.

GARFINKEL, P. E. (2002). Classification and diagnosis of eating disorders. In C. G. FAIRBURN & K. D. BROWNELL (Eds.), *Eating disorders and obesity: A comprehensive handbook* (pp. 155–161). New York: Guilford Press.

GARLAND, C. F., GARLAND, F. C., GORHAM, E. D., LIPKIN, M., NEWMARK, H., et al. (2006). The role of vitamin D in cancer protection. *American Journal of Public Health*, 96, 252–261.

GARMEZY, N. (1983). Stressors of childhood. In N. GARMEZY & M. RUTTER (Eds.), *Stress, coping, and development in children* (pp. 43–84). New York: McGraw-Hill.

GARRITY, T. F. (1981). Medical compliance and the clinician-patient relationship: A review. *Social Science and Medicine*, 15, 215–222.

GATCHEL, R. J. (1980). Effectiveness of two procedures for reducing dental fear: Group-administered desensitization and group education and discussion. *Journal of the American Dental Association*, 101, 634–638.

GATCHEL, R. J. (1996). Psychological disorders and chronic pain: Cause-and-effect relationships. In R. J. GATCHEL & D. C. TURK (Eds.), *Psychological approaches to pain management: A practitioner's handbook* (pp. 33–52). New York: Guilford.

GATCHEL, R. J. (2001). Biofeedback and self-regulation of physiological activity: A major adjunctive treatment modality in health psychology. In A. BAUM, T. A. REVENSON, & J. E. SINGER (Eds.), *Handbook of health psychology* (pp. 95–103). Mahwah, NJ: Erlbaum.

GATCHEL, R. J., PENG, Y. B., PETERS, M. L., FUCHS, P. N., & TURK, D. C. (2007). The Biopsychosocial approach to chronic pain: Scientific advances and future directions. *Psychological Bulletin*, 133, 581–624.

GAUGLER, J. E., MITTELMAN, M. S., HEPBURN, K., & NEWCOMER, R. (2009). Predictors of change in caregiver burden and depressive symptoms following nursing home admission. *Psychology and Aging*, 24, 385–396.

GAUTHIER, J., CÔTÉ, G., & FRENCH, D. (1994). The role of home practice in the thermal biofeedback treatment of migraine headache. *Journal of Consulting and Clinical Psychology*, 62, 180–184.

GEBEL, K., BAUMAN, A., & OWEN, N. (2009). Correlates of non-concordance between perceived and objective measures of walkability. *Annals of Behavioral Medicine*, 37, 228–238.

GEDNEY, J. J., & LOGAN, H. (2006). Pain related recall predicts pain report. *Pain*, 121, 69–76.

GEHI, A. K., ALI, S., NA, B., & WHOOLEY, M. A. (2007). Self-reported medication adherence and cardiovascular events in patients with stable coronary heart disease: The Heart and Soul Study. *Archives of Internal Medicine*, 167, 1798–1803.

GELLER, A. C., COLDITZ, G., OLIVERIA, S., EMMONS, K., JORGENSEN, C., et al. (2002). Use of sunscreen, sunburning rates, and tanning bed use among more than 10,000 US children and adolescents. *Pediatrics*, 109, 1009–1014.

GENDOLLA, G., & WRIGHT, R. (2005). Motivation in social settings studies of effort-related cardiovascular arousal. In J. FORGAS, K. WILLIAMS, & S. LAHAM (Eds.). *Social motivation* (pp. 71–90). New York: Cambridge University Press.

GENTRY, W. D. (1984). Behavioral medicine: A new research paradigm. In W. D. GENTRY (Ed.), *Handbook of behavioral medicine* (pp. 1–12). New York: Guilford.

GENTRY, W. D., & OWENS, D. (1986). Pain groups. In A. D. HOLZMAN & D. C. TURK (Eds.), *Pain management: A handbook of psychological treatment approaches* (pp. 100–112). New York: Pergamon.

GERACE, R. A., & VORP, R. (1985). Epidemiology and behavior. In N. SCHNEIDERMAN & J. T. TAPP (Eds.), *Behavioral medicine: The biopsychosocial approach* (pp. 25–44). Hillsdale, NJ: Erlbaum.

GEREND, M. A., SHEPHERD, J. E., & MONDAY, K. A. (2008). Behavioral frequency moderates the effects of message framing on HPV vaccine acceptability. *Annals of Behavioral Medicine*, 35, 221–229.

GERIN, W., DAVIDSON, K. W., CHRISTENFELD, N. J. S., GOYAL, T., & SCHWARTZ, J. E. (2006). The role of angry rumination and distraction in blood pressure recovery from emotional arousal. *Psychosomatic Medicine*, 68, 64–72.

GERLIN, A. (1999). Health care's deadly secret: Accidents routinely happen. *Philadelphia Inquirer*, pp. A1, A20.

GERVASIO, A. H. (1986). Family relationships and compliance. In K. E. GERBER & A. M. NEHEMKIS (Eds.), *Compliance: The dilemma of the chronically ill* (pp. 98–127). New York: Springer.

GHAED, S. G., & GALLO, L. C. (2007). Subjective social status, objective socioeconomic status, and cardiovascular risk in women. *Health Psychology*, 26, 668–674.

GIACHELLO, A. L., & ARROM, J. O. (1997). Health service access and utilization among adolescent minorities. In D. K. WILSON, J. R. RODRIGUE, & W. C. TAYLOR (Eds.), *Health-promoting and health-compromising behaviors among minority adolescents* (pp. 303–320). Washington, DC: American Psychological Association.

GIBBONS, F. X., GERRARD, M., BLANTON, H., & RUSSELL, D. W. (1998). Reasoned action and social reaction: Willingness and intention as independent predictors of health risk. *Journal of Personality and Social Psychology, 74,* 1164–1180.

GIBBONS, F. X., GERRARD, M., LANE, D. J., MAHLER, H. I. M., & KULIK, J. A. (2005). Using UV photography to reduce use of tanning booths: A test of cognitive mediation. *Health Psychology, 24,* 358–363.

GIBBONS, F. X., MCGOVERN, P. G., & LANDO, H. A. (1991). Relapse and risk perception among members of a smoking cessation clinic. *Health Psychology, 10,* 42–45.

GIBSON, S. J., & CHAMBERS, C. T. (2004). Pain over the life span: A developmental perspective. In T. HADJISTAVROPOULOS & K. D. CRAIG (Eds.), *Pain: Psychological perspectives* (pp. 113–153). Mahwah, NJ: Earlbaum.

GIDRON, Y., BARAK, T., HENIK, A., GURMAN, G., & STEINER, O. (2002). Implicit learning of emotional information under anesthesia. *Cognitive Neuroscience and Neuropsychology, 13,* 139–142.

GIDRON, Y., DAVIDSON, K., & BATA, I. (1999). The short-term effects of a hostility-reduction intervention on male coronary heart disease patients. *Health Psychology, 18,* 416–420.

GIL, K. M., CARSON, J. W., PORTER, L. S., SCIPIO, C., BEDIAKO, S. M., & ORRINGER, E. (2004). Daily mood and stress predict pain, health care use, and work activity in African American adults with sickle-cell disease. *Health Psychology, 23,* 267–274.

GIL, K. M., KEEFE, F. J., SAMPSON, H. A., MCCASKILL, C. C., RODIN, J., & CRISSON, J. E. (1988). Direct observation of scratching behavior in children with atopic dermatitis. *Behavior Therapy, 19,* 213–227.

GIL, K. M., WILSON, J. J., & EDENS, J. L. (1997). The stability of pain coping strategies in young children, adolescents, and adults with sickle cell disease over an 18-month period. *Clinical Journal of Pain, 13,* 110–115.

GILBERSTADT, H., & DUKER, J. (1965). *A handbook for clinical and actuarial MMPI interpretation.* Philadelphia: Saunders.

GILBERT, D. G., & SPIELBERGER, C. D. (1987). Effects of smoking on heart rate, anxiety, and feelings of success during social interaction. *Journal of Behavioral Medicine, 10,* 629–638.

GILES-CORTI, B., BROOMHALL, M. H., KNUIMAN, M., COLLINS, C., DOUGLAS, K., et al. (2005). Increasing walking: How important is distance to, attractiveness, and size of public open space? *American Journal of Preventive Medicine, 28,* 169–176.

GILL, T. M., & FEINSTEIN, A. R. (1994). A critical appraisal of the quality of quality-of-life measurements. *Journal of the American Medical Association, 272,* 619–626.

GILLES, D. M., TURK, C. L., & FRESCO, D. M. (2006). Social anxiety, alcohol expectancies, and self-efficacy as predictors of heavy drinking in college students. *Addictive Behaviors, 31,* 388–398.

GILLESPIE, N. A., NEALE, M. C., JACOBSON, K., & KENDLER, K. S. (2009). Modeling the genetic and environmental aociation between peer group deviance and cannabi use in male twins. *Addiction, 104,* 420–429.

GILPIN, E. A., WHITE, M. M., MESSER, K., & PIERCE, J. P. (2007). Receptivity to tobacco advertising and promotions among young adolescents as a predictor of established smoking in young adulthood. *American Journal of Public Health, 97,* 1489–1495.

GINZBERG, E. (1983). Allied health resources. In D. MECHANIC (Ed.), *Handbook of health, health care, and the health professions* (pp. 479–494). New York: Free Press.

GIPSON, M., LISKEVYCH, T., & SWILLINGER, E. (1996). *Managing your health care: Making the most of your medical resources.* Ventura, CA: Pathfinder.

GIRODO, M., & WOOD, D. (1979). Talking yourself out of pain: The importance of believing that you can. *Cognitive Therapy and Research, 3,* 23–33.

GLADIS, M. M., MICHELA, J. L., WALTER, H. J., & VAUGHAN, R. D. (1992). High school students' perceptions of AIDS risk: Realistic appraisal or motivated denial? *Health Psychology, 11,* 307–316.

GLANZ, K. (2001). Current theoretical bases for nutrition intervention and their uses. In A. M. COULSTON, C. L. ROCK, & E. R. MONSEN (Eds.), *Nutrition in the prevention and treatment of disease* (pp. 83–93). San Diego: Academic Press.

GLANZ, K., & LERMAN, C. (1992). Psychosocial impact of breast cancer: A critical review. *Annals of Behavioral Medicine, 14,* 204–212.

GLASER, R., NEEDLEMAN, B., MALARKEY, W., DICKINSON, S., LEMESHOW, S., et al. (2006). Pain and wound healing in surgical patients. *Annals of Behavioral Medicine, 31,* 165–172.

GLASER, R., THORN, B. E., TARR, K. L., KIECOLT-GLASER, J. K., & D'AMBROSIO, S. M. (1985). Effects of stress on methyltransferase synthesis: An important DNA repair enzyme. *Health Psychology, 4,* 403–412.

GLASGOW, R. E., DAVIDSON, K. W., DOBKIN, P. L., OCKENE, J., & SPRING, B. (2006). Practical behavioral trials to advance evidence-based behavioral medicine. *Annals of Behavioral Medicine, 31,* 5–13.

GLASGOW, R. E., KLESGES, R. C., MIZES, J. S., & PECHACEK, T. F. (1985). Quitting smoking: Strategies used and variables associated with success in a stop-smoking contest. *Journal of Consulting and Clinical Psychology, 53,* 905–912.

GLASGOW, R. E., MCCAUL, K. D., & SCHAFER, L. C. (1986). Barriers to regimen adherence among persons with insulin-dependent diabetes. *Journal of Behavioral Medicine, 9,* 65–77.

GLASGOW, R. E., MCCAUL, K. D., & SCHAFER, L. C. (1987). Self-care behaviors and glycemic control in Type I diabetes. *Journal of Chronic Diseases, 40,* 399–412.

GLASGOW, R. E., ORLEANS, C. T., WAGNER, E. H., CURRY, S. J., & SOLBERG, L. I. (2001). Does the chronic care model serve also as a template for improving prevention? *Milbank Quarterly, 79,* 579–612.

GLASS, D. C. (1977). *Behavior patterns, stress, and coronary heart disease.* Hillsdale, NJ: Erlbaum.

GLASS, D. C., KRAKOFF, L. R., CONTRADA, R., HILTON, W. F., KEHOE, K., et al. (1980). Effect of harassment and competition upon cardiovascular and plasma catecholamine responses in Type A and Type B individuals. *Psychophysiology*, 17, 453–463.

GLYNN, S. M., GRUDER, C. L., & JEGERSKI, J. A. (1986). Effects of biochemical validation of self-reported cigarette smoking on treatment success and on misreporting abstinence. *Health Psychology*, 5, 125–136.

GOADSBY, P. J. (2005). Migraine pathophysiology. *Headache*, 45(Suppl. 1), S14–S24.

GODIN, G., DESHARNAIS, R., JOBIN, J., & COOK, J. (1987). The impact of physical fitness and health-age appraisal upon exercise intentions and behavior. *Journal of Behavioral Medicine*, 10, 241–250.

GODIN, G., DESHARNAIS, R., VALOIS, P., LEPAGE, L., JOBIN, J., & BRADET, R. (1992). *Perceived barriers to exercise among different populations*. Paper presented at the meeting of the Society of Behavioral Medicine, New York.

GODIN, G., VALOIS, P., SHEPHARD, R. J., & DESHARNAIS, R. (1987). Prediction of leisure-time exercise behavior: A path analysis (LISREL V) model. *Journal of Behavioral Medicine*, 10, 145–158.

GODTFREDSEN, N. S., HOLST, C., PRESCOTT, E., VESTBO, J., & OSLER, M. (2002). Smoking reduction, smoking cessation, and mortality: A 16-year follow-up of 19,732 men and women from the Copenhagen Center for Prospective Population Studies. *American Journal of Epidemiology*, 156, 994–1001.

GOEL, M. S., MCCARTHY, E. P., PHILLIPS, R. S., & WEE, C. C. (2004). Obesity among US immigrant subgroups by duration of residence. *Journal of the American Medical Association*, 292, 2860–2867.

GOETZEL, R. Z., & OZMINKOWSKI, R. J. (2008). The health and cost benefits of work site health-promotion programs. *Annual Review of Public Health*, 29, 303–323.

GOFFMAN, E. (1961). *Asylums*. Garden City, NY: Doubleday.

GOLASZEWSKI, T. (2001). Shining lights: Studies that have most influenced the understanding of health promotion's financial impact. *American Journal of Health Promotion*, 15, 332–340.

GOLD, R. S., & SKINNER, M. J. (1996). Judging a book by its cover: Gay men's use of perceptible characteristics to infer antibody status. *International Journal of STD & AIDS*, 7, 39–43.

GOLD, R. S., SKINNER, M. J., & HINCHY, J. (1999). Gay men's stereotypes about who is HIV-infected: A further study. *International Journal of STD & AIDS*, 10, 1–6.

GOLDBACHER, E. M., & MATTHEWS, K. A. (2007). Are psychological characteristics related to risk of the metabolic syndrome? A review of the literature. *Annals of Behavioral Medicine*, 34, 240–52.

GOLDBACHER, E. M., MATTHEWS, K. A., & SALOMON, K. (2005). Central adiposity is associated with cardiovascular reactivity to stress in adolescents. *Health Psychology*, 24, 375–384.

GOLDBERG, E. L., & COMSTOCK, G. W. (1980). Epidemiology of life events: Frequency in general populations. *American Journal of Epidemiology*, 111, 736–752.

GOLDBERG, J. H., & KING, A. C. (2007). Physical activity and weight management across the lifespan. *Annual Review of Public Health*, 28, 145–170.

GOLDEN, S. H., LAZO, M., CARNETHON, M., BERTONI, A. G., SCHREINER, P. J., et al. (2008). Examining a bidirectional association between depressive symptoms and diabetes. *Journal of the American Medical Association*, 299, 2751–2759.

GOLDING, J. F., & CORNISH, A. M. (1987). Personality and life-style in medical students: Psychopharmacological aspects. *Psychology and Health*, 1, 287–301.

GOLDMAN, R. L., RADNITZ, C. L., & MCGRATH, R. E. (2008). Posttraumatic stress disorder and major depression in veterans with spinal cord injury. *Rehabilitation Psychology*, 53, 162–170.

GOLDSTEIN, I. B., JAMNER, L. D., & SHAPIRO, D. (1992). Ambulatory blood pressure and heart rate in healthy male paramedics during a workday and a nonworkday. *Health Psychology*, 11, 48–54.

GOLDSTEIN, L. H. (1990). Behavioural and cognitive-behavioural treatments for epilepsy: A progress review. *British Journal of Clinical Psychology*, 29, 257–269.

GOLDSTON, D. B., KOVACS, M., OBROSKY, D. S., & IYENGAR, S. (1995). A longitudinal study of life events and metabolic control among youths with insulin-dependent diabetes mellitus. *Health Psychology*, 14, 409–414.

GOLDWATER, B. C., & COLLIS, M. L. (1985). Psychologic effects of cardiovascular conditioning: A controlled experiment. *Psychosomatic Medicine*, 47, 174–181.

GOMEL, M., OLDENBURG, B., SIMPSON, J. M., & OWEN, N. (1993). Work-site cardiovascular risk reduction: A randomized trial of health risk assessment, education, counseling, and incentives. *American Journal of Public Health*, 83, 1231–1238.

GONA, P., VAN DYKE, R. B., WILLIAMS, P. L., DANKNER, W. M., CHERNOFF, M. C., et al. (2006). Incidence of opportunistic and other infections in HIV-infected children in the HAART era. *Journal of the American Medical Association*, 296, 292–300.

GONDER-FREDERICK, L. A., COX, D. J., & RITTERBAND, L. M. (2002). Diabetes and behavioral medicine: The second decade. *Journal of Consulting and Clinical Psychology*, 70, 611–625.

GONZALEZ, J. S., PENEDO, F. J., ANTONI, M. H., DURÁN, R. E., FERNANDEZ, M. I., et al. (2004). Social support, positive states of mind, and HIV treatment adherence in men and women living with HIV/AIDS. *Health Psychology*, 23, 413–418.

GONZALEZ, J. S., PEYROT, M., MCCARL, L. A., COLLINS, E. M., SERPA, L., et al. (2008). Depression and diabetes treatment nonadherence: A meta-analysis. *Diabetes Care*, 31, 2398–2403.

GOODALL, T. A., & HALFORD, W. K. (1991). Self-management of diabetes mellitus: A critical review. *Health Psychology*, 10, 1–8.

GORDON, C. M., & CAREY, M. P. (1996). Alcohol's effects on requisites for sexual risk reduction in men: An initial experimental investigation. *Health Psychology*, 15, 56–60.

GORDON, W. A., & DILLER, L. (1983). Stroke: Coping with a cognitive deficit. In T. G. BURISH & L. A. BRADLEY (Eds.), *Coping with chronic disease: Research and applications* (pp. 113–135). New York: Academic Press.

GORIN, A., PHELAN, S., TATE, D., SHERWOOD, N., JEFFERY, R., & WING, R. (2005). Involving support partners in obesity treatment. *Journal of Consulting and Clinical Psychology*, 73, 341–343.

GORIN, A. A., PHELAN, S., WING, R. R., & HILL, J. O. (2004). Promoting long-term weight control: Does dieting consistency matter? *Journal of Obesity Related Metabolic Disorders*, 28, 278–281.

GORTMAKER, S. L., ECKENRODE, J., & GORE, S. (1982). Stress and the utilization of health services: A time series and cross-sectional analysis. *Journal of Health and Social Behavior*, 23, 25–38.

GOTTLIEB, N. H. (1983). The effect of health beliefs on the smoking behavior of college women. *Journal of American College Health*, 31, 214–221.

GOTTLIEB, N. H., & BAKER, J. A. (1986). The relative influence of health beliefs, parental and peer behaviors and exercise program participation on smoking, alcohol use and physical activity. *Social Science and Medicine*, 22, 915–927.

GOTTLIEB, N. H., & GREEN, L. W. (1987). Ethnicity and lifestyle health risk: Some possible mechanisms. *American Journal of Health Promotion*, 2, 37–45, 51.

GOUIN, J.-P., HANTSOOA, L., & KIECOLT-GLASER, J. K. (2008). Immune dysregulation and chronic stress among older adults: A review. *Neuroimmunomodulation*, 15, 251–259.

GRANDES, G., SANCHEZ, A., SANCHEZ-PINILLA, R. O., TORCAL, J., MONTOYA, I., et al. (2009). Effectiveness of physical activity advice and prescription by physicians in routine primary care. *Archives of Internal Medicine*, 169, 694–701.

GRAHAM, J. D., CORSO, P. S., MORRIS, J. M., SEGUI-GOMEZ, M., & WEINSTEIN, M. C. (1998). Evaluating the cost-effectiveness of clinical and public health measures. *Annual Review of Public Health*, 19, 125–152.

GRAY, R., MUKHERJEE, R. A. S., & RUTTER, M. (2009). Alcohol consumption during pregnancy and its effect on neurodevelopment: What is known and what remains uncertain. *Addiction*, 104, 1270–1273.

GREEN, C. J. (1985). The use of psychodiagnostic questionnaires in predicting risk factors and health outcomes. In P. KAROLY (Ed.), *Measurement strategies in health psychology* (pp. 301–334). New York: Wiley.

GREENGLASS, E. R., & NOGUCHI, K. (1996). *Longevity, gender and health: A psychocultural perspective.* Paper presented at the meeting of the International Society of Health Psychology in Montreal.

GREENLAND, P., KNOLL, M. D., STAMLER, J., NEATON, J. D., DYER, A. R., et al. (2003). Major risk factors as antecedents of fatal and nonfatal coronary heart disease events. *Journal of the American Medical Association*, 290, 891–897.

GREENWALD, H. P., BONICA, J. J., & BERGNER, M. (1987). The prevalence of pain in four cancers. *Cancer*, 60, 2563–2569.

GRIFFIN, K. W., FRIEND, R., KAELL, A. T., & BENNETT, R. S. (2001). Distress and disease status among patients with rheumatoid arthritis: Roles of coping styles and perceived responses from support providers. *Annals of Behavioral Medicine*, 23, 133–138.

GRIMLEY, D. M., ANNANG, L., HOUSER, S., & CHEN, H. (2005). Prevalence of condom use errors among STD clinic patients. *American Journal of Health Behavior*, 29, 324–330.

GRITZ, E. R., CARR, C. R., & MARCUS, A. C. (1991). The tobacco withdrawal syndrome in unaided quitters. *British Journal of Addiction*, 86, 57–69.

GROB, G. N. (1983). Disease and environment in American history. In D. MECHANIC (Ed.), *Handbook of health, health care, and the health professions* (pp. 3–22). New York: Free Press.

GRØNBÆK, M., BECKER, U., JOHANSEN, D., GOTTSCHAU, A., SCHNOHR, P., et al. (2000). Type of alcohol consumed and mortality from all causes, coronary heart disease, and cancer. *Annals of Internal Medicine*, 133, 411–419.

GROSSARDT, B. R., BOWER, A. J., GEDA, Y. E., COLLIGAN, R. C., & ROCCA, W. A. (2009). Pessimistic, anxious, and depressive personality traits predict all-cause mortality: The Mayo Clinic Cohort Study of Personality and Aging. *Psycholosomatic Medicine*, 71, 491–500.

GRUBE, J. W., & WALLACK, L. (1994). Television beer advertising and drinking knowledge, beliefs, and intentions among schoolchildren. *American Journal of Public Health*, 84, 254–259.

GRUEN, W. (1975). Effects of brief psychotherapy during the hospitalization period on the recovery process in heart attacks. *Journal of Consulting and Clinical Psychology*, 43, 223–232.

GRUENEWALD, T. L., COHEN, S., MATTHEWS, K. A., TRACY, R., & SEEMAN, T. E. (2009). Association of socioeconomic status with inflammation markers in black and white men and women in the Coronary Artery Risk Development in Young Adults (CARDIA) study. *Social Science and Medicine*, 69, 451–459.

GRUETZNER, H. (1992). *Alzheimer's: A caregiver's guide and sourcebook.* New York: Wiley.

GRUNAU, R. V. E., & CRAIG, K. D. (1987). Pain expression in neonates: Facial action and cry. *Pain*, 28, 395–410.

GRUNBERG, N. E., & BOWEN, D. J. (1985). Coping with the sequelae of smoking cessation. *Journal of Cardiopulmonary Rehabilitation*, 5, 285–289.

GUCCIONE, A. A., FELSON, D. T., ANDERSON, J. J., ANTHONY, J. M., ZHANG, Y., et al. (1994). The effects of specific medical conditions on the functional limitations of elders in the Framingham Study. *American Journal of Public Health*, 84, 351–358.

GUCK, T. P., SKULTETY, F. M., MEILMAN, P. W., & DOWD, E. T. (1985). Multidisciplinary pain center follow-up study: Evaluation with a no-treatment control group. *Pain*, 21, 295–306.

GUMP, B. B., & MATTHEWS, K. A. (1999). Do background stressors influence reactivity to and recovery from acute stressors? *Journal of Applied Social Psychology*, 29, 469–494.

GUMP, B. B., REIHMAN, J., STEWART, P., LONKY, E., & DARVILL, T. (2005). Terrorism and cardiovascular responses to acute stress in children. *Health Psychology, 24,* 594–600.

GUYLL, M., MATTHEWS, K. A., & BROMBERGER, J. T. (2001). Discrimination and unfair treatment: Relationship to cardiovascular reactivity among African American and European American women. *Health Psychology, 20,* 315–325.

GUYTON, A. C. (1985). *Anatomy and physiology.* Philadelphia: Saunders.

HAAKE, M., MÜLLER, H.-H., SCHADE-BRITTINGER, C., BASLER, H. D., SCHÄFER, H. et al. (2007). German Acupuncture Trials (GERAC) for chronic low back pain: Randomized multicenter, blinded, parallel-group trial with 3 groups. *Archives of Internal Medicine, 167,* 1892–1898.

HAAS, F., & HAAS, S. S. (1990). *The chronic bronchitis and emphysema handbook.* New York: Wiley.

HACKETT, M. L., ANDERSON, C. S., HOUSE, A., & HALTEH, C. (2008). Interventions for preventing depression after stroke. *Cochrane Database of Systematic Reviews,* Issue 3, Retrieved (1-30-2010) from http://www.thecochranelibrary.com.

HACKETT, T. P., & WEISMAN, A. D. (1985). Reactions to the imminence of death. In A. MONAT & R. S. LAZARUS (Eds.), *Stress and coping: An anthology* (2nd ed., pp. 248–255). New York: Columbia University Press.

HADJISTAVROPOULOS, T. (2004). Ethics for psychologists who treat, assess, and/or study pain. In T. HADJISTAVROPOULOS & K. D. CRAIG (Eds.), *Pain: Psychological perspectives* (pp. 327–344). Mahwah, NJ: Earlbaum.

HAFEN, B. Q. (1981). *Nutrition, food, and weight control.* Boston: Allyn & Bacon.

HAGEDOORN, M., & MOLLEMAN, E. (2006). Facial disfigurement in patients with head and neck cancer: The role of social self-efficacy. *Health Psychology, 25,* 643–647.

HAGEDOORN, M., SANDERMAN, R., BOLKS, H. N., TUINSTRA, J., & COYNE, J. C. (2008). Distress in couples coping with cancer: A meta-analysis and critical review of role and gender effects. *Psychological Bulletin, 134,* 1–30.

HAJEK, P., STEAD, L. F., WEST, R., JARVIS, M., & LANCASTER, T. (2009). Relapse prevention interventions for smoking cessation. *Cochrane Database of Systematic Reviews,* Issue 1. Retrieved (1-30-2010) from http://www.thecochranelibrary.com. DOI:10.1002/14651858.CD003999.pub3.

HAJJAR, I., KOTCHEN, J. M., & KOTCHEN, T. A. (2006). Hypertension: Trends in prevalence, incidence, and control. *Annual Review of Public Health, 27,* 465–490.

HALEY, W. E. (1998). Alzheimer's disease: A general review. In E. A. BLECHMAN & K. D. BROWNELL (Eds.), *Behavioral medicine and women: A comprehensive handbook* (pp. 546–550). New York: Guilford.

HALL, H. I., SONG, R., RHODES, P., PREJEAN, J., AN, Q., et al. (2008). Estimation of HIV incidence in the United States. *Journal of the American Medical Association, 300,* 520–529.

HALL, M., VASKO, R., BUYSSE, D., OMBAO, H., CHEN, Q., et al. (2004). Acute stress affects heart rate variability during sleep. *Psychosomatic Medicine, 66,* 56–62.

HAMILTON, J. G., LOBEL, M., & MOYER, A. (2009). Emotional distress following genetic testing for hereditary breast and ovarian cancer: A meta-analytic review. *Health Psychology, 28,* 510–518.

HAMILTON, N. A., AFFLECK, G., TENNEN, H., KARLSON, C., LUXTON, D., et al. (2008). Fibromyalgia: The role of sleep in affect and in negative event reactivity and recovery. *Health Psychology, 27,* 490–494.

HAMMOND, S. K., SORENSON, G., YOUNGSTROM, R., & OCKENE, J. K. (1995). Occupational exposure to environmental tobacco smoke. *Journal of the American Medical Association, 274,* 956–960.

HAMPSON, S. E., GOLDBERG, L. R., VOGT, T. M., & DUBANOSKI, J. P. (2006). Forty years on: Teachers' assessments of children's personality traits predict self-reported behaviors and outcomes at midlife. *Health Psychology, 25,* 57–64.

HAMRICK, N., COHEN, S., & RODRIGUEZ, M. S. (2002). Being popular can be healthy or unhealthy: Stress, social network diversity, and incidence of upper respiratory infection. *Health Psychology, 21,* 294–298.

HAN, J. C., & YANOVSKI, J. A. (2008). Intensive therapies for the treatment of pediatric obesity. In E. JELALIAN & R. G. STEELE (Ed.), *Handbook of childhood and adolescent obesity* (pp. 241–260). New York: Springer.

HANSEN, W. B., GRAHAM, J. W., SOBEL, J. L., SHELTON, D. R., FLAY, B. R., & JOHNSON, C. A. (1987). The consistency of peer and parent influences on tobacco, alcohol, and marijuana use among young adolescents. *Journal of Behavioral Medicine, 10,* 559–579.

HANSEN, W. B., RAYNOR, A. E., & WOLKENSTEIN, B. H. (1991). Perceived personal immunity to the consequences of drinking alcohol: The relationship between behavior and perception. *Journal of Behavioral Medicine, 14,* 205–224.

HANSON, C. L., HENGGELER, S. W., & BURGHEN, G. A. (1987). Social competence and parental support as mediators of the link between stress and metabolic control in adolescents with insulin-dependent diabetes mellitus. *Journal of Consulting and Clinical Psychology, 55,* 529–533.

HARBURG, E., ERFURT, J. C., HAUENSTEIN, L. S., CHAPE, C., SCHULL, W. J., & SCHORK, M. A. (1973). Socio-ecological stress, suppressed hostility, skin color, and black-white male blood pressure: Detroit. *Psychosomatic Medicine, 35,* 276–296.

HARDEN, R. N., & BRUEHL, S. P. (2006). Diagnosis of complex regional pain syndrome: Signs, symptoms, and new empirically derived diagnostic criteria. *Clinical Journal of Pain, 22,* 415–419.

HARE, B. D., & MILANO, R. A. (1985). Chronic pain: Perspectives on physical assessment and treatment. *Annals of Behavioral Medicine, 7*(3), 6–10.

HARRIS, D. M., & GUTEN, S. (1979). Health-protective behavior: An exploratory study. *Journal of Health and Social Behavior, 20,* 17–29.

HARRIS, J. L., BARGH, J. A., & BROWNELL, K. D. (2009). Priming effects of television food advertising on eating behavior. *Health Psychology, 28,* 404–413.

HARRIS, J. L., POMERANZ, J. L., LOBSTEIN, T., & BROWNELL, K. D. (2009). A crisis in the marketplace: How food marketing contributes to childhood obesity and what can be done. *Annual Review of Public Health, 30,* 211–225.

HARRIS, J. R., PEDERSON, N. L., MCCLEARN, G. E., PLOMIN, R., & NESSELROADE, J. R. (1992). Age differences in genetic and environmental influences for health from the Swedish Adoption/Twin Study of Aging. *Journal of Gerontology, 47,* P213–220.

HARRISON, K., & MARSKE, A. I. (2005). Nutritional content of foods advertised during the television programs children watch most. *American Journal of Public Health, 95,* 1568–1574.

HARRISON, S. L., MACLENNAN, R., SPEARE, R., & WRONSKI, I. (1994). Sun exposure and melanocytic naevi in young Australian children. *Lancet, 1994,* 1529–1532.

HART, W. (1987). *The art of living: Vipassana meditation.* New York: HarperCollins.

HASKELL, W. L. (1984). Overview: Health benefits of exercise. In J. D. MATARAZZO, S. M. WEISS, J. A. HERD, N. E. MILLER, & S. M. WEISS (Eds.), *Behavioral health: A handbook of health enhancement and disease prevention* (pp. 409–423). New York: Wiley.

HASKELL, W. L., ALDERMAN, E. L., FAIR, J. M., MARON, D. J., MACKEY, S. F., et al. (1994). Effects of intensive multiple risk factor reduction on coronary atherosclerosis and clinical cardiac events in men and women with coronary artery disease: The Stanford Coronary Risk Intervention Project (SCRIP). *Circulation, 89,* 975–990.

HAUG, M. R., & LAVIN, B. (1981). Practitioner or patient—Who's in charge? *Journal of Health and Social Behavior, 22,* 212–229.

HAUSER, W. A., & HESDORFFER, D. C. (1990). *Facts about epilepsy.* Landover, MD: Epilepsy Foundation of America.

HAY, P. P. J., BACALTCHUK, J., STEFANO, S., & KAHYAP, P. (2009). Psychological treatment for bulimia nervosa and binging. *Cochrane Database of Systematic Reviews,* Issue 4. Retrieved (1-30-2010) from http://www.thecochranelibrary.com. DOI:10.1002/14651858.CD000562.pub3.

HAYDEN, J. A., VAN TULDER, M. W., & TOMLINSON, G. (2005). Systematic review: Strategies for using exercise therapy to improve outcomes in chronic low back pain. *Annals of Internal Medicine, 142,* 776–785.

HAYES, R. D., KRAVITZ, R. L., MAZEL, R. M., SHERBOURNE, C. D., DIMATTEO, M. R., et al. (1994). The impact of patient adherence on health outcomes for patients with chronic disease in the Medical Outcomes Study. *Journal of Behavioral Medicine, 17,* 347–360.

HAYES, S. C., & WILSON, K. G. (1995). The role of cognition in complex human behavior: A contextualistic perspective. *Journal of Behavior Therapy and Experimental Psychiatry, 26,* 241–248.

HAYMAN, L. L. (2007). Behavioral medicine across the life course: Challenges and opportunities for interdisciplinary science. *Annals of Behavioral Medicine, 33,* 236–241.

HAYNES, A. B., WEISER, T. G., BERRY, W. R., LIPSITZ, S. R., BREIZAT, A. H., et al. (2009). A surgical safety checklit to reduce morbidity and mortality in a global population. *New England Journal of Medicine, 360,* 491–499.

HAYNES, R. B. (1976). A critical review of the "determinants" of patient compliance with therapeutic regimens. In D. L. SACKETT & R. B. HAYNES (Eds.), *Compliance with therapeutic regimens* (pp. 26–40). Baltimore: Johns Hopkins University Press.

HAYNES, R. B., ACKLOO, E., SAHOTA, N., MCDONALD, H. P., & YAO, X. (2008). Interventions for enhancing medication adherence. *Cochrane Database of Systematic Reviews,* Issue 2. Retrieved (1-30-2010) from http://www.thecochranelibrary.com. DOI:10.1002/14651858.CD000011.pub3.

HAYS, J. C., GOLD, D. T., FLINT, E. P., & WINER, E. P. (1999). Patient preference for place of death: A qualitative approach. In B. DE VRIES (Ed.), *End of life issues: Interdisciplinary and multidimensional perspectives* (pp. 3–21). New York: Springer.

HAYS, J. C., KASL, S. V., & JACOBS, J. C. (1994). The course of psychological distress following threatened and actual conjugal bereavement. *Psychological Medicine, 24,* 917–927.

HAYTHORTHWAITE, J. A., & FAUERBACH, J. A. (2001). Assessment of acute pain, pain relief, and patient satisfaction. In D. C. TURK & R. MELZACK (Eds.), *Handbook of pain assessment* (2nd ed., pp. 417–430). New York: Guilford.

HEAPY, A., OTIS, J., MARCUS, K. S., FRANTSVE, L. M., JANKE, E. A., et al. (2005). Intersession coping skill practice mediaties the relationship between readiness for self-management treatment and goal accomplishment. *Pain, 118,* 360–368.

HEARN, M. D., BARANOWSKI, T., BARANOWSKI, J., DOYLE, C., SMITH, M., et al. (1998). Environmental influences on dietary behavior among children: Availability and accessibility of fruits and vegetables enable consumption. *Journal of Health Education, 29,* 26–32.

HEBB, D. O. (1955). Drives and the C.N.S. (conceptual nervous system). *Psychological Review, 62,* 243–254.

HEINRICH, R. L., COHEN, M. J., NALIBOFF, B. D., COLLINS, G. A., & BONNEBAKKER, A. D. (1985). Comparing physical and behavior therapy for chronic low back pain on physical abilities, psychological distress, and patients' perceptions. *Journal of Behavioral Medicine, 8,* 61–78.

HELGESON, V. S., & COHEN, S. (1996). Social support and adjustment to cancer: Reconciling descriptive, correlational, and intervention research. *Health Psychology, 15,* 135–148.

HELGESON, V. S., COHEN, S., SCHULZ, R., & YASKO, J. (1999). Education and peer discussion group interventions and adjustment to breast cancer. *Archives of General Psychiatry, 56,* 340–347.

HELGESON, V. S., & FRITZ, H. L. (1999). Cognitive adaptation as a predictor of new coronary events after percutaneous transluminal coronary angioplasty. *Psychosomatic Medicine, 61,* 488–495.

HELGESON, V. S., REYNOLDS, K. A., & TOMICH, P. L (2006). A meta-analytic review of benefit finding and growth. *Journal of Consulting and Clinical Psychology, 74,* 797–816.

HELGESON, V. S., SNYDER, P., & SELTMAN, H. (2004). Psychological and physical adjustment to breast cancer over 4 years: Identifying distinct trajectories of change. *Health Psychology, 23,* 3–15.

HELLER, K., PRICE, R. H., & HOGG, J. R. (1990). The role of social support in community and clinical interventions. In B. R. SARASON, I. G. SARASON, & G. R. PIERCE (Eds.), *Social support: An interactional view* (pp. 482–507). New York: Wiley.

HELLSTEN, L., NIGG, C., NORMAN, G., BURBANK, P., BRAUN, L., et al. (2008). Accumulation of behavioral validation evidence for physical activity stage of change. *Health Psychology, 27,* S43–S53.

HENDERSON, B. N., & BAUM, A. (2004). Biological mechanisms of health and disease. In S. SUTTON, A. BAUM, & M. JOHNSTON (Eds.), *The Sage handbook of health psychology* (pp. 69–93). London: Sage.

HENDERSON, G., & PRIMEAUX, M. (1981). Religious beliefs and healing. In G. HENDERSON & M. PRIMEAUX (Eds.), *Transcultural health care* (pp. 185–195). Menlo Park, CA: Addison-Wesley.

HENDLER, N. H. (1984). Chronic pain. In H. B. ROBACK (Eds.), *Helping patients and their families cope with medical problems* (pp. 79–106). San Francisco: Jossey-Bass.

HENDRICK, S. S. (1985). Spinal cord injury and neuromuscular reeducation. In N. SCHNEIDERMAN & J. T. TAPP (Eds.), *Behavioral medicine: The biopsychosocial approach* (pp. 589–614). Hillsdale, NJ: Erlbaum.

HENRY, J. H., LIU, Y-Y., NADRA, W. E., QIAN, C.-G., MORMEDE, P., et al. (1993). Psychosocial stress can induce chronic hypertension in normotensive strains of rats. *Hypertension, 21,* 714–723.

HERBERT, T. B., & COHEN, S. (1993). Stress and immunity in humans: A meta-analytic review. *Psychosomatic Medicine, 55,* 364–379.

HERD, J. A., & WEISS, S. M. (1984). Overview of hypertension: Its treatment and prevention. In J. D. MATARAZZO, S. M. WEISS, J. A. HERD, N. E. MILLER, & S. M. WEISS (Eds.), *Behavioral health: A handbook of health enhancement and disease prevention* (pp. 789–805). New York: Wiley.

HEREK, G. M. (1999). AIDS and stigma. *American Behavioral Scientist, 42,* 1106–1116.

HEREK, G. M., & GLUNT, E. K. (1988). An epidemic of stigma: Public reactions to AIDS. *American Psychologist, 43,* 886–891.

HERMAN, C. P., OLMSTEAD, M. P., & POLIVY, J. (1983). Obesity, externality, and susceptibility to social influence: An integrated analysis. *Journal of Personality and Social Psychology, 45,* 926–934.

HERNDON, E. J., & WANDERSMAN, A. (2004). Prevention. In A. J. CHRISTENSEN, R. MARTIN, & J. M. SMYTH (Eds.), *Encyclopedia of health psychology* (pp. 220–221). New York: Kluwer.

HERSHEY, G. K. K., FRIEDRICH, M. F., ESSWEIN, L. A., THOMAS, M. L., & CHATLIA, T. A. (1997). The association of atopy with a gain-of-function mutation in the (alpha) subunit of the interluken-4 receptor. *New England Journal of Medicine, 337,* 1720–1725.

HESHKA, S., ANDERSON, J. W., ATKINSON, R. L., GREENWAY, F. L., HILL, J. O., et al. (2003). Weight loss with self-help compared with a structured commercial program: A randomized trial. *Journal of the American Medical Association, 289,* 1792–1798.

HFA (Hospice Foundation of America) (2010). *What is hospice?* Retrieved (4-17-2010) from http://www.hospicefoundation.org.

HIGGINS, S. T., HEIL, S. H., & LUSSIER, J. P. (2004). Clinical implications of reinforcement as a determinant of substance use disorders. *Annual Review of Psychology, 55,* 431–461.

HILGARD, E. R. (1967). Individual differences in hypnotizability. In J. E. GORDON (Ed.), *Handbook of clinical and experimental hypnosis* (pp. 391–443). New York: Macmillan.

HILGARD, E. R., & HILGARD, J. R. (1983). *Hypnosis in the relief of pain* (rev. ed.). Los Altos, CA: Kaufmann.

HILL-BRIGGS, F. (2003). Problem solving in diabetes self-management: A model of chronic illness self-management behavior. *Annals of Behavioral Medicine, 25,* 182–193.

HILLSDON, M. M., BRUNNER, E. J., GURALNIK, J. M., & MARMOT, M. G. (2005). Prospective study of physical activity and physical function in early old age. *American Journal of Preventive Medicine, 28,* 245–250.

HINTON, J. (1984). Coping with terminal illness. In R. FITZPATRICK, J. HINTON, S. NEWMAN, G. SCAMBLER, & J. THOMPSON (Eds.), *The experience of illness* (pp. 227–245). London: Tavistock.

HIROTO, D. S., & SELIGMAN, M. E. P. (1975). Generality of learned helplessness in man. *Journal of Personality and Social Psychology, 31,* 311–327.

HITCHCOCK, L. S., FERRELL, B. R., & MCCAFFERY, M. (1994). The experience of chronic nonmalignant pain. *Journal of Pain and Symptom Management, 9,* 312–318.

HLETKO, P. J., ROBIN, S. S., HLETKO, J. D., & STONE, M. (1987). Infant safety seat use: Reaching the hard to reach. *American Journal of Diseases in Children, 141,* 1301–1304.

HO, P. M., SPERTUS, J. A., MASOUDI, F. A., REID, K. J., PETERSON, E. D., et al. (2006). Impact of medication therapy discontinuation on mortality after myocardial infarction. *Archives of Internal Medicine, 166,* 1842–1847.

HOBFOLL, S. E. (1989). Conservation of resources: A new attempt at conceptualizing stress. *American Psychologist, 44,* 513–524.

HODGINS, D. C., LEIGH, G., MILNE, R., & GERRISH, R. (1997). Drinking goal selection in behavioral self-management of chronic alcoholics. *Addictive Behaviors, 22,* 247–255.

HOELSCHER, T. J., LICHSTEIN, K. L., & ROSENTHAL, T. L. (1986). Home relaxation practice in hypertension treatment: Objective assessment and compliance induction. *Journal of Consulting and Clinical Psychology, 54,* 217–221.

HOFFMAN, B. M., PAPAS, R. K., CHATKOFF, D. K., & KERNS, R. D. (2007). Meta-analysis of psychological interventions for chronic low back pain. *Health Psychology, 26,* 1–9.

HOFFMAN, K. E., MCCARTHY, E. P., RECKLITIS, C. J., & NG, A. K. (2009). Psychological distress in long-term survivors of adult-onset cancer: Results from a national survey. *Archives of Internal Medicine, 169,* 1274–1281.

HOGAN, B. E., & LINDEN, W. (2004). Anger response styles and blood pressure: At least don't ruminate about it! *Annals of Behavioral Medicine, 27,* 38–49.

HOGAN, B. E., LINDEN, W., & NAJARIAN, B. (2002). Social support interventions: Do they work? *Clinical Psychology Review, 22,* 381–440.

HOLAHAN, C. J., MOOS, R. H., HOLAHAN, C. K., & BRENNAN, P. L. (1997). Social context, coping strategies, and depressive symptoms: An expanded model with cardiac patients. *Journal of Personality and Social Psychology, 72,* 918–928.

HOLAHAN, C. J., MOOS, R. H., HOLAHAN, C. K., CRONKITE, R. C., & RANDALL, P. K. (2001). Drinking to cope, emotional distress and alcohol use and abuse: A ten-year model. *Journal of Studies on Alcohol, 62,* 190–198.

HOLAHAN, C. K., HOLAHAN, C. J., & BELK, S. S. (1984). Adjustment in aging: The roles of life stress, hassles, and self-efficacy. *Health Psychology, 3,* 315–328.

HOLDEN, C. (1980). Love Canal residents under stress. *Science, 208,* 1242–1244.

HOLDEN, S. D., SHELTON, R. C., & DAVIS, D. D. (1993). Cognitive therapy for depression: Conceptual issues and clinical efficacy. *Journal of Consulting and Clinical Psychology, 61,* 270–275.

HOLMES, D. S. (1993). Aerobic fitness and the response to psychological stress. In P. SERAGANIAN (Ed.), *Exercise psychology: The influence of physical exercise on psychological processes* (pp. 39–63). New York: Wiley.

HOLMES, T. H., & MASUDA, M. (1974). Life change and illness susceptibility. In B. S. DOHRENWEND & B. P. DOHRENWEND (Eds.), *Stressful life events: Their nature and effects* (pp. 45–72). New York: Wiley.

HOLMES, T. H., & RAHE, R. H. (1967). The Social Readjustment Rating Scale. *Journal of Psychosomatic Research, 11,* 213–218.

HOLROYD, K. A. (2002). Assessment and psychological management of recurrent headache disorders. *Journal of Consulting and Clinical Psychology, 70,* 656–677.

HOLROYD, K. A., FRANCE, J. L., NASH, J. M., & HURSEY, K. G. (1993). Pain state as artifact in the psychological assessment of recurrent headache sufferers. *Pain, 53,* 229–235.

HOLROYD, K. A., & PENZIEN, D. B. (1986). Client variables and the behavioral treatment of recurrent tension headache: A meta-analytic review. *Journal of Behavioral Medicine, 9,* 515–536.

HOLT, J. (1995,). Motivating Beth. *American Journal of Nursing, 95,* pp. 60, 62.

HOLT-LUNSTAD, J., BIRMINGHAM, W., HOWARD, A. M., & THOMAN, D. (2009). Married with children: The influence of parental status and gender on ambulatory blood pressure. *Annals of Behavioral Medicine, 38,* 170–179.

HOLT-LUNSTAD, J., BIRMINGHAM, W., & JONES, B. Q. (2008). Is there something unique about marriage? The relative impact of marital status, relationship quality, and network social support on ambulatory blood pressure and mental health. *Annals of Behavioral Medicine, 35,* 239–244.

HOLT-LUNSTAD, J., BIRMINGHAM, W. A., & LIGHT, K. C. (2008). Influence of a "warm touch" support enhancement intervention among married couples on ambulatory blood pressure, oxytocin, alpha amylase, and cortisol. *Psychosomatic Medicine, 70,* 976–985.

HOLT-LUNSTAD, J., JONES, B. Q., & BIRMINGHAM, W. (2009). The influence of close relationships on nocturnal blood pressure dipping. *International Journal of Psychophysiology, 71,* 211–217.

HOLT-LUNSTAD, J., SMITH, T. W., & UCHINO, B. N. (2008). Can hostility interfere with the health benefits of giving and receiving social support? The impact of cynical hostility on cardiovascular reactivity during social support interactions among friends. *Annals of Behavioral Medicine, 35,* 319–330.

HOLTZMAN, S., & DELONGIS, A. (2007). One day at a time: The impact of daily satisfaction with spouse responses on pain, negative affect and catastrophizing among individuals with rheumatoid arthritis. *Pain, 131,* 202–213.

HOLUM, J. R. (1994). *Fundamentals of general, organic, and biological chemistry* (5th ed.). New York: Wiley.

HÖLZL, R., KLEINBÖHL, D., & HUSE, E. (2005). Implicit operant learning of pain sensitization. *Pain, 115,* 12–20.

HOLZMAN, A. D., TURK, D. C., & KERNS, R. D. (1986). The cognitive-behavioral approach to the management of chronic pain. In A. D. HOLZMAN & D. C. TURK (Eds.), *Pain management: A handbook of psychological treatment approaches* (pp. 31–50). New York: Pergamon.

HOMISH, G. G., & LEONARD, K. E. (2008). Spousal influence on general health behaviors in a community sample. *American Journal of Health Behavior, 32,* 754–763.

HOOD, K. K., PETERSON, C. M., ROHAN, J. M., & DROTAR, D. (2009). Association between adherence and glycemic control in pediatric type 1 diabetes: A meta-analysis. *Pediatrics, 124,* e1171–e1179.

HORN, J. C., & MEER, J. (1987, May). The vintage years. *Psychology Today,* pp. 76–84, 89–90.

HOROWITZ, L. M., KRASNOPEROVA, E. M., TATAR, D. G., HANSEN, M. B., PERSON, E. A., et al. (2001). The way to console may depend on the goal: Experimental studies of social support. *Journal of Experimental Social Psychology, 37,* 49–61.

HOUSE, J. S., ROBBINS, C., & METZNER, H. L. (1982). The association of social relationships and activities with mortality: Prospective evidence from the Tecumseh Community Health Study. *American Journal of Epidemiology, 116,* 123–140.

HOUSTON, B. K., BABYAK, M. A., CHESNEY, M. A., BLACK, G., & RAGLAND, D. R. (1997). Social dominance and 22-year all-cause mortality in men. *Psychosomatic Medicine, 59,* 5–12.

HOUSTON, B. K., CHESNEY, M., BLACK, G., CATES, D., & HECKER, M. (1992). Behavioral clusters and coronary heart disease risk. *Psychosomatic Medicine, 54,* 447–461.

HOWARD, G., WAGENKNECHT, L. E., BURKE, G. L., DIEZ-ROUX, A., EVANS, G. W., et al. (1998). Cigarette smoking and progression of atherosclerosis: The Atherosclerosis Risk in Communities (ARIC) Study. *Journal of the American Medical Association, 279,* 119–224.

HOWELL, D. (1986). The impact of terminal illness on the spouse. *Journal of Palliative Care, 2,* 22–30.

HOWREN, M. B., CHRISTENSEN, A. J., KARNELL, L. H., & FUNK, G. F. (2010). Health-related quality of life in head and neck cancer survivors: Impact of pretreatment depressive symptoms. *Health Psychology, 29,* 65–71.

HOWREN, M. B., LAMKIN, D. M. & SULS, J. (2009). Associations of depression with C-reactive protein, IL-1, and IL-6: A meta-analysis. *Psychosomatic Medicine, 71,* 171–186.

HP (Health Psychology, Division 38 of the American Psychological Association) (2010). *About health psychology: Becoming a health psychologist.* Retrieved (5-12-2010) from http://www.health-psych.org.

HRÓBJARTSSON, A., & GØTZSCHE, P. C. (2010). Placebo interventions for all clinical conditions. *Cochrane Database of Systematic Reviews,* Issue 1. Retrieved (1-30-2010) from http://www.thecochranelibrary.com. DOI:10.1002/14651858.CD003974.pub3.

HU, F. B., PERSKY, V., FLAY, B. R., & RICHARDSON, J. (1997). An epidemiological study of asthma prevalence and related factors among young adults. *Journal of Asthma, 34,* 67–76.

HUANG, M., HOLLIS, J., POLEN, M., LAPIDUS, J., & AUSTIN, D. (2005). Stages of smoking acquisition versus susceptibility as predictors of smoking initiation in adolescents in primary care. *Addictive Behavior, 30,* 1183–1194.

HUDCOVA, J., MCNICOL, E., QUAH, C., LAU, J., & CARR, D. B. (2006). Patient controlled opioid analgesia versus conventional opioid analgesia for postoperative pain. *Cochrane Database of Systematic Reviews,* Issue 4. DOI: 10.1002/14651858.CD003348.pub2.

HUEBNER, D. M. &. DAVIS, M. C. (2007). Perceived antigay discrimination and physical health outcomes. *Health Psychology, 26,* 627–634.

HUFFMAN, L. C., & DEL CARMEN, R. (1990). Prenatal stress. In L. E. ARNOLD (Ed.), *Childhood stress* (pp. 141–172). New York: Wiley.

HUGHES, J. R. (2009). How confident should we be that smoking cessation treatments work? *Addiction, 104,* 1637–1640.

HULL, J. G., & BOND, C. F. (1986). Social and behavioral consequences of alcohol consumption and expectancy: A meta-analysis. *Psychological Bulletin, 99,* 347–360.

HUMBLE, C., CROFT, J., GERBER, A., CASPER, M., HAMES, C. G., & TYROLER, H. A. (1990). Passive smoking and 20-year cardiovascular disease mortality among nonsmoking wives, Evans County, Georgia. *American Journal of Public Health, 80,* 599–601.

HUNCHAREK, M., HADDOCK, K. S., REID, R., & KUPELNICK, B. (2010). Smoking a risk factor for prostate cancer: A meta-analysis of 24 prospective cohort studies. *American Journal of Public Health, 100,* 693–701.

HUNKELER, E. M., KATON, W., TANG, L., WILLIAMS, J. W., KROENKE, K., et al. (2006). Long term outcomes from the IMPACT randomised trial for depressed elderly patients in primary care. *British Medical Journal, 332,* 259–263.

HUNT, E. B., & MACLEOD, C. M. (1979). Cognition and information processing in patient and physician. In G. C. STONE, F. COHEN, & N. E. ADLER (Eds.), *Health psychology—A handbook* (pp. 303–332). San Francisco: Jossey-Bass.

HUNT, M. G., MOSHIER, S., & MILONOVA, M. (2009). Brief cognitive-behavioral internet therapy for irritable bowel syndrome. *Behaviour Research and Therapy, 47,* 797–802.

HURKMANS, E., VAN DER GIESEN, F. J., VLIET VLIELAND, T. P. M., SCHOONES, J., VAN DEN ENDE. E. C. H. M. (2009). Dynamic exercise programs (aerobic capacity and/or muscle strength training) in patients with rheumatoid arthritis. *Cochrane Database of Systematic Reviews,* Issue 4. Retrieved (1-30-2010) from http://www.thecochranelibrary.com.

HURLEY, D. (1987). A sound mind in an unsound body. *Psychology Today,* pp. 34–43.

HURLEY, D. (2007, January 16). Diet supplements and safety: Some disquieting data. *New York Times,* pp. F5, F8.

HURWITZ, B. E. (2004). Chronic fatigue syndrome. In A. J. CHRISTENSEN, R. MARTIN, & J. M. SMYTH (Eds.), *Encyclopedia of health psychology* (pp. 45–48). New York: Kluwer.

HURWITZ, E. L., MORGENSTERN, H., & CHIAO, C. (2005). Effects of recreational physical activity and back exercises on low back pain and psychological distress: Findings from the UCLA Low Back Pain Study. *American Journal of Public Health, 95,* 1817–1824.

HUSSUSSIAN, C. J., STRUEWING, J. P., GOLDSTEIN, A. M., HIGGINS, P. A. T., ALLY, D. S., et al. (1994). Germline p16 mutations in familial melanoma. *Nature Genetics, 8,* 15–21.

HUSTAD, J. T. P., BARNETT, N. P., BORSARI, B., & JACKSON, K. M. (2010). Web-based alcohol prevention for incoming college students: A randomized controlled trial. *Addictive Behaviors, 35,* 183–189.

HUSZTI, H. C., & WALKER, C. E. (1991). Critical issues on consultation and liaison. In J. J. SWEET, R. H. ROZENSKY, & S. M. TOVIAN (Eds.), *Handbook of clinical psychology in medical settings* (pp. 165–185). New York: Plenum.

HUTCHINSON, K. E., MCGEARY, J., SMOLEN, A., BRYAN, A., & SWIFT, R. M. (2002). The DRD4 VNTR polymorphism moderates craving after alcohol consumption. *Health Psychology, 21,* 139–146.

HYSON, M. C. (1983). Going to the doctor: A developmental study of stress and coping. *Journal of Child Psychology and Psychiatry, 24,* 247–259.

IHGSC (International Human Genome Sequencing Consortium) (2001). Initial sequencing and analysis of the human genome. *Nature, 409,* 860–921.

IHMELS, M. A., WELK, G. J., EISENMANN, J. C., NUSSER, S. M., & MEYERS, E. F. (2009). Prediction of BMI change in young children with the Family Nutrition and Physical Activity (FNPA) screening tool. *Annals of Behavioral Medicine, 38,* 60–68.

ILFELD, F. W. (1980). Coping styles of Chicago adults: Description. *Journal of Human Stress*, 6, 2–10.

INGERSOLL, K. S., & COHEN, J. (2008). The impact of medication regimen factors on adherence to chronic treatment: A review of literature. *Journal of Behavioral Medicine*, 31, 213–224.

INSEL, P. M., & ROTH, W. T. (1998). *Core concepts in health* (8th ed.). Mountain View, CA: Mayfield.

INUI, T. S., YOURTEE, E. L., & WILLIAMSON, J. W. (1976). Improved outcomes in hypertension after physician tutorials. *Annals of Internal Medicine*, 84, 646–651.

IOM (Institute of Medicine) (2004). *Health literacy: A prescription to end confusion*. Retrieved (6-18-2004) from http://www.iom.edu.

IRONSON, G., FRIEDMAN, A., KLIMAS, N., ANTONI, M., FLETCHER, M. A., et al. (1994). Distress, denial, and low adherence to behavioral interventions predict faster disease progression in gay men infected with human immunodeficiency virus. *International Journal of Behavioral Medicine*, 1, 90–105.

IRONSON, G., & KREMER, H. (2009). Spiritual transformation, psychological well-being, health, and survival in people with HIV. *International Journal of Psychiatry in Medicine*, 39, 263–281.

IRONSON, G., O'CLEIRIGH, C., FLETCHER, M. A., LAURENCEAU, J. P., BALBIN, E., et al. (2005). Psychosocial factors predict CD4 and viral load change in men and women with human immunodeficiency virus in the era of highly active antiretroviral treatment. *Psychosomatic Medicine*, 67, 1013–1021.

IRONSON, G. H., O'CLEIRIGH, C., WEISS, A., SCHNEIDERMAN, N., & COSTA, P. T. (2008). Personality and HIV disease progression: Role of NEO-PI-R openness, extraversion, and profiles of engagement. *Psychosomatic Medicine*, 70, 245–253.

IRVIN, J. E., BOWERS, C. A., DUNN, M. E., & WANG, M. C. (1999). Efficacy of relapse prevention: A meta-analytic review. *Journal of Consulting and Clinical Psychology*, 67, 563–570.

IRVINE, J., BAKER, B., SMITH, J., JANDCIU, S., PAQUETTE, M., et al. (1999). Poor adherence to placebo or amiodarone therapy predicts mortality: Results from the CAMIAT study. *Psychosomatic Medicine*, 61, 566–575.

IRWIN, M., MASCOVICH, A., GILLIN, J. C., WILLOUGHBY, R., PIKE, J., & SMITH, T. L. (1994). Partial sleep deprivation reduces natural killer cell activity in humans. *Psychosomatic Medicine*, 56, 493–498.

IRWIN, M. R., COLE, J. C., & NICASSIO, P. M. (2006). Comparative meta-analysis of behavioral interventions for insomnia and their efficacy in middle-aged adults and in older adults 55+ years of age. *Health Psychology*, 25, 3–14.

IZARD, C. E. (1979). Emotions as motivations: An evolutionary developmental perspective. In H. E. HOWE & R. A. DIENSTBIER (Eds.), *Nebraska Symposium on Motivation 1978* (Vol. 26, pp. 163–200). Lincoln, NE: University of Nebraska Press.

JACCARD, J., & TURRISI, R. (1987). Cognitive processes and individual differences in judgments relevant to drunk driving. *Journal of Personality and Social Psychology*, 53, 135–145.

JACOB, M. C., & KERNS, R. D. (2001). Assessment of the psychosocial context of the experience of chronic pain. In D. C. TURK & R. MELZACK (Eds.), *Handbook of pain assessment* (2nd ed., pp. 362–385). New York: Guilford.

JACOBSEN, P. B., BOVBJERG, D. H., SCHWARTZ, M. D., HUDIS, C. A., GILEWSKI, T. A., & NORTON, L. (1995). Conditioned emotional distress in women receiving chemotherapy for breast cancer. *Journal of Consulting and Clinical Psychology*, 63, 108–114.

JACOBSEN, P. B., & THORS, C. L. (2003). Fatigue in the radiation therapy patient: Current management and investigations. *Seminars in Radiation Oncology*, 13, 372–380.

JACOBSEN, P. B., WIDOWS, M. R., HANN, D. M., ANDRYKOWSKI, M. A., KRONISH, L. E., & FILEDS, K. K. (1998). Posttraumatic stress disorder symptoms after bone marrow transplantation for breast cancer. *Psychosomatic Medicine*, 60, 366–371.

JACOBSON, A. M., HAUSER, S. T., LAVORI, P., WILLETT, J. B., COLE, C. F., et al. (1994). Family environment and glycemic control: A four-year prospective study of children and adolescents with insulin-dependent diabetes mellitus. *Psychosomatic Medicine*, 56, 401–409.

JACOBSON, E. J. (1938). *Progressive relaxation*. Chicago: University of Chicago Press.

JACOBSON, J. A., DANFORTH, D. N., COWAN, K. H., D'ANGELO, T., STEINBERG, S. M., et al. (1995). Ten-year results of a comparison of conservation with mastectomy in the treatment of stage I and II breast cancer. *New England Journal of Medicine*, 332, 907–911.

JACOBY, A., & BAKER, G. A. (2008). Quality-of-life trajectories in epilepsy: A review of the literature. *Epilepsy & Behavior*, 12, 557–571.

JAIN, S., SHAPIRO, S. L., SWANICK, S., R., ROESCH, S. C., MILLS, P. J., et al. (2007). A randomized controlled trial of mindfulness meditation versus relaxation training: Effects on distress, positive states of mind, rumination, and distraction. *Annals of Behavioral Medicine*, 33, 11–21.

JAMES, G. D., YEE, L. S., HARSHFIELD, G. A., BLANK, S. G., & PICKERING, T. G. (1986). The influence of happiness, anger, and anxiety on the blood pressure of borderline hypertensives. *Psychosomatic Medicine*, 48, 502–508.

JAMES, J. E. (2004). Critical review of dietary caffeine and blood pressure: A relationship that should be taken more seriously. *Psychosomatic Medicine*, 66, 63–71.

JAMNER, L. D., & TURSKY, B. (1987). Syndrome-specific descriptor profiling: A psychophysiological and psychophysical approach. *Health Psychology*, 6, 417–430.

JANAL, M. N., GLUSMAN, M., KUHL, J. P., & CLARK, W. C. (1994). On the absence of correlation between responses to noxious heat, cold, electrical, and ischemic stimulation. *Pain*, 403–411.

JANICKI, D. L., KAMARCK, T. W., SHIFFMAN, S., STTON-TYRRELL, K., & GWALTNEY, C. J. (2005). Frequency of spousal interaction and 3-year progression of carotid artery intima medial thickness: The Pittsburgh Healthy Heart Project. *Psychosomatic Medicine, 67,* 889–896.

JANIS, I. L. (1958). *Psychological stress.* New York: Wiley.

JANIS, I. L. (1984). The patient as decision maker. In W. D. GENTRY (Ed.), *Handbook of behavioral medicine* (pp. 326–368). New York: Guilford.

JANIS, I. L., & MANN, L. (1977). *Decision making: A psychological analysis of conflict, choice, and commitment.* New York: Free Press.

JANKE, E. A., HOLROYD, K. A., & ROMANEK, K. (2004). Depression increases onset of tension-type headache following laboratory stress. *Pain, 111,* 230–238.

JANSON-BJERKLIE, S., CARRIERI, V. K., & HUDES, M. (1986). The sensations of pulmonary dyspnea. *Nursing Research, 35,* 154–159.

JANSSENS, T., VERLEDEN, G., DE PEUTER, S., VAN DIEST, I., & VAN DEN BERGH, O. (2009). Inaccurate perception of asthma symptoms: A cognitive–affective framework and implications for asthma treatment. *Clinical Psychology Review, 29,* 317–327.

JARET, P. (1986, June). Our immune system: The wars within. *National Geographic, 169,* 702–735.

JAY, S. M., ELLIOTT, C. H., KATZ, E., & SIEGEL, S. E. (1987). Cognitive-behavioral and pharmacologic interventions for children's distress during painful medical procedures. *Journal of Consulting and Clinical Psychology, 55,* 860–865.

JEANS, M. E. (1983). Pain in children—A neglected area. In P. FIRESTONE, P. J. MCGRATH, & W. FELDMAN (Eds.), *Advances in behavioral medicine for children and adolescents* (pp. 23–37). Hillsdale, NJ: Erlbaum.

JEFFERY, A. N., VOSS, L. D., METCALF, B. S., ALBA, S., & WILKIN, T. J. (2005). Parents' awareness of overweight in themselves and their children: Cross sectional study within a cohort (EarlyBird 21). *British Medical Journal.* Retrieved (11-16-2006) from http://www.bmj.com. DOI:10.1136/bmj.38315.451539.F7.

JEFFERY, R. W. (1998). Prevention of obesity. In G. A. BRAY, C. BOUCHARD, & W. P. T. JAMES (Eds.), *Handbook of obesity* (pp. 819–829). New York: Marcel Dekker.

JEFFERY, R. W., HENNRIKUS, D. J., LANDO, H. A., MURRAY, D. M., & LIU, J. W. (2000). Reconciling conflicting findings regarding postcessation weight concerns and success in smoking cessation. *Health Psychology, 19,* 242–246.

JEMMOTT, J. B., CROYLE, R. T., & DITTO, P. H. (1988). Commonsense epidemiology: Self-based judgments from laypersons and physicians. *Health Psychology, 7,* 55–73.

JEMMOTT, J. B., JEMMOTT, L. S., & FONG, G. T. (1999). Abstinence and safer sex HIV risk-reduction interventions for African American adolescents: A randomized controlled trial. *Journal of the American Medical Association, 279,* 1529–1536.

JENKINS, C. D. (1979). An approach to the diagnosis and treatment of problems of health related behaviour. *International Journal of Health Education, 22*(Suppl. 2), 1–24.

JENKINS, C. D., ZYZANSKI, S. J., & ROSENMAN, R. H. (1979). *The Jenkins Activity Survey for Health Prediction.* New York: The Psychological Corporation.

JENKINS, L. S., & GORTNER, S. R. (1998). Correlates of self-efficacy expectations and prediction of walking behavior in cardiac surgery elders. *Annals of Behavioral Medicine, 20,* 99–103.

JENNINGS, G., NELSON, L., NESTEL, P., ESLER, M., KORNER, P., et al. (1986). The effects of changes in physical activity on major cardiovascular risk factors, hemodynamics, sympathetic function, and glucose utilization in man: A controlled study of four levels of activity. *Circulation, 73,* 30–40.

JENSEN, G. M., & LORISH, C. D. (1994). Promoting patient cooperation with exercise programs. *Arthritis Care and Research, 7,* 181–189.

JENSEN, I. B., BERGSTRÖM, G., LJUNGQUIST, T., & BODIN, L. (2005). A 3-year follow-up of a multidisciplinary rehabilitation for back and neck pain. *Pain, 115,* 273–283.

JENSEN, M. P. (2009). Hypnosis for chronic pain management: A new hope. *Pain, 146,* 235–237.

JENSEN, M. P., CHEN, C., & BRUGGER, A. M. (2003). Interpretation of visual analog scale ratings and change scores. *Journal of Pain, 4,* 407–414.

JENSEN, M. P., HIRSH, A. T., MOLTON, I. R., & BAMER, A. M. (2009). Sleep problems in individuals with spinal cord injury: Frequency and age effects. *Rehabilitation Psychology, 54,* 323–331.

JENSEN, M. P., & KAROLY, P. (2001). Self-report scales and procedures for assessing pain in adults. In D. C. TURK & R. MELZACK (Eds.), *Handbook of pain assessment* (2nd ed., pp. 15–34). New York: Guilford.

JENSEN, M. P., & MCFARLAND, C. A. (1993). Increasing the reliability and validity of pain intensity measurement in chronic pain patients. *Pain, 55,* 195–203.

JENSEN, M. P., ROMANO, J. M., TURNER, J. A., GOOD, A. B., & WALD, L. H. (1999). Patient beliefs predict patient functioning: Further support for a cognitive-behavioral model of chronic pain. *Pain, 81,* 95–104.

JENSEN, M. P., TURNER, J. A., & ROMANO, J. M. (2007). Changes after multidisciplinary pain treatment in patient beliefs and coping are associated with concurrent changes in patient functioning. *Pain, 131,* 38–47.

JETTE, A. M. (1984). Understanding and enhancing patient cooperation with arthritis treatments. In G. K. RIGGS & E. P. GALL (Eds.), *Rheumatic diseases: Rehabilitation and management* (pp. 299–307). Boston: Butterworth.

JOEKES, K., MAES, S., & WARRENS, M. (2007). Predicting quality of life and self-management from dyadic support and overprotection after myocardial infarction. *British Journal of Health Psychology, 12,* 473–489.

JOHANSEN, O., BROX, J., & FLATEN, M. A. (2003). Placebo and nocebo responses, cortisol, and circulating beta-endorphin. *Psychosomatic Medicine, 65,* 786–790.

JOHN, O. P., & GROSS, J. J. (2004) Healthy and unhealthy emotion regulation: Personality processes, individual differences, and life span development. *Journal of Personality, 72,* 1301–1334.

JOHNSON, J. E. (1983). Psychological interventions and coping with surgery. In A. BAUM, S. E. TAYLOR, & J. E. SINGER (Eds.), *Handbook of psychology and health* (Vol. 4, pp. 167–187). Hillsdale, NJ: Erlbaum.

JOHNSON, J. E., & LEVENTHAL, H. (1974). Effects of accurate expectations and behavioral instructions on reactions during a noxious medical examination. *Journal of Personality and Social Psychology, 29,* 710–718.

JOHNSON, J. H. (1986). *Life events as stressors in childhood and adolescence.* Newbury Park, CA: Sage.

JOHNSON, K., ANDERSON, N. B., BASTIDA, E., KRAMER, B. J., WILLIAMS, D., & WONG, M. (1995). Panel II. Macrosocial and environmental influences on minority health. *Health Psychology, 14,* 601–612.

JOHNSON, L. J., MEACHAM, S. L., & KRUSKALL, L. J. (2003). The antioxidants—vitamin C, vitamin E, and carotenoids. *Journal of Agromedicine, 9,* 65–82.

JOHNSON, M. I. (2001). Transcutaneous electrical nerve stimulation (TENS) and TENS-like devices: Do they provide pain relief? *Pain Reviews, 8,* 121–158.

JOHNSON, S. B., FREUND, A., SILVERSTEIN, J., HANSEN, C. A., & MALONE, J. (1990). Adherence-health status relationships in childhood diabetes. *Health Psychology, 9,* 606–631.

JOHNSON, S. B., KELLY, M., HENRETTA, J. C., CUNNINGHAM, W. R., TOMER, A., & SILVERSTEIN, J. H. (1992). A longitudinal analysis of adherence and health status in childhood diabetes. *Journal of Pediatric Psychology, 17,* 537–553.

JOHNSON, W. D., DIAZ, R. M., FLANDERS, W. D., GOODMAN, M., HILL, A. N., et al. (2008). Behavioral interventions to reduce risk for sexual tranmision of HIV among men who have sex with men. *Cochrane Database of Systematic Reviews,* Issue 3. Retrieved (1-30-2010) from http://www.thecochranelibrary.com. DOI:10.1002/14651858.CD001230.pub2.

JOHNSTON, L. D., O'MALLEY, P. M., BACHMAN, J. G., & SCHULENBERG, J. E. (2009). *Monitoring the Future: National survey results on drug use, 1975–2008. Volume I: Secondary school students.* Bethesda, MD: National Institute on Drug Abuse. Retrieved (1-15-2010) from http://www.monitoringthefuture.org.

JOHNSTON, M., MORRISON, V., MACWALTER, R., & PARTRIDGE, C. (1999). Perceived control, coping and recovery from disability following stroke. *Psychology and Health, 14,* 181–192.

JOHNSTON, M., & VÖGELE, C. (1993). Benefits of psychological preparation for surgery: A meta-analysis. *Annals of Behavioral Medicine, 15,* 245–256.

JOHNSTON-BROOKS, C. H., LEWIS, M. A., EVANS, G. W., & WHALEN, C. K. (1998). Chronic stress and illness in children. *Psychosomatic Medicine, 60,* 597–603.

JOHNSTON-BROOKS, C. H., LEWIS, M. A., & GARG, S. (2002). Self-efficacy impacts self-care and HbA1c in young adults with type 1 diabetes. *Psychosomatic Medicine, 64,* 43–51.

JONAS, B. S., & MUSSOLINO, M. E. (2000). Symptoms of depression as a prospective risk factor for stroke. *Psychosomatic Medicine, 62,* 463–471.

JONES, L. R., MABE, P. A., & RILEY, W. T. (1989). Physician interpretation of illness behavior. *International Journal of Psychiatry in Medicine, 19,* 237–248.

JORDAN, K., SCHMOLL, H. J., & AAPRO, M. S. (2007). Comparative activity of antiemetic drugs. *Critical Reviews in Oncology/Hematology, 61,* 162–175.

JORGENSEN, R. S. (2004). Meditation. In A. J. CHRISTENSEN, R. MARTIN, & J. M. SMYTH (Eds.), *Encyclopedia of health psychology* (pp. 165–167). New York: Kluwer.

JORGENSEN, R. S., FRANKOWSKI, J. J., & CAREY, M. P. (1999). Sense of coherence, negative life events, and appraisal of physical health. *Personality and Individual Differences, 27,* 1079–1089.

JOUSILAHTI, P., VARTIAINEN, E., TUOMILEHTO, J., PEKKANEN, J., & PUSKA, P. (1995). Effect of risk factors and changes in risk factors on coronary mortality in three cohorts of middle-aged people in Eastern Finland. *American Journal of Epidemiology, 141,* 50–60.

JOYCE, C. (1984, November). A time for grieving. *Psychology Today,* pp. 42–46.

JUTH, V., SMYTH, J. M., & SANTUZZI, A. M. (2008). How do you feel? Self-esteem predicts affect, stress, social interaction, and symptom severity during daily life in patients with chronic illness. *Journal of Health Psychology, 13,* 884–894.

KABAT-ZINN, J. (1982). An outpatient program in behavioral medicine for chronic pain patients based on the practice of mindfulness meditation: Theoretical considerations and preliminary results. *General Hospital Psychiatry, 4,* 33–47.

KABAT-ZINN, J., LIPWORTH, L., & BURNEY, R. (1985). The clinical use of mindfulness meditation for the self-regulation of chronic pain. *Journal of Behavioral Medicine, 8,* 163–190.

KACZYNSKI, A. T., MANSKE, S. R., MANNELL, R. C., & GREWAL, K. (2008). Smoking and physical activity: A systematic review. *American Journal of Health Behavior, 32,* 93–100.

KAHN, K. L., KEELER, E. B., SHERWOOD, M. J., ROGERS, W. H., DRAPER, D., et al. (1990). Comparing outcomes of care before and after implementation of the DRG-based prospective payment system. *Journal of the American Medical Association, 264,* 1984–1988.

KALICHMAN, S. C. (1998). *Preventing AIDS: A sourcebook for behavioral interventions.* Mahwah, NJ: Erlbaum.

KALICHMAN, S. C., CHERRY, C., CAIN, D., WEINHARDT, L. S., BENOTSCH, E., et al. (2006). Health information on the Internet and people living with HIV/AIDS: Information evaluation and coping styles. *Health Psychology, 25,* 205–210.

KALICHMAN, S. C., & COLEY, B. (1995). Context framing to enhance HIV-antibody-testing messages targeted at African American women. *Health Psychology, 14,* 247–254.

KALICHMAN, S. C., EATON, L., WHITE, D., CHERRY, C., POPE, H., et al. (2007). Beliefs about treatments for HIV/AID and sexual risk behavior among men who have sex with men, 1997–2006. *Journal of Behavioral Medicine, 30,* 497–503.

KALICHMAN, S. C., & NACHIMSON, D. (1999). Self-efficacy and disclosure of HIV-positive serostatus to sex partners. *Health Psychology, 18*, 281–287.

KALICHMAN, S. C., ROMPA, D., & COLEY, B. (1996). Experimental component analysis of a behavioral HIV-AIDS prevention intervention for inner-city women. *Journal of Consulting and Clinical Psychology, 64*, 687–693.

KALIL, A., ZIOL-GUEST, K. M., HAWKLEY, L. C., & CACIOPPO, J. T. (2010). Job insecurity and change over time in health among older men and women. *Journal of Gerontology: Social Sciences, 65B*, 81–90.

KALISH, R. A. (1985). The social context of death and dying. In R. H. BINSTOCK & E. SHANAS (Eds.), *Handbook of aging and the social sciences* (pp. 149–170). New York: Van Nostrand-Reinhold.

KALISH, R. A., & REYNOLDS, D. K. (1976). *Death and ethnicity: A psychocultural study.* Los Angeles: University of Southern California Press.

KALOUPEK, D. G., WHITE, H., & WONG, M. (1984). Multiple assessment of coping strategies used by volunteer blood donors: Implications for preparatory training. *Journal of Behavioral Medicine, 7*, 35–60.

KALSO, E., EDWARDS, J. E., MOORE, R. A., & MCQUAY, H. J. (2004). Opioids in chronic non-cancer pain: Systematic review of efficacy and safety. *Pain, 112*, 372–380.

KAMARCK, T. W., HASKETT, R. F., MULDOON, M., FLORY, J. D., ANDERSON, B., et al. (2009). Citalopram intervention for hostility: Results of a randomized clinical trial. *Journal of Consulting and Clinical Psychology, 77*, 174–188.

KAMARCK, T. W., MULDOON, M. F., SHIFFMAN, S. S., & SUTTON-TYRRELL, K. (2007). Experiences of demand and control during daily life are predictors of carotid atherosclerotic progression among healthy men. *Health Psychology, 26*, 324–332.

KAMEN, L. P., & SELIGMAN, M. E. P. (1989). Explanatory style and health. In M. JOHNSTON & T. MARTEAU (Eds.), *Applications in health psychology* (pp. 73–84). New Brunswick, NJ: Transaction.

KANDEL, D. (1974). Inter- and intragenerational influences of adolescent marijuana use. *Journal of Social Issues, 30*, 107–135.

KANDEL, D., & FAUST, R. (1975). Sequence and stages in patterns of adolescent drug use. *Archives of General Psychiatry, 32*, 923–932.

KANDEL, D. B., WU, P., & DAVIES, M. (1994). Maternal smoking during pregnancy and smoking by adolescent daughters. *American Journal of Public Health, 84*, 1407–1413.

KANGAS, M., BOVBJERG, D. H., & MONTGOMERY, G. H. (2008). Cancer-related fatigue: A systematic and meta-analytic review of non-pharmacological therapies for cancer patients. *Psychological Bulletin, 134*, 700–741.

KANNER, A. D., COYNE, J. C., SCHAEFER, C., & LAZARUS, R. S. (1981). Comparison of two modes of stress measurement: Daily hassles and uplifts versus major life events. *Journal of Behavioral Medicine, 4*, 1–39.

KANNER, R. (1986). Pain management. *Journal of the American Medical Association, 256*, 2110–2114.

KAPLAN, R. M. (2004). Quality of life. In A. J. CHRISTENSEN, R. MARTIN, & J. M. SMYTH (Eds.), *Encyclopedia of health psychology* (pp. 235–239). New York: Kluwer.

KAPLAN, R. M., ATKINS, C. J., & REINSCH, S. (1984). Specific efficacy expectations mediate exercise compliance in patients with COPD. *Health Psychology, 3*, 223–242.

KAPLAN, R. M., & GROESSL, E. J. (2002). Applications of cost-effectiveness methodologies in behavioral medicine. *Journal of Consulting and Clinical Psychology, 70*, 482–493.

KAPLAN, R. M., & KRONICK, R. G. (2006). Marital status and longevity in the United States population. *Journal of Epidemiology and Community Health, 60*, 760–765.

KAPLAN, R. M., ORLEANS, C. T., PERKINS, K. A., & PIERCE, J. P. (1995). Marshalling the evidence for greater regulation and control of tobacco products: A call for action. *Annals of Behavioral Medicine, 17*, 3–14.

KAPLAN, R. M., PATTERSON, T. L., KERNER, D., GRANT, I., et al. (1997). Social support: Cause or consequence of poor health outcomes in men with HIV infection? In G. R. PIERCE, B. LAKEY, I. G. SARASON, & B. R. SARASON (Eds.), *Sourcebook for social support and personality* (pp. 279–301). New York: Plenum.

KAPLAN, R. M., & SIMON, H. J. (1990). Compliance in medical care: Reconsideration of self-predictions. *Annals of Behavioral Medicine, 12*, 66–71.

KAPLAN, R. M., & TOSHIMA, M. T. (1990). The functional effects of social relationships on chronic illnesses and disability. In B. R. SARASON, I. G. SARASON, & G. R. PIERCE (Eds.), *Social support: An interactional view* (pp. 427–453). New York: Wiley.

KAPTEIN, A. A., BIJSTERBOSCH, J., SCHARLOO, M., HAMPSON, S. E., KROON, H. M., & KLOPPENBURG, M. (2010). Using the common sense model of illness perceptions to examine osteoarthritis change: A 6-year longitudinal study. *Health Psychology, 29*, 56–64.

KARLAMANGLA, A. S., SINGER, B. H., & SEEMAN, T. E. (2006). Reduction in allostatic load in older adults is associated with lower all-cause mortality risk: MacArthur Studies of Successful Aging. *Psychosomatic Medicine, 68*, 500–507.

KARLBERG, L., KRAKAU, I., & UNDÉN, A.-L. (1998). Type A behavior intervention in primary health care reduces hostility and time pressure: A study in Sweden. *Social Science and Medicine, 46*, 397–402.

KARLIN, W. A., BRONDOLO, E., & SCHWARTZ, J. (2003). Workplace social support and ambulatory cardiovascular activity in New York City traffic agents. *Psychosomatic Medicine, 65*, 167–176.

KARNIK, R. (2001). The value of lipid lowering in patients with coronary heart disease. *Journal of Clinical and Basic Cardiology, 4*, 31–34.

KAROLY, P. (1985). The assessment of pain: Concepts and procedures. In P. KAROLY (Ed.), *Measurement strategies in health psychology* (pp. 461–516). New York: Wiley.

KASCH, F. W., WALLACE, J. P., & VAN CAMP, S. P. (1985). Effects of 18 years of endurance exercise on the physical work capacity of older men. *Journal of Cardiopulmonary Rehabilitation, 5,* 308–312.

KASL, S. V., & COBB, S. (1966a). Health behavior, illness behavior, and sick role behavior: I. Health and illness behavior. *Archives of Environmental Health, 12,* 246–266.

KASL, S. V., & COBB, S. (1966b). Health behavior, illness behavior, and sick role behavior: II. Sick role behavior. *Archives of Environmental Health, 12,* 531–541.

KATON, W., LIN, E. H. B., & KROENKE, K. (2007). The association of depression and anxiety with medical symptom burden in patients with chronic medical illness. *General Hospital Psychiatry, 29,* 147–155.

KATZ, D. L. (2009). School-based interventions for health promotion and weight control: Not just waiting on the world to change. *Annual Review of Public Health, 30,* 253–272.

KAWACHI, I., COLDITZ, G. A., STAMPFER, M. J., WILLETT, W. C., MANSON, J. E., et al. (1993). Smoking cessation and decreased risk of stroke in women. *Journal of the American Medical Association, 269,* 232–236.

KAYE, S., MCKETIN, R., DUFLOU, J., & DARKE, S. (2007). Methamphetamine and cardiovascular pathology: A review of the evidence. *Addiction, 102,* 1204–1211.

KAZARIAN, S. S., & EVANS, D. R. (2001). Health psychology and culture: Embracing the 21st century. In S. S. KAZARIAN & E. R. EVANS (Eds.), *Handbook of cultural health psychology* (pp. 3–43). San Diego: Academic Press.

KAZDIN, A. E. (2008). Evidence-based treatment and practice. *American Psychologist, 63,* 146–159.

KEATING, N. L., GREEN, D. C., KAO, A. C., GAZMARARIAN, J. A., WU, V. Y., & CLEARY, P. D. (2002). How are patients' specific ambulatory care experiences related to trust, satisfaction, and considering changing physicians? *Journal of General Internal Medicine, 17,* 29–39.

KEEFE, F. J., ABERNATHY, A. P., & CAMPBELL, L. C. (2005). Psychological approaches to understanding and treating disease-related pain. *Annual Review of Psychology, 56,* 601–630.

KEEFE, F. J., & DOLAN, E. (1986). Pain behavior and pain coping strategies in low back pain and myofascial pain dysfunction syndrome patients. *Pain, 24,* 49–56.

KEEFE, F. J., & GIL, K. M. (1985). Recent advances in the behavioral assessment and treatment of chronic pain. *Annals of Behavioral Medicine, 7(3),* 11–16.

KEEFE, F. J., HAUCK, E. R., EGERT, J., RIMER, B., & KORNGUTH, P. (1994). Mammography pain and discomfort: A cognitive-behavioral perspective. *Pain, 56,* 247–260.

KEEFE, F. J., WILLIAMS, D. A., & SMITH, S. J. (2001). Assessment of pain behaviors. In D. C. TURK & R. MELZACK (Eds.), *Handbook of pain assessment* (2nd ed., pp. 170–187). New York: Guilford.

KEEL, P. K. (2010). Anorexia nervosa. In I. B. WEINER & W. E. CRAIGHEAD (Eds.), *The Corsini encyclopedia of psychology* (4th ed., Vol. 1, pp. 113–114). Hoboken, NJ: Wiley.

KEESEY, R. E. (1986). A set point theory of obesity. In K. D. BROWNELL & J. P. FOREYT (Eds.), *Handbook of eating disorders: The physiology, psychology, and treatment of the eating disorders* (pp. 63–87). New York: Basic Books.

KELLY, J. A., & KALICHMAN, S. C. (2002). Behavioral research in HIV/AIDS primary and secondary prevention: Recent advances and future directions. *Journal of Consulting and Clinical Psychology, 70,* 626–639.

KELLY, J. A., KALICHMAN, S. C., KAUTH, M. R., KILGORE, H. G., HOOD, H. V., et al. (1991). Situational factors associated with AIDS risk behavior lapses and coping strategies used by gay men who successfully avoid lapses. *American Journal of Public Health, 81,* 1335–1338.

KELLY, J. A., MURPHY, D. A., SIKKEMA, K. J., MCAULIFFE, T. L., ROFFMAN, R. A., et al. (1997). Randomized, controlled, community-level HIV-prevention intervention for sexual-risk behaviour among homosexual men in U.S. cities. *Lancet, 350,* 1500–1505.

KELLY, J. A., SIKKEMA, K. J., WINETT, R. A., SOLOMON, L. J., ROFFMAN, R. A., et al. (1995). Factors predicting continued high-risk behavior among gay men in small cities: Psychological, behavioral, and demographic characteristics related to unsafe sex. *Journal of Consulting and Clinical Psychology, 63,* 101–107.

KELSEY, J. L., & HOCHBERG, M. C. (1988). Epidemiology of chronic musculoskeletal disorders. *Annual Review of Public Health, 9,* 379–401.

KEMENY, M. E. (2007). Psychoneuroimmunology. In H. S. FRIEDMAN & R. C. SILVER (Eds.), *Foundations of health psychology* (pp. 92–116). New York: Oxford University Press.

KENDALL, P. C., WILLIAMS, L., PECHACEK, T. F., GRAHAM, L. E., SHISSLAK, C., & HERZOFF, N. (1979). Cognitive-behavioral and patient education interventions in cardiac catheterization procedures: The Palo Alto Medical Psychology Project. *Journal of Consulting and Clinical Psychology, 47,* 49–58.

KENDLER, K. S., SCHMITT, E., AGGEN, S. H., & PRESCOTT, C. A. (2008). Genetic and environmental influences on alcohol, caffeine, cannabis, and nicotine use from early adolescence to middle adulthood. *Archives of General Psychiatry, 65,* 674–682.

KENNEDY, S., KIECOLT-GLASER, J. K., & GLASER, R. (1990). Social support, stress, and the immune system. In B. R. SARASON, I. G. SARASON, & G. R. PIERCE (Eds.), *Social support: An interactional view* (pp. 253–266). New York: Wiley.

KENT, G. (1985). Memory of dental pain. *Pain, 21,* 187–194.

KERLIKOWSKE, K., GRADY, D., RUBIN, S. M., SANDROCK, C., & ERNSTER, V. L. (1995). Efficacy of screening mammography: A meta-analysis. *Journal of the American Medical Association, 273,* 149–154.

KERN, M. L., & FRIEDMAN, H. S. (2008). Do conscientious individuals live longer? A quantitative review. *Health Psychology, 27,* 505–512.

KERNS, R. D. (1995). Family assessment and intervention. In P. M. NICASSIO & T. W. SMITH (Eds.), *Managing chronic illness: A biopsychosocial perspective* (pp. 207–244). Washington, DC: American Psychological Association.

444 References

KERNS, R. D., & PAYNE, A. (1996). Treating families of chronic pain patients. In R. J. GATCHEL & D. C. TURK (Eds.), *Psychological approaches to pain management: A practitioner's handbook* (pp. 283–304). New York: Guilford.

KERNS, R. D., TURK, D. C., & RUDY, T. E. (1985). The West Haven-Yale Multidimensional Pain Inventory. *Pain, 23,* 345–356.

KERNS, R. D., & WEISS, L. H. (1994). Family influences on the course of chronic illness: A cognitive-behavioral transactional model. *Annals of Behavioral Medicine, 16,* 116–121.

KETT, J. F. (1977). *Rites of passage: Adolescence in America 1790 to present.* New York: Basic Books.

KETTERER, M. W., BRYMER, J., RHOADS, K., KRAFT, P., KENYON, L., et al. (1996). Emotional distress among males with "syndrome X." *Journal of Behavioral Medicine, 19,* 455–466.

KIANK, C, TACHÉ, Y., & LARAUCHE, M. (2010). Stress-related modulation of inflammation in experimental models of bowel disease and post-infectious irritable bowel syndrome: Role of corticotropin-releasing factor receptors. *Brain, Behavior, and Immunity, 24,* 41–48.

KIECOLT-GLASER, J. K., DURA, J. R., SPEICHER, C. E., TRASK, O. J., & GLASER, R. (1991) Spousal caregivers of dementia victims: Longitudinal changes in immunity and health. *Psychosomatic Medicine, 53,* 345–362.

KIECOLT-GLASER, J. K., FISHER, L. D., OGROCKI, P., STOUT, J. C., SPEICHER, C. E., & GLASER, R. (1987). Marital quality, marital disruption, and immune function. *Psychosomatic Medicine, 49,* 13–34.

KIECOLT-GLASER, J. K., GARNER, W., SPEICHER, C., PENN, G. M., HOLLIDAY, J., & GLASER, R. (1984). Psychosocial modifiers of immunocompetence in medical students. *Psychosomatic Medicine, 46,* 7–14.

KIECOLT-GLASER, J. K., & GLASER, R. (1986). Psychological influences on immunity. *Psychosomatics, 27,* 621–624.

KIECOLT-GLASER, J. K., & GLASER, R. (1995). Psychoneuro-immunology and health consequences: Data and shared mechanisms. *Psychosomatic Medicine, 57,* 269–274.

KIECOLT-GLASER, J. K., GRAHAM, J. E., MALARKEY, W. B., PORTER, K., LEMESHOW, S., & GLASER, R. (2008). Olfactory influences on mood and autonomic, endocrine, and immune function. *Psychoneuroendocrinology, 33,* 328–339.

KIECOLT-GLASER, J. K., LOVING, T. J., STOWELL, J. R., MALARKEY, W. B., LEMESHOW, S., et al. (2005). Hostile marital interactions, proinflammatory cytokine production, and wound healing. *Archives of General Psychiatry, 62,* 1377–1384.

KIECOLT-GLASER, J. K., MARUCHA, P. T., ATKINSON, C., & GLASER, R. (2001). Hypnosis as a modulator of cellular immune dysregulation during acute stress. *Journal of Consulting and Clinical Psychology, 69,* 674–682.

KIECOLT-GLASER, J. K., & WILLIAMS, D. A. (1987). Self-blame, compliance, and distress among burn patients. *Journal of Personality and Social Psychology, 53,* 187–193.

KIENE, S. M., TENNEN, H., & ARMELI, S. (2008). Today I'll use a condom, but who knows about tomorrow: A daily process study of variability in predictors of condom use. *Health Psychology, 27,* 463–472.

KILLEN, J. D., & FORTMANN, S. P. (1994). Craving is associated with smoking relapse: Findings from three prospective studies. *Experimental and Clinical Psychopharmacology, 5,* 137–142.

KILLEN, J. D., TAYLOR, C. B., HAYWARD, C., WILSON, D. M., HAYDEL, K. F., et al. (1994). Pursuit of thinness and onset of eating disorder symptoms in a community sample of adolescent girls: A three-year prospective analysis. *International Journal of Eating Disorders, 16,* 227–238.

KILLEN, J. D., TAYLOR, C. B., TELCH, M. J., SAYLOR, K. E., MARON, D. J., & ROBINSON, T. N. (1986). Self-induced vomiting and laxative and diuretic use among teenagers. *Journal of the American Medical Society, 255,* 1447–1449.

KILO, C., & WILLIAMSON, J. R. (1987). *Diabetes: The facts that let you regain control of your life.* New York: Wiley.

KILPATRICK, D. G., ACIERNO, R., SAUNDERS, B., RESNICK, H. S., BEST, C. L., & SCHNURR, P. P. (2000). Risk factors for adolescent substance abuse and dependence: Data from a national sample. *Journal of Consulting and Clinical Psychology, 68,* 19–30.

KIM, Y., KASHY, D. A., WELLISCH, D. K., SPILLERS, R. L., KAW, C. K., & SMITH, T. G. (2008). Quality of life of couples dealing with cancer: Dyadic and individual adjustment among breast and prostate cancer survivors and their spousal caregivers. *Annals of Behavioral Medicine, 35,* 230–238.

KIM, Y. & SCHULZ, R. (2008). Family caregivers' strains: Comparative analysis of cancer caregiving with dementia, diabetes, and frail elderly caregiving. *Journal of Aging and Health. 2008, 20,* 483–503.

KIMMEL, P. L., PETERSON, R. A., WEIHS, K. L., SIMMENS, S. J., ALLEYNE, S., et al. (1998). Psychosocial factors, behavioral compliance and survival in urban hemodialysis patients. *Kidney International, 54,* 245–254.

KINDELAN, K., & KENT, G. (1987). Concordance between patients' information preferences and general practitioners' perceptions. *Psychology and Health, 1,* 399–409.

KING, A. C., MARCUS, B., AHN, D., DUNN, A. L., REJESKI, W. J., et al. (2006). Identifying subgroups that succeed or fail with three levels of physical activity intervention: The Activity Counseling Trial. *Health Psychology, 25,* 336–347.

KING, G., POLEDNAK, A. P., GILREATH, T., & BENDEL, R. B. (2007). Disparities in smoking cessation among U.S. adults with a history of asthma. *Annals of Behavioral Medicine, 33,* 312–317.

KING, L. A., & MINER, K. N. (2000). Writing about the perceived benefits of traumatic events: Implications for physical health. *Personality and Social Psychology Bulletin, 26,* 220–230.

KIRSCHT, J. P. (1983). Preventive health behavior: A review of research and issues. *Health Psychology, 2,* 277–301.

KITZMANN, K. M., DALTON, W. T., STANLEY, C. M., BEECH, B. M., REEVES, T. P., et al. (2010). Lifestyle interventions for youth who are overweight: A meta-analytic review. *Health Psychology, 29,* 91–101.

KIVIMÄKI, M., FERRIE, J. E., SHIPLEY, M., GIMENO, D., ELOVAINIO, M., et al. (2008). Effects on blood pressure do not explain the association between organizational justice and coronary heart disease in the Whitehall II Study. *Psychosomatic Medicine 70*, 1–6.

KIVIPELTO, M., NGANDU, T., LAATINKAINEN, T., WINBLAD, B., SOININEN, H., & TUOMILEHTO, J. (2006). Risk score for the prediction of dementia risk in 20 years among middle aged people: A longitudinal, population-based study. *Lancet Neurology, 5*, 735–741.

KIVLAHAN, D. R., MARLATT, G. A., FROMME, K., COPPEL, D. B., & WILLIAMS, E. (1990). Secondary prevention with college drinkers: Evaluation of an alcohol skills training program. *Journal of Consulting and Clinical Psychology, 58*, 805–810.

KIYAK, H. A., VITALIANO, P. P., & CRINEAN, J. (1988). Patients' expectations as predictors of orthognathic surgery outcomes. *Health Psychology, 7*, 251–268.

KLAPOW, J. C., SLATER, M. A., PATTERSON, T. L., DOCTOR, J. N., ATKINSON, J. H., & GARFIN, S. R. (1993). An empirical evaluation of multidimensional clinical outcome in chronic low back pain patients. *Pain, 55*, 107–118.

KLATSKY, A. L., FRIEDMAN, G. D., ARMSTRONG, M. A., & KIPP, H. (2003). Wine, liquor, beer, and mortality. *American Journal of Epidemiology, 158*, 585–595.

KLEINJAN, M., VAN DEN EIJNDEN, R. J. J. M., DIJKSTRA, A., BRUG, J., & ENGELS, R. C. M. E. (2006). Excuses to continue smoking: The role of disengagement beliefs in smoking cessation. *Addictive Behaviors, 31*, 2223–2237.

KLEINKE, C. L., & SPANGLER, A. S. (1988). Psychometric analysis of the audiovisual taxonomy for assessing pain behavior in chronic back-pain patients. *Journal of Behavioral Medicine, 11*, 83–94.

KLESGES, R. C., DENOWITZ, N. L., & MEYERS, A. W. (1991). Behavioral and biobehavioral aspects of smoking and smoking cessation: The problem of postcessation weight gain. *Behavior Therapy, 22*, 179–199.

KLESGES, R. C., ECK, L. H., & RAY, J. W. (1995). Who underreports dietary intake in a dietary recall? Evidence from the Second National Health and Nutrition Examination Survey. *Journal of Consulting and Clinical Psychology, 63*, 438–444.

KLESGES, R. C., HADDOCK, C. K., LANDO, H., & TALCOTT, G. W. (1999). Efficacy of forced smoking cessation and an adjunctive behavioral treatment on long-term smoking rates. *Journal of Consulting and Clinical Psychology, 67*, 952–958.

KLESGES, R. C., SHUSTER, M. L., KLESGES, L. M., & WERNER, K. (1992). *The effects of television viewing on metabolic rate in normal weight and obese children.* Paper presented at the meeting of the Society of Behavioral Medicine, New York.

KLESGES, R. C., WINDERS, S. E., MEYERS, A. W., ECK, L. H., WARD, K. D., et al. (1997). How much weight gain occurs following smoking cessation? A comparison of weight gain using both continuous and point prevalence abstinence. *Journal of Consulting and Clinical Psychology, 65*, 286–291.

KLESGES, R. C., ZBIKOWSKI, S. M., LANDO, H. A., HADDOCK, C. K., TALCOTT, G. W., & ROBINSON, L. A. (1998). The relationship between smoking and body weight in a population of young military personnel. *Health Psychology, 17*, 454–458.

KLIMAS, N., KONERU, A. O., & FLETCHER, M. A. (2008). Overview of HIV. *Psychosomatic Medicine, 70*, 523–530.

KLINKENBERG, M., WILLEMS, D. L., ONWUTEAKA-PHILIPSEN, B. D., DEEG, D. J. H., VAN DER WAL, G. (2004). Preferences in end-of-life care of older persons: After-death interviews with proxy respondents. *Social Science & Medicine, 59*, 2467–2477.

KLOSE, K. J., NEEDHAM, B. M., SCHMIDT, D., BROTON, J. G., & GREEN, B. A. (1993). An assessment of the contribution of electromyographic biofeedback as an adjunct therapy in the physical training of spinal cord injured persons. *Archives of Physical Medicine and Rehabilitation, 74*, 453–456.

KNITTLE, J., MERRITT, R. J., DIXON-SHANIES, D., GINSBERG-FELLNER, F., TIMMERS, K. I., & KATZ, D. P. (1981). Childhood obesity. In R. M. SUSKIND (Ed.), *Textbook of pediatric nutrition* (pp. 415–434). New York: Raven Press.

KNOL, M. J., TWISK, J. W. R., BEEKMAN, A. T. F., HEINE, R. J., SNOEK, F. J., & FOUWER, F. (2006). Depression as a risk factor for the onset of type 2 diabetes mellitus. A meta-analysis. *Diabetologia, 49*, 837–845.

KNOWLER, W. C., BARRETT-CONNOR, E., FOWLER, S. E., HAMMAN, R. F., LACHIN, J. M., et al. (2002). Reduction in the incidence of type 2 diabetes with lifestyle intervention or metformin. *New England Journal of Medicine, 346*, 393–403.

KOBASA, S. C., & MADDI, S. R. (1977). Existential personality theory. In R. CORSINI (Ed.), *Current personality theories* (pp. 243–276). Itasca, IL: Peacock.

KOBASA, S. C. O., MADDI, S. R., PUCCETTI, M. C., & ZOLA, M. A. (1985). Effectiveness of hardiness, exercise and social support as resources against illness. *Journal of Psychosomatic Research, 29*, 525–533.

KÖBLITZ, A. R., MAGNAN, R. E., MCCAUL, K. D., DILLARD, A. J., O'NEILL, H. K., & CROSBY, R. (2009). Smokers' thoughts and worries: A study using ecological momentary assessment. *Health Psychology, 28*, 484–492.

KOCH, J. (1977, August). When children meet death. *Psychology Today*, pp. 64–66, 79–80.

KOENIG, L. J., PALS, S. L., BUSH, T., PRATT PALMORE, M., & STRATFORD, D. & ELLERBROCK, T. V. (2008). Randomized controlled trial of an intervention to prevent adherence failure among HIV-infected patients initiating antiretroviral therapy. *Health Psychology, 27*, 159–169.

KÖHLER, T., & HAIMERL, C. (1990). Daily stress as a trigger of migraine attacks: Results of thirteen single-subject studies. *Journal of Consulting and Clinical Psychology, 58*, 870–872.

KOHRT, W. M., KIRWAN, J. P., STATEN, M. A., BOUREY, R. E., KING, D. S., & HOLLOSZY, J. O. (1993). Insulin resistance in aging is related to abdominal obesity. *Diabetes, 42*, 273–281.

KOKKINOS, P. F., NARAYAN, P., COLLERAN, J. A., PITTARAS, A., NOTARGIACOMO, A., et al. (1995). Effects of regular exercise on blood pressure and left ventricular hypertrophy in African-American men with severe hypertension. *New England Journal of Medicine, 333*, 1462–1467.

KOMRO, K. A., MCCARTY, M. C., FORSTER, J. L., BLAINE, T. M., & CHEN, V. (2003). Parental, family, and home characteristics associated with cigarette smoking among adolescents. *American Journal of Health Promotion*, 17, 291–299.

KOOCHER, G. P., O'MALLEY, J. E., GOGAN, J. L., & FOSTER, D. J. (1980). Psychological adjustment among pediatric cancer survivors. *Journal of Child Psychology and Psychiatry*, 21, 163–173.

KOP, W. J. (2003). The integration of cardiovascular behavioral medicine and psychoneuroimmunology: New developments based on converging research fields. *Brain, Behavior, and Immunity*, 17, 233–237.

KOP, W. J., BERMAN, D. S., GRANSAR, H., WONG, N. D., MIRANDA-PEATS, R., et al. (2005). Social network and coronary artery calcification in asymptomatic individuals. *Psychosomatic Medicine*, 67, 343–352.

KORNACK, D. R., & RAKIC, P. (2001). Cell proliferation without neurogenesis in adult primate neocortex. *Science*, 294, 2127–2130.

KORO, C. E., BOURGEOIS, N., BOWLIN, S. J., & FEDDER, D. O. (2004). Glycemic control from 1988 to 2000 among U.S. adults diagnosed with type 2 diabetes. *Diabetes Care*, 27, 17–20.

KOROL, C. T., & CRAIG, K. D. (2001). Pain from the perspectives of health psychology and culture. In S. S. KAZARIAN & E. R. EVANS (Eds.), *Handbook of cultural health psychology* (pp. 241–265). San Diego: Academic Press.

KORSCH, B. M., FINE, R. N., & NEGRETE, V. F. (1978). Noncompliance in children with renal transplants. *Pediatrics*, 61, 872–876.

KOSTEN, T. R., JACOBS, S. C., & KASL, S. V. (1985). Terminal illness, bereavement, and the family. In D. C. TURK & R. D. KERNS (Eds.), *Health, illness, and families: A life-span perspective* (pp. 311–337). New York: Wiley.

KOSTER, A., HARRIS, T. B., MOORE, S. C., SCHATZKIN, A., HOLLENBECK, A. R., et al. (2009). Joint associations of adiposity and physical activity with mortality: The National Institutes of Health-AARP Diet and Health Study. *American Journal of Epidemiology*, 169, 1344–1351.

KRAMER, J. R., LEDOLTER, J., MANOS, G. N., & BAYLESS, M. L. (2000). Stress and metabolic control in diabetes mellitus: Methodological issues and an illustrative analysis. *Annals of Behavioral Medicine*, 22, 17–28.

KRAMER, M. S., LYDON, J., SÉGUIN, L. GOULET, L., KAHN, S. R., et al. (2009). Stress pathways to spontaneous preterm birth: The role of stressors, psychological distress, and stress hormones. *American Journal of Epidemiology*, 169, 1319–1313.

KRANTZ, D. S., & DECKEL, A. W. (1983). Coping with coronary heart disease and stroke. In T. G. BURISH & L. A. BRADLEY (Eds.), *Coping with chronic disease: Research and applications* (pp. 85–112). New York: Academic Press.

KRANTZ, D. S., LUNDBERG, U., & FRANKENHAEUSER, M. (1987). Stress and Type A behavior: Interactions between environmental and biological factors. In A. BAUM & J. E. SINGER (Eds.), *Handbook of psychology and health* (Vol. 5, pp. 203–228). Hillsdale, NJ: Erlbaum.

KRANZLER, H. R., & ANTON, R. F. (1994). Implications of recent neuropsychopharmacologic research for understanding the etiology and development of alcoholism. *Journal of Consulting and Clinical Psychology*, 62, 1116–1126.

KRAUSE, J. S., & CREWE, N. M. (1991). Chronologic age, time since injury, and time of measurement: Effect on adjustment after spinal cord injury. *Archives of Physical Medicine and Rehabilitation*, 72, 91–100.

KRAUSE, J. S., & REED, K. S. (2009). Life satisfaction and self-reported problems after spinal cord injury: Measurement of underlying dimensions. *Rehabilitation Psychology*, 54, 343–350.

KREUTER, M. W., & STRECHER, V. J. (1995). Changing inaccurate perceptions of health risk: Results from a randomized trial. *Health Psychology*, 14, 56–63.

KRIEG, A. M., YI, A.-K., MATSON, S., WALDSCHMIDT, T. J., BISHOP, G. A., et al. (1995). CpG motifs in bacterial DNA trigger direct B-cell activation. *Nature*, 374, 546–549.

KRING, A. M., DAVISON, G. C., NEALE, J. M., & JOHNSON, S. L. (2007). *Abnormal Psychology* (10th ed.). Hoboken, NJ: Wiley.

KRING, A. M., JOHNSON, S. L., DAVISON, G. C., & NEALE, J. M., (2010). *Abnormal Psychology* (11th ed.). Hoboken, NJ: Wiley.

KROENKE, K., & SPITZER, R. L. (1998). Gender differences in the reporting of physical and somatoform symptoms. *Psychosomatic Medicine*, 60, 150–155.

KROHNE, H. W., & SLANGEN, K. E. (2005). Influence of social support on adaptation to surgery. *Health Psychology*, 24, 101–105.

KRUPAT, E. (2004). Patient-provider communication. In A. J. CHRISTENSEN, R. MARTIN, & J. M. SMYTH (Eds.), *Encyclopedia of health psychology* (pp. 204–206). New York: Kluwer.

KSOBIECH, K. (2003). A meta-analysis of needle sharing, lending, and borrowing behaviors of needle exchange program attenders. AIDS *Education and prevention*, 15, 257–268.

KÜBLER-ROSS, E. (1969). *On death and dying*. New York: Macmillan.

KUBZANSKY, L. D., COLE, S. R., KAWACHI, I., VOLONAS, P. & SPARROW, D. (2006). Shared and unique contributions of anger, anxiety, and depression to coronary heart disease: A prospective study in The Normative Aging Study. *Annals of Behavioral Medicine*, 31, 21–29.

KUBZANSKY, L. D., KOENEN, K. C., JONES, C., & EATON, W. W. (2009). A prospective study of posttraumatic stress disorder symptoms and coronary heart disease in women. *Health Psychology*, 28, 125–130.

KUBZANSKY, L. D., KOENEN, K. C., SPIRO, A., VOKONAS, P. S., & SPARROW, D. (2007). Prospective study of posttraumatic stress disorder symptoms and coronary heart disease in the Normative Aging Study. *Archives of General Psychiatry*, 64, 109–116.

KUBZANSKY, L. D. & THURSTON, R. C. (2007). Emotional vitality and incident coronary heart disease: Benefits of healthy psychological functioning. *Archives of General Psychiatry*, 64, 1393–1401.

KUDIELKA, B. M., HELLHAMMER, J., HELLHAMMER, D. H., WOLF, O. T., PIRKE, K.-M., et al. (1998). Sex differences in endocrine and psychological responses to psychosocial stress in healthy elderly subjects and the impact of a 2-week dehydroepiandrosterone treatment. *Journal of Clinical Endocrinology and Metabolism, 83,* 1756–1761.

KUJALA, U. M., KAPRIO, J., SARNA, S., & KOSKENVUO, M. (1998). Relationship of leisure-time physical activity and mortality: The Finnish twin cohort. *Journal of the American Medical Association, 279,* 440–444.

KULIK, J. A., & CARLINO, P. (1987). The effect of verbal commitment and treatment choice on medication compliance in a pediatric setting. *Journal of Behavioral Medicine, 10,* 367–376.

KULIK, J. A., & MAHLER, H. I. M. (1987a). Effects of preoperative roommate assignment on preoperative anxiety and recovery from coronary-bypass surgery. *Health Psychology, 6,* 525–543.

KULIK, J. A., & MAHLER, H. I. M. (1987b). Health status, perceptions of risk, and prevention interest for health and nonhealth problems. *Health Psychology, 6,* 15–27.

KULIK, J. A., & MAHLER, H. I. M. (1989). Social support and recovery from surgery. *Health Psychology, 8,* 221–238.

KULIK, J. A., MOORE, P. J., & MAHLER, H. I. M. (1993). Stress and affiliation: Hospital roommate effects on preoperative anxiety and social interaction. *Health Psychology, 12,* 118–124.

KUNDA, Z. (1990). The case for motivated reasoning. *Psychological Bulletin, 108,* 480–498.

KUNDERMANN, B., SPERNAL, J., HUBER, M. T., KRIEG, J. C., & LAUTENBACHER, S. (2004). Sleep deprivation affects thermal pain thresholds but not somatosensory thresholds in healthy volunteers. *Psychosomatic Medicine, 66,* 932–937.

KURTH, T., GAZIANO, J. M., BERGER, K., KASE, C. S., REXRODE, K. M., et al. (2003). Body mass index and the risk of stroke in men. *Archives of Internal Medicine, 163,* 2557–2662.

KUSAKA, Y., KONDOU, H., & MORIMOTO, K. (1992). Healthy lifestyles are associated with higher natural killer cell activity. *Preventive Medicine, 21,* 602–615.

KUSHNER, M. A. (2009). A review of the empirical literature about child development and adjustment postseparation. *Journal of Divorce & Remarriage, 50,* 496–516.

KUSNECOV, A. W. (2001). Behavioral conditioning of the immune system. In A. BAUM, T. A. REVENSON, & J. E. SINGER (Eds.), *Handbook of health psychology* (pp. 105–115.). Mahwah, NJ: Erlbaum.

KVAAVIK, E., BATTY, G. D., URSIN, G., HUXLEY, R., & GALE, C. R. (2010). Influence of individual and combined health behaviors on total and cause-specific mortality in men and women: The United Kingdom Health and Lifestyle Survey. *Archives of Internal Medicine, 170,* 711–718.

KYROU, I. & TSIGOS, C. (2009). Stress hormones: Physiological stress and regulation of metabolism. *Current Opinion in Pharmacology, 9,* 787–793.

LaBARBA, R. C. (1984). Prenatal and neonatal influences on behavioral health development. In J. D. MATARAZZO, S. M. WEISS, J. A. HERD, N. E. MILLER, & S. M. WEISS (Eds.), *Behavioral health: A handbook of health enhancement and disease prevention* (pp. 41–55). New York: Wiley.

LaBRIE, J. W., PEDERSEN, E. R., EARLEYWINE, M., & OLSEN, H. (2006). Reducing heavy drinking in college males with the decisional balance: Analyzing an element of Motivational Interviewing. *Addictive Behaviors, 31,* 254–263.

LaCHMAN, M. E. (1986). Personal control in later life: Stability, change, and cognitive correlates. In M. M. BALTES & P. B. BALTES (Ed.), *The psychology of control and aging* (pp. 207–236). Hillsdale, NJ: Erlbaum.

LaCROIX, A. Z., LANG, J., SCHERR, P., WALLACE, R. B., CORNONI-HUNTLEY, J., et al. (1991). Smoking and mortality among older men and women in three communities. *New England Journal of Medicine, 324,* 1619–1625.

LAFFREY, S. C. (1986). Normal and overweight adults: Perceived weight and health behavior characteristics. *Nursing Research, 35,* 173–177.

LA GRECA, A. M., & STONE, W. L. (1985). Behavioral pediatrics. In N. SCHNEIDERMAN & J. T. TAPP (Eds.), *Behavioral medicine: The biopsychosocial approach* (pp. 255–291). Hillsdale, NJ: Erlbaum.

LAHEY, B. B. (2009). Public health significance of neuroticism. *American Psychologist, 64,* 241–256.

LAI, D. T. C., CAHILL, K., QIN, Y., & TANG, J.-L. (2010). Motivational interviewing for smoking cessation. *Cochrane Database of Systematic Reviews,* Issue 1. Retrieved (1-30-2010) from http://www.thecochranelibrary.com. DOI:10.1002/14651858.CD006936.pub2.

LAKEIN, A. (1973). *How to get control of your time and life.* New York: New American Library.

LANDRINE, H., & KLONOFF, E. A. (2001). Cultural diversity and health psychology. In A. BAUM, T. A. REVENSON, & J. E. SINGER (Eds.), *Handbook of health psychology* (pp. 851–891). Mahwah, NJ: Erlbaum.

LANE, J. D., PIEPER, C. F., PHILLIPS-BUTE, B. G., BRYANT, J. E., & KUHN, C. M. (2002). Caffeine affects cardiovascular and neuroendocrine activation at work and home. *Psychosomatic Medicine, 64,* 595–603.

LANE, M. A., BAER, D. J., RUMPLER, W. V., WEINDRUCH, R., INGRAM, D. K., et al. (1996). Calorie restriction lowers body temperature in rhesus monkeys, consistent with a postulated anti-aging mechanism in rodents. *Proceedings of the National Academy of Sciences, 93,* 4159–4164.

LANGER, E. J., JANIS, I. L., & WOLFER, J. A. (1975). Reduction of psychological stress in surgical patients. *Journal of Experimental Social Psychology, 11,* 155–165.

LANGER, E. J., & RODIN, J. (1976). The effects of choice and enhanced personal responsibility for the aged: A field experiment in an institutional setting. *Journal of Personality and Social Psychology, 34,* 191–198.

LANGLIE, J. K. (1977). Social networks, health beliefs, and preventive health behavior. *Journal of Health and Social Behavior, 18,* 244–260.

LANTZ, P. M., HOUSE, J. S., MERO, R. P., & WILLIAMS, D. R. (2005). Stress, life events, and socioeconomic disparities in health: Results from the Americans' Changing Lives Study. *Journal of Health and Social Behavior, 46,* 274–288.

LA PLACE, J. (1984). *Health* (4th ed.). Englewood Cliffs, NJ: Prentice Hall.

LARIMER, M. E., & CRONCE, J. M. (2007). Identification, prevention, and treatment revisited: Individual-focused college drinking prevention strategies 1999–2006. *Addictive Behaviors, 32,* 2439–2468.

LARKIN, K. T., KNOWLTON, G. E., & D'ALESSANDRI, R. (1990). Predicting treatment outcome to progressive relaxation training in essential hypertensive patients. *Journal of Behavioral Medicine, 13,* 605–618.

LARKIN, K. T., & ZAYFERT, C. (1996). Anger management training with mild essential hypertensive patients. *Journal of Behavioral Medicine, 19,* 415–433.

LAROCCO, J. M., HOUSE, J. S., & FRENCH, J. R. P. (1980). Social support, occupational stress, and health. *Journal of Health and Social Behavior, 21,* 202–218.

LARSON, N., & STORY, M. (2009). A review of environmental influences on food choices. *Annal of Behavioral Medicine, 38*(suppl.), S56–S73.

LASZLO, J. (1987). *Understanding cancer.* New York: Harper & Row.

LATIMER, A. E., & GINIS, K. A. M. (2005). The importance of subjective norms for people who care what others think of them. *Psychology and Health, 20,* 53–62.

LAU, R. R., & HARTMAN, K. A. (1983). Common sense representations of common illnesses. *Health Psychology, 2,* 167–185.

LAVE, J. R. (1989). The effect of the Medicare prospective payment system. *Annual Review of Public Health, 10,* 141–161.

LAWLER, S. P., & CAMERON, L. D. (2006). A randomized, controlled trial of massage therapy as a treatment for migraine. *Annals of Behavior Medicine, 32,* 50–59.

LAWRENCE, D. B., & GAUS, C. R. (1983). Long-term care: Financing and policy issues. In D. MECHANIC (Ed.), *Handbook of health, health care, and the health professions* (pp. 365–378). New York: Free Press.

LAWHON, D., HUMFLEET, G. L., HALL, H. M., REUS, V. I., & MUÑOZ, R. F. (2009). Longitudinal analysis of abstinence-specific social support and smoking cessation. *Health Psychology, 28,* 465–472.

LAZARUS, A. A. (1971). *Behavior therapy and beyond.* New York: McGraw-Hill.

LAZARUS, R. S. (1999). *Stress and emotion: A new synthesis.* New York: Springer.

LAZARUS, R. S., & FOLKMAN, S. (1984). *Stress, appraisal, and coping.* New York: Springer.

LEAHEY, T. H. (1987). *A history of psychology: Main currents in psychological thought* (2nd ed.). Englewood Cliffs, NJ: Prentice Hall.

LEAKE, R., FRIEND, R., & WADHWA, N. (1999). Improving adjustment to chronic illness through strategic self-presentation: An experimental study on a renal dialysis unit. *Health Psychology, 18,* 54–62.

LEARY, M., TWENGE, J., & QUINLIVAN, E. (2006). Interpersonal rejection as a determinant of anger and aggression. *Personality and Social Psychology Review, 10,* 111–132.

LEARY, M. R., COTTRELL, C. A., & PHILLIPS, M. (2001). Deconfounding the effects of dominance and social acceptance on self-esteem. *Journal of Personality and Social Psychology, 81,* 898–909.

LEBEL, S., ROSBERGER, Z., EDGAR, L., & DEVINS, G. M. (2007). Comparison of four common stressors across the breast cancer trajectory. *Journal of Psychosomatic Research, 63,* 225–232.

LEDESMA, D., & KUMANO, H. (2009). Mindfulness-based stress reduction and cancer: A meta-analysis. *Psycho-Oncology, 18,* 571–579.

LEE, C. (1989). Perceptions of immunity to disease in adult smokers. *Journal of Behavioral Medicine, 12,* 267–277.

LEE, C. D., SUI, X., & BLAIR, S. N. (2009). Combined effects of cardiorespiratory fitness, not smoking, and normal waist girth on morbidity and mortality in men. *Archives of Internal Medicine, 169,* 2096–2101.

LEE, H., BAHLER, R., TAYLOR, A., ALONZO, A., & ZELLER, R. A. (1999). Clinical symptoms of myocardial infarction and delayed treatment-seeking behavior in Blacks and Whites. *Journal of Applied Biobehavioral Research, 3,* 135–159.

LEE, H., & ERNST, E. (2005). Acupuncture analgesia during surgery: A systematic review. *Pain, 114,* 511–517.

LEE, H.-Y., CHEN, Y.-H., CHIU, W.-T., HWANG, J.-S., WANG, J.-D. (2010). Quality-adjusted life-year and helmet use among motorcyclists sustaining head injuries. *American Journal of Public Health, 100,* 165–170.

LEE, M. B., LEIBOWITZ, A., & ROTHERAM-BORUS, M. J. (2005). Cost-effectiveness of a behavioral intervention for seropositive youth. *AIDS Education and Prevention, 17,* 105–118.

LEE, M. B., WU, Z., ROTHERAM-BORUS, M. J., DETELS, R., GUAN, J., & LI, L. (2005). HIV-related stigma among marker workers in China. *Health Psychology, 24,* 435–438.

LEE, W.-H., MORTON, R. A., EPSTEIN, J. I., BROOKS, J. D., CAMPBELL, P. A., et al. (1994). Cytidine methylation of regulatory sequences near the π-class glutathione S-transferase gene accompanies human prostatic carcinogenesis. *Proceedings of the National Academy of Sciences USA, 91,* 11733–11737.

LEEUW, M., GOOSSENS, M. E. J. B., VAN BREUKELEN, G. J., P., DE JONG, J. R., HEUTS, P. H. T. G., et al. (2008). Exposure *in vivo* versus operant graded activity in chronic low back pain paitients: Results of a randomized controlled trial. *Pain, 138,* 192–207.

LEFF, B., BURTON, L., MADER, S. L., NAUGHTON, B., BURL, J., et al. (2005). Hospital at home: Feasibility and outcomes of a program to provide hospital-level care at home for acutely ill older patients. *Annals of Internal Medicine, 143,* 798–808.

LEFFERT, N., & PETERSEN, A. C. (1998). Healthy adolescent development: Risks and opportunities. In P. M. KATO & T. MANN (Eds.), *Handbook of diversity issues in health psychology* (pp. 117–140). New York: Plenum.

LEHRER, P., FELDMAN, J., GIARDINO, N., SONG, H.-Y., & SCHMALING, K. (2002). Psychological aspects of asthma. *Journal of Consulting and Clinical Psychology, 70*, 691–711.

LEIBEL, R. L., ROSENBLUM, M., & HIRSCH, J. (1995). Changes in energy expenditure resulting from altered body weight. *New England Journal of Medicine, 332*, 621–628.

LEIGH, B. C., MORRISON, D. M., TROCKI, K., & TEMPLE, M. T. (1994). Sexual behavior of American adolescents: Results from a U.S. national survey. *Journal of Adolescent Health, 15*, 117–125.

LEINO, P., ARO, S., & HASAN, J. (1987). Trunk muscle function and low back disorders: A ten-year follow-up study. *Journal of Chronic Diseases, 40*, 289–296.

LEITZMANN, M. F., PARK, Y., BLAIR, A., BALLARD-BARBASH, R., MOUW, T., et al. (2007). Physical activity recommendations and decreased risk of mortality. *Archives of Internal Medicine, 167*, 2453–2460.

LEMELIN, E. T., DIEZ ROUX, A. V., FRANKLIN, T. G., CARNETHON, M., LUTSEY, P. L., et al. (2009). Life-course socioeconomic positions and subclinical atherosclerosis in the multi-ethnic study of atherosclerosis. *Social Science and Medicine, 68*, 444–451.

LENGACHER, C. A., JOHNSON-MALLARD, V., POST-WHITE, J., MOSCOSO, M. S., JACOBSEN, P. B., et al. (2009). Randomized controlled trial of mindfulness-based stress reduction (MBSR) for survivors of breast cancer. *Psycho-Oncology, 18*, 1261–1272.

LENNEBERG, E. H. (1967). *Biological foundations of language.* New York: Wiley.

LEONARD, B. E. (1995). Stress and the immune system: Immunological aspects of depressive illness. In B. E. LEONARD & K. MILLER (Eds.), *Stress, the immune system and psychiatry* (pp. 113–136). New York: Wiley.

LEONARD, E. A. (1990, April 9). How the brain recovers. *Newsweek*, pp. 48–50.

LEPORE, S. J. (1997). Social-environmental influences on the chronic stress process. In B. H. GOTTLIEB (Ed.), *Coping with chronic stress* (pp. 133–160). New York: Plenum.

LEPORE, S. J., ALLEN, K. A. M., EVANS, G. W. (1993). Social support lowers cardiovascular reactivity to an acute stressor. *Psychosomatic Medicine, 55*, 518–524.

LEPORE, S. J., GLASER, D. B., & ROBERTS, K. J. (2008). On the positive relation between received social support and negative affect: A test of the triage and self-esteem threat models in women with breast cancer. *Psycho-Oncology, 17*, 1210–1215.

LEPORE, S. J., & HELGESON, V. S. (1998). Social constraints, intrusive thoughts, and mental health after prostate cancer. *Journal of Social and Clinical Psychology, 17*, 89–106.

LEPORE, S. J., REVENSON, T. A., WEINBERGER, S. L., WESTON, P., FRISINA, P. G., et al. (2006). Effects of social stressors on cardiovascular reactivity in Black and White women. *Annals of Behavioral Medicine, 31*, 120–127.

LERMAN, C., AUDRAIN, J., & CROYLE, R. T. (1994). DNA-testing for heritable breast cancer risks: Lessons from traditional genetic counseling. *Annals of Behavioral Medicine, 16*, 327–333.

LERMAN, C., & BERRETTINI, W. (2003). Elucidating the role of genetic factors in smoking behavior and nicotine dependence. *American Journal of Medical Genetics, 118B*, 48–54.

LERMAN, C., CAPORASO, N. E., AUDRAIN, J., MAIN, D., BOWMAN, E. D., et al. (1999). Evidence suggesting the role of specific genetic factors in cigarette smoking. *Health Psychology, 18*, 14–20.

LERMAN, C., CAPORASO, N. E., MAIN, D., AUDRAIN, J., BOYD, N. R., et al. (1998). Depression and self-medication with nicotine: The modifying influence of the dopamine D4 receptor gene. *Health Psychology, 17*, 56–62.

LERMAN, C., HUGHES, C., TROCK, B. J., MYERS, R. E., MAIN, D., et al. (1999). Genetic testing in families with heredity nonpolyposis colon cancer. *Journal of the American Medical Association, 17*, 1618–1622.

LERMAN, C., NAROD, S., SCHULMAN, K., HUGHES, C., GOMEZ-CAMINERO, A., et al. (1996). BRAC1 testing in families with hereditary breast-ovarian cancer: A prospective study of patient decision making and outcomes. *Journal of the American Medical Association, 275*, 1885–1892.

LERMAN, C., TROCK, B., RIMER, B. K., BOYCE, A., JEPSON, C., & ENGSTROM, P. F. (1991). Psychological and behavioral implications of abnormal mammograms. *Annals of Internal Medicine, 114*, 657–661.

LESTER, N., LEFEBVRE, J. C., & KEEFE, F. J. (1994). Pain in young adults: I. Relationship to gender and family history. *Clinical Journal of Pain, 10*, 282–289.

LETT, H. S., BLUMENTHAL, J. A., BABYAK, M. A., STRAUMAN. T. J., ROBINS, C., & SHERWOOD, A. (2005). Social support and coronary heart disease: Epidemiologic evidence and implications for treatment. *Psychosomatic Medicine, 67*, 869–878.

LEVENSON, R. W. (1986). Alcohol, reactivity, and the heart: Implications for coronary health and disease. In K. A. MATTHEWS, S. M. WEISS, T. DETRE, T. M. DEMBROSKI, B. FALKNER, S. B. MANUCK, & R. B. WILLIAMS (Eds.), *Handbook of stress, reactivity, and cardiovascular disease* (pp. 345–364). New York: Wiley.

LEVENSTEIN, S. (2002). Psychosocial factors in peptic ulcer and inflammatory bowel disease. *Journal of Consulting and Clinical Psychology, 70*, 739–750.

LEVENTHAL, E. A., & PROHASKA, T. R. (1986). Age, symptom interpretation, and health behavior. *Journal of the American Geriatrics Society, 34*, 185–191.

LEVENTHAL, H., & CLEARY, P. D. (1980). The smoking problem. A review of research and theory in behavioral risk modification. *Psychological Bulletin, 88*, 370–405.

LEVENTHAL, H., HALM, E., HOROWITZ, C., LEVENTHAL, E. A., & OZAKINCI, G. (2004). Living with chronic illness: A contextualized, self-regulation approach. In S. SUTTON, A. BAUM, & M. JOHNSTON (Eds.), *The Sage handbook or health psychology* (pp. 197–240). London: Sage.

LEVENTHAL, H., LEVENTHAL, E. A., & CONTRADA, R. J. (1998). Self regulation, health, and behavior: A perceptual-cognitive approach. *Psychology & Health, 13*, 717–733.

LEVENTHAL, H., LEVENTHAL, E. A., & VAN NGUYEN, T. (1985). Reactions of families to illness: Theoretical models and perspectives. In D. C. TURK & R. D. KERNS (Eds.), *Health, illness, and families: A life-span perspective* (pp. 108–145). New York: Wiley.

LEVENTHAL, H., PROHASKA, T. R., & HIRSCHMAN, R. S. (1985). Preventive health behavior across the life span. In J. C. ROSEN & L. J. SOLOMON (Eds.), *Prevention in health psychology* (pp. 191–235). Hanover, NH: University Press of New England.

LEVIN, D. N., CLEELAND, C. S., & DAR, R. (1985). Public attitudes toward cancer pain. *Cancer, 56*, 2337–2339.

LEVINE, J. D., GORDON, N. C., & FIELDS, H. L. (1978, September 23). The mechanism of placebo analgesia. *Lancet*, 654–657.

LEVINSON, W., KAO, A., KUBY, A., & THISTED, R. A. (2005). Not all patients want to participate in decision making: A national study of public preferences. *Journal of General Internal Medicine, 20*, 531–535.

LEVY, B. S. & SIDEL, V. W. (2009). Health effects of combat: A life-course perspective. *Annual Review of Public Health, 30*, 123–136.

LEVY, S. M. (1983). The process of death and dying: Behavioral and social factors. In T. G. BURISH & L. A. BRADLEY (Eds.), *Coping with chronic disease: Research and applications* (pp. 425–446). New York: Academic Press.

LEVY, S. M. (1985). *Behavior and cancer*. San Francisco: Jossey-Bass.

LEVY, S. M., HERBERMAN, R. B., WHITESIDE, T., SANZO, K., LEE, J., & KIRKWOOD, J. (1990). Perceived social support and tumor estrogen/progesterone receptor status as predictors of natural killer cell activity in breast cancer patients. *Psychosomatic Medicine, 52*, 73–85.

LEVY-LAHAD, E., WASCO, W., POORKAJ, P., ROMANO, D. M., OSHIMA, J., et al. (1995). Candidate gene for the chromosome 1 familial Alzheimer's disease locus. *Science, 269*, 973–977.

LEWINSOHN, P. M., MERMELSTEIN, R. M., ALEXANDER, C., & MACPHILLAMY, D. J. (1985). The Unpleasant Events Schedule: A scale for the measurement of aversive events. *Journal of Clinical Psychology, 41*, 483–498.

LI (Lamaze International) (2010). *Lamaze healthy birth practices*. Retrieved (4-16-2010) from http://www.lamaze.org.

LI, J. T. C., & O'CONNELL, E. J. (1987). Viral infections and asthma. *Annals of Allergy, 59*, 321–331.

LIBBY, P., RIDKER, P. M., & HANSSON, G. K. (2009). Inflammation in atherosclerosis from pathophysiology to practice. *Journal of the American College of Cardiology, 54*, 2129–2138.

LICHSTEIN, K. L. (1988). *Clinical relaxation strategies*. New York: Wiley.

LICHTENSTEIN, E., & MERMELSTEIN, R. J. (1984). Review of approaches to smoking treatment: Behavior modification strategies. In J. D. MATARAZZO, S. M. WEISS, J. A. HERD, N. E. MILLER, & S. M. WEISS (Eds.), *Behavioral health: A handbook of*

health enhancement and disease prevention (pp. 695–712). New York: Wiley.

LICHTENSTEIN, E., WEISS, S. M., HITCHCOCK, J. L., LEVETON, L. B., O'CONNELL, K. A., & PROCHASKA, J. O. (1986). Task Force 3: Patterns of smoking relapse. *Health Psychology, 5*(Suppl.), 29–40.

LICHTENSTEIN, E., ZHU, S.-H., & TEDESCHI, G. J. (2010). Smoking cessation quitlines: An underrecognized intervention success story. *American Psychologist, 65*, 252–261.

LICHTENSTEIN, P., HOLM, N. V., VERKASALO, P. K., ILIADOU, A., KAPRIO, J., et al. (2000). Environmental and heritable factors in the causation of cancer—Analyses of cohorts of twins from Sweden, Denmark, and Finland. *New England Journal of Medicine, 343*, 78–85.

LICHTMAN, S. W., PISARSKA, K., BERMAN, E. R., PESTONE, M., DOWLING, H., et al. (1992). Discrepancy between self-reported and actual caloric intake and exercise in obese subjects. *New England Journal of Medicine, 327*, 1893–1898.

LIGHTFOOT, M., SWENDEMAN, D., ROTHERAM-BORUS, M. J., COMULADA, W. S., & WEISS, R. (2005). Risk behaviors of youth living with HIV: Pre- and post-HAART. *American Journal of Health Behavior, 29*, 162–171.

LILJAS, B., & LAHDENSUO, A. (1997). Is asthma self-management cost-effective? *Patient Education and Counseling, 32*, S97–S104.

LIN, E. H., & PETERSON, C. (1990). Pessimistic explanatory style and response to illness. *Behavior Research and Therapy, 28*, 243–248.

LINDE, K., STRENG, A., JÜRGENS, S., HOPPE, A., BRINKHAUS, B., et al. (2005). Acupuncture foe patients with migraine: A randomized controlled trial. *Journal of the American Medical Association, 293*, 2118–2125.

LINDEMAN, B. (1976). Widower, heal thyself. In R. H. MOOS (Ed.), *Human adaptation: Coping with life crises* (pp. 275–286). Lexington, MA: Heath.

LINDEN, W., & CHAMBERS, L. (1994). Clinical effectiveness of non-drug treatment for hypertension: A meta-analysis. *Annals of Behavioral Medicine, 16*, 35–45.

LINDEN, W., PHILLIPS, M. J., LECLERC, J. (2007). Psychological treatment of cardiac patients: A meta-analysis. *European Heart Journal, 28*, 2964–2966.

LINDENBERG, C. S., ALEXANDER, E. M., GENDROP, S. C., NENCIOLI, M., & WILLIAMS, D. G. (1991). A review of the literature on cocaine abuse in pregnancy. *Nursing Research, 40*, 69–75.

LINDSAY, J., LAURIN, D., VERREAULT, R., HÉBERT, R., HELLIWELL, B., et al. (2002). Risk factors for Alzheimer's disease: A prospective analysis from the Canadian Study on Health and Aging. *American Journal of Epidemiology, 156*, 445–453.

LINNAN, L. A., EMMONS, K. M., KLAR, N., FAVA, J. L., LAFORGE, R. G., & ABRAMS, D. B. (2002). Challenges to improving the impact of worksite cancer prevention programs: Comparing reach, enrollment, and attrition using active versus passive recruitment strategies. *Annals of Behavioral Medicine, 24*, 157–166.

LINTON, S. J., ALTHOFF, B., MELIN, L., LUNDIN, A., BODIN, L., et al. (1994). Psychological factors related to health, back pain, and dysfunction. *Journal of Occupational Rehabilitation*, 4, 1–10.

LINTON, S. J., & BUER, N. (1995). Working despite pain: Factors associated with work attendance versus dysfunction. *International Journal of Behavioral Medicine*, 2, 252–262.

LIOSSI, C., & HATIRA, P. (1999). Clinical hypnosis versus cognitive behavioral training for pain management with pediatric cancer patients undergoing bone marrow aspirations. *International Journal of Clinical and Experimental Hypnosis*, 47, 104–116.

LIOSSI, C., WHITE, P., & HATIRA, P. (2006). Randomized clinical trial of local anesthetic versus a combination of local anesthetic with self-hypnosis in the management of pediatric procedure-related pain. *Health Psychology*, 25, 307–315.

LIPPKE, S., ZIEGELMANN, J. P., SCHWARZER, R., & VELICER, W. F. (2009). Validity of stage assessment in the adoption and maintenance of physical activity and fruit and vegetable consumption. *Health Psychology*, 28, 183–193.

LISSPERS, J., SUNDIN, Ö., ÖHMAN, A., HOFFMAN-BANG, C., RYDÉN, L., & NYGREN, Å. (2005). Long-term effects of lifestyle behavior change in coronary artery disease: Effects on recurrent coronary events after percutaneous coronary intervention. *Health Psychology*, 24, 41–48.

LITT, M. D., KADDEN, R. M., KABELA-CORMIER, E., & PETRY, N. M. (2009). Changing network support for drinking: Network Support Project 2-year follow-up. *Journal of Consulting and Clinical Psychology*, 77, 229–247.

LITT, M. D., NYE, C., & SHAFER, D. (1995). Preparation for oral surgery: Evaluating elements of coping. *Journal of Behavioral Medicine*, 18, 435–459.

LITTLEWOOD, R. A., VANABLE, P. A., CAREY, M. P., & BLAIR, D. C. (2008). The association of benefit finding to psychosocial and health behavior adaptation among HIV+ men and women. *Journal of Behavioral Medicine*, 31, 145–155.

LIVERMORE, B. (1991, December). What reflexology can do for you. *Self*, p. 50.

LLABRE, M. M. & HADI, F. (2009). War-related exposure and psychological distress as predictors of health and sleep: A longitudinal study of Kuwaiti children. *Psychosomatic Medicine*, 71, 776–783.

LOBEL, M., CANNELLA, D. L., GRAHAM, J. E., DEVINCENT, C., SCHNEIDER, J. & MEYER, B. A. (2008). Pregnancy-specific stress, prenatal health behaviors, and birth outcomes. *Health Psychology*. 27, 604–615.

LOGAN, T. K., COLE, J., & LEUKEFELD, C. (2002). Women, sex, and HIV: Social and contextual factors, meta-analysis of published interventions, and implications for practice and research. *Psychological Bulletin*, 128, 851–885.

LOGUE, A. W. (1991). *The psychology of eating and drinking: An introduction* (2nd ed.). New York: Freeman.

LONETTO, R. (1980). *Children's conceptions of death*. New York: Springer.

LONG, R. T., LAMONT, J. H., WHIPPLE, B., BANDLER, L., BLOM, G. E., BURGIN, L., & JESSNER, L. (1958). A psychosomatic study of allergic and emotional factors in children with asthma. *American Journal of Psychiatry*, 114, 890–899.

LORBER, J. (1975). Good patients and problem patients: Conformity and deviance in a general hospital. *Journal of Health and Social Behavior*, 16, 213–225.

LORBER, W., MAZZONI, G., & KIRSCH, I. (2007). Illness by suggestion: Expectancy, modeling, and gender in the production of psychosomatic symptoms. *Annals of Behavioral Medicine*, 33, 112–116.

LORIG, K., GONZÁLEZ, V. M., LAURENT, D. D., MORGAN, L., & LARIS, B. A. (1998). Arthritis Self-Management Program variations: Three studies. *Arthritis Care and Research*, 11, 448–454.

LORIG, K. R., & HOLMAN, H. R. (2003). Self-management education: History, definition, outcomes, and mechanisms. *Annals of Behavioral Medicine*, 26, 1–7.

LORISH, C. D., RICHARDS, B., & BROWN, S. (1989). Missed medication doses in rheumatic arthritis patients: Intentional and unintentional reasons. *Arthritis Care and Research*, 2, 3–9.

LOUCKS, E. B., LYNCH, J. W., PILOTE, L., FUHRER, R., ALMEIDA, N. D., et al. (2009). Life-course socioeconomic position and incidence of coronary heart disease: The Framingham Offspring Study. *American Journal of Epidemiology*, 169, 829–836.

LOUNSBURY, P. (2004). Cardiovascular rehabilitation. In A. J. CHRISTENSEN, R. MARTIN, & J. M. SMYTH (Eds.), *Encyclopedia of health psychology* (p. 41). New York: Kluwer,

LOVALLO, W. R. (2005). *Stress and health: Biological and psychological interactions*. (2nd ed.). Thousand Oaks, CA: Sage.

LOVEJOY, T. I., & SUHR, J. A. (2009). The relationship between neuropsychological functioning and HAART adherence in HIV-positive adults: A systematic review. *Journal of Behavioral Medicine*, 32, 389–405.

LOW, C. A., STANTON, A. L., & DANOFF-BURG, S. (2006). Expressive disclosure and benefit finding among breast cancer patients: Mechanisms for positive health effects. *Health Psychology*, 25, 181–189.

LOWRY, R., HOLTZMAN, D., TRUMAN, B. I., KANN, L., COLLINS, J. L., & KOLBE, L. J. (1994). Substance use and HIV-related sexual behaviors among U.S. high school students: Are they related? *American Journal of Public Health*, 84, 1116–1120.

LUCINI, D., COVACCI, G., MILANI, R., MELA, G. S., MALLIANI, A., & PAGANI, M. (1997). A controlled study of the effects of mental relaxation on autonomic excitatory responses in healthy subjects. *Psychosomatic Medicine*, 59, 541–552.

LUDESCHER, B., LEITLEIN, G., SCHAEFER, J.-E., VANHOEFFEN, S., BAAR, S., et al. (2009). Changes in body composition in bulimia nervosa: Increased visceral fat and adrenal gland size. *Psychosomatic Medicine*, 71, 93–97.

LUDWICK-ROSENTHAL, R., & NEUFELD, R. W. J. (1993). Preparation for undergoing an invasive medical procedure: Interacting effects of information and coping style. *Journal of Consulting and Clinical Psychology*, 61, 156–164.

LUECKEN, L. J., & GALLO, L. C. (2008). Handbook of physiological research methods in health psychology. Thousand Oaks, CA: Sage.

LUECKEN, L. J., SUAREZ, E. C., KUHN, C. M., BAREFOOT, R. B., BLUMENTHAL, J. A., SIEGLER, I. C., & WILLIAMS, R. B. (1997). Stress in employed women: Impact of marital status and children at home on neurohormone output and home strain. *Psychosomatic Medicine*, 59, 352–359.

LUFT, H. S. (1998). Medicare and managed care. *Annual Review of Public Health*, 19, 459–475.

LUMLEY, J., CHAMBERLAIN, C., DOWSWELL, T., OLIVER, S., OAKLEY, L., & WATSON, L. (2009). Interventions for promoting smoking cessation during pregnancy. *Cochrane Database of Systematic Reviews*, Issue 3. Retrieved (1-30-2010) from http://www.thecochranelibrary.com. DOI:10.1002/14651858.CD001055.pub3.

LUNDBERG, U. (1999). Coping with stress: Neuroendocrine reactions and implications for health. *Noise and Health*, 4, 67–74.

LUNDBERG, U., DOHNS, I. E., MELIN, B., SANDSJÖ, L., PALMERUD, G., et al. (1999). Psychophysiological stress responses, muscle tension, and neck shoulder pain among super-market cashiers. *Journal of Occupational Health Psychology*, 4, 245–255.

LUNDBERG, U., & FRANKENHAEUSER, M. (1999). Stress and workload in men and women in high-ranking positions. *Journal of Occupational Health Psychology*, 4, 142–151.

LUNDIN, R. W. (1987). Locus of control. In R. J. CORSINI (Ed.), *Concise encyclopedia of psychology* (pp. 670–672). New York: Wiley.

LUPARELLO, T. J., LYONS, H. A., BLEECKER, E. R., & MCFADDEN, E. R. (1968). Influences of suggestion on airway reactivity in asthmatic subjects. *Psychosomatic Medicine*, 30, 819–825.

LUTGENDORF, S. K., ANTONI, M. H., IRONSON, G., KLIMAS, N., KUMAR, M., et al. (1997). Cognitive-behavioral stress management decreases dysphoric mood and herpes simplex virus–type 2 antibody titers in symptomatic HIV-seropositive gay men. *Journal of Consulting and Clinical Psychology*, 65, 31–43.

LYKKEN, D. T. (2004). Psychophysiology. In W. E. CRAIGHEAD & C. B. NEMEROFF (Eds.), *The concise Corsini encyclopedia of psychology and behavioral science* (3rd ed., pp. 768–769). Hoboken, NJ: Wiley.

LYNAM, D. R., MILICH, R., ZIMMERMAN, R., NOVAK, S. P., LOGAN, T. K., et al. (1999). Project DARE: No effects at 10-year follow-up. *Journal of Consulting and Clinical Psychology*, 67, 590–593.

LYNCH, J. J. (1990). The broken heart: The psychobiology of human contact. In R. ORNSTEIN & C. SWENCIONIS (Eds.), *The healing brain: A scientific reader* (pp. 75–87). New York: Guilford.

LYNCH, J. W., EVERSON, S. A., KAPLAN, G. A., SALONEN, R., SALONEN, J. T. (1998). Does low socioeconomic status potentiate the effects of heightened cardiovascular responses to stress on the progression of carotid atherosclerosis? *American Journal of Public Health*, 88, 389–394.

MACDONALD, T. K., MACDONALD, G., ZANNA, M. P., & FONG, G. T. (2000). Alcohol, sexual arousal, and intentions to use condoms in young men: Applying alcohol myopia theory to risky sexual behavior. *Health Psychology*, 19, 290–298.

MACIEWJEWSKI, P. K., ZHANG, B., BLOCK, S. D., & PRIGERSON, H. G. (2007). An empirical examination of the stage theory of grief. *Journal of the American Medical Association*, 297, 716–723.

MACKAY, C., & COX, T. (1978). Stress at work. In T. COX (Ed.), *Stress* (pp. 147–173). Baltimore: University Park Press.

MACPHERSON, A., & SPINKS, A. (2009). Bicycle helmet legislation for the uptake of helmet use and prevention of head injuries. *Cochrane Database of Systematic Reviews*, Issue 3. Retrieved (1-30-2010) from http://www.thecochranelibrary.com. DOI:10.1002/14651858.CD005401.pub3.

MADDUX, B. A., SBRACCIA, P., KUMAKURA, S., SASSON, S., YOUNGREN, J., et al. (1995). Membrane glycoprotein PC-1 and insulin resistance in non-insulin-dependent diabetes mellitus. *Nature*, 373, 448–451.

MAES, S., & BOERSMA, S. N. (2004). Applications in health psychology: How effective are interventions? In S. SUTTON, A. BAUM, & M. JOHNSTON (Eds.), *The Sage handbook of health psychology* (pp. 299–325). London: Sage.

MAGES, N. L., & MENDELSOHN, G. A. (1979). Effects of cancer on patients' lives: A personological approach. In G. C. STONE, F. COHEN, & N. E. ADLER (Eds.), *Health psychology—A handbook* (pp. 255–284). San Francisco: Jossey-Bass.

MAGKOS, F., YANNAKOULIA, M., CHAN, J. L., & MANTZOROS, C. S. (2009). Management of the metabolic syndrome and type 2 diabetes through lifestyle modification. *Annual Review of Nutrition*, 29, 223–56.

MAGNI, G., MORESCHI, C., RIGATTI-LUCHINI, S., & MERSKEY, H. (1994). Prospective study on the relationship between depressive symptoms and chronic musculoskeletal pain. *Pain*, 56, 289–297.

MAGUIRE, P. (1985). Barriers to psychological care of the dying. *British Medical Journal*, 291, 1711–1713.

MAHLER, H. I. M., & KULIK, J. A. (1991). Health care involvement preferences and social-emotional recovery of male coronary-artery-bypass patients. *Health Psychology*, 10, 399–408.

MAISEL, N. C., & GABLE, S. L. (2009). The paradox of received social support: The importance of responsiveness. *Psychological Science*, 20, 928–932.

MAISTO, S. A. (2004). Alcoholism. In A. J. CHRISTENSEN, R. MILLER, & J. M. SMYTH (Eds.), *Encyclopedia of health psychology* (pp. 9–13). New York: Kluwer.

MAJ, M. (1990). Psychiatric aspects of HIV-1 infection and AIDS. *Psychological Medicine*, 20, 547–563.

MAJOR, B., RICHARDS, C., COOPER, M. L., COZZARELLI, C., & ZUBEK, J. (1998). Personal resilience, cognitive appraisals, and coping: An integrative model of adjustment to abortion. *Journal of Personality and Social Psychology*, 74, 735–752.

MALKIN, S. (1976). Care of the terminally ill. *Canadian Medical Association Journal*, 115, 129–130.

MALONEY, E. M., BONEVA, R., NATER, U. M., & REEVES, W. C. (2009). Chronic fatigue syndrome and high allostatic load: Result from a population-based case-control study in Georgia. *Psychosomatic Medicine*, 71, 549–556.

MANFREDI, M., BINI, G., CRUCCU, G., ACCORNERO, N., BERADELLI, A., & MEDOLAGO, L. (1981). Congenital absence of pain. *Archives on Neurology*, 38, 507–511.

MANHEIMER, E., WHITE, A., BERMAN, B., FORYS, K., & ERNST, E. (2005). Meta-analysis: Acupuncture for low back pain. *Annals of Internal Medicine*, 142, 651–663.

MANINI, T. M., EVERHART, J. E., PATEL, K. V., SCHOELLER, D. A., COLBERT, L. H., et al. (2006). Daily activity energy expenditure and mortality among older adults. *Journal of the American Medical Association*, 296, 171–179.

MANN, E., & CARR, E. (2006). *Pain management*. Oxford, UK: Blackwell.

MANN, T. (1996). Why do we need a health psychology of gender or sexual orientation? In P. M. KATO & T. MANN (Eds.), *Handbook of diversity issues in health psychology* (pp. 187–198). New York: Plenum.

MANNE, S. L. (1999). Intrusive thoughts and psychological distress among cancer patients: The role of spouse avoidance and criticism. *Journal of Consulting and Clinical Psychology*, 67, 539–546.

MANNE, S. L., BAKEMAN, R., JACOBSEN, P. B., GORFINKLE, K., BERNSTEIN, D., & REDD, W. H. (1992). Adult-child interaction during invasive medical procedures. *Health Psychology*, 11, 241–249.

MANNE, S. L., BAKEMAN, R., JACOBSEN, P. B., GORFINKLE, K., & REDD, W. H. (1994). An analysis of a behavioral intervention for children undergoing venipuncture. *Health Psychology*, 13, 556–566.

MANNE, S. L., JACOBSEN, P. B., GORFINKLE, K., GERSTEIN, F., & REDD, W. H. (1993). Treatment adherence difficulties among children with cancer: The role of parenting style. *Journal of Pediatric Psychology*, 18, 47–62.

MANNE, S., OSTROFF, J. S., & WINKEL, G. (2007). Social-cognitive processes as moderators of a couple-focused group intervention for women with early stage breast cancer. *Health Psychology*, 26, 735–744.

MANNE, S. L., RUBIN, S., EDELSON, M., ROSENBLUM, N., BERGMAN, C., et al. (2007). Coping and communication-enhancing intervention versus supportive counseling for women diagnosed with gynecological cancers. *Journal of Consulting and Clinical Psychology*, 75, 615–628.

MANNE, S. L., & ZAUTRA, A. J. (1990). Couples coping with chronic illness: Women with rheumatoid arthritis and their healthy husbands. *Journal of Behavioral Medicine*, 13, 327–342.

MANTON, K. G. (2008). Recent declines in chronic disability in the elderly U.S. population: Risk factors and future dynamics. *Annual Review of Public Health*, 29, 91–113.

MANUCK, S. B. (1994). Cardiovascular reactivity in cardiovascular disease: "Once more unto the breach." *International Journal of Behavioral Medicine*, 1, 4–31.

MANUCK, S. B., MARSLAND, A. L., KAPLAN, J. R., & WILLIAMS, J. K. (1995). The pathogenicity of behavior and its neuroendocrine mediation: An example from coronary artery disease. *Psychosomatic Medicine*, 57, 275–283.

MARCO, C. A. (2004). Coping. In A. J. CHRISTENSEN, R. MARTIN, & J. M. SMYTH (Eds.), *Encyclopedia of health psychology* (pp. 66–70). New York: Kluwer.

MARCUS, B. H., BOCK, B. C., PINTO, B. M., FORSYTH, L. H., ROBERTS, M. B., & TRAFICANTE, R. M. (1998). Efficacy of an individualized, motivationally-tailored physical activity intervention. *Annals of Behavioral Medicine*, 20, 174–180.

MARCUS, B. H., DUBBERT, P. M., FORSYTH, L. H., MCKENZIE, T. L., STONE, E. J., et al. (2000). Physical activity behavior change: Issues in adoption and maintenance. *Health Psychology*, 19, 32–41.

MARIANO, A. J. (1992). Chronic pain and spinal cord injury. *Journal of Clinical Pain*, 8, 87–92.

MARIN, T. I., CHEN, E., MUNCH, J. A., & MILLER, G. E. (2009). Double-exposure to acute stress and chronic family stress is associated with immune changes in children with asthma. *Psychosomatic Medicine*, 71, 378–384.

MARKES, M., BROKOW, T., & RESCH, K. L. (2006). Exercise for women receiving adjuvant therapy for breast cancer. *Cochrane Database of Systematic Reviews*, Issue 4. DOI:10.1002/14651858.CD005001.pub2.

MARKS, G., RICHARDSON, J. L., GRAHAM, J. W., & LEVINE, A. (1986). Role of health locus of control beliefs and expectations of treatment efficacy in adjustment to cancer. *Journal of Personality and Social Psychology*, 51, 443–450.

MARLATT, G. A. (1983). The controlled-drinking controversy: A commentary. *American Psychologist*, 38, 1097–1110.

MARLATT, G. A., & GORDON, J. R. (1980). Determinants of relapse: Implications for the maintenance of behavior change. In P. O. DAVIDSON & S. M. DAVIDSON (Eds.), *Behavioral medicine: Changing health lifestyles* (pp. 410–452). New York: Brunner/Mazel.

MARON, D. J., & FORTMANN, S. P. (1987). Nicotine yield and measures of cigarette smoke exposure in a large population: Are lower-yield cigarettes safer? *American Journal of Public Health*, 77, 546–549.

MARSHALL, S. J., & BIDDLE, S. J. H. (2001). The transtheoretical model of behavior change: A meta-analysis of applications to physical activity and exercise. *Annals of Behavioral Medicine*, 23, 229–246.

MARSLAND, A. L., BACHEN, E. A., COHEN, S., & MANUCK, S. B. (2001). Stress, immunity, and susceptibility to infectious disease. In A. BAUM, T. A. REVENSON, & J. E. SINGER (Eds.), *Handbook of health psychology* (pp. 683–695). Mahwah, NJ: Erlbaum.

MARSLAND, A. L., MANUCK, S. B., FAZZARI, T. V., STEWART, C. J., & RABIN, B. S. (1995). Stability of individual differences in cellular immune responses to acute psychological stress. *Psychosomatic Medicine, 57,* 295–298.

MARTEAU, T. M., & JOHNSTON, M. (1986). Determinants of beliefs about illness: A study of parents of children with diabetes, asthma, epilepsy, and no chronic illness. *Journal of Psychosomatic Research, 30,* 673–683.

MARTEAU, T. M., JOHNSTON, M., BAUM, J. D., & BLOCH, S. (1987). Goals of treatment in diabetes: A comparison of doctors and parents of children with diabetes. *Journal of Behavioral Medicine, 10,* 33–48.

MARTEAU, T. M., & WEINMAN, J. (2004). Communicating about health threats and treatments. In S. SUTTON, A. BAUM, & M. JOHNSTON (Eds.), *The Sage handbook of health psychology,* (pp. 270–298). London: Sage.

MARTELL, B. A., O'CONNOR, P. G., KERNS, R. D., BECKER, W. C., MORALES, K. H., et al. (2007). Systematic review: Opioid treatment for chronic back pain: Prevalence, efficacy, and association with addiction. *Annals of Internal Medicine, 146,* 116–127.

MARTIN, J. L. (1988). Psychological consequences of AIDS-related bereavement among gay men. *Journal of Consulting and Clinical Psychology, 56,* 856–862.

MARTIN, J. L., & DEAN, L. (1993). Effects of AIDS-related bereavement and HIV-related illness on psychological distress among gay men: A 7-year longitudinal study, 1985–1991. *Journal of Consulting and Clinical Psychology, 61,* 94–103.

MARTIN, P. R., MILECH, D., & NATHAN, P. R. (1993). Towards a functional model of chronic headaches: Investigation of antecedents and consequences. *Headache, 33,* 461–470.

MARTIN, P. R., TODD, J., & REECE, J. (2005). Effects of noise and a stressor on head pain. *Headache, 45,* 1353–1364.

MARTIN, R., DAVIS, G. M., BARON, R. S., SULS, J., & BLANCHARD, E. B. (1994). Specificity in social support: Perceptions of helpful and unhelpful provider behaviors among irritable bowel, headache, and cancer patients. *Health Psychology, 13,* 432–439.

MARTIN, R., JOHNSEN, E. L., BUNDE, J., BELLMAN, S. B., ROTHROCK, N. E., et al. (2005). Gender differences in patients' attributions for myocardial infarction: Implications for adaptive health behaviors. *International Journal of Behavioral Medicine, 12,* 39–45.

MARTIN, R., LEMOS, K., ROTHROCK, N., BELLMAN, S. B., RUSSELL, D., et al. (2004). Gender disparities in common sense models of illness among myocardial infarction victims. *Health Psychology, 23,* 345–353.

MARTINEZ, F. D., WRIGHT, A. L., TAUSSIG, L. M., & The Group Health Medical Associates (1994). The effect of paternal smoking on the birthweight of newborns whose mothers did not smoke. *American Journal of Public Health, 84,* 1489–1491.

MARTINEZ-GOMEZ, D., TUCKER, J., HEELAN, K. A., WELK, G. J., & EISENMANN, J. C. (2009). Associations between sedentary behavior and blood pressure in young children. *Archives of Pediatric and Adolescent Medicine, 163,* 724–730.

MARTIRE, L. M., KEEFE, F. J., SCHULZ, R., READY, R., BEACH, S. R., et al. (2006). Older spouses' perceptions of partners' chronic arthritis pain: Implications for spousal responses, support provision, and caregiving experiences. *Psychology and Aging, 21,* 222–230.

MARTIRE, L. M., LUSTIG, A. P., SCHULZ, R., MILLER, G. E., & HELGESON, V. S. (2004). Is it beneficial to involve a family member? A meta-analysis of psychosocial interventions for chronic illness. *Health Psychology, 23,* 599–611.

MARTIRE, L. M., & SCHULZ, R. (2001). Informal caregiving to older adults: Health effects of providing and receiving care. In A. BAUM, T. A. REVENSON, & J. E. SINGER (Eds.), *Handbook of health psychology* (pp. 477–491). Mahwah, NJ: Erlbaum.

MARVEL, M. K., EPSTEIN, R. M., FLOWERS, K., & BECKMAN, H. B. (1999). Soliciting the patient's agenda: Have we improved? *Journal of the American Medical Association, 281,* 283–287.

MARX, M. H., & HILLIX, W. A. (1963). *Systems and theories in psychology.* New York: McGraw-Hill.

MASLACH, C., & JACKSON, S. E. (1982). Burnout in health professions: A social psychological analysis. In G. S. SANDERS & J. SULS (Eds.), *Social psychology of health and illness* (pp. 227–251). Hillsdale, NJ: Erlbaum.

MASLACH, C., SCHAUFELI, W. B., & LEITER, M. P. (2001). Job burnout. *Annual Review of Psychology, 52,* 397–422.

MASON, J. W. (1975). A historical view of the stress field. *Journal of Human Stress, 1,* 22–36.

MASTERS, K. S. (2004). Religion and health. In A. J. CHRISTENSEN, R. MARTIN, & J. M. SMYTH (Eds.), *Encyclopedia of health psychology* (pp. 249–251). New York: Kluwer.

MASTERS, K. S., HILL, R. D., KIRCHER, J. C., BENSON, T. L. L., & FALLON, J. A. (2004). Religious orientation, aging, and blood pressure reactivity to interpersonal and cognitive stressors. *Annals of Behavioral Medicine, 28,* 171–178.

MASTERS, K. S., SPIELMANS, G. I., & GOODSON, J. T. (2006). Are there demonstrable effects of distant intercessory prayer? A meta-analytic review. *Annals of Behavioral Medicine, 32,* 21–26.

MATA, J., THOMPSON, R. J., & GOTLIB, I. H. (2010). BDNF genotype moderates the relation between physical activity and depressive symptoms. *Health Psychology, 29,* 130–133.

MATARAZZO, J. D. (1982). Behavioral health's challenge to academic, scientific, and professional psychology. *American Psychologist, 37,* 1–14.

MATHEWS, A., & RIDGEWAY, V. (1984). Psychological preparation for surgery. In A. STEPTOE & A. MATHEWS (Eds.), *Health care and human behaviour* (pp. 231–259). London: Academic Press.

MATICKA-TYNDALE, E. (1991). Sexual scripts and AIDS prevention: Variations in adherence to safer-sex guidelines by heterosexual adolescents. *Journal of Sex Research, 28,* 45–66.

MATSON-KOFFMAN, D. M., GOETZEL, R. Z., ANWURI, V. V., SHORE, K. K., ORENSTEIN, D., & LAPIER, T. (2005). Heart-healthy and stroke free: Successful business strategies to prevent cardiovascular disease. *American Journal of Preventive Medicine, 29*, 113–121.

MATTES, R. D., ARNOLD, C., & BORAAS, M. (1987a). Learned food aversions among cancer chemotherapy patients. *Cancer, 60*, 2576–2580.

MATTES, R. D., ARNOLD, C., & BORAAS, M. (1987b). Management of learned food aversions in cancer patients receiving chemotherapy. *Cancer Treatment Reports, 71*, 1071–1078.

MATTHEWS, C. E., CHEN, K. Y., FREEDSON, P. S., BUCHOWSKI, M. S., BEECH, B. M., et al. (2008). Amount of time spent in sedentary behaviors in the United States, 2003–2004. *American Journal of Epidemiology, 167*, 875–881.

MATTHEWS, K. A., & ANGULO, J. (1980). Measurement of the Type A behavior pattern in children: Assessment of children's competitiveness, impatience-anger, and aggression. *Child Development, 51*, 466–475.

MATTHEWS, K. A., & GUMP, B. B. (2002). Chronic work stress and marital dissolution increase risk of posttrial mortality in men from the multiple risk factor intervention trial. *Archives of Internal Medicine, 162*, 309–315.

MATTHEWS, K. A., OWENS, J. F., KULLER, L. H., SUTTON-TYRRELL, K., LASSILA, H. C., & WOLFSON, S. K. (1998). Stress-induced pulse pressure change predicts women's carotid atherosclerosis. *Stroke, 29*, 1525–1530.

MATTHEWS, K. A., SCHWARTZ, J., COHEN, S., & SEEMAN, T. (2006). Diurnal cortisol decline is related to coronary calcification: CARDIA Study. *Psychosomatic Medicine, 68*, 657–661.

MATTHEWS, K. A., ZHU, S., TUCKER, D. C., & WHOOLEY, M. A. (2006). Blood pressure reactivity to psychological stress and coronary calcification in the Coronary Artery Risk Development in Young Adults Study. *Hypertension, 47*, 391–395.

MATTICK, R. P., KIMBER, J., BREEN, C., & DAVOLI, M. (2003). Buprenorphine maintenance versus placebo or methadone maintenance for opioid dependence. *Cochrane Database of Systematic Reviews*, Issue 2. Retrieved (10-5-2006) from http://mrw.interscience.wiley.com. DOI:10.1002/14651858.CD002207.pub2.

MATTSON, M. E., POLLACK, E. S., & CULLEN, J. W. (1987). What are the odds that smoking will kill you? *American Journal of Public Health, 77*, 425–431.

MAUDE-GRIFFIN, P. M., HOHENSTEIN, J. M., HUMFLEET, G. L., REILLY, P. M., TUSEL, D. J., & HALL, S. M. (1998). Superior efficacy of cognitive-behavioral therapy for urban crack cocaine abusers: Main and matching effects. *Journal of Consulting and Clinical Psychology, 66*, 832–836.

MAUKSCH, L. B., DUGDALE, D. C., DODSON, S., & EPSTEIN, R. (2008). Relationship, communication, and efficiency in the medical encounter. *Archives of Internal Medicine, 168*, 1387–1395.

MAYER, W. (1983). Alcohol abuse and alcoholism: The psychologist's role in prevention, research, and treatment. *American Psychologist, 38*, 1116–1121.

MAYNARD, L. M., GALUSKA, D. A., BLANCK, H. M., & SERDULA, M. K. (2003). Maternal perceptions of weight status of children. *Pediatrics, 111*, 1226–1231.

MAYS, V. M., COCHRAN, S. D., & BARNES, N. W. (2007). Race, race-based discrimination, and health outcomes among African Americans. *Annual Review of Psychology, 58*, 201–225.

MAZZE, R. S., SHAMOON, H., PASMANTIER, R., LUCIDO, D., MURPHY, J., et al. (1984). Reliability of blood glucose monitoring by patients with diabetes mellitus. *American Journal of Medicine, 77*, 211–217.

MAZZONI, G., FOAN, L., HYLAND, M. E., & KIRSCH, I. (2010). The effects of observation and gender on psychogenic symptoms. *Health Psychology, 29*, 181–185.

MCADOO, W. G., WEINBERGER, M. H., MILLER, J. Z., FEINBERG, N. S., & GRIM, C. E. (1990). Race and gender influence hemodynamic responses to psychological and physical stimuli. *Journal of Hypertension, 8*, 961–967.

MCALLISTER-SISTILLI, C. G., CAGGIULA, A. R., KNOPF, S., ROSE, C. A., MILLER, A. L., & DONNY, E. C. (1998). The effects of nicotine on the immune system. *Psychoneuroendocrinology, 23*, 175–187.

MCCABE, P. M., GONZALES, J. A., ZAIAS, J., SZETO, A., KUMAR, M., et al. (2002). Social environment influences the progression of atherosclerosis in the watanabe heritable hyperlipidemic rabbit. *Circulation, 105*, 354–359.

MCCABE, S. E., SCHULENBERG, J. E., JOHNSTON, L. D., O'MALLEY, P. M., BACHMAN, J. G., & KLOSKA. D. D. (2005). Selection and socialization effects of fraternities and sororities on US college student substance use: A multi-cohort national longitudinal study. *Addiction, 100*, 512–524.

MCCAFFERY, J. M., FRASURE-SMITH, N., DUBÉ, M. P., THÉEROUX, P., ROULEAU, G. A., et al., (2006). Common genetic vulnerability to depressive symptoms and coronary artery disease: A review and development of candidate genes related to inflammation and serotonin. *Psychosomatic Medicine, 68*, 187–200.

MCCAFFERY, J. M., PAPANDONATOS, G. D., STANTON, C., LLOYD-RICHARDON, E. E., & NIAURA, R. (2008). Depressive symptoms and cigarette smoking in twins form the National Longitudinal Study of Adolescent Health. *Health Psychology, 27*(Suppl.), S207–S215.

MCCAFFERY, J. M., POGUE-GEILE, M. F., MULDOON, M. F., DEBSKI, T. T., WING, R. R., & MANUCK, S. B. (2001). The nature of the association between diet and serum lipods in the community: A twin study. *Health Psychology, 20*, 341–350.

MCCAHON, C. P. (1991). Why did Martha want her husband to deteriorate? *Nursing, 21*(4), 44–46.

MCCAIN, N. L., GRAY, D. P., ELSWICK, R. K., ROBINS, J. W., TUCK, I., et al. (2008). A randomized clinical trial of alternative stress management interventions in persons with HIV infection. *Journal of Consulting and Clinical Psychology, 76*, 431–441.

MCCARTY, D. (1985). Environmental factors in substance abuse: The microsetting. In M. GALIZIO & S. A. MAISTO (Eds.), *Determinants of substance abuse: Biological, psychological, and environmental factors* (pp. 247–281). New York: Plenum.

MCCAUL, K. D., HOCKEMEYER, J. R., JOHNSON, R. J., ZETOCHA, K., QUINLAN, K., & GLASGOW, R. E. (2006). Motivation to quit using cigarettes: A review. *Addictive Behaviors, 31*, 42–56.

McCaul, K. D., & Malott, J. M. (1984). Distraction and coping with pain. *Psychological Bulletin*, 95, 516–533.

McCaul, K. D., Monson, N., & Maki, R. H. (1992). Does distraction reduce pain-produced distress among college students? *Health Psychology*, 11, 210–217.

McClellan, A. T., Arndt, I. O., Metzger, D. S., Woody, G. E., & O'Brien, C. P. (1993). The effects of psychosocial services in substance abuse treatment. *Journal of the American Medical Association*, 269, 1953–1959.

McClintic, J. R. (1985). *Physiology of the human body* (3rd ed.). New York: Wiley.

McConnell, S., Biglan, A., & Severson, H. H. (1984). Adolescents' compliance with self-monitoring and physiological assessment of smoking in natural environments. *Journal of Behavioral Medicine*, 7, 115–122.

McCoy, J. M., & Evans, G. W. (2005). Physical work environment. In J. Barling, E. K. Kelloway, & M. R. Frone (Eds.), *Handbook of work stress* (pp. 219–246). Thousand Oaks, CA: Sage.

McCoy, S. B., Gibbons, F. X., Reis, T. J., Gerrard, M., Luus, C. A. E., & Von Wald Sufka, A. (1992). Perceptions of smoking risk as a function of smoking status. *Journal of Behavioral Medicine*, 15, 469–488.

McCracken, L. M. (2005). Social context and acceptance of chronic pain: The role of solicitous and punishing responses. *Pain*, 113, 155–159.

McCracken, L. M., & Eccleston, C. (2005). A prospective study of pain and patient functioning with chronic pain. *Pain*, 118, 164–169.

McCracken, L. M., Vowles, K. E., & Eccleston, C. (2005). Acceptance-based treatment for persons with complex, long standing chronic pain: A preliminary analysis of treatment outcome in comparison to a waiting phase. *Behaviour Research and Therapy*, 43, 1335–1346.

McCrady, B. S. (1988). Alcoholism. In E. A. Blechman & K. D. Brownell (Eds.), *Handbook of behavioral medicine for women* (pp. 356–368). New York: Pergamon.

McCrady, B. S., & Irvine, S. (1989). Self-help groups. In R. K. Hester & W. R. Miller (Eds.), *Handbook of alcoholism treatment approaches: Effective alternatives* (pp. 153–169). New York: Pergamon.

McDaniel, S., & Campbell, T. L. (1986). Physicians and family therapists: The risk of collaboration. *Family Systems Medicine*, 4, 4–8.

McDaniel, S. H., & Fogarty, C. T. (2009). What primary care psychology has to offer the Patient-Centered Medical Home. *Professional Psychology*, 40, 483–497.

McDonald, R. V., & Siegel, S. (2004). Intra-administration associations and withdrawal symptoms: Morphine-elicited morphine withdrawal. *Experimental and Clinical Psychopharmacology*, 12, 3–11.

McEvoy, S. P., Stevenson, M. R., McCartt, A. T., Woodward, M., Haworth, C., & Palamara, P. (2005). Role of mobile phones in motor vehicle crashes resulting in hospital attendance: A case-crossover study. *British Medical Journal*. Retrieved (11-16-2006) from http://www.bmj.com. DOI:10.1136/bmj.38537.397512.55.

McEwen, B. S. (2006). Sleep deprivation as a neurobiologic and physiologic stressor: Allostasis and allostatic load. *Metabolism Clinical and Experimental*, 55, S20–S23.

McEwen, B. S., & Stellar, E. (1993). Stress and the individual: Mechanisms leading to disease. *Archives of Internal Medicine*, 153, 2093–2101.

McFarlane, A. H., Norman, G. R., Streiner, D. L., & Roy, R. G. (1983). The process of social stress: Stable, reciprocal, and mediating relationships. *Journal of Health and Social Behavior*, 24, 160–173.

McGehee, D. S., Heath, M. J. S., Gelber, S., Devay, P., & Role, L. W. (1995). Nicotine enhancement of fast excitatory transmission in CNS by presynaptic receptors. *Science*, 269, 1692–1696.

McGinnis, J. M., & Lee, P. R. (1995). Healthy People 2000 at mid decade. *Journal of the American Medical Association*, 273, 1123–1129.

McGinnis, J. M., Shopland, D., & Brown, C. (1987). Tobacco and health: Trends in smoking and smokeless tobacco consumption in the United States. *Annual Review of Public Health*, 8, 441–467.

McGrady, A., Conran, P., Dickey, D., Garman, D., Farris, E., & Schumann-Brzezinski, C. (1992). The effects of biofeedback-assisted relaxation on cell-mediated immunity, cortisol, and white blood cell count in healthy adult subjects. *Journal of Behavioral Medicine*, 15, 343–354.

McGrady, A., & Higgins, J. T. (1990). Effect of repeated measurements of blood pressure in essential hypertension: Role of anxiety. *Journal of Behavioral Medicine*, 13, 93–101.

McGrath, P. A., & Gillespie, J. (2001). Pain assessment in children and adolescents. In D. C. Turk & R. Melzack (Eds.), *Handbook of pain assessment* (2nd ed., pp. 97–118). New York: Guilford.

McGrath, P. A., & Hillier, L. M. (1996). Controlling children's pain. In R. J. Gatchel & D. C. Turk (Eds.), *Psychological approaches to pain management: A practitioner's handbook* (pp. 331–370). New York: Guilford.

McGregor, B. A., Antoni, M. H., Boyers, A., Alferi, S. M., Blomberg, B. B., & Carver, C. S. (2004). Cognitive-behavioral stress management increases benefit finding and immune function among women with early-stage breast cancer. *Journal of Psychosomatic Research*, 56, 1–8.

McGuigan, F. J. (1999). *Encyclopedia of stress*. Boston: Allyn & Bacon.

McGuire, F. L. (1982). Treatment of the drinking driver. *Health Psychology*, 1, 137–152.

McGuire, M. T., Wing, R. R., Klem, M. L., Lang, W., & Hill, J. O. (1999). What predicts weight regain in a group of successful weight losers? *Journal of Consulting and Clinical Psychology*, 67, 177–185.

McHugh, R. K., & Barlow, D. H. (2010). The dissemination and implementation of evidence-based psychological treatments. *American Psychologist*, 65, 73–84.

MCILWAIN, H. H., SILVERFIELD, J. C., BURNETTE, M. C., & BRUCE, D. F. (1991). *Winning with arthritis*. New York: Wiley.

MCKAY, J. R., LYNCH, K. G., SHEPARD, D. S., RATICHEK, S., MORRISON, R., et al. (2004). The effectiveness of telephone-based continuing care in the clinical management of alcohol and cocaine use disorders: 12-month outcomes. *Journal of Consulting and Clinical Psychology*, 72, 967–979.

MCKELLAR, J., STEWART, E., & HUMPHREYS, K. (2003). Alcoholics Anonymous involvement and positive alcohol-related outcomes: Cause, consequence, or just a correlate? A prospective 2-year study of 2,319 alcohol-dependent men. *Journal of Consulting and Clinical Psychology*, 71, 302–308.

MCKINLAY, J. B. (1975). Who is really ignorant—Physician or patient? *Journal of Health and Social Behavior*, 16, 3–11.

MD (March of Dimes) (2010). *Birth defects: Quick reference fact sheet*. Retrieved (3-4-2010) from http://www.marchofdimes.com/professionals.

MEAD, M., & NEWTON, N. (1967). Cultural patterning of perinatal behavior. In S. A. RICHARDSON & A. F. GUTTMACHER (Eds.), *Childbearing: Its social and psychological aspects* (pp. 142–244). Baltimore: Williams & Wilkins.

MEADER, N., LI, R., DES JARLAIS, D. C., & PILLING, S. (2010). Psychosocial interventions for reducing injection and sexual risk behaviour for preventing HIV in drug users. *Cochrane Database of Systematic Reviews*, Issue 1. Retrieved (1-30-2010) from http://www.thecochranelibrary.com. DOI:10.1002/14651858.CD007192.pub2.

MECHANIC, D. (1972). Social psychologic factors affecting the presentation of bodily complaints. *New England Journal of Medicine*, 286, 1132–1139.

MECHANIC, D. (1979). The stability of health and illness behavior: Results from a 16-year follow-up. *American Journal of Public Health*, 69, 1142–1145.

MEICHENBAUM, D., & CAMERON, R. (1983). Stress inoculation training: Toward a general paradigm for training coping skills. In D. MEICHENBAUM & M. E. JAREMKO (Eds.), *Stress reduction and prevention* (pp. 115–154). New York: Plenum.

MEICHENBAUM, D., & TURK, D. (1982). Stress, coping, and disease: A cognitive-behavioral perspective. In R. W. J. NEUFIELD (Ed.), *Psychological stress and psychopathology* (pp. 289–306). New York: McGraw-Hill.

MEISER-STEDMAN, R., DALGLEISH, T., GLUCKSMAN, E., YULE, W. & SMITH, P. (2009). Maladaptive cognitive appraisals mediate the evolution of posttraumatic stress reactions: A 6-month follow-up of child and adolescent assault and motor vehicle accident survivors. *Journal of Abnormal Psychology*, 118, 778–787.

MELAMED, B. G., & BUSH, J. P. (1985). Family factors in children with acute illness. In D. C. TURK & R. D. KERNS (Eds.), *Health, illness, and families: A life-span approach* (pp. 183–219). New York: Wiley.

MELAMED, B. G., DEARBORN, M., & HERMECZ, D. A. (1983). Necessary conditions for surgery preparation: Age and previous experience. *Psychosomatic Medicine*, 45, 517–525.

MELAMED, B. G., & SIEGEL, L. J. (1975). Reduction of anxiety in children facing hospitalization and surgery by use of filmed modeling. *Journal of Consulting and Clinical Psychology*, 43, 511–521.

MELCHART, D., STRENG, A., HOPPE, A., BRINKHAUS, B., WITT, C., et al. (2005). Acupuncture in patients with tension-type headache: Randomized controlled trial. *British Medical Journal*. DOI:10.1136/BMJ. 38512.405440.8F.

MELIN, B., LUNDBERG, U., SÖDERLUND, J., & GRANQVIST, M. (1999). Psychological and physiological stress reactions of male and female assembly workers: A comparison between two different forms of work organization. *Journal of Organizational Behavior*, 20, 47–61.

MELLINS, C. A., HAVENS, J. F., MCCASKILL, E. O., LEU, C. S., BRUDNEY, K., & CHESNEY, M. A. (2002). Mental health, substance use and disclosure are significantly associated with the medical treatment adherence of HIV-infected mothers. *Psychology, Health & Medicine*, 7, 451–460.

MELTZER, L. J., JOHNSON, S. B., PAPPACHAN, S., & SILVERSTEIN, J. (2003). Blood glucose estimations in adolescents with type 1 diabetes: Predictors of accuracy and error. *Journal of Pediatric Psychology*, 28, 203–211.

MELZACK, R. (1975). The McGill Pain Questionnaire: Major properties and scoring methods. *Pain*, 1, 277–299.

MELZACK, R., & KATZ, J. (2001). The McGill pain Questionnaire: Appraisal and current status. In D. C. TURK & R. MELZACK (Eds.), *Handbook of pain assessment* (2nd ed., pp. 35–52). New York: Guilford.

MELZACK, R., & KATZ, J. (2004). The gate control theory: Reaching for the brain. In T. HADJISTAVROPOULOS & K. D. CRAIG (Eds.), *Pain: Psychological perspectives* (pp. 13–34). Mahwah, NJ: Erlbaum.

MELZACK, R., & TORGERSON, W. S. (1971). On the language of pain. *Anesthesiology*, 34, 50–59.

MELZACK, R., & WALL, P. D. (1965). Pain mechanisms: A new theory. *Science*, 150, 971–979.

MELZACK, R., & WALL, P. D. (1982). *The challenge of pain*. New York: Basic Books.

MELZACK, R., WEISZ, A. Z., & SPRAGUE, L. T. (1963). Strategems for controlling pain: Contributions of auditory stimulation and suggestion. *Experimental Neurology*, 8, 239–247.

MENDELSON, B. K., & WHITE, D. R. (1985). Development of self-body-esteem in overweight youngsters. *Developmental Psychology*, 21, 90–96.

MENDELSON, T., THURSTON, R. C., KUBZANSKY, L. D. (2008). Affective and cardiovascular effects of experimentally-induced social status. *Health Psychology*, 27, 482–489.

MENEFEE, L. A., HAYTHORNTHWAITE, J. A., CLARK, M. R., & KOENIG, T. (1996, March). *The effect of social responses on pain coping strategies*. Paper presented at the meeting of the Society of Behavioral Medicine, Washington, DC.

MENKES, M. S., MATTHEWS, K. A., KRANTZ, D. S., LUNDBERG, U., MEAD, L. A., et al. (1989). Cardiovascular reactivity to the cold pressor test as a predictor of hypertension. *Hypertension*, 14, 524–530.

MENTE, A., DE KONING, L., SHANNON, H. S., & ANAND, S. S. (2009). A systematic review of the evidence supporting a causal link between dietary factor and coronary heart disease. *Archives of Internal Medicine, 169,* 659–669.

MENTZER, S. J., & SNYDER, M. L. (1982). The doctor and the patient: A psychological perspective. In G. S. SANDERS & J. SULS (Eds.), *Social psychology of health and illness* (pp. 161–181). Hillsdale, NJ: Erlbaum.

MERCADO, A. C., CARROLL, L. J., CASSIDY, J. D., & CÔTÉ, P. (2005). Passive coping is a risk factor for disabling neck or low back pain. *Pain, 117,* 51–57.

MEREDITH, H. V. (1978). *Human body growth in the first ten years of life.* Columbia, SC: The State Printing Company.

MEYER, A. J., NASH, J. D., MCALISTER, A. L., MACCOBY, N., & FARQUHAR, J. W. (1980). Skills training in a cardiovascular health education campaign. *Journal of Consulting and Clinical Psychology, 48,* 129–142.

MEYER, T. J., & MARK, M. M. (1995). Effects of psychosocial interventions with adult cancer patients: A meta-analysis of randomized experiments. *Health Psychology, 14,* 101–108.

MEYEROWITZ, B. E., RICHARDSON, J., HUDSON, S., & LEEDHAM, B. (1998). Ethnicity and cancer outcomes: Behavioral and psychosocial considerations. *Psychological Bulletin, 123,* 47–70.

MEYERS, R. J., MILLER, W. R., SMITH, J. E., & TONIGAN, J. S. (2002). A randomized trial of two methods for engaging treatment-refusing drug users through concerned significant others. *Journal of Consulting and Clinical Psychology, 70,* 1182–1185.

MEZUK, B., EATON, W. W., GOLDEN, S. H., & DING, Y. (2008). The influence of educational attainment on depression and risk of type 2 diabetes. *American Journal of Public Health. 98,* 1480–1485.

MICCINESI, G., FISCHER, S., PACI, E., ONWUTEAKA-PHILIPSEN, B. D., CARTWRIGHT, C., et al. (2005). Physicians' attitudes towards end-of-life decisions: A comparison between seven countries. *Social Science & Medicine, 60,* 1961–1974.

MICHELA, J. L. (1987). Interpersonal and individual impacts of a husband's heart attack. In A. BAUM & J. E. SINGER (Eds.), *Handbook of psychology and health* (Vol. 5, pp. 225–301). Hillsdale, NJ: Erlbaum.

MICHIE, S., ABRAHAM, D., WHITTINGTON, C., MCATEER, J., & GUPTA, S. (2009). Effective techniques in healthy eating and physical activity interventions: A meta-regression. *Health Psychology, 28,* 690–701.

MICHIE, S., & PRESTWICH, A. (2010). Are interventions theory-based? Development of a theory coding scheme. *Health Psychology, 29,* 1–8.

MIGLIORELLI, R., TESÓN, A., SABE, L., PETRACCHI, M., LEIGUARDA. R., & STARKSTEIN, S. E. (1995). Prevalence and correlates of dysthymia and major depression among patients with Alzheimer's disease. *American Journal of Psychiatry, 152,* 37–44.

MIKKELSSON, M., EL-METWALLY, A., KAURIAINEN, H., AUVINEN, A., MACFARLANE, G. J., & SALMINEN, J. J. (2008). Onset, prognosis and risk factors for widespread pain in schoolchildren: A prospective 4-year follow-up study. *Pain, 138,* 681–687.

MILES, F., & MEEHAN, J. W. (1995). Visual discrimination of pigmented skin lesions. *Health Psychology, 14,* 171–177.

MILLAR, M. (2005). The effects of perceived stress on reactions to messages designed to increase health behaviors. *Journal of Behavioral Medicine, 28,* 425–432.

MILLER, B., & CAFASSO, L. (1992). Gender differences in caregiving: Fact or artifact? *Gerontologist, 32,* 498–507.

MILLER, B. D., & WOOD, B. L. (1994). Psychophysiologic reactivity in asthmatic children: A cholinergically mediated confluence of pathways. *Journal of the American Academy of Child and Adolescent Psychiatry, 33,* 1236–1245.

MILLER, C. K., & GUTSCHALL, M. (2009). Arandomized trial about glycemic index and glycemic load improves outcomes among adult with type 2 diabetes. *Health Education & Behavior, 36,* 615–626.

MILLER, G. E. (2009). In search of integrated specificity: Comment on Denson, Spanovic, and Miller (2009). *Psychological Bulletin 135,* 854–856.

MILLER, G. E., CHEN, E., FOK, A. K., WALKER, H., LIM, A., et al. (2009). Low early-life social class leaves a biological residue manifested by decreased glucocorticoid and increased proinflammatory signaling. PNAS *Proceedings of the National Academy of Sciences of the United States of America, 106,* 14716–14721.

MILLER, G. E., GAUDIN, A., ZYSK, E & CHEN, E. (2009), Parental support and cytokine activity in childhood asthma: The role of glucocorticoid sensitivity. *Journal of Allergy and Clinical Immunology, 123,* 824–830.

MILLER, N. E. (1959). Liberalization of basic S-R concepts: Extensions to conflict behavior, motivation, and social learning. In S. KOCH (Ed.), *Psychology: A study of a science* (Vol. 2, pp. 196–292). New York: McGraw-Hill.

MILLER, N. E. (1978). Biofeedback and visceral learning. *Annual Review of Psychology, 29,* 373–404.

MILLER, R. H., & LUFT, H. S. (1994). Managed care plans: Characteristics, growth, and premium performance. *Annual Review of Public Health, 15,* 437–459.

MILLER, S. B., TURNER, J. R., SHERWOOD, A., BROWNLEY, K. A., HINDERLITER, A. L., & LIGHT, K. C. (1995). Parental history of hypertension and cardiovascular response to stress in black and white men. *International Journal of Behavioral Medicine, 2,* 339–357.

MILLER, S. M., BRODY, D. S., & SUMMERTON, J. (1987). Styles of coping with threat: Implications for health. *Journal of Personality and Social Psychology, 54,* 142–148.

MILLER, S. M., & GREEN, M. L. (1984). Coping with stress and frustration: Origins, nature, and development. In M. LEWIS & C. SAARNI (Eds.), *The socialization of emotions* (Vol. 5, pp. 263–314). New York: Plenum.

MILLER, S. M., & MANGAN, C. E. (1983). Interacting effects of information and coping style in adapting to gynecologic stress: Should the doctor tell all? *Journal of Personality and Social Psychology, 45,* 223–236.

MILLER, T. D., BALADY, G. J., & FLETCHER, G. F. (1997). Exercise and its role in the prevention and rehabilitation of cardiovascular disease. *Annals of Behavioral Medicine*, 19, 220–229.

MILLER, T. Q., TURNER, C. W., TINDALE, R. S., POSAVAC, E. J., & DUGONI, B. L. (1991). Reasons for the trend toward null findings in research on Type A behavior. *Psychological Bulletin*, 110, 469–485.

MILLER, W. R. (1989). Increasing motivation for change. In R. K. HESTER & W. R. MILLER (Eds.), *Handbook of alcoholism treatment approaches: Effective alternatives* (pp. 67–80). New York: Pergamon.

MILLER, W. R., & HESTER, R. K. (1980). Treating the problem drinker: Modern approaches. In W. R. MILLER (Ed.), *The addictive behaviors: Treatment of alcoholism, drug abuse, smoking, and obesity* (pp. 11–141). New York: Pergamon.

MILLER, W. R., & HESTER, R. K. (1986). Inpatient alcoholism treatment: Who benefits? *American Psychologist*, 41, 794–805.

MILLER, W. R., MEYERS, R. J., & TONIGAN, J. S. (1999). Engaging the unmotivated in treatment for alcohol problems: A comparison of three strategies for intervention through family members. *Journal of Consulting and Clinical Psychology*, 67, 688–697.

MILLER, W. R., & ROLLNICK, S. (1991). *Motivational interviewing: Preparing people to change addictive behaviors*. New York: Guilford.

MILLER, W. R., & ROSE, G. S. (2009). Toward a theory of motivational interviewing. *American Psychologist*, 64, 527–537.

MILLER JOHNSON, S., EMERY, R. E., MARVIN, R. S., CLARKE, W., LOVINGER, R., & MARTIN, M. (1994). Parent-child relationships and the management of insulin-dependent diabetes mellitus. *Journal of Consulting and Clinical Psychology*, 62, 603–610.

MILLING, L. S., REARDON, J. M., & CAROSELLA, G. M. (2006). Mediation and moderation of psychological pain treatments: Response expectancies and hypnotic suggestibility. *Journal of Consulting and Clinical Psychology*, 74, 253–262.

MILLING, L. S., SHORES, J. S., COURSEN, E. L., MENARIO, D. J., & FARRIS, C. D. (2007). Response expectancies, treatment credibility, and hypnotic suggestibility: Mediator and moderator effects in hypnotic and cognitive-behavioral pain interventions. *Annals of Behavioral Medicine*, 33, 167–178.

MILLS, P. J., & ZIEGLER, M. G. (2008). Sympathetic hormones in health psychology research. In L. LEUKEN & L. C. GALLO (Eds.), *Handbook of physiological research methods in health psychology* (pp. 75–94). Thousand Oaks, CA: Sage.

MINOR, M. A., & SANFORD, M. K. (1993). Physical interventions in the management of pain in arthritis. *Arthritis Care and Research*, 6, 197–206.

MISOVICH, S. J., FISHER, J. D., & FISHER, W. A. (1997). Close relationships and elevated HIV risk behavior: Evidence and possible underlying psychological processes. *Review of General Psychology*, 1, 72–107.

MITTAN, R. J. (2009). Psychosocial treatment programs in epilepsy: A review. *Epilepsy & Behavior*, 16, 371–380.

MITTLEMAN, M. A., MINTZER, D., MACLURE, M., TOFLER, G. H., SHERWOOD, J. B., & MULLER, J. E. (1999). Triggering of myocardial infarction by cocaine. *Circulation*, 99, 2737–2741.

MIZOGUCHI, H., O'SHEA, J. J., LONGO, D. L., LOEFFLER, C. M., MCVICAR, D. W., & OCHOA, A. C. (1992). Alterations in signal transduction molecules in T lymphocytes from tumor-bearing mice. *Science*, 258, 1795–1798.

MOFFET, J. K., TORGERSON, D., BELL-SYER, S., JACKSON, D., LLEWLYN-PHILLIPS, H., et al. (1999). Randomized controlled trial of exercise for low back pain: Clinical outcomes, costs, and preferences. *British Medical Journal*, 319, 279–283.

MOHR, D. C., HART, S., & VELLA, L. (2007). Reduction in disability in a randomized controlled trial of telephone-administered cognitive-behavioral therapy. *Health Psychology*, 26, 554–563.

MOLLOY, G. J., PERKINS-PORRAS, L., STRIKE, P. C. & STEPTOE, A. (2008). Social networks and partner stress as predictors of adherence to medication, rehabilitation attendance, and quality of life following acute coronary syndrome. *Health Psychology*, 27, 52–58.

MOLTON, I. R., SIEGEL, S. D., PENEDO, F. J., DAHN, J. R., KINSINGER, D., et al. (2008). Promoting recovery of sexual functioning after radical prostatectomy with group-based stress management: The role of interpersonal sensitivity. *Journal of Psychosomatic Research*, 64, 527–536.

MONIN, J. K., MARTIRE, L. M., SCHULZ, R., & CLARK, M. S. (2009). Willingness to express emotions to caregiving spouses. *Emotion*, 9, 101–106.

MONIN, J. K., & SCHULZ, R. (2009). Interpersonal effects of suffering in older adult caregiving relationships. *Psychology and Aging*, 24, 681–695.

MONROE, S. M. (2008). Modern approaches to conceptualizing and measuring human life stress. *Annual Review of Clinical Psychology*, 4, 33–52.

MONTGOMERY, D. D. (2004). Biofeedback. In A. J. CHRISTENSEN, R. MARTIN, & J. M. SMYTH (Eds.), *Encyclopedia of health psychology* (pp. 26–28). New York: Kluwer.

MONTGOMERY, G. H., & BOVBJERG, D. H. (2003). Expectations of chemotherapy-related nausea: Emotional and experiential predictors. *Annals of Behavioral Medicine*, 25, 48–54.

MONTI, P. M., ROHSENOW, D. J., SWIFT, R. M., GULLIVER, S. B., COLBY, S. M., et al. (2001). Naltrexone and cue exposure with coping and communication skills training for alcoholics: Treatment process and 1-year outcomes. *Alcoholism: Clinical and Experimental Research*, 25, 1634–1647.

MOORE, B. A., AUGUSTSON, E. M., MOSER, R. P., & BUDNEY, A. J. (2005). Respiratory effects of marijuana and tobacco use in a U.S. sample. *Journal of General Internal Medicine*, 20, 33–37.

MOORE, L. V., ROUX, A. V. D., NETTLETON, J. A., JACOBS, D. R., & FRANCO, M. (2009). Fast-food consumption, diet quality, and neighborhood exposure to fast food: The Multi-Ethnic

Study of Atherosclerosis. *American Journal of Epidemiology*, 170, 29–36.

MOORE, P. J., KULIK, J. A., & MAHLER, H. I. M. (1998). Stress and multiple potential affiliates: Does misery choose miserable company? *Journal of Applied Biobehavioral Research*, 3, 81–95.

MOORE, S. M., BARLING, N. R., & HOOD, B. (1998). Predicting testicular and breast self-examination behaviour: A test of the theory of reasoned action. *Behaviour Change*, 15, 41–49.

MOORE, S. M., CHARVAT, J. M., GORDON, N. H., PASHKOW, F., RIBISL, P., et al. (2006). Effects of a CHANGE intervention to increase exercise maintenance following cardiac events. *Annals of Behavioral Medicine*, 31, 53–62.

MOOS, R. H. (1982). Coping with acute health crises. In T. MILLON, C. GREEN, & R. MEAGHER (Eds.), *Handbook of clinical health psychology* (pp. 129–151). New York: Plenum.

MOOS, R. H., & MOOS, B. S. (2004). Long-term influence of duration and frequency of participation in Alcoholics Anonymous on individuals with alcohol use disorders. *Journal of Consulting and Clinical Psychology*, 72, 81–90.

MOOS, R. H., & SCHAEFER, J. A. (1986). Life transitions and crises: A conceptual overview. In R. H. MOOS (Ed.), *Coping with life crises: An integrated approach* (pp. 3–33). New York: Plenum.

MORA, P. A., HALM, E., LEVENTHAL, H., & CERIC, F. (2007). Elucidating the relationship between negative affectivity and symptoms: The role of illness-specific affective responses. *Annals of Behavioral Medicine*, 34, 77–86.

MORAN, P. M., CHRISTENSEN, A. J., & LAWTON, W. J. (1997). Social support and conscientiousness in hemodialysis adherence. *Annals of Behavioral Medicine*, 19, 333–338.

MORAN, T. E. (2004). Hypnosis. In A. J. CHRISTENSEN, R. MARTIN, & J. M. SMYTH (Eds.), *Encyclopedia of health psychology* (p. 145). New York: Kluwer.

MORELAND, J., & THOMPSON, M. A. (1994). Efficacy of electromyographic biofeedback compared with conventional physical therapy for upper-extremity function in patients following stroke: A research overview and meta-analysis. *Physical Therapy*, 74, 534–547.

MORGENSTERN, J., BUX, D. A., PARSONS, J., HAGMAN, B. T., WAINBERG, M., & IRWIN, T. (2009). Randomized trial to reduce club drug use and HIV risk behaviors among men who have sex with men. *Journal of Consulting and Clinical Psychology*, 77, 645–656.

MORIN, C. M., VALLIÉRES, A., GUAY, B., IVERS, H., SAVARD, J., et al. (2009). Cognitive behavioral therapy, singly and combined with medication, for persistent insomnia. *Journal of the American Medical Association*, 301, 2005–2016.

MORLEY, S., ECCLESTON, C., & WILLIAMS, A. (1999). Systematic review and meta-analysis of randomized controlled trials of cognitive behaviour therapy and behaviour therapy for chronic pain in adults, excluding headache. *Pain*, 80, 1–13.

MORLING, B., & EVERED, S. (2006). Secondary control reviewed and defined. *Psychological Bulletin*, 132, 269–296.

MORRONGIELLO, B. A., CORBETT, M., & BELLISSIMO, A. (2008). "Do as I say, not as I do": Family influences on children's safety and risk behavior. *Health Psychology*, 27, 498–503.

MORROW, G. R., ASBURY, R., HAMMON, S., DOBKIN, P., CARUSO, L., et al. (1992). Comparing the effectiveness of behavioral treatment for chemotherapy-induced nausea and vomiting when administered by oncologists, oncology nurses, and clinical psychologists. *Health Psychology*, 11, 250–256.

MORZORATI, S. L., RAMCHANDANI, V. A., FLURY, L., LI, T.-K., & O'CONNOR, S. (2002). Self-reported subjective perception of intoxication reflects family history of alcoholism when breath alcohol levels are constant. *Alcoholism: Clinical and Experimental Research*, 26, 1299–1306.

MOSELEY, J. B., O'MALLEY, K., PETERSEN, N. J., MENKE, T. J., BRODY, B. A., et al. (2002). A controlled trial of arthroscopic surgery for osteoarthritis of the knee. *New England Journal of Medicine*, 347, 81–88.

MOSER, D. K., RIEGEL, B., MCKINLEY, S., DOERING, L. V., AN, K., & SHEAHAN, S. (2007). Impact of anxiety and perceived control on in-hospital complications after acute myocardial infarction. *Psychosomatic Medicine*, 69, 10–16.

MOSKOWITZ, J. T., FOLKMAN, S., COLLETTE, L., & VITTINGHOFF, E. (1996). Coping and mood during AIDS-related caregiving and bereavement. *Annals of Behavioral Medicine*, 18, 49–57.

MOSKOWITZ, J. T., HULT, J. R., BUSSOLARI, C., & ACREE, M. (2009). What works in coping with HIV? A meta-analysis with implications for coping with serious illness. *Psychological Bulletin*, 135, 121–141.

MOSLEY, T. H., PENZIEN, D. B., JOHNSON, C. A., WITTROCK, D., RUBMAN, S., et al. (1990). *Coping with stress in headache sufferers and no-headache controls*. Paper presented at the meeting of the Society of Behavioral Medicine, Chicago.

MOSS, G. E., DIELMAN, T. E., CAMPANELLI, P. C., LEECH, S. L., HARLAN, W. R., et al. (1986). Demographic correlates of SI assessments of Type A behavior. *Psychosomatic Medicine*, 48, 564–574.

MOYER, A. (1997). Psychosocial outcomes of breast-conserving surgery versus mastectomy: A meta-analytic review. *Health Psychology*, 16, 284–298.

MOYER, A., & FINNEY, J. W. (2002). Outcomes for untreated individuals involved in randomized trials of alcohol treatment. *Journal of Substance Abuse Treatment*, 23, 247–252.

MOYER, C. A., ROUNDS, J., & HANNUM, J. W. (2004). A meta-analysis of massage therapy research. *Psychological Bulletin*, 130, 3–18.

MOZAFFARIAN, D., KATAN, M. B., ASCHERIO, A., STAMPFER, M., & WILLETT, W. C. (2006). Trans fatty acids and cardiovascular disease. *New England Journal of Medicine*, 354, 1601–1613.

MUKAMAL, K. J., & RIMM, E. B. (2001). Alcohol's effects on the risk for coronary heart disease. *Alcohol Research and Health*, 25, 255–261.

MULDOON, M. F., & MANUCK, S. B. (1992). Health through cholesterol reduction: Are there unforeseen risks? *Annals of Behavioral Medicine*, 14, 101–108.

MULDOON, M. F., MANUCK, S. B., & MATTHEWS, K. A. (1990). Lowering cholesterol concentrations and mortality: A quantitative review of primary prevention trials. *British Medical Journal, 301,* 309–314.

MULLAN, F. (1983). *Vital signs: A young doctor's struggle with cancer.* New York: Farrar, Straus, & Giroux.

MULLER, J. E., MITTLEMAN, M. A., MACLURE, M., SHERWOOD, J. B., TOFLER, G. H., et al. (1996). Triggering myocardial infarction by sexual activity: Low absolute risk and prevention by regular physical exertion. *Journal of the American Medical Association, 275,* 1405–1409.

MUMMERY, W. K., SCHOFIELD, G. M., STEELE, R., EAKIN, E. G., & BROWN, W. J. (2005). Occupational sitting time and overweight and obesity in Australian workers. *American Journal of Preventive Medicine, 29,* 91–97.

MURDAUGH, C. L. (1998). Problems with adherence in the elderly. In S. A. SHUMAKER, E. B. SCHRON, J. K. OCKENE, & W. L. MCBEE (Eds.), *The handbook of health behavior change* (2nd ed., pp. 357–376). New York: Springer.

MURPHY, L. B. (1974). Coping, vulnerability, and resilience in childhood. In G. V. COELHO, D. A. HAMBURG, & J. E. ADAMS (Eds.), *Coping and adaptation* (pp. 69–100). New York: Basic Books.

MURPHY, S., & BENNETT, P. (2004). Lifespan, gender and cross-cultural perspectives in health psychology. In S. SUTTON, A. BAUM, & M. JOHNSTON (Eds.), *The Sage handbook of health psychology* (pp. 241–269). London: Sage.

MURPHY-HOEFER, R., HYLAND, A., & HIGBEE, C. (2008). Perceived effectiveness of tobacco countermarketing advertisements among young adults. *American Journal of Health Behavior, 32,* 725–734.

MURRAY, D. M., DAVIS-HEARN, M., GOLDMAN, A. I., PIRIE, P., & LUEPKER, R. V. (1988). Four- and five-year follow-up results from four seventh-grade smoking prevention strategies. *Journal of Behavioral Medicine, 11,* 395–405.

MURRAY, D. M., PIRIE, P., LEUPKER, R. V., & PALLONEN, U. (1989). Five- and six-year follow-up results from four seventh-grade smoking prevention strategies. *Journal of Behavioral Medicine, 12,* 207–218.

MURRELL, J., FARLOW, M., GHETTI, B., & BENSON, M. D. (1991). A mutation in the amyloid precursor protein associated with hereditary Alzheimer's disease. *Science, 254,* 97–99.

MUSCAT, J. E., HARRIS, R. E., HALEY, N. J., & WYNDER, E. L. (1991). Cigarette smoking and plasma cholesterol. *American Heart Journal, 121,* 121–141.

MUSSELMAN, D. L., BOWLING, A., GILLES, N., LARSEN, H., BETAN, E. & PHILLIPS, L. S. (2007). The interrelationship of depression and diabetes. In A. STEPTOE (Ed.), *Depression and physical illness* (pp. 165–194), Cambridge, UK: Cambridge University Press.

MYERS, H. F. (2009). Ethnicity- and socio-economic status-related stresses in context: An integrated review and conceptual model. *Journal of Behavioral Medicine, 32,* 9–19.

MYUNG, S.-K., MCDONNELL, D. D., KAZINETS, G., SEO, H. G., & MOSKOWITZ, J. M. (2009). Effects of Web- and computer-based smoking cessation programs: Meta-analysis of randomized controlled trials. *Archives of Internal Medicine,* 69, 929–937.

NAAR-KING, S., WRIGHT, K., PARSONS, J. T., FREY, M., TEMPLIN, T., LAM, P., & MURPHY, D. (2006). Healthy Choices: Motivation enhancement therapy for health risk behaviors in HIV-positive youth. AIDS *Education and Prevention, 18,* 1–11.

NABI, H., KIVIMAKI, M., SABIA, S., DUGRAVOT, A., LAJNEF, M., MARMOT, M. G., & SINGH-MANOUX, A. (2009). Hostility and trajectories of body mass index over 19 years: the Whitehall II Study. *American Journal of Epidemiology, 169,* 347–354.

NAHVI, S, & COOPERMAN, N. A. (2009). Review: The need for smoking cessation among HIV-positive smokers. AIDS *Education and Prevention, 21,* 14–27.

NAQVI, N. H., RUDRAUF, D., DAMASIO, H., & BECHARA, A. (2007). Damage to the insula disrupts addiction to cigarette smoking. *Science, 315,* 531–534.

NASH, J. M., & THEBARGE, R. W. (2006). Understanding psychological stress, its biological processes, and impact on primary headache. *Headache, 46,* 1377–1386.

NASH, M. R. (2001). The truth and the hype of hypnosis. *Scientific American, 285*(1), 46–53.

NASH, S. S., & SMITH, M. J. (1982). Perception and coordination. In M. J. SMITH, J. A. GOODMAN, N. L. RAMSEY, & S. B. PASTERNACK (Eds.), *Child and family: Concepts in nursing practice* (pp. 1033–1088). New York: McGraw-Hill.

NATHAN, D. M., CLEARY, P. A., BACKLUND, J. Y., GENUTH, S. M., LACHIN, J. M., et al. (2005). Intensive diabetes treatment and cardiovascular disease in patients with type 1 diabetes. *New England Journal of Medicine, 353,* 2643–2653.

NATHAN, P. (1984). Johnson & Johnson's Live for Life: A comprehensive positive lifestyle change program. In J. D. MATARAZZO, S. M. WEISS, J. A. HERD, N. E. MILLER, & S. M. WEISS (Eds.), *Behavioral health: A handbook of health enhancement and disease prevention* (pp. 1064–1070). New York: Wiley.

NATHAN, P. E. (1986). Outcomes of treatment for alcoholism: Current data. *Annals of Behavioral Medicine, 8*(2–3), 40–46.

NAVARRO, A. M., SENN, K. L., MCNICHOLAS, L. J., KAPLAN, R. M., ROPPÉ, B., & CAMPO, M. C. (1998). *Por La Vita* model intervention enhances use of cancer screening tests among Latinas. *American Journal of Preventive Medicine, 15,* 32–41.

NAYAK, S. R., PAI, M. M., PRABHU, L. V., D'COSTA, S., & SHETTY, P. (2006). Anatomical organization of aortic arch variations in India: Embryological basis and review. *Jornal Vascular Brasileiro, 5*(2). DOI:10.1590/S1677-54492006000200004. Retrieved (1-6-2010) from http://www.scielo.br.

NAYLOR, M. T., KEEFE, F. J., BRIGIDI, B., NAUD, S., & HELZER, J. E. (2008). Therapeutic Interactive Voice Response for chronic pain reduction and relapse prevention. *Pain, 134,* 335–345.

NCADI (National Clearinghouse for Alcohol and Drug Information) (2000). *Drugs of abuse.* Retrieved (3-23-2000) from http://www.samhsa.gov.

NCADI (National Clearinghouse for Alcohol and Drug Information) (2006). *National Survey on Drug Use and Health 2005*. Retrieved (12-6-2006) from http://www.samhsa.gov.

NCCAM (National Center for Complementary and Alternative Medicine) (2006). *Health Information*. Retrieved (12-8-2006) from http://nccam.nih.gov.

NCHS (National Center for Health Statistics) (2006). *Health, United States, 2006*. Retrieved (12-3-2006) from http://www.cdc.gov/nchs.

NCHS (National Center for Health Statistics) (2009a). *Health, United States, 2008*. Retrieved (1-5-2010) from http://www.cdc.gov/nchs.

NCHS (National Center for Health Statistics) (2009b). *Summary health statistics for U.S. adults: National Health Interview Survey, 2008*. Retrieved (1-20-2010) from http://www.cdc.gov/nchs.

NEALEY-MOORE, J. B., SMITH, T. W., UCHINO, B. N., HAWKINS, M. W., & OLSON-CERNY, C. (2007). Cardiovascular reactivity during positive and negative marital interactions. *Journal of Behavioral Medicine*, 30, 6, 505–519.

NEGRI, E., LA VECCHIA, C., D'AVANZO, B., NOBILI, A., LA MALFA, R. G., et al. (1994). Acute myocardial infarction: Association with time since stopping smoking in Italy. *Journal of Epidemiology and Community Health*, 48, 129–133.

NEHEMKIS, A. M., & GERBER, K. E. (1986). Compliance and the quality of survival. In K. E. GERBER & A. M. NEHEMKIS (Eds.), *Compliance: The dilemma of the chronically ill* (pp. 73–97). New York: Springer.

NEIGHBORS, C. J., O'LEARY, A., & LABOUVIE, E. (1999). Domestically violent and nonviolent male inmates' responses to their partners' requests for condom use: Testing a social-information processing model. *Health Psychology*, 18, 427–431.

NEMETZ, P. N., ROGER, V. L., RANSOM, J. E., BAILEY, K. R., EDWARDS, W. D., & LEIBSON, C. L. (2008). Recent trends in the prevalence of coronary disease: A population-based autopsy study of nonnatural deaths. *Archives of Internal Medicine*, 168, 264–270.

NESTORIUC, Y., RIEF, W., & MARTIN, A. (2008). Meta-analyis of biofeedback for tension-type headache: Efficacy, specificity, and treatment moderators. *Journal of Consulting and Clinical Psychology*, 76, 379–396.

NETTEN, A., BEBBINGTON, A., DARTON, F., & FORDER, J. (2001) *Care Homes for Older People, Vol. 1*. Retrieved (11-23-10) from http://www.pssru.ac.uk/pdf/chop1.pdf.

NEWCOMB, M. D., & BENTLER, P. M. (1986). Cocaine use among adolescents: Longitudinal associations with social context, psychopathology, and use of other substances. *Addictive Behaviors*, 11, 263–273.

NEWCOMB, M. D., MADDAHIAN, E., & BENTLER, P. M. (1986). Risk factors for drug use among adolescents: Concurrent and longitudinal analyses. *American Journal of Public Health*, 76, 525–531.

NEWLIN, D. B., & THOMSON, J. B. (1991). Chronic tolerance and sensitization to alcohol in sons of alcoholics. *Alcoholism: Clinical and experimental research*, 15, 399–405.

NEWMAN, S. (1984a). Anxiety, hospitalization, and surgery. In R. FITZPATRICK, J. HINTON, S. NEWMAN, G. SCAMBLER, & J. THOMPSON (Eds.), *The experience of illness* (pp. 132–153). London: Tavistock.

NEWMAN, S. (1984b). The psychological consequences of cerebrovascular accident and head injury. In R. FITZPATRICK, J. HINTON, S. NEWMAN, G. SCAMBLER, & J. THOMPSON (Eds.), *The experience of illness* (pp. 179–202). London: Tavistock.

NEWSOM, J. T., MAHAN, T. L., ROOK, K. S., & KRAUSE, N. (2008). Stable negative social exchanges and health. *Health Psychology*, 27, 78–86.

NEWTON, J. L., SHETH, A., SHIN, J., PAIRMAN, J., WILTON, K., et al. (2009). Lower ambulatory blood pressure in chronic fatigue syndrome. *Psychosomatic Medicine*, 71, 361–365.

NEWTON, T. L. (2009). Cardiovascular functioning, personality, and the social world: The domain of hierarchical power. *Neuroscience and Biobehavioral Reviews*, 33, 145–159.

NEWTON-JOHN, T. R. O. (2002). Solicitousness and chronic pain: A critical review. *Pain Reviews*, 9, 7–27.

NEZU, A. M., NEZU, C. M., & PERRI, M. G. (1989). *Problem-solving therapy for depression: Theory, research, and clinical guidelines*. New York: Wiley.

NG, B., DIMSDALE, J. E., SHRAGG, P., & DEUTSCH, R. (1996). Ethnic differences in analgesic consumption for postoperative pain. *Psychosomatic Medicine*, 58, 125–129.

NG, D. M., & JEFFERY, R. W. (2003). Relationships between perceived stress and health behaviors in a sample of working adults. *Health Psychology*, 22, 638–642.

NGUYEN, M., WATANABE, H., BUDSON, A. E., RICHIE, J. P., HAYES, D. F., & FOLKMAN, J. (1994). Elevated levels of an angiogenic peptide, basic fibroblast factor, in the urine of patients with a wide spectrum of cancers. *Journal of the National Cancer Institute*, 86, 356–361.

NHTSA (National Highway Traffic Safety Administration) (2006). *Seat belt use in 2006: Overall results*. Retrieved (1-3-2007) from http://www.nhtsa.gov.

NHTSA (National Highway Traffic Safety Administration) (2008). *Traffic safety facts: Sobriety checkpoints*. Retrieved (3-30-2010) from http://www.nhtsa.gov.

NIA (National Institute on Aging) (2006). *Alzheimer's Information: Causes; Treatment; Understanding Alzheimer's Disease*. Retrieved (12-6-2006) from http://www.nia.nih.gov/alzheimers.

NIAAA (National Institute on Alcohol Abuse and Alcoholism) (1993). *Alcohol and health* (8th Special Report to the U.S. Congress; Publication No. 94-3699). Washington, DC: U.S. Government Printing Office.

NIAAA (National Institute on Alcohol Abuse and Alcoholism) (2006). U.S. *Alcohol Epidemiologic Data Reference Manuals. Alcohol use and alcohol use disorders in the United States: Main findings from the 2001–2002 National Epidemiologic Survey on Alcohol and Related Conditions* (NESARC). Retrieved (3-30-2010) from http://www.niaaa.nih.gov.

NIAAA (National Institute on Alcohol Abuse and Alcoholism) (2009). *Quick facts—Apparent per capita alcohol consumption: National, state, and regional trends, 1850–2007.* Retrieved (1-30-2010) from http://www.niaaa.nih.gov.

NICASSIO, P. M., MEYEROWITZ, B. E., & KERNS, R. D. (2004). The future of health psychology interventions. *Health Psychology, 23,* 132–137.

NICASSIO, P. M., RADOJEVIC, V., WEISMAN, M. H., CULBERTSON, A. L., LEWIS, C., & CLEMMEY, P. (1993). The role of helplessness in the response to disease-modifying drugs in rheumatoid arthritis. *Journal of Rheumatology, 20,* 1114–1120.

NICASSIO, P. M., WALLSTON, K. A., CALLAHAN, L. F., HERBERT, M., & PINCUS, T. (1985). The measurement of helplessness in rheumatoid arthritis: The development of the Arthritis Helplessness Index. *Journal of Rheumatology, 12,* 462–467.

NICHOLSON, A., KUPER, H., HEMINGWAY, H. (2006). Depression as an aetiologic and prognostic factor in coronary heart disease: A meta-analysis of 6362 events among 146,538 participants in 54 observational studies. *European Heart Journal, 27,* 2763–2774.

NICHOLSON, A., ROSE, R., & BOBAK, M. (2010). Associations between different dimensions of religious involvement and self-rated health in diverse European populations. *Health Psychology, 29,* 227–235.

NICOLSON, N. A. (2008). Measurement of cortisol. In L. LEUKEN & L. C. GALLO (Eds.), *Handbook of physiological research methods in health psychology* (pp. 37–74). Thousand Oaks, CA: Sage.

NICKEL, C., KETTLER, C., MUEHLBACHER, M., LAHMANN, C., TRITT, K., et al. (2005). Effect of progressive muscle relaxation in adolescent female bronchial asthma patients: A randomized, double-blind, controlled study. *Journal of Psychosomatic Research, 59,* 393–398.

NISSEN, S. E., NICHOLLS, S. J., SIPAHI, I., LIBBY, P., RAICHLEN, J. S., et al. (2006). Effect of very high-intensity statin therapy on regression of coronary atherosclerosis: The ASTEROID Trial. *Journal of the American Medical Association, 295,* 1556–1565.

NKF (National Kidney Foundation) (2006). *Brochures: Hemodialysis; High Blood Pressure and Your Kidneys; Nutrition and Hemodialysis.* Retrieved (12-6-2006) from http://www.kidney.org.

NKF (National Kidney Foundation) (2010). *A to Z health guide.* Retrieved (4-14-2010) from http://www.kidney.org.

NOACHTAR, S., & BORGGRAEFE, I. (2009). Epilepsy surgery: A critical review. *Epilepsy & Behavior, 15,* 66–72.

NOAR, S. M., BENAC, C. N., & HARRIS, M. S. (2007). Does tailoring matter? Meta-analytic review of tailored print health behavior change interventions. *Psychological Bulletin, 133,* 673–693.

NORAT, T., BINGHAM, S., FERRARI, P., SLIMANI, N., JENAB, M., et al. (2005). Meat, fish, and colorectal cancer risk: The European Prospective Investigation into Cancer and Nutrition. *Journal of the National Cancer Institute, 97,* 906–916.

NORMAN, C. D., MALEY, O., LI, X., & SKINNER, H. A. (2008). Using the Internet to assist smoking prevention and cessation in schools: A randomized, controlled trial. *Health Psychology, 27,* 799–810.

NORMAN, P., CONNER, M., & BELL, R. (1999). The theory of planned behavior and smoking cessation. *Health Psychology, 18,* 89–94.

NORRIS, J., STONER, S. A., HESSLER, D. M., ZAWACKI, T. M., GEORGE, W. H., et al. (2009). Cognitive mediation of alcohol's effect on women's in-the-moment sexual decision making. *Health Psychology, 28,* 20–28.

NORTHCOTE, R. J., FLANNIGAN, C., & BALLANTYNE, D. (1986). Sudden death and vigorous exercise—A study of 60 deaths associated with squash. *British Heart Journal, 55,* 198–203.

NOVACO, R. W. (1975). *Anger control: The development and evaluation of an experimental treatment.* Lexington, MA: Heath.

NOVACO, R. W. (1978). Anger and coping with stress: Cognitive behavioral interventions. In J. P. FOREYT & D. P. RATHJEN (Eds.), *Cognitive behavior therapy: Research and application* (pp. 135–161). New York: Plenum.

NOWACK, K. M. (1989). Coping style, cognitive hardiness, and health status. *Journal of Behavioral Medicine, 12,* 145–158.

NSCIA (National Spinal Cord Injury Association) (2006). *Fact Sheets: Common questions about spinal cord injury; More about spinal cord injury; SCI rehabilitation.* Retrieved (12-8-2006) from http://www.spinalcord.org.

NYSTUL, M. S. (2004). Transcendental meditation. In W. E. CRAIGHEAD & C. B. NEMEROFF (Eds.), *Concise Corsini encyclopedia of psychology and behavioral science* (3rd ed., pp. 998–1000). New York: Wiley.

O'BYRNE, K. K., PETERSON, L., & SALDANA, L. (1997). Survey of pediatric hospitals' preparation programs: Evidence for the impact of health psychology research. *Health Psychology, 16,* 147–154.

O'CALLAGHAN, M. E., & COUVADELLI, B. (1998). Use of self-instructional strategies with three neurologically impaired adults. *Cognitive Therapy and Research, 22,* 91–107.

O'CAMPO, P., BURKE, J. G., CULHANE, J., ELO, I. T., EYSTER, J., et al. (2008). Neighborhood deprivation and preterm birth among non-Hispanic black and white women in eight geographic areas in the United States. *American Journal of Epidemiology, 167,* 155–163.

O'CARROLL, R. E., SMITH, K. B., GRUBB, N. R., FOX, K. A. A., & MASTERSON, G. (2001). Psychological factors associated with delay in attending hospital following a myocardial infarction. *Journal of Psychosomatic Research, 51,* 611–614.

OCKENE, I. S., HEBERT, J. R., OCKENE, J. K., SAPERIA, G. M., STANEK, E., et al. (1999). Effect of physician-delivered nutrition counseling training and an office support program on saturated fat intake, weight, and serum lipid measurements in a hyperlipidemic population: Worcester Area Trial for Counseling in Hyperlipidemia (WATCH). *Archives of Internal Medicine, 159,* 725–731.

OCKENE, J. K., EMMONS, K. M., MERMELSTEIN, R. J., PERKINS, K. A., BONOLLO, D. S., et al. (2000). Relapse and maintenance issues for smoking cessation. *Health Psychology, 19,* 17–31.

OCKENE, J. K., KRISTELLER, J., GOLDBERG, R., AMICK, T. L., PEKOW, P. S., et al. (1991). Increasing the efficacy of physician-delivered smoking interventions. *Journal of General Internal Medicine, 6,* 1–8.

OCKENE, J. K., KRISTELLER, J. L., PBERT, L., HEBERT, J. R., LUIPPOLD, R., et al. (1994). The Physician-Delivered Smoking Intervention Project: Can short-term interventions produce long-term effects for a general outpatient population? *Health Psychology, 13,* 278–281.

OCKENE, J. K., REED, G. W., & REIFF-HEKKING, S. (2009). Brief patient-centered clinician-delivered counseling for high-risk drinking: 4-year results. *Annals of Behavioral Medicine, 37,* 335–342.

O'CLEIRIGH, C., IRONSON, G., WEISS, A., & COSTA, P. T. (2007). Conscientiousness predicts disease progression (CD4 number and viral load) in people living with HIV. *Health Psychology, 26,* 473–480.

O'CONNELL, K. A., GERKOVICH, M. M., BOTT, M. J., COOK, M. R., & SHIFFMAN, S. (2002). The effect of anticipatory strategies on the first day of smoking cessation. *Psychology of Addictive Behaviors, 16,* 150–156.

O'DOUGHERTY, M., & BROWN, R. T. (1990). The stress of childhood illness. In L. E. ARNOLD (Ed.), *Childhood stress* (pp. 325–350). New York: Wiley.

OENEMA, A., BRUG, J., DIJKSTRA, A., DE WEERDT, I., & DE VRIES, H. (2008). Efficacy and use of an Internet-delivered computer-tailored lifestyle intervention, targeting saturated fat intake, physical activity and smoking cessation: A randomized controlled trial. *Annal of Behavioral Medicine, 35,* 125–135.

OGEDEGBE, G., PICKERING, T. G., CLEMOW, L., CHAPLIN, W., SPRUILL, T. M., et al. (2008). The misdiagnosis of hypertension. *Archives of Internal Medicine, 168,* 2459–2465.

O'HARE, T. (2005). Risky sex and drinking contexts in freshman first offenders. *Addictive Behaviors, 30,* 585–588.

ÖHLUND, C., LINDSTRÖM, I., ARESKOUG, B., EEK, C., PETERSON, L.-E., & NACHEMSON, A. (1994). Pain behavior in industrial subacute low back pain: Part I. Reliability: Concurrent and predictive validity of pain behavior assessments. *Pain, 58,* 201–209.

OKOLI, C. T. C., KELLY, T., & HAHN, E. J. (2007). Secondhand smoke and nicotine exposure: A brief review. *Addictive Behaviors, 32,* 1977–1988.

OLBRISCH, M. E., BENEDICT, S. M., ASHE, K., & LEVENSON, J. L. (2002). Psychological assessment and care of organ transplant patients. *Journal of Consulting and Clinical Psychology, 70,* 771–783.

OLDRIDGE, N. B. (1984). Adherence to adult exercise fitness programs. In J. D. MATARAZZO, S. M. WEISS, J. A. HERD, N. E. MILLER, & S. M. WEISS (Eds.), *Behavioral health: A handbook of health enhancement and disease prevention* (pp. 467–487). New York: Wiley.

O'LEARY, A., JEMMOTT, L. S., & JEMMOTT, J. B. (2008). Mediation analysis of an effective sexual risk-reduction intervention for women: The importance of self-efficacy. *Health Psychology, 27*(Suppl.), S180–S184.

OLIVER, G., WARDLE, J., & GIBSON, E. L. (2000). Stress and food choice: A laboratory study. *Psychosomatic Medicine, 62,* 853–865.

OLIVET, L. W. (1982). Basic needs of the hospitalized child. In M. J. SMITH, J. A. GOODMAN, N. L. RAMSEY, & S. B. PASTERNACK (Eds.), *Child and family: Concepts of nursing practice* (pp. 342–408). New York: McGraw-Hill.

O'LOUGHLIN, J., DIFRANZA, J., TYNDALE, R. F., MESHEFEDJIAN, G., MCMILLAN-DAVEY, E., et al. (2003). Nicotine-dependence symptoms are associated with smoking frequency in adolescents. *American Journal of Preventive Medicine, 25,* 219–225.

O'LOUGHLIN, J., KARP, I., KOULIS, T., PARADI, G., & DIFRANZA, J. (2009). Determinants of first puff and daily cigarette smoking in adolescents. *American Journal of Epidemiology, 170,* 585–597.

OLSHANSKY, S. J., CARNES, B. A., & CASSEL, C. (1990). In search of Methuselah: Estimating the upper limits to human longevity. *Science, 250,* 634–640.

ONG, A. D., BERGEMAN, C. S., BISCONTI, T. L., & WALLACE, K. A. (2006). Psychological resilience, positive emotions, and successful adaptation to stress in later life. *Journal of Personality and Social Psychology, 91,* 730–749.

ORFUTT, C, & LACROIX, J. M. (1988). Type A behavior pattern and symptom reports: A prospective investigation. *Journal of Behavioral Medicine, 11,* 227–237.

ORLANDO, M., ELLICKSON, P. L., & JINNETT, K. (2001). The temporal relationship between emotional distress and cigarette smoking during adolescence and young adulthood. *Journal of Consulting and Clinical Psychology, 69,* 959–970.

ORNISH, D., BROWN, S. E., SCHERWITZ, L. W., BILLINGS, J. H., ARMSTRONG, W. T., et al. (1990). Can lifestyle changes reverse coronary heart disease? The Lifestyle Heart Trial. *Lancet, 336,* 129–133.

ORNISH, D., SCHERWITZ, L. W., BILLINGS, J. H., GOULD, K. L., MERRITT, T. A., et al. (1998). Intensive lifestyle changes for reversal of coronary heart disease. *Journal of the American Medical Association, 280,* 2001–2007.

OROZCO, L. J., BUCHLEITNER, A. M., GIMENEZ-PEREZ, G., ROQUÉ I FIGULS, M., RICHTER, B. & MAURICIO, D. (2008). Exercise or exercise and diet for preventing type 2 diabetes mellitus. *Cochrane Database of Systematic Reviews,* Issue 3. Retrieved (1-30-2010) from http://www.thecochranelibrary.com.

ORTH-GOMÉR, K., SCHNEIDERMAN, N., WANG, H.-X., WALLDIN, C., BLOM, M., & JERNBERG, T. (2009). Stress reduction prolongs life in women with coronary disease: The Stockholm Women's Intervention Trial for Coronary Heart Disease (SWITCHD). *Circulation: Cardiovascular Quality and Outcomes, 2,* 25–32.

OSSIP-KLEIN, D. J., BIGELOW, G., PARKER, S. R., CURRY, S., HALL, S., & KIRKLAND, S. (1986). Task Force 1: Classification and assessment of smoking behavior. *Health Psychology, 5*(Suppl.), 3–11.

OUELETTE, S. C., & DIPLACIDO, J. (2001). Personality's role in the protection and enhancement of health: Where the research has been, where it is stuck, how it might move. In A. BAUM, T. A. REVENSON, & J. E. SINGER (Eds.), *Handbook of health psychology* (pp. 175–193). Mahwah, NJ: Erlbaum.

OUIMETTE, P. C., FINNEY, J. W., & MOOS, R. H. (1997). Twelve-step and cognitive-behavioral treatment for substance abuse: A comparison of treatment effectiveness. *Journal of Consulting and Clinical Psychology*, 65, 230–240.

PALERMO, T. M., ECCELSTON, C., LEWANDOWSKI, A. S., WILLIAMS, A. C., & MORLEY, S. (2010). Randomized controlled trials of psychological therapies for management of chronic pain in children and adolescents: An updated meta-analytic review. *Pain*, 148, 387–397.

PALERMO, T. M., WILSON, A. C., PETERS, M., LEWANDOWSKI, A., & SOMHEGYI, H. (2009). Randomized controlled trial of an Internet-delivered family cognitive-behavioral therapy intervention for children and adolescents with chronic pain. *Pain*, 146, 205–213.

PALLONEN, U. E., MURRAY, D. M., SCHMID, L., PIRIE, P., LUEPKER, R. V. (1990). Patterns of self-initiated smoking cessation among young adults. *Health Psychology*, 9, 418–426.

PAOLETTI, P., CAMILLI, A. E., HOLBERG, C. J., & LEBOWITZ, M. D. (1985). Respiratory effects in relation to estimated tar exposure from current and cumulative cigarette consumption. *Chest*, 88, 849–855.

PARK, C. L., EDMONDSON, D., FENSTER, J. R., & BLANK, T. O. (2008). Meaning making and psychological adjustment following cancer: The mediating roles of growth, life meaning, and restored just-world beliefs. *Journal of Consulting and Clinical Psychology*, 76, 863–875.

PARK, D. C., HERTZOG, C., LEVENTHAL, H., MORRELL, R. W., LEVENTHAL, E., et al. (1999). Medication adherence in rheumatoid arthritis patients: Older is wiser. *Journal of the American Geriatric Society*, 47, 172–183.

PARKER, J. C. (1995). Stress management. In P. M. NICASSIO & T. W. SMITH (Eds.), *Managing chronic illness: A biopsychosocial perspective* (pp. 285–312). Washington, DC: American Psychological Association.

PARKER, J. C., FRANK, R. G., BECK, N. C., SMARR, K. L., BUESCHER, K. L., et al. (1988). Pain management in rheumatoid arthritis patients: A cognitive-behavioral approach. *Arthritis and Rheumatism*, 31, 593–601.

PARRISH, B. P., ZAUTRA, A. J., & DAVIS, M. C. (2008). The role of positive and negative interpersonal events on daily fatigue in women with fibromyalgia, rheumatoid arthritis, and osteoarthritis. *Health Psychology*, 27, 694–702.

PARRISH, J. M. (1986). Parent compliance with medical and behavioral recommendations. In N. A. KRASNEGOR, J. D. ARASTEH, & M. F. CATALDO (Eds.), *Child health behavior: A behavioral pediatrics perspective* (pp. 453–501). New York: Wiley.

PARROTT, A. C. (1999). Does cigarette smoking *cause* stress? *American Psychologist*, 54, 817–820.

PARSONS, A. C., SHRAIM, M., INGLIS, J., AVEYARD, P., & HAJEK, P. (2009). Interventions for preventing weight gain after smoking cessation. *Cochrane Database of Systematic Reviews*, Issue 1. Retrieved (1-30-2010) from http://www .thecochranelibrary.com. DOI:10.1002/14651858.CD006219 .pub2.

PARSONS, O. A. (1986). Alcoholics' neuropsychological impairment: Current findings and conclusions. *Annals of Behavioral Medicine*, 8(2–3), 13–19.

PARSONS, T. (1951). *The social system*. New York: Free Press.

PASCOE, E. A. & RICHMAN, L. S. (2009). Perceived discrimination and health: A meta-analytic review. *Psychological Bulletin*, 135, 531–554.

PATERSON, R. J., & NEUFELD, R. W. J. (1987). Clear danger: Situational determinants of the appraisal of threat. *Psychological Bulletin*, 101, 404–416.

PATRICK, A. W., GILL, G. V., MACFARLANE, I. A., CULLEN, A., POWER, E., & WALLYMAHMED, M. (1994). Home glucose monitoring in type 2 diabetes: Is it a waste of time? *Diabetic Medicine*, 11, 62–65.

PATRICK, M. E., & MAGGS, J. L. (2009). Does drinking lead to sex? Daily alcohol–sex behaviors and expectancies among college students. *Psychology of Addictive Behaviors*, 23, 472–481.

PATTERSON, D. R., & JENSEN, M. P. (2003). Hypnosis and clinical pain. *Psychological Bulletin*, 129, 495–521.

PATTERSON, F., KERRIN, K., WILEYTO, E. P., & LERMAN, C. (2008). Increases in anger symptoms after smoking cessation predicts smoking relapse. *Drug and Alcohol Dependence*, 95, 173–176.

PATTERSON, J. M., & GARWICK, A. W. (1994). The impact of chronic illness on families: A family systems perspective. *Annals of Behavioral Medicine*, 16, 131–142.

PATTERSON, S. M., MATTHEWS, K. A., ALLEN, M. T., & OWENS, J. F. (1995). Stress-induced hemoconcentration of blood cells and lipids in healthy women during acute psychological stress. *Health Psychology*, 14, 319–324.

PATTERSON, S. M., ZAKOWSKI, S. G., HALL, M. H., COHEN, L., WOLLMAN, K., & BAUM, A. (1994). Psychological stress and platelet activation: Differences in platelet reactivity in healthy men during active and passive stressors. *Health Psychology*, 13, 34–38.

PATTERSON, T. L., SEMPLE, S. J., SHAW, W. S., YU, E., HE, Y., et al. (1998). The cultural context of caregiving: A comparison of Alzheimer's caregivers in Shanghai, China and San Diego, California. *Psychological Medicine*, 28, 1071–1084.

PATTERSON, T. L., SHAW, W. S., SEMPLE, S. J., CHERNER, M., MCCUTCHAN, J. A., et al. (1996). Relationship of psychosocial factors to HIV disease progression. *Annals of Behavioral Medicine*, 18, 30–39.

PATTISHALL, E. G. (1989). The development of behavioral medicine: Historical models. *Annals of Behavioral Medicine*, 11, 43–48.

PAVLOV, I. P. (1927). *Conditioned reflexes*. New York: Oxford University Press.

PEARLIN, L. I., & SCHOOLER, C. (1978). The structure of coping. *Journal of Health and Social Behavior*, 19, 2–21.

Pearson Assessments (2009). Millon Behavioral Medicine Diagnostic. Retrieved (4-17-2009) from http://www .pearsonassessments.com.

PECHACEK, T. F., FOX, B. H., MURRAY, D. M., & LUEPKER, R. V. (1984). Review of techniques for measurement of smoking behavior. In J. D. MATARAZZO, S. M. WEISS, J. A. HERD, N. E. MILLER, & S. M. WEISS (Eds.), *Behavioral health: A handbook of health enhancement and disease prevention* (pp. 729–754). New York: Wiley.

PECKENPAUGH, N. J. (2007). *Nutrition essentials and diet therapy* (10th ed.). Philadelphia: Saunders.

PEDERSON, L. L. (1982). Compliance with physician advice to quit smoking: A review of the literature. *Preventive Medicine,* 11, 71–84.

PEEK, M. K., CUTCHIN, M. P., SALINAS, J. J., SHEFFIELD, K. M., ESCHBACH, K., et al. (2009). Allostatic load among non-Hispanic whites, non-Hispanic blacks, and people of Mexican origin: Effects of ethnicity, nativity, and acculturation. *American Journal of Public Health,* 99, 1–7.

PEELE, S. (1984). The cultural context of psychological approaches to alcoholism: Can we control the effects of alcohol? *American Psychologist,* 39, 1337–1351.

PEIRCE, R. S., FRONE, M. R., RUSSELL, M., COOPER, M. L., & MUDAR, P. (2000). A longitudinal model of social contact, social support, depression, and alcohol use. *Health Psychology,* 19, 28–38.

PENN, A., & SNYDER, C. A. (1993). Inhalation of sidestream cigarette smoke accelerates development of arteriosclerotic placques. *Circulation,* 88(Part 1), 1820–1825.

PENN, N. E., KAR, S., KRAMER, J., SKINNER, J., & ZAMBRANA, R. E. (1995). Panel VI: Ethnic minorities, health care systems, and behavior. *Health Psychology,* 14, 641–646.

PENNEBAKER, J. W. (1983). Accuracy of symptom perception. In A. BAUM, S. E. TAYLOR, & J. SINGER (Eds.), *Handbook of psychology and health* (Vol. 4, pp. 189–217). Hillsdale, NJ: Erlbaum.

PENNEBAKER, J. W. (1990). *Opening up: The healing power of confiding in others.* New York: William Morrow.

PENNEBAKER, J. W., & WATSON, D. (1988). Blood pressure estimation and beliefs among normotensives and hypertensives. *Health Psychology,* 7, 309–328.

PENNINX, B. W. J. H., GURALNIK, J. M., FERRUCCI, L., SIMONSICK, E. M., DEEG, D. J. H., & WALLACE, R. B. (1998). Depressive symptoms and physical decline in community-dwelling older persons. *Journal of the American Medical Association,* 279, 1720–1726.

PENZIEN, D. B., RAINS, J. C., & ANDRASIK, F. (2002). Behavioral management of recurrent headache: Three decades of experience and empiricism. *Applied Psychophysiology and Biofeedback,* 27, 163–181.

PÉREZ, A., ARIZA, C., SÁANCHEZ-MARTINEZ, F., & NEBOT, M. (2010). Cannabis consumption initiation among adolescents: A longitudinal study. *Addictive Behaviors,* 35, 129–134.

PERKINS, K. A., ROHAY, J., MEILAHN, E. N., WING, R. R., MATTHEWS, K. A., & KULLER, L. H. (1993). Diet, alcohol, and physical activity as a function of smoking status in middle-aged women. *Health Psychology,* 12, 410–415.

PERRI, M. G., ANTON, S. D., DURNING, P. E., KETTERSON, T. U., SYDEMAN, S. J., et al. (2002). Adherence to exercise prescriptions: Effects of prescribing moderate versus higher levels of intensity and frequency. *Health Psychology,* 21, 452–458.

PERRI, M. G., MCALLISTER, D. A., GANGE, J. J., JORDAN, R. C., MCADOO, W. G., & NEZU, A. M. (1988). Effects of four maintenance programs on the long-term management of obesity. *Journal of Consulting and Clinical Psychology,* 56, 529–534.

PERRI, M. G., NEZU, A. M., MCKELVEY, S. F., SHERMER, R. L., RENJILIAN, D. A., & VIEGENER, B. J. (2001). Relapse prevention training and problem-solving training in the long-term management of obesity. *Journal of Consulting and Clinical Psychology,* 69, 722–726.

PERRI, M. G., NEZU, A. M., & VIEGENER, B. J. (1992). *Improving the long-term management of obesity.* New York: Wiley.

PERZ, C. A., DICLEMENTE, C. C., & CARBONARI, J. P. (1996). Doing the right thing at the right time? The interaction of stages and processes of change in successful smoking cessation. *Health Psychology,* 15, 462–468.

PETERSON, L., CROWSON, J., SALDANA, L., & HOLDRIDGE, S. (1999). Of needles and skinned knees: Children's coping with medical procedures and minor injuries for self and other. *Health Psychology,* 18, 197–200.

PETRAITIS, J., FLAY, B. R., MILLER, T. Q., TORPY, E. J., & GREINER, B. (1998). Illicit substance use among adolescents: A matrix of prospective predictors. *Substance Use and Misuse,* 33, 2561–2604.

PETRIE, K. J., BROADBENT, E. A., KLEY, N., MOSS-MORRIS, R., HORNE, R., & RIEF, W. (2005). Worries about modernity predict symptom complaints after environmental pesticide spraying. *Psychosomatic Medicine,* 67, 778–782.

PETRIE, K. J., FONTANILLA, I., THOMAS, M. G., BOOTH, R. J., & PENNEBAKER, J. W. (2004). Effect of written emotional expression on immune function in patients with human immunodeficiency virus infection: A randomized trial. *Psychosomatic Medicine,* 66, 272–275.

PETRIE, K. J., & PENNEBAKER, J. W. (2004). Health-related cognitions. In S. SUTTON, A. BAUM, & M. JOHNSTON (Eds.), *The Sage handbook of health psychology* (pp. 127–142). London: Sage.

PETRY, N. M., BARRY, D., PIETRZAK, R. H., & WAGNER, J. A. (2008). Overweight and obesity are associated with psychiatric disorders: Results from the National Epidemiologic Survey on Alcohol and Related Conditions. *Psychosomatic Medicine,* 70, 288–297.

PETRY, N. M., & MARTIN, B. (2002). Low-cost contingency management for treating cocaine- and opioid-abusing methadone patients. *Journal of Consulting and Clinical Psychology,* 70, 398–405.

PHAC (Public Health Agency of Canada) (2006). *Cardiovascular disease surveillance on-line: Cardiovascular disease hospital separations.* Retrieved (3-26-2007) from http://dsol-smed.phac-aspc.gc.ca.

PHARES, E. J. (1984). *Introduction to personality*. Columbus, OH: Merrill.

PHELAN, S., LIU, T., GORIN, A., LOWE, M., HOGAN, J., et al. (2009). What distinguishes weight-loss maintainers from the treatment-seeking obese? Analysis of environmental, behavioral, and pychosocial variables in diverse populations. *Annals of Behavioral Medicine, 38*, 94–104.

PHELAN, S., & WADDEN, T. A. (2002). Combining behavioral and pharmacological treatments for obesity. *Obesity Research, 10*, 560–574.

PHELAN, S., WING, R. R., RAYNOR, H. A., DIBELLO, J., NEDEAU, K., & PENG, W. (2008). Holiday weight management by successful weight losers and normal weight individuals. *Journal of Consulting and Clinical Psychology, 76*, 442–448.

PHILIPS, C. A. (1989). Rehabilitation of the patient with rheumatoid hand involvement. *Physical Therapy, 69*, 1091–1098.

PHILLIPS, D. P., & BREDDER, C. C. (2002). Morbidity and mortality from medical errors: An increasingly serious public health problem. *Annual Review of Public Health, 23*, 135–150.

PHILLIPS, W. T., KIERNAN, M., & KING, A. C. (2001). The effects of physical activity on physical and psychological health. In A. BAUM, T. A. REVENSON, & J. E. SINGER (Eds.), *Handbook of health psychology* (pp. 627–657). Mahwah, NJ: Erlbaum.

PIASECKI, T. M., KENFORD, S. L., SMITH, S. S., FIORE, M. C., & BAKER, T. B. (1997). Listening to nicotine: Negative affect and the smoking withdrawal conundrum. *Psychological Science, 8*, 184–189.

PIASECKI, T. M., MCCARTHY, D. E., FIORE, M. C., & BAKER, T. B. K (2008). Alcohol consumption, smoking urge, and the reinforcing effects of cigarette. An ecological study. *Psychology of Addictive Behaviors, 22*, 230–239.

PIERCE, J. P., DISTEFAN, J. M., KAPLAN, R. M., & GILPIN, E. A. (2005). The role of curiosity in smoking initiation. *Addictive Behaviors, 30*, 685–696.

PIERCE, J. P., & GILPIN, E. A. (1995). A historical analysis of tobacco marketing and the uptake of smoking by youth in the United States: 1890–1977. *Health Psychology, 14*, 500–508.

PIETTE, J. D., HEISLER, M., & WAGNER, T. H. (2004). Cost-related medication underuse among chronically ill adults: The treatments people forgo, how often, and who is at risk. *American Journal of Public Health, 94*, 1782–1787.

PIGNONE, M., DEWALT, D. A., SHERIDAN, S., BERKMAN, N., & LOHT, K. N. (2005). Interventions to improve health outcomes for patients with low literacy: A systematic review. *Journal of General Internal Medicine, 20*, 185–192.

PILISUK, M. (1982). Delivery of social support: The social inoculation. *American Journal of Orthopsychiatry, 52*, 20–31.

PINES, M. (1979, January). Superkids. *Psychology Today*, pp. 53–63.

PINQUART, M., & SÖRENSEN, S. (2003). Differences between caregivers and noncaregivers in psychological health and physical health: A meta-analysis. *Psychology and Aging, 18*, 250–267.

PINTO, B. M., EAKIN, E., & MARUYAMA, N. C. (2000). Health behavior changes after a cancer diagnosis: What do we know and where do we go from here? *Annals of Behavioral Medicine, 22*, 38–52.

PINTO, R. P., & HOLLANDSWORTH, J. G. (1989). Using videotape modeling to prepare children psychologically for surgery: Influence of parents and costs versus benefits of providing preparation services. *Health Psychology, 8*, 79–95.

PIOTROWSKI, C., & LUBIN, B. (1990). Assessment practices of health psychologists: Survey of APA Division 38 clinicians. *Professional Psychology: Research and Practice, 21*, 99–106.

PITKÄNEN, T., LYYRA, A.-L., & PULKKINEN, L. (2005). Age of onset of drinking and the use of alcohol in adulthood: A follow-up study from age 8–42 for females and males. *Addiction, 100*, 652–661.

PLACE, M. (1984). Hypnosis and the child. *Journal of Child Psychology and Psychiatry, 25*, 339–347.

PMRG (Project Match Research Group) (1998). Matching alcoholism treatments to client heterogeneity: Treatment main effects and matching effects on drinking during treatment. *Journal of Studies on Alcohol, 59*, 631–639.

PNHP (Physicians for a National Health System) (2006). *International health systems*. Retrieved (2-29-2007) from http://www.pnhp.org.

POLESHUCK, E. L., & GREEN, C. R. (2008). Socioeconomic disadvantage and pain. *Pain, 136*, 235–238.

POLIVY, J., & HERMAN, C. P. (2002). If at first you don't succeed: False hopes of self-change. *American Psychologist, 57*, 677–689.

POLLOCK, S. E., CHRISTIAN, B. J., & SANDS, D. (1991). Responses to chronic illness: Analysis of psychological and physiological adaptation. *Nursing Research, 39*, 300–304.

POLONSKY, W. H., ANDERSON, B. J., LOHRER, P. A., APONTE, J. E., JACOBSON, A. M., & COLE, C. F. (1994). Insulin omission in women with IDDM. *Diabetes Care, 17*, 1178–1185.

POMERLEAU, O. F., COLLINS, A. C., SHIFFMAN, S., & POMERLEAU, C. S. (1993). Why some people smoke and others do not: New perspectives. *Journal of Consulting and Clinical Psychology, 61*, 723–731.

POMERLEAU, O. F., & POMERLEAU, C. S. (1989). A biobehavioral perspective on smoking. In T. NEY & A. GALE (Eds.), *Smoking and human behavior* (pp. 69–90). New York: Wiley.

POMERLEAU, O. F., POMERLEAU, C. S., MEHRINGER, A. M., SNEDECOR, S. M., & CAMERON, O. G. (2005). Validation of retrospective reports of early experiences with smoking. *Addictive Behaviors, 30*, 607–611.

POON, E. C., CINA, J. L., CHURCHILL, W., PATEL, N., FEATHERSTONE, E., et al. (2006). Medication dispensing errors and potential adverse drug events before and after implementing bar code technology in the pharmacy. *Annals of Internal Medicine, 145*, 426–434.

POPE, M. K., & SMITH, T. W. (1991). Cortisol excretion in high and low cynically hostile men. *Psychosomatic Medicine, 53*, 386–392.

PORGES, S. W. (1995). Cardiac vagal tone: A physiological index of stress. *Neuroscience and Behavioral Reviews*, 19, 225–233.

PORTER, F. L., MILLER, R. H., & MARSHALL, R. E. (1986). Neonatal pain cries: Effects of circumcision on acoustic features and perceived urgency. *Child Development*, 57, 790–802.

POUND, P., BRITTEN, N., MORGAN, M., YARDLEY, L., POPE, C., et al. (2005). Resisting medicines: A synthesis of qualitative studies of medicine taking. *Social Science & Medicine*, 61, 133–155.

POWELL, K. E., THOMPSON, P. D., CASPERSEN, C. J., & KENDRICK, J. S. (1987). Physical activity and the incidence of coronary heart disease. *Annual Review of Public Health*, 8, 253–287.

POWELL, L. H., & FRIEDMAN, M. (1986). Alteration of Type A behaviour in coronary patients. In M. J. CHRISTIE & P. G. MELLETT (Eds.), *The psychosomatic approach: Contemporary practice of whole-person care* (pp. 191–214). New York: Wiley.

POWER, M., BULLINGER, M., HARPER, A., and The World Health Organization Quality of Life Group (1999). The World Health Organization WHOQOL-100: Tests of the universality of quality of life in 15 different cultural groups worldwide. *Health Psychology*, 18, 495–505.

PRADHAN, E. K., BAUMGARTEN, M., LANGENBERG, P, HANDWERGER, B., GILPIN, A. K., et al. (2007). Effect of mindfulness-based stress reduction in rheumatoid arthritis patients. *Arthritis & Rheumatism*, 57, 1134–1142.

PRADO, G., PANTIN, H., BRIONES, E., SCHWARTZ, S. J., FEASTER, D., et al. (2007). A randomized controlled trial of a parent-centered intervention in preventing substance use and HIV risk behaviors in Hispanic adolescents. *Journal of Consulting and Clinical Psychology*, 75, 914–926.

PRESSMAN, S. D., & COHEN, S. (2005). Does positive affect influence health? *Psychological Bulletin*, 131, 925–971.

PRESSMAN, S. D., MATTHEWS, K. A., COHEN, S., MARTIRE, L. M., SCHEIER, M., et al. (2009). Association of enjoyable leisure activities with psychological and physical well-being. *Psychosomatic Medicine*, 71, 725–732.

PRESTWICH, A., PERUGINI, M., & HURLING, R. (2010). Can implementation intentions and text messages promote brisk walking? A randomized trial. *Health Psychology*, 29, 40–49.

PROCHASKA, J. O., & DICLEMENTE, C. C. (1984). *The transtheoretical approach: Crossing traditional boundaries of therapy*. Homewood, IL: Dow Jones/Irwin.

PROCHASKA, J. O., DICLEMENTE, C. C., & NORCROSS, J. C. (1992). In search of how people change: Applications to addictive behaviors. *American Psychologist*, 47, 1102–1114.

PROKHOROV, A. V., WARNEKE, C., DE MOOR, C., EMMONS, K. M., MULLIN-JONES, M., et al. (2003). Self-reported health status, health vulnerability, and smoking behavior in college students: Implications for intervention. *Nicotine and Tobacco Research*, 5, 545–552.

PUHL, R. M., & LATNER, J. D. (2007). Stigma, obesity, and the health of the nation's children. *Psychological Bulletin*, 133, 557–580.

PULEO, P. R., MEYER, D., WATHEN, C., TAWA, C. B., WHEELER, S., et al. (1994). Use of rapid assay of subforms of creatine kinase MB to diagnose or rule out acute myocardial infarction. *New England Journal of Medicine*, 331, 561–566.

PURCELL, K., WEISS, J., & HAHN, W. (1972). Certain psychosomatic disorders. In B. B. WOLMAN (Ed.), *Manual of child psychopathology* (pp. 706–740). New York: McGraw-Hill.

PUTWAIN, D. W., CONNORS, L., & SYMES, W. (2010). Do cognitive distortions mediate the test anxiety–examination performance relationship? *Educational Psychology*, 30, 11–26.

QUALE, A. J., & SCHANKE, A.-K. (2010). Resilience in the face of coping with a severe physical injury: A study of trajectories of adjustment in a rehabilitation setting. *Rehabilitation Psychology*, 55, 12–22.

QUARTANA, P. J., WICKWIRE, E. M., KLICK, B., GRACE, E., & SMITH, M. T. (2010). Naturalistic changes in insomnia symptoms and pain in temporomandibular joint disorder: A cross-lagged panel analysis. *Pain*, 149, 325–331.

QUERFURTH, H. W., & LAFERLA, F. M. (2010). Alzheimer's disease. *New England Journal of Medicine*, 362, 329–344.

QUICK, J. C. (1999). Occupational health psychology: Historical roots and future directions. *Health Psychology*, 18, 82–88.

QUICK, J. C., QUICK, J. D., NELSON, D. L., & HURRELL, J. J. (1997). *Preventive stress management in organizations*. Washington, DC: American Psychological Association.

QUITTNER, A. L., ESPELAGE, D. L., OPIPARI, L. C., CARTER, B., EID, N., & EIGEN, H. (1998). Role strain in couples with and without a child with a chronic illness: Associations with marital satisfaction, intimacy, and daily mood. *Health Psychology*, 17, 112–124.

RABKIN, J. G., FERRANDO, S. J., SHU-HSING, L., SEWELL, M., & MCELHINEY, M. (2000). Psychological effects of HAART: A 2-year study. *Psychosomatic Medicine*, 62, 413–422.

RADECKI, S. E., & BRUNTON, S. A. (1992). Health promotion/disease prevention in family practice residency training: Results of a national survey. *Family Medicine*, 24, 534–537.

RÆDER, H., JOHANSSON, S., HOLM, P. I., HALDORSEN, I. S., MAS, E., et al. (2006). Mutations in the CEL VNTR cause a syndrome of diabetes and pancreatic exocrine dysfunction. *Nature Genetics*, 38, 54–62.

RÄIKKÖNEN, K., MATTHEWS, K. A., FLORY, J. D., OWENS, J. F., & GUMP, B. B. (1999). Effects of optimism, pessimism, and trait anxiety on ambulatory blood pressure and mood during everyday life. *Journal of Personality and Social Psychology*, 76, 104–113.

RAINFORTH, M. V., SCHNEIDER, R. H., NIDICH, S. I., GAYLORD-KING, C., SALERNO, J. W., & ANDERSON, J. W. (2007). Stress reduction programs in patients with elevated blood pressure: A systematic review and meta-analysis. *Current Hypertension Reports*, 9, 520–528.

RAINS, S. A., YOUNG, V. (2009). A meta-analysis of research on formal computer-mediated support groups: Examining group characteristics and health outcomes. *Human Communication Research*, 35, 309–336.

RAJ, A., AMARO, H., & REED, E. (2001). Culturally tailoring HIV/AIDS prevention programs: Why, when, and how. In S. S. KAZARIAN & E. R. EVANS (Eds.), *Handbook of cultural health psychology* (pp. 195–239). San Diego: Academic Press.

RAMSEY, N. L. (1982). Effects of hospitalization on the child and family. In M. J. SMITH, J. A. GOODMAN, N. L. RAMSEY, & S. B. PASTERNACK (Eds.), *Child and family: Concepts of nursing practice* (pp. 317–341). New York: McGraw-Hill.

RAMPERSAUD, E., MITCHELL, B. D., POLLIN, T. I., FU, M., SHEN, H., et al. (2008). Physical activity and the association of common FTO gene variants with body mass index and obesity. *Archives of Internal Medicine, 168*, 1791–1797.

RAND, C. S., & WEEKS, K. (1998). Measuring adherence with medication regimens in clinical care research. In S. A. SHUMAKER, E. B. SCHRON, J. L., OCKENE, & W. L. MCBEE (Eds.), *The handbook of health behavior change* (2nd ed., pp. 114–132). New York: Springer.

RANDALL, A. K. & BODENMANN, G. (2009). The role of stress on close relationships and marital satisfaction. *Clinical Psychology Review, 29*, 105–115.

RANSOM, S., SACCO, W. P., WEITZNER, M. A., AZZARELLO, L. M., & MCMILLAN, S. C. (2006). Interpersonal factors predict increased desire for hastened death in late-stage cancer patients. *Annals of Behavioral Medicine, 31*, 63–69.

RAPHAEL, B. G. (1999). Hematological disorders. In M. G. EISENBERG, R. L., GLUECKAUF, & H. H. ZARETSKY (Eds.), *Medical aspects of disability: A handbook for the rehabilitation professional* (pp. 273–286). New York: Springer.

RAPPAPORT, N. B., MCANULTY, D. P., WAGGONER, C. D., & BRANTLEY, P. J. (1987). Cluster analysis of Minnesota Multiphasic Personality Inventory (MMPI) profiles in a chronic headache population. *Journal of Behavioral Medicine, 10*, 49–60.

RAPS, C. S., PETERSON, C., JONAS, M., & SELIGMAN, M. E. P. (1982). Patient behavior in hospitals: Helplessness, reactance, or both? *Journal of Personality and Social Psychology, 42*, 1036–1041.

RASMUSSEN, H. N., SCHEIER, M. F., & GREENHOUSE, J. B. (2009). Optimism and physical health: A meta-analytic review. *Annals of Behavioral Medicine, 37*, 239–256.

RATLIFF-CRAIN, J., & BAUM, A. (1990). Individual differences and health: Gender, coping, and stress. In H. S. FRIEDMAN (Ed.), *Personality and disease* (pp. 226–253). New York: Wiley.

RAVEN, B. H., & HALEY, R. W. (1982). Social influence and compliance of hospital nurses with infection control policies. In J. R. EISER (Ed.), *Social psychology and behavioral medicine* (pp. 413–438). New York: Wiley.

RAY, R., SCHNOLL, R. A., & LERMAN, C. (2009). Nicotine dependence. Biology, behavior, and treatment. *Annual Review of Medicine, 60*, 247–260.

RAYMOND, N. R., & D'ERAMO-MELKUS, G. (1993). Non-insulin-dependent diabetes and obesity in the Black and Hispanic population: Culturally sensitive management. *Diabetes Educator, 19*, 313–317.

REBOLLO, I., & BOOMSMA, D. I. (2006). Genetic and environmental influences on Type A behavior pattern: Evidence from twins and their parents in the Netherlands Twin Register. *Psychosomatic Medicine, 68*, 437–442.

REDD, W. H., & JACOBSEN, P. (2001). Behavioral intervention in comprehensive cancer care. In A. BAUM, T. A. REVENSON, & J. E. SINGER (Eds.), *Handbook of health psychology* (pp. 757–776). Mahwah, NJ: Erlbaum.

REDD, W. H., SILBERFARB, P. M., ANDERSEN, B. L., ANDRYKOWSKI, M. A., BOVBJERG, D. H., et al. (1991). Physiologic and psychobehavioral research in oncology. *Cancer, 67*, 813–822.

REDDY, D. M., FLEMING, R., & ADESSO, V. J. (1992). Gender and health. In S. MAES, H. LEVENTHAL, & M. JOHNSTON (Eds.), *International review of health psychology* (Vol. 1, pp. 3–32). New York: Wiley.

REEB, R. N., & BUSH, J. P. (1996). Preprocedural psychological preparation in pediatric oncology: A process-oriented intervention study. *Children's Health Care, 25*, 265–279.

REED, G. M., KEMENY, M. E., TAYLOR, S. E., WANG, H-Y., & VISSCHER, B. R. (1994). Realistic acceptance as a predictor of decreased survival time in gay men with AIDS. *Health Psychology, 13*, 299–307.

REHM, L. P., & NAYAK, N. (2004). Placebo effects. In A. J. CHRISTENSEN, R. MARTIN, & J. M. SMYTH (Eds.), *Encyclopedia of health psychology* (pp. 211–213). New York: Kluwer.

REINEHR, T., DE SOUSA, G., TOSCHKE, A. M., & ANDLER, W. (2006). Long-term follow-up of cardiovascular disease risk factors in children after an obesity intervention. *American Journal of Clinical Nutrition, 84*, 490–496.

REINIS, S., & GOLDMAN, J. M. (1980). *The development of the brain: Biological and functional perspectives*. Springfield, IL: Charles C. Thomas.

REIS, B. Y., BROWNSTEIN, J. S., & MANDL, K. D. (2005). Running outside the baseline: Impact of the 2004 Major League baseball postseason on emergency department use. *Annals of Emergency Medicine, 46*, 386–387.

RENNICK, J. E., JOHNSTON, C. C., DOUGHERTY, G., PLATT, R., & RITCHIE, J. A. (2002). Children's psychosocial responses after critical illnesses and exposure to invasive technology. *Journal of Developmental and Behavioral Pediatrics, 23*, 133–144.

RESNICOW, K., DIIORIO, C., SOET, J. E., BORELLI, B., HECHT, J., & ERNST, D. (2002). Motivational interviewing in health promotion: It sounds like something is changing. *Health Psychology, 21*, 444–451.

REVENSON, T. A., & JELTOVA, I. (2004). Women's health. In A. J. CHRISTENSEN, R. MARTIN, & J. M. SMYTH (Eds.), *Encyclopedia of health psychology* (pp. 336–342). New York: Kluwer.

REVENSON, T. A., & MAJEROVITZ, S. D. (1991). The effects of chronic illness on the spouse: Social resources as stress buffers. *Arthritis Care and Research, 4*, 63–72.

REY, M. J. (1999). Cardiovascular disorders. In M. G. EISENBERG, R. L. GLUECKAUF, & H. H. ZARETSKY (Eds.), *Medical aspects of disability: A handbook for the rehabilitation professional* (pp. 154–184). New York: Springer.

REYNOLDS, D. V. (1969). Surgery in the rat during electrical anesthesia induced by focal brain stimulation. *Science, 164*, 444–445.

RHOADES, R., & PFLANZER, R. (1996). *Human physiology* (3rd ed.). Fort Worth: Saunders.

RHODES, R. E., FIALA, B., & CONNER, M. (2009). A review and meta-analysis of affective judgments and physical activity in adult populations. *Annals of Behavioral Medicine, 38,* 180–204.

RIBISL, K. M., WINKLEBY, M. A., FORTMANN, S. P., & FLORA, J. A. (1998). The interplay of socioeconomic status and ethnicity on Hispanic and White men's cardiovascular disease risk and health communication patterns. *Health Education Research, 13,* 407–417.

RICHARDS, J. S., KEWMAN, D. G., RICHARDSON, E., & KENNEDY, P. (2010). Spinal cord injury. In R. G. FRANK, M. ROSENTHAL., & B. CAPLAN (Eds.). *Handbook of Rehabilitation Psychology* (2nd ed., pp. 9–28). Washington, DC: American Psychological Association.

RICHARDS, J. S., NEPOMUCENO, C., RILES, M., & SUER, Z. (1982). Assessing pain behavior: The UAB Pain Behavior Scale. *Pain, 14,* 393–398.

RICHARDSON, K. M., & ROTHSTEIN, H. R. (2008). Effects of occupational stress management intervention programs: A meta-analysis. *Journal of Occupational Health Psychology, 13,* 69–93.

RICHMAN, L. M., & LEARY, M. R. (2009). Reactions to discrimination, stigmatization, ostracism, and other forms of interpersonal rejection: A multimotive model. *Psychological Review, 116,* 365–383.

RICHTER, M., ECK, J., STRAUBE, T., MILTNER, W. H. R., & WEISS, T. (2010). Do words hurt? Brain activation during the processing of pain-related words. *Pain, 148,* 198–205.

RIETVELD, S., & BROSSCHOT, J. F. (1999). Current perspectives on symptom perception in asthma: A biomedical and psychological review. *International Journal of Behavioral Medicine, 6,* 120–134.

RIGOTTI, N. A., SINGER, D. E., MULLEY, A. G., & THIBAULT, G. E. (1991). Smoking cessation following admission to a coronary care unit. *Journal of General Internal Medicine, 6,* 305–311.

RIKSEN, N. P., RONGEN, G. A., & SMITS, P. (2009). Acute and long-term cardiovascular effects of coffee: Implications for coronary heart disease. *Pharmacology and Therapeutics, 121,* 185–191.

RIMER, B. K. (1998). Interventions to enhance cancer screening: A brief review of what works and what is on the horizon. *Cancer, 83,* 1770–1774.

RIMER, B. K., MCBRIDE, C. M., & CRUMP, C. (2001). Women's health promotion. In A. BAUM, T. A. REVENSON, & J. E. SINGER (Eds.), *Handbook of health psychology* (pp. 519–539). Mahwah, NJ: Erlbaum.

RIMM, D. C., & MASTERS, J. C. (1979). *Behavior therapy: Techniques and empirical findings* (2nd ed.). New York: Academic Press.

RISSER, N. L., & BELCHER, D. W. (1990). Adding spirometry, carbon monoxide, and pulmonary symptom results to smoking cessation counseling: A randomized trial. *Journal of General Internal Medicine, 5,* 16–22.

RITTERBAND, L. M., THORNDIKE, F. P., GONDER-FREDERICK, L. A., MAGEE, J. C., BAILEY, E. T., et al. (2009). Efficacy of an Internet-based behavioral intervention for adults with insomnia. *Archives of General Psychiatry, 66,* 692–698.

RIZVI, A. A. (2009). Cytokine biomarkers, endothelial inflammation, and atherosclerosis in the metabolic syndrome: Emerging concepts. *American Journal of the Medical Sciences, 338,* 310–318.

ROBBINS, L. (1994). Precipitating factors in migraine: A retrospective review of 494 patients. *Headache, 34,* 214–216.

ROBERTO, C. A., LARSEN, P. D., AGNEW, H., BAIK, J., & BROWNELL, K. D. (2010). Evaluating the impact of menu labeling on food choices and intake. *American Journal of Public Health, 100,* 312–318.

ROBERTS, A. H. (1995). The powerful placebo revisited: Magnitude of nonspecific effects. *Mind/Body Medicine, 1,* 35–43.

ROBERTS, C. S., COX, C. E., REINTGEN, D. S., BAILE, W. F., & GILBERTINI, M. (1994). Influence of physician communication on newly diagnosed breast patients' psychologic adjustment and decision-making. *Cancer, 74,* 336–341.

ROBERTSON, L. S. (1986). Behavioral and environmental interventions for reducing motor vehicle trauma. *Annual Review of Public Health, 7,* 13–34.

ROBERTSON, S. M., CULLEN, D. W., BARANOWSKI, J., BARANOWSKI, T., HU, S., & DE MOOR, C. (1999). Factors related to adiposity among children aged 3 to 7 years. *Journal of the American Dietetic Association, 99,* 938–943.

ROBINS, C. J., & HAYES, A. M. (1993). An appraisal of cognitive therapy. *Journal of Consulting and Clinical Psychology, 61,* 205–214.

ROBINSON, J. D., & CINCIRIPINI, P. M. (2006). The effects of stress and smoking on catacholaminergic and cardiovascular response. *Behavioral Medicine, 32,* 13–18.

ROBINSON, L. A., & KLESGES, R. C. (1997). Ethnic and gender differences in risk factors for smoking onset. *Health Psychology, 16,* 499–505.

ROBINSON, T. E., & BERRIDGE, K. C. (2001). Incentive-sensitization and addiction. *Addiction, 96,* 103–114.

ROBINSON, T. E., & BERRIDGE, K. C. (2003). Addiction. *Annual Review of Psychology, 54,* 25–53.

ROBLES, T. F. (2007). Stress, social support, and delayed skin barrier recovery. *Psychosomatic Medicine, 69,* 807–815.

ROBLES, T. F. & KIECOLT-GLASER, J. K. (2003). The physiology of marriage: Pathways to health. *Physiology and Behavior, 79,* 409–416.

RODENHUIS, S., VAN DE WETERING, M. L., MOOR, W. J., EVERS, S. G., VAN ZANDWIJK, N., & BOS, J. L. (1987). Mutational activation of the K-ras oncogene. *New England Journal of Medicine, 317,* 929–935.

RODIN, J. (1981). Current status of the internal-external hypothesis for obesity: What went wrong? *American Psychologist, 36,* 361–372.

RODIN, J. (1985). Insulin levels, hunger, and food intake: An example of feedback loops in body weight regulation. *Health Psychology, 4,* 1–24.

RODIN, J., & BAUM, A. (1978). Crowding and helplessness: Potential consequences of density and loss of control. In A. BAUM & Y. M. EPSTEIN (Eds.), *Human response to crowding* (pp. 390–401). Hillsdale, NJ: Erlbaum.

RODIN, J., & JANIS, I. L. (1979). The social power of health-care practitioners as agents of change. *Journal of Social Issues, 35,* 60–81.

RODIN, J., & LANGER, E. J. (1977). Long-term effects of a control-relevant intervention with the institutionalized aged. *Journal of Personality and Social Psychology, 35,* 897–902.

RODRIGUEZ, C. M. & RICHARDSON, M. J. (2007). Stress and anger as contextual factors and preexisting cognitive schemas: Predicting parental child maltreatment risk. *Child Maltreatment, 12,* 325–337.

RODRIGUEZ, D., ROMER, D., & AUDRAIN-MCGOVERN, J. (2007). Beliefs about the risks of smoking mediate the relationship between exposure to smoking and smoking. *Psychosomatic Medicine, 69,* 106–113.

ROELOFS, J., BOISSEVAIN, M. D., PETERS, M. L., DE JONG, J. R., & VLAEYEN, J. W. S. (2002). Psychological treatments for chronic low back pain: Past, present, and beyond. *Pain Reviews, 9,* 29–40.

ROESCH, S. C., ADAMS, L., HINES, A., PALMORES, A., PEARLIN, V., et al. (2005). Coping with prostate cancer: A meta-analytic review. *Journal of Behavioral Medicine, 28,* 281–293.

ROESCH, S. C., & WEINER, B. (2001). A meta-analytic review of coping with illness: Do causal attributions matter? *Journal of Psychosomatic Research, 50,* 205–219.

ROHLEDER, N., CHEN, E., WOLF, J. M. & MILLER, G. E. (2008). The psychobiology of trait shame in young women: Extending the social self preservation theory. *Health Psychology, 27,* 523–532.

ROHLING, M. L., BINDER, L. M., & LANGHINRICHSEN-ROHLING, J. (1995). A meta-analytic review of the association between financial compensation and the experience and treatment of chronic pain. *Health Psychology, 14,* 537–547.

ROHRBAUGH, M. J., SHOHAM, V., & COYNE, J. C. (2006). Effect of marital quality on eight-year survival of patients with heart failure. *American Journal of Cardiology, 98,* 1069–1072.

ROHSENOW, D. J., MONTI, P. M., RUBONIS, A. V., GULLIVER, S. B., COLBY, S. M., et al. (2001). Cue exposure with coping skills training and communication skills training for alcohol dependence: 6- and 12-month outcomes. *Addiction, 96,* 1161–1174.

ROJO, L., CONESA, L., BERMUDEZ, O., & LIVIANOS, L. (2006). Influence of stress in the onset of eating disorders: Data from a two-stage epidemiologic controlled study. *Psychosomatic Medicine, 68,* 628–635.

ROLLMAN, B. L., BELNAP, B. H., LEMENAGER, M. S., MAZUMDAR, S., HOUCK, P. R., et al. (2009). Telephone-delivered collaborative care for treating post-CABG depression: A randomized controlled trial. *Journal of the American Medical Association, 302,* 2095–2103.

ROLLMAN, G. B. (2004). Ethnocultural variations in the experience of pain. In T. HADJISTAVROPOULOS & K. D. CRAIG (Eds.), *Pain: Psychological perspectives* (pp. 155–178). Mahwah, NJ: Earlbaum.

ROLLS, B. J., MORRIS, E. L., & ROE, L. S. (2002). Portion size of food affects energy intake in normal-weight and overweight men and women. *American Journal of Clinical Nutrition, 76,* 1207–1213.

ROMANO, J. M., TURNER, J. A., & JENSEN, M. P. (1997). The family environment in chronic pain patients: Comparison to controls and relationship to patient functioning. *Journal of Clinical Psychology in Medical Settings, 4,* 383–395.

ROSE, J. S., CHASSIN, L., PRESSON, C. C., & SHERMAN, S. J. (1996). Prospective predictors of quit attempts and smoking cessation in young adults. *Health Psychology, 15,* 261–268.

ROSE, R. J. (1986). Familial influences on cardiovascular reactivity to stress. In K. A. MATTHEWS, S. M. WEISS, T. DETRE, T. M. DEMBROSKI, B. FALKNER, S. B. MANUCK, & R. B. WILLIAMS (Eds.), *Handbook of stress, reactivity, and cardiovascular disease* (pp. 259–272). New York: Wiley.

ROSEN, J. C. (2002). Obesity and body image. In C. G. FAIRBURN & K. D. BROWNELL (Eds.), *Eating disorders and obesity: A comprehensive handbook* (pp. 399–402). New York: Guilford Press.

ROSEN, J. C., & GROSS, J. (1987). Prevalence of weight reducing and weight gaining in adolescent boys and girls. *Health Psychology, 6,* 131–147.

ROSEN, J. C., GRUBMAN, J. A., BEVINS, T., & FRYMOYER, J. W. (1987). Musculoskeletal status and disability of MMPI profile subgroups among patients with low back pain. *Health Psychology, 6,* 581–598.

ROSENBAUM, J. E. (2009). Patient teenagers? A comparison of the sexual behavior of virginity pledgers and matched pledgers. *Pediatrics, 123,* e110–e120.

ROSENFELD, B. (2004). Euthanasia and physician-assisted suicide. In A. J. CHRISTENSEN, R. MARTIN, & J. M. SMYTH (Eds.), *Encyclopedia of health psychology* (pp. 103–104). New York, Kluwer.

ROSENMAN, R. H., BRAND, R. J., SHOLTZ, R. I., & FRIEDMAN, M. (1976). Multivariate prediction of coronary heart disease during 8.5 year follow-up in the Western Collaborative Group Study. *American Journal of Cardiology, 37,* 903–910.

ROSENMAN, R. H., SWAN, G. E., & CARMELLI, D. (1988). Definition, assessment, and evolution of the Type A behavior pattern. In B. K. HOUSTON & C. R. SNYDER (Eds.), *Type A behavior pattern: Research, theory, and intervention* (pp. 8–31). New York: Wiley.

ROSENSTOCK, I. M. (1966). Why people use health services. *Millbank Memorial Fund Quarterly, 44,* 94–127.

ROSENSTOCK, I. M., & KIRSCHT, J. P. (1979). Why people seek health care. In G. C. STONE, F. COHEN, & N. E. ADLER (Eds.), *Health psychology—A handbook* (pp. 161–188). San Francisco: Jossey-Bass.

Roskies, E. (1983). Stress management for Type A individuals. In D. Meichenbaum & M. E. Jaremko (Eds.), *Stress reduction and prevention* (pp. 261–288). New York: Plenum.

Roskies, E., Seraganian, P., Oseasohn, R., Hanley, J. A., Collu, R., et al. (1986). The Montreal Type A Intervention Project: Major findings. *Health Psychology*, 5, 45–69.

Roter, D. L., & Hall, J. A. (1987). Physicians' interviewing styles and medical information obtained from patients. *Journal of General Internal Medicine*, 2, 325–329.

Roter, D. L., & Hall, J. A. (1989). Studies of doctor-patient interaction. *Annual Review of Public Health*, 10, 163–180.

Roter, D. L., Hall, J. A., Mersica, R., Nordstrom, B., Cretin, D., & Svarstad, B. (1998). Effectiveness of interventions to improve patient compliance: A meta-analysis. *Medical Care*, 36, 1138–1161.

Roth, D. L., & Holmes, D. S. (1985). Influence of physical fitness in determining the impact of stressful life events on physical and psychologic health. *Psychosomatic Medicine*, 47, 164–173.

Rotheram-Borus, M. J., Murphy, D. A., Reid, H. M., & Coleman, C. L. (1996). Correlates of emotional distress among HIV+ youths: Health status, stress, and personal resources. *Annals of Behavioral Medicine*, 18, 16–23.

Rothman, A. J., & Salovey, P. (1997). Shaping perceptions to motivate healthy behavior: The role of message framing. *Psychological Bulletin*, 121, 3–19.

Rothman, A. J., & Salovey, P. (2004). Message-framing effects. In A. J. Christensen, R. Martin, & J. M. Smyth (Eds.), *Encyclopedia of health psychology* (pp. 168–169). New York: Kluwer.

Rothman, R. I., Dewalt, D. A., Malone, R., Bryant, B., Shintani, A., et al. (2004). Influence of patient literacy on the effectiveness of a primary care-based diabetes disease management program. *Journal of the American Medical Association*, 292, 1711–1716.

Rothrock, N. E. (2004). Lay referral network. In A. J. Christensen, R. Martin, & J. M. Smyth (Eds.), *Encyclopedia of health psychology* (p. 157). New York: Kluwer.

Rotter, J. B. (1966). Generalized expectancies for the internal versus external control of reinforcement. *Psychological Monographs*, 90(1), 1–28.

Rowe, M. M. (1999). Teaching health-care providers coping: Results of a two-year study. *Journal of Behavioral Medicine*, 22, 511–527.

Roy, B., Diez-Roux, A., Seeman, T., Ranjit, N., Shea, S., & Cushman, M. (2010). Association of optimism and pessimism with inflammation and hemostasis in the Multi-Ethnic Study of Atherosclerosis. Psychosomatic Medicine, 72, 134–140.

Rozanski, A. (2005). Integrating psychologic approaches into the behavioral management of cardiac patients. *Psychosomatic Medicine*, 67(Suppl. 1), S67–S73.

Rozlog, L. A., Kiecolt-Glaser, J. K., Marucha, P. T., Sheridan, J. F., & Glaser, R. (1999). Stress and immunity: Implications for viral disease and wound healing. *Journal of Periodontology*, 70, 786–792.

Rueda, S., Park-Eyllie, L. Y., Bayoumi, A. M., Tynan, A. M., Antoniou, T. A., et al. (2006). Patient support and education for promoting adherence to highly active antiretroviral therapy for HIV/AIDS. *Cochrane Database of Systematic Reviews*, Issue 3. DOI: 10.1002/14651858.CD001442.pub2.

Rugulies, R., Aust, B., & Syme, S. L. (2004). Epidemiology of health and illness: A socio-psycho-physiological perspective. In S. Sutton, A. Baum, & M. Johnston (Eds.), *The Sage handbook of health psychology* (pp. 27–68). London: Sage.

Ruitenberg, A., van Swieten, J. C., Witteman, J. C. M., Mehta, K. M., van Duijn, C. M., et al. (2003). Alcohol consumption and risk of dementia: The Rotterdam Study. *Lancet*, 359, 281–286.

Rundall, T. G., & Wheeler, J. R. C. (1979). The effect of income on use of preventive care: An evaluation of alternative explanations. *Journal of Health and Social Behavior*, 20, 397–406.

Runyan, C. W. (1985). Health assessment and public policy within a public health framework. In P. Karoly (Ed.), *Measurement strategies in health psychology* (pp. 601–622). New York: Wiley.

Russell, M., Peirce, R. S., Chan, A. W. K., Wieczorek, W. F., Moscato, B. S., & Nochajski, T. H. (2001). Natural recovery in a community-based sample of alcoholics: Study design and descriptive data. *Substance Use and Misuse*, 36, 1417–1441.

Ryan, C., Huebner, D., Diaz, R. M., & Sanchez, J. (2009). Family rejection as a predictor of negative health outcomes in White and Latino lesbian, gay, and bisexual young adults. *Pediatrics*, 123, 346–352.

Ryan, R. S., & Travis, J. W. (1981). *The wellness workbook*. Berkeley, CA: Ten Speed Press.

Rybstein-Blinchik, E. (1979). Effects of different cognitive strategies on chronic pain experience. *Journal of Behavioral Medicine*, 2, 93–101.

Rychtarik, R. G., Connors, G. J., Whitney, R. B., McGillicuddy, N. B., Fitterling, J. M., & Wirtz, P. W. (2000). Treatment settings for persons with alcoholism: Evidence for matching clients to inpatient versus outpatient care. *Journal of Consulting and Clinical Psychology*, 68, 277–289.

Rzewnicki, R., & Forgays, D. G. (1987). Recidivism and self-cure of smoking and obesity: An attempt to replicate. *American Psychologist*, 42, 97–100.

Saab, P. G., Llabre, M. M., Schneiderman, N., Hurwitz, B. E., McDonald, P. G., et al. (1997). Influence of ethnicity and gender on cardiovascular responses to active coping and inhibitory-passive coping challenges. *Psychosomatic Medicine*, 59, 434–446.

Saab, P. G., McCalla, J. R., Coons, H. L., Christensen, A. J., Kaplan, R., et al. (2004). Technological and medical advances: Implications for health psychology. *Health Psychology*, 23, 142–146.

Sabia, S., Nabi, H., Kivimaki, M., Shipley, M. J., Marmot, M. G., & Singh-Manoux, A. (2009). Health behaviors from early to late midlife as predictors of cognitive function: The

Whitehall II Study. *American Journal of Epidemiology*, 170, 428–437.

SACCO, R. L., ELKIND, M., BODEN-ALBALA, B., LIN, I.-F., KARGMAN, D. E., et al. (1999). The protective effect of moderate alcohol consumption on ischemic stroke. *Journal of the American Medical Association*, 281, 53–60.

SACCO, W. P., WELLS, K. J., VAUGHAN, C. A., FRIEDMAN, A., PEREZ, S., & MATTHEW, R. (2005). Depression in adults with type 2 diabetes: The role of adherence, body mass index, and self-efficacy. *Health Psychology*, 24, 630–634.

SACK, F. M., BRAY, G. A., CAREY, V. J., SMITH, S. R., RYAN, D. H. (2009). Comparison of weight-loss diet with different compositions of fat, protein, and carbohydrates. *New England Journal of Medicine*, 360, 859–873.

SACKS, D. A., & KOPPES, R. H. (1986). Blood transfusion and Jehovah's Witnesses: Medical and legal issues in obstetrics and gynecology. *American Journal of Obstetrics and Gynecology*, 154, 483–486.

SAFER, M. A., THARPS, Q. J., JACKSON, T. C., & LEVENTHAL, H. (1979). Determinants of three stages of delay in seeking care at a medical clinic. *Medical Care*, 17, 11–29.

SAFREN, S. A., O'CLEIRIGH, C., TAN, J. Y., RAMINANI, S. R., REILLY, L. C., et al. (2009). A randomized controlled trial of cognitive behavioral therapy for adherence and depression (CBT-AD) in HIV-infected individuals. *Health Psychology*, 28, 1–10.

SAHLER, O. J. Z., FAIRCLOUGH, D. L., PHIPPS, S., MULHERN, R. K., DOLGIN, M. J., et al. (2005). Using problem-solving skills training to reduce negative affectivity in mothers of children with newly diagnosed cancer: Report of a multisite randomized trial. *Journal of Consulting and Clinical Psychology*, 73, 272–283.

SALAS-SALVADO, J., FERNANDEZ-BALLART, J., ROS, E., MARTINEZ-GONZÁLEZ, M.-A., FITO, M., et al. (2008). Effect of a Mediterranean diet supplemented with nuts on metabolic syndrome status: One-year result of the PREDIMED randomized trial. *Archives of Internal Medicine*, 168, 2449–2458.

SALLIS, J. F., CERVERO, R. B., ASCHER, W., HENDERSON, K. A., KRAFT, M. K., & KERR, J. (2006). An ecological approach to creating active living communities. *Annual Review of Public Health*, 27, 297–322.

SALLIS, J. F., KING, A. C., SIRARD, J. R., & ALBRIGHT, C. L. (2007). Perceived environmental predictors of physical activity over 6 months in adults: Activity Counseling Trial. *Health Psychology*, 26, 701–709.

SALLIS, J. F., & OWEN, N. (1999). *Physical activity and behavioral medicine*. Thousand Oaks, CA: Sage.

SALLIS, J. F., PATTERSON, T. L., BUONO, M. J., ATKINS, C. J., & NADER, P. R. (1988). Aggregation of physical activity habits in Mexican-American and Anglo families. *Journal of Behavioral Medicine*, 11, 31–41.

SALLIS, J. F., TREVORROW, T. R., JOHNSON, C. C., HOVELL, M. F., & KAPLAN, R. M. (1987). Worksite stress management: A comparison of programs. *Psychology and Health*, 1, 237–255.

SALMON, J., OWEN, N., CRAWFORD, D., BAUMAN, A., & SALLIS, J. F. (2003). Physical activity and sedentary behavior: A population-based study of barriers, enjoyment, and preference. *Health Psychology*, 22, 178–188.

SALVY, S. J., HOWARD, M., READ, M., & MELE, E. (2009). The presence of friends increases food intake in youth. *American Journal of Clinical Nutrition*, 90, 282–287.

SAMHSA(Substance Abuse and Mental Health Services Administration) (2008). *Results from the 2007 National Survey of Drug Use and Health: National findings*. Retrieved (3-30-2010) from http://www.samhsa.gov.

SANDBERG, G. G., & MARLATT, G. A. (1991). Relapse prevention. In D. A. CIRAULO & R. I. SHADER (Eds.), *Clinical manual of chemical dependence* (pp. 377–399). Washington, DC: American Psychiatric Press.

SANDERS, S. H. (1985). Chronic pain: Conceptualization and epidemiology. *Annals of Behavioral Medicine*, 7(3), 3–5.

SANDERS, S. H., BRENA, S. F., SPIER, C. J., BELTRUTTI, D., MCCONNELL, H., & QUINTERO, O. (1992). Chronic low back pain patients around the world: Cross-cultural similarities and differences. *Journal of Clinical Pain*, 8, 317–323.

SANTIAGO, J. V. (1984). Effect of treatment on the long term complications of IDDM. *Behavioral Medicine Update*, 6(1), 26–31.

SARACENO, L., MUNAFÓ, M., HERON, J., CRADDOCK, N., & VAN DEN BREE, M. B. M. (2009). Genetic and non-genetic influences on the development of co-occurring alcohol problem use and internalizing symptomatology in adolescence: A review. *Addiction*, 104, 1100–1121.

SARAFINO, E. P. (1986). *The fears of childhood: A guide to recognizing and reducing fearful states in children*. New York: Human Sciences Press.

SARAFINO, E. P. (1997). *Behavioral treatments for asthma: Biofeedback-, respondent-, and relaxation-based approaches*. Lewiston, NY: Edwin Mellon Press.

SARAFINO, E. P. (2000). Connections among parent and child atopic illnesses. *Pediatric Allergy and Immunology*, 11, 80–86.

SARAFINO, E. P. (2001). *Behavior modification: Principles of behavior change* (2nd ed.). Mountain View, CA: Mayfield.

SARAFINO, E. P. (2004a). Asthma. In A. J. CHRISTENSEN, R. MARTIN, & J. M. SMYTH (Eds.), *Encyclopedia of health psychology* (pp. 19–21). New York: Kluwer.

SARAFINO, E. P. (2004b). Context and perspectives in health psychology. In S. SUTTON, A. BAUM, & M. JOHNSTON (Eds.), *The Sage handbook of health psychology* (pp. 1–26). London: Sage.

SARAFINO, E. P. (2005). *Research methods: Using processes and procedures of science to understand behavior*. Upper Saddle River, NJ: Prentice Hall.

SARAFINO, E. P. (2011). *Self-management: Using behavioral and cognitive principles to manage your life*. Hoboken, NJ: Wiley.

SARAFINO, E. P., & ARMSTRONG, J. W. (1986). *Child and adolescent development* (2nd ed.). St. Paul, MN: West.

SARAFINO, E. P., & DILLON, J. M. (1998). Relationships among respiratory infections, triggers of attacks, and asthma severity in children. *Journal of Asthma*, 35, 497–504.

SARAFINO, E. P., & EWING, M. (1999). The Hassles Assessment Scale for Students in College: Measuring the frequency and unpleasantness of and dwelling on stressful events. *Journal of American College Health, 48,* 75–83.

SARAFINO, E. P., & GOEHRING, P. (2000). Age comparisons in acquiring biofeedback control and success in reducing headache pain. *Annals of Behavioral Medicine, 22,* 10–16.

SARAFINO, E. P., & GOLDFEDDER, J. (1995). Genetic factors in the presence, severity, and triggers of asthma. *Archives of Disease in Childhood, 73,* 112–116.

SARAFINO, E. P., & GRAHAM, J. A. (2006). Development and psychometric evaluation of an instrument to assess reinforcer preferences: The Preferred Items and Experiences Questionnaire. *Behavior Modification, 30,* 835–847.

SARASON, I. G., JOHNSON, J. H., & SIEGEL, J. M. (1978). Assessing the impact of life changes: Development of the Life Experiences Survey. *Journal of Consulting and Clinical Psychology, 46,* 932–946.

SARASON, I. G., LEVINE, H. M., BASHAM, R. B., & SARASON, B. R. (1983). Assessing social support: The Social Support Questionnaire. *Journal of Personality and Social Psychology, 44,* 127–139.

SARASON, I. G., & SARASON, B. R. (1984). *Abnormal psychology* (4th ed.). Englewood Cliffs, NJ: Prentice Hall.

SARASON, I. G., SARASON, B. R., POTTER, E. H., & ANTONI, M. H. (1985). Life events, social support, and illness. *Psychosomatic Medicine, 47,* 156–163.

SARKASIAN, C. A., PROHASKA, T. R., WONG, M. D., HIRSCH, S., & MANGIONE, C. M. (2005). The relationship between expectations for aging and physical activity among older adults. *Journal of General Internal Medicine, 20,* 911–915.

SASTRE, M. T. M., MULLET, E., & SORUM, P. C. (1999). Relationship between cigarette dose and perceived risk of lung cancer. *Preventive Medicine, 28,* 566–571.

SAUNDERS, C. (1986). A philosophy of terminal care. In M. J. CHRISTIE & P. G. MELLETT (Eds.), *The psychosomatic approach: Contemporary practice of whole-person care* (pp. 427–436). New York: Wiley.

SAURO, M. D., & GREENBERG, R. P. (2005). Endogenous opiates and the placebo effect: A meta-analytic review. *Journal of Psychosomatic Research, 58,* 115–120.

SCAMBLER, G. (1984). Perceiving and coping with stigmatizing illness. In R. FITZPATRICK, J. HINTON, S. NEWMAN, G. SCAMBLER, & J. THOMPSON (Eds.), *The experience of illness* (pp. 203–226). London: Tavistock.

SCARMEAS, N., LUCHSINGER, J. A., SCHUPF, N., BRICKMAN, A. M., COSENTINO, S., et al. (2009). Physical activity, diet, and risk of Alzheimer disease. *Journal of the American Medical Association, 302,* 627–637.

SCARR, S., & KIDD, K. K. (1983). Developmental behavior genetics. In P. H. MUSSEN (Ed.), *Handbook of child psychology* (4th ed., Vol. 2, pp. 345–434). New York: Wiley.

SCHACHTER, S. (1971). Some extraordinary facts about obese humans and rats. *American Psychologist, 26,* 129–144.

SCHACHTER, S. (1980). Urinary pH and the psychology of nicotine addiction. In P. O. DAVIDSON & S. M. DAVIDSON (Eds.), *Behavioral medicine: Changing health lifestyles* (pp. 70–93). New York: Brunner/Mazel.

SCHACHTER, S. (1982). Recidivism and self cure of smoking and obesity. *American Psychologist, 37,* 436–444.

SCHACHTER, S., SILVERSTEIN, B., KOZLOWSKI, L. T., PERLICK, D., HERMAN, C. P., & LIEBLING, B. (1977). Studies of the interaction of psychological and pharmacological determinants of smoking. *Journal of Experimental Psychology: General, 106,* 3–40.

SCHAEFER, C., COYNE, J. C., & LAZARUS, R. S. (1981). The health-related functions of social support. *Journal of Behavioral Medicine, 4,* 381–406.

SCHAFER, L. C., GLASGOW, R. E., & MCCAUL, K. D. (1982). Increasing the adherence of diabetic adolescents. *Journal of Behavioral Medicine, 5,* 353–362.

SCHAUFFLER, H. H., & MORDAVSKY, J. K. (2001). Consumer reports in health care: Do they make a difference? *Annual Review of Public Health, 22,* 69–89.

SCHEFFLER, R. M., BROWN, T. T, SYME, L., KAWACHI, I., TOLSTYK. I., & IRIBARREN, C. (2007). Community-level social capital and recurrence of acute coronary syndrome. *Social Science & Medicine, 66,* 1603–1613.

SCHEIER, L. M., & BOTVIN, G. J. (1997). Expectancies as mediators of the effects of social influences and alcohol knowledge on adolescent alcohol use: A prospective analysis. *Psychology of Addictive Behaviors, 11,* 48–64.

SCHEIER, M. F., & CARVER, C. S. (2001). Adapting to cancer: The importance of hope and purpose. In A. BAUM & B. L. ANDERSON (Eds.), *Psychosocial interventions for cancer* (pp. 15–36). Washington, DC: American Psychological Association.

SCHEIER, M. F., CARVER, C. S., & BRIDGES, M. W. (2001). Optimism, pessimism, and psychological well-being. In E. C. CHANG (Ed.), *Optimism and pessimism: Implications for theory, research and practice* (pp. 189–216). Washington, DC: American Psychological Association.

SCHEIER, M. F., MATTHEWS, K. A., OWENS, J. F., SCHULZ, R., BRIDGES, M. W., et al. (1999). Optimism and rehospitalization after coronary artery bypass graft surgery. *Archives of Internal Medicine, 159,* 829–835.

SCHERER, K. R. (1986). Voice, stress, and emotion. In M. H. APPLEY & R. TRUMBULL (Eds.), *Dynamics of stress: Physiological, psychological, and social perspectives* (pp. 157–179). New York: Plenum.

SCHERRER, J. F., GRANT, J. D., DUNCAN, A. E., PAN, H., WATERMAN, B., et al. (2008). Meaured environmental contributions to cannabis abuse/dependence in an offpring of twins design. *Addictive Behaviors, 33,* 1255–1266.

SCHIAFFINO, K. M., SHAWARYN, M. A., & BLUM, D. (1998). Examining the impact of illness representations on psychological adjustment to chronic illnesses. *Health Psychology, 17,* 262–268.

SCHIFFMAN, H. R. (1996). *Sensation and perception: An integrated approach* (4th ed.). New York: Wiley.

SCHIFTER, D. E., & AJZEN, I. (1985). Intention, perceived control, and weight loss: An application of the theory of planned behavior. *Journal of Personality and Social Psychology, 45,* 843–851.

SCHINKE, S. P., FANG, L., & COLE, K. C. (2009). Preventing substance use among adolescent girls: 1-year outcomes of a computerized, mother–daughter program. *Addictive Behaviors, 34,* 1060–1064.

SCHMIEDER, R., FRIEDRICH, G., NEUS, H., RÜDEL, H., & VON EIFF, A. W. (1983). The influence of beta-blockers on cardiovascular reactivity and Type A behavior pattern in hypertensives. *Psychosomatic Medicine, 45,* 417–423.

SCHNALL, P. L., PIEPER, C., SCHWARTZ, J. E., KARASEK, R. A., SCHLUSSEL, Y., et al. (1990). The relationship between "job strain," workplace diastolic blood pressure, and left ventricular mass index: Results of a case-control study. *Journal of the American Medical Association, 263,* 1929–1935.

SCHNALL, P. L., SCHWARTZ, J. E., LANDSBERGIS, P. A., WARREN, K., & PICKERING, T. G. (1998). A longitudinal study of job strain and ambulatory blood pressure: Results from a three-year follow-up. *Psychosomatic Medicine, 60,* 697–706.

SCHNEIDER, A. M., & TARSHIS, B. (1975). *An introduction to physiological psychology.* New York: Random House.

SCHNEIDER, C., PALOMBA, D., & FLOR, H. (2004). Pavlovian conditioning of muscular responses in chronic pain patients: Central and peripheral correlates. *Pain, 112,* 239–247.

SCHNEIDERMAN, N., & HAMMER, D. (1985). Behavioral medicine approaches to cardiovascular disorders. In N. SCHNEIDERMAN & J. T. TAPP (Eds.), *Behavioral medicine: The biopsychosocial approach* (pp. 467–507). Hillsdale, NJ: Erlbaum.

SCHNUR, J. B., & MONTGOMERY, G. H. (2010). A systematic review of therapeutic alliance, group cohesion, empathy, and goal consensus/collaboration in psychotherapeutic interventions in cancer. Uncommon factors? *Clinical Psychology Review, 30,* 238–247.

SCHOENBORN, C. A. (1993). The Alameda Study—25 years later. In S. MAES, H. LEVENTHAL, & M. JOHNSTON (Eds.), *International review of health psychology* (Vol. 2, pp. 81–116). New York: Wiley.

SCHOFIELD, P. (2005). Effects of chronic pain. In P. SCHOFIELD (Ed.), *Beyond pain* (pp. 19–36). London: Whurr.

SCHOOTMAN, M., ANDRESEN, E. M., WOLINSKY, F. D., MALMSTROM, T. K., MILLER, J. P., et al. (2007). The effect of adverse housing and neighborhood conditions on the development of diabetes mellitus among middle-aged African Americans. *American Journal of Epidemiology, 166,* 379–387.

SCHRAA, J. C., & DIRKS, J. F. (1982). Improving patient recall and comprehension of the treatment regimen. *Journal of Asthma, 19,* 159–162.

SCHREIER, H. M. C. & CHEN, E. (2008). Prospective associations between coping and health among youth with asthma. *Journal of Consulting and Clinical Psychology, 76,* 790–798.

SCHREIER, H. M. C., & CHEN, E. (2010). Longitudinal relationships between family routines and biological profiles among youth with asthma. *Health Psychology, 29,* 82–90.

SCHROEDER, S. A. (2005). What to do with a patient who smokes. *Journal of the American Medical Association, 294,* 482–487.

SCHROEVERS, M., RANCHOR, A. V., & SANDERMAN, R. (2006). Adjustment to cancer in the 8 years following diagnosis: A longitudinal study comparing cancer survivors with healthy individuals. *Social Science & Medicine, 63,* 598–610.

SCHUCKIT, M. A. (1996). Recent developments in the pharmacotherapy of alcohol dependence. *Journal of Consulting and Clinical Psychology, 64,* 669–676.

SCHUCKIT, M. A., DAEPPEN, J.-B., DANKO, G. P., TRIPP, M. L., SMITH, T. L., LI, T.-K., et al. (1999). Clinical implications for four drugs of the DSM-IV distinction between substance dependence with and without a physiological component. *American Journal of Psychiatry, 156,* 41–49.

SCHULZ, R. (1976). Effects of control and predictability on the physical and psychological well-being of the institutionalized aged. *Journal of Personality and Social Psychology, 33,* 563–573.

SCHULZ, R., & BEACH, S. R. (1999). Health effects study caregiving as a risk factor for mortality: The caregiver. *Journal of the American Medical Association, 282,* 2215–2219.

SCHULZ, R., CZAJA, S. J., LUSTIG, A., ZDANIUK, B., MARTIRE, L. M., & PERDOMO, D. (2009). Improving the quality of life of caregivers of persons with spinal cord injury: A randomized controlled trial. *Rehabilitation Psychology, 54,* 1–15.

SCHULZ, R., & HANUSA, B. H. (1978). Long-term effects of control and predictability-enhancing interventions: Findings and ethical issues. *Journal of Personality and Social Psychology, 36,* 1194–1201.

SCHUMANN, A., MEYER, D., RUMPF, H.-J., HANNÖVER, W., HAPKE, U., & JOHN, U. (2005). Stage of change transitions and processes of change, decisional balance, and self-efficacy in smokers: A transtheoretical model validation using longitudinal data. *Psychology of Addictive Behaviors, 19,* 3–9.

SCHUNK, D. H., & CARBONARI, J. P. (1984). Self-efficacy models. In J. D. MATARAZZO, S. M. WEISS, J. A. HERD, N. E. MILLER, & S. M. WEISS (Eds.), *Behavioral health: A handbook of health enhancement and disease prevention* (pp. 230–247). New York: Wiley.

SCHUSTER, C. R., & KILBEY, M. M. (1992). Prevention of drug abuse. In J. M. LAST & R. B. WALLACE (Eds.), *Maxcy-Rosenau-Last public health and preventive medicine* (13th ed., pp. 769–786). Norwalk, CT: Appleton & Lange.

SCHUSTER, M. A., STEIN, B. D., HAYCOX, L. H., COLLINS, R. L., MARSHALL, G. N., et al. (2001). A national survey of stress reactions after the September 11, 2001, terrorist attacks. *New England Journal of Medicine, 345,* 1507–1512.

SCHUTTE, K. K., NICHOLS, K. A., BRENNAN, P. L., & MOOS, R. H. (2003). A ten-year follow-up of older problem drinkers: Risk of relapse and implications of successfully maintained remission. *Journal of Studies on Alcohol, 64,* 367–374.

SCHWARTZ, M. D., TAYLOR, K. L., WILLARD, K. S., SIEGEL, J. E., LAMDAN, R. M., & MORAN, K. (1999). Distress, personality, and mammography utilization among women with a family history of breast cancer. *Health Psychology, 18,* 327–332.

Schwarzer, R., Luszczynska, A., Ziegelmann, J. P., Scholz, U., & Lippke, S. (2008). Social–cognitive predictors of physical exercise adherence: Three longitudinal studies in rehabilitation. *Health Psychology, 27*(Suppl.), S54–S63.

Scott, J. L., Halford, W. K., & Ward, B. G. (2004). United we stand? The effects of a couple-coping intervention on adjustment to early stage breast or gynecological cancer. *Journal of Consulting and Clinical Psychology, 72,* 1122–1135.

Scott, K. M., Von Korff, M., Alonso, J., Angermeyer, M. C., Benjet, C., et al. (2008). Childhood adversity, early-onset depressive/anxiety disorders, and adult-onset asthma. *Psychosomatic Medicine, 70,* 1035–1043.

Scott-Sheldon, L. A. J., Kalichman, S. C., Carey, M. P., & Fielder, R. L. (2008). Stress management interventions for HIV+ adults: A meta-analysis of randomized controlled trials, 1989 to 2006. *Health Psychology, 27,* 129–139.

Seaburn, D. B., Morse, D., Mcdaniel, S. H., Beckman, H., Silberman, J., & Epstein, R. (2005). Physician responses to ambiguous patient symptoms. *Journal of General Internal Medicine, 20,* 525–530.

Sears, S. R., & Stanton, A. L. (2001). Physician-assisted dying: Review of issues and roles for health psychologists. *Health Psychology, 20,* 302–310.

Sears, S. R., Stanton, A. L., & Danoff-Burg, S. (2003). The yellow brick road and the Emerald City: Benefit finding, positive reappraisal coping, and posttraumatic growth in women with early-stage breast cancer. *Health Psychology, 22,* 487–497.

Seeman, T. E., & Mcewen, B. S. (1996). Impact of social environment characteristics on neuroendocrine regulation. *Psychosomatic Medicine, 58,* 459–471.

Seeman, T. E., Singer, B. H., Rowe, J. W., Horwitz, R. I., & Mcewen, B. S. (1997). Price of adaptation—allostatic load and its health consequences. *Archives of Internal Medicine, 157,* 2259–2268.

Segerstrom, S. C. (2005). Optimism and immunity: Do positive thoughts always lead to positive effects? *Brain Behavior and Immunity, 19,* 195–200.

Segerstrom, S. C., & Miller, G. E. (2004). Psychological stress and the human immune system: A meta-analytic study of 30 years of inquiry. *Psychological Bulletin, 130,* 601–630.

Seidman, D. F., Westmaas, J. L., Goldband, S., Rabius, V., Katkin, E. S., et al. (2010). Randomized controlled trial of an interactive Internet smoking cessation program with long-term follow-up. *Annals of Behavioral Medicine, 39,* 48–60.

Self, C. A., & Rogers, R. W. (1990). Coping with threats to health: Effects of persuasive appeals on depressed, normal, and antisocial personalities. *Journal of Behavioral Medicine, 13,* 343–357.

Seligman, M. E. P. (1975). *Helplessness: On depression, development, and death.* San Francisco: Freeman.

Seligmann, J., & Sulavik, C. (1992, April 27). Software for hard issues. *Newsweek,* p. 55.

Selye, H. (1956). *The stress of life.* New York: McGraw-Hill.

Selye, H. (1974). *Stress without distress.* Philadelphia: Lippincott.

Selye, H. (1976). *Stress in health and disease.* Reading, MA: Butterworth.

Selye, H. (1985). History and present status of the stress concept. In A. Monat & R. S. Lazarus (Eds.), *Stress and coping: An anthology* (2nd ed., pp. 17–29). New York: Columbia University Press.

Serdula, M. K., Ivery, D., Coates, R. J., Freedman, D. S., Williamson, D. F., & Byers, T. (1993). Do obese children become obese adults? A review of the literature. *Preventive Medicine, 22,* 167–177.

Serfass, R. C., & Gerberich, S. G. (1984). Exercise for optimal health: Strategies and motivational considerations. *Preventive Medicine, 13,* 79–99.

Sesso, H. D., Buring, J. E., Christen, W. G., Kurth, T., Belanger, C., et al. (2008). Vitamins E and C in the prevention of cardiovascular disease in men: The Physician's Health Study II randomized controlled trial. *Journal of the American Medical Association, 300,* 2123–2133.

Severson, H. H. (1993). Smokeless tobacco: Risks, epidemiology, and cessation. In C. T. Orleans & J. Slade (Eds.), *Nicotine addiction: Principles and management.* New York: Oxford University Press.

Shadel, W. G., & Mermelstein, R. (1993). Cigarette smoking under stress: The role of coping expectancies among smokers in a clinic-based smoking cessation program. *Health Psychology, 12,* 443–450.

Shadel, W. G., Shiffman, S., Niaura, R., Nichter, M., & Abrams, D. B. (2000). Current models of nicotine dependence: What is known and what is needed to advance understanding of tobacco etiology among youth. *Drug and Alcohol Dependence, 59*(Suppl.), S9–S22.

Shafey, O., Erikson, M., Ross, H., & Mackay, J. (2009). *The tobacco atlas* (3rd ed.). Atlanta, GA: American Cancer Society. Retrieved (3-27-2010) from http://www.cancer.org.

Shahab, L., & Mcewen, A. (2009). Online support for smoking cessation: A systematic review of the literature. *Addiction, 104,* 1792–1804.

Shain, R. N., Piper, J. M., Newton, E. R., Perdue, S. T., Ramos, R., et al. (1999). A randomized, controlled trial of a behavioral intervention to prevent sexually transmitted disease among minority women. *New England Journal of Medicine, 340,* 93–100.

Shalev, A. Y., Tuval, R., Frenkeil-Fishman, S., Hadar, H., & Eth, S. (2006). Psychological responses to continuous terror: A study of two communities in Israel. *American Journal of Psychiatry, 163,* 667–673.

Shanfield, S. B. (1990). Return to work after an acute myocardial infarction: A review. *Heart & Lung, 19,* 109–117.

Shankar, A., Koh, W.-P., Yuan, J.-M., Lee, H.-P., & Yu, M. C. (2008). Sleep duration and coronary heart disease mortality among Chinese adults in Singapore: A population-based cohort study. *American Journal of Epidemiology* 168, 1367–1373.

SHARMAN, S. J., GARRY, M., JACOBSON, J. A., LOFTUS, E. F., & DITTO, P. H. (2008). False memories for end-of-life decisions. *Health Psychology, 27*, 291–296.

SHAW, R. E., COHEN, F., DOYLE, B., & PALESKY, J. (1985). The impact of denial and repressive style on information gain and rehabilitation outcomes in myocardial infarction patients. *Psychosomatic Medicine, 47*, 262–273.

SHEAR, K., FRANK, E., HOUCK, P. R., & REYNOLDS, C. F. (2005). Treatment of complicated grief: A randomized controlled trial. *Journal of the American Medical Association, 293*, 2601–2608.

SHEARER, H. M., & EVANS, D. R. (2001). Adherence to health care. In S. S. KAZARIAN & E. R. EVANS (Eds.), *Handbook of cultural health psychology* (pp. 113–138). San Diego: Academic Press.

SHERIDAN, K. (1991). Psychosocial services for persons with human immunodeficiency virus disease. In J. J. SWEET, R. H. ROZENSKY, & S. M. TOVIAN (Eds.), *Handbook of clinical psychology in medical settings* (pp. 587–600). New York: Plenum.

SHERMAN, B. F., BONANNO, G. A., WIENER, L. S., & BATTLES, H. B. (2000). When children tell their friends they have AIDS: Possible consequences for psychological well-being and disease progression. *Psychosomatic Medicine, 62*, 238–247.

SHERMAN, J. J., CARLSON, C. R., MCCUBBIN, J. A., & WILSON, J. F. (1997). Effects of stretch-based progressive relaxation training on the secretion of salivary immunoglobulin A in orofacial pain patients. *Journal of Orofacial Pain, 11*, 115–124.

SHERWOOD, A., GIRDLER, S. S., BRAGDON, E. E., WEST, S. G., BROWNLEY, K. A., et al. (1997). Ten-year stability of cardiovascular responses to laboratory stressors. *Psychophysiology, 34*, 185–191.

SHERWOOD, A., MAY, C. W., SIEGEL, W. C., & BLUMENTHAL, J. A. (1995). Ethnic differences in hemodynamic responses to stress in hypertensive men and women. *American Journal of Hypertension, 8*, 552–557.

SHIELDS, C. A., BRAWLEY, L. R., & LINDOVER, T. I. (2005). Where perception and reality differ: Dropping out is not the same as failure. *Journal of Behavioral Medicine, 28*, 481–491.

SHIFFMAN, S. (1986). A cluster-analytic classification of smoking relapse episodes. *Addictive Behaviors, 11*, 295–307.

SHIFFMAN, S., BALABANIS, M. H., PATY, J. A., ENGBERG, J., GWALTNEY, C. J., et al. (2000). Dynamic effects of self-efficacy on smoking lapse and relapse. *Health Psychology, 19*, 315–323.

SHIFFMAN. S., FISCHER, L. B., ZETTLER-SEGAL, M., & BENOWITZ, N. L. (1990). Nicotine exposure among nondependent smokers. *Archives of General Psychiatry, 47*, 333–336.

SHIFFMAN, S., HICKCOX, M., PATY, J. A., GNYS, M., KASSEL, J. D., & RICHARDS, T. J. (1996). Progression from a smoking lapse to relapse: Prediction from abstinence violation effects, nicotine dependence, and lapse characteristics. *Journal of Consulting and Clinical Psychology, 64*, 993–1002.

SHIFFMAN, S., PATY, J. A., GNYS, M., KASSEL, J. D., & ELASH, C. (1995). Nicotine withdrawal in chippers and regular smokers: Subjective and cognitive effects. *Health Psychology, 14*, 301–309.

SHIFFMAN, S., SHADEL, W. G., NIAURA, R., KHAYRALLAH, M. A., JORENBY, D. E., et al. (2003). Efficacy of acute administration of nicotine gum in relief of cue-provoked cigarette craving. *Psychopharmacology, 166*, 343–350.

SHIFFMAN, S., & STONE, A. A. (1998). Introduction to the special section: Ecological momentary assessment in health psychology. *Health Psychology, 17*, 3–5.

SHIMBO, D., CHAPLIN, W., AKINOLA, O., HARRIS, A., ABRAHAM, D., et al. (2007). Effect of anger provocation on endothelium-dependent and -independent vasodilation. *American Journal of Cardiology, 99*, 860–863.

SHIN, S. H., EDWARDS, E. M., & HEEREN, T. (2009). Child abuse and neglect: Relations to adolescent binge drinking in the national longitudinal study of Adolescent Health (AddHealth) Study. *Addictive Behaviors, 34*, 277–280.

SHIPLEY, R. H., BUTT, J. H., HORWITZ, B., & FARBRY, J. E. (1978). Preparation for a stressful medical procedure: Effect of amount of stimulus preexposure and coping style. *Journal of Consulting and Clinical Psychology, 46*, 499–507.

SHNEIDMAN, E. S. (1977). The college student and death. In H. FEIFEL (Ed.), *New meanings of death* (pp. 67–86). New York: McGraw-Hill.

SHOGREN, E. (1988, June 3). Physicians favor death with "dignity." *Philadelphia Inquirer*, p. D14.

SHONTZ, F. C. (1975). *The psychological aspects of physical illness and disability*. New York: Macmillan.

SHOPLAND, D. R., & BROWN, C. (1985). Changes in cigarette smoking prevalence in the U.S.: 1955 to 1983. *Annals of Behavioral Medicine, 7*(2), 5–8.

SHOPLAND, D. R., & BURNS, D. M. (1993). Medical and public health implications of tobacco addiction. In C. T. ORLEANS & J. SLADE (Eds.), *Nicotine addiction: Principles and management* (pp. 105–142). New York: Oxford University Press.

SHUPE, D. R. (1985). Perceived control, helplessness, and choice: Their relationship to health and aging. In J. E. BIRREN & J. LIVINGSTON (Eds.), *Cognition, stress, and aging* (pp. 174–197). Englewood Cliffs, NJ: Prentice Hall.

SHUPER, P. A., & FISHER, W. A. (2008). The role of sexual arousal and sexual partner characteristics on HIV+ MSM's intentions to engage in unprotected sexual intercourse. *Health Psychology, 27*, 445–454.

SIEGEL, L. J., & PETERSON, L. (1980). Stress reduction in young dental patients through coping skills and sensory information. *Journal of Consulting and Clinical Psychology, 48*, 785–787.

SIEGLER, I. C., FEAGANES, J. R., & RIMER, B. K. (1995). Predictors of adoption of mammography in women under age 50. *Annals of Behavioral Medicine, 14*, 274–278.

SIEGMAN, A. W., KUBZANSKY, L. D., KAWACHI, I., BOYLE, S., VOKONAS, P. S., & SPARROW, D. (2000). A prospective study of dominance and coronary heart disease in the Normative Aging Study. *American Journal of Cardiology, 86*, 145–149.

Sierra, F., Hadley, E., Suzman, R., & Hodes, R. (2009). Prospects for life span extension. *Annual Review of Medicine*, 60, 457–469.

Sieverding, M., Matterne, U., & Ciccarello, L. (2010). What role do social norms play in the context of men's cancer screening intention and behavior? Application of the extended theory of planned behavior. *Health Psychology*, 29, 72–81.

Sikkema, K. J. (1998). HIV prevention. In E. A. Blechman & K. D. Brownell (Eds.), *Behavioral medicine and women: A comprehensive handbook* (pp. 198–202). New York: Guilford.

Sikkema, K. J., Hansen, N. B., Ghebremichael, M., Kochman, A., Tarakeshwar, N., et al. (2006). A randomized controlled trial of a coping group intervention for adults with HIV who are AIDS bereaved: Longitudinal effects on grief. *Health Psychology*, 25, 563–570.

Sikkema, K. J., & Kelly, J. A. (1996). Behavioral medicine interventions can improve the quality-of-life and health of persons with HIV disease. *Annals of Behavioral Medicine*, 18, 40–48.

Sikkema, K. J., Kelly, J. A., Winett, R. A., Solomon, L. J., Cargill, V. A., et al. (2000). Outcomes of a randomized community-level HIF prevention intervention for women living in 18 low-income housing developments. *American Journal of Public Health*, 90, 57–63.

Silver, R. L., & Wortman, C. B. (1980). Coping with undesirable life events. In J. Garber & M. E. P. Seligman (Eds.), *Human helplessness: Theory and applications* (pp. 279–375). New York: Academic Press.

Simon, G. E., Katon, W. J., Lin, E. H., Rutter, C., Manning, W. G., et al. (2007). Cost-effectiveness of systematic depression treatment among people with diabetes mellitus. *Archives of General Psychiatry*, 64, 65–72.

Simoni, J. M., Frick, P. A., & Huang, B. (2006). A longitudinal evaluation of a social support model of medication adherence among HIV-positive men and women on antiretroviral therapy. *Health Psychology*, 25, 74–81.

Simoni, J. M., Mason, H. R. C., Marks, G., Ruiz, M. S., Reed, D., & Richardson, J. L. (1995). Women's self-disclosure of HIV infection: Rates, reasons, and reactions. *Journal of Consulting and Clinical Psychology*, 63, 474–478.

Simons-Morton, B., Chen, R., Abroms, L., & Haynie, D. L. (2004). Latent growth curve analyses of peer and parent influences on smoking progression among early adolescents. *Health Psychology*, 23, 612–621.

Simons-Morton, B. G., Hartos, J. L., Leaf, W. A., & Preusser, D. F. (2005). Persistence of effects of the Checkpoints Program on parental restrictions of teen driving privileges. *American Journal of Public Health*, 95, 447–452.

Sims, E. A. H. (1976). Experimental obesity, dietary-induced thermogenesis, and their clinical implications. *Clinics in Endocrinology and Metabolism*, 5, 377–395.

Sindelar, J. L., & Fiellin, D. A. (2001). Innovations in treatment for drug abuse: Solutions to a public health problem. *Annual Review of Public Health*, 22, 249–272.

Skelly, A. H., Marshall, J. R., Haughey, B. P., Davis, P. J., & Dunford, R. G. (1995). Self-efficacy and confidence in outcomes as determinants of self-care practices in inner-city, African-American women with non-insulin-dependent diabetes. *Diabetes Educator*, 21, 38–46.

Skinner, C. S., Campbell, M. K., Rimer, B. K., Curry, S., & Prochaska, J. O. (1999). How effective is tailored print communication? *Annals of Behavioral Medicine*, 21, 290–298.

Skinner, E. A., Edge, K., Altman, J., & Sherwood, H. (2003). Searching for the structure of coping: A review and critique of category systems for classifying ways of coping. *Psychological Bulletin*, 129, 216–269.

Sklar, L. S., & Anisman, H. (1981). Stress and cancer. *Psychological Bulletin*, 89, 369–406.

Skolnick, A. S. (1986). *The psychology of human development*. San Diego: Harcourt Brace Jovanovich.

Sliwinski, M. (2004). Dementia. In A. J. Christensen, R. Martin, & J. M. Smyth (Eds.), *Encyclopedia of health psychology* (pp. 75–77). New York: Kluwer.

Smart, J. L. (1991). Critical periods in brain development. In D. J. P. Barker (Chair, Ciba Foundation Symposium, No. 156), *The childhood environment and adult disease*. New York: Wiley.

Smeets, V. M. J., van Lierop, B. A. G., Vanhoutvin, J. P. G., Aldenkamp, A. P., & Nijhuis, F. J. N. (2007). Epilepsy and employment: Literature review. *Epilepsy & Behavior*, 10, 354–362.

Smith, A. W., & Baum, A. (2003). The influence of psychological factors on restorative function in health and illness. In. J. Suls & K. Wallston (Eds.), *Social psychological foundations of health and illness* (pp. 431–457). Oxford, UK: Oxford University Press.

Smith, C. A., & Wallston, K. A. (1992). Adaptation in patients with chronic rheumatoid arthritis: Application of a general model. *Health Psychology*, 11, 151–162.

Smith, C. E., Fernengel, K., Holcorft, C., Gerald, K., & Marien, L. (1994). Meta-analysis of the associations between social support and health outcomes. *Annals of Behavioral Medicine*, 16, 352–362.

Smith, D. H., Kramer, J. M., Perrin, N., Platt, R., Roblin, D. W., et al. (2008). A randomized trial of direct-to-patient communication to enhance adherence to β-blocker therapy following myocardial infarction. *Archives of Internal Medicine*, 168, 477–483.

Smith, E. L. (1984). Special considerations in developing exercise programs for the older adult. In J. D. Matarazzo, S. M. Weiss, J. A. Herd, N. E. Miller, & S. M. Weiss (Eds.), *Behavioral health: A handbook of health enhancement and disease prevention* (pp. 525–546). New York: Wiley.

Smith, J. B., & Autman, S. H. (1985). The experience of hospitalization. In L. L. Hayman & E. M. Sporing (Eds.), *Handbook of pediatric nursing* (pp. 78–124). New York: Wiley.

Smith, M. T., & Perlis, M. L. (2006). Who is a candidate for cognitive-behavioral therapy for insomnia? *Health Psychology*, 25, 15–19.

SMITH, M. T., PERLIS, M. L., SMITH, M. S., GILES, D. E., & CARMODY, T. P. (2000). Sleep quality and presleep arousal in chronic pain. *Journal of Behavioral Medicine, 23,* 1–13.

SMITH, P. J., BLUMENTHAL, J. A., HOFFMAN, B. M., COOPER, H., STRAUMAN, T. A., et al. (2010). Aerobic exercise and neurocognitive performance: A meta-analytic review of randomized controlled trials. *Psychosomatic Medicine, 72,* 239–252.

SMITH, R. C., & ZIMNY, G. H. (1988). Physicians' emotional reactions to patients. *Psychosomatics, 29,* 392–397.

SMITH, S. S., MCCARTHY, D. E., JAPUNTICH, S. J., CHRISTIANSEN, B., PIPER, M. E., et al. (2009). Comparative effectiveness of 5 smoking cessation pharmacotherapies in primary care clinics. *Archives of Internal Medicine, 169,* 2148–2155.

SMITH, T. W. (1992). Hostility and health: Current status of a psychosomatic hypothesis. *Health Psychology, 11,* 139–150.

SMITH, T. W. (2010). Depression and chronic medical illness: Implications for relapse prevention. In C. S. RICHARDS & M. G. PERRI (Eds), *Relapse prevention for depression* (pp. 199–225). Washington, DC: American Psychological Association.

SMITH, T. W., & ANDERSON, N. B. (1986). Models of personality and disease: An interactional approach to Type A behavior and cardiovascular risk. *Journal of Personality and Social Psychology, 50,* 1166–1173.

SMITH, T. W., CHRISTENSEN, A. J., PECK, J. R., & WARD, J. R. (1994). Cognitive distortion, helplessness, and depressed mood in rheumatoid arthritis: A four-year longitudinal analysis. *Health Psychology, 13,* 213–217.

SMITH, T. W., & GALLO, L. C. (1999). Hostility and cardiovascular reactivity during marital interaction. *Psychosomatic Medicine, 61,* 436–445.

SMITH, T. W., & GALLO, L. C. (2001). Personality traits as risk factors for physical illness. In A. BAUM, T. A. REVENSON, & J. E. SINGER (Eds.), *Handbook of health psychology* (pp. 139–173). Mahwah, NJ: Erlbaum.

SMITH, T. W., GALLO, L. C., GOBLE, L., NGU, L. Q., & STARK, K. A. (1998). Agency, communion, and cardiovascular reactivity during marital interaction. *Health Psychology, 17,* 537–545.

SMITH, T. W., GALLO, L. C., & RUIZ, J. M. (2003). Toward a social psychophysiology of cardiovascular reactivity: Interpersonal concepts and methods in the study of stress and coronary disease. In J. SULS & K. WALLSTON (Eds.), *Social psychological foundations of health and illness* (pp. 335–366). Oxford, UK: Blackwell.

SMITH, T. W., GLAZER, K., RUIZ, J. M., & GALLO, L. C. (2004). Hostility, anger, aggressiveness, and coronary heart disease: An interpersonal perspective on personality, emotion, and health. *Journal of Personality, 72,* 1217–1270.

SMITH, T. W., & MACKENZIE, J. (2006). Personality and risk of physical illness. *Annual Review of Clinical Psychology, 2,* 435–467.

SMITH, T. W., ORLEANS, C. T., & JENKINS, C. D. (2004). Prevention and health promotion: Decades of progress, new challenges, and an emerging agenda. *Health Psychology, 23,* 126–131.

SMITH, T. W., RUIZ, J. M., & UCHINO, B. N. (2000). Vigilance, incentive, and cardiovascular reactivity in social interactions. *Health Psychology, 19,* 382–392.

SMITH, T. W., TURNER, C. W., FORD, M. H., HUNT, S. C., BARLOW, G. K., et al. (1987). Blood pressure reactivity in adult male twins. *Health Psychology, 6,* 209–220.

SMITH, T. W., UCHINO, B. N., BERG, C. A., FLORSHEIM, P., PEARCE, G., et al. (2008). Associations of self-reports versus spouse ratings of negative affectivity, dominance, and affiliation with coronary artery disease: Where should we look and who should we ask when studying personality and health? *Health Psychology 27,* 676–684.

SMITH, T. W., UCHINO, B. N., BERG, C. A., FLORSHEIM, P., PEARCE, G., et al. (2009). Conflict and collaboration in middle-aged and older couples: II. Cardiovascular reactivity during marital interaction. *Psychology and Aging, 24,* 274–286.

SMITH, T. W. & WILLIAMS, P. G. (1992). Personality and health: Advantages and limitations of the five factor model. *Journal of Personality 60,* 395–423.

SMOLDEREN, K. G., SPERTUS, J. A., NALLAMOTHU, B. K., KRUMHOLZ, H. M., TANG, F., et al. (2010). Health care insurance, financial concerns in accessing care, and delays to hospital presentation in acute myocardial infarction. *Journal of the American Medical Association, 303,* 1392–1400.

SMUCKER-BARNWELL, EARLEYWINE, & GORDIS, E. B. (2006). Confirming alcohol-moderated links between cannabis use and dependence in a national sample. *Addictive Behaviors, 31,* 1695–1699.

SMYTH, J. M., & PENNEBAKER, J. W. (2001). What are the health effects of disclosure? In A. BAUM, T. A. REVENSON, & J. E. SINGER (Eds.), *Handbook of health psychology* (pp. 339–348). Mahwah, NJ: Erlbaum.

SMYTH, J. M., WONDERLICH, S. A., HERON, K. E., SLIWINSKI, M. J., CROSBY, R. D., et al. (2007). Daily and momentary mood and stress are associated with binge eating and vomiting in bulimia nervosa patients in the natural environment. *Journal of Consulting and Clinical Psychology, 75,* 629–638.

SNIEHOTTA, F. F., SCHOLZ, U., & SCHWARZER, R. (2005). Bridging the intention-behaviour gap: Planning, self-efficacy, and action control in the adoption and maintenance of physical exercise. *Psychology and Health, 20,* 143–160.

SNOW, L. F. (1981). Folk medical beliefs and their implications for care of patients: A review based on studies among black Americans. In G. HENDERSON & M. PRIMEAUX (Eds.), *Transcultural health care* (pp. 78–101). Menlo Park, CA. Addison-Wesley.

SNOW, V., BARRY, P., FITTERMAN, N., QASEEM, A., WEISS, K., et al. (2005). Pharmacologic and surgical management of obesity in primary care: A clinical practice guideline from the American College of Physicians. *Annals of Internal Medicine, 142,* 525–531.

SNOWDON, D. A., GREINER, L. H., MORTIMER, J. A., RILEY, K. P., GREINER, P. A., & MARKESBERY, W. R. (1997). Brain infarction and the clinical expression of Alzheimer disease. *Journal of the American Medical Association, 277,* 813–817.

SNOWLING, N. J., & HOPKINS, W. G. (2006). Effects of different modes of exercise training on glucose control and risk factors for complications in type 2 diabetic patients: A meta-analysis. *Diabetes Care, 29,* 2518–2927.

SNYDER, D. K., HETMAN, R. E., & HAYNES, S. N. (2005) Evidence-based approaches to assessing couple distress. *Psychological Assessment, 17,* 288–307.

SNYDER, S. H. (1977). Opiate receptors and internal opiates. *Scientific American, 236,* 44–56.

SOBELL, L. C., SOBELL, M. B., LEO, G. I., AGRAWAL, S., JOHNSON-YOUNG, L., & CUNNINGHAM, J. A. (2002). Promoting self-change with alcohol abusers: A community-level mail intervention based on natural recovery studies. *Alcoholism: Clinical and Experimental Research, 26,* 936–948.

SOBELL, L. C., SOBELL, M. B., TONEATTO, T., & LEO, G. I. (1993). What triggers the resolution of alcohol problems without treatment? *Alcoholism: Clinical and Experimental Research, 17,* 217–224.

SOLBERG, L. I., ASCHE, S. E., BOYLE, R., MCCARTY, M. C., & THOELE, M. J. (2007). Smoking and cessation behaviors among young adults of various educational backgrounds. *American Journal of Public Health, 97,* 1421–1426.

SOLÉ-LERIS, A. (1986). *Tranquility and insight.* Boston: Shambhala.

SOLOMON, L. J. (2004). Breast self-examination. In A. J. CHRISTENSEN, R. MARTIN, & J. M. SMYTH (Eds.), *Encyclopedia of health psychology* (p. 33). New York: Kluwer.

SOLOMON, L. J., FLYNN, B. S., WORDEN, J. K., MICKEY, R. M., SKELLY, J. M., et al. (1998). Assessment of self-reward strategies for maintenance of breast self-examination. *Journal of Behavioral Medicine, 21,* 83–102.

SOMERS, T. J., KEEFE, F. J, GODIWALA, N., & HOYLER, G. H. (2009). Psychosocial factors and the pain experience of osteoarthritis patients: New findings and new directions. *Current Opinion in Rheumatology, 21,* 501–506.

SONG, A. V., MORRELL, H. E. R., CORNELL, J. L., RAMOS, M. E., BIEHL, M., et al. (2009). Perceptions of smoking-related risks and benefit a predictors of adolescent smoking initiation. *American Journal of Public Health, 99,* 487–492.

SOO, H., & LAM, S. (2009). Stress management training in diabetes mellitus. *Journal of Health Psychology, 14,* 933–943.

SOO, H., BURNEY, S., & BASTEN, C. (2009). The role of rumination in affective distress in people with a chronic physical illness: A review of the literature and theoretical formulation. *Journal of Health Psychology, 14,* 956–966.

SPARRENBERGER, F., CICHELERO, F. T., ASCOLI, A. M., FONSECA, F. P., WEISS. G., et al. (2009). Does psychosocial stress cause hypertension? A systematic review of observational studies. *Journal of Human Hypertension, 23,* 12–9.

SPECTER, M. (1996, March 3). 10 years later, through fear, Chernobyl still kills in Belarus. *New York Times,* pp. 1, 6.

SPEECE, M. W., & BRENT, S. B. (1984). Children's understanding of death: A review of three components of a death concept. *Child Development, 55,* 1671–1686.

SPEISMAN, J. C., LAZARUS, R. S., MORDKOFF, A., & DAVISON, L. (1964). Experimental demonstration of stress based on ego-defense theory. *Journal of Abnormal and Social Psychology, 68,* 367–380.

SPENCE, J. D., BARNETT, P. A., LINDEN, W., RAMSDEN, V., & TAENZER, P. (1999). Recommendations on stress management. *Canadian Medical Association Journal, 160*(9 Suppl.), S46–S50.

SPENCER, L., PAGELL, F., & ADAMS, T. (2005). Applying the transtheoretical model to cancer screening behavior. *American Journal of Health Promotion, 29,* 36–56.

SPENCER, L., PAGELL, F., HALLION, M. E., & ADAMS, T. B. (2002). Applying the transtheoretical model to tobacco cessation and prevention: A review of the literature. *American Journal of Health Promotion, 17,* 7–71.

SPENCER, S. M., LEHMAN, J. M., WYNINGS, C., ARENA, P., CARVER, C. S., et al. (1999). Concerns about breast cancer and relations to psychosocial well-being in a multiethnic sample of early-stage patients. *Health Psychology, 18,* 159–168.

SPIEGEL, D., BLOOM, J. R., KRAEMER, H. C., & GOTTHEIL, E. (1989). Effect of psychosocial treatment on survival of patients with metastatic breast cancer. *Lancet, 334,* 888–891.

SPIEGEL, D., SANDS, S., & KOOPMAN, C. (1994). Pain and depression in patients with cancer. *Cancer, 74,* 2570–2578.

SPINETTA, J. J. (1974). The dying child's awareness of death: A review. *Psychological Bulletin, 81,* 256–260.

SPINETTA, J. J. (1982). Behavioral and psychological research in childhood cancer. *Cancer, 50,* 1939–1943.

SPOTH, R. L., REDMOND, C., & SHIN, C. (2001). Randomized trial of brief family interventions for general populations: Adolescent substance use outcomes 4 years following baseline. *Journal of Consulting and Clinical Psychology, 69,* 627–642.

SPOTTS, E. L., PRESCOTT, C., & KENDLER, K. (2006). Examining the origins of gender differences in marital quality: A behavior genetic analysis. *Journal of Family Psychology, 20,* 605–613.

SPURGEON, P., BROOME, A., EARLL, L., & HARRIS, B. (1990). Health psychology in a broader context. In P. BENNETT, J. WEINMAN, & P. SPURGEON (Eds.), *Current developments in health psychology* (pp. 331–345). Chur, Switzerland: Harwood.

SQUIRES, D. D., & HESTER, R. K. (2004). Using technical innovations in clinical practice: The Drinker's Check-Up program. *Journal of Clinical Psychology/In Session, 60,* 159–169.

STACY, A. W. (1997). Memory activation and expectancy as prospective mediators of alcohol and marijuana use. *Journal of Abnormal Psychology, 106,* 61–73.

STACY, A. W., ZOGG, J. B., UNGER, J. B., & DENT, C. W. (2004). Exposure to televised alcohol ads and subsequent adolescent alcohol use. *American Journal of Health Behavior, 28,* 498–509.

STADE, B. C., BAILEY, C., DZENDOLETAS, D., SGRO, M., DOWSWELL, T., & BENNETT, D. (2009). Psychological and/or educational interventions for reducing alcohol consumption in pregnant women and women planning pregnancy. *Cochrane Database of Systematic Reviews*, Issue 2. Retrieved (1-30-2010) from http://www.thecochranelibrary.com. DOI:10.1002/14651858.CD004228.pub2.

STAFFORD, L., JACKON, H. J., & BERK, M. (2008). Illness beliefs about heart disease and adherence to secondary prevention regimens. *Psychosomatic Medicine*, 70, 942–948.

STALL, R. D., COATES, T. J., & HOFF, C. (1988). Behavioral risk reduction for HIV infection among gay and bisexual men: A review of results from the United States. *American Psychologist*, 43, 878–885.

STANFORD, E. A., CHAMBERS, C. T., & CRAIG, K. D. (2005). A normative analysis of the development of pain-related vocabulary in children. *Pain*, 114, 278–284.

STANG, P. E., BRANDENBURG, N. A., LANE, M. C., MERIKANGAS, K. R., VON KORFF, M. R., & KESSLER, R. C. (2006). Mental and physical comorbid conditions and days in role among persons with arthritis. *Psychosomatic Medicine*, 68, 152–158.

STANTON, A. L., DANOFF-BURG, S., CAMERON, C. L., BISHOP, M., COLLINS, C. A., et al. (2000). Emotionally expressive coping predicts psychological and physical adjustment to breast cancer. *Journal of Consulting and Clinical Psychology*, 68, 875–882.

STANTON, A. L., ESTES, M. A., ESTES, N. C., CAMERON, C. L., DANOFF-BURG, S., & IRVING, L. M. (1998). Treatment decision making and adjustment to breast cancer: A longitudinal study. *Journal of Consulting and Clinical Psychology*, 66, 313–322.

STANTON, A. L., REVENSON, T. A., & TENNEN. H. (2007) Health psychology: Psychological adjustment to chronic disease. *Annual Review of Psychology*, 58, 565–592.

STEAD, L. F., PERERA, R., BULLEN, C., MANT, D., & LANCASTER, T. (2008). Nicotine replacement therapy for smoking cessation. *Cochrane Database of Systematic Reviews*, Issue 1. Retrieved (1-30-2010) from http://www.thecochranelibrary.com. DOI:10.1002/14651858.CD000146.pub3.

STEFFEN, P. R., MCNEILLY, M., ANDERSON, N., & SHERWOOD, A. (2003). Effects of perceived racism and anger inhibition on ambulatory blood pressure in African Americans. *Psychosomatic Medicine*, 65, 746–750.

STEFFEN, P. R., SMITH, T. B., LARSON, M., & BUTLER, L. (2006). Acculturation to Western society as a risk factor for high blood pressure: A meta-analytic review. *Psychosomatic Medicine*, 68, 386–397.

STEIN, J. A., NEWCOMB, M. D., & BENTLER, P. M. (1987). An 8-year study of multiple influences on drug use and drug use consequences. *Journal of Personality and Social Psychology*, 53, 1094–1105.

STEIN, J. H., KEEVIL, J. G., WIEBE, D. A., AESCHLIMANN, S., & FOLTS, J. D. (1999). Purple grape juice improves endothelial function and reduces the susceptibility of LDL cholesterol to oxidation in patients with coronary artery disease. *Circulation*, 100, 1050–1055.

STEINBERG, L. (1985). Early temperamental antecedents of adult Type A behaviors. *Developmental Psychology*, 21, 1171–1180.

STEINER, H., & CLARK, W. R. (1977). Psychiatric complications of burned adults: A classification. *Journal of Trauma*, 17, 134–143.

STEPTOE, A., & AYERS, S. (2004). Stress, health and illness. In S. SUTTON, A. BAUM, & M. JOHNSTON (Eds.), *The Sage handbook of health psychology* (pp. 169–196).

STEPTOE, A., & BRYDON, L. (2005). Associations between acute lipid stress responses and fasting lipid levels 3 years later. *Health Psychology*, 24, 601–607.

STEPTOE, A., CROPLEY, M., & JOEKES, K. (2000). Task demands and the pressures of everyday life: Associations between cardiovascular reactivity and work blood pressure and heart rate. *Health Psychology*, 19, 46–54.

STEPTOE, A., HAMER, M. & CHIDA, Y. (2007). The effects of acute psychological stress on circulating inflammatory factors in humans: A review and meta-analysis. *Brain, Behavior, and Immunity*, 21, 901–912.

STEPTOE, A., WARDLE, J., VINCK, J., TUOMISTO, M., HOLTE, A., & WICHSTRØM, L. (1994). Personality and attitudinal correlates of healthy and unhealthy lifestyles in young adults. *Psychology and Health*, 9, 331–343.

STERBA, K. R., DEVELLIS, R. F., LEWIS, M. A., DEVELLIS, B. M., JORDAN, J. M., & BAUCOM, D. H. (2008). Effect of couple illness perception congruence on psychological adjustment in women with rheumatoid arthritis. *Health Psychology*, 27, 221–229.

STETSON, B. A., RAHN, J. M., DUBBERT, P. M., WILNER, B. I., & MERCURY, M. G. (1997). Prospective evaluation of the effects of stress on exercise adherence in community-residing women. *Health Psychology*, 16, 515–520.

STEVENS, V. J., GLASGOW, R. E., TOOBERT, D. J., KARANJA, N., & SMITH, K. S. (2002). Randomized trial of a brief dietary intervention to decrease consumption of fat and increase consumption of fruits and vegetables. *American Journal of Health Promotion*, 16, 129–135.

STEWART, D. E., ABBEY, S. E., SHNEK, Z. M., IRVINE, J., & GRACE, S. L. (2004). Gender differences in health information needs and decisional preferences in patients recovering from an acute ischemic coronary event. *Psychosomatic Medicine*, 66, 42–48.

STEWART, W. F., SHECHTER, A., & RASMUSSEN, B. K. (1994). Migraine prevalence: A review of population-based studies. *Neurology*, 44(Suppl. 4), S17–S23.

STEWART-WILLIAMS, S. (2004). The placebo puzzle: Putting together the pieces. *Health Psychology*, 23, 198–206.

STICE, E., CAMERON, R. P., KILLEN, J. D., HAYWARD, C., & TAYLOR, C. B. (1999). Naturalistic weight-reduction efforts prospectively predict growth in relative weight and onset of obesity among female adolescents. *Journal of Consulting and Clinical Psychology*, 67, 967–974.

STICE, E., PRESNELL, K., & SPANGLER, D. (2002). Risk factors for binge eating onset in adolescent girls: A 2-year prospective investigation. *Health Psychology*, 21, 131–138.

STICE, E., SHAW, H., & MARTI, C. N. (2006). A meta-analytic review of obesity prevention programs for children and adolescents: The skinny on interventions that work. *Psychological Bulletin, 132,* 667–691.

STICE, E., SHAW, H., & MARTI, C. N. (2007). A meta-analytic review of eating disorder prevention programs: Encouraging findings. *Annual Review of Clinical Psychology, 3,* 207–231.

STIEG, R. L., & TURK, D. C. (1988). Chronic pain syndrome: Demonstrating the cost-benefit of treatment. *Clinical Journal of Pain, 4,* 58–63.

STILLEY, C. S., BENDER, C. M., DUNBAR-JACOB, J., SEREIKA, S., RYAN, C. M. (2010). The impact of cognitive function on medication management: Three studies. *Health Psychology, 29,* 50–55.

ST. LAWRENCE, J. S., CROSBY, R. A., BRASFIELD, T. L., & O'BANNON, R. E. (2002). Reducing STD and HIV risk behavior of substance-dependent adolescents. A randomized controlled trial. *Journal of Consulting and Clinical Psychology, 70,* 1010–1021.

STOCKTON, W. (1988, March 7). Fresh research tells asthmatics to stay active. *New York Times,* p. C9.

STOCKWELL, T., & TOWN, C. (1989). Anxiety and stress management. In R. K. HESTER & W. R. MILLER (Eds.), *Handbook of alcoholism treatment approaches: Effective alternatives* (pp. 222–230). New York: Pergamon.

STONE, A. A., & NEALE, J. M. (1984). New measure of daily coping: Development and preliminary results. *Journal of Personality and Social Psychology, 46,* 892–906.

STONE, A. A., NEALE, J. M., COX, D. S., NAPOLI, A., VALDIMARSDOTTIR, H., & KENNEDY-MOORE, E. (1994). Daily events are associated with a secretory immune response to an oral antigen in men. *Health Psychology, 13,* 440–446.

STONE, G. C. (1979). Health and the health system: A historical overview and conceptual framework. In G. C. STONE, F. COHEN, & N. E. ADLER (Eds.), *Health psychology—A handbook* (pp. 1–17). San Francisco: Jossey-Bass.

STORY, M., KAPHINGST, K. M., ROBINSON-O'BRIEN, R., & GLANZ, K. (2008). Creating healthy food and eating environments: Policy and environmental approaches. *Annual Review of Public Health, 29,* 253–272.

STRANDBERG, A. Y., STRANDBERG, T. E., PITKKÄLÄ, K., SALOMAA, V. V., TILVIS, R. S., & MIETTINEN, T. A. (2008). The effect of smoking in midlife on health-related quality of life in old age: A 26-year prospective study. *Archives of Internal Medicine, 168,* 1968–1974.

STRAUSS, R. H., & YESALIS, C. E. (1991). Anabolic steroids in the athlete. *Annual Review of Medicine, 42,* 449–457.

STRAW, M. K. (1983). Coping with obesity. In T. G. BURISH & L. A. BRADLEY (Eds.), *Coping with chronic disease: Research and applications* (pp. 219–258). New York: Academic Press.

STRECHER, V. J., KREUTER, M. W., & KOBRIN, S. C. (1995). Do cigarette smokers have unrealistic perceptions of their heart attack, cancer, and stroke risks? *Journal of Behavioral Medicine, 18,* 45–54.

STRECHER, V. J., SHIFFMAN, S., & WEST, R. (2005) Randomized controlled trial of a web-based computer-tailored smoking cessation program as a supplement of nicotine patch therapy. *Addiction, 100,* 682–888.

STRIEGEL-MOORE, R., & RODIN, J. (1985). Prevention of obesity. In J. C. ROSEN & L. J. SOLOMON (Eds.), *Prevention in health psychology* (pp. 72–110). Hanover, NH: University Press of New England.

STRIEGEL-MOORE, R. H. (1997). Risk factors for eating disorders. *Annals of the New York Academy of Sciences, 817,* 98–109.

STROEBE, W., SCHUT, H., & STROEBE, M. S. (2005). Grief work, disclosure and counseling: Do they help the bereaved? *Clinical Psychology Review, 25,* 395–414.

STROEBE, M., SCHUT, H., & STROEBE, W. (2007). Health outcomes of bereavement. *Lancet, 370,* 1960–73.

STRONG, J. P., MALCOM, G. T., MCMAHAN, C. A., TRACY, R. E., NEWMAN, W. P., et al. (1999). Prevalence and extent of atherosclerosis in adolescents and young adults: Implications for prevention from the Pathobiological Determinants of Atherosclerosis in Youth Study. *Journal of the American Medical Association, 281,* 727–735.

STUART, R. B. (1967). Behavioral control of overeating. *Behavior Research and Therapy, 5,* 357–365.

STUNKARD, A. J. (1987). Conservative treatments for obesity. *American Journal of Clinical Nutrition, 45,* 1142–1154.

STYLIANOS, S. K., & VACHON, M. L. S. (1993). The role of social support in bereavement. In M. S. STROEBE, W. STROEBE, & R. O. HANSSON (Eds.), *Handbook of bereavement: Theory, research, and intervention* (pp. 397–410). Cambridge: Cambridge University Press.

SUAREZ, E. C., WILLIAMS, R. B., KUHN, C. M., ZIMMERMAN, E. H., & SCHANBERG, S. M. (1991). Biobehavioral basis of coronary-prone behavior in middle-aged men. Part II: Serum cholesterol, the Type A behavior pattern, and hostility as interactive modulators of physiological reactivity. *Psychosomatic Medicine, 53,* 528–537.

SUCHY, Y. (2009). Executive functioning: Overview, assessment, and research issues for non-neuropsychologists. *Annals of Behavioral Medicine, 37,* 106–116.

SUGARMAN, D. E., & CAREY, K. B. (2007). The relationship between drinking control strategies and college student alcohol use. *Psychology of Addictive Behaviors, 21,* 338–345.

SUI, X., LAMONTE, M. J., LADITKA, J. N., HARDIN, J. W., CHASE, N., et al. (2007). Cardiorespiratory fitness and adiposity as mortality predictors in older adults. *Journal of the American Medical Association, 298,* 2507–2516.

SULLIVAN, M., TANZER, M., STANISH, W., FALLAHA, M., KEEFE, F. J., et al. (2009). Psychological determinants of problematic outcomes following total knee arthroplasty. *Pain, 143,* 123–129.

SULLIVAN, M. D., EDLUND, M. J., STEFFICK, D., & UNÜTZER, J. (2005). Regular use of prescribed opioids: Association with common psychiatric disorders. *Pain, 119,* 95–103.

SULLIVAN, M. J. L., ADAMS, H., TRIPP, D., & STANISH, W. D. (2008). Stage of chronicity and treatment response in patients with musculoskeletal injuries and concurrent symptoms of depression. *Pain*, 135, 151–159.

SULS, J. (1982). Social support, interpersonal relations, and health: Benefits and liabilities. In G. S. SANDERS & J. SULS (Eds.), *Social psychology of health and illness* (pp. 255–277). Hillsdale, NJ: Erlbaum.

SULS, J., & BUNDE, J. (2005). Anger, anxiety, and depression as risk factors for cardiovascular disease: The problems and implications of overlapping affective dispositions. *Psychological Bulletin*, 131, 260–300.

SULS, J., & FLETCHER, B. (1985). The relative efficacy of avoidant and nonavoidant coping strategies: A meta-analysis. *Health Psychology*, 4, 249–288.

SULS, J., MARTIN, R., & LEVENTHAL, H. (1997). Social comparison, lay referral, and the decision to seek medical care. In B. P. BUUNK & F. X. GIBBONS (Eds.), *Health, coping, and well-being: Perspectives from social comparison theory* (pp. 195–226). Mahwah, NJ: Erlbaum.

SULS, J., & MULLEN, B. (1981). Life change and psychological distress: The role of perceived control and desirability. *Journal of Applied Social Psychology*, 11, 379–389.

SULS, J., & SANDERS, G. S. (1988). Type A behavior as a general risk factor for physical disorder. *Journal of Behavioral Medicine*, 11, 210–226.

SULS, J., SANDERS, G. S., & LABRECQUE, M. S. (1986). Attempting to control blood pressure without systematic instruction: When advice is counterproductive. *Journal of Behavioral Medicine*, 9, 567–576.

SUPER, C. N. (1981). Cross-cultural research on infancy. In H. C. TRANDIS & A. HERON (Eds.), *Handbook of cross-cultural psychology: Developmental psychology* (Vol. 4, pp. 17–53). Boston: Allyn & Bacon.

SURTEES, P., WAINWRIGHT, N., LUBEN, R., KHAW, K.-T., & DAY, N. (2003). Sense of coherence and mortality in men and women in the EPIC-Norfolk United Kingdom Prospective Cohort Study. *American Journal of Epidemiology*, 158, 1202–1209.

SURTEES, P. G., WAINWRIGHT, N. W. J., LUBEN, R., KHAW, K-T., & DAY, N. E. (2006). Mastery, sense of coherence, and mortality: evidence of independent associations from the EPIC-Norfolk Prospective Cohort Study. *Health Psychology*, 25, 102–110.

SURWIT, R. S. (1993). Of mice and men: Behavioral medicine in the study of type II diabetes. *Annals of Behavioral Medicine*, 15, 227–235.

SURWIT, R. S., FEINGLOS, M. N., & SCOVERN, A. W. (1983). Diabetes and behavior: A paradigm for health psychology. *American Psychologist*, 38, 255–262.

SUSSER, M., HOPPER, K., & RICHMAN, R. (1983). Society, culture, and health. In D. MECHANIC (Ed.), *Handbook of health, health care, and the health professions* (pp. 23–49). New York: Free Press.

SUSSMAN, S., & SKARA, S. (2004). Smoking prevention. In A. J. CHRISTENSEN, R. MARTIN, & J. M. SMYTH (Eds.), *Encyclopedia of health psychology* (pp. 273–276). New York: Kluwer.

SUTER, P. O., SCHUTZ, Y., & JEQUIER, E. (1992). The effect of ethanol on fat storage in healthy subjects. *New England Journal of Medicine*, 326, 983–987.

SVARSTAD, B. (1976). Physician-patient communication and patient conformity with medical advice. In D. MECHANIC (Ed.), *The growth of bureaucratic medicine* (pp. 220–228). New York: Wiley.

SWAN, G. E., CARMELLI, D., & ROSENMAN, R. H. (1986). Spouse-pair similarity on the California Psychological Inventory with reference to husband's coronary heart disease. *Psychosomatic Medicine*, 48, 172–186.

SWEET, J. J. (1991). Psychological evaluation and testing services in medical settings. In J. J. SWEET, R. H. ROZENSKY, & S. M. TOVIAN (Eds.), *Handbook of clinical psychology in medical settings* (pp. 291–313). New York: Plenum.

SWEET, J. J., ROZENSKY, R. H., & TOVIAN, S. M. (1991). Clinical psychology in medical settings: Past and present. In J. J. SWEET, R. H. ROZENSKY, & S. M. TOVIAN (Eds.), *Handbook of clinical psychology in medical settings* (pp. 3–9). New York: Plenum.

SWIGONSKI, M. E. (1987). *Bio-psycho-social factors affecting coping and compliance with the hemodialysis treatment regimen.* University Microfilms International (Order No. 8803518).

SZAPARY, P. O., BLOEDON, L. T., & FOSTER, G. D. (2003). Physical activity and its effects on lipids. *Current Cardiology Reports*, 5, 488492.

SZAPOCZNIK, J., PRADO, G., BURLEW, A. K., WILLIAMS, R. A., & SANTISTEBAN, D. A. (2007). Drug abuse in African American and Hispanic adolescents: Culture, development, and behavior. *Annual Review of Clinical Psychology*, 3, 77–105

TAGLIACOZZO, D. L., & MAUKSCH, H. O. (1972). The patient's view of the patient's role. In E. G. JACO (Ed.), *Patients, physicians, and illness* (2nd ed., pp. 172–185). New York: Free Press.

TALBOT, F., NOUWEN, A., GINGRAS, J., BÉLANGER, A., & AUDET, J. (1999). Relations of diabetes intrusiveness and personal control to symptoms of depression among adults with diabetes. *Health Psychology*, 18, 537–542.

TANG, N. K. Y., SALKOVSKIS, P. M., HODGES, A., WRIGHT, K. J., HANNA, M., & HESTER, J. (2008). Effects of mood on pain responses and pain tolerance: An experimental study in chronic back pain patients. *Pain*, 138, 392–401.

TANIS, M. (2008). Health-related on-line forums: What's the big attraction? *Journal of Health Communication*, 13, 698–714.

TANNER, J. M. (1970). Physical growth. In P. H. MUSSEN (Ed.), *Carmichael's manual of child psychology* (3rd ed., Vol. 1, pp. 77–155). New York: Wiley.

TANNER, J. M. (1978). *Foetus into man.* Cambridge, MA: Harvard University Press.

TAPERT, S. F., BROWN, G. G., BARATTA, M. V., & BROWN, S. A. (2004). fMRI BOLD response to alcohol stimuli in alcohol dependent young women. *Addictive Behaviors*, 29, 33–50.

TARNOWSKI, K. J., RASNAKE, L. K., & DRABMAN, R. S. (1987). Behavioral assessment and treatment of pediatric burn injuries: A review. *Behavior Therapy*, 18, 417–441.

TATE, D. F. (2008). Application of innovative technologies in the prevention and treatment of overweight in children and adolescents. In E. JELALIAN & R. G. STEELE (Eds.), *Handbook of childhood and adolescent obesity* (pp. 387–404). New York: Springer.

TATE, D. G., MAYNARD, F., & FORCHHEIMER, M. (1993). Predictors of psychologic distress one year after spinal cord injury. *American Journal of Physical Medicine and Rehabilitation, 72,* 272–275.

TAYLOR, B., IRVING, H. M., BALIUNAS, D., ROERECKE, M., PATRA, J., et al. (2009). Alcohol and hypertension: Gender differences in dose–response relationships determined through systematic review and meta-analysis. *Addiction, 104,* 1981–1990.

TAYLOR, B., REHM, J., ROOM, R., PATRA, J., & BONDY, S. (2008). Determination of lifetime injury mortality risk in Canada in 2002 by drinking amount per occasion and number of occasions. *American Journal of Epidemiology, 168,* 1119–1125.

TAYLOR, C. B., BANDURA, A., EWART, C. K., MILLER, N. H. &, DEBUSK, R. F. (1985). Exercise testing to enhance wives' confidence in their husbands' cardiac capability soon after clinically uncomplicated acute myocardial infarction. *American Journal of Cardiology, l55,* 635–638.

TAYLOR, C. B., BRYSON, S., LUCE, K. H., CUNNING, D., DOYLE, A. C., et al. (2006). Prevention of eating disorders in at-risk college-age women. *Archives of General Psychiatry, 63,* 881–888.

TAYLOR, M. D., WHITEMAN, M. C., FOWKES, G. R., LEE, A. J., ALLERHAND, M. & DEARY, I. J. (2009). Five factor model personality traits and all-cause mortality in the Edinburgh Artery Study Cohort. *Psychosomatic Medicine, 71,* 631–641.

TAYLOR, R. S., BROWN, A., EBRAHIM, S., JOLLIFFE, J., NOORANI, H., et al. (2004). Exercise-based rehabilitation for patients with coronary heart disease: Systematic review and meta-analysis of randomized controlled trials. *American Journal of Medicine. 11,* 682–692.

TAYLOR, S. E. (1979). Hospital patient behavior: Reactance, helplessness, or control? *Journal of Social Issues, 35,* 156–184.

TAYLOR, S. E. (1983). Adjustment to threatening events: A theory of cognitive adaptation. *American Psychologist, 38,* 1161–1173.

TAYLOR, S. E., COUSINO KLEIN, L., LEWIS, B. P., GRUNEWALD, T. L., GURUNG, R. A. R., & UPDEGRAFF, J. A. (2000). Biobehavioral responses to stress in females: Tend-and-befriend, not fight-or-flight. *Psychobiological Review, 107,* 411–429.

TAYLOR, S. E., LICHTMAN, R. R., & WOOD, J. V. (1984). Attributions, beliefs about control, and adjustment to breast cancer. *Journal of Personality and Social Psychology, 46,* 489–502.

TAYLOR, S. E., SEEMAN, T. E., EISENBERGER, N. I., KOZANIAN, T. A., MOORE, A. N., et al. (2010). Effects of a supportive or an unsupportive audience on biological and psychological responses to stress. *Journal of Personality and Social Psychology, 98,* 47–56.

TAYLOR, T. R., WILLIAMS, C. D., KEPHER, H., MAKAMBI, K. H., MOUTON, C., et al. (2007). Racial discrimination and breast cancer incidence in US black women: The Black Women's Health Study. *American Journal of Epidemiology, 166,* 46–54.

TEBBI, C. K., CUMMINGS, K. M., ZEVON, M. A., SMITH, L., RICHARDS, M., & MALLON, J. (1986). Compliance of pediatric and adolescent cancer patients. *Cancer, 58,* 1179–1184.

TELAMA, R., YANG, X., VIIKARI, J., VÄLIMÄKI, I., WANNE, O., & RAITAKARI, O. (2005). Physical activity from childhood to adulthood: A 21-year tracking study. *American Journal of Preventive Medicine, 28,* 267–273.

TELL, G. S., POLAK, J. F., WARD, B. J., KITTNER, S. J., SAVAGE, P. J., et al. (1994). Relation of smoking with carotid artery wall thickness and stenosis in older adults: The Cardiovascular Health Study. *Circulation, 90,* 2905–2908.

TENNEN, H., & AFFLECK, G. (1997). Social comparison as a coping process: A critical review and application to chronic pain disorders. In B. P. BUUNK & F. X. GIBBONS (Eds.), *Health, coping, and well-being: Perspectives from social comparison theory* (pp. 263–298). Mahwah, NJ: Erlbaum.

TENNEN, H., AFFLECK, G., ARMELI, S., & CARNEY, M. A. (2000). A daily process approach to coping: Linking theory, research, and practice. *American Psychologist, 55,* 626–636.

TENNEN, H., AFFLECK, G., & ZAUTRA, A. (2006). Depression history and coping with chronic pain: A daily process analysis. *Health Psychology, 25,* 370–379.

TENNEN, H., EBERHARDT, T. L., & AFFLECK, G. (1999). Depression research methodologies at the social-clinical interface: Still hazy after all these years. *Journal of Social and Clinical Psychology, 18,* 121–159.

TENNES, K., & KREYE, M. (1985). Children's adrenocortical responses to classroom activities and tests in elementary school. *Psychosomatic Medicine, 47,* 451–460.

TERI, L., HUGHES, J. P., & LARSON, E. B. (1990). Cognitive deterioration in Alzheimer's disease: Behavioral and health factors. *Journal of Gerontology: Psychological Sciences, 45,* 58–63.

TERRACCIANO, A., LÖCKENHOFF, C. E., ZONDERMAN, A. B., FERRUCCI, L., & COSTA, P. T. (2008). Personality predictors of longevity: Activity, emotional stability, and conscientiousness. *Psychosomatic Medicine, 70,* 621–627.

TERRY, P., & WRIGHT, K. A. (2005). Self-reported driving behaviour and attitudes towards driving under the influence of cannabis among three different user groups in England. *Addictive Behaviors, 30,* 619–626.

TERRY, R. D., OAKLAND, M. J., & ANKENY, K. (1991). Factors associated with adoption of dietary behavior to reduce heart disease risk among males. *Journal of Nutrition Education, 23,* 154–160.

THAYER, J. F., HANSEN, A. L., SAUS-ROSE, E. & JOHNSEN, B. H. (2009). Heart rate variability, prefrontal neural function, and cognitive performance: The neurovisceral integration perspective on self-regulation, adaptation, and health. *Annals of Behavioral Medicine, 37,* 141–153.

THAYER, J. F., & LANE, R. D. (2007). The role of vagal function in the risk for cardiovascular disease and mortality. *Biological Psychology, 74,* 224–242.

THELEN, M. H., FRY, R. A., FEHRENBACH, P. A., & FRAUTSCHI, N. M. (1979). Therapeutic videotape and film modeling: A review. *Psychological Bulletin*, 86, 701–720.

THIRLAWAY, K., & UPTON, D. (2009). *The psychology of lifestyle: Promoting healthy behaviour*. London: Routledge.

THOMAS, A. M., PETERSON, L., & GOLDSTEIN, D. (1997). Problem solving and diabetes regimen adherence by children and adolescents with IDDM in social pressure situations: A reflection of normal development. *Journal of Pediatric Psychology*, 22, 541–561.

THOMBS, B. D., DE JONGE, P., COYNE, J. C., WHOOLEY, M. A., FRASURE-SMITH, N., et al. (2008). Depression screening and patient outcomes in cardiovascular care: A systematic review. *Journal of the American Medical Association*, 300, 2161–2171.

THOMPSON, B., CORONADO, G., SNIPES, S. A., & PUSCHEL, K. (2003). Methodologic advances and ongoing challenges in designing community-based health promotion programs. *Annual Review of Public Health*, 24, 315–340.

THOMPSON, J. K. (1986, April). Larger than life. *Psychology Today*, pp. 38–44.

THOMPSON, S. C. (1981). Will it hurt less if I can control it? A complex answer to a simple question. *Psychological Bulletin*, 90, 89–101.

THOMPSON, S. C., KENT, D. R., THOMAS, C., & VRUNGOS, S. (1999). Real and illusory control over exposure to HIV in college students and gay men. *Journal of Applied Social Psychology*, 29, 1128–1150.

THOMPSON, S. C., & KYLE, D. J. (2000). The role of perceived control in coping with the losses associated with chronic illness. In J. H. HARVEY & E. D. MILLER (Eds.), *Loss and trauma: General and close relationship perspectives* (pp. 131–145). Philadelphia: Bruner/Mazel.

THOMPSON, S. C., NANNI, C., & SCHWANKOVSKY, L. (1990). Patient-oriented interventions to improve communication in a medical office visit. *Health Psychology*, 9, 390–404.

THOMSON, A., & PAGE, L. (2009). Psychotherapies for hypochondriasis. *Cochrane Database of Systematic Reviews*, Issue 4. Retrieved (1-30-2010) from http://www.thecochrane library.com. DOI:10.1002/14651858.CD006520.pub2.

THORESEN, C. E. (1984). Overview. In J. D. MATARAZZO, S. M. WEISS, J. A. HERD, N. E. MILLER, & S. M. WEISS (Eds.), *Behavioral health: A handbook of health enhancement and disease prevention* (pp. 297–307). New York: Wiley.

THORNDIKE, A. N., REGAN, S., MCKOOL, K., PASTERNAK, R. C., SWARTZ, S., et al. (2008). Depressive symptoms and smoking cessation after hospitalization for cardiovascular disease. *Archives of Internal Medicine*, 168, 186–191.

THORNDIKE, A. N., REGAN, S., & RIGOTTI, N. A. (2007). The treatment of smoking by US physicians during ambulatory visits: 1994–2003. *American Journal of Public Health*, 97, 1878–1883.

THUN, M. J., PETO, R., LOPEZ, A. D., MONACO, J. H., HENLEY, S. J., et al. (1997). Alcohol consumption and mortality among middle-aged and elderly U.S. adults. *New England Journal of Medicine*, 337, 1705–1714.

THURSTON, R. C., & KUBZANSKY, L. D. (2009). Women, loneliness, and incident coronary heart disease. *Psychosomatic Medicine*, 71, 836–842.

TIMKO, C. (1987). Seeking medical care for a breast cancer symptom: Determinants of intentions to engage in prompt or delay behavior. *Health Psychology*, 6, 305–328.

TIMS, F. M., FLETCHER, B. W., & HUBBARD, R. L. (1991). Treatment outcomes for drug abuse clients. In R. W. PICKENS, C. G. LEUKEFELD, & C. R. SCHUSTER (Eds.), *Improving drug abuse treatment* (pp. 93–113). Rockville, MD: National Institute on Drug Abuse.

TINDLE, H. A., CHANG, Y., KULLER, L., MANSON, J., ROBINSON, J., et al. (2009). Optimism, cynical hostility, and incident coronary heart disease and mortality in the Women's Health Initiative. *Circulation*, 120, 656–662.

TINDLE, H. A., RIGOTTI, N. A., DAVIS, R. B., BARBEAU, E. M., KAWACHI, I., & SHIFFMAN, S. (2006). Cessation among smokers of "light" cigarettes: Results from the 2000 National Health Interview Survey. *American Journal of Public Health*, 96, 1498–1504.

TINETTI, M. E., BAKER, D. I., MCAVAY, G., CLAUS, E. B., GARRETT, P., et al. (1994). A multifactorial intervention to reduce the risk of falling among elderly people living in the community. *New England Journal of Medicine*, 331, 821–827.

TODD, M., TENNEN, H., CARNEY, M. A., ARMELI, S., & AFFLECK, G. (2004). Do we know how we cope? Relating daily coping reports to global and time-limited retrospective assessments. *Journal of Personality and Social Psychology*, 86, 310–319.

TOMAKA, J. BLASCOVICH, J., KIBLER, J., & ERNST, J. M. (1997). Cognitive and physiological antecedents to threat and challenge appraisal. *Journal of Personality and Social Psychology*, 73, 63–72.

TOMFOHR, L., COOPER, D., MILLS, P., NELESEN, R., & DIMSDALE, J. (2010). Everyday discrimination and nocturnal blood pressure dipping in black and white Americans. *Psychosomatic Medicine*, 72, 266–272.

TONIGAN, J. S., MILLER, W. R., & SCHERMER, C. (2002). Atheists, agnostics and Alcoholics Anonymous. *Journal of Studies on Alcohol*, 63, 534–541.

TORRENS, P. R. (1985). Hospice care: What have we learned? *Annual Review of Public Health*, 6, 65–83.

TORRES, G., & HOROWITZ, J. M. (1999). Drugs of abuse and brain gene expression. *Psychosomatic Medicine*, 61, 630–650.

TORTORA, G. J., & DERRICKSON, B. (2006). *Principles of anatomy and physiology* (11th ed.). New York: Wiley.

TORTORA, G. J., & DERRICKSON, B. (2009). *Principles of anatomy and physiology* (12th ed.). Hoboken, NJ: Wiley.

TOVIAN, S. M. (2004). Health services and health care economics: The health psychology marketplace. *Health Psychology*, 23, 138–141.

TRABIN, T., RADER, C., & CUMMINGS, C. (1987). A comparison of pain management outcomes for disability compensation and non-compensation patients. *Psychology and Health*, 1, 341–351.

TRAPP, B. D., PETERSON, J., RANSOHOFF, R. M., RUDICK, R., MORK, S., & BO, L. (1998). Axonal transection in the lesions of multiple sclerosis. *New England Journal of Medicine, 338,* 278–285.

TREMBLAY, A., WOUTERS, E., WENKER, M., ST.-PIERRE, S., BOUCHARD, C., & DESPRÉS, J.-P. (1995). Alcohol and a high-fat diet: A combination favoring overfeeding. *American Journal of Clinical Nutrition, 62,* 639–644.

TREMBLAY, G. C., & PETERSON, L. (1999). Prevention of childhood injury: Clinical and public health policy challenges. *Clinical Psychology Review, 19,* 415–434.

TRIEF, P. M. (2004). Diabetes mellitus. In A. J. CHRISTENSEN, R. MARTIN, & J. M. SMYTH, *Encyclopedia of health psychology* (pp. 82–85). New York: Kluwer.

TRIVEDI, R. B., AYOTTE, B., EDELMAN, D., & BOSWORTH, H. B. (2008). The association of emotional well-being and marital status with treatment adherence among patients with hypertension. *Journal of Behavioral Medicine, 31,* 489–497.

TROXEL, W. M., BUYSSE, D. J., HALL, M., KAMARCK, T. W., STROLLO, P. J., et al. (2010). Social integration, social contacts, and blood pressure dipping in African-Americans and whites. *Journal of Hypertension, 28,* 265–271.

TROXEL, W. M., & MATTHEWS, K. A. (2004). What are the costs of marital conflict and dissolution to children's physical health? *Clinical and Child Family Psychology Review, 7,* 29–57.

TROXEL, W. M., MATTHEWS, K. A., BROMBERGER, J. T., & SUTTON-TYRRELL, K. (2003). Chronic stress burden, discrimination, and subclinical carotid artery disease in African American and Caucasian women. *Health Psychology, 22,* 300–309.

TRUCHON, M., CÔTÉ, D., FILLION, L., ARSENAULT, B., & DIONNE, C. (2008). Low-back-pain related disability: An integration of psychological risk factors in the stress process model. *Pain, 137,* 564–573.

TRUMBULL, R., & APPLEY, M. H. (1986). A conceptual model for examination of stress dynamics. In M. H. APPLEY & R. TRUMBULL (Eds.), *Dynamics of stress: Physiological, psychological, and social perspectives* (pp. 21–45). New York: Plenum.

TSAI, A. G., & WADDEN, T. A. (2005). Systematic review: An evaluation of major commercial weight loss programs in the United States. *Annals of Internal Medicine, 142,* 56–66.

TSC (Trenton State College) (1992). *Alcohol & drug education program.* Trenton, NJ: Author.

TSUTSUMI, A., KAYABA, K., KARIO, K., & ISHIKAWA, S. (2009). Prospective study on occupational stress and risk of stroke. *Archives of Internal Medicine, 169,* 56–61.

TUCKER, L. A., & CLEGG, A. G. (2002). Differences in health care costs and utilization among adults with selected lifestyle-related risk factors. *American Journal of Health Promotion, 16,* 225–233.

TUGADE, M. M., & FREDRICKSON, B. L. (2004). Resilient individuals use positive emotions to bounce back from negative emotional experiences. *Journal of Personality and Social Psychology, 86,* 320–333.

TUNKS, E., & BELLISSIMO, A. (1991). *Behavioral medicine: Concepts and procedures.* New York: Pergamon.

TUOMISTO, M. T., MAJAHALME, S., KÄHÖNEN, M., FREDRIKSON, M., & TURJANMAA, V. (2005). Psychological stress tasks in the prediction of blood pressure level and need for antihypertensive medication: 9–12 years of follow-up. *Health Psychology, 24,* 77–87.

TURK, D. C. (1996). Biopsychosocial perspective on chronic pain. In R. J. GATCHEL & D. C. TURK (Eds.), *Psychological approaches to pain management: A practitioner's handbook* (pp. 3–32). New York: Guilford.

TURK, D. C. (2001). Physiological and psychological bases of pain. In A. BAUM, T. A. REVENSON, & J. E. SINGER (Eds.), *Handbook of health psychology* (pp. 117–137). Mahwah, NJ: Erlbaum.

TURK, D. C. (2002). Clinical effectiveness and cost-effectiveness of treatments for patients with chronic pain. *Clinical Journal of Pain, 18,* 355–365.

TURK, D. C., BRODY, M. C., & OKIFUJI, E. A. (1994). Physicians' attitudes and practices regarding the long-term prescribing of opioids for non-cancer pain. *Pain, 59,* 201–208.

TURK, D. C., & HOLZMAN, A. D. (1986). Commonalities among psychological approaches in the treatment of chronic pain: Specifying the meta-constructs. In A. D. HOLZMAN & D. C. TURK (Eds.), *Pain management: A handbook of psychological treatment approaches* (pp. 257–267). New York: Pergamon.

TURK, D. C., LITT, M. D., SALOVEY, P., & WALKER J. (1985). Seeking urgent pediatric treatment: Factors contributing to frequency, delay, and appropriateness. *Health Psychology, 4,* 43–59.

TURK, D. C., & MEICHENBAUM, D. (1991). Adherence to self-care regimens: The patient's perspective. In J. J. SWEET, R. H. ROSENSKY, & S. M. TOVIAN (Eds.), *Handbook of clinical psychology in medical settings* (pp. 249–266). New York: Plenum.

TURK, D. C., MEICHENBAUM, D., & GENEST, M. (1983). *Pain and behavioral medicine: A cognitive-behavioral perspective.* New York: Guilford.

TURK, D. C., MONARCH, E. S., & WILLIAMS, A. D. (2004). Assessment of chronic pain sufferers. In T. HADJISTAVROPOULOS & K. D. CRAIG (Eds.), *Pain: Psychological perspectives* (pp. 209–243). Mahwah, NJ: Earlbaum.

TURK, D. C., & RUDY, T. E. (1986). Assessment of cognitive factors in chronic pain: A worthwhile enterprise? *Journal of Consulting and Clinical Psychology, 54,* 760–768.

TURK, D. C., & SALOVEY, P. (1995). Cognitive-behavioral treatment of illness behavior. In P. M. NICASSIO & T. W. SMITH (Eds.), *Managing chronic illness: A biopsychosocial perspective* (pp. 245–284). Washington, DC: American Psychological Association.

TURK, D. C., & STACEY, B. R. (2000). Multidisciplinary pain centers in the treatment of chronic back pain. In J. W. FRYMOYER, T. B. DUCKER, N. M. HADLER, J. P. KOSTUIK, J. N. WEINSTEIN, & T. S. WHITCLOUD (Eds.), *The adult spine: Principles and practice* (2nd ed., pp. 253–274).). Philadelphia: Lippincott Williams & Wilkins.

Turk, D. C., Wack, J. T., & Kerns, R. D. (1985). An empirical examination of the "pain-behavior" construct. *Journal of Behavioral Medicine*, 8, 119–130.

Turk, D. C., & Winters, F. (2006). *The pain survival guide: How to reclaim your life*. Washington: American Psychological Association.

Turk-Charles, S., Gatz, M., Kato, K., & Pedersen, N. L. (2008). Physical health 25 years later: The predictive ability of neuroticism. *Health Psychology*, 27, 369–378.

Turk-Charles, S., Meyerowitz, B. E., & Gatz, M. (1997). Age differences in information-seeking among cancer patients. *International Journal of Aging and Human Development*, 45, 85–98.

Turkkan, J. S., McCaul, M. E., & Stitzer, M. L. (1989). Psychophysiological effects of alcohol-related stimuli: II. Enhancement with alcohol availability. *Alcoholism: Clinical and Experimental Research*, 13, 392–398.

Turner, J. A. (1982). Comparison of group progressive-relaxation training and cognitive-behavioral group therapy for chronic low back pain. *Journal of Consulting and Clinical Psychology*, 50, 757–765.

Turner, J. A., Clancy, S., McQuade, K. J., & Cardenas, D. D. (1990). Effectiveness of behavioral therapy for chronic low back pain: A component analysis. *Journal of Consulting and Clinical Psychology*, 58, 573–579.

Turner, J. A., Clancy, S., & Vitaliano, P. P. (1987). Relationships of stress, appraisal and coping, to chronic low back pain. *Behavior Research and Therapy*, 25, 281–288.

Turner, J. R., & Hewitt, J. K. (1992). Twin studies of cardiovascular response to psychological challenge: A review and suggested future directions. *Annals of Behavioral Medicine*, 14, 12–20.

Turner, J. R., Ward, M. M., Gellman, M. D., Johnston, D. W., Light, K. C., & van Doornen, L. J. P. (1994). The relationship between laboratory and ambulatory cardiovascular activity: Current evidence and future directions. *Annals of Behavioral Medicine*, 16, 12–23.

Tyler, D. C. (1990). Patient-controlled analgesia in adolescents. *Journal of Adolescent Health Care*, 11, 154–158.

Uchino, B. N. (2004). *Social support and physical health: Understanding the health consequences of physical health*. New Haven, CT: Yale University Press.

Uchino, B. N. (2006). Social support and health: A review of physiological processes potentially underlying links to disease outcomes. *Journal of Behavioral Medicine*, 29, 377–387.

Uchino, B. N., Berg, C. A., Smith, T. W., Pearce, G., & Skinner, M. (2006). Age-related differences in ambulatory blood pressure during daily stress: Evidence for greater blood pressure reactivity with age. *Psychology and Aging*, 21, 231–239.

Uchino, B. N., & Garvey, T. S. (1997). The availability of social support reduces cardiovascular reactivity to acute psychological stress. *Journal of Behavioral Medicine*, 20, 15–27.

Uchino, B. N., Holt-Lunstad, J., Bloor, L. E., & Campo, R. A. (2005). Aging and cardiovascular reactivity to stress: Longitudinal evidence for changes in stress reactivity. *Psychology and Aging*, 20, 134–143.

Uchino, B. N., Holt-Lunstad, J., Uno, D., Betancourt, R., & Garvey, T. S. (1999). Social support and age-related differences in cardiovascular function: An examination of potential mediators. *Annals of Behavioral Medicine*, 21, 135–142.

Uchino, B. N., Smith, T. W., Holt-Lunstead, J., Campo, R. A., & Reblin, M. (2007). Stress and illness. In J. T. Cacioppo, L. G. Tassinary, & G. G. Bertson (Eds.), *Handbook of psychophysiology* (pp. 608–632). New York, NY: Cambridge University Press.

Uhl, G. R., Liu, Q.-R., Drgon, T., Johnson, C., Walther, D., et al. (2008). Molecular genetics of successful smoking cessation. *Archives of General Psychiatry*, 65, 683–693.

Ullrich, P. (2004). Testicular self-examination. In A. J. Christensen, R. Martin, & J. M. Smyth (Eds.), *Encyclopedia of health psychology* (pp. 315–316). New York: Kluwer.

Umberson, D., Williams, K., Powers, D. A., Liu, H., & Needham, B. (2006). You make me sick: Marital quality and health over the life course. *Journal of Health and Social Behavior*, 47, 1–16.

UNAIDS (Joint United Nations Programme on HIV/AIDS) (2004). *Questions & answers*. Retrieved (5-3-2004) from http://www.unaids.org.

UNAIDS (Joint United Nations Programme on HIV/AIDS) (2006). *AIDS epidemic update*. Retrieved (12-8-2006) from http://www.unaids.org.

UNAIDS (Joint United Nations Programme on HIV/AIDS) (2009). *AIDS epidemic update, 2009*. Retrieved (1-11-2010) from http://www.unaids.org.

Underhill, K., Montgomery, P., & Operario, D. (2008). Abstinence-plus programs for HIV infection prevention in high-income countries. *Cochrane Database of Systematic Reviews*, Issue 1. Retrieved (1-30-2010) from http://www.thecochranelibrary.com. DOI:10.1002/14651858.CD007006.

Urban, B. J., France, R. D., Steinberger, E. K., Scott, D. L., & Maltbie, A. A. (1986). Long-term use of narcotic/antidepressant medication in the management of phantom limb pain. *Pain*, 24, 191–196.

USBC (United States Bureau of the Census) (1971). *Statistical Abstract of the United States: 1971*. (92nd ed.). Washington, DC: U.S. Government Printing Office.

USBC (United States Bureau of the Census) (1995). *Statistical Abstract of the United States: 1994* (114th ed.). Washington, DC: U.S. Government Printing Office.

USBC (United States Bureau of the Census) (2006). *Statistical Abstract of the United States: 2006*. Retrieved (12-3-2006) from http://www.census.gov.

USBC (United States Bureau of the Census) (2010). *Statistical Abstract of the United States: 2009*. Retrieved (1-5-2010) from http://www.census.gov.

USDA (United States Department of Agriculture) (2005). *Dietary guidelines for Americans 2005*. Retrieved (4-9-2010) from http://www.health.gov.

USDHHS (United States Department of Health and Human Services) (1981). *Medicines and you* (Publication No. NIH 81-2140). Washington, DC: U.S. Government Printing Office.

USDHHS (United States Department of Health and Human Services) (1985). *Charting the nation's health: Trends since 1960* (Publication No. PHS 85-1251). Washington, DC: U.S. Government Printing Office.

USDHHS (United States Department of Health and Human Services) (1986a). *Clinical opportunities for smoking intervention: A guide for the busy physician* (Publication No. NIH 86-2178). Washington, DC: U.S. Government Printing Office.

USDHHS (United States Department of Health and Human Services) (1986b). *The health consequences of involuntary smoking: A report of the Surgeon General* (Publication No. CDC 87-8398). Washington, DC: U.S. Government Printing Office.

USDHHS (United States Department of Health and Human Services) (1987). *Vital statistics of the United States, 1984: Life tables* (Publication No. PHS 87-1104). Washington, DC: U.S. Government Printing Office.

USDHHS (United States Department of Health and Human Services) (1990). *Alcohol and health* (Publication No. ADM 90-1656). Rockville, MD: National Institute on Alcohol Abuse and Alcoholism.

USDHHS (United States Department of Health and Human Services) (1995). *Health United States: 1994* (Publication No. PHS 95-1232). Washington, DC: U.S. Government Printing Office.

USDHHS (United States Department of Health and Human Services) (2004). *Healthy workforce: 2010*. Retrieved (7-16-2004) from http://www.prevent.org.

USDL (United States Department of Labor) (2010). *Occupational outlook handbook, 2010–11*. Retrieved (1-5-2010) from http://www.bls.gov.

USSHER, J., KIRSTEN, L., BUTOW, P., & SANDOVAL, M. (2006). What do cancer support groups provide which other supportive relationships do not? The experience of peer support groups for people with cancer. *Social Science & Medicine, 62,* 2565–2576.

VALOIS, R. F., ADAMS, K. G., & KAMMERMANN, S. K. (1996). One-year evaluation results from CableQuit: A community cable television smoking cessation pilot program. *Journal of Behavioral Medicine, 19,* 479–499.

VAN DE VEN, M. O. M., ENGELS, R. C. M. E., OTTEN, R., & VAN DE EIJNDEN, R. J. J. M. (2007). A longitudinal test of the theory of planned behavior predicting smoking onset among asthmatic and non-asthmatic adolescents. *Journal of Behavioral Medicine, 30,* 435–445.

VAN DULMEN, A. M., & BENSING, J. M. (2002). Health promoting effects of the physician-patient encounter. *Psychology, Health & Medicine, 7,* 289–300.

VAN KESSEL, K., MOSS-MORRIS, R., WILLOUGHBY, E., CHALDER, T., JOHNSON, M. H., & ROBINSON, E. (2008). A randomized controlled trial of cognitive behavior therapy for multiple sclerosis fatigue. *Psychosomatic Medicine, 70,* 205–213.

VAN TILBURG, M. A. L., MCCASKILL, C. C., LANE, J. D., EDWARDS, C. L., BETHEL, A., et al. (2001). Depressed mood is a factor in glycemic control in type 1 diabetes. *Psychosomatic Medicine, 63,* 551–555.

VAN 'T LAND, H., VERDURMEN, J., TEN HAVE, M., VAN DORSSELAER, S., BEEKMAN, A., & DE GRAAF, R. (2010). The association between arthritis and psychiatric disorders: Results from a longitudinal population-based study. *Journal of Psychosomatic Research, 68,* 187–193.

VAN'T SPIJKER, A., TRIJSBURG, R. W., & DUIVENVOORDEN, H. J. (1997). Psychological sequelae of cancer diagnosis: A meta-analytic review of 58 studies after 1980. *Psychosomatic Medicine, 59,* 280–293.

VARNI, J. W., & BABANI, L. (1986). Long-term adherence to health care regimens in pediatric chronic disorders. In N. A. KRASNEGOR, J. D. ARASTEH, & M. F. CATALDO (Eds.), *Child health behavior: A behavioral pediatrics perspective* (pp. 502–520). New York: Wiley.

VARNI, J. W., JAY, S. M., MASEK, B. J., & THOMPSON, K. L. (1986). Cognitive-behavioral assessment and management of pediatric pain. In A. D. HOLZMAN & D. C. TURK (Eds.), *Pain management: A handbook of psychological treatment approaches* (pp. 168–192). New York: Pergamon.

VARNI, J. W., & THOMPSON, K. L. (1986). Biobehavioral assessment and management of pediatric pain. In N. A. KRASNEGOR, J. D. ARASTEH, & M. F. CATALDO (Eds.), *Child health behavior: A behavioral pediatrics perspective* (pp. 371–393). New York: Wiley.

VARTANIAN, L. R., HERMAN, C. P., & WANSINK, B. (2008). Are we aware of the external factors that influence our food intake? *Health Psychology, 27,* 533–538.

VECCHIO, P. C. (1994). Attitudes to alternative medicine by rheumatology outpatient attenders. *Journal of Rheumatology, 21,* 147–147.

VEDHARA, K., COX, N. K. M., WILCOCK, G. K., PERKS, P., HUNT, M., et al. (1999). Chronic stress in elderly carers of dementia patients and antibody response to influenza vaccination. *Lancet, 353,* 627–631.

VEIT, R., BRODY, S., & RAU, H. (1997). Four-year stability of cardiovascular reactivity to psychological stress. *Journal of Behavioral Medicine, 20,* 447–460.

VELLA, E. J., KAMARCK, T. W., & SHIFFMAN, S. (2008). Hostility moderates the effects of social support and intimacy on blood pressure in daily social interactions. *Health Psychology, 27*(Suppl). S155–S162.

VENER, A. M., & KRUPKA, L. R. (1990). AIDS knowledge and attitudes revisited (1987–1989). *American Biology Teacher, 52,* 461–466.

VENN, J. R., & SHORT, J. G. (1973). Vicarious classical conditioning of emotional responses in nursery school children. *Journal of Personality and Social Psychology, 28,* 249–255.

VERBRUGGE, L. M. (1985). Gender and health: An update on hypotheses and evidence. *Journal of Health and Social Behavior*, 26, 156–182.

VERTINSKY, P., & AUMAN, J. T. (1988). Elderly women's barriers to exercise, Part I: Perceived risks. *Health Values*, 12(4), 13–19.

VEUGELERS, P. J., & FITZGERALD, A. L. (2005). Effectiveness of school programs in preventing childhood obesity: A multilevel comparison. *American Journal of Public Health*, 95, 432–435.

VIANE, I., CROMBEZ, G., ECCLESTON, C., DEVULDER, J., & DECORTE, W. (2004). Acceptance of the unpleasant reality of chronic pain: Effects upon attention to pain and engagement with daily activities. *Pain*, 112, 282–288.

VINCENT, J.-L. (2003). Nosocomial infections in adult intensive-care units. *Lancet*, 361, 2068–2077.

VINEY, L. L., WALKER, B. M., ROBERTSON, T., LILLEY, B., & EWAN, C. (1994). Dying in palliative care units and in hospital: A comparison of the quality of life of terminal cancer patients. *Journal of Consulting and Clinical Psychology*, 62, 157–164.

VINOKUR, A. D., THREATT, B. A., VINOKUR-KAPLAN, D., & SATARIANO, W. A. (1990). The process of recovery from breast cancer for younger and older patients: Changes during the first year. *Cancer*, 65, 1242–1254.

VITALIANO, P. P., RUSSO, J., BREEN, A. R., VITIELLO, M. V., & PRINZ, P. N. (1986). Functional decline in the early stages of Alzheimer's disease. *Journal of Psychology and Aging*, 1, 41–46.

VITALIANO, P. P., ZHANG, J., & SCANLAN, J. M. (2003). Is caregiving hazardous to one's physical health? A meta-analysis. *Psychological Bulletin*, 129, 946–972.

VIVEKANANTHAN, D. P., PENN, M. S., SAPP, S. K., HSU, A., & TOPOL, E. J. (2003). Use of antioxidant vitamins for the prevention of cardiovascular disease: Meta-analysis of randomized trials. *Lancet*, 361, 2017–2023.

VLAEYEN, J. W. S., KOLE-SNIJDERS, A. M., BOEREN, R. G. B., & VAN EEK, H. (1995). Fear of movement/(re)injury in chronic low back pain and its relation to behavioral performance. *Pain*, 62, 363–372.

VOGELZANGS, N., KRITCHEVSKY, S. E., BECKMAN, A. T. F., NEWMAN, A. B., SATTERFIELD, S., et al. (2008). Depressive symptoms and change in abdominal obesity in older persons. *Archives of General Psychiatry*, 65, 1386–1393.

WADDEN, T. A., & ANDERTON, C. H. (1982). The clinical use of hypnosis. *Psychological Bulletin*, 91, 215–243.

WADDEN, T. A., BROWNELL, K. D., & FOSTER, G. D. (2002). Obesity: Responding to the global epidemic. *Journal of Consulting and Clinical Psychology*, 70, 510–525.

WAITZKIN, H., & STOECKLE, J. D. (1976). Information control and the micropolitics of health care: Summary of an ongoing research project. *Social Science and Medicine*, 10, 263–276.

WALBURN, J., VEDHARA, K., HANKINS, M., RIXON, L., WEINMAN, J. (2009). Psychological stress and wound healing in humans: A systematic review and meta-analysis. *Journal of Psychosomatic Research*, 67, 253–271.

WALITZER, K. S., & CONNORS, G. J. (2007). Thirty-month follow-up of drinking moderation training for women: A randomized clinical trial. *Journal of Consulting and Clinical Psychology*, 75, 501–507.

WALKER, L. S., WILLIAMS, S. E., SMITH, C. A., GARBER, J., VAN SLYKE, D. A., & LIPANI, T. A. (2006). Parent attention versus distraction: Impact on symptom complaints by children with and without chronic functional abdominal pain. *Pain*, 122, 43–52.

WALLACE, L. M. (1986). Communication variables in the design of pre-surgical preparatory information. *British Journal of Clinical Psychology*, 25, 111–118.

WALLSTON, B. S., ALAGNA, S. W., DEVELLIS, B. M., & DEVELLIS, R. F. (1983). Social support and physical illness. *Health Psychology*, 2, 367–391.

WALLSTON, K. A., WALLSTON, B. S., & DEVELLIS, R. (1978). Development of the Multidimensional Health Locus of Control (MHLC) Scales. *Health Education Monographs*, 6, 161–170.

WALSH, J. C., LYNCH, M., MURPHY, A. W., & DALY, K. (2004). Factors influencing the decision to seek treatment for symptoms of myocardial infarction: An evaluation of the self-regulatory model of illness behavior. *Journal of Psychosomatic Research*, 56, 67–73.

WALTERS, S. T., VADER, A. M., HARRIS, T. R., FIELD, C. A., & JOURILES, E. N. (2009). Dismantling motivational interviewing and feedback for college drinkers. *Journal of Consulting and Clinical Psychology*, 77, 64–73.

WANG, F., SCHULTZ, A. B., MUSICH, S., MCDONALD, T., HIRSCHLAND, D., & EDINGTON, D. W. (2003). The relationship between National Heart, Lung, and Blood Institute weight guidelines and concurrent medical costs in a manufacturing population. *American Journal of Health Promotion*, 17, 183–189.

WANSINK, B., VAN ITTERSUM, K., & PAINTER, J. E. (2006). Ice cream illusions: Bowls, spoons, and self-served portion sizes. *American Journal of Preventive Medicine*, 31, 240–243.

WARD, S. E., GOLDBERG, N., MILLER-McCAULRY, V., MUELLER, C., NOLAN, A., et al. (1993). Patient-related barriers to management of cancer pain. *Pain*, 52, 319–324.

WARDLE, F. J., COLLINS, W., PERNET, A. L., WHITEHEAD, M. I., BOURNE, T. H., & CAMPBELL, S. (1993). Psychological impact of screening for familial ovarian cancer. *Journal of the National Cancer Institute*, 85, 653–657.

WARDLE, J., & CARNELL, S. (2009). Appetite is a heritable phenotype associated with adiposity. *Annals of Behavioral Medicine*, 38(Suppl.), S25–S30.

WARDLE, J., HAASE, A. M., STEPTOE, A., NILLAPUN, M., JONWUTIWES, K., & BELLISLE, F. (2004). Gender differences in food choice: The contribution of health beliefs and dieting. *Annals of Behavioral Medicine*, 27, 107–116.

WARGA, C. (1987, August). Pain's gatekeeper. *Psychology Today*, pp. 50–56.

WARREN, J. M., HENRY, C. J. K., & SIMONITE, V. (2003). Low glycemic index breakfasts and reduced food intake in preadolescent children. *Pediatrics*, 112, e414–e419.

WATERLAND, R. A., & MICHELS, K. B. (2007). Epigenetic epidemiology of the developmental origins hypothesis. *Annual Review of Nutrition*, 27, 363–388.

WATSON, M., HAVILAND, J. S., GREER; S., DAVIDSON, J., & BLISS, J. M. (1999). Influence of psychological response on survival in breast cancer: A population-based cohort study. *Lancet*, 354, 1331–1336.

WATSON, M., & RAMIREZ, A. (1991). Psychological factors in cancer prognosis. In C. L. COOPER & M. WATSON (Eds.), *Cancer and stress: Psychological, biological, and coping studies* (pp. 47–72). New York: Wiley.

WEBB, M. S., VANABLE, P. A., CAREY, M. P., & BLAIR, D. C. (2009). Medication adherence in HIV-infected smokers: The mediating role of depressive symptoms. AIDS *Education and Prevention*, 21, 94–105.

WEBB, T. L., & SHEERAN, P. (2006). Does changing behavioral intentions engender behavior change? A meta-analysis of the experimental evidence. *Psychological Bulletin*, 132, 249–268.

WEIDNER, G., KOHLMANN, C.-W., DOTZAUER, E., & BURNS, L. R. (1996). The effect of academic stress on health behaviors in young adults. *Anxiety, Stress, and Coping*, 9, 123–133.

WEIDNER, G., & MESSINA, C. R. (1998). Cardiovascular reactivity to mental stress. In K. ORTH-GOMER, M. CHESNEY, & N. K. WEGNER (Eds.), *Women, stress, and heart disease* (pp. 219–236). Mahwah, NJ: Erlbaum.

WEINER, S. J., BARNET, B., CHENG, T. L., & DAALEMAN, T. P. (2005). Processes for effective communication in primary care. *Annals of Internal Medicine*, 142, 709–714.

WEINHARDT, L. S., CAREY, M. P., JOHNSON, B. T., & BICKHAM, N. L. (1999). Effects of HIV counseling and testing on sexual risk behavior: Meta-analytic review of published research, 1985–1997. *American Journal of Public Health*, 89, 1397–1405.

WEINMAN, J. (1990). Health psychology: Progress, perspectives and prospects. In P. BENNETT, J. WEINMAN, & P. SPURGEON (Eds.), *Current developments in health psychology* (pp. 9–33). Chur, Switzerland: Harwood.

WEINMAN, J., EBRECHT, M., SCOTT, S., WALBURN, J., & DYSON, M. (2008). Enhanced wound healing after emotional disclosure intervention. *British Journal of Health Psychology*, 13, 95–102.

WEINRIB, A. (2004). General adaptation syndrome. In A. J. CHRISTENSEN, R. MARTIN, & J. M. SMYTH (Eds.), *Encyclopedia of health psychology* (pp. 118–119). New York: Kluwer.

WEINSTEIN, A. R., SESSO, H. D., LEE, I.-M., REXRODE, K. M., COOK, N. R., et al., (2008). The joint effects of physical activity and body mass index on coronary heart disease risk in women. *Archives of Internal Medicine*, 168, 884–890.

WEINSTEIN, N. D. (1982). Unrealistic optimism about susceptibility to health problems. *Journal of Behavioral Medicine*, 5, 441–460.

WEINSTEIN, N. D. (1987). Unrealistic optimism about susceptibility to health problems: Conclusions from a community-wide sample. *Journal of Behavioral Medicine*, 10, 481–500.

WEINSTEIN, N. D. (1988). The precaution adoption process. *Health Psychology*, 7, 355–386.

WEINSTEIN, N. D. (2000). Perceived probability, perceived severity, and health-protective behavior. *Health Psychology*, 19, 65–74.

WEINSTEIN, N. D., & KLEIN, W. M. (1995). Resistance of personal risk perceptions to debiasing interventions. *Health Psychology*, 14, 132–140.

WEIR, R., BROWNE, G., ROBERTS, J., TUNKS, E., & GAFNI, A. (1994). The Meaning of Illness Questionnaire: Further evidence for its reliability and validity. *Pain*, 58, 377–386.

WEISS, E. C., GALUSKA, D. A., KHAN, L. K., & SERDULA, M. K. (2006). Weight-control practices among U.S. adults, 2001–2002. *American Journal of Preventive Medicine*, 31, 18–24.

WEISS, J. W., MERRILL, V., & GRITZ, E. R. (2007). Ethnic variation in the association between weight concern and adolescent smoking. *Addictive Behaviors*, 32, 2311–2316.

WERNER, E. E., & SMITH, R. S. (1982). *Vulnerable but invincible: A study of resilient children.* New York: McGraw-Hill.

WERNICK, R. I. (1983). Stress inoculation in the management of clinical pain: Applications to burn pain. In D. MEICHENBAUM & M. E. JAREMKO (Eds.), *Stress reduction and prevention* (pp. 191–217). New York: Plenum.

WEST, S. G., LIGHT, K. C., HINDERLITER, A. L., STANWYCK, C. L., BRAGDON, E. E., & BROWNLEY, K. A. (1999). Potassium supplementation induces beneficial cardiovascular changes during rest and stress in salt sensitive individuals. *Health Psychology*, 18, 229–240.

WESTERDAHL, J., OLSSON, H., MÅSBÄCK, A., INGVAR, C., JONSSON, N., et al. (1994). Use of sunbeds or sunlamps and malignant melanoma in Southern Sweden. *American Journal of Epidemiology*, 140, 691–699.

WESTMAAS, J. L., & JAMNER, L. D. (2006). Paradoxical effects of social support on blood pressure reactivity among defensive individuals. *Annals of Behavioral Medicine*, 31, 238–247.

WHIPPLE, M. O., LEWIS, T. T., SUTTON-TYRRELL, K., MATTHEWS, K. A., BARINAS-MITCHELL, E., et al. (2009). Hopelessness, depressive symptoms, and carotid atherosclerosis in women: The Study of Women's Health Across the Nation (SWAN) heart study. *Stroke*, 40, 3166–3172.

WHITAKER, R. C., WRIGHT, J. A., PEPE, M. S., SEIDEL, K. D., & DIETZ, W. H. (1997). Predicting obesity in young adulthood from childhood and parental obesity. *New England Journal of Medicine*, 337, 869–873.

WHITE, A. M., KRAUS, C. L., MCCRACKEN, L. A., & SWARTZWELDER, H. S. (2003). Do college students drink more than they think? Use of a free-pour paradigm to determine how college students define standard drinks. *Alcoholism: Clinical and Experimental Research*, 27, 1750–1756.

WHITE, A. R., RAMPES, H., & CAMPBELL, J. L. (2006). Acupuncture and related interventions for smoking cessation. *Cochrane Database of Systematic Reviews*, Issue 1. Retrieved (11-20-2006) from http://mrw.interscience.wiley.com. DOI:10.1002/14651858.CD000009.pub2.

WHITE, B., DRIVER, S., & WARREN, A. M. (2010). Resilience and indicators of adjustment during rehabilitation from a spinal cord injury. *Rehabilitation Psychology*, 55, 23–32.

WHITEHEAD, W. E., BUSCH, C. M., HELLER, B. R., & COSTA, P. T. (1986). Social learning influences on menstrual symptoms and illness behavior. *Health Psychology*, 5, 13–23.

WHITFIELD, K. E., WEIDNER, G., CLARK, F., & ANDERSON, N. B. (2002). Sociodemographic diversity and behavioral medicine. *Journal of Consulting and Clinical Psychology*, 70, 463–481.

WHO (World Health Organization) (1999). *World health report*. Retrieved (2-28-2000) from http://www.who.org.

WHO (World Health Organization) (2000). *World health report 2000—health systems: Improving performance*. Retrieved (4-11-2010) from http://www.who.int.

WHO (World Health Organization) (2004). *The Atlas of Heart Disease and Stroke*. Retrieved (11-19-2010) from www.who.int.

WHO (World Health Organization) (2005). *Snapshots of health systems*. Retrieved (1-20-2010) from http://www.who.int.

WHO (World Health Organization) (2006). *World health statistics*. Retrieved (12-3-2006) from http://www.who.int.

WHO (World Health Organization) (2007). *Fact sheets: Asthma, Diabetes, and Epilepsy*. Retrieved (3-20-2007) from http://www.who.int/mediacentre/factsheets.

WHO (World Health Organization) (2008). *The global burden of disease, 2004 Update*. Retrieved (1-24-2010) from http://www.who.int.

WHO (World Health Organization) (2009). *World health statistics*. Retrieved (1-5-2010) from http://www.who.int.

WHO (World Health Organization) (2010). *Chronic obstructive pulmonary disease* (COPD). Retrieved (3-29-2010) from http://www.who.int.

WHO (World Health Organization) (2010b). *Epilepsy*. Retrieved (11-19-2010) from www.who.int.

WHO (World Health Organization) (2010c). *Skin Cancers*. Retrieved (11-19-2010) from www.who.int.

WHO/Europe (World Health Organization Regional Office for Europe) (2006) *Health for all* (HFA) *database*. Retrieved (12-8-2006) from http://www.euro.who.int.

WHO/Europe (World Health Organization Regional Office for Europe) (2010) *Health for all* (HFA) *database*. Retrieved (3-28-2010) from http://www.euro.who.int/hfadb.

WICKSELL, T. K., MELIN, L., LEKANDER, M., & OLSSON, G. L. (2009). Evaluating the effectiveness of exposure and acceptance strategies to improve functioning and quality of life in longstanding pediatric pain—A randomized controlled trial. *Pain*, 141, 248–257.

WIDEMAN, M. V., & SINGER, J. E. (1984). The role of psychological mechanisms in preparation for childbirth. *American Psychologist*, 39, 1357–1371.

WIEBE, D. J., & MCCALLUM, D. M. (1986). Health practices and hardiness as mediators in the stress-illness relationship. *Health Psychology*, 5, 425–438.

WIEBE, J. S. (2004). Patient adherence. In A. J. CHRISTENSEN, R. MARTIN, & J. M. SMYTH (Eds.), *Encyclopedia of health psychology* (pp. 200–204). New York: Kluwer.

WIELGOSZ, A. T., FLETCHER, R. H., MCCANTS, C. B., MCKINNIS, R. A., HANEY, T. L., & WILLIAMS, R. B. (1984). Unimproved chest pain in patients with minimal or no coronary disease: A behavioral phenomenon. *American Heart Journal*, 108, 67–72.

WIENS, A. N., & MENUSTIK, C. E. (1983). Treatment outcome and patient characteristics in an aversion therapy program for alcoholism. *American Psychologist*, 38, 1089–1096.

WIJEYSUNDERA, H. C., MACHADO, M., FARAHATI, F., WANG, X., WITTEMAN, W., et al. (2010). Association of temporal trends in risk factors and treatment uptake with coronary heart disease mortality, 1994–2005. *Journal of the American Medical Association*. 303, 1841–1847.

Wikipedia (2010). *Human anatomical terms: Anatomical variations*. Retrieved (1-6-2010) from http://en.wikipedia.org.

WILBERT-LAMPEN, U., LEISTNER, D., GREVEN, S., POHL, T., SPER, S., et al. (2008). Cardiovascular events during World Cup soccer. *New England Journal of Medicine*, 358, 475–483.

WILCOX, V. L., KASL, S. V., & BERKMAN, L. F. (1994). Social support and physical disability in older people after hospitalization: A prospective study. *Health Psychology*, 13, 170–179.

WILKINSON, G. (1987). The influence of psychiatric, psychological and social factors on the control of insulin-dependent diabetes mellitus. *Journal of Psychosomatic Research*, 31, 277–286.

WILKOWSKI, B. M. & ROBINSON, M. D. (2008). The cognitive basis of trait anger and reactive aggression: An integrative analysis. *Personality and Social Psychology Review*, 12, 3–21.

WILLI, C., BODENMANN, P., GHALI, W. A, FARIS, P. D., & CORNUZ, J. (2007). Active smoking and the risk of type 2 diabetes: A systematic review and meta-analysis. *Journal of the American Medical Association*, 298, 2654–2664.

WILLIAMS, C. J. (1990). *Cancer biology and management: An introduction*. New York: Wiley.

WILLIAMS, D. A., & KEEFE, F. J. (1991). Pain beliefs and the use of cognitive-behavioral coping strategies. *Pain*, 46, 185–190.

WILLIAMS, D. R. (2003). The health of men: Structured inequalities and opportunities. *American Journal of Public Health*, 93, 724–731.

WILLIAMS, K. A., KOLAR, M. M., REGER, B. E., & PEARSON, J. C. (2001). Evaluation of a wellness-based mindfulness stress reduction intervention: A controlled trial. *American Journal of Health Promotion*, 15, 422–432.

WILLIAMS, P. G. (2004). Hypochondriasis. In A. J. CHRISTENSEN, R. MARTIN, & J. M. SMYTH (Eds.), *Encyclopedia of health psychology* (pp. 145–146). New York: Kluwer.

WILLIAMS, P. G., SMITH, T. W., GUNN, H., & UCHINO, B. N. (2010). Personality and stress: Individual differences in exposure, reactivity, recovery, and restoration. In R. J. CONTRADA & A. BAUM (Eds.), *Handbook of stress science*. New York: Springer Publishing.

WILLIAMS, P. G., SUCHY, Y., & RAU, H. K. (2009). Individual differences in executive functioning: Implications for stress regulation. *Annals of Behavioral Medicine*, 37, 126–40.

WILLIAMS, R. B. (2008). Psychosocial and biobehavioral factors and their interplay in coronary heart disease. *Annual Review of Clinical Psychology*, 4, 349–65.

WILLIAMS, R. B., MARCHUK, D. A., GADDE, K. M., BAREFOOT, J. C., GRINCHNIK, K., et al. (2001). Central nervous system serotonin function and cardiovascular resonses. *Psychosomatic Medicine*, 63, 300–305.

WILLIAMS, R. B., SUAREZ, E. C., KUHN, C. M., ZIMMERMAN, E. A., & SCHANBERG, S. M. (1991). Biobehavioral basis of coronary-prone behavior in middle-aged men. Part I: Evidence for chronic SNS activation in Type As. *Psychosomatic Medicine*, 53, 517–527.

WILLIAMS, R. J., MCDERMITT, D. R., BERTRAND, L. D., & DAVIS, R. M. (2003) Parental awareness of adolescent substance use. *Addictive Behaviors*, 28, 803–809.

WILLIAMS-PIEHOTA, P., PIZARRO, J., SCHNEIDER, T. R., MOWAD, L., & SALOVEY, P. (2005). Matching health messages to monitor-blunter coping styles to motivate screening mammography. *Health Psychology*, 24, 58–67.

WILLIAMSON, D. A., CUBIC, B. A., & FULLER, R. D. (1992). Eating disorders. In S. E. TURNER, K. S., CALHOUN, & H. E. ADAMS (Eds.), Handbook of clinical behavior therapy (2nd ed., pp. 355–372). New York: Wiley.

WILLIS, L., THOMAS, P., GARRY, P. J., & GOODWIN, J. S. (1987). A prospective study of response to stressful life events in initially healthy elders. *Journal of Gerontology*, 42, 627–630.

WILLS, T. A. (1986). Stress and coping in early adolescence: Relationships to substance use in urban school samples. *Health Psychology*, 5, 503–529.

WILLS, T. A., & FEGAN, M. F. (2001). Social networks and social support. In A. BAUM, T. A. REVENSON, & J. E. SINGER (Eds.), *Handbook of health psychology* (pp. 209–234). Mahwah, NJ: Erlbaum.

WILLS, T. A., SANDY, J. M., & YEAGER, A. M. (2002). Stress and smoking in adolescence: A test of directional hypotheses. *Health Psychology*, 21, 122–130.

WILPER, A. P., WOOLHANDLER, S., LASSER, K. E., MCCORMICK, D., BOR, D. H., & HIMMELSTEIN, D. U. (2009). Health insurance and mortality in US adults. *American Journal of Public Health*, 99, 2289–2295.

WILSON, D. P., & ENDRES, R. K. (1986). Compliance with blood glucose monitoring in children with type 1 diabetes mellitus. *Behavioral Pediatrics*, 108, 1022–1024.

WILSON, G. T., LOEB, K. L., WALSH, B. T., LABOUVIE, E., PETKOVA, E., et al. (1999). Psychological versus pharmacological treatments for bulimia nervosa: Predictors and processes of change. *Journal of Consulting and Clinical Psychology*, 67, 451–459.

WILSON, W., ARY, D. V., BIGLAN, A., GLASGOW, R. E., TOOBERT, D. J., & CAMPBELL, D. R. (1986). Psychosocial predictors of self-care behaviors (compliance) and glycemic control in non-insulin-dependent diabetes mellitus. *Diabetes Care*, 9, 614–622.

WINCZE, J. P. (1977). Sexual deviance and dysfunction. In D. C. RIMM & J. W. SOMERVILL (Eds.), *Abnormal psychology*. New York: Academic Press.

WINDSOR, R. A., LOWE, J. B., PERKINS, L. L., SMITH-YODER, D., ARTZ, L., et al. (1993). Health education for pregnant smokers: Its behavioral impact and cost benefit. *American Journal of Public Health*, 83, 201–206.

WINETT, R. A., KING, A. C., & ALTMAN, D. G. (1989). *Health psychology and public health: An integrative approach*. New York: Pergamon.

WING, R. R., EPSTEIN, L. H., NOWALK, M. P., & LAMPARSKI, D. M. (1986). Behavioral self-regulation in the treatment of patients with diabetes mellitus. *Psychological Bulletin*, 99, 78–89.

WING, R. R., & JEFFERY, R. W. (1999). Benefits of recruiting participants with friends and increasing social support for weight loss and maintenance. *Journal of Consulting and Clinical Psychology*, 67, 132–138.

WING, R. R., & POLLEY, B. A. (2001). Obesity. In A. BAUM, T. A. REVENSON, & J. E. SINGER (Eds.), *Handbook of health psychology* (pp. 263–279). Mahwah, NJ: Erlbaum.

WINIKOFF, B. (1983). Nutritional patterns, social choices, and health. In D. MECHANIC (Ed.), *Handbook of health, health care, and the health professions* (pp. 81–98). New York: Free Press.

WINKLEBY, M. A., FLORA, J. A., & KRAEMER, H. C. (1994). A community-based heart disease intervention: Predictors of change. *American Journal of Public Health*, 84, 767–772.

WINETT, R. A., ANDERSON, E. S., WOJCIK, J. R., WINETT, S. G., & BOWDEN, T. (2007). Guide to health: Nutrition and physical activity outcomes of a group-randomized trial of an Internet-based intervention in churches. *Annals of Behavioral Medicine*, 33, 251–261.

WINTERS, R. (1985). Behavioral approaches to pain. In N. SCHNEIDERMAN & J. T. TAPP (Eds.), *Behavioral medicine: The biopsychosocial approach* (pp. 565–587). Hillsdale, NJ: Erlbaum.

WIRTZ, P. H., ULRIKE, E., EMINI, L., RÜDISÜLI, K., GROESSBAUER, S., et al. (2006). Anticipatory cognitive stress appraisal and the acute proagulant stress response in men. *Psychosomatic Medicine*, 68, 851–858.

WITKIEWITZ, K., & MARLATT, G. A. (2004). Relapse prevention for alcohol and drug problems: That was Zen, this is Tao. *American Psychologist*, 59, 224–235.

WITRYOL, S. L. (1971). Incentives and learning in children. In H. W. REESE (Ed.), *Advances in child development and behavior* (Vol. 6, pp. 2–61). New York: Academic Press.

WITTROCK, D. A., & MYERS, T. C. (1998). The comparison of individuals with recurrent tension-type headache and headache-free controls in physiological response, appraisal, and coping with stressors: A review of the literature. *Annals of Behavioral Medicine*, 20, 118–134.

WOLCHIK, S. A., SCHENCK, C. E., & SANDLER, I. N. (2009). Promoting resilience in youth from divorced families: Lessons learned from experimental trials of the new beginnings program. *Journal of Personality* 77, 1833–1868.

WOLF, S., & WOLFF, H. G. (1947). *Human gastric function* (2nd ed.). New York: Oxford University Press.

WOLPE, J. (1958). *Psychotherapy by reciprocal inhibition*. Stanford, CA: Stanford University Press.

WOLPE, J. (1973). *The practice of behavior therapy* (2nd ed.). New York: Pergamon.

WONDERLICH, S. A., & FREIBURGER, P. (2004). Set-point theory. In A. J. CHRISTENSEN, R. MARTIN, & J. M. SMYTH (Eds.), *Encyclopedia of health psychology* (pp. 268–269). New York: Kluwer.

WOOD, M. D., VINSON, D. C., & SHER, K. J. (2001). Alcohol use and misuse. In A. BAUM, T. A. REVENSON, & J. E. SINGER (Eds.), *Handbook of health psychology* (pp. 281–318). Mahwah, NJ: Erlbaum.

WOODGATE, J. & BRAWLEY, L. R. (2008). Self-efficacy for exercise in cardiac rehabilitation: Review and recommendations. *Journal of Health Psychology, 13*, 366–387.

WOODS, A. M., & BIRREN, J. E. (1984). Late adulthood and aging. In J. D. MATARAZZO, S. M. WEISS, J. A. HERD, N. E. MILLER, & S. M. WEISS (Eds.), *Behavioral health: A handbook of health enhancement and disease prevention* (pp. 91–100). New York: Wiley.

WOODS, M. P., & ASMUNDSON, G. J. G. (2008). Evaluating the efficacy of graded *in vivo* exposure for the treatment of fear in patients with chronic back pain: A randomized controlled clinical trial. *Pain, 136*, 271–280.

WOODWARD, N. J., & WALLSTON, B. S. (1987). Age and health care beliefs: Self-efficacy as a mediator of low desire for control. *Psychology and Aging, 2*, 3–8.

WOOSTER, R., BIGNELL, G., LANCASTER, J., SWIFT, S., SEAL, S., et al. (1995). Identification of the breast cancer susceptibility gene BRCA2. *Nature, 378*, 789–792.

WORTMAN, C. B., & DUNKEL-SCHETTER, C. (1979). Interpersonal relationships and cancer: A theoretical analysis. *Journal of Social Issues, 35*, 120–155.

WORTMAN, C. B., & DUNKEL-SCHETTER, C. (1987). Conceptual and methodological issues in the study of social support. In A. BAUM & J. E. SINGER (Eds.), *Handbook of psychology and health* (Vol. 5, pp. 63–108). Hillsdale, NJ: Erlbaum.

WRIGHT, A. A., ZHANG, B., RAY, A., MACK, J. W., TRICE, E., et al. (2008). Associations between end-of-life discussions, patient mental health, medical care near death, and caregiver bereavement adjustment. *Journal of the American Medical Association, 300*, 1665–1673.

WRIGHT, L., & FRIEDMAN, A. G. (1991). Challenge of the future: Psychologists in medical settings. In J. J. SWEET, R. H. ROZENSKY, & S. M. TOVIAN (Eds.), *Handbook of clinical psychology in medical settings* (pp. 603–614). New York: Plenum.

WU, J-N., HO, S. C., ZHOU, C., LING, W-H., CHEN, W-Q., et al. (2009). Coffee consumption and risk of coronary heart diseases: A meta-analysis of 21 prospective cohort studies. *International Journal of Cardiology, 137*, 216–225.

WULFERT, E., WAN, C. K., & BACKUS, C. A. (1996). Gay men's safer sex behavior: An integration of three models. *Journal of Behavioral Medicine, 19*, 345–366.

WURTELE, S. K., & MADDUX, J. E. (1987). Relative contributions of protection motivation theory components in predicting exercise intentions and behavior. *Health Psychology, 6*, 453–466.

XU, J., & ROBERTS, R. E. (2010). The power of positive emotions: It's a matter of life or death—Subjective well-being and longevity over 28 years in a general population. *Health Psychology, 29*, 9–19.

YALI, A. M., & REVENSON, T. A. (2004). How changes in population demographics will impact health psychology: Incorporating a broader notion of cultural competence into the field. *Health Psychology, 23*, 147–155.

YANEZ, B., EDMONDSON, D., STANTON, A. L., PARK, C. L., KWAN, L., et al. (2009). Facets of spirituality as predictors of adjustment to cancer: Relative contributions of having faith and finding meaning. *Journal of Consulting and Clinical Psychology, 77*, 730–741.

YANKAH, E., & AGGLETON, P. (2008). Effects and effectiveness of life skills education for HIV prevention in young children. *AIDS Education and Prevention, 20*, 465–495.

YATES, L. B., DJOUSSÉ, L., KURTH, T., BURING, J. E., & GAZIANO, J. M. (2008). Exceptional longevity in men: Modifiable factors associated with survival and function to age 90 years. *Archives of Internal Medicine, 168*, 284–290.

YONG, H.-H., & BORLAND, R. (2008). Functional beliefs about smoking and quitting activity among adult smokers in four countries: Findings from the International Tobacco Control Four-Country Survey. *Health Psychology, 27*, S216–S223.

YOUNG, D. R., VOLLMER, W. M., KING, A. C., BROWN, A. J., STEVENS, V. J., et al. (2009). Can individuals meet multiple physical activity and dietary behavior goals? *American Journal of Health Behavior, 33*, 277–286.

YOUNG, K., & ZANE, N. (1995). Ethnocultural influences in evaluation and management. In P. M. NICASSIO & T. W. SMITH (Eds.), *Managing chronic illness: A biopsychosocial perspective* (pp. 163–206). Washington, DC: American Psychological Association.

YUSUF, S., HAWKEN, S., ÔUNPUU, S., DANS, R., AVEZUM, A., et al. (2004). Effect of potentially modifiable risk factors associated with myocardial infarction in 52 countries (the INTERHEART Study): A case-control study. *Lancet, 364*, 937–952.

ZACK, M., POULOS, C. X., FRAGOPOULOS, F., WOODFORD, T. M., & MACLEOD, C. M. (2006). Negative affect words prime beer consumption in young drinkers. *Addictive Behaviors, 31*, 169–173.

ZAMBOANGA, B. A., LEITKOWSKI, L. K., RODRÍGUEZ, L., & CASCIO, K. A. (2006). Drinking games in female college students: More than just a game? *Addictive Behaviors, 31*, 1485–1489.

ZARSKI, J. J. (1984). Hassles and health: A replication. *Health Psychology, 3*, 243–251.

ZAUTRA, A. J., BURLESON, M. H., SMITH, C. A., BLALOCK, S. J., WALLSTON, K. A., et al. (1995). Arthritis and perceptions of quality of life: An examination of positive and negative affect in rheumatoid arthritis patients. *Health Psychology, 14*, 399–408.

ZELLER, M. H., & MODI, A. C. (2008). Psychosocial factors related to obesity in children and adolescents. In E. JALALIAN & R. G. STEELE (Eds.), *Handbook of childhood and adolescent obesity* (pp. 25–42). New York: Springer.

ZHANG, B., WRIGHT, A. A., HUSKAMP, H. A., NILSSON, M. E., MACIEJEWSKI, M. L., et al. (2009). Health care costs in the last week of life. *Archives of Internal Medicine, 169,* 480–488.

ZHANG, T-Y., & MEANEY, M. J. (2010). Epigenetics and the environmental regulation of the genome and its function. *Annual Review of Psychology, 61,* 439–466.

ZHU, S.-H., STRECH, V., BALABANIS, M., ROSBROOK, B., SADLER, G., & PIERCE, J. P. (1996). Telephone counseling for smoking cessation: Effects of single-session and multiple-session interventions. *Journal of Consulting and Clinical Psychology, 64,* 202–211.

ZIEGELSTEIN, R. C., KIM, S. Y., KAO, D., FAUERBACH, J. A., THOMBS, B. D., et al. (2005). Can doctors and nurses recognize depression in patients hospitalized with an acute myocardial infarction in the absence of formal screening? *Psychosomatic Medicine, 67,* 393–397.

ZIMBARDO, P. G. (1970). The human choice: Individuation, reason, and order versus deindividuation, impulse, and chaos. In W. J. ARNOLD & D. LEVINE (Eds.), *Nebraska symposium on motivation, 1969* (Vol. 17, pp. 237–307). Lincoln, NE: University of Nebraska Press.

ZIMMER, J. G., JUNCKER, A. G., & MCCUSKER, J. (1985). A randomized controlled study of a home health care team. *American Journal of Public Health, 75,* 134–141.

ZINMAN, B. (1984). Diabetes mellitus and exercise. *Behavioral Medicine Update, 6*(1), 22–25.

ZISOOK, S., PETERKIN, J. J., SHUCHTER, S. R., & BARDONE, A. (1995). Death, dying, and bereavement. In P. M. NICASSIO & T. M. SMITH (Eds.), *Managing chronic illness: A biopsychosocial perspective* (pp. 351–390). Washington, DC: American Psychological Association.

ZOLA, I. K. (1973). Pathways to the doctor—From person to patient. *Social Science and Medicine, 7,* 677–689.

PHOTO CREDITS

CHAPTER 1

Page 3: Bettman/Corbis Images. Page 5: John Verano, National Museum of Natural History; courtesy Smithsonian Institution. Page 6: From R. Melzack and P. Wall (1965). "Pain mechanisms: A new theory." Science, 150: 971–979. Page 9: Digital Vision/Getty Images. Page 13: Gilles Mingasson/Getty Images News and Sport Services.

CHAPTER 2

Page 29: Mauro Fermariello/Photo Researchers. Page 33: ©Photosani, supplied by www.shutterstock.com. Page 41: David H. Wells/Corbis Images. Page 43: Jim Mahoney/The Image Works. Page 45: Richard T. Nowitz/Photo Researchers, Inc.

CHAPTER 3

Page 53: ©Carols Seller, supplied by www.shutterstock.com. Page 61: Pat Benic/Corbis-Bettmann. Page 76: F. Andrasik, D. D. Blake, & M. S. McCarran, A biobehavioral analysis of pediatric headache, child health behavior: A behavioral pediatrics perspective, 1986, Figure 18.1, Wiley.

CHAPTER 4

Page 88: ©Morgan Lane Photography, supplied by www.shutterstock.com. Page 89: ©AP/Wide World Photos. Page 94: Bob Daemmrich/The Image Works.

CHAPTER 5

Page 104: David Sacks/The Image Bank/Getty Images, Inc. Page 118: ©Monkey Business Images, supplied by www.shutterstock.com. Page 125: ©AP/Wide World Photos. Page 130: Tony Michaels/The Image Works.

CHAPTER 6

Page 142: Reprinted by the permission of the American Cancer Society, Inc. from www.cancer.org. All rights reserved. Page 147: ©Monkey Business Images. Supplied by www.shutterstock.com. Page 153: ©Joseph Sohm/Visons of America/Corbis.

CHAPTER 7

Page 166: Don Mason/Corbis Images. Page 174: T. R. Tharp/Corbis Images. Page Page 176: PhotoDisc, Inc. Page 179: Stephen Wilkes/The Image Bank/Getty Images. Page 184: David Young-Wolff/PhotoEdit. Page 190: Ariel Skelly/Corbis Images. Page 193: ©AVAVA, supplied by www.shutterstock.com.

CHAPTER 8

Page 197: ©Dean Mitchell, supplied by www.shutterstock.com. Page 202: ©Mangostock, supplied by www.shutterstock.com. Page 210: LWA-Stephen Welstead/Corbis Images.

CHAPTER 9

Page 223: Culver Pictures, Inc. Page 225: ©Beerkoff, supplied by www.shutterstock.com. Page 228: ©Alexander Raths, supplied by wwwishutterstock.com. Page 237: Monkey Business Images, supplied by www.shutterstock.com. Page 246: Al Campanie/The Image Works.

CHAPTER 10

Page 254: Corbis-Bettmann. Page 262: ©Holbox, supplied by www.shutterstock.com. Page 268: ©Monkey Business Images, supplied by www.shutterstock.com. Page 270: Alan Delaney/Stone/Getty Images.

CHAPTER 11

Page 276: Collection of the New-York Historical Society (negative #5707). Page 289: ©Yuri Arcurs, supplied by www.shutterstock.com. Page 290: AJPhoto/Photo Researchers.

CHAPTER 12

Page 298: Rob Lewine/Corbis Images. Page 305: Richard Ellis/The Image Works. Page 313: Barros & Barros/The Image Bank/Getty Images.

CHAPTER 13

Page 331: AJ Photos/Hop American/Photo Researchers. Page 340: Edwige/Photo Researchers. Page 343: Newscom. Page 348: Getty Images.

APPENDIX

Page 377: Susumu Nishinaga/Photo Researchers.

FIGURES AND TABLES CREDITS

Table 2.4: From T. Holmes & R. Rahe (1967). The Social Readjustment Rating Scale. *Journal of Psychosomatic Research*, 11, 213–218.

Table 2.6: Adapted from E. P. Sarafino & M. Ewing (1999). The Hassles Assessment Scale for Students in College: Measuring the frequency and unpleasantness of and dwelling on stressful events. *Journal of American College Health*, 48, 75–83. Reprinted by permission of the author.

Figure 3–6: From F. Andrasik, D. D. Blake, & M. S. McCarran (1986). A biobehavioral analysis of pediatric headache. In N. A. Krasnegor, J. D. Arasteh, & M. F. Cataldo (Eds.), *Child health behavior: A behavioral pediatrics perspective.* Copyright © 1986 by John Wiley & Sons, Inc.

Table 4.4: From R. W. Novaco (1978). Anger and coping with stress: cognitive and behavioral interventions. In J. P. Foreyt & D. P. Rathjen (Eds.), *Cognitive behavioral therapy: Research and application.* Copyright © 1978 by Plenum Press.

Figure 5–2: Adapted from M. H. Becker & I. M. Rosenstock (1984). Compliance with medical advice. In A. Steptoe & A. Mathews (Eds.), *Health care and human behavior.* Copyright © 1984 by Academic Press.

Figure 8–2: From M. A. Safer, Q. J. Tharps, T. C. Jackson, & H. Leventhal (1979). Determinants of three stages of delay in seeking care at a medical clinic. *Medical Care*, 17, 11–29.

Figure 9–2: Adapted from E. A. Anderson (1987). Preoperative preparation for cardiac surgery facilitates recovery, reduces psychological distress, and reduced the incidence of acute postoperative hypertension. *Journal of Consulting and Clinical Psychology*, 55, 513–520. Copyright © 1987 by the American Psychological Association; adapted by permission of the author.

Figure 9–3: From S. M. Miller & C. E. Mangan (1983). Interacting effects of information and coping style in adapting to gynecological stress: Should the doctor tell all? *Journal of Personality and Social Psychology*, 45, 223–236. Copyright © 1983 by the American Psychological Association; reprinted by permission of the author.

Figure 9–4: From E. P. Sarafino & J. W. Armstrong (1986). *Child and adolescent development* (2nd ed.). St. Paul, MN: West Publishing Co. Copyright © 1986 by Edward P. Sarafino and James W. Armstrong; reprinted by permission of the authors.

Figure 10–7: From R. Melzack (1975). The McGill Pain Questionnaire: Major properties and scoring methods. *Pain*, 1, 277–299. Copyright © 1975 by Elsevier Science Publishers.

Figure 12–1: Adapted from R. H. Moos (1982). Coping with acute health crises. In T. Millon, C. Green, & R. Meagher (Eds.), *Handbook of clinical health psychology.* Copyright © 1982 by Plenum Press.

Figure 12–2: From J. R. Holum (1994). *Fundamentals of general, organic, and biological chemistry* (5th ed.). Copyright © 1994 by John Wiley & Sons, Inc.; reprinted by permission of the publisher.

Figure 13–3: From American Cancer Society (2010). *Cancer facts and figures*, 2010. Atlanta: American Cancer Society, Inc. Retrieved (10-14-2010) from http://www.cancer.org. Reproduced by permission of the American Cancer Society.

Figure A–2: Drawings from E. H. Lenneberg (1967, Figure 4.6). *Biological foundations of language.* Copyright © 1967 by John Wiley & Sons, Inc.; reprinted by permission of the publisher. Drawings based on photographs from J. L. Conel (1939–1963). *The postnatal development of the human cerebral cortex* (Vols. 1–7). Reproduced by permission of Harvard University Press.

Figure A–9: From S. R. Nayak, M. M. Pai, L. V. Prabhu, S. D'Costa, & P. Shetty. (2006) Anatomical organization of aortic arch variations in India: Embryological basis and review. *Jornal Vascular Brasileiro*, 5(2). DOI:10.1590/S1677-54492006000200004. Used by permission.

AUTHOR INDEX

SUBJECT INDEX